Ward 8—Precinct 1

City of Boston

List of Residents 20 years of Age and Over

(Females Indicated by Dagger) as of April 1, 1924

Unknown

Alpha Editions

This edition published in 2020

ISBN : 9789354027802

Design and Setting By
Alpha Editions
email - alphaedis@gmail.com

Ward 8—Precinct 1

CITY OF BOSTON.

LIST OF RESIDENTS
20 YEARS OF AGE AND OVER

(FEMALES INDICATED BY DAGGER)

AS OF

APRIL 1, 1924

HERBERT A. WILSON, } Listing
JAMES F. EAGAN, } Board.

CITY OF BOSTON—PRINTING DEPARTMENT

Page.	Letter	FULL NAME.	Residence, April 1, 1924.	Occupation.	Supposed Age.	Reported Residence April 1, 1923. Street and Number

Beacon Street

	Letter	FULL NAME.	Residence	Occupation	Age	Reported Residence
	A	Endicott Francis M	35	retired	44	here
	B	Greely Agnes—†	35	chambermaid	34	"
	C	Hartnett Annie—†	35	cook	40	"
	D	Haven Florence E—†	35	housewife	40	"
	E	McGlauflin Pearl—†	35	nurse	32	S Hamilton
	F	Russell Nora—†	35	laundress	25	13 Hereford
	G	Waldron Cecelia—†	35	waitress	27	here
	H	Adams Mary C—†	36	housewife	45	"
	K	Garfad Emma—†	36	cook	40	"
	L	Horgan Mary—†	36	waitress	25	Waban
	M	Loudon Julia—†	36	chambermaid	40	here
	N	Blake Ann L—†	37	housewife	38	"
	O	Blake John A	37	banker	40	"
	P	Cameron Elizabeth—†	37	nurse	65	"
	R	Dolan Katherine—†	37	laundress	50	"
	S	Frisk Ingabork—†	37	maid	23	"
	T	Given Elizabeth—†	37	nurse	43	"
	U	Havstron Anna—†	37	maid	23	"
	V	Rowley Jessie—†	37	"	35	Florida
	W	Swanson Julia—†	37	cook	34	53 Chestnut
	X	Crossland Florence—†	37½	nurse	38	Franconia N
	Y	Samuels Ruth—†	37½	student	27	New Hampshire
	Z	Sullivan Alice—†	37½	housekeeper	40	here
	A	Bjorkland Elizabeth—†	38	maid	40	"
	B	Cahill Marie—†	38	cook	39	191 Com av
	C	Johnson Hilma—†	38	maid	35	21 "
	D	Lynch Nellie—†	38	waitress	40	here
	E	Winthrop Ann—†	38	housewife	84	"

Bowdoin Street

	Letter	FULL NAME.	Residence	Occupation	Age	Reported Residence
	F	Albert Antonio	1 & 3	dishwasher	31	20 Bulfinch
	G	Arruda Phyllis—†	1 & 3	chambermaid	38	Natick
	H	Belco Andrew J	1 & 3	molder	35	3 Bowdoin
	K	Clifford Osland	1 & 3	salesman	31	California
	L	Comer Phillip	1 & 3	machinist	68	Maine
	M	Coresky Michael	1 & 3	barber	32	26 Hancock
	N	Crawford Amelia—†	1 & 3	chambermaid	42	Young's Hotel
	O	Dedunsky Donald	1 & 3	counterman	26	Springfield

2

Bowdoin Street—Continued

P	Findlen Harold V	1 & 3	tallyman	37	46 Green
R	Flagg George E	1 & 3	shipper	46	3 Bowdoin
S	Gagnon Lazare	1 & 3	laborer	50	New Brunswick
T	Gill George	1 & 3	draughtsman	29	Ohio
U	Jasikaiski Adam	1 & 3	baker	36	3 Bowdoin
V	Lafrance Joseph	1 & 3	waiter	24	Revere
W	Lenewick Toney	1 & 3	cook	27	3 Bowdoin
X	Lomos Amistano	1 & 3	millhand	31	Taunton
Y	Lovell Fredrick	1 & 3	clerk	45	Canada
Z	Lucy Clara—†	1 & 3	housewife	61	here
A	Lucy Samuel	1 & 3	lodging house	61	"
B	Malone Charles L	1 & 3	busboy	42	W Medford
C	McFarland Peter	1 & 3	laborer	63	3 Bowdoin
D	Mekoni Mary—†	1 & 3	waitress	24	3 "
E	Moran Daniel V	1 & 3	carpenter	41	3 "
F	Muscluk Michael	1 & 3	cook	34	here
G	Rosenfield Max	1 & 3	salesman	35	3 Bowdoin
H	Smith Alfred	1 & 3	cook	40	52 Chandler
K	Smith Alick	1 & 3	upholsterer	28	3 Bowdoin
L	Stetson George B	1 & 3	lather	45	Maine
M	Verreult Wilfred	1 & 3	longshoreman	20	"
O	Anderson Charles	7	lodging house	60	Mass Gen Hosp
P	Anderson Oscar	7	penmaker	29	Foxboro
R	Erekson John	7	painter	36	New Hampshire
S	Fiscut George	7	steamfitter	37	625 Tremont
T	Hammond Charles A	7	electrician	70	here
U	Juno Josephine—†	7	checker	20	Maine
V	Marotta John	7	barrelmaker	23	Woburn
W	Melnick Michial	7	laborer	37	New Hampshire
X	Napolitono Salvadore	7	"	44	here
Y	O'Brien John	7	expressman	26	103 Brookline
Z	Sullivan Jeremiah	7	longshoreman	30	here
A	Sullivan John J	7	teamster	28	"
B	Bines Ester—†	9	housewife	44	"
C	Bines Samuel	9	truckman	41	"
E	Hackett Catherine M—†	9	clerk	26	Revere
F	Hackett John T	9	salesman	32	Medford
G	Bines Ruth—†	9	housekeeper	27	here
K	Pedersen Jens L	9	machinist	41	"
L	Amerio John F	9	lobster dealer	69	"
M	Garta Frank	9	actor	55	Winthrop

Bowdoin Street—Continued

Letter	Full Name	Residence, April 1, 1924	Occupation	Supposed Age	Reported Residence, April 1, 1923
N	Gray Charles H	9	salesman	61	here
O	Laverty Tresa—†	9	housekeeper	78	"
P	Laverty William H	9	molder	75	"
R	Sweeney Hugh M	9	paperhanger	73	"
S	Brisky David	9	newspaperman	35	"
T	Brisky Zoe—†	9	housewife	42	"
U	Sullivan Beulah L—†	9	"	23	23 Dartmouth
V	Sullivan Fred J	9	chauffeur	25	23 "
W	Jesseau Edna—†	9	housewife	28	here
X	Jesseau William	9	mechanic	29	"
Y	Owen Walter	9	machinist	52	"
Z	Haltman David	9	truck driver	32	37 Joy
A	Hattman Huldah—†	9	tel operator	26	Vermont
B	DeNutte Charlotte—†	9	waitress	36	Brighton
C	Hamilton Harriet M—†	9	cook	42	here
D	Jennings John H	9	coalworker	42	Chelsea
E	Albert Fannie—†	9	housewife	26	here
F	Albert Martin	9	shipper	28	"
G	Avellis William	11	barber	25	56 Chambers
H	Benett Gasper	11	bootblack	45	here
K	Carroll John	11	dishwasher	60	7 Bowdoin
L	Cottle Marie—†	11	housewife	35	here
M	Curran Elizabeth—†	11	lodging house	45	"
N	Drazba Alexander	11	watchman	44	"
O	Forgrthy John F	11	janitor	44	"
P	Heiland Gustave	11	carpenter	35	9 Green
R	Jordan Eli	11	lodging house	70	here
S	Mackay Fred	11	engineer	55	"
T	Martin John	11	laborer	44	Maine
U	Molkie Edward	11	actor	52	here
V	Saellowske Joseph	11	shoeworker	35	"
W	Squinter Munzio	11	barber	46	41 Chambers
X	Sterdevent Westley	11	foreman	56	here
Y	Travis Thomas	11	counterman	39	"
Z	Warren Herbert	11	meatcutter	32	New Brunswick
A	Zapasik William	11	student	32	here
B	Zagoro Ralph	11	laborer	25	249 Hanover
C	Burrill Anna—†	13	housewife	29	3 Bulfinch
D	Burrill Arthur	13	fireman	42	here
E	Carr Frank	13	tinsmith	58	"
F	Countvay Marie—†	13	lodging house	59	"

Bowdoin Street—Continued

G	Deveau Agnes—†	13	waitress	23	3 Bulfinch
H	Falnon Samuel	13	cook	34	here
K	Garrick John S	13	laborer	43	12 Staniford pl
L	McCann John	13	"	38	9 Staniford
M	Parsons Arthur	13	watchman	42	here
N	Parsons Mabel—†	13	waitress	38	"
O	Rafuse Avery	13	shoecutter	35	"
P	Robinson Arthur	13	tinsmith	61	"
R	Smith Charles H	13	laborer	36	9 Bulfinch
S	Waterman Lena—†	13	waitress	48	here
T	Arma Mohamed	15	pedler	38	"
U	Cormitintino John	15	tinsmith	27	66 Causeway
V	DeFlor James	15	cook	27	here
W	Doody James E	15	furniture work'r	53	"
X	Dreugeha Speros	15	cook	30	3 Bowdoin
Y	Fladger Louis	15	"	25	here
Z	Foti Thomas	15	shoeworker	30	"
A	George Kosmos	15	"	25	"
B	Henderson Charles	15	tinsmith	50	"
C	King Sadie M—†	15	lodging house	38	"
D	Mira Louis	15	cook	38	"
E	Shannon John H	15	barber	52	58 Howard
F	Stanton George F	15	steamfitter	65	here
G	Boonsjas Richard	17	baker	29	"
H	Bruno Arthur	17	taxi driver	28	Illinois
K	Fax William	17	"	40	Maine
L	Ferrario Benjamin	17	laborer	23	Revere
M	Hale Edson	17	chauffeur	40	Newton
N	Howard Fred J	17	clerk	78	here
O	List Harry	17	machinist	39	"
P	List Sarah—†	17	housewife	39	"
S	Martin Charles E	17	porter	49	Lynn
R	McNamara Henry M	17	roofer	40	here
T	Miner Murray	17	tradesman	28	"
U	Moolivni Morio	17	cabinetmaker	24	Dedham
V	Morse Leo	17	counterman	21	here
W	Mortell Anna—†	17	waitress	25	Canada
X	Packard Gladys M—†	17	housekeeper	30	Fairhaven
Y	Pearson John A	17	clerk	31	here
Z	Sears Jack	17	counterman	21	Canada
A	Simione Adolf	17	machinist	25	Springfield

5

Bowdoin Street—Continued

B	Simione Armond	17	student	22	Southbridge
C	Strain Catherine—†	17	waitress	40	"
D	Sullivan William J	17	clerk	40	here
E	Swanson Earnest	17	rigger	32	"
F	Tailor Stanley	17	restaurantman	24	"
G	Tremblay Harry	17	seaman	25	Canada
H	Warren Carl E	17	janitor	70	Brockton
K	Baker John	19	cook	28	25 Bowdoin
L	Branigan John	19	counterman	38	here
M	Doherty John	19	tailor	52	2 Cambridge
N	Dwinell Alice M—†	19	lodging house	49	here
O	Dwinell George H	19	cashier	48	"
P	Farrell John	19	fishcutter	54	"
R	Gilder Daniel	19	counterman	37	"
S	Griffin Frank	19	boilermaker	37	Connecticut
T	Griffin Harold	19	machinist	24	"
U	Lonovik Julia—†	19	stitcher	28	5½ Barton
V	MacDonald Anna—†	19	waitress	36	here
W	MacGloughlin Charles	19	janitor	54	15 Bowdoin
X	Mahoney James	19	printer	30	19 Savin
Y	Parkhurst Edward	19	civil engineer	62	here
Z	Slack Joseph F	19	U S A	40	"
A	Sutton Albert	19	letter carrier	63	"
B	Webster George	19	patternmaker	71	"
C	Antonion Thomas	21	bootblack	39	"
D	Burleigh John	21	cook	50	"
E	Danforth Herbert	21	waiter	46	"
F	Dee George	21	teamster	48	Andover
G	Devlin Daniel	21	waiter	38	270 Col av
H	Dingler Oscar	21	"	58	New Hampshire
K	Ferry Catherine—†	21	waitress	35	here
L	Graham Minnie—†	21	lodging house	42	"
M	Hanley Jeremiah	21	waiter	48	"
N	Harrison John	21	painter	43	"
O	McIvers Peter J	21	retired	72	Maine
P	Murphy James	21	cook	55	here
R	Pesonen William	21	painter	41	35 Lynde
S	Venyes George	21	waiter	45	here
T	Booris Harry	23	salesman	25	Haverhill
U	Carey Thomas H	23	"	35	New Jersey
V	Chamberlain Albert	23	machinist	32	Brockton

Bowdoin Street—Continued

	w	Chamberlain Timothy	23	clerk	61	New Bedford
	x	Foley William J	23	molder	25	New Hampshire
	y	Gordon James J	23	lodging house	24	New York
	a	Main James A	23	papercutter	37	New Hampshire
	a¹	McDonald James	23	cook	23	Connecticut
	b	Murphy John J	23	waiter	42	New Jersey
	c	Riley William F	23	shoemaker	45	Lynn
	d	Spaulding Albert	23	garageman	26	here
	e	Spoor James	23	clerk	27	Malden
	f	Baidley Henry	25	physician	58	here
	g	Curtis George S	25	janitor	67	"
	h	Curtis Hattie—†	25	lodging house	58	"
	k	Kelley James H	25	clerk	73	New York
	l	Minue George	25	"	35	here
	m	Minan James	25	engineer	40	"
	p	Ramsay Charles	25	lawyer	50	"
	n	Ring Edward	25	paperhanger	45	"
	o	Ring Helen—†	25	housewife	44	"
	r	Abianis Joseph	27	cook	28	New York
	s	Cuneo Michael	27	laborer	52	here
	t	Cunningham Nellie—†	27	tailoress	45	"
	u	Kaleel Michael	27	clerk	27	New York
	v	Pai Visha	27	student	25	here
	w	Scott Dora A	27	lodging house	38	"
	w¹	Soje Amalia—†	27	bookkeeper	28	"
	x	Soule Henry	27	"	28	"
	y	Taylor Rose—†	27	housewife	23	England
	z	Taylor Sidney	27	laborer	28	"
	b	Vermilyia Roy G	27	clerk	25	New York
	c	Atwood Frank	29	"	71	here
	d	Buoninest John	29	"	40	New York
	e	Egan William	29	meatcutter	35	Roslindale
	f	Holmgreen Lena—†	29	dressmaker	42	here
	g	Hunter Fred	29	clerk	54	"
	k	Maltars James G	29	welder	33	New Hampshire
	h	McCarthy John	29	chauffeur	25	here
	l	Reynolds Edward	29	machinist	35	"
	m	Sartory Henry	29	painter	61	"
	n	Sawyer Elmwood	29	clerk	36	"
	o	Smith George E	29	machinist	28	"
	p	Antonioli Giacomo	31	cook	29	60 Bowdoin

Bowdoin Street—Continued

R	Brown Michael	31	elevatorman	72	Illinois
S	Cafferty James J	31	laborer	44	here
T	Carbaneau John B	31	"	58	23 Bowdoin
U	Carbaneau Laurence	31	"	23	23 "
V	Carroll Thomas	31	"	23	Illinois
W	Cavicchi Antonio	31	salesman	49	23 Bowdoin
X	Cavicchi Malvina—†	31	housewife	46	23 "
Y	Cornell David	31	salesman	21	Scotland
Z	Cote Onesime	31	laborer	60	here
A	Derry Ernest	31	salesman	28	Worcester
C	Dixon Robert E	31	bookkeeper	41	Canada
B	Duff William G	31	meatcutter	22	here
D	Emerson Lillian M—†	31	cashier	43	Medford
E	Gianelli Aurilie	31	laborer	46	13 Cambridge
F	Hayward Ellis E	31	janitor	43	Somerville
G	Hayward James W	31	shipper	27	"
H	Johnson Caroline—†	31	lodging house	26	23 Bowdoin
K	Johnson Harry W	31	shipper	43	23 "
L	Kimball Frank	31	laborer	64	here
M	Trask Marjorie—†	31	stenographer	20	Cambridge
N	Briggs Ernest E	33	clergyman	43	here
O	Burton Spence	33	"	42	"
P	Converse Duncan	33	"	72	"
R	Dale Oliver B	33	"	36	"
S	Field Charles N	33	"	75	"
T	Fitz Frank	33	"	45	"
U	Powell Fred C	33	"	60	"
V	Viall Kenneth	33	"	30	"
W	Williams Granville M	33	"	32	"
X	Johnson John C	33	"	45	"
Y	Palmer Roland	33	"	32	"
Z	Turney William C	33	"	38	"
B	Ambrose Andrew S	37	salesman	36	"
C	Balshin Joseph	37	waiter	25	37 Union Park
D	Balshin Samuel	37	meatcutter	28	37 "
E	Baumsee Samuel	37	salesman	50	New York
F	Benkalsky Stanley S	37	proprietor	31	37 Lynde
G	Bergh Edward	37	inspector	31	Connecticut
H	Botch George	37	clerk	44	here
K	Chapman Arthur S	37	salesman	24	"
L	Chapman Bessie—†	37	housewife	48	"

Bowdoin Street—Continued

M	Chapman Robert S	37	manager	54	here
N	Edmunds Nathenel	37	detective	35	"
O	Elamer Joseph J	37	salesman	29	New York
P	Faucett Frank A	37	"	52	here
R	Francis Frank	37	"	35	"
S	Gates Claude—†	37	housewife	23	"
T	Gates Evelyn—†	37	"	50	"
U	Gates Wendall M	37	elevators	28	E Princeton
V	Gluntz Bermark	37	designer	30	274 Blue Hill av
W	Gordon Wendall	37	lawyer	35	here
X	Gustofson Adolf	37	engineer	31	Sweden
Y	Hershieft Albert	37	watchman	30	24 Beacon
Z	Kerrigan Mary—†	37	waitress	21	30 Hancock
A	Klyman Harry	37	clerk	20	Lawrence
B	Klyman Isadore	37	salesman	27	Revere
C	Klyman John	37	clerk	24	here
D	Lisk George F	37	electrician	37	Millbury
E	Marion Louis	37	music dealer	27	37 Union Park
F	McFadden Peter J	37	salesman	35	910 E Fourth
G	McMahon Eileen—†	37	waitress	21	Ohio
H	Pandulier Peter	37	chef	30	Lynn
K	Pauvis Paul	37	restaurateur	24	"
L	Petronas Peter	37	counterman	26	Haverhill
M	Rosenfield Joseph	37	waiter	26	37 Union Park
N	Rosenfield Philip	37	salesman	28	Peabody
O	Shockat George	37	shoeworker	30	here
P	Sullivan Timothy	37	carpenter	45	Worcester
R	Tripp Nellie—†	37	shoeworker	29	Maine
S	Tripp William F	37	clerk	29	"
T	Tufts Ray	37	plumber	25	Mexico
U	White Helen—†	37	waitress	28	here
V	Whitten James	37	solicitor	50	"
W	Azzolina Ernest	39	musician	21	New York
X	Ballou John	39	special police	32	here
Y	Bernstein Harry	39	electrician	36	"
Z	Casey Harry	39	lawyer	30	37 Bowdoin
A	Cohn Alexander	39	news agent	30	here
B	Damon Amon	39	carpenter	47	8 Bulfinch pl
C	Frazer Albert	39	checker	52	62 Fuller
D	Frost John	39	welder	40	here
A	Gleason Edward	39	musician	26	New York

Bowdoin Street—Continued

		FULL NAME	Residence April 1, 1924	Occupation	Supposed Age	Reported Residence April 1, 1923
B	Gold Gustave	39	musician	23	New York
C	Hotton Charles	39	salesman	40	here
D	Margolis Jacob	39	"	37	Chelsea
E	Nemrow Barnet	39	"	26	here
F	Nemrow Harry	39	"	28	"
G	Pearlstein Louis	39	"	34	"
H	Pike Michael	39	accountant	44	Illinois
K	Rude John	39	musician	25	New York
L	Shapiro David	39	hatmaker	26	here
M	Shapiro John	39	salesman	31	26 Abbot
N	Shay Frank	39	"	28	Ohio
O	Sibeck Frederick	39	musician	24	New York
P	Silberg Max	39	butcher	27	6 Bulfinch
R	Smith Merritt	39	musician	30	New York
S	Southerland Harry	39	janitor	42	here
T	Westbrook Benjaman	39	musician	45	New York
U	Wilson George	39	watchmaker	41	here
V	Burke Kathleen—†	41	cashier	29	New York
W	Burke Marion—†	41	"	24	"
X	Carney Thomas L	41	electrician	41	here
Y	Chay Frank	41	salesman	31	New York
Z	Connelly Peter	41	clerk	50	here
A	Coven Isaac	41	"	30	64 Bowdoin
B	Coven Louis	41	"	32	64 "
C	Crowley Richard	41	teacher	33	39 Allston
D	Dumphy Richard A	41	machinist	38	Malden
E	Ericson Oscar H	41	"	36	34 Temple
F	Gershon Abraham	41	clerk	27	243 Callender
G	Gershon Frank	41	"	30	243 "
H	Gershon Julius	41	hotelkeeper	61	243 "
K	Hannafri James	41	clerk	38	here
L	LaRoy Charles	41	chauffeur	36	Quincy
M	Levine Myer	41	newsdealer	34	156 Leverett
N	McNall William J	41	telegrapher	27	Andover
O	Miller Isadore	41	pedler	34	here
P	Paulsner Grace—†	41	stenographer	27	31 Romsey
R	Shapero Harry	41	printer	32	here
S	Snyder Morris	41	postal clerk	29	Philadelphia
T	Taylor Fred	41	conductor	45	here
U	White George	41	machinist	42	Malden
V	Barron Charles	43	engineer	65	18 Allston

Bowdoin Street— Continued

w	Barron Maud —†	43	waitress	28	18 Allston
x	Breed Charles	43	brakeman	25	Williamstown
y	Brown Drusilla Q—†	43	housekeeper	64	here
z	Brown Elwood A	43	merchant	62	"
a	Brown Jessie S—†	43	housekeeper	60	"
b	Donehue Mary—†	43	bookkeeper	40	"
c	Fagan John E	43	manufacturer	60	Middleboro
d	Fagan Josephine—†	43	housewife	50	"
e	McGowan John J	43	special police	38	New Hampshire
e¹	Mitchell Charles	43	druggist	48	here
f	Murch Leon I	43	clerk	32	Maine
g	Potter Joseph	43	conductor	30	Williamstown
h	Ryder George	43	multigrapher	38	here
k	Beal Belle—†	45	stenographer	40	Randolph
l	Francis Margaret—†	45	usher	63	here
m	Gilman Alice G—†	45	housekeeper	63	41 Hancock
n	Hoffman Charles P	45	salesman	45	New York
o	Pinkham Mary E—†	45	teacher	37	Franklin
p	Potter Mary K—†	45	artist	69	here
r	Swansey Lillian—†	45	saleswoman	42	"

Cambridge Street

w	Boyle John	30	coal carrier	48	142 Cambridge
x	Cohen Sarah—†	30	housekeeper	46	142 "
y	Cohen Wolf	30	antique dealer	78	142 "
z	Gulevich Nicol	30	laborer	33	Maine
a	Messhuk Sarhar	30	"	29	142 Cambridge
b	Novack Michael	30	rag sorter	40	142 "
c	Raman George	30	dishwasher	32	142 "
h	Bowlen John	42	baker	50	here
k	Brock Warner E	42	printer	60	28 Bowdoin
g	Foster James	42	dishwasher	50	Brockton
p	Betts Emma—†	62	housewife	42	7 Chambers
r	Betts George L	62	laundryman	36	7 "
s	Bowman Caroline A—†	62	housewife	64	here
t	Bowman George B	62	manager	61	"
t¹	Morray Walter	62	laborer	40	Vermont
v	Beaton David	66	"	56	here
w	Beaton Edith—†	66	housewife	48	"

Cambridge Street—Continued

X	Chesholm Helen—†	66	waitress	41	here
Y	Deschutsner Edward	66	cigarmaker	22	Worcester
Z	Douglass Annie—†	66	housemaid	43	45 Buckingh'm
A	Flynn Delia—†	66	laundress	50	here
B	Hanrahan William	66	lodging house	57	"
C	Johnson John	66	laborer	45	Maine
D	Jones Annie—†	66	waitress	42	here
E	Jones John	66	laborer	55	"
F	Kapler Alexander	66	porter	20	Cambridge
G	Lannon John	66	carpenter	52	here
H	Manning Thomas	66	blacksmith	49	32 Warren
K	McCrossin Hugh	66	metalworker	60	New Hampshire
L	Sheen James	66	porter	63	171 Charles
M	Stockbridge Lydia—†	66	housewife	71	here
N	Wholey Patrick	66	cook	49	788 Beacon
O	Buckley Patrick	68	laborer	39	35 Lynde
P	DeLisse James J	68	engineer	34	here
R	DeLisse Joseph I	68	salesman	43	"
T	Dolge Antony	68	machinist	34	"
S	Downling Forbes	68	watchman	56	"
U	Elms Mary I—†	68	lodging house	33	"
V	Fitzgerald Charles O	68	mason	68	"
W	Hanson Thomas	68	baker	33	"
X	Manning Martin	68	laborer	56	"
Y	McKelvie John A	68	cook	50	"
Z	Rose Frank	68	chef	34	8 Bowdoin
A	Rose Helen—†	68	waitress	32	8 "
B	Vigneault Armand	68	woodsman	23	New Hampshire
C	Weston Rena—†	68	chambermaid	49	here
E	Arnott Thomas	76	lineman	42	5 Merriam
F	Bertrand Charles	76	fireman	36	Rhode Island
G	Carter Richard	76	laborer	40	New Brunswick
H	Chapdelian Jacob	76	roofer	52	9 Staniford pl
K	Chisholm Harry	76	molder	52	here
L	Desmond Daniel J	76	checker	55	135 Cambridge
M	Dolovan James	76	papermaker	44	New Hampshire
N	Donlon John	76	laborer	39	"
O	Gervais William C	76	painter	52	Vermont
P	Gregorie George	76	lodging house	58	here
R	Johnson Augustus	76	laborer	51	"
S	McCarthy James	76	hotel clerk	48	Woburn

Cambridge Street—Continued

Page.	Letter.	FULL NAME.	Residence, April 1, 1924.	Occupation.	Supposed Age.	Reported Residence, April 1, 1923. Street and Number.
	T	McLaughlin John T	76	laborer	40	Lowell
	U	Pierce Arthur M	76	"	68	25 Bowdoin
	V	Provencher Joseph	76	buffer	44	here
	W	Provencher Olvine—†	76	housekeeper	37	"
	Z	Brohlin William	82	electrician	34	Brookline
	A	Duffault John	82	cook	60	Canada
	B	Howell Herbert	82	chemist	77	66 Cambridge
	C	McLaughlin John	82	roofer	72	262 "
	D	Meehan William	82	"	56	14 S Russell
	E	Nolan John J	82	shoemaker	71	here
	F	Perrin John	82	laborer	33	"
	G	Phelps William	82	longshoreman	67	66 Cambridge
	H	Robinson Alexander	82	plasterer	67	here
	K	Shea Jeremiah	82	blacksmith	53	Woburn
	L	Sliney Albert L	82	laborer	43	here
	M	Sutter Joseph	82	shoemaker	61	"
	N	Arcaro Peter	84	polisher	32	"
	O	Ayash Zayeh	84	pedler	27	22 Staniford
	P	Balzek Felix	84	laborer	29	Newton
	R	Barrasso Louis	84	clerk	23	here
	S	Bercuanu Vasik	84	porter	43	Pennsylvania
	T	Buyko Michael	84	laborer	45	here
	U	Cosek Harry	84	presser	29	Cambridge
	V	Doran Nicholas	84	carpenter	49	Connecticut
	W	Fullone Joseph	84	plaster	31	Lawrence
	X	Hadley William	84	chauffeur	40	Cambridge
	Y	Hanley John	84	fireman	61	here
	Z	Hanseen Christian	84	chauffeur	35	Brookline
	A	Hanseen Ruth—†	84	housewife	27	"
	B	Lesnik John	84	laborer	29	here
	C	MacNally Thomas	84	"	44	178 Harris'n av
	D	Mann James	84	carpenter	64	Quincy
	E	McSweeney Terence	84	laborer	43	Revere
	F	Quinlan Frank	84	chauffeur	38	here
	G	Sergey Joseph	84	bookbinder	48	"
	H	Sherbuck Angeline—†	84	housewife	29	"
	K	Sherbuck Charles	84	baker	32	"
	L	Varden Henry	84	porter	61	131 Court
	M	Wax Anna—†	84	housewife	35	here
	N	Wax Samuel	84	cigarmaker	40	"
	O	White John	84	shipper	55	Somerville

Cambridge Street—Continued

P	Zaslavsky Jacob	84	pedler	30	here
Y	Mroszczyk Joseph	110	carpenter	57	"
Z	Mroszczyk Victoria—†	110	housewife	41	"
A	Goulin Elizabeth—†	110	"	26	"
B	Landers Mary M—†	110	"	54	"
C	Murphy John J	110	printer	36	"
D	Minnihan Daniel P	110	teamster	48	"
E	Minnihan Margaret M—†	110	housewife	60	"

Derne Street

G	Leighton Frederick	2	caretaker	40	Maine
H	Swan Elizabeth B—†	2	housekeeper	57	here
K	Swan Martha C—†	2	"	54	"
L	Swan Mary B—†	2	"	50	"
M	Alden Oakly W	4	agent	70	"
N	Burnham Charles	4	salesman	55	19 Hancock
O	French Annie—†	4	tiemaker	54	here
P	Kyeracos Louis	4	restaurateur	34	"
S	McClellan James A	4	letter carrier	47	"
R	McClellan John	4	baker	55	"
T	Wells Elford L	4	machinist	50	"
U	Woodford Alice—†	4	housekeeper	50	"
V	Coats Sylvester R	6	hotelkeeper	57	"
W	Coismill John	6	barber	28	18 Temple
X	Currier Lorenzo G	6	clerk	23	Haverhill
Y	Dobbins Samuel	6	meatcutter	58	here
Z	Gallagher William L	6	manager	62	7 Common
A	Heydman Thomas J	6	contractor	58	here
B	Penny Charles L	6	shoeworker	58	New Hampshire
C	Polgary Lewis	6	printer	28	229 St Botolph
D	Warren Walter	6	radio mechanic	38	Everett
E	Sweeney Joseph M	10	manager	35	Connecticut
F	Crosby Albert H	10	florist	30	Minnesota
G	Greenleaf Louis S	10	salesman	28	New York
H	Sanford Curtis A	10	elevators	45	Springfield
K	Skelly John J	10	engineer	27	Connecticut
L	Estes Michael	12	chauffeur	30	50 Allston
M	Goldman Daniel	12	blacksmith	50	here
N	Ireland Ida L—†	12	housekeeper	55	"

Derne Street—Continued

o	Ireland Ora M	12	blacksmith	63	here
p	McAuley Alexander	12	clerk	55	"
r	McCroan John	12	salesman	30	"
s	Finochetti Louis	12A	proprietor	55	"
t	Bessaraba John	14	porter	32	"
u	Bursmith James L	14	clerk	43	70 Revere
v	Farrar Estelle E—†	14	proofreader	57	here
w	Gould Daniel J	14	laborer	52	"
x	Gould Henry R	14	ironworker	40	"
y	Gould Minnie—†	14	housekeeper	49	"
z	Herlihy John J	14	machinist	69	"
a	McAfee William	14	cabinetmaker	59	"
b	Murray Edward G	14	clerk	25	Somerville
c	Nelson Edward	14	printer	51	here
d	Pavlink Thomas	14	porter	37	"
e	Saunders Patrick	14	"	46	"
f	Swanson Andrew	14	steamfitter	52	"
h	Archer Gleason L	18	dean	45	"
k	Snyder Henry S	18	treasurer	65	"
l	Lung Annie—†	26	laundress	42	"
m	Lung Charlie W	26	laundryman	62	"
n	Mathis Ernest L	26	student	26	8 Revere
o	Mathis Lynda—†	26	housewife	24	8 "

Hancock Street

a	Allbee Burton	1	mason	50	here
b	Campbell Alexander	1	fireman	67	"
c	Campbell James A	1	laborer	35	35 Lynde
d	Collins James	1	"	50	273 Commerc'l
e	Cutler Ely	1	real estate	34	here
f	Diorio Andrew	1	stonecutter	35	Lowell
g	Driscoll Bartholomew	1	laborer	60	13½ Howard
h	Erickson Theodore	1	shoemaker	73	75 Charles
k	Fragos John	1	laborer	25	35 Tremont
l	George Tony	1	"	36	102 Cambridge
m	Givens Edward	1	"	41	Lawrence
n	Goodwin Herbert P	1	lodging house	58	here
o	Gray Maud—†	1	laundress	35	"
p	Harvey John	1	cook	59	"

Page.	Letter.	FULL NAME.	Residence, April 1, 1924.	Occupation.	Supposed Age.	Reported Residence, April 1, 1923. Street and Number.	Date.

Hancock Street—Continued

R	Higgins Mary—†	1	laundress	42	here
S	Hocsceta Peter	1	laborer	29	84 Green
T	Joidas John	1	"	54	here
U	Joidas Joseph	1	"	27	"
V	Keahes Peter	1	"	23	7 Chandler
W	Kulninch Harry	1	"	40	9 Hancock
X	Landon Ida F—†	1	saleswoman	50	here
Y	Leahy John	1	carpenter	59	"
Z	Long Martin	1	printer	37	"
A	Manning James	1	laborer	46	"
C	McCarty Peter A	1	printer	45	27 Myrtle
B	Mulville Horace	1	restaurateur	53	here
D	Mortaugh Matthew	1	laborer	44	131 Chambers
E	Nevins Charles	1	"	45	7 "
F	Peterson Olon	1	chauffeur	42	Concord
G	Randell Warren	1	elevatorman	47	here
H	Silver Frank	1	laborer	42	"
K	Smith Katherine—†	1	maid	42	10 Cambridge
L	Stewart Alexander	1	teamster	48	15 Harvard
M	Sullivan John J	1	laborer	45	New York
N	Tenerodi Conti	1	"	43	here
O	Williams Arthur	1	meatcutter	34	48 Cottage
P	Wilson Frank	1	laborer	31	131 Chambers
R	Chmarack Ornigue	3	window cleaner	29	here
S	Chornew Blazil	3	cook	43	"
T	Deduck Michael	3	machinist	35	Springfield
U	Dempsey James	3	laborer	45	76 Cambridge
V	Hayes Mary—†	3	waitress	27	Cambridge
W	Kelley Joseph	3	laborer	48	32 Staniford
X	Kulikowsky Joseph	3	lodging house	40	here
Y	Leroy Louis	3	tailor	40	Providence R I
Z	Mitchell Frank	3	fireman	43	Waterbury Ct
A	Mulligan Catherine—†	3	retired	65	here
B	Ribachuck Kyzma	3	dishwasher	33	40 Spring
C	Sirachuk Sidor	3	laborer	33	here
D	Vinageros Arthur	3	civil engineer	64	"
E	Whalen Edward B	3	machinist	27	"
F	Whalen Helen—†	3	housewife	24	"
G	Wilhunsky Jozet	3	laborer	35	"
H	Wiohnevriky John	3	"	29	"
L	Bonder Harry	5	"	33	140 Leverett

Page.	Letter.	FULL NAME.	Residence, April 1, 1924.	Occupation.	Supposed Age.	Reported Residence, April 1, 1923. Street and Number.

Hancock Street—Continued

	M	Cronin Patrick	5	laborer	49	here
	K	Cutamehnk Samuel	5	dishwasher	40	37 Lynde
	N	DeJulio Nicolas	5	tailor	50	here
	O	Dergaieva Elizabeth—†	5	lodging house	31	3 Hancock
	P	Dergaieva Joseph	5	machinist	41	here
	R	Garlad Joseph	5	waiter	36	300 Wash'n
	S	Hanson Henry	5	machinist	42	here
	T	Kelly John J	5	porter	45	"
	U	Leveland William	5	salesman	34	"
	V	Nepper Nicholas	5	machinist	35	3 Hancock
	W	Ranber Jack	5	porter	26	49 Saunders
	X	Rich Edward	5	baker	67	here
	Y	Rind William E	5	paperhanger	68	Maine
	Z	Welch Harry	5	cook	30	12 Hancock
	A	Wobst Fredrick	5	porter	37	here
	B	Yalzuskin Peter	5	laborer	32	7 Minot
	C	Zarkavik Steven	5	porter	40	12 Staniford
	D	Cleman Samuel	6	tailor	49	here
	E	Cloutiel Natpolan	6	laborer	47	"
	F	Johnson Carl	6	stevedore	47	"
	G	Johnson Marie—†	6	housekeeper	45	"
	H	Leeds William	6	contractor	32	"
	K	Lopkin Ella—†	6	housekeeper	29	"
	L	Lopkin John	6	tailor	31	"
	M	Carr Frank	7	cigarmaker	54	"
	N	Crooks Rose L—†	7	housekeeper	58	"
	O	Crooks William J	7	lather	64	"
	P	Granoff Abraham	7	clerk	23	"
	R	Hancock Herman	7	shoeworker	35	Lynn
	S	Harris William	7	cook	45	here
	T	Miiler Samuel	7	restaurateur	32	"
	U	Mooney Maurice	7	engineer	52	"
	V	Rubin Samuel	7	salesman	40	"
	W	Schecter Jacob	7	"	22	"
	X	Sears Frank	7	painter	58	Texas
	Y	Timbler Fred	7	cigarmaker	57	Atlanta Ga
	Z	Tranter Bertram K	7	R R man	48	here
	A	Wezleicki Macystuw	7	machinist	40	"
	B	Blake Robert	8	laborer	28	Gloucester
	C	Blood Hazen D	8	salesman	44	here
	D	Blood Mary E—†	8	lodging house	35	"

Hancock Street—Continued

E	Goldman Isaac	8	tailor	46	here
F	Gray James	8	plasterer	22	Scotland
G	Gray Robert	8	"	28	"
H	Irish James	8	engineer	34	"
K	Lawder Harry W	8	waiter	28	767 Tremont
L	O'Brien Michael	8	printer	37	here
M	Racicot Eugene	8	painter	41	"
N	Racicot Margaret—†	8	waitress	31	"
O	Robinson Catherine—†	8	"	38	"
P	Robinson James W	8	elevatorman	72	"
R	Shafter Arthur	8	clerk	54	"
S	Sheridan Alice—†	8	housewife	37	507 Beacon
T	Sheridan William	8	fireman	34	507 "
U	Stone Henry	8	retired	71	here
W	Tarle Gertrude—†	9	bookkeeper	22	"
X	Tarle Henry	9	pressman	55	"
Y	Tarle Leah—†	9	housewife	50	"
Z	Tarle Samuel	9	salesman	28	"
A	Brown Abraham	9	musician	22	35 McLean
B	Brown Esther—†	9	bookkeeper	27	35 "
C	Brown Harry	9	salesman	52	35 "
D	Brown Irving	9	"	25	35 "
E	Brown Rose—†	9	housewife	47	35 "
F	Schofield Agnes—†	9	"	66	34 Myrtle
G	Schofield Gertrude—†	9	clerk	25	34 "
H	Schofield William	9	"	27	34 "
K	Poulos Demanto	9	housewife	33	here
L	Poulos Pantazs	9	fruit	37	"
M	Poulos Peter	9	"	43	"
N	Barry David	10	printer	39	Malden
O	Consales Peter A	10	physician	26	Somerville
P	Grise Aral P	10	chemist	42	here
R	McCormack John	10	machinist	45	"
S	McManus Frank	10	manager	22	156 Centre
T	Peltier William	10	waiter	21	here
U	Robinson John	10	lodging house	27	"
V	Robinson Mildred—†	10	housewife	23	"
W	Stout William	10	clergyman	80	"
X	Andrews Eugene	11	laborer	68	"
Y	Billings William C	11	clerk	50	11 Bowdoin
Z	Elder Jessie—†	11	lodging house	40	here

Hancock Street—Continued

A	Flynn Dennis	11	special police	40	here
A¹	Lawler Thomas J	11	physician	60	"
B	Lynch Martin J	11	watchman	47	"
C	McLaughlin Danial	11	janitor	60	61 Joy
D	Silverman Max	11	pressman	38	19 S Russell
E	Brown Henry	12	salesman	37	Haverhill
F	Burns Bernard A	12	"	58	here
G	Cavanaugh Vincent	12	draughtsman	27	63 Austin
H	Cole Irving	12	carpenter	44	Maine
K	Denning Gertrude H—†	12	housekeeper	49	here
L	Duncanson Sarah—†	12	waitress	35	26 Temple
M	Elovitz Samuel	12	shoemaker	39	here
N	Henegen Mary—†	12	waitress	52	1 Myrtle
O	Henegan Timothy	12	clerk	69	1 "
P	Lothrop Fannie M—†	12	housewife	73	94 Bowdoin
R	Lothrop James W	12	retired	68	94 "
S	McGloan Mary—†	12	compositor	50	here
T	McGorcen Frank	12	laborer	65	9 Chambers
U	Pendleton Oren L	12	secretary	22	Maine
V	Perry Mary—†	12	housewife	86	Nova Scotia
W	Perry Nichols T	12	lodging house	67	here
X	Prescott William	12	painter	55	26 Temple
Y	Reynolds Edward	12	waiter	35	here
Z	Stickney Frederick M	12	orderly	28	27 Hancock
A	Walker Annie—†	12	postal clerk	50	here
B	Cunningham Frank	13	clerk	32	"
C	Jackson Mary E—†	13	lodging house	42	"
D	Kosch John	13	newsdealer	35	"
E	Lee Mary—†	13	houseworker	44	"
F	O'Connor Lawrence	13	laborer	30	"
G	Page Helen L—†	14	housewife	42	"
K	Lynch Mary A—†	14	waitress	37	"
L	Tripp Harry E	14	expressman	28	"
M	Tripp Mary E—†	14	housewife	29	"
N	Kolodziej Anna E—†	14	"	27	"
O	Kolodziej Michel	14	clerk	29	"
P	Linehan Gertrude M—†	14	housewife	32	"
R	Linehan Joseph F	14	undertaker	67	"
S	Linehan Margret—†	14	clerk	27	"
T	Quinlan Thomas F	14	upholsterer	60	"
U	Jezierski Bronislas A	14	clerk	35	"

Hancock Street—Continued

v	Jezierski Julia C—†	14	housewife	31	here
w	Kogos Minnie—†	14	"	41	"
x	Mintz Harry	14	laborer	35	"
y	Palischuk Samual	14	pressman	32	"
a	Campbell Jennie—†	14	waitress	33	"
b	Simen Emma R—†	14	clerk	28	"
c	Simen John W	14	machinist	60	"
d	Simen Karen—†	14	housewife	54	"
e	Simmons Eva—†	14	"	40	"
f	Simmons James	14	grocer	45	"
g	Adams Gladys—†	15	housewife	33	"
h	Adams Grace—†	15	houseworker	50	"
k	Adams Jay Roger	15	musician	45	"
l	Ambrosio Robert	15	laborer	30	"
m	Connor Frank	15	"	38	"
n	Contos Charles	15	fruit	38	"
o	Doherty Josiah	15	elevatorman	50	"
p	Folsom Isa—†	15	seamstress	55	"
r	Snow Frank L	15	clerk	60	"
s	Hines Sarah E—†	16	superintendent	60	"
t	MacLeod Mary—†	16	attendant	30	Halifax N S
u	Small Kathlene—†	16	"	30	here
v	Chalkee Albert S	17	meatcutter	22	Canada
w	Cook William	17	chef	61	39 Cambridge
x	DeLance Franklin	17	waiter	22	Waterford Ct
y	Higgins Hanna—†	17	housekeeper	60	51 Temple
z	Kotonski Hugh	17	meatcutter	24	Providence R I
a	Slater Elizabeth—†	17	dressmaker	28	Canada
b	Watkins William	17	baker	39	England
c	Zolotoz Samuel	17	salesman	35	20 Hancock
d	Burrill Emily F—†	18	housewife	46	Europe
e	Fowler Edith—†	18	artist	38	67 Chestnut
f	Fowler Susan—†	18	houseworker	78	67 "
h	McDonald Alice—†	18	"	22	Middleboro
k	Stein Albert A	18	druggist	41	here
l	Stein Celia—†	18	housewife	35	"
m	Stroyman Barned	18	student	25	"
n	Greenberg Joseph	18	storekeeper	47	"
o	Greenberg Julia—†	18	housewife	46	"
p	Brown George	19	furrier	30	47 Hancock
r	Connors Michael J	19	packer	45	here

Hancock Street—Continued

s	Dickinson Blanche—†	19	housekeeper	27	here
t	Dickinson Ethel M—†	19	"	50	"
u	Dickinson Harold S	19	salesman	30	"
v	Handy John	19	student	25	Maine
w	Higgins Lydia S—†	19	housewife	70	here
x	Lippie Dante	19	clerk	50	Lowell
y	Lyons John	19	artist	30	Revere
z	Martin Sylvia—†	19	student	23	Maine
a	Quinlan Edward J	19	student	23	Bristol Ct
b	Tyler Earl	19	"	25	Maine
c	Weinroub Harry	19	manager	30	47 Hancock
d	Cate Stanley H	20	electrician	33	here
e	Clement Helen—†	20	bookkeeper	40	"
f	Davis Mabel—†	20	shoestitcher	27	30 Hancock
g	Gleason Margaret—†	20	seamstress	50	25 "
h	Griffin Alice M—†	20	secretary	30	Danvers
k	Jackson Dora M—†	20	housekeeper	68	here
l	Jackson Frank O	20	retired	72	"
m	Kuhn Herbert R	20	lawyer	31	Brookline
n	Langley Benjamin F	20	engineer	47	here
o	MacKeown Thomas C	20	baker	48	Lowell
p	Mahoney Abbie C—†	20	waitress	38	here
r	Mahoney Daniel A	20	clerk	40	"
s	Perkins Frank O	20	engineer	53	"
t	Shafftman Benjamin	20	insurance	40	10 Hancock
u	Woodrow Bertha—†	20	cashier	30	Berlin N H
v	Bryant Ida M—†	21	clerk	64	19 Hancock
w	Butler Winifred E—†	21	houseworker	40	15 Allston
x	Clark Annie M—†	21	saleswoman	64	Billerica
y	Fuller Howard E	21	lawyer	31	here
z	Isenbeck Gustave	21	real estate	23	Peabody
e	Loomis Mary—†	21	chambermaid	53	here
a	Mullen Jeremiah	21	porter	65	Westwood
b	North William	21	polishmaker	65	17 Hancock
c	Ricard Annett—†	21	housewife	36	Canada
d	Ricard Joseph	21	cook	42	"
f	Aipins Fannie—†	22	retired	70	here
g	Anderson Nancy—†	22	"	78	"
h	Armistead Mary E—†	22	housekeeper	61	"
k	Brooks Martha—†	22	retired	70	"
l	Brown Hulda—†	22	"	67	"

Hancock Street—Continued

M	Brown Matilda—†	22	retired	71	here
N	Christian Catherine—†	22	"	67	"
O	Cousins Martha—†	22	"	75	Newburyport
P	Deering Maria—†	22	"	71	here
R	Fynes Isabel—†	22	"	68	"
S	Hatfield Alice—†	22	"	50	"
T	Johnson Agnes—†	22	"	81	2 Concord pl
U	Johnson Victoria—†	22	"	50	Springfield
V	Jowziff Anna—†	22	"	65	here
W	Lester Margaret—†	22	"	71	"
X	Matthews Marcissa—†	22	"	84	Medford
Y	Merrick Anna—†	22	"	75	6 Mill
Z	Nelson Fannie—†	22	"	60	here
A	Taylor Agnes—†	22	retired	71	94 Camden
B	Bain Bessie—†	23	saleswoman	43	44 Pinckney
C	Barker Walter E	23	manager	46	here
D	Foley Warren G	23	waiter	79	"
E	Madden Thomas	23	lineman	33	Manchester
F	Merrill John M	23	engineer	66	here
G	Ross Frederick F	23	shipper	48	10 Joy
H	Rouillard Cora L—†	23	landlady	41	here
K	Sargent Charles T	23	clerk	75	"
L	Watson John F	23	retired	83	"
M	Cusie s Aidille E—†	24	pianist	37	"
N	Fine Morris	24	clerk	29	"
O	Hadley Fred M	24	trainman	64	"
P	Kerien Mena K—†	24	stitcher	48	"
V	Lyon Edward H	24	clerk	69	"
W	McMillan Hugh C	24	electrician	52	"
R	Morse Nellie P—†	24	secretary	56	"
S	Morse Nettie P—†	24	housekeeper	56	"
X	Murphy Neal J	24	bellboy	21	Milton
T	Robinson Blanche S—†	24	typist	59	here
U	Robinson Frank P	24	salesman	58	"
Y	Swan Arthur H	24	inspector	39	"
Z	Connor Mary L—†	25	nurse	44	"
A	Cox Thomas	25	stitcher	40	Bangor Me
B	Heath Charles A	25	salesman	48	here
C	Heath Elizabeth M—†	25	landlady	41	"
D	Kenney Arthur L	25	chef	52	"
E	Lee James H	25	carpenter	54	Quincy

Hancock Street—Continued

F	Ross George	25	foreman	43	here
G	Sliney Katherine—†	25	waitress	52	"
H	Smith George M	25	engineer	38	Harrisburg Pa
K	Stevens Elizabeth M—†	25	waitress	37	here
L	Taylor Jane—†	25	examiner	22	"
M	Thompson Alfred	25	artist	48	20 Pinckney
N	Abraham Sarah—†	26	dressmaker	27	22 Staniford
O	Antonaros Michael	26	waiter	34	here
P	Collins Bernice—†	26	waitress	25	Portland Me
R	Hannon Margaret—†	26	maid	50	27 Hollis
S	MacDonald Agnes—†	26	tel operator	30	8 Worcester sq
T	Myles Alice—†	26	housewife	30	here
U	Myles Gertrude—†	26	"	26	"
V	Myles Robert	26	carpenter	26	"
W	Myles Walter	26	"	30	"
X	Orkin John	26	jeweler	51	"
Y	Orkin Rose—†	26	housewife	46	"
Z	Pynn John	26	carpenter	43	"
A	Pynn Mabel—†	26	housekeeper	46	"
D	Reps John	26	student	35	Cambridge
B	Sweetland Emma—†	26	housekeeper	35	Newfoundland
C	Sweetland Hubert	26	laborer	37	"
E	Torsney Patrick	26	gardener	48	here
F	Brennan Joseph E	27	salesman	32	Rhode Island
G	Collins James	27	clerk	50	here
H	Corbett Frank L	27	"	30	Malden
K	Doival Edward	27	cook	28	New York
L	Dooley Anna—†	27	saleswoman	32	here
M	Dorris Micheal J	27	overseer	40	"
N	Doyle Margaret—†	27	seamstress	45	45 Hancock
O	Drinkwater Edward J	27	bookkeeper	35	24 "
P	Dunphy Mary—†	27	stenographer	25	here
R	Fessenden James	27	clerk	59	"
S	Hamilton Edward	27	cook	30	Buffalo N Y
T	Holloway Catherine—†	27	landlady	48	here
U	Muller Albert	27	laborer	28	51 Hancock
V	O'Toole Patrick	27	clerk	73	here
W	Pase William	27	pugilist	24	Montreal Canada
X	Van Norman Everett	27	laborer	27	New York
Y	Wells Susie J—†	27	retired	60	here
Z	Whipple Frank A	27	laborer	50	Charlestown

Hancock Street—Continued

A	Wunderlind Frederick	27	physician	35	Connecticut
B	Yovick Anthony	27	waiter	30	3 N Anderson
C	Akin Louie	28	trainman	35	here
D	Boland Anna—†	28	houseworker	43	"
E	Brown Walter E	28	auditor	37	"
F	Camsil Angie—†	28	saleswoman	48	"
G	Caramanico Daniel	28	lawyer	32	"
H	Jacobson Wolf	28	agent	27	"
K	Jewell Alice—†	28	houseworker	63	"
L	Jewell Edward	28	salesman	64	"
M	Jones Clifton	28	retired	66	"
N	Lamb Grace—†	28	houseworker	38	"
O	Lamb James	28	druggist	44	"
P	Pearce William B	28	retired	79	"
R	Rose Frank	28	leatherworker	32	Newport R I
S	Vincent Charles	28	machinist	40	here
T	Vincent Eva—†	28	housewife	40	Newburyport
U	Avery Emily—†	29	factoryworker	23	250 Mass av
V	Battles Margaret—†	29	retired	83	here
W	Breathan Annett—†	29	"	73	"
X	Campion James	29	towerman	70	"
Y	Campion Martha—†	29	cashier	60	"
Z	Carpenter Eva—†	29	domestic	42	30 Hancock
A	Cassidy Frank	29	metalworker	55	here
B	Chisholm John	29	clerk	50	"
C	Cummings James	29	"	50	"
D	David Richard R	29	laborer	27	New York
E	Dulginson Carl	29	mason	50	19 Hancock
F	Fisher Juel—†	29	waitress	25	here
G	Getchel Anna—†	29	typesetter	80	"
H	Gilson Edward	29	conductor	54	"
K	Hawkins Geraldine—†	29	waitress	27	"
L	Haynes Charles	29	watchman	63	"
M	Hess John	29	carpetlayer	50	"
N	Karevenco Stephen	29	cook	30	"
O	Korner Jacob	29	shoeworker	42	52 Chambers
P	Labou Morris	29	"	34	Maine
R	Lokes William	29	printer	29	Framingham
S	Maguire James	29	waiter	70	here
T	Martin Joseph	29	special police	50	"
U	McMahon Nora—†	29	stenographer	32	"

Hancock Street—Continued

v	McNeal Archibald	29	printer	43	32 Burrell
w	Mooney Catherine—†	29	dressmaker	32	98 Bowdoin
x	Morse Charles	29	mason	32	here
y	Morse Helen—†	29	landlady	26	"
z	Osgood George	29	waiter	30	31 Temple
A	Projedska Rose—†	29	manicurist	20	98 Bowdoin
B	Ray Harold	29	clerk	50	here
c	Raymond Beatrice—†	29	"	26	"
c	Tucker Alice—†	29	secretary	40	"
E	Washburn Letty—†	29	saleswoman	50	"
F	White Lottie—†	29	clerk	21	98 Bowdoin
G	Wolk Benjamin	29	tailor	35	36 Floyd
H	Adams Roy	30	waiter	28	here
K	Ainsley Benjamin	30	salesman	22	Allston
L	Bennett William	30	R R man	68	here
M	Cornish Clifford C	30	manager	36	Blackstone H
N	Flinn Helen—†	30	nurse	38	11 Queensberry
o	Gilleck Mary—†	30	cook	34	6 Staniford
P	Gilleck Phillip	30	steward	40	6 "
R	Goodman Joseph	30	restaurateur	35	Providence R I
s	Harding Mary—†	30	clerk	32	37 Bowdoin
T	Karp Abraham	30	salesman	22	63 Campbell av
U	Leonard Carrie—†	30	waitress	27	here
v	Ratnoff Anna—†	30	telegrapher	28	"
w	Ratnoff Max	30	student	28	"
x	Silver Benjamin	30	salesman	25	Georgia
y	Smith Frank	30	"	28	here
z	Vigdor Wolfe	30	"	33	Everett
A	Willner Aarron	30	"	23	Revere
B	Woods Fred C	30	bricklayer	58	New Bedford
c	Woods Nellie—†	30	housekeeper	53	"
D	Wynne Richard	30	physician	52	here
E	Collins Fred H	32	expressman	41	Randolph
F	Girraca Frank	32	"	27	133 Eliot
G	Lapoint Bertha—†	32	clerk	23	90 Marion
H	Larkin Anthony	32	teamster	24	295 W Fourth
K	McAuley Elizabeth—†	32	housewife	27	67 Hancock
L	McAuley Frances H—†	32	saleswoman	25	67 "
M	McAuley John W	32	salesman	34	67 "
N	McAuley Kathleen B—†	32	saleswoman	23	67 "
o	McAuley Mary M—†	32	operator	26	67 "

Hancock Street—Continued

P	Rogers Mabel V—†	32	waitress	31	6 Hancock
R	Sethman Andrew O	32	decorator	39	154 Warren av
S	Sethman Anna E—†	32	housewife	38	154 "
T	Trembly Florence—†	32	waiter	25	30 Hancock
U	Will Alden T	32	radioworker	33	Chelsea
V	Will Harnett	32	clerk	24	65 Hancock
W	Bennett Arthur W	33	milliner	68	Natick
X	Foss Fay W	33	clerk	43	here
Y	Foss Helen W—†	33	landlady	39	"
Z	Gatsos John	33	student	25	"
A	George Arthur	33	meat cutter	40	Greece
B	Ham Francis N	33	lineman	21	Worcester
C	MacIsaac Ira	33	bookkeeper	32	33 Pinckney
D	Morrison Louis N	33	mechanic	48	35 Union Park
E	Nalwaka Peter	33	clerk	21	here
F	Porter Ernest	33	cashier	56	"
G	Rush Durward C	33	lineman	21	Henniker N H
H	Shurin John	33	tailor	30	55½ Allen
K	Swensen Carl	33	retired	70	16 Temple
L	Treamer Scott	33	clerk	26	here
M	Armetage Mabel—†	34	nurse	40	"
N	Blanchard Joseph	34	draughtsman	21	Chelsea
O	Chamfoux Raymond L	34	civil engineer	25	Pawtucket R I
P	Davis Frances—†	34	clerk	50	here
R	Foss Robert O	34	"	30	"
S	Kozloff Victor R	34	advertising	59	39 Hancock
T	Moses Max	34	salesman	35	here
U	Murdock Maude—†	34	secretary	40	24 Pinckney
V	O'Rourke William C	34	student	45	here
W	Robinson Walter H	34	agent	62	"
X	Savage Charles A	34	printer	38	"
Y	Snow Herbert F	34	baggagemaster	65	"
Z	Stone Charles	34	hospitalworker	54	"
A	Suett Addie F—†	34	saleswoman	50	"
B	Wilkins Dorothy E—†	34	student	21	"
C	Wilkins Gwendolyn E—†	34	housewife	42	"
D	Berthoud Ferdinand	35	author	45	Springfield
E	Bigelow E Sherman, jr	35	nurse	57	Hartford Ct
F	Blaikie Bessie E—†	35	clerk	45	Canada
G	Burby Grace H—†	35	"	35	Cambridge
H	Daden Sadie—†	35	bookbinder	26	Canada

Hancock Street—Continued

K	Fisher Ella—†	35	housewife	55	here
L	Fisher Walter L	35	bookkeeper	57	35 Hancock
M	Kimball Hester M—†	35	clergyman	53	Pittsfield N H
N	Le Barron Arthur G	35	salesman	67	Springfield
O	Maguire Edward G	35	barber	45	here
P	Marston George F	35	retired	70	"
R	Rutherford Harry W	35	clerk	48	"
S	Shepherd Alfred D	35	"	26	Canada
T	Shepherd Alfred H	35	porter	55	Nova Scotia
U	Shepherd Cecil R	35	storekeeper	22	Canada
V	Wills Edith M—†	35	landlady	53	here
W	Keegan Mary B—†	36	housekeeper	30	"
X	Prior James E	36	doctor	60	"
Y	Prior Marie A—†	36	housewife	55	"
Z	Rice Andrew	36	teacher	24	35 Temple
A	Rice Bertha W—†	36	"	47	35 "
B	Young Effie—†	36	missionary	65	35 "
C	Randlett Josephine G—†	36	milliner	57	here
D	Bartevian Gregory	36	merchant	37	W Newton
E	Bartevian Vera—†	36	housewife	30	"
F	Chisholm Alexandra A—†	36	nurse	35	Audubon rd
G	Fessenden John L	36	clerk	24	38 Hancock
H	Hellen Lillian M—†	36	housewife	53	here
K	Hellen Samuel H	36	coal dealer	61	"
L	Bigelow Cora—†	36	lawyer	57	"
M	Bigelow Irene E—†	36	housewife	85	"
N	Bradlee Clara D—†	36	housekeeper	50	"
O	Bradlee Helen W—†	36	lawyer	35	"
P	Dupee Hadasah—†	36	housewife	58	New York
R	MacDonald Esther—†	36	"	92	here
S	McHale Patrick	36	student	21	"
T	Newell Emma—†	36	milliner	60	"
U	McKenna Catherine—†	36	housewife	30	"
V	McKenna John	36	teacher	30	"
W	Gilman Edith—†	36	housewife	42	"
X	Gilman George W	36	engineer	22	"
Y	Gilman William H	36	shoe dealer	52	"
Z	Parmelee Matilda—†	36	dry goods	60	"
A	Parmelee Orra—†	36	housewife	43	"
B	Gallivan Thomas W	36	bookkeeper	48	"
C	White Alice A—†	36	housewife	52	"

Hancock Street—Continued

D	White Fred H	36	superintendent	64	here	
E	Kennedy Josephine—†	36	waitress	45	"	
F	Roberts Henry J	36	conductor	46	"	
G	Steves Jarvis S	36	signalman	45	"	
H	Steves Seymour	36	electrician	21	New Brunswick	
K	Allen Edward H	37	physician	55	here	
L	Allen Linda—†	37	housewife	50	"	
M	Allen Nathanial D	37	student	20	"	
N	Sutherland Agusta—†	37	houseworker	50	"	
O	Beseke Herman	38	retired	55	"	
P	Camp Harriet M—†	38	agent	50	"	
R	Cohen Max	38	shoe dealer	38	"	
S	Condosses Arthur	38	salesman	33	"	
T	Davis William	38	contractor	50	"	
U	Dosick Ralph	38	tailor	31	"	
V	Friedman Jacob C	38	salesman	43	"	
W	Green Mason A	38	editor	74	"	
X	Karyyeans George	38	candymaker	28	"	
Y	Mospan Fred	38	salesman	37	"	
Z	Ried John	38	tailor	30	37 Hancock	
A	Ross James	38	retired	70	here	
B	Thema Pantello	38	salesman	45	"	
C	Woods Annie—†	38	stenographer	35	"	
D	Woods Patrick H	38	clerk	55	"	
E	Zembler Louis	38	salesman	35	"	
F	Zilg Alois	38	retired	60	"	
G	Zilg Bridget—†	38	housewife	53	"	
H	Zilg Francis	38	shipper	23	"	
K	Zilg Kathyrn H—†	38	manager	26	"	
L	Caplan David	39	manufacturer	74	"	
M	Caplan Ida—†	39	housekeeper	70	"	
N	Caplan James	39	manager	29	"	
O	Caplan Leah—†	39	housekeeper	23	"	
P	Grossman Benjimin L	39	foreman	33	"	
R	Grossman Helen A—†	39	housewife	32	"	
S	Bertram Ada R—†	40	"	47	"	
T	Blackwood Harold	40	student	27	Maine	
U	Cammon Hazel—†	40	waitress	26	here	
V	Glidden Earlin	40	restaurateur	54	"	
W	Glidden Harriet—†	40	housewife	50	"	
X	Hardy William	40	newsdealer	34	"	

Hancock Street—Continued

Y	Hinckey Micheal	40	bookkeeper	57	here
z	Litchfield Fred	40	clerk	35	"
A	Moulton Helen—†	40	retired	47	Vermont
B	Munroe James F	40	librarian	69	here
C	Perry Lewis	40	druggist	67	"
D	Powers Morris	40	bacteriologist	37	Providence R I
E	Robinson Helen—†	40	housemaid	30	60 Temple
F	Robinson Lawrence	40	automobiles	32	60 "
G	Stevens Oliver	40	insurance	38	49 Hancock
H	Welch Helen—†	40	housekeeper	42	Somerville
K	Whalen Charles	40	student	32	Manchester N H
L	Boulos George	41	laundryworker	28	here
M	Garvin Frank	41	waiter	28	"
N	Goodhue Goerge	41	electrician	50	"
O	Hemphill Dela—†	41	waitress	23	"
P	Hemphill Grace—†	41	"	21	"
R	Hemphill Ruth—†	41	"	24	"
S	Hicks George	41	clerk	38	"
T	Marks Edith—†	41	stenographer	33	"
U	McMasters Frank	41	chef	30	"
V	Morris Alice M—†	41	housewife	46	"
W	Nixon Fredrick	41	student	32	"
X	Nute Arthur	41	chauffeur	34	"
Y	Smart Edward	41	shipper	53	"
Z	Thorn Lillian—†	41	housekeeper	42	"
A	Brown Peter	43	chauffeur	22	"
B	Desrochers Laura—†	43	factory worker	20	"
C	Haliway Edward	43	watchman	61	"
D	Johnes William	43	mechanic	50	"
E	Kirkland Agnes—†	43	operator	30	"
F	Kirkland Barney	43	U S A	43	"
G	Miller John	43	porter	63	"
H	Peters Francis	43	window washer	21	"
K	Turin Simon	43	butcher	34	"
L	Varoque Jane—†	43	factory worker	22	"
M	Anderson Albert	45	plumber	20	Wilmington
N	Durant George W	45	accountant	23	Rockland
O	Glick Morris	45	salesman	35	here
P	Holdman William P	45	leatherworker	22	"
R	Hunt John S	45	janitor	63	"
S	Hunt Robert R	45	elevatorman	31	"

Hancock Street—Continued

T	Law Louise—†	45	elocutionist	45	Maine
U	Philbrook Ormand H	45	carpenter	42	here
V	Pollard Robert S	45	leatherworker	39	Woburn
W	Swann Walter	45	blacksmith	34	7 Upton
X	Taylor Bertrand W	45	lawyer	24	here
Y	Taylor John L	45	photo printer	54	"
Z	Weinstein Morris	45	salesman	40	"
A	Young Michael	45	waiter	39	72 Myrtle
B	Carudonno Joseph	47	student	29	here
C	Crawford G Edward	47	chef	29	"
D	Crawford Jean H—†	47	stenographer	20	"
E	Kelley Alice C—†	47	housewife	45	"
F	Kelley Thomas H	47	salesman	48	"
G	Orkin Harry	47	"	37	"
H	Rosen Phillip	47	"	28	"
K	Bowden Albert L	49	stonecutter	64	"
L	Bowden Almira—†	49	housekeeper	48	"
M	Chiaramante Felix	49	correspondent	55	42 Bowdoin
N	Fine Joseph	49	clerk	28	here
O	Freeman Harold	49	accountant	24	"
P	Freeman Maude B—†	49	housewife	22	"
R	Heinemelman Paul G	49	shipper	20	New Brunswick
S	Hendersen William R	49	engineer	58	here
T	Mason Harold S	49	clerk	32	"
U	Mason Joseph B	49	compositor	37	"
V	Minehan James	49	detective	32	31 Allston
W	Papagelis Charles	49	merchant	31	here
X	Barile Lenard	49	barber	30	"
Y	Ritcey Winfred L—†	49	coffee roaster	25	Nova Scotia
Z	Rosenberg Iasac	49	broker	32	here
A	Scanlon George	49	manager	31	"
B	Staff Peter	49	"	32	"
C	Stenborg Irene—†	49	bookkeeper	22	Revere
D	Stenborg Marion—†	49	housewife	21	"
E	Lamski Bruno U	49	cleaner	35	8 Bulfinch
F	Allen Bessie R—†	51	nurse	29	33 Mt Vernon
G	Cassidy William J	51	superintendent	45	Brookline
H	Coundrey Howard	51	musician	23	Lynn
K	Deion Charles	51	mechanic	28	New Hampshire
L	Deion Jennie—†	51	nurse	25	"
M	Donovan Elizabeth—†	51	chambermaid	33	33 Mt Vernon

Page.	Letter.	Full Name.	Residence, April 1, 1924.	Occupation.	Supposed Age.	Reported Residence, April 1, 1923. Street and Number.

Hancock Street—Continued

	x	Ellis Jessie—†	51	nurse	37	33 Mt Vernon
	o	La Roy James L	51	bookkeeper	30	here
	p	Orcutt Ralph S	51	mechanic	35	"
	r	Stanley Ada M—†	51	housekeeper	63	"
	s	Stanley Alma M—†	51	"	27	69 Hancock
	t	Stanley Garnet U	51	salesman	42	69 "
	u	White Benjimin W	51	musician	29	Springfield
	v	Allen Samuel P	53	real estate	78	here
	w	Burlingame Walter F	53	clerk	53	"
	x	Dean Alexander T	53	salesman	55	"
	y	Elliot Eliza H—†	53	housekeeper	56	"
	z	Gilmore David	53	real estate	48	"
	a	Morris Edward L	53	bookkeeper	81	"
	b	Russell Agnes—†	53	housekeeper	53	"
	c	Allen John	57	engineer	45	21 Temple
	d	Cullen Charles V	57	paperhanger	48	here
	e	Dubrau William F	57	clerk	51	"
	f	Dubrau William F, jr	57	"	21	"
	g	Keltie Robert B	57	"	35	Malden
	h	Towle Agnes E—†	57	housekeeper	36	here
	k	Towle Charles E	57	physician	52	"
	l	Weiand Albert	57	professor	55	Chicago Ill
	o	Addleman Olga E—†	61	clerk	32	here
	p	Brogna Ralph	61	laborer	32	"
	r	Carter Annette—†	61	stenographer	35	"
	s	Fulton Susan D—†	61	accountant	36	10 Pinckney
	t	Hunter Walter	61	"	35	28 Hancock
	u	Langmaid Lillian F—†	61	housekeeper	37	Maine
	v	Langmaid Thomas	61	machinist	37	"
	w	MacAlister Elizabeth J—†	61	stenographer	39	14 Pinckney
	x	Riley Lena—†	61	"	36	here
	y	Wesche Emma—†	61	housewife	39	"
	z	Wesche Reinhard R	61	electrician	38	"
	a	Barcley Robert	63	engineer	49	New York
	b	Bolen George	63	salesman	43	here
	c	Dyar Perlie A	63	merchant	67	"
	d	Englund Gustav	63	tailor	35	132 W Newton
	e	Hailey Mabel H—†	63	bookkeeper	44	Cambridge
	f	Jones Charles	63	druggist	47	here
	g	Jones Clarie—†	63	housewife	48	Arlington
	h	Hannen Alice—†	63	housekeeper	40	Denver Col

Hancock Street—Continued

K	Henderson Beatrice—†	63	stenographer	27	Derry N H
L	Morrison Jennie—†	63	housekeeper	71	here
M	O'Hare John T	63	insurance agent	50	Cambridge
N	Reed Ruth V—†	63	secretary	33	Brookline
O	Rowe Lucy P—†	63	clerk	59	here
P	Shaver Earl	63	architect	35	Canada
R	Shaver Ellen—†	63	housewife	30	"
S	Smith Alonzo H	63	clergyman	49	here
T	Smith Florence V—†	63	housewife	48	"
U	Stearns Helen H—†	63	clerk	39	Brookline
V	Anderson Alice J—†	65	bookkeeper	29	Somerville
W	Burnham Harold E	65	student	23	Maine
X	Cook Arnold	65	clerk	28	New York
Y	Dominy Nathaniel M	65	student	27	162 Newbury
Z	Eaton Ethel M—†	65	clerk	32	Andover
A	Gates Gilbert	65	restaurateur	60	here
B	Goddard Barbara C—†	65	secretary	24	Newton
C	Goddard Paul M	65	broker	27	"
D	Hahn David	65	student	20	New Bedford
E	Kempton Amelda S—†	65	bookkeeper	69	here
F	Offutt Ellen J—†	65	clerk	40	"
G	Papkin Barney	65	student	20	New Bedford
H	Tomb George W	65	architect	34	here
K	Yeager Hugh F	65	clerk	35	New Bedford
L	Yeager Lena F—†	65	nurse	32	"
M	Bailey Minnie A—†	67	teacher	35	here
N	Herbert George	67	shipper	63	"
O	Hills Catherine—†	67	tailoress	65	"
P	Johnson George W	67	switchman	50	"
R	Kendrick Murray	67	clerk	26	Canada
S	Leach Etta—†	67	stitcher	65	here
T	McMurdo Beecher	67	clerk	20	Moncton N B
U	McMurdo John W	67	"	27	36 Temple
V	Phillips Charles	67	painter	65	here
W	Phillips Nellie—†	67	housewife	60	"
X	Rogerson Robert	67	lawyer	42	"
Y	Slack Stella J—†	67	housekeeper	40	Brookline
Z	Smith Helen—†	67	clerk	22	here
A	Williams Lawrence	67	porter	30	Cambridge
B	Benson Herbert H	69	retired	59	Florida
C	Fehr Henry	69	waiter	27	Mass Gen Hosp

Hancock Street—Continued

D	Hawkins John B	69	clerk	20	here
E	Putnam Frances—†	69	teacher	60	"
F	Shasta Theodore S	69	student	23	Cambridge
G	Thomas William	69	watchman	65	here
H	Tweedy Pensy S—†	69	housekeeper	57	"
K	Van Iderstine Minnie—†	69	"	57	"
L	Wires Alden	69	clerk	21	Rockport
M	Barcley Alexander H	71	tinsmith	51	here
N	Forgan Eliza K—†	71	housekeeper	70	"
O	Gallant Adeline—†	71	stenographer	23	Canada
S	Johnson Rasmus	71	laborer	52	here
T	Lawrence Walter F	71	toolmaker	67	"
U	MacLeod Helen—†	71	stenographer	21	Denver Col
V	MacLeod Ida—†	71	cashier	51	"
P	Shultz John R	71	clerk	37	here
R	Smith Emerson	71	musician	37	"
W	White Charles H	71	merchant	64	"
X	White Elizabeth N—†	71	housekeeper	57	"
Y	Dunbar Annie—†	73	"	40	"
Z	Fraser Christine—†	73	"	26	"
A	Hardy Helna—†	73	"	45	182 Com av
B	Hardy Milton	73	salesman	50	182 "
C	Highland Thelma—†	73	student	21	21 Joy
D	Leavitt Ralph	73	"	21	Portsmouth N H
E	Murdock Dorothy—†	73	stenographer	20	21 Joy
F	Pierce Edward	73	clerk	21	61 Hancock
G	Triwen May—†	73	teacher	40	here
H	Condon Katherine—†	75	waitress	30	"
K	Converse Ida J—†	75	housewife	36	"
L	Converse Samuel	75	manager	33	"
M	Forrest Allan	75	waiter	40	"
N	Gardaman Allan H	75	student	29	Philadelphia
O	Hudson Willard A	75	investigator	23	Providence R I
P	Jones Grace J—†	75	waitress	44	Egypt
R	Kingman Albert P	75	student	36	here
S	McLean Alexander	75	retired	84	Florida
T	McLean Ida—†	75	housewife	65	"
U	Tiffany Charles H	75	manager	60	here
V	Wade Joseph H	75	teamster	45	220 Mass av
W	Wade Margaret—†	75	cook	45	220 "

Page	Letter	Full Name.	Residence, April 1, 1924.	Occupation.	Supposed Age.	Reported Residence, April 1, 1923. Street and Number.

Joy Street

Y	O'Neill Elizebeth—†	1	housewife	63	here
Z	O'Neill Herbert W	1	chemist	25	Fall River
A	O'Neill John A	1	musician	30	here
B	O'Neill Thomas H	1	janitor	59	"
E	Champlin Edgar R	5	banker	65	400 Com av
F	Champlin Katherine—†	5	housewife	64	400 "
G	Hannigan Annie J—†	5	"	60	Lexington
H	Hannigan John E	5	lawyer	56	"
K	Tierney Winifred—†	5	housekeeper	68	"
L	Coffee Annie—†	5	waitress	45	Milton
R	Finn Margaret A—†	5	housekeeper	45	21 Canton av
M	Forde Eva C—†	5	governess	36	Milton
N	McElwain Alexander	5	reporter	22	535 Beacon
O	McElwain Helen B—†	5	retired	22	535 "
P	McElwain Helen H—†	5	housekeeper	55	Philadelphia
S	Barry Caroline—†	5	"	50	here
T	Barry Elizabeth—†	5	housewife	42	"
U	Gallagher Mary—†	5	maid	32	"
V	Brackett Clara—†	5	housekeeper	50	"
W	Conalogue Helen—†	5	maid	22	"
X	Foster Catherine—†	5	none	65	"
Y	Foley Margaret—†	5	maid	23	Ireland
Z	Pierce Caroline—†	5	housewife	58	here
A	Coolidge Helen W—†	5	housewife	64	Asia
B	Coolidge William W	5	lawyer	65	"
C	Emalundson Aillen—†	5	maid	24	21 Bexley rd
D	Emalundson Annie—†	5	"	21	Brookline
E	Mills Susan L—†	5	retired	58	Asia
F	Austin Calvin	5	president	70	here
G	Austin Julia—†	5	housewife	69	"
H	Griffiths Hannah—†	5	maid	38	England
K	Brennan Edith—†	5	housewife	38	here
L	Brennan James	5	banker	43	"
M	Driscoll Mary—†	5	maid	60	336 Marlboro
N	McCloskey Mary E—†	5	"	38	here
O	Brown Thomas H	5	trustee	36	"
P	Budd Emma—†	5	housewife	47	"
R	Budd William	5	butler	44	"
S	Swift Valley G—†	5	housewife	40	"
T	DeCourcey Charles	5	clerk	66	"

34

Joy Street—Continued

U	DeCourcey Elizabeth—†	5	retired	55	here
V	Eaton Gertrude B—†	5	housekeeper	30	"
W	Morgan Elsie N—†	5	"	46	"
X	Morgan William F	5	trustee	46	"
X¹	Dalford Lawrence A	5	janitor	46	186 Devonshire
Y	Wright Alice L—†	5	housewife	40	Quincy
Z	Wright Henry O	5	engineer	44	"
B	Brown Stella—†	6	maid	22	46 Beacon
C	Cummings Charles K	6	student	22	here
D	Cummings Charles K	6	architect	52	"
E	Cummings Ethel—†	6	student	20	"
F	Cummings Francis H	6	"	24	"
G	Cummings Lydia T—†	6	housewife	47	"
H	Doherty Katherine—†	6	maid	36	"
K	Egan Mary—†	6	"	36	"
L	Lane Margaret—†	6	"	47	"
M	Murphy Julia—†	6	cook	27	"
N	O'Connor Katherine—†	6	laundress	50	"
O	White Margaret—†	6	maid	26	Ireland
R	Barry Charles G	11	clerk	45	here
S	Barry Martha E—†	11	housewife	45	"
T	Carleton Francis E	11	clerk	30	"
U	Jewett Annie—†	11	housewife	80	"
V	Johnson Amy B—†	11	retired	40	16 Pinckney
W	Lemon Ada—†	11	housewife	58	here
X	Lemon Edward L	11	editor	62	"
Y	Mears Mary C—†	11	retired	77	"
Z	Milliken Grace E—†	11	clerk	35	16 Pinckney
A	Begin Joseph	11½	clerk	28	Canada
B	Carigan Valmore	11½	student	30	here
C	Donahue William	11½	"	24	23 Pinckney
D	Grey Henry P	11½	general worker	54	here
E	Horsman August M	11½	clerk	32	"
F	Horsman Grace M—†	11½	housewife	32	"
G	Maxwell Carl	11½	salesman	45	"
H	McDonald Lerie—†	11½	clerk	23	Nova Scotia
K	Montgomery Katherine—†	11½	waitress	40	here
L	Stewart Anna—†	11½	clerk	23	Nova Scotia
M	Falger Carrie—†	15	industri'l work'r	37	22 Ashburton pl
N	Geisinger Roy W	15	printer	24	New York
O	Leighton Harriet—†	15	newspaper	23	here

Joy Street—Continued

P	Maloney Eva J—†	15	clerk	33	here
R	Peterson Helen M—†	15	waitress	25	Quincy
S	Richardson Robert	15	painter	53	here
T	Shaw Robert E	15	bookbinder	20	New York
U	Vines Eleanor—†	15	lodging house	46	212 W Springfield
W	Bean Metta—†	19	social worker	37	here
X	Thompson Louise B—†	19	student	39	"
Y	McGaw Agnes—†	19	housewife	75	"
Z	McGaw John	19	carpenter	53	"
A	Brigham Curtis D	19	chemist	41	"
B	White Charles W	19	inspector	38	"
C	White Gladys—†	19	housewife	33	"
D	Carpenter Annie G—†	19	clerk	59	"
E	Chapman Samuel	21	inspector	31	"
F	Datin Mary—†	21	saleswoman	40	"
G	Ebann Caroline M—†	21	housekeeper	35	"
H	Fowler Anna—†	21	saleswoman	25	"
K	Fowler Earl	21	salesman	26	"
L	Glennon Mildred—†	21	accountant	50	"
M	Goldthwaite Elizebeth—†	21	saleswoman	56	"
N	VonGlahn Emma—†	21	"	38	"
O	Bremer Gustave	23	houseman	48	Sweden
P	Comer Mae—†	23	clerk	25	here
R	Comer Maria—†	23	housekeeper	60	"
S	Edstrom Carl A	23	carpenter	60	"
T	Edstrom Ellen L—†	23	housewife	52	"
U	Jackson William	23	printer	30	19 Joy
V	Maguire Austin J	23	janitor	50	24 "
W	McDonald Bert	23	bookbinder	22	Canada
X	McKenna Lucy—†	23	finisher	21	here
Y	Nowers Francis L	23	manager	32	Chelsea
Z	Purday Rena F—†	23	waitress	23	692 Tremon
A	Scallan James	23	janitor	61	15 Chamber
B	Shribman Maurice	23	waiter	23	Lakewood N
C	White Charles	23	salesman	30	New York
D	Ginsberg Amby	25	newsdealer	28	here
E	Ginsberg Jacob	25	"	35	"
F	Whelpley Edward H	37	mechanic	28	"
G	Whelpley Evelyn—†	37	housewife	30	"
H	Branzburg Bessie—†	37	"	31	"
K	Branzburg Max	37	cabinetmaker	36	"

Joy Street—Continued

Letter	Full Name	Residence	Occupation	Age	Reported Residence
L	Harrison Henry	37	tailor	46	here
M	Harrison Jennie —†	37	dressmaker	35	"
N	Harrison Sarah—†	37	fitter	40	"
O	Kitover John	37	leatherworker	41	"
P	Kitover Molly—†	37	housewife	42	"
R	Glickson Minnie—†	37	"	60	"
S	Glickson Oscar	37	upholsterer	30	19 Myrtle
T	Glickson Rae—†	37	housewife	30	Salem
U	Glickson Samuel	37	retired	65	here
V	Gokey Esther—†	37	housewife	49	"
W	Gokey William O	37	expressman	48	"
X	Slotkes Esther—†	37	clerk	35	46 Revere
Y	Slotkes Eva—†	37	housewife	63	46 "
Z	Slotkes Louis	37	retired	70	46 "
A	Slotkes Sarah—†	37	clerk	25	46 "
B	Foley Eleanor—†	37	bookbinder	24	here
C	Foley James E	37	salesman	32	"
D	Foley Mary—†	37	clerk	27	"
E	Gayton Ellen—†	37	retired	86	"
F	Shapiro Annie—†	37	housewife	22	Few Hampshire
G	Shapiro Edward	37	pedler	22	6 Bulfinch pl
H	Butcher Margaret—†	39	houseworker	51	here
K	Dean Catherine E—†	39	saleswoman	26	"
L	Walton Charles	39	chauffeur	45	53 Hancock
M	Hall John	39	painter	35	Dover N H
N	Hall Mary—†	39	housewife	32	"
O	Lapp Frank	39	salesman	27	36 Myrtle
P	Lapp Minnie—†	39	housewife	23	36 "
R	Meyers Benjamin	39	musician	31	here
S	Meyers Rose—†	39	housewife	27	"
U	Davis Agnes—†	41	"	39	"
V	Davis Charles M	41	longshoreman	55	"
W	Jensen Peter	41	"	60	"
X	Goldberg Ethel—†	41	houseworker	48	"
Y	Goldberg Hyman	41	student	20	"
Z	Goldberg Jacob	41	"	24	"
A	Weinstein Marion—†	41	housewife	26	"
B	Weinstein Samuel	41	manufacturer	28	Malden
C	Resnick Dora—†	41	housewife	38	65 Joy
D	Resnick Jacob	41	tailor	45	65 "
E	Resnick Samuel	41	"	31	65 "

Joy Street—Continued

	Letter	FULL NAME	Residence	Occupation	Age	Reported Residence
	F	Yanofsky Bessie—†	41	dressmaker	30	here
	G	Yanofsky Harry C	41	manufacturer	29	"
	H	Yanofsky Hilda—†	41	saleswoman	26	"
	K	Yanofsky Nathan	41	retired	70	"
	L	Yanofsky Pauline—†	41	stenographer	21	"
	M	Yanofsky Rose—†	41	housekeeper	23	"
	N	O'Connor Mary A—†	41	maid	43	43 Joy
	O	Sullivan Catherine—†	41	housewife	40	43 "
	P	Sullivan John	41	laborer	45	43 "
	R	Norton Raymond	43	chauffeur	24	Arlington
	S	Norton Ruth—†	43	housewife	23	"
	T	Golinsky Barnard	43	dentist	23	here
	U	Golinsky Bessie—†	43	housewife	47	"
	V	Wishnick Abraham	43	grocer	28	"
	W	Wishnick Lillian—†	43	housewife	26	"
	X	Rosenthal Fannie—†	43	"	36	"
	Y	Rosenthal Harry	43	letter carrier	38	"
	Z	Levine Bella—†	43	dressmaker	24	"
	A	Levine Hyman	43	bookbinder	20	"
	B	Levine May—†	43	housewife	56	"
	C	Gill Edward J	43	caretaker	53	"
	D	Gill Hannah J—†	43	housewife	45	"
	F	Minsky Anna—†	45	"	33	"
	G	Minsky Nathan	45	cigarmaker	35	"
	H	Pearlman Pauline—†	45	bookkeeper	27	"
	K	Pearlman Rachael—†	45	housekeeper	65	"
	L	Pearlman Simon D	45	tailor	64	"
	M	Waxman Hinda—†	45	housekeeper	50	"
	N	Waxman Hyman	45	sexton	52	"
	O	Waxman Samuel	45	salesman	21	"
	P	Cohen Max	45	coatmaker	39	"
	R	Cohen Minnie—†	45	housekeeper	39	"
	S	Wiener Joseph	45	student	22	"
	U	Leppo Annie—†	47	housewife	58	"
	V	Leppo Henry	47	blacksmith	62	"
	W	Leppo Hyman	47	upholsterer	21	"
	X	Leppo Jacob	47	"	24	"
	Y	Goldman Eva—†	47	housekeeper	35	51 Anderson
	Z	Goldman Jacob	47	tailor	44	51 "
	A	Witkin Bleuome—†	47	housekeeper	68	here
	B	Witkin Jacob	47	shipper	34	"

Joy Street—Continued

c	Witkin Maurice J	47	cigarmaker	38	here
D	Witkin Samuel	47	attorney	37	"
F	Smith Alexander	47	junk dealer	45	"
E	Smith Anna—†	47	bookkeeper	22	"
G	Smith Flora—†	47	housewife	40	"
H	Clark Franklin L	51	stereotyper	45	"
K	Clark Majorie—†	51	housewife	47	"
L	Judd Elizabeth R—†	51	"	49	"
M	Judd Fredrick E	51	representative	72	"
N	Rathbun Sarah—†	51	houseworker	83	"
O	Keenan Elizabeth—†	51	housewife	38	"
P	Keenan Michael J	51	painter	38	"
R	Broe Elizebeth C—†	51	clerk	26	47 S Russell
S	Broe George M	51	"	36	47 "
T	Broe John J	51	U S customs	39	47 "
U	Berntsen Harold J	53	salesman	35	here
V	Berntsen Marie—†	53	cook	38	"
W	Silva Alice—†	53	housewife	23	29 Hancock
X	Silva Frank	53	clerk	23	29 "
Y	Chaliks Catherine—†	53	housewife	32	here
Z	Chaliks Mitchell	53	cook	41	"
A	Chaliks Mitchell W	53	busboy	21	"
B	Finlayson Mary—†	53	waitress	42	"
C	Greenstein Max	53	student	21	"
D	Herman Frank	53	salesman	50	"
E	Mackintosh Emma—†	53	housewife	55	"
F	Mackintosh Grant	53	engineer	60	"
G	Mackintosh Maud—†	53	secretary	30	"
H	Wright Chester I	55	salesman	30	"
K	Wright Mabel B—†	55	housewife	28	"
L	Mitchell Mary—†	55	waitress	34	"
M	Sodano Madalyne—†	55	housewife	29	"
N	Sodano Santo	55	engraver	30	"
O	Maguire Patrick J	55	retired	74	"
P	McFarland Mary J—†	55	saleswoman	46	"
R	Roberts Catherine E—†	55	housewife	23	"
S	Roberts Florence—†	55	houseworker	22	"
T	Roberts George E	55	paperruler	24	"
U	Roberts Herbert M	55	foreman	50	"
V	Nickerson Daniel E	55	carpenter	76	"
W	Nickerson Hannah—†	55	housewife	66	"

Joy Street—Continued

X	Krigel Francis	55	housewife	55	here
Y	Krigel John J	55	tailor	54	"
Z	Carter Wilfred	55	cook	35	"
A	Keyes Charles J	59	chauffeur	33	"
B	Keyes Jennie—†	59	housewife	63	"
C	Keyes William H	59	fireman	75	"
D	Kelley Fredrick	59	janitor	60	"
E	Kelley Nellie—†	59	housewife	50	"
F	Williams Florence—†	59	tailoress	48	"
G	Kelley Alicia J—†	59	houseworker	71	"
H	Phelan Edward F	59	clerk	36	"
K	Thorn Albert C	61	laborer	38	235 Broadway
L	Thorn Minnie A—†	61	laundress	34	235 "
M	Cameron Joseph	61	painter	28	Halifax N S
N	Curran William	61	plumber	50	here
O	Wiswall Jennie—†	61	houseworker	52	"
P	Rosnitsky Ida—†	65	clerk	21	"
R	Rosnitsky Mollie—†	65	storekeeper	65	"
S	Rosnitsky Ruth—†	65	saleswoman	20	"
T	Ponce Harriet—†	65	clerk	22	"
U	Ponce Hyman	65	jeweler	30	"
V	Ponce Joseph	65	tailor	65	"
W	Ponce Lillian—†	65	clerk	25	"
X	Harris Sarah—†	65	housewife	20	"
Y	Harris William	65	foreman	23	"
Z	Selant Charles	65	clerk	20	2 Poplar
A	Selant Dora—†	65	tobacco stripper	41	2 "
B	Weinstein Sarah—†	65	housewife	31	3 Ottawa
C	Weinstein William	65	teamster	32	3 "
D	DeMartin Frances—†	67	housewife	37	1 Charles
E	DeMartin Timothy	67	real estate	38	1 "
F	Platzman Celia—†	67	housewife	42	72 Revere
G	Platzman Nathan	67	tailor	48	72 "
H	Zack Esther—†	67	housewife	28	49 Allen
K	Zack Morris	67	shoelaster	31	49 "
L	Rosso Joseph	67	barber	40	here
M	Rosso Josephine—†	67	housewife	37	"
N	Taylor Nellie—†	69	"	47	"
O	Crutchfield Mary—†	69	"	45	"
P	Minor Catherine—†	69	housekeeper	91	"
R	Moore Emma—†	69	housewife	83	Westerly R I

Joy Street—Continued

Letter.	FULL NAME.	Residence, April 1, 1924.	Occupation.	Supposed Age.	Reported Residence, April 1, 1923. Street and Number.
T	Cutter Margarita J—†	71	social worker	22	425 Harvard
U	Houde William	71	clerk	32	Medford
V	Lincoln Miriam—†	71	social worker	24	93 Taylor
W	Pendelton Alice—†	71	real estate	35	52 Garden
X	Robbins William	71	clerk	34	Newton
Y	Donelli Lino	73	cook	36	here
Z	Kracon Frank	73	tailor	35	Concord N H
A	Madigan William T	73	cook	33	Providence R I
B	Neville Joseph	73	salesman	50	42 Brattle
C	Stewart Julia—†	73	housewife	50	here
D	Tobin John	73	laborer	48	Cambridge
F	Grant George	79	salesman	54	here
G	Grant Mary—†	79	houseworker	50	"
H	Ouelletti Catherine—†	79	housewife	44	"
K	Ouelletti Joseph	79	laborer	41	"
L	Pizziminti Gaitano	79	buyer	34	"
M	Pizziminti Mary—†	79	housewife	25	"
N	Reiodon Frederick	79	machinist	53	"
O	Goren Elizabeth—†	81	bookkeeper	20	"
P	Goren Etta—†	81	storekeeper	40	"
R	Goren Sarah—†	81	houseworker	22	"
S	Lichenstein Louis	81	clerk	29	67 Joy
T	Lichenstein Pauline—†	81	housewife	26	67 "
U	Segal Charles	81	tailor	55	67 "
V	Segal Rose—†	81	housewife	53	67 "
W	Drucker Samuel	81	tailor	36	here
X	Drucker Sarah—†	81	housewife	37	"
Y	Sudak Joseph	81	window cleaner	26	"
A	Wickham Catherine—†	83	housewife	47	"
B	Wickham James E	83	laborer	47	"
C	Harrington Mary—†	83	waitress	40	"
D	Reardon James F	83	tailor	64	"
D¹	Reardon Mary A—†	83	housewife	60	"

Mt Vernon Place

Letter.	FULL NAME.	Residence, April 1, 1924.	Occupation.	Supposed Age.	Reported Residence, April 1, 1923. Street and Number.
B	Gray Hope—†	7	housekeeper	35	here
C	Gray Samuel S	7	merchant	75	"
D	McDonald Margaret—†	7	housewife	48	Vineyard Haven
E	McDonald Ronald	7	janitor	51	"

Mt Vernon Street

K	Pettis Edna H—†	20	housekeeper	56	here
L	Baker Charlotte H—†	20	retired	69	"
M	Blanchard Charles B	20	banker	57	2 Walnut
N	Blanchard Cornelia L—†	20	housewife	57	2 "
O	Fottler Jacob	20	retired	80	here
P	McLean Mary—†	20	housewife	40	Malden
R	McLean Miriam—†	20	housekeeper	21	"
S	Stevens William S B	20	retired	60	here
T	Greenleaf Mary L—†	20	housekeeper	65	"
U	Clarke Carrie B—†	20	"	58	"
V	Clarke Elihue B	20	salesman	60	"
X	Nickerson Harriet—†	20	housekeeper	60	"
Y	Stevens Grace S—†	20	"	58	"
Z	Pickering Henry G	20	lawyer	75	"
A	Southgate Elizabeth A—†	20	housekeeper	68	"
B	Appleton William S	20	retired	51	"
C	Hopkins John	20	"	68	"
D	Hopkins William	20	"	65	"
E	Hardy Bertha—†	20	housekeeper	28	Brookline
F	Ackroyd Walter	22	salesman	62	here
G	Blanchard Frances A—†	22	bookkeeper	35	Brookline
H	Bolster Charles H	22	student	28	here
K	Desmond Catherine—†	22	"	45	New York
L	Gould Florence A—†	22	bookkeeper	33	"
M	Hinckley Louise H—†	22	"	39	here
N	Hinckley Margaret C—†	22	clerk	28	"
O	Matson Harold B	22	salesman	35	New York
P	Mulhern Frances G—†	22	bookkeeper	35	65 Hancock
R	Mulhern Louise T—†	22	clerk	38	65 "
S	Noonan Nellie F—†	22	"	32	72 Pinckney
T	Norris Catherine—†	22	housekeeper	48	4 Union pk
U	Norris Frank	22	janitor	50	4 "
V	Payne Sarah A—†	22	retired	87	here
W	Powers Maye W—†	22	housekeeper	50	"
X	Roberts Rena—†	22	tel operator	30	Chelsea
Y	Sears Stephen F	22	student	48	here
Z	Spinden Herbert A	22	surgeon	47	"
A	Ward Arthur S	22	salesman	30	Chelsea
B	Weber John J	22	"	48	here
D	Conlan Julia M—†	26	bookkeeper	24	"

Mt Vernon Street—Continued

E	Flaherty Barbara F—†	26	cook	28	here
F	Guild Courtney	26	printer	60	"
G	Guild Sarah L—†	26	housekeeper	61	"
H	McDonagh Annie—†	26	waitress	27	"
K	Connolley Mary—†	28	cook	28	Brookline
L	Curtis Frances—†	28	housekeeper	56	here
L¹	Curtis Harriet S—†	28	social worker	43	"
z¹	Curtis Isabella—†	28	"	51	"
z²	Curtis Margaret—†	28	"	40	"
M	Ogara Margaret—†	28	chambermaid	60	"
N	Back Helen R—†	31	bookkeeper	27	63 Hancock
O	Baker Roy W	31	engineer	32	New York
P	Bellfontaine Isaac	31	steelworker	21	Halifax N S
R	Bowen Charles E	31	cook	44	Providence R I
S	Chambers Flora A—†	31	housewife	50	71 Hancock
T	Chambers Gilson R	31	painter	54	71 "
U	Friberg Eino	31	student	22	43 Falmouth
V	Hall Rachael—†	31	operator	27	265 Lamartine
W	King Millie—†	31	accountant	42	Somerville
X	Matthews Richard M	31	designer	64	75 Hancock
Y	Warner Joseph	31	clerk	23	Halifax N S
z	Wells George H	31	student	22	Tufts College
A	Dromey Bridget—†	32	waitress	30	"
B	Moors Ethel P—†	32	housewife	50	"
C	Moors John F	32	broker	60	"
D	Sheehan Bridget—†	32	cook	30	"
E	Steele Sarah—†	32	chambermaid	38	"
F	Bell Letitia R—†	33	housewife	35	Brookline
G	Bell Warner H	33	printer	58	"
H	Burnie Avis P—†	33	housewife	39	64 Revere
K	Burnie Douglas P	33	chef	33	64 "
L	Chase William A	33	meatcutter	46	Gloucester
M	Greaves Herbert	33	textile worker	47	Watertown
N	Gunnarson Gustaf A	33	draughtsman	36	Lowell
O	Hurnhan Catherine M—†	33	housekeeper	63	37 Temple
P	Hustis H Cuthbert	33	architect	37	Salem
R	Jordan Perley P	33	salesman	38	6 Ridgemont
S	Small Alfred K	33	engineer	65	18 Pinckney
T	Small Clara W—†	33	housewife	57	18 "
U	Wilder W Dean	33	printer	22	Springfield
V	Fuller Gilbert E	34	banker	40	79 Mt Vernon

Mt Vernon Street—Continued

w	Fuller Sidney M	34	merchant	37	79 Mt Vernon
x	Brennan Joseph W	35	porter	57	here
y	Clark Mabel—†	35	clerk	46	42 Worcester sq
z	Connell Edward J	35	auditor	35	Brookline
A	Durning Frances—†	35	retired	60	76 Hancock
B	Hartwell Christie A—†	35	housewife	56	98 Bowdoin
C	Hartwell Eugene W	35	retired	53	98 "
D	LeCouetre Elizabeth—†	35	"	65	here
E	Mollison Martin	35	salesman	30	"
F	Phinney Charles A	35	retired	70	Dedham
G	Stetson Olive—†	35	housekeeper	55	73 Pinckney
H	Townsend Edward	35	salesman	53	Providence R I
K	Flint George M	37	agent	41	here
L	Flint Myra G—†	37	housewife	40	"

Myrtle Street

N	Callahan Mary—†	1	shoeworker	40	9 Allston
O	Corey Sanford	1	shipper	34	97 Pinckney
P	Gred Peter	1	upholsterer	27	Scotland
R	Holden Emma—†	1	housekeeper	56	97 Pinckney
S	Morrison Arnold	1	salesman	52	Medford
T	Payson Edgar R	1	clerk	35	97 Pinckney
U	Reynolds Bertha—†	1	social worker	48	93 Revere
V	Reynolds Frank W	1	clerk	31	Manchester
W	Sparrow Emma—†	1	retired	50	24 Joy
X	Styles Hinton	1	reporter	32	Newton
Y	Alden Clara S—†	2	bookkeeper	67	here
Z	Allamade Andrew	2	salesman	38	"
A	Foye Fredrick	2	printer	49	"
B	Holbrook John B	2	salesman	37	Bridgeport Ct
C	Maynard Mattie M—†	2	housekeeper	66	here
D	Noble John	2	waiter	37	2 Temple
E	Boyle Andrew	4	"	28	New Hampshire
F	Foy Alice L—†	4	waitress	26	11 Myrtle
G	Foy Ella M—†	4	saleswoman	30	11 "
H	Hurley Timothy A	4	salesman	36	here
K	Maloney Frank J	4	lawyer	48	"
L	Ritcey Hattie M—†	4	housewife	58	"

Myrtle Street—Continued

Letter	FULL NAME	Res.	Occupation	Age	Reported Residence
M	Ritcey William S	4	waiter	54	here
N	Crocker Frank B	5	clerk	45	"
O	Johnson Delia—†	5	lodging house	49	"
P	Worsley Fredrick	5	manager	45	"
R	Toye John J	5	clerk	60	"
S	Toye Margaret T—†	5	housewife	58	"
T	Parker Catherine—†	5	"	58	"
U	Parker Chipman G	5	cook	65	"
V	Parker Leo C	5	clerk	29	"
W	Dunn Agnes—†	5	housewife	66	"
X	Dunn Bertha O—†	5	housekeeper	29	"
Y	Dunn John T	5	clerk	44	"
Z	Wehrle Theodore H	5	"	47	43 Peter Parley rd
A	Williams Frederick G	7	carpenter	65	here
B	Williams Jessie—†	7	housewife	49	"
C	Noble Addie—†	7	cook	55	"
D	Smith John C	7	salesman	25	"
E	Danforth Mabel—†	7	housewife	40	"
F	Danforth William E	7	salesman	55	"
G	Morton Steven	7	engineer	43	"
H	Gracey Mabel—†	7	waitress	37	"
K	Soenksen Carle	7	valet	36	"
L	Poly Angelo	7	salesman	27	"
M	Poly Caroline—†	7	hairdresser	24	"
N	Poly Mary—†	7	housewife	60	"
O	Clark George W	7	manager	24	Cambridge
P	Sullivan Maud—†	7	housewife	56	here
R	Young Carrol	7	metalworker	24	Dover N H
S	Young Catherine—†	7	housewife	20	"
T	Herderhurst Elmer	7	salesman	36	Medford
U	Herderhurst Rose—†	7	housewife	24	"
V	Kaddy Margaret—†	7	"	33	here
W	Kaddy Roy	7	machinist	35	"
X	Sewell Fannie—†	7	housewife	40	"
Y	Sewell Harry	7	manager	44	"
Z	Myers Elizabeth M—†	8	housekeeper	67	"
A	Perkins Louis A	8	editor	70	"
B	Sexton Charles T	8	lawyer	28	"
C	Steele Asa S	8	janitor	65	"
D	Willis David	8	painter	62	Lexington
E	Grady Daniel	9	fruit	50	here

Myrtle Street—Continued

F	Grady Elizabeth—†	9	housewife	51	here
G	Morgan Josephine—†	9	"	39	"
H	Morgan Robert H	9	restaurant man	32	"
K	Dalton Mary—†	9	housewife	70	"
L	Kelly Annie—†	9	buyer	30	"
M	Boyle Angie—†	9	hairdresser	33	"
N	Swenbeck Lydia—†	9	housewife	60	"
O	Swenbeck Paul L	9	chef	53	"
P	Merchant Sophie—†	9	housewife	38	"
R	Stienfield Max	9	machinist	25	U S N
S	Ruttan Monica S—†	9	housewife	47	33 Myrtle
T	Ruttan Richard R	9	cashier	49	33 "
U	Lewis Carrie F—†	9	waitress	39	here
V	Ryan Timothy J	9	clerk	40	Chelsea
W	Andrews Emily—†	9	housewife	40	here
X	Andrews George J	9	seaman	20	"
Y	Andrews Harry C	9	manager	45	"
Z	Andrews Valentine A—†	9	stenographer	21	"
A	Brewer Beatrice—†	9	housewife	33	"
B	Brewer Joseph W	9	janitor	33	"
C	Mowry Preston W	9	distributer	39	"
D	Nutter Richard C	9	stitcher	38	"
E	Roberts Esther—†	9	bookkeeper	23	"
F	Sternes Sarah L—†	9	housekeeper	45	"
G	Shea Joseph	9	printer	34	"
H	Shea Susan I—†	9	housewife	33	"
K	Appleton Elliott W	10	machinist	35	Springfield
L	Grant Alice—†	10	clerk	22	here
M	Grant Frank	10	janitor	51	"
N	Grant Frank E	10	machinist	27	"
O	Grant Lillian—†	10	clerk	24	"
P	McNabb Everett	10	carpenter	53	"
R	Tyler Richard	10	gardener	69	"
S	Barrows Edward	11	rubberworker	65	"
T	Campbell Ella M—†	11	housewife	62	"
U	Gibson Gene—†	11	dressmaker	24	New York
V	Gibson Harry	11	laundryman	30	"
W	Grover Charles	11	cook	25	here
X	Healy Emma A—†	11	artist model	70	Maine
Y	Neil John	11	laborer	48	Atlanta Ga
Z	Timmons Peter	11	salesman	57	here

Letter	Full Name	Residence, April 1, 1924	Occupation	Supposed Age	Reported Residence, April 1, 1923. Street and Number.

Myrtle Street—Continued

A	Williams Hattie—†	11	maid	70	here
C	Rand Sarah—†	12	housekeeper	65	"
D	Rand Winifred—†	12	nurse	29	"

Ridgeway Lane

F	Pierson Carl	21	tailor	46	here
G	Shea John	21	"	54	"
H	Shilling Gustaf	21	"	50	"
K	Condit Gidion B	23	retired	56	"
L	Mitcehll Benjamin	25	printer	39	"
M	Mitchell Francis—†	25	housewife	40	"
N	Bass Abraham	25	salesman	53	9 Temple
O	Bass Minie—†	25	housewife	40	9 "
P	Lamia James	25	candymaker	39	here
R	Lamia Rose—†	25	housewife	30	"
S	Mull Mary—†	25	"	58	"
T	Mull William	25	cigarmaker	55	"
U	Weiner Eva—†	25	stenographer	23	"
V	Weiner Louis	25	ragman	47	"
W	Weiner Minie—†	25	housewife	47	"
X	Weiner Morris	25	student	21	"
Y	Matthews James E	27	laborer	50	"
Z	Matthews Mary C—†	27	housewife	29	"
A	Drake Elizabeth L—†	27	"	62	"
B	Drake James E	27	janitor	65	"
C	Gorndahl Margaret—†	27	waitress	38	"
D	Murphy Helen A—†	27	operator	26	"
E	Murphy Mary—†	27	houseworker	60	"
F	Sordillo Edward L	27	salesman	22	112 Salem
G	Sordillo Madeline E—†	27	housewife	20	Randolph

Temple Street

H	Douglas Leon	2	laborer	36	Pittsburgh Pa
K	Dunnaine Fred	2	cook	24	New Bedford
L	Faught John W	2	laborer	33	22 Dwight
M	Faurner Joseph	2	cook	40	here
N	Fisher John	2	"	40	"

Page.	Letter.	FULL NAME.	Residence, April 1, 1924.	Occupation.	Supposed Age.	Reported Residence April 1, 1923. Street and Number.

Temple Street—Continued

o	Gallager Joseph W	2	cook	25	here
p	Georgette George	2	molder	47	"
r	McNair John	2	cook	25	"
s	Zarrella Angelo M	2	barber	27	29 Baldwin
t	Breslin Mary—†	4	clerk	29	17 Hancock
u	Felino Joseph	4	barber	39	Medford
v	Gillispie John	4	janitor	47	86 Revere
w	Higgins Thomas	4	painter	40	4 Bulfinch pl
x	Jackson Lelia	4	machinist	53	here
y	Kicema Blanche—†	4	housekeeper	27	1 James
z	Kicema Phillip	4	tailor	29	1 "
a	Kline Charles	4	sign painter	29	11 Hubbard
b	Miler Paul	4	calendarman	46	here
c	Miller Victoria—†	4	housewife	33	"
c	Niman Eli	4	carpenter	33	"
e	Novers Silvester	4	waiter	42	Rhode Island
f	Wing Abner	4	dentist	42	here
g	Wing Deborah—†	4	student	33	"
h	Darling William W	5	letter carrier	60	"
k	Davis Robert	5	clerk	29	"
l	Lambert Anna—†	5	housekeeper	69	"
m	Cook Blanche—†	5	clerk	33	"
n	Cook Edward J	5	"	45	"
o	McCone Madge—†	5	housekeeper	43	"
p	Smailey Max	5	manager	46	"
r	Ajian Louis	6	storekeeper	32	"
s	Ames Alfred	6	boatbuilder	43	"
t	Brown Harry	6	waiter	46	"
u	Buckley John	6	engineer	52	102 Revere
v	Carney Bartholemew	6	optician	30	21 Bowdoin
w	Foley Frank	6	carpenter	33	Bridgewater
x	Frost George	6	expressman	32	here
y	Gifford John B	6	waiter	35	Worcester
z	Gifford Lillian—†	6	waitress	28	"
a	Gray Josephine—†	6	lodging house	39	45 Hancock
b	Gray William	6	machinist	37	45 "
c	Irving Bella—†	6	waitress	35	here
d	Kelley Mary—†	6	"	36	"
e	Matouskey Edward	6	molder	25	18 Temple
f	McNally Thomas	6	shoeworker	26	30 "
k	Powers Alexander	6	laborer	20	Newfoundland

Temple Street Continued

L	Powers William	6	laborer	22	Newfoundland
G	Remeior Gilbert	6	truckman	52	here
H	Remeior Gilbert, jr	6	teamster	21	"
M	Rice George	6	fireman	44	45 Hancock
N	Walsh Gerald	6	laborer	20	Newfoundland
O	Armstrong Margaret—†	7	housekeeper	60	here
P	Hooker Joseph E	7	woolworker	44	"
R	Johnson Axel F	7	helper	28	"
S	Johnson Bernard	7	metalworker	56	"
T	Lunge Max	7	painter	30	Revere
U	Mudge Norman H	7	meatcutter	32	82 Myrtle
V	O'Shea Michael	7	laborer	47	18 Temple
W	Ryan Thomas J	7	counterman	33	here
X	Sabrins Martin	7	rigger	40	"
Y	Smith William	7	laborer	51	"
Z	Spitz Hyman	7	painter	25	Revere
A	Dodge Agnes—†	9	saleswoman	50	Maine
B	Fetherston Edward J	9	paperhanger	52	here
C	Fetherston Floyd	9	housewife	36	"
D	Green Herman	9	carpenter	52	Quincy
E	Massell Samuel	9	laborer	38	here
F	O'Mally Austin	9	chauffeur	32	"
G	Pellerin Martin	9	porter	52	Providence R I
H	Putman Clyde	9	chauffeur	35	Lynn
K	Rodzokewitz Antonio	9	cook	31	here
L	St Pierce Joseph	9	machinist	28	"
M	Serofinasicz Antoni	9	baker	40	"
N	Veazie Maurice	9	salesman	59	"
O	Watson George	9	"	60	18 Temple
P	Wyman Samuel T	9	retired	78	here
R	Rifkin Abraham	11	physician	29	"
S	Rifkin Rose—†	11	housewife	27	"
T	Lakin Abraham	11	salesman	34	"
U	Lakin Sophie—†	11	housewife	27	"
V	Ferguson Clifford M	11	musician	27	39 Somerset
W	Ferguson Gertrude—†	11	housewife	25	39 "
X	Mosson Irving	11	cook	30	Canada
Y	Mosson Milton	11	carpenter	30	"
Z	Ritcy Maurice	11	cook	28	"
A	Wiseman Ida—†	11	housewife	31	here
B	Wiseman Morris	11	tailor	50	"

Temple Street—Continued

c	Rosenblatt Alice—†	11	housekeeper	63	here
d	Rosenblatt Nathan	11	salesman	60	"
e	Springer Morris	11	"	48	"
f	Block Miriam—†	11	operator	22	"
g	Block Rachael—†	11	housekeeper	37	"
h	Barlow Hatty—†	11	housewife	34	"
k	Barlow Myer	11	salesman	37	"
l	Silverman Joseph	11	real estate	28	21 McLean
m	Mauricae Bertha—†	11	housewife	32	here
n	Maurice Samuel	11	salesman	32	"
o	Brown Annie—†	11	saleswoman	48	"
p	Jacobs David	11	lawyer	31	"
r	Jacobs Samuel	11	"	29	"
s	Mansfield Ruth—†	11	saleswoman	28	"
t	Green Louie	11	tailor	39	"
u	Green Rebecca—†	11	tailoress	43	"
w	Dolan Patrick	14	laborer	35	Manchester N H
x	Emmons George H	14	retired	60	169 Charles
y	Emmons Margaret—†	14	lodging house	59	169 "
a	Flynn Daniel	14	painter	50	New Hampshire
a[1]	Foutch Emma—†	14	Salvation Army	59	Connecticut
b	Greene Morris	14	waiter	35	here
c	Powell Alexander	14	painter	35	New Hampshire
d	Powell William	14	"	40	"
e	Slavin Lillian—†	14	housewife	34	Calais Me
f	Slavin Thomas	14	laborer	45	"
g	Wallace Patrick	14	"	21	here
h	Barker Mary—†	15	stitcher	47	"
k	Barker William	15	mattressmaker	57	"
l	Borick Stephen	15	machinist	27	Cleveland O
m	Conover Erving	15	clerk	36	here
n	Conover Vivian G	15	printer	40	"
o	Cronin Daniel	15	liveryman	34	Chelsea
p	Gregoire Horace	15	machinist	24	New Hampshire
r	Hennessy Etta M—†	15	housewife	32	here
s	Hennessy Leonard C	15	manager	30	"
t	Little Frank	15	taxidermist	31	"
u	Long George	15	engineer	50	New Hampshire
v	Markey Raymond	15	laborer	25	Maine
w	Markham Michael	15	houseman	43	here
x	O'Mara Walter	15	counterman	24	"

Temple Street—Continued

Letter.	Full Name.	Residence, April 1, 1924.	Occupation.	Supposed Age.	Reported Residence, April 1, 1923. Street and Number.
y	Robertson George	15	counterman	45	here
z	Cary Earnest	16	instructor	45	Hanover N H
a	Chalmers Flora E—†	16	lodging house	62	here
b	Chase Roy	16	plumber	40	"
c	Frasier Allen	16	mason	41	19 Temple
d	Herrick Oren H	16	painter	50	Danbury N H
e	Leary Earl P	16	window washer	30	New York City
f	Lycette Arthur G	16	clerk	26	51 Hancock
g	Murphy William E	16	shoeworker	52	New York City
h	Rogers Michael	16	laborer	25	5 Staniford
k	Sabine Howard C	16	printer	33	Hudson
l	Turner Earnest W	16	janitor	50	Clinton Me
m	Young Peter	16	clerk	25	New Hampshire
n	Dolphin Martin	18	farmer	46	Still River Me
o	Littlefield Melbourne	18	laborer	20	Pittsfield Me
p	McKenna Frank C	18	B F D	38	25 S Russell
r	McKenna Mary E—†	18	housewife	43	25 "
s	Zucouska Martin M	18	teamster	23	28 Lawn
t	Aiken Augustus	19	chef	76	here
u	Caulfield William H	19	cigarmaker	54	"
v	Derkin Edward	19	cook	37	"
w	Fannel Austin	19	carpenter	24	"
x	Fannel Joseph	19	restaurateur	27	26 Temple
y	Gray William H	19	contractor	43	here
z	Halprin Jacob	19	paperhanger	33	"
a	Juro Joseph	19	salesman	28	7 Cotting
b	Largey Fred	19	restaurateur	35	Augusta Me
c	Menzer Lawrence	19	musician	33	here
d	Mull Isaac	19	cigarmaker	55	"
e	Ross Elizabeth J—†	19	lodging house	53	"
f	Shevlin Patrick	19	mason	59	11 Chambers
g	Silverman David	19	tailor	42	here
h	Smith Elmer H	19	clerk	21	"
k	Smith John	19	laborer	50	"
l	Stephens William H	19	"	55	Foxcroft Me
m	Collins Anna—†	20	collector	34	here
n	Hawly John F	20	physician	65	"
o	Hawly Minnie T—†	20	housewife	61	"
p	Kelly Elsie—†	20	maid	34	"
r	Kinny Asa	20	carpenter	50	"
s	Leary Dennis	20	conductor	34	"

Page.	Letter.	FULL NAME.	Residence, April 1, 1924.	Occupation.	Supposed Age.	Reported Residence April 1, 1923. Street and Number

Temple Street—Continued

s¹	McGowan Daniel V	21	druggist	44	10 Marie
T	Sidlinger Albert K	21	broker	34	169 Charles
U	Sidlinger Annie—†	21	housewife	32	169 "
V	Rosenstein Fannie—†	21	"	42	here
W	Rosenstein Morris	21	pedler	48	"
X	Villard Dora—†	21	housekeeper	45	"
Y	Klein Morris	21	butcher	42	56 Spring
Z	Klein Sadie—†	21	housewife	36	56 "
B	Coit Dorothy—†	22	teacher	34	here
C	Coit Lucetta H—†	22	"	47	"
D	Coit Mary C—†	22	secretary	28	"
E	Coit Mary L—†	22	housewife	86	"
F	Coit Robert	22	architect	62	"
G	Coit Robert S	22	lawyer	26	"
H	Roucher Mary—†	23	housewife	58	103 Chamb
K	Roucher Peter	23	elevatorman	54	103 "
L	Cohen Bessie—†	23	housewife	48	here
M	Cohen Isaac	23	salesman	51	"
N	Greenberg Annie—†	23	housewife	45	"
P	Greenberg Isaac	23	salesman	28	"
O	Greenberg Israel	23	"	30	"
R	Greenberg Louie	23	pressman	45	"
S	Moranti Amelia—†	23	housewife	43	20 Lynde
T	Moranti Charles	23	barber	47	20 "
U	Moranti Marchie	23	chauffeur	27	20 "
V	Moranti Mary—†	23	clerk	23	20 "
X	Yee Lun	24	laundryman	53	here
Y	Winters Blanche G—†	24A	clerk	24	"
Z	Winters Charlotte—†	24A	housewife	43	"
A	Winters Roy J	24A	engineer	23	"
B	Galvin William	24A	waiter	30	"
C	Murphy Thomas	24A	chef	60	"
D	Paris Annie—†	24A	housewife	50	20 Temple
E	Rice Elizabeth—†	24A	cook	40	here
F	Burgin Eli	25	salesman	52	"
G	Burgin Ida—†	25	teacher	24	"
H	Burgin Milla—†	25	housewife	49	"
K	Goldfine Bella—†	25	retired	55	"
L	Goldfine Frank	25	pedler	55	"
M	Miller Minnie—†	25	housewife	35	"
N	Miller Morris	25	salesman	48	"

Temple Street—Continued

O	Brown Mary A—†	25	housewife	53	here
P	Brown Robert S	25	porter	59	"
R	Wilson Gray	25	watchman	46	"
S	Rosenband Adolph	25	barber	53	15 Lyman
T	Rosenband Dora—†	25	housewife	50	15 "
U	Rosenband Julia—†	25	musician	20	15 "
V	Rosenband Lillian—†	25	stenographer	20	here
X	Bruno Americo	26	tailor	45	"
Y	Chell John	26	houseman	47	"
Z	Crockford Alexander J	26	clerk	55	"
A	Davis Harry	26	"	28	"
B	Groves Mary E—†	26	housewife	47	"
C	Handler Abraham	26	tailor	46	"
D	Hendrickson Alonzo	26	salesman	35	Walpole
E	Levin Benjamin	26	tailor	32	20 Rose
F	Mahoney Charles J	26	trainman	45	here
G	Morgan William	26	chauffeur	33	Quebec
H	Plevenski Benjamin	26	tailor	35	here
K	Quarison James	26	chauffeur	35	"
L	Sandres Demetrios I	26	chef	38	"
M	Whittaker Harold	26	textile worker	45	46 Lowell
N	Wilson Mary—†	26	housekeeper	72	here
O	Albert Fannie—†	27	tailoress	40	"
P	Rotman Mary—†	27	housewife	50	"
R	Rotman Morris	27	furrier	55	"
S	Miller Eva—†	27	housewife	48	"
T	Miller Israel	27	grocer	48	"
U	Miller Rose—†	27	none	20	"
V	Miller Samuel	27	lawyer	25	"
W	Kane Ellen—†	27	housewife	50	"
X	Kane Patrick	27	shipper	65	112 Thornton
Y	Kallivas Rose—†	27	housewife	31	Lynn
Z	Kallivas Stephen S	27	fruit	36	"
B	Abbell Arthur S	28	cook	58	here
C	Bumpus Albert W	28	metalworker	52	"
D	Burns Guesippe	28	laborer	24	"
E	Doyle Daniel J	28	carpenter	26	"
F	Doyle Ruth—†	28	housewife	22	"
G	Dunn William J	28	printer	51	"
H	Feldman Benjamin	28	tailor	36	"
K	Jealson Frank W	28	shoecutter	51	"

Temple Street—Continued

L	Jealson Jennie—†	28	housewife	50	here
M	Kames Morris	28	laborer	22	"
N	Lavender John A	28	machinist	38	"
O	Malone John	28	farmer	59	"
P	McHugh Sarah—†	28	cook	53	"
R	Mesianco Fred T	28	salesman	32	"
S	Vail Charles W	28	landlord	48	"
T	Vail George W	28	laborer	52	"
V	Ahearn Katharine M—†	30	housewife	50	"
W	Allen Thomas	30	gardener	48	"
X	Antelano Joseph W	30	salesman	36	"
Y	Brown Alexander	30	roofer	70	"
Z	Cleveland Ralph M	30	cook	40	"
A	Dempsey Alban	30	porter	52	"
B	Donavan Nellie—†	30	shoecutter	36	"
C	Gallagher Martha—†	30	maid	48	"
D	Hudson William S	30	musician	50	"
E	Lampron Henry	30	mechanic	38	"
F	Mossman Titus	30	clerk	28	"
G	Sheehan John L	30	"	50	"
H	Watkins Arnold C	30	chef	27	"
K	Watkins Bernice—†	30	clerk	28	"
L	Constantineau Joseph	31	barber	67	35 Revere
M	Constantineau Laura—†	31	furworker	60	35 "
N	Dale Estella—†	31	housewife	28	Detroit Mic
O	Dale William J	31	engraver	38	"
P	Hayes Roy E	31	manager	46	here
R	Hayes Virginia L—†	31	housewife	36	"
S	Currin William H	31	laborer	28	"
T	Hambury Benjiman	31	buyer	22	"
U	Hambury Freda—†	31	housewife	54	"
V	Hambury Soloman	31	clerk	60	"
W	Bennett Alice S—†	31	"	54	"
X	Barnwell Bridget A—†	31	housewife	45	"
Y	Morrisroe John J	31	freighthandler	40	"
Z	Pollander Joseph N	31	typist	36	635 Tremon
A	Pollander Lillian J—†	31	housewife	38	635 "
B	Bennett Albert	32	electrician	40	here
C	Conner Alexander	32	supervisor	39	Somerville
D	Cronin Michael J	32	clerk	26	48 Temple
E	Hunnelman Milton	32	carpenter	30	here

Temple Street—Continued

	Letter	FULL NAME	Residence April 1, 1924	Occupation	Supposed Age	Reported Residence April 1, 1923
F	Laganes John D		32	cook	32	12 School
G	Lehr Fred		32	steamfitter	35	here
H	Lonergan Agnes—†		32	housewife	33	Framingham
K	Lonergan John J		32	metalworker	37	"
L	Masson John A		32	chef	65	here
M	Muzzy Charles W		32	laborer	60	"
N	Pefiozle Albert		32	cook	27	12 School
O	Thurber Stanley		32	orderly	32	here
P	Witcher Chauncey D		32	engineer	57	"
R	Currier Loda—†		33	saleswoman	25	Leominster
S	Earls Ira		33	engineer	30	here
T	Green William E		33	teller	64	"
U	McNally Anna—†		33	secretary	33	"
V	McNally Leo J		33	shipper	37	"
W	Monick Paul		33	mattressmaker	26	New York
X	Mullin James		33	longshoreman	25	7 Haynes
Y	Ross Thomas		33	garageworker	33	56 Temple
Z	Stevens Homer J		33	none	24	here
A	Stevens John M		33	salesman	49	"
B	Stevens John G		33	electrician	20	"
C	Stevens Mary A—†		33	houseworker	47	"
D	Ginty Edward		34	salesman	35	"
E	Moran Rose—†		34	fitter	31	"
F	Murphy Giles		34	laborer	42	"
G	O'Connor Nora E—†		34	housekeeper	43	"
K	Regan Mary A—†		34	tel operator	23	46 Morris
H	Ryan Julia—†		34	bookbinder	21	Halifax N S
L	Scott Agnes—†		34	designer	35	here
M	Smith George H		34	lawyer	51	Cambridge
N	Thompson Frank		34	salesman	34	here
O	Werner Rudolph		34	toolmaker	21	Germany
P	Aberti Angelina—†	35 & 37	student	23	here
R	Aultman Elsie—†	35 & 37	"	39	"
S	Baker Alice H—†	35 & 37	"	35	Andover
T	Barker Frances—†	35 & 37	social worker	40	here
U	Bennett Bertha—†	35 & 37	student	45	New York
V	Bermer Gladys—†	35 & 37	"	29	here
W	Blackstock Constana—†	35 & 37	"	33	England
X	Blanchard Mary—†	35 & 37	housewife	75	here
Y	Brigham Doris—†	35 & 37	student	21	"
Z	Calado Alice—†	35 & 37	"	25	Somerville

Temple Street—Continued

A	Coleman Marion—†	35 & 37	student	27	here
B	Craig Mabel—†	35 & 37	"	28	43 Salcombe
C	Curry Olive—†	35 & 37	"	26	Pittsburgh Pa
D	Dotzon Laura—†	35 & 37	"	30	Maryland
E	Fazer Dorothy—†	35 & 37	"	21	here
F	Fraley Helen—†	35 & 37	"	25	Rochester Me
G	Fundi Elizabeth—†	35 & 37	matron	61	here
H	Greer Lillian—†	35 & 37	student	36	China
K	Griffith Margaret—†	35 & 37	social worker	26	68 Warrenton
L	Halford Ruth A—†	35 & 37	student	31	here
M	Hammers Irene—†	35 & 37	"	23	"
N	Hange Lillie—†	35 & 37	"	39	San Francisco
O	Hannah Mary—†	35 & 37	"	28	Framingham
P	Hawkes Dora M—†	35 & 37	secretary	32	here
R	Hayton Maggie—†	35 & 37	student	25	New Bedford
S	Hodgson Eileen—†	35 & 37	"	28	Portland Me
T	Holinshead Helen—†	35 & 37	"	21	Buffalo N Y
U	Humphrey Gertrude—†	35 & 37	"	48	Philadelphia
V	Hunter Daisy A—†	35 & 37	matron	48	here
W	Johnston Jessie—†	35 & 37	nurse	37	"
X	Jones Serena—†	35 & 37	student	22	"
Y	Kentfield Anna—†	35 & 37	"	31	China
Z	Kitajina Tsuya—†	35 & 37	"	32	Japan
A	Leonard Mary—†	35 & 37	"	23	Portland Me
B	Lucas Dorothy—†	35 & 37	"	24	here
C	MacKay Mary—†	35 & 37	clerk	31	68 Warrenton
D	MacLeod Mary—†	35 & 37	lawyer	34	here
E	Mann Gladys—†	35 & 37	student	25	Lynnfield
F	McBride Elizabella—†	35 & 37	"	48	here
G	McMurphy Charles A	35 & 37	houseman	56	Laconia N H
H	McMurphy Mary—†	35 & 37	housewife	56	"
K	Meanor Ethel—†	35 & 37	student	26	Pennsylvania
L	MerLu Chang—†	35 & 37	"	36	here
M	Nickerson Arrilla—†	35 & 37	bushelwoman	55	"
N	Pearson Dorothy—†	35 & 37	student	24	324 Bay State rd
O	Pearson Sarah—†	35 & 37	clerk	38	Connecticut
P	Ritter Amy—†	35 & 37	student	28	Allentown Pa
R	Robinson Ethel R—†	35 & 37	"	31	here
S	Sager Bess—†	35 & 37	"	35	"
T	Shannon Mary—†	35 & 37	"	44	Kansas
U	Slackey Bertha—†	35 & 37	"	42	Japan

Temple Street—Continued

v	Stimpson Mary J—†	35 & 37	housewife	81	here
w	Stone Florence—†	35 & 37	tel operator	25	"
x	Stone Lillian—†	35 & 37	clerk	37	"
z	Taft Elizabeth—†	35 & 37	student	36	"
y	Tang Mary R—†	35 & 37	"	25	China
A	Taylor Alma—†	35 & 37	student	34	here
B	Temple Teresa—†	35 & 37	stenographer	35	New York
D	Thompson Florence K—†	35 & 37	housewife	50	here
D	Thompson Mary C—†	35 & 37	"	77	"
E	Wallace Avis—†	35 & 37	student	28	Lewiston Me
F	Welliam Gertrude—†	35 & 37	"	35	here
G	Wells Dorothy—†	35 & 37	"	26	"
H	Whetro Jeannette—†	35 & 37	"	21	Cleveland O
K	Whitaker Isabel—†	35 & 37	"	27	here
L	White Lola—†	35 & 37	"	27	"
M	Wirth Julia—†	35 & 37	stenographer	24	New York City
N	Wirth Cornelia—†	35 & 37	student	28	here
O	Wooden Nellie—†	35 & 37	"	35	"
P	Blackbird Gardner	36	printer	55	22 Temple
R	Burns Richard	36	"	45	here
S	Gibbons Anna—†	36	seamstress	50	30 Blossom
T	Hill Elsie C—†	36	housewife	45	22 Temple
U	Johnson John, jr	36	porter	21	22 "
V	Kennedy John J	36	laborer	23	Portland Me
W	Lucy Cornelius V	36	painter	40	"
X	Machio Bartholomew	36	waiter	45	here
Y	Mollet Jacob	36	chef	28	"
Z	Musidelli Anthony	36	porter	25	New York
A	Pedro Joseph	36	laborer	25	"
B	Shortell Joseph	36	stableman	60	50A Green
C	Williams John	36	janitor	60	Vermont
D	Bagdoian Jacob B	38	student	22	New Hampshire
E	Galvin Grace G—†	38	school teacher	22	here
F	Galvin John J	38	waiter	50	"
G	Galvin Mary G—†	38	housewife	50	"
H	Gorin Simon	38	pedler	55	New York
K	Haley Clarice—†	38	housewife	30	Chelsea
L	Haley Leroy	38	salesman	40	"
M	McIntyre Sarah—†	38	scrubwoman	51	here
N	Murphy Arthur	38	stableman	55	"
O	Pollard Alden	38	porter	43	"

Temple Street—Continued

P	Tucker Fred A	38	machinist	44	here
R	Tyler Sherman	38	waiter	60	"
S	Bailey Henry R	39	clergyman	38	"
T	Bailey Mabel D—†	39	housewife	37	"
U	Mitchell Mary H—†	39	housekeeper	53	Lincoln Neb
V	Bartlett Walter	40	clerk	48	here
W	Deehan Charles	40	skipper	32	"
X	Donovan Walter R	40	student	27	Worcester
Y	Friedman Joseph	40	tailor	37	here
Z	Kempton Eva M—†	40	textile mender	29	North Adam
A	Laplante Charles H	40	railway mail	36	here
B	Leggett Parker A	40	bookkeeper	44	"
C	Lowney Herbert	40	chauffeur	23	"
D	McGregor Anna—†	40	housewife	42	"
E	McGregor Daniel G	40	stereotyper	44	"
F	Moss William	40	cashier	50	"
G	Parker Elizabeth E—†	40	housekeeper	45	"
H	Sheldon Dorothy M—†	40	clerk	30	"
K	Covert Mabel—†	44	nun	34	"
L	Culby Florence—†	44	"	50	"
M	Garcia Carmen—†	44	"	20	Porto Rico
N	Holmes Muriel—†	44	"	20	here
O	Hubbard Alice—†	44	"	25	"
P	Kimball Myra S—†	44	"	40	"
R	Ley Wilhilmina—†	44	"	35	"
S	Merrick Ruth—†	44	clerk	23	12 Glenville
T	Petrie Elsie—†	44	housemaid	20	Vermont
U	Sainsbury Winifred—†	44	nun	32	here
V	Slaymaker Harriet—†	44	retired	75	"
W	Tibbetts Dorothy—†	44	nun	30	"
X	Barrett Peter P	48	cashier	62	38 Temple
Y	Davidson Alfred	48	watchman	60	here
Z	MacKenzie Herbert	48	porter	34	58 Temple
A	Nickett Eva—†	48	waitress	40	Quebec
B	Piccordi Joseph	48	contractor	74	23 Bowdoin
C	Ronimus Samuel W	48	porter	70	169 Cambrid
D	Rosen William	48	woodturner	40	45 McLean
E	Dooley Joseph	50	printer	67	here
F	Miller Alice A—†	50	housewife	45	"
G	Miller Theodore C	50	optometrist	60	"

Temple Street—Continued

K	McAuliffe Albert T	52	shoemaker	23	Brockton
L	McAuliffe Dolly—†	52	housewife	52	"
M	McAuliffe Thomas J	52	shoemaker	54	"
N	McAuliffe William F	52	"	27	"
O	Daley Elsie E—†	52	dressmaker	38	here
P	DeVoe Emma L—†	52	housekeeper	54	2 Myrtle
R	Hill Annie S—†	52	"	70	38 Temple
S	Jones Percy F	52	manager	48	38 "
V	Cameron Louis	54½	student	32	243 W Newton
W	Collins Ralph	54½	merchant	33	here
X	Gordon Edmond	54½	shoemaker	28	243 W Newton
X¹	Moser William	54½	weaver	33	19 Hancock
Y	Roy Fred J	54½	carpenter	33	51 Winchester
Z	Roy Josephine—†	54½	housewife	32	51 "
B	Wallace John	54½	waiter	28	Newton
E	Bartlett Alfred	56	stationer	52	here
F	Bertholet Joseph	56	pressman	40	"
G	Coyne Emma J—†	56	housewife	43	"
H	Coyne John M	56	engineer	43	"
K	Donovan Stephen	56	clerk	63	"
L	Slater Joseph	56	cigarmaker	57	"
M	Snow Henry	56	inspector	34	55 Temple
N	Walsh Timothy J	56	investigator	37	here
P	Brigham Frank H	58	cigarmaker	38	"
R	Figley Howard J	58	salesman	34	New Orleans La
S	Figley Stella F—†	58	saleswoman	22	"
T	Flaherty Emma E—†	58	stenographer	33	here
U	Flaherty John A	58	salesman	37	"
V	Gilbert Fred W, jr	58	"	35	Somerville
W	Hale Charlotte L—†	58	saleswoman	38	47 Hancock
X	Hale Samuel	58	salesman	40	47 "
Y	Luzinski Frank P	58	policeman	25	Salem
Z	McSherry Harold L	58	clerk	23	St John N B
A	Michaud John	58	cigarmaker	52	here
B	Michaud Susan—†	58	housewife	55	"
D	Bowngar Nicholas	60	bellboy	22	38 Hancock
E	Chick Madaline—†	60	housekeeper	69	here
F	Duhig Catherine—†	60	clerk	21	Ireland
G	Duhig William	60	student	35	7 Emmons
H	King Frank	60	retired	71	12 Hancock

Temple Street—Continued

K	Lee Lawrence	60	painter	21	107 Myrtle
L	Livadary Emily—†	60	stitcher	36	here
M	Moriello Patrick D	60	elevatorman	25	Lowell
N	Walter Harry E	60	painter	33	Cambridge

Walnut Street

P	Hartford Harriette—†	2	housekeeper	69	here
R	Williams Dora—†	2	school teacher	45	"
S	Langdon George W	2	inspector	60	"
T	Langdon Helen—†	2	housewife	60	"
U	Blanchard Lillias—†	2	teacher	50	"
V	Sweeney Helen B—†	2	manager	48	"
W	Tailor Elizabeth M—†	2	lawyer	50	"
X	Grady Alice—†	2	insurance agent	48	"
Y	Staniford Francis	2	retired	60	"
Z	Farrell Albert	2	guide	63	"
A	Hunt Emma—†	2	housewife	57	"
B	Hunt George	2	manager	51	"
C	Welch Lucy M—†	2	social worker	53	"
D	Keys Carrie M—†	4	matron	65	"
E	Bowman Gardner	4	salesman	70	"
F	Burnham Harry L	4	lawyer	45	"
G	McMullin Alban	4	manager	50	98 Chestnut
H	Holbrook Abby—†	4	housewife	86	here
K	Holbrook Ann—†	4	stenographer	50	"
L	Holbrook Anntonett—†	4	manager	45	"
M	Starr Lydia A—†	4	seamstress	64	"
N	Morse Alice J—†	4	art teacher	50	"
O	Canavan Charlotte A—†	4	housewife	68	"
P	Canavan Ruth—†	4	manager	39	"
R	Russell Fred	4	fruit	65	"
S	Ware Robert A	4	bookkeeper	65	"
T	Conner Madaline—†	6	housewife	60	"
U	Emlah James	6	manager	55	"
V	Godfrey Sophie—†	6	housewife	85	"
W	Hazelton Alice—†	6	"	51	"
X	Hazelton Norman	6	lawyer	55	"
Y	Hines Irene—†	6	teacher	35	"
Z	Hodgkins Florence—†	6	housewife	50	"

Walnut Street—Continued

A	Rockwell Henry	6	manager	50	here
B	Rockwell Jessie—†	6	housewife	50	"
C	Singleton Florence—†	6	"	48	"
D	Zerrahn Carl	6	insurance agent	60	"
E	Cushing Florence—†	8	housewife	70	"
F	Durgan Margaret—†	8	maid	30	"
G	Gray Mary—†	8	"	50	Ireland
H	Hickey Catherine—†	8	"	30	here
K	Griffin Margaret—†	10	"	40	"
L	Morash Carrie—†	10	parlormaid	40	"
M	Ryan Nellie—†	10	maid	45	"
N	Sullivan Penelope—†	10	"	21	"
O	Watson Margaret—†	10	cook	30	"
P	Winthrop Elizabeth—†	10	housewife	75	"
R	Hanlon Mary—†	14	maid	30	"
S	McPurell Helen—†	14	"	21	"
T	Russell Martha—†	14	cook	27	England
U	Sedgewick Ellery	14	editor	50	here
V	Sedgewick Mable—†	14	housewife	50	"
W	Sullivan Ellen—†	14	maid	27	"

Ward 8—Precinct 2

CITY OF BOSTON.

LIST OF RESIDENTS
20 YEARS OF AGE AND OVER

(FEMALES INDICATED BY DAGGER)

AS OF

APRIL 1, 1924

HERBERT A. WILSON, } *Listing*

JAMES F. EAGAN, } *Board.*

CITY OF BOSTON—PRINTING DEPARTMENT

Anderson Place

A	Feinstein Celia—†	1	housewife	25	Malden
B	Feinstein Harry	1	waiter	32	"
C	Miller Max	1	cigarmaker	28	53 Spring
D	Miller Minnie—†	1	housewife	23	53 "
E	Metro Ada—†	1	"	28	here
F	Metro Charles	1	circus man	32	"
G	Metro Thomas	1	laborer	24	"
H	Strong Estelle B—†	2	maid	56	78 Carver
L	Gannarman Esther—†	2	laundry worker	27	here
M	Wax Lena—†	2	housekeeper	58	"
N	O'Donnell Charles	2	expressman	38	30 Nashua
O	Kaufman Anna—†	2	housekeeper	52	here

Anderson Street

R	Nason Mary A—†	4	housewife	58	here
S	Mason Robert J	4	inspector	58	"
T	Doherty Agnes—†	4	clerk	20	"
U	Doherty Catherine—†	4	"	21	"
V	Doherty John	4	carpenter	29	"
W	Doherty John	4	porter	60	"
X	Doherty Margrett—†	4	housewife	55	"
Y	Doherty Mary—†	4	operator	26	"
Z	Doherty Rose—†	4	stenographer	25	"
A	Oharo Sarah—†	6	housewife	50	"
B	Armstrong Janie—†	6	"	60	"
C	Casey Elizabeth—†	6	"	70	"
D	Peterson Ferdinand	6	porter	57	"
E	Sullivan Rose—†	8	housewife	64	Chicago Ill
F	Sullivan Rose—†	8	tel operator	27	"
G	Sullivan Thomas H	8	machinist	30	"
H	Brown George E	10	laborer	45	Lynn
K	Henessy John J	10	clerk	40	Worcester
L	McCarthy Cornelius	10	waiter	60	here
M	McDevitt Thomas	10	clerk	50	"
N	Sullivan Norah—†	10	housewife	42	"
O	Wofharsky Abraham	14	clerk	20	7 Russell pl
P	Wofharsky Bessie—†	14	housewife	43	7 "
R	Wofharsky Harry	14	clerk	67	7 "

Anderson Street—Continued

Letter.	FULL NAME.	Residence, April 1, 1924.	Occupation.	Supposed Age.	Reported Residence, April 1, 1923. Street and Number.
s	Cohen Jacob	14	chauffeur	39	here
T	Cohen Sophie—†	14	housewife	36	"
U	Goldberg Bella—†	14	clerk	22	"
V	Goldberg Elena—†	14	housewife	50	"
W	Goldberg Jacob	14	storekeeper	48	"
Y	Klaymen Gertrude—†	16	housewife	42	"
Z	Klaymen Jacob	16	tailor	45	"
A	Pollock Beckie—†	16	housewife	50	"
B	Pollock David	16	chauffeur	26	"
C	Pollock Harry	16	baker	52	"
D	Dropkin Joseph	16	painter	61	"
E	Lemkin Charles	16	"	44	"
F	Lemkin Sarah—†	16	housewife	42	"
H	Branavich Frances—†	18	"	26	58 Cliff
K	Branavich John	18	waiter	27	58 "
L	Winer Esidore	18	tailor	27	48 Garden
M	Winer Esta—†	18	housewife	25	48 "
N	Snider David	18	tailor	44	here
O	Snider Morris	18	salesman	21	"
P	Snider Rebecca—†	18	housewife	38	"
S	Swatz Abraham	20	tailor	31	18 W Cedar
T	Swatz Mary—†	20	housewife	30	18 "
U	Sherman Phillip	20	pedler	44	here
V	Sherman Rose—†	20	housewife	43	"
W	Levine Abraham	20	chauffeur	29	60 Auburn
X	Levine Rose—†	20	housewife	25	60 "
Z	Lexenberg Fannie—†	24	housewife	39	here
A	Lexenberg Louis	24	storekeeper	43	"
B	Brenner Benjamin	24	laborer	35	"
C	Brenner Frances—†	24	housewife	30	"
D	Finberg Mary—†	24	"	28	"
E	Finberg Morris	24	laborer	29	"
F	Barron Frank L	24	"	28	"
G	Barron Josephine—†	24	housewife	24	15 N Russell
H	Marcus Goldie—†	24	"	27	here
K	Marcus William	24	tailor	33	"
L	Cohen Bertha—†	24	housewife	38	77A Revere
M	Cohen Florence—†	24	bookkeeper	21	77A "
N	Rasner Fannie—†	24	housewife	26	here
O	Rasner Max	24	watchmaker	28	"
P	Johnston Mary—†	28	housewife	29	"

Anderson Street—Continued

	Letter	Full Name	Residence	Occupation	Age	Reported Residence
	R	Kadetsky Fannie—†	28	housewife	29	here
	S	Smallivotz Freda—†	28	"	33	"
	T	Smallivotz Phillip	28	painter	42	"
	U	Pruskin Harry	28	tailor	38	"
	V	Pruskin Rosie—†	28	housewife	35	"
	W	Hickner Dorah—†	28	"	36	"
	X	Hickner Harry	28	teamster	37	"
	Y	Lappo Morris	28	laborer	35	Hartford Ct
	Z	Lappo Sarah—†	28	housewife	27	"
	A	Gillman Lillian—†	28	housewife	25	23 Willard
	B	Gillman Morris	28	laborer	24	23 "
	C	Gladden Viola—†	28	housewife	20	here
	D	Gladden Walter	28	longshoreman	22	"
	E	Orel Sarah—†	28	housewife	32	"
	F	Orel Saul	28	laborer	33	"
	G	Reddick Charles	28	"	49	"
	H	Reddick Josephine —†	28	decorator	21	"
	K	Reddick Minnie—†	28	housewife	46	"
	L	Reddick William	28	laborer	23	"
	M	Brown John	28	"	29	"
	N	Brown Mary—†	28	housewife	27	"
	O	Brown William	28	laborer	30	"
	P	Silverman Himan	28	painter	40	"
	R	Silverman Selia—†	28	housewife	40	"
	S	Johnston Elizabeth—†	28	candymaker	24	"
	T	Johnston Elizabeth M—†	28	housewife	50	"
	U	Johnson Andrew	28	clerk	27	"
	V	Johnson Margrett—†	28	housewife	28	"
	W	Jones Mary—†	28	cook	50	"
	X	Mathews Charles H	28	clerk	32	"
	Y	Henderson Lois—†	30	"	28	Chelsea
	A	Pasqua Fred	30	fruit	57	here
	B	Pasqua Joseph	30	storekeeper	21	"
	C	Pasqua Mary—†	30	housekeeper	25	"
	D	Pasqua Mary C—†	30	"	47	"
	E	Pasqua Phillip F	30	watchman	28	"
	F	Yackolow Annie—†	30	housewife	27	Chelsea
	G	Yackolow Lois P	30	tailor	34	"
	H	Grossberg Ida—†	32	housekeeper	62	here
	K	Grossberg Max	32	merchant	24	"
	L	Stepansky Harold	32	upholsterer	38	"

Anderson Street—Continued

M	Stepansky Milia—†	32	housewife	37	here
N	Strommer Nathan	32	tailor	38	"
O	Rubin Fannie—†	32	housewife	49	"
P	Rubin Louis	32	junk dealer	50	"
R	Egelnick Louis	32	tailor	38	42 Anderson
S	Egelnick Mary—†	32	housewife	35	42 "
T	Dubeshter Abraham	32	salesman	30	here
U	Dubeshter Fannie—†	32	housewife	33	"
X	Maxwell Archibald	34	automobiles	30	"
Y	Maxwell Emma—†	34	housewife	30	"
Z	Pearl Victoria—†	34	saleswoman	27	"
A	Filene Louis	34	electrician	35	"
B	Krasner Abraham	34	teacher	80	"
C	Krasner Elizabeth—†	34	housewife	60	"
D	Krasner Evelyn—†	34	dressmaker	21	"
E	Krasner Louis	34	truck driver	20	"
F	Goldman Eva—†	34	housekeeper	48	"
G	Goldman Joseph	34	automobile tops	24	"
H	Dreyfus Anna—†	34	housewife	40	"
K	Dreyfus Jacob	34	paperboy	20	"
L	Dreyfus Max	34	paperhanger	45	"
M	Dreyfus Melvin	34	student	21	"
N	Niss Abraham	34	tailor	49	"
O	Niss Morris	34	milkman	24	"
P	Niss Rosie—†	34	housewife	47	"
R	Shulman Ida—†	34	housekeeper	35	"
T	Miller Benjamin	36	roofer	38	"
U	Miller Clara—†	36	housewife	36	"
V	Letters James	36	carpenter	27	"
W	Letters Louise—†	36	housewife	22	"
Y	Podbersky Celia—†	36	"	30	"
Z	Podbersky Isadore	36	waiter	25	"
A	Evzen Dora—†	36	housewife	35	"
B	Evzen Morris	36	tailor	39	"
C	Michelon Alice—†	36	housewife	44	"
D	Michelon Antonio	36	salesman	36	"
E	Sadofsky Anna—†	36	housewife	42	New York
F	Sadofsky Morris	36	tailor	42	"
G	Iswick Gentie—†	36	housewife	53	Russia
H	Iswick Isreal	36	tailor	55	33 Anderson
K	Hershon Barnett	40	bartender	49	here

Anderson Street—Continued

L	Hershon Mildred	40	housewife	48	here
M	Hershon Pauline—†	40	saleswoman	20	"
N	Talisman William	40	weaver	43	Chelsea
O	Nash James	40	student	28	here
R	Kaplan Mary—†	40	housewife	38	"
S	Kaplan Samuel	40	framemaker	38	"
T	Benett Ralph W	40	paperhanger	41	15 Ailston
U	Hardy Gwendolyn—†	40	elevatorman	34	106 Newton
V	Breslouf Lillian—†	40	housewife	30	here
W	Breslouf Solomon	40	rubberworker	32	"
X	Byrne Elizabeth—†	40	housekeeper	69	"
Y	Cassidy Catherine—†	40	stitcher	37	"
Z	Daltry Edward J	40	teamster	42	"
A	Lane Emily—†	40	dishwasher	64	"
B	Smith Charles C	42	laborer	52	"
C	Smith Sarah—†	42	housewife	47	"
D	Pierce Josephine—†	42	emp agency	48	85 Myrtle
E	Girdlestone Florence—†	42	housekeeper	52	Everett
E¹	Stewart Emma S—†	42	boxmaker	44	"
F	Stewart Sophia—†	42	retired	80	"
G	Case Eva—†	42	housekeeper	50	642 Dor av
H	Doody Delia—†	42	cook	45	160 Com av
K	Pierce William	42	iceman	44	here
L	Dick Elizabeth—†	46	counterwoman	29	60 Myrtle
M	Dick William	46	waiter	34	60 "
N	Carter Caroline—†	58	retired	81	here
O	Carter Caroline L—†	58	manager	38	"
P	Carter Charlotte O—†	58	none	80	"
R	Grover George G	58	lecturer	39	57 Myrtle
S	Skach Herbert S	58	student	21	New York

Auburn Court

W	King Ada—†	1	cook	65	58 Howard
X	Peterson Annie—†	1	"	45	49 W Cedar
Y	Murray Katherine—†	1	maid	28	95 "
Z	Murray Margaret—†	1	"	23	95 "
E	Treen Joseph	3	carpenter	50	33 Dennis
F	Young William	3	"	45	69 Dwight
G	McCormack John	3	"	35	49 Waltham

Auburn Court—Continued

H	McFee David	3	cook	54	15 Temple
K	Watson Thomas	3	laborer	65	1244 Wash'n
L	Sands Elizabeth—†	4	housekeeper	55	176 Cambridge
M	Sands Mary C—†	4	stenographer	22	176 "

Cambridge Street

D	Shoales Alfred B	120	engineer	63	here
E	Shoales Lydia—†	120	housewife	43	"
F	Quattrochi Letterio	120	printer	41	"
G	Quattrochi Tresa—†	120	housewife	39	"
H	Sayer Lucy—†	120	"	70	"
K	Barry Annie—†	120	"	34	"
L	Barry William F J	120	carpenter	34	"
O	Howard Frank	126	artist	67	"
P	Howard Louisa—†	126	housewife	46	"
R	Mellen Catherine E—†	126	"	45	"
S	Mellen William	126	packer	46	"
Y	Bussey Harry M	142	chauffeur	24	Cohoes N Y
Z	Bussey Mary M—†	142	housewife	34	"
A	Carnes John O	142	longshoreman	42	68 Cambridge
B	Daly Charles L	142	houseman	42	here
C	Dunham James	142	cook	38	"
D	Dunham Mable J—†	142	housewife	38	"
E	Finn Ruth O—†	142	chambermaid	26	Wellesley
F	Fitzgerald Annie—†	142	houseworker	30	Athol
G	Fitzgerald Edward	142	painter	46	"
H	Flynn Ethel E—†	142	waitress	30	20 Auburn
K	Hines James F	142	lather	45	13 Cambridge
L	Jean Adelard V	142	painter	42	Canton
M	Leeson John	142	printer	38	72 Myrtle
N	Leeson Mary—†	142	houseworker	85	72 "
O	Mangiarulo Eony	142	blacksmith	47	Chicago Ill
P	Nelson Alice—†	142	alterations	29	Athol
R	Pring John	142	longshoremen	35	Watertown
S	Pring May—†	142	bookkeeper	38	"
T	Reese Annie—†	142	houseworker	34	New York
U	Reese Louis	142	dishwasher	28	"
V	Roscher Contine—†	142	chambermaid	27	Wellesley
G	Johnson Mary—†	166	houseworker	40	here

Cambridge Street—Continued

H	Kirkland Felix	166	milkman	22	New York	
K	Pearson Edward	166	laborer	50	here	
L	Ross James	166	"	35	"	
M	Vincent Estele —†	166	housewife	27	"	
N	Vincent Harry	166	laborer	30	"	
T	Addassi Beigio	176	tailor	37	Connecticut	
U	Mereborgei Mary —†	176	housekeeper	39	"	
W	McIsaac Joseph	176	laborer	59	here	
X	McIsase Lilian —†	176	housewife	48	"	
Y	Degan Margaret †	176	"	30	Somerville	
Z	Degan Thomas	176	laborer	38	"	
A	O'Connell Mary—†	176	cook	52	here	
B	Driscoll Edward	176	laborer	40	"	
C	Driscoll William	176	porter	42	"	
D	O'Mara Thomas J	176	clerk	28	4 Temple	
E	Clifford John J	176	shipper	24	here	
F	Clifford Margaret —†	176	housewife	24	"	
H	Fortes Hilda—†	176	"	26	New York	
K	Fortes Peter	176	laborer	30	"	
L	McNeil Florence—†	176	housewife	32	here	
M	McNeil Hugh	176	laborer	32	"	
O	Haran Margaret —†	182	housekeeper	39	N Russell pl	
P	Ebbetts Delia— †	182	housewife	44	here	
R	Ebbetts William H	182	painter	55	"	
S	Fuller Stanley E	182	salesman	45	538 Newbury	
T	Dascoli Domoniek	182	tinsmith	26	100 Wash'n	
U	Dascoli James	182	"	30	65 Billerica	
V	Dascoli Mary —†	182	housewife	22	65 "	
W	Solo Cosmino	182	laborer	35	65 "	
X	Johnson Jennie †	182	housewife	27	97 W Cedar	
Y	Smith John F	182	chemist	37	here	
Z	Smith Mabel —†	182	housewife	36	"	
G	Higgins Catherine † rear	200	"	27	315 Cambridg	
H	Higgins George "	200	chauffeur	38	315 "	
K	Eagen Catherine—† "	200	houseworker	45	315 "	
L	Eagen Robert "	200	chauffeur	22	315 "	
M	Rodgerson Edward D "	200	teamster	37	here	
N	Rodgerson Esther—† "	200	housewife	38	"	
O	Rodgerson John "	200	teamster	33	30 St John	
P	Gallagher Charles "	200	"	22	here	
R	Gallagher John "	200	"	25	"	

Cambridge Street—Continued

s	Stephens Catherine—† rear	200	houseworker	45	here
T	Stephens Elizabeth—† "	200	housewife	55	"
U	Savage Domonic "	200	mechanic	29	"
V	Smith Suzanne—† "	200	houseworker	74	"
W	Smith Earl W "	200	teamster	25	"
X	Smith Ida—† "	200	houseworker	39	"
A	Brown John H	202	helper	70	"
P	Fallon Mary—†	218	housekeeper	48	"
R	Perry Margaret—†	218	"	67	"
S	Perry William T	218	painter	63	"
T	Roberts Charles	218	cook	66	"
U	La Naio Elizabeth—†	218	houseworker	49	"
V	La Naio Frederick	218	carpenter	54	"
W	La Naio Lillian—†	218	candymaker	27	"
X	Fallon Catherine—†	218	actress	24	"
Y	Fallon Sarah—†	218	houseworker	46	"
Z	Fallon William	218	teamster	22	"
C	Marsh George	222	chauffeur	35	"
D	Marsh Mabel—†	222	houseworker	32	"
E	Watson Lottie—†	222	"	62	"
F	Fallon Mary C—†	222	"	25	"
L	Boyd Charles	226	painter	50	"
M	Martin Maud—†	226	houseworker	45	"
N	Butler John W	226	shipper	63	"
O	Butler Mable A—†	226	houseworker	33	"
P	Connelly Helen—†	226	"	45	"
R	Connelly James	226	machinist	21	"

Coburn Court

T	Richards Crawford	3	laborer	44	here
U	Richards Gertrude—†	3	housewife	36	"
V	Wells Carolina—†	3	"	70	"
W	Mason Joseph	3	laborer	67	"
X	Smith Alice—†	3	housekeeper	55	"

Garden Street

B	Coodlitz Clara—†	15	housekeeper	27	here
C	Coodlitz Victor	15	shoemaker	30	"

Garden Street—Continued

D	Rottenberg Alice—†	15	housekeeper	28	here
E	Rottenberg Hyman	15	hairdresser	29	"
F	Sherman Goldie—†	15	housekeeper	40	"
G	Sherman Jacob	15	presser	43	"
H	Monteiro Antonia—†	15	housekeeper	43	"
K	Monteiro Petro	15	rubberworker	46	"
L	Howard Herbert	18	sailor	26	Philadelphia
M	Linwood Garfield—†	18	housewife	43	262 Cambridg
N	Hootnick Anna—†	18	"	33	here
O	Hootnick Morris	18	carpenter	34	"
P	Epstein Celia—†	18	bookkeeper	20	"
R	Epstein Joseph	18	storekeeper	61	"
S	Epstein Fannie—†	18	"	50	"
T	Yankelowitz Max	18	painter	33	"
U	Yankelowitz Rose—†	18	housewife	32	"
V	Spack Harry	18	carpenter	68	"
W	Spack Mollie—†	18	housewife	68	"
X	Praskunnick Helen—†	18	"	35	"
Y	Praskunnick Michael	18	manager	32	"
Z	Stuneteky John	18	waiter	42	"
E	Eldridge Emma—†	20	housewife	47	"
F	Eldridge Sylvanust	20	janitor	73	"
G	Jenkins Jennie—†	20	cook	50	"
H	Tucker William	20	laborer	40	"
K	Kopple Mollie—†	20	housekeeper	28	27 N Anderso
L	Kopple Yale	20	tailor	32	27 "
M	Goberman Jennie—†	20	housewife	60	here
N	Goberman Morris	20	pedler	65	"
O	Spector Abraham	20	teamster	40	77 Revere
P	Spector Sadie—†	20	housewife	35	77 "
R	Secovitz George	20	laborer	30	here
S	Secovitz Pauline—†	20	dishwasher	25	"
T	Matcher Abraham	20	tailor	25	"
U	Matcher Bessie—†	20	housewife	24	"
V	Snowbecker Alice—†	20	"	30	"
W	Snowbecker George	20	laborer	35	"
Y	Scrivner Anna—†	22	domestic	46	"
Z	Scrivner William M	22	janitor	44	"
A	Gray Annie—†	23	housekeeper	50	3 Lindall pl
B	Pierce Walter	23	laborer	25	here
C	West Christina—†	23	housekeeper	60	"

Garden Street—Continued

D	Wilson George W	23	laborer	50	here
D¹	Ippolito Constance—†	24	housewife	52	"
E	Ippolito John	24	general worker	54	"
F	Lewis Benjiman	25	manager	26	"
G	Lewis Frances—†	25	housekeeper	23	"
H	Hershberg David	25	mattressmaker	30	"
K	Hershberg Polly—†	25	housekeeper	26	"
L	Florance Benjiman	25	mattressmaker	35	"
M	Florance Molly—†	25	housekeeper	25	"
N	Farren Cassie—†	26	general worker	45	"
O	Farren Tersa—†	26	cook	52	"
P	Laundry Joseph E	26	carpenter	44	"
R	Smith George F	27	laborer	47	"
S	Smith Victoria—†	27	housekeeper	35	"
T	Foster Fillis—†	27	"	32	39 Grove
U	Florance Lena—†	27	"	50	here
V	Israel Anna—†	27	"	37	"
W	Israel David	27	leather	39	"
X	Bornstein Annie—†	27	housekeeper	50	"
Y	Bornstein Barney	27	pedler	54	"
Z	Goodman Charlott—†	27	housekeeper	25	"
A	Goodman Joseph	27	shoemaker	27	"
B	Welisblatt Bessey—†	27	housekeeper	49	247 Chambers
C	Welisblatt Israel	27	painter	25	247 "
D	Weinbaum Harry	27	advertising	21	here
E	Weinbaum Meyer	27	metal dealer	43	"
F	Weinbaum Tillie—†	27	housekeeper	41	"
G	Orent Abraham	27	laborer	25	64 Revere
H	Orent Bertha—†	27	dressmaker	41	64 "
K	Orent Mary—†	27	"	23	64 "
L	Orent Ruth—†	27	hatmaker	24	64 "
M	Rosenthal Anna—†	27	housewife	28	25 Allen
N	Rosenthal Jacob	27	shoemaker	30	25 "
O	Iwdes Eva—†	28	housewife	50	20 Anderson
P	Iwdes Mary—†	28	clerk	22	46 "
S	Andrews Etta—†	28	housewife	45	here
T	Andrews Walter W	28	carpetlayer	63	"
U	Spector Anna—†	30	housewife	30	"
V	Spector Myer	30	tailor	36	"
W	Mogul Lena—†	30	housewife	35	"
X	Mogul Morris	30	egg candler	35	"

Garden Street—Continued

Y	Lewis Rebecca—†	30	housewife	25	here
z	Lewis Rubin	30	insurance agent	26	"
A	Ezers Abramham	30	tailor	30	"
B	Ezers Anna—†	30	housewife	28	"
E	Block Abraham	33	storekeeper	58	"
F	Block Annette—†	33	waitress	22	New York
G	Block Jacob	33	upholsterer	20	here
H	Block Lillian—†	33	housekeeper	50	"
K	Comensky Alexander	33	clerk	25	25 Lynde
L	Comensky Frances—†	33	housekeeper	22	25 "
M	Goldberg Nathan	33	tailor	35	here
N	Goldberg Tilly—†	33	housekeeper	35	"
O	Levine Celia—†	33	"	50	38 N Russell
P	Levine Nathan	33	tailor	50	38 "
R	Fox Ida—†	34	housewife	50	here
S	Fox Joseph	34	jeweler	54	"
T	Bernthal Ida—†	34	housewife	46	"
T¹	Bernthal Nathan	34	tailor	48	"
U	Sawyer Hyman	34	shoemaker	64	"
V	Sawyer Jennie—†	34	housewife	65	"
X	Clark Allen	36	clerk	24	Northampton
Y	Watfauicz Joseph	36	artist	27	Gloucester
Z	Bolton Lawrence J	36	director	26	here
A	McCully Ray	36	student	23	"
B	Franklin Rosa—†	37	housekeeper	31	"
B¹	Thomas Catherine—†	37	houseworker	61	"
C	Watts Arnard E	37	laborer	33	13 Irving
D	Goldman Harry	37	upholsterer	25	134 Chambers
E	Goldman Lilly—†	37	housekeeper	22	134 "
F	Biatok James	37	salesman	27	here
G	Biatok Martha—†	37	housekeeper	25	"
H	Slate Hyman	37	machinist	52	"
K	Slate Rose—†	37	housekeeper	30	"
L	Gonsalves Mary—†	37	tailoress	47	"
M	Mack Mary—†	37	housekeeper	25	"
N	Swartz David	37	laborer	36	31 Auburn
O	Swartz Molly—†	37	housekeeper	34	31 "
P	Lipisky Harry	37	pedler	42	here
R	Lipisky Mary—†	37	housekeeper	36	"
S	Perkins Bertha—†	37	matron	35	"
T	Perkins John	37	laborer	34	"

Garden Street—Continued

u	Hellin Lena—†	37	housekeeper	36	here
v	Stern Jacob	38	clerk	36	"
w	Stern Jennie—†	38	housekeeper	63	"
x	Stern Morris	38	bookbinder	25	"
y	Eisman Freda—†	38	housekeeper	48	Russia
z	Cohen Mary—†	38	housewife	33	16 Blossom
a	Cohen Nathan	38	pressman	33	16 "
b	Stiman David	38	machinist	28	here
c	Stiman Dora—†	38	housewife	28	"
d	Candow Grace—†	41	candyroller	25	47 Garden
e	Candow Ida—†	41	housekeeper	58	47 "
f	McShery Mary—†	41	"	70	47 "
g	Cohen Rose—†	41	"	40	31 Phillips
h	Stockman Goldie—†	41	"	32	here
k	Stockman Phillip	41	violin teacher	34	"
l	Finsilver Annie—†	41	housekeeper	24	9 Anderson
m	Finsilver Samuel	41	tailor	25	9 "
n	Aldeman Alexander	41	painter	24	here
o	Aldeman Bella—†	41	housekeeper	23	"
p	Karinski Nathan	41	painter	26	"
r	Karinski Sarah—†	41	housekeeper	25	"
s	Kaplan Bessie—†	41	"	30	"
t	Kaplan David	41	tinsmith	32	"
u	Barritz Ida—†	41	housekeeper	30	"
v	Barritz Morris	41	tailor	32	"
w	Sussman Eva—†	41	housekeeper	27	"
w¹	Sussman Saul	41	printer	27	"
y	Desmond Ida—†	41	housekeeper	33	"
x	Desmond William	41	painter	41	"
a	Gillespie Catherine A—†	42	housewife	33	23 Irving
b	Gillespie Michael	42	packer	43	23 "
c	Mulligan Elizabeth—†	42	housekeeper	64	Brookline
d	Mulligan Elizabeth J—†	42	"	65	70 Pinckney
e	Bantton William	42	porter	56	here
f	O'Neil Anna—†	42	chambermaid	35	"
m	Koeller Gladys—†	44	housekeeper	20	"
n	Koeller Minnie—†	44	"	41	"
o	McLaughlin Alice—†	44	"	45	"
p	Philipson Bridget—†	44	"	45	"
r	Philipson Henry	44	ice cream	41	"
u	Scacak John	45	laborer	42	2 Anderson pl

Garden Street—Continued

v	Taylor Charles F	45	chauffeur	25	49 Garden
w	Taylor Harriet L—†	45	houseworker	26	49 "
x	McGlinchey Charles	45	laborer	42	11 School
y	McGlinchey Isabelle—†	45	houseworker	42	11 "
z	Kirkham Annie—†	45	housewife	35	Bangor Me
A	Kirkham Leonard	45	porter	36	"
B	Mokrovalsky Samuel	45	laborer	36	here
C	Smoich Annie—†	45	housekeeper	38	"
D	Holmes Esther—†	45	housewife	37	"
E	Holmes Percival	45	porter	50	"
F	Mazzuchelli Angelo	45	pedler	45	Italy
G	Mazzuchelli Teresa—†	45	housewife	39	"
H	Lewis Georgia—†	45	general worker	43	Winchester
K	Margolin Frieda—†	46	housewife	27	here
L	Margolin Samuel	46	cutter	27	"
M	Block Louis J	46	shipper	35	"
N	Block Rachel—†	46	housewife	34	"
O	Eworetsky Gertrude—†	46	"	36	"
P	Eworetsky Samuel	46	tailor	46	"
R	Carbone Anthony	46	salesman	45	"
S	Potman Annie—†	47	houseworker	42	31 Temple
T	Potman Ariel	47	boxmaker	21	31 "
U	Potman Levi D	47	egg inspector	47	31 "
V	Haggerty Gertrude I—†	47	housewife	27	here
W	Haggerty William W	47	steamfitter	33	"
X	Sniper Isadore—†	47	capmaker	30	"
Y	Sniper Rebecca—†	47	housewife	25	"
A	Penn George	47	laborer	30	16 Barton
B	Penn Sophie—†	47	housewife	26	16 "
C	Mellen Aaron	47	capmaker	25	here
C¹	Mellen Freda—†	47	houseworker	60	"
D	Lanza Joseph	47	carpenter	34	75 Endicott
E	Lanza Mary—†	47	housewife	21	75 "
F	Kessler Doris—†	47	clerk	21	here
G	Kessler Joseph	47	tailor	46	"
H	Kessler Pauline—†	47	houseworker	44	"
K	Lottie Mollie—†	47	kitchenworker	38	11 Blossom
L	Levine Gertrude—†	48	housekeeper	24	here
M	Levine Harry	48	chauffeur	30	"
N	Chayet Jacob	48	student	23	"
O	Chayet Jennie—†	48	housewife	42	"

Garden Street—Continued

P	Chayet Max	48	tailor	45	here
R	Chayet Minnie—†	48	stenographer	20	"
S	Cullen Harry	48	machinist	39	"
T	Cullen Lottie—†	48	housewife	35	"
U	Finkle Lena—†	48	housekeeper	30	"
V	Finkle Max	48	upholsterer	31	"
W	MacArthur Mary—†	48	bookkeeper	35	New York
X	Perkins Theresa—†	49	houseworker	47	here
Y	Schultz Clara—†	49	"	29	53 Garden
Z	Schultz Louis	49	collector	39	53 "
A	Taylor Charlotte—†	49	nurse	28	here
A¹	Taylor Lillian—†	49	general worker	45	"
B	Bynoe Eva—†	49	cleaner	49	"
C	Bynoe Walden	49	operator	29	"
E	Cohen Benjamin	50	tailor	30	"
F	Cohen Mary—†	50	housewife	29	"
G	Kravitz Fannie—†	50	"	49	"
H	Kravitz Julius	50	bookbinder	22	"
K	Kravitz Louis	50	tailor	54	"
L	Engle Fannie—†	50	housewife	36	"
M	Engle Philip	50	cutter	37	"
N	Goodman Benjamin	50	policeman	27	"
O	Goodman Celia—†	50	housewife	26	"
O¹	Hyman Henry	50	operator	23	Salem
P	Hyman Joseph	50	salesman	20	"
R	Levi Benjamin	50	boxmaker	30	here
S	Levi Dora—†	50	housewife	27	"
T	Sparks Philip	50	carpenter	45	"
U	Norton Helen F—†	51	clerk	28	Norwood
V	Conant Wallace L	51	musician	45	6 Goodwin pl
W	Greene Emma—†	51	secretary	48	here
X	Mullen Annie—†	52	housekeeper	55	115 Myrtle
Y	Mullen Kitty—†	52	factory worker	35	115 "
Z	Mullen Thomas	52	hostler	58	115 "
A	Finkel Edith—†	52	housewife	25	here
B	Finkel Harry	52	teamster	29	"
C	Lazarus Harry	52	salesman	24	"
D	Lazarus Minnie—†	52	housewife	23	"
E	Stone Lena—†	52	"	58	"
F	Oxman Etta—†	52	"	24	"
G	Oxman Saul	52	salesman	24	"

Garden Street—Continued

H	Sacks Bessie—†	52	housewife	23	here
K	Sacks Jacob	52	tailor	27	"
L	Baker Lena—†	52	housewife	20	72 Revere
M	Baker Robert	52	cutter	23	72 "
N	Pappas Ada—†	52	housewife	41	here
O	Pappas John	52	machinist	43	"
P	Sivinority Katie—†	52	stitcher	24	"
R	Cocyk John	52	laborer	35	"
S	Chambers Clark	53	general worker	49	"
T	Bonfanti Frank	53	baker	39	3 Blossom ct
U	Bonfanti Mary—†	53	houseworker	30	3 "
V	Rosenberg Etta D—†	53	housewife	26	2 Parkman
W	Rosenberg Maurice	53	chauffeur	29	2 "
X	Ableman Jacob	53	salesman	27	135 Myrtle
Y	Pearlman Bertha—†	53	houseworker	29	135 "
Z	Pearlman Israel	53	leathercutter	30	135 "
A	Buzek Robert	53	actor	38	here
B	Ormsby Corinne—†	53	housewife	34	"
C	Ormsby William S	53	conductor	63	"

Hoyt Place

P	Pioppo Mary—†	2	housewife	51	here
R	Pioppo Munzill	2	rubberworker	45	"
S	Pylypink Mary—†	2	housewife	33	"
T	Pylypink Michael	2	cook	32	"
U	Baronsky James	2	dishwasher	29	"
V	Galanzy Yelovon	2	"	25	"
W	Lukolski Peter	2	"	49	"
X	Yomoyuk Michael	2	"	49	"

Irving Street

Z	Ryan Maria M—†	3	housewife	42	here
A	Ryan William	3	millworker	53	"
B	Robinson Alice—†	3	housewife	23	"
C	Robinson Herbert	3	mechanic	28	"
D	Olsen Florence—†	3	housewife	44	"
E	Olsen Harry	3	cabinetmaker	59	"

Irving Street—Continued

F	Blaustein Jacob—†	13	bagmaker	49	36 Garden
G	Berman Annie—†	13	housewife	48	152 Chambers
H	Berman Keener	13	pedler	52	152 "
K	Berman Lottie—†	13	bookkeeper	21	152 "
L	Iroof Benjaman	13	blacksmith	44	here
M	Iroof Rose—†	13	housewife	39	"
N	Kadoff Joseph	13	shoemaker	45	"
O	Kadoff Mollie—†	13	housewife	42	"
R	Fay Martha—†	14	music teacher	61	"
S	Ferranti Graziano	14	fruit	53	"
T	Ferranti Phylies—†	14	housewife	40	"
U	Ferranti Theresa—†	14	feeder	21	"
V	Fredd Ester—†	14	housewife	63	"
W	Fredd Nathan	14	printer	27	"
X	Fredd Suzanne E—†	14	stenographer	33	"
Y	Goldman Celia—†	14	housewife	51	"
Z	Goldman Louis	14	tailor	55	"
A	Remick Mary E—†	14	housewife	34	"
B	Remick William E	14	fireman	32	"
C	Barry Anna—†	14	housewife	24	"
D	Barry John	14	plumber	29	25 Revere
E	Tangherlini Emil	14	machinist	29	56 Temple
F	Tangherlini Rose—†	14	housewife	27	56 "
G	Kolman Annie—†	14	"	26	here
H	Kolman Jacob	14	bagmaker	26	"
K	Mortlock James	15	carpenter	42	27 Anderson
L	Mortlock Nonie—†	15	housewife	25	27 "
M	Addis Abraham	15	foreman	56	here
N	Addis Dinah—†	15	housewife	46	"
O	Addis Hyman	15	student	22	"
P	Fineman Harry	15	metalworker	25	"
R	Fineman Ida—†	15	housewife	23	12 McLean ct
S	Pritzker Rebecca—†	15	"	40	Canada
T	Pritzker Solomon	15	laborer	43	"
U	Zeigler Paul	15	porter	48	here
V	Zeigler Tracey—†	15	housewife	30	"
W	Centorino Antonet—†	16	"	46	"
X	Centorino Domick	16	fruit	47	"
Y	Venturini Ezechiele	16	storekeeper	38	"
Z	Venturini Mary—†	16	housewife	37	"
A	Bowdoin Elizabeth—†	16	"	44	"

Irving Street—Continued

B	Bowdoin Fredrick	16	chauffeur	24	here
C	Bowdoin Iven	16	cook	52	"
D	Burns Mary—†	16	housewife	29	"
E	Burns William	16	laborer	31	"
F	Payne Mary—†	17	housewife	45	"
G	Kniskeck Cora—†	17	"	39	"
H	Kniskeck Nathan	17	upholster	38	"
K	Gamunck Esther—†	17	student	20	"
L	Gamunck Rose—†	17	housewife	40	"
M	Gamunck Samuel	17	pedler	48	"
N	Feldman Samuel	17	merchant	58	"
O	Kriger Alice—†	17	housewife	25	"
P	Kriger Samuel	17	printer	31	"
R	Kantor Lillian—†	17	housewife	22	Europe
S	Kantor Louis	17	manager	28	18 Fayston
T	Berenson Hyman	17	waiter	23	here
U	Luper Angel	17	laborer	29	190 Chambe
U1	Milden David	17	waiter	40	here
V	Schniederman Benjaman	17	tailor	40	"
W	Schniederman Bessie—†	17	bookkeeper	20	"
X	Schniederman Esther—†	17	housewife	40	"
Y	Schniederman Samuel	17	upholsterer	25	"
Z	Campbell Grace J—†	17	tel operator	24	"
A	Campbell John D	17	carpenter	57	"
B	Campbell Nora—†	17	housewife	59	"
C	Miller Jennie—†	17	"	48	"
D	Miller Lillian—†	17	stenographer	22	"
E	Miller Samuel	17	meatcutter	50	"
F	Gallagher Harry	18	waiter	45	692 Tremon
G	Carangelo Frank	18	tailor	40	here
H	Carangelo Rose—†	18	housewife	34	"
K	McQuaid Francis J	18	laborer	38	42 S Russell
L	McQuaid Frieda—†	18	housewife	25	Monson
M	Merceri Mathew	18	soapcutter	21	"
O	Sagall George	19	bookkeeper	21	here
P	Sagall Joseph	19	storekeeper	61	"
R	Sagall Rose—†	19	housekeeper	59	"
S	Pletts Anthony	21	laborer	64	"
T	Jager Astor	22	collector	45	"
U	Jager Dagny—†	22	housewife	46	"
V	Fishman Celia—†	22	"	32	"

Irving Street—Continued

w	Fishman Morris	22	stitcher	33	here
x	Bermann David	22	tinsmith	41	"
y	Bermann Rachel—†	22	housewife	38	"
z	Feldman Abraham	22	tailor	38	"
A	Feldman Rose—†	22	housewife	34	"
B	Raymond Alma H—†	23	housekeeper	64	"
C	Raymond Frederick M	23	salesman	45	"
D	Raymond Nina J—†	23	housewife	36	Norwood
E	Newman Dora—†	23	"	54	here
F	Newman George L	23	draughtsman	28	"
G	Candon Ida—†	23	houseworker	37	47 Garden
H	Hozid Annie—†	23	housewife	34	here
K	Hozid Jacob M	23	printer	35	"
L	Levey Dora G—†	23	housewife	23	50 Allen
M	Levey Maurice J	23	printer	26	59 Hollander
N	Schroeder Helen—†	23	housewife	38	here
O	Schroder William	23	electrician	40	"
P	Allen Ivory L	23	conductor	40	"
R	Allen Lucy—†	23	housewife	35	"
S	Palkans Pauline—†	23	waitress	36	Chelsea
T	Shurkes Helen—†	23	"	34	"
U	Staskywicz Adolph	23	proprietor	33	17 Barton
V	Staskywicz Pauline—†	23	housewife	28	17 Parkman
X	Ross Robert	24	salesman	30	New Haven Ct
Y	Ross Sarah—†	24	housewife	26	"
Z	Nathan Elizabeth—†	24	"	27	here
A	Nathan Samuel	24	plumber	33	"
B	Cooper Elmer	24	waiter	60	19 S Russell
C	Marcus Bertha—†	24	housewife	38	Cambridge
D	Marcus Samuel	24	salesman	38	"
F	Richman Isaac	26	tailor	44	here
G	Richman Mary—†	26	housewife	42	"
H	Clarfield Harris	26	laborer	58	"
K	Clarfield Rachel—†	26	housewife	50	"
L	Charam David	26	newsboy	20	"
M	Charam Jacob	26	carpenter	48	"
N	Charam Sarah—†	26	housewife	46	"
O	Hagen Maud—†	28	cook	39	"
P	Davney Alice—†	28	"	43	"
R	Dickson Daniel	30	laborer	48	"
S	Williams Charles	30	"	48	"

Irving Street—Continued

T	Simmons Henry	30	porter	49	here
U	Thomas Aline—†	30	waitress	23	"
V	Thomas Charlotte—†	30	maid	55	"
W	Thomas Mary—†	30	cook	40	"
X	Thomas Francis	30	retired	70	"
Y	Wiggins Joseph	30	laborer	65	"
Z	Dubreuil Edward A	31	superintendent	54	"
A	Dubreuil Rose—†	31	housewife	42	"
C	Charette Frederick	31	cook	35	1689 Wash'n
B	Charette Olive—†	31	waitress	37	1689 "
D	Masse Albert	31	clerk	42	48 Green
E	Novogrodske Isaac	31	meatcutter	28	13 Parkman
F	Hultman Oscar	31	Hebrew teacher	45	here
G	Silver Samuel	31	presser	29	"
H	Silver Sylvia—†	31	housewife	22	"
K	Helman Max	31	laborer	29	33 Irving
L	Helman Sadie—†	31	housewife	29	33 "
M	Freedman Bessie—†	31	housekeeper	30	here
N	Freedman Harry L	31	engineer	34	"
O	Gates George A	31	chauffeur	29	"
P	Tennyson Margarett—†	31	housekeeper	39	"
R	Tennyson Thomas	31	fireman	50	"
S	Floreskul Onafrie	31	baker	30	63 Phillips
T	Floreskul Rose—†	31	housewife	26	63 "
U	Korrelsky Nicholas	31	porter	28	63 "
V	Rosin Charles	31	shoemaker	47	here
W	Rosin Ida—†	31	housekeeper	47	"
X	Leroft William	32	fishcutter	55	"
Y	Locks Michael	32	electrotyper	33	"
Z	McCartney Eva—†	32	housekeeper	35	"
A	McCartney Joseph	32	boilermaker	35	"
B	Rumbolt Louis	32	barber	30	Beverly
C	Tobin Henry	32	gardener	51	22 Myrtle
D	Lee Annie—†	33	housewife	43	here
E	Lee Mary—†	33	waitress	22	"
F	Lee Michael	33	janitor	61	"
G	Hayes James	33	cook	35	18 Allston
H	Hayes Mary—†	33	housekeeper	33	18 "
K	Chicofsky Jacob	33	tailor	26	here
L	Chicofsky Mary—†	33	housewife	23	"
M	Bestall Alma—†	33	matron	56	"

Irving Street—Continued

Letter.	FULL NAME.	Residence	Occupation.	Age	Reported Residence
N	Putlack Bertha—†	33	housewife	27	here
O	Putlack Samuel	33	shoeworker	33	"
P	Shore Annie—†	33	housekeeper	50	"
R	Shore Fannie—†	33	stenographer	20	"
S	McCue Henry	33	painter	21	"
T	Seale Annie—†	33	housewife	45	"
U	Seale Herbert	33	painter	44	"
V	Beshansky Annie—†	33	houseworker	56	"
W	Beshansky Arthur	33	raincoats	26	"
X	Beshansky Dora—†	33	housewife	26	"
Y	McKay Christina—†	33	houseworker	68	"
Z	Poczebot Annie—†	33	housewife	30	18 Lynde
A	Poczabot Vincent	33	factory worker	29	18 "
B	Byrne Alice M—†	34	housewife	57	here
C	Byrne Thomas W	34	advertising	26	"
D	Corcoran Martin J	34	watchman	52	"
E	Coughlin Frank	34	carpenter	42	"
F	Josylson Joseph	34	salesman	50	"
G	Kelley John W	34	shipper	27	71 Bunker Hill
H	O'Neil Bartholomew	34	paver	67	here
K	Righton John J	34	machinist	45	"
L	Walsh Edward J	34	waiter	37	"
M	Brown Rosa—†	36	clerk	44	"
N	Lake John	36	janitor	54	"
O	Lee Lavina—†	36	retired	22	838 Wash'n
P	Lee William B	36	sweeper	34	838 "
R	Moore Isabella—†	36	retired	82	here
S	Perry Frederick	36	storekeeper	27	"
S¹	Perry Jesse	36	porter	35	"
T	Perry Lucy—†	36	clerk	53	"
U	Perry William	36	janitor	30	"
V	Smith Lavina—†	36	clerk	43	44 Irving
W	Green Allan	38	kitchenman	49	here
X	Johnston John	38	dishwasher	63	"
Y	Perry Silvia—†	38	housewife	45	"
Z	Perry William	38	janitor	50	"
A	Moore Samuel A	39	salesman	26	"
B	Small Eva—†	39	clerk	22	"
C	Smolevitz Sarah—†	39	housewife	47	"
D	Lerner Celia—†	39	housekeeper	42	"
E	Lerner Jacob	39	tailor	42	"

Irving Street—Continued

F	Garber Pauline—†	39	dressmaker	23	here
G	Novagradsky Fella—†	39	waitress	25	Russia
H	Shnider Martha—†	39	housekeeper	60	here
K	Allston Bessie L—†	39	housewife	32	"
L	Allston Redci D	39	waiter	38	"
M	Rho Margaret—†	40	housewife	60	"
N	Mullin Daniel	40	janitor	50	"
O	Mullen James	40	teamster	20	"
P	Mullen Mary A—†	40	housewife	45	"
R	Foster Mildred—†	40	saleswoman	30	"
S	Greer Charles	40	laborer	26	"
T	Seaver Elizabeth—†	41	housewife	50	"
U	Seaver Joseph	41	engineer	58	"
V	Spazman Gertrude—†	41	retired	30	"
W	Spazman Harris	41	junk dealer	80	"
X	Spazman Rose—†	41	housewife	60	"
Y	Quinter Joseph	41	carpenter	37	"
Z	Quinter Rose—†	41	housewife	32	"
A	Barroll Mary—†	41	"	32	"
B	Barroll Maurice	41	tailor	35	"
C	Rose Maurice	41	"	26	"
D	Fitzgerald Annie—†	42	housewife	41	"
E	Russell William H	42	painter	62	"
F	Day Bertha M—†	43	housewife	39	"
G	Desmond Grace—†	43	saleswoman	45	"
H	Hanlon Edward O	43	chimney clean'r	62	"
K	Hoag Edmund C	43	cook	49	"
L	Moffett Mary—†	43	housewife	41	"
M	Moffett Patrick	43	horseshoer	41	"
N	Grose Agnes V—†	43	housewife	52	"
O	Grose William F	43	mechanic	57	"
P	Steele Agnes—†	43	housewife	52	"
R	Steele Charles	43	wire weaver	60	"
S	Steele Charles W	43	clerk	28	"
T	Steele Edward O	43	"	24	"
U	Steele Jessie M—†	43	bookbinder	30	"
V	Brown Elizabeth—†	44	housecleaner	23	Georgia
W	Cottrell Mary—†	44	housewife	53	here
X	Harris Mary—†	44	"	78	23 Garden
Y	Hall James	44	laborer	42	23 "

Irving Street—Continued

Letter	Full Name	Residence	Occupation	Age	Reported Residence
z	Parsnip William	44	furniture mover	45	19 Garden
A	Sullivan Charles H	44	mechanic	44	here
B	Bendell Lena—†	45	housewife	39	"
C	Bendell Max	45	butcher	42	"
D	Kaplan Abraham	45	junk dealer	60	"
E	Kaplan Annie—†	45	housewife	57	"
F	Kaplan Harry	45	moving pictures	27	"
G	Milgroom Esther—†	45	housewife	30	"
H	Milgroom John	45	chauffeur	32	"
K	Rothman Charles	45	salesman	28	"
L	Hirshchovitz Jacob	45	tailor	55	"
M	Hirshchovitz Minnie—†	45	housewife	54	"
N	Hirshchovitz Samuel	45	salesman	33	"
O	Myers Bessie—†	46	housewife	40	"
P	Myers Morris	46	salesman	23	"
R	Gatz Jennie—†	46	housewife	38	"
S	Gatz Joseph	46	tailor	45	"
T	Tax Ida—†	46	housewife	29	"
U	Tax Samuel	46	raincoats	32	"
V	Shub Charles	47	salesman	25	"
W	Shub Eli—†	47	repairer	54	"
X	Shub Fannie—†	47	housewife	55	"
Y	Chalker Annie—†	48	"	39	"
Z	Chalker William D	48	cook	38	"
A	Prescott Benjamin	48	auto tepmaker	29	"
B	Prescott Rose—†	48	housewife	24	"
C	Kramer Lena R—†	48	"	26	"
D	Kramer Samuel W	48	druggist	30	"
E	Chisholm George D	52	operator	51	"
E¹	Chisholm Mary L—†	52	housewife	47	"
F	Peterson Albion	52	salesman	37	200 Cambridge
G	Peterson Arthur	52	"	38	200 "
H	Peterson Mathilda—†	52	housewife	75	200 "
K	Condon Catherine—†	52	"	61	here
L	Condon Thomas F	52	salesman	35	"
N	Edwards Albert H	54	"	65	46 S Russell
O	Edwards Catherine—†	54	dressmaker	67	46 "
P	Monahan Julia—†	54	cook	36	here
R	Shenick Edith—†	54	housewife	58	"
S	Shenick James	54	tinsmith	62	"

Irving Street—Continued

T	Kelley Daniel J	54	retired	72	here
U	Kelley Jennie S—†	54	housewife	62	"
V	Whalen Edward J	54	clerk	48	Miami Fla

Joy Street

W	Brooks George A	12	grocer	52	here
X	Brooks Netta A—†	12	housewife	38	"
Y	Robbins Grace A—†	12	"	39	54 Temple
Z	Robbins Irene L—†	12	clothcutter	45	54 "
A	Sherman Augusta H	12	clerk	28	16 Bradford lane
B	Sherman Roger W	12	salesman	31	5s Montclair av
D	Bicknell James F	14	laborer	69	here
E	Buckley Frederick	14	salesman	38	"
F	Buckley Joseph D	14	manager	43	"
G	Freeman John	14	laborer	28	"
H	Gilman Edward	14	salesman	75	"
K	McCullian Annie—†	14	waitress	32	"
L	McEachern Daniel	14	toolmaker	29	"
M	Marshall Robert J	14	clerk	39	"
N	Smith Myra L—†	14	housekeeper	55	"
O	White Charles F	14	waiter	29	Maine
P	Wiley Eva M—†	14	cook	57	here
R	Bailey Mary—†	16	collector	50	"
S	Briggs Clarence	16	policeman	34	"
T	Costa George	16	waiter	25	New York
U	Craig William H	16	student	22	Southbridge
V	Haley Stephen	16	checker	31	Brookline
W	Johnson George	16	cook	32	here
X	McConnell Warren	16	"	29	Wash'n D C
Y	Mehkelsen Soren	16	mechanic	28	Concord
Z	Peirce Stephen	16	salesman	25	5 Hancock
A	Rogers Annie—†	16	housewife	40	here
B	Rogers Phineas	16	engineer	46	"
C	Schufield Hiram	16	retired	90	"
D	Haley Jasen C	18	porter	35	109 Pinckney
E	Malone Frank E	18	engineer	24	24 Mt Vernon
F	Malone George	18	operator	39	Maine
C	Malone Mary J—†	18	housekeeper	52	24 Mt Vernon
H	Munore Mary—†	18	cook	25	here

24

Joy Street—Continued

Letter	Full Name	Residence, April 1, 1924	Occupation	Supposed Age	Reported Residence, April 1, 1923. Street and Number
K	Powell Lawrence	18	musician	25	England
L	Sullivan Cornelius	18	manager	45	Newburyport
M	Bartlect Helen M—†	20	salesman	48	here
N	Bowers Jeffery D	20	carpenter	79	60 Myrtle
O	Doherty Margaret J—†	20	housewife	47	10 Pinckney
P	Fowler Charles H	20	attendant	38	3 "
R	Matthews Moses	20	tailor	40	8 Myrtle
S	Waite Charles	20	pipefitter	52	here
T	Waite Emma—†	20	retired	50	"
U	Carlson George E	22	bricklayer	47	"
V	Evans Walter A	22	retired	60	"
W	Fraser Roberta G—†	22	storekeeper	53	"
X	Kantervily Joseph	22	bookkeeper	34	"
Y	Reynolds Louise—†	22	clerk	29	"
Z	Simonds Mabel A—†	22	"	59	"
A	Tapp Henrietta—†	22	housewife	56	"
B	Cassidy Francis	24	student	20	New York City
C	Harrington Alfred	24	collector	31	Worcester
D	LeDrew Lucie—†	24	housekeeper	27	Nova Scotia
E	LeDrew Willis	24	manager	41	"
F	McQuord Rita—†	24	saleswoman	30	here
G	O'Brien Catherine—†	24	housewife	33	73 Pinckney
H	O'Brien Thomas	24	policeman	32	58 Temple
K	Perkins Eliot	24	student	24	Maine
L	Rankin Amy—†	24	housewife	42	11 Myrtle
M	Rankin Frank	24	laborer	63	11 "
N	Spinney Edith—†	24	housewife	44	Canada
O	Spinney Frank	24	teamster	43	"
P	Yarston John	24	machinist	28	"
R	Bodkin Margaret—†	36	clerk	24	Kentucky
S	Brownell Elizabeth—†	36	"	24	New Jersey
T	Grannett Mary B—†	36	retired	40	Cambridge
U	Leland Gordon	1st r 36	salesman	26	"
V	Leland Priscilla—†	1st " 36	housewife	23	"
W	Palmer Lemuel	1st " 36	artist	29	Springfield
X	Snow Homer	1st " 36	reporter	27	54 Cedarlane way
Y	Snow Muriel—†	1st " 36	housewife	25	54 "
Z	Anderson Corine—†	1st " 36	designer	31	here
A	Poor Jane—†	2d " 36	manager	34	"
C	Sargent Carl	2d " 36	salesman	28	Leominster
B	Sargent Florence—†	2d " 36	teacher	26	"

Joy Street—Continued

D	Wiren George	2d r 36	artist	29	54 S Russell
E	Townsend Prescott	3d " 36	"	29	here
F	Carter Charles C	38	van driver	59	"
G	Carter Harriett F—†	38	clerk	30	"
H	Carter Mary E—†	38	housewife	53	"
M	Gilbert Cathrine—†	44	"	70	76 W Cedar
N	Gilbert Charles	44	storekeeper	54	76 "
O	Gropman Asher	44	carpenter	49	Chelsea
P	Gropman Fannie—†	44	housewife	49	"
R	Gropman Harry	44	salesman	23	"
S	Barrow Minnie—†	44	housewife	28	here
T	Kann Annie—†	44	"	45	"
U	Kann Bernard	44	tailor	50	"
V	Stearns Jennie—†	44	housewife	58	"
W	Stearns Max	44	chauffeur	21	"
X	Stearns Rosie—†	44	stenographer	23	"
Y	Goldberg Harry	44	tailor	25	"
Z	Goldberg Herman	44	clerk	50	"
A	Goldberg Ida—†	44	housewife	52	"
B	Balkin Celia—†	44A	cigar stripper	28	"
C	Pertes Mary—†	44A	housewife	60	"
D	Schneider Abraham	44A	salesman	23	"
E	Snow Ruth—†	44A	housewife	25	"
F	Snow William	44A	laborer	32	"
G	Corrigan Catherine—†	44A	seamstress	63	"
H	Harrington Helen—†	44A	factory worker	35	"
K	Farley Helen—†	44A	housekeeper	31	"
L	Dentali John	44A	cook	26	"
M	Dentali Lena—†	44A	housewife	25	"
N	Valuletti Gromondo	44A	cook	66	"
O	Valuletti Louise—†	44A	housekeeper	56	"
P	Shkow Mary—†	44A	housewife	44	"
R	Shkow Max	44A	laborer	42	"
S	Ahern Mary C—†	44A	elevatorwoman	21	"
T	Ahern Nora—†	44A	housewife	50	"
U	Ahern William H	44A	chauffeur	22	"
V	Titorchwok Henry	44A	laborer	27	"
W	Titorchwok Mary—†	44A	housewife	27	"
X	Larangelo Frank	44A	shoemaker	37	"
Y	Larangelo Grace—†	44A	housewife	34	"
B	Givan Margaret—†	50	waitress	26	"

Joy Street—Continued

Letter	Full Name	Residence	Occupation	Age	Reported Residence
C	Muir Elizabeth—†	50	housewife	38	here
D	Scanlon Nellie—†	50	housekeeper	38	"
E	Roucher Andrew	50	laborer	29	5 Goldsmith pl
F	Roucher Anna—†	50	housewife	33	5 "
G	Arthur Albert	50	laborer	31	128 Pembroke
H	Arthur Margaret—†	50	housewife	31	128 "
K	King Charles	50	steamfitter	47	here
L	King Sue—†	50	housewife	41	"
M	Smith Thomas	50	pedler	37	"
O	Cousins Frances L—†	52	housewife	38	4 Brown's ct
P	Cousins Nathen L	52	teamster	30	4 "
R	Shepard Martin	52	"	34	Maine
S	Shepard Vena M—†	52	waitress	29	"
U	Moore James E	52	watchman	51	14 Temple
V	Moore Jennie E—†	52	housewife	53	14 "
W	Alden Marie E—†	52	"	27	22 Allston
X	Alden Walter A	52	salesman	38	22 "
Y	Burnes Richard	52	foreman	35	here
Z	Winn Dora—†	52	stitcher	65	"
A	Swanson Jennie—†	52	housewife	35	Georgia
B	Swanson Leslie	52	auto mechanic	37	"
C	Lusignan Edna R—†	52	housewife	39	Cambridge
D	Lusignan George E	52	painter	38	"
E	Guyette Elizabeth—†	52	housewife	34	here
F	Guyette Erle	52	painter	33	"
G	Jenson Henry	52	chauffeur	27	"
H	Jenson Jacob	52	retired	63	"
K	Armstrong George	52	janitor	48	"
L	Armstrong Gertrude—†	52	housewife	48	"
M	Armstrong Irwin	52	laborer	66	6 Staniford pl
N	Millard Harry	52	machinist	27	New Hampshire
O	Millard Mary—†	52	houseworker	24	"
P	Millett Cushing C	52	tinsmith	41	here
R	Kollings Theresa—†	52	saleswoman	21	28 Allen
T	Ripley Agnes—†	52	housewife	37	18 Gertrose
U	Ripley Charles	52	cook	46	18 "
V	Elliott Charles	70 & 72	salesman	55	here
W	Pierni John	70 & 72	instruments	20	81 Cotting
X	Resnick Annie—†	70 & 72	housewife	38	here
Y	Resnick Jacob	70 & 72	baker	40	"
Z	Feld Esther—†	70 & 72	housewife	38	"

Joy Street—Continued

A	Feld Jacob	70 & 72	tailor	39	here
B	Trieber Pearl —†	70 & 72	housewife	24	"
C	Trieber William	70 & 72	furrier	26	"
D	Newman Meyer	70 & 72	tailor	30	"
E	Newman Rose—†	70 & 72	housewife	28	"
F	Atkins Harry D	70 & 72	furrier	28	"
G	Atkins Marion—†	70 & 72	housewife	22	"
H	Kantor Harry	70 & 72	clerk	45	"
K	Kantor Rose—†	70 & 72	housewife	33	"
L	Uneef Pauline—†	70 & 72	"	40	"
M	Uneef Status	70 & 72	waiter	48	"
N	Cohen Arnold	70 & 72	salesman	22	"
O	Cohen David	70 & 72	buyer	25	"
P	Cohen Ida—†	70 & 72	housewife	47	"
R	Cohen Morris	70 & 72	glazier	48	"
S	A'Hearn Nora—†	70 & 72	cook	40	"
T	Haskell Mary—†	70 & 72	waitress	35	"
U	Bloom Samuel	70 & 72	pedler	27	10 Bower
V	Bloom Sarah—†	70 & 72	housewife	23	33 Havelock
W	Wasserman Joseph	70 & 72	tailor	60	here
X	Wasserman Rose—†	70 & 72	housekeeper	21	"
Y	Verblin Elizabeth—†	70 & 72	housewife	25	15 Irving
Z	Verblin Harry	70 & 72	stitcher	37	15 "
A	Green Hyman	70 & 72	shoecutter	35	here
B	Green Rose—†	70 & 72	housewife	30	"
C	Rollo Ellen—†	70 & 72	"	45	Scotland
D	Rollo James	70 & 72	barber	41	"
E	Tankin Alexander	70 & 72	grocer	29	here
F	Tankin Sarah—†	70 & 72	housewife	24	"
G	Lauria John	70 & 72	tailor	35	"
H	Lauria Leah—†	70 & 72	housewife	33	"
K	Gruber Philip	70 & 72	paperhanger	35	"
L	Gruber Sarah—†	70 & 72	housewife	42	"
M	Kasperovitch John	70 & 72	janitor	28	83 Brighton
N	Griffin Patrick	82	watchman	60	here
O	Leary Mary—†	82	housekeeper	50	"
P	Secondori Annie—†	82	housewife	30	"
R	Secondori Spartaco	82	machinist	39	"
S	Perrin Elizabeth—†	86	packer	47	"
T	Snow George M	86	retired	73	"
U	Snow Sidney H	86	counterman	48	"

28

Joy Street—Continued

v	Snow Theresa—†	86	housewife	42	here	
w	Pakundaki Constantine	86	clerk	39	"	
x	Pakundaki Santina—†	86	housekeeper	38	"	

Myrtle Street

c	Andrews Lewis P	19	salesman	39	here
d	Armstrong William F	19	chiropodist	58	"
e	Babbitt George H	19	bank clerk	40	"
f	Bancroft Robert L	19	stenographer	67	"
g	Barnes Alfred O	19	merchant	75	"
h	Barrett Louis F	19	clerk	42	"
k	Barry James H	19	printer	45	"
l	Bean Charles H	19	accountant	54	"
m	Bean Eugene F	19	lunchroom	35	51 Temple
n	Berger Edmund A	19	student	25	here
o	Bingle George	19	"	29	Salem
p	Blanchard Wilson	19	clerk	46	here
r	Bowman John E	19	clergyman	57	New Hampshire
s	Brintwall William P	19	cashier	45	here
t	Bryant Stephen R	19	shipper	70	"
u	Bryant Willis G	19	janitor	54	"
v	Cadue Eugene E	19	salesman	75	239 Mass av
w	Clark Lyman O	19	clerk	57	here
x	Condon Henry M	19	draughtsman	53	32 Woodford
y	Connolly John J	19	letter carrier	52	here
z	Connor John J	19	clerk	45	75 Charles
a	Curran William T	19	telegrapher	26	here
b	Currier Wilton L	19	lawyer	59	"
c	Damon Charles E	19	clerk	72	"
d	Dando William A	19	postal clerk	52	"
e	Dimock John C	19	cutter	55	"
f	Drew Walter G	19	produce	69	"
g	Dudley Joseph A	19	"	45	"
h	Dugan Edward	19	salesman	46	"
k	Dunmore Edward M	19	agent	64	"
l	Farron Thomas A	19	letter carrier	58	"
m	Federman Maurice	19	salesman	36	Medford
n	Flower Francis N	19	restaurateur	71	here
o	Flynn Daniel F	19	clerk	64	"

Myrtle Street—Continued

P	Francis Fred F	19	salesman	44	here
R	Gillis Archibald A	19	steamfitter	40	"
S	Grant Julius	19	cigarmaker	41	"
T	Greeley Charles G	19	printer	68	Stoneham
U	Grimes George F	19	lawyer	34	here
V	Hall George J	19	tel worker	45	"
W	Hamilton James M	19	engineer	44	"
X	Haskell Francis F	19	retired	43	"
Y	Hazard John G	19	salesman	44	"
Z	Healy Francis A A	19	insurance agent	41	51 Temple
A	Hocking Winifred	19	salesman	25	32 Boulevard ter
B	Huntington Fred T	19	photographer	51	here
C	James William D	19	chemist	42	"
D	Jennings William T	19	janitor	49	72 Carney
E	Johnson August	19	tailor	51	here
F	Johnson William M	19	clerk	49	"
G	Johnson William W	19	elevatorman	42	"
H	Johnson Fachariah T	19	tinsmith	75	"
K	Kaulback James P	19	clerk	68	"
L	Keenan Anthony V	19	real estate	44	"
M	Keevin Edward E	19	agent	49	"
N	Kelley Michael B	19	shipper	61	Chelsea
O	Kelley Rutherford J	19	civil engineer	26	here
P	King James	19	salesman	39	"
R	Laliberte John N	19	clerk	28	"
S	Laurence William L	19	teacher	36	35 Pinckney
T	Lehan Timothy J	19	clerk	53	8 Rutherford a
U	Levin Simon L	19	insurance agent	39	here
V	Libel Charles	19	salesman	38	"
W	Lorey Adolph	19	casemaker	66	"
X	Lawson Alex W	19	salesman	64	"
Y	Luscambe Richard L	19	druggist	71	29 Col rd
Z	MacGlashan Richard A	19	salesman	33	here
A	Madigan William E	19	"	53	"
B	Mahoney Richard J	19	clerk	51	Medford
C	Manning George J	19	chauffeur	46	here
D	Marble Ezra	19	salesman	64	"
E	March Louis	19	"	41	"
F	Marks Isaac	19	designer	46	"
G	Marks Joseph S	19	laborer	48	130 Greenwoo
H	Marston George W	19	carpenter	54	here

Myrtle Street—Continued

k	Maynard Charles A	19	dentist	63	here
l	McAdams Robert	19	clerk	40	56 Saratoga
m	McAskill Syrene B	19	retired	61	here
n	McCarthy Andrew H	19	clerk	34	Sharon
o	McCarthy Edward A	19	manager	53	here
p	McCoy Richard A	19	postal clerk	45	"
r	McDonnell Edward S	19	packer	52	"
s	McGillen John B	19	postal clerk	49	78 Chelsea
t	McGrath Harold S	19	candymaker	49	here
u	Mellon Harold E	19	manager	27	"
v	Morrison George H	19	engineer	82	"
w	Murdock Juliun H	19	draughtsman	30	"
x	Murphy Henry J	19	collector	71	"
y	Nesson David	19	salesman	37	"
z	O'Brien John H	19	"	30	"
a	Payne Arthur M	19	clerk	54	"
b	Perkins Richard E	19	manufacturer	56	"
c	Phillips Henry E	19	cashier	48	
d	Pierson Bert F	19	salesman	25	131 Franklin
e	Plummer Morton W	19	emp agency	51	here
f	Pollock Jacques J	19	real estate	34	"
g	Proctor Thomas F	19	watchmaker	71	"
h	Quinn William F	19	clerk	46	"
k	Ramsdell Eugene C	19	teacher	74	"
l	Reid Thomas J	19	dentist	41	"
m	Rogers James	19	clerk	60	"
n	Rome Abraham C	19	lawyer	29	"
o	Rosenberg Nathan	19	engraver	40	"
p	Ryan Albert B	19	salesman	54	"
r	Sampson Charles F L	19	truckman	46	"
s	Sawyer William P	19	lawyer	44	"
t	Scheiring Louis L	19	printer	53	"
u	Stewart Samuel A	19	clerk	61	"
v	Straizel Charles J	19	weaver	30	"
w	Strock John M	19	artist	52	"
x	Tenney Franklin A	19	machinist	44	"
y	Tingley James F	19	retired	56	"
z	Varney Frank P	19	superintendent	50	"
a	Warren Frank E	19	clerk	51	"
b	Waters James C	19	drug clerk	27	"
c	Webb Henry H	19	metalworker	65	"

Myrtle Street—Continued

D	Wentzell Ralph S	19	clerk	40	here
E	Wilder John F	19	cashier	68	"
F	Woodhed Harry S	19	newspaperman	28	Portland Me
N	Petcove Abraham	26	chauffeur	49	here
O	Petcove Mammie—†	26	housekeeper	36	"
P	Cloutier Elizabeth A—†	26	"	56	23 Irving
R	Cloutier Joseph W	26	clerk	53	34 Temple
S	McGinnis Sarah F—†	26	housekeeper	70	23 Irving
T	Kaplan Louis A	26	photographer	37	34 W Cottage
U	Kaplan Sadie—†	26	housekeeper	28	34 "
V	Gordon Annie—†	26	"	38	here
W	Gordon Oscar J	26	storekeeper	44	"
X	Risner Louis	26	butcher	29	"
Y	Pearse Almond	26	shipper	51	"
Z	Pearse Lillian—†	26	housekeeper	27	"
A	Pearse Rose—†	26	"	48	"
B	Ahern Sarah—†	26	"	52	"
C	Murdock Hattie—†	26	"	35	46 S Russell
D	Murdock William R	26	baker	56	46 "
E	Ahern Katherine—†	26	stenographer	25	here
F	Kantarous Gus	26	bootblack	28	"
G	Kantos Louis	26	fruit	50	"
H	Poulos Constatina—†	26	housekeeper	40	"
K	Poulos Stephen	26	storekeeper	40	"
M	Balcom Margaret M—†	27	housewife	62	"
N	Butler William O	27	packer	72	17 Hancock
O	Fotelis Nicholas P	27	shoecutter	31	148 Kneeland
P	Gardner Delia S—†	27	housewife	60	here
R	MacDonnell Michael A	27	salesman	29	"
S	McNeill Edith J—†	27	housewife	30	48 S Russell
T	McNeill Romie J	27	shipper	34	48 "
U	Mullally Mary E—†	27	waitress	24	Canada
V	Murphy Norman A	27	butler	25	Littleton
W	Wolcott Levi B	27	salesman	54	Medford
X	Wolcott Ruth A—†	27	designer	56	"
Y	Lung Sam	28	laundryman	34	here
A	McGahan Anna—†	28½	operator	24	"
B	McGahan Laurence	28½	laborer	49	"
C	McGahan Margarete—†	28½	housekeeper	48	"
D	McGahan Margarete V—†	28½	stenographer	23	"
E	McGahan Mary F—†	28½	multigrapher	20	"

Myrtle Street—Continued

Letter.	Full Name.	Residence, April 1, 1924.	Occupation.	Supposed Age.	Reported Residence, April 1, 1925. Street and Number.
F	Cohen Louis	28½	cigarmaker	42	here
G	Cohen Ray—†	28½	housekeeper	40	"
H	Entin Elizabeth—†	28½	"	28	"
K	Entin Joseph	28½	paperhanger	34	"
L	Flouer Ellen—†	28½	housekeeper	56	42 Anderson
M	Jager Ellen V—†	28½	"	21	91 Revere
N	Jager Holger N	28½	mechanic	24	9 "
O	Casey Elizabeth—†	29	housewife	22	Cambridge
P	Casey John E	29	musician	22	"
R	Gallaher John T	29	porter	54	here
S	Gallaher Mary A—†	29	cook	58	"
T	Mott Gertrude—†	29	saleswoman	48	Cambridge
U	Mott William H	29	special police	48	"
V	Kimball Anna V—†	29	housewife	35	22 Bulfinch
W	Kimball Ernest A	29	ticket seller	35	22 "
X	Rosen Bessie—†	29	housewife	34	here
Y	Rosen Samuel	29	plumber	35	"
Z	Granger Ethel—†	29	cook	30	Connecticut
A	Ordway Carina—†	29	school teacher	32	26 Linden pl
B	Ordway Katherine—†	29	secretary	26	Cambridge
C	Ordway Laura E—†	29	housewife	69	Stony Brook
D	Stevens Anne—†	29	secretary	51	Belmont
E	Stevens Elizabeth—†	29	clerk	55	"
F	Stevens Sarah K—†	29	masseuse	66	"
H	Degman Thomas	31	foreman	55	here
K	Greenleaf George W	31	janitor	67	"
L	Kenny Edward	31	machinist	45	"
M	McCormack Agnes M—†	31	housewife	61	"
N	Moore Charles H	31	lawyer	43	"
O	Powers William	31	R R man	44	"
S	Bellfontaine Helen—†	32	housekeeper	36	"
T	Bellfontaine Victor	32	boxmaker	34	"
U	Costello Patrick	32	watchman	57	"
V	Giossi Leo	32	cook	29	"
W	Griffin Agnes—†	32	waitress	48	"
X	La Pierre Joseph	32	elevatorman	27	"
Y	La Pierre Linus	32	laborer	23	"
Z	Miller Mary J—†	32	domestic	47	"
A	Dwyer Bridget—†	32	housekeeper	60	"
B	Dwyer John V	32	chauffeur	20	"
C	Dwyer Timothy	32	teamster	56	"

8—2

Myrtle Street—Continued

D	Dwyer Timothy F	32	clerk	23	here
E	Sargent John	32	mechanic	35	"
F	Sargent Mary—†	32	housekeeper	33	"
G	Fusto Maria—†	33	housewife	46	137 Salem
H	Spina Charles	33	retired	46	137 "
K	Breslin Daniel J	33	chauffeur	30	36 Myrtle
L	Breslin Edna L—†	33	housewife	27	36 "
M	McGowan Flora—†	33	"	54	here
N	McGowan Mary M—†	33	saleswoman	25	"
O	McGowan William J	33	"	62	"
P	Elovitz Mary—†	33	packer	22	"
R	Orkin Benjamin	33	hatmaker	46	"
S	Orkin Goldie—†	33	housewife	40	"
T	Calloniatis Angela—†	33	houseworker	26	85 Myrtle
U	Calloniatis Efstratios	33	retired	70	85 "
V	Calloniatis Evagelos	33	proprietor	32	85 "
W	Gioshes George T	33	bootblack	30	29 "
X	Gioshes Olga—†	33	housewife	24	29 "
Y	Ford Ella E—†	34	housekeeper	50	61 Falmouth
Z	Conrad Bennet	34	carpenter	46	52 Temple
A	Conrad Laura—†	34	housekeeper	43	here
B	Crandall Julia—†	34	"	43	"
C	Dean Jesse M	34	storekeeper	62	65 St Botolph
D	Dean Mary S—†	34	housewife	61	65 "
E	Geary John P	34	mechanic	29	here
F	Green Benjamin J	34	real estate	34	"
G	Wing May—†	34	housekeeper	29	"
H	Zagaretta Theresa—†	35	housewife	36	"
K	Zagaretta Vincent	35	barber	47	"
L	Mersicano Frank	35	laborer	50	"
M	Mersicano Isabella—†	35	housewife	52	"
N	Mersicano Mary—†	35	clerk	23	"
O	Easchimn Amil	35	laborer	55	"
P	Easchimn Mary—†	35	bookkeeper	22	"
R	Easchimn Rose—†	35	housewife	52	"
S	Mersicano Mary—†	35	"	25	"
T	Mersicano Nicholas	35	waiter	29	"
U	DePasqual Charles	35	barber	34	"
V	DePasqual Santa—†	35	vestmaker	32	"
W	Hussey George W	35	merchant	59	"
X	Hussey Mary E—†	35	housewife	51	"

Myrtle Street—Continued

Y	Billings Anna C—†	35	housewife	34	here
Z	Billings Ervin N	35	clerk	55	"
A	Mersicano John	35	waiter	27	"
B	Mersicano Mary—†	35	packer	26	11 North
D	Archibald David	36	cook	54	17½ Centre
E	Berry Gordon T	36	electrician	23	16 Joy
F	Berry Nellie P—†	36	housekeeper	40	16 "
G	Dubois Annie—†	36	housewife	67	here
H	Dubois Telesphore	36	clerk	84	"
K	Goodwin Bean	36	laborer	45	"
L	Goodwin Viva—†	36	cook	42	"
M	Monson Niles	36	clerk	45	"
N	Monroe Anna—†	36	storekeeper	36	Canada
O	Monroe Havelock	36	ironworker	40	New Hampshire
P	Monroe Leland	36	carpenter	22	Canada
R	Monroe Shannon	36	"	43	11 Myrtle
S	Grillo Conrad	36	correspondent	26	Revere
T	Grillo Rose—†	36	retired	25	"
U	Thomas Marion F—†	36	"	32	here
V	Thomas Stanley E	36	metalworker	32	"
W	Clarke James A	36	bookkeeper	48	"
X	Clarke Mary—†	36	retired	43	"
Y	Savard Ida M—†	36	"	43	"
Z	Savard Joseph E	36	cigarmaker	50	"
C	Kornblum Jacob	38	storekeeper	45	"
D	Kornblum Mollie—†	38	housewife	42	"
E	Levine Annie—†	54	"	48	"
F	Levine Morris	54	tailor	55	"
G	Agusta Sophia—†	54	baker	31	30 Temple
H	Goldberg Clara—†	54	retired	60	here
K	Goldberg Myer	54	cigarmaker	35	"
L	Malend Sarah—†	54	raincoats	25	Chelsea
M	Lenkosky John	54	laborer	21	553 Hunt'n av
N	Lenkosky Stella—†	54	cook	42	553 "
P	Byrne Mary—†	57	clerk	47	13 Auburn
S	Richardson Gertrude E—†	57	housewife	28	here
T	Richardson Harry M	57	engineer	54	"
U	Ellsay Charles	57	chauffeur	29	607 Dor av
V	Levine Maurice	57	foreman	28	here
W	Levine Rose—†	57	housewife	22	"
X	Lazaris Antonio P	57	clerk	41	44 Cambridge

Myrtle Street—Continued

Y	Lazaris Lena—†	57	housewife	28	44 Cambridge
Z	Gargan Bridget—†	57	"	52	here
A	Gargan John A	57	deputy sealer	44	"
B	Gargan Mary F—†	57	packer	53	"
C	Gargan Thomas L	57	collector	41	"
D	Harsenian Oscar	57	student	28	37 Joy
E	Simons Alice—†	57	housewife	32	47 Temple
F	Simons Harry	57	meatcutter	28	47 "
G	Caragianes Bessie—†	58	housekeeper	34	here
H	Caragianes William	58	storekeeper	35	"
K	Steinberg Ida—†	58	housekeeper	45	116 Myrtle
L	Steinberg Minna—†	58	bookkeeper	22	116 "
M	Steinberg Samuel	58	tailor	55	116 "
N	Billings Erma—†	58	waitress	29	here
O	Bradbury Walter	58	decorator	34	"
P	Calvert Harry	58	counterman	29	"
R	Carty James A	58	manager	32	"
S	Carty May—†	58	housekeeper	32	"
T	Kapelos Peter	58	storekeeper	29	"
U	Krag Consitina—†	58	housekeeper	30	"
V	Krag Nicholas	58	storekeeper	34	"
W	Ravelas George	58	shoeworker	24	46 Vine
X	Harris Catherine—†	58	housekeeper	28	here
Y	Harris Peggy—†	58	candymaker	23	"
A	Harris Theodore	58	storekeeper	35	"
C	Whitcross Catherine—†	59	housewife	37	415 Col av
D	Whitcross Edmund H	59	elevatorman	38	415 "
E	Schneider Julia—†	59	housewife	35	here
F	Schneider Morris	59	tailor	38	"
G	Hurwitz Bessie—†	59	dressmaker	28	"
H	Hurwitz Nathan	59	cigarmaker	30	"
K	Hurwitz Sarah—†	59	housekeeper	59	"
L	Cooper Annie—†	59	housewife	28	83 Fayston
M	Cooper Harry	59	jeweler	30	83 "
N	Byer Annie—†	59	housewife	34	here
O	Byer Louis	59	carpenter	35	"
P	Belnkl Etta—†	59	housewife	52	"
R	Belnkl Louis	59	laborer	55	"
S	Morochnick Abraham	59	paperhanger	26	"
T	Morochnick Ida—†	59	housewife	22	"
U	Payser Rose J—†	59	checker	38	"

Myrtle Street--Continued

v	Pelch Mary—†	59	housewife	37	New York
w	Pelch Paul	59	window cleaner	41	"
x	Thomas Benjamin F	59	painter	46	here
y	Thomas Evelyn—†	59	housewife	42	"
a	Olich Anna—†	60	housewife	24	29 Hancock
b	Olich John	60	clerk	27	29 "
c	Ducheck George	60	busboy	21	here
d	Ducheck Helen—†	60	housewife	31	"
e	Ducheck John	60	busboy	24	"
f	Ducheck William	60	waiter	36	"
g	Sweeney Annie—†	60	waitress	45	"
h	Sweeney Peter	60	steamfitter	52	"
k	Larrivee George E	60	compositor	30	Cochituate
l	Larrivee Ruby—†	60	housewife	26	"
m	Landa Ralph	60	clerk	20	here
n	Blender Samuel	60	paperhanger	39	"
o	Blender Edith A—†	60	housewife	34	"
p	Palmer George	60	chauffeur	30	108 Staniford
r	Palmer Margaret—†	60	housekeeper	27	128 "
s	Brooker Dora—†	60	housewife	32	21 Hancock
t	Brooker Samuel	60	tailor	46	21 "
u	Smith Edgar L	60	hatter	56	25 Temple
v	Smith Sadie—†	60	milliner	34	25 "
w	Kane Alice—†	60	housewife	23	98 Princeton
x	Kane Frederick H	60	salesman	27	112 Thornton
y	MacGeachey Lillian A—†	61	social worker	30	here
a	MacGeachey Zella—†	61	housekeeper	50	"
b	Farley Mary E—†	61	housewife	72	"
c	Dewey Elizabeth W—†	61	teacher	20	229 Newbury
d	Dewey Harriette W—†	61	housewife	52	229 "
e	Dewey Henry B	61	manager	59	229 "
f	Dewey Katherine B—†	61	teacher	25	229 "
g	Taylor Margaret—†	61	student	36	62 Pinckney
h	Apollonio Elizabeth—†	61	"	21	Providence R I
k	Apollonio Hortense E—†	61	housewife	53	Milton
l	Apollonio Theron A	61	banker	57	"
m	Kostarelos Anna—†	62	housewife	23	here
n	Kostarelos Peter	62	manager	45	"
o	Schneider Abraham	62	"	32	Detroit Mich
p	Schneider Dora—†	62	housewife	31	"
r	Firing Anna—†	62	dressmaker	25	40 Revere

Myrtle Street—Continued

s	Matis Dora—†	62	milliner	36	72 Revere
t	Rosen Anna—†	62	housewife	40	here
u	Meier George F	62	chef	52	"
v	Meier Laura—†	62	housewife	43	"
w	Tatelbaum Minnie—†	62	dressmaker	30	"
x	Drakos Georgie—†	62	factory worker	23	"
y	Kostarelos Panos	62	pedler	39	"
z	Kostarelos Thresa—†	62	housewife	31	"
A	Gilbert Peter	63	storekeeper	67	"
B	Gilbert Sophie—†	63	housekeeper	65	"
C	Cook George	63	textileman	68	"
D	Ludmersky Joseph	63	tailor	31	"
E	Ludmersky Vita—†	63	housewife	30	"
F	Smith Celia—†	63	housekeeper	23	"
G	Smith David	63	druggist	25	"
H	Malinsky Pauline—†	63	housekeeper	25	"
K	Malinsky Ruben	63	tailor	60	"
L	Roper Catherine—†	63	housewife	52	"
M	Roper Charles	63	machinist	52	"
N	Griffin Margaret—†	63	housewife	32	"
O	Griffin William C	63	pressman	47	"
P	Collins James E	63	teamster	49	"
R	Collins Mary F—†	63	clerk	23	"
S	Collins Mary J—†	63	housewife	52	"
T	Sawyer Mary E—†	63	tel operator	35	"
v	Covino Alice—†	64	housewife	30	26 Allston
w	Covino Joseph	64	bookkeeper	28	26 "
x	Rosenberg Bella—†	64	housewife	24	here
y	Rosenberg Julius	64	guard	25	"
z	Goldberg Benjamin	64	jeweler	45	"
A	Goldberg Rose—†	64	housewife	43	"
B	Rothonberg Carl	64	pressman	40	39 Chambers
C	Gould Dora—†	64	housewife	35	here
D	Gould Jacob	64	cabinetmaker	41	"
E	Bell George P	64	salesman	21	"
F	Bell Margaret—†	64	waitress	38	"
G	Flagg Annie—†	64	housekeeper	66	"
H	Jones Helen—†	66	"	38	"
K	Jones Joshua	66	secretary	42	"
L	Fritz Louis	66	student	20	"
M	Fritz Morris	66	painter	55	"

Myrtle Street—Continued

Letter	Full Name	Res.	Occupation	Age	Reported Residence
N	Fritz Rebecca—†	66	housewife	48	here
O	Rodkin Anna—†	66	stenographer	24	"
P	Rodkin Julia—†	66	housewife	55	"
R	Rodkin Samuel	66	artist	30	"
S	Rodkin Sarah—†	66	bookkeeper	28	"
T	Winner Isadore	66	salesman	26	"
U	Ginsberg Anita—†	66	bookkeeper	20	"
V	Ginsberg Morris	66	jeweler	48	"
W	Ginsberg Sarah—†	66	housewife	46	"
X	Getselovitz Abraham	66	tailor	42	"
Y	Getselovitz Hyman	66	upholsterer	20	"
Z	Getselovitz Lena—†	66	housekeeper	40	"
A	Gofung Borouch O	68	attorney	41	"
B	Stephens James F	68	cigarmaker	55	"
C	Stephens Pauline—†	68	nurse	54	"
D	Danielson Elizebeth—†	68	housewife	48	"
E	Danielson John O	68	janitor	24	"
F	Danielson Sven A	68	superintendent	62	"
G	Danielson Walter E	68	manager	20	"
H	Tibbetts Clifford W	68	clerk	23	"
K	Tibbetts Elizebeth—†	68	tailoress	53	"
L	Tibbetts Paul J	68	clerk	20	"
M	Tibbetts William	68	superintendent	53	"
O	Pappas Bessie—†	68	housewife	33	"
P	Pappas Thomas	68	baker	46	
R	Hart Rose—†	69	housewife	39	860 Col av
S	Hart Walter J	69	clerk	43	860 "
T	Smolins Florence—†	69	housewife	23	31 St Lukes rd
U	Smolins Israel	69	salesman	31	31 "
V	Cohen Annie—†	69	saleswoman	25	here
W	Cohen Benjamin	69	carpenter	60	"
X	Cohen Gertrude—†	69	salesman	24	"
Y	Cohen Golden—†	69	clerk	25	"
Z	Cohen Lena—†	69	"	28	"
A	Cohen Mary—†	69	saleswoman	26	"
B	Cohen Morris	69	student	22	"
C	Cohen Sadie—†	69	typist	23	"
D	Johnson Beda—†	69	maid	34	"
E	Johnson Elizebeth—†	69	tailoress	40	"
F	Samovitz Helen—†	69	housekeeper	43	"
G	Hedberg George	69	conductor	31	Worcester

Myrtle Street—Continued

H	Rolche Annie—†	69	housekeeper	29	here
K	Rolche Frank	69	baker	30	"
L	Busck Elica—†	69	housewife	48	"
M	Busck George	69	musician	40	"
N	Miller Frances—†	69	housewife	23	20 Auburn
O	Miller Morris	69	manager	24	7 Hancock
P	Kramer Leon	69	gas fixtures	26	32 "
R	Kramer Sarah—†	69	dressmaker	26	32 "
S	Evans Albert R	70	salesman	23	Canton
T	Evans Gladys—†	70	housekeeper	22	"
U	Keep William	70	tailor	68	672 Tremont
V	Canning Elizabeth—†	71	seamstress	44	here
W	Canning Teresa—†	71	operator	42	"
X	Slabinsky Annie—†	71	housewife	48	"
Y	Slabinsky Barney	71	shoemaker	50	"
Z	Slabinsky Phillip	71	printer	20	"
A	Krovitz Ida—†	71	housekeeper	60	"
B	Krovitz Tillie—†	71	vestmaker	28	"
C	Yaker Fannie—†	71	housekeeper	26	"
D	Sorenti Anthony	71	salesman	27	45 Garden
E	Sorenti Edward	71	shoemaker	30	45 "
F	Sorenti Frank	71	retired	56	45 "
G	Sorenti Mildred—†	71	housekeeper	21	181 Norfolk a
A	Sorenti Peter	71	assembler	20	45 Garden
B	Sorenti Rose—†	71	housewife	56	45 "
C	Slabinsky Aaron	71	tailor	48	here
D	Slabinsky Fannie—†	71	housewife	44	"
F	Barber Catherine—†	73	waitress	40	35 Revere
G	Collins Anna—†	73	cook	47	35 "
H	Cunningham Sadie—†	73	waitress	35	35 "
K	Stone Charles	73	salesman	65	35 "
L	Cady Corria	73	repairman	48	New York
M	Huntley Charles W	73	teamster	65	here
N	Marcello Anthony	73	plasterer	38	"
O	Marcello Florence—†	73	housewife	36	"
P	Leonard Paul	73	waiter	28	"
R	Rathburn Ethel—†	73	cashier	39	"
S	Krivitsky Bessie—†	73	housewife	34	"
T	Krivitsky Samuel	73	butcher	37	"
U	Samuels William	73	laster	56	"
V	Thonopulos Tena—†	73	housewife	30	"

Myrtle Street—Continued

Letter	Full Name	Residence April 1, 1924	Occupation	Supposed Age	Reported Residence April 1, 1923
W	Thonopulos Thomas	73	pedler	37	here
X	Lavens Teresa —†	74	waitress	30	"
Y	Rumbolt Margaret—†	74	"	28	"
Z	Adams Katherine—†	74	housewife	23	17 Raven
A	Adams Thomas	74	chauffeur	30	17 "
B	Malo Joseph E	74	barber	50	here
C	Malo Julia B—†	74	housewife	44	"
D	O'Brien Mary E—†	74	"	42	"
E	O'Brien Thomas F	74	U S N	43	"
F	Ralston Florence H—†	74	housewife	27	"
G	Ralston William J	74	chauffeur	28	"
H	Conway Kathrine—†	74	waitress	37	"
K	Hersfeld Abraham	74	printer	30	32 McLean
L	Hersfield Sarah—†	74	housewife	30	32 Chambers
M	Johnson William H	74	laborer	20	here
N	Stevens Mary—†	74	domestic	42	"
O	Fierlefyn Lewis	74	painter	39	"
P	Fierlefyn Lillian—†	74	housewife	45	"
R	Sargent Mortimer	76	insurance	43	"
S	Flagg Helen L—†	76	clerk	22	"
T	Flagg Helen M—†	76	"	43	"
U	McDonald Anna—†	76	waitress	42	"
V	Wing Gertrude—†	76	housekeeper	29	"
W	Wing Irene—†	76	bookkeeper	23	"
X	Wing Lilly—†	76	housewife	60	"
Y	McGowan Mary M—†	76	"	33	"
Z	McGowan William L	76	salesman	33	"
A	Girard Hilda—†	76	saleswoman	27	32 Hancock
B	Nowell Mary E—†	76	domestic	45	32 "
C	Blumenfeld Frances—†	76	housewife	20	31 Anderson
D	Blumenfeld Lewis	76	salesman	26	43 N Anderson
E	Chamberland Elizabeth—†	76	housewife	65	here
F	Jackman John A	76	clerk	38	"
G	Wright Ernest B	76	laborer	54	55 Joy
H	Wright Jane M—†	76	domestic	49	55 "
K	Flynn Katherine—†	76	waitress	40	here
L	Dean Abbott M	77	student	23	Cambridge
M	Dean Elizabeth B—†	77	teacher	23	Quincy Ill
N	Hinkle Charles A	77	merchant	28	114 Mt Vernon
O	Hoskins Harold	77	engineer	25	4 W Cedar
P	Howell Mary—†	77	housekeeper	70	114 Mt Vernon

Myrtle Street—Continued

R	Stillwell John B	77	clerk	22	Quincy Ill
S	Warren Frank D	77	publisher	27	4 Cedar
T	Benjamin Milton	78	salesman	41	here
U	Dunn Kenneth	78	"	21	19 Myrtle
V	Feeney Vincent	78	"	20	19 "
W	Klein Zoltan	78	draughtsman	32	here
X	Loiselle Josephine—†	78	housekeeper	48	New York City
Y	Loiselle Ulysses P	78	salesman	50	"
Z	Milton Thomas	78	waiter	35	here
A	Murphy Marie—†	78	stenographer	29	"
B	Nichols Craig	78	watchman	31	"
C	Scharfman Morris	78	printer	26	"
D	Shea Michael J	78	"	36	"
E	Summer Bradish P	78	plumber	46	"
F	Harrison Arthur E	79	janitor	42	California
G	Harrison Mary—†	79	housewife	28	"
H	Apostles George A	79	fruit	31	here
K	Cartunia George	79	"	43	"
L	McDonald Daniel	79	carpenter	60	New Hampshire
M	Prescott Althea—†	79	housewife	56	here
N	Prescott Walter	79	lawyer	58	"
O	Golden Harry	79	physician	27	"
P	Goldenberg Annie—†	79	housewife	62	"
R	Goldenberg Isac	79	retired	62	"
S	Tucker Joseph	79	engineer	32	"
T	Tucker Minnie—†	79	housewife	29	"
U	Halpern Bessie—†	79	"	59	26 Auburn
V	Halpern Jacob	79	bookkeeper	61	26 "
W	Halpern Samuel	79	cutter	32	26 "
X	Weiner Louis	79	salesman	29	26 "
Y	Weiner Samuel	79	"	32	26 "
Z	Weiner Tina—†	79	housewife	28	Beachmont
A	Coughlin William J	79	ticket agent	53	here
B	Thorp Alice I—†	79	cashier	50	"
C	Whitehouse Frank W	79	salesman	45	"
D	Bournmayer Gregory	80	fruit	41	"
E	Brouberg Frederick W	80	student	30	72 Myrtle
F	Conloners Nelor	80	fruit	42	here
G	Powell Ella—†	80	housewife	60	"
H	Powell George E	80	printer	22	"
K	Powell Thomas W	80	manager	66	"

Myrtle Street—Continued

L	Rounds May—†	80	bookkeeper	40	here
M	Toumbakis Louis	80	waiter	37	"
N	Toumbakis Peter	80	candymaker	26	"
O	Voyias Charles	80	salesman	27	"
P	Widerhand Louis	80	fireman	65	"
R	Zaimis Stilianos	80	fruit	35	"
S	Belknap Elizabeth—†	81	housewife	43	Dedham
T	Belknap Robert E	81	salesman	47	"
U	Bjoison Ingeborg—†	81	nurse	23	267 Com av
V	Griffin Peter F	82	salesman	54	80 N Cedar
W	Sharkey Ada J—†	82	housewife	38	80 "
X	Sharkey John L	82	janitor	36	80 "
Y	Holmes Wallace	82	cook	54	here
Z	Malone Christine—†	82	housewife	38	64 Revere
A	Malone Matthew	82	janitor	43	64 "
B	Harris Charles E	82	teacher	36	here
C	Harris Helen M—†	82	housewife	36	"
D	Rosenfield Abraham L	82	sign writer	34	"
E	Rosenfield Lena—†	82	housewife	31	"
F	Kaufman Andrew	82	toolmaker	37	"
G	Kaufman Anna—†	82	housewife	38	"
H	Rideout Earnest	82	inspector	30	"
K	Rideout Elsie—†	82	housewife	26	"
L	Kuznuk Frances—†	82	"	24	"
M	Kuznuk Joseph	82	carpenter	29	"
N	Hastings Florence V—†	82	housewife	31	"
O	Hastings George M	82	inspector	36	"
P	Giroux Elsie U—†	82	housewife	24	"
R	Giroux Louis O	82	cook	20	"
S	Connolly Margaret—†	83	maid	25	"
T	Homans Edith—†	83	housewife	27	"
U	Homans William P	83	lawyer	45	"
V	Cummings Bertha—†	84	clerk	27	Worcester
W	Kagan Abraham B	84	real estate	50	here
X	Kagan Anna—†	84	student	20	"
Y	Kagan Dora—†	84	bookkeeper	22	"
Z	Kagan Lena—†	84	housewife	45	"
A	Gelb Anna—†	84	"	45	"
B	Gelb Benjamin	84	newspaperman	35	"
C	Gelb Susa—†	84	clerk	25	"
D	Bennett Bessie—†	84	housekeeper	27	"

Page	Letter	Full Name.	Residence, April 1, 1924.	Occupation.	Supposed Age.	Reported Residence, April 1, 1923. Street and Number.

Myrtle Street—Continued

	E	Bennett Herman	84	photographer	35	here
	F	Bennett Louis	84	salesman	55	"
	G	Bennett Samuel	84	clerk	31	"
	H	Waxman Ester—†	84	housewife	54	"
	K	Waxman Hyman	84	tailor	34	"
	L	McCarthy Anna—†	85	housewife	56	5 Hancock
	M	Whalen Edward	85	laborer	40	here
	N	Whalen Mary—†	85	housewife	35	"
	O	Isber Bessie—†	85	"	48	"
	P	Isber Israel	85	lawyer	26	"
	R	Isber William	85	student	25	"
	S	Calvettie Arthur	85	cutter	22	5 Hancock
	T	Calvettie Kathrine—†	85	housewife	20	5 "
	U	Grossblatt Bessie—†	85	"	34	here
	V	Grossblatt Isidore	85	jeweler	37	"
	W	Latsey Andrew	85	storekeeper	28	"
	X	Latsey Katherine—†	85	housewife	25	"
	Y	McDonald Vera—†	85	saleswoman	35	"
	Z	Cooper Emily—†	85	student	22	35 Temple
	A	Davis Dorothy—†	85	"	32	35 "
	B	Trotter Charlotte—†	85	"	32	New York
	C	Chisolm Caroline—†	85	waitress	30	here
	D	McKay Mary—†	85	"	26	"
	E	Gorman Daisey—†	85	"	37	"
	F	Morgan John	85	laborer	38	"
	G	Dickson Laura—†	85	housewife	28	"
	H	Dickson Stanley	85	student	26	"
	K	Dunnell Caroline—†	86	housewife	58	Pennsylvania
	L	Dunnell Jacob	86	student	23	4 W Cedar
	M	Dunnell William W	86	"	28	4 "
	N	Newberry John S	87	instructor	40	here
	O	Newberry Rossamond—†	87	housewife	36	"
	P	Biggar Oscar	88	painter	48	"
	R	Corodova Elmore	88	engineer	60	"
	S	Drury Henry	88	clerk	30	72 W Cedar
	T	Gould Edward F	88	salesman	50	here
	U	Hetch Eva—†	88	florist	25	"
	V	Hetch Joseph	88	printer	30	"
	W	Hetch Morris	88	florist	40	"
	X	Hopkins Margaret—†	88	bookbinder	25	Revere
	Y	Mabee Dorothy—†	88	saleswoman	22	Canada

Myrtle Street—Continued

Letter	Full Name	Residence	Occupation	Age	Reported Residence
z	Maxwell Maragret—†	88	salesman	28	Canada
A	Mullen Josephine—†	88	housekeeper	38	here
B	O'Brien John A	88	hotelman	40	"
C	Rosen Isaac	88	tailor	35	"
D	Berringer Alfred	89	clerk	45	
E	Blanchard Cora—†	89	"	40	New Hampshire
F	Jeffrey Frederick	89	marketman	59	here
G	Jeffrey Nora—†	89	housewife	60	"
H	Leach AnnieJ—†	89	retired	64	"
K	Raymond Jessie—†	89	"	75	90 Myrtle
L	Latter David T	89	tailor	30	New Hampshire
M	White Albert	89	retired	74	here
N	Harvey Alice E—†	90	housewife	37	"
O	Harvey Phillips	90	engineer	50	"

Phillips Street

Letter	Full Name	Residence	Occupation	Age	Reported Residence
P	Adams Charles	2	stableman	47	here
R	Crawford Daniel J	2	porter	25	Camden N J
S	Love Zachary T	2	"	29	here
T	Smith Sylvia L—†	2	scrubwoman	73	"
U	Towles George	2	fireman	80	"
V	Wheaton Wendella—†	2	houseworker	47	"
W	Dukacs Mollie—†	3	housewife	45	"
X	Dukacs Ruth—†	3	rubberworker	21	"
Y	Snider Jacob	3	barber	43	Malden
Z	Snider Sadie—†	3	storekeeper	37	"
A	Apple Benjamin	3	tailor	31	here
B	Apple Ida—†	3	housewife	29	"
C	Hoffman Morris	3	tailor	48	"
D	Chusad Charles	3	clerk	36	"
E	Chusad Sadie—†	3	housewife	32	"
F	Jaspan Fannie—†	3	"	37	"
G	Jaspan Max	3	jeweler	42	"
H	Zion Fannie—†	3	capmaker	20	"
K	Palatnck Ida—†	3	housewife	58	59 Phillips
L	Palatnck Phillips	3	shoemaker	58	59 "
M	Wallace Anna—†	3	housewife	23	90 W Cedar
N	Wallace Isdore	3	painter	26	90 "
O	Raymond Minnie—†	3	housewife	31	here

Phillips Street—Continued

p	Raymond Morris	3	tailor	34	here
R	Hughes Fannie M—†	3	housewife	41	270 Bay State rd
s	Hughes John F	3	foreman	40	270 "
T	Hughes Elmont	3	tramster	21	270 "
u	Boris Aaron	4	meatcutter	23	63 Bickford
v	Boris Fannie—†	4	housewife	44	63 "
w	Swartz Celia—†	4	"	37	37 S Russell
x	Swartz Morris	4	tailor	42	37 "
y	Artenstein Mary—†	4	housewife	28	here
z	Artenstein Max	4	grocer	35	"
A	Fishman Ettel—†	4	housewife	31	"
B	Fishman Jacob	4	shoemaker	31	"
c	Kaufman Charles	5	pedler	38	"
D	Kaufman Rebecca—†	5	housewife	33	"
E	Kaufman Beatrice—†	5	housemaid	37	"
F	White Julius	5	helper	20	"
G	White Louis	5	meatcutter	21	"
H	White Rose—†	5	housewife	58	"
K	White Samuel	5	locksmith	60	"
L	Crafin Benjamin	5	storekeeper	35	"
M	Crafin Sarah—†	5	housewife	35	"
N	Krosnogar Vitel—†	5	"	76	"
o	Bloom Esther—†	5	"	35	"
P	Bloom Louis	5	pedler	35	"
R	Borin Harry	6	barber	28	"
s	Borin Rose—†	6	housewife	27	"
T	Ligams Phillip	6	plumber	27	"
u	Ligams Sarah—†	6	housewife	27	"
v	Polansky Harry	6	tailor	42	"
w	Polansky Rose—†	6	housewife	38	"
x	Stern Anna—†	6	"	45	25 Blossom
y	Stern Samuel	6	tinsmith	42	25 "
z	Ivory Elizabeth—†	7	housekeeper	62	10 Salem
A	Peterson Dellia—†	7	laundryworker	54	1 N Anderson
B	McKernan Mary—†	7	houseworker	50	here
c	McCourt Charles	7	woolworker	40	"
D	McCourt Sarah J—†	7	houseworker	60	"
E	McDonald Edith—†	7	housewife	46	"
F	McDonald Thomas J	7	cooper	35	"
G	Stack Catherine B—†	7	housewife	38	"
H	Stack John J	7	waiter	45	"

Phillips Street—Continued

K	Rothberg Eva—†	13	housewife	60	here
L	Rothberg Goldie—†	13	"	38	"
M	Rothberg Samuel	13	storekeeper	40	"
N	Krinsky Max	13	"	21	"
O	Krinsky Myer	13	painter	50	"
P	Krinsky Rebecca—†	13	housewife	50	"
R	Baker Jennie—†	13	"	21	Malden
S	Baker Joseph	13	electrician	25	"
T	Solelman Esther—†	13	housewife	40	here
U	Solelman Max	13	tailor	50	"
V	Foster Bessie—†	13	housewife	46	38 Garden
W	Foster Samuel	13	carpenter	50	38 "
X	Cohen Ida—†	13	housewife	32	here
Y	Cohen Israel	13	cutter	32	"
Z	Magar Morris	13	auto mechanic	38	"
A	Gilman Rosie—†	13	housewife	38	"
B	Grosser John	13	machinist	31	"
C	Grosser Katharine—†	13	housewife	29	"
D	Levine Benjamin	13	tailor	26	"
E	Levine Lillian—†	13	housewife	26	"
F	Huff Edith—†	15	"	21	11 Cambridge
G	Huff William C	15	janitor	22	11 "
H	Silverstein Abraham	15	retired	60	11 "
K	Silverstein Jennie—†	15	housewife	60	here
L	Campbell Margaret—†	15	cleaner	63	"
M	Riggs John W	15	garageman	44	"
N	Riggs Mary A—†	15	housewife	42	"
O	Henderson Alice—†	17	"	51	"
P	Henderson Frederick H	17	laborer	25	"
R	Henderson Gertrude—†	17	factory worker	28	"
S	Henderson James B	17	postal clerk	27	"
T	Henderson James H	17	porter	52	"
U	Henderson Richard E	17	janitor	21	"
W	Davidson Phillip L	19	salesman	28	Pennsylvania
X	Pinney Humphrey	19	"	31	New York
Y	Paul Elliot H	19	author	33	36 Garden
A	Beyers George	20	janitor	55	here
B	Daltry Ellen—†	20	housewife	68	"
C	Dabosky Mary—†	20	"	70	"
G	Hines John	20	waiter	40	New Bedford
H	McGee Charles	20	janitor	63	here

Phillips Street—Continued

K	Nelson Dora—†	20	housewife	50	here	
M	Roundtree David	22	coalheaver	42	42 Grove	
N	Narraveth Edward	22	pedler	41	75 Phillips	
U	Miller Elizabeth—†	22	housewife	30	12 Warwick	
W	Adler Bella—†	24	"	53	here	
X	Adler Bengamin	24	carpenter	50	"	
Y	Levine Samuel	24	retired	68	"	
Z	Press Rose—†	24	housewife	38	"	
A	Press Samuel	24	presser	35	"	
B	Adamchuck James	24	baker	29	48 Revere	
C	Adamchuck Mary—†	24	housewife	20	48 "	
D	Wienstein Bertha—†	24	"	24	here	
E	Wienstein Hyman	24	tailor	26	"	
F	Catalina Joseph	24	electrician	32	New York City	
G	Cohen Samuel	24	retired	65	here	
K	Primack Bertha—†	25	housewife	32	"	
L	Primack Harry	25	meatcutter	27	"	
M	Solor Annie—†	25	housewife	27	1 Anderson pl	
N	Solor Morris	25	shoemaker	28	1 "	
O	Jacobson Jacob	25	laborer	50	Worcester	
P	Kaplan Julius	27	"	29	"	
R	Katz Annie—†	27	dressmaker	22	103 Chambers	
S	Rabenovitz David	27	tailor	35	here	
T	Rabenovitz Lillian—†	27	housewife	29	"	
U	Borodsky Selia—†	27	"	65	Chelsea	
V	Stern Dora—†	27	"	38	Reading	
W	Stern Samuel	27	shoemaker	42	"	
X	Gamerman Ida—†	27	housewife	37	here	
Y	Gamerman Samuel	27	meatcutter	43	"	
Z	Ameris Annie—†	27	housewife	38	"	
A	Rabinovitz Rita—†	28	housewife	26	Brockton	
B	Rabinovitz Samuel	28	pedler	31	27 Phillips	
C	Newman Abraham	28	retired	55	Russia	
D	Kerner Mollie—†	28	housewife	45	here	
E	Kerner Phillip	28	carpenter	50	"	
F	Kerner Samuel	28	baker	20	"	
G	Goldberg Benjamin	28	glazier	40	"	
H	Goldberg Jennie—†	28	housewife	44	"	
K	Goldberg Sarah—†	28	housekeeper	22	"	
L	Israel Charles	28	butcher	25	"	
M	Isreal Etta—†	28	housewife	20	"	

Phillips Street—Continued

o	Davis Hellen—†	29	housewife	43	here
p	David Robert W	29	printer	53	"
r	Kruminsky Bernard	29	painter	54	"
s	Kruminsky Esther—†	29	saleswoman	21	"
t	Kruminsky Rebecca—†	29	housewife	49	"
u	Beshansky Bessie—†	29	"	29	"
v	Beshansky Hyman	29	laborer	45	"
w	Clark Alexander H	29	"	33	"
x	Clark Julia—†	29	housewife	29	"

Pinckney Street

A	Bean Susan—†	3	librarian	35	here
B	Goodman Albert A	3	cook	35	"
C	Livingston Archibald B	3	cabinetmaker	53	"
D	Livingston Carrie M—†	3	housewife	42	"
E	Morrisey John	3	salesman	56	"
F	Ames Daniel E	5	treasurer	43	"
G	Carter Apphia—†	5	housewife	51	"
H	Carter Arthur B	5	secretary	57	"
K	Beansang Eileen—†	9	housewife	26	"
L	Beansang John	9	janitor	37	"
M	Bowman Ada M—†	9	none	36	"
N	Clark Cora E—†	9	clerk	52	"
O	Durham Elizabeth P—†	9	none	50	"
P	Outterson George	9	engineer	60	"
R	Rosenbaum Albert	9	tailor	62	"
S	Rosenbaum Emma—†	9	housekeeper	50	"
T	Brown Alice—†	11	writer	62	"
U	Reed Maria G—†	11	housekeeper	70	"
V	Rich Evelyn—†	11	"	75	"
W	Cleveland Alfred E	13 & 15	chemist	50	"
X	Cleveland Olive—†	13 & 15	housekeeper	33	"
Y	Fahey Mary—†	13 & 15	maid	28	"
Z	Judd Marian H—†	13 & 15	housekeeper	52	"
A	Nichols Edith J—†	13 & 15	housekeeper	55	"
B	Hastings Dorothy—†	13 & 15	"	33	"
C	Hastings Leslie	13 & 15	real estate	39	"
D	McDonough Margaret—†	13 & 15	maid	23	827 Broadway
E	Dervell Mary A—†	13 & 15	treasurer	36	here

8—2   49

Pinckney Street—Continued

F	Reardon Bernice E—†	13 & 15	teacher	37	here
G	Burke Nellie—†	13 & 15	maid	22	Brookline
H	Wheeler Annie B—†	13 & 15	housewife	55	here
K	Wheeler George H	13 & 15	agent	58	"
L	Rausoules Marguerite—†	13 & 15	maid	24	Brookline
M	Russell Charlotte—†	13 & 15	housekeeper	28	here
N	Russell Otis	13 & 15	lawyer	30	"
O	Cameron Annie—†	17	waitress	38	"
P	Fenton Edward	17	lawyer	28	12 Hancock
R	Flannery Mary E—†	17	housewife	35	here
S	Higgins Lota—†	17	cook	55	"
T	Newton Lyda—†	17	retired	95	"
U	Sawyer Adelida—†	17	milliner	70	"
V	Mann Elizabeth—†	19	matron	50	"
W	McCann Katharine—†	19	houseworker	43	"
X	Leone Giovanni	21	restaurateur	37	"
X¹	Brawford James	23	salesman	35	"
Y	Brown Anna—†	23	retired	80	"
Z	Cleary John	23	accountant	29	"
A	Cleary Margaret—†	23	saleswoman	31	"
B	Coombs Inez—†	23	milliner	26	"
C	Fratus Margaret—†	23	tailoress	40	"
D	Galvin Maritime	23	student	25	"
E	Gillette Emma—†	23	bookkeeper	50	"
F	Holt Celeste—†	23	retired	80	"
G	Hutchinson Harry	23	printer	31	"
H	Isnor Mabel—†	23	landlady	29	"
K	Jones Florence—†	23	bookkeeper	45	"
L	Keene George	23	accountant	60	"
M	Leonard James	23	clerk	57	"
N	Luce Robert	23	salesman	69	"
O	McCormack Edward J	23	engineer	41	"
P	McGrail Thomas	23	student	24	"
R	Mitchell George	23	machinist	29	"
S	Murphy Gerald	23	student	24	"
T	Nutting Lawrence	23	laborer	45	"
U	Nutting Louise—†	23	cashier	40	"
V	Quilivan Theodore	23	student	26	"
W	Ross John	23	trainman	43	"
X	Seidensicker Clara—†	23	milliner	53	"
Y	Smith Alvin	23	laborer	24	"

Pinckney Street—Continued

Letter	Full Name	Residence	Occupation	Age	Reported Residence
z	Smith Daisy—†	23	bookkeeper	55	here
A	Smith Margaret—†	23	cashier	22	"
B	Sullivan John	23	broker	55	"
C	Sullivan Nellie—†	23	school teacher	38	"
D	Trombly Florence—†	23	housewife	50	"
E	Downes Frances E—†	25	housekeeper	47	"
F	Eggleston Pierce J	25	fireman	37	"
G	Fisher Arthur J	25	salesman	44	"
H	Kerrigan William F	25	glasscutter	43	"
K	Ramsey Theresa A—†	25	housekeeper	60	"
L	Ramsey Theresa F—†	25	bookkeeper	38	"
M	Aldrich Caroline—†	27	retired	60	Portland Me
N	Dayton Corella—†	27	housewife	58	here
O	Dayton Herbert W	27	treasurer	51	"
P	Delay John W	27	florist	59	"
R	Harrington Alice—†	27	clerk	31	"
S	Pritchard Madline—†	27	housewife	24	Portland Me
T	Pritchard William	27	U S A	35	here
U	Yamanikas Michael	27	chef	37	"
V	Burrill Charles L	29	treasurer	62	"
W	Burrill Clara—†	29	housewife	49	"
X	Marshall Jessie—†	29½	"	42	"
Y	Marshall William	29½	manufacturer	42	"
A	Howarth Donald G	31	student	22	"
B	Howarth Fanny C—†	31	housewife	60	"
C	Howarth Marjorie—†	31	nurse	29	"
D	Sheldon Lura E—†	31	housewife	33	"
E	Sheldon Russell S	31	physician	38	"
F	Ayers Fredrick	31	clerk	47	"
G	Bruce Josephine—†	31	proprietor	50	"
H	Cook Caroline—†	31	lawyer	50	"
K	Hewey Hudson A	31	operator	25	Wash'n D C
L	Bridgemon Mary—†	33	clerk	55	86 Myrtle
M	Ely Grace D—†	33	"	23	Wash'n D C
M¹	MacLanaphan Rebecca N—†	33	student	32	Methuen
N	Tirrell Arthur L	33	broker	43	38 Westland av
O	Tirrell Laurel W—†	33	housewife	35	38 "
P	Dickinson Beatrice E B—†	35	accountant	50	here
R	Lawson Douglas	35	laborer	35	New York
S	Parker Alice E—†	35	housewife	59	here
T	Parsons Elizabeth C—†	35	housekeeper	59	"

Pinckney Street—Continued

U	Rice Florence M L—†	35	housekeeper	48	here
V	Rice Fred I	35	steamfitter	68	"
W	Cram Robert N	37	architect	30	"
X	McCoy Andrew T	37	electrician	60	"
Y	McCoy Emeley L—†	37	housewife	72	"
Z	Peck Lucius	37	salesman	26	"
A	Ronden Jose	37	student	23	"
B	Armes Fritzi—†	39	housewife	33	"
C	Armes Lyman	39	advertiser	33	"
D	Smith Alexander	41	chef	52	"
E	Smith Marcella—†	41	housewife	38	"
F	Maguire Grace—†	41	student	24	"
G	Maguire Inocentia—†	41	dressmaker	29	"
H	Maguire Louise—†	41	milliner	27	"
K	Crowley Jerome J	41	packer	63	"
L	Ryan Mary A—†	41	housewife	68	"
M	Ryan Walter J	41	reporter	43	"
N	Alford Lillian R—†	41	housewife	35	"
O	Alford Nathan	41	lawyer	38	"
P	Peterson Julia E—†	41	storekeeper	50	27 Robinwood av
R	Twombly Florence—†	41	buyer	50	72 "
S	Twombly Gertrude—†	41	clerk	44	72 "
T	Farren Catherine—†	43	housekeeper	75	here
U	Hart Beatrice—†	43	restaurant man	36	"
V	Hart Frank A	43	watchman	50	"
W	Horton Ann—†	43	saleswoman	34	Taunton
X	Horton Earl	43	cook	30	"
Y	Johnson Florence—†	43	designer	47	here
Z	Johnson Seth	43	retired	63	"
A	MacEachern Marie—†	43	factory worker	30	"
B	Macinnis Sarah—†	43	restaurantman	50	"
C	McDonald Olive B—†	43	lodging house	42	"
D	Proctor Wilbur	43	tel worker	22	"
E	Simons Ida—†	43	housekeeper	24	New Hampshire
F	Simons William	43	clerk	29	"
G	Sims Harry	43	designer	65	here
P	Little Elsie D—†	45	housewife	40	"
R	Little William J	45	artist	58	"
S	Mansolff Alfred	45	architect	30	"
H	Abby Frank P	47	broker	49	24 Haviland
K	Jones John D	47	music teacher	70	21 W Cedar

Pinckney Street—Continued

Letter.	FULL NAME.	Residence	Occupation	Age	Reported Residence
L	Jones Mollie I—†	47	embroiderer	40	here
M	Kelley Horace R	47	auditor	68	"
N	Kibbie Leonard R	47	manager	33	"
O	Kibbie William H B	47	metalworker	71	"
T	McCoy William T	47	insurance agent	50	115 Pinckney
U	Moore Martha J—†	47	secretary	68	here
V	Rich William A	47	retired	68	"
W	Tailor Florence A—†	47	housekeeper	45	"
X	Tailor Henry A	47	manager	50	"
Y	Adams Mary M—†	49	seamstress	22	"
Z	Brault Lawrence	49	salesman	48	"
A	Burke John S	49	manager	37	Chicago Ill
B	Burke Lillian K—†	49	housewife	28	"
C	Calloway George	49	clerk	66	here
D	Elliott John R	49	fish dealer	52	"
E	Garrity Josephine M—†	49	clerk	45	"
F	Goldenberg Rose—†	49	dressmaker	30	"
G	Hartnett Stephen P	49	clerk	35	"
H	Houghton George W	49	"	66	"
K	Kearney Neil	49	bank clerk	33	"
L	Leitch Helen G—†	49	housewife	48	"
M	Leitch Samuel	49	clerk	54	"
N	MacDonald Florence—†	49	bookkeeper	25	"
O	McClintock Henry E	49	clerk	32	"
P	Moore Zina S—†	49	waiter	34	"
R	Nealand Frank	49	clerk	40	"
S	Prue Rockwood S	49	collector	30	"
T	Sullivan Michael F	49	laborer	55	"
U	Sullivan Neil J	49	salesman	50	"
V	Campbell Arthur D	51	decorator	36	Brookline
W	Campbell Elizabeth—†	51	housewife	37	"
X	Dearborn Sara F—†	51	"	70	"
Y	Enman Helen—†	51	nurse	46	"
Z	Codman Charles R	53	broker	29	here
A	Codman Theodora D—†	53	housewife	28	"
B	Colvin Rebecca—†	53	nurse	23	"
C	Vose Evans	55	manager	31	42 Pinckney
D	Vose Winifred E—†	55	housewife	28	42 "
E	Beckett George P	57	salesman	50	New York
F	Cullen Teresa—†	57	nurse	52	here
G	Downing Daniel F	57	clerk	45	"

Pinckney Street— Continued

H	Gallivan Morris	57	printer	43	here
K	Hallett Laura—†	57	housekeeper	60	"
L	Hedley Priscilla—†	57	clerk	40	"
M	LeBlanc Edesse—†	57	dressmaker	40	"
N	Murphy Adeline—†	57	school teacher	40	825 Beacon
O	Priestly George	57	waiter	39	here
P	Randles Alice W—†	57	housekeeper	65	"
R	Randles Joseph	57	clockmaker	65	"
S	Staples Florence E—†	57	bookkeeper	38	"
T	Staples Nathaniel W	57	accountant	40	"
U	Sullivan Mary—†	57	secretary	36	"
V	Trefethen Norman	57	clerk	24	Lynn
W	Dorthey Hugh W	59	salesman	28	here
X	Holton Albert H	59	buyer	59	"
Y	Holton Evalena H—†	59	housewife	54	"
Z	Ryan Joseph	59	printer	41	"
A	Sheck Adelia G—†	59	housewife	47	"
B	Sheck Charles E	59	yardmaster	59	"
C	Teele William	59	painter	74	"
D	Crowley Catherine—†	61	bookkeeper	45	"
E	Duncan Robert N	61	salesman	60	"
F	Finley Katherine—†	61	bookkeeper	45	"
G	LeClair Catherine B—†	61	housewife	61	"
H	LeClair Fred E	61	retired	62	"
K	Mahan Mary J—†	61	clerk	45	"
L	Rawles Caroline—†	63	housekeeper	74	"
M	Rawles James D	63	retired	68	"
N	Sanford Florence—†	63	bookkeeper	32	"
O	Cutter Frederick S	65	retired	71	"
P	Cutter Lelia—†	65	housewife	62	"
R	Moran Laide—†	65	nurse	48	"
S	Otis Mable I—†	65	bookkeeper	52	"
T	Peterkin Mary J—†	65	domestic	23	"

Revere Street

U	Garrigan Olive—†	4	housewife	26	here
V	Garrigan Peter R	4	plasterer	32	"
W	Gathemann Adolph A	6	salesman	44	64 W Cedar
X	Gathemann Mabel S—†	6	housewife	48	64 "

Revere Street—Continued

Y	Merrill Charles A	8	engineer	64	here
Z	Merrill Emily L—†	8	housewife	62	"
A	Conty Idea—†	9	"	26	"
B	Conty Louis	9	storekeeper	31	"
C	Sherman Abraham	9	chauffeur	28	"
D	Shuman Israel B	9	operator	24	"
E	Sherman Tillie—†	9	housewife	46	"
F	William Albert E	9	veteran	76	"
G	Williams Ruth—†	9	housewife	72	"
H	Markowsky Lena—†	9	"	21	"
K	Markowsky Oscar	9	student	23	"
L	Brown Harry	9	cigarmaker	37	"
M	Brown Rose—†	9	housewife	35	"
N	Bryant Andrew A	9	laborer	65	"
O	Tanner Minnie—†	9	houseworker	60	"
P	Hayes Anna M—†	9	housewife	43	"
R	Hayes Fredrick W	9	clerk	43	"
S	Levine Abraham	9	chauffeur	27	36 Quincy
T	Levine Pauline—†	9	housewife	23	36 "
U	Jeffrie John	11	porter	39	here
V	Perigo Mable—†	11	housewife	42	"
W	Perigo Orrin W	11	clerk	43	"
X	Themea Manuel	11	waiter	38	114 W Springfield
Y	Jacobs Abraham	11	salesman	29	here
Z	Jacobs Julius	11	fruit	52	"
A	Jacobs Minnie—†	11	housewife	49	"
B	Jacobs Sarah—†	11	"	23	"
C	Bodner Esther—†	11	"	38	49 Chambers
D	Bodner Julius	11	jeweler	42	49 "
E	Murphy Louis	11	counterman	24	Everett
F	Young Alfred W	11	manager	42	33 Myrtle
G	Young Julia M—†	11	housewife	39	33 "
H	Randall Albert	13	R R man	37	here
K	Grey Celia—†	13	housewife	39	"
L	Grey Fredrick	13	grocer	47	"
M	Grey Samuel H	13	"	20	"
N	Rudin Anna—†	13	housewife	29	"
O	Rudin Samuel	13	tailor	33	"
P	Goldman Bella—†	13	housewife	60	"
R	Finer Max	13	capmaker	43	"
S	Finer Rebecca—†	13	housewife	43	"

Revere Street—Continued

U	Gordon Bertha—†	15	housewife	35	here
V	Gordon Solomon	15	storekeeper	42	"
W	Synofsky Ida—†	15	housewife	44	"
X	Synofsky Samuel	15	coppersmith	58	18 Revere
Y	Lezberg Dave	15	storekeeper	21	here
Z	Lezberg Ida—†	15	housewife	58	"
A	Lezberg Jacob	15	salesman	22	"
B	Goldman Benjamin	15	tailor	29	"
C	Goldman Sarah—†	15	housewife	26	"
D	Soltz Annie—†	15	"	31	"
E	Soltz Jacob	15	chauffeur	33	"
F	Miller Bessie—†	15	housewife	26	"
G	Miller Francis—†	15	boxmaker	25	"
H	Miller Harry	15	meatcutter	27	"
K	Miller Letha—†	15	factory worker	23	"
L	Miller Ruth—†	15	"	21	"
M	Cidulka Mollie—†	15	houseworker	38	"
N	Yiding Nina—†	15	clerk	35	69 Myrtle
O	Bravman Edith—†	15	housewife	33	here
P	Bravman Louis	15	raincoats	33	"
S	Goldblat Fannie—†	19	housewife	25	"
T	Goldblat Haskell	19	contractor	28	"
U	Temple Israel	19	tailor	41	"
V	Temple Ira—†	19	housewife	38	"
W	Roth Morris I	19	clerk	42	"
X	Roth Pauline—†	19	housewife	37	"
Y	Ginsberg Rebbecca—†	19	"	38	"
Z	Ginsberg Samuel	19	upholsterer	41	"
A	Cohen David A	19	student	20	"
B	Cohen Jacob	19	shoedealer	46	"
C	Cohen Jennie R—†	19	housewife	43	"
D	Grotsky Harry	19	capmaker	60	"
E	Grotsky Rebbecca—†	19	housewife	50	"
F	Portnoff Ella—†	19	operator	27	China
G	Portnoff Mitchell	19	packer	28	"
H	Swerling Arthur	19	salesman	29	here
K	Swerling Ida—†	19	housewife	26	"
L	Modist Joseph	19	painter	36	"
M	Modist Rose—†	19	housewife	27	"
N	Izzard Ethell—†	21	"	38	"
O	Izzard James	21	coal dealer	53	"

Revere Street—Continued

	Letter	Full Name	Residence	Occupation	Age	Reported Residence
	P	Ozer Esther—†	21	housewife	37	here
	R	Ozer Hyman	21	grocer	43	"
	S	Belsky Bessie—†	21	housewife	35	"
	T	Belsky Phillips	21	tailor	45	"
	U	Horwitz Albert	21	storekeeper	35	"
	V	Horwitz Rose—†	21	housewife	33	"
	W	Diamond Ida—†	21	houseworker	58	"
	X	Diamond Morris	21	tailor	58	"
	Y	Finkel Hyman	21	manager	25	"
	Z	Finkel Rose—†	21	housewife	24	"
	A	Wiesenfeld Ida—†	23 & 25	"	32	"
	B	Wiesenfeld Morris	23 & 25	designer	36	"
	C	Wall Saul	23 & 25	baker	34	"
	D	Wall Sofie—†	23 & 25	housewife	33	"
	E	Blustin Fannie—†	23 & 25	"	29	"
	F	Blustin Paul	23 & 25	tailor	34	"
	G	Freedman Jennie—†	23 & 25	housewife	36	"
	H	Freedman Morris	23 & 25	tailor	35	"
	K	Goldman Martin	23 & 25	auto mechanic	23	34 Anderson
	L	Goldman Minnie—†	23 & 25	housewife	21	36 Myrtle
	M	Pearlstein Max	23 & 25	school teacher	24	here
	N	Pearlstein Mollie—†	23 & 25	housewife	23	"
	O	Pearlstein Jennie—†	23 & 25	"	38	"
	P	Pearlstein Robert	23 & 25	tailor	40	"
	R	Golb Morris	23 & 25	"	29	47 Allen
	S	Golb Rose—†	23 & 25	housewife	23	40 Spring
	T	O'Connell Nora—†	23 & 25	hatmaker	25	here
	U	O'hern Frank D	23 & 25	janitor	42	"
	V	O'hern Katherine—†	23 & 25	housewife	37	"
	W	Krute Jack	23 & 25	coffee roaster	29	"
	X	Krute Rose—†	23 & 25	housewife	27	"
	Y	Blacklow Rose—†	29 & 31	"	28	19 S Russell
	Z	Blacklow Sam	29 & 31	salesman	29	19 "
	A	Pully Joseph	29 & 31	dishwasher	56	Cambridge
	B	Shore Harry	29 & 31	capmaker	40	here
	C	Shore Rose—†	29 & 31	housewife	28	"
	D	Stein Jennie—†	29 & 31	"	28	"
	E	Stein Morris	29 & 31	tailor	32	"
	F	Goldstein Sadie—†	29 & 31	housewife	27	"
	G	Goldstein Samuel	29 & 31	tailor	34	"
	H	Finer David	29 & 31	"	31	"

Revere Street—Continued

K	Finer Leah—†	29 & 31	housewife	28	here
L	Redlar Barney	29 & 31	shoemaker	33	"
M	Redlar Sadie—†	29 & 31	housewife	29	"
N	Downey Mary—†	29 & 31	"	35	"
O	Downey Michael	29 & 31	laborer	38	"
P	Dobroskin Fannie—†	29 & 31	housewife	35	"
R	Dobroskin Isac	29 & 31	watchmaker	38	"
S	Minor Helen—†	29 & 31	housewife	45	"
T	Minor William	29 & 31	waiter	49	"
U	Kargitiz James	29 & 31	bootblack	40	"
V	Kargitiz Stella—†	29 & 31	housewife	37	"
W	Dury Emmie C—†	30	"	47	"
X	Bodge Minnie—†	33	cook	35	"
Y	Crosby Helen S—†	33	housewife	28	"
Z	Crosby William A	33	professor	30	"
D	Bosthwick David	35	laborer	52	Nova Scotia
E	Young Ernest	35	"	42	"
F	Young Lena—†	35	housewife	38	"
G	Kanispros Despenia—†	35	"	35	here
H	Kanispros George	35	clerk	39	"
K	Scott Robert C	35	student	31	New Hampshire
L	Rosen Max	37	grocer	44	here
M	Rosen Sarah—†	37	housewife	45	"
N	Curtis Nason	37	laborer	38	89 Revere
O	Curtis Rose—†	37	housewife	42	89 "
P	Frank Jack	37	salesman	29	here
R	Carroll John	37	laborer	28	"
S	Carroll Katherine—†	37	bookkeeper	23	"
T	Carroll Mary—†	37	housewife	70	"
U	Carroll William	37	laborer	25	"
V	Barmack Mois	37	"	28	Egypt
W	Harvey Bertha—†	37	factory worker	25	here
X	Harvey Dave	37	laborer	55	"
Y	Harvey Elizebeth—†	37	housewife	48	"
Z	Bornstein Sarah—†	37	factory worker	25	"
A	Spill Harry	37	tailor	28	"
B	Spill Rose—†	37	housewife	28	"
C	Brooks Anna—†	37	"	47	"
D	Brooks Harry	37	barber	36	"
E	Brooks Joe	37	"	30	"
F	Deery Margaret—†	37	housewife	38	"

Revere Street—Continued

G	Steric John	37	brakeman	34	here
H	Adams Andrew	37	storekeeper	27	99 Myrtle
K	Adams Mary—†	37	housewife	63	Southbridge
L	Adams Peter	37	none	74	"
M	George Andrew	37	storekeeper	26	New Hampshire

Rollins Place

N	Hurwitz Abraham	1	tailor	55	here
O	Hurwitz Ida—†	1	housewife	50	"
P	Hurwitz David	1	machinist	33	"
R	Hurwitz Martha—†	1	housewife	31	"
S	Barton Agnes—†	2	"	29	New York City
T	Barton Robert	2	agent	29	"
U	Jackson Elizabeth—†	3	housewife	48	here
V	Jackson Ralph T	3	architect	44	"
W	Richards Edith—†	4	secretary	38	69 W Cedar
X	Richards Sadie—†	4	housewife	58	Chelmsford
Y	Richards Sybil—†	4	decorator	35	69 W Cedar
A	Littell Lucy—†	5	none	62	222 Marlboro
B	Howe James S	6	student	38	49 Grove
C	Taber Frances—†	6	housewife	25	here
D	Taber Wendell	6	real estate	32	"

Smith Court

E	Meehan Mary—†	2	domestic	53	here
F	Meehan Thomas	2	chef	54	"
G	Rock Clements	2	laborer	57	147 Cambridge
H	Currier Frances—†	2	housewife	39	here
K	Currier Fredrick	2	painter	49	"
L	Stark Jennie	2	cook	39	"
M	Stark John D	2	chef	50	"
N	Salerno Sadie—†	2	housewife	22	Halifax
O	Salerno Thomas	2	laborer	24	"
R	Cormier Mary—†	3	seamstress	52	here
S	Fitzallen Vennetta—†	3	domestic	70	71 Joy
T	Witherspoon Nana—†	3	housekeeper	65	here
U	Witherspoon William A	3	laborer	40	"

Smith Court—Continued

v	Joyce Henry T	4	clerk	44	here
w	Joyce Sarah—†	4	housewife	42	"
x	Goodman Fannie—†	4	"	28	"
y	Goodman Samuel	4	merchant	30	"
z	Thall Ethel—†	4	housewife	30	163 Everett a
A	Thall Morris	4	tailor	32	163 "
B	Wise Hannah—†	4	housewife	43	here
c	Wise Isdore	4	merchant	51	"
D	Cherry Elsie A—†	5	housewife	60	"
E	Cherry William R	5	plasterer	63	"
F	Cockrell William	5	fireman	37	"
H	Hilton Alfarata—†	7	housewife	23	"
K	Hilton Seavens W	7	illustrator	25	22 St Botolph

South Russell Street

L	Higgins Lillian—†	4	inspector	23	here
M	Higgins Margaret—†	4	housekeeper	59	"
N	Reardon Lucy—†	4	housewife	29	"
O	Livine Abram	8	merchant	38	"
P	Livine Dora—†	8	housewife	32	"
R	Brier Mary—†	8	"	40	"
S	Brier Max	8	grocer	37	"
T	Springer Frank	8	tailor	51	Malden
T¹	Springer Jennie—†	8	housewife	50	"
U	Walton Stephen	8A	whitewasher	61	here
v	Harding Frank	9	garageworker	39	"
w	Harding Nellie—†	9	housewife	61	"
x	Larkin Joseph	9	gardener	47	"
y	Larkin Mary—†	9	housewife	45	"
z	Delany John	9	watchman	50	23 Irving
A	Burns Agnes—†	9	seamstress	54	here
B	Sartini Edith—†	9	dressmaker	21	"
c	Sartini Esther—†	9	housewife	48	"
D	Sartini James	9	rubberworker	32	"
D¹	Sartini Lena—†	9	saleswoman	23	"
E	Wright Fred	9	pressman	58	"
F	Laffin Agnes—†	11	clerk	21	177 Shawmut av
G	Laffin Mary—†	11	housewife	53	177 "
K	Metting Frank	11	real estate	35	here

South Russell Street—Continued

Letter.	Full Name.	Residence	Occupation.	Age	Reported Residence
L	Metting Henrietta—†	11	housewife	30	here
M	Louis Harry	11	laborer	50	"
N	Spencer Sadie—†	11	cook	45	"
O	Fine Morris	12	junk dealer	47	91 Poplar
P	Salaman Gartruth—†	12	housewife	48	106 Union Park
R	Forman Michael	12	salesman	26	here
S	Forman Rose—†	12	housewife	55	"
T	Forman Sam U	12	salesman	23	"
U	Goldberg Hilda—†	12	saleswoman	24	19 N Anderson
V	Swartz Jannie—†	12	housewife	48	here
W	Swartz Phillip	12	tailor	48	"
X	Haylar Edith M—†	13	secretary	27	"
Y	Haylar Laura—†	13	housewife	49	"
Z	Horn Frances M—†	13	bookkeeper	24	14 Glenville av
A	Bissell Elizabeth—†	13	social worker	28	New York City
B	Bissell Emma—†	13	houseworker	71	"
C	Lee Marian—†	13	bookkeeper	26	Peabody
D	Bond Lindly A	13	bank clerk	30	Cambridge
G	Nelson Joseph	14	chauffeur	37	here
H	Nelson Nellie—†	14	housewife	35	"
K	Burns Joseph	14	pedler	42	"
L	Reilly Beatrice—†	14	housewife	33	"
M	Reilly Morris C	14	chauffeur	34	"
N	Perlis Harry	14	painter	35	"
O	Perlis Rebecca—†	14	housewife	33	"
R	McGonagle Annie—†	15	"	52	"
S	McGonagle James	15	stagehand	48	"
T	McGonagle James J	15	pressfeeder	22	"
U	McGonagle Minnie—†	15	housewife	53	"
W	Bates Alfred	16	laborer	21	"
X	Bates George	16	"	65	"
Y	Bates Julia—†	16	packer	23	"
Z	Bates Mary—†	16	housewife	60	"
A	Silvester Louis	16	laborer	33	"
B	Silvester Louise—†	16	housewife	33	"
C	Derry Caroline I—†	16	"	38	"
D	Derry William T	16	rubberworker	46	"
E	Fitzjarald Thomas H	16	waiter	34	Worcester
F	Kane Margaret—†	16	housewife	21	E Cambridge
G	O'Connor Alice—†	16	factory worker	30	16 N Russell
H	O'Connor Alice—†	16	housekeeper	60	E Cambridge

South Russell Street—Continued

K	Levy Henry	17	tailor	40	here
L	Levy Rae—†	17	housewife	35	"
M	Santosuosso Joseph A	17	shoemaker	30	49 Joy
M¹	Wisegold Clara—†	17	housewife	54	here
N	Wisegold Samuel	17	pedler	54	"
O	Hoffman Ida—†	17	tailoress	22	"
P	Levine Annie—†	17	housewife	50	"
R	Shapiro Coleman	17	tailor	60	Revere
S	Shapiro Sarrah—†	17	housewife	60	here
T	Davidson Annie—†	17	"	27	"
U	Davidson Harry	17	salesman	28	"
V	Stearn Rose—†	17	housewife	32	"
W	Stearn Samuel	17	tailor	50	"
Y	Danella Ida—†	17	housewife	35	11 Milford
Z	Danella Michael	17	butcher	37	11 "
A	Cullis Julius	17	cigarmaker	44	here
B	Cullis Katie—†	17	housewife	38	"
C	Ellis Theodor	18	shipper	39	22 Main
D	Fallon Thomas H	18	engineer	53	48 Howard
E	Hayes John	18	janitor	40	here
F	Levirone Louis	18	poolroom	52	"
H	Mahoney Thomas	18	laborer	50	24 Cambridge
G	Miller Charles	18	plumber	45	here
K	Roache Michael J	18	agent	55	Lowell
L	Sweet Nellie—†	18	housekeeper	46	here
M	Walkin John	18	artist	60	Chelsea
N	Arahchek Adolph	19	laborer	30	15 Minto
O	Berkshire George	19	physician	59	Silver Lake N H
P	Bradbury Samuel	19	machinist	45	42 S Russell
R	Comal Peter	19	waiter	26	Worcester
S	Cypolopoulous Constance	19	"	28	"
T	Farren Margaret—†	19	houseworker	60	15 Chambers
U	Goulding Joseph	19	iceman	38	here
V	Gramm Edward	19	laborer	28	"
W	Handzon Paul	19	student	32	"
X	Kaufman Fred	19	cook	56	"
Y	Salin Wendella—†	19	houseworker	42	"
Z	Smith Josephine—†	19	laundryworker	36	Worcester
A	Smith Wilson	19	laundryman	45	"
B	Walton William H	19	retired	58	Chicago Ill
C	Doherty Agnes—†	21	housewife	37	here

South Russell Street—Continued

D	Doherty Bernard	21	cook	36	here
E	Grant John	21	laborer	21	Ireland
F	Wallace Patrick	21	"	40	27 S Russell
G	Antin Clara—†	23	teacher	24	Waltham
H	Franz Gertrude—†	23	"	23	Holyoke
K	Frey Andrie—†	23	"	37	32 Appleton
L	Manning Margaret—†	23	typist	52	52 Raven
M	Poucet Emily—†	23	hairdresser	30	France
O	Brown William	27	farmer	75	25 S Russell
P	Jones Arthur	27	carpenter	53	here
R	Jones Bridget—†	27	housewife	58	"
S	Sullivan John	27	steamfitter	50	"
T	Taylor Robert	27	tailor	70	"
U	Backus Grace E—†	29	tel operator	32	"
V	Hines Celia—†	29	housekeeper	65	"
W	Seidman Joseph	29	printer	42	"
X	Leary Caroline E—†	31	stenographer	23	"
Y	Leary Charles J	31	clerk	35	"
Z	Leary Ella V—†	31	stenographer	28	"
A	Leary James J	31	retired	67	"
B	Leary Mary F—†	31	bookkeeper	30	"
C	Burke Alice I—†	33	school teacher	24	Sanford Me
D	Clarke Bertha—†	33	housewife	31	here
E	Clarke Burton	33	architect	42	"
F	Harrington Katheryn—†	33	stenographer	26	13 S Russell
G	Mott Leroy W	33	electrician	28	Medford
H	Mott Margaret E—†	33	stenographer	27	13 S Russell
K	Reilly Winnifred—†	33	school teacher	37	New Bedford
L	Rosenfield Isadore	33	architect	30	112 Poplar
M	Rosenfield Leora K—†	33	housewife	26	112 "
N	Vincent Theresa A—†	33	nurse	37	here
O	Wynne Mary E—†	33	housekeeper	61	"
P	Lannan Anna—†	34	"	48	42 Garden
R	Lannan Anna T—†	34	tel operator	24	42 "
S	Lannan John J	34	teamster	60	42 "
T	Bloom Fannie—†	34	housewife	29	here
U	Bloom Jacob	34	tailor	32	"
V	Bloom Manie—†	34	tailoress	24	Russia
W	Fare Fannie—†	34	housewife	36	here
X	Fare Myere	34	butcher	41	"
Y	Portman Abram	34	tailor	35	"

South Russell Street—Continued

z	Portman Ida—†	34	housewife	29	here	
A	Dovi Josephine—†	34	housewife	46	5 Leverett	
B	Dovi Sam	34	barber	44	5 "	
C	Murliss Eva—†	34A	housewife	28	Russia	
D	Murliss Samuel	34A	antique dealer	37	56 Allen	
E	Blake Esther—†	34A	housewife	22	here	
F	Blake Harry D	34A	meatcutter	31	"	
G	Prager Mary—†	34A	housewife	26	"	
H	Prager Morris	34A	tailor	28	"	
K	Fishera George	34A	barber	31	"	
L	Fishera Helen—†	34A	housekeeper	27	"	
M	Ponack Abraham	34A	student	23	"	
N	Ponack Barnett	34A	tailor	45	"	
O	Ponack Mollie—†	34A	housewife	45	"	
P	Snyder Celia—†	35	"	46	"	
R	Snyder Harry	35	tailor	48	"	
S	Snyder Joseph	35	machinist	23	"	
T	Snyder Samuel	35	secretary	21	"	
U	Podubny Flora—†	35	housewife	30	"	
V	Podubny Thomas	35	baker	32	"	
W	Spellman Anna—†	36	housewife	39	"	
X	Spellman James	36	teamster	56	"	
Y	Glassman Bessie—†	36	housewife	38	37 S Russell	
Z	Glassman Hyman	36	painter	39	37 "	
A	Mendel Ida—†	36	tailoress	23	16 Blossom	
B	Prendible Helen A—†	36	needleworker	32	here	
C	Prendible Ross	36	retired	63	"	
D	Burnstien Goldie—†	36	housewife	28	"	
E	Burnstien Samuel	36	florist	29	"	
F	Ludenfield Ida—†	36	housekeeper	56	"	
G	Ludenfield Jacob	36	laborer	24	"	
H	Ludenfield Rebecca—†	36	candymaker	22	"	
K	Kirshen Etta—†	36	housewife	45	"	
L	Kirshen Isaac	36	tailor	54	"	
M	Ryter Abraham	36	merchant	33	54 Allen	
N	Ryter Cecelia—†	36	housewife	24	here	
O	Thoresen Gerhard E B	37	janitor	24	101 Mt Vernon	
P	Thoresen Sophia—†	37	bookkeeper	25	101 "	
R	Hurwich Leah—†	37	housewife	31	58 Johnston rd	
S	Hurwich Louis	37	superintendent	37	129 Hutchings	
T	Shohan Jacob B	37	student	26	6 Intervale	

South Russell Street—Continued

U	Shohan Marcia—†	37	dietitian	26	6 Intervale
V	Ward Peggy—†	37	housekeeper	35	here
W	Cohen Irving	38	plumber	36	"
X	Cohen Sadie—†	38	housewife	29	"
Y	Schwartz Lizzie—†	38	"	39	"
Z	Schwartz Louis	38	tailor	40	"
A	Bloom Ethel—†	38	retired	60	Russia
B	Schnider Joseph	38	blacksmith	38	here
C	Schnider Nellie—†	38	housewife	36	"
D	Wilker Bessie—†	38	"	38	"
E	Wilker Jacob	38	tinsmith	72	"
F	Bullard Grace B—†	39	housewife	23	3 Goodwin pl
G	Bullard Parker O	39	banker	25	3 "
H	Skelding Anthony D	39	journalist	38	here
K	Skelding Marian—†	39	housewife	38	"
L	Lavena Joseph	40	barber	42	"
M	Lavena Josephine—†	40	housewife	39	"
N	Cooper Sumner J	40	accountant	25	"
O	Kupperberg Rose—†	40	housekeeper	47	"
P	Cohen Ella—†	40	"	56	"
R	Cohen Isador	40	teacher	58	"
S	Cohen Lyna—†	40	saleswoman	23	"
T	Friedman Baila—†	40	"	50	"
U	Forbush Helen M—†	41	housewife	57	33 S Russell
V	Forbush Horace	41	retired	80	33 "
W	Hogue Bernard J	41	student	21	Brookline
X	Moon James S	41	"	22	"
Y	Mabie Hazel—†	42	housewife	27	6 Hancock
Z	Mabie Leonard	42	carpenter	39	6 "
A	McKay George	42	skipper	28	St John N B
B	McKay Myrtle—†	42	housewife	25	"
C	Flanders Benjamin A	42	lawyer	31	70 Batavia
D	Flanders Edwin D, jr	42	policeman	33	70 "
E	Flanders Minnie E—†	42	housewife	25	Hudson N H
F	Strong Mable—†	42	social worker	25	18 Anderson
G	Vagiass Anna—†	42	housewife	40	here
H	Davidson Barratt	43	manufacturer	33	"
K	Davidson Ruth—†	43	housewife	29	"
L	Parker Alice—†	44	secretary	30	Melrose
M	Parker Lena W—†	44	"	27	"
N	Townsend Gertrude—†	44	assistant	31	here

South Russell Street—Continued

o	Vignoles Arthur H	44	architect	27	here
p	Vignoles Margaret M—†	44	housewife	26	"
r	Warren Hilda—†	44	nurse	33	"
s	Warren Winifred B—†	44	teacher	35	"
t	Nix James E	46	clerk	38	"
u	O'Brien John F	46	teamster	58	"
v	O'Brien Mary A—†	46	housewife	58	"
w	Aldrich Frances V—†	46	housekeeper	38	Brookline
x	McGrady Beatrice—†	47	waitress	40	here
y	Griffin Catherine—†	47	housewife	47	85 Myrtle
z	Griffin Lawrence	47	checker	48	85 "
a	Newell Mary F—†	47	music teacher	62	here
b	Moran Mary—†	47	houseworker	55	"
c	Contantino Angelo	48	laborer	26	"
d	Corkum Bennet S	48	piano tuner	23	Canada
e	Downey Mary—†	48	housewife	65	here
f	Downey Willard G	48	clerk	21	Pennsylvania
g	Gamwell Edward F	48	writer	55	here
h	Greenberg Louis	48	student	21	Newport R I
k	Mooman Richard H	48	clerk	35	'here
l	Williams Dora—†	48	waitress	28	Canada
m	Williams Frank	48	cook	30	"
n	Jackson Sidney M	49	barber	39	here
o	Miller Jennie R—†	49	housewife	54	"
p	Hubbard Dora E—†	49	"	68	"
r	Hubbard Effie R—†	49	cashier	44	"
s	Hubbard Myron W	49	clerk	77	"
t	Pratt Malvina—†	49	housewife	51	"
u	Pratt Wilfred R	49	student	20	"
v	Pratt Winifred D—†	49	cigarmaker	51	"
w	Aldrick Julia—†	49	cook	50	13 S Russell
x	Backus Charles K	50	shipper	32	here
y	Backus Gustavas G	50	cook	45	"
z	Backus Mary G—†	50	secretary	34	"
a	Backus Susen C—†	50	housewife	65	"
b	Bacon Beatrice—†	52	"	30	54 S Russell
c	Bacon William	52	clerk	30	54 "
d	Barrett Pringle	52	editor	23	32 Newbury
e	Strain Dorothy—†	52	clerk	23	here
f	Van Dyer Esther—†	52	student	20	Wash'n D C
g	Van Dyer Frances—†	52	"	20	Brooks House

Page.	Letter.	FULL NAME.	Residence, April 1, 1924.	Occupation.	Supposed Age.	Reported Residence, April 1, 1923. Street and Number.

South Russell Street—Continued

H	White Lucy E—†	52	clerk	27	here
K	Bolles Florence I—†	54	nurse	27	Wellesley
L	Dodge Mary B—†	54	school teacher	27	91 Revere
M	Jansen Josephine C—†	54	stenographer	25	Belmont
N	Washburn Charlotte—†	56	social worker	26	Dayton O
O	Bangs Marjorie—†	56	secretary	27	New York
P	Foroden Alice P—†	56	student	24	Pennsylvania
R	Hamlin Ruth E—†	56	"	22	Ohio
S	LaTinte Chyisa R	56	salesman	30	15 Glenville av
T	LaTinte Yvetta S—†	56	teacher	25	Maine
U	Morse John P	56	clerk	27	here
V	Towle Mildred L—†	56	student	20	Waltham
W	Washburn Annie—†	56	secretary	24	Mass Gen Hosp
X	Whittington Dorothy—†	56	student	25	Ohio

Ward 8—Precinct 3

CITY OF BOSTON.

LIST OF RESIDENTS
20 YEARS OF AGE AND OVER

(FEMALES INDICATED BY DAGGER)

AS OF

APRIL 1, 1924

HERBERT A. WILSON, } *Listing*
JAMES F. EAGAN, } *Board.*

CITY OF BOSTON—PRINTING DEPARTMENT

Page.	Letter.	FULL NAME.	Residence, April 1, 1924.	Occupation.	Supposed Age.	Reported Residence, April 1, 1923. Street and Number.

Anderson Street

A	Turk Annie—†	3 & 5	housewife	68	here
B	Turk Frank	3 & 5	retired	27	"
C	Turk James	3 & 5	chauffeur	25	"
D	Lividoti Mary—†	3 & 5	housewife	29	"
E	Lividoti Thomas	3 & 5	chauffeur	29	"
F	Katz Rose—†	3 & 5	housewife	34	"
G	Katz William	3 & 5	millworker	34	"
H	Lavidor Lena—†	3 & 5	housewife	31	"
K	Sholler Albert	3 & 5	shoeworker	26	"
L	Langone Hattie—†	7	housewife	44	"
M	Preo Ralph	7	roofer	26	"
N	Bowen Helen—†	7	boxmaker	24	"
O	Dorman Nellie—†	7	housewife	45	"
P	Finkelstein Rose—†	7	"	50	"
R	Finkelstein Rubin	7	dyer	53	"
S	Goldberg Minnie—†	7	housewife	48	18 Market
T	Nimberg Boris	7	retired	63	here
U	Nimberg Elise—†	7	housekeeper	20	"
V	Nimberg Esther—†	7	dressmaker	24	"
W	Nimberg Ida—†	7	"	26	"
X	Ranefsky Rose—†	7	storekeeper	48	"
Y	Rudnick Izzy	7	mattressmaker	24	"
Z	Paty Bessie—†	7	saleswoman	22	"
A	Paty Louis	7	tailor	47	"
B	Paty Rose—†	7	housewife	45	"
C	Goldberg Ethel—†	7	"	30	"
D	Goldberg Samuel	7	painter	35	"
E	Ellis Bessie—†	7	housewife	24	24 Brighton
F	Ellis William	7	barber	29	24 "
G	Griffin Catherine—†	7	housewife	47	3 Phillips
H	Griffin Frances—†	7	stenographer	24	3 "
K	Ahern Bridget—†	9	housewife	70	130 Myrtle
L	Ahern John	9	rubberworker	63	130 "
M	Ahern Phillip	9	laborer	33	130 "
N	Nebdor Rose—†	9	housewife	39	114 Chambe
O	Nedbor Samuel	9	brassworker	39	114 "
P	Liberman Aaron	9	shoeworker	28	26 Minot
R	Sharap Rose—†	9	housewife	50	here
S	Bloom Gertrude—†	9	"	21	"
T	Bloom Harry	9	salesman	30	"

2

Page	Letter	Full Name.	Residence, April 1, 1924.	Occupation.	Supposed Age.	Reported Residence, April 1, 1923. Street and Number.

Anderson Street—Continued

u	Cogen Isadore	9	tailor	38	here
v	Cogen Lena—†	9	housewife	36	"
w	Melnich Bessie—†	9	rubberworker	20	"
x	Melnich Malhe—†	9	housewife	60	"
y	Shapio Rose—†	9	"	28	17 Parkman
z	Shapio Samuel	9	pressman	34	17 "
a	Shuman Rebecca—†	9	housewife	22	23 Joy
b	Shuman Samuel	9	marketman	30	23 "
d	Goldman Abraham	9	ironworker	41	here
e	Goldman Ida—†	9	housewife	42	"
f	Goldman Sarah—†	9	shoeworker	21	"
g	Dizais Bordeu	11	laborer	21	"
h	Jackson Frank	11	"	25	"
k	Jackson Richard	11	"	22	"
l	Perry Izedor	11	"	46	"
m	Perry Maud—†	11	housewife	40	"
n	Catolani Anna—†	13	"	55	"
o	Catolani Robert	13	candymaker	29	"
p	Catolani Rose—†	13	housekeeper	20	"
r	Cullen Aaron	13	pressman	22	"
s	Cullen Celia—†	13	dressmaker	30	"
t	Cullen Goldie—†	13	"	23	"
u	Cullen Jenney—†	13	"	27	"
v	Cullen Rose—†	13	housewife	66	"
w	Fox Myer	13	teamster	48	66 Allen
x	Goodman Harry	13	barber	29	66 "
y	Goodman Martha—†	13	housewife	27	66 "
a	Schulz Frank	27	laborer	21	here
b	Taylor Jacob	27	pedler	60	"
c	Taylor Morris	27	clerk	23	"
d	Taylor Rebecca—†	27	housewife	60	"
e	Franklin Ester—†	27	"	28	"
f	Franklin Harry	27	tailor	40	"
g	Hersch Abraham	27	"	40	"
h	Hersch Jennie—†	27	housewife	40	"
k	Pollock Hyman	27	painter	23	"
m	Handel Rose—†	27	housewife	30	"
n	Handel Samuel	27	molder	37	"
o	Dubrofkin Ida—†	29	housewife	55	"
p	Dubrofkin Jacob	29	storekeeper	55	"
r	Dubrofkin Samuel	29	salesman	20	"

Anderson Street—Continued

s	Steinberg Bessie—†	29	housewife	44	here
T	Steinberg Harry	29	student	21	"
U	Steinberg Hyman	29	shoe dealer	52	"
V	Steinberg Sule	29	student	24	"
W	Waretuick Annie—†	29	saleswoman	20	"
X	Waretuick Harry	29	tailor	28	"
Y	Waretuick Solomen	29	presser	55	"
Z	Waretuick Tessie—†	29	housewife	50	"
A	Sidman Belle—†	31	"	25	"
B	Sidman Edward	31	engineer	27	"
C	Cohen Freida—†	31	housewife	52	"
D	Cohen John	31	printer	30	"
E	Cohen Max	31	pedler	56	"
F	Cohen Samuel	31	printer	25	"
G	Port Anna—†	31	bookkeeper	26	"
H	Port Benjamin	31	plumber	25	"
K	Port Gertrude—†	31	housewife	46	"
L	Port Max	31	pedler	52	"
N	Weinstein Morris	33	"	32	Chelsea
O	Weinstein Sarah—†	33	housewife	28	"
P	Neupal Ida—†	33	"	32	here
R	Neupal Morris	33	pedler	32	"
S	Barbmark David	33	shoemaker	26	Cambridge
T	Iseck Mary—†	33	housewife	38	here
U	Iseck Samuel	33	machinist	38	"
V	Orkin Gussie—†	33	housewife	34	"
W	Warchosky Fannie—†	33	"	32	"
X	Warchosky Harry	33	shoemaker	33	"
Z	Kaplan Rebecca—†	33	housewife	29	128 Brighton
A	Kaplan Wolf	33	polisher	34	128 "
C	Vegal Charles	35	tailor	48	here
D	Vegal Ida—†	35	housewife	43	"
E	Vegal Lena—†	35	stenographer	23	"
F	Gusenoff David	35	furniture	48	"
G	Gusenoff Ida—†	35	housewife	45	"
H	Gusenoff Sarah—†	35	saleswoman	21	"
K	Goodman Ida—†	35	housewife	30	"
L	Goodman Samuel	35	tailor	44	"
M	Leibman Frances—†	37	clerk	20	"
N	Leibman Ida—†	37	housewife	42	"
O	Leibman Max	37	bookbinder	48	"

Anderson Street—Continued

P	Foster Elizabeth—†	37	saleswoman	22	here
R	Foster Isreal	37	ironworker	55	"
S	Foster Leah—†	37	housewife	52	"
T	Foster Mary—†	37	saleswoman	21	"
U	Green Dora—†	37	housewife	50	"
V	Green Henry	37	truckman	26	Detroit Mich
W	Green Hyman	37	tailor	54	here
X	Taterow Isadore	37	"	29	"
Y	Steinberg Beulah—†	37	nurse	28	New York
Z	Steinberg Etta—†	37	housewife	55	here
A	Steinberg Max	37	storekeeper	62	"
B	Steinberg Samuel	37	salesman	21	"
C	Johnson Annie—†	39	housewife	50	"
D	Rickson Clarence	39	chauffeur	23	22 Newcomb
E	Slater Bessie—†	39	chambermaid	20	48 Phillips
F	Koupchik Hyman	39	tailor	55	here
G	Koupchik Ida—†	39	stenographer	21	"
H	Koupchik Polly—†	39	housewife	55	"
K	Levy Dina—†	39	cashier	20	33 Anderson
L	Levy Nathan	39	shipper	21	33 "
M	Levy Rose—†	39	bookkeeper	23	33 "
N	Levy Sarah—†	39	housewife	50	33 "
O	Cutler Dora—†	39	"	32	20 Poplar
P	Cutler Morris	39	storekeeper	43	20 "
R	Brown Eliza—†	41	houseworker	29	45 Garden
S	Cooper Barbara—†	41	"	48	here
T	Cooper Benjamin	41	laborer	47	"
U	Hickerson Charles	41	"	27	45 Garden
V	Chonontowitz Samuel	41	butcher	24	Europe
W	Hurwitz Boris	41	painter	31	here
X	Hurwitz Ethel—†	41	housewife	23	"
Y	River David	41	plumber	31	24 Anderson
Z	River Minnie—†	41	housewife	27	24 "
A	Jonath Ida—†	41	"	27	30 "
B	Jonath William	41	bookbinder	33	30 "
C	Desmond Patrick J	41	plumber	45	here
D	Schieff Bessie—†	41	housewife	25	Revere
E	Schieff Hyman	41	butcher	27	"
F	Brewster Charles J	43	laborer	50	here
G	Colby Julia G—†	43	waitress	57	"
H	Cohen Annie—†	43	housewife	49	Russia

Anderson Street—Continued

K	Cohen Max	43	upholsterer	21	21½ Allen
L	Cohen Morris	43	shoemaker	50	21½ "
M	Cohen Rubin	43	upholsterer	24	21½ "
N	Helfenbaum Louis	43	tailor	55	here
O	Helfenbaum Sarah—†	43	housewife	53	"
P	Phillips Etta V—†	43	"	23	"
R	Phillips Sidney E	43	salesman	27	Taunton
S	Vernick Albert	43	shoemaker	53	here
T	Vernick Annie—†	43	housewife	50	"
U	Vernick Rosilind—†	43	clerk	20	"
W	McMann Charlotte C—†	49	housewife	66	"
X	McMann John J	49	blacksmith	68	"
Y	Barron Bridget—†	51	housewife	48	34 Anderson
Z	Barron Margaret—†	51	houseworker	46	34 "
A	Siciliano Amelio	51	stonecutter	54	26 Battery
B	Venezio Ellen—†	51	housewife	27	3 Parkman
C	Venezio Gennaro	51	laborer	33	3 "
D	Franklin Jacob	51	painter	30	here
E	Madfis Ethel—†	51	housewife	25	"
F	Madfis Frank	51	furrier	32	"
G	Whicoff George	51	waiter	31	"
H	Whicoff Olimpia—†	51	housewife	28	"
K	Rivitz Bessie—†	51	leather worker	35	"
L	Rivitz Morris	51	butcher	33	"
M	Rivitz Rose—†	51	houseworker	32	"
N	Rivitz Yettie—†	51	bookkeeper	25	"
P	Wanders Hans H	57	engineer	31	"
R	Apthorp Harrison	57	real estate	34	"
S	Apthorp Marion S—†	57	housewife	23	"
T	Parker Gordon	57	merchant	34	78 Revere
U	Parker Mary S—†	57	housewife	28	78 "
V	Chester Elizabeth—†	61	social worker	51	here
W	Pierce Catherine—†	61	clerk	22	Brookline
X	Peirce Norma L—†	61	secretary	47	here

Bellingham Place

Y	Magoun Marie H—†	1	housewife	51	here
Z	Magoun Roger	1	student	20	"
A	Magoun William W	1	manager	48	"

Bellingham Place—Continued

B	Chase Jessie A—†	2	tutor	58	here
C	Chase Robert S	2	artist	55	"
D	Briggs Arthur C	3	manager	50	"
E	Chamberlain Clara E—†	3	nurse	48	"
F	Wright Louise C—†	3	housewife	36	"
G	Wright William H	3	comptroller	45	"

Cambridge Street

M	Goldberg Celia—†	236	housewife	26	55 Phillips
N	Goldberg Paul	236	tailor	30	55 "
O	Zavesky Morris	236	watchmaker	31	New Hampshire
P	Sheingold Freda—†	236	housewife	31	here
R	Sheingold Israel	236	carpenter	37	"
S	Saya Paul	236	insurance	35	"
T	Saya Victoria—†	236	housewife	36	"
U	Vicari Antonio	238	tailor	45	16 Leverett
V	Vicari Josephine—†	238	housewife	44	16 "
W	Massaro Domenic	238	secretary	23	here
X	Massaro Frank V	238	barber	59	"
Y	Massaro Sarah—†	238	housewife	50	"
Z	De Rose Geradio	238	stonecutter	44	"
A	De Rose Mary—†	238	housewife	24	"
B	Trombetta Angelo—†	238	"	38	"
C	Trombetta Mario	238	butcher	39	"
F	Oginz Isaac	244	storekeeper	40	"
G	Oginz Martha—†	244	housewife	40	"
H	Weiner Harry	244	tailor	45	90 W Cedar
K	Weiner Ida—†	244	housewife	45	90 "
L	Cafalo Genevaso	244	tailor	33	here
M	Cafalo Mary—†	244	housewife	28	"
N	Frenzo Louis	244	chauffeur	28	"
O	Frenzo Mary—†	244	housewife	57	"
P	Frenzo Marianna—†	244	"	22	"
S	Kirios Andrew	246	bootblack	48	Salem
T	Kirios Ellen—†	246	housewife	35	"
U	Dolph Albert	246	bookbinder	28	here
V	Dolph Anna—†	246	housewife	21	"
W	Fraidin Mark	246	paperhanger	42	Russia
X	Fraidin Nellie—†	246	housewife	40	"

Cambridge Street—Continued

Y	Shecher Fannie—†	246	housewife	37	here	
Z	Shecher Morris	246	tailor	50	"	
A	Shecher Sarah—†	246	housewife	28	72 Allen	
B	Shecher William	246	tailor	35	California	
C	Kibrick Bessie—†	246	housewife	34	here	
D	Kibrick Joseph	246	storekeeper	38	"	
E	Kessler Mary—†	246	housewife	38	"	
F	Sherman Samuel	246	pedler	35	"	
G	Goven Barney	246	coatmaker	31	"	
H	Goven Dora—†	246	housewife	26	"	
K	Powell Anna A—†	252	"	44	"	
L	Powell Benjamin F	252	constable	50	"	
M	Powell Godfrey H	252	janitor	70	"	
N	Watkins Jennette—†	252	houseworker	48	"	
O	Watkins John H	252	waiter	52	"	
P	Gladden Bertha—†	256	housewife	40	"	
R	Gladden Frederick	256	janitor	67	"	
S	Pierce Antonio	256	porter	22	"	
V	Conlon Patrick	262	"	48	Cambridge	
W	Hays Michael	262	laborer	65	here	
X	House Charles	262	janitor	57	"	
Y	Luke John	262	"	50	"	
Z	Russell Louis	262	"	57	"	
A	Watts Harriet A—†	262	housewife	70	"	
B	Watts Louis E W	262	upholsterer	60	"	
C	Williams John	262	laborer	48	Cambridge	
D	Williams Mary—†	262	maid	42	Chicago Ill	
E	Brown Josephine—†	266	housewife	45	here	
F	Brown William	266	laborer	45	"	
G	Cain Emma—†	266	housewife	65	"	
H	Cotter Harry	266	stevedore	25	"	
K	Jackson James	266	laborer	50	"	
L	Lawles Sarah—†	266	maid	54	"	
M	Smith William	266	sailor	30	S Carolina	
N	Thompson Gean	266	laborer	40	Cambridge	
O	Chandler Victoria—†	270	housewife	49	here	
P	McKenlon Howard	270	laborer	40	50 Phillips	
R	Thomas Sarah—†	270	housewife	64	here	
U	Darragh Anna—†	282	"	29	Everett	
V	Darragh Richard	282	salesman	31	Cambridge	
W	Finn Arthur	282	"	29	here	

Cambridge Street—Continued

x	Finn Elena—†	282	housewife	30	here
y	Maccini Emma—†	282	operator	23	"
z	Maccini Frank	282	laborer	62	"
a	Godfrey Frances—†	282	housewife	33	"
b	Godfrey Walter	282	carpenter	30	"
d	Carlow Rose—†	286	housewife	38	"
e	Carlow William	286	salesman	45	"
f	Griffin Fannie—†	286	housewife	42	"
g	Griffin Harry	286	longshoreman	52	"
k	Green Lucile—†	288	housewife	27	"
l	Green William H	288	sailor	46	"
m	Harris Mary—†	288	housewife	60	"
n	Johnston Clifton	288	porter	22	"
o	Lipman James	288	laborer	56	"
p	Smith Albert	288	fireman	59	"
r	Young Joseph	288	retired	78	"
h	Henderson Clarence E	312	waiter	31	"
k	Henderson Gertrude E—†	312	housewife	30	"
l	Parker Augustus L	312	chauffeur	26	"
m	Parker John	312	porter	54	"
p	Gallagher Margaret—†	314	housekeeper	21	"
n	Gallagher Elizabeth—†	314	student	22	"
o	Gallagher John	314	mason	70	"
r	Gallagher Mary—†	314	houseworker	68	"
s	McGunnis Patrick	314	laborer	68	"
t	Bosberry Edward	314	ironworker	65	"
u	Terry John	314	retired	70	"
v	Welch Richard	314	florist	62	"

Champney Place

x	Carpenter Albert	1	salesman	30	here
y	Carpenter Betty—†	1	housewife	28	"
z	Davenport Muriel—†	1	clerk	25	"
a	Wheeler Mary—†	1	teacher	38	"
b	Wilson Marion K—†	2	housewife	27	"
c	Wilson Walter A	2	student	28	"
d	Libby Edith—†	2	clerk	34	"
e	Pratt Fannie A—†	2	teacher	30	"
f	Pratt Mary G—†	2	"	29	"

Page	Letter	Full Name	Residence, April 1, 1924	Occupation	Supposed Age	Reported Residence, April 1, 1923. Street and Number.

Champney Place—Continued

	G	Eastman Charlotte—†	3	clerk	51	here
	H	Eastman Gertrude—†	3	nurse	38	"
	K	Fay Edgar E	3	manager	60	"
	L	Fay Janet T—†	3	stenographer	23	Italy
	M	Fay Olivia T—†	3	housekeeper	63	"
	N	Howard Alice—†	3	housewife	26	here
	O	Howard Charles	3	clerk	28	"
	P	Brackett Carlton R	4	artist	40	"
	R	Freeman Sylvia—†	4	social worker	30	"
	S	Gardner Edith F—†	4	secretarian	40	"
	T	Gardner Alice L—†	4	librarian	26	Connecticut
	U	Gifford Anna S—†	4	editor	26	here
	V	Gifford Eleanore D—†	4	manager	27	Wendell

Charles Street

	X	Shevlin Anna W—†	119	housekeeper	45	Somerville
	Y	Shevlin Helen—†	119	stenographer	21	"
	Z	Allen Elizabeth—†	119	housewife	58	here
	A	Allen Elizabeth M—†	119	saleswoman	23	"
	B	Allen Mary J—†	119	stenographer	33	"
	C	Allen Maud F—†	119	clerk	20	"
	D	Allen William	119	coachman	59	"
	E	Allen William J	119	plumber	29	"
	F	Doyle George F	119	fireman	45	"
	G	Doyle Mary E—†	119	housewife	43	"
	H	Duggan Paul	119	clerk	42	"
	K	Garrity Patrick	119	carpenter	40	"
	L	Sullivan Annie F—†	119	housewife	63	"
	M	Sullivan Catherine M—†	119	bookkeeper	37	"
	N	Sullivan Dennis J	119	clerk	63	"
	O	Sullivan Edward J	119	"	33	"
	P	Blood John	121	engineer	35	"
	R	Dickey Mabel—†	121	stenographer	35	69 Pinckney
	S	Forsey Thomas	121	painter	25	22 Myrtle
	T	Gaywood Frank	121	janitor	50	here
	U	Guarente Helen—†	121	student	21	"
	V	Nelson Lillian—†	121	lodging house	48	"
	W	Russell Elizabeth—†	121	writer	40	Weston
	X	Shoemaker Orlando	121	civil engineer	30	Philadelphia

Page.	Letter.	Full Name.	Residence, April 1, 1924.	Occupation.	Supposed Age.	Reported Residence, April 1, 1923. Street and Number.

y	Smith Gardner	121	clerk	25	here
z	Thoresan Gerard	121	artist	50	22 River
B	Gregg John	123	chauffeur	40	32 Green
c	Gregg Mary—†	123	housewife	42	32 "
d	Koorkian Leo	123	butcher	36	121 Beacon
e	McKay John	123	janitor	30	Cambridge
f	Plumber Fred	123	cook	52	here
g	Plumber Maud—†	123	clerk	30	"
h	Renick Charles	123	salesman	29	New York
k	Renick Rae—†	123	housewife	23	"
l	Carey Carolyn—†	125	"	36	Vermont
m	Carey Daniel J	125	clerk	48	"
n	Collins Kenneth R	125	manager	26	69 Pinckney
o	Collins Martha M—†	125	housewife	25	69 "
p	Harrington Ellen—†	125	housekeeper	60	Salem
r	Harrington George H	125	salesman	34	"
s	Means Agnes B—†	125	housewife	55	Manchester
t	Means James	125	adjuster	60	"
u	Means James M	125	salesman	29	"
v	Pond Thomas T	125	agent	24	St Louis
w	Pond Virginia—†	125	housewife	22	"
x	Clarke Berton S	127	architect	42	33 S Russell
y	Clarke Lillian S—†	127	housewife	31	33 "
z	Williams Muriel—†	127	retired	36	Brookline
A	Faber Arthur	127	engineer	38	"
B	Faber Zoe—†	127	journalist	33	"
c	Larkins Carolyn D—†	127	director	24	Worcester
d	Larkins Mary H—†	127	houseworker	47	"
e	Allen George	129	verger	59	here
f	Allen Laura—†	129	housewife	51	"
g	Allen Phillip B	129	manager	27	"
h	Healey Herman E	129	verger	37	"
k	Ruffin George A	129	bookkeeper	56	"
l	Bowgauht Valentine—†	131	nurse	21	Mass Gen Hosp
m	Bresnahan John	131	houseman	69	169 Charles
n	DelRossi Antonio	131	"	35	215 Brimmer
o	Demsy Thomas	131	laborer	54	311 Cambridge
p	Dreyer Nils L	131	elevatorman	63	Framingham
r	Emmons Reginald F	131	salesman	30	20 Pinckney
s	Evans William	131	wrecker	43	107 Myrtle
t	Goodwin Thomas	131	machinist	45	here

Charles Street—Continued

U	Knoop Henry C	131	valet	37	311 Cambridge
V	Knoop Jean—†	131	housewife	47	311 "
W	O'Shea Jeremiah	131	porter	63	311 "
Y	Cuzner Frederick George	133	caterer	42	here
Z	Cuzner Jennie—†	133	housewife	40	"
A	Talbot Catherine—†	133	houseworker	66	"
B	Talbot John	133	chauffeur	37	"
E	Bolton Thomas E	137	machinist	33	"
F	Conway Abbie—†	137	housewife	58	"
G	Conway Michael	137	tinsmith	61	"
H	Barth Hortense—†	137	housewife	28	79 Myrtle
K	Barth William H	137	trimmer	32	79 "
L	Kenney Catherine—†	137	housewife	40	here
M	Kenney Edward H	137	starter	46	"
O	Courlang Abraham	139	operator	47	"
P	Courlang Margaret—†	139	housewife	44	"
R	Witzman Dora—†	139	"	40	"
S	Witzman Max	139	2d h'd dealer	40	"
T	Corrigan Francis J	139	waiter	39	"
U	Corrigan Mary—†	139	housewife	38	"
V	Dermody Katherine S—†	141 & 143	waitress	39	"
W	Dermody Margaret T—†	141 & 143	"	36	"
X	Apstein Moses	141 & 143	waiter	47	Chelsea
Y	Kroot Louis H	141 & 143	salesman	37	"
Z	Kroot Rosie—†	141 & 143	housewife	38	"
A	Daley Elizabeth J—†	141 & 143	saleswoman	50	here
B	Daley John H	141 & 143	clerk	62	"
C	Daley Mary A—†	141 & 143	housekeeper	73	"
D	Ely John M	141 & 143	repairman	50	115 Charles
E	Hibb Wilbert A	141 & 143	caretaker	55	Manchester
F	Lambides Costar G	141 & 143	storekeeper	34	here
L	Gromelaky George	141 & 143	"	34	"
G	Haldoryses John	141 & 143	candymaker	55	172 Cambridge
H	Nagle Catherine M—†	141 & 143	housewife	49	here
K	Nagle Thomas E	141 & 143	clerk	49	"
O	Shaughnessey Charles	145	instructor	55	"
P	Shaughnessey Charles, jr	145	salesman	28	"
R	Shaughnessey Harold J	145	creditman	23	"
S	Shaughnessey James	145	draughtsman	22	"
T	Shaughnessey Marion—†	145	stenographer	27	"
U	Shaughnessey Mary J—†	145	housewife	55	"

Charles Street—Continued

v	Kirland Charles	145	tailor	44	85 Phillips
w	Kirland Fannie—†	145	housewife	41	85 "
x	Lydotes Harry	145	furniture	32	here
y	Quirk Annie—†	145	housekeeper	75	"
z	Teahan Daniel J	145	watchman	68	"
a	Teahan Mary—†	145	housekeeper	75	"
g	Goodfellow Catherine—†	149	candymaker	36	"
h	Scally Josephine—†	149	saleswoman	36	"
k	Hughes Anna—†	149	forewoman	28	301 Cambridge
l	Hughes Elizabeth—†	149	tel operator	24	301 "
n	Silverman Elizabeth—†	151	housewife	61	here
o	Silverman Etta—†	151	houseworker	26	"
p	Silverman Minnie W—†	151	teacher	24	"
r	Silverman Simon	151	real estate	63	"
s	James Laura—†	151	maid	26	92 Kendall
t	Rudd Dwight	151	broker	31	here
u	Rudd Eugenia G—†	151	housewife	26	"
v	Bellow Robert E	151	bookkeeper	39	"
w	Memmolo Anthony	151	machinist	39	"
x	Memmolo Frances—†	151	housewife	38	"
z	Mallon Ellen A—†	155	"	54	"
a	Penfield Annie S—†	155	"	55	"
b	Chapnick Viola—†	157	"	23	New York
c	Troy Gertrude—†	157	clerk	25	"
d	Neely James	157	janitor	34	92 Revere
e	Neely Nora—†	157	housewife	29	92 "
f	Leonard James F	157	clerk	52	here
g	Leonard John F	157	paver	59	"
h	Bailey Mabel—†	157	factory worker	33	"
k	Hutchings Ellen—†	157	housekeeper	62	"
l	Hutchings Marjore—†	157	clerk	24	"
m	Krovitz Myer	157	salesman	38	"
n	Krovitz Regina—†	157	housewife	28	"
o	Whelan Julia—†	157	"	38	11 S Russell
p	Whelan Lawrence	157	packer	40	11 "
r	Tattlebaum Fannie—†	157	housewife	23	118 Quincy
s	Tattlebaum Myer	157	tailor	28	118 "
t	Clayman Celia—†	157	bookkeeper	22	118 ElmHill av
u	Clayman Fannie—†	157	"	25	118 "
v	London Samuel	157	laborer	41	127 Garden
w	London Sarah—†	157	housewife	40	127 "

Charles Street—Continued

x	Stephens Mildred—†	159	housewife	43	Revere
y	Stephens Morris	159	student	21	"
z	Stephens Simon	159	antiques	48	"
A	Hutchings Elizabeth—†	159	saleswoman	21	here
B	Hutchings Kenneth	159	mechanic	20	"
c	Regonas John	159	salesman	35	37 Bowdoin
D	Van Rijssel Josephine—†	159	stitcher	30	37 "
E	Savage Arthur H	159	teamster	39	4 Levant
F	Savage Eliza M—†	159	housewife	31	4 "
G	Furman Joseph	159	tailor	26	53 N Russell
H	Furman Sarah—†	159	housewife	26	Chelsea
K	Bartlett Bertha—†	159	"	34	here
L	Bartlett Henry	159	clerk	33	"
M	Brennan Anna—†	159	stitcher	21	39 Bowdoin
N	Rose Bessie—†	159	housewife	24	here
O	Rose Nathan	159	clerk	27	"
P	Kaplan Harry	159	"	32	"
R	Kaplan Rose—†	159	housewife	28	"
S	Cullen Margaret—†	159	shirt presser	44	"
T	Emparoto Daniel	159	salesman	22	New York
U	Emparoto Mary—†	159	stitcher	20	"
x	Arnold Albert	161	clerk	69	Cambridge
Y	Arnold Bessie—†	161	housewife	49	"
z	Whitehill Florence M—†	161	"	42	Wellesley
A	Whitehill Walter M	161	engineer	42	"
B	Williams Flora G—†	161	housewife	72	"
C	Daley John F	163	porter	54	here
D	DeWinton James A	163	"	64	"
E	Dillon Annie J—†	163	housewife	60	"
F	Dillon James W	163	retired	58	"
G	Lang Elizabeth B—†	163	tailoress	64	"
H	Burnside William S	165	carpenter	50	38 Williams
K	Drake Clement W	165	clerk	36	here
L	Gallagher James	165	shoemaker	57	Lynn
M	Hoitt Katherine C—†	165	housewife	52	here
N	Hoitt Walter B	165	drawtender	64	"
O	McDonald William S	165	barber	51	"
P	Noone Patrick J	165	painter	50	169 Charles
R	O'Connor William	165	clerk	51	125 "
S	Sullivan Michael J	165	painter	76	here
U	Brannick Sarah V—†	167	cook	42	"

14

Charles Street—Continued

V	Cates Vergina—†	167	nurse	24	Winthrop
W	Howard Abigail—†	167	"	27	Quincy
X	Lorrant Eva—†	167	"	30	Milton
Y	Quinn Delia A—†	167	"	45	here
A	Sawyer Dorothy—†	167	"	25	Gloucester
A¹	Staples Edith—†	167	"	28	Lynn
B	Tilton Constine—†	167	"	30	"
C	Erl Herbert	169	carpenter	64	here
D	Josie Roswell H	169	electrician	28	139 Chambers
E	McDonald John A	169	laborer	45	Canada
F	Mullen Mary E—†	169	housewife	41	139 Chambers
G	Samuson Charles	169	printer	62	here
H	Simpson George	169	salesman	69	"
K	Childs Henry	171	laborer	26	Maine
L	Cooney Patrick	171	"	38	here
M	Elliot Phillip	171	"	47	Maine
N	McMann Fred	171	porter	43	Fall River
O	Vincent Mary C—†	171	housewife	56	here
P	Vincent Mary F—†	171	clerk	22	"

Gilson Court

B	Smith Edward	8	clerk	20	37 Millet
C	Smith Mildred—†	8	housekeeper	22	Brookline
D	Peterson Mary E—†	14	saleswoman	32	here
E	Scribner Charles	14	instructor	27	"
F	Vincent Elizebeth—†	14	bookkeeper	25	"

Goodwin Place

G	Berger Bessie—†	1	housewife	60	here
H	Berger James A	1	student	22	"
K	Saxe Fanny—†	1	housewife	62	"
L	Saxe Joseph	1	clerk	62	"
M	Gruber Barney	1	letter carrier	31	"
N	Gruber Elizabeth—†	1	bookkeeper	28	"
O	Gruber Minnie—†	1	housewife	57	"

Goodwin Place—Continued

P	Allen Ruth—†	2	secretary	25	here
R	Miller Gertrude E—†	2	clerk	24	"
S	Railey Ruth—†	2	nurse	35	"
T	Ray Mary C—†	2	teacher	28	"
U	Rambeau Grace E—†	2	stenographer	41	W Medway
V	Rambeau Harry E	2	clerk	34	Brookline
W	Gregson Arthur	2	secretary	30	Arlington
X	Gregson Julia—†	2	stenographer	25	"
Y	Matthews Ethel M—†	3	housewife	49	8 Idlewild
Z	Matthews Maria E—†	3	retired	75	8 "
A	Hadler Hetty E—†	3	housewife	48	Malden
B	Hadler Nathan E	3	salesman	48	"
C	Crawford Hazel M—†	3	social worker	26	51 Garden
D	Sharpley Emily—†	3	nurse	46	Wollaston
E	Sharpley Ethel—†	3	social worker	57	97 Pinckney
F	Danby Anna—†	4	housewife	73	here
G	Danby Elizabeth—†	4	saleswoman	35	"
H	Kelley Margaret—†	4	houseworker	50	"
K	Petro Bessie—†	4	"	35	"
M	King Dorothy—†	5	housewife	26	"
N	King William	5	real estate	27	"
O	Breed Marjorie L—†	5	housewife	30	Colorado
P	Breed William M	5	salesman	32	Newton
R	Smith Grace M—†	5	examiner	38	here
S	Foster Marjore L—†	5	clerk	34	"
T	Lombard Lou—†	5	"	32	"
U	Nichols Rhoda—†	6	student	21	Wellesley
V	Sturgis Ruth—†	6	secretary	23	"
W	Harding Eleanor B—†	6	housewife	29	here
X	Harding John	6	reporter	35	"
Y	Stabler Dorothy—†	6	housewife	34	"
Z	Stabler Harold W	6	batteryman	26	"
A	Elwell Lucille—†	6	nurse	30	Gloucester
B	Olmstead Jean M—†	6	editor	24	Newton
C	Currin Mary—†	7	dressmaker	61	here
D	Ferris Catherine—†	7	retired	55	"
E	McGoughlin Mary—†	7	stitcher	50	"
F	Whittier George	7	collector	73	"

Grove Street

H	Navisky Benjamin	3	clerk	20	here
K	Navisky Lena—†	3	houseworker	45	"
L	Navisky Meyer	3	merchant	51	"
M	Navisky Moses	3	clerk	21	"
N	Genoesa Leo	5	barber	55	"
O	Intress Jacob	5	mason	38	"
P	Intress Mollie—†	5	houseworker	32	"
R	Finer Louis	5	painter	33	"
S	Finer Sarah—†	5	houseworker	32	"
T	Mazar Albert	5	clerk	23	"
U	Mazar Dora—†	5	houseworker	52	"
V	Mazar Joseph	5	tailor	52	"
W	Feldman Sarah—†	5	houseworker	46	"
X	Stone Reta—†	5	"	67	"
A	Glazar Annie—†	rear 5	"	23	Russia
B	Glazar Barnard	" 5	carpenter	30	"
C	Glazar Sophie—†	" 5	houseworker	20	"
C¹	Berry David	" 5	pressman	28	21 Parkway
D	Berry Minnie—†	" 5	houseworker	24	21 "
E	Goldman Annie—†	" 5	"	25	here
F	Goldman Hyman	" 5	baker	27	"
G	Berman Louis	" 5	tailor	39	"
H	Berman Rebecca—†	" 5	houseworker	36	"
K	Feldman Barnett	" 5	tailor	42	"
L	Rutman Goldie—†	" 5	houseworker	27	"
M	Rutman Jacob	" 5	cabinetmaker	33	"
O	Zeidman Louis	6	chauffeur	35	"
P	Zeidman Minnie—†	6	housewife	35	"
R	Fulransky Esther—†	6	"	42	"
S	Fulransky Nathan	6	tailor	44	"
T	Chianpa Ginaro	6	laborer	28	"
T¹	Chianpa Raffaele	6	roofer	24	"
U	Manzelli Antonio	6	"	34	"
V	Manzelli Carolina—†	6	housewife	34	"
W	Goldberg Lizzie—†	7	houseworker	65	"
X	Goldberg Simon	7	shoemaker	66	"
Y	Grabinowitz Cirsto	7	laborer	50	"
Z	Kiminsky Fred	7	"	37	"
A	Kiminsky Minnie—†	7	houseworker	35	"
B	Smith Frank	7	laborer	42	"

Page.	Letter.	FULL NAME.	Residence, April 1, 1924.	Occupation.	Supposed Age.	Reported Residence, April 1, 1923. Street and Number.

Grove Street—Continued

c	Handrahan Ralph	7	janitor	48	21 Parkman
d	Shepard James	7	"	46	here
e	Smith Thomas	7	painter	47	"
f	Price Hyman	7	tailor	35	"
g	Price Tillie—†	7	houseworker	32	"
h	London Sarah—†	7	"	50	"
k	Rosenbloom Bessie—†	7	"	43	"
l	Rosenbloom John	7	tailor	48	"
m	Roseman Kate—†	7	houseworker	42	"
n	Roseman Louis	7	tailor	48	"
o	Lamonica Constantino	7	laborer	55	"
p	Lamonica James	7	machinist	24	"
r	Lamonica John	7	"	26	"
s	Lamonica Mary—†	7	houseworker	52	"
t	Lamonica Paulina—†	7	milliner	22	"
u	Roseman Hyman	7	electrician	24	"
w	Frisch Jennie—†	8	housewife	33	Germany
x	Frisch Lawrence	8	dentist	34	"
y	Troston Samuel	8	tailor	40	here
z	Trostin Sarah—†	8	housewife	30	"
a	Weinberg Benjamin	8	tailor	33	Russia
b	Weinberg Minnie—†	8	housewife	46	"
c	Zuckerman Etta—†	8	"	44	here
d	Feldman Bessie—†	9	"	50	"
e	Feldman Nathan	9	teacher	52	"
g	Roche Angerina—†	9	housewife	33	112 Prince
h	Roche Frank	9	laborer	35	112 "
k	Teperow Bessie—†	9	housewife	52	here
l	Teperow Jacob	9	laborer	56	"
n	Mouriello Antonio	10	plasterer	39	"
o	Mouriello Louisa—†	10	housewife	36	"
p	Gilman Celia—†	10	"	35	73 Revere
r	Gilman John	10	tailor	38	73 "
s	Rubenstein Bessie—†	10	housewife	37	here
t	Rubenstein Sasha	10	merchant	42	"
v	Mageerer Anna—†	11	housewife	25	"
w	Mageerer Solomon S	11	painter	26	"
x	Robinovitz Celia—†	11	housewife	21	"
y	Johnston Elian—†	11	"	46	3 Leonard's ct
z	Johnston Helmar	11	painter	46	3 "
a	Sears Bertha—†	11	housewife	50	here

Grove Street—Continued

B	Sears Samuel	11	inspector	57	here
C	Barrott Alvenia—†	11	housewife	30	134 Halleck
D	Barrott Frederick	11	painter	30	134 "
E	Matell Sullen C	11	chauffeur	30	Cambridge
F	Uppenhim David	11	tailor	40	here
G	Audrozze Artur	11	jeweler	36	"
H	Audrozze Eva—†	11	housewife	35	"
K	Viall Anna—†	11	nurse	55	"
L	Viall John	11	retired	70	"
M	Paris Hinda—†	12	housewife	56	Revere
N	Paris Lewis	12	pedler	56	"
P	Simon Bettie—†	12	housewife	40	here
R	Simon Phillip	12	tailor	44	"
S	Lebofsky Isreal	12	"	40	"
T	Lebofsky Lena—†	12	housewife	38	"
U	Perry Albert	12	chauffeur	50	40 S Hunt'n av
V	Perry Martha—†	12	houseworker	44	40 "
W	Wereszko Frances—†	13	housewife	28	here
X	Wereszko Joseph	13	laborer	29	"
Y	Molosky Agnes—†	13	housewife	28	"
Z	Molosky John	13	dishwasher	30	"
A	Misskie Boris	13	carpenter	25	"
B	Volansky Gertrude—†	13	housewife	48	"
C	Volansky Max	13	jeweler	50	"
D	Crouse Aron	13	tailor	60	"
E	Crouse Sarah—†	13	housewife	57	"
F	Segal Bessie—†	13	"	24	"
G	Segal Eva—†	13	bookkeeper	22	"
H	Segal Fred	13	storekeeper	46	"
K	Starr Celia—†	13	housewife	42	"
L	Starr David	13	painter	43	"
M	Seresky Samuel	13	tailor	31	"
N	Seresky Sophia—†	13	housewife	30	"
O	Bank Jennie—†	13	"	45	"
P	Bank Samuel	13	tailor	47	"
S	Balls George	14	janitor	51	"
T	Balls Lucy—†	14	housewife	49	"
U	Payne Clement	14	laborer	37	"
V	Payne Inec—†	14	housewife	36	"
W	Slader Florence—†	14	"	35	"
X	Slader James R	14	porter	38	"

Page.	Letter.	FULL NAME.	Residence, April 1, 1924.	Occupation.	Supposed Age.	Reported Residence, April 1, 1923. Street and Number.

Grove Street—Continued

	Letter	FULL NAME	Res.	Occupation	Age	Reported Residence
	Y	Fleming Ethel—†	14	housewife	29	9 Anderson
	Z	Fleming Mason	14	upholsterer	32	9 "
	A	Dombrosky Nicklos	15	laborer	42	22 Wall
	B	Thomas George	15	cook	26	22 "
	C	Herman Isaac	15	laborer	36	here
	D	Herman Sherry—†	15	housewife	36	"
	E	Regenstreif Frances—†	15	"	31	"
	F	Regenstreif Louis	15	tailor	31	"
	G	Hurwitz Fannie—†	15	housewife	26	35 Grove
	H	Hurwitz Israel	15	carpenter	26	35 "
	K	Summers Celia—†	15	housewife	52	35 "
	M	Grup Sarah—†	15	"	28	here
	N	Grup William	15	tailor	34	"
	O	Deluca Angelian—†	15	housewife	36	"
	P	Deluca Biagio	15	butcher	40	"
	R	Lazer Jacob	16	expressman	38	"
	S	Lazer Sarah—†	16	housewife	32	"
	T	Griscoe John	16	laborer	41	"
	U	Griscoe Sadie—†	16	housewife	31	"
	V	Edghill Estill—†	16	"	32	Cambridge
	W	Edghill Herman	16	laborer	27	"
	X	Wolcott Dudley	16	cook	30	here
	Y	Wolcott Eveline—†	16	housewife	23	"
	A	Cooper Elizabeth—†	17	housewife	30	"
	B	Cooper Harry	17	shoe repairer	40	"
	C	Randall Elizabeth—†	17	housewife	40	"
	D	Randall Louis	17	presser	40	"
	E	Silver Morris	17	tailor	37	"
	F	Silver Rebecca—†	17	housewife	28	"
	G	Kramer Samuel	17	chauffeur	29	"
	H	Kramer Sarah—†	17	housewife	26	"
	L	Cooper Hyman	18	tinsmith	44	"
	M	Cooper Sarah—†	18	housewife	44	"
	N	Penansky Fannie—†	18	"	52	"
	O	Penansky Hyman	18	shipper	58	"
	P	Chaflin Bessie—†	18	housewife	31	"
	R	Chaflin Morris	18	tailor	37	"
	S	Capp Ernest	20	watchman	39	"
	T	Capp Helen—†	20	housewife	37	"
	U	Patterson Margaret—†	20	housekeeper	58	315 Benningt'n
	V	Goodman David	20	janitor	50	here

Grove Street—Continued

w	Goodman Rosie—†	20	housewife	50	here	
x	Jaffe George	20	boilermaker	26	156 Chambers	
y	Jaffe Ida—†	20	housewife	25	156 "	
z	Trabazan Mary—†	20	"	56	here	
a	Trabazan Nicholas	20	kitchenman	48	"	
b	Morse Harold	28	truckman	21	54 Revere	
c	Morse John H	28	stevedore	60	54 "	
d	Berkovitz Mary—†	28	housewife	28	130 Brighton	
e	Berkovitz Samuel	28	storekeeper	28	130 "	
f	Kostetzky Hyman	28	tailor	60	here	
g	Kostetzky Rebecca—†	28	housewife	63	"	
h	Farbush Bessie—†	28	"	36	76A Leverett	
k	Farbush Solomon	28	tailor	38	76A "	
l	Feingold Benjamin	28	hatmaker	25	76A "	
m	Cohen Ida—†	28	housewife	57	here	
n	Labofsky Fannie—†	28	"	24	"	
o	Labofsky Morris	28	painter	30	"	
p	Gormack Hyman	28	boxmaker	30	59 Phillips	
r	Gormack Sophie—†	28	housewife	28	59 "	
s	Lendfield Gertrude—†	28	"	29	here	
t	Lendfield Samuel	28	meatcutter	29	"	
u	Seigal Meyer	28	tailor	28	84 Myrtle	
v	Seigal Sophie—†	28	housewife	27	84 "	
w	Almeda Manuel	28	freighthandler	35	170 Chelsea	
x	Almeda Mary—†	28	housewife	40	170 "	
y	Duesbury Henrietta—†	29	"	53	here	
a	Koretsky Celia—†	29	"	48	"	
b	Koretsky David	29	bookbinder	49	"	
c	Koretsky Esther—†	29	saleswoman	23	"	
d	Fleishman Bessie—†	29	housewife	26	"	
e	Fleishman David	29	tinsmith	26	"	
f	Shore Bessie—†	29	housewife	53	"	
g	Shore Frank	29	tailor	56	"	
h	Marcus Maxwell	29	manager	40	"	
k	Marcus Rebecca—†	29	housewife	35	"	
l	Morrison Dora—†	29	"	29	80 Phillips	
m	Morrison James	29	student	30	80 "	
n	Kaplin Louis	29	pedler	35	here	
o	Kaplin Rose—†	29	housewife	30	"	
p	Sims Ethel—†	29	"	49	39 Sullivan	
r	Sims Morris	29	tailor	58	39 "	

Grove Street—Continued

s	Martenof Helen—†	29	housewife	25	here
T	Martenof Henry	29	cook	29	"
U	Greenberg Irving	30 & 32	musician	22	"
V	Greenberg Sarah R—†30 & 32		housewife	55	"
W	Walker Annie—†	30 & 32	"	26	"
X	Walker John E	30 & 32	clerk	27	"
Y	Seal Even	30 & 32	foreman	39	"
Z	Seal Violet—†	30 & 32	housewife	27	"
A	Goldberg Benjamin	30 & 32	tailor	37	"
B	Goldberg Rose—†	30 & 32	housewife	37	"
C	Krovocuk Isador	30 & 32	shoeworker	35	Brockton
D	Krovocuk Rose—†	30 & 32	housewife	25	"
E	Matz Fannie—†	30 & 32	retired	64	here
F	Zigman Kate—†	30 & 32	housewife	32	27 N Anderson
G	Levenet Frank	30 & 32	tailor	30	here
H	Goldstein Harry	30 & 32	"	28	"
K	Goldstein Lena—†	30 & 32	housewife	24	"
L	Smith Samuel	30 & 32	clerk	28	"
M	Swift John L	30 & 32	electrician	29	Hartford Ct
N	Levenetz Stephen	30 & 32	cook	28	here
O	Levenetz Vera—†	30 & 32	housewife	24	"
s	Gottsman Sarah—†	31	housekeeper	35	"
T	Miller Elizabeth—†	31	housewife	23	"
U	Miller Harry	31	manager	29	"
W	Cohen Ida—†	31	housewife	29	"
X	Cohen Morris	31	tailor	34	"
Y	Prague Lillian—†	31	housewife	22	"
Z	Prague Oscar	31	laborer	25	"
A	Solomon Morris	31	shoemaker	57	"
B	Solomon Sarah—†	31	housewife	53	"
C	Tanzer Anna—†	31	"	26	"
D	Tanzer David	31	manager	26	"
E	Weise Arnold	31	shoemaker	30	"
F	Weise Esther—†	31	housewife	24	"
H	Gennison John	33	laborer	48	"
K	Gennison Minnie—†	33	housewife	43	"
G	Ashman Benjamin	33	storekeeper	46	"
G¹	Ashman Ida—†	33	"	45	"
L	Cunningham James	33	clerk	42	"
M	Cunningham Mary—†	33	housewife	45	"
N	Sharaf Bessie—†	33	"	23	54 Poplar

Page.	Letter.	Full Name.	Residence, April 1, 1924.	Occupation.	Supposed Age.	Reported Residence, April 1, 1923. Street and Number.

Grove Street—Continued

o	Sharaf Israel	33	pedler	23	9 Anderson
p	Fisher Sadie—†	33	housewife	34	here
p¹	Fisher William	33	tailor	36	"
r	Bourne Julia A—†	34	houseworker	50	"
s	Bourne Sydney	34	painter	21	"
t	Miller Charles	34	waiter	26	"
u	Kaminsky Carl	34	printer	27	"
v	Kaminsky Sarah—†	34	housewife	24	"
w	Cohen Harvey	34	mechanic	23	"
x	Silverman Annie—†	34	charwoman	45	"
y	Silverman Harry	34	mechanic	21	"
z	Shaffer Samuel	34	clerk	30	New York
a	Courtney William	34	"	35	Cambridge
c	Portnoy David	34	milkman	23	15 Revere
d	Portnoy Jennie—†	34	housewife	21	15 "
e	Ackerman John	34	salesman	27	here
f	Fuschetti Concetta—†	34	housewife	62	"
g	Fuschetti Genmaro	34	jeweler	64	"
h	Fushetty Carlman	35	"	23	"
k	Fushetty Josephine—†	35	housewife	23	"
l	Farbish Ethel—†	35	"	45	"
m	Farbish John	35	salesman	22	"
n	Farbish Morris	35	tailor	48	"
o	Swalnick Benjamin	35	carpenter	34	"
p	Swalnick Ida—†	35	housewife	32	"
r	Cohen Harry	35	capmaker	29	New York
s	Cohen Minnie—†	35	dressmaker	22	11 Marble
u	Miller Bertha—†	35	"	20	Russia
v	Miller Leo	35	tailor	46	"
w	Miller Rebecca—†	35	housewife	44	"
x	Entin Bertha—†	35	"	28	here
y	Entin Samuel	35	tailor	27	"
z	Charam Annie—†	35	housewife	40	"
a	Charam Nathan	35	carpenter	43	"
b	Charam Samuel	35	student	20	"
c	Karsten Julia—†	35	housewife	49	"
d	Karsten Otto	35	laborer	54	"
e	Zarogianis Annie—†	35	housewife	40	"
f	Zarogianis Peter	35	manager	45	"
g	Eastman Caroline—†	37	housewife	40	"
h	Eastman Daniel	37	longshoreman	49	"

Page.	Letter.	Full Name.	Residence, April 1, 1924.	Occupation.	Supposed Age.	Reported Residence, April 1, 1923. Street and Number.

Grove Street—Continued

	K	Crawford Ella—†	37	housewife	32	13 Irving
	L	Crawford William	37	teamster	32	13 "
	M	Alfadus Oscar F	37	longshoreman	32	20 Grove
	N	Freeman Iverna—†	37	laundress	26	20 "
	O	Smith Georgiana—†	37	matron	55	20 "
	S	Foilb Fannie—†	38	housewife	62	here
	T	Foilb Louis	38	pedler	62	"
	U	Vitale Louis	38	shoemaker	56	"
	V	Lodsitz Ida—†	38	housewife	37	35 Grove
	W	Lodsitz Samuel	38	tailor	39	35 "
	X	Mednick Annie—†	38	housewife	28	Malden
	Y	Mednick Michael	38	shoecutter	31	"
	Z	Levine Alexander	38	junk dealer	36	here
	A	Levine Rose—†	38	housewife	30	"
	B	Weiner Isadore	38	tinsmith	44	"
	C	Weiner Sarah—†	38	housewife	42	"
	D	Yosovitz Annie—†	38	"	32	"
	E	Yosovitz Harry	38	tailor	37	"
	F	Harris Ida—†	38	dishwasher	32	"
	G	Harris Russell T	38	fireman	35	"
	H	Bowser Louisa—†	39	housekeeper	46	"
	K	Stewart John	39	laborer	58	"
	L	Savage Martin	39	"	25	"
	M	Savage Rose—†	39	housewife	46	"
	N	Savage Samuel	39	clerk	22	"
	O	Wavrous Charles	39	baker	37	10 Parkman
	P	Wavrous Fannie—†	39	housewife	37	10 "
	R	Brooks Jacob	39	butcher	22	Russia
	S	Brooks Samuel	39	tailor	40	here
	T	Brooks Sarah—†	39	housewife	38	"
	U	Scriber Daniel	40	painter	66	"
	V	Goldberg Philip	40	meatcutter	25	"
	W	Goldberg Sarah—†	40	housewife	50	"
	X	Klayman Jacob	40	tailor	48	"
	Y	Klayman Rose—†	40	housewife	46	"
	Z	Goldstein Rose—†	40	"	53	"
	A	Goldstein Victor	40	tailor	53	"
	B	Levine Annie—†	40	operator	24	"
	C	Levine Fannie—†	40	"	22	"
	D	Levine Pauline—†	40	"	28	"
	E	Levine Zelda—†	40	housewife	60	"

Grove Street—Continued

F	Lucas Harry	40	furniture	38	here
G	Zigelbaum Isaac	40	tailor	48	"
H	Zigelbaum Tilly—†	40	housewife	45	"
K	Lipshitz Isaac	40	painter	65	"
L	Lipshitz Jennie—†	40	housewife	62	"
M	Weinfeld Bessie—†	40	"	36	"
N	Weinfeld Morris	40	collector	45	"
O	Groom John	40	rubbercutter	27	86 W Cedar
P	Groom Nellie—†	40	housewife	27	86 "
R	Grove Francesca—†	41	"	31	here
S	Grove Philip	41	shoemaker	32	"
T	Geller Harry	41	tailor	42	"
U	Geller Sarah—†	41	housewife	32	"
V	Glass Freda—†	41	"	27	"
W	Glass Jacob	41	tailor	35	"
X	Cohen Max	41	carpenter	50	"
Y	Cohen Rose—†	41	housewife	47	"
Z	Cohen Sarah—†	41	forewoman	21	"
B	Green Ellen—†	42	cleaner	37	"
C	Mocosta John	42	laborer	35	Cambridge
D	Siegel Abraham	42	tailor	42	here
E	Siegel Dora—†	42	housewife	42	"
F	Atlas Abraham	42	tailor	41	"
G	Atlas Gussie—†	42	housewife	39	"
H	Buckss Frank	42	bookbinder	22	"
K	Buckss Sarah—†	42	housewife	48	"
L	Buckss Sussman	42	tailor	48	"
M	Nelson Barnet	42	furfinisher	36	246 Cambridge
N	Nelson Ida—†	42	housewife	36	246 "
O	Golden Sidney	42	rubberworker	35	here
P	Golden Sylvia—†	42	housewife	27	"
R	Lederout Albertine—†	42	"	37	52 Garden
S	Lederout Charles	42	shoemaker	44	52 "
T	Giove Nunzio	43	"	35	here
U	Giove Tritto—†	43	housewife	28	"
V	Leon Abraham	43	tailor	39	"
W	Leon Leah—†	43	housewife	33	"
X	Soucy Alcide	43	laborer	47	"
Y	Soucy Katherine—†	43	housewife	33	"
Z	Feldman Jennie—†	43	"	35	"
A	Feldman Morris	43	painter	32	"

Grove Street—Continued

c	Brown Anna—†	44	housewife	34	42 Grove
d	Brown William	44	janitor	36	42 "
e	Isenstein Jacob	44	mattressmaker	26	here
f	Isenstein Paul	44	teacher	62	"
g	Isenstein Rose—†	44	housewife	49	"
h	Edner Joseph	44	spice packer	27	"
k	Edner Tilly—†	44	housewife	20	"
l	Corcoran Catherine—†	45	"	42	"
m	Corcoran Thomas	45	grocer	53	"
n	McKay Anna F—†	45	housewife	25	"
o	McKay James E	45	laborer	24	"
p	McLaughlin Mary E—†	45	waitress	32	"
r	McLaughlin Philip	45	retired	60	"
s	McLaughlin Rose M—†	45	cook	34	"
t	Carney Cassie—†	45	domestic	38	"
u	Ford Cecelia—†	45	housewife	37	"
v	Ford Henry F	45	guard	37	"
w	McElhinney Daniel	45	engineer	56	New York
x	Leavens Robert	45	superintendent	42	here
y	Leavens Rose—†	45	housewife	34	"
z	Hobbs Louise A—†	46	artist	40	"
a	lettman Matilda—†	46	maid	30	W Indies
b	Byers Corinne W—†	49	housewife	28	77 Mt Vernon
c	Byers Wheaton B	49	manufacturer	30	77 "
e	Cheeseman Kate—†	49	student	21	New York
g	Rogers Caroline S—†	53	housewife	29	N Andover
h	Rogers Horatio	53	physician	27	381 Hammond
k	Wilson Mary G—†	53	housekeeper	73	W Newton
l	Fiathfull Stanley E	53	merchant	44	here
m	Jacobs May—†	53	housekeeper	35	"

Lindall Place

a	Coleman William H	1	jobber	52	27 Garden
b	Wilson Jennie—†	1	houseworker	26	here
c	Wilson John A	1	chauffeur	26	"
d	Oliver Earnest, jr	1	"	25	"
e	Oliver Earnest	1	teamster	45	"
f	Oliver Mollie—†	1	houseworker	45	"
g	Landers George W	1	carpenter	57	"

Letter	Full Name.	Residence, April 1, 1924.	Occupation.	Supposed Age.	Reported Residence, April 1, 1923. Street and Number.

Lindall Place—Continued

H	Drake Leona—†	3	laundryworker	25	here
K	Whiting Lillian—†	3	houseworker	46	"
L	Hampton Sarah—†	3	"	39	"
M	Aarons Addie—†	3	"	35	"
N	Aarons Alexander	3	laborer	45	"
O	Moxie Sallie—†	3	houseworker	66	"
P	Williamson Eva—†	8	"	40	Cambridge
R	Clarke Eugen	8	porter	38	here
S	Clark Nellie—†	8	houseworker	37	"
T	Harris Florence—†	8	"	22	"
U	Nash Emily—†	10	"	102	Georgia
V	Nash Irine—†	10	"	39	"
W	Nash King	10	mason	45	"
X	Bunton Alexander	10	laborer	39	here
Y	Bunton Rachel—†	10	houseworker	41	"
Z	Gough Mable—†	10	"	26	"
A	Gough Peter	10	butler	30	"
C	Smallwood Maria—†	12	houseworker	77	"
D	Smallwood William	12	carpenter	109	"
E	Wilson Herman	12	laborer	50	"
F	Wilson Mary—†	12	houseworker	45	"
G	Hasel Frances—†	12	"	42	"
H	Leslie Maria—†	12	"	63	"
K	Smith Ida—†	12	"	46	"
L	Watson Andrew E	12	laborer	53	"
M	Watson Mary—†	12	houseworker	47	"
N	King Barnard	14	mover	41	"
O	Leboue Mary—†	14	houseworker	35	"
R	Johnson Frank	14	teamster	49	"
T	Butt Mary—†	16	houseworker	52	"
U	Silkes Catherine—†	16	"	31	"
W	Robertson Margaret—†	16	"	50	"
X	Bean Mary—†	16	"	72	"
Y	Martin Julia—†	16	"	69	"

Myrtle Street

Z	Cohen Fannie—†	97	housewife	35	here
A	Cohen Isreal	97	carpenter	35	"
B	Humes Randolph	97	elevatorman	44	"

Myrtle Street—Continued

Page.	Letter.	FULL NAME.	Residence, April 1, 1924.	Occupation.	Supposed Age.	Reported Residence, April 1, 1923. Street and Number.
	c	Flicop Carl	97	furrier	26	48 Hampden
	D	Flicop May—†	97	housewife	22	48 "
	E	Flicop Gertrude—†	97	"	25	here
	F	Flicop Max	97	electrician	30	"
	G	Myer Julia—†	97	housewife	31	"
	H	Myer Theodore	97	waiter	31	"
	K	Greenberg Etta—†	97	housewife	26	"
	L	Greenberg Joseph	97	hardware	26	"
	M	Neistadt Sarah—†	97	housekeeper	48	"
	N	Donovan James	97	messenger	57	"
	O	Donovan Mary—†	97	housewife	59	"
	P	Naida George	97	cook	28	"
	R	Naida Pauline—†	97	housewife	26	"
	S	Hallet Edgar P	97	inspector	42	"
	T	Hallet Harriet A—†	97	housewife	38	"
	U	Holt Frederick	98	painter	59	"
	V	Holt Mary J—†	98	housewife	45	"
	W	Kouroyen George	98	painter	52	"
	X	Kouroyen Polymner—†	98	housewife	48	"
	Y	Wolfe Charlotte—†	98	bookkeeper	21	"
	Z	Wolfe Dora—†	98	housewife	44	"
	A	Wolfe Joseph	98	tailor	50	"
	B	Fruchter Max	98	"	35	"
	C	Rosenthal Morris	98	"	32	"
	D	Rosenthal Sadie—†	98	housewife	28	"
	E	Berkowitch Leah—†	98	"	48	"
	F	Berkowitch Phillip	98	tailor	44	"
	G	Baccas Catherine—†	99	housewife	35	"
	H	Baccas Peter	99	candymaker	34	"
	L	Klyman Anna—†	99	housewife	34	"
	M	Klyman Louis	99	tailor	35	"
	N	Levine Samuel	99	chauffeur	32	"
	O	Levine Sophie—†	99	housewife	29	"
	P	Baker Edith—†	99	bookkeeper	25	"
	R	Leavitt George	99	teacher	28	"
	S	Leavitt Isreal	99	chiropodist	61	"
	T	Leavitt Matilda—†	99	bookkeeper	21	"
	U	Leavitt Sarah—†	99	housewife	50	"
	V	White Max	99	cutter	32	33 Garden
	W	White Sarah—†	99	housewife	27	33 "
	X	Weiner Bessie—†	99	"	34	here

Letter.	Full Name.	Residence, April 1, 1924.	Occupation.	Supposed Age.	Reported Residence, April 1, 1923. Street and Number.

Myrtle Street—Continued

Letter.	Full Name.	Residence, April 1, 1924.	Occupation.	Supposed Age.	Reported Residence, April 1, 1923.
Y	Weiner Jacob	99	chauffeur	35	here
Z	Wolf Anna—†	99	housewife	27	48 Hampden
A	Wolf Hyman	99	butcher	29	48 "
B	Humes Nettie—†	99½	housewife	33	here
C	Tatilbum Harry	99½	tailor	34	"
D	Tatilbum Lena—†	99½	housewife	32	"
E	Rosen Fannie—†	99½	"	38	"
F	Rosen Samuel	99½	musician	44	"
G	Davis Anna—†	99½	bookkeeper	20	"
H	Davis Hyman	99½	tailor	43	"
K	Davis Minnie—†	99½	housewife	42	"
L	Padis Eftihia—†	99½	housekeeper	49	"
M	Padis Nicholas	99½	shoemaker	49	"
N	Clark Julia—†	100	housekeeper	35	"
O	Seidman Ida—†	100	housewife	54	"
P	Seidman Jacob	100	photographer	54	"
R	Seidman Sarah—†	100	stenographer	22	"
S	Chermer Peter	100	tailor	40	"
T	Cherner Rebecca—†	100	housewife	40	"
U	Bonick Aaron	100	shoecutter	26	"
V	Bonick Harry	100	salesman	21	"
W	Bonick Ida—†	100	housewife	45	"
X	Bonick Samuel	100	tailor	47	"
Y	Matthews Elizebeth—†	101	housekeeper	22	"
Z	Matthews Richard E	101	clerk	21	"
A	Matthews Richard S	101	"	53	"
B	Dunbar Jessie A—†	101	jeweler	46	"
C	Axtell Alfred J	101	clerk	33	"
D	Axtell Edith—†	101	stenographer	33	"
E	Clark Alice R—†	101	housekeeper	53	"
F	Clark Helen S—†	101	clerk	25	"
G	Deering James H	102	barber	76	"
H	Deering Joseph	102	clerk	25	"
K	Deering Mary—†	102	housewife	49	"
L	Fessenden Zelda—†	102	saleswoman	35	"
M	Foster Mildred—†	102	"	44	"
N	Shuman Harry	102	retired	65	"
O	Shuman Laura—†	102	housewife	48	"
P	Goldman Albert B	102	lawyer	33	"
R	Goldman Annie R—†	102	housekeeper	68	"
S	Goldman Tessie—†	102	clerk	26	"

Page.	Letter.	FULL NAME.	Residence, April 1, 1924.	Occupation.	Supposed Age.	Reported Residence, April 1, 1923. Street and Number.

Myrtle Street—Continued

T	Treadwell Emily M—†	103	retired	60	Brookline
U	Shepard Winthrop R	103	salesman	34	Medford
W	Wilson Arthur	104	janitor	54	here
X	Wilson Arthur L	104	starter	29	"
Y	Wilson Esther—†	104	housewfe	55	"
Z	Wilson John H	104	clerk	20	"
A	Rabkin Celia—†	104	housewife	46	43 Revere
B	Rabkin Morris	104	student	21	43 "
C	Rabkin Myer	104	bookbinder	48	43 "
D	Bornstein Edward	104	printer	32	here
E	Bornstein Etta—†	104	saleswoman	25	"
F	Bornstein Sadie—†	104	housewife	27	"
G	Bornstein Sarah—†	104	housekeeper	52	"
H	Epstein Morris	104	junk dealer	52	"
K	Epstein Rose—†	104	housewife	50	"
L	Ruby Louis B	104	furrier	32	"
M	Ruby Shirley T—†	104	housewife	23	"
N	Bulmer Marie—†	105	nurse	27	Brookline
O	Chadwick Grace—†	105	"	26	Marblehead
P	Jordan Ruth—†	105	secretary	23	Portland Me
R	Ralph Virginia—†	105	"	22	Maine
S	Sullivan Hazel—†	105	nurse	28	Plymouth
T	Thibolt Margaret—†	105	"	26	Maine
V	Goorvich Max	106	machinist	30	here
W	Goorvich Rebecca—†	106	housewife	26	"
X	Musy Marcel	106	butler	29	51 Beacon
Y	Musy Margaret—†	106	housewife	26	51 "
Z	Goldman Lewis	106	hardware	42	here
A	Goldman Pauline—†	106	housewife	34	"
B	Scheroff Jennie—†	106	storekeeper	29	"
C	Scheroff Max	106	U S A	32	"
D	Waldman Fannie—†	106	housewife	47	"
E	Waldman Lewis	106	carpenter	48	"
F	Wise Annie—†	106	housewife	52	"
G	Wise John	106	watchmaker	53	"
H	Azapes Barney	106	capmaker	45	"
K	Azapes Bessie—†	106	housekeeper	38	"
L	Safeon Harry	106	tailor	30	"
M	Paderson Morris	106	shipper	39	"
N	Paderson Sophia—†	106	housewife	39	"
O	Comins Fannie—†	106	"	31	"

Myrtle Street—Continued

	Letter	Full Name	Residence	Occupation	Age	Reported Residence
	P	Comins Samuel	106	printer	31	here
	R	Friedlander David	106	butcher	43	"
	S	Friedlander Dora—†	106	housewife	45	"
	T	Jenkenson Harold R	107	druggist	45	"
	U	Lynch Joseph J	107	watchman	61	Medford
	V	McGeorge Margaret—†	107	housekeeper	62	here
	W	McGeorge Marion—†	107	"	26	"
	X	Verge Freeman	107	watchman	40	Somerville
	Y	Chisholm Catherine—†	108	dressmaker	43	here
	Z	Adelson Mary—†	108	housewife	40	"
	A	Adelson Samuel I	108	furniture	51	"
	B	Adelson Ida—†	108	housekeeper	80	2 Anderson pl
	C	Adelson Maler	108	retired	81	2 "
	D	Sexton Elizabeth—†	108	packer	47	here
	E	Devores Hyman	108	salesman	44	61 Revere
	F	Devores Mary—†	108	housekeeper	45	61 "
	G	Davis Gladys—†	108	"	24	here
	H	Davis Rebecca—†	108	housewife	55	"
	K	Stewart Frederick H	108	U S N	41	"
	L	Richder David	108	salesman	40	"
	M	Richder Dora—†	108	housekeeper	34	"
	N	Swartz Bessie—†	108	stitcher	22	"
	O	Swartz Celia—†	108	"	20	"
	P	Swartz Louis	108	tailor	49	"
	R	Swartz Rebecca—†	108	housekeeper	48	"
	S	Slater Annie—†	108	housewife	47	"
	T	Slater Frank	108	longshoreman	62	"
	U	Hacker Alice L—†	108	housewife	26	116 Myrtle
	V	Hacker Orrin F	108	student	30	116 "
	W	Green Bertha—†	108	housewife	25	37 Anderson
	X	Green Harry	108	clerk	29	37 "
	Y	Reubens Anna—†	108	nurse	32	76 W Cedar
	Z	Daniels Alice F—†	108	housewife	29	52 Joy
	A	Daniels Griffith F	108	student	29	52 "
	B	Chadwick Burton L	108	collector	26	Florida
	C	Freeman Georgie—†	108	operator	56	"
	D	Steinfield Gertrude—†	108	"	20	here
	E	Steinfield Rose—†	108	manager	41	"
	F	Newcomb Anna W—†	108	housekeeper	61	"
	G	Taylor Waldo A	108	carpenter	69	"
	H	Jenny Frances—†	109	housekeeper	29	New York

Myrtle Street—Continued

K	Jenny Reginald	109	salesman	25	Brookline
L	Thomas Helen G—†	109	editor	34	here
M	Trowbridge Miriam—†	109	housekeeper	22	"
N	Lishinsky David	112	rags	59	"
O	Lishinsky Sophia—†	112	housewife	47	"
P	Silva Amelia—†	112	housekeeper	34	E Stratham
R	Silva Mathew	112	papercutter	50	"
S	Baer Esther—†	112	housewife	20	46 S Russell
T	Baer Joseph	112	manager	28	46 "
U	Locke Austin P	112	jobber	51	here
V	Locke Mary—†	112	housewife	49	"
W	Chillei Mary—†	112	housekeeper	45	"
X	Chillei Rubin	112	capmaker	46	"
Y	Baker Gussie—†	112	housewife	26	"
Z	Baker Nathan	112	carpenter	38	"
A	Christian Frank	112	waiter	39	"
B	Christian Helene—†	112	housewife	27	"
C	Block Dora—†	112	"	27	"
D	Block Isreal	112	agent	31	"
E	Entner Adolf	112	manufacturer	49	"
F	Entner Bessie—†	112	housewife	47	"
G	Entner Rose—†	112	housekeeper	22	"
H	Corbett Ethel—†	112	housewife	28	"
K	Corbett William M	112	chauffeur	30	"
L	Eaton Ralph M	115	instructor	30	94 Chestnut
N	Foster Carl O	116	merchant	37	New Bedford
V	Foster Elizabeth—†	116	housewife	27	"
O	Huckel Dorothea—†	116	"	36	Pennsylvania
P	Huckel Earle	116	student	38	"
R	Aldrich Mary L D—†	116	librarian	52	Providence R I
S	Aldrich Suzanne—†	116	stenographer	24	98 Chestnut
T	Bosworth Willis—†	116	housekeeper	50	New York
U	Gahn Annie—†	116	"	45	Quincy
W	Packard Grace—†	116	nurse	30	Melrose
X	Butterfield Emley—†	117	housekeeper	60	4 Chestnut
Y	Butterfield Thirza—†	117	storekeeper	35	4 "
Z	Carroll Theresa—†	117	maid	27	484 Blue Hill av
A	Eaton Hortense—†	117	housekeeper	28	94 Chestnut
B	Foster Isabell—†	117	editor	30	91 Pinckney
C	Rhodes Marion—†	117	"	30	91 "
D	Logan Nellie—†	118	maid	38	8 Louisburg sq

Myrtle Street—Continued

E	Styles Annie—†	118	nurse	28	New York
F	Tacher Thomas	118	broker	27	261 Beacon
G	Tacher Vera—†	118	housewife	27	261 "
H	McIver Mary—†	124	maid	20	Canada
K	Potter Howard	124	manager	34	here
L	Potter Leanore—†	124	housewife	32	"
M	Winsor Clara—†	124	maid	25	"
N	Anderson Sven—†	125	housewife	24	Bangor Me
O	Anderson Mabel	125	bookbinder	30	Houlton Me
P	Flynn Thomas J	125	inspector	39	8 Anderson
R	Murphy Alice L—†	125	stenographer	20	8 "
S	Murphy Mary C—†	125	elevatormwan	37	8 "
T	Cohen Goldie—†	125	housekeeper	62	here
U	Cohen Hyman	125	retired	77	"
V	Cohen Max	125	chauffeur	21	"
W	Cohen Morris	125	manager	26	"
Y	Haddock Charles D	126	clerk	20	"
Z	Haddock Mary H—†	126	housewife	45	"
A	Haddock Stephen D	126	waiter	48	"
B	Kagan Rebecca—†	127	housekeeper	35	"
C	Campbell Emily E—†	127	"	30	Brookline
D	MacCarthy Gertrude—†	127	"	52	here
E	MacCarthy Henery	127	clerk	36	"
F	MacCarthy Mary—†	127	saleswoman	40	"
H	Code Grant H	127	teacher	28	"
K	Code Marion—†	127	housewife	27	"
L	Jones Margaret—†	128	"	77	"
M	Jones Margaret E—†	128	"	48	"
N	Ryan Dennis	128	laborer	61	"
O	Ryan Mary L—†	128	housewife	58	"
P	Walsh Catherine L—†	128	inspector	34	"
R	Kagan Belle—†	129	housekeeper	40	"
S	Pepper Margaret A—†	129	saleswoman	36	"
T	Shea Margaret A—†	129	housekeeper	50	"
U	Primick Jennie—†	129	housewife	60	"
V	Primick Nathan	129	real estate	60	"
W	Lucas Abraham S	129	tailor	38	"
X	Lucas Clara—†	129	housewife	34	"
Y	Furman Abraham	129	storekeeper	42	"
Z	Furman Lena—†	129	housewife	35	"
A	D'Errico Fannie—†	129	"	43	"

Page.	Letter.	FULL NAME.	Residence, April 1, 1924.	Occupation.	Supposed Age.	Reported Residence, April 1, 1923. Street and Number.

Myrtle Street—Continued

	Letter	FULL NAME	Res.	Occupation	Age	Reported Residence
	B	D'Errico Hector	129	clerk	41	here
	C	Parkhurst Ellen—†	130	janitress	65	"
	D	Griffin Catherine—†	130	bookkeeper	35	"
	E	Murphy Annie—†	130	saleswoman	62	"
	F	Murphy Joseph	130	gardener	60	"
	H	McDonald Annie—†	130	housewife	32	Saxonville
	K	McDonald William H	130	chauffeur	38	Westwood
	L	Donavon Mary—†	130	inspector	36	122 Mt Vernon
	M	Gerad James R	130	salesman	26	Cambridge
	N	Kilcup Harry S	130	clerk	43	18 Hancock
	O	Kilcup Katherine S—†	130	forewoman	37	18 "
	P	McArdle Edith T—†	130	tel operator	23	here
	R	McArdle Mary G—†	130	housewife	59	"
	S	Halliday Annie E—†	131	housekeeper	65	"
	T	Levis Elbert	131	manager	40	"
	U	Nagle James	131	"	37	"
	V	Cherry Annie—†	132	housewife	40	"
	W	Cherry Charles	132	laborer	42	"
	X	Rosen Jacob	132	salesman	26	Chelsea
	Y	Rubin Mary—†	132	housewife	45	"
	Z	Wallack Abraham D	132	salesman	33	here
	B	Wallack Violette—†	132	housewife	29	"
	A	Winn Sarah—†	132	"	60	"
	C	Kanevitz Harry	132	meatcutter	30	"
	D	Kanevitz Minnie—†	132	housewife	28	"
	E	Levenson Miah	132	tailor	26	160 Harold
	F	Hart Charles	132	laborer	55	23 Irving
	G	Hart Mary—†	132	housewife	40	23 "
	H	Halladay Ethel L—†	133	"	26	here
	K	Halladay Henry G	133	clerk	51	"
	L	Leonard Gertrude H—†	133	housekeeper	44	"
	M	Paine Frances—†	133	advertising	30	New York
	N	Walmsley Elizabeth—†	133	housekeeper	40	England
	O	Chiplovitz George	135	salesman	32	here
	P	Chiplovitz Wolf	135	retired	54	"
	R	Chiplovitz Barney	135	shoeworker	26	"
	S	Chiplovitz Rebecca—†	135	housewife	52	"
	T	Pasol Benjamin	135	fruit	30	"
	U	Pasol Mary—†	135	housewife	23	"
	V	Abrams Louis	135	tailor	39	"
	W	Abrams Rose—†	135	housewife	35	"

Myrtle Street—Continued

x	Trigg Benjamin	136	clerk	65	here
y	Trigg Maude—†	136	housewife	58	"
z	Lane Alice J—†	136	"	54	"
a	Lane Edward	136	chauffeur	61	"
b	Lane Edward C, jr	136	clerk	25	"
c	Lane George F	136	laborer	21	"
d	Lane John C	136	clerk	26	"
e	McKenna Anna—†	136	housewife	22	"
f	McKenna Josephine—†	136	"	48	"
g	McKenna Patrick F	136	janitor	55	"
h	McKenna William A	136	clerk	25	"
k	Granz Agnes—†	136	housewife	54	"
l	Granz Louis	136	cutter	56	"

Phillips Court

m	Francis Tibitha—†	4	housewife	80	14 Lindall pl
n	Johnson William	4	janitor	40	here
o	Taylor Viny—†	5	housewife	35	256 Cambridge
p	Taylor William	5	teamster	38	256 "
r	Simpson Ella—†	5	housewife	28	here
s	Clark Benjamin	5	teamster	64	68 Phillips

Phillips Street

w	Ferguson Alice—†	40	housekeeper	57	here
x	Morton Hattie—†	40	"	60	182 Cambridge
y	Morton Stella—†	40	houseworker	30	182 "
z	Goren Barney	40	laborer	50	here
a	Goren Molly—†	40	housewife	48	"
c	Ciampa Anthony	42	laborer	21	"
d	Ciampa Louis	42	"	20	"
e	Vardaro Frank	42	"	40	"
f	Vardaro Mary—†	42	housewife	42	"
g	Greenberg Fannie—†	42	"	45	"
h	Greenberg Jacobs	42	carpenter	52	"
k	Freeman Ely	42	paperhanger	44	"
l	Freeman Goldie—†	42	tailoress	20	"
m	Freeman Ida—†	42	"	21	"

Phillips Street—Continued

Letter	Full Name	Residence, April 1, 1924	Occupation	Supposed Age	Reported Residence, April 1, 1923. Street and Number.
N	Freeman Mary—†	42	housewife	42	here
P	Ellisman Tillie—†	44	houseworker	70	22 N Russell
R	Jacobs Mollie—†	44	tailoress	28	here
S	Firestine Anna—†	44	housewife	73	"
T	Firestine Minnie—†	44	housekeeper	51	"
U	Firestine Samuel	44	tailor	73	"
V	Goldberg Morris	44	laborer	27	337 Charles
W	Goldberg Rachel—†	44	housewife	24	337 "
X	Hurwitz Ida—†	44	"	52	7 Parkman
Y	Hurwitz Julius	44	laborer	60	7 "
Z	Solomon Azer	44	tailor	77	7 "
B	Crutchfield Mary—†	48	housewife	57	here
C	Jenison Georgiana—†	48	"	49	"
D	Jenison James H	48	teamster	52	"
E	Gray Annie—†	48	housekeeper	49	"
F	Jones Thomas S	48	laborer	55	"
G	Nelson Albert	48	"	35	New York
H	O'Neal Charles	48	"	24	40 S Hunt'n av
K	O'Neal Christobel—†	48	housewife	24	40 "
L	Slater Eli	48	laborer	28	here
M	Halloway Sidney	50	houseworker	40	16 Blossom ct
N	Wilson Josephine—†	50	housewife	37	here
O	Deboise Martha A—†	50	housekeeper	73	"
P	Jones Anna—†	50	housewife	39	"
R	Kelley John F	50	painter	59	"
S	Chalfen Bessie—†	51	housewife	34	"
T	Chalfen Morris	51	merchant	36	"
U	Schiraga Morris	51	tinsmith	42	"
V	Schiraga Pauline—†	51	housewife	42	"
W	Schiraga Sarah—†	51	clerk	21	"
X	Hyman Anna—†	51	housewife	38	"
Y	Hyman Philip	51	laster	38	"
Z	Resnick Barney	51	tailor	33	"
A	Resnick Sarah—†	51	housewife	35	"
B	Newell Max	51	tailor	44	"
C	Newell Rose—†	51	housewife	39	"
D	Levitt Jacob	51	retired	70	"
E	Levitt Sarah—†	51	housewife	60	"
F	Gallas Nathan	51	baker	32	"
G	Gallas Sarah—†	51	housewife	36	"
H	Cohen Louis	51	storekeeper	36	"

Page.	Letter.	Full Name.	Residence, April 1, 1924.	Occupation.	Supposed Age.	Reported Residence, April 1, 1923. Street and Number.

Phillips Street—Continued

K	Cohen Mary—†	51	housewife	36	here
M	Patterson John J	52	laborer	41	New York
N	Turner Arthur	52	"	50	here
O	Turner Ellen—†	52	housewife	60	"
P	Davis Joseph	52	laborer	64	"
R	Davis Rachel—†	52	housewife	52	"
S	Bond Albert	52	laborer	59	"
T	Bond Sara—†	52	housewife	61	"
U	James Mary—†	52	"	34	"
V	James Samuel F	52	laborer	32	"
X	Galla Jacob	53 & 55	tailor	39	"
Y	Galla Rebecca—†	53 & 55	housewife	30	"
Z	Winigen Jacob	53 & 55	storekeeper	60	"
A	Winigen Racheal—†	53 & 55	"	60	"
B	Goldberg Annie—†	53 & 55	housewife	45	11 Grove
C	Goldberg Joseph	53 & 55	student	22	11 "
D	Goldberg Max	53 & 55	blacksmith	49	11 "
E	Blyer Eva—†	53 & 55	housewife	38	here
F	Blyer Max	53 & 55	tailor	45	"
G	Kluka George	53 & 55	cook	29	"
H	Kluka Mary—†	53 & 55	housewife	26	"
K	Newman Morris	53 & 55	tailor	25	"
L	Newman Tillie—†	53 & 55	housewife	26	"
M	Cohen Barnett	53 & 55	salesman	25	"
N	Cohen Estelle—†	53 & 55	housewife	24	"
O	Rosetcha Amelia—†	53 & 55	"	28	"
P	Rosetcha Anthony	53 & 55	cook	28	"
T	Rosenfeld Max	59	storekeeper	50	"
U	Rosenfeld Sadie—†	59	housewife	45	"
V	Cohen Annie—†	59	"	25	"
W	Cohen Samuel	59	teamster	35	"
X	Kramer Joseph	59	laborer	30	"
Y	Kramer Mary—†	59	housewife	26	"
Z	Braverman Jacob	59	metalworker	31	"
A	Braverman Leana—†	59	housewife	26	"
C	Zaharoff Pauline—†	59	housekeeper	30	"
D	Letuk Julia—†	59	housewife	29	"
E	Letuk Micheal	59	painter	30	"
F	Richman Rebecca—†	59	housewife	28	Chelsea
G	Richman Samuel	59	laborer	31	"
H	Goldman Annie—†	60	housewife	29	Revere

Page.	Letter.	FULL NAME.	Residence, April 1, 1924.	Occupation.	Supposed Age.	Reported Residence, April 1, 1923. Street and Number.

Phillips Street—Continued

K	Goldman Morris	60	druggist	30	Revere
L	Dolnick Annie—†	60	housewife	40	here
M	Dolnick Max	60	tailor	45	"
N	Dolnick Philip	60	dentist	23	"
O	Grover Aron	60	tailor	44	"
P	Grover Bessie—†	60	housewife	39	"
R	Smith Louis	60	buffer	49	"
S	Kopp Dora—†	60	housewife	45	"
T	Kopp Morris	60	baker	50	"
U	Bloom Annie—†	61	housewife	46	72 Barton
V	Bloom Philip	61	tailor	55	72 "
W	Bantick Sarah—†	61	housekeeper	68	here
X	Shapiro Ida—†	61	"	28	"
Y	Winer Aarah	61	boilermaker	60	"
Z	Winer Bessie—†	61	housewife	52	"
A	Hoffman Anna—†	62	"	75	"
B	Hoffman Philip	62	retired	75	"
C	Rosenberg Harry	62	salesman	40	"
D	Segal Eva—†	62	retired	24	"
E	Segal Ida—†	62	"	—	"
F	Segal Sarah—†	62	housekeeper	64	"
G	Howard Daniel W	62	porter	54	"
H	Howard Marion A—†	62	housewife	30	"
K	Perry Irving	62	porter	35	"
L	Perry Mary—†	62	housewife	33	"
M	Green Ida—†	63	"	32	"
N	Green Nathan	63	tailor	32	"
O	Richstein Bessie—†	63	housewife	28	Chelsea
P	Richstein Samuel	63	agent	29	"
R	Shatz Harry	63	clerk	26	here
S	Shatz Nellie—†	63	housewife	26	"
T	Currie Cecil	63	cook	28	Texas
U	Currie Lottie—†	63	housewife	28	22 Yarmouth
V	Shankle John E	63	janitor	31	Wash'n D C
W	Fisher Ellen—†	64	housekeeper	43	13 Anderson
X	Goldman Samuel	64	tailor	40	here
Y	Goldman Sarah—†	64	housewife	37	"
Z	Cooper Harry	64	tailor	24	France
A	Cooper Rebecca—†	64	housekeeper	64	Russia
B	Robbins Edith—†	64	housewife	30	here
C	Robbins Jacob	64	tailor	35	"

Page.	Letter.	FULL NAME.	Residence, April 1, 1924.	Occupation.	Supposed Age.	Reported Residence, April 1, 1923. Street and Number.

Phillips Street—Continued

E	Ravreby Abraham	65	student	21	here
F	Ravreby Fannie—†	65	housewife	61	"
G	Ravreby John	65	chauffeur	24	"
L	Lamkin Jennie—†	65	housewife	23	78 Phillips
M	Lamkin Leo	65	grocer	26	78 "
O	Goldstein Dora—†	67	housewife	57	here
P	Goldstein Hyman	67	retired	58	"
R	Cohen Benjamin	67	plumber	28	"
S	Cohen Mollie—†	67	houseworker	25	"
T	Diner Rose—†	67	factory worker	24	27 Temple
U	Manhiern Gertrude—†	67	housewife	36	Malden
V	Goldberg Annie—†	67	"	42	here
W	Goldberg Joseph	67	laborer	42	"
Y	Clark Benjamin	68	teamster	62	"
Z	Moore David	68	janitor	24	"
A	Moore Lena—†	68	housewife	43	"
B	Urdang Sarah—†	68	"	68	"
C	Urdang Wolf	68	junk dealer	70	"
D	Patt Ida—†	68	housekeeper	32	"
E	Dusirvis Julia—†	68	mattressmaker	45	"
F	Baker Ada—†	68	bookkeeper	22	"
G	Baker Etta—†	68	housekeeper	49	"
H	Mechifaron Stephen	68	carpenter	33	"
K	Mechifaron Teny—†	68	housewife	28	"
L	Gittleman Ida—†	68	"	45	"
M	Gittleman Isadore	68	student	22	"
N	Gittleman William	68	tailor	45	"
O	Adolson George	69	laborer	38	"
P	Berkman Benjamin	69	janitor	35	"
R	Kline Molly—†	69	housewife	23	"
S	Kline Samuel	69	machinist	24	91 Intervale
T	Wiener Samuel	69	clerk	22	here
U	Billistock Granum	69	tailor	40	"
V	Billistock Rose—†	69	housewife	40	"
X	Skinner Annie M—†	70	"	34	Milton
Y	Skinner Charles H	70	janitor	35	"
Z	Langson Jennie—†	70	housekeeper	31	88 W Cedar
A	Brown Benjamin	70	junk dealer	47	here
B	Brown Sarah—†	70	housewife	43	"
C	Shapiro Sadie—†	70	"	29	"
D	Shapiro Samuel	70	chauffeur	27	"

Phillips Street—Continued

E	Spector Harry	70	pedler	22	here
F	Spector Ida—†	70	housekeeper	44	"
G	Berman Soloman	70	tailor	61	"
H	Miller Eva—†	70	housewife	24	"
K	Miller Morris	70	tailor	24	"
L	Dixon Harriet—†	70	housewife	25	"
M	Dixon Randall	70	laborer	39	"
N	Ward Charles	70	chauffeur	40	"
O	Ward May—†	70	housewife	43	"
P	Olson John	70	laborer	30	"
R	Bookman Annie—†	71	housewife	45	"
S	Bookman Isaac	71	tailor	47	"
T	Fishman Sarah—†	71	housewife	24	"
U	Orkin Louis	71	sexton	60	"
V	Winer Isreal	71	tailor	33	"
W	Winer Rebecca—†	71	housewife	30	"
X	Cohen Fannie—†	71	"	31	"
Y	Cohen Nathan	71	clerk	33	"
Z	Mogelson Ethel—†	71	stitcher	25	"
C	Fishman Abraham	73	florist	20	86 W Cedar
D	Fishman Benjamin	73	accountant	24	86 "
E	Fishman Minnie—†	73	cook	49	86 "
F	Weinstein Anna—†	73	housewife	55	here
G	Weinstein Isaac	73	shoecutter	24	"
H	Weinstein Louis	73	shoemaker	65	"
K	Birfeld Isador	73	tailor	27	"
L	Birfeld Lena—†	73	housewife	24	"
M	Fineberg Aleck	73	tailor	40	Russia
N	Fineberg Rose—†	73	housewife	35	"
O	Green Anna—†	73	"	23	Brookline
P	Green Max	73	storekeeper	30	"
R	Meister Sarah—†	73	housekeeper	55	"
S	Weinstein Harry	73	shoeworker	29	"
T	Weinstein Lena—†	73	housewife	26	"
U	Gray Barnard	74	janitor	63	"
V	Gray Louis	74	plumber	46	"
W	Gray Morris	74	"	28	"
X	Gray Rosie—†	74	housewife	60	"
Y	Lydeotes Andrew	74	fruit	33	145 Charles
Z	Lydeotes Mary—†	74	housewife	28	145 "
A	Zistman Rosie—†	74	housekeeper	48	here

Phillips Street—Continued

B	Zistman Samuel	74	laborer	27	here
C	Grossman Harry	74	tailor	28	"
D	Grossman Rosie	74	housekeeper	65	"
E	Katz Lilla—†	74	housewife	41	"
F	Katz Rubin	74	tailor	43	"
G	Wittinberg Eva—†	74	housewife	30	"
H	Wittin berg Harry	74	painter	35	"
K	Robinson Arthur	75	laborer	36	"
L	Robinson Mary—†	75	cook	35	"
M	Sachnovitz Ida—†	75	housewife	38	"
N	Ingram Lula—†	75	laundress	25	18 Dartmouth pl
O	Foskey Clary—†	76	housewife	40	here
P	Foskey Harvey	76	freighthandler	40	"
R	Gomes Jennie—†	76	maid	30	"
S	Gordon Louis	76	junk dealer	34	"
T	Gordon Sofie—†	76	housewife	37	"
X	Rockport Bessie—†	76	"	48	"
Y	Rockport Samuel	76	laborer	29	"
Z	Richamond Fannie—†	76	housewife	37	200 Quincy
A	Richamond Jacob	76	laborer	36	200 "
C	Norman Henry	77	clergyman	79	here
D	Ginsberg Herman	77	salesman	31	85 Phillips
E	Ginsberg Mary—†	77	housewife	29	85 "
F	Karpelovitch Celia—†	77	"	49	85 "
G	Hall Charles	77	porter	39	here
H	Hall Ida—†	77	waitress	38	"
M	Rubin Etta—†	78	housewife	23	"
N	Rubin Jacob	78	storekeeper	23	"
O	Zidman Harry	78	tailor	43	"
P	Zidman Jennie—†	78	housewife	40	"
R	Winer Morris	78	shoemaker	38	"
S	Berkman David	78	tailor	30	72 Byron
T	Berkman Sarah—†	78	housewife	27	72 "
U	Berne Gertrude—†	78	dressmaker	24	44 Phillips
V	Hussian Arshalonis—†	78	housewife	30	Russia
W	Braxton Joseph	78	laborer	35	Lynn
X	Fishbam Jacob	78	laundryman	40	here
Z	Mattel Max	79	shoemaker	45	"
A	Mattel Rebecca—†	79	housewife	42	"
B	Zimmerman Max	79	painter	45	"
C	Zimmerman Rose—†	79	housewife	40	"

Phillips Street—Continued

D	Cohen David A	79	restaurateur	34	Chelsea
E	Cohen Sadie—†	79	housewife	27	"
F	Matal Joseph	80	tailor	26	79 Phillips
G	Matal Ray—†	80	housewife	20	79 "
H	Zide Abraham	80	carpenter	42	14 Spring
K	Zide Lillie—†	80	housewife	41	14 "
L	Lipsky Anna—†	80	"	40	here
M	Lipsky Max	80	shoemaker	42	"
N	Libis Phillip	80	tailor	35	31 Auburn
O	Libis Pollie—†	80	housewife	33	31 "
R	Litcofsky Annie—†	81	"	36	here
S	Litcofsky Phillip	81	chauffeur	36	"
T	Kaplan Gertrude—†	81	housewife	36	"
U	Kaplan Samuel	81	presser	37	90 W Cedar
V	Ferrari Frances—†	81	cook	64	here
W	Ferrari Margaret—†	81	"	44	"
X	Cleyton Ida—†	82	housewife	45	"
Y	Foster Fred	82	U S N	25	Canada
Z	Foster Henry	82	laborer	35	California
A	Berman Abraham	82	tailor	50	here
B	Berman Rose—†	82	housewife	41	"
C	Roseman Esta—†	82	"	53	Russia
D	Roseman Phillip	82	pedler	55	"
G	Burnadett Mary—†	83	houseworker	68	here
H	Porpanova Josephine—†	83	housewife	36	"
K	Porpanova Veto	83	barber	56	"
L	Winer Max	83	shoemaker	33	"
M	Winer Sadie—†	83	housewife	33	"
N	Goodman Celia—†	83	"	43	"
O	Goodman David	83	salesman	54	"
P	Goodman Harry	83	artist	22	"
R	Goodman Louis	83	sign painter	24	"
S	Bryan Adele—†	85	houseworker	46	Winthrop
T	Bronetsky Alice—†	85	housewife	41	32 Spring
U	Bronetsky Samuel	85	tailor	50	32 "
V	Shtrcahman Barney	85	junk dealer	47	64 Phillips
W	Shtrachman Rebecca—†	85	housewife	46	here
X	Levine Jennie—†	85	"	30	"
Y	Levine Louis	85	carpenter	38	"
A	Kleine Annie—†	86	housewife	40	33 Myrtle
B	Kleine David	86	tailor	47	33 "

Letter.	FULL NAME.	Residence, April 1, 1924.	Occupation.	Supposed Age.	Reported Residence, April 1, 1923. Street and Number.

Phillips Street—Continued

C	Berinsky Louis	86	tailor	30	here
D	Berinsky Mary—†	86	housewife	27	"
E	Karazin Louis	86	junk dealer	72	"
F	Karazin Sarah—†	86	housewife	72	"
G	Williams Joseph	86	teamster	32	"
H	Williams Susie—†	86	housewife	45	"
K	Goldman Isaac	86	junk dealer	52	53 Allen
L	Goldman Rose—†	86	housewife	50	53 "
N	Cohen Abraham	86	chemist	21	here
O	Cohen Toba—†	86	housewife	50	"
R	Gleklen Henry F	86	moving pictures	21	"
S	Gleklen Rose—†	86	housewife	43	"
T	Gleklen Samuel	86	laborer	43	"
U	McCrensky David	86	salesman	23	Somerville
V	Pecker Benjamin	86	junk dealer	38	here
W	Plecker Etta—†	86	housewife	35	"
X	Rutman David	86	junk dealer	50	"
Y	Rutman Louis	86	tailor	20	"
Z	Rutman Sarah—†	86	housewife	50	"
A	Rutman Annie—†	86	"	25	"
B	Rutman Charles	86	carpenter	29	"
C	Spegal Max	86	shoemaker	30	"
D	Spegal Sarah—†	86	housewife	30	"
G	Carol Joseph	90	teamster	35	Quincy
H	Katz Phillip	90	storekeeper	41	here

Pinckney Street

A	Aiken Grace—†	67	secretary	22	1053 Beacon
B	Aiken Mabel—†	67	"	26	1053 "
C	Campbell Mary—†	67	retired	40	here
D	Dockery John A	67	agent	35	"
E	Dow Francis W	67	merchant	50	New York
F	Grant Alice M—†	67	housekeeper	25	here
G	Grant John J	67	lawyer	47	"
H	Hurlburt Catherine M—†	67	importer	40	"
K	Lanman Everett L	67	physician	26	Ohio
L	Roome Bessie M—†	67	importer	40	here
M	Sherburne Lois—†	67	secretary	30	Rockport
N	Brigham Robert	69	buyer	24	here

Pinckney Street—Continued

O	Brownell Grace—†	69	teacher	29	89 Pinckney	
P	Cole William A	69	lawyer	36	here	
R	Condon Edward C	69	salesman	28	"	
S	Drew Luke H	69	"	53	"	
T	Foley Minnie L—†	69	housekeeper	49	"	
U	Hall Edward W	69	manager	43	Braintree	
V	Hall Grace E—†	69	secretary	43	"	
W	Hobson Dorothy M—†	69	accountant	37	here	
X	Parsons Gertrude K—†	69	bookkeeper	40	260 Newbury	
Y	Titus Henry A	69	retired	80	here	
Z	Bennett William	71	bookkeeper	35	"	
A	Bowers Kenneth B	71	clerk	23	Fall River	
B	Davy William	71	"	50	Atlantic	
C	Johnson Axel A	71	molder	50	here	
D	Johnson Charlotte—†	71	housekeeper	65	"	
E	Rabbette Leo	71	photographer	25	"	
F	Stebbins Muron	71	bookkeeper	32	"	
G	Sutton Beatrice—†	71	"	35	"	
H	Cody Annie—†	73	housekeeper	45	76 Chestnut	
K	Foley Francis	73	student	20	76 "	
L	Justis Clarence	73	clergyman	30	Vermont	
M	Keating Francis	73	dentist	26	76 Chestnut	
N	Kelley Elizabeth—†	73	saleswoman	22	35 Mt Vernon	
O	Lockwood Charles	73	clerk	25	76 Chestnut	
P	Mooney Lee	73	student	25	Ohio	
R	Norwood Helene—†	73	waitress	25	76 Chestnut	
S	Peckham John	73	student	22	76 "	
T	Shea Agnes—†	73	bookkeeper	25	Providence R I	
U	Shea Henry	73	clerk	25	"	
V	Warren Howard	73	preacher	30	Vermont	
W	Auld Caroline—†	75	housekeeper	59	here	
X	Bell Helen—†	75	"	70	"	
Y	Bonney Chester E	75	clerk	31	"	
Z	Brown Clara—†	75	"	40	Portland Me	
A	Davis Elizebeth—†	75	teacher	40	here	
B	Garrison Litia—†	75	stenographer	30	"	
C	Gunning Jennie—†	75	clerk	41	"	
D	Pope Henrietta—†	75	architect	50	"	
E	Riley Ella—†	75	dietitian	38	"	
F	Titcomb Everett	75	musician	39	"	
G	Bennett Nellie—†	77	governess	40	"	

Pinckney Street—Continued

Letter.	Full Name.	Residence	Occupation	Age	Reported Residence
H	Jordan Gertrude—†	77	housekeeper	36	here
K	Jordan Leland	77	U S N	40	"
L	Maynard Robert W	79	merchant	44	"
M	McGovern Annie—†	79	housekeeper	40	"
N	Bowman George E	81	editor	52	"
O	Brown Phoebe—†	81	housekeeper	36	"
P	Caverly Albert H	81	superintendent	50	"
R	Clark Franklin P	81	clerk	24	3 Mt Vernon
S	Clark Samuel O	81	"	26	Connecticut
T	Edmonds Walter S	81	contractor	50	here
U	Hallowell Eleanor—†	81	bookkeeper	25	"
V	Marvin William B	81	salesman	25	Portsmouth N H
W	McLaughlin Irene—†	81	clerk	25	New Hampshire
X	Painter Florence M—†	81	secretary	46	Boston
Y	Penny Beatrice—†	81	clerk	24	New York
Z	Shea H Gregory	81	student	22	"
A	Titcomb Eleanor D—†	81	housewife	46	here
B	Vinnicomb Herbert	81	steward	45	"
C	Wheeler Lucius B	81	salesman	30	"
D	Woodbury Edward I	81	student	21	Iowa
E	Clarke Josephine B—†	83	housewife	69	37 Pinckney
F	Clarke William B	83	custodian	75	37 "
G	Fullam David	83	clerk	50	New York
H	Hayden Francis A	83	"	45	"
K	Pettes Helen F—†	83	housewife	62	66 Chestnut
O	Berle Rudolf	85	lawyer	25	here
P	Campbell Andrew	85	merchant	40	43 Pinckney
R	Campbell Gertrude—†	85	stenographer	35	43 "
S	Franks William	85	salesman	28	here
T	Lochrie Howard	85	"	22	"
U	Mitchel Edward G	85	painter	58	"
V	Mitchel Ethel D—†	85	housewife	51	"
W	Reed Robert C	85	retired	72	"
X	Wilde Donald	85	printer	25	"
Y	Woods Florence—†	85	housewife	60	87 Pinckney
Z	Darling Elizabeth C—†	87	antiques	38	Newbury Vt
A	Chase Anita D—†	87	musician	39	63 Mt Vernon
D	Goodland Roger	89	secretary	45	10 Dartmouth
E	McDuffee Frank E	89	carpenter	56	here
F	McDuffee Mary A—†	89	housewife	46	"
G	Noble Caroline E—†	89	bookkeeper	58	"

		FULL NAME.	Residence, April 1, 1924.	Occupation.	Supposed Age.	Reported Residence, April 1, 1923. Street and Number.

Pinckney Street—Continued

H	Atwood Catherine—†	91	inspector	28	here
L	Church Helen—†	91	housewife	74	"
K	Congdon Louise—†	91	architect	25	"
M	Curtis Alice T—†	91	writer	50	"
N	Frantz Margret P—†	91	social worker	28	"
O	Gilman Esther A—†	91	housewife	45	"
P	Gilman Frank H	91	superintendent	45	"
R	Heizer Helen—†	91	clerk	30	"
U	Jardene Margret—†	91	artist	23	"
S	Johesen Sarah—†	91	agent	25	109 Pinckney
T	Jones Katheline—†	91	bookkeeper	40	here
V	Osgood Cora D—†	91	agent	25	"
W	Reed Grace—†	91	instructor	40	Europe
X	Williamson Ada C—†	91	teacher	45	here
Y	Hintiager Euielie—†	93	housekeeper	49	"
Z	Meier Pauline—†	93	maid	27	"
A	Murray Jessie G—†	93	housekeeper	60	"
B	Wyman Henry A	93	lawyer	63	"
C	Balcom Bell—†	95	housewife	57	"
D	Douglass Mary—†	95	clerk	65	"
E	Gray Helen S—†	95	"	23	"
F	Haven Sophia E—†	95	housewife	60	"
G	Leavitt Laura E—†	95	stenographer	47	97 Pinckney
H	Phillips Grace—†	95	bookkeeper	35	here
K	Shaughness Anna M—†	95	"	61	"
L	Sheldon Lillian F—†	95	teacher	64	"
M	Doherty Wayland F	97	lawyer	48	"
N	Gillis Sadie—†	97	paster	25	52 Pinckney
O	Mahoney John P	97	merchant	48	52 "
P	McGurk Alice—†	97	nurse	30	52 "
R	McLaughlin Albert	97	salesman	25	Cambridge
S	Patte Clara—†	97	buyer	50	here
T	Terrell Gene—†	97	"	45	"
U	Washburn Henry	97	salesman	45	52 Pinckney
V	Wells Maude—†	97	forewoman	36	52 "
W	Westover Alice—†	97	clerk	37	52 "
X	White Carl P	97	salesman	39	52 "
X¹	White Lillian P—†	97	housewife	37	52 "
Y	Woodward Sarah J—†	97	housekeeper	64	52 "
A	Robinson Margaret T—†	101	advertising	39	New Jersey
C	Breed William N	105	physician	30	402 Marlboro

Pinckney Street—Continued

D	Diedrichs Erik	105	manager	34	36 W Cedar
E	Diedrichs Jane—†	105	housewife	38	here
F	Lewis Kenneth H	105	broker	49	230 Beacon
G	Bates Emily—†	107	housekeeper	64	here
H	Brennan Alice M—†	107	retired	61	Keene N H
K	Cowdrey Elsie R—†	107	accountant	45	here
L	Evans Charlotte R—†	107	saleswoman	42	London Eng
M	Fauteaux Louise W—†	107	student	23	Colorado
N	Kelly Mary T—†	107	nurse	45	here
O	Kinsman Anne L—†	107	librarian	30	19 Gardner
P	McKittrick John	107	clerk	21	Cambridge
R	Ramsey Annie A—†	107	retired	53	Newton
S	Stearns Myra D—†	107	"	60	here
T	Crawford Sallie W—†	109	housewife	26	Randolph
U	Crawford Seth T	109	lawyer	35	"

Primus Avenue

V	Verity May—†	7	reporter	27	157 Charles
W	Townsend DePeyster	7	retired	50	New York
Y	Macveigh Gertrude—†	7	stenographer	23	Cambridge
Z	Macveigh Wayne D	7	janitor	24	"
A	Paul Rosa G—†	7	reporter	25	3 Goodwin pl

Revere Street

M	Tallent Herbert T	39	cashier	21	here
N	Tallent Mary—†	39	housewife	48	"
O	Tallent Sue M—†	39	operator	23	"
P	Ableman Bertha—†	39	housewife	21	"
R	Ableman Zelig N	39	shoeworker	29	"
S	Ger Wolf	39	jeweler	43	"
T	Ger Zlata—†	39	housewife	43	"
U	Weiss Fannie—†	39	"	42	33 Irving
V	Fiering Abraham M	39	salesman	26	here
W	Fiering Charles M	39	laborer	24	"
X	Fiering Isreal I	39	"	23	"
Y	Simonds Frank	39	pedler	52	"

Revere Street—Continued

z	Weiss Morris	39	watchmaker	45	33 Irving
B	Wiggins Alfred T	40	janitor	32	50 Revere
C	Wiggins Catherine—†	40	domestic	28	50 "
D	Esselson Arron	40	cabinetmaker	45	here
E	Esselson Olga—†	40	housewife	40	"
F	Massiff Herman	40	tailor	34	"
G	Massiff Rebecca—†	40	housewife	30	"
H	Ringer Annie—†	40	"	35	"
K	Ringer Samuel	40	tailor	38	"
L	Haysel Dora—†	40	housewife	37	"
M	Haysel Samuel	40	butcher	41	"
N	Berti Lena—†	40	housewife	40	"
O	Berti Oresti	40	cook	50	"
P	Cardinale Amadio	40	"	35	"
R	Dillon Rose—†	40	houseworker	37	"
S	Zipple Alice—†	41	housewife	46	"
T	Zipple Carl	41	presser	56	"
U	Ginsburg Elizabeth—†	41	housewife	75	"
V	Ginsburg Harris	41	shoe dealer	45	"
W	Ginsburg Percy	41	printer	31	"
X	Feinsilver Ethel—†	41	housewife	58	"
Y	Feinsilver Morris	41	laborer	65	"
Z	Goldberg Celia—†	41	bookkeeper	22	"
A	Goldberg Hyman	41	tailor	45	"
B	Goldberg Morris	41	salesman	20	"
C	Goldberg Rose—†	41	housewife	40	"
D	Knight John C	43	buffer	43	"
E	Knight Mary—†	43	housewife	42	"
F	Kreamer Jacob	43	clerk	58	"
G	Kreamer Sofie—†	43	housewife	50	"
H	Granovsky Eva—†	43	clerk	20	"
K	Granovsky Gertrude—†	43	housewife	48	25 Revere
L	Granovsky Samuel	43	tailor	50	25 "
M	Beckman Fannie—†	43	housewife	45	here
N	Beckman Irving	43	student	24	"
O	Beckman Louis	43	"	23	"
P	Beckman Paul	43	tailor	46	"
R	Rosenthal Jennie—†	45	housewife	40	"
S	Rosenthal Max	45	cigarmaker	40	"
T	Fegelman Eva—†	45	housewife	46	"
U	Fegelman Frances—†	45	dressmaker	21	"

Revere Street— Continued

v	Fegelman Goldie —†	45	dressmaker	23	here
w	Fegelman Hyman	45	presser	48	"
x	Boland Dora—†	45	housewife	43	"
y	Boland Joseph	45	tailor	49	"
z	Feldman Lena—†	45	saleswoman	21	"
A	Adler Bessie—†	45	housewife	43	"
B	Adler Jacob	45	tailor	52	"
C	Logan Ruth L—†	46	cook	36	Woburn
D	Mulvey Charles	46	auto mechanic	32	"
E	Levy Annie—†	47	housewife	42	here
F	Levy Phillip	47	carpenter	42	"
H	Wald Jenny—†	47	housewife	41	"
K	Wald Louis	47	tailor	43	"
L	Herwitz Ethel—†	47	housewife	26	"
M	Herwitz Jacob	47	storekeeper	30	"
N	Smekos Antonio	48	counterman	38	146 Chambers
O	Zozula Archie	48	auto mechanic	31	146 "
P	Zozula Elsie—†	48	housewife	30	146 "
R	Weinsman Dora—†	48	"	50	here
S	Weinsman Elizabeth—†	48	stenographer	22	"
T	Derfel Barney	48	newsdealer	23	"
U	Derfel Rose—†	48	housewife	45	"
W	Piper Philip	48	cleanser	22	28 Anderson
X	Marcus Helen—†	48	dressmaker	35	Malden
Y	Schneider Beckie—†	49	saleswoman	21	here
Z	Schneider Bessie—†	49	housewife	51	"
A	Schneider Nathan	49	tailor	60	"
B	Goldberg Bessie—†	49	housewife	34	"
C	Goldberg Charles	49	waiter	34	"
D	Lezberg Fannie—†	49	housewife	58	"
E	Lezberg Ida—†	49	dressmaker	24	"
F	Lezberg Louis	49	butcher	29	"
G	Lezberg Zissie—†	49	retired	56	"
H	Zung Manuel	49	student	21	"
K	Zung Rubin	49	tailor	46	"
L	Zung Sarah—†	49	housewife	41	"
M	Ching Sam	50	laundryman	40	Malden
O	Walsh John E	50	engineer	58	157 Charles
P	Walsh Margaret B—†	50	housewife	48	157 "
S	Reed George	50	laborer	21	here
T	Reed Richard	50	"	22	"

Revere Street—Continued

Page.	Letter.	FULL NAME.	Residence, April 1, 1924.	Occupation.	Supposed Age.	Reported Residence, April 1, 1923. Street and Number.
	U	McDonagh Elizabeth—†	51	saleswoman	31	here
	V	McDonagh James	51	laborer	33	"
	W	Beder Dora—†	51	housewife	31	"
	X	Beder Joseph	51	tailor	33	"
	Y	Springer Ada—†	51	housewife	23	Chelsea
	Z	Springer Louis	51	printer	25	"
	A	Anderson Margaret—†	52	storekeeper	35	141 Charles
	B	Gillis Marjorie—†	52	"	38	141 "
	C	Stockton Lucy—†	52	retired	35	here
	D	Pierce Elizabeth W—†	52	housewife	32	"
	E	Pierce Starr McG	52	advertising	46	"
	G	Burke Anna—†	55	waitress	31	108 Myrtle
	H	Burke Geogie—†	55	housekeeper	24	Newfoundland
	K	Burke Hazel—†	55	waitress	27	108 Myrtle
	L	Epstien Rose—†	55	housewife	50	here
	M	Cohen Mollie—†	55	"	36	"
	N	Cohen Ruben	55	painter	37	"
	O	O'Connor Julia M—†	55	housewife	40	"
	P	O'Connor Thomas W	55	florist	47	"
	R	Rudin Ida—†	55	housewife	30	"
	S	Rudin Samuel	55	cigarmaker	45	"
	T	Cohen Harry	55	pedler	37	"
	U	Cohen Sadie—†	55	housewife	36	"
	V	Volensky Eva—†	55	"	26	"
	W	Volensky Morris	55	ironworker	28	"
	W¹	Jordan Harris R	55	waiter	23	"
	X	Odian Livingston C	55	postal clerk	41	"
	Y	Odian Millicent E—†	55	housewife	35	"
	Z	Thornton Frank	55	cook	38	Worcester
	A	Kirshy George	61	iceman	36	here
	B	Kirshy Hilma—†	61	housewife	27	"
	C	Dodge Maude—†	61	waitress	40	"
	D	Yellin Mendil	61	salesman	29	52 Allen
	E	Yellin Sarah—†	61	housewife	28	52 "
	F	Hyde Dora—†	61	"	30	here
	G	Hyde Max	61	tailor	32	"
	H	Rubenfein Joseph	61	pedler	55	"
	K	Rubenfein Rebbecca—†	61	housewife	55	"
	L	Devores Hyman	61	manufacturer	41	"
	M	Devores Mary—†	61	housewife	41	"
	N	Swartz Hyman	61	boxmaker	28	30 Staniford

Revere Street—Continued

o	Swartz Ida—†	61	housewife	24	27 Temple
p	Garber Esther—†	61	"	39	here
r	Garber Joseph	61	laborer	28	"
u	Wood George L	64	retired	83	"
v	Wood Mary—†	64	housewife	76	"
w	Wood Quenton	64	theatricalman	39	84 Elm
x	Young Jessie—†	64	cook	57	here
y	Banker Herbert	64	salesman	23	206 Woodrow av
z	Banker Louis	64	auto topmaker	31	206 "
A	Banker Sadie—†	64	housewife	26	206 "
B	Banker Sarah—†	64	stitcher	26	206 "
c	Low Marion—†	64	restaurateur	31	89 Myrtle
D	Wadsworth Catherine—†	64	"	27	89 "
E	Neiberg John E	64	salesman	27	here
F	Neiberg Julia—†	64	housewife	27	"
G	White Jennie—†	64	bookkeeper	24	"
H	White Rose—†	64	housewife	54	"
K	Zembler Celia—†	64	"	30	"
L	Zembler Harry	64	salesman	38	
M	Carney Bessie—†	64	houseworker	58	108 Myrtle
N	Libby Sadie—†	64	waitress	35	108 "
o	Stanley Lena J—†	64	housekeeper	34	Maine
R	Bogart Earl	65	inspector	35	Cambridge
s	Bogart Gertrude—†	65	housewife	29	"
T	Prescott Mary J—†	66	matron	65	here
U	Sliney Catherine A—†	66	retired	57	"
V	Sliney Edward L	66	clerk	28	"
W	Sliney Matilda F—†	66	housewife	58	"
X	Haseltine Emery	67	salesman	34	Brookline
Y	Haseltine Nester D—†	67	housewife	30	71 Waldeck
z	Murry David E	67	clerk	30	Brookline
A	Murry Jane—†	67	housewife	27	Medford
B	Penn Mildred—†	67	"	30	New Hampshire
c	Penn Ramon A	67	decorator	29	here
D	Perry Osborne R	67	salesman	50	Milton
E	Hughes Thomas	68	engineer	50	here
F	Mack Anna—†	68	stenographer	22	"
G	Mack Annie—†	68	housekeeper	55	"
H	Mack Catherine—†	68	stenographer	24	"
K	Mack Thomas	68	accountant	28	"
L	West John	68	retired	70	"

Revere Street—Continued

M	Alden John G	69	architect	40	Brookline
N	Carret James W	69	salesman	47	"
P	Quinby Sarah P—†	69	housewife	54	Waban
R	Quinby Thedore E	69	editor	60	"
S	Williams Ira J, jr	69	lawyer	24	Philadelphia Pa
T	Winsor Charles P	69	engineer	27	Concord
U	Furbush May L—†	70	housewife	31	here
V	Furbush Ralph A	70	blacksmith	33	"
W	Tobin Abbie A—†	70	clerk	52	12 Walnut
X	Mandell Edith—†	70	stitcher	25	here
Y	Mandell May—†	70	housewife	50	"
Z	Mandell Molly—†	70	storekeeper	20	"
A	Mandell Morris	70	salesman	30	"
B	McBride Catherine—†	70	housewife	28	Worcester
C	McBride Thomas S	70	salesman	27	"
D	Emmons George E	70	chauffeur	33	here
E	Emmons Josephine—†	70	housewife	28	"
E¹	Leahy Theresa—†	70	clerk	23	"
F	Vail Beverly	70	mechanic	24	28 Temple
G	Vail Mary—†	70	housewife	20	28 "
H	Wilde James	70	painter	46	Canada
K	Kaye Cecil	70	repairman	26	"
L	Kaye Ella—†	70	housewife	20	"
M	Smith Beatrice—†	70	furrier	23	101 Chestnut
N	Closon Edith M—†	70	housewife	20	Leominster
O	Kieley Thomas J	70	chauffeur	52	here
P	Standish Celia—†	70	housewife	45	"
R	Standish Miles	70	printer	58	"
S	Barchard Annie—†	71	waitress	38	Providence R I
T	James Emma L—†	71	houseworker	62	Cohasset
U	McLane Edgar	71	painter	64	Lawrence
V	McMaster Lyle—†	71	artist	60	69 Myrtle
W	Patisteas John	71	waiter	65	18 Joy
X	Patisteas Mitchell N	71	draughtsman	35	18 "
Y	Rae Margaret—†	71	saleswoman	45	Newton
Z	Robertson Catherine—†	71	cook	35	"
A	Waterman Edith—†	71	houseworker	48	Hanover
B	Waterman Elizabeth—†	71	"	68	"
C	Woodbury John	71	painter	61	Lowell
D	Dawes Fred	72	janitor	70	here
E	Johnson Lousia—†	72	nursemaid	28	"

Revere Street — Continued

F	McNamee Lena—†	72	housewife	49	here
G	Scollan Catherine—†	72	stenographer	21	"
H	Converse Blanche †	72	cook	38	Somerville
K	Soule Olive—†	72	model	23	Brockton
L	Izenstein Rachael—†	72	retired	76	here
M	Segal Ida—†	72	housewife	50	"
N	Segal Joseph	72	physician	28	"
O	Segal Morris	72	manufacturer	53	"
R	England John A	73	painter	42	Chelsea
S	Manousas Germaine—†	73	housewife	26	521 Mass av
T	Manousas James	73	restaurateur	38	521 "
U	Silverman Abraham	73	fruit	49	here
V	Silverman Francis—†	73	housewife	47	"
W	Angofsky Morris	73	merchant	48	4 Revere
X	Angofsky Sarah—†	73	housewife	44	4 "
Y	London Dora—†	73	"	48	here
Z	London Elizabeth—†	73	bookkeeper	23	"
A	London Jacob	73	pressman	50	"
B	Johnson Agnes—†	74	housewife	30	"
C	Johnson Albert J	74	carpenter	29	"
D	Ward Cecil A	74	longshoreman	23	"
E	Bondaruk John	74	baker	30	18 N Anderson
F	Frankel Harry	74	clerk	52	here
G	Frankel Minnie—†	74	housewife	50	"
H	Calley Nelson R	74	student	29	Cambridge
K	Tileston John B	74	advertising	21	Sharon
L	Cullen Frank	75	tailor	50	81 Revere
N	Donegan Catherine—†	75	houseworker	60	here
O	Donegan Margaret —†	75	"	65	"
M	Dykes Albert	75	gunmaker	36	England
P	Greene Mary H—†	75	dressmaker	62	here
R	Roberts Ella—†	75	missionary	56	"
S	Curtis Benjamin F	76	publisher	61	"
T	Curtis Carol—†	76	artist	26	"
U	Curtis Helen—†	76	student	24	"
V	Curtis Mary—†	76	housewife	61	"
W	Fitzmaurice Agnes—†	77	maid	25	"
X	Foster Frances H—†	77	housewife	28	"
Y	Foster Reginald C	77	broker	32	"
Z	Pepper Mary—†	77A	housewife	38	"
A	Pepper Patrick	77A	laborer	41	"

Revere Street—Continued

	Letter	Full Name	Res.	Occupation	Age	Reported Residence
	B	Kagan Isaac B	77A	tailor	47	here
	C	Kagan Jacob	77A	bookkeeper	21	"
	D	Kagan Sarah—†	77A	housewife	45	"
	E	Gabar Elizabeth—†	77A	"	38	"
	F	Gabar Samuel	77A	dressmaker	42	"
	G	Flannery Catherine T—†	77A	clerk	35	"
	H	Flannery Mary A—†	77A	houseworker	55	"
	K	Segal Jennie—†	77A	housewife	22	86 W Cedar
	L	Segal Samuel	77A	salesman	26	50 Poplar
	M	Gaudelet Catherine—†	77A	houseworker	57	here
	N	Gaudelet Madeline—†	77A	operator	28	"
	O	Gaudelet Marion—†	77A	"	32	"
	P	Rudcke Della—†	77A	housewife	40	"
	R	Rudcke Fredrick	77A	steward	45	"
	S	Sugar Annie—†	77A	housewife	33	"
	T	Sugar William	77A	clerk	34	"
	U	Brown Dorothy K—†	78	housewife	35	143 Kilsyth rd
	V	Brown LaRue	78	lawyer	40	143 "
	W	Omansky Bessie—†	79	housewife	64	here
	X	Omansky Max I	79	contractor	31	"
	Y	Omansky Robert	79	manufacturer	63	"
	Z	Omansky David L	79	cutter	29	"
	A	Omansky Jacob	79	cabinetmaker	58	"
	B	Omansky Mildred—†	79	houseworker	24	"
	C	Berger Bessie—†	79	"	42	80 Phillips
	D	Berger David	79	storekeeper	42	80 "
	G	Greene Carlos	79	retired	64	here
	E	Greene Michael E	79	salesman	32	"
	F	Greene Minnie E—†	79	secretary	26	"
	H	Greene Rose—†	79	housewife	54	"
	K	Greene Thomas H	79	lawyer	25	"
	L	DeLuca Annie J—†	80	housewife	32	"
	M	Cohen Eva—†	80	cigarstriper	52	"
	N	Mason Benedict F	80	chauffeur	21	4 Anderson
	O	Mason Mary E—†	80	tel operator	21	61 W Cedar
	P	Graves Joseph B	80	machinist	36	here
	R	Graves Mary—†	80	housewife	36	"
	S	Aronson Ida—†	80	"	55	"
	T	Aronson Isaac	80	salesman	55	"
	U	Doten Beatrice—†	81	student	22	Worcester
	V	Doten Edith—†	81	"	50	"

Revere Street Continued

w	Hannis Annie M—†	81	houseworker	60	21 W Cedar
x	Northrop Consula—†	81	student	23	Vermont
y	Sayward Vincent R	81	dentist	45	21 W Cedar
z	Walker Charles E	81	watchmaker	40	21 "
A	Young Alice M—†	81	stenographer	45	21 "
B	Levine Belle—†	82	saleswoman	23	here
C	Levine Hyman J	82	salesman	40	"
D	Levine Israel	82	contractor	67	"
E	Levine Rebecca G—†	82	corsetiere	38	"
F	Levine William S	82	salesman	26	"
K	Fenton Anett—†	83	houseworker	29	"
L	Fenton John E	83	artist	39	"
G	Hay Aimme—†	83	housekeeper	27	"
H	Hay Duncan M	83	salesman	31	"
M	Lafferty James J	83	lather	51	"
N	Lafferty Mary—†	83	houseworker	53	"
P	Duncan Harriett A—†	85	retired	64	"
R	Hodges Alice M—†	85	housekeeper	59	"
S	Hodges Gertrude L—†	85	librarian	54	"
T	Hodges Grace—†	85	housekeeper	47	"
U	Hodges Leonard L	85	retired	89	"
V	Chadbourne Augustas C	86	collector	60	"
W	Coughlin Maurice J	86	superintendent	41	"
X	Daniels Charles E	86	secretary	42	"
Y	Graham Ellen—†	86	emp agency	53	"
Z	Keene Edward A	86	painter	60	"
A	Kikorian Karkro H	86	pharmacist	35	"
C	Lane Mary E—†	86	cook	46	74 Revere
D	Power William	86	waiter	66	here
E	Sarafian Karing A	86	student	31	"
F	Wright Effie G—†	86	bookkeeper	47	"
G	Bennett Laura E—†	87	housewife	71	"
H	Bennett Nellie F—†	87	housekeeper	64	"
K	Humphrey Nellie F—†	89	housewife	60	"
L	Nevins Lillian—†	89	saleswoman	35	"
M	O'Leary William	89	inspector	45	"
N	Thaxter Eben B	89	superintendent	60	"
O	Hurley Elizabeth S—†	90	cashier	27	106 Revere
P	Hurley Lawrence	90	shipper	60	106 "
R	Hurley Sarah J—†	90	housewife	55	106 "
S	Mccartney Mary—†	90	nurse	60	106 "

Revere Street—Continued

T	Wright Dorothy—†	90	nurse	24	103 Charles
U	Wright Eliza L—†	90	housewife	57	103 "
V	Wright Harriet G—†	90	student	20	103 "
W	Gorey Lena C—†	90	stenographer	33	here
X	Gorey Mary—†	90	housekeeper	60	"
Y	Crispin Gilbert	91	carpenter	39	"
Z	Malnborg Karl	91	engineer	31	"
A	Pease Margaret M—†	91	housewife	27	"
B	Pease Robert A	91	lawyer	30	"
C	Southard Frances M—†	91	advertising	26	"
D	Wattles Hazel M—†	91	clerk	30	"
E	Rafferty Catherine F—†	92	housewife	60	"
F	Rafferty James J	92	storekeeper	68	"
G	Gardner George E	92	meatcutter	64	Beverly
H	Gardner Lydia A—†	92	housewife	59	"
K	McAuliffe Cecelia C—†	92	bookkeeper	26	here
L	McAuliffe Eugene F	92	U S Gov't	34	"
L¹	McAulliffe Margaret J—†	92	housewife	60	"
M	McAulliffe Susan M—†	92	tel operator	24	"
N	Campbell Catherine—†	92	waitress	28	"
O	Campbell Ellen—†	92	housewife	67	"
P	Campbell Margaret—†	92	bookkeeper	30	"
R	Campbell Susan—†	92	houseworker	24	"
S	Austin Mary N—†	93	missionary	58	"
T	Bacon Eva M—†	93	stenographer	45	Waverley
U	Barker Lillian F—†	93	housekeeper	50	here
V	Buckley Chester L	93	manager	33	Rodway N J
W	Capper Parker F	93	engineer	60	here
X	Davis Wayne E	93	salesman	34	Canada
Y	Fox Helen L—†	93	nurse	44	New Hampshire
Z	French Lena G—†	93	bookkeeper	44	Plainsville
A	Fuller Jessie E—†	93	student	32	"
B	Gamon William W	93	clerk	24	Wollaston
C	Haskins Caroline—†	93	nurse	28	here
D	Howarth Victoria D—†	93	teacher	34	"
E	Johnson John A	93	clerk	24	New York
F	Pierce Melba G—†	93	secretary	25	here
G	Ward Frederic B	93	treasurer	39	Somerville
H	Wilson Sussan E—†	93	secretary	45	here
K	Wright Cornelia R—†	93	social worker	62	"

Revere Street—Continued

L	McKenna Mary A—†	99	student	33	here
M	McKenna William M	99	contractor	64	"
N	McKenna William M. jr	99	"	34	"
O	Ball Eloise J—†	101	housekeeper	45	"
P	Ball Harold A	101	clerk	26	Waltham
R	Mulvaney John	101	salesman	30	Salem
S	Eustis Margaret R—†	103	housewife	33	here
T	Eustis Richard S	103	physician	37	"
U	McGaugh Mary—†	103	nurse	23	"
V	McLellan Christina—†	103	domestic	22	Canada
W	White Charles A	105	music teacher	67	here
X	White Isabelle—†	105	"	52	"

Revere Street Place

Y	Small Alfred W	1	treasurer	61	here
Z	Small Charlotte K—†	1	housewife	50	"
A	Kendrick Laura M—†	1	teacher	63	"
B	Small Ruth J—†	1	retired	33	"
C	Davidson Katherine L—†	2	housewife	30	Illinois
D	Davidson Kenneth L M	2	engineer	27	"
E	Reed David A	2	architect	34	here
F	Reed Margaret W—†	2	housewife	32	"
G	Waterman Anne C—†	3	"	53	"
H	Waterman Thomas T	3	architect	23	"
K	Cromwell Lucile L—†	4	housewife	35	"
L	Cromwell Richard	4	journalist	47	"
M	Rogers Anna—†	5	housekeeper	54	"
N	Rogers Margaret—†	5	designer	55	"
O	Farmer Gertrude L—†	6	social worker	56	"
P	Pickard Emma O—†	6	emp agency	55	"
R	Ellicott Evans B	7	salesman	36	"
S	Ellicott Lillis—†	7	housewife	27	"
T	Little John D	7	salesman	26	"
U	Little Margaret J—†	7	housewife	26	"

Silver Place

Y	Ferri Andrew	3	laborer	27	here
W	Movan Joseph	3	"	47	Cambridge
X	Movan Margret—†	3	housewife	45	"
Y	Bergozini Louise—†	3	"	67	here
Z	Ferrari Louise—†	3	"	26	"
A	Tasho Bessie—†	3	"	24	"
B	Tasho Peter	3	laborer	27	"
C	Bayard Alexena—†	5	housewife	50	"

Strong Place

D	Donizio Michael	1	laborer	59	here
E	Enos Annie—†	1	housewife	48	"
F	Enos Guido	1	laborer	42	"
G	Vickey Edward	2	"	20	"
H	Vickey Sadie—†	2	housewife	40	"
K	Violante Carmine	3	laborer	63	"
L	Violante Cloventa—†	3	housewife	50	"
N	Malanson Berenice W—†	5	"	37	90 Revere
O	Malanson James H	5	physician	47	90 "
P	Grant Bertha R—†	6	housewife	44	here
R	Grant Dorthy—†	6	bookkeeper	21	"
S	Griffen Robert	6	laborer	48	"
T	Leinton Anderson	6	"	45	"
U	Marconis Joseph	7	"	50	"
V	Marconis Mary—†	7	housewife	39	"
W	Novok Kate—†	7	cook	40	"
X	Viduna Minney—†	7	housewife	42	29 Poplar

West Cedar Street

Y	Ballou Edward P	37	mason	42	Magnolia
Z	Goulter Helen H—†	37	teacher	36	here
A	Goulter Mary E—†	37	retired	55	"
B	Smith Lillian A—†	37	teacher	36	"
C	Smith William B	37	proprietor	60	"
D	Homes Cornelia B—†	39	housewife	44	"
E	Homes John B	39	physician	46	"

West Cedar Street—Continued

Letter	Full Name	Residence	Occupation	Age	Reported Residence
F	Brown Abbie F—†	41	authoress	50	here
G	Brown Clara N—†	41	retired	80	"
H	Brown Ethel C—†	41	artist	46	"
K	Brooks Constance—†	43	housewife	33	"
L	Brooks Edward	43	photographer	36	"
M	Frazer Christine—†	43	domestic	35	Canada
N	McCauley Catherine—†	43	"	36	15 Pinckney
O	Howland Edward	45	banker	39	here
P	Howland Eleanor C—†	45	housewife	33	"
R	Jones Katie—†	45	domestic	40	"
S	Strangway Segrid—†	45	"	22	Brookline
X	Asler Douglas F	47	furniture	40	here
T	Butters Carlton C	47	accountant	50	"
U	Lancaster Southworth	47	R R man	29	"
V	Mudge Angelina K—†	47	teacher	45	"
W	Noyes Minnie E—†	47	retired	45	"
Y	Richardson Leslie—†	47	"	28	"
Z	Richardson Sara H—†	47	"	58	"
A	Rust Katherine R—†	47	"	45	"
B	Hannington Bella—†	55	housewife	32	"
C	Hannington David	55	cigarmaker	33	"
D	Arrick Etta—†	55	housewife	28	"
E	Arrick Hyman	55	chauffeur	38	"
E¹	Silverstein Harry	55	lawyer	26	"
F	Silverstein Kaufman	55	hawker	54	"
G	Silverstein Molly—†	55	housewife	48	"
H	Hobbs Charles L	55	chauffeur	36	"
K	McGonagle Patrick	55	laundryman	39	77A Revere
L	Harrison Racheal—†	55	housewife	45	here
M	Arkin Mary—†	57	"	40	"
N	Arkin Nathan	57	carpenter	40	"
O	Magnan Michael	57	clerk	45	"
P	Ostrovsky Ida—†	57	housewife	60	"
R	Ostrovsky Isreal	57	carpenter	70	"
S	Ostrovsky Louis	57	lawyer	24	"
T	Whycoff Alexander	57	cook	34	"
U	Whycoff Annie—†	57	housewife	23	"
V	Smith John S	57	expressman	39	131 Charles
W	Smith Mae—†	57	housewife	42	131 "
X	Kaye Balfour W	57	mechanic	30	Rhode Island
Y	Sheafe Harold	57	student	23	New York

West Cedar Street—Continued

z	Buffman Abraham	57	printer	26	Chelsea
A	Buffman Elizabeth—†	57	housewife	24	"
B	Parker Alice F—†	57	stenographer	32	43 Pinckney
c	Sayers Frances—†	57	"	32	Stoughton
D	MacDonald Ella M—†	57	saleswoman	29	here
E	Brown Jane—†	59	housekeeper	65	"
F	Brown Maria—†	59	attendant	45	Fruit st
G	O'Brien Catherine—†	59	housewife	51	here
H	O'Brien Catherine E—†	59	stitcher	30	"
K	O'Brien Micheal J	59	retired	54	"
L	Leaney Catherine—†	59	attendant	45	"
M	Leaney Frances—†	59	counterwoman	20	"
N	Leaney Joseph F	59	teamster	26	"
O	McCafferey Susan—†	59	houseworker	54	Quincy House
P	Morin Albert	59	roofer	37	here
R	Morin Ernest	59	chauffeur	29	"
S	Morin Henri	59	plumber	27	"
T	Morin Rose—†	59	housewife	70	"
U	Berry Harriett—†	60	retired	35	"
V	Richardson Charolett—†	60	housewife	22	"
W	Richardson Wyman	60	physician	30	"
X	Garrett Alice H—†	60	housewife	55	2 Brimmer
Y	Garrett Hardy G	60	manufacturer	65	2 "
Z	Pierce Edward P, jr	60	merchant	34	here
A	Pierce Ruth—†	60	housewife	29	"
B	Gill Nellie—†	61	"	40	32 W Cedar
C	Graham Joseph P	61	manager	21	here
D	Graham Mary J—†	61	housekeeper	53	"
E	Graham William F A	61	clerk	23	"
F	Foley John J	61	watchman	62	"
G	Foley Mary A—†	61	housewife	60	"
H	Young Mary H—†	61	tel operator	32	"
K	Lee Elizabeth A—†	61	housewife	32	"
L	Lee John P	61	postal clerk	38	"
M	Riley Anna—†	61	houseworker	61	133 Charles
N	Riley Catherine—†	61	tel operator	23	133 "
O	Church Elizabeth C—†	62	clerk	50	here
P	Church Helen M—†	62	"	55	"
R	Gaylord Gladys—†	62	housekeeper	30	New York
S	MacIlwain George E	62	retired	45	here
T	MacIlwain Helen H—†	62	housewife	40	"

West Cedar Street—Continued

U	Smith Edith A—†	62	housewife	45	here
V	Smith Elizabeth C—†	62	student	20	"
W	Smith Fred S	62	insurance agent	50	"
X	Churchill Sarah N—†	63	buyer	40	"
Y	Coughlin Cyrus	63	advertising	31	121 Appleton
Z	Coughlin Elizabeth—†	63	housewife	36	Cambridge
A	Harris Laura—†	63	domestic	34	"
B	Newell Julia H—†	63	retired	60	89 Pinckney
D	Morse Alice C—†	63	housewife	37	here
E	Morse Frank E	63	teacher	67	"
C	Townsend Edith R—†	63	housewife	31	New York
F	Newell Dorcey C	64	houseman	37	66 W Cedar
G	Newell Jane—†	64	housewife	36	66 "
H	Hoffman May F—†	64	"	45	here
K	Hoffman Robert S	64	insurance agent	47	E Weymouth
L	Clark Arthur W	64	physician	28	171 Marlboro
M	Clark Doris B—†	64	housewife	28	Brookline
N	McMillin Helen—†	64	publisher	30	New Hampshire
O	Remick Helen—†	64	saleswoman	26	"
P	Shirleff Elizabeth—†	64	artist	25	"
R	Jones Eleanor C—†	64	housewife	33	here
S	Jones Reginald F	64	banker	45	"
T	Bear Bruce M	66	writer	25	Cuba
V	Cyle Marion C—†	66	dressmaker	42	here
U	Dalton Thomas W	66	salesman	54	"
W	Hull Mary—†	66	housewife	27	"
X	Hull William D	66	choreman	27	"
Y	Herman George	66	fireman	50	"
Z	Herman George W, jr	66	clerk	23	"
A	Herman Mary L—†	66	secretary	45	"
B	Herman Theresa—†	66	housewife	45	"
C	Dwight George E	66	salesman	53	"
D	Hilling Joseph	66	"	21	"
E	Bain Josephine—†	67	housewife	22	26 Hemenway
F	Bain Lawrence	67	student	23	621 Com av
G	Ropes Caroline S—†	67	manager	47	here
H	McLean Helen—†	67	housewife	35	"
K	McLean John	67	accountant	43	"
L	Hamblin Elizabeth—†	67	manager	27	"
M	Carey Dennis T	68	cook	37	"
N	Caswell John G	68	"	60	"

West Cedar Street—Continued

o	Caswell John T	68	chauffeur	28	here
p	Crosby Mary C—†	68	housekeeper	74	"
r	Harlow Cora L—†	68	seamstress	61	"
s	Hennessey Frank J	68	porter	26	"
v	McConnell William	68	coachman	59	"
w	Quinn Ruth—†	68	clerk	26	"
t	Rahn Albert H	68	chemist	49	"
u	Rahn Ethel F—†	68	housewife	44	"
x	Tansey Michael J	68	laborer	42	"
y	Hopkins Constance—†	69	chemist	22	4 Champney
z	Brown Gertrude E—†	69	supervisor	41	Cambridge
a	Hagerty Cora M—†	69	nurse	38	"
b	Collins Leila—†	69	retired	71	Illinois
c	Dudley Catherine—†	69	saleswoman	23	4 Champney
d	Dudley Margaret—†	69	stenographer	22	Portland Me
e	Freeman Elizabeth—†	69	librarian	24	Northampton
f	McArdle Katherine—†	70	maid	43	here
g	McIntosh Henry	70	clerk	60	"
h	Merrigan James F	70	plumber	47	"
k	Murray Anna E—†	70	clerk	27	"
l	Murray Richard J	70	deputy sheriff	67	"
m	O'Connell John J	70	janitor	62	"
n	Porter Charles J	70	rattanworker	72	"
o	Porter James J	70	laborer	67	"
p	Roach John P	70	clerk	51	"
r	Sullivan Robert W	70	watchman	66	"
s	Welch John J	70	clerk	59	"
t	Campbell Walter E	71	student	22	Illinois
u	Skidmore Louis H	71	"	27	"
v	MacLain Grace R—†	71	secretary	27	Belmont
w	Mason Olive—†	71	"	27	here
x	Wilkins Zora P—†	71	"	40	"
y	Burke Phylis—†	71	"	25	"
z	Reed Marion—†	71	teacher	25	"
a	Butter Rae—†	72	waitress	28	194 W Canton
b	Gignac Victor	72	window dresser	26	36 Concord
c	Gosse Nancy—†	72	clerk	20	102 Revere
d	Hanson Richard	72	shipper	26	here
e	Hopkins John	72	"	35	37 Chambers
f	Hopkins Margaret—†	72	housekeeper	47	102 Revere
g	Kennedy Ruth—†	72	waitress	23	13 James

West Cedar Street—Continued

H	Lent Bertha—†	72	waitress	21	61 Rockwell
K	Matthews Alexander	72	insurance agent	31	95 W Cedar
L	Morrison Josie—†	72	tel operator	28	168 W Canton
M	Ross Frank F	72	clerk	59	168 "
N	Ward Julia—†	72	waitress	28	194 "
O	Wardell Evelyn G—†	72	housewife	48	here
P	Wardell George J	72	houseman	50	"
R	Roberts Sarah E—†	73	retired	70	"
S	Woodman Charles H	73	broker	60	"
T	Woodman Vinnie L—†	73	housewife	60	"
U	Walsh Arthur	74	shipper	58	"
V	Walsh Mary—†	74	housewife	48	"
W	McGonagle Edward L	74	clerk	26	36 Allston
X	McGonagle Helen E—†	74	housewife	29	36 "
Y	Gilboy Barbara—†	74	"	45	here
Z	Gilboy George	74	janitor	50	"
A	Murphy Helen—†	74	housewife	63	"
B	Murphy James H	74	instructor	21	"
C	Murphy John J	74	coachman	65	"
D	McDermott Delia—†	74	housekeeper	49	36 Myrtle
E	McDermott Helen—†	74	"	65	36 "
F	McHugh Helen—†	74	bookkeeper	25	36 "
G	McHugh Peter	74	salesman	35	36 "
H	Capon Charles T	75	designer	40	Europe
K	Capon Ruth J—†	75	housewife	33	1 Sentry Hill pl
L	Cohen Philip	76	mechanic	27	57 W Cedar
M	Cohen Sophia—†	76	housewife	24	57 "
N	Short Alice B—†	76	stenographer	25	here
O	Short Joseph H	76	elevatorman	27	"
P	Short Mary—†	76	housekeeper	68	"
R	Galvin Harry	76	retired	76	"
S	Rubin Annie—†	76	housewife	39	"
T	Rubin David	76	retired	45	"
U	Rice Clara—†	76	housewife	32	"
V	Rice Isadore	76	tailor	39	"
W	Carp Frances—†	76	housekeeper	22	"
X	Carp Jacob	76	merchant	23	80 Devon
Y	Carp Sarah—†	76	clerk	20	here
Z	Gray Ida —†	76	housewife	47	"
A	Gray Louis	76	storekeeper	50	"
B	Cutler Rebecca—†	76	housewife	37	"

West Cedar Street—Continued

c	Cutler Samuel	76	truckman	38	here
d	Berenstin Sadie—†	76	housewife	27	27 Parkman
e	Berenstin William	76	shipper	32	7 "
f	Ostrosky Abraham	76	printer	32	here
g	Ostrosky Gertrude—†	76	housewife	27	"
h	Teitelbaum Adolf	76	restaurateur	39	"
k	Teitelbaum Rose—†	76	housewife	39	"
l	Basmajian Charles	76	laborer	21	"
m	Basmajian Esther—†	76	housekeeper	45	"
n	Morris Annie—†	76	housewife	36	"
o	Morris Arthur M	76	salesman	40	"
s	Goldman Harry	80	tailor	40	98 W Cedar
t	Goldman Ida—†	80	housewife	37	98 "
u	Karchmer Joseph	80	upholsterer	36	45 Garden
v	Karchmer Lillian—†	80	housewife	35	45 "
w	Sigel Mollie—†	80	"	29	here
x	Sigel Morris	80	tailor	33	"
c	Heresoff Bessie—†	81	housewife	50	"
d	Heresoff Mandell	81	retired	60	"
e	Cover Abraham	81	repairman	43	"
f	Cover Gasi—†	81	housewife	55	90 W Cedar
g	Cover Rebecca—†	81	stitcher	26	90 "
h	Isenberg Rebecca—†	81	cigarmaker	28	"
k	Isenberg Samuel	81	retired	50	"
l	Simon Dora—†	81	housewife	35	"
m	Simon Morris	81	tailor	39	"
n	Simon Charles	81	shoemaker	35	"
o	Simon Dora—†	81	housewife	35	"
p	Tanzer Annie—†	81	"	30	"
r	Tanzer William	81	manager	29	"
s	Chin Charles	82	laundryman	75	"
t	Cats Sarah—†	82	housewife	37	"
u	Gilman Joseph	82	merchant	33	Chelsea
v	Gilman Mary—†	82	housewife	30	"
w	Smilg Harry	82	shoemaker	32	41 Garden
x	Smilg Rebecca—†	82	housewife	29	41 "
y	Yuman Solman	82	teacher	42	here
z	Yuman Yetta—†	82	housewife	39	"
a	Lipschitz Jacob	82	pedler	39	15 Spring
b	Oshry Barney	82	merchant	73	here
c	Bessin David	82	insurance agent	33	37 Fowler

West Cedar Street—Continued

Letter	Full Name	Res.	Occupation	Age	Reported Residence
ɔ	Marder Barnet	82	tailor	41	31 Auburn
ɛ	Marder Jennie—†	82	housewife	36	31 "
ɟ	Pollard David	82	pedler	30	here
ɟ	Pollard Rebbecca—†	82	housewife	25	"
ɪ	Geimach George	82	furniture	44	"
ʞ	Geimach Sophie—†	82	housewife	38	"
ʟ	Melvin Florra—†	84	clerk	34	125 Myrtle
ɪ	Oshry Bessie—†	84	housewife	62	here
ɾ	Oshry Jacob	84	storekeeper	64	"
ɔ	Cohen Florence—†	84	saleswoman	21	"
ɔ	Cohen Lewis	84	salesman	45	"
ɛ	Cohen Martha—†	84	housewife	45	"
ʃ	Beloststsky Bessie—†	84	"	47	"
ʌ	Beloststsky Nathan	84	pedler	53	"
	Carp Max	86	merchant	60	"
	Hesselgren Elena—†	86	housewife	60	"
ʔ	Parker Forrest E	86	carpenter	22	17 Harvard
	Parker Gertrude—†	86	housewife	24	83 Joy
	Goldman Lippe	86	tailor	40	Russia
ɪ	Goldman Ida—†	86	housewife	48	135 Chambers
	Goldman Lewis	86	tailor	53	135 "
	Cone Edward	86	"	34	here
	Cone Emma—†	86	housewife	29	"
	Aken Benjamin	86	painter	36	1521 Wash'n
ɪ	Jesin Dora—†	86	housewife	45	13 Harrison av
	Jesin Harry	86	window cleaner	35	13 "
	Morrison Charles	87	butcher	23	Holyoke
	Morrison Sadie—†	87	housewife	22	"
	Lassiter Isac	87	porter	40	here
ɪ	Sherman Anna—†	87	housewife	44	55 Auburn
ɛ	Sherman Samuel	87	musician	55	55 "
ʔ	Brodsky Elie	87	storekeeper	40	here
ɔ	Brodsky Esta—†	87	housewife	28	"
	Levitt Gertrude—†	87	"	26	Revere
ɛ	Levitt Samiul	87	waiter	33	"
ʃ	Cohen Abraham	87	poultry	30	here
ɾ	Cohen Rose—†	87	housewife	29	"
ɾ	Sweetman John J	87	laborer	45	Chelsea
ɾ	Rosen Lena—†	87	clerk	25	here
ɾ	Rosen Maurice	87	draughtsman	23	"
ɛ	Rosen Max	87	tailor	52	"

West Cedar Street—Continued

Y	Rosen Pearl—†	87	housewife	50	here	
Z	Utchenik George	88	grocer	60	"	
A	Utchenik Jacob	88	"	26	"	
B	Rosen Edith—†	88	saleswoman	20	"	
C	Rosen Harry	88	tailor	58	"	
D	Rosen Leah—†	88	housekeeper	22	"	
E	Rosen Sarah—†	88	housewife	58	"	
F	Winer Furman	88	janitor	70	"	
G	Winer Minnie—†	88	housewife	60	"	
H	Miller Ethel—†	88	"	36	"	
K	Miller Jacob	88	painter	38	"	
L	Sebell Rebecca—†	88	housekeeper	60	"	
M	Sebell Samuel	88	merchant	26	"	
N	Alter David	88	mechanic	41	"	
O	Alter Jennie—†	88	housewife	40	"	
P	Cohen Annie—†	88	"	44	"	
R	Cohen Morris	88	polisher	48	"	
T	Trainor Gertrude—†	89	housewife	32	Revere	
U	Trainor Morris	89	butcher	34	"	
V	Lurie Fannie—†	89	candymaker	40	here	
W	Lurie Ida—†	89	housewife	80	"	
Y	Heartz Fannie—†	89	"	43	"	
X	Heartz Hyman	89	tinsmith	45	"	
Z	Cohen Harry	89	salesman	35	"	
A	Cohen Phillip	89	"	29	"	
B	Cohen Tila—†	89	housewife	60	"	
C	Chernak Ida—†	90	dressmaker	25	91 Leveret
D	Portman Abraham	90	shoeworker	33	91 "
E	Portman Ester—†	90	housewife	30	91 "
G	Krupnick Peter	90	capmaker	36	72 Joy
H	Krupnick Rose—†	90	housewife	35	72 "
K	Altman Freda—†	90	"	22	61 Lucerne
L	Altman Louis	90	carpenter	26	77 Brighto.
M	Goodman Ester—†	90	housewife	28	here
N	Goodman William	90	baker	38	"
O	Bergman Bella—†	90	housewife	36	"
P	Bergman David	90	butcher	39	"
R	Mykyton Katie—†	90	housekeeper	30	"
S	Wallace William	90	machinist	35	New York
T	Hartman Rose—†	90	housewife	39	here
U	Hartman Walter	90	book agent	41	"

West Cedar Street—Continued

v	Katz Abraham	90A	pickle dealer	32	162 Chambers
v	Katz Jennie—†	90A	dressmaker	27	162 "
x	Weinstein Rose—†	90A	housekeeper	32	162 "
y	Naglin Abraham	90A	tailor	33	34 Grove
z	Naglin Bessie—†	90A	housewife	37	34 "
A	Swartz Rose—†	90A	"	31	17 Eaton
B	Swartz Samuel	90A	tailor	28	17 "
C	Dubina Harry	90A	laborer	32	here
D	Dubina Sophie—†	90A	housewife	28	"
E	Kleymann Harry	91	shoemaker	50	"
F	Kleymann Sarah—†	91	housewife	40	"
G	King Edith—†	91	"	32	"
H	King Pereth	91	pedler	37	"
K	Gold Goldie—†	91	housewife	28	"
L	Gold Louis	91	tailor	40	"
J	Lipkin Max	91	watchmaker	41	"
N	Lipkin Sadie—†	91	housewife	38	"
O	Gold Abraham	92	shoemaker	68	"
P	Gold Sarah—†	92	housewife	60	"
R	Patkewitz Josephine—†	92	dressmaker	52	"
S	Cohen Louis	92	pedler	32	"
T	Cohen Sarah—†	92	housewife	35	"
U	Bix James	92	salesman	22	"
V	Bix Minnie—†	92	housewife	52	"
V	Bix Zelark	92	tailor	67	"
X	Lefkovitz Dora—†	92	housewife	30	"
Y	Lefkovitz Jacob	92	buttonmaker	34	"
Z	Blood Harland A	92	mech dentist	30	105 W Springfield
A	Blood Mary J—†	92	waitress	29	Nashua N H
B	Bradsky Rose—†	92	housewife	39	here
C	Bradsky Samuel	92	painter	44	"
D	Rudd Mollie—†	92	housewife	43	"
E	Rudd Samuel	92	tailor	42	"
G	Sylvestruk Alexander	92	waiter	29	35 Allen
H	Sylvestruk Rose—†	92	housewife	28	here
K	Gerald Bessie F—†	93	retired	27	105 Charles
L	Lapley Anna G—†	93	"	45	Clifton
M	Lewis Anna E—†	93	"	43	Brookline
N	Garvey Ada—†	95	housewife	32	here
O	Garvey Patrick	95	nurse	47	"
P	Jones Edwan	95	"	22	Beverly

West Cedar Street—Continued

R	Silcoff Michael	95	machinist	30	96 W Cedar
S	Lanes Bessie—†	96	housewife	52	here
T	Lanes Morris	96	tailor	56	"
U	Tsutsui Kada K	96	janitor	30	"
V	Uzar Gertrude—†	96	housewife	42	"
W	Uzar Morris	96	tailor	46	"
X	Abromovitz Louis	96	coal dealer	24	51 Allen
Y	Abromovitz Racheal—†	96	housewife	23	51 "
Z	Katz Eva—†	96	"	23	here
A	Katz Irving	96	carpenter	28	"
B	Greenberg Myer	96	tailor	29	New York
C	Greenberg Rose—†	96	housewife	25	"
D	Shuman Bessie—†	96	housekeeper	27	32 Spring
E	Shuman Max	96	boxmaker	33	here
F	Williams Aldred J	97	laborer	57	"
G	Williams Aldred J	97	"	33	"
H	Williams Mary—†	97	housewife	54	"
K	Vegoda Morris	98	baker	45	51 Waumbeck pk
L	Vegoda Rachael—†	98	housewife	23	51 "
M	Cohen Abraham	98	baker	56	here
N	Cohen Annie—†	98	housewife	50	"
O	Cohen Morris	98	clerk	23	"
P	Miller Joseph	98	laborer	34	13 Parkman
R	Miller Rose—†	98	housekeeper	33	13 "
S	Angelovitz Morris	98	tailor	40	Russia
T	Angelovitz Rose—†	98	housekeeper	40	"
U	Timmerman Albert	98	fishcutter	24	here
V	Timmerman Ida—†	98	housekeeper	22	"
W	Myer Albert	98	butcher	24	Germany
X	Myer Carl	98	"	28	96 W Cedar
Y	Myer Mary—†	98	housewife	27	96 "
Z	Adleman Ida—†	98	"	36	353 Charles
A	Adleman Leon	98	metalworker	39	353 "
D	Westley Carrie—†	102	waitress	45	here
E	Westley Melvin	102	laborer	20	"
F	Johnson William	102	"	55	"
G	Cronin Mary—†	102	waitress	50	"
H	Ingleton Isaac	102	laborer	64	"
K	Sheinfeld Elizebeth—†	102	housewife	62	"
L	Sheinfeld Jacob	102	presser	65	"
M	Ryan Mary—†	102	housewife	49	Lynn

West Cedar Street—Continued

N	Crowmell John B	102	merchant	53	here
O	Crowmell Katherine A–†	102	housewife	53	"
P	Bird Blanche—†	102	elevatorwoman	38	"
P¹	DiCosta Eva—†	102	housewife	57	"
R	Sam Mary—†	104	cook	35	"
S	Harper Elizebeth—†	104	stitcher	48	"
T	Madden Peter	104	laborer	32	Jamaica Plain
U	Murphy Annie—†	104	housewife	35	here
V	Murphy John P	104	laborer	39	"
W	Gordon Mary—†	104	stitcher	50	Lynn
X	O'Donnell Elizebeth—†	104	housewife	55	here
Y	O'Donnell Phillip	104	mason	60	"
Z	Sragire Ida—†	104	housewife	63	"
A	Larsen William	104	fireman	46	"
B	Murry Mary—†	104	housewife	54	"
C	Hill Ellen—†	104	"	48	276 C
D	Hill George	104	painter	66	276 "
E	Ransom Josephine C—†	104	housewife	53	here
G	Muligan William	106	laborer	40	"
H	Hewey Addie C—†	106	housewife	58	Winthrop
K	Hewey Earl A	106	chauffeur	27	"
L	Hewey Grace H—†	106	housewife	26	"
M	Spector Liana—†	106	"	33	here
N	Spector Noah	106	laborer	33	"

Ward 8—Precinct 4

CITY OF BOSTON.

LIST OF RESIDENTS
20 YEARS OF AGE AND OVER

(FEMALES INDICATED BY DAGGER)

AS OF

APRIL 1, 1924

HERBERT A. WILSON, } Listing

JAMES F. EAGAN, } Board.

CITY OF BOSTON—PRINTING DEPARTMENT

Page.	Letter.	FULL NAME.	Residence, April 1, 1924.	Occupation.	Supposed Age.	Reported Residence, April 1, 1923. Street and Number.

Acorn Street

	A	Lynch Alice—†	1	domestic	34	Springfield
	A¹	Mahoney Margaret—†	1	"	29	Scotland
	B	Minns Elizabeth—†	1	retired	61	here
	C	Minns Grace W—†	1	"	65	"
	D	Cutler Dorothy—†	1A	stenographer	23	Hotel Kempton
	E	Fraine Edith—†	1A	"	24	274 Newbury
	F	Ayers Grace—†	1A	secretary	35	here
	G	Clark Catherine—†	1A	housewife	67	"
	H	Fletcher Lucy M—†	1A	nurse	50	"
	K	Bywell Catherine—†	2	domestic	38	"
	L	Gay Josephine—†	2	retired	64	"
	M	Lodemehl Olga—†	2	domestic	24	"
	N	Scelley Margaret—†	2	"	30	Brookline
	O	Davenport Charles M	3	lawyer	45	here
	P	Hoyle Alexander	3	architect	41	"
	R	DeCourcy Marie—†	4	domestic	35	"
	S	Lyon George A	4	banker	45	"
	T	Lyon Majorie W—†	4	housewife	40	"
	U	Norton Charles L	5	professor	52	"
	V	Norton Dorothy—†	5	student	22	"
	W	Norton Frances S—†	5	housewife	53	"
	X	Norton John T	5	instructor	25	"
	Y	Howe Edna H—†	6	housewife	44	"
	Z	Howe Irving B	6	shoe dealer	46	"
	A	Alline Louise M—†	7	retired	81	"
	B	Chalden Lena—†	8	domestic	24	"
	C	Lowe George H, jr	8	manufacturer	37	"
	D	Lowe Ruth E—†	8	housewife	37	"

Beacon Street

	E	Ericson Karen—†	39	cook	33	here
	F	Gustafson Annie—†	39	chambermaid	23	"
	G	Johnson Hannah—†	39	waitress	34	410 Beacon
	H	Johnson Ruth—†	39	parlormaid	24	119 Perkins
	K	Lyman Elizabeth—†	39	housewife	40	here
	L	Lyman Ronald	39	manufacturer	40	"
	M	Parker George	39	secretary	35	"
	N	Sullivan Annie—†	39	laundress	33	"

Beacon Street—Continued

o	Allen Marion—†	40	retired	38	here
p	Barber Anna—†	40	manager	38	"
r	Hartwell Margaret—†	40	"	21	40 Berkeley
s	Hinman Mary—†	40	"	32	here
t	Newell Nettie—†	40	housekeeper	48	"
u	Barlow Robert S	41	lawyer	52	"
v	Speare Aleca—†	41	housekeeper	50	"
w	Byrne Margaret—†	42 & 43	maid	50	"
x	Clooney John	42 & 43	waiter	31	"
y	Conway Delia—†	42 & 43	cook	45	"
z	Conway Martin	42 & 43	waiter	27	"
a	Cowle Alice F—†	42 & 43	maid	25	"
b	Crehan Michael	42 & 43	waiter	25	"
w	Byrne Margaret—†	42 & 43	maid	50	"
x	Clooney John	42 & 43	waiter	31	"
y	Conway Delia—†	42 & 43	cook	45	"
z	Conway Martin	42 & 43	waiter	27	"
a	Cowle Alice F—†	42 & 43	maid	25	"
b	Crehan Michael	42 & 43	waiter	25	"
c	Deane Desmond	42 & 34	"	29	New York
d	DeLovry Edward	42 & 43	"	23	Navy
e	Gregory Mary—†	42 & 43	maid	48	Somerville
f	Hernon Mary—†	42 & 43	"	22	here
g	Markey Edward P	42 & 43	valet	37	"
h	McDonald Beatrice—†	42 & 43	maid	26	"
k	McDonald Katherine—†	42 & 43	"	24	"
l	McGovern Margaret—†	42 & 43	"	25	"
m	McLaughlin Mary-†	42 & 43	"	49	Mass Gen Hosp
n	Schribman Daniel	42 & 43	waiter	21	Salem
o	Barret Mary—†	44	cook	45	here
p	Burton Jennie—†	44	maid	54	England
r	Cummings Annie—†	44	waitress	40	here
s	Dixey Ellen C—†	44	retired	70	"
t	Flaherty Mary—†	44	maid	22	"
u	Manning Emily—†	44	laundress	50	"
v	Moriarity Margaret—†	44	chambermaid	22	"
w	Tappan Mary A—†	44	retired	68	"
x	Campbell Katie—†	45	maid	55	"
y	Murray Edward	45	chauffeur	40	"
z	Vyncker Herma—†	45	parlormaid	43	Wash'n D C
a	Vyncker Joseph	45	butler	42	"

Beacon Street—Continued

B	Wadsworth Elizabeth—†	45	housewife	55	New York
C	Alexander Carl	46	houseman	35	Brookline
D	Bonnet Louise—†	46	maid	33	New York
E	Carlson Beda—†	46	"	21	Brookline
F	Griffiths Hugh	46	steward	40	here
G	Griffiths Selma—†	46	chambermaid	35	"
H	Johnson Anna—†	46	waitress	35	Bay State rd
K	Jordan Jane—†	46	housewife	35	here
L	Jordan Robert	46	merchant	39	"
M	O'Toole Mary—†	46	cook	40	Brookline
N	Stedman Henry	48	physician	65	here
O	Hood Chauncy W	48	lawyer	45	"
P	May Ralph	48	banker	39	"
R	Hayes Hammond V	48	engineer	62	"
S	Anthony Nathan	48	broker	49	"
T	Foss Edwin C	48	merchant	57	"
U	Crooks Phillip S	48	"	42	"
V	Parker George A	48	state police	36	"
X	Winship Blanton	48	U S A	53	France
Y	Sprague Seth	48	retired	60	here
Z	Stevens Arthur W	48	real estate	36	"
A	Seman Howard	48	banker	53	"
B	Perkins Nathaniel	48	merchant	53	"
C	Davis Livingston	48	broker	40	"
D	Dyer Arthur H	48	salesman	71	"
E	Schlesenger Barthold	48	merchant	42	"
H	Brown Charles W, jr	48	salesman	27	"
K	Barlow Charles L	48	lawyer	46	"
L	Anthony Arthur C	48	broker	55	"
L¹	Carlton William L	48	clerk	40	"
M	Grafton Harry, jr	48	salesman	33	"
N	Hunt Horace C	48	real estate	40	"
O	Steer Gertrude A—†	48	secretary	23	"
P	Steer Maria A—†	48	housekeeper	39	"
R	Steer Thomas	48	superintendent	53	"
S	Being Mary—†	49	waitress	29	Brookline
T	Brennan Norah—†	49	laundress	50	113 Beacon
U	Coakley Helen—†	49	cook	60	47 Falmouth
V	Coen Molly—†	49	kitchenmaid	28	here
W	McCarthy Mary—†	49	chambermaid	23	"
X	O'Malley Mary—†	49	parlormaid	32	New Hampshire

Letter.	FULL NAME.	Residence, April 1, 1924.	Occupation.	Supposed Age.	Reported Residence, April 1, 1923. Street and Number.

Beacon Street—Continued

v	Putnam Elizabeth—†	49	housewife	62	here
z	Putnam William	49	lawyer	62	"
a	Romkey Carrie—†	49	chambermaid	31	"
c	Cronin Daniel	51	coachman	50	"
d	Crowley Julia—†	51	maid	48	"
e	Curtis Allen	51	broker	62	"
f	Curtis Evelyn—†	51	housewife	52	"
g	Machain Fernand	51	butler	41	"
h	Musy Marcel	51	"	38	"
k	Olson Alma—†	51	maid	45	"
l	Swenson Hannah—†	51	cook	60	"
m	Maguire Julia—†	52	maid	50	"
n	Murphy Michael D	52	letter carrier	35	"
o	O'Brien Margaret—†	52	maid	27	"
r	Bergman Louise—†	54	"	24	"
s	Brolin Manolf	54	houseman	22	"
t	Ek Hilda—†	54	cook	21	Navy Yard
u	Higgins Laurence	54	teacher	27	here
v	Higgins Marion L—†	54	housewife	51	"
w	Mays Jessie E—†	54	"	38	"
x	Mays Percy C	54	chauffeur	36	"
y	Rentel Augusta—†	54	housekeeper	44	"
z	Bradwin Herbert	55	butler	33	"
a	Dexter Gordon	55	trustee	50	"
b	Hughes Margaret—†	55	chambermaid	34	"
c	Laycell Christine—†	55	cook	27	84 Beacon
d	Niland Catherine—†	55	parlormaid	26	312 Com av
e	Tolmey Mary—†	55	housekeeper	43	here
f	Barry Mary—†	56	chambermaid	48	"
g	Bigelow William L	56	physician	74	"
h	McAleer Margaret—†	56	housekeeper	30	"
k	McNamara Margaret—†	56	cook	35	68 Beacon
l	Shepard Herold D	56	nurse	25	68 St Germain
m	Black George	57	real estate	80	here
n	Fraser Mary—†	57	chambermaid	72	"
o	Grant Christine—†	57	"	45	"
p	Gunbie Francis	57	valet	32	"
r	Rocrarite Isolena—†	57	laundress	34	"
s	Steckell Martha—†	57	cook	30	"
t	Tachessi Sonoda	57	butler	32	"
u	Calnan Margaret T—†	58	maid	40	23 Com av

5

Page.	Letter.	Full Name.	Residence, April 1, 1924.	Occupation.	Supposed Age.	Reported Residence April 1, 1923. Street and Number.

Beacon Street—Continued

	v	Connell Mary H—†	58	maid	43	here
	w	Daley Mary J—†	58	"	50	Lancaster
	x	Fraser Lydia J—†	58	"	50	34 Isabella
	y	MacEachern Florence J—†	58	"	40	23 Com av
	z	Warren John	58	physician	49	here
	a	Warren John C	58	"	81	"
	d	MacBride Georgina E—†	59	teacher	52	"
	e	MacBride Bessie—†	59	"	46	"
	f	MacBride Lucy—†	59	housekeeper	65	"
	g	Ayer Isabelle—†	59	manufacturer	45	"
	h	Ham Lottie—†	59	housekeeper	40	"
	k	Peabody Charlotte E—†	59	editress	24	"
	l	Very Eleanor—†	59	writer	22	1295 Com av
	m	Chapin Horace D	60	lawyer	75	here
	n	Lehane Bridget—†	60	maid	30	"
	o	Sullivan Margaret—†	60	cook	60	Brookline
	p	McQueen Sarah—†	61	"	50	"
	r	Morrison Margaret—†	61	chambermaid	45	here
	s	Nystrom Elsa—†	61	waitress	40	Quincy
	t	Lawton Cornelia—†	61	housewife	60	"
	u	Lawton Herbert	61	merchant	63	"
	v	Nourse Leland D	62	superintendent	68	here
	w	Nourse Minnie R—†	62	housewife	47	"
	y	Batchelder Grace L—†	62	"	54	"
	z	Batchelder John L	62	merchant	56	"
	a	Hall John H	62	butler	59	Canada
	b	Hall Mildred E—†	62	cook	48	"
	c	Bemis Marion W—†	62	housekeeper	54	here
	d	O'Connor Mary—†	62	maid	42	"
	e	Stephenson Arabella—†	62	cook	43	"
	f	Deste Eliese—†	62	housekeeper	40	"
	g	Deste Julian	62	merchant	70	"
	h	Laven Julia—†	62	cook	40	Newton
	k	Little Joanna—†	62	housekeeper	65	here
	l	Little Luther	62	merchant	71	"
	m	Morrison Marian—†	62	maid	56	"
	n	Buchanan Ellen—†	63	parlormaid	45	Brookline
	o	Buckley Catherine—†	63	seamstress	45	here
	p	Gallagal Alice—†	63	laundress	45	Brookline
	r	Kelley Ellen—†	63	cook	40	"

Beacon Street—Continued

s	Sturgis Alice—†	63	retired	55	here
T	Sturgis Evelyn—†	63	"	50	"
U	Sturgis Frances C—†	63	housekeeper	60	"
V	Sturgis Mabel—†	63	artist	58	"
W	Wood Catherine—†	63	chambermaid	45	Brookline
X	Beck Ida—†	64	maid	37	298 Beacon
Y	Bowler Julia—†	64	"	30	3 Fairfield
Z	Briggs Loyde V	64	physician	65	here
A	Briggs Mary C—†	64	housewife	60	"
B	Degoumois Mary—†	64	maid	39	Switzerland
C	Stewart Elizabeth—†	64	"	37	Brookline
F	Denny John W	66	retired	76	here
G	Meredith James M	66	real estate	74	"
K	Pridchard Joseph W	66	retired	70	"
L	Crosbey Edward H	66	journalist	65	"
M	Crosbey Medora R—†	66	housewife	60	"
N	Ely Philip R	66	retired	66	Nahant
O	Brown Herbert W C	66	architect	64	here
R	Mallory Charles	66	clergyman	76	25 Chestnut
S	Mallory Katherine F—†	66	housewife	72	25 "
T	Longfellow Alex W	66	plumber	69	here
U	Sheldon Benjinen	66	retired	72	"
V	Swedd Harry B	66	architect	38	"
W	Whistler Ross T	66	publisher	29	"
X	Haven Parkman B	66	architect	65	"
Y	Dittrich Emil	66	superintendent	54	"
Z	Dittrich Ingburg—†	66	housewife	48	"
A	Rice Durant	66	clerk	34	Cambridge
B	Smith Robert E	66	broker	42	Wisconsin

Branch Street

G	Dillingham Frank W	17	artist	60	here
H	Dillingham Paul W	17	student	24	"
K	Dillingham Sarah A—†	17	houswife	61	"
L	Welsh Frank	17	watchman	58	Newport N H
M	Brewster Daniel O	17A	teacher	41	here

Cedarlane Way

o	Johnson Bertha G—†	14	clerk	23	Brockton
p	Gillette Helen H—†	14	bacteriologist	30	here
r	Sparrell Suzane E F	14	bookkeeper	50	"
s	Cole Carrie B—†	14	clerk	46	"
t	Rogers Alllison —†	16	"	29	"
u	Hartwell Alena—†	16	housewife	44	"
v	Hartwell Francis W	16	designer	58	"
w	Hatch Julia B—†	16	clerk	48	"
x	Cambell Margaret—†	16	dressmaker	50	"
y	Watson Moses	18	janitor	64	"
a	Kingdon Mabel G—†	18	secretary	40	18 W Cedar
b	Thayer Mary A—†	18	librarian	57	here
c	Delano Helen L—†	18	nurse	45	33 Highgate
d	Sparks Susan C—†	18	secretary	41	264 Bay State rd
e	Bassett Gertrude S—†	18	housewife	57	here

Charles Street

h	Allen Albin M	7	merchant	54	here
k	Allen Josephine E—†	7	housewife	54	"
l	Frank William	7	printer	48	Connecticut
m	Hirschberg Samual	7	jeweler	53	here
n	Kelly Thomas E	7	contractor	52	"
o	Lynch Patrick	7	chauffeur	24	New York
p	Philbrick Hattie N G—†	7	solicitor	69	here
r	Acunto Stephen A	9	fruit	30	63 Chestnut
s	DeLuca Joseph	9	"	23	63 "
t	Edward Charles A	9	retired	72	here
u	Edward Gertrude E—†	9	secretary	38	"
v	Hutchinson Maragret—†	9	retired	69	"
w	Leahy David J	9	salesman	39	"
x	Robbins Walter	9	clerk	46	"
z	Briggs Thelma—†	15	retired	61	California
a	Davis Minot F	15	physician	62	here
b	Chase William H	15	retired	79	"
c	Deway Martha L—†	15	"	56	"
d	Stricklan Carl L	15	clerk	33	"
e	Mahoney Bertha E—†	15	manager	40	"
f	Mahoney Ruth E—†	15	social worker	35	"

Charles Street—Continued

G	Byers William L	15	salesman	27	Princeton
H	Fretheam Marie—†	15	nurse	35	New York
S	Brickley Edith C—†	37	hairdresser	28	here
T	Brickley James	37	policeman	32	"
U	Hill Emma—†	37	clerk	24	"
V	Hill Franklin P	37	florist	66	"
W	Hill Franklin P, jr	37	grocer	22	"
X	Hill Lizza—†	37	housewife	53	"
Y	Hill Mildred—†	37	clerk	24	"
Y¹	McCoy Margaret—†	37	laundress	35	"
A	Burnham Lillian—†	39	housewife	42	"
B	Fitzgerald Richard R	39	banker	26	"
C	Tream Daisy—†	39	director	35	"
E	Atkins Albert H	45	artist	44	"
H	Eisenburg Adolph	49	physician	37	"
K	Diamond Peter J	49	broker	37	Manchester
L	Morse John R	49	clerk	22	"
O	Temple Samuel	53	merchant	32	here
P	Temple Ruth—†	53	housewife	32	"

Chestnut Street

S	Bartol Charlotte H—†	1	housewife	54	here
T	Bartol Janet—†	1	student	21	"
U	Bartol John W	1	physician	60	"
V	Bohen Maria—†	1	domestic	42	"
W	Dever Catherine—†	1	"	33	Ireland
X	Donovan Agnes—†	1	"	44	here
Y	Hegarty Catherine—†	1	"	41	"
Z	Lyndes Jenny—†	1	"	72	"
A	Nolan Sarah—†	1	"	35	"
B	Walsh Josephine—†	1	"	38	"
E	Ames Fannie B—†	4	retired	80	44 St James av
F	Chase Charles M	4	"	72	here
G	Chase Edith S—†	4	housekeeper	39	"
H	Crosby Edith A—†	4	artist	44	44 St James av
K	Crosby Raymond M	4	"	50	44 "
L	Elliott James W	4	broker	59	14 Carver
M	Elliott Martha H—†	4	housewife	52	14 "
N	Elms Helen T—†	4	housekeeper	29	here

Page	Letter	Full Name	Residence, April 1, 1924.	Occupation.	Supposed Age.	Reported Residence, April 1, 1923. Street and Number.

Chestnut Street—Continued

	Letter	Full Name	Residence	Occupation	Age	Reported Residence
	o	Ward Elizabeth O—†	4	teacher	30	Brookline
	p	Hathaway Helen L—†	5	shoe stitcher	37	here
	r	Hathaway William E	5	janito·	41	"
	s	Lewis Myron P	5	commissioner	42	33 Com av
	t	Moore Spurgeon	5	houseman	23	18 Williams
	u	McCloud Christie—†	5	domestic	50	Winchester
	v	McNeil Eda M—†	5	nurse	37	Watertown
	w	Robbins Edward B	5	retired	80	here
	x	Robbins Elise—†	5	clerk	37	"
	y	Leonard Mary F—†	5	housekeeper	72	"
	z	Emery Annita P—†	5	housewife	49	333 Com av
	a	Emery Willett, jr	5	student	21	Cambridge
	b	Howard Sophie—†	5	domestic	70	"
	d	Askenasy Herman F	5	retired	69	here
	e	Askenasy Nellie E—†	5	housewife	54	"
	f	Foley Julia T—†	6 & 8	housekeeper	38	Lowell
	g	Foley Patrick J	6 & 8	butler	39	"
	h	Garvonni Flora—†	6 & 8	domestic	25	here
	k	Green Charlotte—†	6 & 8	housewife	46	"
	l	Green Edwin F	6 & 8	engineer	50	"
	m	Jones Benjamin F	6 & 8	student	25	"
	n	Martin Alice F—†	6 & 8	domestic	26	107 Chestnut
	n¹	Nichols Grace E—†	6 & 8	none	48	107 "
	o	Southworth Franklin C	6 & 8	student	30	Natick
	p	Boyce Sarah—†	7	domestic	35	116 Com av
	r	Flanagan Anna—†	7	"	26	109 "
	s	Kneeland Bridget—†	7	"	30	109 "
	t	Smith Elizabeth—†	7	"	38	109 "
	u	Wigglesworth Edward	7	physician	36	109 "
	v	Wigglesworth Sarah—†	7	housewife	31	109 "
	w	Canty Catherine—†	9	domestic	55	here
	x	Gordon Hannah M—†	9	"	58	160 Beacon
	y	Wendam Florence—†	9	housekeeper	54	here
	z	Whitevell Nathalie—†	9	"	60	"
	a	Codman Mary J—†	10	housewife	42	"
	b	Codman Stephen S	10	architect	52	"
	c	Kenney Mary—†	10	domestic	29	"
	d	O'Neill Bridget—†	10	"	20	Ireland
	e	King Anne P—†	11	housekeeper	50	here
	f	King Caroline W—†	11	"	52	"
	g	Juselius Ida—†	11	domestic	20	Cambridge

Page.	Letter.	FULL NAME.	Residence, April 1, 1924.	Occupation.	Supposed Age.	Reported Residence, April 1, 1923. Street and Number.

Chestnut Street—Continued

	H	MacInnes Etta—†	11	domestic	27	Cambridge
	K	Nilson Pauline—†	11	"	57	"
	L	Goddard Alice H—†	12	housewife	61	here
	M	Goddard Amory	12	broker	24	"
	N	Goddard George W	12	student	21	"
	O	Heffernan Mary—†	12	domestic	24	Brookline
	P	Holmes Thomas W	12	draughtsman	56	here
	R	Sullivan Margaret—†	12	domestic	42	"
	S	Wellington Louis B	13	broker	55	"
	T	Wellington Louise—†	13	housewife	55	"
	U	Brady Margaret—†	14	domestic	22	Dover
	V	Carroll Annie—†	14	"	39	Lexington
	W	Cumming Alexina—†	14	nurse	24	here
	X	Hunnewell Emeline T—†	14	housewife	37	"
	Y	Hunnewell James M	14	lawyer	43	"
	Z	Kinnear Ruby—†	14	domestic	21	Scotland
	A	Scott Evelyn—†	14	nurse	20	Brookline
	B	Thompson Margaret—†	14	domestic	29	416 Com av
	C	Dunn Nora—†	15	"	60	here
	D	Hassett Mary—†	15	"	45	"
	E	Leahy Nellie—†	15	"	21	"
	F	Means James H	15	physician	35	"
	G	Means Marion J—†	15	housewife	35	"
	H	Noonan Catherine—†	15	domestic	28	Cohasset
	K	Cunningham Mary—†	16	"	40	here
	L	Foley Margaret—†	16	"	35	"
	M	Steele Annie—†	16	"	37	"
	N	Tyler Mary O—†	16	housewife	69	"
	O	Anderson Betty—†	17	domestic	55	"
	P	Anderson Julia E—†	17	"	54	"
	R	Bartol Elizabeth H—†	17	housekeeper	82	"
	S	Hedquist Hannah—†	17	domestic	44	"
	T	Daly Cathrine—†	18	"	32	Arlington
	U	Doyle Rebecca—†	18	"	34	175 Marlboro
	V	Price Margaret—†	18	"	35	Milton
	W	Winslow Arthur	18	merchant	63	here
	X	Winslow Cameron, 2d	18	"	27	Wash'n D C
	Y	Winslow Mary L—†	18	housewife	62	here
	Z	Winslow Sarah H—†	18	housekeeper	30	"
	A	McGee Mary—†	19	domestic	40	246 Marlboro
	B	McLellen Catherine—†	19	"	23	Canada

Chestnut Street—Continued

B¹	McLellen Celia—†	19	domestic	22	Canada
C	Norton Elizabeth—†	19	housekeeper	57	here
D	Chisholm Sarah—†	20	domestic	57	"
E	Cushing Grafton D	20	lawyer	59	"
F	MacDonald Mary E—†	20	domestic	60	"
G	Frye Alice E—†	21	housekeeper	65	"
H	Frye Edmund B	21	banker	36	"
K	Frye Elizabeth H—†	21	retired	40	"
L	Frye Mary A—†	21	"	42	"
M	Hanson Hilda—†	21	domestic	45	"
N	Ryan Catherine—†	21	"	30	"
O	Croke Margaret—†	22	"	58	"
P	Warren Edward R	22	retired	59	"
R	Warren Marion P—†	22	housewife	50	"
S	Adamoski Gertrude—†	23	"	40	"
T	Adamoski Timothie	23	musician	40	"
U	Crowley Anna—†	23	domestic	32	"
V	Donovan Annie—†	24	"	35	83 Mt Vernon
W	Maloney Mary—†	24	"	50	Brookline
X	McLean Margaret—†	24	"	38	Concord
Y	Suter John W	24	clergyman	62	here
Z	Foster Kendall W	25	student	24	"
A	Foster Lydia K—†	25	janitress	49	"
B	Kendall Anna—†	25	housewife	88	"
C	Boynton Dalton	25	clerk	35	"
D	Boynton Pauline H—†	25	housewife	41	"
E	Denton Susan E—†	25	houseworker	66	"
F	Jennings Harriett T—†	25	retired	66	"
G	Mitchell James W	25	insurance	64	"
H	Mitchell Ruth P—†	25	housewife	41	"
K	Walker Catherine S—†	25	"	54	"
L	Walker Edward P	25	manager	28	"
M	Walker Margaret—†	25	librarian	30	"
N	Merrill Charles	25	banker	50	City Club
O	Peirce Frederick N	25	"	39	Newton
P	Carlson Matilda—†	26	domestic	26	Brookline
R	Hawley Anna—†	26	housewife	40	here
S	Hawley George	26	merchant	50	"
T	Lundin Merrie—†	26	domestic	40	Worcester
U	Winquist Edith M—†	26	waitress	21	Wellesley
V	Evans Wilmont	28	banker	60	here

Chestnut Street—Continued

w	Clark Susan D—†	29A	housewife	66	here
x	Keough William B	29A	retired	69	"
y	Morrison Margaret—†	29A	domestic	55	"
z	Purtell Hannah E—†	29A	"	60	"
A	Sweeney Mary—†	29A	"	50	"
B	Burns Rose—†	30	"	21	57 Chestnut
C	Driscoll Margaret—†	30	"	22	57 "
D	Edgell Elsie—†	30	housekeeper	35	57 "
E	Keene Mary—†	30	domestic	25	57 "
F	Roberts Helen—†	30	nurse	21	57 "
G	Wheeler Alice—†	30	"	30	57 "
H	Burr Alice E—†	31	housewife	57	here
K	Burr Herman M	31	retired	67	"
L	Burr Mary H—†	31	student	25	"
M	Donovan Mary—†	31	domestic	43	"
N	Hannon Catherine—†	31	"	30	"
O	Monahan Bridget J—†	31	"	38	"
P	Murphy Bridget—†	31	"	50	Cambridge
R	Reidy Mary—†	31	"	36	Ireland
S	Johnson Elizabeth—†	32	housekeeper	60	here
T	Johnson Eric St J	32	physician	46	"
U	Johnson Harriet—†	32	instructor	40	"
V	Johnson Leslie A	32	merchant	55	"
W	Adams Brooks	33	retired	72	"
X	Adams Evelyn—†	33	housewife	68	"
Y	Colby Margaret—†	33	domestic	45	Weymouth
Z	Coyle Ellen—†	33	"	44	here
A	Dayton Mary—†	33	"	45	"
B	Graves Frances—†	33	"	38	"
C	Phillips Alice—†	33	"	45	"
D	Scofield Nora—†	33	"	52	"
E	Wellington Arthur W	35	merchant	53	"
F	Wellington Evelyn L—†	35	housewife	46	"
G	Bates Natica I—†	37	housekeeper	36	"
H	Courteney Celia—†	37	chambermaid	22	"
K	Healey Hannah—†	37	cook	40	"
L	McCaffery Julia—†	37	nursemaid	40	"
M	Whehan Delia—†	37	waitress	29	"
N	McDonald Margaret—†	38	domestic	24	Nova Scotia
O	McLeod Annie—†	38	cook	45	here
P	Morrison Agnes—†	38	nurse	21	"

Page.	Letter.	FULL NAME.	Residence, April 1, 1924.	Occupation.	Supposed Age.	Reported Residence, April 1, 1923. Street and Number.

Chestnut Street—Continued

R	Osgood Margaret C—†	38	housewife	52	here
S	Osgood Robert B	38	surgeon	57	"
T	Anderson Enis—†	39	governess	23	Brookline
U	Anderson Hulda—†	39	cook	50	"
V	Eiseman Helen—†	39	housewife	30	496 Com av
W	Eiseman Sydney	39	merchant	37	496 "
X	Swanson Inja—†	39	waitress	26	Brookline
Y	Ahlund Emma—†	40	domestic	45	here
Z	Morris Frieda—†	40	"	40	"
A	Morris Grover	40	chauffeur	38	"
B	Palmgren Sigride—†	40	domestic	40	"
C	Spring John	40	merchant	50	"
D	Spring Louis C—†	40	housekeeper	43	"
E	Dodge Edwin S	41	architect	48	"
F	Dodge Margaret H—†	41	housewife	48	"
G	Finucane Edward	41	chef	26	Lowell
H	Pierri Victoria—†	41	domestic	46	20 Appleton
K	Ramella Enrico	41	butler	35	here
L	Campbell Mary A—†	42	domestic	24	Newton
M	McKinnon May—†	42	"	23	here
N	Parker Charles H	42	trustee	53	"
O	Parker Winifred E—†	42	housekeeper	43	"
P	Walhstron Annette—†	42	domestic	37	"
R	Cunningham Anna N—†	43	housewife	45	"
S	Cunningham Henry V	43	lawyer	55	"
T	Cunningham Henry V, jr	43	student	22	"
U	Cunningham John M	43	lawyer	28	"
V	Cunningham Winifred A—†	43	student	24	"
W	Fallon Kate—†	43	domestic	45	"
X	Dumorties Anne—†	44	housekeeper	47	"
Y	Dumorties Leo P—†	44	domestic	22	"
Z	Eldridge Criside—†	44	housekeeper	45	"
A	Eldridge Edward H	44	real estate	55	"
B	Clancy Celia—†	45	domestic	26	421 Marlboro
C	Greeley Delia—†	45	"	21	Portland Me
D	Greene Catherine—†	45	housewife	62	here
E	Greene Edward M	45	physician	63	"
F	Macomber Mary S—†	46	housekeeper	55	"
G	McDiarmid Jesse—†	47	domestic	55	New Hampshire
H	Murphy Catherine—†	47	"	55	here
K	Winslow Anna W—†	47	retired	24	"

14

Chestnut Street—Continued

L	Winslow Eleanor S—†	47	retired	22	here
M	Winslow George S	47	real estate	62	"
N	Winslow Mary W—†	47	housewife	53	"
O	Curran Hannah M—†	48	cook	36	"
P	O'Hara Ellen—†	48	domestic	52	"
R	Woods Harriett—†	48	housekeeper	56	"
S	Woods Joseph F	48	merchant	60	"
T	Woods Joseph W	48	student	22	"
U	Galvin Margaret—†	49	domestic	60	"
V	Pitman Catherine—†	49	housewife	62	"
W	Pitman Harold A	49	broker	62	"
X	Sheehan Catherine—†	49	domestic	40	"
Y	Brewer Georgie G—†	50	secretary	52	"
Z	Everhart Helen—†	50	student	21	Falmouth
A	Fogg Caroline—†	50	"	22	Bangor Me
B	Randolph Grace—†	50	maid	40	here
C	Walker Elizabeth—†	50	student	22	New Haven Ct
D	Clark Mary A—†	51	retired	67	here
E	MacNamara Mary—†	51	domestic	30	320 Beacon
F	Robinson Jennie D—†	51	retired	57	here
G	Sullivan Hannah—†	51	domestic	24	Beverly
H	Woodberry Mary—†	51	retired	55	here
K	Clancy Mary—†	52	maid	26	41 Alberta
L	Cram Elizabeth—†	52	housewife	50	here
M	Cram Ralph A	52	architect	60	"
N	Foley Margarite—†	52	cook	35	Newburyport
O	Larsen Hilda—†	53	domestic	24	12 Arlington
P	Mapes Anna L—†	53	housewife	44	here
R	Mapes James J	53	student	21	"
S	Mapes Victor	53	playwright	52	"
T	Olsen Olga—†	53	domestic	34	Norway
U	Peterson Edith—†	53	"	25	here
V	Daly Julia—†	54	maid	21	Wellesley
W	Duggan Catherine—†	54	cook	34	Maine
X	Fahey Mary—†	54	maid	26	Weston
Y	Wheeler Annie—†	54	housewife	28	here
Z	Wheeler Edward	54	broker	47	"
A	Callaghan Marie—†	55	domestic	33	"
B	Canney Nora—†	55	"	33	"
C	Tucker Herbert A	55	broker	62	"
D	Tucker Mary—†	55	housewife	50	"

Page.	Letter.	FULL NAME.	Residence, April 1, 1924.	Occupation.	Supposed Age.	Reported Residence, April 1, 1923. Street and Number.

Chestnut Street—Continued

	E	Woods Catherine—†	55	domestic	35	here
	F	Buchanan Jessie—†	56	cook	35	Nova Scotia
	G	Buchanan Tena—†	56	maid	30	"
	H	Hamn Agnes—†	56	"	45	Concord
	K	Rousmaniere Edmun S	56	clergyman	65	here
	L	Rousmaniere Mary S—†	56	houseworker	43	"
	M	Rousmaniere Sophie K—†	56	housewife	58	"
	N	Illsley Ruth—†	57	domestic	24	101 Chestnut
	O	McDonald Mabel—†	57	"	24	Canada
	P	Prince Majorie—†	57	housewife	37	101 Chestnut
	R	Prince Norton P	57	manager	35	101 "
	S	Taylor Julia—†	57	domestic	23	Ireland
	T	Chandler Joseph	57A	architect	52	here
	U	Clark Eleona W—†	57A	housewife	38	"
	V	Clark Henry P	57A	steamfitter	50	"
	W	McCloud Mary—†	58	maid	26	258 Beacon
	X	McCullough Sadie—†	58	nurse	27	here
	Y	McGregor Mary—†	58	housekeeper	45	Nova Scotia
	Z	Swanson Hulda—†	58	cook	31	Milton
	A	Warner Mary H—†	58	housewife	45	here
	B	Warner Rodger S	58	lawyer	47	"
	D	Hoppin Eliza M—†	60	retired	75	"
	E	O'Connor Catherine—†	60	domestic	36	Ireland
	F	Parker Ellen G—†	60	housekeeper	65	here
	G	Clark J Redman	61	broker	39	68 Chestnut
	H	Coddington Alice P—†	61	retired	74	68 "
	K	Hoyt Mabel M—†	61	"	50	78 Charles
	O	Cuddy Catherine—†	62	maid	52	here
	L	DeBlois Elizabeth—†	62	student	21	"
	M	DeBlois George S	62	trustee	56	"
	N	DeBlois Mary—†	62	housewife	49	"
	P	Finn Anna—†	62	maid	30	New York
	R	Rooney Anna—†	62	cook	45	here
	S	Danforth Jennie G—†	63	housewife	52	"
	T	Danforth Pauline—†	63	teacher	27	"
	V	Fairchild Helen M—†	63	housewife	34	6 Brimmer
	U	Fairchild John C	63	broker	50	58 Charles
	W	Adams Ella L—†	64	housewife	42	here
	X	Adams Karl	64	lawyer	48	"
	Y	Collin Ellen—†	64	waitress	45	"
	Z	Daly Hattie—†	64	cook	45	Lexington

Chestnut Street—Continued

A	Metcalf Margarete—†	64	maid	46	here
B	Kimbill Benjamin	66	lawyer	75	"
C	Kimbill Elizabeth—†	66	housewife	30	"
D	Boyd Carrie—†	66	"	32	N Carolina
E	Boyd Jounis	66	janitor	33	"
F	Howe Alice—†	66	housewife	35	here
G	Howe Warner	66	merchant	40	"
K	Fitz Emma—†	66	retired	55	"
L	Bangs Mary—†	66	"	40	"
M	Ramsey Helen—†	66	"	35	"
N	Hills Elizabeth—†	66	painter	60	"
O	Hills Laura—†	66	"	40	"
P	Herene Mary—†	68	cook	40	"
R	Smith George G	68	physician	40	"
S	Smith Ruth D—†	68	housewife	35	"
T	Taylor Catherine—†	68	maid	21	Ireland
U	Duffield Elizabeth—†	68	clerk	25	New Jersey
V	Matteson Elizabeth—†	68	"	25	Rhode Island
W	Tamburini Arnaldo	68	artist	40	New York
X	Baker Edith M—†	70	housewife	50	here
Y	Baker Richard K	70	salesman	27	"
Z	Baker Roland M	70	postmaster	59	"
A	Molloy Anna J—†	70	maid	22	321 Market
B	Molloy Barbara H—†	70	cook	29	23 Hawthorne
C	Cabot Amy—†	72	housekeeper	30	here
D	Cabot Frederick	72	judge	50	"
E	Weidolf Ellen—†	72	cook	24	Sweden
F	Frothingham Ellenore—†	74	housekeeper	60	here
G	Frothingham Thomas	74	trustee	59	"
H	Hay Caroline W—†	74	houseworker	58	"
K	Bruce Margarete—†	76	waitress	50	"
L	Cherry Elizabeth—†	76	maid	28	"
M	Ciker Estella—†	76	waitress	25	40 St Stephen
N	Defonda Madeline—†	76	tailor	48	here
O	Harris Mary—†	76	retired	70	Cambridge
P	Hennings Henry	76	salesman	35	New York
R	Hennings Julia—†	76	housewife	27	"
S	Howe Jenette—†	76	teacher	35	79 Charles
T	Jackman Ann—†	76	housekeeper	70	here
U	Jackman Elizabeth—†	76	governess	24	"
V	Morten Ella—†	76	clerk	35	Connecticut

8—4

Page.	Letter.	FULL NAME.	Residence, April 1, 1924.	Occupation.	Supposed Age.	Reported Residence, April 1, 1923. Street and Number.

Chestnut Street—Continued

w	Pillsbury Adlade—†	76	merchant	70	here
x	Wheeller Chritener—†	76	teacher	60	Belmont
y	Wilson Elmer—†	76	clerk	48	here

Joy Street

A	Nichols Frederick	2	secretary	60	here
B	Nichols Sarah D—†	2	houseworker	58	"
D	Abbot Emma—†	8	waitress	38	"
E	Abbot Nina—†	8	cashier	31	"
F	Abbot Wallace	8	waiter	43	"
G	Bronspiel Abraham	8	student	24	New Bedford
H	Edgar Nellie—†	8	clerk	36	27 Myrtle
K	French Susan—†	8	"	38	New Hampshire
L	Honica Alice—†	8	"	33	here
M	Modell Charles	8	radio worker	26	"
N	Morffet Florence—†	8	houseworker	29	14 Pinckney
O	Morffet Peter	8	clerk	41	14 "
P	Sorica Alfred	8	student	23	New Hampshire
R	Anderson Ruby L—†	10	"	27	Brookline
S	Davenport Arthur	10	watchman	43	here
T	Elkins Herbert F	10	insurance agent	31	51 Hancock
U	Elkins Mary—†	10	clerk	23	51 "
V	Hansone Axel E	10	shipper	57	33 Pinckney
W	Maree Josephine—†	10	proofreader	54	16 Joy
X	Mason William M	10	clerk	64	33 Pinckney
Y	Scannell John F	10	plumber	73	57 "
Z	Treat Joseph B	10	clerk	32	20 Joy
A	Webster Charles H	10	sexton	73	33 Pinckney
B	Rolph Bessie—†	10½	retired	57	here

Louisburg Square

C	Foote Doris R—†	1	housewife	30	here
D	Foote George L	1	musician	38	"
E	LeMoal Jennie—†	1	housewife	24	New Jersey
F	LeMoal Yoes	1	butler	24	"
G	Lopez Emanuel	1	chef	37	"
H	Thoburn Stanley	2	student	25	Pennsylvania

18

Louisburg Square—Continued

Letter	Full Name	Residence	Occupation	Age	Reported Residence
k	Davidson Julia —†	3	maid	33	here
m	Mien Jean B	3	chef	40	"
n	Morrison Arria F—†	3	housewife	37	"
o	Morrison Della—†	3	governess	35	"
l	Morrison Horace	3	inspector	40	"
p	Healey Winfred—†	4	maid	25	"
r	Tuttle Grace G—†	4	housewife	35	"
s	Tuttle Henry C	4	lawyer	40	"
t	Kennedy Bertha—†	5	waitress	25	"
u	Kennedy Catherine—†	5	cook	28	"
v	Wadsworth Lucy G—†	5	housewife	76	"
w	Bassett Josephine—†	6	"	37	"
x	Bassett Josiah C	6	lawyer	50	"
y	MacRitchie Mabel—†	6	cook	30	Brookline
z	Post Bertha—†	6	maid	35	"
A	Greenwood Levi H	7	manufacturer	52	here
B	Greenwood Margaret—†	7	social worker	26	"
c	Greenwood Mary A—†	7	housewife	48	"
D	Olson Marie—†	7	waitress	35	Manchester
E	Raftery Alice—†	7	maid	55	"
F	Sheehan Bridget—†	7	cook	35	here
G	O'Donnell Catherine—†	8	maid	27	118 Beacon
H	Vanderbilt Emmaline—†	8	housewife	20	New York
K	Vanderbilt William H	8	broker	23	Newport
L	Conway Margaret—†	8	maid	40	Salem
M	Draper Henry	9	butler	35	Somerville
N	Erickson Helen —†	9	teacher	24	England
O	Gavin Catherine—†	9	cook	42	Manchester
P	Johnson Arthur F	9	lawyer	42	here
R	Johnson Joanne—†	9	housewife	34	"
S	Murdock Christine—†	9	maid	40	New York
T	Bradlee Frances B—†	10	retired	73	here
U	Casey Julia A—†	10	companion	65	"
V	Gustafson Esther—†	11	cook	35	Manchester
W	Winkley Hobart W	11	librarian	65	here
X	Winkley Margaret H—†	11	housewife	53	"
Y	Drinan Margaret—†	12	maid	40	152 Mt Vernon
z	McDonald Flora—†	12	nurse	60	here
A	Metcalf Elizabeth P—†	12	housewife	28	"
	Metcalf Thomas N	12	advertising	41	"
c	Walsh Ellen—†	12	cook	60	152 Mt Vernon

Louisburg Square—Continued

	Letter	Full Name	Residence	Occupation	Age	Reported Residence
	D	Decost Ada—†	13	maid	28	Brookline
	E	Fitzgerald Nellie—†	13	nursemaid	50	here
	F	Lowder Marion—†	13	waitress	32	395 Beacon
	G	Rollins Sherwood	13	banker	29	India
	H	Minns Susan—†	14	housekeeper	84	here
	K	Blackmur Eleanor—†	16	social worker	31	59 River
	L	Ide Elizabeth W—†	16	housekeeper	70	here
	M	Ide Lilla D—†	16	"	56	"
	N	Richardson Anna R—†	16	"	46	59 River
	O	Allender Louise—†	17	"	43	Wash'n D C
	P	Ambrose Grace—†	17	nun	60	here
	R	Appleyard Marian—†	17	nurse	33	Newark N J
	S	Berg Lina—†	17	handicraft	40	here
	T	Berry Amy—†	17	artist	50	"
	U	Bobbett Mary A—†	17	nun	50	"
	V	Bowen Dorothy—†	17	clerk	29	Orange N J
	W	Broomhall Margaret—†	17	artist	29	New York
	X	Carrier Agnes—†	17	houseworker	20	Dedham
	Y	Chandler Evaline—†	17	nun	63	here
	B	Crockett Martha E—†	17	"	48	"
	A	Curry Eliza—†	17	retired	65	"
	C	Davis Emma—†	17	nun	39	"
	D	Dickinson Claire—†	17	"	31	"
	E	Dillon Minnie—†	17	"	64	"
	F	Ellenwood Fred	17	janitor	63	"
	G	Gregory Susan A—†	17	nun	53	"
	H	Judson Madeline—†	17	"	63	"
	K	Knowles Frances—†	17	"	50	"
	L	Lee Geraldine—†	17	"	27	"
	M	Lonus Louise—†	17	"	70	"
	N	MacLeod Frances—†	17	"	76	"
	O	Matthews Sarah—†	17	"	66	"
	P	Pearson Ella—†	17	"	72	"
	R	Price Madeline—†	17	"	37	"
	S	Trufant Gertrude—†	17	"	56	"
	T	Tuffs Eleanor—†	17	"	52	"
	U	Walker Maud—†	17	"	40	"
	V	Warfield Helen M—†	17	"	54	"
	W	Warren Louise—†	17	"	49	"
	X	Wyllys Florence—†	18	housekeeper	40	"
	Y	Collins Mary—†	20	laundress	52	"

Louisburg Square—Continued

z	Heard Eliza B—†	20	housewife	55	here
A	Heard Henry R	20	retired	49	"
B	Heard Rosaliz I—†	20	housekeeper	77	"
C	Judge Mary—†	20	cook	36	"
D	O'Loughlin Abbey—†	20	seamstress	37	"
E	Riley Mary—†	20	waitress	29	413 Beacon
G	Quinn Frederick A	22	manufacturer	53	here
F	Quinn John W	22	mechanic	24	"
H	Quinn Mary J—†	22	housewife	50	"

Mt Vernon Street

B	Barker Charles E	42	superintendent	49	here
C	Barker Dora N—†	42	housewife	50	"
D	Rush Josephine R—†	42	tel operator	43	"
E	Saunders Caroline—†	42	secretary	51	"
F	Marble Charles B	42	editor	38	"
G	Marble Mary F—†	42	housewife	36	"
H	Ellison Isabella H—†	42	retired	57	"
K	Harris Edward L	42	manager	51	"
L	Harris Edward R	42	student	20	"
M	Harris Maud R—†	42	housewife	45	"
N	Miller Caroline H—†	42	"	46	"
O	Miller George E	42	broker	51	"
P	Gordon Charles S	42	retired	45	"
R	Matthews Julius	42	advertising	65	"
S	Matthews Nellie—†	42	housewife	62	"
T	Davis Harold S	42	lawyer	40	"
U	Ritchie Rosa G—†	42	housewife	68	"
V	Dowd Catherine G—†	43	matron	40	"
W	Ellis Jenny E—†	43	"	42	"
X	Hayes Frank A	43	janitor	30	"
Y	Hayes Maud L—†	43	houseworker	29	79 Highland
Z	Rood Jean G—†	43	matron	60	here
A	Hunt Carrie—†	44	housewife	50	"
B	Hunt Thomas	44	lawyer	50	"
C	Lockwood Emma—†	44	cook	50	"
D	McDonald Nellie—†	44	maid	60	"
E	Shaughnessy Helen—†	44	"	23	Brookline
F	Mahoney Frank	45	janitor	33	here

Mt Vernon Street—Continued

G	Parker Helen S—†	46	housewife	48	81 Mt Vern
H	Parker James A	46	broker	54	81 "
K	Sealy Fanny—†	46	maid	32	81 "
M	Foley Abbie—†	48	"	40	here
N	Mocklar Delia—†	48	waitress	30	90 Beacon
O	Tobin Maria—†	48	cook	40	1 Acorn
P	Ware Margaret W—†	48	retired	50	here
R	Whitman Effie—†	48	"	53	"
S	Deverny Annie—†	49	maid	45	Brookline
T	Lang Howard W	49	trustee	44	here
U	Lang Maud—†	49	housewife	48	"
V	McLean Anna—†	49	cook	42	"
W	Pasquale Luigi	49	chauffeur	36	"
X	Morrissey John J	50	letter carrier	51	"
Y	Morrissey Louise L—†	50	housewife	50	"
Z	Morrissey Marion—†	50	editor	22	"
A	Thatcher Martha—†	51	maid	43	"
B	Thatcher Mary—†	51	housekeeper	41	"
C	Rycroft Charles J	53	inspector	47	"
F	Kennedy Isadora H—†	53	housekeeper	62	Melrose
G	Kennedy Lewis H	53	clerk	27	"
H	Pillsbury Mary—†	53	librarian	41	here
K	Mulligan Mary—†	55	cook	29	"
L	Nichols Elizabeth F—†	55	housewife	78	"
M	Nichols Marian C—†	55	secretary	50	"
N	Nichols Rose S—†	55	architect	52	"
P	Turkington Grace A—†	57	artist	31	"
R	Keller Carl T	57	accountant	51	"
S	Howells Mildred—†	57	artist	31	"
T	Doane Ralph H	57	architect	36	"
V	Aldrich Lillian E—†	59	housewife	71	"
W	Campbell Delia—†	59	cook	38	"
X	Hennessy Nellie—†	59	maid	37	"
Y	Hoffman Isabel C—†	59	"	51	"
A	Whetherhultz Allen	61	janitor	32	"
B	Bartlett Gertrude—†	61	retired	44	"
C	Little Nora—†	61	cook	36	"
D	Conway Sarah—†	61	maid	54	"
E	Frazar Mary—†	61	retired	75	"
F	Herbert Katherine—†	61	maid	48	"
G	Peirce Laura F—†	61	housewife	78	"

Mt Vernon Street—Continued

H	Talcott Lucy—†	61	maid	24	here
K	Carson Vera—†	61	"	38	"
L	Weare Charles A	61	retired	72	"
M	Weare Lillie C—†	61	housewife	65	"
N	Woun Margaret—†	61	cook	63	"
O	Boody Romaine	61	newswriter	25	"
P	DePalge Marie—†	62	nurse	24	"
R	McLeod Grace—†	62	cook	50	Brookline
S	Weeks Annie—†	62	maid	22	Canada
T	Wilson Germaine B—†	62	housewife	37	here
U	Wilson Phillip D	62	physician	38	"
V	Sweet Henry N	63	broker	60	"
X	Dupdale Henry A	63	valet	42	"
D	Arnold Sarah E—†	64	secretary	45	"
E	Collins Caroline M—†	64	housewife	69	"
F	Collins Walter H	64	clerk	74	"
G	Cooke Paul K—†	64	merchant	30	1006 Beacon
K	Cram Charles M	64	lawyer	55	here
H	Crocker Orilla A—†	64	housewife	75	"
L	Edwards John W	64	physician	56	287 Marginal
M	Farwell Robert B	64	civil engineer	53	here
N	Fiske Emma B—†	64	auditor	45	"
O	Robbins Anne M—†	64	stenographer	69	"
P	Whetherhult Martha—†	65	housewife	30	"
R	Crehore Alice B—†	65	"	64	295 Beacon
S	Crehore Morton S	65	treasurer	66	295 "
T	Ryan Anastasia—†	65	maid	32	Brookline
U	Baker Lillian—†	65	clerk	66	here
V	Wilcox Agnes—†	65	housewife	33	"
W	Wilcox Rolland C	65	architect	36	"
X	Merrick Pauline—†	65	housewife	61	"
Y	Hughes Julia H—†	65	housekeeper	29	"
Z	McIver Flora—†	65	housewife	66	"
A	Moses Sally P—†	65	real estate	41	"
B	Tilton Elizabeth—†	65	retired	56	"
C	Crocker Courtenay	65	lawyer	43	"
D	Ropes Alice—†	65	retired	39	"
E	Ropes Charlotte—†	65	music teacher	36	"
F	Crawford Mary C—†	65	real estate	51	"
G	Bradley Agnes S—†	66	housekeeper	31	"
H	Cooke Mary E—†	66	governess	41	Randolph

Mt Vernon Street—Continued

K	Kertz Louise—†	66	waitress	31	here
L	Shurtleff Arthur A	66	architect	53	"
M	Shurtleff Margaret—†	66	housewife	44	"
N	Weber Emile J	67	merchant	49	"
O	Weber Florence G—†	67	housewife	48	"
P	Malcotti Ida—†	67	domestic	25	"
R	Sewell Juanita H—†	67	retired	42	"
S	Philbrick Anna—†	67	"	78	"
T	Poor Mary M—†	67	"	50	"
U	Fombaron Marie—†	67	teacher	50	"
V	Watson Elizabeth S—†	67	housewife	67	"
W	Watson Florence—†	67	retired	60	"
X	Watson Thomas A	67	"	70	"
Y	Beard Elisa W—†	67	"	49	121 Marlboro
Z	Beard Mary—†	67	nurse	47	here
A	Beard Theodora—†	67	social worker	53	"
B	Turner Charles M	68	treasurer	43	"
C	Turner Elise—†	68	housewife	70	"
D	Carlson Edith—†	69	housemaid	20	Brookline
E	Craig Hellen M—†	69	housewife	60	here
F	Craig James W	69	banker	28	"
G	Ekberg Carl	69	butler	38	"
H	Ekberg Gerda—†	69	cook	38	"
K	Hall Esther—†	69	laundress	30	"
L	Sterling Marian—†	69	housemaid	60	"
N	Clark George	71	clerk	40	"
O	Leman Ella—†	71	housekeeper	60	"
P	Orr Clifford B	71	student	23	"
R	Pasko Kate—†	71	houseworker	50	"
S	Patchare Edwin	71	banker	60	"
T	Pevy Lester	71	clerk	40	"
U	Brien Margaret—†	73	cook	26	"
V	Curley Julia—†	73	laundress	50	"
W	Duval Hermine—†	73	dressmaker	54	"
X	Ford Annie—†	73	housemaid	30	Concord
Y	Mitchall Mary—†	73	waitress	26	here
Z	Wheelwright Mary C—†	73	housekeeper	45	"
A	Galacas Frederick R	74	insurance agent	50	"
B	Galacar Rosmond—†	74	housewife	46	"
C	Anderson Ingeborg—†	75	maid	25	Malden
D	Clancey Margaret—†	75	waitress	30	138 Beacon

Mt Vernon Street—Continued

E	Draper Benjamin H B	75	manufacturer	39	138 Beacon
F	Draper Queena—†	75	housewife	39	138 "
G	Geghan Delia—†	75	cook	30	138 "
H	Orr Jennie—†	75	waitress	24	138 "
K	Smith Juletta—†	75	nurse	23	138 "
P	Weston Betty—†	77	retired	22	here
R	Weston Byron	77	salesman	28	"
S	Weston Edith D—†	77	housekeeper	50	"
M	Hersey Heloise E—†	78	housewife	69	"
N	McEachen Sadie—†	78	maid	40	"
O	McKay Bessie—†	78	cook	52	71 Peter Parley rd
T	Doyle Catherine—†	79	laundress	32	621 Tremont
U	Gray Horace—†	79	housewife	50	here
V	Martin Bridget—†	79	waitress	30	Ireland
W	Murphy Rose—†	79	cook	50	Worcester
X	Bradley George M	80	salesman	45	here
Y	Cooke Atkins N	80	clerk	82	"
Z	Falardeau Reina M—†	80	music teacher	28	60 Pinckney
A	Hodge Harry M	80	clerk	50	here
B	Low Maria B—†	80	housewife	66	"
C	Low William C	80	salesman	69	"
D	Martin Adelaide M—†	80	secretary	60	44 Pinckney
E	Nay Ann S—†	80	housewife	34	here
F	Nay Winthrop S	80	real estate	35	"
G	Savelle Edith A—†	80	secretary	38	"
H	Whitcher Florence A—†	80	clerk	58	"
K	Wilson Ina B—†	80	"	58	"
L	Appleton Mary—†	81	housekeeper	66	310 Com av
M	Marks Mary—†	81	cook	45	310 "
N	McLennan Mary—†	81	waitress	29	Worcester
O	Blaney David	82	student	22	here
P	Blaney Dwight	82	artist	69	"
R	Blaney Edith—†	82	housewife	56	"
S	Blaney Margaret—†	82	student	25	"
T	Callahan Katherine F—†	82	domestic	34	"
U	Mahoney Mary—†	82	maid	24	"
V	Roberts Mary—†	82	cook	43	"
W	Cronin Mary—†	83	waitress	33	Brookline
X	Hart Margaret—†	83	maid	26	Cambridge
Y	Hegarty Annie—†	83	laundress	54	here
Z	Lawson Josephine—†	83	cook	36	Springfield

Mt Vernon Street—Continued

A	Sears Francis P	83	banker	55	here
B	Sears Maria—†	83	housewife	30	"
C	Sullivan Margaret—†	83	waitress	30	"
D	Swanson Rhoda—†	83	nurse	30	"
E	Hall Hilda A—†	85	cook	43	"
F	Johnston Ingrid—†	85	waitress	41	Sweden
G	Myers Ellen—†	85	maid	40	here
H	Sears Annie L—†	85	retired	60	"
K	Sears Evelyn J—†	85	"	48	"
L	Sears Mary P—†	85	"	58	"
M	Smith John	85	coachman	50	"
N	Sporrong Hannah—†	85	maid	50	"
O	Hillsmith Clara—†	86	housewife	35	"
P	Hillsmith Clarence	86	manufacturer	40	"
R	Gale Anna—†	86	housewife	48	"
R¹	Gale Edward	86	architect	50	"
S	Pope Charles K	86	student	23	"
T	Pope Elizabeth K—†	86	housewife	55	"
U	Pope Walter F	86	secretary	69	"
V	Pope William A	86	student	20	"
W	Balfe Mary J—†	87	cook	40	58 Lonsdale
X	Callinan Margaret—†	87	maid	40	here
Y	McNamarre Susan—†	87	waitress	35	"
Z	Paine Frank C	87	architect	33	"
Z¹	Paine Virginia—†	87	housewife	30	"
A	Wilson Jessie—†	87	maid	25	"
B	Fay Sarah B—†	88	housewife	68	Falmouth
C	Freivold Josephine—†	88	maid	48	304 Berkeley
D	Fritz Hulda—†	88	houseworker	49	here
E	Murphy Mary J—†	88	housekeeper	52	"
F	Rogers Isabel—†	88	houseworker	69	"
G	Tornfelt Ellen—†	88	housekeeper	42	"
H	Andrews Thomas	89	caretaker	36	Plymouth
K	Hornblower Hattie—†	89	housewife	57	Arlington
L	Hornblower Henry	89	broker	60	"
M	Bradley Charles F	90	retired	71	here
N	Bradley Mary E—†	90	housekeeper	53	"
O	Emery Annie K—†	90	none	58	"
P	Mubuman Margaret—†	90	maid	24	"
R	Ferguson Robert	91	banker	35	"
S	McKinnon Anastasia—†	92	maid	27	Canada

Mt Vernon Street—Continued

T	Williams Esther B—†	92	housewife	60	here
U	Williams Oliver E	92	broker	65	"
V	Williams Oliver E, jr	92	student	24	"
W	Williams Thomas	92	"	21	"
X	Brown Jennie—†	93	housewife	40	"
Y	Brown Sydney	93	chauffeur	41	"
Z	Brownlee Helen—†	93	maid	32	"
A	Dwyer Martha—†	93	cook	45	"
B	Smith Corinne E—†	93	housewife	48	"
C	Smith Frances G—†	93	student	20	"
D	Smith Joseph L	93	artist	62	"
E	Smith Rebecca S—†	93	housekeeper	22	"
F	Flynn Anna—†	94	maid	38	136 Marlboro
G	French Helen—†	94	housewife	45	here
H	French Hollis	94	engineer	53	"
K	Walsh Mary—†	94	maid	23	"
L	Chaffey Edwin	95	caretaker	43	"
M	Garfield Edith T—†	95	housewife	25	"
N	Garfield James	95	lawyer	33	"
O	Simson Isabelle—†	95	housewife	54	Brookline
P	Simson John D	95	manufacturer	25	"
R	Shaw Alice deV—†	95	housewife	39	here
S	Shaw Herbert B	95	clerk	36	"
T	Babcock Mary K—†	95	housewife	60	193 Salem
U	Babcock Samuel G	95	clergyman	72	496 Com av
V	Hincks Anne P—†	95	social worker	51	here
W	Dewey Jessica M—†	95	housewife	43	54 Pinckney
X	Dewey Walter E	95	accountant	45	54 "
Y	Lee Joseph	96	social worker	60	here
Z	Lee Joseph, jr	96	writer	22	"
A	Lee Susan M—†	96	teacher	23	"
Y	Cushman Josephine—†	98	student	21	34 Lime
Z	Cushman Mary R †	98	housewife	50	34 "
A	Cushman Robert	98	lawyer	51	34 "
B	Kunhardt George E	100	merchant	62	here
C	Kunhardt Harriot—†	100	student	23	"
D	Kunhardt Martha—†	100	housewife	55	"
E	Lawless Alice—†	100	maid	35	136 Beacon
F	Hansen Alma—†	102	student	27	here
G	Lynch Emily—†	102	housewife	38	"
H	Lynch Harry P	102	salesman	52	"

Mt Vernon Street—Continued

K	Wollett Christine—†	104	artist	39	here
L	Wollett Julia D—†	104	housewife	62	"
M	Wollett Sidney D	104	sculptor	35	"
O	Knapp Ethel M—†	110	storekeeper	41	18 W Cedar
P	Williams Alfred S	112	merchant	51	here
R	Williams Corinne H—†	112	student	23	"
S	Williams Maude K—†	112	housewife	47	"
X	Hillard Julia—†	116	housekeeper	87	"
Y	Hillard Sarah—†	116	"	85	"
Z	Knapp Martha W—†	116	"	54	"
A	Flayderman Edward	118	physician	24	Cambridge
B	Warren Elizabeth B—†	118	artist	32	18 W Cedar
C	Hunt Frank S	118	clerk	35	here
D	Turner John	118	engineer	34	Weston
F	Clements Collins C	118	author	25	Harvard
G	Hillyer Robert	118	"	25	Weston
H	Dunham Ruby—†	118	housewife	44	2 Brimmer

Pinckney Street

K	Derrah Thomas L	4	retired	57	here
L	Ham Agnes C—†	4	housekeeper	59	"
M	Ham John L	4	carpenter	69	"
N	Harrington Jeremiah T	4	printer	56	"
O	Hoel William H	4	janitor	68	"
P	Kendall Edward	4	salesman	52	"
R	Mackin Frederick E	4	"	70	"
S	Merton Margaret—†	4	dressmaker	54	"
T	Palmer Frances H—†	4	housewife	54	61 Chestnut
U	Palmer William L	4	geneologist	55	61 "
V	Smith Sarah E—†	4	dressmaker	55	here
W	Traverse Anthony J	4	barber	45	"
X	Paeff Anna N—†	6	music teacher	24	"
Y	Paeff Bashka—†	6	sculptor	27	"
Z	Paeff Fannie—†	6	housewife	60	"
A	Paeff Lewis	6	broker	65	"
B	Paeff Reba—†	6	student	21	"
C	Fong June	8	laundryman	42	"
E	Barnes Frank E	10	salesman	59	51 Hancock
F	Barnes Lucy E—†	10	saleswoman	46	51 "

Pinckney Street—Continued

G	Cleveland Frank E	10	salesman	63	here
H	Duncan James R	10	"	32	Newark N J
K	Feldman Hyman	10	draughtsman	28	Providence R I
L	Haggert John J	10	banker	43	243 Dor av
M	Haynes Charles F	10	lawyer	29	Lynn
N	King Nora—†	10	waitress	33	here
O	Lewis George R	10	painter	37	"
P	Mayo Henry A	10	chauffeur	40	"
R	Mayo Nellie I—†	10	housekeeper	38	"
S	Robbins Florence—†	10	dressmaker	41	54½ Temple
T	Robbins Walter E	10	tailor	51	54½ "
U	Allen Emma A—†	12	accountant	40	here
V	Geer Elizabeth L—†	12	school teacher	64	"
W	Geer Frank W	12	insurance agent	59	"
X	Geer Grace W—†	12	artist	69	"
Y	Abercrombie Margaret L–†	14	housekeeper	35	"
Z	Brown George E	14	insurance agent	67	60 Pinckney
A	Finney Harry W	14	broker	46	Barnstable
B	Healey John	14	retired	50	Pittsfield
C	Hill Florence—†	14	housekeeper	65	here
D	Hill Kate—†	14	librarian	63	"
E	McMullen Daniel	14	laborer	45	"
F	Pierce Florence—†	14	clerk	22	Dover N H
G	Small Frederick S	14	retired	76	22 Mt Vernon
H	Clark Esther—†	16	housewife	54	New Orleans
K	Clark Esther—†	16	clerk	20	"
L	Clark Nathaniel	16	manager	58	"
M	Harwood Agnes—†	16	clerk	55	Brookline
N	Hayes Helen—†	16	"	25	Pepperal
O	Stevenson Thomas	16	proofreader	69	Arlington
P	Sutherland John M	16	carpenter	58	here
R	Sutherland Lillian V—†	16	housewife	54	"
S	Sutherland Mary A—†	16	student	20	"
T	Burkett Belle—†	18	housekeeper	48	228 Newbury
U	Cahill Timothy	18	waiter	38	here
V	Cleaves Mary L—†	18	bookkeeper	30	"
W	Coffin Nora H—†	18	clerk	40	60 Pinckney
X	Cowan Charles	18	laborer	48	here
Y	Eckhart Ruth A—†	18	student	33	Brookline
Z	Kent Grace—†	18	saleswoman	28	New York
A	Sparling Clyde V	18	student	22	"

Pinckney Street—Continued

B	Fitzgibbons Robert	20	policeman	28	Cambridge
C	Harding Fred	20	fireman	25	St John N B
D	Hurley Bessie—†	20	saleswoman	22	here
E	Hurley Elizabeth—†	20	housekeeper	48	"
F	Lum King	20	laborer	30	New York
G	March David M	20	printer	27	Worcester
H	Petris Mary E—†	20	domestic	24	Taunton
K	Brooks Arthur C	22	author	30	here
L	Brooks Lousa K—†	22	bookkeeper	25	"
M	Brooks Mary J—†	22	housewife	65	"
N	Brooks William F	22	bookkeeper	75	"
O	Fennell Nora V—†	24	clerk	28	Hamilton
P	Lingard Olga—†	24	teacher	36	13 Louisburg sq
R	Parkhurst Dorothy—†	24	housewife	35	13 "
S	Neil Edmund C	30	professor	52	here
T	Neil Grace G—†	30	housekeeper	47	"
U	Holcombe Martha J—†	30	housewife	55	"
V	Holcombe Theodore G	30	secretary	25	"
W	Ayer Flora H—†	30	"	31	"
X	Hopson Pauline—†	30	clerk	35	"
Y	Morse Clara A—†	30	secretary	57	"
Z	Patrick Sarah L—†	30	stenographer	60	"
A	Chamberlain Allen	30	journalist	56	"
B	Chamberlain Grace M—†	30	housewife	56	"
C	Jenkins Charles D	36	inspector	60	"
D	Jenkins Josephine K—†	36	housewife	59	"
E	Jenkins Lawrence D	36	writer	34	"
F	Cragin Jean—†	36	accountant	45	Allston
G	Swain Mary L—†	36	secretary	46	"
H	Butler Charlotte W—†	36	artist	30	here
K	Butler Frances J—†	36	"	31	"
L	Forristall Charles L	40	roofer	50	"
M	Forristall Katherine—†	40	housekeeper	48	"
N	McNamee Helen J—†	40	bookkeeper	21	"
O	Allen Gordon	42	architect	47	"
P	Allen Harriott K—†	42	housewife	31	"
R	Blaisdell Glen R	44	salesman	26	"
S	Blaisdell Israel	44	clerk	36	"
T	Brown Charles S	44	bookkeeper	64	"
U	Brown Nina E—†	44	writer	62	"
V	Johnson Charlotte—†	44	housewife	25	Franklin

Pinckney Street—Continued

Letter.	FULL NAME.	Residence, April 1, 1924	Occupation.	Supposed Age.	Reported Residence, April 1, 1923. Street and Number.
w	Johnson Phillip R	44	lawyer	28	Franklin
x	Niles George R	44	tailor	45	here
y	Waterman Abbie J—†	44	housewife	69	"
z	Waterman Frank A	44	retired	71	"
A	Yerdon Etta—†	44	"	60	"
B	Kendall Barbara—†	46	student	43	"
C	Kendall Frederick—†	46	housewife	56	"
D	Sweeney Mary—†	46	domestic	22	Newburyport
E	Doyle Anna—†	48	housewife	43	here
F	Doyle Matthew	48	waiter	49	"
G	Gifford Gordon B	48	inspector	33	"
H	Gill Thomas H	48	clerk	47	"
K	Goldthwaite Willis	48	music teacher	50	"
L	Magoun Arthur	48	salesman	55	"
M	Mealey James F	48	cook	39	Florida
N	Pickett Frederick	48	printer	50	here
O	Brown Edith B—†	50	housekeeper	54	"
P	Kimball Mary F—†	50	retired	76	"
R	Delano Myrtle E—†	• 52	"	34	421 Marlboro
S	Dresser Mabel T—†	52	saleswoman	45	421 "
T	Jackson Caleb S	52	vice president	52	421 "
U	Sargent Adelaide J—†	52	housekeeper	80	Virginia
V	Klebs Sarah M—†	54	therapeutist	24	here
W	Halway Alice M—†	54	housewife	54	"
X	Halway Walter S	54	accountant	54	"
Y	Bensen Anna F—†	54	domestic	28	22 Prospect
Z	Droppers Cora R—†	54	teacher	23	64 W Cedar
A	Haskell Adelaide—†	56	housewife	30	99 Pinckney
B	Haskell Kenneth	56	lawyer	44	99 "
C	Kinsman Everett P	56	janitor	50	here
D	Kinsmore Marguerite—†	56	housewife	45	"
E	Watson Lawrence J	56	salesman	45	99 Pinckney
F	Bird Clara—†	58	lodging house	45	Cambridge
G	Brown Alice—†	58	bookkeeper	24	Ipswich
H	Donnelly Gale	58	salesman	48	Rochester N Y
K	Emmons Florence—†	58	housekeeper	50	83 Pinckney
L	Emmons Irwin	58	clerk	50	83 "
M	Epps John A	58	sign painter	55	here
N	Epps Judith—†	58	housewife	55	"
O	Goodstone Samuel	58	student	25	Pittsburgh Pa
P	Jarvis Robert	58	"	22	New Hampshire

Pinckney Street—Continued

R	Randalls Gertrude—†	58	nurse	24	Mass Gen Hosp
S	Roberts Royal	58	salesman	30	Wisconsin
T	Scott Ella—†	58	nurse	24	Mass Gen Hosp
U	Smith Andrew	58	salesman	50	New Jersey
V	Willis Walter	58	clerk	25	"
W	Bailey James W	60	lawyer	55	here
X	Brown George E	60	broker	67	"
Y	Edwards Harold M	60	advertising	40	"
Z	Gleason Henry C	60	dentist	53	"
A	Glencross Libby—†	60	saleswoman	32	"
B	Guild Herbert L	60	draughtsman	58	"
C	Hazelton William P	60	teacher	43	"
D	Kelly George F	60	broker	48	"
E	Kenney Emma M—†	60	lodging house	72	"
F	Kenney Henry M	60	retired	76	"
G	Wheatley Charles S	60	"	42	New Hampshire
H	Dodge Lilith W—†	62	housekeeper	30	here
K	Drowbridge Edward A	62	salesman	56	"
L	Estabrook John A	62	retired	72	"
M	Lord Adelaide E—†	62	housekeeper	65	"
N	Morse James T	62	retired	82	"
O	Pike Martha W—†	62	"	60	California
P	Wilbur Eva P—†	62	bookkeeper	36	here
R	Worthen Louisa W—†	62	social worker	35	"
S	Boudreau May—†	64	saleswoman	40	"
T	Boyle Betty—†	64	accountant	30	"
U	Eaton Arthur W	64	retired	70	"
V	Nelson Alice—†	64	housewife	54	"
W	Nelson Horatio	64	retired	74	"
X	Seymour Nettie—†	64	bookkeeper	25	Foxboro
Y	White Emma—†	64	"	60	here
A	White Lucy—†	64	"	65	"
B	Huntington Catherine S—†	66	teacher	36	"
C	Bailey Winifred—†	68	cook	24	44 Warwick
D	Parmenter Caroline W—†	68	housewife	30	here
E	Parmenter Derric C	68	physician	34	"
F	Turner Charles N	68	chauffeur	42	"
G	Crosby Marie—†	70	tel operator	24	83 Pinckney
H	Flynn Margaret—†	70	teacher	29	83 "
K	Fontaine Edgar	70	clerk	34	83 "
L	Getchell Ashton	70	manager	39	83 "

Pinckney Street—Continued

Letter.	FULL NAME.	Residence, April 1, 1924.	Occupation.	Supposed Age.	Reported Residence, April 1, 1923. Street and Number.
M	Mahoney Edna—†	70	secretary	25	83 Pinckney
N	Murphy Raymond	70	bookkeeper	24	Cambridge
O	Rivinius Augusta—†	70	lodging house	49	83 Pinckney
P	Smith Elmer	70	engineer	45	here
R	Swan Elizabeth—†	70	clerk	55	Florida
S	White Alice F—†	70	"	43	83 Pinckney
T	Barnaby John C	72	engineer	32	here
U	Brakely Brice	72	chauffeur	33	73 Pinckney
V	Briggs LeRoy J	72	"	33	here
W	Briggs Maria S—†	72	housekeeper	64	"
X	Cheney William	72	clergyman	72	105 Pinckney
Y	Coggeshall Thomas	72	banker	32	New York
Z	Dynes William	72	salesman	34	Vancouver
A	Minton Telfayer	72	secretary	64	here
B	Reed Charles	72	retired	72	"
C	Rueter Peter	72	engineer	32	Ohio
D	Sedgwick John H	72	editor	55	64 Mt Vernon
E	Seymour Rhoda—†	72	saleswoman	40	New Jersey
F	Bennett March G	74	manager	55	here
G	Henderson William	74½	architect	32	"
H	Allen George M	76	clerk	38	90 Pinckney
K	Blake Alfred	76	lawyer	27	New Hampshire
L	Brien James O	76	waiter	24	here
M	Fryer Mary—†	76	lodging house	59	"
N	Musgrove Cathrine—†	76	clerk	29	"
O	Rosen Abraham	76	printer	30	"
P	Sewall George N	76	clerk	42	18 Pinckney
R	Taylor George H	76	bookkeeper	44	here
S	Wrightson Cecil H	76	printer	45	"
T	Cuningham Stephen J	78	letter carrier	42	"
U	Gillette Annie B—†	78	housewife	56	"
V	Gillette Benjamin B	78	musician	59	"
W	Graham Caroline S—†	78	teacher	64	New York
X	Hamilton Berdie—†	78	student	30	N Carolina
Y	Hamilton Guy	78	"	32	"
Z	Keddie Albert	78	clerk	65	Melrose
A	Kopeland William	78	waiter	65	here
B	Wyatt Frederick E	78	master mariner	55	"
C	Greene Warwick	80	vice president	44	"
D	Macearchan Bessie—†	80	maid	38	Cambridge
E	MacInnis Mary—†	80	housekeeper	40	60 Quail

Pinckney Street—Continued

F	Baity Caorie—†	82	maid	24	Florida
G	Baity Jessie—†	82	"	22	here
H	Huntress George, jr	82	manufacturer	45	"
K	Huntress Gertrude—†	82	housewife	38	"
L	Thompson Mary—†	82	cook	31	Framingham
M	Thompson Thomas	82	student	29	"
N	Atwater Arlan R	84	vice treasurer	34	86 Pinckney
O	Atwater Conway—†	84	housewife	32	86 "
P	Haynes Lillian—†	84	maid	23	3 Wabon
R	Hughes Mary—†	84	nurse	23	here

Spruce Street

T	Edwards Mary—†	1	cook	45	here
U	Farquhar Frances—†	1	housewife	46	"
V	Farquhar Frederick	1	agent	46	"
W	Long Dorothy—†	1	maid	27	Nova Scotia
X	Nickerson Daniel	3	clerk	35	here
Y	Nickerson Hazel—†	3	housewife	29	"
Z	Hopkins Guida—†	3	secretary	35	851 Beacon
A	Hutchins Carol	3	agent	70	2 Walnut
B	Hutchins Florence—†	3	housewife	70	2 "
C	Ramsayer Annie G—†	3	retired	53	here
D	Green Clara—†	3	authoress	55	"
E	Green Nora—†	3	artist	61	"
F	Stewart Erwen	3	broker	32	22 W Cedar
G	Waldo Frederick	3	manager	40	22 "
H	Shaw Marion—†	3	artist	45	22 "
K	Craven Allen B	3	decorator	45	here
L	Horton Lydard	3	specialist	50	"
M	Cromett Eva—†	3	housewife	35	"
N	Cromett Orran J	3	agent	38	"
O	Peacock Anna—†	3	housewife	29	"
P	Peacock Harold	3	physician	35	"
R	Griffith Hugh	rear 3	steward	35	"
S	Griffith Zelma—†	" 3	housewife	36	"

Walnut Street

Letter	Full Name	Residence	Occupation	Age	Reported Residence
T	Crommett Elizabeth—†	1	domestic	40	here
U	Duggan Catherine—†	1	"	32	"
V	Mason Ellen F—†	1	retired	76	"
W	Mason Ida M—†	1	"	66	"
X	Moriarity Catherine—†	1	domestic	32	304 Marlboro
Y	Moriarity Nellie—†	1	"	32	Brookline
Z	Bowker Dexter	3	salesman	75	here
A	Bowman Edwin S	3	buyer	52	"
B	Foley Julia M—†	3	"	40	Hotel Touraine
C	Gardener Caroline—†	3	housewife	54	here
D	Gardner Lewis B	3	engraver	54	"
E	Goodmore Eliza—†	3	retired	56	Vermont
F	Hess Oscar C	3	collector	46	here
G	Housh Frank E	3	manufacturer	50	"
H	Housh Harriet—†	3	housewife	54	"
K	Manson George F	3	lawyer	58	"
L	Mayo Elizabeth—†	3	clerk	35	W Somerville
M	Raftery Harold	3	student	23	here
N	Reynolds Stanley C	3	agent	24	"
O	Stevens Beatty	3	advertising	40	121 Chestnut
P	White Leon H	3	cashier	45	here
R	Battle Jeannie—†	5	domestic	49	"
S	Libby Virginia—†	5	"	48	"
U	Clasbee Agnes C—†	9	secretary	40	Waltham
V	Martin Theresa—†	9	treasurer	40	Dorchester
W	Matthews Landon	9	decorator	31	here
X	Robie Lula—†	9	bookkeeper	41	"
Y	Segar George B	9	clerk	27	Brookline
Z	Underwood Mary E—†	9	secretary	32	here
A	Ways Carl K	9	manager	27	"
B	Cumming Edith P—†	11	lawyer	32	"
C	Davis Clifford R	11	agent	31	"
D	Davis Hazel H—†	11	housewife	29	"
E	Dion Eva L—†	11	clerk	29	Watertown
F	Duce Julia A—†	11	agent	30	here
G	O'Keefe Annie J—†	11	housekeeper	47	Maine
H	Preston Mary—†	11	housewife	50	here
K	Root Malcolm M	11	agent	35	"

Walnut Street—Continued

	Letter.	FULL NAME.	Residence	Occupation.	Age	Reported Residence
	L	Steinbach Edward S	11	engineer	36	here
	M	Brickett Christina—†	13	cook	57	"
	N	Holland Jennie—†	13	seamstress	56	Magnolia
	O	Walker Howard C	13	architect	65	here
	P	Walker Mary—†	13	housewife	63	"

West Cedar Street

	Letter.	FULL NAME.	Residence	Occupation.	Age	Reported Residence
	S	Eliot Abigail A—†	2	student	31	here
	T	Eliot Christopher R	2	banker	68	"
	R	Eliot Mary M—†	2	housewife	64	"
	U	McDonagh Rose—†	2	maid	48	"
	V	Whitman Marjorie—†	3	housewife	24	England
	W	Whitman William	3	publisher	24	"
	X	Wilkes Arthur	3	butler	36	"
	Y	Wilkes Elizabeth N—†	3	housewife	39	"
	Z	Boss Charles A	4	salesman	23	New London
	A	Edwards Arthur B	4	"	38	89 Pinckney
	B	Holden Joshua B	4	banker	59	128 Chestnut
	C	Paddock Arthur K	4	school teacher	58	30 "
	D	Pitkin Charles L	4	architect	40	here
	E	Royse Mary L—†	4	housewife	68	"
	F	Royse Vere	4	lodging house	62	"
	G	Weiss Hans	4	truant officer	39	"
	H	Woodworth Arthur V	4	school teacher	58	38 Chestnut
	K	Jones Eliot N	5	lawyer	49	here
	L	Jones Theodora B—†	5	housewife	45	"
	M	Kerrigan Mary—†	6	cook	29	62 Beacon
	N	Long Harriet—†	6	housewife	27	here
	O	Long William B	6	banker	38	"
	P	McGonigle Bridget—†	6	waitress	30	"
	R	O'Donnell Katharine—†	6	nursemaid	26	"
	S	Toland Rose—†	6	"	21	"
	T	Baker Sarah W—†	7	housewife	83	"
	U	DeCamp Edith F—†	7	teacher	55	"
	V	Lowney Annie—†	8	maid	52	"
	W	Lowney Elizabeth—†	8	cook	50	"
	X	Nutter Adeline R—†	8	housewife	89	"
	Y	Nutter George R	8	lawyer	60	"
	Z	Dubois Louise—†	9	governess	22	Belmont

West Cedar Street—Continued

A	Matales Alfred	9	manufacturer	38	here
B	Matales Constance—†	9	housewife	33	"
C	McCormick Maud—†	9	cook	27	Brookline
D	Smith Anna—†	9	waitress	26	Cambridge
E	Wadsworth Adelaide E—†	10	housewife	79	here
F	Walsh Ellen E—†	10	maid	54	24 Lawrence
G	Woodward Marion—†	10	nurse	36	here
H	Bird Elizabeth H—†	11	housewife	35	"
K	Bird Paul P	11	manager	45	"
L	McKinnon Laura—†	11	cook	30	20 Charles River sq
M	Garceau Albert	12	lawyer	53	here
N	Garceau Minnie B—†	12	housewife	47	"
O	Georgetti Adel—†	12	maid	65	"
P	Cameron Ida—†	13	waitress	20	Somerville
R	Hiebell Agnes—†	13	cook	40	New York
S	Hoar Dorothy B—†	13	housewife	30	"
T	McCann Louise—†	13	nurse	34	Lowell
U	Wheelwright John T	14	lawyer	69	279 Dartmouth
V	Wheelwright Mabel—†	14	housewife	47	279 "
W	Gardiner Eugenia—†	15	retired	71	here
X	Lorden Margaret—†	15	nurse	36	33 Mt Vernon
Y	Snelson Susan—†	15	housekeeper	45	here
Z	Clark Mary F—†	16	student	27	"
A	McNaughton Ellen—†	16	cook	27	9 Hereford
B	Nicholson Katherine—†	16	waitress	32	here
C	Richardson Homar B—†	16	housewife	57	"
D	Chase Anne—†	17	cook	46	Barnstable
E	Hornblower Elenor G—†	17	housewife	27	here
F	Hornblower Ralph	17	broker	33	"
G	McIsaac Katherine—†	17	domestic	23	Cambridge
H	Allen Frederick	18	printer	70	here
K	Blair Mary P—†	18	teacher	50	"
L	Crawford Isabelle—†	18	clerk	36	"
M	Crawford Julia—†	18	"	50	"
N	Dewese Ethel—†	18	artist	40	"
P	Finnott John F	18	caretaker	30	43 Mt Vernon
O	Foss Amy—†	18	social worker	40	here
R	Gant Marie L—†	18	student	23	31 Norway
S	Greeley Charlotte—†	18	housewife	70	here
T	Horner Clara—†	18	social worker	45	"
U	MacLeod Mary—†	18	nurse	30	"

West Cedar Street—Continued

V	McGrath Ethel—†	18	artist	48	here
W	McGrath Saul E	18	retired	58	"
X	McLaughlin John J	18	real estate	26	"
Y	Michener Mary—†	18	social worker	48	"
Z	Moore Frederick	18	banker	58	"
A	Moore Jane F—†	18	housewife	46	"
F	Smith Elecra—†	18	stenographer	58	"
G	Speelman Marie—†	18	student	28	26 Derne
B	Taylor Abbie F—†	18	housewife	63	here
C	Tetlow Helen R—†	18	teacher	47	"
D	Tinnerman Donald	18	clergyman	28	72 Mt Vernon
E	Tinnerman Lois—†	18	housewife	26	33 Norway
H	Baker Elizabeth J—†	19	teacher	46	here
K	Bird Anna B L—†	19	housewife	51	"
L	Bird Henry W	19	trustee	51	"
M	Boretti Ruth T—†	19	social worker	42	"
N	Cheney Mabel E—†	19	clerk	43	"
O	Clain Jessica H—†	19	"	42	"
P	Eager Julia A—†	19	"	45	"
R	Guild Florence—†	19	bookkeeper	46	"
S	Hall Virginia—†	19	genealogist	57	"
T	Mitchell Cora—†	19	retired	62	"
U	Powers Lilian D—†	19	stenographer	41	"
V	Spike Emily L—†	19	bookkeeper	50	"
W	Turner Ethel M—†	19	librarian	38	"
X	Warren Elisabeth B—†	19	illustrator	37	"
Y	McKenna Mary A—†	21	housekeeper	25	99 Revere
Z	McKenna William N	21	contractor	63	99 "
A	McKenna William N, jr	21	"	33	99 "
A¹	Connelly Christine—†	23	nurse	49	Hingham
B	Icabo Julia—†	23	cook	37	Cambridge
C	Sherburne Edward N	23	retired	43	here
D	Sherburne Mary G—†	23	housewife	41	"
E	Newman Ellen—†	25	nurse	60	"
F	Pierce Gabrielle—†	25	housewife	35	"
G	Prandergast Delia—†	25	clerk	25	Brookline
L	Crocker Emma L—†	27	housewife	61	here
M	Crocker George U	27	lawyer	61	"
N	Crocker Josephine—†	27	student	20	"
H	Anderson Olga—†	29	cook	25	107 Bay State rd
K	Benson Cerin—†	29	waitress	27	here

Page	Letter	Full Name.	Residence, April 1, 1924.	Occupation.	Supposed Age.	Reported Residence, April 1, 1925. Street and Number.

West Cedar Street—Continued

	o	Reed Chester A	29	retired	63	here
	p	Reed Fannie B—†	29	housewife	60	"
	r	Clark Davis W, jr	31	architect	40	"
	s	Clark Fannie J—†	31	housewife	60	"
	t	Clark William A	31	merchant	38	"

Willow Street

	u	Smith Beverley	9	caretaker	31	here
	v	Smith Ethel—†	9	housewife	28	"
	x	King Alice—†	17	"	36	"
	y	King James E	17	newspaperman	33	"
	z	Blaney Hannah—†	19	retired	63	"

Ward 8—Precinct 5

CITY OF BOSTON.

LIST OF RESIDENTS
20 YEARS OF AGE AND OVER

(FEMALES INDICATED BY DAGGER)

AS OF

APRIL 1, 1924

HERBERT A. WILSON, } Listing

JAMES F. EAGAN, } Board.

CITY OF BOSTON—PRINTING DEPARTMENT

Beacon Street

B	Makohin Jacob	68	retired	43	here	
C	Makohin Sue F—†	68	housewife	32	"	
D	Peterson Caroline D—†	68	retired	54	"	
E	Peterson Walter	68	coal dealer	60	"	
F	Ward Annie—†	68	domestic	45	"	
G	Black Elizabeth—†	68	"	43	155 Beacon	
H	Floete Mary T—†	68	housekeeper	50	California	
K	Olympeprieur Joan—†	68	maid	46	Brookline	
L	Walters Harriet—†	68	cook	45	107 Cabot	
M	Colle Elisa—†	68	domestic	50	here	
N	Cushing Caroline E—†	68	housekeeper	60	"	
O	Tucker Mary—†	68	cook	39	"	
P	Achterberg Minna—†	68	domestic	33	410 Beacon	
R	Brown Beatrice—†	68	"	23	Brookline	
S	Lyman Frank W	68	superintendent	42	S America	
T	Lyman Frieda B—†	68	housewife	38	"	
U	Lyman Jesse P	68	president	62	here	
V	Lyman Mary G—†	68	housewife	57	"	
W	Ostergren Lottie—†	68	domestic	38	"	
X	Flaherty Minnie—†	68	"	25	"	
Y	Green Delia—†	68	cook	29	8 Otis pl	
Z	Page Alice H—†	68	housekeeper	65	here	
A	Carter Mary—†	68	domestic	35	Brookline	
B	Lonergan Katherine—†	68	"	35	"	
C	McIntyre Alfred	68	publisher	37	"	
D	McIntyre Helen H—†	68	housekeeper	25	New Jersey	
E	Ellis Charles A	68	retired	65	here	
F	Walsh Alice M—†	68	domestic	44	"	
G	Walsh Mary A—†	68	housekeeper	49	"	
H	Anderson May—†	68	domestic	31	425 Com av	
K	Bergstrom Alva—†	68	"	26	here	
L	Merrill Edwin A	68	broker	50	"	
M	Merrill Sarah L S—†	68	housewife	48	"	
N	Howe Polly—†	68	"	24	490 Com av	
O	Howe William D	68	student	24	490 "	
P	MacDonald Frances—†	68	domestic	21	Brookline	
R	Mackenzie Mary—†	68	cook	50	Framingham	
S	Williams Eva M—†	68	nurse	45	Newtonville	
T	Back Bessie—†	68	cook	49	here	
U	Riely Annie M—†	68	retired	74	"	

Beacon Street—Continued

v	Riely William J	68	retired	74	here
w	Merrill Martha S—†	68	housewife	47	"
x	Merrill Sherburn M	68	retired	52	"
y	Wansberg Emma—†	68	domestic	29	"
z	Bagley Frederick P	68	manager	60	"
A	Bagley Grace H—†	68	housewife	56	"
B	MacLeod Laura—†	68	domestic	23	68 Com av
D	Mann Mary S—†	68	housewife	60	here
E	Greeley Grace G—†	68	"	51	410 Beacon
F	Greeley Norman F	68	trustee	53	410 "
G	Johnson Edith—†	68	domestic	25	Brookline
H	Kresek Alice—†	68	cook	46	"
K	Murphy Ellen—†	70	domestic	35	97 Beacon
L	Sullivan Mary—†	70	"	40	Brookline
M	Taft Edward A	70	lawyer	40	"
N	Taft Gertrude P—†	70	housewife	36	New York City
O	Beebe Frank H	71	retired	65	here
P	Bothwell Agnes—†	71	domestic	45	"
R	Clendining Jemima—†	71	"	63	"
S	McGrath Delia—†	71	"	65	"
T	Robinson Maude—†	71	housekeeper	60	"
U	Sullivan Annie—†	71	domestic	25	Newton
W	Amery Francis	73	banker	32	here
X	Amery Margaret—†	73	housewife	30	"
Y	Burke Nellie—†	73	nurse	29	"
Z	Gavin Alice—†	73	chambermaid	32	"
A	Murphy Mary—†	73	cook	38	"
B	Appleton William	74	physician	65	"
C	Flynn Elizabeth A—†	74	domestic	63	"
D	Foley Marcella—†	74	"	60	"
E	Cousins Alice—†	75	cook	54	"
F	Fitz Henrietta S—†	75	housewife	75	"
G	Goldborough Luccatta—†	75	housekeeper	60	"
H	Moran Mary—†	75	chambermaid	51	"
K	Shannon Anna—†	75	maid	43	"
L	Shannon Margaret—†	75	waitress	52	"
M	Darcy Julia—†	76	domestic	25	439 Marlboro
N	Dooley Ellen—†	76	"	40	here
O	Iasigi Annie G—†	76	retired	60	"
P	O'Connor Katherine—†	77	chambermaid	28	"
R	O'Connor Mary—†	77	cook	45	"

Beacon Street—Continued

s	Sigourney Edith—†	77	student	27	here
T	Sigourney Katherine—†	77	"	28	"
U	Sigourney Louise—†	77	housewife	56	"
V	Clancy Margarete—†	78	domestic	45	"
W	Edwards Catherine—†	78	teacher	26	"
X	Hall Laura—†	78	housewife	45	"
Y	Sears Madaline—†	78	retired	60	"
Z	MacDonald Mary—†	79	cook	42	298 Beacon
A	Shannon Marion—†	79	chambermaid	41	202 "
B	Sohier Eleanor—†	79	housekeeper	39	here
C	Sohier Elizabeth P—†	79	housewife	76	"
D	Sohier William D	79	lawyer	65	"
E	Wallis Harriet—†	79	seamstress	65	"
F	Burke Julia—†	80	domestic	60	"
G	Cote Rose—†	80	nurse	40	"
H	Faulkner Fannie M—†	80	retired	72	"
K	Hayes Margarete—†	80	domestic	55	"
L	Maher Nora—†	80	"	42	"
M	Sullivan Mary E—†	80	"	55	"
O	Dorr Henry G	82	retired	60	"
T	Grinell Charles E W	82	manager	50	"
P	Hanley John H	82	"	52	"
R	Hanley Mary E—†	82	housewife	60	"
S	Hession Eleanor W—†	82	stenographer	20	"
U	Ahern Margaret—†	84	domestic	34	"
V	Anderson Eleanor—†	84	"	30	"
W	Bucknole Jessie—†	84	"	40	"
X	Callahan Julia—†	84	"	45	"
Y	Fletcher Maxwell	84	houseman	30	"
Z	Jesburt Oloff—†	84	domestic	50	"
A	Lawson Ida—†	84	"	35	"
B	MacDonald Margaret—†	84	"	32	93 Mt Verno
C	McQuiggan Elizabeth—†	84	"	39	here
D	Raymond Margaret—†	84	"	40	"
E	Thayer Bayard	84	merchant	55	"
F	Thayer Nathaniel	84	lawyer	25	"
G	Thayer Ruth—†	84	none	27	"
H	Sears Henry F	86	retired	62	"
K	Sears Jean I—†	86	housewife	52	"
M	Johasson Anna—†	88	secretary	41	41 S Russell
N	Doucette Angelina—†	89	waitress	30	7 Chestnut

Beacon Street—Continued

Letter.	FULL NAME.	Residence, April 1, 1924	Occupation.	Supposed Age.	Reported Residence, April 1, 1923.
O	Flaherty Margaret—†	89	nurse	27	Manchester
P	Heaney Mary—†	89	laundress	40	"
R	MacDonald Catherine—†	89	maid	32	"
S	Putnam George	89	banker	34	here
T	Putnam Kathrine—†	89	housewife	32	"
U	Wimmer Anna—†	90	domestic	40	"
V	Ahearn Margaret—†	91	maid	35	"
V	Bennit Annie—†	91	cook	30	"
X	Emmons Helen—†	91	housewife	45	"
Y	Emmons Robert	91	retired	53	"
Z	Kane Nora—†	91	maid	23	"
A	Murphy Katie—†	91	chambermaid	33	"
B	O'Hare Mary—†	91	waitress	33	"
C	Straller Hedwig—†	91	maid	40	"
D	Brooks Clara—†	92	none	60	"
E	Ludwig Caroline—†	92	secretary	39	"
F	Lynch Mazzie—†	92	domestic	30	"
G	Mahoney Elizabeth—†	92	"	26	"
H	McFarland Mary—†	92	"	22	"
K	Petterson Betty—†	92	"	60	"
N	Bryant Nana M—†	94	retired	50	"
M	Gibson Ledore—†	94	none	35	"
O	Clark Thomas A	95	butler	30	"
P	Crosby Henrietta M—†	95	housewife	52	"
R	Crosby Stephen V R	95	broker	54	"
S	Doughty Constance—†	95	maid	30	225 Beacon
T	Grant Lucy—†	95	laundress	55	here
U	Kelley Catherine—†	95	chambermaid	40	"
V	Lisk Catherine—†	95	maid	35	"
W	McDonald Elizabeth—†	95	chambermaid	40	"
X	Scott Margaret—†	95	cook	42	"
Y	Burnham Johanna H—†	96	housekeeper	60	California
Z	Burnham Nina H—†	96	retired	34	"
A	Cullen Delia—†	96	domestic	55	Brookline
B	Farrell Nora—†	96	"	40	Watertown
C	Finnerty Ellen—†	96	"	45	Brookline
D	Johnson Elsie—†	96	"	31	Sweden
E	Mallay Katherine—†	96	"	43	California
F	Page Walter	96	butler	40	"
G	Dermody Annie—†	97	chambermaid	30	here
H	Dwyer Margaret—†	97	maid	26	Dedham

Page.	Letter.	FULL NAME.	Residence, April 1, 1924.	Occupation.	Supposed Age.	Reported Residence, April 1, 1923. Street and Number.

Beacon Street—Continued

K	Fleming Mary—†	97	waitress	26	255 Com av
L	Motley Miriam—†	97	housewife	45	here
M	O'Neill Delia—†	97	cook	35	"
N	Riley Annie—†	97	laundress	35	Hanover
O	Drinan Ellen—†	98	domestic	50	here
P	Machain George	98	butler	35	"
R	Machain Therese—†	98	domestic	35	219 Hamilton
S	Millar Louise—†	98	"	28	here
T	Murphy Catherine—†	98	"	50	"
U	Pickman Dudley L	98	retired	70	"
V	Pickman Dudley L, jr	98	lawyer	35	Europe
W	Pickman Ellen R—†	98	retired	68	here
X	Doran Daniel J	99	butler	46	"

Beaver Street

Z	Pearson Harold	15–19	chauffeur	33	here
A	Tonberg Carl	15–19	"	32	"
B	Livermore Harris	21–25	agent	40	"
C	Livermore Mildred—†	21–25	housewife	38	"
D	Langan Thomas	27–29	chauffeur	50	"
E	Langan Winifred E—†	27–29	stenographer	23	"
H	Parker Elizabeth—†	31–35	housewife	63	"
K	Parker Elizabeth—†	31–35	secretary	36	"
L	Parker Cornelia—†	31–35	artist	29	"
F	Wenmark Gertrude—†	31–35	housewife	32	"
G	Wenmark William	31–35	chauffeur	35	"

Brimmer Street

O	Doyle Marie R—†	2	housewife	38	here
P	Sharkey Elizabeth—†	2	teacher	26	"
R	Sharkey May A—†	2	editor	50	"
S	Sharkey Thaddeus	2	student	21	"
T	Talcott Melinda—†	2	editor	54	"
U	Fairfield Herbert G	2	insurance	53	101 Chestnut
V	Payne Arthur W	2	manager	52	here
W	Payne Carlotta—†	2	housewife	52	"
X	Pearson Hugh F	2	engineer	26	London Eng

Brimmer Street—Continued

Letter.	FULL NAME.	Residence, April 1, 1924.	Occupation.	Supposed Age.	Reported Residence, April 1, 1923. Street and Number.
A	Ormsby Alvin S	4	retired	50	California
B	Ormsby Rose E—†	4	housewife	74	Iowa
D	Field Caroline I—†	4	"	65	here
E	Field Robert H	4	news writer	55	"
F	Hanson Anna—†	5	cook	45	405 Com av
G	Paine John B, jr	5	student	21	Weston
H	Sandberg Augusta—†	5	waitress	52	125 Bay State rd
K	Codman John	5	real estate	25	90 Mt Vernon
L	Codman William C	5	"	60	90 "
M	Clarke Susan L—†	5	housewife	43	15 Brimmer
N	Furey Nellie—†	5	cook	34	15 "
O	Eliot Carol—†	5	nurse	25	here
P	Eliot Mary Y—†	5	housewife	55	"
R	Thayer Sadie—†	5	housemaid	30	37 Eliot
S	Trull Henrietta D—†	6	secretary	45	18 W Cedar
T	Trull Mary A—†	6	housewife	75	18 "
U	Trull Mary R—†	6	teacher	49	18 "
V	Trull Washington B	6	physician	85	18 "
W	Burroughs Caroline—†	6	housewife	77	18 "
X	Hobart Anna T—†	6	housekeeper	64	here
Y	Turner Frances E—†	6	librarian	55	"
Z	Cowell Eugene I	6	salesman	38	52 Charlesgate E
A	Robbins Harry C	6	"	33	Somerville
C	Flint John G	7	bookkeeper	21	here
D	Creamer Mary—†	8	chambermaid	48	Wakefield
E	Hourihan Nellie—†	8	cook	45	1575 Beacon
F	Lang Frances N—†	8	housewife	84	here
G	Lang Margaret R—†	8	"	56	"
H	McSharry Mary—†	8	maid	24	"
K	Ames Helen—†	9	housewife	60	"
L	Gilligan Mary—†	9	cook	40	Brookline
M	Leaf Hannah—†	9	waitress	29	here
N	McKay Alice—†	9	nurse	36	Watertown
O	Peterson Freda—†	9	chambermaid	45	here
P	Datcher Mary—†	10	maid	38	"
R	Reardon Mary—†	10	cook	41	"
T	Viaux Florence—†	10	housekeeper	45	"
S	Viaux Frederick H	10	retired	75	"
U	Viaux Victor	10	lawyer	49	"
V	Diskan Mary—†	11	waitress	36	"
W	Kane Annie—†	11	cook	42	"

Brimmer Street — Continued

x	Wheelwright Mary—†	11	housewife	89	here
x¹	Johnston Elizabeth—†	12	maid	26	Brookline
y	Munroe Elizabeth W—†	12	secretary	25	here
y¹	Munroe James P	12	manufacturer	61	"
z	Munroe Katherine W—†	12	housewife	61	"
c	Johnson Edla—†	14	maid	22	21 Marlboro
d	Johnson Ellen—†	14	cook	24	Brookline
e	Rogers Edwin A	14	manufacturer	65	here
f	Rogers Harriet G—†	14	housewife	55	"
g	Rogers Mildred R—†	14	secretary	32	"
k	Brown Frank C	16	architect	47	"
l	Brown Mabel S—†	16	housewife	45	"
m	Flaherty Julia—†	17	waitress	24	"
n	Flannary Frances—†	17	chambermaid	24	"
o	Hill Adam S	17	clerk	27	"
p	Hill Arthur D	17	lawyer	55	"
r	Hill Henrietta McL—†	17	housewife	50	"
s	Lydon Annie—†	17	maid	22	"
t	O'Hare Catherine—†	17	cook	40	"
u	Booker Frances—†	18	maid	23	Brookline
v	Place Marion—†	18	housewife	47	226 Bay State rd
w	Place Walter S	18	broker	51	226 "
x	Twyne Martha—†	18	cook	34	226 "
z	Bradley Leverett	20	broker	42	here
a	Bradley Susan H—†	20	housewife	73	"
b	Bradley Walter H	20	manufacturer	40	"
c	McDonald Sarah—†	20	cook	58	Lynn
d	Sutherland Margaret—†	20	maid	35	here
e	Cronin Julia—†	21	cook	47	"
f	Houghton Carrie—†	21	nurse	50	"
g	Mahoney Mary—†	21	waitress	35	"
h	Paine Helen—†	21	housewife	73	"
k	Paine Sarah—†	21	"	84	"
n	Codman Margarette B—†	24	"	40	"
o	Neffe Mae—†	25	nurse	42	"
p	Wells Albert B	25	optician	50	"
r	Wells Ethel—†	25	housewife	45	"
s	Howe Fannie O—†	26	"	54	"
t	Howe Mark DeW	26	editor	59	"
u	Howe Quincy	26	publisher	24	"
v	McClay Elizabeth—†	26	maid	38	"

Brimmer Street—Continued

w	Shea Bertha—†	26	cook	38	here
x	Oliver Andrew	27	teacher	54	"
y	Oliver Charles E	27	manufacturer	55	"
z	Oliver Edward P	27	accountant	50	"
a	Oliver Edwin L	27	physician	48	"
b	Oliver Susan L—†	27	housewife	84	"
c	Oliver Susan L—†	27	teacher	43	"
d	Evans Robert	28	clergyman	32	New York
e	Murfitt Emma—†	28	housekeeper	74	Michigan
f	Smith Alberta—†	28	"	51	"
g	Van Allen William H	28	clergyman	58	here
h	Coady Rebecca—†	29	waitress	39	"
k	Foley Minnie—†	29	cook	35	310 Com av
l	Howe Anne S—†	29	housewife	43	here
m	Howe Thorndike D	29	leather dealer	42	"
n	McFadden Grace—†	29	laundress	47	"
p	Forrest Bridget—†	31	cook	46	"
p¹	Forrest Margaret—†	31	housekeeper	44	"
r	Tarbell Arthur P	31	retired	69	"
s	McKinnon Mary—†	33	cook	38	"
t	Mercer Marjory—†	33	nurse	22	455 Cambridge
u	Putnam Delano F	33	lawyer	34	here
v	Putnam Dorothy—†	33	housewife	38	"
w	Steele Mary—†	33	waitress	27	"
x	Codman Catherine A—†	35	housewife	65	"
y	Connolly Annie—†	35	cook	30	"
z	Cushing Frances—†	35	laundress	34	"
a	Kelley Katherine—†	35	waitress	30	"
b	Madden Catherine—†	35	chambermaid	38	"
c	Erickson Agnes—†	37	waitress	32	Everett
d	Wells Irene—†	37	housewife	36	here
f	Brown Edward P	41	lawyer	27	"
g	Holmes Rachel E—†	41	waitress	26	119 W Brookline
h	O'Donnell Katherine—†	41	cook	40	2 Gloucester
k	Quinn Mary—†	41	laundress	73	Milton
l	Shean Mary—†	41	chambermaid	27	Beverly
m	Ware Mary L—†	41	housewife	65	here
n	Ereikainen Anna—†	44	maid	32	"
o	Morrison Emily—†	44	housewife	31	"
p	Ware Charles E	49	agent	40	"
r	Ware Elizabeth L—†	49	housewife	38	"

Brimmer Street—Continued

s	Frew Anna—†	50	cook	40	Brookline
t	Melholm Margaret—†	50	housekeeper	35	Cambridge
u	Peabody Frances—†	50	none	36	here
v	Felton Samuel	52	banker	35	"
w	Gibbons Nellie—†	52	maid	32	"
x	O'Rourke Mary—†	52	"	30	"
y	Whitcomb Carol S—†	52	housewife	49	31 Pilgrim rd
z	Whitcomb Howard	52	broker	53	31 "
a	Crowley Nora—†	54	cook	47	14 W Cedar
b	Walker Guy, jr	54	salesman	26	here
c	Lowell Alfred	56	lawyer	34	"
d	McCarthy Anna—†	56	cook	40	Somerville
f	McLean Mary—†	58	maid	32	England
g	Richman Arthur R	58	broker	26	here
h	Richman Arthur T	58	manager	56	"
k	McDonald Alzina—†	69	housekeeper	45	"
n	Pevear Ina C—†	71	housewife	37	"
o	Pevear Munroe R	71	engineer	47	"

Byron Street

s	Aydelotte Mabel D—†	2	housewife	44	here
t	Denney Sim C	2	student	28	"
u	Towle Annie F—†	2	maid	55	Brookline
v	Harding Charles	3	merchant	43	here
w	Harding Harriet—†	3	housewife	44	"
d	Noonan John A	10	clerk	26	"
e	Noonan Kathrine A—†	10	housewife	54	"
f	Noonan William J	10	chauffeur	54	"
g	Noonan William J, jr	10	clerk	24	"
l	Connolly Nellie—†	12 & 13	housewife	37	"
k	Connolly Patrick J	12 & 13	chauffeur	41	"
m	Burke James F	14	coachman	49	"
n	McDonald Daniel	15	"	40	"

Cedarlane Way

o	Gilligan James H	32	steamfitter	52	here
p	Gilligan Ralph	32	teamster	22	"

Cedarlane Way—Continued,

R	McGahey Anna E—†	34	housewife	38	here
S	McGahey Catherine—†	34	housekeeper	61	"
T	McGahey Robert	34	floorlayer	33	"
U	McGahey William	34	laborer	36	"
V	Kennedy Mary—†	36	cook	46	"
W	McCool Jennie—†	36	maid	35	"
X	Walker Ann—†	44	housewife	28	"
Y	Walker Joseph	44	merchant	32	"
Z	Mason Christine M—†	46	student	32	Springfield
A	Wilkins Margaret—†	46	"	29	Nebraska
B	Gudy Marjorie—†	46	decorator	29	here
C	Gudy Nanie—†	46	teacher	53	"
D	Pratt Marion D—†	48	secretary	33	39 Newbury
E	Jones Anne—†	48	housewife	51	here
F	Jones Ellen E—†	48	artist	35	"
G	Jones Marion—†	48	"	23	"
H	Nielsen Genne—†	48	teacher	46	"
K	Hill Ruth—†	50	editor	33	"
L	Stone Edward D	50	draughtsman	22	"
M	Cusick William	50	architect	32	"
N	McDonough Clarence J	50	"	22	"

Charles Street

X	Edmands Louise—†	38	clerk	38	here
Y	Adams Elizabeth—†	38	housewife	35	"
Z	Adams Sherred W—†	38	teacher	40	"
A	Joyce Althea C—†	38	housewife	38	44 Charles
B	Joyce Peter J	38	manufacturer	38	44 "
E	Drown Betty—†	42	weaver	24	Philadelphia
F	Drown Mary B—†	42	housewife	62	"
G	deFlorez Fannie—†	42	"	32	here
H	deFlorez Louis	42	salesman	36	"
K	Vogelgesang Sheppard	42	student	21	"
L	Neale Floyd	42	manager	37	New York
N	McDermott William T	44	real estate	37	here
O	Wright Anna—†	44	housewife	49	23 S Russell
P	Wright William	44	sawmaker	51	23 "
V	Baker Amos P	48	retired	79	here
W	Jardel Josephine M—†	48	housewife	61	"

Charles Street—Continued

B	Knowles John A	58	cotton broker	47	Cohasset
L	Fernald Fred C	69	lawyer	30	here
M	Fernald Lilian H—†	69	housewife	28	"
N	Hunting Joseph H	69	sexton	54	"
O	Hunting Mary F—†	69	housewife	45	"
P	Joslin Mary R—†	71	houseworker	47	"
R	Joslin Rebecca R—†	71	housekeeper	55	"
S	Adams Curtiss	73	painter	35	"
T	Bartlett John	73	engineer	60	50 Clarendon
U	Bremner Harry	73	jeweler	50	here
V	Carver Edward	73	butler	35	153 Beacon
W	Connors Catherine—†	73	retired	60	here
X	Custeau Julia—†	73	waitress	23	"
Y	Deering Joseph	73	clerk	25	237 Princeton
Z	Farrell Alice—†	73	housewife	38	here
A	Farrell Thomas	73	collector	42	"
B	Murry Harry	73	leather worker	40	"
C	White Mathew	73	janitor	50	"
F	Brouillette Frances—†	75	housewife	24	77A Charles
G	Brouillette Jean D	75	chemist	26	77A "
D	Macomber Doris—†	75	housewife	46	here
E	Macomber Walter	75	artist	30	Waltham
H	Orr Clement W	75	manager	34	1A Acorn
K	Orr Margaret G—†	75	houseworker	34	1A "
L	Richards Bertha—†	75	housewife	64	Scituate
M	Sumner May A—†	75	"	45	"
O	Mullane William J	77	storekeeper	48	117 Pinckney
P	Gardner Margaret C—†	77A	houseworker	52	New Hampshire
R	Gardner Roy R	77A	teacher	51	"
S	Needham Caroline F—†	77A	"	60	here
T	Piston Catherine N—†	77A	housewife	31	"
T¹	Piston Walter H	77A	musician	30	"
U	Simmons Eva L—†	77A	social worker	44	92B Pinckney
Y	Colt Amy L—†	79	none	20	96 Mt Vernon
Z	Colt Charles C	79	newspapers	22	Cambridge
A	DeBeauvivier Andre	79	teacher	27	47 Hancock
B	Fishelson Max	79	florist	32	here
C	Fishelson Rebecca—†	79	housewife	29	"
D	Hartman Henry E	79	teacher	27	47 Hancock
E	Kennard Irma—†	79	housewife	45	here
F	Libby John M	79	electrician	31	5 Paulding

Charles Street—Continued

G	Snow Thomas	81	retired	50	here
H	Haggerty John	81	janitor	75	"
K	Parks Bessie—†	81	domestic	43	319 Tremont
L	Parks Walter C	81	window cleaner	32	319 "
M	Goss Fredrick	81	tailor	76	here
N	Goss Victoria—†	81	housewife	60	"
O	Mahoney James J	81	painter	50	"
P	Mahoney Margaret—†	81	houseworker	35	"
S	Hart John H	83	laborer	55	"
T	Hart Mary E—†	83	housewife	55	"
U	Hart James A	83	teamster	25	"
V	Hart Mary—†	83	clerk	22	"
W	Ames Louise L—†	84	housewife	41	"
X	Ames Owen B	84	physician	47	"
Y	Bonner Adlena—†	84	nurse	33	"
Z	Coleman Abigail—†	84	retired	71	"
A	Crowhurst Mary—†	84	bookkeeper	47	"
B	Dorman Ella—†	84	nurse	29	"
C	Hall Ida—†	84	housekeeper	62	"
D	Haywood Victoria—†	84	nurse	34	"
E	Holdahl Stena—†	84	dietitian	33	St Paul Minn
F	Kendall Edward	84	retired	78	here
G	Shaw Louise—†	84	"	60	"
H	Witter Clarence J	84	clerk	51	"
K	Witter Lilla—†	84	housewife	45	"
M	Caswell Margaret—†	86	writer	34	"
N	Caswell Muriel—†	86	"	31	"
O	Fod Charles	86	engineer	49	Salem
P	Hall Harriet E—†	86	collector	65	here
R	Loomis Charles O	86	physician	67	"
S	Loomis Sue E—†	86	housewife	49	"
T	Parker Charles A	86	reporter	48	"
U	Ruggles Mary A—†	86	secretary	42	"
V	Stewart Belle—†	86	houseworker	46	"
W	Atkinson Richard	88	architect	65	Troy N Y
X	Cotty Jessie—†	88	bookkeeper	40	Plymouth
Y	Devine Frances—†	88	nurse	40	Lynn
Z	Dole Annie—†	88	housekeeper	75	here
A	Glass Sarah—†	88	nurse	38	Arkansas
B	Homer Alfred	88	organist	26	here
C	Johnson Statari—†	88	nurse	24	Mass Gen Hosp

Charles Street—Continued

D	Morill Edith—†	88	bookkeeper	48	here
E	Shea Katherine—†	88	nurse	45	Illinois
F	Thomas Janette—†	88	"	30	here
G	West Helen—†	88	bookkeeper	33	Arizona
H	Whitney Myra—†	88	nurse	42	here
L	Bellis Mary—†	90	maid	21	"
N	Sutherland Jean—†	90	"	23	"
M	Tuttle Katherine—†	90	"	22	"
O	Welsh Julia—†	90	"	22	"
S	Anderson Margaret—†	92	nurse	22	"
T	Ball Marsia A—†	92	"	21	"
U	Brown Bessie C—†	92	matron	35	"
V	Brown Lucia—†	92	"	54	"
W	Burns Ethel—†	92	maid	21	Ireland
X	Carter Marie P—†	92	nurse	22	here
Y	Flynn Mary M—†	92	"	23	"
Z	Forsander Edith—†	92	"	21	"
A	Glean Agnes E—†	92	"	21	"
B	Goggin Margaret—†	92	maid	30	"
C	Hall Charlotte J—†	92	nurse	23	"
D	Haskins Lena E—†	92	"	22	"
E	Johnson Theodora—†	92	maid	50	170 Charles
F	Jones George J	92	houseman	58	here
G	Lambert Lillian—†	92	maid	24	Brockton
H	Lambert Muriel—†	92	"	20	New Brunswick
K	MacLeod Irene J—†	92	nurse	21	here
L	Menand Adelaide J—†	92	"	22	"
M	Merrell Charlotte—†	92	"	22	"
N	Miller Helen G—†	92	maid	21	Nova Scotia
O	Moore Ella D—†	92	nurse	23	here
P	Nash Charlotte—†	92	"	25	"
R	Park Sybil M—†	92	maid	21	City Hospital
S	Raymond Annie—†	92	"	57	170 Charles
T	Riggs Nellie E—†	92	nurse	21	here
U	Romkey Nellie—†	92	"	20	"
V	Wall Joan—†	92	maid	50	170 Charles
W	Wigglesworth Anna L—†	92	nurse	22	here
X	Wilson Della B—†	92	maid	23	72 Clarendon
Y	Bryant Charles	94	salesman	65	here
Z	Miller Cecelia F—†	94	bookkeeper	32	"
A	Miller Gertrude J—†	94	dressmaker	34	"

Charles Street—Continued

B	Miller Joseph	94	tailor	70	here
C	Miller Joseph T	94	letter carrier	30	"
D	Miller Lawrence E	94	salesman	28	"
E	Paynor Louis	94	"	35	"
F	Stringer Charles	94	antiques	60	"
G	Brown Annie I—†	96	housewife	42	121 Beacon
H	Brown Paul F	96	artist	51	121 "
K	Jones Mildred S—†	96	superintendent	57	here
L	LaBelle Louis	96	retired	55	"
M	LaBelle Mary—†	96	housewife	60	"
N	Palmer Seraph E—†	96	retired	82	"
O	Perry Serena F—†	96	"	77	41 Pinckney
P	Reynolds Ida G—†	96	clerk	40	83 "
R	Ross Lena—†	96	"	40	here
S	Shepard Caroline T—†	96	housekeeper	53	"
U	Boyden Florence D—†	98	stenographer	50	"
V	Codman William	98	real estate	65	"
W	Haley Josephine T—†	98	housekeeper	21	"
X	McCana John	98	salesman	40	Somerville
Y	Sanborn Addie C—†	98	bookkeeper	50	here
Z	Singer Gertrude—†	98	clerk	36	"
A	Talbot Julia—†	98	dressmaker	55	"
B	Schultz Samuel A	99	tailor	42	"
O	Leverson Jacob	99	laborer	45	42 Cambridge
P	Miller William	99	nurse	28	Revere
R	Murray Bridget—†	99	housekeeper	40	here
C	Grogan Anna—†	99	tel operator	22	91 Jamaica
D	Grogan Catherine—†	99	stenographer	24	91 "
E	Grogan Hannah R—†	99	housewife	54	91 "
F	Grogan James R	99	shipper	56	91 "
G	Grogan Margaret—†	99	storekeeper	26	91 "
H	Hartin Alice—†	99	houseworker	52	here
K	Hartin Anna F—†	99	"	32	"
L	Kenney Patrick	99	molder	42	"
M	McGuirk Patrick	99	"	50	"
N	Sherry Edward	99	laborer	75	"
S	Chin Kwong	99A	laundryman	42	"
U	Spilane Margaret—†	101	storekeeper	46	"
V	Von Blomberg Adelheid	101	teacher	61	"
V¹	Von Blomberg Eva—†	101	"	68	"
W	Burke James A	101	steamfitter	35	"

Charles Street—Continued

X	Connors Alice J—†	101	houseworker	37	here
Y	Connors Horace G	101	salesman	34	"
Z	Connors Josephine—†	101	housekeeper	70	"
B	Anderson Ava B—†	102	"	65	"
C	Aurelio William G	102	teacher	55	"
D	Clapp Mary L—†	102	housekeeper	60	"
E	Craig Alfred S	102	engineer	28	"
F	Gibbon Eleanor—†	102	dressmaker	80	"
G	Lever Emma V—†	102	retired	64	"
H	Pierpont Annie—†	102	bookkeeper	57	"
K	Sinclair Lillian—†	102	dressmaker	40	W Hanson
L	Webber Annie—†	103	houseworker	41	Malden
M	Douglass Florence—†	103	"	35	here
N	Morrison Ruby—†	103	"	35	"
O	Dulles Eleanor L—†	103	student	28	New York
P	Huntington Emily H—†	103	"	28	San Francisco
R	Doherty Edward	103	stableman	62	15 Monument av
S	Doherty Margaret T—†	103	housewife	42	15 "
T	Kaufman Annie J—†	103	"	42	here
U	Kaufman Samuel	103	machinist	45	"
W	Rowe Ernest B	105	lawyer	32	109 Charles
X	Rowe Grace B—†	105	housewife	24	109 "
Y	Palmer Franklin H	105	broker	40	Brookline
Z	Austin Alice—†	105	artist	61	384 Boylston
A	Austin Leonora—†	105	teacher	63	122 Hunt'n a
B	Adams Helen J—†	105	houseworker	38	46 Cedarlane way
C	O'Toole Emma—†	105	hairdresser	49	46 "
D	Jansen Harriet—†	107	housewife	22	50 Peterboro
E	Smith Caroline—†	107	houseworker	77	50 "
F	Sigourney Augusta—†	107	housewife	26	Belmont
G	Sigourney David	107	broker	28	"
H	Carter Edward D	107	banker	42	10 Hemenway
K	Carter Wilmia D—†	107	housewife	38	10 "
L	Desmond Anna—†	107	secretary	25	41 S Russell
M	Durell Elsie A—†	109	housewife	34	here
N	Durell Ralph B	109	manufacturer	34	"
O	Thayer Lucy C—†	109	buyer	30	40 Com av
P	Hobart Charles H	109	correspondent	23	79 Charles
R	Hobart Ethel G—†	109	advertising	42	79 "
S	Trease Hurxthal F	109	engineer	24	Canton O
T	Trease Marjorie E—†	109	housewife	27	"

Charles Street—Continued

U	Coolidge Allison—†	110	housewife	24	here
V	Coolidge Charles A	110	lawyer	29	"
W	McKinnon Catherine—†	110	chambermaid	22	54 Com av
X	Grinnell Blanche S—†	110	housekeeper	56	Scituate
Y	Grinnell Charles T	110	manufacturer	59	"
Z	Webber Eugene L	110	manager	47	here
A	Webber Pamelia G—†	110	housekeeper	49	"
B	Morse Caroline E—†	110	school teacher	66	"
D	Power Ethel B—†	112	editor	35	"
E	Raymond Eleanor—†	112	architect	35	"
F	Raymond Josephine M—†	112	housewife	73	"
G	Raymond Rachel C—†	112	decorator	29	"
K	Brassard Laura M—†	118	tel operator	28	"
L	Campbell Rose—†	118	cook	47	Nova Scotia
M	Clifford Hope A—†	118	saleswoman	49	here
N	Forrest William D	118	author	54	"
O	Graves Mabel S—†	118	dressmaker	51	"
P	Graves Rupert A	118	builder	56	"
R	Higgins John J	118	boatmaker	57	"
S	Ilsley Letitia—†	118	housekeeper	78	"
T	Larson Hilmer	118	attendant	38	"
U	LeGard Gladys—†	118	waitress	32	"
V	Linnell Augustine—†	118	dressmaker	52	"
W	Sabin Edwin A	118	music teacher	65	"
X	Bennett Jessie—†	120	nurse	35	"
Y	Cunningham John	120	janitor	58	"
Z	Dailey Margaret—†	120	saleswoman	43	"
A	Elliott Susan M—†	120	retired	70	"
B	Frost Angelina—†	120	housekeeper	79	"
C	Kerigan Marie—†	120	dressmaker	35	"
D	Moran Bessie T—†	120	milliner	48	"
E	Moran Ella M—†	120	decorator	50	"
F	Moran Mary—†	120	housekeeper	76	"
G	Paul George	120	chauffeur	40	"
H	Watts Elizabeth—†	120	stenographer	56	"
M	Dunton Florence P—†	132	housekeeper	43	Spencer
L	Safford Margarita—†	132	saleswoman	44	175 Dartmouth
N	Ferguson James	132	student	20	Plymouth
O	Mabbett Harry I	132	manufacturer	37	"
P	Smith Frances E—†	134	housewife	22	Cambridge
R	Smith Frank F	134	physician	29	"

8—5

Charles Street—Continued

s	Odlin Emily C—†	134	housewife	47	56 Charlesgate East
T	Odlin Joseph	134	broker	46	56 "
G	Abbott Jessie—†	170	attendant	28	here
H	Allen Callie B—†	170	student	39	Michigan
K	Anderson Selina —†	170	nurse	38	here
L	Barrett Eva F—†	170	"	25	Milton
M	Beaman Alice—†	170	"	25	Waltham
N	Blackmer Katherine—†	170	"	23	Melrose
P	Bremner Ruby—†	170	attendant	22	here
O	Brennan Rose—†	170	maid	41	"
R	Carter Bridie—†	170	nurse	32	"
S	Crosby Nellie—†	170	housekeeper	44	Wellesley
T	Crowley Mary—†	170	waitress	44	here
T¹	Cunningham Mary—†	170	nurse	44	"
U	David Florence E—†	170	"	23	619 Com av
V	Dowland Anna—†	170	"	23	here
W	Ellis Gladys—†	170	student	25	Kansas
X	Farrell Mollie A—†	170	nurse	30	Maine
Y	Fitzgerald Eleanor—†	170	"	23	32 Fruit
Z	Gaulin Albertine—†	170	waitress	31	Worcester
A	Glynn Annie—†	170	laundress	23	73 "
C	Goode Annie—†	170	maid	50	here
D	Goodwin Rose B—†	170	nurse	24	Melrose
E	Gorman Agnes—†	170	matron	40	here
B	Grant Sarah—†	170	laundress	48	"
F	Gray Annie D—†	170	nurse	21	Melrose
G	Gribben Natalie—†	170	"	25	734 Columbia rd
H	Grollig Clara P—†	170	"	32	here
K	Harney Mary—†	170	maid	29	Salem
L	Hayden Mary—†	170	nurse	33	here
M	Healey Mazie—†	170	"	25	"
N	Helmstetter Gevena—†	170	"	30	"
O	Hurley Annie—†	170	matron	50	"
P	Huth Esther—†	170	nurse	26	"
R	Johnson Lillian P—†	170	student	21	"
S	Johnson Theodora—†	170	attendant	50	"
T	Kelleher Teresa J—†	170	nurse	29	202 W Newton
U	Leach Geneva—†	170	supervisor	25	Nashville Tenn
V	Leavitt Mabel—†	170	nurse	23	Somerville
W	Lockwood Maud E—†	170	"	21	Melrose
X	Long Florence—†	170	student	29	Illinois

Charles Street—Continued

Letter.	FULL NAME.	Res.	Occupation.	Age	Reported Residence
Y	Mack Mary—†	170	laundress	54	here
z	MacQuarrie Christine —†	170	supervisor	26	"
A	Massley Mary—†	170	waitress	21	Medfield
B	McAuliffe Annie—†	170	maid	50	here
C	McDonald Catherine—†	170	"	23	75 Clarendon
D	McDonald Ida H—†	170	nurse	30	Maine
E	McGloughton Kate—†	170	laundress	36	here
F	McGuire Loretta—†	170	nurse	26	"
G	Morrisey Florence—†	170	anesthetist	40	"
H	Morrissey Mary—†	170	laundress	45	"
K	Mungorin Mary—†	170	seamstress	48	"
L	Nelson Emma—†	170	instructor	26	Colorado
M	Ouran Ina—†	170	nurse	23	Ipswich
N	Padelford Doris—†	170	dietician	23	Connecticut
O	Patton Agnes G—†	170	clerk	28	32 Fruit
P	Potter Helen O—†	170	superintendent	36	35 N Anderson
R	Raymond Annie—†	170	attendant	57	here
S	Reynolds Bessie—†	170	maid	40	"
T	Ryan Nora—†	170	nurse	32	25 Astor
U	Ryder Jessie E—†	170	clerk	40	Vermont
V	Scannell Mary J—†	170	maid	40	New York
W	Shea Emma—†	170	supervisor	36	Somerville
Y	Smiley Rodena—†	170	nurse	27	here
Z	Smith Olive E—†	170	"	23	Melrose
X	Sparkhawk Margaret —†	170	"	20	Waltham
A	Sullivan Annie—†	170	laundress	60	Westwood
B	Sullivan Mary J—†	170	nurse	30	Waltham
C	Teed Frances M—†	170	laundress	62	553 Wash'n
D	Trijko Alice —†	170	maid	20	E Dedham
E	Vance Ina B—†	170	anesthetist	26	Brookline
F	Wall Joan—†	170	maid	50	here
G	Wilkerson Myrtle B—†	170	student	26	Kansas
H	Winters Frances L—†	170	anesthetist	23	32 Fruit

Charles River Square

Letter.	FULL NAME.	Res.	Occupation.	Age	Reported Residence
K	Goldthwait Jessie S R—†	1	housewife	56	here
L	Goldthwait Joel E	1	physician	57	"
M	Goldthwait Margrett R—†	1	student	24	"
N	McAlinden Bridget—†	1	housemaid	26	16 Bynner

19

Charles River Square—Continued

O	MacDonald Emma—†	1	housemaid	21	here
P	McNeil Mary—†	1	cook	40	Canada
R	Gurnett Daniel W	3	banker	40	here
S	Gurnett Mary E—†	3	housewife	36	"
T	Heggins Catherine—†	3	maid	33	"
U	Quincy Edmond	4	student	20	Cambridge
V	Quincy Mary—†	4	retired	49	here
W	Santeen Angelo	4	cook	30	Sudbury
X	Greenslat Ella S H—†	5	housewife	50	here
Y	Greenslat Ferris	5	publisher	49	"
Z	MacDonald Margrett—†	5	maid	36	"
A	MacIsaac Clementina—†	5	cook	50	"
B	Long Bridie—†	6	"	23	9 Shepherd a
C	Smith Roseman H—†	6	retired	40	here
D	Stoney Louisa—†	6	school teacher	35	"
E	Atherton Louise—†	7	housewife	42	"
F	Atherton Percey	7	lawyer	45	"
K	Linton Emmie—†	8	waitress	30	Cambridge
G	Vose Elizabeth—†	8	retired	46	here
H	Vose Louis	8	manufacturer	50	"
L	Albert Amelia—†	9	nurse	43	"
M	Gilbert Elizebeth—†	9	housewife	23	"
N	Gilbert Percival	9	banker	38	"
O	Lardner Margret—†	9	cook	35	72 Marlboro
P	Costello Delia—†	10	"	25	Brookline
R	Donegan Margrett—†	10	"	25	22 Brimmer
S	Foret Louise—†	10	nurse	25	here
T	Pillbury Hellen F—†	10	retired	38	"
U	Pillbury Samuil H	10	lawyer	48	"
V	MacIsaac Catherine M—†	12	maid	23	Canada
W	Maclaurin Alice—†	12	retired	45	here
X	McDonald Margaret—†	12	maid	48	91½ Concord
Y	Keyes Idelle—†	14	retired	70	here
Z	Kimball Idelle M C—†	14	"	39	"
A	Kimball William O	14	banker	46	"
B	Spaulding Maud—†	14	maid	28	"
C	Coale Elizabeth—†	15	housewife	60	"
D	Coale George O G	15	lawyer	67	"
E	Desmond Anna—†	15	cook	28	"
F	MacIntyre Wanda—†	15	maid	23	12 Charles River sq
G	Miller James	16	manufacturer	50	here

Charles River Square—Continued

Letter.	FULL NAME.	Residence	Occupation	Age	Reported Residence
H	Miller Margret W—†	16	retired	33	here
K	Morrison Helen—†	16	waitress	30	"
L	Vance Christina K—†	16	nurse	28	"
M	Young Margaret—†	16	cook	20	Brookline
N	Beamish Mary—†	18	maid	34	here
O	Hopkins Helen B—†	18	retired	50	"
P	Hopkins Woolsey R	18	scout master	30	"
R	Gay Joan—†	19	cook	32	285 Marlboro
S	Knox Alaxender	19	student	22	here
T	Knox Edith—†	19	housewife	50	"
U	Knox Samuel G	19	engineer	60	"
V	Paige Jessie S—†	19	waitress	25	285 Marlboro
W	Allen Seabury W	20	physician	47	here
X	Allen Winnie—†	20	retired	40	"
Y	Bauer Julia—†	20	cook	24	Brookline
Z	Clark Ellen—†	20	maid	28	Cambridge
C	Spring Rommey	21	lawyer	60	"
A	MacKay Mary—†	22	maid	26	"
B	McLean Catherine—†	22	cook	28	"
D	Stuart Agnes B—†	22	retired	33	"
E	Stuart Harrold C	22	physician	32	"
F	Gavin Delia—†	23	cook	46	Brookline
G	McDermitt Marie—†	23	waitress	22	"
H	Robinson Arthur L, jr	23	manufacturer	29	here
K	Robinson Hortense—†	23	housewife	31	"

Chestnut Street

Letter.	FULL NAME.	Residence	Occupation	Age	Reported Residence
M	Griffin James J	65	chauffeur	26	here
O	Smith Charles	67	"	58	"
P	Smith Mary W—†	67	housewife	52	"
R	Williston Constance—†	67A	teacher	51	40 Com av
S	Durborow Lawrence	67A	advertising	39	Indiana
T	Durborow Sara—†	67A	housewife	35	"
U	Tetlow Elizabeth H—†	67A	teacher	49	here
V	Baker Isabel—†	67A	retired	54	"
A	Fordan Jenney—†	77	housewife	42	"
B	Fordan John	77	chauffeur	55	"
F	Perkins Dorlores—†	81	housewife	24	"
G	Perkins Thomas C	81	banker	52	"

Chestnut Street—Continued

H	Kennard Asa W	82	jeweler	53	here
K	Kennard John P	82	broker	21	"
M	Orswell Jessamine J—†	82	housekeeper	44	Providence l
O	Gilman Alice I—†	82	secretary	27	here
P	Gilman Benjamin I	82	"	72	"
R	Gilman Cornelia D—†	82	housewife	61	"
S	Brigham Eleanor—†	82	music teacher	41	"
T	Matthews Margaret —†	82	housekeeper	62	"
U	Winters Mary R—†	82	secretary	40	"
W	Vialle Ruth—†	82	cashier	42	"
Y	Powers Edward W	82	engineer	38	80 Mt Vern
Z	Heard Alice—†	82	artist	56	here
B	Curtis Lucy—†	82	secretary	30	"
C	Symonds Jessie H—†	82	teacher	47	"
D	Symonds Sally C—†	82	secretary	22	"
F	Pleadwell Amy—†	82	artist	45	"
G	Shepherd Margaret E—†	82	housewife	33	S Lincoln
H	Shepherd Percival D	82	salesman	35	"
K	Collova Santa	83	chauffeur	29	here
L	Ridgley Charles	83	merchant	31	"
O	Crowley Ellen—†	86	housekeeper	72	"
P	Crowley Mary—†	86	dressmaker	35	"
R	Pink Aloysious S	86	clerk	22	"
S	Pink Elizabeth—†	86	housewife	55	"
T	Pink Henry A	86	shipper	25	"
U	Pink Joseph	86	harnessmaker	61	"
V	Pink Joseph A	86	clerk	32	"
W	Ames Jane—†	87	housewife	56	"
X	Ames John L	87	physician	61	"
Y	Ames John L, jr	87	clerk	28	"
Z	Ames Muriel—†	87	student	23	"
A	Beale Arthur M	88	lawyer	49	"
B	Beale Louise D—†	88	housewife	43	"
C	Miller Helen M—†	88	housekeeper	72	"
F	Elliott William	93	coachman	43	"
G	Manney Charles F	94	composer	45	"
H	Hayward Frances—†	94	artist	58	"
K	Alden John	94	broker	24	Portland Me
L	Bishop Barbara E—†	94	housekeeper	48	here
M	Broe James A, jr	94	insurance agent	24	Portland Me
N	Whalen Esther —†	94	secretary	27	New York Cit

Chestnut Street— Continued

P	Elliott Cecilia—†	95	housewife	33	here
R	Buckingham Mary—†	96	teacher	55	"
S	Gilman Margaret—†	96	"	57	Italy
T	Robbins Catherine E—†	97	housewife	48	here
U	Robbins Frank	97	chauffeur	48	"
V	Clark Caroline O—†	98	housewife	71	"
W	Clark Louise—†	98	teacher	47	"
X	Keller Harrison	98	music teacher	32	"
Y	Moffat Adelene—†	98	artist	62	Italy
Z	Stanton Lucy—†	98	teacher	48	82 Chestnut
A	Whittier Amy R—†	98	"	51	here
B	Wheelock Helen—†	98	housekeeper	77	"
C	Bachelder Samuel	100	lawyer	65	"
D	Foster Margaret J—†	100	housekeeper	75	"
E	Tisdale Archibald R	100	lawyer	50	"
F	Wheelwright Grace—†	100	author	60	"
G	Dormer Isabella—†	101	housewife	43	125 Myrtle
H	Dormer John W	101	janitor	47	125 "
K	Conant Nellie F—†	101	housewife	50	here
L	Coggshall Carrie L—†	101	"	50	"
M	Hartwell Effie E M—†	101	housekeeper	60	"
N	Kimball Madeleine—†	101	student	26	"
O	Dalton Ellen B—†	101	retired	40	"
P	Dalton Elsie L—†	101	housekeeper	55	"
R	Amrey Lena—†	101	"	50	"
S	Crocker Frank W	101	student	26	"
T	Crocker George H	101	retired	70	"
U	Crocker Hellen W—†	101	housewife	52	"
W	Mann Gertrude—†	101	retired	50	New York
X	Shaley Mary—†	101	cook	48	here
Y	Herrick Alice—†	101	student	21	"
Z	Herrick Margaret—†	101	housewife	48	"
A	Herrick Robert F	101	lawyer	58	"
C	Chauvent Annie L A—†	101	housekeeper	66	"
D	Converse Barbara W—†	101	housewife	23	"
E	Converse Roger W	101	banker	24	"
F	Dacey Grace—†	101	nurse	30	Salem
G	Pearson Mary—†	101	cook	30	Cambridge
H	Saltonstall Frances A—†	101	housekeeper	55	7 Chestnut
H¹	Saltonstall Nathaniel	101	student	21	7 "
K	Russell Catherine—†	101	housewife	40	here

Chestnut Street—Continued

L	Commy Mary—†	101	maid	32	9 Louisburg sc	G
M	Sheppard Marion—†	101	housekeeper	50	here	H
N	Bowen Nellie—†	101	maid	28	"	K
O	Burnham Clement	101	student	29	"	L
P	Burnham Myra S—†	101	housekeeper	55	"	M
S	Coppola Louis	102	artist	35	"	N
T	Ambrose Nettie M—†	104	housekeeper	48	"	O
V	Baker Mary J—†	104	clerk	50	"	P
U	Baker Sarah E—†	104	tailoress	50	"	R
W	Fitzgerald Helen—†	104	waitress	45	"	S
X	Parker Samuel D	104	manufacturer	54	"	
Y	McCarthy Annie W—†	106	housewife	67	"	U
Z	McCarthy Charles C	106	lawyer	39	"	
A	McCarthy Julia E—†	106	housekeeper	38	"	
B	McCarthy Thomas F	106	retired	66	"	
C	Noyes Annie A—†	106	housekeeper	52	"	
D	Trask Mary G—†	106	"	71	"	
E	Andrews Barrett	107	banker	35	"	
F	Andrews Margaret—†	107	housewife	44	New York	
G	Persson Per B	107	butler	25	Sweden	
H	Wigglesworth Edward	109	physician	46	here	
K	Wigglesworth Sarah—†	109	housewife	40	"	
L	Condit Louise—†	124	housekeeper	28	400 Com av	
M	Condit Mary L—†	124	housewife	50	400 "	
N	Condit Sears B	124	manufacturer	51	400 "	
O	Holden Joshua B	128	broker	47	here	
P	Holden Mabel B—†	128	housewife	42	"	
R	Holden Mabel L—†	128	student	20	"	
S	Mason Emeline E—†	128	advertising	46	82 Chestnut	
T	Taylor Bertha V—†	128	housewife	29	19 Beacon	
U	Taylor Harry M	128	broker	38	19 "	
V	Bruce Mary S—†	128	teacher	56	here	
W	Burt Sarah B—†	128	housekeeper	83	"	
X	Durand Mary B—†	128	"	57	"	
Y	Wilkins Louisa A—†	128	housewife	23	Fall River	
Z	Wilkins Raymond S	128	lawyer	32	Salem	
A	Sherman George M	128	clothier	54	here	
B	Sherman Jeannette C—†	128	housewife	52	"	
D	Dynes Olga B—†	128	"	41	Montserrat Mo	
E	Dynes Thomas W	128	salesman	41	"	
F	Merrill Abner	128	lawyer	35	here	

Chestnut Street—Continued

G	Gray Elizabeth F—†	128	housewife	42	here
H	Willis Clara F—†	128	retired	51	"
K	Sand Max L	128	treasurer	51	"
L	Tuckerman Anne—†	128	housekeeper	58	Ipswich
M	Wilkins Helen P—†	128	"	34	here
N	Wilkins Jennie S—†	128	"	63	"
O	Haskell Henry H	128	retired	55	W Newton
P	Haskell Marcia H—†	128	student	21	New London Ct
R	Haskell Marian L—†	128	housewife	54	W Newton
S	Fay Amy C—†	128	buyer	35	here
T	Rockwood Albert W	128	lawyer	32	Wakefield
U	Rockwood Lucia—†	128	housewife	28	"
V	Allison Marion—†	128	"	52	here
W	Allison Nathaniel	128	physician	55	"
X	Wilkins Arthur G	128	merchant	34	69 Charlesgate East
Y	Gaston William	128	lawyer	33	here
Z	Fuller Mary—†.	130	nurse	35	Atlanta Ga
A	Kilcoyne Mary—†	130	maid	29	Brookline
B	McKenna Isoline—†	130	housewife	28	Atlanta Ga
C	McKenna William J	130	manufacturer	32	Beverly Farms
D	Shea Abbie—†	130	cook	45	Brookline
E	Gillis Celia—†	132	maid	40	382 Com av
E¹	Munroe Christina—†	132	cook	50	382 "
F	Sears Lila W—†	132	housewife	48	308 "
G	Sears Zenas	132	shoemaker	57	308 "
H	King May S—†	134	housekeeper	56	here
K	Slater Charles B	134	manufacturer	64	"
L	Slater Olive L—†	134	housewife	50	"
M	Bigelow Chandler	142	wool sorter	22	"
N	Bigelow Henry F	142	architect	46	"
O	Bigelow Nelson	142	banker	22	"
P	Bigelow Susan T—†	142	housewife	38	"
R	Brigham Celia—†	142	laundress	50	"
S	Burke Edmund	142	draughtsman	22	"
T	Headstrom Fritz	142	butler	30	"
U	Lenihan Julia—†	142	maid	27	"
V	Lennon Catherine C—†	142	seamstress	31	"
W	McCallion Mary—†	142	cook	27	"
X	Young Frank L	144	steward	45	"
Y	Young Louise E—†	144	housewife	37	"

Embankment Road

z	Gagen Annie—†	20	cook	37	here
A	Morse Ednah R—†	20	housewife	53	"
B	Haynes Muriel S—†	22	retired	42	"
C	Patrick Annie—†	30	cook	44	"
D	White Florence—†	30	housewife	45	"
E	White Helen—†	30	student	22	"
F	White Henry K	30	retired	50	"
G	White Josephine—†	30	student	20	"
H	Frizel Mary E—†	32	dressmaker	51	Melrose
K	Kendall Clara I—†	32	housewife	75	here
L	Kendall Henry P	32	manufacturer	46	"
M	O'Connor Annie—†	32	cook	48	"

Lime Street

N	Furness Laura—†	4	housekeeper	66	here
N¹	Furness Rebekah T—†	4	artist	69	"
O	McAskell Joana—†	4	cook	45	"
P	Munroe Mary—†	4	chambermaid	28	Nova Scotia
R	Greeley Ruth—†	5	social worker	45	here
S	Wells Ruth L—†	5	housekeeper	61	"
T	Church Mary E—†	9	retired	50	"
U	Hastings Nora—†	9	waitress	28	Worcester
V	Paul Annie—†	9	retired	50	here
W	Borgesen Lydia—†	10	waitress	22	"
X	Borgesen Sigvart J	10	busboy	20	Norway
Y	Crandon LeRoy G	10	physician	50	here
Z	Crandon Mina S—†	10	housewife	35	"
A	Sherwood Katherine—†	11	retired	45	"
B	Silsbury Martha—†	12	artist	64	"
C	Fowkles Lucien J	16	student	26	"
D	Platt Richard B	16	music teacher	46	"
F	Haley Elizabeth R —†	20	housewife	37	Newton
G	Haley John J	20	secretary	40	"
H	Lang Lilla W	20	housewife	27	195 Audubon rd
K	Lang William W	20	lawyer	28	195 "
L	Johnson Ellen C—†	20	housekeeper	34	261 Marlboro
M	Warren Sylvia—†	20	social worker	27	261 "
N	Richards Archibald E	20	broker	40	Chicago Ill

Lime Street—Continued

o	Lovell Helen D—†	20	housewife	23	Weston
p	Lovell Philip G	20	salesman	28	"
R	Ellis Thomas H	20	banker	38	Brooklyn N Y
s	Guy Arthur S	20	salesman	35	48 Beacon
T	McKey Edward V	20	banker	35	48 "
V	Wainwright Grace M—†	20	housekeeper	64	Marstons Mills
w	Wainwright Maude B—†	20	secretary	32	"
x	Donovan Alfred F	20	manufacturer	27	Lynn
Y	Donovan Ellen—†	20	housewife	25	"
B	Brady John W	20	physician	47	Cambridge
c	Agnew Sarah O—†	20	social worker	54	New York City
E	Walker Sarah—†	20	housekeeper	31	Medford
F	Walker William A	20	janitor	35	"
G	Christinsen Alice—†	21	nurse	36	here
H	Desmond Margaret—†	21	cook	48	Ireland
K	Harwood Bartlett	21	lawyer	30	here
L	Harwood Sabra B—†	21	housewife	28	"
M	McIntyre Margaret—†	21	waitress	25	"
o	Cooper Henry S	23	student	28	70 Beacon
N	Cooper Katherine—†	23	housewife	28	70 "
P	Fisher Ida—†	23	nurse	35	70 "
R	Folley Nellie—†	23	cook	40	70 "
s	Walsh Katherine—†	23	domestic	23	Brookline
U	Ahlm Inez—†	25	"	21	6 Brimmer
V	Fernald Dora—†	25	"	23	here
w	Palfrey Francis W	25	physician	47	"
x	Palfrey Lucy D—†	25	housewife	38	"
Y	Christiansen Thorwald	26	jeweler	63	"
z	Atkinson Richard S	26	retired	70	"
A	Cleveland Henry G	26	craftsman	77	"
B	Panis Samual G	26	jeweler	42	"
c	Van Beechten Gretel—†	26	teacher	25	New York
D	Van Beechten Robert D	26	"	27	"
F	Graves James O	30	carpenter	63	20 Lime
G	Frederickson Walborg—†	31	waitress	24	here
H	Sears Helen W—†	31	housewife	25	"
K	Sears Samuel P	31	lawyer	28	"
M	Bliss Elsie—†	34	maid	40	Brookline
N	Conway Mary—†	34	"	21	"
o	Roberts Ada—†	34	housewife	53	here
P	Roberts Oden	34	lawyer	53	"

Lime Street—Continued

	R	Roberts Sumner M	34	student	25	here
	S	Tevnan Julia—†	34	maid	24	Brookline
	S¹	Walley Gertrude—†	34	"	46	Norwood
	T	O'Brien Josephine—†	36	"	30	Winchester
	U	Wells Livermore—†	36	housewife	48	here
	V	Wells Thomas	36	student	23	"
	W	Rhoades Mary—†	38	domestic	74	"

Mt Vernon Square

	X	Cameron Katherine E—†	1	domestic	21	here
	Y	Davidson Bertha J—†	1	housewife	30	"
	Z	Davidson George B	1	chauffeur	41	"
	A	Hubbard Catherine F—†	2	housewife	60	Brookline
	B	Hubbard Edward A	2	architect	34	"
	C	Hubbard Eleanore E—†	2	teacher	38	"
	D	Anderson Lillian—†	3	nurse	23	here
	E	Grinnell Frank W	3	lawyer	50	"
	F	Grinnell Isabel M—†	3	housewife	44	"

Mt Vernon Street

	K	Anderson Alvin E	101	janitor	32	Connecticut
	L	Anderson Sarah—†	101	housewife	35	"
	M	Hayes Margaret L—†	101	retired	52	here
	N	Barnard Lucy P—†	101	housewife	45	"
	O	Barnard William L	101	secretary	46	"
	P	Keenan Delia A—†	101	domestic	56	"
	R	Ryce Helen K—†	101	retired	52	New Hampshire
	S	Battelle Sarah W—†	101	housekeeper	46	here
	T	Kennan Mary J—†	101	maid	21	"
	U	Colburn Elinor M—†	103	student	21	"
	V	Colburn Hardy R	103	"	23	"
	W	Colburn Harry H	103	physician	50	"
	X	Colburn Mae E—†	103	housewife	46	"
	Y	McAuley Murdo	103	retired	60	"
	Y¹	Rockett James F	103	auditor	45	"

Mt Vernon Street—Continued

z	Stevens Mary A—†	103	compositor	55	here
A	Mason Max	105	draughtsman	32	71 Mt Vernon
B	Roeth Martha E—†	105	retired	69	here
C	Scarlett William R	105	buyer	66	"
D	Goodnow Nellie—†	107	bookkeeper	50	"
E	Holman Nora K—†	107	social worker	50	"
F	Jackson Lavinia—†	107	housekeeper	40	"
G	Maclennan Mary—†	107	cook	30	"
H	Peaks Gertrude—†	107	retired	60	"
K	Baker Marie—†	109	"	70	90 Pinckney
L	Murphy Frank S	109	grocer	61	here
M	Murphy Lillian B—†	109	housewife	39	"
O	Bruce Betsie L—†	122A	"	51	"
P	Bruce John H	122A	mason	52	"
R	Reed George S	122A	clerk	42	"
S	Miller Clifford G	124	salesman	33	"
T	Miller Valerie V—†	124	housewife	35	"
U	Collins Ellen L—†	124	retired	70	"
V	Harriman Delphine P—†	124	statistician	51	"
Y	Buckley Nora—†	129	waitress	40	Hingham
Z	Gillis Mary—†	129	cook	35	here
A	Lamb Rosanna—†	129	retired	80	"
B	Bourne Frank A	130	architect	45	"
C	Bourne Gertrude—†	130	housewife	45	"
D	McGowan Annie—†	130	domestic	45	"
E	Gardiner June G—†	131	housewife	68	"
F	O'Brien Elizabeth A—†	131	cook	30	"
G	O'Brien Nellie T—†	131	waitress	22	"
H	Houghton Anna—†	133	"	20	Ireland
K	Houghton Sarah—†	133	cook	30	Brookline
L	Wheelwright Anita—†	133	retired	65	here
M	Ford Margaret—†	135	nurse	40	"
N	Harlow Edward D	135	banker	46	"
O	Harlow Elsie M—†	135	housewife	43	"
R	Marron Julia—†	140	"	28	New York
S	Marron Peter	140	janitor	31	"
T	DeBlois Esther A—†	140	housewife	40	here
U	Foley Mary—†	140	domestic	37	295 Com av
V	Sullivan Helen L—†	140	housekeeper	52	here
W	Nugent Hannah—†	140	domestic	40	"
X	Van Wyck Benjamin S	140	manufacturer	37	"

Mt Vernon Street—Continued

Y	Van Wyck Evelyn H—†	140	housewife	29	here	
Z	Shurtleff Gertrude H—†	140	"	52	"	
A	Shurtleff Howard L	140	manufacturer	65	"	
B	Bowditch Mary O—†	140	retired	39	"	
C	Blodgett Ellen P—†	140	housewife	31	"	
D	Blodgett William	140	merchant	39	"	
E	Carlson Vera—†	140	domestic	28	Quincy	
F	Shurtleff Ernest W	140	merchant	46	here	
G	Shurtleff Gertrude S—†	140	student	22	"	
H	Reed James H	140	manufacturer	45	Brookline	
K	Peden Elizabeth—†	140	nurse	45	here	
L	Anton Lena—†	144	domestic	60	"	
M	Beal Lillian D—†	144	housewife	47	"	
N	Beal Willis P	144	student	21	"	
O	Gleason Katherine—†	144	domestic	43	Brookline	
P	Foley Nellie—†	146	"	23	"	
R	Herrick Robert F, jr	146	manufacturer	30	here	
S	Herrick Thelma—†	146	housewife	23	"	
T	O'Donnell Fannie—†	146	domestic	29	"	
U	Parker Elizabeth S—†	148	housewife	43	"	
V	Parker William S	148	architect	46	"	
W	Killduff Mary—†	150	domestic	30	"	
X	McLean Catherine—†	150	"	20	Brookline	
Y	O'Donnell Elizabeth—†	150	"	21	211 Com av	
Z	Parker John S	150	salesman	34	391 "	
A	Parker Violet O—†	150	housewife	31	391 "	
B	Chin Cheng	152	domestic	30	New York	
C	Regula Anna—†	152	"	33	"	
D	Zinsser Hans	152	physician	45	"	
E	Zinsser Ruby H—†	152	housewife	39	"	
G	McNair Jean—†	156	domestic	50	here	
F	Pecker Annie J—†	156	retired	65	"	
H	Pickering Martha—†	156	domestic	50	Brookline	
K	Eaton Frederick W	158	lawyer	45	here	
L	Eaton Jeane W—†	158	housewife	48	"	
M	Giotty Sarah—†	158	domestic	35	"	
N	McLean Margaret—†	158	"	39	"	
O	Tierney Annie—†	158	"	40	"	
P	Freeman Helen—†	160	retired	60	"	
R	Jones Anna F—†	160	domestic	30	"	
S	Kane Margaret—†	160	"	22	"	

Otis Place

T	Bradshaw Jennie—†	1	waitress	23	Lowell
U	Lee Georgie—†	1	housewife	53	here
V	Lee James S	1	architect	53	"
W	Logan Margaret—†	1	maid	22	"
X	McMillan Jessie—†	1	cook	45	"
Y	Carlson Fannie—†	2	nurse	50	"
Z	Coyne Julia—†	2	waitress	35	"
A	Fay Hester—†	2	housewife	30	"
B	Fay Samuel P	2	banker	40	"
C	Hollis Charlotte—†	2	chambermaid	35	"
D	O'Sullivan Mary—†	2	cook	35	"
E	Dingwell Elizabeth—†	4	houseworker	50	"
F	Roberts Mary A—†	4	housewife	69	"
G	Briggs Isabell—†	5	author	70	"
H	Folette Mary B—†	5	"	50	"
K	Heald Donald R	5	janitor	33	Maine
L	Heald Marion G—†	5	houseworker	25	"
M	Gaugengigl Ignatz M	5	artist	69	here
N	Connors Bridget—†	6	maid	23	222 Com av
O	Lebrun Metilda—†	6	governess	42	California
P	Munn Harriet—†	6	housewife	35	New York
R	Munn John R	6	merchant	45	"
S	Renahan Helen—†	6	cook	35	79 Richfield
T	Thackara Elizabeth—†	7	clerk	43	here
U	Wells Louisa A—†	7	housekeeper	51	"
V	Loring Charles G	8	architect	42	"
W	Loring Katharine P—†	8	housewife	32	"
X	Filene Edward A	12	storekeeper	50	"
Y	Taya Takeshi	12	utilityman	40	"
Z	Holmes Priscilla S—†	14	domestic	38	6 Lawrence
A	MacLean Catherine—†	14	"	38	6 "
B	O'Malley Elizabeth—†	14	cook	26	264 Bay State rd
C	Whitney Margaret F G—†	14	housewife	66	here

Pinckney Street

D	Fulks Ethel M—†	88	housewife	34	Cambridge
E	Fulks George W	88	banker	36	"
F	Wetherell Bryant D	88	physician	35	146 Mt Vernon

Pinckney Street—Continued

G	Wetherell Mildred—†	88	housewife	27	146 Mt Vern
H	Burke Helen—†	90	maid	34	here
K	Parker Ross	90	clothier	52	"
L	Parker Ruth B—†	90	housewife	40	"
M	Sakane Choichi	90	cook	26	"
N	Anderson Charles	92	clerk	75	"
O	Bigley William	92	bookkeeper	34	61 Chestnut
P	Broman Heldge	92	chauffeur	38	68 "
R	Bryson Emily—†	92	nurse	32	here
S	Golden Hugh H	92	proprietor	54	"
T	Haggerty Arthur	92	chauffeur	45	"
U	Morrisette Cecile—†	92	nurse	28	"
V	Reid Malcolm	92	salesman	49	"
W	Thebault Nellie—†	92	housekeeper	33	"
X	Thebault Paul H	92	teamster	34	"
Y	Titus Mildred—†	92	nurse	28	"
Z	Williams Lester	92	waiter	35	Albany N Y
A	Crawford Harold	92A	secretary	38	2 Goodwin pl
B	Rebensdorf Ludwig	92A	engineer	34	2 "
C	Saunders Lewis	92A	salesman	52	here
D	Saunders Lewis W	92A	clerk	23	"
E	Saunders Susan L—†	92A	housewife	47	"
F	Moore Delphine—†	92A	"	45	Detroit Mich
G	Moore George H	92A	publisher	50	"
H	Brooks Helen A—†	92A	musician	67	here
K	Brooks Mary M—†	92A	retired	57	"
L	Puffer Emma J—†	92A	lawyer	37	"
M	Philbrick Eliphalet	92A	manager	63	"
N	Philbrick Gertrude T—†	92A	housewife	50	"
O	Greeley George E	92A	clerk	58	10 Newbury
P	Stacy Charles A	92A	salesman	52	here
R	School Sarah A—†	92B	bookkeeper	32	"
S	Sherlock Nellie—†	92B	"	26	"
T	McDonough Helen—†	94	cook	29	"
U	O'Rourke Margaret—†	94	maid	20	"
V	Porter Ellen S H—†	94	housewife	51	"
W	Porter John B	94	keeper	59	"
X	Spooner Florence—†	96	retired	75	"
Y	Flint Lucy W—†	98	"	78	"
Z	Harrison Mabel—†	98	cook	22	"
A	Townsend Charles	98	clerk	22	"

Pinckney Street—Continued

B	King Stanley	100	manufacturer	41	here
C	Robinson Sally—†	109	housewife	47	England
D	Bullard Harold	111	retired	46	here
E	Bullard Mary R—†	111	houseworker	76	"
F	Davison Hope—†	111	teacher	60	"
G	Oneill Catherine—†	111	dressmaker	31	"
H	Oneill Margaret—†	111	housekeeper	74	"
K	Oneill Margaret—†	111	"	30	"
L	Paterson Marie R—†	111	"	70	105 Pinckney
M	Randall Neal D	111	accountant	37	99 "
N	Weeks Laura—†	111	bookkeeper	50	109 "
O	Andrews Glennie—†	112	cook	22	New Brunswick
P	Bellevue Flora—†	112	chambermaid	21	Framingham
R	Moroni Andrew	112	steward	53	here
S	Moroni Sarah—†	112	housekeeper	50	"
T	Powell William	112	valet	35	"
U	Stafani Cocasca—†	112	chambermaid	21	Framingham
V	Stern Chandler	112	architect	36	here
W	Allen Russell G	112	salesman	45	"
X	Hutchinson Frank	112	architect	45	"
Y	Numeubruk Otto	112	engineer	40	"
Z	Herman William	112	physician	35	Baltimore Md
A	Gay Howard	112	advertising	69	here
C	Rossetta Owen	112	artist	38	Brookline
D	Brooks Francis	112	banker	29	"
E	Metz John	112	salesman	29	"
F	Talac Francis J	112	banker	35	here
G	Boyd William	112	student	29	Wash'n D C
H	Montgomery Stewart	112	lawyer	36	here
K	Buck John	112	physician	28	Mass Gen Hosp
L	Orb Joseph	112	"	29	"
M	White Paul	112	"	38	"
N	Grant Henry J	112	retired	68	here
O	Gamel Ivers	112	painter	26	"
P	Prescott Albert	112	musician	59	"
R	Prescott Charles	112	retired	69	Medford
S	Bacon James	112	lawyer	45	here
T	Worthington John	112	plumber	37	44 Charles
U	Bullock Rufus	112	retired	69	here
V	Brewer Edward	112	broker	38	"
W	Felton William	112	banker	30	Cambridge

8—5

Pinckney Street—Continued

x	Stubb Osmond	112	banker	30	here
y	Updike Daniel B	112	publisher	57	"
z	Jones Clayton	112	musician	59	"
A	Adams Cynthia E—†	113	housekeeper	55	Brookline
B	Light Mary F—†	113	retired	76	here
c	Stevens Elizabeth C—†	113	"	82	"
D	Bell George C	115	printer	41	"
E	Bullock John M	115	cigarmaker	52	"
F	Bullock Nina—†	115	housewife	52	"
G	Burgevin Marc C	115	salesman	29	Milford
H	Doherty Bertha—†	115	housewife	36	here
K	Doherty John A	115	salesman	38	"
L	Hosmer Charles	115	jeweler	29	Springfield
M	Jackson Edith—†	115	housewife	42	here
N	Jackson Frank	115	conductor	45	"
O	Sargent Bernice—†	115	artist	25	"
P	Walsh Katherine—†	117	housewife	50	"
R	Walsh William	117	retired	75	"
s	Ames Lois W—†	119	secretary	24	"
T	Garey Mary E—†	119	housekeeper	65	"
U	Garey Pauline M—†	119	teacher	45	"
V	Morse Grace E—†	119	proofreader	47	"
W	Walsh Edmond F	121	physician	42	"
X	Walsh Ellen V—†	121	housewife	71	"
Y	Walsh Michael J	121	retired	72	"
z	McKay Agnes—†	123	housewife	58	"
A	McKay Patrick	123	waiter	62	"
B	Wilde George H	127	agent	43	"
C	Wilde Isabelle—†	127	housewife	47	"
D	Cronin Cornelius H	129	contractor	56	"
E	Cronin Elizebeth A—†	129	housewife	50	"
F	Cronin Francis L	129	student	26	"
G	Cronin James G	129	clerk	24	"
H	Cronin John J	129	salesman	30	"
K	King Delia—†	129	cook	35	"

Revere Street

M	Anderson Arnold	102	electrician	30	here
N	Anderson Mary—†	102	housewife	35	"
O	Burt Gene—†	102	nurse	29	84 Charles

Revere Street—Continued

P	Green James	102	mechanic	60	here
R	Kattileson Olaf	102	houseman	65	"
S	Kaye Byron	102	mechanic	26	"
U	McKinnon Lucy—†	102	waitress	25	Canada
V	Merrill John	102	mechanic	60	Springfield
W	O'Brien Nellie—†	102	cook	40	here
X	Rogers Mary—†	102	retired	60	84 Revere
T	Tector James	102	doorman	49	107 Charles
Y	Murray Marie—†	104	maid	33	here
Z	Roberts Isac L	104	physician	54	"
A	Roberts Marie J—†	104	housewife	50	"
B	Turner Carrie—†	104	dressmaker	64	"
C	Gleason Anna V—†	106	housekeeper	49	1295 Com av
D	Gleason Benjamin W	106	physician	53	1295 "
E	Gleason Mary E—†	106	housewife	74	California
F	Austin Matilda—†	108	retired	82	here
G	Blevins Mary—†	108	laundress	34	"
H	Bradbury Fannie—†	108	retired	88	"
K	Brooks Mary A—†	108	"	89	"
L	Brown Maria E—†	108	"	88	"
M	Byrnes Thomas E	108	janitor	60	"
N	Cawley Nancy J—†	108	retired	82	"
O	Chandler Francena P—†	108	housekeeper	72	"
P	Childs Chester M	108	houseman	55	"
R	Clark Frances M—†	108	retired	70	"
T	Cobleigh Ellen—†	108	"	88	"
S	Cochrane Nellie—†	108	"	72	"
U	Cook Charlotte P—†	108	"	75	"
V	Cook Helen M—†	108	"	82	"
W	Cressy Mary J—†	108	"	80	"
X	Currier Josephine—†	108	"	82	"
Y	Cushman Julia—†	108	"	83	"
Z	Davis Delia—†	108	"	72	"
A	Ditson Caroline—†	108	"	72	"
B	Downe Susan A—†	108	"	72	"
C	Edmonds Georginna—†	108	"	73	"
D	Farwell Sarah J—†	108	"	84	"
E	Grammar Betsey B—†	108	"	74	"
F	Grant Caroline C—†	108	"	93	"
G	Green Anna—†	108	"	88	"
H	Green Lucy F—†	108	"	86	"

Revere Street—Continued

K	Greenleaf Henrietta—†	108	retired	85	here
L	Haynes Mary F—†	108	"	82	"
M	Houghton Eliza—†	108	"	85	"
N	Howe George	108	engineer	58	Somerville
O	Howe Julia A—†	108	retired	84	here
P	Howe Annie S—†	108	"	81	"
R	Howes Julia—†	108	"	84	"
S	Jamesson Harriet B—†	108	"	84	"
T	Johnson Josephine A—†	108	"	80	"
U	Keith Isabel—†	108	"	71	"
V	Lane Clara E—†	108	"	73	"
W	Lang Ellen E—†	108	"	81	"
X	Lewis Mary M—†	108	"	78	"
Y	Murphy William	108	engineer	55	"
Z	Norton Margaret E—†	108	retired	78	"
A	Olcott Ellea—†	108	"	76	"
B	Peterson Emma—†	108	"	76	"
C	Poole Charlotte—†	108	"	78	"
D	Poole Louisa R—†	108	"	78	"
E	Pratt Celia L—†	108	"	82	"
F	Reed Elisa—†	108	"	86	"
G	Reid Mary E—†	108	"	86	"
H	Rich Ada M—†	108	"	72	"
K	Richardson Harriett—†	108	"	72	"
L	Roberts Dora E—†	108	matron	50	"
M	Conant Grace W—†	117	composer	62	"
N	McDonald William L	117	retired	88	"
O	Stowell Mary A—†	117	music teacher	55	"
P	Wilbur Sidney A	117	retired	80	"
R	Pratt Edna M—†	141	housewife	39	"
S	Pratt Russel R	141	coal dealer	43	"

River Street

T	Emerson Ella C—†	16	saleswoman	45	here
U	Davis Edward H	16	research work	31	"
V	Killourn Henrietta A—†	16	clerk	42	Winthrop
W	Sawyer Vera L—†	16	secretary	37	"
X	Benson Dorothy M—,	16	housewife	54	here
Y	Benson Willard	16	insurance agent	50	"

River Street—Continued

z	Hallinan Charles J	16	clerk	30	43 S Russell
A	Lally Gertrude M—†	16	stenographer	26	here
B	Lally Mary F—†	16	"	29	"
D	Turner William B	22	banker	55	"
E	Moore Joseph F	22	retired	60	"
F	Moore Susan—†	22	housewife	55	"
G	Bowditch Lillian—†	22	"	60	"
H	Bowditch Nathanio	22	lawyer	62	"
K	Lutz Alma—†	22	stenographer	25	"
L	Smith Mary—†	22	"	30	"
M	Mead Mary P—†	22	"	55	"
N	Brigham Harry H	22	lawyer	61	"
O	Brigham Mary C—†	22	housewife	47	"
P	Garrett Christina H—†	22	teacher	35	"
R	Robinson Helen—†	22	"	50	"
S	Thoresen John	22	janitor	47	"
X	Day Agnes B—†	32	housewife	54	"
Y	Emerson Ineze G—†	32	writer	42	"
Z	Nevens Byron D	32	clerk	35	"
A	Nevens Edna D—†	32	housewife	30	"
B	Enright Jane F—†	33	housekeeper	30	"
C	Enright John	33	designer	35	"
D	Samuda Benjamin	34	butler	28	"
E	Wylde John	34	steamship agt	58	"
F	Wylde John I	34	"	30	"
G	Wylde Kate—†	34	housewife	45	"
H	Bruice Josephine—†	35	waitress	57	31 Pinckney
K	Young Alise—†	35	"	52	81 River
L	Clark Ransom	36	lawyer	40	here
M	Lucile Clara—†	36	retired	34	"
N	Rosenkvist Olga—†	36	maid	20	Sweden
O	Parker Frederick, jr	37	physician	33	New York City
P	Parker Marie C—†	37	housekeeper	25	"
R	Frankfurter Felix	37	physician	33	here
S	Frankfurter Marion—†	37	housekeeper	30	"
X	Henebry Annie—†	49	"	55	"
Y	Henebry Thomas	49	laborer	60	"
A	Begford Freda—†	50	cook	32	"
B	Porter Frances W—†	50	housewife	76	"
C	Porter Frances R—†	50	clerk	37	"
D	Porter Mary O—†	50	housewife	58	"

River Street—Continued

E	Baker Arthur M	52	banker	59	here
F	Baker Elizebith F—†	52	secretary	29	"
G	Baker Helen C—†	52	housewife	50	"
H	Hanson Signa—†	52	maid	37	Newburyport
L	Crane Blanch A—†	56	housewife	41	here
M	Crane Newton	56	mechanic	56	"
N	Dabney Ellen—†	56	retired	61	"
O	Dabney Sarah H—†	56	"	62	"
P	Deneroand Maria D—†	56	teacher	39	"
R	Lincoln Bertha M—†	56	housekeeper	48	"
S	Lyons Thomas J	56	U S A	46	"
T	Welch Mary A T—†	56	housewife	53	"
U	Welch Mary L—†	56	clerk	23	"
V	Welch Michael J	56	retired	56	"
X	Savage Alace—†	59	housewife	39	"
Y	Savage Frank F	59	accountant	37	"
Z	Walling Archy C	59	engineer	36	"
A	Walling Ethel D—†	59	housewife	36	"
B	McIver Elizabeth P—†	59	housekeeper	36	106 Marlboro
C	McIver Monroe A	59	physician	33	402 "
D	Cox Lena M—†	59	dressmaker	30	here
E	Kilton Esther L—†	59	"	30	"
F	Nason Margret W—†	63	housekeeper	35	"
G	Nason Thomas W	63	secretary	35	"
H	Warren Halen—†	63	housekeeper	44	"
K	Baldwin Amelia M—†	71	decorator	47	"
M	Somes Clementine—†	85	housekeeper	38	"
N	Somes Dana	85	architect	40	"

West Cedar Street

O	Evans Charles	20	retired	71	here
P	Evans Henrietta E—†	20	"	66	"
R	Hastings Caroline T—†	22	housewife	53	"
S	Hastings Edward R	22	clerk	30	"
T	Hastings Mildred—†	22	housekeeper	33	"
U	Richard Mary—†	22	"	66	"
V	Terrell Sarah—†	22	retired	84	"
W	Emerson Frances V—†	24	"	69	"
X	Watson Lillian A—†	24	housekeeper	40	"

West Cedar Street—Continued

Letter	Full Name	Residence	Occupation	Age	Reported Residence
Y	Patterson Gordon F	26	accountant	47	here
Z	Patterson Helen B—†	26	housewife	42	"
A	Eldridge Ruth—†	28	"	49	"
B	Burns Elizabeth—†	30	domestic	28	Newton Centre
C	Forbes Maude H—†	30	housewife	46	here
D	Forbes William S	30	manufacturer	52	"
E	Forbes William S, jr	30	"	22	"
F	Mallory Margaret—†	30	domestic	38	Newton
G	McCormack Anna—†	32	"	20	Ireland
H	Montague Henry W	32	broker	60	here
K	Montague Louise—†	32	housewife	60	"
L	Ferguson Katharine M—†	34	housekeeper	22	Ipswich
M	Goodrich Mary—†	34	retired	77	here
N	Rothwell Bernard J	34	miller	64	"
O	Rothwell Henrietta —†	34	housewife	56	"
S	Courtney Margaret—†	36	domestic	23	247 Com av
P	Griswold Penelope—†	36	housewife	29	here
R	Griswold Rodger	36	architect	34	"
T	Tracey Mary—†	36	"	21	Ireland
V	Cooke Ernest J	38	chauffeur	31	here
W	Cooke Margaret—†	38	housewife	60	"
X	Cooke William	38	waiter	63	"
Y	Cooke Alfred W	38	steamfitter	34	"
Z	Cooke Annie F—†	38	housewife	30	"
B	Burke Mary—†	42	maid	30	"
C	Kilham Jane H—†	42	housewife	50	"
D	Kilham Jeanette—†	42	decorator	25	"
E	Kilham Walter H	42	architect	42	"
F	Murphy Hannah—†	42	housekeeper	56	"
G	Bowman Morris	44	student	23	Cambridge
H	Crocker Clara B—†	44	housewife	41	Brookline
K	Crocker Courtenay	44	lawyer	43	"
L	Gildea Morris	44	student	24	Medford
M	Manley Alice K—†	44	social worker	53	Milton
N	Schiling Walter	44	student	22	Cambridge
O	Wicks Gertrude—†	44	"	24	Quincy
P	Cutter Charles G	46	retired	63	here
R	Parker Edith—†	46	housekeeper	57	"
S	Brooks Louise W—†	48	retired	45	"
T	Kivlan Margaret—†	48	cook	48	"
U	Scanlon Anna E—†	48	housekeeper	39	Milton

West Cedar Street—Continued

v	Dolan Catherine M—†	50	lawyer	36	here
w	Dolan Mary A—†	50	clerk	45	"
x	Dixwell Catherine—†	52	housewife	67	"
y	Dixwell John	52	physician	75	"
z	Curley Bridget—†	54	housekeeper	48	"
a	Paul Maria—†	54	"	47	"
b	Paul William	54	restaurateur	31	"
c	Wallace Allen P	54	"	42	"
d	Bassett Alice H—†	56	physician	55	"
e	Bassett Sara W—†	56	author	51	"
f	Cummings Gertrude—†	56	housekeeper	51	"
g	Hay Mary—†	56	cook	55	Brookline
h	Bean Horace	58	insurance agent	58	here
k	Bean Marion—†	58	housewife	58	"
l	Blake Albert W	58	manufacturer	53	Lynn
m	Blake Mable W—†	58	housewife	51	"
n	Blake Margery D—†	58	none	23	"
o	Welch Walter D	58	manufacturer	42	"
p	Cudworth Grace F—†	58	healer	44	here
r	Cudworth Luther P	58	"	46	"
s	Roper Louise—†	58	domestic	30	140 Mt Vernon

West Hill Place

t	Filene Theresa—†	1	housewife	46	here
u	Filene Lincoln	1	merchant	55	"
v	Baker Bebe—†	2	housekeeper	30	"
w	Baker Harold W	2	physician	42	"
x	Gillam Katherine—†	2	maid	40	"
y	Murray Frances—†	2	"	33	6 Gloucester
a	Chadbourne Henry R	3	manager	52	here
b	Chadbourne Gertrude F—†	3	housewife	37	"
b¹	Conlon Mary—†	3	cook	44	Brookline
c	Chase Margaret P—†	4	student	28	here
d	Chase Marion M—†	4	housewife	49	"
e	Powers Mary—†	4	maid	38	"
f	Sullivan Teresa—†	4	"	24	88 Bay State rd
g	Green Sarah H—†	5	housewife	45	here
h	Corcoran Alice—†	6	maid	21	Winthrop
k	Dexter Constance V R—†	6	housewife	23	Lancaster

West Hill Place—Continued

Letter	Full Name	Residence	Occupation	Age	Reported Residence
L	Dexter William	6	lawyer	26	65 Marlboro
M	Kelley Mary—†	6	maid	30	Brookline
N	Lydon Annie—†	6	cook	24	207 Com av
O	Harding Edward	7	physician	36	here
P	Harding Geraldine L—†	7	housewife	30	"
R	Marsden Katherine—†	7	cook	23	"
S	West John	8	engineer	38	"
T	West Martha I—†	8	housewife	39	"
U	Lane Henry R	8	manager	38	"
V	Lane Lucy S—†	8	housewife	36	"
W	Tomlinson Elizabeth C—†	8	teacher	51	"
X	Tomlinson Irving C	8	"	51	"
Y	Turner Helen—†	8	housekeeper	38	"
Z	Lawrence John	8	retired	65	Groton
A	Lawrence Martha P—†	8	housewife	62	"
C	Coolidge Elsa—†	10	"	32	here
E	Hill Frances—†	10	"	86	"
D	Hooper Mary F—†	10	"	48	"

Ward 8—Precinct 6

CITY OF BOSTON.

LIST OF RESIDENTS
20 YEARS OF AGE AND OVER

(FEMALES INDICATED BY DAGGER)

AS OF

APRIL 1, 1924

HERBERT A. WILSON, } *Listing*

JAMES F. EAGAN, } *Board.*

CITY OF BOSTON—PRINTING DEPARTMENT

Page.	Letter.	FULL NAME.	Residence, April 1, 1924	Occupation.	Supposed Age.	Reported Residence April 1, 1923. Street and Number.

Arlington Street

	F	Sacca Joseph	140	shoemaker	41	here
	G	Casey Albert	166	carpenter	45	Cambridge
	H	Grinnell Elizabeth—†	166	housewife	25	767 Tremont
	K	Grinnell George	166	metalworker	34	767 "
	L	Lovejoy Hedvig—†	166	dressmaker	49	New Hampshire
	M	Roche Amy—†	166	housewife	30	50 Lawrence
	N	Roche Henry	166	manager	35	50 "
	O	Weinch Chester	166	crossing tender	62	here
	P	Weinch Sarah—†	166	housewife	50	"
	R	Wentworth Clara—†	166	housekeeper	52	"

Bay Street

	S	Owen Maurice	1	salesman	41	11 Joy

Boylston Place

	U	Pariseau Joseph	4	porter	51	Bedford

Boylston Street

	Z	Le Febure Effie—†	264	housewife	44	Somerville
	A	Le Febure Fred J	264	janitor	40	"
	E	Magrath George B	274	physician	53	here
	G	Henschel Flavia—†	278	housewife	28	"
	H	Henschel Siegfried	278	tailor	36	"
	K	Strain Daniel J	278	artist	77	"
	O	Preston Martha E—†	286	housewife	48	"
	P	Preston Patrick	286	janitor	48	"

Broadway

	A	Quilici Amelia	67	housewife	49	here
	B	Quilici Peter	67	baker	47	"
	L	Zacchini Emilia—†	81	housewife	38	"
	M	Zacchini Louis	81	storekeeper	38	"

Broadway—Continued

	Letter	FULL NAME	Residence, April 1, 1924	Occupation	Supposed Age	Reported Residence, April 1, 1923. Street and Number
	N	Baldi Louisa—†	81	housekeeper	31	21 Kirkland
	O	Baldi Luigi	81	laborer	32	21 "
	Y	Drury John P	97	plumber	51	here
	Z	Loury David	97	hostler	43	"
	Z¹	Lowry Letitia—†	97	housekeeper	43	"
	C	Meehan John	99	plater	42	here
	P	Chacane Eva—†	124	housewife	26	Framingham
	R	Chacane Koco	124	restaurateur	30	"
	S	Varney George H	124	glazier	39	here
	T	Varney Martha—†	124	housewife	27	"
	U	De Boli Joseph	124	butcher	44	63 Emerald
	V	Giordano Gaetano	124	barber	35	63 "
	W	Giordano Mary—†	124	housewife	35	63 "
	Z	May Bernhard	128	mechanic	23	here
	A	May Ella F—†	128	housewife	61	"
	B	Cakridas Constance—†	128	"	40	"
	C	Cakridas George	128	salesman	45	"
	D	Cakridas John	128	"	40	"
	E	Merquipis Helen—†	128	housewife	29	"
	F	Merquipis Sperirs	128	salesman	32	"
	H	Lee Pong	135	laundryman	22	96 Carver
	K	Lee Tong	135	"	62	96 "
	N	De Checo Margarite—†	149	tailoress	33	here
	O	Delagarda Christina—†	149	housekeeper	60	"
	P	Belaqua Mary—†	149	housewife	34	"
	R	Belaqua Vincent	149	janitor	31	"
	S	Dempsey Mary E—†	149	housewife	50	"
	T	Dempsey Patrick T	149	tailor	49	"
	V	Donato Joseph	159	conemaker	38	Concord
	W	Donato Sarah—†	159	housewife	36	"
	X	Barret Florence—†	159	waitress	23	here
	Y	Barret John	159	garageman	24	"
	Z	Markowitz Esther—†	159	housewife	60	"
	A	Markowitz Frank	159	rabbi	65	"
	B	Markowitz Rose—†	159	saleswoman	26	"
	C	Beeman Frank R	159	waiter	47	251 Dover
	D	Sullivan Besse—†	159	housewife	39	320½ Tremont
	E	Sullivan Henry J	159	plumber	39	321½ "
	F	Cortes Michael	159	porter	50	here
	G	Cortes Sarah—†	159	housewife	56	"
	H	Impalla Peter	159	clerk	24	"

3

Broadway—Continued

K	Caracappa Delphamy—†	159	tailoress	29	here
L	Caracappa Girolamo	159	tailor	31	"
M	Alabrandi Jane—†	159	housewife	35	"
N	Alabrandi Philip	159	barber	40	"
O	Catino Margarite—†	159	tailoress	42	"
P	Catino William	159	barber	42	"

Carver Street

Z	Young Jennie—†	26	housewife	40	here
A	Young Julian	26	printer	41	"
B	Cahmbers Gertrude—†	26	bus woman	47	"
C	Tilton Lillian W—†	26	housekeeper	45	"
D	Morrissey Ellen—†	26	"	69	"
F	Bye Grace—†	28	"	41	"
B	Baker Isabel—†	28	seamstress	51	"
H	Baker William	28	painter	58	"
K	Bona George	35	carpenter	43	Maine
L	Carroll James	35	painter	45	4 Warrenton
M	Condry Margaret—†	35	houseworker	45	Copley Plaza
N	Flowers Thomas	35	counterman	48	here
O	Hickey Michael J	35	clerk	55	"
P	Kuhn Robert	35	nurse	43	202 B'way
R	Martino Peter	35	tailor	65	here
S	Murphy William	35	clerk	22	Providence R
T	Page George R	35	brickmason	62	here
U	Solone Louis	35	clerk	23	1489 Col av
V	Spencer William	35	"	32	38 Ruggles
Z	Maitland John	36	engineer	56	here
W	Cosnedi Auguste	37	cook	59	42 Warrenton
X	DeJoie Victor	37	mechanic	29	here
Y	Havey John	37	laborer	40	Quincy
A	Parvy John	37	"	23	Brockton
B	Semeur Clemence—†	37	houseworker	73	here
C	Simmon Alfred	37	waiter	39	"
D	Spencer Edwin	37	mechanic	30	Canada
E	Whitty George	37	teamster	39	288 Bowen
F	Benson Gertrude—†	38	housekeeper	42	here
G	Benson Ida—†	38	"	50	"
H	Chisholm William D	38	salesman	64	"

4

Carver Street—Continued

K	Lincoln Emma—†	38	housewife	52	here
L	Lincoln Henry B	38	foreman	58	"
M	Maitland Mary—†	38	housewife	65	"
N	Moore Charles	38	painter	50	"
O	Oakes Henry	38	laborer	61	346 Tremont
P	Sweeney Dennis	38	court officer	63	here
R	Thompson James	38	janitor	55	67 Fayette
S	Whidden Frank	38	salesman	76	100 Carver
T	Chadwick Redmond N	39	waiter	53	here
U	Clarke Frank	39	hatter	52	"
V	Kay Noble	39	laborer	64	"
W	Kelley Ellen—†	39	houseworker	30	"
X	Mills Carry—†	39	parlor maid	42	"
Y	Murphy John	39	polisher	47	"
Z	O'Leary Michael	39	porter	26	"
A	Sullivan Daniel	39	baker	38	"
B	Abbott Mary A—†	48	housewife	59	"
C	Barlow Richard A	48	salesman	65	"
D	Graves John T	48	laborer	50	California
E	Graves Mary—†	48	housewife	35	"
F	O'Keefe John J	48	laborer	55	350 Tremont
G	Reardon John P	48	"	57	here
H	Sheridan Thomas C	48	shipper	45	"
K	Sroerski John	48	machinist	27	"
L	Williams Bertha—†	48	waitress	44	"
N	Kelley Mary A—†	51	matron	55	"
O	Starbuck Margaret C—†	51	clerical	40	1056 Com av
P	Sullivan Frank J	51	veterinarian	50	here
R	Courtney David	52	machinist	60	52 Carver
S	Donahue Thomas	52	laborer	60	68 "
T	Maher Mark	52	upholsterer	66	107 Myrtle
U	Malloy John	52	carpenter	60	52 Carver
V	McInerney James	52	window cleaner	64	54 "
W	McInerney Michael	52	"	56	54 "
X	Milling Ellen—†	52	housewife	43	52 "
Y	Milling Thomas	52	waiter	48	52 "
Z	Hayes Thomas W	53	grocer	45	here
A	Buckley Cornieliues	54	janitor	72	"
B	Cox James	54	"	40	"
C	Gallagher Annie E—†	54	dressmaker	35	"
D	Hajiro George	54	cook	30	65 Eliot

Carver Street—Continued

E	Hurley Annie—†	54	housekeeper	59	here
F	Jacobs Otto	54	waiter	35	"
G	Kastuedes Phillip	54	cook	35	"
H	Knight Oscar	54	engineer	43	12 St Charles
K	Lawler Joseph	54	watchman	73	here
L	O'Neil Henry	54	painter	50	Springfield
M	Terleos John	54	baker	26	New York City
N	Walsh John	54	laborer	45	here
O	Brereton Elizabeth—†	55	housekeeper	46	"
P	Brereton John	55	clerk	48	"
R	Kelliher Cornelious	55	watchman	56	"
S	Sullivan Dennis	55	chef	55	"
T	Young John	55	laborer	60	"
U	Adams Charles J	56	blacksmith	54	Detroit Mich
V	Baril Frederick J	56	laborer	40	here
W	Barry Jeremiah J	56	"	49	"
X	Cawley Timothy	56	"	55	Lowell
Y	Johnson George H	56	"	41	Norton
Z	Kinney Henry	56	blacksmith	56	Malden
Z¹	Kinsman Benjamin F	56	painter	54	151 Warren av
A	Piligian Paul H	56	student	20	New Hampshire
B	Worcester Charles S	56	waiter	72	336 Tremont
C	Pastorelli Anthony A	57	clerk	45	here
D	Pastorelli Christina M—†	57	houseworker	70	"
E	Pastorelli Leopold	57	retired	76	"
F	Pastorelli Martha C—†	57	stenographer	40	"
G	Bertolli Adolph	58	cook	40	"
H	Bertolli Amilio	58	"	39	"
K	Bertolli Julia —†	58	housewife	36	"
K¹	Griffin Mary A—†	58	waitress	51	"
L	Griffin Michael F	58	expressman	50	"
M	Bretolli John	58	laborer	72	"
N	Canatja John	58	shoemaker	39	New York
O	Manetti Louise—†	58	housewife	63	here
P	Scaramela Fiolante	58	shoemaker	50	"
S	Dini Harry	60	baker	31	5 Newburn pl
T	Dini Lawrence	60	laborer	25	5 "
U	Dini Susie—†	60	houseworker	23	5 "
V	Vizzari Frank	60	baker	39	Italy
W	Mootafian Charles	60	real estate	35	here
X	Mootafian Elmes—†	60	housewife	27	"

Carver Street—Continued

Y	Coyne James	60	waiter	30	New Hampshire
z	Egan George	60	porter	32	"
A	Stiller Anna G—†	60	housewife	36	here
B	Stiller Nathan	60	salesman	38	"
E	Agostino Lawrenzi	61	ice cream	42	"
D	Agostino Mary—†	61	houseworker	41	"
F	Allegrini Darino	61	cook	36	"
G	Gambogi Amelio	61	laborer	29	"
H	Marchi Mary—†	61	houseworker	52	"
K	Marchi Peter	61	baker	44	27 Kirkland
L	Baldi Nicola	61	ice cream	37	here
M	Baldi Pia—†	61	housewife	27	"
N	Berch Stephen	62	harnessmaker	58	50 Carver
O	Blake George	62	teamster	30	50 "
P	Hartnett James P	62	marbleworker	54	50 "
R	Hope Stanley	62	waiter	25	50 "
S	Murphy Thomas	62	watchman	55	50 "
T	Slatery William	62	laborer	24	50 "
U	Smith George E	62	cook	44	50 "
V	Trautvetter Margaret E—†	62	housekeeper	45	50 "
W	Byrne Mary E—†	63	houseworker	48	here
X	Dodge John L	63	clerk	74	"
Y	Fox Priscilla—†	63	cook	50	"
Z	Hubert Christopher	63	barber	62	"
A	Mansfield James	63	violinmaker	79	New York City
B	McNeil Margaret—†	63	cashier	45	here
C	Neiley Ward E	63	engineer	54	"
D	Shine Eugene	63	watchman	54	"
E	Stevens Harry	63	"	45	62 Carver
G	Allen Arthur W	65	laborer	50	here
H	Allen Ruby—†	65	waitress	23	21 Dover
K	Cook William	65	laborer	26	Fitchburg
L	Despre Eugina—†	65	cook	45	here
M	Friedman John C	65	carpenter	23	Chicago Ill
N	McGinnis Catherine—†	65	houseworker	75	here
O	Monroe John	65	laborer	47	New York City
P	O'Brien John	65	"	25	here
R	Robbins Ellsworth W	65	"	30	5 Pine
X	Boland William	71	waiter	55	New York City
Y	Caretti Carlo	71	cook	52	70 Carver
Z	Downs Herbert R	71	dishwasher	60	36 Church

Carver Street—Continued

A	Grevelund John	71	engineer	39	354 Tremont
B	Harrigan James	71	tailor	42	here
C	Jones William	71	actor	60	"
D	Nutting Frederick	71	watchman	59	12 Emerald
E	O'Callaghan John	71	elevatorman	22	Ireland
F	O'Connell John	71	porter	55	here
G	O'Connell Patrick	71	"	35	"
H	O'Connell William	71	"	36	"
K	Reed James	71	"	60	"
L	Sullivan John J	71	watchman	45	"
M	Sullivan John J, jr	71	painter	26	"
N	Sullivan Mary—†	71	housekeeper	48	"
O	Bell John	73	salesman	53	"
P	Bell Mary—†	73	cook	50	"
R	Caspian John	73	baker	39	"
S	Cronin Hannah—†	73	housewife	48	"
T	Cronin John	73	laborer	53	"
U	Cronin Michael	73	clerk	21	"
V	Furley William P	73	laborer	52	Cambridge
W	Jackson Harry	73	cook	65	65 Eliot
X	Lonergon William	73	laborer	52	Malden
Y	McGilvary Angus	73	salesman	62	here
Z	O'Connor Jeremiah	73	laborer	47	"
A	O'Connor Patrick	73	waiter	44	"
B	Sikker George	73	timekeeper	21	19 Corning
C	Simone Posquale	73	dishwasher	62	here
D	Bolan Thomas	75	printer	40	"
E	Johnson Frederick	75	inspector	50	"
F	Lynch Timothy J	75	waiter	60	"
G	McGuire James	75	"	50	"
H	Pollinger Charles	75	decorator	55	"
K	Scanlon John	75	clerk	45	"
L	Shea John P	75	chauffeur	31	"
N	Shea Nora V—†	75	housekeeper	60	"
M	Shea Senoro E—†	75	saleswoman	26	"
O	Turner Benjamin	75	salesman	50	"
P	Brady John	77	porter	20	Ireland
R	Curran John	77	retired	70	84 Carver
S	Groman Joseph	77	chauffeur	30	84 "
T	Lyons Thomas	77	porter	20	Ireland
U	O'Shea Mary—†	77	housekeeper	50	84 Carver

Carver Street—Continued

Letter	FULL NAME	Res.	Occupation	Age	Reported Residence
v	O'Shea Timothy	77	stagehand	21	84 Carver
x	Tanner James	77	carpenter	65	35 "
y	Willes Thomas	77	retired	80	Dedham
L	Clark Leo J	79	waiter	45	here
M	Coy John E	79	laborer	50	Worcester
N	Dawson William	79	cook	24	Buffalo N Y
o	Gibbler Christian	79	baker	50	19 Common
P	O'Connor Timothy	79	chauffeur	42	here
R	Parker Hannah—†	79	housekeeper	48	"
s	Pipechorn Arthur	79	dishwasher	21	1419 Col av
T	Sullivan Ellen—†	79	housewife	52	here
u	Sullivan James A	79	storekeeper	30	"
v	Sullivan Joseph T	79	salesman	20	"
w	Sullivan Margaret A—†	79	clerk	25	"
x	Sullivan Mary E—†	79	"	27	"
x¹	Sullivan Timothy	79	laborer	56	"
y	Silver Annie—†	81	waitress	37	"
z	Radica Justine—†	81	housewife	38	"
A	Radica Natalie	81	laborer	48	"
B	Maloof David	81	shoeworker	38	Ashland
c	Maloof Debui—†	81	housewife	39	"
D	Amando Galli	81	cook	33	here
E	Amando Mary—†	81	housewife	30	"
G	Burke Ellen—†	83	waitress	34	Faulkner Hosp
H	Keating James	83	crackermaker	40	11 Concord sq
K	Kenney John	83	stevedore	45	here
L	Kenney Williams	83	stagehand	38	"
M	Preissler Frank	83	chef	37	"
N	Savage Mary L—†	83	waitress	48	"
o	Shanahan James	83	painter	56	35 Waltham
P	West Charles H	83	roofer	74	here
R	West Louisa H—†	83	stenographer	24	"
u	Manning Elizabeth—†	85	housewife	57	71 Berkeley
v	Manning Henry J	85	chauffeur	54	71 "
w	Mullane Frances M—†	85	dietitian	29	here
x	Pine Helen M—†	85	teacher	50	"
y	Courtney John	86	retired	60	Providence R I
z	Fagree John	86	laborer	30	16 Boston
A	Founier Henry	86	waiter	24	New Bedford
B	Founier Vera—†	86	clerk	21	"
c	Garrigan James	86	janitor	33	61 Court

Carver Street—Continued

D	Garrigan Margaret—†	86	housewife	28	61 Court
E	Kyuokas George	86	waiter	24	10 Haverhill
F	Mulett Lawrence	86	barber	38	here
F¹	Scopel John	86	chef	33	16 Boston
G	Sturrock Isabell—†	86	housewife	52	41 Garden
H	Sturrock William	86	fireman	58	41 "
K	Yonkes Charles	86	chef	29	Marion
L	Doherty John	88	yardman	56	here
M	Falli Humbert	88	musician	45	90 Carver
N	Hayes Mary J—†	88	housewife	48	here
O	Hayes William	88	bricklayer	54	"
P	Shine John	88	letter carrier	50	"
R	Shine John, jr	88	clerk	21	"
S	Turner Andrew	88	watchman	75	"
T	Jones Harriet—†	89	housewife	44	72 Clarendon
U	Jones Pascal	89	mechanic	52	72 "
V	Van Tassell Julia—†	89	manager	41	85 Carver
W	Vannah Charles W	89	bookkeeper	50	here
X	Moran Beatrice E—†	89	saleswoman	40	"
Y	Berneditte Memi	90	cook	51	161 Broadway
Z	Ferrari Charles	90	"	50	90 Carver
A	Ferrari Ernestina —†	90	housewife	38	here
B	Lajjaro Julias	90	mechanic	26	Lowell
C	Piga Eugene	90	barber	38	here
D	Donavan Helen—†	94	houseworker	51	"
E	Gorman Edith—†	94	housewife	39	Bridgewater
F	Gorman Edward	94	stonecutter	31	"
G	Kalvert William	94	waiter	40	New York Cit
H	McGilvary Georgiana—†	94	housewife	27	17 Ceylon
K	McGilvary Robert	94	foreman	38	17 "
L	Riferio Sylvia —†	94	saleswoman	29	here
M	Riferio William	94	chef	31	"
N	Smith Grace A —†	94	housewife	34	"
O	Smith Joseph	94	pianomaker	41	"
P	Vogel Frank	94	tailor	74	"
T	Baker Susan H —†	100	housekeeper	69	"
U	Beradine Eugene	100	chef	56	"
V	Ireland Charles W	100	operator	33	Bangor Me
W	Kearns Joseph	100	laborer	34	"
X	Lans Joseph	100	salesman	36	here
Y	Mandeville Ethel —†	100	housekeeper	40	"

Letter.	Full Name.	Residence, April 1, 1924.	Occupation.	Supposed Age.	Reported Residence, April 1, 1923. Street and Number.

Carver Street—Continued

A	Magnani Dulio	104	porter	36	Winchester
B	Magnani Theresa —†	104	housewife	34	Hotel Vendome
C	Grant Frank M	104	engineer	70	here
D	Coury Anna—†	104	dressmaker	45	"
E	Barabella Joseph	104	waiter	28	New York City
F	Kontopoulos John	104	laborer	39	here
G	Canellopoulos Catherine—†	104	housewife	43	"
H	Canellopoulos Nicholas	104	storekeeper	46	"

Church Street

K	McKenzie Amelia—†	5	housekeeper	79	here
L	Anderson Henry	5	druggist	65	"
M	Locker Clara—†	5	housewife	73	"
N	Bardo Demitree—†	5	housekeeper	30	"
N¹	Lew Tim	7	laundryman	34	"
O	Arimondi Lawrence	8	waiter	36	"
P	Hornbeck Josephine—†	8	clerk	20	"
P¹	Hornbeck Nicholas B	8	waiter	52	"
R	Hornbeck Theresa—†	8	housewife	46	"
S	Bradley Elizabeth—†	10	housekeeper	65	"
T	Callahan Elizabeth—†	10	clerk	36	"
U	Callahan James	10	collector	32	3 Wall
V	Hull Susan—†	10	retired	74	here
W	Coleman James	11	dishwasher	60	"
X	Gorman John	11	porter	55	"
Y	Lockhart John	11	metalworker	45	"
Z	MacNeil Mary—†	11	housewife	50	"
A	McInnis Duncan	11	machinist	24	"
B	McMinn Malcolm	11	"	26	"
C	McMinn Robert	11	repairman	23	"
D	Pyott Colin	11	boilermaker	39	"
E	Sousa Toney	11	operator	38	"
F	Grant Nettie—†	13	housewife	64	"
G	Grant Thomas	13	laborer	56	"
H	Mason James W	13	"	42	Cambridge
K	Mason Mary E—†	13	housewife	48	"
M	Hurley Margaret—†	24	"	52	here
N	Hurley Michael	24	watchman	58	"
O	Richards Florence F—†	24	librarian	62	"

Church Street—Continued

p	Cronin Annie—†	24	housekeeper	47	here
R	Reardon Timothy C	24	elevatorman	48	"
s	Glynn Delia—†	24	seamstress	56	"
T	Glynn Mary J—†	24	dressmaker	60	"
U	Glynn Nellie—†	24	housewife	50	"
V	Morris Fred	24	cook	35	"
W	Morris Mary—†	24	housekeeper	34	"
X	Watson John B	24	clerk	78	"
Y	Wiley Carrie H—†	24	saleswoman	49	"
Z	Wiley Frank S, jr	24	motorman	45	"
A	Wiley Frank S	24	cab driver	78	"
B	Wilder Mary E—†	24	librarian	69	"
C	Stephens Frank	24	chauffeur	27	"
D	Geary Sadie E—†	24	hairdresser	33	"
E	Geary Susana—†	24	housekeeper	63	"
H	Kearney Frank E	32	repairman	23	New York City
K	Barbosa Anna—†	32	housewife	35	Somerville
L	Barbosa John	32	longshoreman	35	"
M	Downey John	32	draughtsman	24	here
N	Fay Gertrude—†	34	nurse	23	Dedham
O	Hayes Estelle—†	34	social worker	21	Hingham
P	McCrady Jane R—†	34	"	46	here
R	McCrady Mary C—†	34	"	79	"
S	Tompkins Clara—†	34	"	36	"
U	Almgreen Axel	36	basketmaker	70	"
V	Hanon Mary—†	36	laundress	35	"
W	Moriarity Bessie—†	36	technician	25	"
X	Moriarty Nora—†	36	housewife	70	"
Y	Twoomey Michael	36	laborer	60	"
B	Connor Delia—†	41	domestic	35	"
C	Hill Annie—†	41	housewife	33	"
D	Hill John	41	laborer	43	"
G	Bradley Harry	45	auto washer	38	756 Wash'n
H	Bradley Julia—†	45	housewife	36	756 "
N	Dowd Charles F	51	steamfitter	48	here
O	Dowd Daniel	51	porter	54	"
P	Dowd Henry	51	meatcutter	58	"
R	Dowd Julia—†	51	housewife	54	"
V	Candle Arthur	64	salesman	21	"
W	Cavanaugh Alice—†	64	housewife	36	"
X	Cavanaugh Joseph	64	hotelworker	35	"

Church Street—Continued

Y	Crowell Annie —†	64	housewife	63	here
Z	Crowell Charles S	64	clerk	30	"
A	Hoag Louis	64	laborer	48	"
B	Langbein Emil	64	butcher	30	"
C	Stevenson Louise —†	64	housewife	32	"
D	Stevenson Sidney	64	cable splicer	32	"
E	Wright John	64	salesman	50	"
F	Clifford Daniel	66	retired	50	"
G	Clifford Mary—†	66	housewife	52	"
H	Cronin Patrick	66	laborer	35	Haverhill
K	Dwyer Dennis	66	"	38	here
L	Hurley James	66	bricklayer	22	Oregon
M	Hurley Thomas	66	laborer	45	here
N	McGorrill Myles	66	bushelman	60	38 Fordham rd
O	McKenna Patrick	66	laborer	50	here
R	Benedict Joseph	68	tailor	55	"
S	Burns Michael	68	laborer	24	Ireland
T	Flynn Martin	68	"	23	Lowell
U	King Walter	68	insurance agent	58	here
V	McElory James	68	shipper	40	"
W	O'Shea Mary—†	68	lodging house	74	"
X	Sanford Harold	68	laborer	35	"
Y	Sanford Louis	68	"	38	"
A	Peabody David	70	"	60	78 Carver
B	Schlicke George C	70	clockmaker	40	78 "

Corning Street

K	Bayless Charles	25-37	student	28	Michigan
L	Bayless Hazel—†	25-37	housewife	27	"
M	Richards Eliza—†	25-37	retired	81	here
N	Richards Lillian—†	25-37	secretary	58	"
O	VanDemark Marion—†	25-37	housewife	21	Ohio
P	VanDemark Martin	25-37	clergyman	32	"
R	Ciffill John T	30	rigger	59	Maine
S	Copeland Grace A—†	30	housekeeper	45	Waltham
T	McGlyna Arthur	30	clerk	32	Maine
U	Moran James	30	laborer	32	261 Shawmut av
V	Moran Margaret—†	30	houseworker	55	261 "
W	Orcutt Ernest	30	truckman	24	359 Tremont

Corning Street—Continued

X	Page Arthur	30	janitor	23	Newton
Y	Page Kathrine—†	30	houseworker	22	"
Z	Antonio Anthony	32	laborer	36	393 Shawmut av
A	Campbell Roy J	32	clerk	23	New York Cit
B	Caughey Andrew	32	tailor	52	Providence R
C	Connor Timothy	32	"	69	here
D	Dhiomandi George	32	barber	40	"
E	Gibson Joseph E	32	truckman	26	Vermont
F	Harwood William H	32	painter	35	1 Warrenton
G	MacGraw Margaret—†	32	waitress	22	Canada
G¹	MacGraw Mildred—†	32	"	21	"
H	McCarthy Margret—†	32	housekeeper	42	Lynn
K	Saunders Annie—†	32	"	43	Canada
L	Saunders Gordon	32	cook	59	"
M	Craik May—†	43	housewife	36	Fitchburg
N	Craik Norman	43	clerk	49	"
O	Orwaco Harry	43	laborer	33	here
P	Orwaco Mary—†	43	housewife	30	"
S	Anderson John	47	cook	40	New York
T	Brown Natalie—†	47	housemaid	29	here
U	Brown Robert P	47	porter	34	"
V	Gatewood William	47	longshoreman	36	2 Compton
W	Hewitt Charles W	47	janitor	49	here
X	Jordan Eben	47	clerk	43	80 Compton
Y	Morris Robert C	47	janitor	27	New York City
Z	Smallwood Fannie—†	47	housekeeper	48	here
A	Smallwood Joshua B	47	factory worker	55	"
B	Suggs Merrett	47	longshoreman	59	"
C	Vedder Wilfred	47	cook	24	New York City
D	William Arrie	47	sugarmaker	23	New York
E	William Mabelle—†	47	housemaid	35	New York City
F	Bannestor Thomas	49	cook	20	233 Northampton
G	Chisholm Dudley	49	stableman	48	here
H	Demby Elsa—†	49	housemaid	26	"
K	Dumas Victor	49	butler	58	"
L	Floyd Charles S	49	janitor	34	"
M	Neal Clarance	49	"	24	"
N	Perkins George	49	longshoreman	52	"
O	Pugh Sylvester—†	49	housemaid	58	"
P	Roane Nathan	49	longshoreman	30	28 Village
R	Zigiler William	49	janitor	35	29 Greenwich pk

Corning Street—Continued

Letter	FULL NAME.	Residence, April 1, 1924.	Occupation.	Supposed Age.	Reported Residence, April 1, 1923. Street and Number.
s	Bailey Gorden	51	porter	24	32 Bradford
t	Bowen McDonald	51	laborer	41	Canada
u	Braxton George	51	porter	44	28 Albion
v	Clark Allen	51	laborer	39	here
w	Edwards Cyril	51	"	23	New York
x	Foster James	51	student	28	here
y	Hinds Albert	51	laborer	38	"
z	Hinds Eldica—†	51	housewife	37	"
a	Nile Herbert	51	laborer	30	Canada
b	Thomas Hezekiah	51	"	29	New York
c	Dann Warren H	57	fireman	47	New York City
d	McGivney Eliza—†	57	restaurant wkr	46	15 Dover
e	McGivney Philip	57	restaurantman	47	15 "
f	Morrissey Thomas	57	laborer	47	15 "
h	Lundberg Frank D	57	teamster	52	here
k	Lundberg Grace—†	57	housekeeper	39	"
m	Redwin Katherine—†	59	clerk	60	"
n	Shady Mary—†	59	housewife	26	65 Corning
o	Shady Stanley	59	janitor	30	65 "
p	Kozinpa Dmytro	59	laborer	35	here
r	Kozinpa Mary—†	59	housewife	42	"
s	Dzwiniarski Andrew	59	porter	22	Peabody
t	Kudruk Alexander	59	"	33	43 Corning
u	Sztogryn Katherine—†	59	housewife	28	43 "
v	Sztogryn Steven	59	janitor	30	43 "
w	Casey Margret—†	59	houseworker	63	here
y	Homans Andrew	61	janitor	40	"
z	Homans Edna—†	61	housewife	35	"
a	Ginsberg Bessie—†	61	"	50	"
b	Ginsberg Eva—†	61	milliner	21	"
c	Ginsberg Joseph	61	pedler	50	"
d	Pugliano Antonio	61	tailor	45	"
e	Pugliano Katherine—†	61	housewife	32	"
f	Randall Amanda—†	61	housekeeper	50	"
g	Johnson Frank	63	paver	67	"
h	Johnson Mary—†	63	housekeeper	57	"
k	Lopes Mabel—†	63	domestic	29	"
l	Lopes Thomas	63	longshoreman	31	"
m	Byko Frances—†	63	housekeeper	29	"
n	Byko Stephen	63	factory worker	34	"
o	Zwarich Mary—†	63	housekeeper	28	52 Porter

Corning Street—Continued

P	Zwarich Roman	63	restaurantman	30	52 Porter
R	Cronin John	63	laborer	50	56 Compton
S	Wright Luke	63	"	46	here
T	Coonan Loretta—†	65	tel operator	25	43 Corning
U	Tierney Henry	65	shipfitter	34	43 "
V	Tierney Margaret—†	65	matron	50	43 "
W	Hunchuk Kalenik	65	laundry worker	40	here
X	Hunckuk Katie—†	65	housekeeper	30	"
Y	Freedman Charles	65	laborer	40	"
Z	Lynch Annie—†	65	kitchenmaid	48	44 Kirkland
A	Andrews Frank	67	storekeeper	28	New Bedford
B	Athincos George	67	baker	36	303 Shawmut av
C	Berten Maude—†	67	waiter	43	43 Dwight
D	Carmelos Steven	67	porter	32	241 Arlington
E	Chehanes Charles	67	"	35	445 Shawmut av
F	Gonnares William	67	"	53	225 Harris'n a
G	Kalea Antonio	67	cook	32	Somerville
H	Lekbalo Joseph	67	baker	36	Brockton
K	McNeill Wallace	67	salesman	57	39 Warren av
L	Ruchos Vasil	67	storekeeper	30	207 W Fifth
M	Spelos Angleo	67	fruit	40	303 Shawmut av
N	Spelos Annie—†	67	housewife	30	303 "
O	Tnnessoy Dennis	67	porter	60	90 Hudson

Edgerly Place

A	Foley Nora M—†	10	janitor	39	here
B	Savage Esther—†	10	housekeeper	78	"
C	Savage Eugene	10	cook	58	"
D	Breen Bridget—†	10	house cleaner	50	"
E	Breen Mary—†	10	bookkeeper	24	"
F	Plaisted Roscoe M	14	retired	77	"
G	Marcus Hannah—†	14	housekeeper	57	"
H	Kelly Bridget A—†	14	"	44	"
K	Kelly John J	14	porter	44	"
L	Griffin Catherine—†	16	housekeeper	41	"
M	Griffin John L	16	laborer	41	"
N	Ferrari Bridget—†	16	housekeeper	42	"
O	Ferrari Charles P	16	stagehand	22	"

Edgerly Place—Continued

P	James Anna E—†	16	housekeeper	20	here
R	James Clarence J	16	chauffeur	22	"
S	James Minnie—†	16	housekeeper	48	"

Eliot Street

V	Lahalle Joseph	21 & 23	butcher	53	here
W	Lahalle Julia—†	21 & 23	housewife	49	"
X	Lahalle Louis	21 & 23	retired	84	"
Y	Villeboex Edward	21 & 23	carpenter	63	"
Z	Wagner Frederick	21 & 23	teamster	36	"
A	Oliva Alfred	21 & 23	porter	20	"
B	Oliva Daniel	21 & 23	garmentworker	32	"
C	Oliva Eugene	21 & 23	printer	25	"
D	Oliva George	21 & 23	porter	21	"
E	Oliver Judith M—†	21 & 23	school teacher	26	"
F	Oliver Louisa—†	21 & 23	housewife	60	"
G	Meredith Grace J—†	25 & 27	"	50	480 Shawmut av
H	Meredith Morgan	25 & 27	trainman	56	480 "
K	Gordon James	25 & 27	cook	38	here
L	Martin Hannah R—†	25 & 27	foundryman	49	"
M	Catalani Adolph	25 & 27	cook	45	"
N	Catalani Mary—†	25 & 27	housewife	45	"
O	Giannelli Ettore	25 & 27	cook	27	"
P	Menconi John	25 & 27	storekeeper	44	"
R	Orsi Egidio	25 & 27	cook	25	"
S	Tucaretti Edward	25 & 27	"	35	Italy
X	Tenn Himm	38	laundryman	52	here

Fayette Street

C	Barnett Lillian—†	3	housekeeper	27	here
D	Fissuites Angelo	3	chef	29	"
E	Jefferson George	3	counterman	29	"
F	Liepo Tony	3	barber	38	"
G	Miska Samuel	3	storekeeper	35	Albania
H	Novellia Mike	3	hotelworker	35	Greece
K	Bronson Axel	5	dishwasher	70	here

Fayette Street—Continued

Letter	FULL NAME	Residence	Occupation	Age	Reported Residence
L	Brown George W	5	painter	52	here
M	Carlson Edward	5	cook	41	Wellesley
N	Dunn Timothy	5	roofer	35	Reading
O	Griffin Michael	5	storekeeper	65	here
P	Kelley Nellie—†	5	housekeeper	41	Ireland
R	Mullen Annie—†	5	"	47	"
S	Mullen Patrick	5	fireman	57	here
T	Petrucia Christinia I—†	5	checker	44	"
U	Mary Margaret S—†	6	housekeeper	44	"
V	Neary Thomas E	6	drawtender	45	"
W	Davey Margaret L—†	6	housekeeper	51	"
X	Davey Thomas R	6	waiter	53	"
Y	Bruno Anthony	7	tailor	45	"
Z	Larson Gus	7	machinist	31	"
A	Mahoney Timothy J	7	engineer	43	"
B	Murphy Daniel	7	rubberworker	28	Ireland
C	Murphy Michael	7	porter	29	"
D	Sennott William	7	"	33	Nova Scotia
E	Shea Hanna—†	7	housekeeper	37	92 Compton
F	Shea Jeremiah	7	porter	39	here
G	Shea Patrick	7	coal heaver	48	"
H	Aitken James	8	laborer	36	Scotland
K	Harkins Elizabeth H—†	8	housekeeper	31	here
L	Harkins John	8	boilermaker	37	"
M	Higgins Charles M	8	janitor	22	Falmouth
O	Gorman Patrick	8	watchman	68	here
N	Green Mary Ann—†	8	waitress	50	"
P	Rydbeck Blanch—†	8	housekeeper	43	"
R	Hartnett Margaret—†	8	saleswoman	30	"
S	Hartnett William J	8	inspector	45	"
T	Lonergan Elizabeth A—†	8	housekeeper	40	"
U	Clifford John J	8	clerk	45	"
V	Clifford Margaret—†	8	candymaker	42	"
W	Clifford Margaret L—†	8	retired	68	"
X	Fitzgerald Henry G	8	manager	56	"
Y	Lonergan Elizabeth—†	8	housekeeper	40	"
Z	Lonergan Thomas	8	chauffeur	45	"
A	McLaughlin Dennis F	9	"	31	"
B	McLaughlin Eugene F	9	clerk	35	"
C	McLaughlin Mary—†	9	housekeeper	40	"
D	Green Emma—†	10	domestic	53	86 Warrenton

Fayette Street—Continued

E	Green John M	10	engineer	57	86 Warrenton
F	Riley Mamie—†	10	housekeeper	28	22 Melrose
G	Riley Robert	10	laborer	40	22 "
H	Egan Christine M—†	10	inspector	39	here
K	Egan Marie A—†	10	"	21	"
L	Bradley Alice—†	11	dishwasher	45	"
M	Lawton Harry	11	plasterer	64	"
N	Pavitt Caroline—†	11	housekeeper	56	"
O	Sauliner Albert F	11	carpenter	58	"
P	Stacey James	11	restaurateur	30	"
R	Sutherland Isabella—†	11	saleswoman	35	"
S	White Alphonso	11	painter	40	"
T	Lyons Katherine—†	12	chambermaid	45	"
U	Lyons Nellie—†	12	"	32	Adams House
V	Myers Mary E—†	12	housekeeper	75	here
W	Cook Delia—†	12	laundress	60	"
X	Hayes James L	12	stagehand	23	"
Y	Hayes Margaret M—†	12	housekeeper	20	"
Z	Sweeney Abbie—†	12	"	72	"
B	White Elizabeth—†	14	"	45	"
C	White Lester A	14	steamfitter	21	"
D	Casey James J	14	truckman	32	"
E	Casey Mary—†	14	housekeeper	40	"
F	Casey Michael J	14	student	29	"
G	Casey Timothy P	14	furniture mover	38	"
H	Ingegners Angelina—†	14	housekeeper	39	"
K	Ingegners Angelo	14	barber	45	"
M	Alexander Bertlandt	16	waiter	30	"
N	Gorski John	16	laborer	25	New York
O	McIssac John	16	waiter	23	St John N B
P	McNeil Cornelius	16	porter	21	"
R	Murphy Frederick W	16	clerk	45	here
S	Twohey Louis	16	watchman	50	Philadelphia
T	Vahey Charles	16	cook	27	here
U	Weir Georgine—†	16	stenographer	21	"
V	Weir Jessie A—†	16	housekeeper	55	"
W	Weir John	16	laborer	55	"
X	Montague Cathrine A-†	17	housekeeper	71	"
Y	Montague Frank G	17	lawyer	30	"
Z	Montague George A	17	civil engineer	39	"
A	Montague Hugh	17	mason	75	"

Fayette Street—Continued

B	Montague Mary E—†	17	housekeeper	36	here
C	Andrews William	18	watch repairer	60	"
D	Broderick Michael	18	porter	35	"
E	Doherty Robert	18	tender	48	"
F	Juniar Arthur	18	shoemaker	55	"
G	Lawler Lue	18	janitor	35	"
H	Monahan Eugene	18	chairmaker	50	"
K	Moriarty Timothy	18	porter	55	"
L	O'Brien Edward	18	"	60	"
M	Sullivan Mary C—†	18	housekeeper	55	"
N	Walsh Michael	18	expressman	40	"
P	Allen Jane—†	20	housekeeper	65	"
R	Grant Chrysalite—†	20	"	25	56 Middlesex
S	Hulmboldt Charles L	22	cleaner	38	here
T	Ricke Bertha C—†	22	saleswoman	64	"
U	Ricke Emma A—†	22	housekeeper	61	"
V	Ricke Helen L—†	22	clerk	25	"
W	Ricke Lena C—†	22	housekeeper	48	"
X	Ricke Otto H	22	clerk	53	"
A	Healey James J	25	cook	67	"
B	McNaughton Ismay—†	25	housewife	23	"
C	McNaughton Mary—†	25	charwoman	54	"
D	McNaughton Norman	25	tailor	64	"
E	Meehan William	25	plumber	50	"
F	Cardwell Raymond W	26	actor	24	"
G	Forest Eugene N	26	designer	24	"
H	Corcoran Timothy A	27	chauffeur	39	"
K	Purcell Hanna J—†	27	housewife	62	"
L	Purcell John J	27	clerk	45	"
M	Purcell Mary S—†	27	stenographer	42	"
N	Purcell Michael V	27	janitor	72	"
P	Fay James M G	29	genealogist	37	"
R	Griggs Marie B—†	29	treasurer	39	486 Boylston
S	McCormack Helen E—†	29	illustrator	26	61 Grampian way
T	Scott Dorothy M—†	29	proprietor	23	100 Norway
U	Scott Mary E—†	29	"	48	100 "
V	Thieme Anthony	29	artist	35	Dedham
W	Bresnahan Ellen—†	30	housewife	36	here
X	Bresnahan Thomas	30	laborer	36	"
Y	Flynn Isabel—†	30	housewife	43	"
Z	Costello Bartholemew F	32	clerk	31	"

Fayette Street—Continued

A	Costello James M	32	electrician	24	here
B	Costello Michael J	32	clerk	37	"
C	Costello Thomas F	32	"	34	"
D	Porter Jacke E	33	salesman	28	Nova Scotia
E	Swaney Morris F	33	"	24	Providence R I
F	Calliste Alexander	34	mason	26	here
G	Ceckair Rosella—†	34	dressmaker	43	"
H	Noel Wellington	34	carpenter	35	"
K	Donovan Dennis	35	laborer	44	23 Joy
L	Hogan Charles A	35	plumber	70	here
M	Murphy Catherine—†	35	housekeeper	52	"
N	Trudeau Marie—†	35	stenographer	30	"
O	Dalton Robert J	37	policeman	27	"
P	Grankow Frank	37	restaurateur	65	"
R	Langley Frank X	37	barber	50	"
S	Langley Nellie F—†	37	housekeeper	42	"
T	Shannon Patrick	37	mattressmaker	65	"
U	Talbot Mary F—†	37	operator	20	"
V	Breen Catherine—†	39	housekeeper	45	"
W	Johnson Harold H	39	longshoreman	37	"
X	Larson Delia—†	39	cook	50	"
Y	O'Connor Edgar	39	auto mechanic	34	Millville
Z	Perry Edward	39	chef	65	Lynn
A	Wilson Edward K	39	mechanic	41	Maynard
B	Wilson Josephine C—†	39	housewife	42	"
C	Collins Bernard J T	42	engineer	31	New York
D	Collins May J—†	42	housewife	30	Scotland
E	Sullivan Joseph P	42	clerk	50	here
F	Towle Joseph	42	mason	40	"
G	Towle Susan M—†	42	bookkeeper	35	"
L	Burke John T	46	chairmaker	56	"
M	Burke Josephine—†	46	housewife	55	"
N	Collins James	46	laborer	70	"
O	Corcoran Cathrine J—†	46	housewife	68	"
P	Driscoll James T	46	leatherworker	74	"
R	Driscoll Mary E—†	46	housewife	67	"
S	Hamilton Mary A—†	46	hattrimmer	63	"
T	Moran Agustus	46	waiter	52	"
U	Carr Margaret G—†	48	cook	50	Brigham Hosp
V	Crammer Max	48	student	28	N Adams
W	Libby Charles	48	carpenter	37	Lynn

Fayette Street—Continued

X	Maxis Kosmay	48	collector	35	178 Col av
Y	Spence Claude	48	cook	42	546 "
Z	Spence Rachel—†	48	housewife	39	546 "
A	Sullivan Elizabeth A—†	48	domestic	74	36 Gray
B	Walsh Annie—†	48	kitchenmaid	35	9 Cortes
C	Clarke Elizabeth—†	50	housewife	63	here
D	Clarke Joseph M	50	elevatorman	37	"
E	Clarke Stephen	50	cook	65	"
H	Grady Mary—†	50	"	59	"
F	Cook Alfred F	50	janitor	76	"
G	Cook Mary—†	50	domestic	56	"
K	Bell Mary A—†	52	clerk	57	"
L	Cavanaugh Fannie—†	52	domestic	70	"
M	Frazer Margaret—†	52	housewife	65	"
N	Frazer Mary—†	52	leatherworker	45	"
O	McDonald Sabina—†	52	"	50	"
P	Quiring Gustave A	54	decorator	59	"
R	Quiring Joanna—†	54	housekeeper	56	"
S	Quiring Julia C—†	54	housewife	55	"
U	Caraman Jennet—†	56	"	65	"
V	Lewis Florence—†	56	domestic	50	"
W	Morrison Alma—†	56	tel operator	30	"
X	Sampson Wilfred	56	painter	32	Canada
Y	Waldron Margaret—†	56	seamstress	45	here
Z	Walsh Margaret—†	56	housekeeper	50	"
B	Long Edward	62	chauffeur	39	"
C	Long Mary—†	62	housewife	37	"
D	Harkins James G	62	ship calker	44	"
E	Harkins Sarah B—†	62	housewife	41	"
F	Botter Lillian—†	64	housekeeper	50	New Mexico
G	Gillespie Mary—†	64	cook	40	14 Blanchard
H	Kelley Daniel H	64	bookkeeper	23	14 "
K	Kelley Gertrude—†	64	housewife	20	14 "
L	Watson Richard	64	engineer	23	Manchester Ct
N	Cahill Nellie—†	66	storekeeper	30	here
O	Cahill Timothy J	66	freighthandler	28	"
P	Savage Hannah—†	66	housekeeper	50	"
R	Morey Hannah—†	68	housewife	55	"
S	Morey James V	68	ironmolder	59	"
T	Morey Maude—†	68	saleswoman	27	"
U	Morey Russell T	68	mechanic	25	"

Fayette Street—Continued

v	Clifford Anna—†	70	housewife	40	here
w	Clifford Michael	70	laborer	65	"
x	Millett George	70	salesman	23	"
y	Millett Theresa—†	70	housewife	21	"
z	O'Connor Timothy	72	shoecutter	50	"
A	O'Donnell Bartholomew	72	stagehand	24	"
B	O'Donnell Margaret—†	72	housewife	56	"
C	O'Donnell Thomas F	72	salesman	22	"
D	O'Donnell William J	72	shipper	28	"
E	Dwyer Frederick	74	painter	50	"
F	Mellen John J	74	"	56	"
G	Mellen Margaret—†	74	saleswoman	25	"
H	Mellen Nellie—†	74	housewife	56	"
K	Mellen Patrick F	74	stockkeeper	21	"

Grenville Place

O	English Maria J—†	1	cook	45	here

Jefferson Street

U	Negus William	11	waiter	40	here
V	Runford Anna—†	11	housewife	50	"
W	Stangus John	11	waiter	31	"
X	Nelson Esther—†	11	housewife	30	"
Y	Nelson John E	11	porter	41	"
Z	Hopkins Mary—†	11	dressmaker	54	"
B	Boynton Lester	14	bellboy	23	Nashua N H
C	Burns Maud—†	14	actress	35	Buffalo N Y
D	Burns William	14	chauffeur	30	"
E	Corcogne John	14	barber	60	here
F	Ellis Samuel	14	cook	28	Bangor Me
G	Fielding Harry	14	actor	60	Nahant
H	Fielding Margaret—†	14	actress	60	"
K	Kennedy Isobel—†	14	housekeeper	47	Philadelphia
L	Kennedy John T	14	laundryman	47	157 W Brookline
M	Kolet Joseph	14	tailor	50	New York City
N	Libby Charles	14	porter	24	82 Waltham
O	McLean Charles	14	food checker	30	Ireland

Page	Letter	Full Name.	Residence, April 1, 1924.	Occupation.	Supposed Age.	Reported Residence, April 1, 1923. Street and Number.	

Jefferson Street—Continued

P	Parkinson Henry	14	painter	30	New Bedford	
R	Russell Catherine—†	14	actress	30	Portland Me	
S	Russell Charles	14	actor	35	"	
T	Walding Lillian—†	14	agent	40	Wayland	
U	Walding Louis A	14	mechanic	47	"	

Kirkland Street

V	Falcioni Amelia—†	1	housewife	25	here
W	Falcioni Charles	1	cook	30	"
Y	Barburo John	3	laborer	50	"
Z	Falcione Carmela—†	3	housewife	24	"
A	Falcione John	3	cook	28	"
B	McConnon Eva—†	3	housewife	25	"
C	McConnon John	3	laborer	30	"
D	Giliberti Casimio	5	"	40	"
E	Giliberti Jennie—†	5	housewife	42	"
F	Dessauer Ella—†	7	"	50	"
G	Dessauer Julius	7	storekeeper	70	"
K	Falcione Joseph	9	laborer	37	"
L	Falcione Lewis	9	"	21	"
M	Falcione Nicola	9	cook	60	"
N	Renzetti Almerend—†	9	housewife	34	"
O	Renzetti Elverino	9	laborer	40	"
P	Neice Lottie—†	10	houseworker	60	"
R	Walters Bert	10	waiter	66	"
S	Kryskow Joseph	10	carpenter	38	"
T	Kryskow Veronika—†	10	cook	31	"
U	Sedliff Katherine—†	10	"	25	Chelsea
V	Barnett Grace—†	10	housekeeper	20	New York Cit
W	Barnett Robert	10	chauffeur	28	"
X	Stanziani Ersena—†	11	housewife	32	here
Y	Stanziani Pasaualf	11	laborer	32	"
Z	Biasella Clarinda—†	11	housewife	25	"
A	Biasella Pasquale	11	cook	30	"
B	Cevolani Adrianna—†	12	housewife	30	26 Kirkland
C	Cevolani Joseph	12	cook	30	26 "
D	Sabitene Alfonse	12	"	36	here
E	Sabitene Annie—†	12	housewife	36	"
F	Micchi Mary—†	12	"	51	"

Kirkland Street—Continued

G	Micchi Vincent	12	waiter	45	here
H	Zaccardi John	13	laborer	21	"
K	Scopellite Antonio	13	"	40	"
L	Laureanco Anthony	14	watchman	60	"
M	Laureanco Delia—†	14	housewife	45	"
N	Thompson Edward	15	cook	50	"
O	Thompson Lillian—†	15	housewife	38	"
P	Lantz Catherine—†	15	"	63	"
U	Ciampaglia Antonio	16	meatcutter	52	10 Middlesex
S	Ciampaglia Charles	16	waiter	24	44 Bennet
T	Ciampaglia Lucy—†	16	housewife	48	10 Middlesex
V	Mosesso Joseph	16	cook	46	34 Kirkland
W	Mosesso Joseph	16	meatcutter	23	94 Village
Y	Mateika Lena—†	16	housewife	43	here
Z	Mateika William	16	cook	33	"
A	Guidoni Mary—†	17	housewife	24	"
B	Saxe Annie—†	17	"	47	"
C	Saxe Morris	17	laborer	49	"
D	Aja Camilo	18	"	29	"
E	Aja Maria—†	18	housewife	29	"
F	Bonanigo Frank	18	laborer	31	"
G	Dinino Joseph	18	"	35	"
H	Perello Julia—†	19	housewife	42	"
K	Perello Sabatore	19	laborer	68	"
L	Furcs Eugenis	19	"	35	"
M	Furcs Mary—†	19	housewife	36	"
N	Carrio Anita—†	20	"	25	"
O	Carrio Frank	20	laborer	27	"
P	English Daniel	20	"	34	"
R	Ormston Mary—†	20	housewife	79	"
S	Taylor Christinia—†	20	brushmaker	75	"
U	Kareers Aheleas	21	laborer	50	"
V	Giordano Joseph	22	"	37	"
W	Pusicusk Albert	22	"	42	"
X	Pusicusk Mary—†	22	housewife	40	"
Y	Matick Mary—†	22	"	38	"
Z	Assato Annie—†	23	"	33	"
A	Assato Nicholas	23	laborer	31	"
B	Lentini John	23	"	36	"
C	Lentini Rose—†	23	housewife	37	"
D	Lisandro Aurelia—†	23	"	46	"

Kirkland Street—Continued

E	Lisandro Lewisi	23	cook	43	here
F	Sassa Anthony	24	candymaker	30	25 Morton
G	Sassa Victoria—†	24	housewife	24	434 Bowdoin
H	Gentelea Dominick	24	fireman	28	here
K	Perello Ceasar	24	cook	59	"
L	Perello Mary—†	24	dressmaker	28	"
M	Puglisi Frances—†	24	housekeeper	37	"
N	Korklinewski Anthony—†	25	laborer	45	30 Kirkland
O	Korklinewski Pauline—†	25	housewife	50	30 "
R	Bombaci Salvatóre	26	kitchenman	25	36 Prince
S	Di Giovanni Adele—†	26	dressmaker	21	here
T	Di Giovanni Dora—†	26	housewife	41	"
U	Di Giovanni Guy	26	painter	56	"
V	Marcelli Joseph	26	cook	34	"
W	Terano Peter	26	"	30	"
X	Donato Joseph	27	laborer	46	"
Y	Donato Mary—†	27	housewife	34	"
Z	Salvatore Dominica—†	27	"	25	"
A	Salvatore Lembo	27	laborer	30	"
B	Slessi Angelina—†	27	housewife	37	"
C	Slessi Philip	27	laborer	32	"
D	Columbo Thomas	28	tinsmith	35	"
E	Di Sciullo Dominic	28	cook	55	"
F	Rosa Michael	28	laborer	35	Hartford
G	Magaldi Marie—†	28	housewife	26	526 Newbury
H	Bartell John	29	laborer	40	here
K	Scarlotelli Oreste	29	"	42	"
M	Di Giovanni Albert	30	clerk	35	Holbrook
N	Di Giovanni Mary—†	30	housewife	29	"
O	Giletti Secondo	30	cook	30	22 Common
P	Pacella Joseph	30	"	33	22 "
R	Pacella Mary—†	30	housewife	30	22 "
S	Anastasi Camelia—†	30	"	27	here
T	Anastasi John	30	factory worker	36	"
U	Woloszyn Nicholas	31	laborer	40	"
X	Inginire Frances—†	32	housewife	28	"
Y	Inginire Pasquale	32	laborer	34	"
Z	Di Salvo Nicholas	32	cook	29	"
A	DiSalvo Olinda—†	32	housewife	26	"
B	Palmieri John	32	waiter	24	"
C	DiSalvo Carmela—†	32	housewife	29	"

Kirkland Street—Continued

Letter	FULL NAME.	Residence	Occupation	Age	Reported Residence
D	DiSalvo Dominic	32	laborer	29	here
E	Mosseso Renaldi	33	cook	24	"
F	Zaccardi Joseph	33	"	45	"
G	Zaccardi Matilda—†	33	housewife	34	"
H	Zaccardi Nicolas	33	cook	38	"
K	Apolone Vincenzo	34	dishwasher	30	Portland Me
L	Campagler Charles	34	cook	49	here
M	Campagler Esther—†	34	housewife	46	"
N	Culle Bernard	34	dishwasher	35	"
O	Lolles Constantino	34	cook	30	Portland Me
R	Ditullio Andrea	36	laborer	48	here
S	Sulfeero Annie—†	36	housewife	45	42 Kirkland
T	Sulfeero Nunzio	36	laborer	55	42 "
U	Oudey Catherine—†	36	housewife	29	118 Hudson
V	Oudey Howard	36	laborer	28	118 "
Y	Semchuk Anna—†	38	housewife	29	here
Z	Semchuk Michael	38	laborer	39	"
B	Mazurkych Harry	40	"	45	"
C	Szaday Katherine—†	40	housewife	35	"
D	Szaday Michael	40	laborer	36	"
E	Pimdlski Juzfe—†	40	dishwasher	36	"
L	Carlson Gustav	48	laborer	21	"
M	Haskell Philip	48	"	20	1069 Wash'n
N	Howe Charles	48	"	44	here

Knox Street

Letter	FULL NAME.	Residence	Occupation	Age	Reported Residence
O	Sartini Eugenio	9	ice cream	37	here
P	Sartini Julia—†	9	housewife	39	"
R	Noonan Jeremiah	9	laborer	47	"
S	Noonan Theresa—†	9	housewife	50	"
T	Martin Mary—†	9	"	47	"
U	Fletcher Albert	11	laborer	51	"
V	Fletcher Elizabeth—†	11	housewife	51	"
W	King George H	11	chauffeur	25	"
X	King Mary J—†	11	housewife	56	"
Y	Lindsay Mary E—†	11	"	52	"
Z	Lindsay Robert F	11	chauffeur	30	"
A	Ross John	11	locksmith	55	"

Knox Street—Continued

	B	Augustus John	15	cook	24	21 Kirkland
	C	Augustus Madeline—†	15	waitress	25	21 "
	D	Dillon Elizabeth—†	15	housewife	35	5 Church
	E	Dillon James J	15	printer	38	5 "

Lyndeboro' Place

	F	Donovan Daniel B	1	plumber	54	here
	G	Donovan Mary V—†	1	housewife	54	"
	L	Cook Alice E—†	4	school teacher	35	"
	M	Deane Dorothy L—†	4	social worker	35	"
	N	French Marion E—†	4	secretary	26	26 Charles
	O	Palmer Alice—†	4	dietitian	30	here

Melrose Street

	P	Donahue Mary—†	1	laundress	40	here
	R	Frazer Mary—†	1	dressmaker	50	"
	S	McCreahan John	1	laborer	38	"
	T	Murphy Cornelius	1	engineer	42	"
	U	O'Connor Nellie—†	1	cook	50	"
	V	O'Neil John	1	porter	40	342 Tremont
	W	O'Neil Julia—†	1	housekeeper	50	here
	X	Baker Edwin L	1A	painter	49	"
	Y	Baker Kenneth L	1A	chauffeur	21	"
	Z	Baker Martha—†	1A	housewife	42	"
	A	Baker Winfield S	1A	mechanic	23	"
	B	Leone Ortenzio—†	1A	housekeeper	58	"
	C	Prince Joseph	1A	tailor	42	"
	D	Prince Teresa—†	1A	housewife	34	"
	G	Conlin Katherine—†	2	cook	55	"
	H	Donoghue Bridget—†	2	"	69	"
	K	Kelley William J	2	longshoreman	47	Portland Me
	L	Kett John	2	laborer	55	here
	M	Stevens George C	2	chauffeur	69	"
	N	Stevens Mary G—†	2	housewife	69	"
	O	Collins Catherine—†	3	cook	36	"
	P	Hunt Phillip	3	waiter	70	35 Melrose
	R	Maloney Bridget—†	3	cook	50	here

Melrose Street—Continued

Letter	Name	Res	Occupation	Age	Reported Residence
s	McCarthy James	3	mechanic	55	New York
T	Murray John	3	carpenter	55	36 Church
U	O'Malley Mary—†	3	housemaid	50	Lawrence
V	O'Meara Abbey—†	3	housewife	35	here
W	O'Meara Michael	3	laborer	38	"
X	Ryan Julia—†	3	housekeeper	70	35 Fayette
Y	Day Patrick	4	laborer	40	616 Tremont
Z	Donohue Catherine—†	4	housewife	40	616 "
A	Nolan Patrick	4	retired	49	here
B	Stearns John J	4	laborer	65	616 Tremont
D	Carney Roger	6	"	24	Ireland
E	Corrigan Frederick	6	plater	40	N Attleboro
F	Long Thomas	6	laborer	33	here
G	McGonigle William	6	machinist	24	Ireland
H	McLoughlin Neil	6	fireman	23	"
K	Mullin Katherine—†	6	housewife	36	here
L	Mullin Neil	6	cook	35	"
M	Asdot Annie—†	7	housewife	38	"
N	Asdot Rudolph	7	silverman	40	"
P	Domaldo Jennie—†	7	none	60	"
R	Domaldo Joseph	7	cook	29	"
S	Domaldo Mary—†	7	housewife	23	"
O	Fran Michael	7	laborer	40	"
T	Courtney Mary—†	7	housekeeper	45	16 Melrose
U	Breen Bridget—†	8	"	60	here
V	Kaufman Eva—†	8	housewife	23	"
W	Kaufman Harry	8	stagehand	25	"
X	Ward David—†	8	baker	61	"
Y	Ward Elizabeth—†	8	housewife	65	"
Z	Cronin John A	8	painter	55	"
A	Cronin Mary A—†	8	secretary	21	"
B	Lawson Gertrude—†	9	housekeeper	65	"
C	Linehan Daniel P	9	printer	71	"
D	Linehan Mary J—†	9	housewife	62	"
E	Coleman Mary—†	9	laundress	60	"
F	White Ellen—†	9	waitress	53	"
G	Doptos Stanley	10	cook	27	12 Clarendon
H	Graber Mary—†	10	housewife	31	here
K	Kirkpatrick Adeline—†	10	laundress	52	23 Melrose
L	Kirkpatrick Edward H	10	cook	54	23 "
M	McCarthy John J	10	janitor	53	here

Melrose Street—Continued

N	McGillavary Vincent	10	carpenter	40	Egypt
O	Pivine Harry	10	cook	25	Worcester
P	Quinn Mary—†	10	pantry worker	56	here
R	Sparrow Estha—†	10	stenographer	21	"
S	Wilson Celia—†	10	housewife	48	"
T	Wilson Seth	10	laborer	45	"
U	McCreahan Ellen—†	11	housekeeper	58	"
V	McCreahan Patrick J	11	laborer	25	"
W	Doherty James P	11	"	45	"
X	Doherty Margaret—†	11	housewife	39	"
Y	O'Brien James J	11	clerk	23	"
Z	O'Brien Mary—†	11	housekeeper	50	"
A	O'Brien William F	11	stagehand	34	"
B	Sullivan James	11	laborer	46	"
C	Cohen Bertha—†	11A	housekeeper	28	42 Newman
D	Cohen Jacob	11A	proprietor	35	42 "
E	Peterson Jenny—†	11A	housewife	29	414 E Eighth
F	Peterson William	11A	policeman	29	414 "
G	Giannotti Emilo	11A	tailor	29	here
H	Giannotti Lucia—†	11A	cook	27	"
L	Pernici Annie—†	14	housewife	38	"
M	Pernici Louis	14	cook	39	"
N	Falcione Joseph	14	"	29	"
O	Faicione Luciano	14	chef	24	"
P	Martello Anthony	14	kitchenworker	61	"
R	Perelli Dominic	14	cook	26	"
S	Perelli Emilieno	14	"	54	"
T	Perelli Theodora—†	14	housewife	52	"
U	Agabite Italo	14	kitchenworker	27	Italy
V	Jianotti Americo	14	manager	32	here
W	Jianotti Concetta—†	14	housewife	34	"
X	Foley Annie—†	15	housekeeper	40	"
Y	Foley Timothy	15	retired	85	"
Z	Landry John H	15	carpenter	30	"
A	Limmer Abbie—†	15	housewife	38	"
B	Limmer Carl	15	letter carrier	45	"
C	Pelham Flora—†	15	housewife	55	"
D	Pelham Simon A	15	roofer	67	"
E	MacDougall Alexander	16	painter	62	"
F	MacDougall Stella—†	16	housewife	65	"
G	Buchanon Mary C—†	16	"	45	575 Tremont

Melrose Street—Continued

Letter.	FULL NAME.	Residence, April 1, 1924.	Occupation.	Supposed Age.	Reported Residence, April 1, 1923. Street and Number.
H	Buchanon Neil	16	carpenter	62	575 Tremont
K	Davidson Mary—†	16	cleaner	50	here
L	Barton John	17	artist	26	25 Melrose
M	Collum Theresa A—†	17	housekeeper	50	here
N	Bresnahan Hannah—†	17	"	55	"
O	Bresnahan Josephine C—†	17	packer	27	"
P	Shea James P	17	bill poster	29	"
R	Sullivan Dennis	17	laborer	49	"
S	Bowie Sarah—†	18	housekeeper	68	"
T	Groves Edward	18	laborer	30	31 Harwich
U	Pheysic Nelson	18	"	40	27 Fabin
V	Welch Emil C—†	18	housewife	23	Atlanta Ga
W	Welch James	18	laborer	23	"
X	Wooding George	18	"	35	here
A	March Helen—†	21	housewife	20	New York City
B	Rubin Anna—†	21	artist	20	here
C	Rubin Ivan	21	metalworker	44	"
D	Dramis Arthur	22	furrier	21	"
E	Dramis Cusmo C	22	salesman	48	"
F	Dramis Walter	22	textile worker	23	"
G	Dramis Wilhemina—†	22	housewife	46	"
H	Mozart John	22	polisher	38	21 Melrose
K	Noonan Bridget—†	22	housewife	49	here
L	Noonan Grace—†	22	tel operator	21	"
M	Noonan Katherine—†	22	stenographer	22	"
N	Burke Michael	23	laborer	45	12 Staniford
O	Claxton James	23	painter	60	Chelsea
P	Cook Bernard	23	teamster	52	94 Carver
R	Cook Louise—†	23	housewife	35	94 "
S	Daijawsku Japaw	23	laborer	22	18 Kneeland
T	Flynn Michael	23	"	54	Revere
U	Glover William	23	waiter	38	30 Appleton
V	Keefe William	23	laborer	50	W Newton
W	Koulalis Nickolis	23	"	35	9 Gustin
X	Nickolas James	23	busboy	45	here
Y	Shortall William	23	laborer	60	81 Shawmut av
Z	Taproporulon Elerzerion	23	"	35	12 Kneeland
A	Tossis Alexander	23	"	36	here
B	Hennessy Katherine M—†	24	bookkeeper	49	"
C	Hennessy Mary L—†	24	school teacher	51	"
D	Mostofsky Joseph	25	printer	60	"

Melrose Street—Continued

E	Mishna John V	25	printer	35	here
F	Mishna Marie J—†	25	housewife	25	"
G	Stroglis Costos	25	shoemaker	42	"
H	Stroglis Smateer—†	25	housewife	40	"
K	Murray Margaret—†	26	housekeeper	50	"
L	Twooney Mary—†	26	"	59	"
M	Ryan George	26	teamster	48	"
N	Ryan Katherine—†	26	housekeeper	40	"
O	Connors Bartholomew	26	roofer	25	"
P	Connors Mary—†	26	housewife	55	"
R	Baker Margaret—†	27	nurse	59	561 Mass av
S	Cheyne Catherine—†	27	housewife	38	Fabyan N H
T	Cheyne William	27	upholsterer	51	"
U	Collins James H	27	engineer	49	Stockton Cal
V	Dorval Joseph	27	laborer	21	Franklin N H
W	Hamel John	27	carpenter	66	here
X	Kelley Agnes—†	27	clerk	35	Bermuda
Y	Kelley Walter	27	"	35	"
Z	McAvoy Edward F	27	retired	70	80 Windsor
A	Mullins Edward	27	carpenter	45	Milford
B	Murphy William F	27	foreman	62	here
C	Ray Moses	27	carpenter	32	Franklin N H
D	Renault Francis	27	clerk	52	Brockton
E	Fitzgerald Mary—†	28	retired	65	here
F	Kohlstedt Henry C	28	cook	35	"
G	Kohlstedt Nellie—†	28	clerk	33	"
H	Stenstrom Carl	28	student	30	146 Mass av
K	Stenstrom Singne—†	28	masseur	40	146 "
L	Crowley Julia—†	31	garmentworker	55	here
M	Crowley Mary—†	31	"	59	"
N	Galvin Catherine—†	31	housekeeper	44	"
O	Galvin Richard F	31	clerk	46	"
P	Gilmartin Catherine—†	31	housewife	50	"
R	Gilmartin Elizabeth—†	31	packer	29	"
S	Gilmartin James	31	shoemaker	50	"
T	Gilmartin John J	31	houseman	40	"
T¹	Gilmartin Mary V—†	31	housekeeper	40	"
U	Carboy Catherine—†	33	"	55	52 Melrose
V	Carboy John	33	stagehand	29	52 "
W	Carboy William	33	roofer	34	52 "
X	Madison Edward	34	cook	47	here

Melrose Street—Continued

Y	Madison Margaret—†	34	housekeeper	35	here
Z	Meehan Catherine—†	34	waitress	32	Cambridge
A	Abrahams Matilda—†	35	maid	40	here
B	Anderson Marie—†	35	cook	42	"
C	Bergeson Augusta—†	35	"	40	"
D	Hoar James	35	laborer	54	"
E	Hoar James J	35	clerk	22	"
F	Hoar Mary—†	35	housekeeper	54	"
G	Hoar Nora—†	35	"	24	"
H	Musselman Charles	35	student	28	New York
K	Pettee Georgianna—†	35	none	70	here
M	Land Bertha—†	37	housekeeper	74	"
N	Saloman Louise L—†	37	housewife	45	"
O	Saloman Saul M	37	salesman	47	"
R	Foley John B	39	laborer	42	26 Winchester
S	Lymneous Charles	39	cook	42	here
T	Lymneous Zony—†	39	housewife	40	"
U	Ferris Catherine—†	39	"	26	"
V	Ferris James	39	chauffeur	26	"
W	Shea Thomas M	39	laborer	58	"
Y	Purvis Effie—†	41	housewife	32	"
Z	Purvis William	41	waiter	35	"
A	Stokes James	41	watchman	40	"
D	Basque Wilfred A	44	painter	30	22 Main
E	Harris Oscar G	44	salesman	63	here
F	Straub Joseph	44	restaurantman	26	24 Cortes
G	O'Connor John	46	cook	46	58 Melrose
H	O'Connor Agnes—†	46	housekeeper	46	58 "
K	Potage Alice—†	46	"	23	here
L	Potage Christofor J	46	tailor	29	"
N	Nolan Lawrence	52	waiter	49	79 Albion
O	Nolan Maria D—†	52	housekeeper	49	79 "
P	Loilartas Alexander	52	laborer	65	33 "
R	Loilartas Eva—†	52	housekeeper	70	33 "
S	Dyer Annie T—†	52	stitcher	70	here
T	Cate Margret—†	54	finisher	29	"
U	Ferrara Clementine—†	54	housekeeper	35	"
V	Ferrara Constantine	54	tailor	44	"
W	Kollias John	54	laborer	40	Lynn
X	Kollias Victoria—†	54	housewife	30	"
Y	Simmi Dante	54	cook	32	here

Melrose Street—Continued

z	Simmi Eufrasia—†	54	housekeeper	26	here
A	Simmi Fiorini	54	cook	29	"
E	Jastremsky Alice—†	56	housewife	22	60 Leverett
C	Jastremsky Bazil	56	designer	32	60 "
D	Baysimsky Clement	56	porter	30	60 "
F	Limneos Helen—†	56	housewiie	29	39 Melrose
G	Limneos Nikolas	56	cook	35	39 "
H	Ribatto Charles	56	mason	37	here
K	Ribatto Mary—†	56	housewife	32	"
L	Jenks Louise A L—†	58	book dealer	61	"
N	Scannell Mary—†	58	retired	55	"
O	Rielly Bridget—†	60	housewife	35	"
P	Rielly James	60	laborer	40	"
R	Manning Elizebeth—†	60	scrubwoman	38	"
S	Manning Michael	60	laborer	45	"
T	McDonald Amy—†	60	stitcher	48	"
U	McDonald Clarence	60	shipper	22	"
V	Berry John	62	tailor	60	New Hampshire
W	Chandler Mollie—†	62	scrubwoman	50	here
X	Goubeau Josephine—†	62	lodging house	63	"
Y	Goubeau Leon	62	machinist	35	"
Z	Holland Helen—†	62	retired	77	"
A	Marchant Louise—†	62	buttonholes	70	"
B	Mitchell Thomas	62	laborer	70	"
C	Nights Mary A—†	62	houseworker	30	560 Tremont
D	Moser Isabella—†	64	housekeeper	78	here
E	Canfield Catherine A—†	64	seamstress	69	"
F	Corthell Alice D—†	64	housekeeper	45	"
G	Shaffer Eva—†	64	housewife	21	Brazil S A
H	O'Connor Catherine—†	64	retired	75	here
K	O'Connor Catherine—†	64	housewife	45	"
L	Winn James	64	laborer	35	"

Newbern Place

B	McQuaide Hugh J	7	laborer	46	here
C	McQuaide Mary—†	7	housewife	38	"
D	Frazzoni Joseph	7	cook	36	"
E	Frazzoni Noemi—†	7	housewife	30	"
F	Lotti Ezio	7	cook	32	"

Newbern Place—Continued

G	Lotti Samuel	7	kitchenman	29	here
H	Luvisi Fred	7	"	23	"
K	Speroni Giacamo	7	butcher	55	"
L	Speroni Zita—†	7	housewife	48	"
M	Bowen John	7	laborer	38	"
N	Nagle Mary—†	7	housewife	39	"
O	Nagle Patrick	7	cook	39	"
P	Joyce Catherine—†	7	checker	45	"
R	Griffin Margret—†	7	housewife	60	"
S	Griffin Patrick	7	silver polisher	48	"
T	Scaramella Giralamo	7	cook	48	"
U	Baldi Elvira—†	7	housewife	26	"
V	Baldi Giacomo	7	factoryhand	31	"
W	Dini Alfred	7	kitchenman	42	"
X	Puccini Elivis	7	stonecutter	43	"
Y	Puccini Lucey—†	7	housewife	33	"
Z	Waht Hans	7	factoryhand	52	"
A	Malerbi Georgia—†	7	housewife	23	Italy
B	Malerbi Giacomo	7	factoryhand	26	"
C	Tanelli Dante	7	porter	30	New Hampshire
D	Bertolaccini Brunna—†	7	housewife	33	81 Broadway
E	Bertolaccini Vassilo	7	butcher	37	81 "

Newman Place

L	French Henry E	1	cabinetmaker	64	Revere

Park Square

N	Clark Myra E—†	2	storekeeper	48	here
O	Crouley Elizabeth—†	2	hairdresser	45	"
P	Flanders Ella—†	2	decorator	45	"
R	Herrtz Peter	2	tailor	55	"
S	Meserer Minnie—†	2	hairdresser	53	"
T	O'Toole Emma—†	2	"	38	"
U	Rooney Margaret—†	2	"	48	"
V	Webber Margaret—†	2	"	40	"
W	Berkman Aaron	3	student	23	429 Mass av
X	Hoffman Irwin D	3	"	23	Dorchester

Park Square—Continued

Y	Lundberg Dors—†	3	student	22	Brookline
Z	Lundberg Marie—†	3	housekeeper	50	"
C	Alley Everett	7 & 8	clerk	60	here
D	Bosher Charles C	7 & 8	retired	62	"
E	Dewing Arthur G	7 & 8	student	21	Hanover N H
F	Drew Edward H	7 & 8	retired	71	here
G	Flannery Florence C—†	7 & 8	tel operator	26	"
H	Flannery John W	7 & 8	superintendent	47	"
K	Foss Wallace H	7 & 8	"	67	"
L	Goodwin Montgomery M	7 & 8	clerk	63	"
M	Poulson Harper W	7 & 8	stationer	62	"
N	Sheldon Nelson L	7 & 8	lawyer	63	Brookline
O	Skinner Charles C	7 & 8	clerk	73	here
P	Sowle Humphrey L	7 & 8	accountant	66	"
R	Cook Emily—†	9A	housewife	54	California
S	Cook Ethel M—†	9A	artist	30	"
T	Chick Ivery E—†	14	housewife	29	Somerville
U	Chick Justin I	14	manager	31	"
V	Goodridge Grace D—†	14	stenographer	40	349 Col av
W	Gustin Henry O	14	superintendent	51	here
X	Gustin Olive A—†	14	housewife	35	"
Y	Gustin Richard H	14	salesman	28	"
Z	Hilton Flora A—†	14	housekeeper	31	Maine
A	Hilton Roscoe C	14	janitor	39	"
B	Johnson William F	14	"	66	here
C	Sullivan John A	14	elevatorman	66	"

Porter Street

K	Pappas Speiroi	8	pedler	60	here
L	Burlison William S	8	salesman	74	"
M	Dickerson Lillian—†	8	presser	40	"
N	Grosse Edward V	8	barber	35	Havana Cuba
O	Grosse Mary—†	8	housewife	56	here
P	Scipione Florence—†	8	"	38	"
R	Scipione Frank A	8	tailor	40	"
U	Lockhart Alfred	10	porter	38	23 Greenwich pk
V	Lockhart Rose—†	10	housewife	34	23 "
W	Mack Stella—†	10	"	55	here
X	Harris John	12	choreman	50	"

Porter Street—Continued

	Letter	FULL NAME	Residence	Occupation	Age	Reported Residence
	Y	Kioski Pauline—†	12	housewife	35	here
	A	Collins Esther—†	14	printer	21	"
	B	Collins William	14	chauffeur	25	"
	C	Joseph Ella—†	14	housewife	57	"
	D	Pitlo Robert B	14	waiter	53	"
	E	West Alexander	14	cook	76	36 Melrose
	F	Martin Alexander	16	janitor	49	here
	G	Martin Rose E—†	16	housewife	47	"
	H	Ross Caroline—†	16	"	75	Providence R I
	K	Grooms Henrietta—†	18	"	56	here
	L	Grooms John W	18	janitor	58	"
	M	Caskey James	20	porter	62	1 Dartmouth pl
	N	Grier George	20	hotelworker	27	Portland Me
	O	Harrison Leopold	20	porter	21	Jamaica W I
	P	Lynch George	20	"	28	47 Piedmont
	R	Moore George	20	laborer	36	23 Melrose
	S	Moore Stella—†	20	housewife	35	23 "
	T	Moran Herbert	20	porter	28	20 Fayette
	U	Morrison Dora—†	20	housekeeper	46	here
	V	Morrison Thomas	20	janitor	48	"
	W	Woods Otto	20	laborer	29	47 Piedmont
	X	Jeffreys Arthur H	22	packer	42	here
	Y	Jeffreys Ida H—†	22	housewife	44	"
	Z	Lewis Annie L—†	22	"	61	"
	A	Murray Oscar	22	chauffeur	45	"
	B	Rouse Levonia A	22	"	25	Cleveland Ohio
	C	Rouse Louise—†	22	housewife	23	"
	F	Lovett Edward C	28	cook	53	here
	G	Lovett Fannie—†	28	housewife	52	"
	K	Hoag Ida—†	32	"	42	92 Castle
	L	Bertagna Placido	34	plasterer	31	here
	M	Verreschi Vincent	34	"	26	"
	O	Carli Barbara—†	38	stenographer	20	"
	P	Carli Marion—†	38	housewife	58	"
	R	Frati Bruno—†	38	"	22	"
	S	Frati Elidamo	38	waiter	27	"
	T	Harrington William N	40	cook	54	18 Dartmouth pl
	U	Washington Robert	40	waiter	48	36 Melrose
	X	Shiba William	44	"	29	here
	Y	Bowman Katherine—†	45	laundress	71	38 Melrose
	Z	Monte Manuel	45	shoeworker	34	24 Albion

Porter Street—Continued

A	Capozzi Frank	45	tailor	32	100 Village
B	Capozzi Pauline—†	45	housewife	28	100 "
C	Nanac Joseph	45	factory worker	25	here
D	Nanac Katherine—†	45	housewife	24	"
E	Berretta Addone	46	waiter	33	2 Yarmouth
F	Bogni Richard	46	bricklayer	33	here
G	Bogni Rosa—†	46	housewife	29	"
H	Bonardi Joseph	46	cook	29	"
K	Negretto Frank	46	laborer	42	"
L	Pagani Guilio	46	waiter	35	"
M	Attinonsie Andrea—†	47	housewife	51	284 Sumner
N	Welch Julia—†	47	"	70	here
O	Welch William F	47	chauffeur	25	"
P	Welch William R	47	laborer	69	"
R	Chopyk Josephine—†	47	housewife	32	"
S	Chopyk Stephen	47	factoryworker	33	"
T	Shafranska Alexandria—†	47	housewife	36	"
U	Shafranska Micheal	47	laborer	39	"
V	Briney Catherine—†	47	housewife	46	"
W	Briney William	47	waiter	43	"
X	Lubacsiwski Andrew	47	cook	30	"
Y	Lubacsiwski Catherine—†	47	housewife	27	"
Z	O'Leary James	47	waiter	54	8 Groton
A	Maurelle Blanche Z—†	48	steam presser	47	here
B	Taylor George	48	porter	73	"
C	Taylor Mattie—†	48	housewife	42	"
D	Duncan Arthur	49	baker	24	Hartford Ct
E	Singletary Flora—†	49	factory worker	49	here
F	Cronik Anthony	49	polisher	39	"
G	Cronik Tesse—†	49	housewife	42	"
H	Kolsnick Stephen	49	garageman	21	"
L	Barlone Clotillda—†	49	hemstitcher	25	34 Melrose
K	Barlone Domonie	49	chauffeur	27	34 "
M	Prisco Marie—†	49	housewife	22	34 "
N	Prisco Prospero	49	shoe worker	23	34 "
O	Paczchock Annie—†	49	housewife	30	here
P	Paczchock Dinytro	49	cook	34	"
R	Zarwodnick Peter	49	factory worker	40	"
S	Harrison Louise—†	50	domestic	35	"
T	Bana Domano	50	laborer	20	Portugal
U	Bana Florence—†	50	"	40	S Carver

Porter Street—Continued

v	Bana Joseph	50	laborer	33	Portugal
w	Gonealies Julio	50	"	22	here
x	Goncalves Julius	50	"	22	"
y	Pina Florence	50	"	40	S Carver
z	Pina Joseph J	50	"	33	Portugal
a	Roz Domenk	50	laborer	20	"
b	Pizura Peter	50	"	35	here
c	Pizuro Tina—†	50	housekeeper	30	"
d	Zura Peter	50	laborer	33	"
e	Zura Tena—†	50	housewife	33	"
g	Rosi Annas	52	laborer	38	Canton
h	Rosi Charles	52	retired	98	"
k	Rosi Mary—†	52	housewife	24	"
l	Kuse Domenico	52	cook	40	here
m	Rogowsky Anna—†	52	housewife	31	"
n	Smith Anna—†	52	"	45	"
o	Smith Michael	52	machinist	44	"
p	Gardikis James	58	cook	36	54 Carver
r	Knoblauch Charles	58	waiter	52	New York
s	Knoblauch Elizabeth—†	58	housekeeper	47	"
t	Papas William	58	cook	58	"
u	Revelies Louis	58	"	44	Gloucester
v	Tsunis James	58	shoemaker	40	29 Dover
w	Tsunis Mary—†	58	housewife	27	29 "
x	Vlachres John A	58	cook	34	54 Carver

Shawmut Avenue

g	Crugnola Arlaudena—†	67	housewife	32	here
h	Crugnola Vito	67	shoecutter	34	"
k	Delucia Dominico	67	tailor	27	60 Castle
l	Milano Florence—†	67	stitcher	42	60 "
m	Arias Louis	67	waiter	27	here
n	Arias Peter	67	cook	37	"
o	Arias Teresa—†	67	housewife	35	"
p	Gadoline Mario	67	baker	26	10 Middlesex
r	Rodesta Toney	67	"	28	here
s	Zanotti Josephine—†	67	housewife	26	"
t	Zanotti Louis	67	laborer	28	"
u	Oliva Gaetan	67	cook	47	"

Shawmut Avenue—Continued

v	Oliva Gilda—†	67	embroiderer	21	here
w	Oliva Teodore—†	67	housewife	33	"
x	Aspesi Mary—†	67	candymaker	42	"
y	Aspesi Vincent	67	cook	42	"
z	Andreoli Alexander	67	"	39	"
A	Andreoli Victoria—†	67	housewife	39	"
B	Brugnoni Andrew	67	student	20	"
c	Daino Alexander	67	waiter	32	"
D	Daino Mary—†	67	housewife	26	"
E	Ferrari Joseph	67	cook	37	3 Kirkland
F	Lew Charlie	67½	laundryman	54	Milford
G	DiMaio Patrick	67½	tailor	33	67 Dover
H	Shapiro Catherine—†	67½	domestic	46	here
K	Burbona Francesca—†	67½	cook	50	"
L	Labella Joseph	67½	tailor	25	8 Wheeler
M	Lockhart John	69	porter	65	here
N	McDonough Philip	69	"	35	"
P	Curtis Benjamin	73	cook	35	"
R	Girmino Rose—†	73	housewife	21	30 Kirkland
S	Girmino Sapiro	73	laborer	35	30 "
T	Foley Elizabeth—†	73	candymaker	27	Ireland
U	Teehan Dennis	73	laborer	54	here
V	Teehan Patrick	73	"	21	"
W	Inferrera Antonio	73	baker	36	104 Carver
X	Inferrera Jennie—†	73	housewife	28	104 "
Y	Foley James	75	janitor	50	12 Corning
Z	Lyons John	75	laborer	63	here
B	Sullivan Charles	75	"	49	"
C	Sullivan Elizabeth—†	75	housekeeper	44	"
D	Barnes Joseph	77–81	laborer	39	"
E	Beeman Chauncey E	77–81	secretary	33	"
F	Beeman Cora B—†	77–81	housewife	29	"
G	Benish Edna V—†	77–81	"	27	"
H	Benish Frank	77–81	clergyman	27	"
K	Betts Clifford	77–81	laborer	62	Malden
L	Boadon Wilfred	77–81	"	29	Somerville
M	Cardone Charles	77–81	"	36	Fall River
M¹	Carson Richard	77–81	"	24	Oakland Cal
N	Chaney Neilson	77–81	"	21	here
O	Clemens John	77–81	"	32	England
P	Connor John	77–81	"	58	Brunswick M

Shawmut Avenue—Continued

R	Connor Timothy	77–81	laborer	69	32 Corning
s	Coutour John J	77–81	"	20	here
T	Doherty Joseph W	77–81	"	44	New York City
U	Downey Thomas	77–81	"	39	Albany N Y
V	Evans David E	77–81	student	31	here
W	Evans Grace E	77–81	housewife	30	"
X	Fisk Ferdinand G	77–81	laborer	70	60 School
Y	Fowle Franklin	77–81	"	50	here
Z	Glazier Ella B—†	77–81	housewife	30	"
A	Glazier Glenn	77–81	clergyman	26	"
B	Griffin Norman	77–81	laborer	26	"
C	Hand Edward	77–81	"	52	New York City
D	Hurley William E	77–81	"	42	here
E	Johnson Warren	77–81	"	45	Richmond Va
F	Kelly James F	77–81	"	40	Augusta Me
G	King Martin	77–81	"	53	here
H	Lunard William	77–81	"	57	Andover
K	Mahoney Charles	77–81	"	38	New Haven Ct
L	Mahoney John	77–81	"	50	here
M	Mahoney William H	77–81	"	34	Oakland Cal
N	Marks Hugo C	77–81	"	25	Detroit Mich
O	McArthur George	77–81	"	48	Buffalo N Y
P	Meyer Harley	77–81	"	26	Dubuque Ia
R	Morris John	77–81	"	48	City Hospital
S	Mosely James	77–81	"	73	here
T	Moulton Erastus B	77–81	"	55	"
U	Muller Lester	77–81	"	30	St Louis Mo
V	Richards John A	77–81	"	40	Reading
W	Saunders Morton	77–81	"	24	Bangor Me
X	Sorenson Oae	77–81	"	41	695 East Seventh
Y	Studley Edward	77–81	"	61	Boothbay Me
Z	Sullivan Jeremiah J	77–81	"	39	39 Staniford
A	Sullivan Timothy	77–81	"	32	Bridgewater
B	Thomas Harriet J—†	77–81	housewife	23	here
C	Thomas John W	77–81	clergyman	29	"
D	Thompson Louis	77–81	laborer	50	Montreal Can
E	Vining George H	77–81	"	54	Syracuse N Y
F	White Neil	77–81	clerk	28	here
G	Wiegand Carl W	77–81	laborer	32	Suffolk County
H	Williams Herbert	77–81	"	35	England
K	Woodes Herschell	77–81	"	63	Lowell

Shawmut Avenue—Continued

L	Wylie James	77–81	laborer	67	here	
N	Barnard Addie—†	85	janitress	60	"	
O	Beardsley George	85	printer	25	"	
P	Beardsley Hazel—†	85	housewife	23	"	
R	Fagan Mary—†	85	nurse	60	"	

Shawmut Street

T	Bartolo Pietro	4	laborer	29	Italy	
U	Forti Albert	4	waiter	24	here	
V	Bambogi Guilio	4	cook	28	"	
W	Guitianette Effrem	4	"	25	"	
X	Pacini Demetrio	4	"	42	"	
Y	Pacini Julia—†	4	housewife	42	"	
Z	Piecotti Romeo	4	laborer	26	"	
A	O'Brien Edward J	6	auctioneer	66	"	
B	O'Brien Edward J, jr	6	clerk	37	Brookline	
F	Quealey Emma L—†	17	"	36	here	
G	Quealey Honara—†	17	dressmaker	40	"	
H	Quealey Katherine—†	17	typist	31	"	
K	Quealey Louise—†	17	housekeeper	38	"	
L	Quealey Mathew H	17	clerk	37	"	
N	Jones Henderson	19	waiter	59	"	
O	Parker Ruth V—†	19	housekeeper	50	"	
P	Graham Gertrude—†	20	housewife	26	"	
R	Graham Samuel	20	porter	27	"	
S	Sylva Francis	20	laborer	34	19 Rose	
T	Sylva John	20	"	49	here	
U	Britto Martin P	20	"	51	"	
V	Brooks George	20	"	36	Atlanta Ga	
W	Kelly Mary—†	21	cook	50	here	
X	McGonagle Annie—†	21	waitress	40	"	
Y	McInnis Eliza—†	21	housekeeper	40	"	
Z	Smith Elizabeth—†	21	chambermaid	60	"	
A	Thomas Fanny—†	21	cook	58	"	
B	Williams Mary—†	21	"	60	"	
C	Sullivan James A	22	stone pointer	44	"	
D	Sullivan Margaret E—†	22	housekeeper	75	"	
E	Eames Herbert E	23	cattle dealer	62	"	

Shawmut Street— Continued

F	Eames Mable W—†	23	domestic	49	here
G	Hobbs Edith W—†	25	weaver	40	"
H	Richardson Lonlie—†	25	handweaver	35	"

South Cedar Place

K	Finisti John J	2	chef	40	Framingham
L	Cook Nora—†	2	housekeeper	60	Brookline
M	Hayes Bridget A—†	2	"	60	here
N	Hayes John J	2	elevatorman	65	"
O	Hayes Joseph P	2	chauffeur	28	"

Stuart Street

W	Bennett Rufus H	129	engineer	60	here
Y	Giracca Emma—†	133	housewife	48	"
Z	Giracca Harry	133	laborer	23	"
A	Landry Anna—†	133	factory worker	23	Canada
B	Marquis Clara—†	133	housewife	46	here
C	Marquis Paul	133	machinist	45	"
D	Heffernan Daniel J	133	lineman	21	"
E	Heffernan John	133	laborer	45	"
F	Heffernan Mary—†	133	housewife	43	"
G	Wise Augustus	133	bookbinder	45	"
H	Wise Emily—†	133	housewife	34	"
K	Jenkins Annie E—†	133	"	49	"
L	Jenkins Oliver L	133	actor	67	"
M	Delory Ella E—†	133	housewife	41	"
N	Reed Frank L	133	salesman	45	"
O	Steward Bethel—†	133	housewife	34	"
P	Steward James	133	mechanic	35	"
R	Blanchard Ina F—†	133	laundress	50	"
T	Sweeney Annie—†	139	dishwasher	45	"
U	Lamis Mary—†	139	housewife	27	"
V	Lamis William	139	waiter	36	"
W	Kennedy Delia—†	139	housewife	64	"
X	Kennedy James P	139	retired	79	"
Y	Kennedy Joseph P	139	clerk	24	"
Z	MacDonald Inez—†	139	waitress	29	"

Stuart Street—Continued

A	Kekeris John	141	tailor	50	here
B	Sullivan Helen—†	141	reel winder	30	"
C	Sullivan James	141	telephoneman	30	"
D	Sullivan John A	141	student	21	"
E	Sullivan John W	141	collector	45	"
F	Sullivan Josephine—†	141	housewife	40	"
G	Gallagher Evelyn—†	141	restaurantman	40	"
H	O'Connell Elizabeth—†	141	"	40	"

Townsend Place

T	Bates Abigail—†	8	housewife	70	here
U	Bates Charles	8	carpenter	65	"
V	Lyman Elizabeth—†	8	housewife	64	60 Warrentor
W	Murray Eleanor E—†	8	cook	57	here

Tremont Street

D	Delery Josephine—†	231	housekeeper	46	here
E	Delery Oscar	231	boxmaker	65	"
F	Manookian Karekin E	231	real estate	36	"
G	Tirell Louise A—†	231	housekeeper	55	"
L	Crossett Marion—†	245	cashier	25	1213 Beacon
M	Duff Vera K—†	245	saleswoman	26	Montreal Can
N	Fields Herbert	245	merchant	32	Providence R
O	Harrington Daniel J	245	clerk	58	here
P	Harrington Elinor J—†	245	housewife	52	"
R	Holdridge Clifford N	245	salesman	48	New York City
S	Howard Pearl—†	245	actress	28	"
T	Jenkins Josephine F—†	245	housewife	38	here
U	McCabe Frank	245	garagekeeper	48	Hyannisport
V	O'Meara Daniel	245	actor	30	New York City
W	Rattajo Christos A	245	physician	39	21 Hollis
X	Regan James P	245	proprietor	42	here
Y	Roberts Frank A	245	superintendent	50	"
Z	Stahl George A	245	retired	70	"
A	Stowell Fredericks	245	counterman	28	35 Blaine av
B	Walsh Joseph A	245	salesman	38	31 Mt Ida rd
D	Bova Leo E	253 & 255	manager	63	here

Letter	Full Name	Residence, April 1, 1924	Occupation	Supposed Age	Reported Residence, April 1, 1923. Street and Number.
	Tremont Street—Continued				
E	Fisher Janet—†	253 & 255	housekeeper	46	here
F	Romane Ernest	253 & 255	busboy	26	"
G	Smiddle Frank	253 & 255	dishwasher	25	"
H	Wilson Herbert	253 & 255	houseman	25	"
N	Kantaros Christos	275	bootblack	55	"
O	Gray Charles A	285	publisher	37	106 Belvidere
P	Mitsakos Demetrious	285	physician	50	280 Tremont
R	Casey John	285	steamfitter	44	29 Hollis
S	Gogin Ida A—†	285	housewife	37	Medford
T	Gogin James B	285	foreman	42	"
U	Jones Anna—†	285	usher	39	29 Hollis
V	Sousa Amelia—†	285	housewife	41	29 "
W	Edwards Jessie L—†	285	housekeeper	44	143 W Newton
X	Edwards Robert M	285	electrician	49	143 "
Y	Anderson Beatrice—†	285	housekeeper	24	Canada
Z	Anderson James P	285	machinist	31	New Brunswick
A	Natanson Louis	285	salesman	29	232 Magnolia
B	Natanson Rose—†	285	housekeeper	22	232 "
D	Fish Delbert	293	machinist	48	here
E	Fish Rose—†	293	housekeeper	44	"
F	Lyons James M	293	machinist	64	"
G	Lyons Mary J—†	293	housekeeper	63	"
H	Berkland Bertha—†	293	housewife	48	"
K	Knight Fannie B—†	293	"	68	"
M	Wright Margaret—†	297	housekeeper	63	"
N	Woodhead Ellen—†	297	"	61	"
O	Woodhead Frank	297	clerk	58	"
P	Hasten Caroline M—†	297	garmentworker	53	668 Tremont
R	Arding George W	297	fishcutter	55	668 "
S	Hamel Beata—†	297	housewife	39	30 Fayette
T	Hamel Joseph J	297	carpenter	46	30 "
U	Hall Delia—†	297	housewife	64	27 Melrose
V	Hall Fred	297	garageman	66	27 "
W	Kinsman Mildred—†	297	strawworker	49	here
X	Magee Eldora—†	297	"	56	"
Y	Ford Augustin	297	clerk	45	"
Z	Stevens Louise—†	297	laundress	53	"
A	Butler Addie—†	297	nurse	54	"
B	Butler Walter	297	agent	59	"
C	Leathers Fred	297	barber	62	"
D	Leathers Stella—†	297	housewife	62	"

Tremont Street—Continued

	Letter	FULL NAME	Residence	Occupation	Age	Reported Residence
	E	Ball Alice—†	297	housewife	31	here
	F	Ball Ara E	297	clerk	39	"
	G	Hamilton Jessie—†	297	factory worker	53	"
	H	Nicholson Minerva—†	297	garment worker	47	"
	N	Lanigell Frank H	315	clerk	37	Somerville
	O	Lee Ernest F	315	proprietor	50	here
	P	Millner James N	315	contractor	68	Somerville
	X	Cobb Anna—†	326	housekeeper	65	here
	Y	Cobb Clara—†	326	"	40	"
	Z	Royle Roland	326	painter	55	"
	A	Newell Helen F—†	326	housekeeper	65	"
	B	Newell William E	326	waiter	59	"
	B¹	Bedor Mary—†	326	housewife	60	"
	C	Gallant Abbie—†	326	elevatorwoman	40	"
	D	Brown Arthur F	326	retired	65	"
	E	Brown Fannie I—†	326	stitcher	60	"
	F	Brown Leon E	326	machinist	30	"
	G	Fisher Elizabeth I—†	326	inspector	39	1 Dakota
	H	Fisher William A	326	fireman	56	1 "
	L	Burke Francis L—†	328	waiter	56	here
	M	Freni Mary—†	328	rubbermaker	25	38 Putnam
	N	Ginko Louis	328	butcher	32	Chelsea
	O	Lansberry Bertha—†	328	dressmaker	23	Malden
	P	Lyons Michael	328	janitor	45	here
	R	Mandigo Clara—†	328	domestic	52	Rutland
	S	Stone Ella G—†	328	physician	59	here
	T	Stone Frederick	328	stockbroker	35	"
	U	Berry Stephen	330	retired	59	"
	V	Douglas Daniel A	330	laborer	49	"
	W	Hurd Edward	330	painter	58	"
	X	Morrison Lexie—†	330	housekeeper	53	"
	Y	Stewart Harry	330	teamster	44	"
	Z	Alphin Leonard F	331	manager	41	"
	A	Alphin Mary R—†	331	housewife	40	"
	B	Chester William E	331	manager	58	"
	C	Finn Robert E	331	poolroom	29	254 Tremont
	D	Keenan Joseph	331	manager	29'	here
	E	Kelly James F	331	actor	41	Jersey City N J
	F	Kelly James J	331	billposter	38	6 Warrenton
	G	Kipp Adeline—†	331	actress	34	315 Tremont
	H	Kipp Joseph	331	actor	49	315 "

Tremont Street—Continued

к	Latoy Harry	331	actor	38	Natick
l	Lee Edna—†	331	actress	30	New York City
m	Libbey Hermina—†	331	housekeeper	40	here
n	Libbey Walter	331	bellboy	28	"
o	Murray Alexander	331	stagehand	42	27 Hollis
p	Reynolds Agnes—†	331	housewife	24	Chicago Ill
r	Ross Harry A	331	stagehand	42	New York City
s	Rourke Joseph A	331	engineer	56	82 Carver
t	Arzoomanian Yerimiah G	332	agent	41	Salem
u	Bertolaccini Lucy—†	332	housewife	40	here
v	Bertolaccini Ulisse	332	cook	40	"
w	Lucchesi Natale	332	busboy	24	"
y	Abbott Austin	333	blacksmith	68	"
z	Clamp Mary A—†	333	clerk	34	"
a	Clamp Richard B	333	"	37	"
b	Daniell Frank E	333	bookkeeper	55	31 Common
c	Gervais Arthur B	333	agent	48	Nashua N H
d	Mooney Fredrick	333	laborer	42	here
e	Purcell Walter H	333	printer	42	Weymouth
f	Truell William	333	shipper	26	here
g	Visuroyoily Louis	333	shoemaker	30	"
h	Selice Angelina—†	334	housewife	28	"
k	Selice Pasqulie	334	chauffeur	35	"
l	Pettenati Frederick	334	cook	32	Portland Me
m	Pettenati Mary—†	334	housewife	33	"
n	Wylie Mildred—†	334	"	49	23 Corning
o	Wylie Standish P	334	painter	48	23 "
p	Altomaro Salvatore	335	designer	21	50 Colonial av
r	Bricker Louis	335	tailor	28	131 Jersey
s	Brown Charles C	335	mechanic	43	Watertown
t	Cavanna Madelina—†	335	housewife	41	Nantasket
u	Hamel Paul A	335	foreman	27	Ottawa Can
v	Heneberry Rose—†	335	housewife	45	Halifax N S
w	Heneberry Thomas	335	carpenter	48	"
x	Higgens Walter L	335	laborer	28	Lowell
y	Jurgenson Helena—†	335	housewife	59	59 Dwight
z	Kates Logan H	335	chiropodist	33	E Malone N Y
a	Kozanis George N	335	cook	33	New Bedford
b	Rivet Claudia—†	335	singer	27	Lowell
c	Baker Louis	336	laborer	44	here
d	Bouner Roland	336	cabman	63	Montpelier Vt

Page	Letter	Full Name.	Residence, April 1, 1924.	Occupation.	Supposed Age.	Reported Residence, April 1, 1923. Street and Number.	Page.

Tremont Street—Continued

E	Calef Edward B	336	retired	75	here
F	Joseph Mary—†	336	housekeeper	55	"
G	Krug Charles	336	cook	53	"
H	Cronin David	337	laborer	48	1 Hancock
K	Douglas Nellie C—†	337	stitcher	65	Worcester
L	Halin Ehsan	337	laborer	42	New York City
M	McCarthy Thomas	337	clerk	34	here
N	Miller Harry N	337	rubberworker	30	Hudson
O	Davis Margaret—†	338	waitress	23	New Hampshire
P	Lang John	338	waiter	22	359 Tremont
R	Powers John	338	clerk	25	Somerville
S	Sullivan Gertrude—†	338	housekeeper	40	here
T	Sullivan John A	338	presser	48	"
U	Sullivan John F	338	teamster	45	Everett
V	Dunn Michael	339	retired	76	here
W	Green Albert C	339	broker	45	"
X	Hyde Joseph B	339	salesman	57	"
Y	Arsenault Frank	340	laborer	30	Pittsburg Pa
Z	Coles George	340	elevatorman	57	335 Tremont
A	Corcoran Charles H	340	cook	65	38 Warrenton
B	English William	340	retired	60	Hopkinton
C	Grover Marshall	340	"	53	35 Tremont
D	Jones Henry	340	mechanic	40	12 Oak
E	Keyes Charles	340	meat cutter	73	335 Tremont
F	La Force John	340	metalworker	51	335 "
G	Slicer Ella—†	340	housekeeper	55	335 "
H	Van Gilder Katherine—†	340	"	32	335 "
K	Bell Hattie E—†	341	cashier	23	Canada
L	Brenner Leo	341	salesman	35	Lynn
M	Coleman James	341	laborer	65	here
N	Hollenbeck Charles	341	"	24	Cleveland
O	Hechinger Josephine—†	341	bookbinder	52	here
P	Love William	341	accountant	49	Canada
R	Ringer George D	341	cook	22	Cleveland
S	Sampson George	341	clerk	53	here
T	Sherrer Martin	341	shipper	60	495 Broadway
U	White George	341	florist	43	here
V	White Marie L—†	341	housewife	29	"
W	Burcke Thomas	342	salesman	31	New York City
X	Forst Alba B	342	laborer	41	Cambridge
Y	Geary Thomas	342	teamster	23	New York City

48

Tremont Street—Continued

z	Martins Mary—†	342	housewife	43	here
A	Martins Marcizo	342	fireman	45	"
B	Martins Thomas	342	machinist	36	New Haven Ct
C	McKenna William	342	laborer	53	here
D	Miller Oscar	342	cook	40	Providence R I
E	Rodgers Thomas	342	laborer	28	Nova Scotia
F	Walsh William	342	"	21	Canada
G	Walter Army	342	baker	25	Sweden
H	Ardoff John	343A	garment cutter	28	here
K	Cleave Joseph	343A	porter	30	New York City
L	McNally Anna—†	343A	housewife	34	Portsmouth N H
M	McNally Thomas F	343A	machinist	37	"
N	Reardon Catherine—†	343A	housewife	40	here
O	Reardon James	343A	ironworker	41	"
P	Reardon Walter	343A	salesman	24	"
R	Romano Alice—†	343A	domestic	30	"
S	Bromberger Hannah—†	344	housekeeper	83	"
T	Hassan Charles	344	dishwasher	50	"
U	Johnson Emil	344	laborer	25	Sweden
V	Kavadas Gertrude—†	344	housewife	32	here
W	Kavadas John E	344	cook	36	"
X	Bucklus George D	345A	salesman	35	2 Dillaway
Y	Davis Walter	345A	laborer	30	2 "
Z	Francis Bolina—†	345A	housewife	40	here
A	Kolos George	345A	waiter	21	"
B	Kostinana Costas	345A	bellboy	25	"
C	Raymond Edward E	345A	dishwasher	25	Providence R I
D	McDonald Bernard	346	guard	23	1 Cazenove
E	McGrath Francis	346	shoeworker	25	Dover N H
F	Neilson Soren	346	ironworker	37	New York City
G	Olson Andrew G	346	shoemaker	64	here
H	Fisher Ella—†	347A	waitress	40	Lowell
K	Foley Markus	347A	baker	40	365 Tremont
L	Jackson Joseph	347A	mason	59	here
M	Joseph Frank	347A	laborer	50	"
N	Luscomb James	347A	cook	50	365 Tremont
O	McGilvary Arthur	347A	laborer	40	here
P	McGilvary Mary	347A	seamstress	30	"
R	Patnude Catherine—†	347A	housewife	56	"
S	Veno Fred	347A	carpenter	60	358 Tremont
T	Victory James	347A	baker	63	Portland Me

Tremont Street—Continued

U	Bradley Mark W	348	laborer	26	here
V	Cavanaugh Mary—†	348	houseworker	50	"
W	Evans Joseph	348	cook	28	"
X	Grant Elizabeth—†	348	housekeeper	49	14 Highland
Y	Guagasha Frank	348	mechanic	24	here
Z	McDonaugh Thomas	348	chauffeur	26	"
A	Mitchell Herbert	348	bellboy	22	"
B	Mitchell Priscilla—†	348	housewife	20	"
C	Portos Stanley	348	cook	20	"
D	Conoley Michael	349	laborer	58	"
E	Courtney James	349	"	70	48 Montgomery
F	Hall Charles	349	"	40	here
G	Hart Thomas	349	roofer	58	352 Tremont
H	Lawless Cristopher P	349	watchman	40	here
K	Lawless Ellen M—†	349	housewife	41	"
L	Lawrence Ida—†	349	seamstress	45	"
M	McGrath John	349	laborer	40	"
N	Morrisay Ellen—†	349	domestic	45	"
O	Nagle Thomas J	349	timekeeper	56	94 Appleton
P	O'Brien John P	349	painter	45	400 Third
R	Winn Frank J	349	watchman	45	here
S	Burkhart George	350	glazier	42	"
T	Cleveland Lalia—†	350	laundryworker	24	203 Broadway
U	Gammon Liza—†	350	retired	66	6 Warrenton
V	Haywood Fred	350	manager	38	New York City
W	Herlihy John	350	engineer	60	here
X	Holland John	350	cook	24	"
Y	Holland William	350	shipper	62	"
Z	Labare Walter	350	chauffeur	35	"
A	Martel Sarah—†	350	housewife	23	"
B	Martel William C	350	houseman	38	"
C	Norton Frank	350	cook	55	"
D	Suess Annie—†	350	housekeeper	42	22 Cortez
E	Tarbox Everett	350	chauffeur	26	203 Broadway
G	Anderson Peter	352	laborer	60	Portland Me
H	Ballantine Annie—†	352	cook	60	Stoughton
K	Bland James	352	laborer	35	here
L	Davis James	352	"	54	Somerville
M	Dunkley Peter	352	carpenter	65	here
N	Heinicke Moses	352	laborer	55	"
O	Matson John	352	riveter	50	Providence R I

Tremont Street—Continued

Letter.	FULL NAME.	Residence, April 1, 1924	Occupation.	Supposed Age.	Reported Residence, April 1, 1923. Street and Number.
P	Mattermo John J	352	cook	42	Fitchburg
R	Nielson John	352	laborer	35	here
S	Perry Charles	352	cook	25	"
T	Polsky Joseph	352	"	30	Fitchburg
U	Weinglen Fred	352	"	36	N Adams
V	Blanchette Emilie—†	354	housewife	68	here
W	Blanchette Nai	354	laborer	66	"
X	Brennan Richard W	354	bookbinder	69	New York City
Y	Broderick Edwards A	354	boilermaker	59	Cambridge
Z	Cabbot Julius	356	fireman	27	Artic R I
A	Farrell Theresa—†	356	housekeeper	53	here
B	Kubber George	356	counterman	34	Detroit Mich
C	Lyons William T	356	stereotyper	80	here
D	Stone Ann E—†	356	nurse	71	"
E	Tidlund Albert	356	chef	26	"
G	Malcolm Annie—†	358	saleswoman	40	"
H	Malcolm Katherine—†	358	housewife	65	"
K	Menaguain Barroir	358	cook	25	Lynn
L	Pearson Neil	358	fireman	64	58 Porter
M	Baker Eva—†	359	housewife	32	here
N	Baker Walter H	359	manager	43	"
R	Brown William	359	watchman	36	"
O	Burke John F	359	electrician	28	Gorham N H
P	Champlin Frank L	359	shoemaker	50	California
S	Hymere Stanley	359	waiter	20	here
T	Mally John A	359	marblesetter	45	7 Hanson
U	Sturdevant Earnest	359	fireman	38	here
V	Davis George	360½	chauffeur	61	"
W	Hand Frank J	360½	carpenter	50	"
X	McDermott Thomas	360½	foreman	63	"
Y	Papanastassin Earnest	360½	waiter	28	"
Z	Smith Wilfred R	360½	counterman	35	222 Shawmut av
A	Whiting Frank B	360½	teamster	62	here
B	Bailey William	361	laborer	23	"
C	Diamond Leland	361	bellboy	21	"
D	Baldi Daniel	362	screenmaker	52	"
E	Baldi Eletta—†	362	housewife	51	"
F	Spilios Annie—†	362	"	28	30 Corning
G	Spilios Louis	362	porter	35	30 "
H	Alden Elizabeth—†	362	housewife	47	Everett
K	Mangene Sarah—†	362	"	47	here

Tremont Street—Continued

M	Brown Albert	363	carpenter	50	here
N	Cuiahne John	363	chef	47	"
O	Fenton Alice—†	363	cook	55	Newton
P	Finney Ethel H—†	363	musician	40	here
R	Mednitsky Rose—†	363	domestic	21	New York Ci
S	Monahan Catherine—†	363	cook	42	65 Carver
T	Roy Alice—†	363	waitress	21	Lewiston Me
U	Sawyer Albert	363	laborer	62	here
V	Sturdevant George	363	elevatorman	48	"
W	Richards Julia M—†	364	housewife	42	"
X	Richards William H	364	waiter	45	"
Y	Bonaccorsi Alfred	364	barber	34	"
Z	Bonaccorsi Nina—†	364	housewife	38	"
A	Brown Ernestina—†	364	saleswoman	30	"
B	Brown Louis	364	clerk	48	"
C	Beede Annie—†	365	housekeeper	55	"
D	Cabrab Manuel I	365	laborer	42	Providence F
E	Allen James E	366	barber	54	here
F	Alston Margret—†	366	cook	24	160 W Springfield
G	Alston William	366	"	24	160 "
H	Brown Robert	366	"	72	13 Church
K	Henry George	366	waiter	24	160 W Springfield
L	Hillyer Ross	366	barber	32	here
M	Jones Clarence J	366	postal clerk	26	"
N	McDonald William	366	waiter	36	163 W Springfield
P	Calapi Philipa—†	367A	pantsmaker	55	here
O	Calapi Plato	367A	grocer	22	"
R	Gangarossa Joseph	367A	barber	65	"
S	Gangarossa Margaret—†	367A	housewife	35	"
T	Barela Mary—†	367A	"	40	"
U	Earley Thomas	368A	saladmaker	36	13 Groton
V	Frazer Mary A—†	368A	housekeeper	22	13 Corning
W	Frazer Walter	368A	counterman	28	13 "
X	Harrington John G	368A	saladmaker	50	13 "
Y	Harrington Margaret—†	368A	housekeeper	48	13 "
Z	Harrington Margaret T—†	368A	film winder	23	13 "
A	Harris Daniel J	368A	accountant	24	Lynn
B	Pacticcio Terrance	368A	dishwasher	40	13 Corning
C	Regan Francis	368A	longshoreman	38	13 "
E	Cocurello Frank	369A	cook	54	here
F	Cocurello Mary—†	369A	dressmaker	42	"

Tremont Street—Continued

Letter.	FULL NAME.	Residence, April 1, 1924.	Occupation.	Supposed Age.	Reported Residence, April 1, 1923.
G	Alizio Joseph	369A	barber	49	here
H	Alizio Mary—†	369A	housewife	47	"
K	Bartholmew Edward T	370	storekeeper	67	"
L	Bartholmew Emma S—†	370	housekeeper	64	"
P	Cummings Fred C	374	laborer	50	285 Tremont
R	Hart Edward	374	clerk	40	30 Isabella
S	Simonds Louise A—†	374	housekeeper	54	285 Tremont
T	Collins Frank	375	watchman	40	here
U	Dakagirian Ationes	375	kitchen worker	50	19 Corning
V	Ganaun Antonio	375	lodging house	56	67 "
W	Hanvin Manock	375	porter	48	76 "
X	Killian James	375	fireman	44	93 Tyler
Y	Killian Katherine—†	375	housewife	40	93 "
Z	Rounsefell Ethel—†	375	elevatorwoman	21	Canada
A	Rucci Constance—†	376	tailor	36	479 Hanover
B	Rucci Dominick	376	storekeeper	41	479 "
D	Asiugolos Petter E	378	painter	28	179 Harris'n av
E	Bergin Edward	378	laborer	32	160 W Seventh
F	Brusalle John	378	"	28	3 Warrenton
G	Nicholas Gilberthe K—†	378	housekeeper	30	3 "
H	Nicholas John K	378	tailor	30	3 "
K	Seruton Andrew J	378	painter	42	Portland Me
L	Stavros Louis P	378	laborer	30	here
M	Tsakeres Nicholas P	378	cook	32	"
N	Tsakeres Panagiata—†	378	housekeeper	33	"
O	Xenakis Michell E	378	tailor	33	464 Tremont
P	Givonetti Alberto	379	"	40	here
R	Givonetti Dora—†	379	housewife	33	"
S	Rivolta Guiseppe	379	butcher	50	"
T	Faherty Bertha E—†	379	housewife	23	695 Tremont
U	Faherty John J	379	chauffeur	30	695 "
V	Maxwell Bertha—†	379	waitress	26	Belmont
W	Sirunian Anthy—†	379	housewife	42	Watertown
X	Sirunian Garabed	379	plumber	36	"
Z	Duffey Nellie—†	381	housewife	30	here
A	Duffey Patrick	381	janitor	35	"
B	Galvin Francis	381	billposter	27	"
C	Shea Kathrine—†	381	housewife	65	"
D	Shea Nora—†	381	boxmaker	28	"
E	Thebideau Charles A	381	printer	35	"
F	Thebideau Helen—†	381	housewife	35	"

Tremont Street—Continued

G	Foley Henry J	381	billposter	40	here
H	Foley John E	381	"	43	"
L	Diakow Peter	383	shoemaker	42	Chelsea

Warrenton Place

P	Paporis Arthur	5	tailor	55	here
R	Riley Mary—†	5	scrubwoman	45	Providence F
T	Lee Annie—†	7	housekeeper	55	here
S	Sills Delia—†	7	kitchenworker	43	"
U	Sweeney Josephine—†	11	"	58	"
V	Sweeney Michael A	11	hostler	58	"
W	Kennedy Catherine—†	11	seamstress	50	"
X	Grady Bridget—†	11	housewife	51	Hull
Y	Grady Frances—†	11	clerk	20	"
Z	Grady John H	11	fireman	60	"
A	Brooks Mary—†	11	laundress	40	here
B	Farah George	11	cook	27	29 Harvard
C	Farah Nazra—†	11	stitcher	27	157 Tyler
D	Grimanellis Olga—†	11	housewife	22	here
E	Grimanellis Vasilois	11	laborer	40	"
G	Hoar Margaret—†	11	scrubwoman	50	"
H	Hoar Nellie—†	11	"	51	"
K	Moriarty Mary—†	11	"	50	80 Village
L	Alex Edith—†	11	clerk	30	here
M	Alex John	11	laborer	41	"

Warrenton Street

O	Brannan Edward	60	cook	44	36 Warrenton
P	Brannan Mary—†	60	housewife	40	36 "
R	Johnson Lyman	60	machinist	31	Canada
S	Johnson Mary—†	60	housewife	30	"
T	McCarthy Dennis	60	railroad police	38	here
U	McCarthy Katherine—†	60	housekeeper	38	"
V	McKenna James	60	watchman	48	"
W	Carle Joseph S	62	ice cream	49	"
X	Cushman Frank	62	editor	68	"
Y	Hall Siles	62	hotel clerk	66	"

Warrenton Street — Continued

z	Lawford Charles E	62	paperhanger	70	here
A	Caldwell Harriet —†	63	missionary	22	"
B	Fennell Jennie —†	63	"	35	Everett
c	Hubbart James W	63	clergyman	48	here
D	Hubbart Marie E —†	63	"	51	"
E	Read Joseph	63	missionary	28	"
F	Richards Amy —†	63	"	45	"
G	Sammis Marian —†	63	"	35	Wisconsin
H	Spaulding Dora —†	63	"	52	here
K	Spece Earl	63	"	43	"
L	Zerbe Clarence	63	"	32	Wisconsin
M	Zerbe Helen M —†	63	"	28	"
N	Baker Charles J	64	laborer	28	here
O	Boucher Richard	64	switchman	62	"
P	Brook Hickman G	64	notary public	58	"
R	Driscoll John	64	plasterer	72	12 Dillaway
S	Fogarty Michael	64	carpenter	63	here
T	Kackerkas Kossos	64	barber	41	62 Carver
U	Lanane Clifford	64	cook	21	72 Waltham
V	Lyons James H	64	laborer	67	12 Dillaway
W	McAllester Patrick J	64	clerk	51	here
X	McDuff Daniel	64	machinist	62	82 Carver
Y	McKay Wesley	64	carpenter	40	Wash'n D C
z	Small William	64	accountant	36	here
A	Swinnerton William H	64	butler	35	"
B	Tworing Joseph F	64	student	23	Adams
c	Brennan Dorothy —†	66	ticket taker	26	27 Hollis
D	Cavanaugh Daniel	66	carpenter	32	27 "
E	Cline Allen S	66	chauffeur	26	here
F	Devoe Ethel —†	66	hairdresser	26	27 Hollis
G	Durant Rose —†	66	shoeworker	28	27 "
H	Fong Harold	66	student	22	27 "
K	Jacobs Lulla —†	66	saleswoman	48	28 "
L	Kerwood William	66	expressman	40	here
M	McMulland Margaret —†	66	retired	50	Providence R I
N	Morrisett Mary —†	66	waitress	40	here
O	Pitts Mary E —†	66	housekeeper	53	27 Hollis
P	Salamie Salmon W	66	pedler	26	here
R	Vanolenburgh Morris	66	waiter	50	"
S	Ackerson Adella M —†	68	secretary	40	"
T	Allen Lillian —†	68	waitress	30	"

Page	Letter	Full Name.	Residence, April 1, 1924.	Occupation.	Supposed Age.	Reported Residence, April 1, 1923. Street and Number.

Warrenton Street—Continued

	U	Bean Esther M—†	68	stenographer	24	here
	V	Beaton Mary E—†	68	"	24	"
	W	Bedders Saima L—†	68	"	20	New Hampshire
	X	Belcher Mildred A—†	68	"	23	Mansfield
	Y	Bibighaus Bessie M—†	68	student	27	here
	Z	Birmingham Mae—†	68	waitress	23	New Hampshire
	A	Blanchard Florence E—†	68	nurse	24	Keene N H
	B	Blanchard Helen J—†	68	"	24	"
	C	Boorman Myrtle—†	68	clerk	23	Rochester N Y
	D	Brain Alice—†	68	waitress	35	here
	E	Britton Gladys—†	68	milliner	27	Maine
	F	Brooks Alice M—†	68	comptometrist	30	here
	G	Brown Edna M—†	68	typist	24	"
	H	Brown Margery—†	68	stenographer	23	Coventry R I
	K	Budd Louise C—†	68	student	23	here
	L	Caldwell Retta L—†	68	stenographer	26	"
	M	Carmichael Sadie E—†	68	bookkeeper	27	"
	N	Carver Lillian F—†	68	stenographer	21	Brant Rock
	O	Cline Louise H—†	68	"	22	here
	P	Coombs Helen L—†	68	artist	28	"
	R	Copp Charles	68	fireman	50	"
	S	Cowles Annette M—†	68	physician	54	"
	T	Cullinan Katherine—†	68	stenographer	21	New Hampshire
	U	Cullinan Mary F—†	68	"	26	here
	V	Dahlquest Beda M—†	68	clerk	22	"
	W	Dickey Elizabeth A—†	68	student	22	Spearfish S D
	X	Doane Margaret—†	68	clerk	27	here
	Y	Dunster Frances S—†	68	tel operator	23	"
	Z	Fitzmaurice Margaret L—†	68	typist	23	Brockton
	A	Flynn Mary—†	68	cook	40	here
	B	Fuller Alice C—†	68	clerk	29	"
	C	Gallagher Dorris—†	68	bookkeeper	22	"
	D	Gallagher Sarah—†	68	stenographer	22	"
	E	Gardner Mae B—†	68	clerk	29	Fall River
	F	Goldsmith Gladys—†	68	bookkeeper	25	here
	G	Ham Muriel—†	68	sewing teacher	24	"
	H	Hanrahan Elizabeth—†	68	stenographer	25	Brooklyn N Y
	K	Harriman Ione J—†	68	clerk	24	here
	L	Harris Mary—†	68	stenographer	20	Warsaw N Y
	M	Haskell Agnes—†	68	"	20	here
	N	Huff Minnie—†	68	student	27	"

Warrenton Street—Continued

Letter.	FULL NAME.	Residence, April 1, 1924.	Occupation.	Supposed Age.	Reported Residence, April 1, 1923. Street and Number.
o	Jennings Hannah —†	68	milliner	28	Lawrence
p	Johnson Ethel A—†	68	saleswoman	25	here
r	Johnson Greta—†	68	waitress	21	"
s	Jones Gertrude—†	68	housekeeper	40	Syracuse N Y
t	Joyce Nora—†	68	waitress	25	here
u	Lahan Ruth E D—†	68	student	21	Connecticut
v	Laurie Helen R—†	68	tailoress	22	Andover
w	Lener Esther V—†	68	clerk	21	here
x	Lewis Ethel B—†	68	"	22	Connecticut
y	Lewis Hilda P—†	68	"	25	here
z	MacCondach Josephine —†	68	chambermaid	50	"
A	MacDonald Rena—†	68	clerk	23	"
B	MacInnis Marjorie—†	68	stenographer	20	Brookside N S
c	MacKinnon Arta—†	68	"	20	Melrose
D	MacLeay Margaret—†	68	"	23	here
E	MacLeod Daisy A—†	68	dressmaker	27	Canada
F	MacNeil Nellie—†	68	chambermaid	55	here
G	Maloney Mary E—†	68	tel operator	24	Somerville
H	McCarthy Annie—†	68	dishwasher	40	here
K	McDonald Maud—†	68	clerk	27	"
L	McEwen Lillian B—†	68	"	24	Wollaston
M	McInnis Katherine—†	68	"	25	here
N	McKinnon Minnie G—†	68	"	23	"
o	Meserve Dora L—†	68	secretary	21	Taunton
P	Munsey Belle—†	68	chambermaid	55	here
R	Murray Mary—†	68	"	64	"
s	Myrick Annie E—†	68	matron	55	"
T	Norton Doris M—†	68	secretary	22	S Hanover
u	Noyes Frank C	68	engineer	44	here
v	Ouellette Helen—†	68	milliner	22	"
w	Palmer Esther—†	68	student	29	Derry N H
x	Paulin Mary—†	68	waitress	28	here
y	Pollack Rachel—†	68	stenographer	26	"
z	Powers Mae M—†	68	clerk	26	"
A	Price Hilda—†	68	"	24	Nova Scotia
B	Putnam Helen—†	68	student	26	New Hampshire
c	Rayden Annie—†	68	cook	52	here
D	Ryder Marguerite E—†	68	saleswoman	23	Northfield
E	Salman Margaret—†	68	dishwasher	66	here
F	Sanderson Greta—†	68	stenographer	21	"
G	Sanger Florence—†	68	bookkeeper	20	"

Warrenton Street—Continued

H	Sheridian Dorothea S—†	68	dietitian	38	149 Mass av
K	Silva Anna T—†	68	bookkeeper	24	here
L	Stuart Lily M—†	68	clerk	27	"
M	Sword Ruth—†	68	stenographer	22	Northfield
N	Thomas Evelyn M—†	68	clerk	21	here
O	Thurston Frances E—†	68	"	25	"
P	Tiffany Harriett W—†	68	teacher	26	"
R	Todd Louise E—†	68	typist	27	"
S	Tuttle Mildred A—†	68	stenographer	24	"
T	Wolfe Evangeline—†	68	student	24	Plainville
U	Woodworth Laura—†	68	"	20	here
V	Wyer Margaret G—†	68	housekeeper	45	"
W	Young Lorena—†	68	teacher	29	Kansas Mo
X	Douglass Clarence	76	sexton	65	here
Y	Douglass Mary M—†	76	housewife	58	"
C	Bell George R	86	painter	48	here
D	Canny Anna—†	86	clerk	35	21 Winslow
E	Desaulniers Frederick	86	molder	40	20 Warren av
F	Desaulniers Mary—†	86	waitress	38	20 "
G	Garon George E	86	machinist	42	here
H	Joy Martin T	86	meatcutter	38	256 E
K	Manzie Thomas M	86	mechanic	48	86 Westville
L	McCachern Emma—†	86	clerk	35	Cambridge
M	Pierce John	86	watchman	38	85 Warren av
N	Scurtis Thomas	86	storekeeper	35	228A Tremon
O	Shea Lottie—†	86	nurse	36	here
P	Spruce Anna—†	86	waitress	28	56 Cabot
R	Spruce Burt M	86	switcher	35	56 "
S	Sweet Josephine—†	86	dressmaker	43	30 Wabon
V	Harvey Clarence	88	storekeeper	44	here
Y	Tait Herbert	88	truckman	32	"
Z	Cannon James	88	storekeeper	48	"
A	Hays Charles W	88	salesman	65	"
B	Carpenter Horace D	88	elevatorman	72	"
C	Conlon Mary—†	88	dressmaker	48	22 Dore
D	Ferris Mary—†	88	seamstress	31	here
E	Ferris Susanna—†	88	"	43	"
F	Smith Robert	88	janitor	50	"
G	Federici Joseph	88	laborer	40	"
H	Ottino Anna—†	88	housekeeper	45	"

58

Warrenton Street—Continued

K	Sears Anna—†	88	housekeeper	42	here
L	Sears Joseph	88	clerk	45	"
M	Clayton George	88	painter	45	"
N	Cressey Leland	88	janitor	32	"
O	Garvey Mary—†	90	housekeeper	70	"
P	McNamara Mary—†	90	"	48	"
R	Dube Luke	90	carpenter	46	5 Paul
S	Kelijain Charles	90	storekeeper	37	1 Hilley sq
T	Nickas Mary—†	90	housekeeper	31	1 "
V	Sullivan Deborah—†	90	domestic	49	here
W	Brown Nicholas	90	clerk	42	7 Common
X	Kiriagis Louis	90	cook	24	Providence R I
Y	Fitzgerald Margaret A—†	90	waitress	35	24 Montgomery
Z	Herrick Caroline—†	90	stitcher	38	78 Carver
A	Murphy Louise—†	90	chambermaid	44	here
B	Flansburg Mary—†	90	housekeeper	44	"
C	Earnshaw Margaret A—†	90	"	64	"
D	Earnshaw Thomas R	90	weaver	71	"
E	Eames Anna B—†	90	housekeeper	54	"
F	Eames William H	90	laborer	56	"
G	Richards Anne—†	90	housekeeper	32	"
H	Richards Napoleon	90	laborer	32	"
K	Bowton Della—†	90	housekeeper	32	"
L	Bowton John A	90	policeman	28	"
M	Murphy Helen L—†	90	clerk	20	"
N	Hamel Frank	90	carpenter	49	10 Melrose
O	Agestini Paul	90	waiter	27	here
P	Gambogi Felice—†	90	cook	37	"
R	Giusti Charles	90	"	36	"
S	Giusti Mary—†	90	housekeeper	32	"
T	Malvireuti Daniels	90	cook	23	"
U	Montenegro Lina—†	90	housekeeper	65	"
V	Montenegro Rose—†	90	dressmaker	36	"
W	Kelley Dennis P	90	laborer	63	"
X	Gallut Mary L—†	90	clerk	28	"
Y	Gallut Purre	90	waiter	38	"
C	Carver Frances—†	103	housewife	45	214 Col av
D	Carver Frank C	103	salesman	50	214 "
E	Tilson Leroy	103	laborer	74	here

Wheeler Street

N	McDonough Mary E—†	4	housewife	42	here
O	McDonough Philip P	4	forester	40	"
P	Lockhart John	4	porter	70	"
R	Lockhart Victoria—†	4	housekeeper	27	"
S	Contestabile Frank	9	pastry cook	28	"
T	Contestabile Josephine—†	9	housekeeper	58	"
U	Contestabile Patrick	9	ice cream	22	"
V	Leporati Giovanni	9	marketman	40	"
W	Pulcini Servrino	9	cook	32	
Y	Towns Ester—†	11	housekeeper	26	73 Compton
A	Jingozian Karakin	11	shoemaker	32	95 Bolton
B	Jingozian Simon	11	repairman	29	New York City
C	Grosvenor Bertha—†	13	housekeeper	31	here
D	Grosvenor William	13	laborer	30	"
E	Edwards Alonzo	13	porter	55	"
F	Edwards Ethel—†	13	housekeeper	40	"
G	Bootely Jennie—†	13	"	25	"
H	Bootely William	13	porter	26	"
K	Rogers Albion O	15	carpenter	72	"
O	Souther Frank	19	retired	80	"
P	Brown Anna—†	19	housekeeper	40	"
R	Mancuro Mary—†	19	"	45	"
V	Sutton Arthur	23	laborer	29	138 Castle
W	Sutton Wilhelmina—†	23	housekeeper	29	22 Dartmouth
X	Williams Alonzo	23	porter	40	here
Y	Williams Elva—†	23	housekeeper	39	"
Z	Cavanaugh Anna—†	23	"	52	"
A	Cavanaugh Maurice	23	painter	74	"
B	Hurmes Nicholas	25	coal dealer	45	"
C	Bowser George	25	laborer	60	73 Emerald
D	Frattasio Frank	27	"	51	here
E	Frattasio Teresa—†	27	housewife	42	"
F	Frattasio Bambina—†	27	"	51	"
G	Frattasio Donato	27	cook	48	"
H	Falcione Jenny—†	29	housewife	25	"
K	Falcione Patrick	29	cook	30	"
L	Perella Antony	29	coal dealer	40	"
M	Perella Bambina—†	29	housewife	43	"
N	Falcione Annie—†	29	"	33	"
O	Falcione Rocco	29	cook	40	"

Wheeler Street—Continued

P	Beane Anna—†	31	housewife	33	here
R	Beane Harry	31	carpenter	55	"
S	Bennett Louis	31	tailor	60	"
T	Bennett Pauline—†	31	housewife	33	"
U	Danovetch Emillian	31	carpenter	29	Canton
V	Yatsko Max	31	restaurantman	38	9 Upton
W	Zikin Mary—†	31	housekeeper	33	63 Corning
X	Zikin Walter	31	longshoreman	35	63 "

Winchester Street

B	Perella Domonick	4	foreman	26	here
C	Perella Mary—†	4	housewife	24	"
D	Perfetti Giovanni	4	tailor	37	"
E	Perfetti Pellegrino—†	4	housewife	27	"
F	Politakis Peter	4	laborer	38	"
G	Politakis Stella—†	4	housewife	36	"
H	Bora Carolina—†	4	"	50	"
K	Bora Enrico	4	cook	40	"
L	Chiochette Gioseppe	4	"	40	"
M	Rummler Alma H—†	4	stockings	29	"
N	Rummler Edward C	4	toolmaker	23	"
O	Rummler Emielia—†	4	housewife	59	"
P	Rummler Paul	4	chef	64	"
R	Vidal Aline—†	4	housewife	42	"
S	Vidal Gustave	4	cook	42	"
T	Sullivan Hannah—†	9	housewife	54	"
U	Sullivan Julia E—†	9	packer	23	"
V	Dalzall Mary—†	9	housewife	56	"
W	Dalzall Samuel	9	porter	70	"
X	Reid Albert J	9	stagehand	25	"
Y	Reid Ellen M—†	9	factory worker	38	"
Z	Reid Margaret B—†	9	housewife	60	"
A	Reid Patrick J	9	laborer	33	"
B	Kisilinsky Katherine—†	9	housewife	25	18 Winchester
C	Kisilinsky Stephen	9	laborer	29	18 "
D	Contestabile Antonio	9	cook	36	here
E	Crampaglio Luigino	9	"	25	"
F	DiGiovanni Nicola	9	"	36	"
G	DiSalvo Vendurino	9	"	33	"

Page	Letter	Full Name.	Residence, April 1, 1924.	Occupation.	Supposed Age.	Reported Residence, April 1, 1923. Street and Number.

Winchester Street—Continued

H	Zaccardi Angelo	9	cook	44	here
K	Zaccardi Untina—†	9	housewife	40	"
L	DiGiovani Unrico	9	cook	23	Naples Italy
N	Scordella Sabaten—†	9	"	49	here
M	Scordella Vergeanzi—†	9	housewife	42	"
O	Cenci Dominick	9	cook	65	"
P	Cenci Immacolata—†	9	housewife	24	"
R	Cenci Nicolas	9	waiter	30	"
S	Perrella Peter	9	cook	25	"
T	Cartanell Joseph	9	fireman	43	"
U	Matteo Maria—†	9	housewife	35	"
V	Matteo Raffaele	9	cook	35	"
W	Gracia Mary—†	9	housewife	50	"
X	Folco Joseph	9	kitchenman	53	"
Y	Folco Mary—†	9	housewife	59	"
Z	Martell John	9	cook	45	"
A	Perella Dominick	9	busboy	26	"
B	Perella John	9	cook	57	"
C	Perella Mariano	9	kitchenman	52	"
D	Flaherty Annie—†	10	housewife	45	"
E	Flaherty Timothy	10	shipper	47	"
F	Downey Catherine—†	10	housekeeper	45	"
G	Downey James	10	roofer	25	"
H	Downey John J	10	leatherworker	20	"
K	Downey Margaret—†	10	embroiderer	24	"
L	Cavicchi Matilda—†	10	housekeeper	46	"
M	Ottoania Otto	10	cook	41	"
S	Blake James J	14	chauffeur	26	Lowell
T	Blake Theresa—†	14	housewife	27	98 Park
U	Sava Athena—†	14	"	34	366 Col av
V	Sava Basil	14	timekeeper	45	366 "
W	Renaro Michael	14	manufacturer	45	here
X	Renaro Rose—†	14	housewife	37	"
Z	Colombine Grace—†	16	"	28	"
A	Colombini Joseph	16	garageman	32	"
B	Bertini Ada—†	16	dressmaker	24	"
C	Bertini Andrew	16	cook	44	"
D	Bertini Nello	16	"	30	"
E	Cicchini Mario	16	waiter	29	"
F	Giastucci Paola	16	cook	35	Italy
G	Orsi Amedeo	16	"	39	here

Winchester Street—Continued

Letter.	Full Name.	Residence, April 1, 1924.	Occupation.	Supposed Age.	Reported Residence, April 1, 1923. Street and Number.
H	Orsi Leoretta—†	16	housewife	33	here
K	Sema John	16	cook	43	"
L	Sema Mary—†	16	housewife	33	"
M	Macogni Carlo	16	plasterer	60	"
N	Macogni Elisa—†	16	housewife	55	"
O	Macogni Joseph	16	plumber	36	"
P	Macogni Renata—†	16	housewife	27	"
S	Burns Patrick	18	caretaker	45	"
T	Burns Theresa—†	18	housewife	36	"
U	Peter John	18	shoemaker	37	"
V	Weyand Anthony	18	electrician	30	"
W	Hazen George	18	sailor	25	14 Winchester
X	Payson Mary—†	18	housewife	50	14 "
Y	Payson Peter	18	laborer	65	14 "
Z	Maneuso Domenico	18	shoemaker	50	here
A	Maneuso Febia—†	18	housewife	46	"
B	Muldoon Annie J—†	18	"	52	"
C	Muldoon Patrick J	18	porter	57	"
D	Pandelfino Phillippa—†	18	housewife	42	"
E	Pandelfino Placido	18	barber	51	"
F	Piccione John	18	laborer	28	104 Carver
G	Piccione Sarah—†	18	housewife	28	104 "
H	Alizio Anthony	18	waiter	26	Italy
K	Alizio Maria—†	18	housewife	26	"
L	Davis Margarite—†	18	printer	30	257 Shawmut av
N	Farellaso John	19	waiter	24	239 Broadway
O	Gazola Joseph	19	cook	35	here
P	Gazola Mary—†	19	housewife	34	"
R	Changi Americo	19	busboy	21	"
S	Changi Joseph	19	hotelman	30	"
T	DiMariano Charles	19	dishwasher	38	"
U	DiSalva Joseph	19	cook	44	"
V	Palmier Cleonici—†	19	housewife	35	"
W	Palmier David	19	cook	36	"
X	Annechini Gaetano	19	laborer	22	Naples Italy
Y	DaLuca William	19	dishwasher	40	here
Z	Palmier James	19	cook	36	"
A	Palmier Madeline—†	19	housewife	30	"
B	Palmier Martin	19	cook	30	"
E	Ahern Margaret—†	22	milliner	23	"
F	Ahern Mary—†	22	housekeeper	63	"

Winchester Street— Continued

G	Clifford John	22	steamfitter	22	here
H	Clifford Margaret—†	22	houseworker	50	"
K	Griffin Bridget—†	24	housewife	49	"
L	Griffin John H	24	watchman	55	"
M	Griffin John J	24	meatcutter	21	"
N	Griffin Thomas J	24	clerk	23	"
O	Foley John F	24	laborer	46	"
P	O'Neil Abbie—†	24	houseworker	58	"
R	McElmoyle Edward	24	elevatorman	48	"
S	McElmoyle Sarah—†	24	housewife	43	"
T	McLean Mary—†	26	houseworker	42	9 Jefferson
U	Dywer Patrick	26	laborer	60	here
V	O'Reardon John	26	baggageman	45	739 Melrose
W	O'Reardon Katherine—†	26	housewife	40	39 "
Y	Martin Henry	30	storekeeper	65	here
Z	Martin Jeanne—†	30	"	55	"
A	Byrne Mary F—†	30	houseworker	45	"
B	Doyle Ellen M—†	30	"	75	"
C	Doyle Mary E—†	30	clerk	45	"
D	Snow Alice M—†	30	dressmaker	50	"
E	Snow Sarah—†	30	houseworker	80	"
F	Harrison Alice—†	31	housewife	38	"
G	Harrison John	31	rubberworker	58	"
H	Burke Annie—†	31	housewife	80	"
K	Burke Charles	31	laborer	56	"
L	Ellison Annie—†	31	factory worker	40	"
N	Clark Eliot	33	laborer	25	"
O	Hodges Samuel	33	"	39	"
P	Holder Clement	33	"	51	"
R	Myers Leah—†	33	housewife	40	"
S	Myers Thomas A	33	cook	52	"
U	McChoy Palmouse	35	laborer	29	"
V	Packer Luther	35	"	24	"
W	Packer Rebecca—†	35	housewife	21	"
X	Thomas Arthur	35	printer	42	Providence R
B	Colbert Catherine—†	39	housekeeper	62	26 Emerald
C	Diezel Rene	39	clerk	30	Lowell
G	Bisbee Anne I—†	45	housewife	33	here
H	Bisbee Charles A	45	jointer	44	"
K	Williams Anna—†	45	housewife	40	"
L	Williams James	45	cook	46	"

Winchester Street—Continued

o	Regan Katherine—†	49	school teacher	55	here
p	Regan Mary N—†	49	"	54	"
R	Ellis John	51	shipfitter	30	"
s	Field Arthur	51	fireman	30	Newtonville
T	Field Mabel—†	51	housewife	28	"
U	Gould Bertram H	51	mechanic	38	56 Carver
v	Gould Helen M—†	51	housekeeper	35	56 "
w	Kelley Patrick	51	laborer	60	here
x	Lynch Clyde	51	truck driver	40	56 Carver
y	Lynch Lottie C—†	51	draper	39	56 "
z	Scherm Rudolph	51	cigarmaker	53	2 Asylum

Ward 8—Precinct 7

CITY OF BOSTON.

LIST OF RESIDENTS
20 YEARS OF AGE AND OVER

(FEMALES INDICATED BY DAGGER)

AS OF

APRIL 1, 1924

HERBERT A. WILSON, } *Listing*

JAMES F. EAGAN, } *Board.*

CITY OF BOSTON—PRINTING DEPARTMENT

Arlington Street

A	McKinnon Annie—†	1	maid	24	here
B	McKinnon John D	1	janitor	65	Nova Scotia
C	Murphy Mary—†	1	cook	62	Newburyport
D	St Thomas Mary—†	1	teacher	40	here
E	Ayers William F	2	merchant	45	"
F	Baldwin Lucy—†	2	retired	60	122 Newbury
G	Baldwin Margaret—†	2	housekeeper	35	122 "
H	Barrett Clara G—†	2	"	50	here
K	Baungarten Alma—†	2	clerk	35	"
L	Brookfield George P	2	draughtsman	32	279 Pleasant
M	Hall Anna—†	2	cook	47	Malden
N	Haxton Jennie—†	2	teacher	35	here
O	Higgins Harold	2	salesman	22	Arlington
P	Ladd Durant F	2	"	35	Salem
R	Malcolmson Aida—†	2	housewife	55	205 Berkeley
S	Malcolmson Allen	2	colormaker	55	205 "
T	Montague Carrie—†	2	housewife	45	here
U	Montague George E	2	salesman	55	"
V	Shaw Caroline N—†	2	teacher	35	"
W	Shaw John T	2	retired	70	"
X	Strong Rose—†	2	"	40	Winthrop
Y	Uberroth Mary G—†	2	housewife	40	Brookline
Z	Uberroth Prestin H	2	U S N	50	"
A	Codman Alfred E	3	broker	21	here
B	Codman Lydia—†	3	dressmaker	40	"
C	Hudsen Emly—†	3	cook	36	"
D	MacDonald Mary E—†	3	maid	33	Brookline
E	Chaystof Charlotte—†	4	teacher	34	here
F	Dyer Nellie—†	4	"	45	"
G	Johnson Gladys—†	4	"	36	"
H	Lee Gereldine—†	4	"	30	"
K	McClintock Mary T—†	4	"	45	"
L	McCullough Marjorie—†	4	maid	45	"
M	Nortain Helen—†	4	teacher	45	"
N	Park Annie—†	4	maid	29	"
R	Hamilton Mary—†	5A	retired	45	Brookline
S	Almy Dean J	5A	salesman	26	W Newton
T	Almy Isabella V—†	5A	housewife	21	521 Mass av
V	Brace Gwendoline—†	7	maid	25	here
W	Callahan Margaret—†	7	cook	42	Brookline

Arlington Street—Continued

X	Cole Arthur	7	caretaker	50	here
Y	Cole Emma—†	7	"	45	"
Z	Gillis Elizebeth—†	7	maid	34	"
A	Howes Mildred—†	7	nurse	24	Malden
B	MacDonald Christinna—†	7	maid	26	Brookline
C	MacDonald Flaurence—†	7	"	24	here
D	McCarthy Hannah—†	7	"	60	"
E	Tenant Charles	7	butler	48	"
F	Walker Charles C	7	lawyer	53	"
G	Walker Helene—†	7	housewife	24	"
L	Bradley Joseph G	11	broker	44	312 Beacon
M	Bradley Mabel W—†	11	housewife	40	312 "
N	Fay Ellen—†	11	cook	50	here
O	Kelly Mary—†	11	maid	30	Ireland
P	Mooney Anna M—†	11	"	32	Somerville
R	Morrison Nora—†	11	"	38	126 Beacon
S	Mullany Mary—†	11	"	27	Concord
T	Bremner Margaret—†	12	"	31	here
U	Dalton Marie—†	12	"	36	"
V	Fudland Gulie—†	12	"	21	Sweden
W	Johnson Helga—†	12	"	21	8 Fairfield
X	Sears Sarah C—†	12	retired	66	here

Beacon Street

Z	Lathrop Howard	101	physician	58	here
A	Lathrop Sarah Y—†	101	housewife	85	"
B	McCleod Belle—†	101	maid	50	"
C	McKensie Isabelle—†	101	"	45	"
D	Carlson Gurlie—†	102	"	29	10 Abbott
E	Guild Mary E—†	102	retired	66	here
F	Guild Samuel E	102	"	73	"
G	Falk Mathilda—†	103	maid	48	Magnolia
H	Ginn Marguerita C—†	103	student	25	here
K	McLeod Alice—†	103	maid	20	Nova Scotia
L	Robb Frances—†	103	housewife	61	here
M	Robb Hunter	103	physician	60	"
N	Dauce Ellen—†	104	domestic	50	135 Bay State rd
O	Minot James J	104	banker	32	here
P	Minot Miriam S—†	104	housewife	28	"

3

Beacon Street—Continued

R	Janes Margaret—†	105	maid	32	Brookline
S	Connors Hannah—†	106	domestic	29	here
T	Coolidge John F	106	artist	65	"
U	Coolidge Mary A P—†	106	housewife	46	"
V	Farrell Cathrine—†	106	domestic	30	"
W	McEachern Margaret—†	106	"	35	"
X	Merrick Elizabeth—†	106	"	50	"
Y	Moran Teresa—†	106	"	29	"
Z	O'Shea Bridget—†	106	"	50	"
A	Bradley Fredrick W	107	retired	84	"
B	Connolly Margaret—†	107	cook	50	"
C	Gough Annie—†	107	maid	22	Ireland
D	McLeod Barbara—†	107	nurse	45	here
E	McWilliams Anna—†	107	housekeeper	60	"
F	McWilliams Mary—†	107	maid	45	"
G	Smith Sarah—†	107	nurse	50	"
H	Beal Boylston A	108	ambassador	55	"
K	Beal Elizebeth—†	108	student	24	"
L	Beal Elsie—†	108	housewife	50	"
M	Branda Thursa—†	108	domestic	37	"
N	Ewing Margaret—†	108	"	23	Scotland
O	Hanley Elizebeth—†	108	"	34	here
P	Harrington Henery	108	butler	22	"
R	MacEachen Sarah—†	108	domestic	60	"
S	Mercier Alice—†	108	"	46	England
T	Artman Florence—†	109	student	28	New Haven Ct
U	Cooper Ava J—†	109	housewife	21	New York
V	Duke Lorna—†	109	secretary	21	110 Newbury
W	Ewing Lucile—†	109	student	21	Canada
X	Gauld Elizabeth A—†	109	housewife	21	110 Newbury
Y	Godfrey Lulu M—†	109	school teacher	37	205 Hunt'n av
Z	Hamilton Edwin C, jr	109	student	21	Maine
A	Hamilton Millias L—†	109	housewife	52	"
B	Keeler Marion F—†	109	teacher	22	Brookline
C	Mathews Andrew C	109	agent	21	Vermont
D	Mattson Hulda—†	109	housewife	25	413 Beacon
E	Mattson Martin	109	engineer	75	107 Selwyn
F	Mattson Olgo—†	109	housewife	64	107 "
G	Nicolet Theodore A	109	agent	21	Vermont
H	Rhodes Harold	109	clerk	37	Winchester
K	Smith James C	109	engineer	26	Maine

Beacon Street — Continued

L	Stevens Louisa B—†	109	retired	51	7 Walnut
M	Stewart Elizabeth C—†	109	housewife	31	N Carolina
N	Stewart Gustarvus	109	U S N	37	New York
O	Guy Anna—†	110	domestic	22	219 Beacon
P	Niles Sarah F—†	110	retired	70	here
R	Anderson Lena—†	110	maid	29	"
S	Brady Mary—†	111	waitress	27	"
T	Shea Helen—†	111	cook	40	"
U	Webb Marcia—†	111	housewife	36	"
V	Webb Stewart	111	manufacturer	40	"
W	Boland Catherine A—†	112	nurse	40	"
X	Bradlee Alice—†	112	retired	84	"
Y	Bradlee Sarah—†	112	housewife	59	"
Z	Curran Bridget—†	112	domestic	40	"
A	Flynn Margaret—†	112	"	25	Scituate
B	Mulhern Mary—†	112	"	37	here
C	Sharkey Catherine—†	112	nurse	50	"
D	Duane Harry	113	confectioner	48	Brookline
E	Duane Harry, jr	113	student	21	"
F	Duane Isabelle—†	113	housewife	49	"
G	Hoyner Sarah—†	113	maid	55	102 Beacon
H	Kane Isabelle—†	113	"	25	Brookline
K	O'Hern Annie—†	113	"	48	Swampscott
L	O'Hern Joseph	113	butler	38	"
M	Lothrop Alice—†	114	housewife	50	here
N	McDonald Margaret—†	114	domestic	47	"
P	Porter Charles A	116	physician	58	"
R	Porter Isabel—†	116	student	21	"
S	Porter Margaret—†	116	"	20	"
T	Porter Margaret D—†	116	housewife	49	"
U	Grey Chesley	117	butler	29	"
V	Harris Alice—†	117	cook	40	"
W	Lyons Catherine—†	117	housewife	52	"
X	Lyons Henry	117	student	22	"
Y	Lyons Henry I	117	secretary	57	"
Z	Lyons Margaret—†	117	student	25	"
A	Armstrong Minnie—†	118	domestic	38	131 Beacon
B	Collins Annie—†	118	"	50	Fitchburg
C	Cornell Casmer	118	butler	55	here
D	King Alice S—†	118	housewife	50	"
E	McCormick Winifred—†	118	domestic	45	"

Page.	Letter.	Full Name.	Residence. April 1, 1924.	Occupation.	Supposed Age.	Reported Residence, April 1, 1923. Street and Number.

Beacon Street—Continued

	F	O'Connor Alice †	118	domestic	35	here
	G	Whalen Mary †	118	"	52	"
	H	Hebert Marietta †	119	housewife	54	Haverhill
	K	Hebert Natalie †	119	artist	21	"
	L	Hebert Placide	119	manufacturer	64	"
	M	Hebert Placide A	119	"	27	"
	N	Hebert Polly †	119	artist	24	"
	O	Hebert Violet †	119	"	23	"
	P	Townsend Alma †	119	maid	50	Brookline
	R	Townsend George	119	butler	60	"
	S	Buckley Margaret †	120	domestic	35	here
	T	Cullen Anne †	120	"	37	"
	U	Gallagher Mary †	120	"	35	"
	V	Gumbleton Elizabeth †	120	"	60	"
	W	Kidder Charles A	120	banker	63	"
	X	Kidder Josephine B †	120	none	66	"
	Y	Leonard Bridget †	120	domestic	55	71 Mozart
	Z	Merigan Peter	120	houseman	24	here
	A	Dimond Hugh J	121	real estate	39	"
	B	Fraser William J	121	retired	78	"
	C	Gibson Charles	121	"	38	"
	D	Hickman Anna †	121	"	73	"
	E	Nixon Edward F	121	milliner	50	"
	F	Nixon Mary J †	121	buyer	43	"
	G	Pollel Charles	121	janitor	63	"
	H	Harkins Margaret †	122	domestic	37	"
	K	Sears Eleonora R †	122	retired	42	"
	L	Sears Frederick R	122	"	69	"
	N	Brown Mary †	125	maid	40	"
	O	Carey Anne †	125	"	35	"
	P	Forester Agnes †	125	"	40	"
	R	McLeod Maragret †	125	"	28	"
	S	Murphy Mary †	125	"	45	"
	T	Sullivan Mary †	125	"	26	"
	U	Welsh Barbara †	125	housewife	35	"
	V	Welsh Edward S	125	lawyer	36	"
	W	Hutchinson Laura †	126	domestic	60	"
	X	Lamb Aimee †	126	artist	31	"
	Y	Lamb Annie L †	126	housewife	67	"
	Z	Lamb Edith D †	126	student	22	"
	A	Lamb Horatio A	126	retired	74	"

Beacon Street—Continued

	Letter	Full Name	Residence	Occupation	Age	Reported Residence
B	Lamb Rosamond—†	126	student	25	here
C	McPherson Catherine—†	126	domestic	45	61 Bay State rd
D	Mulholland Bridget—†	126	"	45	here
E	Reardon Catherine—†	126	"	39	"
F	Byrne Katherine—†	127	maid	30	Needham
G	Frothingham Lucy—†	127	housewife	53	here
H	Frothingham Theodore	127	retired	76	"
K	McDonald Jessie—†	127	maid	30	"
L	Sullivan Kate—†	127	cook	52	1 Marlboro
M	Good Agnes—†	128	domestic	29	here
N	Hobbs Franklin W	128	maufacturer	56	"
O	Hobbs Jane W—†	128	housewife	52	"
P	Hobbs Rebekah—†	128	student	22	"
R	Johnson Ellen C—†	128	domestic	32	Swampscott
S	St Paul Jeanne M—†	128	housekeeper	35	here
T	Threfenthal Lina—†	128	domestic	35	"
U	McClintock Euphema—†	129	teacher	51	"
V	Aagaard Katherine—†	130	nurse	39	"
W	Cooledge Arthur C	130	librarian	58	"
X	Cooledge Randolph	130	retired	95	"
Y	Doherty Theresa—†	130	domestic	31	"
Z	Neill Helen S—†	130	secretary	46	"
A	Powell Julia—†	130	domestic	25	"
B	Reynolds Mary—†	130	"	28	"
C	Sheehan Hannah—†	130	"	30	"
D	Sullivan Mary—†	130	"	40	"
E	Conconnon Katherine—†	131	maid	24	"
F	Hutchins Hurd	131	salesman	30	"
G	Hutchins John	131	merchant	32	"
H	Hutchins John E	131	retired	65	"
K	Hutchins Olivia E—†	131	housewife	55	"
L	Mahoney Nellie—†	131	maid	23	"
M	McDonohon Sarah—†	131	"	30	"
N	Sears Clara—†	132	housewife	60	"
O	Sears Knevit—†	132	retired	80	"
P	Shannon Nellie—†	132	domestic	46	"
R	Bundy Harvey	133	lawyer	36	373 Marlboro
S	Bundy Katherine D—†	133	housewife	34	373 "
T	Monton Marcelle—†	133	nurse	25	Lexington
U	Mulkerrie Bridget—†	133	maid	22	Readville
V	Mulkerrie Mary—†	133	"	23	66 Com av

Beacon Street—Continued

w¹	Murphy Anna—†	133	maid	43	373 Marlboro
w	Zanolith Candida—†	133	"	57	here
x	Gunneson Mary—†	134	domestic	45	"
y	Kimball Otis	134	retired	74	"
z	McNeil Mary—†	134	domestic	48	"
a	Peterson Mary—†	134	"	40	"
b	Sheridan Bertha—†	134	"	40	"
d	Barbarin Louise—†	136	"	30	"
e	Brooks Frederick	136	retired	65	"
f	Dobbin Ellen—†	136	domestic	32	"
g	Monahan Anna—†	136	"	28	"
h	O'Leary Nora—†	136	"	31	"
k	Sohier Elaine—†	136	housewife	25	"
l	Sohier William D, jr	136	banker	32	"
m	Gibson Charles H	137	author	49	"
n	Gibson Rosemond W—†	137	housewife	77	Nahant
o	O'Connell Elizabeth—†	137	maid	32	here
p	Shankler Frances—†	137	"	35	"
r	Sullivan Margaret—†	137	"	30	"
s	Hayes Mary—†	138	housewife	40	"
t	Kelley Margaret—†	138	domestic	30	"
u	McDonald Katherine—†	138	"	30	"
v	Rice Susanna—†	138	"	43	Concord
w	Sullivan Katherine—†	138	"	40	here
x	Bartlett Ralph S	139	lawyer	56	"
y	Batty Franklin T	139	physician	66	"
z	Davis Laura L—†	139	housewife	50	"
a	Dean Nathaniel W	139	salesman	45	"
b	Mason Frederick C	139	investigator	45	36 Fairfield
c	Loring Robert	140	physician	50	here
d	Codman Annie N—†	141	housewife	50	"
e	Codman Edward D	141	lawyer	55	"
f	Gibons Christine—†	141	maid	38	"
g	Meehan Bridget—†	141	"	42	"
h	Olsen Hilda—†	141	"	40	"
k	Abbott Ann—†	142	student	22	"
l	Andrews Robert	142	architect	60	Brookline
m	Boyd Mary—†	142	student	21	here
n	Brown Albert J	142	steward	60	"
o	Chapman Heloise—†	142	secretary	35	"
p	Chippie Charles	142	broker	70	"

Beacon Street—Continued

R	Clark Ellery	142	lawyer	55	here
S	Farnham Catherine—†	142	student	31	Maine
T	Graves Gertrude—†	142	retired	40	here
U	Mills Agnes—†	142	artist	30	"
V	Pepper Elezebeth—†	142	housekeeper	55	"
W	Preston Winifred—†	142	retired	55	"
X	Walker Alice—†	142	student	35	"
Y	Whitney Louise—†	142	retired	32	"
Z	Curtis Mary B—†	143	housewife	50	"
A	Fairfield Nellie—†	143	maid	28	"
B	Frazier Annie—†	143	"	60	"
C	McKenzie Frances—†	143	"	60	"
D	Garden Mabel—†	144	domestic	28	"
E	LeBeau Sarah—†	144	"	60	"
F	Luvett Alice—†	144	"	27	"
G	McGinley Richard	144	butler	21	"
H	Moseley Charlotte—†	144	student	22	"
K	Moseley Frederick S	144	retired	72	"
L	Moseley Helen—†	144	"	49	"
M	Pinckney Carrie—†	144	domestic	48	"
N	Stanley Eva—†	144	"	36	"
O	Galligher Elizabeth—†	145	cook	37	"
P	Longford Sarah—†	145	waitress	32	"
R	Lucy Mary J—†	145	laundress	45	"
S	Lurley Delia—†	145	maid	37	"
T	Monahan Annie—†	145	nurse	43	"
U	Moore Edward D	145	butler	29	"
V	Morrisey Grace—†	145	maid	24	"
W	Whitman Adelaide—†	145	housewife	31	"
X	Whitman Hendricks	145	merchant	42	"
Y	Barrett Mary—†	146	domestic	20	Ireland
Z	Barry Marion—†	146	"	50	here
A	Burke Walter	146	houseman	28	"
B	Field Elizebeth—†	146	domestic	33	Needham
C	Hunnewell Gertrude—†	146	housewife	30	here
D	Hunnewell Henry	146	retired	60	"
E	Hunnewell Mary—†	146	"	60	"
F	Hunnewell Mary—†	146	housewife	28	"
G	Long Catherine—†	146	domestic	30	Ireland
H	McGuire Ellen—†	146	"	25	here
K	Skehill Catherine—†	146	"	22	Dover

Beacon Street— Continued

L	Anderson Olga—†	147	domestic	45	here
M	Bgorn Gerda—†	148	"	39	"
N	Johnson Ruth—†	148	"	20	Sweden
O	Pierson Anna—†	148	"	30	here
P	Warren George	148	coal dealer	50	"
S	Barron Mary—†	150	governess	28	"
T	Crowley Elizebeth—†	150	domestic	60	"
U	Dickson Lavina—†	150	"	32	"
V	Fuller Alvine T	150	manufacturer	46	"
W	Fuller Viola—†	150	housewife	38	"
X	Kelleher Mary—†	150	domestic	50	"
Y	Lovogan Mary—†	150	"	24	"
Z	Madden Catherine—†	150	nurse	50	"
A	Maloney Bridget—†	150	domestic	20	"
B	Scully Anne—†	150	"	40	"
C	Shea Bridget—†	150	"	30	1 Gloucester
D	Sullivan Ellen T—†	150	"	42	here
E	Connelly Katherine—†	151	maid	29	"
F	Day Bessie—†	151	"	24	"
G	Johnson Annie—†	151	cook	23	New Hampshire
H	Motley John L	151	lawyer	45	here
K	Motley Nancy E—†	151	housewife	30	"
L	Pendeville Nellie—†	151	maid	50	"
M	Carver Edward	153	butler	55	"
N	Hogan Ellen—†	153	maid	45	"
O	McSweeney Katherine—†	153	"	45	"
P	Sturgis Alanson	153	architect	31	"
R	Sturgis Clipston	153	"	63	"
S	Sturgis Esther—†	153	housewife	62	"
T	Sturgis Mary—†	153	"	30	"
U	Foley Annie—†	154	domestic	35	"
V	Ford Nora—†	154	"	30	"
W	Hawe Lotta K—†	154	retired	65	"
X	Hawe Octavius T	154	physician	71	"
Y	Keenan Mary—†	154	domestic	50	"
Z	Maroney Thomas	154	chauffeur	42	"
A	O'Donahue Catherine—†	154	domestic	48	"
B	Ellison Ida—†	155	waitress	25	"
C	Griffiths Lucy—†	155	maid	30	"
D	Olson Caroline—†	155	"	25	"
E	Warden Elinor D—†	155	housewife	42	"

Beacon Street—Continued

F	Farnsworth Lucy—†	157	housewife	61	here
G	Farnsworth William	157	merchant	69	"
H	Luby Agnes—†	157	maid	30	"
K	McDoughner Margaret—†	157	"	21	"
L	O'Hara Elizabeth—†	157	"	40	"
M	O'Leary Mary—†	157	waitress	40	"
N	Johnson Augusta—†	159	maid	64	"
O	Ohlson Anna—†	159	"	44	"
P	Ohlson Hulda—†	159	"	41	"
R	Pearson Hanna—†	159	waitress	42	"
S	Weld Edith—†	159	housewife	60	"
T	Clark Edward	160	houseman	22	424 Mass av
U	Elliot Lillian—†	160	secretary	40	here
V	Walker Mabel S—†	160	housewife	60	"
W	Watts Ida—†	160	domestic	38	"
X	Manny Elizabeth C—†	161	housewife	25	New York
Y	Manny Ralph P	161	salesman	28	"
E	Collins Bridget—†	163	maid	27	Wash'n D C
F	Evans David	163	physician	50	here
G	Evans Rosemond—†	163	housewife	45	"
H	Griffin Alice—†	163	maid	30	"
K	McCarthy Katherine—†	163	cook	50	"
L	Mendel Daisy—†	163	governess	35	"
M	Green Katherine—†	164	domestic	58	"
N	Homans Helen A—†	164	retired	77	"
O	Homans Katherine A—†	164	housewife	48	"
P	Homans Marian J—†	164	"	42	"
R	Martin Jane—†	164	domestic	60	"
S	McGongle Jennie—†	164	"	56	"
T	McLaughlin Mary—†	164	"	55	"
U	McSweeney Nora—†	164	"	30	"
V	Bottomley John T	165	physician	53	"
W	Bottomley May—†	165	housewife	43	"
X	Casey Mary—†	165	nurse	40	"
Y	Keliher Annie—†	165	maid	23	Lincoln
Z	Kelley Annie—†	165	"	23	6 Joy
A	Martin Anna L—†	165	cook	52	here
B	Finn Nora—†	166	domestic	54	"
C	Hegarty Mary—†	166	seamstress	41	"
D	Hutchins Edward	166	lawyer	33	"
E	Hutchins Edward W	166	"	73	"

Beacon Street—Continued

	Letter	Full Name	Residence	Occupation	Age	Reported Residence
	F	Hutchins Susan B—†	166	housewife	64	here
	G	Mulligan Mary—†	166	domestic	42	"
	H	Vance Anna—†	166	"	32	"
	K	Barrett Elmer W	167	bookkeeper	36	142 Beacon
	L	Cloutman Mary A—†	167	operator	58	here
	M	Mahoney Dennis J	167	buyer	51	"
	N	Mahoney Joseph V	167	reporter	21	"
	O	Mahoney Maey A—†	167	"	51	"
	P	Nugent Margaret A—†	167	secretary	42	"
	R	Nugent Susan H—†	167	teacher	47	"
	S	O'Brien Annie E—†	167	reporter	27	"
	T	O'Brien Gertrude G—†	167	teacher	47	"
	U	Erickson Regina—†	168	laundress	38	Swampscott
	V	Erlando John E T	168	butler	50	Illinois
	W	Fearing George R	168	banker	54	here
	X	Fearing George R. 3d	168	salesman	26	"
	Y	Fearing Hester S—†	168	housewife	45	"
	Z	Hafoabe Astrid—†	168	maid	20	Norway
	A	Nelson Betty—†	168	cook	51	here
	B	Peterson Calla—†	168	maid	31	72 Com av
	C	Ruch Juliett—†	168	"	38	256 Beacon
	D	Barry Nellie—†	169	cook	45	here
	E	Burke Elizabeth—†	169	maid	30	"
	F	Clark Edward A, jr	169	broker	25	"
	G	Clark Elizabeth F—†	169	retired	50	"
	H	Clark Goeffrey R	169	broker	21	"
	K	Clark Helen O	169	none	20	"
	L	Gorman Elizabeth—†	169	cook	25	"
	M	Harrington Edith—†	169	waitress	30	"
	N	Johnston Minnie—†	170	maid	28	"
	O	Koshland Abraham	170	merchant	55	"
	P	Koshland Estelle W—†	170	housewife	46	"
	R	Koshland Stephen A	170	student	22	"
	S	Larson Magnus	170	houseman	50	"
	T	Lee Mathea—†	170	cook	45	"
	U	Stotz Lydia M—†	170	seamstress	44	"
	V	Kelley Nellie—†	171	cook	35	New York
	W	Moors Arthur W	171	banker	64	here
	X	Moors Virginia—†	171	housewife	55	"
	Y	O'Hara Catherine—†	171	laundress	51	"
	Z	O'Sullivan Josephine—†	171	waitress	27	285 Com av

Beacon Street—Continued

A	Traynor Margaret—†	171	maid	60	here
B	Anderson Maria—†	172	"	40	"
C	Bostrom Lottie—†	172	cook	55	"
D	Fallon Julia—†	172	maid	45	"
E	Hammond Elizabeth B–†	172	housewife	87	"
F	Peterson Hilda—†	172	maid	43	"
G	Shelby Mary—†	172	laundress	65	"
H	Sullivan Mary—†	172	maid	44	"
K	Cain Sadie—†	173	waitress	30	Nova Scotia
L	Cox Channing H	173	governor	45	here
M	Cox Mary E—†	173	housewife	44	"
N	Gillis Christine—†	173	cook	23	Nova Scotia
O	McNiel Rose—†	173	nurse	30	here
P	Dowd Annie—†	174	cook	40	New York
R	Hammerton Lucy—†	174	maid	65	here
S	McGuiness Annie—†	174	waitress	48	Nova Scotia
T	Rodman Emma—†	174	housewife	77	here
U	Minot Hanoro—†	175	"	55	New York
V	Minot Joseph G	175	real estate	60	"
W	Barron Mary—†	176	cook	32	here
X	Curran Margaret—†	176	maid	24	172 Marlboro
Y	Fenwood Annie—†	176	waitress	22	Ireland
Z	Gray John C	176	lawyer	45	here
A	Riley Helen—†	176	laundress	50	"
B	Roach Nanno—†	176	maid	50	"
C	Clark Marie—†	177	nurse	25	"
D	Gallagher Helen—†	177	laundress	24	Cambridge
E	Locke Edward A	177	physician	49	here
E¹	Locke Elizabeth F—†	177	housewife	46	"
F	McPhee Mary A—†	177	waitress	23	"
G	Oakes Ella M—†	177	cook	49	"
K	Ball Julia L—†	179	governess	40	109 Com av
L	Carr Ann—†	179	cook	30	253 Marlboro
M	Clancy Philomena—†	179	waitress	25	here
N	Sears Susan J—†	179	housewife	40	"
O	Sears William R	179	lawyer	54	"
P	Sullivan Margaret—†	179	maid	25	"
S	Burnell Beatha—†	181	governess	50	"
T	DeMenocal Beatrice C–†	181	housewife	42	"
U	DeMenocal Daniel A	181	banker	42	"
V	O'Leary Margaret—†	181	cook	33	"

Beacon Street—Continued

w	O'Niel Nora—†	181	waitress	23	here
x	Duttan Josephine—†	182	maid	43	France
y	Murnane Anna—†	182	"	52	248 Marlboro
z	Murphy Margaret—†	182	cook	45	New York
A	Parkman Henry, jr	182	agent	30	here
B	Parkman Margaret—†	182	housewife	51	"
C	Reagan Nellie—†	182	maid	27	106 Marlboro
D	Rotch Arthur	182	student	25	here
E	Shilliday Annie—†	182	waitress	35	34 Dalton
F	Conroy Mary—†	183	cook	35	here
G	Gleason Mabel W—†	183	housewife	50	"
H	Gleason Walter H	183	real estate	50	"
K	Nee Mary—†	183	maid	30	"
L	Ward Catherine—†	183	waitress	28	"
M	Barry Mary—†	184	cook	30	277 Clarendo
N	Carey Katherine—†	184	maid	25	here
O	Cooledge Amory	184	merchant	29	"
P	Cooledge Jefferson	184	banker	30	"
R	Cooledge William A	184	student	22	"
S	Drummy Nora—†	184	maid	40	"
T	Fenton Patrick H	184	butler	42	"
U	Lyons Mary—†	185	cook	60	"
V	McCarthy Kathleen—†	185	maid	35	"
W	Stepanek Otto	185	butler	31	"
X	Warren Bently W	185	lawyer	58	"
Y	Warren Helen W—†	185	housewife	54	"
Z	Anderson Elleonora—†	186	waitress	45	"
A	Gardner Esther—†	186	housewife	60	"
B	Gardner George P	186	merchant	60	"
C	Idman Ingred—†	186	maid	21	"
D	Johnson Matilda—†	186	cook	24	Brookline
E	King Minnie—†	186	maid	50	here
F	Larsen Anna—†	186	"	26	Norway
G	Osis Mildred—†	186	laundress	33	here
H	Seabie Esther—†	186	maid	24	"
K	Brennen Helen—†	187	waitress	40	"
M	McDonald Margaret—†	187	nurse	30	"
N	McQueen Jessie—†	187	maid	26	"
O	Mixter Charles G	187	physician	40	"
P	Mixter Helen—†	187	housewife	37	"
R	Monahan Mary—†	187	cook	28	"

Beacon Street—Continued

s	Hedlund Anna—†	188	maid	32	here
t	Ideman Mary—†	188	cook	26	227 Com av
u	O'Neil May—†	188	waitress	28	here
v	Walsh Mary—†	188	laundress	30	224 Beacon
w	Wigglesworth Sarah W—†	188	housewife	67	here
x	Janssen Paul	189	cook	68	19 Myrtle
z	Townsend Robert E	189	real estate	55	3 Plymouth
a	Townsend Robert E, jr	189	salesman	31	3 "
b	Ambrose Nellie—†	190	waitress	29	109 Chestnut
c	Dwyer Ellen—†	190	maid	20	Ireland
d	McHugh Nora—†	190	cook	34	here
e	Ronan Mary—†	190	maid	30	"
f	Ward Alma O—†	190	housekeeper	40	"
g	Ward Richard	190	merchant	44	"
h	Young Elizabeth M—†	190	nurse	29	"
k	Hooper Justine V—†	191	housewife	35	"
l	Hooper Roger F	191	lawyer	35	"
m	Southwick Jane W—†	191	governess	58	"
n	Walton Frances C—†	191	cook	33	"
o	White Mary—†	191	maid	29	"
p	Arvidson Agusta—†	192	cook	53	424 Marlboro
r	Dorr Ada H—†	192	housewife	49	here
s	Dorr Alfred	192	merchant	58	"
t	Dorr Hancock	192	broker	25	"
u	King Adelaide—†	192	maid	22	233 Marlboro
v	O'Donnell Sarah—†	192	waitress	25	here
w	Hammond Grace L—†	193	housekeeper	49	"
x	Hammond Samuel	193	retired	64	"
y	Joy Julia—†	193	houseworker	50	"
z	Giroux Edward	194	cook	34	46 Pinckney
a	Lecours Emil	194	butler	29	Swampscott
b	Roope George W	194	merchant	55	Newtonville
c	Roope Martha—†	194	housewife	45	"
d	Jones Beatrice—†	195	none	22	here
e	Jones Daniel F	195	surgeon	55	"
f	Jones Mary R—†	195	housewife	53	"
g	MacDonald Christine—†	195	waitress	22	"
h	MacDougall Annie—†	195	laundress	43	"
k	MacPherson Margaret—†	195	maid	50	"
l	Askew Jesse—†	196	cook	25	86 Northampton
m	Askew Oscar	196	butler	24	86 "

Beacon Street—Continued

N	Boos Margaret T E—†	196	housewife	50	here
O	Boos William F	196	physician	53	"
P	King Bridget—†	197	laundress	29	"
R	King Margaret M—†	197	cook	38	"
S	O'Connor Delia—†	197	waitress	38	"
T	Preece Janet—†	197	maid	57	"
U	Stoddard Eoline S—†	197	housewife	59	"
V	Stoddard George H	197	treasurer	68	"
W	Stoddard Margaret—†	197	none	30	"
Y	Kemit Ethel—†	199	waitress	28	"
Z	Lavin Nora—†	199	cook	39	"
A	Whitmore Mary B—†	199	housewife	38	"
B	Whitmore Wyman	199	surgeon	44	"
C	Young Mary D—†	199	maid	35	"
D	Allen Freeman	200	physician	53	"
E	Allen Mary E—†	200	housewife	50	"
F	Gough Ellie—†	200	waitress	22	Ireland
O	Holmes Sara—†	200	nurse	45	here
H	McGuire Molly—†	200	cook	52	Newton
K	Nauglor Margaret J—†	200	maid	53	Nova Scotia
L	Powers Mary—†	200	laundress	39	here
M	Pfaelyer Blanche W—†	202	housewife	51	"
N	Pfaelyer Franklin T	202	retired	52	"
O	Pfaelyer Franklin T, jr	202	clerk	24	"
P	Takahashi Kinichi	202	butter	43	New York
R	Burke Mary—†	204	cook	54	Cambridge
S	Jewell Margaret H—†	204	housewife	58	here
T	Murphy Julia—†	204	waitress	56	"
U	Sheehan Annie—†	204	maid	32	"
V	Campell Lester	205	student	24	"
W	Croxford Paul	205	"	23	"
X	Goodall Harry W	205	physician	47	"
Y	Fiske Constance—†	206	housewife	26	115 Com av
Z	Fiske Gardner H	206	salesman	30	115 "
A	Woodford Margaret—†	206	maid	26	Somerville
B	Woodford Mary—†	206	cook	30	"
C	Dodge Anna—†	208	housewife	36	here
D	Dodge Lawrence	208	broker	37	"
E	Holland Abbie—†	208	waitress	24	"
F	McDonald Jessie—†	208	cook	34	"
G	Parker Mary—†	208	maid	34	"

Beacon Street—Continued

H	Johnson Aljhild V	209	cook	32	here
K	Johnson Murdock M	209	laundryman	52	"
L	Johnson Ruth P—†	209	housewife	49	"
M	Wallquist Sigrid M—†	209	waitress	27	"
N	Meaney Annie—†	210	nurse	33	Milton
O	Morrison Margaret—†	210	cook	30	Beverly Farms
P	Newbold Jefferson	210	merchant	38	"
R	Newbold Katherine H—†	210	housewife	31	"
S	Norton Mary—†	210	maid	24	169 Beacon
T	Shea Julia—†	210	waitress	29	Ireland
U	Bradlee Elizabeth—†	211	housewife	60	here
V	Bradlee Frederick J	211	banker	64	"
W	Bradlee Malcolm	211	broker	21	"
X	Bradlee Sargent	211	real estate	24	"
Y	Burke Mary H—†	211	cook	21	"
Z	McDonnell Margaret—†	211	maid	26	"
A	Murphy Mary E—†	211	waitress	27	"
B	Blake Frederick	212	treasurer	52	"
C	Blake John B, jr	212	student	22	371 Com av
D	Blake Marie—†	212	housekeeper	48	here
E	Blake Robert F	212	engineer	46	"
F	McEachern Jennie—†	212	maid	22	"
G	Brewster George W W	213	physician	58	"
H	Brewster Helen H—†	213	housewife	52	"
K	McKinnon Mary—†	213	cook	39	"
L	Nicholson Margaret—†	213	waitress	32	"
A	Jack Frederick L	215	physician	60	"
B	Manuel Carolina—†	215	housekeeper	40	"
C	Steward Jenney—†	215	cook	40	"
D	Bradley Helen A—†	216	housekeeper	29	"
E	Bradley Mary T—†	216	student	22	"
F	Bradley Richard	216	"	21	"
G	Bradley Richard M	216	real estate	63	"
H	Bradley Sarah M—†	216	student	26	"
K	Doherty Rose—†	216	maid	43	"
L	May Annie—†	216	cook	50	"
M	Smith Minnie—†	216	waitress	23	"
N	Haize Victoria—†	217	governess	34	"
O	James Elery S	217	broker	30	"
P	James Louise—†	217	housewife	23	"
R	McWilliam Christin—†	217	maid	32	"

Page.	Letter.	FULL NAME.	Residence, April 1, 1924.	Occupation.	Supposed Age.	Reported Residence, April 1, 1923. Street and Number.

Beacon Street—Continued

	s	Moroney Margaret—†	217	waitress	33	here
	T	Splaine Ella—†	217	cook	48	"
	U	Burke Charlotte—†	218	laundress	60	303 Dartmou
	V	Fitz Edith—†	218	housekeeper	35	here
	W	Fitz Elizabeth—†	218	housewife	65	"
	X	Galvin Annie—†	218	maid	38	"
	Y	Gustavson Gertrude—†	218	"	21	Sweden
	Z	Johnson Sophie—†	218	cook	61	here
	A	Walsh Margaret—†	218	maid	30	"
	B	Cole Harry	219	chauffeur	28	"
	C	Mixter Samuel J	219	retired	68	"
	D	Mixter Wilhelmina—†	219	housewife	63	"
	E	Tuesley Emma F—†	219	housekeeper	44	"
	F	Bradford Edith F—†	220	housewife	60	"
	G	Bradford Edward H	220	physician	75	"
	H	Bradford Robert F	220	student	21	"
	K	Carney Rose—†	220	cook	40	11½ Belvider
	L	Haynes Elizabeth—†	220	maid	40	here
	M	Nolan Margaret—†	220	waitress	50	"
	N	Coombs Margaret—†	221	maid	32	Canada
	O	Curran Mary L—†	221	"	33	here
	P	Geoghegan Mary—†	221	cook	40	"
	R	Osgood Fannie—†	221	retired	41	"
	S	Osgood Hannah T—†	221	housewife	71	"
	T	Riordan Margaret—†	221	waitress	28	"
	U	Clarke Roxanna—†	222	housewife	50	"
	V	Humphrey Annie—†	222	housekeeper	55	Lexington
	W	Humphrey Stetson	222	manager	35	"
	X	Storrs Fred N	222	accountant	31	here
	Y	Williams Isabelle G—†	222	treasurer	55	"
	Z	Colloran Josephine—†	223	cook	27	"
	A	McKinnon Jennette C—†	223	maid	22	"
	B	Murphy Elizabeth—†	223	nurse	40	"
	C	Plummer Morgan H	223	merchant	30	"
	D	Plummer Susan L—†	223	housewife	28	"
	E	Prendergast Elizabeth M—†	223	waitress	50	"
	G	Reidy Elizabeth—†	225	maid	20	"
	H	Stewart Charles	225	manager	50	"
	K	Stewart Elizabeth—†	225	housewife	50	"
	L	Thornton Mary—†	225	cook	25	"
	N	Codman Ernest A	227	surgeon	54	"

Page.	Letter	FULL NAME.	Residence, April 1, 1924.	Occupation.	Supposed Age.	Reported Residence, April 1, 1923. Street and Number.

Beacon Street—Continued

o	Codman Katherine B—†	227	none	54	here
p	Hamilton Alice—†	227	physician	54	"
R	Haven Mary E—†	228	retired	84	"
s	Ross Ellen H—†	228	"	75	"
T	Ruane Dellia—†	228	maid	24	Readville
v	Sheehy Margaret—†	228	cook	41	5 Chestnut
v	Collins Katherine—†	229	"	50	here
w	Connolly Mary—†	229	waitress	23	"
x	Houghton Annie—†	229	maid	22	"
y	Rowe Anna P—†	229	governess	50	"
z	Sears Richard	229	broker	56	"
A	Sears Susan D—†	229	housewife	36	"
B	Shepard Frances J—†	230	"	38	16 Keswick
c	Shepard Luther D	230	physician	52	16 "
D	Mansfield Annie—†	231	housewife	83	here
E	Mansfield Samuel	231	retired	85	"
F	Waters Catherine—†	231	domestic	34	77 Beacon
G	Wright Erwin	231	physician	61	here
H	Gooding William J	232	chauffeur	41	Beverly
K	Sorensen Anna—†	232	maid	53	here
L	McWagh Eliza—†	233	"	40	"
o	Mulrey Nora—†	233	cook	40	"
M	Whiteside Alexander	233	lawyer	49	"
N	Whiteside Edith—†	233	housewife	47	"
P	Stone Charles A	234	merchant	56	"
R	Stone Mary E—†	234	housewife	56	"
s	Dwight Joseph	235	retired	40	"
T	Dwight Margaret—†	235	"	34	"
v	Dwight Sarah—†	235	"	73	"
v	Lynch Elizabeth—†	235	cook	27	Wash'n D C
w	MacDonald Jenny—†	235	maid	31	127 Beacon
y	Carr Alice—†	237	teacher	30	Waban
z	Duggan William	237	clerk	23	here
A	Maran Francis	237	"	23	"
B	Maratte Emelie—†	237	housewife	70	"
c	Maratte Emelie—†	237	"	35	"
D	Millenck Eliose—†	237	cook	31	"
E	Ross Henry	237	clerk	44	139 Marlboro
F	Sawyer Edith L—†	237	saleswoman	50	here
G	Fenno Florence—†	238	retired	24	"
H	Fenno Lawrence	238	"	58	"

Beacon Street—Continued

K	Fenno Marion S—†	238	retired	23	here
L	Bachand Yuanne—†	239	student	23	"
M	Carr Alice—†	239	teacher	39	167 Beacon
N	Cotter Frederick	239	physician	57	here
P	Cotter Jane B—†	239	housewife	55	"
O	Cotter Jean—†	239	student	20	"
R	McMillan Egnar—†	239	housewife	40	184 Beacon
S	Slone Mary—†	239	cook	50	4 Boardman av
T	Abbott Catherine—†	240	housewife	53	here
U	Abbott Gordon	240	banker	62	"
V	Nicholson Johnena—†	240	maid	32	"
W	Sullivan Catherine—†	240	"	26	"
X	Burke Margaret—†	241	cook	38	"
Y	Mortley Frederick	241	banker	49	"
Z	Mortley Margaret—†	241	housewife	42	"
A	Ulrich Minnie—†	241	maid	27	New York
D	Curtis Charles P	244	lawyer	62	here
E	Curtis Ellen A—†	244	housewife	54	"
F	Curtis Ellen S—†	244	retired	24	"
G	Haggerty Margaret—†	244	maid	40	"
H	Lyons Ellen M—†	244	cook	51	58 Beacon
K	Reilly Catherine—†	244	maid	30	312 Dartmouth
L	Slamin Catherine—†	244	"	53	here
M	Beaton Jennie—†	245	cook	38	"
N	Ridge Annie—†	245	maid	28	420 E Sixth
O	Hickey Elizabeth—†	246	"	26	here
P	Mullens John	246	janitor	43	"
R	Norton Theresa—†	246	maid	23	124 Berkeley
S	Spence Margaret—†	246	cook	34	Concord
T	Wing Daniel G	246	banker	50	here
U	Wing Josephine—†	246	housewife	50	"
V	Abbetts Florence—†	247	cook	38	"
W	King Henry	247	banker	26	229 Marlboro
X	King May—†	247	housewife	24	229 "
Y	O'neal Mary—†	247	maid	43	here
Z	Sinksons Betrice—†	247	"	45	"
A	Bancroft Elinor—†	249	housewife	34	"
B	Bancroft Elsie—†	249	"	63	"
C	Dowling Katherine—†	249	maid	54	"
D	McGreely Annie—†	249	cook	66	"
E	Mitchell Ellean—†	249	maid	44	"

Beacon Street—Continued

F	Mitchell Phillip W	250	manager	23	New York
G	Caswell Pauline—†	251	housewife	48	here
H	Caswell William	251	engineer	50	"
K	Conwey Marguate—†	251	maid	30	"
L	Manion Norah—†	251	cook	41	"
M	Murphy Jessey—†	251	maid	23	"
N	Connelly Mary—†	252	cook	34	"
O	Gilbert Viola—†	252	maid	38	"
P	McMillian Annie—†	252	"	45	"
R	Nash Mary C—†	252	retired	92	"
T	Allen Annie—†	255	housewife	53	"
U	Allen Brice	255	retired	63	"
V	Golding Chatreen—†	255	housewife	53	"
W	Golding Richard	255	policeman	54	"
X	Young Roy	256	janitor	30	Canada
Y	Seeley Fannie B—†	256	retired	55	here
A	Greeley Marion—†	256	"	40	"
B	Duffy Mary—†	256	cook	35	291 Marlboro
C	Maxwell Ella—†	256	housewife	58	Duxbury
D	Maxwell Frank R	256	manager	60	"
E	O'Donnell Madge—†	256	maid	24	Brookline
H	Church Gladys—†	259	secretary	34	here
K	Robie Mirian—†	259	retired	46	"
L	Sugarman Ziporah—†	259	secretary	51	"
M	Marshell Annie—†	259	student	21	"
N	Tobie Mary—†	259	housewife	72	"
O	Tobie Mary—†	259	"	34	"
P	Tobie Walter	259	salesman	32	"
R	Houghton Henry	259	student	21	"
S	Houghton Henry O	259	laborer	55	"
T	Stevens Charlotte—†	259	housewife	35	"
U	Stevens James	259	physician	50	"
V	Perkins Florence T—†	259	housewife	54	Malden
W	Perkins George W	259	editor	55	"
X	Gibbs Elenor—†	259	housewife	45	here
Y	Gibbs Elenor—†	259	student	20	"
Z	Gibbs Henry	259	merchant	55	"
A	Lockwood Frederick	259	clerk	30	"
B	Lockwood Mabel—†	259	housewife	50	"
C	Browne Emily W—†	259	artist	34	New York
D	Browne Margaret F—†	259	"	39	288 Marlboro

Page.	Letter.	FULL NAME.	Residence, April 1, 1924.	Occupation.	Supposed Age.	Reported Residence, April 1, 1923. Street and Number.

Beacon Street—Continued

	E	Stevens Cordelia B—†	259	writer	63	288 Marlboro
	F	Stevens David	259	editor	63	288 "
	G	Boardman Emma—†	259	clerk	30	here
	H	Kinnan Catherine—†	259	maid	27	"
	K	Putnam Antistass—†	259	housewife	50	"
	L	Appleton Helen—†	259	retired	59	"
	M	Creigin George	259	physician	55	374 Marlboro
	N	Creigin Louise—†	259	housewife	55	374 "
	O	McLean Florence—†	259	maid	24	here
	P	Houghton Harry	259	retired	70	"
	R	Nelson Martina—†	259	maid	55	"
	S	Willard Helen—†	259	housewife	50	"
	T	Hall Fredzrick G	260	artist	47	"
	U	Rickson Alfred F	260	janitor	59	"
	V	Whalen Mary E—†	260	maid	49	"
	W	Rogers Albert	261	physician	55	"
	X	Rogers Martha—†	261	housewife	50	"
	Y	Burns Agnes—†	261	secretary	47	"
	Z	Burns Alma—†	261	teacher	40	"
	A	Burns Anna A—†	261	housewife	84	"
	B	Drew Adelaide—†	261	"	50	"
	C	Drew Frederick	261	physician	50	"
	D	Humphreys Marean—†	261	housewife	30	Milton
	E	Humphreys Richard	261	clerk	30	"
	F	Hager Albert	261	salesman	50	Marlboro
	G	Hager Elsie—†	261	housewife	50	here
	K	Humphrey Ellen L—†	262	retired	79	"
	L	Driscoll Margaret—†	263	cook	26	"
	M	Keohane Liano—†	263	maid	27	"
	N	Rackman Dortley M—†	263	housewife	33	"
	O	Rackman Francis	263	physician	35	"
	R	Hickey May—†	265	cook	36	"
	S	Lincoln Alexander	265	lawyer	50	"
	T	Lincoln Eleanor A—†	265	housewife	43	"
	U	Lussier Lydin—†	265	maid	33	"
	V	Collin Julia—†	266	"	38	"
	W	Edwards Hanna M—†	266	retired	60	"
	X	Edwards Robert J	266	"	71	"
	Y	Johnson Hannah—†	266	cook	38	"
	Z	Olin Agnes—†	266	maid	52	"
	A	Perono Delfino	266	butler	46	"

Beacon Street—Continued

B	Canty Nora—†	267	maid	45	here
C	Hodges Charles	267	agent	26	Brookline
D	Hodges Gladys F—†	267	housewife	38	Pennsylvania
E	McAvoy Catherine—†	267	cook	40	Maine
F	Faringham Elana—†	269	housewife	29	here
G	Faringham Theodore	269	teacher	30	"
H	Galiwae Catherine—†	269	maid	35	"
K	Maricha Grace—†	269	cook	30	Canada
L	Carew Margaret—†	270	maid	30	here
M	Carroll Minnie—†	270	"	39	"
N	Hagerty Mary—†	270	"	29	"
O	Keane Bridget—†	270	"	55	"
P	Klein Bertha—†	270	"	50	"
R	Knox James L	270	retired	47	"
S	Munay Hannah—†	270	maid	45	"
T	Selfridge Arthur J	270	lawyer	64	"
W	Carney Minnie—†	274	maid	45	"
X	Crane Nellie—†	274	"	21	"
Y	Farley Susan—†	274	"	45	"
Z	Higginson Corina—†	274	housewife	50	"
A	Higginson Francis L	274	broker	82	"
B	McDonough Annie—†	274	maid	30	"
C	McDonough Margaret—†	274	"	21	"
D	Riley Mary—†	274	"	30	"
E	Scanell Mary—†	274	"	25	"
F	Shillaber Katherine B—†	275	retired	58	"
G	Shillaber William C	275	"	73	"
H	Taylor Mary M—†	276	housewife	40	"
K	Taylor William O	276	journalist	52	"
L	Tracey Margaret—†	276	cook	26	10 Fairfield
M	Carchain Mary—†	277	maid	60	here
N	Glynn Delia—†	277	cook	55	Cambridge
O	Lowell Beatris—†	277	housewife	55	here
P	McCarthy Treasia—†	277	maid	53	"
R	Walker Ida—†	277	"	34	Cohasset
S	Amory Elizabeth G—†	278	housekeeper	79	here
T	Amory George G	278	retired	49	"
U	O'Connor Mary—†	278	maid	50	"
V	Slavin Mary—†	278	cook	52	"
W	Sullivan Mary—†	278	maid	39	"
X	Clifford Margauate—†	279	"	32	Ireland

Beacon Street—Continued

Y	Davis Catherine—†	279	housewife	48	here
Z	Davis Lincoln	279	physician	50	"
A	Davis Lincoln, jr	279	student	20	"
B	Driscoll Catherine—†	279	cook	50	"
C	Boutiller Adel—†	280	"	40	"
D	McAskill Mary T—†	280	maid	21	"
E	Reardon Mary—†	280	"	28	330 Com av
F	Streeter Alice C—†	280	housewife	42	here
G	Streeter Edward C	280	physician	49	"
H	Doyle Celia—†	281	cook	35	"
K	Kelley Winifred †	281	maid	23	"
L	Lewis George	281	clerk	27	"
M	Rouke Julia P—†	281	maid	38	"
O	Bush Emer—†	283	retired	50	"
P	Bush Marguate—†	283	"	35	"
R	Bush May—†	283	"	45	"
S	Hayes Lillian—†	283	maid	26	30 Marlboro
T	O'Brien Mary—†	283	cook	27	here
U	Keohane Hannah—†	284	maid	30	New Bedford
U¹	Ledder Mary—†	284	"	38	60 Pond
V	Lochner Ernestina—†	284	"	21	here
W	McKnight Rachel—†	284	nurse	44	"
X	Rueter Bertha G—†	284	housewife	51	"
Y	Rueter Margot C—†	284	"	32	"
Z	Rueter William G	284	manufacturer	34	"
B	Shmitt Anna—†	284	maid	53	"
C	Werner Marie—†	284	"	30	"
D	Duncan Annie—†	285	domestic	52	"
E	MacDonald Agnes—†	285	"	50	Rhode Island
F	Stork Annie—†	285	waitress	46	120 Com av
G	Stork Lavinia—†	285	domestic	48	185 Marlboro
H	Young Charlotte W †	285	housewife	73	here
L	Fay John H	287	student	24	"
M	Fay Katherine D B †	287	housewife	64	"
N	Gallagher Ellen F †	287	domestic	58	"
O	Kelliher Margaret M †	287	"	33	
P	Kilduff Margaret—†	287	"	26	183 Com av
R	McCarthy Winifred †	287	"	23	here
S	Doyle Annie †	288	maid	25	133 Com av
T	Gilmore Alice B †	288	housekeeper	50	Europe
U	Manning Barbari †	288	maid	22	553 Wash'n

Beacon Street—Continued

v	Manning Catherine —†	288	cook	24	104 St James av
w	Thomas Alice L —†	288	student	21	Europe
x	Thomas Katherine L—†	288	''	22	''
y	Farr Ada M—†	289	housewife	51	7 Walnut
z	Leland Ella A—†	289	retired	68	495 Col av
z¹	Lugden Carrie E —†	289	stenographer	40	7 Walnut
A	Milner Lillias —†	289	domestic	36	7 ''
C	Zavoico Basil B	289	student	23	here
D	Buote Agnes—†	290	nurse	23	330 Com av
E	Dick Evans R. jr	290	broker	36	New York
F	Dick Jane T—†	290	housewife	32	''
G	O'Connor Annie—†	290	cook	39	Brookline
H	Shea Mary—†	290	maid	26	''
K	Hennessy Bedina —†	291	domestic	38	here
L	Lane Daniel W	291	councilor	50	''
M	Lane Susan M —†	291	housewife	70	''
N	Warren Margaret—†	291	domestic	45	Maine
O	Clarey Sarah—†	292	maid	45	''
P	MacIsaaic Mary—†	292	''	26	''
R	McCall Mary—†	292	''	42	171 Beacon
S	Stackpole Kathrine —†	292	housewife	48	here
T	Stackpole Lewis	292	lawyer	49	"
U	Amory Gertrude L —†	293	housewife	56	"
V	Amory Harcourt	293	vice president	68	"
W	Amory Harcourt, jr	293	salesman	29	"
X	Amory John S	293	clerk	24	"
Y	Amory Susannah—†	293	housewife	24	"
Z	Callahan Catherine—†	293	domestic	35	"
A	Connelly Ellen—†	293	''	32	"
B	Mulraney Sarah—†	293	''	55	"
C	Frothingham Anna C—†	294	housewife	60	"
D	Frothingham Paul	294	clergyman	59	"
F	Clark Myron G —†	295 & 297	fireman	42	"
F	Russell LeBaron	295 & 297	banker	45	"
G	Vincent Breth	295 & 297	physician	40	"
H	Ely Elizabeth B—†	295 & 297	housewife	51	"
K	McLoud Catherine—†	295 & 297	domestic	40	"
L	Bagley Bridget —†	295 & 297	''	24	"
M	Bissell Eva—†	295 & 297	stenographer	45	"
N	Hesson Mary —†	295 & 297	domestic	24	"
O	Hill George S	295 & 297	physician	55	"

Beacon Street—Continued

P	Burns James H	295 & 297	janitor	71	here
R	Metcalf Abbie –†	295 & 297	domestic	56	"
S	Porter Elizabeth B—†	295 & 297	housewife	72	"
T	Hultman Elizabeth—†	295 & 297	"	45	"
U	Hultman Eugene	295 & 297	director	55	"
V	Sullivan Mary—†	295 & 297	domestic	50	"
W	Daggett Evelyn–†	295 & 297	housewife	68	"
X	Feeney Mary—†	295 & 297	domestic	35	"
Y	Warner Blanche–†	295 & 297	housewife	60	"
Z	Warner Frank E	295 & 297	retired	65	"
z¹	Warner Richard	295 & 297	newsdealer	28	"
A	McGrail Mary—†	295 & 297	domestic	25	"
B	Murray Isabel—†	295 & 297	nurse	41	"
C	Sears Mary C—†	295 & 297	housewife	50	"
D	Prescott George J	295 & 297	clergyman	76	"
E	Prescott Lucille—†	295 & 297	housewife	54	"
F	Daggett Eleanor W—†	295 & 297	"	56	"
G	Smith Mabel—†	295 & 297	domestic	40	"
H	Bowker Charlotte—†	295 & 297	housewife	62	"
K	Dowd Marie—†	295 & 297	domestic	35	"
L	Clarke Harriett–†	295 & 297	housewife	50	"
M	Clarke Robert J	295 & 297	real estate	56	"
N	Walsh Nora—†	295 & 297	domestic	35	"
O	Southworth Mary E—†	295 & 297	housewife	50	"
P	Sharp Virginia G–†	295 & 297	"	60	"
R	Burgess Celia—†	295 & 297	"	65	"
S	Burgess Charles G—†	295 & 297	merchant	72	"
T	Burgess James A	295 & 297	clerk	42	"
U	Dwyer Helen—†	295 & 297	domestic	35	"
V	Bramhall Eleanor–†	295 & 297	housewife	45	"
X	Monks Grace—†	295 & 297	social worker	37	"
Y	Monks Jane—†	295 & 297	housewife	65	"
Z	Randell Louise—†	295 & 297	nurse	65	"
A	Clancy Catherine—†	296	waitress	24	"
B	Donovan Margaret—†	296	maid	60	"
C	Foley Catherine—†	296	"	42	"
D	Foley Mary—†	296	"	45	"
E	Holmes Edward J	296	lawyer	51	"
F	Holmes Mary S—†	296	housewife	46	"
G	Dabuery Frederick L	298	clerk	23	"
H	Dabuery George	298	lawyer	43	"

Letter.	Full Name.	Residence, April 1, 1924.	Occupation.	Supposed Age.	Reported Residence, April 1, 1923. Street and Number.

Beacon Street—Continued

Letter.	Full Name.	Residence, April 1, 1924.	Occupation.	Supposed Age.	Reported Residence, April 1, 1923. Street and Number.
K	Dabuery Mary F—†	298	housewife	35	here
L	Dabuery Thomas N	298	student	21	"
M	Lavender Fannie L—†	299	retired	40	"
N	Cummings Margaret—†	300	housekeeper	47	230 Clarendon
O	Johansen Nicoline B—†	300	companion	52	230 "
P	MacDonald Katherine-†	301	domestic	46	here
R	Williams Hugh	301	physician	51	"
S	Cuniff Catherine—†	302	housekeeper	31	"
T	Storer Grace—†	302	housewife	45	"
U	Storer Malcomb	302	physician	50	"
V	Colley Annie M—†	303	domesic	25	"
W	Howe Melia E—†	303	housewife	50	"
X	Howe Walter C	303	physician	52	"
Y	Brown Adelade—†	304	housewife	52	"
Z	Brown William H	304	lawyer	64	"
A	Cody Catherine—†	304	cook	42	"
B	Dwyer Lillian—†	304	waitress	23	"
C	McSweeney Nellie—†	304	maid	27	"
D	Lord Carol—†	305	student	21	"
E	Lord Frederick T	305	physician	48	"
F	Lord Mabel—†	305	housewife	54	"
G	Doherty Catherine—†	306	waitress	45	"
H	Richardson Fannie—†	306	retired	87	"
K	Richardson William	306	lawyer	65	"
L	Courteney Frances—†	307	domestic	24	"
M	MacDonald Christine—†	307	"	35	"
N	McGann Elizabeth—†	307	housewife	42	"
O	McGann Pierce	307	physician	42	"
P	O'Brien Winifred—†	309	domestic	39	"
R	O'Donnell Mary—†	309	"	45	"
S	Rogers Clara K—†	309	housewife	80	"
T	Rogers Henry M	309	lawyer	85	"
U	Levis Catherine—†	310	laundress	45	Rhode Island
V	Mitchell Catherine—†	310	maid	27	"
W	Mitchell Mary—†	310	"	22	"
X	Richmond Joshua B	310	retired	80	"
Y	Richmond Yosafa—†	310	housewife	70	"
Z	Walsh Elizabeth—†	310	cook	50	"
A	Crossman Annie—†	311	housewife	55	here
B	Crossman John A	311	janitor	63	"
D	Flaherty Catherine—†	313	waitress	38	Ireland

Beacon Street—Continued

E	Stanton Charles F	313	lawyer	43	here
F	Stanton Ethel B—†	313	housewife	48	"
G	Coleman Ruth—†	314	artist	35	Gloucester
H	Heath Warren	314	broker	40	Brookline
K	Shlick Charlotte—†	314	housewife	35	here
L	Shlick Leo	314	engineer	40	"
M	Stuart Carolyn—†	314	housewife	25	Brookline
N	Stuart Lawrence	314	manager	35	"
O	Drain Catherine—†	316	maid	55	247 Marlboro
P	Powers George H	316	physician	47	here
R	Powers Madeline D—†	316	housewife	40	"
S	Stuart Elizabeth—†	316	maid	48	"
U	Brady Agnes T—†	318	"	35	"
V	O'Reilly Mary—†	318	cook	34	"
W	Palmer Bradley W	318	lawyer	58	"
X	Tinlin Helen—†	318	maid	28	"
Y	Baven Anne R—†	319	student	24	"
Z	Baven Stephen	319	merchant	54	"
A	Kelleher Margaret—†	319	cook	60	20 Gloucester
B	Kelleher Nellie—†	319	maid	32	Ireland
C	McSweeney Annie—†	319	waitress	38	"
D	Pratt Frances E—†	319	retired	78	here
E	Hildreth Alma E—†	320	"	51	"
F	Hildreth Henry A	320	"	52	"
G	Nolan Rose—†	320	maid	20	Scotland
H	Ward Rebecca—†	320	cook	52	here
K	Eagleston Muriel A—†	321	student	20	128 Chestnut
L	Judkins George W	321	broker	42	128 "
M	Judkins Lillian—†	321	housewife	42	128 "
N	Gardiner Alice—†	322	"	65	here
O	Gardiner Robert H	322	lawyer	65	"
P	Hart Margaret—†	322	cook	52	"
R	Mulvey Margaret—†	322	maid	30	"
S	Roche Mary A—†	322	domestic	58	"
T	Jones Albert M	323	publisher	52	"
U	Jones Grace H—†	323	housewife	45	"
V	Wilber Alger N	323	butler	34	New Hampshire
W	Cleary Margaret—†	324	nurse	40	here
X	Croll Albert I	324	merchant	65	"
Y	Croll Sara H—†	324	housewife	65	"
Z	DeFriez Grace—†	324	"	38	"

Beacon Street—Continued

Letter	Full Name.	Residence, April 1, 1924.	Occupation.	Supposed Age.	Reported Residence, April 1, 1923. Street and Number.
A	Gill Delia—†	324	maid	35	here
B	Harrington Nellie—†	324	waitress	47	"
C	Jackson Valentine	324	houseman	35	"
D	Parlon Nellie—†	324	cook	38	258 Marlboro
E	Goldthwaite Rose—†	325	nurse	49	381 "
F	Hill Blanche C—†	325	housewife	58	here
G	Hill Josiah F	325	banker	60	"
H	Hill Theoroa—†	325	student	21	"
K	Porter Catherine—†	325	maid	28	"
L	Bickford Fannie—†	326	governess	45	"
M	Brown Clara—†	326	housewife	47	"
N	Brown Martin A	326	merchant	50	"
O	McNeill Minnie—†	326	cook	30	"
P	Gallagher Elizabeth—†	327	maid	35	24 Com av
R	Hutchins Constantin	327	retired	74	here
S	Hutchins Mary S—†	327	housewife	72	"
T	Kuhn Florence J—†	327	nurse	40	"
U	Lyon Adelaide—†	327	cook	50	"
V	Mahoney Catherine—†	327	"	45	"
W	McCarthy Mary—†	327	"	55	"
Y	Bailey Rose—†	329	maid	24	"
Z	Cousins Annie—†	329	cook	44	"
A	Lillie Amy H—†	329	housewife	62	"
B	Lillie John	329	retired	78	"
C	Lillie Louise H—†	329	student	30	"
D	Lillie Rosamond—†	329	"	24	"
E	Caldwell Ida—†	330	maid	57	"
F	Coulter Susan—†	330	"	40	"
G	Fay Elizabeth—†	330	housewife	72	"
H	Grem Matilda—†	330	maid	42	"
K	MacCre Mary—†	330	waitress	48	21 Com av
L	Urquhart Annie—†	330	cook	45	here
M	Martin Antonia E—†	331	secretary	50	330 Dartmouth
N	Prescod Alietha—†	331	maid	40	330 "
O	Rolfe Helen G—†	331	housewife	48	330 "
P	Rolfe William A	331	physician	52	330 "
R	Leonard Carl P	332	merchant	45	here
S	Leonard Marie—†	332	housewife	40	"
T	Madison Catherine—†	332	maid	35	"
U	Nelson Walborg—†	332	nurse	25	"
V	Ottoson Erlin—†	332	waitress	28	"

Beacon Street—Continued

w	Thompson Marie—†	332	laundress	50	here
x	Baker Leonora—†	333	none	41	"
y	Baker Lynette—†	333	housewife	43	"
z	Brennan Joseph	333	choreman	26	"
A	Brennan May—†	333	cook	21	"
B	Moore Florence—†	333	retired	66	"
C	Dalton Frances—†	335	housewife	50	"
D	Dalton Mary—†	335	retired	45	"
E	Monahan Delia—†	335	maid	45	"
F	Murry Roselia—†	335	cook	40	Wakefield
G	Connelly Elizabeth—†	337	"	25	here
H	Driscoll Hanna—†	337	maid	50	"
K	Hannon Winafred—†	337	"	28	"
L	Thorndike Albert	337	broker	63	"
M	Thorndike Mary I—†	337	housewife	52	"
N	Thorndike Rosanna D—†	337	secretary	25	"
O	Cavanaugh Mary—†	339	maid	34	Brookline
P	Davis Bancroft	339	lawyer	54	here
R	Davis Charlotte J—†	339	housewife	42	"
S	Mahony Mary—†	339	cook	39	Newton
T	O'Brien Katherine—†	339	maid	32	here
U	Sullivan Mary—†	339	"	40	"
V	Amory Mary R—†	341	housewife	51	"
W	Amory William	341	broker	51	"
X	Mahoney Julia—†	341	maid	28	"
Y	Kimball Day	343	lawyer	30	"
Z	Brennan Mary—†	345	maid	23	333 Beacon
A	Connelly Barbara—†	345	cook	25	Winchester
B	Whitney Colete—†	345	housewife	36	here
C	Whitney Handasyde	345	lawyer	45	"
D	Chick Issac	347	banker	55	"
E	Chick Jennie H—†	347	housewife	50	"
F	Muldoon Margaret—†	347	waitress	35	"
G	Murphy Annie—†	347	maid	25	"
H	O'Brien Catherine—†	347	cook	35	"

Berkeley Street

L	Jaques Hariet S—†	282	retired	66	here
M	Jaques Louise—†	282	housewife	31	"

Berkeley Street—Continued

R	Curr Bertha T—†	282	housewife	53	here
S	Curr Guy M	282	enigneer	53	"
T	Dunham Alice—†	282	retired	53	"
U	Dunham William H	282	musician	65	"
V	Gavett Ann R—†	282	retired	75	"
W	Cochran Sallie C—†	282	"	65	"
X	Miller Margaret O—†	282	"	45	"
Y	Miller Mary A—†	282	"	70	"
Z	Shattuck Alice—†	282	"	50	"
A	Merrill Clara B—†	282	"	50	"
B	Perkins Annie A—†	282	housewife	59	"
C	Perkins Ellen C—†	282	student	25	"
D	Perkins Frederick H	282	insurance agent	59	"
E	Perkins Louis L	282	student	22	"
H	Rogers Gretchen W—†	282	retired	40	"
K	Rogers Mary T—†	282	"	70	"
M	Hook Caroline B—†	282	housewife	50	"
N	Hook Charles H	282	broker	58	"
O	Olmstead James M	282	lawyer	72	"
P	Baldwin Annie O—†	282	retired	61	"
R	Lawton Frederick	282	judge	70	"
S	Power Alice M—†	282	clerk	55	"
T	Power Clara L—†	282	"	53	"
V	Selfridge Annie F—†	282	housewife	59	"
W	Selfridge George S	282	lawyer	59	"
X	Hall Carolina R—†	282	housewife	40	"
Y	Hall William L	282	manufacturer	50	"
Z	Kimball Louise E—†	282	housekeeper	54	"
A	McKay Helen E—†	282	housewife	58	"
B	McKay William E	282	manager	59	"
C	McKay Wilson E	282	salesman	31	"
D	Yeager Frances P—†	282	manager	55	"
E	Brock Jennie—†	299	waitress	38	"
F	Brock Julia—†	299	domestic	27	"
G	Caglia Joseph	299	butler	26	Italy
H	Fullerton Margaret—†	299	domestic	25	here
K	Gibbons Mary—†	299	"	38	"
L	Hidstrom Eva—†	299	"	38	"
M	Winthrop Frederick	299	broker	54	"
N	Winthrop Sarah T—†	299	housewife	39	"
R	MacKenzie Margaret—†	302	governess	35	"

Berkeley Street—Continued

s	MacLeod Katherine—†	302	domestic	20	here
t	Peabody Harold	302	retired	50	"
v	Peabody Marian L—†	302	housewife	50	"
v	Terne Deborah—†	302	cook	50	"
w	Boyle Margaret—†	303	domestic	27	"
x	Coolidge Edith L—†	303	housewife	50	"
y	Coolidge Harold J	303	lawyer	56	"
z	Coolidge Harold J, jr	303	student	20	"
A	Donovan Patrick	303	houseman	60	"
B	Farrell Agnes—†	303	domestic	46	37 Beacon
C	Linehan Margaret—†	303	"	35	here
D	O'Donahue Hannah—†	303	"	56	"
E	O'Donnell Mary—†	303	"	26	"
F	O'Neill Nellie—†	303	"	26	"
G	Pollock Bertha—†	303	cook	48	Lowell
H	MacDonald Annie—†	304	"	25	here
K	Nelson Anna G—†	304	domestic	25	"
L	Taylor Charles H	304	editor	55	"
M	Taylor Charles H, jr	304	"	26	"
N	Taylor Margurite F—†	304	housewife	50	"

Clarendon Street

o	Colwell Elizebeth W—†	260	teacher	36	here
P	Todd Mabel E—†	260	"	40	"
R	White Pearl—†	260	"	55	"
T	Allen Helen V—†	260	housewife	40	"
U	Allen James F	260	janitor	39	"
V	Simonds Henry F	260	manufacturer	35	"
W	Simonds Mary E—†	260	laundress	38	"
X	Weeks Gertrude C—†	260	housewife	63	390 Com av
Y	Weeks Warren R P	260	real estate	66	390 "
Z	Perkins Elizabeth N—†	260	retired	70	here
A	Parrish Mabel—†	260	housewife	51	"
B	Parrish Rossman	260	bookbinder	51	"
C	Taylor Nellie—†	260	maid	29	"
D	Ganly Josephine—†	260	"	47	92 Beacon
E	Loring Helen—†	260	housewife	73	here
F	Sweeney Margaret—†	260	cook	60	"
K	Adams Mary F—†	260	housekeeper	75	"

Page.	Letter.	FULL NAME.	Residence, April 1, 1924.	Occupation.	Supposed Age.	Reported Residence, April 1, 1923. Street and Number.

Clarendon Street—Continued

L	Chisholm Grace E—†	260	maid	48	here
M	Marshall Mary F—†	260	"	50	24 Walpole
N	Williamson Anna—†	260	cook	58	here
G	Morgan Ellen—†	260	retired	41	"
O	Filkins Bertha K—†	261	matron	36	"
P	Niergarth Anna—†	261	waitress	31	Illinois
R	Aldrich Dorothy W—†	263	housewife	37	here
S	Aldrich William T	263	architect	39	"
T	Fouhy Elizabeth—†	263	waitress	35	"
U	Madden Bridie—†	263	maid	24	9 Brimmer
V	Megrew George	265	manager	50	here
W	Megrew Louise G—†	265	housewife	48	"
X	Quill Katherine—†	265	maid	48	"
Y	Quill Margaret—†	265	waitress	42	"
Z	Davis Elizabeth—†	267	clerk	45	"
A	Luce Stephen B	267	student	36	"
B	Ladd Anna C—†	270	housewife	45	"
C	Ladd Maynard	270	physician	51	"
D	Watson Edith—†	270	housekeeper	43	"
E	Watson Neil	270	butler	50	"
G	Brown Margaret—†	274	cook	35	"
H	Burnett Margaret—†	274	maid	40	"
K	Endicott Ellice E—†	274	housewife	32	"
L	Endicott William	274	banker	59	"
M	Maloney Mary J—†	274	maid	21	"
N	Robcheau Emma—†	274	"	38	"
O	Butler Catherine F—†	275	"	47	"
P	Winslow Frederick B	275	physician	50	"
R	Winslow Mary—†	275	housewife	47	"
S	Green Mary—†	277	cook	38	Cambridge
T	Johnson Sarah—†	277	chambermaid	42	here
U	Parker Frederick	277	coal dealer	59	Bedford
V	Parker Henry B	277	"	31	"
W	Parker Mary—†	277	housewife	57	"
X	Sullivan Barbara—†	277	maid	27	here
Y	Barbour Rosamond P—†	278	housewife	38	"
Z	Barbour Thomas	278	zoologist	40	"
A	Boutinou Ninette—†	278	maid	29	France
B	Drury May—†	278	"	30	here
C	Gallagher Margaret—†	278	"	33	"
D	Herlihy Julia—†	278	"	40	"

8—7

Clarendon Street—Continued

E	O'Malley Kathleen—†	278	maid	30	here
F	O'Rourke Mary—†	278	"	28	"
G	Power Katherine—†	278	"	34	"
H	Goring Henrietta—†	279	housekeeper	50	"
K	Tarr Rebecca J—†	279	nurse	39	"
L	Fallon Peggy—†	285	maid	22	Waltham
M	Gilligan Sarah—†	285	waitress	25	here
N	Hall Dorothy B—†	285	housewife	35	"
O	Hall John L	285	lawyer	45	"
P	McDonald Mary—†	285	maid	20	Belmont
R	Passera Hortuese—†	285	governess	30	here
S	Peterson Madalina—†	285	cook	27	"
T	Stephens Rebecca—†	285	nurse	35	"
U	Taylor Margaret—†	285	laundress	60	"

Commonwealth Avenue

A	Kingston Albert	3	butler	37	here
B	Low Mary—†	3	cook	45	"
C	McCormack Annie—†	3	chambermaid	35	"
D	Qualey Anna—†	3	waitress	30	Brookline
E	Carey Margaret—†	5	kitchenmaid	22	here
F	Frost Della—†	5	parlormaid	35	"
G	Granville Catherine—†	5	laundress	45	"
H	Murphy Mary—†	5	waitress	34	"
K	Quinn Annie—†	5	maid	40	"
L	Quirk Annie—†	5	cook	45	"
M	Riordan Josephine—†	5	chambermaid	47	"
N	Weston Margaret—†	5	maid	48	"
O	Johnson Fannie H—†	7	housewife	50	"
P	Johnson Rosamond B—†	7	none	23	"
R	Armstrong Linda—†	9	housekeeper	45	"
S	Hayes Maragret—†	9	cook	42	"
T	Hollis James	9	butler	54	"
U	Mars Laura—†	9	housewife	88	"
V	Norcross Granville H	9	real estate	65	"
W	Brown Jacob F	11	merchant	59	"
X	Brown Mariette C—†	11	housewife	41	"
Y	Haughton Malcolm G	13	broker	58	"
Z	Houghton Marian S—†	13	housewife	58	"

Commonwealth Avenue—Continued

Letter.	Full Name.	Residence, April 1, 1924.	Occupation.	Supposed Age.	Reported Residence, April 1, 1923. Street and Number.
A	Livingston Elizabeth—†	13	chambermaid	34	here
B	Coveney Maragret—†	15	maid	27	"
C	Fitzgerald Mary—†	15	laundress	40	"
D	Hennesy Mary—†	15	chambermaid	40	"
E	Johnson Minnie—†	15	cook	25	"
F	Joyce Delia—†	15	maid	27	"
G	Mannix Nellie—†	15	"	35	"
H	Murphy Margaret—†	15	laundress	30	"
K	Nilson Sophie—†	15	cook	48	"
L	Glynn Julia—†	17	"	36	"
M	Jinks Margaret—†	17	laundress	36	"
N	Lawless Mary M—†	19	housemaid	32	"
O	Lawless Nora F—†	19	"	29	"
P	Murphy Bridget—†	19	cook	33	"
R	Gray Hanna—†	21	maid	27	New York
T	Wood Edith B—†	25	housewife	29	here
U	Carey Ellen—†	27	cook	50	"
V	Daly Catherine—†	27	waitress	29	"
W	Lothrop Annie M—†	27	housewife	88	"
X	Lothrop Mary B—†	27	housekeeper	53	"
Y	Lothrop Thornton K	27	lawyer	45	"
Z	Shaw Jane W—†	31	housewife	53	"
A	Shaw Samuel P	31	banker	46	"
B	Stockton Howard	31	lawyer	82	"
C	Stockton Howard, jr	31	"	46	"
D	Ellicott Minnie—†	33	housewife	33	22 Bulfinch
E	Ellicott William G	33	sexton	41	22 "
G	Salinger Dorothy—†	33	librarian	24	Brookline
H	Salinger Richard B	33	advertising	28	"
K	Ranck May—†	33	housewife	49	9 W Hill pl
L	Ranck Than V	33	editor	49	9 "
M	Brady Elizabeth A—†	33	housewife	66	here
N	Brady Emily A—†	33	school teacher	29	"
O	Pond Abbott S	33	broker	36	35 Congress
P	Higginson Charles	33	"	28	Brookline
R	Barry Mary—†	35	maid	23	Mattapan
S	McLeod John	35	butler	30	Gloucester
T	Snelling Eva D	35	housewife	48	151 Com av
U	Snelling Rodman P	35	maufacturer	60	151 "
V	Tourgee Goldie L—†	37	housewife	37	Everett
W	Tourgee William H	37	shipper	40	"

Commonwealth Avenue—Continued

x	Choate Lucy E—†	37	housewife	47	127 Newbury
y	Keen Nellie B—†	37	"	45	39 Pinckney
z	Keen William C	37	milliner	54	39 "
e	French Ruth H—†	37	housewife	43	New Hampshire
f	Waters Sarah L—†	37	secretary	29	Fall River
g	Bullard Ellen—†	39	housewife	50	here
h	Credon Agnes—†	39	cook	35	33 Cordis
k	Duffy Alice—†	41	maid	45	here
l	Duffy Annie F—†	41	"	38	212 Com av
m	Duffey Theresa—†	41	cook	43	here
n	King Charles A	41	retired	73	"
o	King Marjorie—†	41	housewife	45	"
p	Clavelle Albertine—†	43	governess	53	"
r	McEntyre John	43	houseman	41	Maine
s	Rosenthal Louis	43	merchant	43	here
t	Rosenthal Mabel—†	43	housewife	35	"
w	Everett Clara P—†	45	"	20	111 Marlboro
x	Everett Henry C	45	manufacturer	32	111 "
y	Swett Mabel N—†	45	housewife	52	Winchester
z	Swett Warren G	45	manager	57	"
a	Richardson Carrie M—†	45	housewife	61	464 Com av
b	Richardson George	45	retired	61	464 "
c	Kemball Beatrice—†	45	housewife	34	Hingham
d	Sylvester Edith—†	45	retired	39	Brookline
f	Bullard Emily—†	47	housewife	64	here
g	Bullard John T	47	retired	60	"
h	Bullard Lydia—†	47	social worker	27	"
k	Moran Catherine—†	47	waitress	23	New Bedford
l	Everett Henry C	49	merchant	60	here
m	Houlihan Nellie—†	49	chambermaid	35	"
n	Kennedy Mary—†	49	laundress	50	"
o	Neary Margarett—†	49	waitress	26	117 Com av
p	Regan Catherine J—†	49	cook	45	here
r	Browne Annie—†	51	maid	35	"
s	Colgan Mary—†	51	cook	60	"
t	Joyce Catherine—†	51	laundress	40	"
u	Monks George G	51	student	25	"
v	Monks George H	51	retired	71	"
w	Monks John P	51	student	23	"
x	Monks Olga H—†	51	housewife	50	"
y	Dwire Marie—†	55	maid	35	192 Marlboro

Commonwealth Avenue—Continued

Letter.	Full Name.	Residence, April 1, 1924.	Occupation.	Supposed Age.	Reported Residence, April 1, 1923. Street and Number.
z	Flagg Eleanor—†	55	housewife	40	192 Marlboro
A	Flagg Elisha	55	physician	55	192 "
B	McClay Elizabeth J—†	57	seamstress	42	here
C	McMaster Helen—†	57	chambermaid	43	"
D	Armstrong Walter	59	butler	38	Yarmouth
E	Bisson Desire	61	"	28	here
F	Decosta Marie—†	63	cook	51	45 Beacon
G	Donnelly Edward C	63	advertising	60	here
H	Donnelly Mary J—†	63	housewife	45	"
K	Mahoney Catherine L—†	63	retired	70	86 Glen rd
M	Edberg Gerda—†	107	laundress	35	here
N	Forbes Alice B—†	107	housewife	77	"
O	Forbes James M	107	retired	79	"
P	Gilligan Margaret—†	107	maid	30	"
R	McHale Anna—†	107	waitress	25	"
S	Mitchell Katie—†	107	maid	23	"
T	Moran Ann—†	107	chambermaid	24	"
U	O'Shea Marion—†	107	maid	22	"
V	Rice Catherine—†	107	cook	33	"
W	Burke Catherine—†	109	maid	25	"
X	Dinneen Margaret—†	109	cook	46	"
Y	Kelliher Margaret—†	111	waitress	36	"
Z	Sampson Gertrude—†	111	housewife	53	"
A	Waldron Nora—†	111	maid	40	"
B	Cooney Ellen—†	113	cook	54	297 Col av
C	Frothingham Harriet A—†	113	housewife	55	here
D	Frothingham Randolph	113	lawyer	43	"
E	Smith Sophia—†	113	waitress	59	"
F	Grinnan Frances A—†	115	none	24	"
G	Lyons Katherine—†	115	parlormaid	55	437 Marlboro
M	McHugh Margaret—†	115	cook	60	Cambridge
H	Morss Ethel R—†	115	housewife	56	here
K	Morss Everett	115	manufacturer	59	"
L	Morss Everett, jr	115	student	23	"
N	Russell Walter	115	butler	38	Texas
O	Hitchcock Esther M—†	117	housewife	52	here
P	Hitchcock Evelyn E—†	117	none	30	"
R	Fielding Nellie—†	119	parlormaid	23	"
S	Ford John	119	houseman	55	"
T	Hurley Catherine—†	119	laundress	40	"
U	Kiernan Mary—†	119	cook	40	"

Commonwealth Avenue—Continued

v	Russell Gertrude—†	119	housewife	41	here
w	Russell Richard S	119	banker	43	"
x	Sugru Margaret—†	119	waitress	25	"
y	White Katherine—†	119	kitchenmaid	22	"
z	Doddy Julia—†	121	parlormaid	27	576 Wash'n
A	Fisk George S	121	clergyman	55	here
B	Hagerty Mary—†	121	cook	35	375 Beacon
C	MacIntyre Christine—†	121	chambermaid	40	130 Chandle
D	Anderson August	123	clerk	24	here
E	Dromey Margaret—†	123	waitress	29	"
F	Dromey Minnie—†	123	laundress	39	"
G	Hartnett Katherine—†	123	nurse	40	"
H	McNamara Bridget—†	123	chambermaid	40	"
K	Mitchell Jennie—†	123	parlormaid	37	"
L	Perkins Anna W—†	123	retired	80	"
M	Regan Jane—†	123	cook	34	"
N	Barry Leonie D—†	125	housewife	43	"
O	Blanchard Harriet E—†	125	retired	79	14 Burr
P	Dabney Nannie H—†	125	"	45	here
R	Dureyea Anna—†	125	clerk	50	365 Marlbor
S	Guibard Alberta—†	125	physician	48	here
T	Guibard Frederick	125	lawyer	48	"
U	White Helen—†	125	retired	43	365 Marlbor
V	White Martin	125	salesman	50	365 "
W	Faelton Carl	127	professor	77	365 "
X	Faelton Reinhold	127	"	68	365 "
Y	Hayes Clermont	127	secretary	37	365 "
Z	Quinn Katherine—†	129	waitress	35	here
A	Quinn Mary—†	129	parlormaid	50	"
B	Shea Mary—†	129	cook	45	"
D	Callahan Mazie—†	133	housekeeper	58	"
E	Dempsey Abigail—†	133	housewife	50	"
F	Dempsey Ethel—†	133	none	25	"
G	Dempsey George C	133	merchant	50	"
H	Dempsey Justin	133	none	23	"
K	Druggett Susan—†	133	cook	35	"
L	McCall Mary F—†	135	laundress	30	"
M	McCarthy Nora—†	135	nurse	30	"
N	McLaughlin Martin	135	butler	54	New Hampshire
O	Sullivan Katherine—†	135	cook	45	Brookline
P	Henry Marie—†	151	"	30	1255 Blue Hill av

		Full Name	Residence, April 1, 1924.	Occupation.	Supposed Age.	Reported Residence, April 1, 1923. Street and Number.

Commonwealth Avenue—Continued

		Full Name	Res.	Occupation.	Age	Reported Residence
R		Lamreaux Florence—†	151	principal	40	247 Berkeley
S		McLean Katherine—†	151	cook	30	here
T		Clarkin Agnes R—†	161	none	28	"
U		Clarkin Marie M—†	161	student	21	"
V		Fitzroy Mary—†	161	housewife	50	"
W		Cannon Annie—†	163	chambermaid	30	"
X		Hurly Katherine—†	163	cook	45	113 Com av
Y		Kidder Elizabeth—†	163	housewife	72	here
Z		McDonald Isabel—†	163	waitress	35	153 Ruthven
A		Connolly Mary—†	165	parlormaid	28	199 Bay State rd
B		King Nora—†	165	waitress	27	here
C		Rooney Mary—†	165	cook	50	Brookline
D		Vaillant Alice—†	165	housewife	46	here
F		Vaillant George, jr	165	student	22	"
E		Vaillant George W	165	broker	46	"
G		Vaillant Marion—†	165	teacher	24	"
H		Brodrick Margaret—†	167	maid	38	"
K		Laugnane Annie—†	167	waitress	38	"
L		Mackey Margaret—†	167	maid	50	"
M		Murray Katherine—†	167	cook	48	"
N		Webster Frank G	167	broker	83	"
O		Webster Mary—†	167	housewife	82	"
P		Fay Grace E—†	169	"	56	"
R		McGeoghegan Margaret—†	169	waitress	23	6 Com av
S		Nilson Wilhelmina—†	169	cook	50	Milton
T		Dexter Susan—†	171	retired	84	here
U		MacDonald Jenney—†	171	parlormaid	20	Canada
V		McWilliams Nellie—†	171	waitress	27	here
W		Ross Sarah G—†	171	cook	48	"
X		Lavin Delia—†	173	parlormaid	28	464 Beacon
Y		O'Brien Winifred J—†	173	cook	28	here
Z		Parker Edith S—†	173	housewife	44	"
A		Parker John H	173	architect	50	"
B		White Nora—†	173	waitress	26	"
C		Bartlett Florence R—†	175	housewife	52	"
D		Bartlett Stephen L	175	merchant	60	"
E		Bremster Isabel—†	175	maid	39	"
F		Coor Doch	175	butler	38	"
G		Hyman Laura—†	175	laundress	35	"
H		Paine Mary—†	175	cook	53	"
K		Adams Charles F	177	lawyer	55	"

Commonwealth Avenue—Continued

		FULL NAME.	Residence, April 1, 1924	Occupation.	Supposed Age.	Reported Residence, April 1, 1923. Street and Number.
L		Adams Frances L—†	177	housewife	52	here
M		Geary Annie—†	177	cook	55	"
N		Lynch Nellie—†	177	waitress	40	"
O		Sweeney Agnes—†	177	laundress	43	"
P		Sweeney Margaret—†	177	maid	35	"
S		Donnelly Helen—†	181	waitress	32	49 Beacon
T		Dupee Arthur	181	merchant	52	here
U		Dupee Clara E—†	181	housewife	48	"
V		Hogarty Mary—†	181	cook	40	27 Parkton rd
W		O'Brien Anna—†	181	laundress	50	New Hampshire
X		O'Brien Katherine—†	181	chambermaid	35	224 Com av
Y		Sullivan Katherine—†	181	kitchenmaid	24	Beverly Farms
Z		Bergerson Mariana—†	183	governess	40	here
A		Clancy Margaret—†	183	waitress	29	"
B		Coyne Margaret—†	183	laundress	50	"
C		English Mary—†	183	maid	34	"
D		Hargadon Mary—†	183	kitchenmaid	22	"
E		Lynch Elizabeth—†	183	chambermaid	22	Ireland
F		McGrail Sarah—†	183	parlormaid	28	31 Mass av
G		Merriam Frank	183	trustee	73	here
H		Merriam Theresa B—†	183	housewife	67	"
K		Merriam Theresa L—†	183	retired	43	"
L		Sheerin Rose—†	183	cook	29	"
M		Willis Agnes E—†	191	retired	65	"
N		Willis Sadie—†	191	housewife	29	"
O		Willis William J	191	janitor	32	"
P		Jennucci Carlo	191	chauffeur	39	24 Haviland
R		Jennucci Rose E—†	191	dressmaker	39	24 "
S		Little Arthur	191	architect	42	here
T		Little Jessie W—†	191	housewife	50	"
U		Amory Lilly C—†	191	retired	69	"
V		Amory Roger	191	trustee	37	"
W		Campbell Mary P—†	191	parlormaid	38	"
X		McCloskey Margaret—†	191	cook	51	412 Beacon
Y		Murray Sarah—†	191	waitress	24	Ireland
Z		Harris Elizabeth—†	191	"	28	86 Marlboro
A		McCalder Flora—†	191	cook	50	Brookline
B		Potter Bessie—†	191	retired	54	here
D		Anderson Jennie—†	191	waitress	40	Europe
E		Velluc Marie—†	191	governess	44	Cambridge
F		Carlson Hulda—†	191	cook	42	90 Marlboro

Commonwealth Avenue—Continued

Letter.	FULL NAME.	Residence, April 1, 1924.	Occupation.	Supposed Age.	Reported Residence, April 1, 1923. Street and Number.
G	Saltonstall Gladys—†	191	housewife	36	here
H	Saltonstall John L	191	broker	45	"
K	Shackelton Lucy—†	191	maid	43	Medfield
L	Woodcocks Eleanor—†	191	"	37	here
M	Caldwell Elizabeth—†	191	waitress	44	"
N	Ellingsen Freda—†	191	chambermaid	55	"
O	Frazer Catherine—†	191	maid	55	"
P	Higginson Ida—†	191	retired	86	"
R	Boratra Henrietta—†	191	governess	25	"
S	McCauley Nora—†	191	parlormaid	22	411 Com av
T	McNulty Winifred—†	191	chambermaid	27	here
U	Stockton Margaret H—†	191	housewife	35	280 Beacon
V	Stockton Philip	191	banker	45	280 "
W	Walsh Josephine—†	191	waitress	22	Brookline
X	Connelly Mary—†	191	secretary	40	here
Y	Hogan Margaret—†	191	cook	30	"
Z	McQuade Mary—†	191	waitress	40	63 Beacon
A	Putnam Elizabeth—†	191	retired	48	here
B	Lyman Eleanor L—†	191	housewife	23	"
C	Lyman George H	191	broker	30	"
D	Lynch Rita—†	191	cook	20	"
E	Robb Margaret—†	191	nursemaid	27	"
K	Cochrane Elfreda—†	197	governess	22	"
F	Doherty Katherine—†	197	nurse	27	7 Chestnut
G	Duffy Alice—†	197	chambermaid	43	here
H	Flaherty Annie—†	197	cook	49	94 Winthrop
L	Peek Carol	197	chauffeur	26	Vermont
M	Rotch Arthur G	197	manager	43	here
N	Rotch Helen G—†	197	housewife	41	"
O	Wholey Bridie—†	197	parlormaid	24	"
P	Christie Andrew	199	butler	45	"
R	Murray Ellen—†	199	chambermaid	56	"
S	Sprague Elizabeth S—†	199	housewife	48	"
T	Sprague Gordon	199	student	20	"
U	Sprague Phineas S	199	"	24	"
V	Sprague Phineas W	199	merchant	44	"
W	Sullivan Julia—†	199	parlormaid	38	"
X	Vary Emma S—†	199	secretary	28	"
Y	Gilmore Julia—†	203	housewife	52	"
Z	Kerr William	205	houseman	35	"
A	McGrath Mary—†	205	chambermaid	50	"

Commonwealth Avenue—Continued

	Letter.	Full Name.	Residence, April 1, 1924.	Occupation.	Supposed Age.	Reported Residence April 1, 1923. Street and Number.
	B	McNulty Jane—†	205	cook	55	here
	C	Newhall Minnie—†	205	parlormaid	35	Brookline
	D	Davis Jennie—†	207	"	38	Cambridge
	E	Dickie Pansy—†	207	chambermaid	35	here
	F	Lawrence Laura A—†	207	housewife	55	"
	G	Riley Annie—†	207	cook	40	"
	H	Bowen Annie—†	211	chambermaid	23	"
	K	Feeley Mary—†	211	cook	60	"
	L	Kiley Nora—†	211	waitress	32	114 Beacon
	M	Mason Fannie C—†	211	none	62	here
	N	McMillen Mary—†	211	laundress	65	"
	O	Murray Anna—†	211	parlormaid	39	535 Beacon
	P	Cullinane Kate—†	213	chambermaid	49	here
	R	Leahy Katherine—†	213	cook	44	"
	S	MacDonald Bessie—†	213	waitress	43	79 Beacon
	T	Ward James	213	houseman	57	here
	U	White Gertrude R—†	213	none	58	"
	V	Boyle Nellie—†	215	laundress	54	"
	W	Cook Harry	215	butler	30	7 Batavia
	X	Covert George	215	chauffeur	37	here
	Y	Girol Marie—†	215	chambermaid	36	117 Com av
	Z	Harrison Mary—†	215	seamstress	38	here
	A	Higginson Francis L, jr	215	banker	47	"
	C	McDonough Delia—†	215	waitress	35	"
	B	Moran Katherine—†	215	cook	45	"
	D	Peabody Ruth—†	215	housekeeper	37	"
	E	Sheridan Theresa—†	215	kitchenmaid	32	W Newton
	F	Beatty Margaret—†	217	chambermaid	24	Brookline
	G	Curley Edward D	217	superintendent	37	here
	H	Curran Annie—†	217	kitchenmaid	24	"
	K	Doherty Margaret—†	217	housemaid	24	Lynn
	L	Foley Nora—†	217	"	55	here
	M	McLaughlin Cassie—†	217	laundress	62	"
	N	Mulkerin Mary—†	217	housemaid	25	"
	O	Morrow John	223	houseman	35	"
	P	Pearson Venla—†	223	maid	30	"
	R	Wilson Alma—†	223	cook	50	101 Chestnut
	V	Ilsner Anna—†	225	maid	46	Nova Scotia
	T	McDonald Annie—†	225	"	55	here
	U	McGowan Catherine—†	225	"	52	"
	S	Richardson William L	225	physician	81	"

Page	Letter	FULL NAME.	Residence, April 1, 1924.	Occupation.	Supposed Age.	Reported Residence, April 1, 1923. Street and Number.

Commonwealth Avenue—Continued

	w	Bartlett Mary F—†	227	housewife	70	here
	x	Johnson Anna E—†	227	maid	39	"
	y	MacDonald Margaret—†	227	"	56	"
	z	Campbell Lillian—†	229	"	38	Brookline
	A	Lyman Herbert	229	manufacturer	55	here
	B	Lyman Ruth W—†	229	housewife	45	"
	c	Matson Nellie—†	229	cook	40	"
	D	Richmond Mary—†	229	governess	45	212 Beacon
	E	Butler Mary W—†	231	housewife	54	here
	F	Butler Miriam—†	231	none	23	"
	G	Butler William M	231	manufacturer	60	"
	H	Davitt Mary—†	231	laundress	44	68 Montgomery
	K	Donelan Mary—†	231	maid	20	Manchester
	L	Eakins George	231	houseman	34	here
	M	Gillis Mary B—†	231	maid	38	Brookline
	N	Jones Georgie—†	231	governess	38	here
	o	Sullivan Norah T—†	231	maid	23	Brookline
	P	Scanlan Jane—†	233	housekeeper	62	here
	R	Bramwell Faithful A—†	235	housewife	36	"
	s	Bramwell Gerald A	235	manufacturer	41	"
	T	Christopherson Magnhild C—†	235	nurse	39	Norway
	U	Seeckstrom Ellen M—†	235	maid	38	Brookline

Dartmouth Street

	v	Boit Edward	303	student	21	Cambridge
	w	Boit Jennie—†	303	retired	50	"
	x	Boit Julia—†	303	"	51	"
	y	Boit Julia D—†	303	housewife	73	"
	z	Nellis Helen—†	303	maid	30	here
	A	Woods Margaret—†	303	"	45	66 Com av
	B	Attridge Mary—†	306	"	48	222 Prince
	c	Guthrie William	306	janitor	28	130 Myrtle
	D	O'Melia Agnes—†	306	maid	36	274 Beacon
	E	Dinwaschter Margaret—†	312	governess	35	here
	F	Dreyfus Carl	312	merchant	49	"
	G	Dreyfus Sylvia G—†	312	housewife	30	"
	H	Farrell Margaret—†	312	chambermaid	28	Ireland
	K	Martinson Bertha—†	312	cook	38	here
	L	Doyle Daniel	314	houseman	50	Somerville

Dartmouth Street—Continued

Letter	Full Name	Residence, April 1, 1924	Occupation	Supposed Age	Reported Residence, April 1, 1923. Street and Number.
M	Foley Nellie—†	314	maid	35	here
N	Luttenback Marie E—†	314	"	37	"
O	McDermott Delia—†	314	"	30	"
P	O'Donnell Agnes—†	314	cook	48	"
R	Reid John	314	butler	38	"
S	Stackpole Laura—†	314	housewife	42	"
T	Stackpole Pierpont L	314	lawyer	49	"
U	Ayer Charles F	315	"	57	"
V	Ayer Theodora E—†	315	housewife	40	"
W	Houlton Rose—†	315	maid	21	215 Com av
X	Jones Catherine—†	315	"	24	Scotland
Y	Kandola Hilma—†	315	cook	40	here
Z	Madigan Catherine—†	315	laundress	40	"
A	McDonald Anna—†	315	maid	48	"
B	Moriarty Daniel	315	houseman	45	28 Isabella
C	Norris John	315	butler	25	23 Forest Hills
D	O'Day Jeannette—†	315	maid	25	here
E	O'Hearn John	315	butler	36	"
F	Aba Ellen—†	317	retired	75	"
G	Allen Joseph	317	cook	45	Cambridge
H	Atkinson Frederick	317	butler	38	180 Com av
K	Battles Gertrude—†	317	maid	40	18 Hunt'n av
L	Browne Catherine—†	317	"	55	315 Dartmouth
M	Clark Alice S—†	317	"	43	220 Clarendon
N	Clark Harry E	317	agent	42	here
O	Hubert Helen—†	317	housewife	65	"
P	Hubert Orwin C	317	retired	65	"
R	Hulima Cora E—†	317	"	60	"
S	Nowea Allena—†	317	housewife	27	"
T	Parsons Albert	317	cook	21	India
U	Savati Jeannette—†	317	secretary	45	Providence R I
V	Thomas Gertrude—†	317	waitress	25	Brookline
W	White Eva—†	317	maid	30	here
X	Wiggan Arthena—†	317	housewife	42	"
Y	Coyne Margaret—†	319	waitress	25	"
Z	Donald Delia—†	319	cook	28	"
A	Goodrich Madilane—†	319	housewife	50	"
B	Goodrich Wise W	319	musician	60	"
C	Sherman Mary E—†	319	maid	40	"
D	Danielson Bertha—†	321	waitress	26	"
E	Foran Alice—†	321	cook	40	"

44

Dartmouth Street—Continued

	Letter.	FULL NAME.	Residence	Occupation	Age	Reported Residence
	F	Moore Mary E—†	321	caretaker	45	here
	G	Neary Anna—†	321	maid	21	"
	H	Johnson Ellen—†	326	chambermaid	27	"
	K	Ladd Catherine B—†	326	housewife	36	"
	L	Ladd William E	326	physician	43	"
	M	McCuspic Christina—†	326	cook	40	37 Lawrence
	N	Nicholson Annie—†	326	nurse	23	491 Beacon
	O	Shea Mary—†	326	waitress	27	New York
	P	Daugherty Rose—†	328	domestic	40	214 Com av
	R	Donohue Nora—†	328	"	42	306 Beacon
	S	Flatley Mary—†	328	"	35	121 Bay State rd
	T	Quill Julia—†	328	"	47	218 Beacon
	U	Sawyer Georgia P—†	328	none	51	here
	V	Sawyer Henry B	328	vice president	52	"
	W	Van Seslar James S	330	physician	38	"
	X	Van Seslar Sophia G—†	330	housewife	32	"
	Y	Rourke Mary—†	330	retired	79	72 Gardner
	Z	Gade Caroline—†	330	housewife	41	New York
	A'	Gade Horace N	330	banker	46	"
	B	Sino Celia—†	330	cook	45	"
	C	Doubleday Clark O	330	dentist	36	72 Gardner
	D	Doubleday Mary R—†	330	housewife	37	72 "
	E	Etckonn Theresa—†	330	caretaker	38	here
	F	Johnson Gladys—†	330	retired	36	"
	G	Johnson Julia—†	330	"	68	"
	H	McEnnany Jennie—†	330	cook	43	"
	K	Morse Alice B—†	330	housewife	43	"
	L	Morse Cabot J	330	retired	55	"
	M	Morse Cabot J, jr	330	salesman	22	"
	N	Fay Joseph	330	retired	47	5 Chester
	O	Fay Margaret—†	330	housewife	45	5 "
	P	Keat Julia—†	330	waitress	24	230 Clarendon
	R	Macarty Catherine—†	330	cook	65	5 Chester

Exeter Street

	Letter.	FULL NAME.	Residence	Occupation	Age	Reported Residence
	T	Hendreckson Catherine J—†	1	cook	34	Rhode Island
	U	Hendreckson Martin J	1	chauffeur	36	"
	V	Park Anna—†	1	housewife	34	330 Dartmouth
	W	Park Gertrude M—†	1	"	60	330 "

Page.	Letter.	FULL NAME.	Residence, April 1, 1924.	Occupation.	Supposed Age.	Reported Residence, April 1, 1923. Street and Number.

Exeter Street—Continued

X	Park Phillip	1	student	28	New Bedford
Y	Anderson Florence W—†	2	housekeeper	64	here
A	Crowley Elizabeth—†	3	cook	26	"
B	Doyle Mary—†	3	laundress	32	Ireland
C	O'Neill Catherine—†	3	waitress	29	here
D	Sowerby Sarah—†	3	governess	40	"
E	Sprague Henry B	3	manager	36	"
F	Sprague Louise H—†	3	housewife	34	"
G	Dearing Evelyn E—†	5	student	27	525 Newbury
H	Gardner Catherine—†	5	housewife	38	7 Exeter
K	Donelan Margaret—†	7	housemaid	23	Wash'n D C
L	Whitney Henry L	7	clerk	38	Milton
M	Whitney Rosamond H—†	7	housewife	29	259 Beacon
N	Hungerford Dorothy—†	7	student	32	here
O	Hungerford Esther W—†	7	housewife	61	"
P	Sears David	7	banker	21	Brookline
R	Sears Ellen—†	7	housewife	22	"
S	Crowell Lillie B—†	9	"	64	here
T	Crowell Ruby M—†	9	housekeeper	34	"
U	Grilli Silvio	9	butler	30	"
V	Pierce Charles C	10	manager	52	"
W	Burke Nellie—†	11	housemaid	28	Brookline
X	Falvy Mary—†	11	"	58	here
Y	McFarland Mary—†	11	"	42	"
Z	Pemperton Annie—†	11	retired	60	"
A	Sandstead Estha—†	11	housemaid	28	"
B	Shaw Sarah—†	11	housewife	50	"
C	Waters Ellen—†	11	housemaid	32	"
E	Handy Alden	16	student	23	"
F	Handy Frank A	16	clerk	54	"
G	Handy Mary G—†	16	housewife	54	"
H	Fall Bertha—†	17	housemaid	46	Brookline
K	Fall Fred C	17	butler	45	"
L	Whitman Ellen—†	17	housewife	80	here
M	Whitman Harry B	17	clerk	40	"
N	Durkin Katherine—†	18	housemaid	35	"
O	Farrell Mary—†	18	laundress	35	"
P	Farrell Nellie—†	18	cook	54	"
R	Frank Isabella—†	18	governess	33	"
S	Frost Donald N	18	lawyer	45	"
T	Frost Mary—†	18	housewife	41	"

Letter.	FULL NAME.	Residence, April 1, 1924.	Occupation.	Supposed Age.	Reported Residence, April 1, 1923. Street and Number.

Exeter Street—Continued

Letter	FULL NAME	Residence	Occupation	Age	Reported Residence
U	Kelly Mary—†	18	waitress	34	Brookline
V	Tracy Marion—†	18	housemaid	34	here
W	Devens Ellen W—†	19	none	60	"
X	Wendell Caroline—†	19	retired	60	"
Y	Hall Maria H—†	19	"	50	Milton
Z	Wendell Alice—†	19	housewife	48	here
A	Wendell Mark R	19	manager	50	"
B	Stephenson Susanna—†	19	retired	75	"
D	Hodge Mary R—†	19	"	48	"

Fairfield Street

Letter	FULL NAME	Residence	Occupation	Age	Reported Residence
E	Burns Bridget—†	8	chambermaid	60	Cambridge
F	Cronin Dorothy—†	8	housemaid	20	here
G	Glennen Anna G—†	8	waitress	26	"
H	Jackson Rebecca—†	8	housewife	70	"
K	Kelly Jane—†	8	housemaid	36	"
L	Kelly Mary—†	8	cook	53	"
M	Wilcox Mary—†	8	retired	64	"
N	Kelly Annie—†	10	housemaid	26	"
O	McNulty Mary—†	10	laundress	26	"
P	Simon Alvin	10	manager	46	"
R	Simon Anna—†	10	housewife	42	"
S	Simon Robert	10	student	22	"
T	Stern Lucy—†	10	cook	36	California
U	Coolidge Ellen W—†	12	social worker	58	here
V	McCauley Margaret—†	12	cook	33	"
W	Peck Lillie M—†	12	social worker	35	"
X	Conroy Delia—†	16	chambermaid	50	"
Y	Morse John T	16	retired	84	"
Z	Patterson Catherine—†	16	maid	50	"
A	Sullivan Ellen—†	16	waitress	50	"
B	Sullivan Mary—†	16	cook	49	"
C	Morrison Christine—†	18	housemaid	24	"
D	Walker Corrine S—†	18	housewife	28	"
E	Walker Harold D	18	architect	36	"
F	Allen Elizabeth B—†	20	housewife	75	"
G	Allen Francis R	20	architect	79	"
H	Lavin Annie—†	20	chambermaid	26	"
K	McElroy Annie—†	20	laundress	45	"

Fairfield Street—Continued

L	Mulcahy Joanna—†	20	cook	50	here
M	Walsh Catherine—†	20	waitress	52	"
N	Cain Elizabeth—†	22	chambermaid	50	"
O	Luc Jennie—†	22	maid	45	"
P	Murphy Minnie—†	22	cook	40	"
R	Norris John	22	butler	23	England
S	Thayer Pauline—†	22	housewife	62	here

Marlborough Street

A	Begley Catherine—†	1	maid	30	here
B	Brown Irene T—†	1	housewife	64	"
C	Brown Joseph F	1	broker	31	"
D	Brown Joseph T	1	retired	76	"
E	Brown Martha T—†	1	"	39	"
F	Hannon Mary F—†	1	maid	25	114 Com av
G	Nurey Mary—†	1	cook	60	here
H	Conway Annie J—†	2	waitress	35	"
K	Conway Mary A—†	2	cook	37	"
L	Waterman Claire—†	2	housewife	50	"
M	Waterman George A	2	physician	51	"
N	Badger Jane W—†	3	housewife	28	"
O	Badger Walter I	3	lawyer	32	"
P	Foley Sarah—†	4	waitress	24	"
R	Hurley Annie—†	4	cook	48	"
S	McLane Bertha—†	4	maid	32	"
T	Thompson Nellie—†	4	laundress	40	"
U	Toland Mary—†	4	maid	25	"
V	Weld Elizabeth—†	4	clerk	33	"
W	Weld Francis	4	merchant	30	"
X	Weld Linsay	4	laborer	25	"
Y	Weld Margaret—†	4	bookkeeper	24	"
Z	Weld Marion C—†	4	housewife	50	"
A	Doubleday Arthur W	5	dentist	46	"
B	Doubleday Florence F—†	5	housewife	40	"
C	Horspool Amelia S—†	6	housekeeper	45	"
D	Horspool George H	6	valet	50	"
E	Shaw Louis A	6	inventor	40	"
F	Weed Evangeline—†	7	teacher	28	"

48

Marlborough Street—Continued

G	Bennett Edna N—†	7	housewife	35	Philadelphia
H	Betton Grace—†	7	"	58	here
K	Rabe Edith R—†	7	physician	22	"
L	Basham Bertha G—†	7	housewife	42	19 Exeter
M	Basham Gladys V—†	7	musician	22	19 "
N	Chase Aderlaid C—†	8	artist	52	here
O	Chase William C	8	architect	55	"
P	Fouhy James P	8	caretaker	36	New York
R	Fouhy Pearl E—†	8	"	28	"
S	Sheehy Catherine—†	8	maid	35	here
T	Bourque Eielde G—†	9	"	21	Canada
U	Clement Mary A—†	9	retired	78	Cambridge
V	Flatley Sarah—†	9	cook	42	here
W	Riley Rose—†	9	maid	30	"
X	Browning Clara—†	10	none	56	"
Y	Main Annie C—†	10	maid	38	"
Z	Main Mary—†	10	"	27	Scotland
A	Massey Jean—†	10	housekeeper	38	here
B	Massey William	10	houseman	42	"
C	McKechnie Annie—†	10	cook	21	Brookline
D	McRoberts Agnes—†	10	"	45	here
E	Perry Arthur	10	banker	67	"
F	Perry Emma—†	10	none	64	"
G	White Mary B—†	10	maid	21	"
H	Best Camelia M—†	11	housewife	26	Maine
K	Best Francis J	11	manager	35	"
L	MacSween Margaret—†	11	housewife	27	Somerville
M	MacSween Neil	11	janitor	34	"
N	Allen Margaret E—†	12	secretary	60	here
O	Folsom Amy—†	12	none	56	"
P	Gillis Ellen—†	12	cook	56	"
R	Jackson Marion C—†	12	retired	77	"
S	Maynes Katherine T—†	12	waitress	47	Ireland
T	Morse Francis R—†	12	retired	74	here
U	Sullivan Julia—†	12	maid	27	"
V	Cunningham Rose A—†	13	"	33	272 Marlboro
W	Gordon Isabella—†	13	nurse	56	here
X	Keily Magaret—†	13	maid	45	114 Com av
Y	Raymond Jonathan L	13	merchant	29	here
Z	Raymond Paulien P—†	13	housewife	30	"
A	Shea Mary—†	13	maid	43	"

Marlborough Street—Continued

B	Sullivan Agnes—†	13	maid	33	here
C	Bowen James W	14	broker	62	"
D	Bowen John T	14	physician	67	"
E	Kane Annie—†	14	housekeeper	63	"
F	Griffin Annie—†	15	cook	45	Brookline
G	Kennedy Norah—†	15	maid	24	279 Beacon
H	O'Brien Nellie—†	15	"	24	here
K	Rich Gertrude L—†	15	housewife	50	Europe
L	Rich Phyllis—†	15	retired	28	"
M	Alexander Charles E	16	editor	46	here
N	Baylor Annie—†	16	musician	48	Brookline
O	Frost Cornelia—†	16	housekeeper	63	here
P	Hough Edith—†	17	maid	47	"
R	King Alice—†	17	housewife	64	"
S	King Samuel G	17	broker	67	"
T	MacLoud Effie—†	17	maid	27	"
U	MacLoud Mary—†	17	"	26	"
V	Skinner Belle F—†	18	none	30	"
W	Skinner Carl H	18	jeweler	53	"
X	Armstrong Helen—†	19	maid	60	"
Y	Cashman Mary—†	19	cook	34	"
Z	Gray Reginald	19	lawyer	30	"
A	Gray Rose L—†	19	housewife	64	"
B	Keohane Mary—†	19	maid	62	"
C	MacQueen Julie—†	19	"	64	"
E	Weir Catherine F—†	19	"	60	"
F	Linzee Elizabeth—†	20	retired	60	"
G	McEachen Catherine A—†	20	domestic	48	P E I
H	Wright Maria G—†	20	"	55	here
K	Bokland Ranihold	21	houseman	42	"
L	Clark Mary V—†	21	retired	83	"
M	Murray Edward M	21	student	21	"
N	Murray Eleanor V—†	21	housewife	55	"
O	Murray Mary V—†	21	student	22	"
P	Murray Morris	21	physician	72	"
R	Jenkins Alice D—†	22	none	48	"
S	Jenkins MacGregor	22	publisher	50	"
T	Joyce Jenny—†	22	nurse	30	"
U	Kelley Catherine—†	22	maid	26	"
V	Murphy Mary—†	22	cook	38	"
W	Aldrich Davis C	24	clerk	23	Cambridge

Marlborough Street—Continued

x	Aldrich Merrett J	24	student	25	Cambridge
y	Cuzner Eva M—†	24	housekeeper	51	here
z	Cuzner John H	24	clerk	51	"
A	Hobart Philip W	24	salesman	33	"
B	Hobart Richard B	24	"	35	"
c	McClough Robert G	24	lawyer	56	"
D	Rock John	24	physician	32	"
E	Carter Bertha—†	25	"	30	"
F	Estes Mary A—†	25	housewife	50	"
G	Graham Annie G—†	25	clerk	32	"
H	Honeiz Florence—†	25	housewife	32	"
K	Lawton Alice M—†	25	writer	25	New York
L	Wenstrom Mary—†	25	housewife	46	here
M	Wenstrom Olof	25	broker	52	"
N	Walsh Annie T—†	26	domestic	25	Brookline
O	Walsh Catherine E—†	26	"	27	"
P	White Charles P	26	clerk	23	here
R	White Grace P—†	26	retired	50	"
S	Boone John W	27	janitor	39	"
T	Boone Mary A—†	27	housewife	38	"
U	Andrew Annie B—†	28	retired	53	"
V	Andrew George C	28	manufacturer	55	"
W	Andrew Sumner B	28	salesman	24	"
X	Johnson Geneva—†	28	domestic	36	Newton
Y	Mitchell Edna J—†	28	"	24	Wash'n D C
Z	Davis James V	29	salesman	56	here
A	Green Maytie—†	29	retired	25	"
B	Kogos John	29	salesman	56	"
c	Lane John W	29	teacher	50	"
D	McCarron Joseph C	29	contractor	41	"
E	Stone Walter E	29	broker	63	"
F	Dillon Mary A—†	30	domestic	44	247 Beacon
G	Dwyer Catherine—†	30	"	24	247 "
H	Minot George R	30	physician	30	247 "
K	Minot Marion W—†	30	housekeeper	33	247 "
L	Scully Ellen—†	30	domestic	42	247 "
M	Tooth Julia—†	30	nurse	44	247 "
N	Buckminister Mary A—†	31	housewife	47	271 Dartmouth
O	Buckminister William R	31	lawyer	50	271 "
R	Chinn Matilda—†	31	maid	55	Wash'n D C
P	DiSomma Gizio F	31	student	28	Cambridge

Marlborough Street—Continued

s	Jeffers Elizabeth —†	31	maid	28	New York
T	Miller Mary A—†	31	housewife	72	271 Dartmou
U	Adams Jessie—†	32	domestic	50	here
V	Buchanan Harriet—†	32	"	38	P E I
W	Johnson Joseph	32	janitor	58	here
X	Kaufman Carl F	32	retired	70	"
Y	Kaufman Elizabeth C—†	32	housewife	48	"
Z	MacInnis Christine—†	32	domestic	45	"
A	MacInnis Effie—†	32	"	38	"
B	Matheson Mamie—†	32	"	21	Nova Scotia
C	Bramer Mabel R—†	33	student	21	here
D	Bramer Mable—†	33	housewife	40	"
E	Bramer Parker S	33	broker	45	"
G	Buckley Geraldine—†	37	nurse	30	"
H	Hollohan Frances—†	37	maid	40	"
K	Hollohan Mary—†	37	"	43	"
L	Peck Charles R	37	clergyman	35	"
M	Peck Helen A—†	37	housewife	35	"
N	Gray Amy—†	39	"	63	"
O	Gray Russell	39	retired	73	"
P	Nelin Catherine—†	39	maid	55	"
R	Shanahan Annie—†	39	"	41	"
S	Gabry Ida—†	53	"	45	"
T	Keilty Mary—†	53	"	35	"
U	Kelley Mary—†	53	"	35	"
V	Lane Emma G—†	53	housewife	40	"
W	Lane Katherine W—†	53	retired	25	"
X	McDonough Ellen—†	53	maid	50	"
Y	Lyman Susan C—†	57	secretary	32	"
Z	Codman Anna K—†	59	housewife	52	"
A	Codman Russell S	59	broker	61	"
B	Codman Russell S, jr	59	salesman	28	"
C	Murphy Mary J—†	59	maid	31	"
D	Ryan Josephine F—†	59	"	28	"
E	Hurley Ellen M—†	61	"	35	"
F	Luce Elizabeth—†	61	housewife	80	"
G	Beatty Mary—†	63	nurse	25	"
H	Connelly Catherine—†	63	maid	21	"
K	Danahy Hannah E—†	63	"	32	"
L	Tobin Norah B—†	63	cook	28	"
M	Weld Rudolph	63	broker	40	"

Marlborough Street—Continued

Letter	Full Name	Res.	Occupation	Age	Reported Residence
N	Weld Sylvia—†	63	housewife	30	here
O	Dexter Edith W—†	65	"	53	"
P	Dexter Philip	65	lawyer	57	"
R	Blaisdell Stella K—†	66	domestic	32	"
S	Burns Sarah—†	66	"	28	"
T	Sturgis James M	66	salesman	51	"
U	Sturgis Lucy—†	66	social worker	47	"
V	Sturgis Margaret R—†	66	retired	90	"
W	Clark Carnzu—†	67	housewife	37	"
X	Clark George O	67	physician	45	"
Y	Walsh Margaret E—†	67	maid	25	"
Z	Woodward Beatrice M—†	67	cook	22	"
A	Woodward William H	67	butler	26	"
B	Gallagher Katherine—†	68	housewife	33	181 Bay state rd
C	Collins Catherine—†	70	domestic	39	here
D	Fahey Julia—†	70	"	40	"
E	Sullivan Delia—†	70	"	29	"
F	Sullivan Katherine—†	70	"	32	"
G	Weld Bernard C	70	merchant	56	"
H	Weld George S	70	"	25	"
K	Weld Mabel S—†	70	housewife	56	"
L	Clark Herbert	71	broker	61	"
M	Clark Joseph P	71	physician	63	"
O	Boardman Carrie L—†	73	housewife	30	"
P	Boardman Reginald	73	broker	42	"
R	Concannon Margaret—†	74	domestic	25	"
S	Shea Mary E—†	74	housewife	30	"
T	Shea William H	74	lawyer	60	"
U	Shea William J	74	student	20	"
V	Bayley Harriet—†	75	housewife	40	"
W	Bayley Helen—†	75	student	21	"
X	Bayley James C	75	banker	50	"
Y	Guild Grace—†	76	nurse	33	"
Z	Weyburn Lyon	76	lawyer	45	"
A	Weyburn Ruth A—†	76	housewife	32	"
B	Anderson Chrissie—†	77	maid	23	"
C	Carr Elizabeth—†	77	"	40	"
D	Greene Delia—†	77	"	25	"
E	Jackson Charles	77	retired	46	"
F	Jackson Elizabeth—†	77	housewife	40	"
G	Green Charles M	78	physician	73	"

Marlborough Street—Continued

H	Watson Catherine—†	79	housewife	40	here
K	Watson John	79	broker	24	"
L	Watson Paul B	79	lawyer	55	"
M	Watson Paul B. jr	79	"	30	"
N	Coleman Bessie—†	80	domestic	40	Milton
O	Donegan Alice T—†	80	"	25	87 Marlboro
P	Everett Madeline W—†	80	housewife	33	49 Com av
R	Everett Richard M	80	broker	40	49 "
S	Houlihan Nora—†	80	domestic	39	416 Beacon
T	Loring Augustus P	81	banker	28	here
U	Loring Rosmond—†	81	housewife	30	"
V	Brady Mary—†	82	domestic	36	"
W	Coolidge Charles A	82	architect	65	"
X	Coolidge Julia—†	82	housewife	69	"
Y	Dean Frederick E	82	salesman	45	China
Z	Dean Julia S—†	82	housewife	28	"
A	Heboty Julia—†	82	domestic	27	here
B	Hurley Catherine—†	82	"	40	"
C	Morrisey Catherine—†	82	"	38	"
D	Cumming Elizabeth—†	83	retired	35	"
E	Cumming Laurence	83	student	24	"
F	McGillivary Florence—†	83	maid	26	"
G	Stanton Katherine—†	83	retired	45	"
H	Waller Nellie—†	83	housewife	70	"
K	Holland Susan—†	85	laundress	78	"
L	Keating Nellie—†	85	cook	42	"
M	Mifflin George H	85	publisher	44	Connecticut
N	Mifflin Jennie H—†	85	housewife	60	here
O	Murphy Margaret—†	85	waitress	48	"
P	Quirk Ellen—†	85	maid	45	"
R	Ericson Ingrid—†	86	domestic	43	"
S	Joy Marie L—†	86	retired	80	"
T	O'Brien Annie—†	86	domestic	26	Newfoundla
U	Silvander Elizabeth—†	86	"	26	Cambridge
V	Trenholm Ella—†	86	"	65	here
W	Barney James D	87	physician	45	"
X	Barney Margaret—†	87	housewife	40	"
Y	Donovan Minnie—†	88	domestic	36	Brookline
Z	Kappell Florilina—†	88	"	34	"
A	Kelly Bridget A—†	88	"	34	209 Beacon
B	Mitton Arthur G	88	lawyer	38	Brookline

Marlborough Street—Continued

c	Mitton Edith—†	88	housewife	32	Brookline
D	Ridge Annie—†	88	domestic	40	46 Beacon
E	Ryan Nellie—†	88	"	35	70 Clarendon
F	Bullard Mary R—†	89	housewife	58	here
G	Bullard William W	89	physician	70	"
H	Shone Catherine E—†	89	housewife	40	3 Hillside av
K	Shone John W	89	policeman	48	3 "
L	Burgeson Edith—†	90	domestic	22	New York
M	Burr Alice M—†	90	housewife	66	here
N	Burr Isaac L	90	banker	63	"
O	Crump Alice—†	90	domestic	39	New York
P	Ferguson Norman	90	chauffeur	23	here
R	Gothe Jennie—†	90	domestic	38	Sweden
S	Hanson Gunman J	90	butler	38	here
T	Helo Sophia—†	90	domestic	30	"
U	Peterson Betty—†	90	"	22	461 Walnut av
V	Maley Elizabeth K—†	92	retired	39	here
W	Sullivan Mary E—†	92	"	56	268 Brookline av
X	Roane Blanche—†	92	bookkeeper	47	here
Y	Pond Ruth—†	92	teacher	26	Brookline
Z	Stoddard Linda T—†	92	clerk	51	here
A	Vinal Eaton W	92	retired	75	"
B	Vinal Ella J—†	92	clerk	47	"
C	Flint Susie—†	92	retired	54	"
E	Nicholson Kenneth J	92	janitor	72	"
F	Anderson Maria—†	103	maid	46	"
G	Curtis Anita G—†	103	housewife	29	"
H	Curtis Richard C	103	lawyer	29	"
K	McCarthy Mary—†	103	maid	22	"
L	McKenzie Bella—†	103	cook	37	20 Com av
M	Nolan Teresa—†	103	waitress	39	here
N	Clinton Annie—†	104	cook	50	Malden
O	Fisk Charles H	104	lawyer	51	382 Com av
P	Fisk Connelia—†	104	student	25	382 "
R	Flynn Rose—†	104	domestic	34	382 "
S	Lee Frances—†	105	teacher	38	here
T	Bowen Catherine—†	106	cook	38	"
U	Colbert Margaret—†	106	maid	27	Brookline
V	Lynch Alice—†	106	"	25	New Hampshire
W	Putnam Louisa H—†	106	student	29	Europe
X	Putnam Marion—†	106	housewife	65	here

Marlborough Street—Continued

Y	Putnam Marion C—†	106	physician	30	Europe
Z	Nema Selma—†	107	housekeeper	36	here
A	Wilson Amanda—†	107	"	40	Milton
B	Cameron Annie—†	108	"	61	here
C	Putnam Annie C—†	108	retired	84	"
D	Putnam Charles W	108	teacher	34	"
E	Putnam Imogene H—†	108	housewife	30	"
F	Putnam Lucy W—†	108	"	81	"
G	Delano Ruth—†	109	"	46	"
H	Demmon Marcia—†	109	"	75	"
K	Higgins Katherine—†	109	housekeeper	41	"
L	Deolis Elizabeth—†	110	cook	44	"
M	French Edith L—†	110	housewife	35	Randolph
N	French Herbert F	110	accountant	56	"
O	Gildea Margaret—†	110	laundress	27	here
P	Murray Katherine—†	110	domestic	37	New York
R	Barnes Charles	111	merchant	45	here
S	Frier Louisa—†	112	housekeeper	50	New York
T	Person Matilda—†	112	"	56	"
U	Sherrill Franklin G	112	merchant	40	"
V	Sherrill Maria K—†	112	housewife	66	"
W	Davis Mary W—†	113	"	78	here
X	Gillis Elizabeth A—†	113	maid	51	"
Y	Hoey Mary—†	113	"	56	"
Z	Sheehan Elsia—†	113	cook	58	"
A	Carney Betty—†	114	domestic	25	1 Willoughby pl
B	Ellsworth Margaret A—†	114	"	30	here
C	Folsom Anna S—†	114	retired	76	"
D	Folsom Ellen M—†	114	"	74	"
E	Folsom Martha W—†	114	housewife	78	"
F	Burke Hilda—†	115	cook	45	"
G	Carlson Christina—†	115	maid	47	"
H	Nelson Hilda—†	115	"	38	"
K	Silsbee Arthur	115	broker	70	"
L	Stramhlad Hilda—†	115	maid	40	"
M	Leary Maria—†	116	cook	60	"
N	Pitkin Edith E—†	116	artist	37	"
O	Pitkin Mabel W—†	116	housewife	63	"
P	Pitkin Margaret—†	116	artist	37	"
R	Pitkin William	116	real estate	34	"
S	Pitkin William H	116	retired	86	"

Letter.	Full Name.	Residence, April 1, 1924.	Occupation.	Supposed Age.	Reported Residence, April 1, 1923. Street and Number.

Marlborough Street—Continued

Letter.	Full Name.	Residence, April 1, 1924.	Occupation.	Supposed Age.	Reported Residence, April 1, 1923. Street and Number.
T	Ward Rose—†	116	domestic	23	Providence R I
V	Blake Maria—†	118	"	60	here
W	Furrey Katherine—†	118	"	28	Palm Beach
X	Gallahere Josephine—†	118	"	28	here
Y	Stevenson Lee—†	118	housewife	40	"
Z	Stevenson Robert	118	retired	50	"
A	Carroll Mae—†	119	maid	25	"
B	Cooper Nellie—†	119	"	25	"
C	Leferre Anita—†	119	"	38	"
D	McManus Beatrice—†	119	waitress	28	"
E	Motley Edward	119	banker	44	"
F	Motley Harriett S—†	119	housewife	38	"
G	Whalen Mary—†	119	cook	27	"
H	Martin Annie—†	120	domestic	28	"
K	McLeod Margaret—†	120	"	23	"
L	Smith Ethel B—†	120	housewife	42	"
M	Smith Richard	120	physician	42	"
N	Carey Georgie—†	121	housewife	68	"
O	Dinneen Helen—†	121	maid	23	48 Mt Vernon
P	Prouse Muriel—†	121	housewife	32	England
R	Beiston Delia—†	122	domestic	24	here
S	Leach Katherine—†	122	"	26	"
T	Mead Louis	122	physician	50	"
U	Mead Mary E—†	122	housewife	50	"
V	Priest Emily—†	122	nurse	22	"
W	Priest George F	122	student	20	"
X	Burns Katherine—†	123	maid	26	"
Y	Callahan Margaret—†	123	"	34	"
Z	Callahan Mary—†	123	"	26	"
A	Johnson Edward C	123	retired	84	"
B	Murphy Agnes—†	123	maid	31	"
C	Orlandini Vittorio	123	lawyer	44	"
D	Rohan John	123	nurse	34	"
E	Sullivan Annie—†	123	maid	24	Brookline
F	Dempsey Elenia—†	124	domestic	30	Medford
G	Garrity Bridie—†	124	"	27	here
H	Guild Charlotte—†	124	housewife	50	"
K	O'Neil Catherine—†	124	domestic	30	"
L	Kinsman Elizabeth—†	125	housewife	32	"
M	Kinsman Lawrence	125	janitor	35	"
N	Poor Florence—†	125	housewife	51	"

Marlborough Street—Continued

o	Breen Nellie—†	126	domestic	34	here
p	McDermont Catherine—†	126	"	33	Brookline
r	Salmon Margaret—†	126	"	28	68 Marlboro
s	Turnbull Charles D	126	retired	60	here
t	Turnbull Lena—†	126	artist	23	"
u	Turnbull Maria P—†	126	housewife	62	"
v	Turnbull Mary D—†	126	retired	84	"
w	Ward Annie V—†	126	nurse	44	"
x	Chamberlain Edward M	127	retired	43	"
y	Garfield Irvin McD	127	lawyer	53	"
z	Madigan Julia—†	127	laundress	28	New York
a	Murray Margaret—†	127	maid	30	Cambridge
b	Saunders Orpha—†	127	nurse	26	48 Dartmout
c	Warren Elizabeth—†	127	maid	25	211 Bay State rd
d	Warren Julia—†	127	"	22	Brookline
e	O'Shea Kathleen—†	128	domestic	24	"
f	O'Shea Mary—†	128	"	26	"
g	Page Calvin G	128	physician	54	here
h	Page Marie D—†	128	housewife	48	"
k	Morris Paul	129	janitor	52	"
l	Flynn Mary L—†	130	domestic	23	N Scituate
m	Killain Margaret—†	130	"	34	Manchester
n	Parker Caroline—†	130	"	23	New York
o	Wheeler Agnes G—†	130	housewife	25	95 Mt Vern
p	Wheeler Alexander	130	lawyer	34	95 "
r	Endicott Henry	131	"	48	Weston
s	Endicott Katherine S—†	131	housewife	47	"
t	Griffin Mary—†	131	cook	35	"
u	Slade Elizabeth—†	131	maid	45	"
v	White Helena—†	131	waitress	25	"
w	Allen Alberta L—†	132	housewife	68	here
x	Allen Frederick B	132	clergyman	83	"
y	Allen Hildegarde—†	132	secretary	38	"
z	Allen Mary J—†	132	retired	89	"
a	Allen Rebecca G—†	132	"	54	"
b	Davis Anna—†	132	domestic	40	240 Dartmou
c	Eames Cora A—†	132	nurse	55	here
d	Flynn Annie—†	132	domestic	34	80 Beacon
e	McSweeney Agnes—†	132	"	36	110 Bay State rd
f	Gray Morris	133	lawyer	60	here
g	Bayley Edward B	134	merchant	56	"

Marlborough Street—Continued

H	Bayley Mary R—†	134	housewife	54	here
K	Driscoll Margaret F—†	134	domestic	40	"
L	Jackson Alice—†	134	"	50	"
M	Kelly Agnes—†	134	"	37	"
N	Kelly Mary—†	134	"	32	"
O	McLeod Annie—†	134	"	46	"
P	Shattuck Elizabeth T—†	135	housewife	77	"
R	Shattuck Frederick C	135	physician	76	"
S	Shattuck George C	135	"	44	"
T	Shattuck Henry L	135	lawyer	44	"
U	Ford Rose—†	136	domestic	34	"
V	Griffin Sarah—†	136	"	30	"
W	Lynch Catherine—†	136	"	44	40 Fenway
X	Philler Nellie—†	136	housewife	76	here
Y	Landers Katherine—†	138	domestic	27	"
Z	Wendell Gwendolyn—†	138	housewife	36	"
A	Wendell John W	138	merchant	40	"
B	French Phillip	138	real estate	48	"
C	Thompson Jessie—†	138	domestic	42	Wakefield
D	Manning Maria P—†	138	housewife	59	here
E	Manning Wayland	138	trustee	54	"
F	Binney Edith M—†	138	housewife	61	"
G	McDonald Mary R—†	138	domestic	39	here
H	Forbes Janet W—†	140	housekeeper	65	"
K	Harris Harriett—†	140	playwright	58	Weymouth
L	Harris Mabel W—†	140	saleswoman	40	Natick
M	Willard Mabel C—†	140	secretary	61	116 Mt Vernon
N	Willard Mabel W—†	140	stenographer	42	92 Marlboro
O	Flynn Catherine—†	142	domestic	24	18 Louisburg sq
P	Minot Elizabeth—†	142	housewife	29	here
R	Minot William	142	trustee	38	"
S	Murphy Mary—†	142	domestic	22	Newton
T	Butler Katie—†	144	"	32	here
U	Dolan Margaret—†	144	"	29	"
V	Hopkins James C	144	architect	50	"
W	Hopkins Mary—†	144	housewife	48	"
X	Taylor Lizzie—†	144	domestic	60	"
Y	Connolly Thersa—†	146	"	22	Medford
Z	Kendal Ethel P—†	146	housewife	43	here
A	Kendal Waldo	146	banker	47	"
B	Quinn Annie—†	146	domestic	22	Brookline

Marlborough Street—Continued

C	Bowles Adelaide H—†	148	housewife	60	here
D	Bowles Francis T	148	retired	62	"
E	Burden Nellie—†	148	domestic	30	New York
F	Connolly Mary—†	148	"	30	here
G	Endicott William C	163	lawyer	55	Danvers
H	Crowinshield Francis B	164	retired	50	here
K	Flynn Margaret—†	166	domestic	23	"
L	Flynn Nellie—†	166	"	38	"
M	Hallisey Bessie—†	166	"	35	"
N	Marks Margaret F—†	166	nurse	51	"
O	Sullivan Mary—†	166	domestic	48	"
P	Whitwell Frederick S	166	lawyer	61	"
R	Whitwell Gertrude—†	166	housewife	48	"
S	Whitwell Mary C—†	166	retired	84	"
T	Rosenthal Eugene	167	merchant	46	"
U	Rosenthal Sadie—†	167	housewife	41	"
V	Chase Alice—†	168	"	64	"
W	Connolly Cecila—†	168	domestic	22	"
X	Geary Nellie—†	168	"	29	121 Com av
Y	McDonough Katherine—†	168	"	30	here
Z	Sinclair Mary—†	169	housekeeper	48	"
A	Allen Charles W	170	printer	76	"
B	Allen Elenor J—†	170	housewife	60	"
C	Pendergast Delia—†	170	domestic	24	"
D	Quin Margaret—†	170	"	60	90 Appleton
E	Clark Preston	171	manager	55	Cohasset
F	Benson Anna—†	172	maid	37	91 Roslindale av
G	Holmgren Alma C—†	172	domestic	44	California
H	Rackeman Charles S	172	lawyer	70	282 Berkeley
K	Rackeman Fannie S—†	172	housewife	70	282 "
L	Wahlstedt Alma C—†	172	domestic	49	California
M	Morse Charles F	173	retired	80	Falmouth
N	Donohue Elizebeth—†	174	domestic	36	New York
O	Gitchel Edna—†	174	nurse	50	New Hampshire
P	Glidden Anna C—†	174	teacher	35	here
R	Glidden Anna W—†	174	housewife	75	"
S	Glidden Joseph	174	merchant	52	Maine
T	Maguire Nellie—†	174	domestic	54	Cambridge
U	Bugier Beatrice—†	175	maid	24	259 Marlboro
V	Thorndike Harry	175	retired	60	here
W	Thorndike Lucy—†	175	housewife	55	"

Marlborough Street—Continued

x	Ellis Effie—†	176	housekeeper	72	here
y	Fehily Hannah—†	176	domestic	36	Ireland
z	Maher Katherine—†	176	"	60	here
A	Lockwood Hamilton DeF	177	accountant	56	"
B	Lockwood Hamilton DeF, jr	177	student	21	"
C	Lockwood Maria W—†	177	housewife	51	"
D	Smith Belle H—†	178	"	45	3 Wyoming
E	Smith Otis	178	dentist	41	3 "
F	Clancy Sarah—†	179	maid	24	183 Com av
G	Clark Elizabeth—†	179	"	25	here
H	Curtis Anna—†	179	housewife	65	"
K	Fay Mary—†	179	cook	40	33 Chestnut
L	Kelly Jean—†	179	laundress	40	here
M	Sheeran Mary—†	179	maid	35	"
O	Cassidy Elizabeth—†	181	"	30	New York
P	Nolan Mary—†	181	"	50	here
R	Shea Margaret—†	181	"	23	Ireland
S	Thorndike Alice—†	181	housewife	34	here
T	Thorndike Florence—†	181	"	73	"
U	Fahey Mary—†	182	domestic	29	Brookline
V	Hart May—†	182	"	28	26 Com av
W	Meade Jennie—†	182	"	40	288 Beacon
X	Russell Charles T	182	trustee	42	here
Y	Russell Louise R—†	182	housewife	44	"
Z	Coyne Delia—†	183	cook	45	"
A	Dulles Margaret—†	183	waitress	30	"
B	Manning Hannah—†	183	maid	28	"
C	Wheeler Ellen H—†	183	housewife	63	"
D	Wheeler Henry	183	lawyer	67	"
E	Fogarty Anna—†	184	domestic	56	"
F	Gallaher Ellen—†	184	"	65	"
G	Scully Margart—†	184	"	29	"
H	Shaw Gertrude S—†	184	housewife	76	"
K	Shaw Parkman	184	retired	72	"
L	Grew Annie—†	185	housewife	80	"
M	Grew Randolph	185	retired	50	"
N	Sullivan Barbara—†	186	domestic	26	Connecticut
O	Worcester Blanche—†	186	housewife	50	here
P	Worcester Elwood	186	clergyman	60	"
R	Worcester Gurden—†	186	editress	26	"
S	MacRae Mary—†	188	domestic	69	"

Marlborough Street—Continued

T	McLeod Florence —†	188	domestic	45	here
U	McLeod Sybil—†	188	"	47	"
V	McPhail Mary —†	188	"	36	"
W	Minot Henry W	188	salesman	28	"
X	Minot James J	188	physician	71	"
Y	Langerfelt Lottie— †	189	nurse	25	Hingham
Z	McCarron Bridget —†	189	maid	28	Cambridge
A	McCarthy May—†	189	"	39	14 Gloucester
B	Porter Alexander, jr	189	trustee	51	9 Lime
C	Porter Elizabeth B —†	189	housewife	38	9 "
D	Regan Hannah—†	189	maid	22	Cambridge
E	St George Nellie †	189	nurse	45	9 Lime
F	Bangs Anna—†	190	housewife	50	here
G	Bangs Francis R	190	lawyer	52	"
H	Hanley Mary—†	190	housemaid	29	"
K	Toomey Lily—†	190	waitress	30	"
L	Hollingsworth Valentine	191	merchant	40	"
M	O'Neil Nellie—†	191	maid	24	186 Com av
N	Eyring Caroline —†	192	governess	33	88 Beacon
O	Flynn Mary—†	192	maid	25	402 Marlboro
P	Howes Henry S	192	merchant	47	88 Beacon
R	Howes Lillian M—†	192	housewife	38	88 "
S	Riley Jennette —†	192	cook	50	Fall River
T	Burke Nora M—†	193	maid	21	here
U	Cheever David	193	physician	45	"
V	Cheever Jane W—†	193	housewife	40	"
W	Greet Elsie —†	193	nurse	30	"
X	Griffin Ellen—†	193	laundress	45	"
Y	McHugh Mary —†	193	maid	27	"
Z	Nolan Mary A—†	193	cook	27	"
A	DeVeau Frederick J	194	lawyer	34	Cambridge
B	Furfey Edith G †	194	housewife	33	here
C	Furfey James A	194	dentist	50	"
D	Furfey Robert M	194	student	23	"
E	Smith Charles W	194	salesman	54	101 Newbury
F	Chandler Alice †	195	housewife	70	here
G	Chandler Frank	195	retired	79	"
H	Chandler Henry D	195	architect	40	"
K	Looney Bridie †	195	maid	28	Ireland
M	Curtis Lawrence	197	broker	75	here
N	O'Brien Hannah †	197	cook	28	"

Marlborough Street—Continued

Letter.	FULL NAME.	Residence April 1, 1924.	Occupation.	Supposed Age.	Reported Residence, April 1, 1923. Street and Number.
o	Saxby George	197	butler	68	here
p	Sullivan Katherine —†	197	maid	30	"
R	Porter James A	199	janitor	67	"
T	MacAdam Catherine E—†	199	maid	56	"
V	Inches Annie —†	199	housekeeper	55	
W	Courtney Margaret —†	199	maid	54	25 Cortis
X	Fallon Margaret—†	199	"	36	here
Y	Warren Louisa—†	199	housekeeper	55	"
Z	Seyfarth Herman B	220	mechanic	21	"
C	Strong Cyrus W	220	manufacturer	53	"
D	Strong Maria B—†	220	housekeeper	63	"
F	Smith Alice W—†	220	housewife	48	"
G	Smith Frank S	220	retired	65	"
H	Brackett Jeffrey R	220	"	62	"
K	Brackett Susan K—†	220	housewife	62	"
L	Nason Frederick E	220	treasurer	38	124 St James
M	Eaton Harold B	222	physician	37	here
N	Eaton Helen S—†	222	teacher	36	"
O	Eaton Margaret S—†	222	housewife	38	"
P	Audubon Johanna—†	222	maid	63	"
R	Whitney Alice F—†	222	retired	77	"
S	Atherton Isabelle R—†	222	"	68	"
T	Parker Dora—†	222	maid	22	"
U	Hodge Sally B—†	222	none	45	"
W	Howard Francis A	222	broker	53	295 Com av
X	Howard Sarah B—†	222	retired	85	295 "
Y	Thomas Emilie—†	224	housewife	56	here
Z	Thomas John P	224	janitor	56	"
A	Brewster John F	224	broker	69	"
B	Brewster Martha C—†	224	housewife	56	"
C	Brewster Mary—†	224	none	26	"
D	Perkins Harold W	224	retired	60	"
E	Young Harry H	224	treasurer	55	"
F	Young Lillian R—†	224	housewife	54	"
G	Carey Nora—†	224	cook	34	"
H	Lindsay Caroline—†	224	retired	72	"
K	Kettle Claude L	224	"	73	"
L	Kettle Elizabeth—†	224	housewife	70	"
M	Ripley Constance B—†	224	none	48	163 Beacon
N	Ripley Julia R—†	224	"	21	163 "
O	Warren Edwin H	224	teacher	60	here

Marlborough Street—Continued

P	Warren Elinor—†	224	housewife	42	here
R	Burrage Alice—†	225	"	42	"
S	Burrage Clarence V	225	manager	47	"
T	Kissack William E	225	butler	24	Cape Cod
U	MacKay Anna—†	225	maid	29	here
V	MacKay Ina—†	225	"	32	"
W	Campbell Mary—†	226	"	28	6 Myrtle
X	Ragle Benjamin H	226	physician	35	112 Marlboro
Y	Ragle Margaret—†	226	housewife	30	112 "
Z	Sheehan Margaret—†	226	maid	24	112 "
A	Teehan Catherine—†	226	"	24	112 "
B	MacOlgan Mary—†	227	"	45	here
C	Minot Lucy F—†	227	housewife	66	"
D	Monigal Mary—†	227	maid	46	"
E	Pearson Rebecca—†	227	"	40	"
F	Whitney Louise E—†	228	none	65	"
G	Whitney Lyman F	228	engineer	34	"
H	Drudy Delia—†	229	maid	26	107 Com av
K	Follett Austin W	229	merchant	45	Attleboro
L	Follett Marion R—†	229	housewife	42	"
M	Foy Nonie—†	229	maid	30	310 Beacon
N	Donnellan Delia—†	230	waitress	43	here
O	MacAusland Dorothy—†	230	housewife	38	"
P	MacAusland William R	230	physician	41	"
R	McNulty Anna—†	230	nurse	27	"
S	Berkstrom Ella V—†	231	cook	27	"
T	Erickson Alfhild—†	231	maid	41	"
U	Sawyer Clifford D	231	retired	50	"
V	Sawyer Gertrude B—†	231	housewife	48	"
W	Sharp Anna M—†	231	maid	35	486 Hammond
X	Herrity Margaret—†	232	"	30	here
Y	Whitney Georgiana—†	232	none	64	"
Z	Bolton Arthur S	233	cook	32	New York
A	Bolton Mary—†	233	maid	28	"
B	Gagnon Mary L—†	233	clerk	21	"
C	Gough Alfred C	233	butler	30	"
D	Gough Maude E—†	233	maid	28	"
E	Ryan Helen—†	233	nurse	42	"
F	Spalding Beatrice C—†	233	housewife	47	"
G	Spalding Eliot	233	trustee	47	"
H	Wills Marion—†	233	governess	37	Canada

Marlborough Street—Continued

	Letter	FULL NAME	Residence, April 1, 1924	Occupation	Supposed Age	Reported Residence, April 1, 1923. Street and Number
	K	Whitford Emma M—†	234	housewife	48	23 Bay State rd
	L	Whitford James	234	janitor	42	23 "
	M	Dorr Elsie—†	235	clerk	45	here
	N	Dorr Mary—†	235	retired	60	"
	O	Hayes Cathrine—†	235	cook	35	"
	P	Orr Mary—†	235	maid	40	"
	R	Ahearn Julia—†	236	domestic	30	"
	S	Jeffries Clemence E—†	236	housewife	62	"
	T	Jeffries William A	236	broker	68	"
	U	Walsh Alice—†	236	domestic	31	"
	V	Begley Jennie—†	237	waitress	21	Brookline
	W	Burns Frederick S	237	physician	49	here
	X	Burns Josephine L—†	237	housewife	55	"
	Y	Grew Edward W	238	real estate	56	"
	Z	Grew Ruth D—†	238	housewife	50	"
	Z¹	Grew Ruth D—†	238	student	22	"
	A	Weeks Elizabeth—†	238	maid	60	"
	B	Tompkins Ina G—†	239	housewife	44	Brockton
	C	Tompkins Seeley K	239	clergyman	43	"
	D	Conroy Delia—†	240	maid	33	here
	E	Hutchins Emma—†	240	retired	70	"
	F	Hutchins Harriet H—†	240	"	73	"
	G	Hutchins Mary H—†	240	"	61	"
	H	MacDonald Catherine—†	240	maid	38	"
	K	Amory Margery S—†	241	clerk	26	"
	L	McDonough Mary—†	241	maid	30	"
	M	Moran Catherine—†	241	cook	34	"
	N	Moran Mary—†	241	waitress	36	"
	O	Burke Delia—†	242	maid	36	"
	P	Davis Margaret—†	242	cook	40	"
	R	Furey Delia—†	242	waitress	34	"
	S	Tappan Elizabeth—†	242	none	69	"
	T	Graves Alice M—†	244	"	49	"
	U	Graves Sydney C	244	student	22	"
	V	Graves William P	244	physician	46	"
	W	Fitzpatrick Mary—†	245	maid	46	"
	X	Gately Elizabeth—†	245	waitress	28	"
	Y	Linehan Margurite—†	245	maid	62	441 Shawmut av
	Z	Minot Elizabeth C—†	245	housekeeper	72	here
	A	Minot Louisa S—†	245	housewife	82	"
	B	Riley Mary—†	245	cook	60	249 Beacon

8—7

Marlborough Street—Continued

c	Floyd Cleveland	246	physician	43	here
d	Floyd Harriet—†	246	housewife	47	"
e	MacDonald Mary—†	246	cook	47	"
f	Raymond Edna—†	246	nurse	25	"
g	Dexter Franklin	247	physician	66	"
h	Dexter Jane—†	247	housewife	52	"
k	Plower Margaret—†	247	maid	43	"
l	Walsh Joanna—†	247	laundress	48	"
m	Barnet Howard J	248	merchant	36	"
n	Barnet Ruth H—†	248	housewife	32	"
o	Finn Ellen—†	249	cook	50	"
p	Norcross Susanna—†	249	housewife	70	"
r	Powers Jennie—†	249	maid	29	11 Arlington
s	Sullivan Hannah—†	249	"	66	here
t	Appleton Francis H	251	retired	76	"
u	Ford Nora—†	251	maid	33	"
v	Hargadon Adelia—†	251	waitress	28	"
w	Hargadon Margaret A—†	251	cook	58	"
x	Byrne Winifred—†	252	maid	25	Newton
y	Donlon Agnes—†	252	cook	50	here
z	Slaven Jessie—†	252	nurse	35	"
a	Talbot Elizabeth—†	252	housewife	40	"
b	Talbot James R	252	physician	49	"
c	Buchanan Annie—†	253	waitress	35	"
d	Curtis Helen F—†	253	housewife	85	"
e	Mersereau Ruth—†	253	nurse	37	"
f	Grew Ethel H—†	254	housewife	46	"
g	Grew Henry S	254	banker	48	"
h	Grew Henry S, jr	254	student	23	"
k	Clark Elizabeth—†	255	maid	51	"
l	Hennessey Ellen—†	255	"	59	"
m	King Anna—†	255	cook	40	10 Fairfield
n	Townsend Elizabeth—†	255	clerk	25	here
o	Townsend Marion—†	255	housewife	58	"
p	Townsend Rose—†	255	clerk	25	"
r	Townsend William S	255	broker	60	"
s	Barry Helen—†	256	cook	54	"
t	Kiernan Katherine—†	256	maid	31	"
u	McColgan Catherine—†	256	"	44	"
v	Sweetser Ida—†	256	none	69	"
w	Harrington Cathrine—†	257	laundress	28	"

Letter	Full Name	Residence, April 1, 1924.	Occupation.	Supposed Age.	Reported Residence, April 1, 1923. Street and Number.

Marlborough Street—Continued

Letter	Full Name	Residence, April 1, 1924.	Occupation.	Supposed Age.	Reported Residence
x	Martin Winifred—†	257	cook	30	53 Hereford
y	Post John R	257	retired	50	here
z	Post Mabel R—†	257	housewife	45	"
A	Post Mary—†	257	clerk	20	"
B	Walsh Mary—†	257	waitress	30	11 Brookline
c	Ahlborn Alice—†	258	none	54	here
D	Ahlborn Emil	258	artist	44	"
E	Ahlborn Emily—†	258	retired	79	"
F	Barry Delia—†	258	laundress	28	"
G	Graham Mary—†	258	cook	40	"
H	Davidson Florence—†	259	maid	30	39 Chestnut
K	Gately Mollie—†	259	waitress	27	39 "
L	Leger Heloise—†	259	maid	56	61 Com av
M	McDonough Cathrine—†	259	cook	25	9 F
N	O'Connor Elizabeth—†	259	maid	21	Ireland
o	Richardson Ellen P—†	259	retired	82	here
P	Welch Elizabeth—†	259	maid	35	40 Com av
R	White Camilla M—†	259	housewife	31	39 Chestnut
s	White Charles J	259	physician	55	here
T	White Olivia A—†	259	housewife	57	"
U	Beebe Edwin P	261	retired	80	Brookline
v	Forrest Marion—†	261	maid	25	135 Mindon
w	MacIver Joanne—†	261	cook	24	Brookline
x	MacSween Margaret—†	261	maid	27	Somerville
y	O'Brien James	261	banker	27	Marlboro
z	Obzendan Lillian H—†	261	clerk	21	New York
A	Wright Lillian—†	261	maid	38	Brookline
B	Galivan Mary—†	272	"	30	here
c	Mink Mabel—†	272	none	50	"
D	Mink Oliver	272	manager	76	"
E	Ridge Ann—†	272	maid	30	"
F	Coughlin Mary—†	274	"	26	Cambridge
G	Donlon Margaret—†	274	"	45	251 Newbury
H	Gannett Gertrude—†	274	housewife	45	here
K	Gannett William W	274	physician	70	"
L	Appleton Maude A—†	275	clerk	51	"
M	Appleton Samuel	275	retired	78	"
N	Isakson Esther—†	275	maid	36	"
o	Johnson Emma—†	275	waitress	31	"
P	Pierce Charlotte—†	275	clerk	51	"
R	Skozland Elsie—†	275	maid	42	"

Page.	Letter.	FULL NAME.	Residence, April 1, 1924.	Occupation.	Supposed Age.	Reported Residence, April 1, 1923. Street and Number.

Marlborough Street—Continued

s	Johnson Agnes—†	277	waitress	50	here
T	Keller Emma—†	277	cook	48	"
U	Kennedy Mabel—†	277	maid	20	"
V	Loring Augustus P	277	lawyer	66	"
W	Loring Ellen—†	277	housewife	63	"
X	Chase Fannie S—†	279	"	49	"
Y	McCormack Jessie—†	279	cook	28	"
Z	McCormack Margaret-†	279	waitress	30	"

Ward 8—Precinct 8

CITY OF BOSTON.

LIST OF RESIDENTS
20 YEARS OF AGE AND OVER

(FEMALES INDICATED BY DAGGER)

AS OF

APRIL 1, 1924

HERBERT A. WILSON, } Listing
JAMES F. EAGAN, } Board.

CITY OF BOSTON—PRINTING DEPARTMENT

Page.	Letter.	Full Name.	Residence, April 1, 1924.	Occupation.	Supposed Age.	Reported Residence April 1, 1923. Street and Number

Arlington Street

	c	Hicks Francis T	18	painter	65	here

Berkeley Street

	L	Killoran Annie—†	229	chiropodist	39	here
	M	Lewis Benjamin	229	dentist	47	"
	P	Bailey Hollis R	237	lawyer	72	"
	R	Bailey Mary P—†	237	housewife	73	"
	S	Barrett Margaret M—†	237	stenographer	20	Philadelphia
	T	Bill Lucinda—†	237	retired	75	here
	U	Bird Frank M	237	"	70	Canton
	V	Bird Grace—†	237	housewife	60	"
	W	Burgoine Beatrice—†	237	domestic	22	Canada
	X	Burns Belle E—†	237	teacher	37	here
	Y	Cleaveland Elizabeth—†	237	retired	50	California
	Z	Conger Mabel D—†	237	director	48	Galesburg Il
	A	Cumnock Mujamer W—†	237	housewife	50	here
	B	Cumnock Ruth—†	237	social worker	37	"
	C	Cushing Julia W—†	237	housewife	50	Lunenburg
	D	Dearborn Sarah—†	237	retired	65	here
	E	Dexter Emma G—†	237	housewife	66	"
	F	Dexter George B	237	merchant	69	"
	G	Dillon Emilie C—†	237	manager	42	"
	H	Dillon Michael F	237	salesman	46	"
	K	Domett Carrie S—†	237	housewife	61	"
	L	Domett Kenneth S	237	treasurer	37	"
	M	Drumm James F	237	merchant	60	Brookline
	N	Drumm Katharine K—†	237	housewife	58	"
	O	Duff Alice H—†	237	retired	75	here
	P	Dunham Grace J—†	237	secretary	50	Winthrop
	R	Dyer Annie—†	237	retired	50	Claremont N
	S	Eddy Gean—†	237	"	50	Brookline
	T	Field Albert M	237	"	60	Taunton
	U	Field Charlotte—†	237	student	20	"
	V	Fisher John R	237	accountant	70	Brookline
	W	Fisher Salome P—†	237	housewife	52	"
	X	Fitts Annie—†	237	"	40	S Duxbury
	Y	Fitts Frank E	237	salesman	45	"
	Z	Fordyce Edmond A	237	broker	48	here

2

Berkeley Street—Continued

Letter.	FULL NAME.	Residence, April 1, 1924.	Occupation.	Supposed Age.	Reported Residence, April 1, 1923. Street and Number.
A	Galvin Adeline—†	237	domestic	28	83 Warren av
B	Grammer Henrietta C—†	237	housewife	55	here
C	Green Mabel—†	237	housekeeper	45	Concord N H
D	Greenleaf Ellen M—†	237	housewife	69	Springfield
E	Greenleaf Lyman B	237	retired	70	"
F	Grubb Ellen F—†	237	housewife	59	Philadelphia
G	Grubb Mary E—†	237	"	51	"
H	Higgins Eudeva P—†	237	"	60	Taunton
K	Higgins Lewis E	237	retired	71	"
L	Hollis Edward F	237	salesman	49	here
M	Hubbard Mary L—†	237	housewife	81	Weston
N	Hunt Alice B—†	237	"	70	here
O	Lewisson William V	237	salesman	68	83 Pinckney
P	Loring Abby R—†	237	retired	65	Weston
R	Loring Edward H	237	"	60	"
S	Macomber Fanny—†	237	housewife	60	here
W	McKenna Margaret—†	237	domestic	30	Cambridge
X	McNeil Alice—†	237	nurse	40	here
T	Mead Kate A—†	237	retired	82	"
U	Merrill Mary—†	237	"	47	"
V	Merrill Susan—†	237	"	45	"
Y	Morrill Helen—†	237	"	60	"
Z	Murphy Margaret—†	237	domestic	25	62 Ainsworth
A	Nash Mary H—†	237	retired	55	here
B	Newell Gertrude—†	237	domestic	30	Hull
C	Nichols Annie—†	237	librarian	70	here
D	Olsen Sigrid—†	237	domestic	35	"
E	Page Elizabeth C—†	237	housewife	44	"
F	Page Rufus W	237	merchant	52	"
G	Patterson Florence M—†	237	saleswoman	45	New York
H	Pearce Katherine—†	237	retired	45	California
K	Russell Annie—†	237	"	60	Somersworth N H
L	Schneider Elizabeth—†	237	writer	40	Methuen
M	Seymour Edward	237	salesman	40	here
N	Seymour Florence—†	237	retired	60	"
O	Shepherd George	237	salesman	45	"
P	Shepherd Katherine—†	237	housewife	40	"
R	Smith Sarah P—†	237	"	65	Taunton
S	Smith Walter N	237	retired	68	"
T	Steinbach Abby—†	237	"	60	here
U	Thomson Margaret—†	237	housewife	60	Andover

Berkeley Street—Continued

v	Thomson T Dennie	237	broker	60	Andover	
w	Toulouse Ellen—†	237	nurse	40	Cambridge	
x	Warren Alice R—†	237	housewife	47	here	
y	Warren Edward A	237	salesman	60	Sharon	
z	Warren Edward W	237	broker	45	here	
A	Warren Elizabeth—†	237	housewife	55	Sharon	
B	Weaver Gwendolyn—†	237	student	21	Oregon	
C	Webster Martha—†	237	retired	99	here	
D	Whitman Ellen—†	237	"	60	Rhode Island	
E	Gravel Della—†	247	housewife	41	New York	
F	Gravel Thomas	247	janitor	64	"	
G	La Moreaux Florence—†	247	school teacher	45	here	
H	Carney Elizabeth A—†	249	housewife	59	"	
K	Green Joseph	249	butler	65	"	
L	Osborne George	249	professor	85	"	
M	Witte Elizabeth—†	249	teacher	40	"	

Boylston Street

z	Ellison Thomas	383	photographer	50	here	
A	Cormick Florence C—†	383	clerk	55	"	
B	Ryan Margaret E—†	383	housewife	58	"	
M	Coogan Joseph A	421	physician	65	"	
N	DeLue Frank S	421	"	55	"	
O	Goodman Nathan M	421	"	55	"	
P	Hardie John A	421	dentist	50	"	
R	Keys John W	421	"	58	"	
S	Krauss James	421	physician	58	"	
T	Lynch Richard A	421	"	35	"	
U	Moore John H	421	"	60	"	
V	Perry Gale	421	"	45	"	
W	York Richard S	421	"	66	"	
x¹	O'Brien Edward P	429	gasfitter	41	Bath Me	
Y	O'Brien Minnie E—†	429	hairdresser	52	here	
z	O'Brien William A	429	clerk	47	"	
A	Hadlock Margaret—†	429	hairdresser	43	Bath Me	
C	Connah Duglas J	431	artist	55	here	
E	Miller Charles E, jr	431	salesman	41	"	
F	Miller M Beatrice—†	431	housewife	31	"	
P	Jones Annette—†	541	"	60	"	

Boylston Street —Continued

R	Tower Kate D †	541	retired	65	here
S	Denig Blanche A †	541	physician	63	"
T	Holt Edith F—†	541	housewife	45	1111 Boylston
U	Holt Harry D	541	salesman	53	1111 "
W	Rea Leota P—†	541	housewife	40	here
V	Rea Sidney F	541	superintendent	58	"
X	Macy William F	541	real estate	56	"
Y	MacDonald Catherine—†	541	dressmaker	47	"
Z	Gregory Ella—†	541	retired	73	"
A	Grinnell Susan B—†	541	"	65	"
B	Pratt Fannie B —†	541	"	97	"
C	Atherton Percy L	541	composer	55	"
D	Atherton Walter	541	architect	60	"
H	Mays Martha E—†	543	housewife	44	"
K	Mays Theodore	543	janitor	46	"
N	Webb Albert E	543	physician	45	"
O	Amadon Arthur F	543	"	65	"
P	Amadon Bertha S—†	543	clerk	24	"
R	Amadon Mary E—†	543	housewife	60	"
S	Franklin Mary E—†	543	teacher	58	"
T	Watson Frances I—†	543	"	28	"
U	Gormely Annie—†	543	cook	50	"
V	Lombard Susan S—†	543	retired	84	"
W	Fogler Gertrude—†	543	teacher	45	"
X	Wall Alice—†	543	none	45	"
Y	Tupper Nona D—†	543	decorator	46	"
Z	Clark Pauline H—†	543	none	50	"
A	Clark William T	543	retired	63	"
B	Morrill Olney S	543	teller	30	"
C	Traver Mary E—†	543	clerk	42	"
D	Anagnos Demetrias	543	broker	35	"
E	Calnan Josephine M—†	543	housekeeper	39	"
F	Snyder Jacob D	543	physician	47	"
G	Felton Minerva L—†	543	teacher	52	"
H	Felton Ruth—†	543	"	26	"
K	Lincoln Catherine—†	543	"	44	"
L	Ellicott Josephine —†	543	none	60	"
M	Woodworth Helen I—†	543	physician	61	"
R	Randall Sarah A—†	551	bookkeeper	62	"
S	Wright Mabel R—†	551	practitioner	53	"
N	Haynes Edith—†	601	osteopath	40	"

Boylston Street—Continued

o	Haynes Perry	601	artist	55	here
p	Morse Stanley	601	"	22	"
r	Anderson Frederick	603	janitor	30	"
s	Anderson Lillian G—†	603	housewife	30	"
v	Douglas Ella B—†	645	waitress	35	"
w	Gordon George A	645	clergyman	71	"
x	Gordon Ruth M—†	645	teacher	29	"
y	Gordon Susan M—†	645	housewife	67	"
z	Murray Jessie G—†	645	cook	25	"
c	Berry Sadie—†	651	modiste	35	"
o	Carroll Albert E	675	manufacturer	54	"
p	Carroll Annetta H—†	675	housewife	47	"
v	Holland Frances M—†	687	dressmaker	70	"
w	Shea Helen L—†	687	therapeutist	46	"
x	Shea Henry W	687	"	49	"
y	Bertrand Luccinne—†	687	milliner	34	112 Hunt'n av
z	Graves Frances—†	687	physician	37	here
b	Holland Lillian A—†	687	saleswoman	50	"
l	Sousa John J	711	superintendent	32	"
m	Sousa Julia V—†	711	housewife	28	"
n	Thorpe Edward E	711	oculist	65	"
w	Lee George C	729	merchant	55	"

Clarendon Street

s	Roberts Harry L	212	physician	65	here
t	Page Henrietta—†	212	retired	78	"
u	Cox Jennie C—†	212	"	45	"
y	Jewell Abby N—†	212	housewife	56	"
z	Mortimer Louise—†	212	practitioner	50	"
a	Paulfrey Phebe—†	212	accountant	40	"
b	Childs Suzanne—†	212	housewife	60	"
c	Childs Walter H	212	merchant	72	"
d	Nickerson Harriet—†	212	housewife	40	"
e	Nickerson Harry L	212	chemist	40	"
f	Cheney Benjamin P	212	retired	58	"
h	Jambrill Louise—†	212	teacher	45	Brookline
k	Chester Frank B	212	physician	55	here
l	Kempton Grace C—†	212	teacher	60	"
o	Clough Alice—†	220	healer	43	"

Clarendon Street—Continued

Letter.	FULL NAME.	Residence	Occupation	Age	Reported Residence
P	Clough Harry	220	clerk	50	here
R	Knox Madie—†	220	housewife	40	"
S	Knox William R	220	healer	45	"
U	Bird Nora—†	232	maid	35	Cambridge
V	Dixon Robert B	232	physician	67	here
W	Dixon Sarah G—†	232	housewife	62	"
X	Fitzgerald Martha—†	232	cook	33	Cambridge
Y	Rubins Mildred—†	232	secretary	20	here
Z	Callahan Mary—†	233	cook	60	Somerville
A	LeBlanc Mary—†	233	waitress	22	Brookline
B	Sherrill Barbara H—†	233	housewife	23	"
C	Sherrill Henry K	233	clergyman	33	"
D	Swift Emily—†	233	nurse	35	Winchester
E	Aldrich Gertrude—†	234	artist	46	here
F	Ashley Louise—†	234	nurse	51	"
G	Baker Harry	234	accountant	29	"
H	Dermody Mary L—†	234	teacher	48	"
K	Fellows Janet K—†	234	secretary	29	"
L	Fellows Willis B	234	salesman	29	"
M	Houghton Victoria—†	234	housekeeper	38	"
N	Houghton William E	234	clerk	29	"
O	King Lena—†	234	nurse	26	"
P	Marley Marie—†	234	"	24	"
R	Meehan Mary A—†	234	housekeeper	24	29 Clayton
S	Nichols Paul	234	teacher	36	here
T	Regan John W	234	"	49	"
U	Regan Mary V—†	234	housewife	39	"
V	Shea Margaret—†	234	statistician	52	"
W	Shea Mary E—†	234	retired	49	"
X	Thorpe Charlotte—†	234	bookkeeper	26	"
Y	Thorpe Nettie—†	234	retired	56	"
Z	Berry Marguerite—†	236	housewife	28	"
A	Berry Walter T	236	mechanic	32	"
G	Colman Susan A—†	236	retired	71	"
B	Jenkins Carrie J—†	236	chiropodist	64	"
C	Moulton Edith F—†	236	housekeeper	47	"
D	Moulton Harriett E—†	236	housewife	81	"
E	Moulton John R	236	salesman	43	"
F	Moulton Suzanne P—†	236	teacher	46	"

Commonwealth Avenue

H	Donlan Charles E	2	physician	50	here
K	Danielson DeForest—†	4	housewife	50	"
L	Doyle Mary—†	4	domestic	45	"
M	Durjie Mary—†	4	"	50	"
N	Peterson Edith—†	4	"	25	"
O	Wistrand Celia—†	4	"	50	"
P	Binney George H	6	physician	38	"
R	Binney Susan A—†	6	housewife	31	"
S	Craigea Annie—†	6	domestic	23	Scotland
T	Johnston Louise—†	6	"	28	here
U	Kehoe Mollie—†	6	"	26	"
V	Kenelly Agnes—†	6	"	40	"
W	Livingston Alexis—†	6	"	30	Nova Scotia
Y	McLoud Dolly—†	6	"	24	Canada
X	McLoughlin Catherine—†	6	"	24	76 Com av
Z	Murphy Mary—†	6	"	26	Dedham
A	Wilson Violet G—†	6	nurse	31	here
B	Currier Guy W	8	lawyer	55	"
C	Currier Lucy P—†	8	student	23	"
D	Currier Marie—†	8	housewife	54	"
E	Currier Richard	8	student	26	"
F	Keefe Kathrine—†	8	domestic	50	"
G	McGoghegan Alice—†	8	"	30	"
H	Nelson Katherine—†	8	"	55	Milton
K	Foster Frederick	10	director	43	here
L	Allen Alice R—†	12	housewife	58	"
M	Allen Eleanor W—†	12	treasurer	40	"
N	Allen Thomas	12	retired	70	"
O	Carroll Mary—†	12	domestic	50	"
P	Dinneen Delia—†	12	"	35	Ireland
R	Finn Margaret M—†	12	"	52	here
S	Perkins Delia—†	12	"	35	"
T	Reardon Dennis D	12	chauffeur	60	"
U	Tracy Margaret—†	12	domestic	22	Ireland
V	Alexander Leslie—†	14	"	22	Brookline
W	Cotter Nellie—†	14	"	45	482 Beacon
X	McDonald Mary—†	14	"	50	Nova Scotia
Y	Murry Myrtle—†	14	"	32	here
Z	Pollard Elise W—†	14	housewife	55	"
A	Pollard Fredrick W	14	lawyer	32	"

Commonwealth Avenue—Continued

Letter	Full Name	Res.	Occupation	Age	Reported Residence
B	Pollard Pricila—†	14	student	20	here
C	Whittier Alberta—†	16	retired	61	"
D	Gallaher Bessie—†	18	domestic	30	"
E	Gallaher Nellie—†	18	"	29	"
F	Taylor Emily—†	18	"	50	"
G	Winslow Carrie—†	18	housewife	58	"
H	Winslow Herbert F	18	broker	60	"
K	Ahler Olga—†	20	nurse	45	"
L	Bain Margaret—†	20	domestic	25	"
M	Carmon Hughida—†	20	nurse	39	"
N	Idman Marie—†	20	domestic	31	"
O	McKenzie Isabel—†	20	retired	36	"
P	Russell Margaret P—†	20	"	65	"
R	Fanning Mary—†	22	domestic	25	"
S	Graham Rebecca—†	22	"	42	"
T	Motley Eleanor—†	22	housewife	77	"
U	Motley Warren	22	lawyer	40	"
V	Sullivan Nora—†	22	domestic	30	30 Marlboro
W	Wall Joana—†	22	"	57	Ireland
X	Keegan Sarah—†	24	"	20	481 Com av
Y	Lorden Hannah—†	24	"	50	here
Z	Lowell James H	24	lawyer	31	"
A	Lowell Mary E—†	24	housewife	50	"
B	McCabe Mary—†	24	domestic	24	"
C	McLoughlin Annie—†	24	"	56	"
D	Denehy Hannah—†	26	"	50	"
E	Sturgis Anita—†	26	clerk	26	"
F	Sturgis Mildred F—†	26	housewife	50	"
G	Sturgis Susett—†	26	clerk	30	"
H	Brown Emma F—†	28	housewife	59	Brookline
K	Brown Joseph B	28	broker	67	"
L	Carlton Guy E	28	banker	40	here
M	Creadon Eleanor—†	28	clerk	37	"
N	Donnelly June—†	28	teacher	48	"
O	Gilpatrick Arthur	28	manager	57	"
P	Gilpatrick Mina A—†	28	housewife	56	"
R	Johnson Ethel—†	28	clerk	35	40 Com av
S	Johnson Florence—†	28	domestic	42	here
T	Shewell George D	28	salesman	23	Pennsylvania
U	Smith M Proctor	28	"	31	New York
V	Taube Arvid	28	"	30	"

Commonwealth Avenue—Continued

w	Weeks Dorothy W—†	28	instructor	31	here
x	Wood Alice —†	28	teacher	48	2 Arlington
y	Wood Elizabeth M—†	28	"	51	here
z	Cotter Nora—†	30	domestic	26	"
A	Daly Agnes—†	30	"	29	"
B	Keating Jane—†	30	"	40	292 Beacon
D	Parkman Frances—†	30	housewife	60	here
C	Parkman Henry	30	treasurer	73	"
E	Sheehan Katherine—†	30	domestic	32	"
F	Corrigan Sarah—†	32	"	40	Nova Scotia
G	Coyle Winifred—†	32	"	31	81 Mt Vernon
H	McKenna Ellen—†	32	"	65	28 Montgomery
K	McKibben Emily—†	32	retired	45	here
L	McKibbin John	32	"	87	"
M	Barnicle Katie—†	34	domestic	36	389 Marlboro
R	Nelson Ludwig	34	"	50	here
N	O'Brion Mary —†	34	"	35	"
O	Tyler Bartlett	34	salesman	26	"
P	Tyler Carrie—†	34	housewife	56	"
S	Tyler William	34	professor	60	"
T	Brown Ellen—†	36	domestic	31	"
U	Colleran Josephine—†	36	"	26	"
V	Drew Julia—†	36	"	41	"
W	Hunnewell Minna —†	36	retired	39	"
X	Hunnewell Walter	36	broker	43	"
Y	Kelley Mary—†	36	domestic	51	"
Z	McLaughlin Anna—†	36	"	37	"
A	McLaughlin Celia—†	36	"	27	"
B	Sullivan Barbara—†	36	"	26	"
C	Clark Rosamond	38 & 40	social worker	40	"
D	Doane Marion E—†	38 & 40	retired	40	"
E	Gould Alice B —†	38 & 40	"	42	"
F	Greene Mary E —†	38 & 40	teacher	40	"
G	Greene Rina M—†	38 & 40	"	40	"
H	Johnson Ethel M —†	38 & 40	commissioner	35	"
K	Merryweather Juliana —†	38 & 40	manager	40	"
L	Tuttle Jennie—†	38 & 40	"	50	"
M	Tuttle Lucy —†	38 & 40	"	40	"
N	Weeks Gertrude—†	38 & 40	teacher	51	11 Tetlow
O	White Marian L—†	38 & 40	secretary	27	here
P	Horton Frances—†	44	retired	77	"

Commonwealth Avenue—Continued

	Letter	FULL NAME	Residence	Occupation	Age	Reported Residence
	R	Howley Annie —†	44	domestic	38	here
	S	McDonough Kate—†	44	"	50	"
	T	Nolan Bessie —†	44	"	64	"
	U	Robbins Phillis—†	44	housewife	40	"
	V	Haran Mary A—†	46	domestic	28	405 Com av
	W	Hopkins Theresa B—†	46	retired	77	here
	X	McKaskill Lena—†	46	domestic	37	332 Beacon
	Y	Sullivan Theresa —†	46	"	40	here
	Z	Whalen Mary—†	46	"	50	"
	B	Bliss Harriet—†	50	retired	69	"
	C	Carpenter Julia—†	50	"	65	Providence R I
	D	Clark Mary—†	50	nurse	25	Winthrop
	E	Cole Alice —†	50	retired	45	here
	F	Conrad Myrtle—†	50	nurse	25	664 Wash'n
	G	Duffy Mary—†	50	manager	24	here
	H	Jones Jennie B—†	50	retired	79	Providence R I
	K	Laughlin Harriet—†	50	"	69	here
	L	McNair Marie L—†	50	"	50	"
	M	Moloney Elizabeth—†	50	domestic	40	Worcester
	N	Soule Richard H	50	retired	69	here
	O	Sturgis Martha—†	50	"	75	"
	P	Tenney Julia M—†	50	housewife	79	"
	R	Tenney William M	50	manufacturer	81	"
	S	Thatcher Louise—†	50	retired	50	"
	T	Withers Grace—†	50	nurse	30	Wareham
	U	Ducette Sophie—†	52	domestic	24	here
	V	Grant Eleanor M—†	52	"	48	"
	W	Redding Delia—†	52	"	30	"
	X	Sharp Arthur R	52	treasurer	60	"
	Y	Sharp Arthur R, jr	52	student	22	"
	Z	Sharp Mary S—†	52	housewife	75	"
	A	Sharp William E	52	student	20	"
	B	Beaton Sadie—†	54	domestic	26	Canada
	C	Brewster Frank	54	lawyer	65	here
	D	Brewster Mary F—†	54	housewife	55	"
	E	McDonald Katherine—†	54	domestic	35	"
	F	McMillen Katherine—†	54	"	21	Nova Scotia
	G	Mulcahy Hanah—†	54	"	50	428 Col av
	H	Sharp Helen—†	54	retired	60	here
	K	Collins Nellie—†	56	domestic	50	"
	L	Driscoll Julia—†	56	"	48	"

Commonwealth Avenue—Continued

M	Francis Frances C—†	56	housewife	53	here
N	Francis George T	56	engineer	62	"
O	Francis Henry S	56	student	22	"
P	Hurley Mary A—†	56	domestic	48	Cambridge
R	Austin Agnes—†	58	housekeeper	38	here
S	Gustafson Thyre—†	58	domestic	23	Sweden
T	Rowe Henry S	58	trustee	78	here
U	Parker Herman	60	merchant	60	"
V	Parker Lillian P—†	60	housewife	40	"
W	Percival Evelyn—†	60	"	30	"
X	Percival Jennie P—†	60	retired	70	"
Y	Percival Lawrence	60	jeweler	45	"
Z	Duncan George	62	retired	79	"
A	Kaddy Elizabeth—†	62	domestic	57	"
B	Kigan Katherine—†	62	"	51	"
C	McRae Jessie—†	62	"	49	"
D	Ruff Arthur	62	butler	51	"
E	Bond Theresa—†	64	retired	30	"
F	George Dorothy—†	64	clerk	20	330 Newbury
G	George Mary—†	64	housewife	43	330 "
H	George Vesper	64	painter	45	330 "
K	Greenwood Alma—†	64	teacher	35	here
L	Hobbs Mary L—†	64	agent	35	Concord N H
M	McAuley Joseph	64	janitor	30	Nova Scotia
N	Page Lillian—†	64	teacher	40	here
O	Richardson Marion—†	64	student	20	138 Newbury
P	Thromantono Ricardo	64	clerk	35	here
S	Johnson Thomas J A	68	manufacturer	47	Europe
T	O'Neil Frank	68	chauffeur	22	E Cambridge
U	Ball Julia S—†	68	retired	60	here
V	Chappell Mary H—†	68	"	65	"
W	Converse Emma T—†	68	housewife	52	"
X	Converse Frederick	68	composer	52	"
Y	Converse Virginia—†	68	teacher	23	"
Z	Monsen Linken—†	68	domestic	28	"
A	Ramseyer Marie—†	68	housekeeper	43	"
B	Cushing Elizabeth—†	70	housewife	22	"
C	Cushing Haywood W	70	physician	68	"
D	Cushing Martha—†	70	housewife	65	"
E	Donovan Josephine—†	70	domestic	26	"
F	Mitchell Annie—†	70	"	30	"

Commonwealth Avenue—Continued

G	Trihy Johanna—†	70	domestic	52	here
H	Brewer Fannie R—†	72	retired	59	"
K	Dusten Charlotte—†	72	domestic	56	"
L	McLeod Helena—†	72	cook	45	Beverly
M	McManus Annie—†	72	domestic	35	Brookline
N	Tomilson Minnie—†	72	"	40	292 Beacon
O	Dowling Josephine—†	74	"	45	here
P	Dunn Hanah—†	74	"	40	"
R	Gardner Harrison	74	student	22	"
S	Gardner Phillip	74	broker	51	"
T	Gardner Virginia A—†	74	housewife	49	"
U	Cannon Agnes—†	76	domestic	21	Ireland
X	Oleary Mary—†	76	"	40	here
Y	Phelps John S	76	physician	56	"
V	Reardon Nellie—†	76	retired	45	"
W	Reardon Timothy J	76	physician	50	"
Z	Tobin Mary A—†	76	none	35	"
B	Choong Myung Ko	78	student	21	Dover
C	Porter Marie L—†	78	teacher	40	"
D	Kelley Florence M—†	78	housewife	43	51 Audubon rd
E	Kelley William C	78	manager	54	51 "
A	Childs Ellen—†	80	retired	55	here
B	Dilloway William E L	80	lawyer	73	"
C	Loughlin Katherine A—†	80	housekeeper	50	"
D	Bossom Elizabeth A—†	82	secretary	49	"
E	Crossman Luther C	82	mechanic	42	Seattle Wash
F	Dugan Frances D—†	82	teacher	32	Brookline
G	Everett Caroline V—†	82	"	33	33 W Cedar
H	Gorman Anna G—†	82	social worker	29	Holyoke
K	Holmes Margaret—†	82	manager	29	here
L	Hoole Anna F—†	82	student	23	Maine
M	Hoole Mary E—†	82	secretary	58	"
N	Plummer Mary A—†	82	"	56	here
O	Williams Fred E	82	manager	63	"
P	Woodworth Albert G	82	retired	50	"
R	Woodworth Ellen V—†	82	housewife	50	"
S	Angell Hellen—†	84	"	45	"
T	Angell W Randolph	84	physician	45	"
U	King Gordan	84	manager	42	182 Com av
V	Wilkinson Arthur C	84	broker	42	here
W	Morrison Leslie	86	retired	77	"

Commonwealth Avenue—Continued

Letter	FULL NAME	Residence	Occupation	Age	Reported Residence
X	Casey Margaret—†	114	laundress	58	here
Y	Forbes Charles S	114	journalist	43	"
Z	Forbes Ethel A—†	114	artist	43	"
A	Forbes Isabel C—†	114	housewife	71	"
B	Donoghue Louisa—†	116	waitress	38	11 Gloucester
C	Hanlon Leona W—†	116	maid	22	Auburndale
D	Sullivan Catherine—†	116	cook	49	82 Mt Vernon
E	Johnson Anna T—†	118	housewife	33	here
F	Johnson David J	118	physician	45	"
G	O'Neil Georgiana—†	118	none	39	"
H	Tuttle Bertha E—†	118	retired	35	23 Beacon
K	McBean Lydia A—†	120	maid	54	here
L	Peabody Amelia—†	120	artist	33	"
M	Raphael Margaret A—†	120	laundress	52	"
N	Scott Annie—†	120	maid	39	"
O	Wright Margaret E—†	120	"	56	"
P	Baskin Lily—†	122	"	23	"
R	Corrigan Sarah—†	122	cook	26	"
S	Kelly Michael	122	butler	47	"
T	Lawrence Frederic C	122	student	24	"
U	Lawrence Julia—†	122	housewife	71	"
V	Lawrence William	122	bishop	73	"
W	Patterson Christina—†	122	maid	27	"
X	Holman Frank H	124	houseman	64	"
Y	Taylor James R, jr	124	physician	45	"
Z	Taylor Mabel S—†	124	housewife	34	"
A	Gray Ellen W—†	126	"	43	"
B	Gray Francis	126	broker	57	"
C	Mullen Hannah—†	126	laundress	56	117 Com av
D	O'Connell Katherine—†	126	maid	31	139 Bay State rd
E	Scott Jean—†	126	cook	43	here
F	Bond Charles L	128	superintendent	25	"
G	Bond Isabella B—†	128	housewife	60	"
H	Stearns Edith B—†	128	none	38	"
K	Boyer Rachel—†	130	maid	32	"
L	Houkom Aster—†	130	"	20	"
M	Richie Margaret—†	130	"	28	46 Bower
N	Snelling May—†	130	cook	44	here
O	Snelling William	130	butler	42	"
P	Thorndyke Alden A	130	retired	60	"
R	Thorndyke Elizabeth—†	130	none	21	"

Commonwealth Avenue—Continued

s	Thorndyke Grace H —†	130	housewife	50	here
t	Thorndyke Thayer	130	clerk	32	"
u	Martin John J	132	banker	50	"
v	Martin Mary—†	132	housewife	48	"
w	Martin Robert C	132	student	23	"
x	Atherton Ellen M—†	144	housewife	42	"
y	Atherton Frederick	144	merchant	67	"
z	Jelly Arthur C	144	physician	71	"
a	LeBaron Grace—†	144	teacher	25	"
b	Osgood Arthur H	144	dentist	65	"
c	Osgood Elizabeth M—†	144	housewife	26	"
d	Osgood Herman A	144	physician	32	"
e	Osgood Lizzie J—†	144	housewife	60	"
f	Anderson Hulda—†	146	laundress	57	"
g	Fabyan Edith—†	146	housewife	46	"
h	Fabyan Frances W	146	broker	50	"
k	Fabyan Wright, jr	146	"	23	"
l	Hunt Henretta —†	146	maid	50	"
m	Robertson Beatrice—†	146	"	40	"
n	Sullivan Hannah—†	146	"	26	Ireland
o	Sullivan Mary—†	146	cook	40	here
s	Johnson Therese—†	148	maid	35	"
p	Swift George H	148	merchant	46	"
r	Swift Lucile—†	148	housewife	44	"
t	Goodwin Eleanor—†	150	"	50	"
u	Goodwin Eleanor—†	150	"	23	"
v	Goodwin William H	150	salesman	25	"
w	Kennard Lucy—†	150	cook	40	"
x	Sherwin Anne I—†	150	teacher	40	"
y	Sherwin Edward V	150	retired	39	"
z	Sherwin Isabel F—†	150	housewife	78	"
a	Thaler Alvina—†	150	maid	38	"
b	Adams Anna—†	152	"	37	"
c	Marshall Mary G—†	152	housekeeper	50	"
d	McAllister Margaret—†	152	maid	54	"
e	Rooney Bessie—†	152	"	45	"
f	Whittington Isabel—†	152	"	40	"
g	Amory Ethel E—†	160	retired	56	"
h	Austin Mary H—†	160	housewife	56	"
k	Benton Mary A—†	160	"	77	"
l	Buskey Cecil S	160	clerk	27	"

Page	Letter	Full Name	Residence, April 1, 1924	Occupation	Supposed Age	Reported Residence, April 1, 1923, Street and Number

Commonwealth Avenue—Continued

	Letter	Full Name	Residence	Occupation	Age	Reported Residence
	M	Campbell Annie—†	160	waitress	30	here
	N	Chard Thomas S	160	retired	78	"
	O	Clark Joseph H	160	"	86	"
	P	Crawford Eva J—†	160	housewife	70	"
	R	Crawford Jay B	160	lawyer	73	"
	S	Crump Julia S—†	160	retired	87	"
	T	Cummings Jennie—†	160	"	56	"
	U	Cusick John	160	baker	45	"
	V	Dennis Emma J—†	160	retired	57	"
	W	Devlin Kate—†	160	cook	30	"
	X	Doherty Annie—†	160	"	50	"
	Y	Doherty Bridget—†	160	maid	30	"
	Z	Donohue Mary—†	160	waitress	50	"
	A	Dunn Elizabeth—†	160	maid	34	"
	B	Emerson Edna—†	160	housewife	51	"
	C	Emerson William T R	160	physician	56	"
	D	Gibbons Ellen—†	160	cook	30	"
	E	Harkins Rose—†	160	waitress	50	"
	F	Harris Ellen M—†	160	retired	65	"
	G	Hobson Fannie—†	160	"	36	"
	K	Lynch Mary—†	160	cook	55	"
	L	Margery Annie—†	160	maid	32	"
	M	McDonnell Sarah—†	160	"	50	Lowell
	N	McGrain Matthew E	160	porter	61	here
	O	McLaughlin Bridget—†	160	cook	28	"
	P	McLaughlin Katherine—†	160	maid	38	"
	R	McLaughlin Mary—†	160	waitress	22	"
	S	McLaughlin Sadie—†	160	maid	31	"
	T	McLaughlin Sadie—†	160	waitress	30	"
	U	McLeod Agnes—†	160	maid	37	"
	V	McLeod Elizabeth J—†	160	housekeeper	53	"
	W	Murdock Carrie E—†	160	retired	68	"
	X	Murdock Hattie—†	160	"	73	"
	H	Naughton Elizabeth—†	160	"	68	"
	Y	O'Donnell Ellen—†	160	maid	55	"
	Z	Parker Henry F	160	music critic	56	"
	B	Pierce Franklin K	160	manager	44	"
	C	Pierce Philemia E—†	160	housewife	44	"
	D	Porter Nellie—†	160	maid	40	"
	A	Powden Hazel—†	160	retired	31	"
	E	Stebbins Agnes M—†	160	"	40	"

Commonwealth Avenue—Continued

Letter.	FULL NAME.	Residence, April 1, 1924.	Occupation.	Supposed Age.	Reported Residence, April 1, 1923. Street and Number.
F	Stephens Martha W—†	160	retired	83	here
G	Nebil Lewis W	160	baker	57	"
K	Walker Mabel J—†	160	retired	58	"
H	Whitney Frank O	160	"	63	"
L	Wilicomb Martha A—†	160	"	77	"
M	Aldworth Sarah—†	172	maid	39	"
N	Beaton Molly—†	172	"	40	"
O	Corvelo Pasquale	172	houseman	29	"
P	Ehrlich Henry	172	physician	58	"
R	Ehrlich Louis H	172	student	21	"
S	Ehrlich Sally H—†	172	housewife	47	"
T	Ehrlich Samuel H	172	student	20	"
U	Johnson Elizabeth—†	172	maid	37	"
V	Brackett Eleanor—†	174	secretary	28	"
W	Brackett Fanny E—†	174	housewife	64	"
X	Brackett Harriet G—†	174	nurse	44	"
Y	Brackett Willard G	174	retired	78	"
Z	Meachan Ellen L—†	174	"	80	"
A	Mulligan Helen—†	174	maid	30	106 Marlboro
B	Walsh Mary—†	174	cook	32	8 Gloucester
C	Winslow Winthrop C	174	merchant	63	here
D	Houghton Camelia M—†	176	housewife	56	"
E	Houghton Harriet—†	176	nurse	26	"
F	Houghton Henry L	176	physician	55	"
F¹	Houghton Henry L, jr	176	student	23	"
G	Lancaster Harland F	176	"	20	"
H	Leahy Norah—†	176	waitress	33	8 Gloucester
K	Ollis Delia—†	176	cook	50	here
L	Dillingham Florence B †	178	housewife	52	"
M	Dillingham Pauline B—†	178	student	24	"
N	Dillingham Pitt	178	clergyman	70	"
O	Hemenway Abbie E—†	178	cook	62	65 St Botolph
P	McLean Jessie—†	178	maid	30	Norwood
R	Norman Mildred H—†	178	secretary	32	65 St Botolph
S	Surphlus Martha—†	178	maid	20	238 Com av
T	Woodbury Benjamin C	178	physician	38	69 W Cedar
U	Woodbury Gertrude O—†	178	housewife	38	69 "
W	Foulicham Anis	182	student	23	22 Newbury
X	Meshaka Albert N	182	salesman	30	England
Y	Meshaka Najub N	182	merchant	40	here
Z	Ostrander Harry	182	dentist	35	"

Commonwealth Avenue—Continued

A	Pratt Helen O—†	182	nurse	45	Corey Hill Hosp	
B	Weisner Edwin J	182	musician	33	Watertown	
C	Weisner Louise I—†	182	housewife	43	"	
D	Broadhurst Thomas	184–188	cook	24	here	
E	Green Patrick J	184–188	watchman	45	"	
F	Osborne Shelly B	184–188	dentist	40	"	
G	Donahue Sarah B–†	184–188	housekeeper	42	"	
H	Richardson Lucy C–†	184–188	housewife	89	"	
K	Lakeman Daniel W	184–188	clerk	46	"	
M	Wood Josephine H–†	184–188	housewife	45	"	
O	Briggs Helen L—†	184–188	"	48	"	
P	Hawley Mary G—†	184–188	"	50	"	
R	Dana Isabella H—†	184–188	"	78	"	
S	Goodhue Grace W–†	184–188	"	45	"	
T	Goodhue Merrill	184–188	clerk	27	"	
W	Neal Caroline F—†	184–188	retired	60	"	
Z	Kendrick Grace W–†	184–188	secretary	40	182 Com av	
A	Warren Annie C—†	184–188	retired	78	here	
C	MacKinnon Anna–†	184–188	nurse	50	"	
D	Wood Emma—†	184–188	housewife	48	"	
E	Frost Annie J—†	184–188	"	45	"	
F	Beech Ruth A—†	184–188	"	72	"	
G	Connor Ellen A—†	184–188	nurse	48	"	
H	Inches Henrietta C–†	184–188	housewife	48	"	
K	Reynolds Walter F	184–188	lawyer	56	"	
L	Stoney Katherine–†	184–188	none	34	"	
M	Stoney Katherine D—†	184–188	housewife	45	"	
O	Doherty Frances—†	184–188	maid	25	"	
R	Warner Margaret–†	184–188	retired	45	"	
S	Lamson Mary E—†	184–188	"	70	"	
T	Kraft Joseph	184–188	manager	59	"	
U	Kraft Josephine—†	184–188	secretary	24	"	
V	Kraft Mary K—†	184–188	housewife	59	"	
W	Haven Sally B—†	184–188	"	60	"	
X	Burke Hannah—†	184–188	maid	60	"	
Y	Iasigi Marie V—†	184–188	housewife	60	"	
Z	Dunphy Elizabeth B—†	184–188	none	28	"	
B	Lincoln Serafinia L–†	184–188	housewife	65	"	
C	Hudson Emilie—†	184–188	"	48	96 Bay State rd	
D	Hudson Samuel H	184–188	lawyer	60	96 "	
F	Robeson Frances–†	184–188	housewife	63	here	

Commonwealth Avenue—Continued

Letter.	FULL NAME.	Residence, April 1, 1924.	Occupation.	Supposed Age.	Reported Residence, April 1, 1923. Street and Number.
K	Barker Florence H—†	190	nurse	46	here
L	Clancy Norah—†	190	maid	24	Newton
M	Prince Charles B	190	merchant	47	here
N	Prince Halldis—†	190	housewife	39	"
O	Anderson Bridget—†	192	maid	45	"
P	Byrne Margaret—†	192	"	27	Cambridge
R	Fay Frank B	192	retired	68	here
S	Fay Mary C—†	192	housewife	55	"
T	Foley May B—†	192	maid	27	"
U	Vandeventer Ethel F—†	192	none	30	"
V	Blackwood Elizabeth—†	196	maid	47	380 Com av
V	Young Elizabeth—†	196	"	37	here
X	Sullivan Annie—†	198	housekeeper	52	"
Y	Storrs Elizabeth W—†	200	"	51	"
Z	Callahan Nellie—†	202	cook	42	"
A	Geoghegan Julia—†	202	maid	27	Milton
B	Robey Isabel—†	202	housewife	48	here
C	Robey William H	202	physician	48	"
D	Jennings Helen—†	204	maid	44	"
E	Culleton Mary E—†	206	"	35	"
F	Erhardt Wilhelmina—†	206	"	38	"
G	Hebb Dorcas—†	206	nurse	52	"
H	Register Albert L, jr	206	salesman	26	"
K	Register Alice S—†	206	housewife	52	"
L	Register Barbara S—†	206	none	22	"
M	Riley Irmine A—†	206	maid	24	"
N	Simmons Elizabeth F—†	206	housewife	81	"
O	Neill Annetta S—†	208	"	47	Cambridge
P	Neill Earnest	208	student	20	"
R	Conway Katherine—†	212	maid	39	52 Brimmer
S	Gibson Emily R—†	212	housewife	72	here
T	MacHugo Marie—†	212	cook	56	"
U	McCormick Molly—†	212	maid	37	"
V	Pease Ella G S—†	214	retired	73	"
W	Quincy George G	214	merchant	70	"
X	Quincy Mary B—†	214	housewife	46	"
Y	Quincy Mary C S—†	214	"	90	"
Y¹	Hargadon Beatrice—†	216	maid	23	41 Chestnut
Z	Lally Mary A—†	216	"	37	33 "
B	Long Ellen—†	216	cook	60	here
C	MacAusland Andrew A	218	physician	38	"

19

Commonwealth Avenue—Continued

D	MacAusland Catherine B—†	218	housewife	38	here
E	Meaney Delia—†	218	maid	30	33 Chestnut
F	Quinn Mary—†	218	"	33	here
G	Raferty Annie—†	218	"	30	"
H	Walker Lula—†	218	nurse	30	"
K	Mullally Sarah—†	220	cook	68	"
L	Tarbell Annie T—†	220	housewife	68	"
M	Weigand Emma—†	220	maid	56	"
N	Guild Helen—†	222	none	49	"
O	Guild Mary—†	222	housekeeper	52	"
P	Guild Mary C—†	222	housewife	79	"
R	Halloran Norah—†	222	cook	32	"
S	McLellan Alexina—†	222	maid	24	Newton
T	Whittemore George C	222	retired	67	here
U	Paul Walter E	224	physician	60	104 Marlboro
V	Joyce Mary—†	226	maid	23	here
W	McDonald Mary—†	226	cook	40	130 Mass av
X	Rattrey Nellie—†	226	maid	28	here
Y	Swain Harriet F—†	226	housewife	55	"
Z	Swain Howard T	226	physician	55	"
A	Dion Bertha D—†	228	sculptress	23	482 Beacon
B	Dion Emma—†	228	housekeeper	58	482 "
C	Dion John L	228	retired	51	482 "
D	King Lena—†	228	nurse	26	234 Clarendo
E	Pullen Leon W	228	salesman	43	Quincy
F	Pullen Rose A—†	228	housewife	43	"
G	Russell Catherine—†	228	stenographer	23	Springfield
H	Boyden Charles	230	broker	44	here
K	Boyden Harriet H E—†	230	housewife	40	"
L	Murphy Bridget—†	230	cook	50	"
M	Reardon Margaret—†	230	laundress	32	Brookline
N	Schnell Ida—†	230	maid	30	here
O	Splaine Norah—†	230	"	30	"
P	Neilson Natalie—†	232	cook	42	Brookline
R	Ostman Nanna—†	232	maid	34	Sweden
S	Shea Caroline J—†	232	retired	69	here
T	Shea Francis	232	manufacturer	64	"
U	Shea Helen E—†	232	retired	67	"
V	Garritt Elizabeth M—†	234	"	57	"
W	Meanning Mary—†	234	maid	45	"
X	Tracey Norah—†	234	cook	45	"

Commonwealth Avenue—Continued

Letter.	FULL NAME.	Residence, April 1, 1924.	Occupation.	Supposed Age.	Reported Residence, April 1, 1923. Street and Number.
Y	Beckford Frances—†	236	clerk	44	271 Dartmouth
z	Doyle Henry L	236	merchant	52	here
A	Doyle Mabel C—†	236	housewife	50	"
B	Hoxie Bertha B—†	236		42	271 Dartmouth
C	Hoxie Edward E	236	architect	48	271 "
D	Miller Susan M—†	236	maid	56	Milton
E	Mitchell Margaret—†	238	"	21	9 Park Lane
F	Mitchell Mary—†	238	"	23	15 "
G	Washburn Alfred H	238	physician	27	New York
H	Allen Herbert S	240	lawyer	42	here
K	Allen Kathryn E—†	240	housewife	31	"
L	Allen Rollin H	240	real estate	71	"
M	Allen Ruth—†	240	artist	36	"
N	Allen Sarah B—†	240	housewife	65	"
O	Campbell Mary—†	240	maid	45	"
P	Rich Charles	240	butler	55	"

Dartmouth Street

Letter.	FULL NAME.	Residence, April 1, 1924.	Occupation.	Supposed Age.	Reported Residence, April 1, 1923. Street and Number.
T	Greene Joseph	271	fireman	28	here
V	Gardner Abby M—†	271	none	74	"
X	Osgood Frances M—†	271	"	50	"
C	Loring Margaret F—†	271	"	79	"
D	Loring Thacher	271	retired	79	"
G	Harlow Ella H—†	271	none	69	"
H	Harlow Jonathan E	271	retired	71	"
K	Burrage Harry L	271	broker	52	"
L	Burrage Mabel A—†	271	housewife	37	"
M	Arnold Allen	271	retired	65	"
N	Loring Marjorie—†	271	none	44	"
V	LaFranche Gertrude F—†	271	"	39	"
W	LaFranche Louis C	271	manager	42	"
X	Wells Emily W—†	271	none	70	"
Z	Smith Bertha E—†	271	"	49	"
A	Jones Frederick K M	271	agent	67	"
B	Jones Helen M—†	271	housewife	67	"
C	Ladd Ella C—†	271	none	68	"
D	Smith Daisey E—†	271	"	50	"
E	Frankenstein Lina H—†	271	"	44	"
N	Newcomb Hortense A—†	279	teacher	50	"

Page.	Letter.	FULL NAME	Residence, April 1, 1921.	Occupation.	Supposed Age.	Reported Residence April 1, 1923. Street and Number

Dartmouth Street—Continued

o	Cheney Robert C	279	physician	29	here
p	Morrison Mary L—†	279	saleswoman	52	"
r	Ruby Ann—†	279	retired	86	"
u	Kelly Frederick E	280	architect	40	Cambridge
v	Plaisted Olive E—†	280	stenographer	66	here
w	Moulton Carolyn—†	280	retired	62	"
z	Reid William J	282	manager	41	"
a	Thornton Rosalie—†	282	teacher	44	"
b	Thurman Eliza C—†	282	retired	46	"
c	Andren Thekla—†	282	social worker	48	"
e	Farnham Adele F—†	283	housewife	45	"
f	Farnham Louis S	283	watchman	50	"

Exeter Street

h	Cutkill Mary—†	25	maid	50	here
k	Groghan Katherine—†	25	"	31	"
l	Kelley Delia—†	25	"	35	"
m	Manyan Marion—†	25	"	40	"
n	McDonald Elizabeth—†	25	"	28	"
o	Tobin Joanna—†	25	"	50	"

Fairfield Street

s	Goldie Mary A—†	30	maid	30	here
t	Higgins Sarah—†	30	"	30	Brookline
u	McGillvary Agnes—†	30	"	28	52 Brimmer
v	McGurn Sarah—†	30	"	40	here
w	Rantoul Lucy—†	30	housewife	52	"
x	Rantoul Neal	30	banker	50	"
y	Thayer Charles I	32	retired	69	"
z	Thayer Florence A M—†	32	housewife	66	"
a	Thayer Marjorie—†	32	none	43	"
b	Aldrich Eleanor—†	34	housewife	46	"
c	Aldrich Talbot	34	broker	51	"
d	Berube Lena—†	34	maid	25	"
e	Nilson Emma—†	34	"	35	Brockton
f	Burt Fannie H—†	36	tel operator	51	223 Newbury
g	Clark Katherine L—†	36	clerk	45	223 "

Fairfield Street—Continued

H	Crosby Lydia A—†	36	bookkeeper	44	223 Newbury
K	Ensgtrom Karl G	36	salesman	25	223 "
L	Neibling Betty U—†	36	saleswoman	25	Newark N J
M	Pond Elsie M—†	36	printer	28	Natick
N	Ratthei Edward A	36	operator	43	223 Newbury
O	Ratthei Nellie L—†	36	saleswoman	43	223 "
P	Riddle Mary M—†	36	instructor	67	223 "
S	Burns Alfred A	40	engineer	36	here
T	Burns Frances S—†	40	housewife	30	"
U	Payne Bena—†	42	maid	24	13 Arnold
V	Walsh Catherine—†	42	retired	82	here
W	Walsh Catherine R—†	42	housewife	40	"
X	Walsh Joseph P	42	lawyer	46	"

Newbury Street

E	Fox Thomas A	4	architect	55	here
F	Morris Charles	6	janitor	50	"
H	Mason Gertrude E—†	8	manager	54	"
L	Baird Nelle R—†	10	retired	46	"
M	Crittenden Robert L	10	merchant	50	"
N	Randall Abel M	10	draughtsman	28	"
O	Randall Hazel—†	10	teacher	23	"
P	Randall Nellie H—†	10	housekeeper	50	"
R	Temple Rosabelle—†	10	teacher	50	"
S	Whitman Winslow	10	broker	50	"
T	Driscoll Elizabeth—†	11	housewife	35	50 Gainsboro
U	Driscoll Timothy	11	painter	36	50 "
V	Gibbs William R	11	importer	60	here
W	Marti John	11	caretaker	31	"
X	Orsett Roy	11	salesman	40	Belmont
Y	Wild Ralph M	11	student	28	Switzerland
A	Edrop Marion S—†	13	housewife	40	New York City
B	Edrop Percy T	13	clergyman	41	"
C	Stafford Sarah C—†	13	retired	78	"
D	Kelley Nellie—†	14	maid	38	here
E	Mitchell Maude L—†	14	housekeeper	45	"
G	Dudley Adalina—†	16	teacher	47	"
H	Post Abner	16	physician	70	"
K	Post Laura N—†	16	housewife	79	"

Page.	Letter.	FULL NAME.	Residence, April 1, 1924.	Occupation.	Supposed Age.	Reported Residence, April 1, 1923. Street and Number.

Newbury Street—Continued

	L	Nolan Cora M L—†	18	hairdresser	53	here
	M	Nolan Robert E	18	bookkeeper	22	"
	N	Thorndike Townsend W	20	physician	54	"
	O	Anderson Margaret—†	22	buyer	33	"
	P	Barnard Lizzie F S—†	22	none	69	"
	R	Charwater Emilie—†	22	stenographer	43	"
	S	Curley John	22	chauffeur	27	89 Auckland
	T	Ellis Harold	22	accountant	30	N Attleboro
	U	Nixon Philip J	22	floorwalker	55	here
	V	Eaton Alice—†	24	artist	80	"
	W	Eaton Martha—†	24	nurse	60	"
	X	Flanders Elizabeth—†	24	teacher	35	"
	Y	Gillespie Ida—†	24	milliner	45	"
	Z	Hill Harriett E—†	24	dressmaker	59	18 Newbury
	A	Hopkins James	24	agent	60	here
	B	Snow Thomas C	24	retired	61	"
	C	Gatley Margaret—†	26 & 28	housewife	56	"
	D	Gatley Thomas H	26 & 28	janitor	59	"
	F	Hanson Minnie—†	29	caretaker	55	"
	H	Donahue Delia E—†	31	teacher	50	"
	K	Foster Joseph	31	retired	62	Portsmouth
	L	Foster Josephine—†	31	housewife	50	"
	M	Greenleaf Ida E—†	31	retired	59	here
	N	Greenleaf Nellie L—†	31	"	62	"
	O	Leach Anna—†	31	"	58	New York
	P	Leach Edith—†	31	"	52	"
	U	McCarthy Mary J—†	31	housekeeper	58	here
	R	Moulton Elizabeth L—†	31	"	70	"
	S	Rogers Jeanne—†	31	housewife	43	39 Milford
	T	Rogers Richard S	31	real estate	54	39 "
	V	Strong Julia H—†	31	retired	68	127 Newbury
	X	Dube Anna—†	33	dressmaker	39	here
	Y	Hallett Florence I—†	33	painter	65	Cambridge
	Z	Rogers Anne E S—†	33	housewife	42	here
	A	Rogers Jacob C	33	real estate	49	"
	G	Hunt Ernest W	39	manager	45	140 Boylston
	H	Hunt Frances E—†	39	dressmaker	38	140 "
	K	Clifford Elizabeth—†	39	housekeeper	70	7 Newbury
	L	Devine James L	39	clerk	55	7 "
	M	Slightholm Clara R—†	39	housewife	39	Mexico
	N	Slightholm William	39	mechanic	45	"

Letter.	Full Name.	Residence, April 1, 1924.	Occupation.	Supposed Age.	Reported Residence, April 1, 1923. Street and Number.

Newbury Street—Continued

Letter.	Full Name.	Residence, April 1, 1924.	Occupation.	Supposed Age.	Reported Residence, April 1, 1923.
N	Buckingham Garland A	39	decorator	29	35 Hammond pl
O	McAuliffe Margaret—†	39	manicurist	25	196 Dartmouth
P	McAuliffe Molly—†	39	hairdresser	32	196 "
R	Gravel Della—†	41	maid	38	New York
B	Henshaw Joseph P B	77	insurance	68	here
C	Smith Sarah—†	77	maid	24	"
D	Goddard Mary L—†	79	retired	85	"
E	Sears Emma E—†	79	none	57	"
F	Sears Mary C—†	79	artist	59	"
G	Stone Frank	79	merchant	45	Maine
H	Stone Letha—†	79	housewife	35	"
L	Connelly Delia—†	81	cook	32	here
K	Costello Mary—†	81	maid	23	"
M	Cushing Sarah P—†	81	retired	74	"
O	Alien Clara W—†	85	"	74	139 Newbury
P	Ayer Constance—†	85	social worker	30	Chatham
R	Rudd Rosel P—†	85	artist	31	here
S	Seaton George W	85	clerk	36	"
T	Tavender Augusta S—†	85	teacher	40	"
U	Woodman Emerette R—†	85	housekeeper	54	"
W	Bailey Lydia A—†	93	"	54	638 Tremont
X	Bailey William R	93	engineer	65	638 "
Y	Carlson May—†	93	milliner	24	127 Newbury
Z	Lovering Anna—†	93	teacher	50	here
A	Raullett Alice—†	93	teacher	68	"
B	Burton Flora—†	95	social worker	45	"
C	MacDonald Harriett—†	95	clerk	45	12 Newbury
D	Munster Christine S—†	95	housewife	54	here
E	Munster George J	95	merchant	56	"
G	Lord Everett W	99	teacher	52	"
H	Lord Myrtle K—†	99	housewife	47	"
K	Lord Samuel L	99	student	21	"
N	Redpath Lide A—†	110	retired	73	"
O	White Mabel F—†	110	"	68	164 Newbury
P	Leach Mabel—†	111	student	43	here
R	Simmons William	111	"	40	"
S	Thayer Albert	111	artist	50	"
T	Thayer Mary—†	111	housewife	53	"
U	French Mary L—†	112	none	59	"
V	Jordan Helen C—†	112	teacher	25	"
W	Jordan Nellie R—†	112	none	53	"

Newbury Street—Continued

x	Lathe Mary M—†	112	none	74	49 Hunt'n av
y	McKee Millie W—†	112	"	57	here
z	Rand Mabel H—†	112	milliner	58	"
A	Cornish Ruth C—†	114	buyer	22	"
B	Maccalduff Dorothy C—†	114	none	22	"
C	Maccalduff Joseph	114	barber	48	"
D	Maccalduff Mary—†	114	housewife	47	"
E	Roll Jacob L	114	salesman	50	"
G	Kimball Caroline E—†	116	housekeeper	60	"
H	Remick Alexandria D—†	116	none	47	"
K	Remick Timothy	116	merchant	85	"
L	Collins John J	117	lawyer	61	"
M	Collins Lilla A—†	117	housewife	60	"
N	Collins Mary E—†	117	none	30	"
O	Cook Catherine E—†	117	maid	50	"
P	Ward Nora C—†	117	"	28	"
R	McDermott Agnes—†	118	domestic	22	"
S	McDermott Mary—†	118	"	33	"
T	McDermott Teresa—†	118	maid	25	"
U	Ross Sarah B C—†	118	retired	89	"
V	Coleran Ellan—†	119	cook	65	"
W	Gilies Effie—†	119	maid	21	Nova Scotia
X	Underwood Mabel W—†	119	none	58	here
Y	Underwood Mary R—†	119	"	56	"
Z	Underwood Sophia A—†	119	"	75	"
A	Cook Sarah P—†	120	teacher	45	"
B	Fobes Mildred M—†	120	"	41	"
C	Kimball Belle—†	120	none	60	"
D	Kneeland Mary—†	120	"	50	"
E	Lawrence Alice G—†	120	"	49	72 Sumner
F	Lawrence William H	120	professor	55	72 "
G	Perrons Jessie—†	120	none	50	here
H	Rivers Helen—†	120	"	60	"
K	Roberts Grace—†	120	"	55	"
L	Shipman Emma S—†	120	teacher	45	"
M	Stickney Marjorie—†	120	secretary	27	Wash'n D C
N	Williamson Manganetta—†	120	none	60	here
O	Adams Louise—†	121	"	51	1081 Beacon
P	Baker Lula—†	121	nurse	50	222 "
R	Davanzati Alfredo	121	decorator	35	Italy
S	Davanzati Enrichetta—†	121	housewife	30	"

Newbury Street—Continued

	Letter	Full Name	Residence	Occupation	Age	Reported Residence
	T	Gardner Alice—†	121	none	51	here
	U	Hackett Blanche—†	121	bookkeeper	46	"
	V	Haynes Gertrude—†	121	housekeeper	57	Manchester
	W	Haynes Guy N	121	starter	35	"
	X	Kimball Isabel—†	121	music teacher	60	297 Dartmouth
	Y	McCabe Edith M—†	121	nurse	35	here
	Z	Small Watters	121	retired	60	St John N B
	A	White Harriett—†	121	"	70	here
	B	Wikel Henry H	121	instructor	55	39 Brattle
	C	Budlong Edith—†	122	teacher	35	here
	D	Gookin Carie W—†	122	retired	71	"
	E	Gookin Kate R—†	122	"	69	"
	F	Kimball Elizabeth H—†	122	"	71	"
	G	Payne Katharine—†	122	housewife	68	"
	H	Wales Alice S—†	122	retired	51	10 Kenmore
	K	Morse Fannie D—†	123	"	75	here
	L	Neal Harriett A—†	123	teacher	60	"
	M	Cabot Elizabeth G—†	124	retired	50	"
	N	Catlin Helen M—†	124	manager	64	"
	O	Clapp Edith R—†	124	"	44	"
	P	Lewis Mary—†	124	nurse	50	"
	R	Ottendorff Blanche P—†	124	housewife	78	142 Beacon
	S	Ottendorff Eleanor P—†	124	teacher	28	142 "
	T	Ottendorff Emil P	124	artist	58	142 "
	U	Russell John R	124	clerk	83	here
	V	Shepard Sally S—†	124	retired	67	"
	W	Stuart Helen A—†	124	teacher	53	"
	X	Williamson Hildegard—†	124	retired	45	California
	Y	Beals Bertha T—†	125	housewife	55	here
	Z	Beals Edward M	125	merchant	56	"
	A	Beals Edward M, jr	125	student	22	"
	B	Beals Madeline T—†	125	none	23	"
	C	Meliotes George N	125	cook	26	Medfield
	D	Meliotes Margurite—†	125	housewife	26	"
	E	Bullard Mary S—†	126	teacher	50	here
	F	Chaswell Emma J—†	126	"	61	"
	G	Currier Matilda T—†	126	retired	58	Switzerland
	H	Hunt Harry R	126	trustee	57	here
	K	Hunt Mariah H—†	126	retired	83	"
	L	Reed Mary E—†	126	"	47	Allston
	M	Dorson William	127	manager	52	here

Page.	Letter.	FULL NAME.	Residence, April 1, 1924.	Occupation.	Supposed Age.	Reported Residence, April 1, 1923. Street and Number.

Newbury Street—Continued

N	Sands Arthur L	127	student	28	here
O	Sands Ella L—†	127	none	60	"
S	Goeil Blanche—†	128	secretary	30	"
T	Rice Nellie S—†	128	milliner	48	"
P	Smith Alice H—†	128	housewife	40	"
R	Smith Howard B	128	janitor	41	"
U	Delaney Mary—†	129	maid	61	"
V	Richards Francis H	129	trustee	55	"
W	Scannell Elizabeth—†	129	maid	68	"
X	Matheson Sarah M—†	130	housekeeper	60	"
Y	Williams Hubart J	130	physician	43	"
Z	Mills Ida T—†	131	real estate	52	553 Wash'n
A	Washburn Ada A—†	131	housewife	50	here
B	Washburn Leon W	131	retired	73	"
C	MacKenzie Elizabeth C—†	132	domestic	23	101 Chestnut
D	Martin Josephine L—†	132	"	61	Cambridge
E	Olaff Mary—†	132	"	63	86 Chandler
F	Smith Fitz Henry, jr	132	lawyer	50	here
G	Smith Marion E—†	132	housewife	45	"
L	Bensley Christien J—†	135	"	35	"
M	Bensley William	135	salesman	40	"
O	Crowell Harold	136	bookkeeper	27	Canaan N H
N	Ford Margaret E—†	136	housekeeper	70	here
P	Franklin Mitchell	136	student	22	Cambridge
R	Franklin Virginia W—†	136	"	22	"
S	Levine William	136	retired	70	22 Newbury
T	Mason Annie—†	136	domestic	48	here
U	Moody Elizabeth D—†	136	retired	75	"
V	Shuler-Shutz Henrietta—†	136	"	74	22 Newbury
W	Stebbins race E—†	136	"	55	Portland Me
X	Tolman Lydia H—†	136	"	69	here
Y	Bryne James	137	"	57	553 Wash'n
Z	Caukins John C	137	"	37	here
A	Chamberland Emiley—†	137	teacher	30	"
B	Harbough Annie L—†	137	housekeeper	58	"
C	Hardy Annie K—†	137	secretary	45	"
D	Kamp Bessie—†	137	bookkeeper	28	"
E	Pritchard John H	137	architect	35	73 Pinckney
F	Thorpe Durant	137	manager	60	12 Newbury
G	Thorpe Fannie—†	137	housewife	53	12 "
H	Nolte Julus	137	civil engineer	40	Brooklyn N Y

Newbury Street—Continued

	Letter	FULL NAME	Residence April 1, 1924	Occupation	Supposed Age	Reported Residence April 1, 1923
	K	Connolly Nellie—†	138	housekeeper	38	here
	L	Gilbert Isabelle E—†	138	none	67	"
	M	Gilchrist Leslie O—†	138	"	73	"
	N	Hill Irene T—†	138	"	60	"
	O	LaLauny Sing	138	laundryman	40	24 Terrace
	P	Lyon Carolyn—†	138	secretary	26	Brookline
	R	Vinton Annie P—†	138	retired	68	here
	S	Webber Elizabeth—†	138	clerk	24	Holyoke
	T	Allen Clara—†	139	retired	66	here
	U	Bird Charles G	139	auditor	71	"
	V	Bird Emma—†	139	housewife	54	"
	W	Churchill William	139	artist	60	"
	X	Fenton William T	139	retired	54	"
	Y	Rose Henry	139	architect	40	"
	Z	Sloan George	139	artist	56	"
	A	Smith Agnes—†	140	housekeeper	60	"
	B	Smith Helena A—†	140	housewife	30	"
	C	Smith Morrill A	140	retired	60	"
	E	Atwood Ida H—†	143	teacher	63	"
	F	Atwood Sophie—†	143	housekeeper	42	"
	G	Burdett James H	143	retired	60	"
	H	Miller Hans	143	cook	38	"
	N	O'Sullivan Anna—†	149	physician	40	"
	S	Hopper Susan T—†	149	housekeeper	75	"
	T	Hurley Catherine—†	149	housemaid	38	"
	U	Black Clifton D	150	manager	60	"
	V	Bradstreet Harry R	150	broker	55	"
	W	Brown William B	150	artist	40	"
	X	Cornell Lewis J	150	instructor	30	"
	Y	Finlay Francis L	150	"	30	"
	Z	Graves Albert S	150	manufacturer	44	"
	A	Ingraham Donald	150	"	35	"
	B	Peabody Charles R	150	broker	55	625 Com av
	C	Thayer Rodney	150	retired	35	here
	D	Vaughan Wanton	150	broker	55	"
	E	Lloyd Alfred A	153	agent	41	"
	F	Lloyd Alice L—†	153	housewife	40	"
	G	Lloyd Florence M—†	153	stenographer	20	"
	K	Carey Helena J—†	154	dressmaker	54	Brookline
	L	Clapp Clara J—†	154	retired	73	here
	M	Cronin Helen L—†	154	milliner	38	Brookline

Page.	Letter.	FULL NAME.	Residence, April 1, 1924.	Occupation.	Supposed Age.	Reported Residence, April 1, 1923. Street and Number.

Newbury Street—Continued

N	O'Brien Andrew T	154	farmer	51	Trinity pl
O	Coffin Mary L—†	154	teacher	55	here
P	Perron Eustis	155	student	27	"
S	Elms Mary H—†	156	housewife	51	"
T	Elms Roy	156	teller	41	"
U	Stone Frances H—†	156	retired	70	"
V	Eaton Bertha L—†	156	secretary	59	"
X	Kent Edward N	157	dentist	49	158 Newbury
Y	Kent Gertrude B—†	157	housekeeper	28	158 "
Z	Marshall Harry H	157	laboratory	45	here
B	MacEachern Emaline—†	158	none	42	100 Hunt'n av
C	Roberts Edna P—†	158	housewife	44	100 "
D	Roberts Frank E	158	physician	44	100 "
E	Chapin Mary E T—†	158	healer	51	here
F	Willard Amy A—†	158	social worker	34	"
G	Willard James L	158	broker	42	"
H	Willard Mary E R—†	158	none	69	"
K	Whittemore Charles A	158	lawyer	60	"
L	Whittemore Elinor—†	158	violinist	29	"
M	Whittemore Elsie—†	158	nurse	32	"
N	Whittemore Martha—†	158	musician	24	"
O	McLaughlin Mary A—†	159	dressmaker	67	"
P	O'Brien Catherine—†	159	"	50	"
R	Williams Arthur H	159	real estate	47	578 Newbury
S	Williams Laura B—†	159	housewife	46	578 "
W	Farman Mabel E—†	160	librarian	56	here
X	Perkins Mary A—†	160	teacher	55	"
Y	Hamilburg Ira	160	manufacturer	24	"
Z	Hamilburg Jennie—†	160	none	47	"
A	Hamilburg Joseph	160	waiter	22	"
B	Hamilburg Morris J	160	manufacturer	49	"
C	Wood Thomas W, jr	160	dentist	63	"
C¹	Oestmann Martha	160	dietitian	46	"
E	Denning Joan H—†	161	retired	41	"
F	Wead Frederick N	161	architect	41	"
G	Wead Kate H—†	161	housekeeper	66	"
H	Hayden Louise—†	161	retired	55	"
L	Pope Adelaide L—†	163	"	86	"
X	Pope Augusta C—†	163	"	78	"
M	Pope Emily F—†	163	"	78	"
O	Pope Luella F—†	163	artist	60	"

Newbury Street— Continued

P	Simmons Mary—†	163	cook	63	here
R	Brown Harry E	164	agent	49	"
S	Brown May—†	164	housewife	40	"
T	Frazer Matilda A—†	164	teacher	42	"
U	Quirk Mary M—†	164	housekeeper	50	"
V	Quirk Mathew	164	clerk	50	"
W	Rouillon Mary A—†	164	teacher	35	New York
X	Hayward George D	165	merchant	34	here
Y	Hayward Mabel S—†	165	housewife	63	"
Z	Hinds Laura I—†	165	waitress	49	"
A	McNaughton Annie—†	165	cook	62	"
B	McNaughton Mary E—†	165	maid	62	"
C	Brackett Elliot G	166	surgeon	63	"
D	Brackett Katherine P—†	166	retired	60	"
E	Johnson Ella F—†	167	housewife	77	"
F	Johnson Frederick	167	retired	43	Honolulu
G	Johnson Frederick W	167	physician	70	here
H	Knowlton Emma F—†	168	retired	70	"
K	Knowlton Jessie—†	168	secretary	40	"
L	Roberts Ethel M—†	168	"	30	"
M	Roberts Mertilla F—†	168	housekeeper	50	"
N	Rochford Grace E—†	168	physician	40	"
P	Brodeur Benjamin H	170	caretaker	50	"
R	Brodeur Margurite—†	170	"	45	"
T	Dorsey Mary—†	172	nurse	26	Braintree
V	Glennan Margret—†	172	cook	46	here
W	Hannon Kathleen—†	172	nurse	25	"
U	McDowell Annie—†	172	"	70	"
X	Payn-Sills Violet—†	172	"	38	Arlington
Y	North Abbie—†	173	housewife	55	here
Z	North Isaac	173	banker	60	"
A	Nowell Charlotte E—†	173	retired	65	496 Com av
B	Tuxbury Cora—†	173	"	62	496 "
C	Coleman Marion—†	173	"	45	here
D	Heath Allen	173	clerk	21	"
E	Heath Victor	173	merchant	50	4 Somerset
F	Sheppard Annie F—†	174	housekeeper	40	433 Col av
G	Sheppard Charles A	174	janitor	50	433 "
H	Van Schaick John	174	editor	50	Wash'n D C
K	Curtis Joseph H	175	architect	84	here
L	Jameson Caroline I—†	175	secretary	45	"

Newbury Street—Continued

M	Merrifield Albert	175	watchman	75	here
N	Merrifield Eila—†	175	housewife	65	"
O	Pratt Mary S—†	175	housekeeper	58	"
P	Stoddard Gertrude E—†	175	secretary	36	"
S	Barron John M	177	clerk	28	261 Newbury
T	Bennett Annie W—†	177	housewife	60	7 "
U	Bennett John A	177	judge	75	7 "
V	Croswell Emily L—†	177	social worker	54	7 "
W	Davis Harry R	177	clerk	25	Cambridge
X	Goodrich Amy E L—†	177	"	51	154 Newbury
Y	Goodrich Lucy H—†	177	housewife	76	154 "
Z	Goodwin Lucy—†	177	secretary	56	here
A	Grad Conrad W	177	clerk	23	261 Newbury
B	Kane Elizabeth H—†	177	housekeeper	55	here
C	Langerman Maurice	177	clerk	25	New York
D	Lyons William J	177	chemist	25	here
E	Parker Maud—†	177	nurse	35	"
F	Raymond Mary J—†	177	secretary	50	"
G	Sears Edward	177	retired	70	9 Newbury
H	Sears Isabella—†	177	housewife	65	9 "
K	Shenkman David	177	salesman	30	New York
L	Watson Charles B	177	clerk	32	261 Newbury
N	York Joseph	179	janitor	28	here
R	Bassett Gordon	205	clerk	33	"
S	Buker Clarence	205	salesman	45	207 Newbury
T	Caruthers Norman	205	clerk	25	England
U	Comiskey James	205	teacher	30	Hartford Ct
V	Foster Deane	205	student	21	here
W	Gleason Hall	205	clerk	60	Medford
X	Grant Helen—†	205	"	25	here
Y	Kellogg Robert	205	"	25	"
Z	Mears Mary—†	205	housekeeper	60	"
A	Stevens Gladys—†	205	agent	26	Cleveland O
B	Walsh Emily—†	205	milliner	48	here
C	Walsh Helen—†	205	"	50	"
H	Easton Elwood T	209	physician	48	"
K	Easton Merle L—†	209	student	21	"
L	Easton Millet D	209	"	21	"
M	Easton Sarah L—†	209	housewife	48	"
N	Mason Jane H—†	209	maid	45	"
O	Pearson Carrie I—†	209	attendant	64	Brookline

Newbury Street— Continued

P	Bridges Albert	210	janitor	40	here
R	Bridges Laura—†	210	housekeeper	35	"
S	George Charles T	211	utilityman	24	"
T	George Katherine—†	211	housekeeper	61	"
U	Beebe Herbert L	212	manager	59	"
V	Beebe Inez M—†	212	dressmaker	59	"
W	Chase Bella M—†	212	clerk	55	"
X	Gray Marjorie—†	212	secretary	42	"
Y	Gray Susan S—†	212	retired	75	"
Z	Jenkins Ina—†	212	clerk	55	139 Newbury
A	MacAusland Druscilla—†	212	housewife	56	here
B	MacAusland George	212	instruments	62	"
C	Phetteplace Jessie C—†	212	retired	69	Providence R I
D	Southerland Helen—†	212	clerk	50	230 Newbury
E	Swift Ellen H—†	212	music teacher	55	139 "
F	Whittemore Arbby C	212	treasurer	65	here
G	Cahill Michael F	213	manufacturer	60	"
H	Gallup Etta—†	213	clerk	48	"
K	Goddard Florence—†	213	secretary	40	"
L	Lahee Henry C	213	manager	60	Cambridge
M	Loy Launclot	213	banker	50	here
N	Macomber Frank M	213	merchant	52	"
O	Nicholson Ellen F—†	213	housekeeper	75	"
P	Roberts Daniel C	213	retired	56	"
R	Slater Robert	213	author	51	"
S	Smith Walter J	213	agent	50	"
T	Betz Andrew L	214	chemist	30	Philadelphia
U	Borglum Monica—†	214	student	20	Simmons College
V	Farrell Leroy	214	"	22	here
W	Hoyt Carter	214	clerk	24	"
X	Seaver Althea—†	214	dressmaker	38	"
Y	Seaver Walter E	214	manager	34	"
Z	Smith Spencer	214	salesman	24	Springfield
A	Sofio Josephine—†	214	secretary	20	New York
B	Villaret Gustave, jr	214	U S A	34	here
C	Rogers Emily—†	215	housewife	57	"
D	Rogers Frank C	215	teller	57	"
E	Caverly Esther—†	216	cashier	37	"
F	Davis Madiline—†	216	housekeeper	36	"
G	Devlin Edward	216	retired	73	"
H	Fox Mary A—†	216	milliner	40	207 Newbury

Newbury Street—Continued

K	Hughes Nora—†	216	hairdresser	35	here
L	Morrison Gertrude—†	216	secretary	28	"
M	Tucker Josephine—†	216	housekeeper	38	"
N	Wills Bessie—†	216	retired	60	194 Marlboro
O	Wills William E	216	"	70	194 "
P	Anderson Walter	217	machinist	22	301 Newbury
S	Cann Laurence M	217	salesman	30	14 Melville av
R	Hogle Raymond F	217	clerk	39	223 Newbury
T	Keegan Elizabeth—†	217	dressmaker	40	here
U	Murray Frank C	217	creditman	54	"
V	Murray William A	217	stockman	43	"
W	Pridmore Joseph W	217	broker	32	"
X	Smith Carl M	217	real estate	39	"
Y	Smith Ella B—†	217	housewife	40	"
Z	Sturtevant Edwin W	217	clerk	32	223 Newbury
A	Swasey Raymond B	217	"	32	here
B	Wagner Herman	217	"	24	301 Newbury
C	Barney Hana—†	218	stenographer	55	here
D	Beaufort Evelyn—†	218	student	30	Minnesota
E	Chamberlain Elsie—†	218	instructor	42	here
F	Chamberlain Henry M	218	salesman	50	"
G	Crossen Florence—†	218	student	35	Ohio
H	Files Minnie A—†	218	nurse	65	Copley Sq Hotel
K	Hallett Harriet—†	218	artist	67	California
L	Lathrop Marion—†	218	musician	70	here
M	Manning Mary A—†	218	housekeeper	50	"
N	Ripley Grace—†	218	dressmaker	40	Brookline
O	Smith Sarah R—†	218	artist	45	Leominster
P	Usher Hanah—†	218	teacher	45	Ludlow Hotel
R	Wampler Esther—†	218	student	30	Connecticut
S	Courtenay Thomas	219	school teacher	40	164 St Botolph
T	George Paul	219	chauffeur	29	here
U	Houghton Victria—†	219	housewife	37	234 Clarendon
U¹	Houghton William	219	bookkeeper	30	234 "
V	Otis Elizabeth W—†	219	"	60	211 Newbury
W	Otis Joseph C	219	retired	59	211 "
X	Pope Agnes M—†	219	secretary	24	New York
Y	Pope Marion B—†	219	housewife	58	Hotel Brunswick
Z	Shaw Clara—†	219	nurse	35	here
A	Coyle Katherine—†	220	cook	35	"
B	Foss Granville	220	maufacturer	56	"

Letter.	FULL NAME.	Residence, April 1, 1924.	Occupation.	Supposed Age.	Reported Residence, April 1, 1923. Street and Number.

Newbury Street— Continued

Letter.	FULL NAME.	Residence, April 1, 1924.	Occupation.	Supposed Age.	Reported Residence, April 1, 1923. Street and Number.
C	Foss Hattie C—†	220	retired	53	here
D	Hay Agnes—†	220	maid	25	"
E	Simonds Caroline A—†	220	retired	91	"
F	Wilde Alice—†	220	maid	42	"
G	Flint George H	221	salesman	60	"
H	Flint Mary—†	221	dressmaker	60	"
K	Hanson Frank D	221	retired	54	"
L	Hanson Harriet H—†	221	housewife	78	"
M	Hanson Lida H—†	221	"	49	"
N	Lord Myrtle—†	221	saleswoman	45	"
O	Lord Samuel H	221	purser	51	"
P	MacGregor Eva M—†	221	dressmaker	40	"
R	MacGregor Robert	221	carpenter	50	"
S	Fitts Gertrude V—†	222	dietitian	27	Quincy
T	Holland Beatrice—†	222	nurse	26	Newton
U	Lally Margurite—†	222	"	33	Waltham
V	Moor Helen—†	222	"	29	here
W	Wadlin Mabel—†	222	"	31	"
X	Carlin Nellie—†	223	bookkeeper	28	Somerville
Y	Cutting Lavia—†	223	"	26	97 Norfolk
Z	Kunepher Charles A	223	weaver	53	258 Newbury
A	Kunepher Hattie—†	223	housewife	50	258 "
B	Robinson Emma—†	223	dressmaker	62	258 "
C	Arkin Dianna—†	224	waitress	35	here
D	Arkin Eva—†	224	"	30	"
E	Bryant Horace	224	salesman	35	Somerville
F	Cobb Frederick L	224	"	50	Vermont
G	DeGooch Arthur W	224	lawyer	50	here
H	McLellan Douglas	224	merchant	26	466 Com av
K	Standish Florence—†	224	cook	45	here
L	Standish Fred A	224	"	56	"
M	Woodberry Lois—†	224	baker	35	"
N	Call Mary A—†	225	nurse	42	Brookline
O	Berard Chauncey A	225	manager	29	here
P	Farnham Henry P	225	merchant	41	36 Fairfield
R	Hinchliffe Edith—†	225	nurse	36	Brookline
S	O'Neil Harry B	225	salesman	27	here
T	Powers James J	225	accountant	27	"
U	Preston Sarah A—†	225	housewife	62	"
V	Price Devorah C—†	225	bookkeeper	36	"
W	Small Fred E	225	clerk	48	36 Fairfield

Newbury Street—Continued

x	Thomas Elizabith A—†	225	retired	45	here
y	Ulrich Ervin J	225	draughtsman	29	Chicago Ill
z	Yates Emily—†	225	housewife	62	36 Fairfield
a	Yates Reuben	225	jeweler	65	36 "
b	Doherty Mathew F	226	clerk	27	Lynn
c	Gates George B	226	foreman	60	Providence R I
d	LeGruner Jeanne—†	226	teacher	42	"
e	McDougall Grover C	226	janitor	28	Canada
f	McDougall Mary E—†	226	domestic	60	"
g	Sullivan James A	226	retired	65	here
h	Sullivan Josephine G—†	226	none	50	"
k	Sullivan Mary F—†	226	"	60	"
l	Wilczek Harold V	226	importer	55	51 Exeter
m	Bowman Doreen W—†	227	housewife	25	349 Newbury
n	Bowman Edward F	227	physician	27	282 "
o	Dunham Steward P	227	salesman	23	282 "
p	Howley Mary—†	227	domestic	37	282 "
r	Howley Ulysies	227	waiter	37	282 "
s	Bunce Alice—†	228	student	32	Newton
t	Cotton Iona—†	228	"	38	Michigan
u	Kibby Alice—†	228	stenographer	35	here
v	Myers Charles W	228	chairmaker	50	Nova Scotia
w	Myers Ethel—†	228	housekeeper	40	"
x	Abbott Alice—†	229	housewife	60	Needham
y	Abbott Arthur	229	retired	65	"
z	Ash Margery—†	229	bookkeeper	24	136 Hunt'n av
a	Childs Eva—†	229	accountant	53	here
b	Cottle Emma—†	229	housekeeper	54	"
c	Dunn Louise—†	229	teacher	26	"
d	Garland William	229	electrician	25	33 Breed
e	Millman Donald	229	clerk	28	22 Dor av
f	Ralston Monte—†	229	nurse	30	here
g	Beale Olive E—†	230	housewife	47	"
h	Beale Wilber F	230	broker	56	"
k	Daggett Herbert F	230	manufacturer	56	"
l	Fogarty Catherine M—†	230	nurse	40	"
m	Gwinnell Elizabeth—†	230	clerk	35	"
p	Nixson Dorothy—†	230	"	43	"
n	Penney Mildred—†	230	"	40	"
o	Sugrue Agnes M—†	230	nurse	45	"
r	Whitnall Jesse	230	clerk	41	"

Letter.	Full Name.	Residence, April 1, 1924.	Occupation.	Supposed Age.	Reported Residence, April 1, 1923. Street and Number.

Newbury Street—Continued

s	Bowman Caroline E—†	231	housewife	33	160 Strathmore rd
t	Bowman Wordsworth W	231	salesman	33	160 "
v	Castro Gerome	232	butler	23	New York
w	Romano Sesson	232	cook	24	"
x	Sternes Harold	232	architect	30	"
y	Sternes Leonie—†	232	artist	28	"
u	Albert Florence B—†	234	clerk	23	here
z	Clukey Love P—†	234	hairdresser	44	"
a	Cragie Charles A	234	bookmaker	72	"
b	Cragie Helen B—†	234	stenographer	26	"
c	Dowd Charles E	234	student	22	Fall River
d	Fairbanks Ella—†	234	artist	70	here
e	Glefield Charlotte G—†	234	teacher	26	Maine
f	McLean Mary E—†	234	student	24	Pennsylvania
g	Norton Ethel—†	234	bookkeeper	30	here
h	O'Brien Edward D	234	electrician	49	Bangor Me
k	O'Brien Lizzie S—†	234	housewife	50	"
l	Secor Helen P—†	234	nurse	30	here
m	Silk John L	234	draughtsman	30	Pittsfield
n	Wadwell Ethal—†	234	nurse	28	here
o	Wilson Cora L—†	234	clerk	28	Deerfield N H
p	Cole Grant	236	manager	26	here
r	Corbin Donald C	236	merchant	26	New York
s	Downey John J	236	engineer	27	Maine
t	Kolt Oscar C	236	draughtsman	29	here
u	Reynolds Flora C—†	236	housewife	58	"
v	Reynolds Wilbur A	236	dentist	64	"
w	Wikson Leon W	236	papermaker	33	Lisbon N H
x	Cann Annie L—†	238	manager	58	here
y	Hamley Florence M—†	238	bookkeeper	35	"
z	Hidden Julia A—†	238	teacher	53	"
a	Monahan Annie A—†	238	caretaker	44	Malden
b	Monahan Dennis T	238	"	42	"
c	Pike Carrie E—†	238	bookkeeper	63	here
d	Procter Abbie C—†	238	nurse	71	"
e	Simons Charlotte M—†	238	"	35	198 Dartmouth
f	Smith May W—†	238	teacher	57	here
g	Wilber Lizzie A—†	238	nurse	66	"
h	Wildes Blanche—†	238	"	43	198 Dartmouth
k	Eldridge Theresa—†	240	maid	55	here
l	MacAusland Millicent—†	240	retired	67	"
m	MacAusland William	240	"	69	"

Ward 8—Precinct 9

CITY OF BOSTON.

LIST OF RESIDENTS
20 YEARS OF AGE AND OVER

(FEMALES INDICATED BY DAGGER)

AS OF

APRIL 1, 1924

HERBERT A. WILSON, } Listing
JAMES F. EAGAN, } Board.

CITY OF BOSTON—PRINTING DEPARTMENT

Beacon Street

A	Barron Clarence W	334	editor	68	here
B	Blake William	334	choreman	61	"
C	Conville Anna—†	334	maid	32	"
D	Donovan Catherine—†	334	"	29	"
E	Gately Ellen—†	334	laundress	60	"
F	Harper Josephine—†	334	cook	55	"
G	Nichobburg Lars	334	nurse	32	"
H	O'Brien Raymond	334	secretary	25	"
K	Swanson Hilda—†	334	maid	36	"
L	Swenson Anna—†	334	waitress	57	"
M	Chesboro Edith—†	336	none	20	"
N	Coughlan Minnie—†	336	maid	35	"
O	Devine Barbara—†	336	"	30	"
P	Devine Mary—†	336	"	35	Ireland
R	Sleeper Elsie C—†	336	none	40	here
S	Sleeper Stephen W	336	broker	45	"
T	Ferguson Sadie—†	338	maid	35	227 Com av
U	Johnson Signe—†	338	"	28	here
V	Keyes Emily E —†	338	none	50	"
W	Keyes George T	338	manufacturer	55	"
X	McKay Hannah —†	338	maid	45	"
Y	Creighton Albert M	340	manufacturer	40	"
Z	Creighton Margaret—†	340	none	38	"
A	Gorman Catherine—†	340	maid	35	Lynn
B	Hoban Catherine—†	340	"	30	here
C	Holmes George	340	butler	36	46 Beacon
D	Rubury Delia—†	340	nurse	45	here
E	Skeffington Mary—†	340	cook	45	"
F	Gardner Dorothy D—†	342	none	32	"
G	Johnson Ida C—†	342	maid	36	"
H	Neilson Louise—†	342	"	50	"
K	Nelson Ingred—†	342	cook	49	"
L	Thompson Catherine —†	342	nurse	45	"
M	Barbour Edmund D	344	retired	83	"
N	Ray Sarah E—†	344	housekeeper	50	"
P	Converse Costello C	348	retired	74	"
R	Converse Mary I—†	348	cook	60	"
S	Eiseman Luderick	350	merchant	61	"
T	Palen Katherine—†	350	housekeeper	31	"
U	Duffily Anne—†	351	"	45	"

2

Beacon Street—Continued

v	Linnehan Mary—†	351	domestic	50	here
w	Straton Anne W—†	351	retired	65	"
x	Anderson Augusta—†	352	domestic	40	"
y	Bancroft Hugh	352	publisher	44	"
z	Bancroft Jane—†	352	housewife	40	"
a	McLaughlin Helen †	352	domestic	32	"
b	Sheehan Mary—†	352	"	28	Somerville
c	Wenham Mary—†	352	nurse	38	here
d	Foote Mary E—†	353	retired	80	"
e	Shanahan Helen—†	354	housekeeper	45	"
f	Vaughan Ellen—†	354	housewife	70	"
g	Vaughan William W	354	lawyer	75	"
h	Bangs Edith—†	355	none	56	"
k	McCauley Mary E—†	356	nurse	21	Canada
l	MacEcachein Jessie—†	356	domestic	28	"
m	MacGough Margaret—†	356	"	20	here
n	Reggio Marion S—†	356	housewife	34	"
o	Reggio William A	356	physician	36	"
p	Rardy Mary—†	357	domestic	33	"
r	Stephenson Robert H	357	broker	86	"
s	Sullivan Julia—†	357	domestic	50	"
t	Stone Clara O—†	359	retired	70	"
u	Beal Ida G—†	361	"	68	"
v	Connell Nora—†	361	domestic	28	"
w	McPartland Mary—†	361	"	39	"
x	Murphy Margaret—†	361	"	35	Somerville
y	O'Connell Mary—†	361	"	33	Haverhill
z	Hills Edward A	363	president	81	here
a	Kane Catherine—†	363	domestic	35	"
b	Riorden Anne—†	363	"	27	"
c	Stephens Julie—†	365	retired	60	"
d	Devens Arthur L	367	banker	43	"
e	Devens Wenonah—†	367	housewife	40	"
g	Brown Katherine—†	371	domestic	22	Newton
h	Harding William P	371	manager	56	400 Com av
k	Kane Nora A—†	371	domestic	27	Cambridge
l	Kelly Nora—†	371	"	34	Ireland
m	DeCosta Elizabeth—†	375	"	40	Cambridge
n	Gray Edward L	375	student	24	here
o	Gray Geraldine—†	375	retired	45	"
p	O'Donnell Rose—†	375	domestic	40	283 Beacon

Beacon Street—Continued

R	Temple Margurite—†	377	housewife	32	here
S	Temple William F	377	physician	72	"
T	Temple William F, jr	377	"	35	"
U	Courtney Nellie F—†	379	domestic	23	"
V	Kane Mary—†	379	"	24	Brookline
W	Leahy Mary A—†	379	"	33	here
X	O'Neil Adela P—†	379	housewife	50	"
Y	O'Neil Richard F	379	physician	50	"
Z	O'Neil Richard F, jr	379	student	20	"
A	Smith William H	379	physician	52	"
B	Otis Edward O	381	"	75	"
C	Otis Edward O, jr	381	mechanic	24	"
D	Otis John F	381	clerk	25	"
E	Coakley Anne—†	383	domestic	65	"
F	Green Delhia C—†	383	"	44	"
G	Jackson Charles L	383	retired	76	"
H	Mulligan Catherine—†	383	domestic	38	"
K	Gay Ellen F—†	385	none	56	"
L	Sheridan Annie T—†	385	domestic	42	"
M	Sullivan Annie—†	385	"	46	"
N	Hennessey Unis T—†	386	housekeeper	35	Canada
O	Inches Charles E	386	broker	38	here
P	Inches Margaret—†	386	housewife	35	"
R	Holton Eleanor P—†	387	"	48	"
S	Holton Henry H	387	broker	48	"
T	McSweeney Margaret—†	387	domestic	34	"
U	O'Neil Catherine—†	387	"	28	"
V	Bowditch Margaret—†	388	teacher	31	"
W	McKinnon Jennie—†	388	nurse	30	"
X	Pearmain Alice—†	388	housewife	60	"
Y	Pearmain Sumner B	388	broker	60	"
Z	Bartlett Elizabeth M—†	389	domestic	32	"
A	Goodhue Gertrude—†	389	housewife	32	"
B	Goodhue Lawrence C	389	lawyer	32	"
C	McLellan Lillian—†	389	domestic	28	"
D	Goodwin Fredrick H	390	lawyer	51	Dover
E	Goodwin Julia—†	390	housewife	40	"
F	Laker Winifred—†	390	maid	27	Cambridge
G	Murphy Nora—†	390	domestic	25	Maine
H	Riorden Mary—†	390	"	28	Ireland
K	Campbell Ethel G—†	391	housewife	30	here

Beacon Street—Continued

L	Campbell Robert J	391	janitor	36	here
M	Evans Jennie—†	391	none	56	"
N	Vermyne Emma—†	391	retired	74	"
O	Collins Mary C—†	391	none	52	Cambridge
R	Chickering Anne R—†	392	housewife	62	here
S	Chickering John J	392	retired	70	"
T	Stackpole Alice—†	393	"	57	"
W	Stackpole Bessie—†	395	housekeeper	65	"
X	Stackpole Grace—†	395	student	25	"
Y	Brown Davenport	396	broker	44	"
Z	Brown Maria M—†	396	housewife	44	"
A	Heavy Catherine T—†	396	housekeeper	27	"
B	Shuman Edward A	397	banker	45	"
C	Shuman Mary K—†	397	housewife	40	"
D	Parson Charlotte—†	398	retired	70	"
E	Parson Lucy—†	398	"	66	"
F	Dexter Rose L—†	400	none	60	"
G	Smith Josephine—†	400	housekeeper	45	Concord
H	Nutman Doris E—†	401	student	21	here
K	Nutman Ernest E	401	carpenter	57	"
L	Nutman Elizabeth E—†	401	housewife	56	"
M	Nutman Harris E	401	dentist	24	"
N	Binney Harriet C—†	403	housewife	38	"
O	Binney Horace	403	physician	48	"
P	McAlleer Mary E—†	405	retired	57	"
S	Stone Phillip	407	"	51	"
T	Gordon William	408	salesman	35	"
U	Dexter Mary—†	409	housewife	40	"
V	Dexter William E	409	retired	47	"
W	DesMarais Joseph D	410	hairdresser	62	"
X	DesMarais Marie—†	410	housewife	53	"
Y	Falvey Charles A	411	broker	45	"
Z	Falvey Margaret—†	411	housewife	35	"
A	Dowse Fanny—†	412	none	65	"
B	Dowse Margaret—†	412	housewife	65	"
C	Dowse William B	412	lawyer	72	"
D	Minot Francis	413	architect	32	Falmouth
E	Minot Isabel—†	413	housewife	37	"
F	Blake Mabel B—†	414	"	62	here
G	Blake William O	414	retired	65	"
H	Word Anita S—†	415	none	61	"

Beacon Street— Continued

K	Word Caroline E—†	415	retired	67	here
L	Word Marion P—†	415	none	58	"
O	Boudenie Carmen—†	416	governess	22	"
M	Bremer John L	416	professor	45	"
N	Bremer Mary C—†	416	housewife	35	"
P	Doherty Annie—†	416	domestic	28	"
R	Doherty Bridget—†	416	"	25	"
S	McGeough Mary—†	416	"	40	"
T	Quigley Catherine—†	416	"	40	"
U	Andersen Minnie—†	417	waitress	50	"
V	Landfors Anna—†	417	maid	55	"
W	Ness Ingarbord—†	417	cook	45	"
X	Storrow Helen—†	417	housewife	60	"
Y	Storrow James J	417	banker	60	"
Z	Casserly Sarah—†	418	domestic	29	Cohasset
A	Dorsey Julia—†	418	"	30	here
B	Endicott Katharine—†	418	none	41	"
C	Endicott Louisa C—†	418	housewife	69	"
D	Endicott Samuel C	418	teacher	44	"
E	McKay Bessie—†	418	cook	55	"
F	Roddy Nellie—†	418	domestic	25	"
G	Ryan Margaret—†	418	"	30	"
H	Seifert Lena—†	418	laundress	60	"
K	Kelley Elizabeth—†	419	maid	26	"
L	O'Sullivan Catherine—†	419	cook	36	"
M	Sherburne Charles H	419	manager	50	"
N	Sherburne Josephine—†	419	housewife	54	"
O	Ahern Nora—†	420	domestic	28	30 W Cedar
P	Berg Annie—†	420	"	40	here
R	Ferguson Mary M—†	420	"	40	"
S	McLeod Margaret J—†	420	"	45	"
T	McLeod Margaret M—†	420	"	39	"
U	Metie Elizabeth—†	420	"	25	"
V	Peterson Marie—†	420	"	30	Cambridge
W	Slip Amber—†	420	governess	40	here
X	Wolbach Anna W—†	420	housewife	40	"
Y	Wolbach Simeon B	420	professor	41	"
Z	Worthington William H	420	broker	24	"
A	McCarthy Catherine—†	421	cook	40	"
B	McDonald Catherine—†	421	maid	27	"
C	McMichael Louise—†	421	retired	50	"

Beacon Street—Continued

Letter	Full Name	Residence	Occupation	Age	Reported Residence
D	Scott Isabel—†	421	waitress	24	Sudbury
E	Carlson Estred—†	422	domestic	22	here
F	Jones Leo	422	footman	26	172 Hyde Park av
G	Leland Frances E—†	422	housewife	58	here
H	Leland Lester	422	merchant	58	"
K	Murphy Kate—†	422	maid	50	"
L	Pascoe Richard H	422	butler	41	"
M	Peterson Emma—†	422	domestic	35	"
N	Thornkelson Charlotte—†	422	"	50	"
O	Healy Nora—†	423	cook	29	"
P	Kelliher Margaret—†	423	waitress	30	"
R	Ladd Eugene F	423	retired	62	"
S	Ladd Violet P—†	423	housewife	54	"
T	Lynch Mary—†	423	maid	32	"
U	MacMillan Elizabeth—†	424	domestic	75	"
V	Morgan Mary—†	424	cook	30	"
W	Nilan Elizabeth—†	424	waitress	56	"
X	Williams Alice B—†	424	housewife	85	"
Y	Barrell Charles C	425	physician	54	"
A	Murray Rose—†	425	waitress	35	"
A¹	O'Donahue Nora—†	425	maid	32	"
B	Ronayne Mary—†	425	cook	60	"
C	Fitzgerald Mary—†	426	domestic	45	"
D	Leonard Maria—†	426	"	40	"
E	Mullens Delia F—†	426	"	40	"
F	Sears George G	426	physician	64	"
G	Sears Ruth W—†	426	housewife	48	"
H	Goulding Eugenie M—†	427	"	38	"
K	Goulding Timothy	427	physician	51	"
L	Patingill Craig L	427	accountant	31	"
M	Sawyer Donald	427	clerk	25	"
N	Barnes Caroline L—†	429	housekeeper	57	"
O	Barnes Marie L—†	429	"	41	"
P	Duffy Mary—†	431	cook	42	Manchester N H
R	Morgan Nellie—†	431	maid	37	"
S	Rice Arthur N	431	lawyer	45	here
T	Rice Cora L—†	431	housekeeper	74	"
U	Dobbins Robert	435	optometrist	74	338 Com av
V	Dobbins Robert, jr	435	real estate	39	338 "
W	Curtis Louis	441	banker	33	447 Beacon
X	Curtis Mary—†	441	housewife	26	447 "

Beacon Street—Continued

Y	Glinn Dellia—†	441	nurse	27	France
Z	Macloud Enna—†	441	maid	20	Brookline
A	Macloud Sadie—†	441	"	26	90 Fenway
B	McPhee Catherine—†	441	cook	50	Canada
C	Newell Franklin S	443	physician	52	here
D	Pascoe Gwenn—†	443	maid	22	"
E	Pascoe Philadelphia F—†	443	housekeeper	44	"
F	Pascoe William S	443	watchman	40	"
G	Hardy Alphias—†	445	housekeeper	82	"
H	Hardy Mary C—†	445	artist	45	"
K	Holt Emma—†	445	waitress	40	"
L	Spencer Bridget—†	445	cook	43	"
M	Toner Susan—†	445	maid	50	"
N	Brown Frances—†	447	cook	64	Hingham
O	Ilfeld Lawrence	447	merchant	34	Brookline
P	Ilfeld Margaret—†	447	housewife	27	"
R	McKiernan Alice—†	447	waitress	23	"
S	O'Connor Marie—†	447	laundress	38	407 Beacon
T	Bliss John W	448	salesman	35	Vermont
U	Clarke Frederic C	448	"	25	here
V	Daniels Louis	448	"	45	"
W	Derrick Charles F	448	postal clerk	55	"
X	Dillon John S	448	dentist	40	"
Y	Dillon William	448	accountant	55	"
Z	Eldridge Ralph K	448	superintendent	33	834 Com av
A	Hodgdon Alvy E	448	physician	38	490 Beacon
B	Horn Henry J	448	importer	30	Winchester
C	Main Harry	448	manager	40	here
D	Mann Frederick	448	publisher	65	"
E	Mathey Nicholas W	448	manufacturer	50	Lynn
F	Meggett John M	448	salesman	55	Newton
G	Oben Floyd C	448	"	30	Vermont
H	Roberts Henry E	448	importer	55	Winchester
K	Spiller Harry C	448	banker	50	here
L	Sprague Rufus W	448	physician	75	"
M	Wheeler William H	448	importer	42	"
N	Wiersum Clarance G	448	manufacturer	32	Michigan
O	Briggs Ada L—†	449	housewife	66	here
P	Briggs Fredrick H	449	manufacturer	58	"
R	Bell Marion—†	450	none	40	"
S	Brown Amy—†	450	domestic	35	"

Beacon Street—Continued

Letter.	Full Name.	Residence	Occupation.	Age	Reported Residence
T	Donovan Hanna—†	450	domestic	45	here
U	Fenno Edward N	450	banker	70	"
V	Fenno Edward N, jr	450	"	45	"
W	Fenno Henry B	450	"	50	"
X	Fenno Nellie—†	450	housewife	70	"
Y	Logan Bridget—†	450	domestic	20	Ireland
Z	McGeary Bessie—†	450	"	69	here
A	McGorty Sarah—†	450	"	34	"
B	O'Brien Hanna—†	450	"	43	"
C	Rice Margaret—†	450	"	34	"
D	Bowles Helen—†	451	housekeeper	24	Germany
E	Devlin Bridie—†	451	maid	22	Ireland
F	McKenner Christine—†	451	cook	32	here
G	Stewart Cecile	451	retired	60	"
H	Burke Mary—†	452	domestic	50	Brookline
K	MacKinnon Maud—†	452	"	26	"
L	McCarthy Mary—†	452	"	43	Somerville
M	Sullivan Mary—†	452	cook	45	371 Beacon
N	Thayer Alice W—†	452	housewife	53	535 "
O	Thayer Frank H	452	manufacturer	60	535 "
P	Ladd Mary H—†	453	retired	71	here
R	Riley Mary—†	453	waitress	28	100 Mt Vernon
S	Sawyer Emely L—†	453	housekeeper	66	here
T	Carlson Ebba—†	454	domestic	29	N Cambridge
U	Larson Tekla—†	454	"	31	here
U¹	Nickerson Nellie R—†	454	housewife	67	"
V	Nickerson William E	454	manufacturer	69	"
X	Gill Elizabeth—†	456	domestic	60	"
Y	Kerney Mary—†	456	"	40	"
Z	Matthews Amory S	456	musician	34	"
A	Matthews Ellen B—†	456	housewife	68	"
B	Matthews Nathan	456	lawyer	70	"
C	Taylor Anna—†	456	domestic	21	Maine
D	Workman Marion—†	456	"	35	34 Gray
E	Byers Barbara—†	457	maid	56	here
F	Byers Isabel—†	457	"	38	"
G	Emerson Sarah—†	457	retired	50	Watertown
H	Farwell John W	457	broker	81	here
K	Summers Mary—†	457	cook	50	7 Mt Vernon pl
L	Leary Julia—†	458	domestic	45	Cambridge
M	McKenney Mary—†	458	"	65	Waltham

Beacon Street - Continued

	N	McKeon Rose—†	458	domestic	38	233 Beacon
	O	Myles Hilda—†	458	"	45	here
	P	Prince Fannie L—†	458	housewife	65	"
	R	Prince Morton	458	physician	70	"
	S	Witberg Aagot—†	458	domestic	42	"
	U	Blocker Elsie—†	460	"	42	Michigan
	V	Davenport Camelia—†	460	housewife	60	here
	W	Davenport George H	460	retired	72	"
	X	Kiley Mary—†	460	domestic	39	"
	Y	Leonard Martha—†	460	"	35	Hamilton
	Z	McKay Elizabeth—†	460	"	50	Andover
	B	Hourihan Katherine—†	462	"	49	here
	C	Jackson Charles C	462	retired	80	"
	D	Jackson Frances—†	462	housewife	75	"
	E	Quigley Elizabeth—†	462	domestic	49	"
	F	Sheehan Helena—†	462	"	30	"
	G	Sheehan Julia—†	462	"	28	"
	K	Curtis Fanny L—†	464	housewife	58	"
	L	Curtis Lawrence	464	lawyer	30	"
	M	Curtis Louis	464	banker	75	"
	N	Feeney Nora—†	464	domestic	25	Cambridge
	O	Fitzgerald Margaret—†	464	seamstress	55	39 Gray
	P	Johnson Josephine—†	464	laundress	60	110 Col av
	R	Laughlin Bridget—†	464	cook	60	here
	S	McAvoy Annie—†	464	domestic	42	148 Terrace
	T	O'Brien Fred W	465	physician	42	here
	U	Parker George S	467	manufacturer	56	"
	V	Parker Grace M—†	467	housewife	46	"
	X	Jacques William W	469	physician	68	France
	Y	Johnston Fannie G—†	469	secretary	35	"
	Z	Knight Alice—†	469	maid	30	Brookline
	A	Oakley May—†	469	cook	30	"
	B	Lawrence Harris H	470	broker	45	here
	C	Lawrence Theodora E—†	470	housewife	39	"
	D	Quigley Katherine—†	470	domestic	45	132 Marlboro
	E	Quigley Mary—†	470	"	42	132 "
	F	Donovan Annie—†	471	maid	39	here
	G	Jones Caroline M—†	471	housekeeper	80	"
	H	Mahoney Mary—†	471	maid	50	"
	K	O'Donnell Bridget—†	471	"	35	"
	L	Carty Beatrice—†	472	domestic	34	"

Beacon Street — Continued

Letter.	FULL NAME.	Residence, April 1, 1924.	Occupation.	Supposed Age.	Reported Residence, April 1, 1923. Street and Number.
M	Hall Ellen N—†	472	none	56	here
N	Hall Harry S	472	retired	65	"
O	Hall Henry S, jr	472	banker	28	"
P	Hall Lydia L—†	472	housewife	24	"
R	McKervey Jennie—†	472	domestic	38	"
S	O'Donoghue Mary—†	472	"	48	"
T	Eastman Ruth—†	473	stenographer	20	Arlington
U	Smith John H	473	physician	55	Cambridge
V	Abbott Elizabeth G—†	474	nurse	60	here
W	Hart Francis R	474	banker	56	"
X	Hart Francis R, jr	474	student	22	"
Y	Hart Gwendolyn—†	474	retired	24	"
Z	Hart Helen B—†	474	housewife	56	"
A	Hobbey Louise W—†	474	none	51	"
B	Maxwell Elizabeth J—†	474	domestic	34	"
C	Sanders Edward H	474	butler	39	"
D	Monteith Annie T—†	475	housekeeper	60	"
E	Monteith Evelyn—†	475	secretary	28	"
F	Frothingham Langdon	476	retired	55	"
G	Frothingham Olga—†	476	housewife	39	"
H	McDonnell Mary—†	476	domestic	24	Medford
K	Shiel Beatrice—†	476	"	25	611 Com av
L	Briggs Flora T—†	477	housewife	38	here
M	Briggs Joseph A	477	physician	50	"
N	Brown Catherine—†	477	maid	42	"
O	Hamilton Isabelle—†	478	domestic	25	Milton
P	Hooper Adeline—†	478	none	40	here
R	Hooper Gertrude—†	478	housewife	69	"
S	Hooper Gertrude—†	478	student	21	"
T	Hooper James R	478	banker	70	"
U	Johnson Gerda—†	478	domestic	25	"
V	Wallen Irene—†	478	"	21	Cambridge
X	Appleton Lucy—†	479	physician	75	here
Y	Appleton Samuel H	479	retired	77	"
Z	Bauer Oscar S	479	merchant	42	"
A	Bradt Florence A—†	479	retired	47	"
B	Terhune Ella P—†	479	housewife	38	168 Newbury
C	Terhune Everit B	479	publisher	48	168 "
D	Hurley Helen—†	480	domestic	25	here
E	Rosenthal Louise—†	480	housewife	35	"
F	Rosenthal Morris	480	merchant	45	"

11

Beacon Street—Continued

G	Carroll Isabell R—†	481	stenographer	48	here
H	Clarken Rose—†	481	"	46	"
K	Blake Henry S	481	retired	52	49 Mass av
L	Blake Lucie M—†	481	housewife	40	405 Marlboro
M	Agren Hilda—†	481	maid	35	Sweden
N	Serrat Harold D	481	insurance agent	41	Malden
O	Davis John W	481	banker	35	here
P	Davis Reta B—†	481	housewife	35	"
R	Bird Lorenzo	482	chef	45	34 Ridgemont
S	Schneider Eunice E—†	482	housewife	42	Brookline
T	Schneider Louis H	482	editor	66	"
W	Carlson Augusta N—†	483	physician	38	here
Z	Brant Austin	483	"	40	"
A	Brant Lille P—†	483	housewife	30	"
D	Atwood Blanche L—†	483	physician	31	"
B	Cossey Grace M—†	483	surgeon	41	"
C	Day Florence F—†	483	housekeeper	48	"
H	Williams Gerva A—†	483	housewife	37	"
K	Williams John T	483	physician	38	"
O	Mason Eunice I—†	483	housewife	37	"
P	Mason Nathaniel	483	physician	48	"
V	Medalia Eugenia—†	483	housewife	40	"
W	Medalia Leon S	483	physician	42	"
Y	Dadmun Eliza J—†	483	"	50	520 Boylston
Z	Beirs Carl	483	"	29	here
E	Kerr Isabelle D—†	483	"	35	"
H	Smithwich Marsena P	483	"	56	"
K	Croll Clarence G	483	salesman	54	"
M	Nichols Emma T—†	483	housewife	64	"
N	Nichols John L	483	treasurer	67	"
O	Hare Charles H	483	physician	58	"
P	Larkin William C	483	chauffeur	45	"
S	Grogan Margaret V—†	483	physician	33	"
T	Rosenfield Harold H	483	"	30	818 Harris'n av
U	Brooks Edith M—†	483	"	47	here
W	Whitbeck Andrew P	483	merchant	50	"
A	Moulton Allen T	483	physician	33	"
B	Clapp Anoitt—†	483	retired	70	"
D	Coon Marion—†	483	physician	42	"
F	Hyde Harold V	483	"	37	"
G	Daniels William	483	"	45	Brookline

Beacon Street—Continued

K	Phillips George P	483	dentist	37	here
L	Smith VanDorn C	484	salesman	25	"
M	Bullard Annie E—†	486	housewife	48	Connecticut
N	Bullard Washington I	486	banker	43	"
O	Lowney Mamie—†	486	domestic	25	here
P	Monahan Nellie—†	486	"	35	336 Beacon
R	Stone Alice—†	488	housewife	74	here
S	Stone Charles W	488	teacher	70	"
T	Stone Elsa W—†	488	"	32	"
U	Ballou Mary A—†	490	housekeeper	60	146 Mass av

Boylston Street

B	Coleman Lelia A—†	803	domestic	35	here
C	Henderson Alexander	803	retired	91	"
D	Henderson Janet W—†	803	none	50	"
E	Conant Carrie O—†	803	housewife	50	"
F	Conant Theodore S	803	retired	43	"
G	Feeney Mary E—†	803	domestic	61	"
H	Lambert Mary A—†	803	"	71	"
K	Burke Anne M—†	803	dressmaker	46	"
L	Catharin Catherine L—†	803	artist	52	"
M	Hardwick Rose S—†	803	teacher	45	"
N	Shea Mary—†	803	secretary	36	"
O	Cronin Nora—†	803	domestic	35	Cambridge
P	Field Elsie C—†	803	retired	50	here
R	Field Fannie—†	803	"	60	"
S	Churchill Florence—†	803	"	50	"
T	Mellin Ellen M—†	803	housekeeper	67	"
U	Winsor Louisa M—†	803	retired	79	"
E	Bruce Lillian—†	827	dressmaker	48	"
F	Crocker Frederick	827	bookkeeper	40	Nahant
G	Graham Allen	827	manufacturer	40	3 Monroe ter
H	Graham Isabella—†	827	housewife	40	3 "
K	Norwood Alice—†	827	tel operator	21	Ipswich
L	Cooper Frank J	827	salesman	24	here
M	Laughlin Thomas O	827	elevatorman	50	"
	Syran Helen E—†	827	housewife	45	"
O	Syran Jennie A—†	827	retired	84	"
P	Syran William H	827	foreman	51	"

Boylston Street—Continued

R	Farnum Ida F J—†	827	none	52	here
S	Whiting George F	827	undertaker	62	"
T	Curran Anne I—†	827	hairdresser	49	456 Parker
U	Curran Chrales P	827	salesman	26	456 "
V	Curran Edwin J	827	reporter	27	456 "
W	Curran Richard J	827	student	22	456 "
X	Shanley Jane F—†	827	housekeeper	46	456 "
Y	Taft Lillian L—†	829	manufacturer	55	here
Z	Cavanaugh Frances—†	829	retired	64	"
A	Kearney Margaret M—†	829	dressmaker	62	"
B	Murray Helen T—†	829	retired	60	"
C	Shorten Jane—†	829	"	70	"
D	Alexander Esther M—†	839	nurse	29	"
E	Ambrose Nora—†	839	"	40	"
F	Anderson Janet—†	839	"	49	"
G	Armstrong Grace—†	839	"	36	"
H	Beame Edith M—†	839	"	29	"
K	Beers Mary—†	839	"	30	"
L	Benoit Louise—†	839	"	27	"
M	Bond Anna B—†	839	"	49	"
N	Boswall Emily O—†	839	"	56	"
O	Brooks Emma—†	839	"	56	"
P	Cambell Jeanette—†	839	"	41	"
R	Cullan Anna—†	839	"	39	"
S	Cunningham Caroline C–†	839	"	31	"
T	Davis Margaret—†	839	"	40	"
U	Dole Sarah M—†	839	"	53	133 W Springfield
V	Dyas Mary—†	839	"	37	here
W	Eaton Olive G—†	839	"	37	"
X	Enderhill Alice—†	839	"	39	"
Y	Everbeck Lilly E—†	839	housekeeper	51	"
Z	Finnegan Margaret E—†	839	nurse	32	"
A	Foss Mary E—†	839	"	49	"
B	Freeman Sarah M—†	839	"	41	"
C	Ganage Ida M—†	839	"	33	"
D	Gile Katherine—†	839	"	51	"
E	Gookin Katherine—†	839	"	33	"
F	Grierson Margaret—†	839	"	39	"
G	Harney Ella—†	839	"	33	"
H	Harris Minerva—†	839	"	26	"
K	Hilton Annie J—†	839	"	49	"

Boylston Street—Continued

L	Hudson Sarah —†	839	nurse	34	here
M	Jackson Laurette—†	839	"	31	"
N	Jonini Lois—†	839	"	40	"
O	Joyce Bertha C—†	839	"	32	"
P	Littlefield Alvaretto—†	839	"	51	"
R	Lyungquist Anna V—†	839	"	28	"
T	MacKay Ella—†	839	"	29	"
U	MacKay Maude—†	839	"	36	"
V	MacKenzie Anna—†	839	"	42	"
W	Macnab Agnes—†	839	"	54	"
X	Maltby Annie—†	839	"	55	"
Y	Manning Marion—†	839	"	46	"
Z	McCarthy Annie—†	839	"	55	"
S	McIntosh Katherine—†	839	"	54	"
A	Newcomb Martha J—†	839	"	46	"
B	O'Connor Katherine—†	839	"	41	"
C	Park Nancy O—†	839	"	29	"
D	Phipps Ora M—†	839	"	29	"
E	Poole Florance—†	839	"	29	"
F	Powers Alice M—†	839	"	39	"
G	Reagan Anna F—†	839	"	27	"
H	Reagan Bridget A—†	839	"	47	"
K	Rosenberg Esther—†	839	"	39	"
L	Ryan Mary B—†	839	"	45	"
M	Shepard Ella—†	839	"	43	"
N	Shepard Rosa—†	839	"	37	"
O	Sherin Elizabeth—†	839	"	40	"
P	Stabo Jean—†	839	"	31	"
R	Sullivan Margaret T—†	839	"	31	"
S	Sullivan Margaret M—†	839	"	26	"
T	Sylvester Edith E—†	839	"	45	"
U	White Mary B—†	839	"	47	"
V	Willis Frances—†	839	"	46	"
W	Wills Elizabeth—†	839	"	46	"
X	Wood Janet P—†	839	"	36	"
Z	Barstow Annie D—†	845	retired	50	"
A	Clark Rufus R	845	elevatorman	70	Pembroke
B	Tully Ida—†	845	dressmaker	42	here
C	Smith Howard H	845	physician	50	"
D	Smith Louise E—†	845	housewife	50	"
E	Ahern Ellen—†	845	housekeeper	40	"

Boylston Street—Continued

F	Kip Charles H	845	broker	57	here
G	Morrison George B	845	retired	55	"
H	Baker Frank O	845	tanner	73	"
K	Burbank Margaret L—†	845	dermatologist	58	"
L	Landie Anna—†	845	retired	79	"
M	Landie James T	845	salesman	35	"
N	Spencer Emma L—†	845	dermatologist	38	"
O	Lambeth Katherine—†	845	maid	50	"
P	Thayer Grace—†	845	housewife	50	"
R	Thayer Henry J	845	banker	65	"
T	Guez Gaston	845	teacher	38	"
S	Guez Margaret D—†	845	dressmaker	38	"
U	Benson Albert E	845	teacher	53	"
V	Benson Susan F—†	845	housekeeper	51	"
W	Arnold Leroy	845	teacher	35	"
X	Blake Isabelle—†	845	retired	85	"
Y	Smith Louise—†	845	housewife	50	"
Z	Henzi Bertha L—†	845	governess	36	"
A	Henzi Herman	845	cook	37	"
T	Finnigan James	905	inspector	55	Millis
U	Gibbons James W	905	paymaster	49	here
V	Gibbons Jessie—†	905	housewife	45	"
W	Masters John F	905	broker	55	"
X	Donovan William J	905	inspector	44	"
Y	O'Brien John E	905	salesman	36	Brooklyn N
Z	O'Neil Harry J	905	inspector	36	here
A	Taylor Jennie—†	905	housewife	50	"
B	Wilson Angeline—†	905	"	64	"
C	Wilson Arthur	905	teacher	44	"
D	Berg Max	905	salesman	40	"
E	Mackenstraw Charles J	905	clerk	26	Cambridge
F	Preble Mary A—†	905	bookkeeper	40	here
G	Wing Dorothy—†	905	housewife	48	"
H	Wing Harry M	905	manager	48	"
K	Erb Amy—†	905	"	28	500 Boylston
L	Esson Catherine—†	905	clerk	26	W Newton
M	Hunt Martha J—†	905	dressmaker	40	here
N	Keugler Lois—†	905	secretary	30	"
O	Snow Emma R—†	905	dressmaker	58	"
P	Filton Clara E—†	905	housewife	59	"
R	O'Neil Edmund F	907	machinist	22	"

Boylston Street—Continued

s	O'Neil Ellen—†	907	housewife	45	here
t	French Albert P	907	salesman	38	"
u	Holden Martha J—†	907	housewife	57	"
v	Geary Patrick	907	chauffeur	40	Brookline
w	Partington Emma J—†	907	housewife	58	Winthrop
x	Partington Hilda B—†	907	bookbinder	34	"
b	Ramsdell Addie F—†	913	housewife	54	here
c	Paradise Josephine—†	913	nurse	45	"
d	Upton Annie—†	913	housewife	50	"
e	Upton Rodney L	913	merchant	51	"
h	Ambrose John	925A	valet	38	"
k	Cochran John L	925A	merchant	41	"
l	Hooper Samuel H	925A	banker	51	"
m	Hubbard Gorham	925A	"	31	"
n	McDuffee Charles H	925A	merchant	44	"
o	McSargent George	925A	lawyer	45	"
p	Meaney Thomas F	925A	merchant	56	"

Commonwealth Avenue

a	Emmons Nathaniel H	245	retired	84	here
b	McGinley Susan—†	245	parlormaid	26	"
c	O'Donnell Catherine—†	245	cook	30	"
d	Simmons Channing C	245	physician	48	"
e	Simmons Eleanor—†	245	housewife	44	"
h	Donovan Catherine—†	248	cook	65	"
k	Driscoll Catherine—†	248	waitress	50	"
l	Kent Alice C—†	249	housewife	55	"
m	Kent Edward L	249	banker	34	"
p	Ellis Augustus H	252	retired	72	"
r	Josselyn Angelina S—†	252	"	78	"
s	Sweeney Annie—†	253	cook	38	"
t	Cruft Eunice M—†	254	retired	52	"
u	Cruft Frances C—†	254	"	49	"
v	Fenno Brooks	255	broker	70	"
w	Fenno Brooks, jr	255	salesman	26	"
x	Fenno Mary—†	255	housewife	45	"
y	Hayes Nora—†	255	cook	40	86 Beacon
z	Murphy Delia—†	255	chambermaid	20	Ireland
a	Murphy Nora—†	255	waitress	26	here

Commonwealth Avenue—Continued

B	Daunt Nellie—†	256	maid	43	here
C	Leeson Mildred D—†	256	retired	41	"
D	Leeson Robert A	256	manufacturer	47	"
E	McDermott Mary—†	256	cook	40	Brookline
F	Shepley Freda—†	256	governess	32	here
G	Buckley Norah—†	257	laundress	40	"
H	Cochrane Francis D	257	manufacturer	45	"
K	Cochrane Remall McK-†	257	housewife	42	"
L	Conners Margaret—†	257	chambermaid	32	"
M	Cusack Mary—†	257	nursemaid	35	"
N	Kenney Nellie—†	257	seamstress	28	23 Com av
O	Walsh Catherine—†	257	parlormaid	28	here
P	Fox Carmen E—†	258	retired	60	Harvard
T	McDonald Mary—†	262	seamstress	50	here
U	Shea James A	262	janitor	55	"
Z	Ames Fannie H—†	267	housewife	36	"
A	Foley Nellie—†	267	parlormaid	26	"
B	Linscock Amanda—†	267	waitress	45	"
C	Claflin Carrie S—†	269	housewife	65	"
D	Claflin William H	269	paper dealer	69	"
E	Currie Elizabeth M—†	270	housewife	30	Somerville
F	Currie Harold V	270	superintendent	30	"
G	Boland Benedict F	270	physician	30	818 Harris'n a
H	Lynch James J	270	"	30	here
X	Fraser Archibald McK	270	"	41	"
Y	Austin A Everett	270	"	63	"
D	Hunt Robert B	270	"	37	"
E	Proctor James H	273	real estate	56	"
F	Proctor Thomas E, 2d	273	contractor	26	"
G	Jackson Dora W—†	274	retired	56	"
H	Kimball Maude B—†	274	"	46	"
K	Taylor Ella C—†	274	"	65	"
L	McHugh Bessie M—†	276	housewife	44	New Jersey
M	McHugh John J	276	clerk	44	"
N	Adams Abbie L—†	278	retired	60	here
O	Adams Samuel G	278	merchant	61	"
P	Fitzgerald Catherine—†	278	cook	35	"
R	McDonald Mary J—†	278	maid	22	22 Hubbard r(
S	Conway James J	280	houseman	49	276 Com av
T	Searle Cora A—†	280	retired	65	here
U	Searle Richard W	280	merchant	33	"

Commonwealth Avenue—Continued

Letter.	Full Name.	Residence, April 1, 1921.	Occupation.	Supposed Age.	Reported Residence, April 1, 1923.
v	Proctor Ellen A—†	282	retired	81	here
w	Stimpson Sarah M—†	282	companion	78	"
x	Boyle Catherine—†	283	cook	30	"
y	Boyle Delia—†	283	laundress	28	"
z	Couffon Yvonne—†	283	governess	23	"
a	Koshland Edith—†	283	housewife	36	"
b	Koshland Jesse	283	merchant	49	"
d	McGovern Mary—†	283	parlormaid	29	"
c	McGowan Catherine—†	283	chambermaid	28	"
e	Guck Katrenia—†	284	maid	55	"
f	McKee Bessie P—†	284	retired	65	"
g	McKee William L	284	merchant	63	"
h	Armstrong Harriet B—†	285	maid	35	Stockbridge
k	Bradbury Harriet J—†	285	retired	60	here
l	McDonald Jennie—†	285	chambermaid	26	"
m	McGee Bridget—†	285	cook	30	"
n	Morse Katherine—†	286	retired	84	"
o	Tweedie Jessie—†	286	cook	63	"
p	Welch Michael	286	retired	80	"
r	Brown May—†	287	kitchenmaid	30	Scotland
s	McKinnon Sarah—†	287	cook	57	here
t	McLeod Christine—†	287	parlormaid	43	"
u	McLeod Hannah—†	287	laundress	50	119 Com av
v	Sanders Frederick E	287	houseman	43	here
w	Sears Herbert M	287	retired	57	"
x	Bowers Paul	288	clerk	26	"
y	Cairns Minnie E—†	288	retired	61	"
z	Lamb Ernest	288	merchant	40	"
a	Estabrook Benjamin	290	"	34	"
b	Estabrook Henry W	290	"	68	"
c	Estabrook Nellie A—†	290	retired	63	"
e	Donegan Belle —†	290	maid	32	Southboro
f	Connell Mary—†	290	"	40	here
g	Lilly Frances E—†	290	retired	70	443 Marlboro
h	Brown Elizabeth B—†	290	"	71	here
k	Jack Mary B—†	290	cook	52	"
l	Jack May—†	290	maid	39	"
m	Donagen Hannah—†	290	cook	50	"
n	Mahoney Nellie—†	290	maid	45	"
o	Stackpole Katherine C-†	290	retired	60	"
p	Johnson Margaret M—†	290	housewife	55	"

Page.	Letter.	FULL NAME.	Residence, April 1, 1924.	Occupation.	Supposed Age.	Reported Residence, April 1, 1923. Street and Number.

Commonwealth Avenue—Continued

	R	Johnson Marion N—†	290	janitor	67	here
	U	Fitzgerald Mary—†	293	maid	40	58 Beacon
	V	Greene Louise A—†	293	housewife	52	here
	T	Hoff Bainbridge—†	293	retired	78	"
	W	Hunt Daniel L	293	physician	55	"
	X	Hunt Ruth H—†	293	housewife	53	"
	Y	Keresy Elizabeth—†	293	maid	40	"
	Z	Hollis Elizabeth H—†	293	retired	46	"
	A	Hollis Leonora H—†	293	"	80	"
	B	Hollis Leonora M—†	293	"	42	"
	C	Hollis Lide T—†	293	"	44	"
	D	Fremont Smith Dorothea—†	293	"	68	"
	E	Fremont Smith Maurice	293	physician	30	"
	F	McDonald Norrine—†	293	housekeeper	40	Somerville
	G	Cameron Catherine—†	293	"	45	here
	H	Stratton Charles E	293	lawyer	77	"
	K	Bent Powell	293	insurance agent	50	Weston
	L	Gordon Sadie—†	293	maid	38	Milton
	M	Morrison Bertha W—†	293	chaperon	38	Weston
	N	Johnson Clara A—†	294	maid	30	here
	O	Tower Elizabeth F—†	294	retired	60	"
	P	Tower Elizabeth H—†	294	"	87	"
	U	Ross Christine—†	295	housekeeper	58	"
	V	Rowe Allen W	295	chemist	45	"
	W	Sutherland John P	295	physician	70	"
	X	McCarthy Nora B—†	295	housekeeper	60	"
	Y	Montgomery Edward M	295	dentist	50	"
	Z	LeBlanc Alice—†	295	maid	35	Brookline
	A	Little James L	295	architect	49	here
	B	Little Leonora S—†	295	housewife	46	"
	C	Cahill Katherine G—†	296	housekeeper	44	20 Hemenway
	D	Hartigan Jennie—†	296	cook	60	Newton
	E	Robinson Harry E	296	retired	51	here
	F	Beckman Greta—†	297	chambermaid	22	96 Beacon
	G	Frye Bertha—†	297	waitress	34	Brookline
	H	MacDonald Jemima—†	297	nurse	42	96 Beacon
	K	Proctor Charles A	297	retired	50	96 "
	L	Proctor Grace H—†	297	housewife	42	96 "
	M	Swedine Elma—†	297	cook	43	96 "
	N	Hart Thomas N	298	retired	95	here
	O	McCarthy Margaret—†	298	maid	61	"

Commonwealth Avenue—Continued

Letter.	Full Name.	Residence	Occupation.	Age	Reported Residence
P	O'Keefe Mary—†	298	maid	50	here
R	Connolly Mary—†	300	cook	39	Brookline
S	Linnell John W	300	retired	58	"
T	Linnell Mary F—†	300	"	58	"
U	McGarrity Margaret—†	300	maid	32	"
V	Faber Lena J—†	302	housekeeper	40	here
W	Ashley John	303	butler	46	"
X	Barker Frank	303	"	46	"
Y	Thomas Gertrude F—†	303	housewife	58	"
Z	Thomas Isaac R	303	merchant	60	"
A	Young Ellen—†	304	cook	43	"
D	Lavers Margaret—†	305	chambermaid	45	"
B	McKenzie Margaret—†	305	laundress	55	"
C	McNeeley Elizabeth—†	305	parlormaid	65	"
E	O'Brien Annie—†	305	cook	65	"
F	Mosley Benjamin P	306	broker	42	303 Com av
G	Mosley Elizabeth—†	306	retired	32	303 "
H	Mullens Elizabeth—†	306	maid	28	303 "
K	O'Rourke Mary—†	306	"	29	303 "
L	Healy Dennis	308	janitor	30	here
M	Thompson Peter H	308	physician	51	"
N	Dyer Nellie—†	308	retired	71	"
O	Carpenter Annie B—†	308	housewife	52	"
P	Carpenter Frank	308	merchant	52	"
R	Day Annie F—†	308	retired	63	"
S	Day Nathan B	308	lawyer	59	"
T	Day Sarah L—†	308	retired	66	"
U	Sargent Constance C—†	308	housewife	47	"
V	Sargent Joseph	308	lawyer	51	"
W	Sargent Joseph, jr	308	clerk	23	"
X	Paul Elizabeth—†	308	retired	51	"
Y	Paul Harriet—†	308	"	36	"
Z	Roberts Dora—†	308	"	55	465 Audubon rd
A	Webster Andrew G	308	real estate	70	here
B	Webster Elizabeth F—†	308	retired	65	"
C	Gray Helen B—†	308	"	53	"
D	Keefe Nora—†	308	maid	50	Chestnut Hill
E	Slade Margaret B—†	308	retired	60	"
F	Lindmark Ida—†	308	maid	27	Watertown
G	Thayer Thirza—†	308	retired	65	271 Dartmouth
K	Chaney Franklin V	313	manufacturer	49	390 Com av

Page.	Letter.	Full Name.	Residence, April 1, 1924.	Occupation.	Supposed Age.	Reported Residence, April 1, 1923. Street and Number.

Commonwealth Avenue—Continued

	L	Chaney Katherine P—†	313	housewife	45	390 Com av
	M	MacLean Christine—†	313	maid	24	Brookline
	N	Nieman Carl E	313	chauffeur	52	43 Union Park
	O	Nieman Hilma M—†	313	cook	45	43 "
	P	Burrage Albert C	314	merchant	65	here
	R	Burrage Alice—†	314	housewife	60	"
	S	Clifford Mary—†	314	domestic	24	"
	T	Lankialis Andrew	314	chauffeur	38	"
	U	Wise George W	314	valet	36	"
	V	Baylies Lincoln	315	manufacturer	31	"
	W	Baylies Mary—†	315	housewife	30	"
	X	Hagerty Martha—†	315	maid	41	"
	Y	Morley Nellie—†	315	waitress	51	"
	Z	O'Leary Rebecca—†	315	cook	29	"
	A	Rowe Edith—†	315	nurse	28	"
	B	Tukey Mary M—†	315	governess	45	"
	C	Chick Ruth F—†	317	housewife	34	"
	D	Chick William C	317	banker	40	"
	E	Daley Lillian E—†	317	waitress	29	"
	F	Kilduff Mary—†	317	cook	30	"
	G	Robinson Susan F—†	317	nurse	36	"
	H	Vincent Katherine—†	317	maid	45	
	K	Anderson Hulda—†	318	domestic	35	308 Marlboro
	L	Dwyer Margaret—†	318	"	23	Brookline
	M	Hobbs Conrad	318	merchant	45	here
	N	Hobbs Jessie L—†	318	housewife	45	"
	O	Manning Margaret—†	318	domestic	28	30 W Cedar
	P	Thorson Anna—†	318	nurse	32	here
	R	Kennedy Bridget A—†	318	cook	59	"
	S	Leonard Helen C—†	319	housewife	34	"
	T	Leonard Russell H	319	manufacturer	35	"
	U	Malone Jenney F—†	319	waitress	34	"
	V	Wagenknecht Christine—†	319	nurse	30	"
	W	Emmons Lucy V—†	320	teacher	54	"
	X	Otis Ada M—†	320	bookkeeper	51	"
	Y	Sanborn Adalyn H—†	320	housewife	49	"
	Z	Sanborn George P	320	physician	49	"
	A	Stacey Louise F—†	320	domestic	41	"
	B	Boyle Margaret—†	321	maid	28	"
	C	Eiseman Gertrude W—†	321	housewife	35	"
	D	Eiseman Julius	321	merchant	58	"

Commonwealth Avenue—Continued

Letter	Full Name	Residence	Occupation	Age	Reported Residence
E	Matheson Margaret—†	321	maid	35	here
F	Walker Margaret—†	321	cook	50	76 Wheatland av
G	Sands Gertrude—†	322	none	40	here
H	Warren Bessie—†	322	cook	37	29 Batavia
K	Warren William J	322	butler	44	29 "
L	Curran Julia—†	323	cook	51	here
M	French George B	323	retired	64	"
N	Sweeney Katherine E—†	323	maid	38	"
O	Thomas Adelaide A—†	323	retired	70	"
P	Thomas Frank	323	"	77	"
R	Hogen-Burger Godfried L	324	physician	65	416 Marlboro
S	Keyes John H	324	clerk	49	Brookline
T	Keyes Mary A—†	324	housekeeper	50	"
U	Scoville Eva—†	324	housewife	34	Winchester
V	Scoville Orville M	324	broker	45	"
W	Smith Edna—†	324	musician	34	California
X	Smith Herbert W	324	"	45	"
Y	Howes Alice M—†	325	housewife	41	Cohasset
Z	Howes Ernest G	325	tanner	52	here
A	Kobe Tokusabus A	325	houseman	45	Cohasset
B	Kumlander Anna J—†	325	waitress	30	"
C	Pearson Nanny C—†	325	maid	35	Brookline
D	Stewart Margaret—†	325	cook	46	Framingham
E	Tinkham George H	326	congressman	51	here
F	Benson Elizabeth—†	327	maid	48	260 Clarendon
G	Bystrom Selma—†	327	"	37	Framingham
H	Carlson Vilhelmina—†	327	cook	47	Milton
K	Dumaresq Frederika S-†	327	housewife	54	New Hampshire
L	Dumaresq Herbert	327	retired	70	"
M	Jentzal Vera—†	327	maid	40	Manchester
N	Ellis Addie—†	328	domestic	40	here
O	Hatch Lucy P—†	328	retired	50	"
P	Hatch Maria E—†	328	"	60	"
R	Verge Susan—†	328	domestic	20	"
S	Goltra Sydney	329	engineer	28	New York
T	King Catherine—†	329	maid	32	here
U	Macurda William H	329	merchant	38	"
V	Magher Ellen J—†	329	secretary	35	281 Dartmouth
W	Murphy Eva—†	329	retired	50	23½ Myrtle
X	Williams Harvey L	329	clerk	23	here
Y	Donnelly Ellen—†	330	domestic	28	163 Bay State rd

Commonwealth Avenue—Continued

z	Doyle Mary—†	330	domestic	25	Southboro
A	Peterson Christine—†	330	"	41	here
B	Phelan George E	330	custodian	52	Concord
C	Stackpole Frank N	330	manufacturer	68	here
D	Stackpole Minna J—†	330	housewife	51	"
E	Cronin Ellen—†	332	domestic	53	Connecticut
F	McLaughlin Mary J—†	332	"	51	Needham
G	Upham Marcella—†	332	housewife	70	here
H	Randall Fannie L—†	333	manager	60	"
L	Bullivant Stanley	333	merchant	40	"
M	Bullivant Susan R—†	333	housewife	45	"
N	Bullivant William M	333	merchant	65	"
O	Bowen Pauline—†	333	maid	21	Nova Scotia
P	Rothwell William H	333	real estate	65	here
R	Mackay Florence—†	333	housewife	40	"
S	Mackay Gordon	333	dentist	50	"
T	LeBlanc Marie—†	333	domestic	50	"
U	Nash Martha W—†	333	retired	76	"
V	Bangs Georgianna—†	333	"	80	"
W	McBride Jenina—†	333	housewife	38	Brookline
X	McBride Maurice A	333	manager	45	"
Y	Munroe Alice I—†	333	housewife	50	373 Com av
Z	Munroe William I	333	lawyer	55	373 "
A	Donnelly Amy F—†	333	retired	55	here
B	Moran Katherine—†	333	"	35	"
C	Dole Augustus L	333	real estate	65	"
D	Dole Helen A—†	333	housewife	50	"
E	Bent Arthur S	333	student	23	"
F	Bent Mary—†	333	retired	55	"
G	Bent Mildred—†	333	osteopath	26	"
H	Townsend Ida J—†	333	retired	50	"
K	Smith Marcel N	333	jeweler	60	"
L	Smith Nellie H—†	333	housewife	60	"
M	Mills Mary B—†	333	retired	65	"
N	Buffam Sarah B—†	333	housewife	40	"
O	Buffum Walter M	333	lawyer	63	"
P	Corneau Barton	333	"	45	"
R	Corneau Octavia R—†	333	housewife	40	"
S	Greeley Anna M—†	333	retired	50	"
T	Greeley Helen A—†	333	"	50	"
U	Lodge Ida J—†	333	housewife	60	"

Commonwealth Avenue—Continued

v	Lodge John T	333	merchant	45	here
w	Stackpole Roxanna—†	333	retired	45	"
x	Fowle Alice P—†	333	housewife	50	366 Com av
y	Fowle Leonard	333	retired	60	366 "
z	Barnum Caroline M—†	333	housewife	45	here
A	Barnum Dana D	333	president	55	"
B	Smith Delia P—†	333	retired	52	"
c	Simonds Mary E—†	333	"	55	"
D	Orcutt Louise T—†	333	housewife	45	"
E	Orcutt Phillip D	333	author	25	"
F	Orcutt William D	333	"	50	"
G	Wolcott Clara G—†	333	retired	65	"
H	Bradley Anna—†	333	waitress	26	"
K	Carr Catherine—†	333	"	27	"
L	Crowley Mary—†	333	scrubwoman	65	"
M	McGuire Mary—†	333	cook	40	Vermont
N	Mulcahy Margaret—†	333	waitress	30	here
o	Quinn Gertrude—†	333	"	30	Pittsfield
P	Simuda Abraham	333	dishwasher	35	here
R	Stowell Lucy—†	333	maid	45	"
s	Sullivan Annie—†	333	domestic	23	39 Peter Parley rd
T	Turnquist Ida—†	333	"	55	here
U	Cadigan Nellie—†	334	cook	30	"
v	King Catherine—†	334	domestic	22	19 Abbot
w	Murphy Alice F—†	334	stenographer	23	here
x	Sullivan Margaret T—†	334	housewife	37	"
y	Sullivan William H	334	tailor	40	"
z	Brown Gertrude L—†	336	secretary	35	Brookline
A	O'Grady Celia—†	336	retired	48	Dedham
B	Rowson Caroline M—†	336	housewife	48	"
c	Rowson Francis H	336	clerk	49	"
D	Woody Regina J—†	336	housewife	29	Chestnut Hill
E	Bournett Anna—†	337	dressmaker	22	New York
F	Darling Lula—†	337	housekeeper	48	here
G	Davis Frieda—†	337	authoress	23	"
H	Davis Louise—†	337	retired	45	"
K	Falvey John F	337	broker	54	"
L	Gray Donald	337	chemist	50	"
M	Johnston Fred	337	salesman	30	"
N	Kerlin Walter	337	clerk	30	"
o	Filton Arthur	337	merchant	45	"

Commonwealth Avenue—Continued

P	Turnquist Burt	337	reporter	24	here
R	Dillworth Anna L—†	338	hairdresser	45	Brookline
S	Dillworth Charles H	338	lawyer	48	"
T	Dillworth Daniel C	338	real estate	59	"
U	Dillworth Eleanor J—†	338	housekeeper	40	"
V	Dillworth Mary E—†	338	hairdresser	50	"
W	MacDonald Margaret—†	339	domestic	30	here
X	Norris Anne C—†	339	housewife	44	"
Y	Norris James F	339	chemist	52	"
Z	Norris Priscilla—†	339	manager	24	"
A	Blakley Elizabeth—†	340	cook	35	Concord
B	Douse Charles F	340	retired	80	here
C	Gifford Carleton S	340	clerk	47	"
D	Gifford Raymah D—†	340	housewife	47	"
E	Hopkins Laura—†	340	domestic	24	Brookline
F	Taylor Ella—†	340	nurse	53	Florida
G	Brown Mary—†	341	waitress	51	here
H	Cavanaugh Maria—†	341	cook	60	"
K	Gorman Mary—†	341	maid	53	"
L	Rice Josephine E—†	341	housewife	85	"
M	Tully Mary—†	341	laundress	47	Ireland
N	Williams George H	342	retired	66	here
O	Colby Florence—†	343	nurse	39	"
P	Cooney Nellie—†	343	waitress	30	4 Marlboro
R	Crocker Annie B—†	343	housewife	79	here
S	Crocker Muriel—†	343	retired	39	"
T	Green Annie G—†	343	laundress	40	"
U	Lowney Margaret—†	343	cook	30	260 Beacon
V	Shea Catherine L—†	343	retired	84	here
W	Eliis Elizabeth M—†	344	nurse	23	407 Marlboro
X	Ott George J	344	physician	56	407 "
Y	Ott Mary R—†	344	housewife	42	407 "
Z	Bangs Harold	346	salesman	50	Brookline
A	Curier Dorothy—†	346	clerk	22	373 Com av
B	Curier Nellie—†	346	retired	53	373 "
C	Dow Eleanor L—†	346	bookkeeper	26	New York
D	Dow Nettie R—†	346	housewife	44	146 Mass av
E	Hadcock Beatrice—†	346	school teacher	40	65 Pinckney
F	Livingston Samuel	346	janitor	50	Brookline
H	Lucas Mabel C—†	346	music teacher	53	91 Westland av
G	Lucas Mabel E—†	346	practitioner	33	91 "

	Letter	Full Name	Residence, April 1, 1924.	Occupation.	Supposed Age.	Reported Residence, April 1, 1923. Street and Number.
	K	Miller Lyda—†	346	bookkeeper	20	Brookline
	L	Penick Margarett—†	346	school teacher	30	203 Com av
	M	Van DeMark Lucy—†	346	nurse	38	New York
	N	Crowley Annie F—†	347	domestic	34	here
	O	O'Brien Angelina—†	347	"	26	"
	P	Ratchesky Abram C	347	banker	45	"
	R	Ratchesky Edith S—†	347	housewife	35	"
	S	Swanson Cecilia—†	347	domestic	36	"
	T	White Kathaleen M—†	347	"	24	Ireland
	U	Smith Caroline P—†	348	housewife	49	here
	V	Smith Henry P	348	retired	69	"
	W	Smith Rachel D—†	348	student	21	"
	X	Hanley Edward J	349	"	21	299 Newbury
	Y	Murphy Edward D	349	"	21	299 "
	Z	Russell Joseph E	349	"	21	299 "
	A	Sullivan Clarence P	349	"	21	299 "
	B	Blaine Minnie—†	350	housewife	41	here
	C	Coffin Rockwell A	350	physician	50	"
	D	Earle Ralph S	350	lawyer	40	"
	E	Henderson Francis F	350	physician	39	"
	F	Kellogg Frederick L	350	"	50	"
	G	Manning James	350	salesman	50	1673 Com av
	H	Killacky Margaret—†	351	cook	30	222 Newbury
	K	Lyman Caroline A—†	351	housewife	63	here
	L	Lyman George H	351	retired	73	"
	M	Robinson Mary—†	351	waitress	41	"
	N	Robinson Sarah—†	351	domestic	28	"
	O	Breslin Nora K—†	352	cook	55	"
	P	Payne Ernestine—†	352	housewife	64	"
	R	Payne John H	352	oculist	64	"
	S	Currie Joseph J	353	metalworker	39	19 Queensberry
	T	Curry Lucy—†	353	housewife	32	19 "
	U	Leland Alice P—†	354	physician	66	here
	V	Ames Blanche—†	355	housewife	45	"
	W	Ames Oakes	355	professor	49	"
	X	Ames Pauline—†	355	student	22	"
	Y	Doherty Catherine—†	355	domestic	50	"
	Z	Hennessy Elizabeth—†	355	"	31	"
	A	Lucey Albina—†	355	waitress	47	"
	B	Mahoney Nora—†	355	domestic	35	"
	C	Whelton Nora—†	355	"	46	"

Commonwealth Avenue—Continued

Page	Letter	Full Name	Residence, April 1, 1924.	Occupation.	Supposed Age.	Reported Residence, April 1, 1923. Street and Number.

Commonwealth Avenue—Continued

E	Reed Arthur	358	janitor	43	here
F	Reed Velina—†	358	maid	38	"
G	Stinson Martha—†	358	housewife	74	"
H	Adams Samuel J	360	janitor	56	"
K	Mitchell Evelin—†	360	physician	42	"
L	Adler John F	362	superintendent	50	4 Haviland
M	Hansen Ernest	362	retired	45	14 Greenville
N	Malcolm John D	362	mechanic	50	621 Beacon
O	Malcolm Laura—†	362	tel operator	30	621 "
P	Martin Anna—†	362	housewife	29	here
R	Phanton George	362	waiter	30	New York
S	Allen George H	362	insurance agent	70	here
T	Allen Sarah P—†	362	housewife	60	"
U	Hughes Mary—†	362	maid	21	Malden
V	McDonald Agnes—†	362	housewife	48	here
W	McDonald Samuel J	362	physician	49	"
X	Boardman Anna—†	362	housewife	60	197 Beacon
Y	Boardman William S	362	physician	65	197 "
Z	Kepler Aura E—†	362	student	23	here
A	Kepler Charles O	362	physician	55	"
B	Kepler Effie S—†	362	none	53	"
C	Foerster Emma—†	362	nurse	45	New York
D	Morgan Alma—†	362	housewife	26	here
E	Morgan David P	362	chemist	29	"
F	West Mary—†	362	maid	40	"
H	Doyle Lettitia—†	366	housewife	60	"
K	Tiernan Margaret C—†	366	clerk	48	"
L	Arkin Louis	366	physician	47	"
M	Campbell Agnes—†	366	housewife	58	"
N	Campbell Hellan M—†	366	nurse	33	"
O	Hayden Mary E—†	366	housewife	76	"
P	Wilson Agnes—†	366	maid	62	"
R	Blackburn Alice—†	366	housewife	47	"
S	Wood Irving	366	retired	79	"
T	Goulding Louis R	366	architect	52	"
U	Goulding Maria W—†	366	housewife	51	"
W	Humphey Clara B—†	366	cook	30	Brookline
X	MacDonald Meda—†	366	nurse	25	here
Y	Wesselhaeft Conrad	366	physician	39	"
Z	Wesselhaeft Frances G—†	366	housewife	35	"
A	Coburn Harry A	366	retired	57	"

Commonwealth Avenue—Continued

	Letter.	Full Name.	Residence	Occupation.	Age	Reported Residence
	B	Fay Harry A C	366	salesman	43	here
	C	Fay William E	366	physician	65	"
	D	Lewis Henrietta J—†	366	nurse	61	"
	E	Cashamn Alvina—†	366	maid	26	430 Center
	F	Finkelstien Harry	366	physician	42	here
	G	Finkelstien Rosa A—†	366	housewife	37	"
	H	Hunter Jennie—†	366	nurse	28	"

Fairfield Street

	Letter.	Full Name.	Residence	Occupation.	Age	Reported Residence
	A	Daniels Alanson L	1	banker	55	here
	B	Daniels Frances P—†	1	housewife	55	"
	C	Hanley Nellie—†	1	maid	35	"
	D	McDonald Bessie—†	1	"	23	"
	E	O'Connell Margaret—†	1	"	45	"
	F	Duffley Mary—†	3	cook	55	63 Wensley
	G	Emmons Margaret Y—†	3	housewife	47	here
	H	Emmons William B	3	retired	45	"
	K	Logan Mary A—†	3	maid	38	85 Mt Vernon
	L	Matheson Margaret—†	3	cook	60	here
	M	Hollingsworh Mary C—†	5	housewife	50	"
	N	Boyed Louise—†	7	maid	50	"
	O	Campbell Jessie—†	7	"	25	Nova Scotia
	P	Garity Nellie—†	7	cook	45	here
	R	Louett Elizabeth—†	7	housewife	50	"
	S	Louett Robert	7	physician	60	"
	T	McBride Anna—†	7	waitress	30	"
	U	Bates Rosalee C—†	9	"	41	61 Bradford
	V	Cutts Lucia B—†	9	retired	69	Wash'n D C
	W	Nolan Catherine—†	9	cook	52	49 Ashland
	X	Norman Ida L—†	9	maid	44	9 Cassnet
	Y	Pratt Anita P—†	9	retired	71	Wash'n D C
	Z	Brown Mary—†	21	housekeeper	37	Cambridge
	A	Cryan Mary T—†	21	parlormaid	28	England
	B	Doherty Bridget H—†	21	cook	40	6 Hecla
	C	Forbes Mary J—†	21	waitress	35	147 Marlboro
	D	Jaques Dora H—†	21	secretary	27	here
	E	Keane Agnes—†	21	maid	32	"
	F	Koudrat Michael C	21	houseman	38	"
	G	O'Neil Mary—†	21	laundress	52	"

Page.	Letter.	FULL NAME.	Residence, April 1, 1924.	Occupation.	Supposed Age.	Reported Residence, April 1, 1923. Street and Number.

Fairfield Street—Continued

H	Robinson Marion—†	21	secretary	30	California
K	Sullivan Ellan—†	21	maid	49	here
L	Wood Ellan A—†	21	housewife	58	"
M	Wood William M	21	manufacturer	60	"
N	Ainslee Emma E—†	29	teacher	40	"
O	Fisher Amy A—†	29	secretary	41	"
P	Folmsbee Beulah—†	29	editress	30	"
R	Hicks Edward P	29	salesman	48	"
S	Hicks Maud G—†	29	teacher	44	"
T	Mead Victoria—†	29	maid	35	"
V	Sprague Charlotte S—†	33	housewife	64	"
W	Congdon Annie L—†	35	retired	52	"
X	Drake James M	37	publisher	60	"
Y	White Katherine—†	37	cook	25	Sharon
Z	Dennis Fannie A—†	39	housewife	62	here
A	Hines Alfred E	39	printer	68	"
B	Bell Walter N	41	mechanic	22	47 Falmouth
C	Boucher George	41	salesman	29	770 Boylston
D	Darah Anna—†	41	clerk	23	47 Falmouth
E	Fairchild Ethel—†	41	housewife	35	here
F	Fairchild Joseph	41	clerk	33	"
G	Knopp Bruce	41	cook	27	Portland Me
H	Larson William	41	cashier	25	41 Falmouth
K	Murphy Fabisla—†	41	clerk	26	219 Newbury
L	Murphy Ferne—†	41	"	23	219 "
M	Murphy Hope—†	41	"	25	219 "
N	Naples Andrew R	41	barber	29	65 Worcester
O	Parker Ella—†	41	clerk	21	457 Mass av
P	Quigg Leo	41	janitor	25	45 Falmouth
R	Robertson Agnes—†	41	retired	60	54 St Stephen
S	Robertson Edith—†	41	"	63	54 "
T	Roof Harold	41	tester	28	399 Newbury
U	Seller Harold W	41	dentist	25	431 Boylston

Gloucester Street

Y	Bresnahan Mary—†	1	maid	28	here
Z	Bresnahan Nellie—†	1	"	35	"
A	Chonis Mary—†	1	"	26	Cambridge
B	Cunningham Julia—†	1	cook	45	Ireland

Letter	Full Name.	Residence, April 1, 1924.	Occupation.	Supposed Age.	Reported Residence, April 1, 1923. Street and Number.

Gloucester Street—Continued

c	Finn Julia—†	1	maid	35	here
d	Fuller Flora A—†	1	housewife	66	"
e	Halsey Martha F—†	1	"	39	"
f	Halsey Oscar L	1	merchant	49	"
h	Concanan Mary—†	3	maid	26	"
k	Denny Charlotte H—†	3	housewife	35	"
l	Denny George B	3	physician	36	"
m	Quinn Hattie—†	3	maid	30	"
o	McEnany Agnes—†	5	housewife	70	Hotel Brunswick
p	McEnany Herbert	5	salesman	28	"
r	Cheney Charles	6	treasurer	28	Cambridge
s	Cheney Sylvia—†	6	housewife	26	"
t	Greenough Malcolm	7	retired	70	here
u	Greenough Malcolm W	7	student	20	"
v	McKenzie Mary—†	7	maid	30	Milton
w	Mullen Annie—†	7	"	36	here
x	Mullen Jane—†	7	"	32	W Newton
y	Malloy Anna—†	8	housewife	31	New York
z	Malloy James H	8	janitor	35	"
a	Ayer Hattie M—†	8	manager	50	Brockton
b	Flaherty Jennie—†	8	maid	40	Maine
c	Lowe Pauline—†	8	housekeeper	30	Brookline
d	Brown Francis—†	8	housewife	23	Waban
e	Brown Waldo	8	manager	28	"
f	Miller Blanche—†	8	housekeeper	38	"
g	Beach Alice M T—†	8	housewife	65	here
h	Beach Edwin H	8	real estate	70	"
k	McEntee Marguerite—†	8	cook	29	"
l	Nolan Margurite—†	8	waitress	22	"
m	Cronin Nellie T—†	8	maid	41	Watertown
n	Kennedy Delia—†	8	cook	48	Lynn
o	Tapley Alice P—†	8	housekeeper	66	here
p	Doherty Grace—†	8	cook	36	224 Beacon
r	Gillan Rose—†	8	waitress	52	30 Clarendon
s	Ericson Louise—†	8	maid	50	Belmont
t	Fletcher Annie I—†	8	nurse	55	390 Com av
u	Olson Elise—†	8	cook	55	Waltham
v	Loman Emma—†	8	maid	25	Brockton
w	Maclelan Bell—†	8	waitress	32	239 Marlboro
x	Spalding Dora—†	8	housekeeper	65	New Hampshire
y	Spalding Mary S—†	8	"	76	"

Gloucester Street—Continued

Page.	Letter.	FULL NAME.	Residence, April 1, 1924.	Occupation.	Supposed Age.	Reported Residence, April 1, 1923.
	z	Haley Annie M—†	9	cook	36	here
	A	Lavin Annie G—†	9	maid	25	"
	B	Small Margaret C—†	9	housekeeper	50	"
	C	Amory Amey—†	10	"	28	118 Bay State rd
	D	Amory Harold	10	brakeman	36	Dedham
	E	McCarthy Nora—†	10	waitress	31	328 Portsmouth
	F	Mooney Nellie—†	10	maid	35	Brookline
	G	Morgan Mary A—†	10	cook	37	New York
	H	Potter Siligl T—†	11	housewife	59	271 Dartmouth
	K	Arnold Edmund V	12	layer	51	here
	K¹	Arnold Pearl B—†	12	housewife	50	"
	L	Collins Mary—†	12	cook	56	Everett
	M	Desmond Annie—†	12	maid	48	Brookline
	N	Lownes Anna—†	12	waitress	27	here
	O	Higgins Mary—†	13	maid	33	"
	P	O'Brien Nellie—†	13	"	34	"
	R	Stewart Catherine—†	13	"	24	Newton
	S	Tufts Mary D—†	13	housewife	59	here
	T	Jaques Herbert	14	merchant	35	491 Beacon
	U	Jaques Mary T—†	14	housewife	38	491 "
	V	Matheson Rod—†	14	cook	50	491 "
	W	Nicholson Margurite—†	14	nurse	35	491 "
	X	Bartlett Mathew	15	broker	42	here
	Y	Bartlett Serita—†	15	housewife	38	"
	z	Fay Mary—†	15	maid	35	"
	A	Murphy Julia—†	15	"	30	"
	B	Stanton Marie—†	15	"	26	"
	C	Anderson Emily—†	17	"	38	"
	D	Farhm Hilda—†	17	waitress	38	"
	E	Hunt Abby W—†	17	housewife	70	"
	F	Hunt Belle—†	17	"	60	"
	G	Johnson Gertrude—†	17	maid	40	"
	H	O'Connell Delia—†	17	"	42	"
	K	Thomas Caroline W—†	20	housewife	60	"
	L	Thomas Washington B	20	retired	64	"
	M	Abbot E Stanley	29	physician	60	"
	N	Baker Cassius H	29	clerk	33	"
	O	Bitzer Elizabeth T—†	29	housewife	38	"
	P	Bitzer Robert	29	professor	46	"
	R	Hoeffel Gerald	29	physician	31	Mass Gen Hospital
	S	Kohsman Bertha L—†	29	secretary	27	here

Gloucester Street—Continued

T	Kohsman Clarice M—†	29	accountant	24	here
U	McCarthy Joseph	29	laundryman	29	"
V	Morison Robert C	29	clerk	34	"
W	Raymond Howard C	29	social worker	34	"
X	Bigelow Albert S	30	retired	78	"
Y	Kelly Annie—†	30	cook	40	"
Z	McLaughlin Celia—†	30	maid	25	"
A	Carter Andrew F	31	engineer	41	35 W Cedar
B	Carter Ethel R—†	31	housewife	31	35 "
C	Craig Nettie—†	31	maid	35	Florida
D	Roberts Emily—†	31	"	60	Brookline
E	Connoly Thresa—†	32	laundress	30	"
F	Dervin Mary—†	32	cook	40	Dedham
G	Hamlin Dorothy D—†	32	housewife	45	here
H	Hamlin Elizebeth—†	32	student	20	"
K	Hamlin Paul M	32	real estate	48	"
L	O'Rourke Catherine—†	32	waitress	29	"
M	Sullivan Bridie—†	32	maid	28	"
N	Campbell Catherine—†	33	"	32	33 Fairfield
O	Campbell Mary—†	33	"	29	33 "
P	White Nora K—†	33	housewife	57	here
R	Cole Charles H	34	manufacturer	51	90 St Mary's
S	Cole Grace F—†	34	housewife	27	90 "
T	Beal Ida D—†	36	housekeeper	69	here
U	Durham Ethel—†	42	secretary	40	2004 Centre
V	Fisher Mary—†	42	housekeeper	50	Wellesley
W	Handy Florence—†	42	clerk	30	Norwood
X	Jewett Catherine A—†	44	housekeeper	26	Newburyport
Y	Cunningham John H	46	physician	46	here
Z	Gannon Ellen—†	46	housekeeper	44	"
A	Gannon Thomas J	46	packer	43	"
B	Monroe Donald	46	physician	40	"
C	Townsend Artenas	46	lawyer	38	"
D	Webster Frederick	46	physician	38	"
F	Smith Sahra B—†	48A	housekeeper	57	"
G	Donahue Anna D—†	48A	dressmaker	36	"
H	Donahue Ida—†	48A	"	35	"
M	Crosby LaBurtte—†	49	housewife	52	Minnesota
N	Crosby Wilson G	49	retired	63	"
O	Crosby Wilson L	49	student	22	211 Newbury
P	May Mary—†	49	maid	26	Brookline

Gloucester Street—Continued

R	Carter John P	50	laborer	50	61 Chestnut
S	Keller Dora A—†	50	stenographer	56	Georgia
T	Sugden Arthur L	50	clerk	39	61 Chestnut
U	Thomas Jules	50	waiter	42	61 "
V	Thomas Marie L—†	50	housewife	41	61 "
W	Viereck Mary—†	50	clerk	46	61 "
X	Kehoe Cecile F—†	51	housewife	37	here
Y	Kehoe Eugene F	51	salesman	52	"

Hereford Street

Z	Derby George L	7	physician	46	here
A	Derby Mary B—†	7	housewife	42	"
B	Dewire Bridie—†	7	maid	35	"
C	Hurley Julia—†	7	nurse	40	"
E	Casey Julia—†	11	maid	22	295 Com av
F	Hardy Alice—†	11	housewife	45	295 "
G	Hardy Charles A	11	retired	50	295 "
H	Hardy Virginia—†	11	student	22	295 "
K	Mullen Rose—†	11	cook	40	295 "
L	Carey Nellie—†	12	maid	40	here
M	Duggan Theresa—†	12	domestic	41	Brookline
N	Greeley Margaret—†	12	"	39	here
O	Kelly Marian—†	12	"	38	Brookline
P	Storrow James J, jr	12	executive	31	here
R	Storrow Margaret R—†	12	housewife	27	Brookline
S	Hubbard Alice D—†	13	"	65	Milton
T	Hubbard Charles J	13	student	21	"
U	Hubbard Charles Y	13	real estate	67	"
V	Carroll Nellie—†	14	maid	36	214 Beacon
W	Freeman Elizabeth B—†	14	retired	78	here
X	Leonard Annie—†	14	cook	40	19 Glen rd
Y	Edwards Alice L—†	15	housewife	49	here
Z	Edwards Joseph O	15	salesman	26	"
A	Edwards William L	15	physician	59	"
B	Costello Julia—†	16	cook	60	Dedham
C	McGuiness Christiana—†	16	maid	38	66 Chestnut Hill av
D	Spellman Anna—†	16	"	35	Dedham
E	Wells Gertrude H—†	16	retired	77	here
F	Belknap Charles	17	manufacturer	44	"

Hereford Street—Continued

G	Belknap Helen R —†	17	housewife	40	here
H	Mangan Julia—†	18	cook	35	381 Marlboro
K	Scott Arnold	18	lawyer	46	here
L	Scott Mabel—†	18	housewife	46	"
M	Welby Annie—†	18	waitress	32	"
N	Welby Margaret—†	18	nurse	32	"
O	Bishop Sarah—†	20	"	49	14 Worcester
P	Hayes Catherine J—†	20	cook	31	179 Marlboro
R	Hunnewell Arnold W	20	clerk	33	179 Beacon
S	Hunnewell Mary C—†	20	housewife	34	179 "
T	Hurley Nellie—†	20	waitress	32	179 "
U	Nally Annie—†	20	maid	45	179 "
W	Whitimore Parker	29	retired	51	here
X	Ahern Mary—†	31	maid	21	899 Beacon
Y	Baird Alice—†	31	nurse	50	899 "
Z	Clark Frances S—†	31	housewife	31	here
A	Clark Franklin H	31	banker	34	"
B	Connolly Catherine—†	31	cook	50	899 Beacon
D	Curtin Margaret M—†	40	domestic	40	here
E	Gavin Annie—†	40	"	35	"
F	Jennings Mary—†	40	nurse	28	West Indies
G	Lane Annie—†	40	domestic	45	here
H	Markham Annie—†	40	"	27	181 Marlboro
K	McKean Margaret S—†	40	housewife	31	13 Com av
L	McKean Quincy A	40	broker	33	13 "
M	McKenna Ellen—†	40	domestic	34	19 W Newton
N	Neary Agnes B—†	40	"	50	here
O	Reagan Ellen G—†	40	"	33	"
P	Reagan Julia J—†	40	"	45	"
R	Sargent Henry J	40	agent	34	"
S	Sargent Jane W—†	40	retired	68	"
T	Lynch Annie M—†	45	"	68	"
U	Lynch Maude A—†	45	teacher	43	"
V	Lynch Maurice B	45	lawyer	45	"
W	Mahoney Bridget—†	45	cook	40	"
X	Jackson John E	46	merchant	48	"
Y	Jackson Madeline S—†	46	housekeeper	36	"
Z	McDonald Ellen A—†	46	domestic	28	"
A	Hensle Julius J	46	manager	44	"
B	Hensle Louise L—†	46	housekeeper	40	"
C	Hatlow Elizabeth—†	46	nurse	50	"

Page.	Letter.	FULL NAME.	Residence, April 1, 1924.	Occupation.	Supposed Age.	Reported Residence, April 1, 1923. Street and Number.

Hereford Street—Continued

	D	Caskey Lacey D	46	curator	43	here
	E	Caskey Mary—†	46	housewife	43	"
	F	Burroughs Edith—†	47	"	65	"
	G	Burroughs George	47	real estate	55	"
	H	Stauga Mary R—†	48	housekeeper	55	"
	K	Stauga Max	48	salesman	48	"
	L	Wilson Frank S	48	engineer	57	14 Cumberland
	M	Boardman Elizabeth D—†	49	housewife	41	here
	N	Boardman Gerald S	49	broker	42	"
	O	Agent Royal H	50	salesman	42	Springfield
	P	Connolly Fred	50	"	41	here
	R	Leahy William	50	"	23	New Hampshire
	S	Sullivan Eva B—†	50	housekeeper	38	here
	T	Toohy Carroll	50	salesman	23	Fall River
	U	Cavell Roger	51	manager	23	Somerville
	V	Coombs Charles	51	salesman	36	here
	W	Hinton John	51	machinist	51	"
	X	Robinson Earle	51	clerk	23	"
	Y	Taylor Myrtle—†	51	housekeeper	35	"
	Z	Swift Newton	52	teacher	52	"
	A	Swift Susan M—†	52	"	53	"
	B	Fallon Eugene	52	clerk	40	Niagara Falls
	C	Paris William	52	salesman	28	285 Newbury
	D	Ryan Elizabeth A—†	52	retired	58	285 "
	E	Dow Abbie R—†	52	"	65	here
	G	Mahoney Nellie—†	53	nurse	40	"
	H	McGuinnis Annie—†	53	maid	28	"
	K	Ryan Sarrah—†	53	"	35	"
	L	Souter Helen E—†	53	housewife	47	"
	M	Souter Robert	53	physician	53	"
	N	Walsh Nellie—†	53	cook	30	"
	R	Ding Fred	62	laundryman	27	Watertown
	S	Fee Louis	62	"	29	California

Marlborough Street

	U	Kelleher Catherine—†	282	domestic	25	here
	V	Kennedy Agnes—†	282	"	28	"
	W	Kennedy Mary—†	282	"	29	"
	X	McCaddeer Beatrice—†	282	"	25	"

Marlborough Street – Continued

Y	Warren Helen T —†	282	housewife	34	here
Z	Warren Samuel D	282	manufacturer	36	"
A	Lingren Sophie—†	284	domestic	28	"
B	Lundenfeld Elvira—†	284	"	25	"
C	Peterson Christine—†	284	"	35	"
D	Hickey Dorothy B—†	285	housewife	43	"
E	Hickey James G	285	proprietor	66	"
F	Hickey Mary M—†	285	retired	29	"
G	Brown Mary—†	286	maid	30	"
H	Stone James S	286	physician	50	"
K	Stone Selma—†	286	housewife	50	"
L	Mactaggart Elsie B F—†	287	"	59	"
M	Mactaggart John B	287	retired	63	"
N	Nelson Hilda—†	288	nurse	25	31 Gloucester
O	Olson Anna—†	288	domestic	36	Sweden
P	Turner Helen J —†	288	housewife	35	31 Gloucester
R	Turner Howard	288	manufacturer	45	31 "
S	Courtnay Mary—†	289	domestic	24	here
T	Homans Abigail—†	289	housewife	44	"
U	Homans Robert	289	lawyer	50	"
V	Langford Elizabeth—†	289	domestic	38	"
W	McKenna Catherine—†	289	"	38	"
X	Monahan Julia—†	289	"	31	"
Y	Slattery Charles L	290	clergyman	56	"
Z	Slattery Sarah L—†	290	housewife	45	122 Com av
A	Connor Minnie—†	291	domestic	23	here
B	Cummings Josephine—†	291	"	44	"
C	Curtis Charles P, jr	291	lawyer	60	"
D	Curtis Edith C—†	291	housewife	34	"
E	Horgan May—†	291	domestic	20	"
F	McCarthy Catherine —†	291	"	28	"
G	Oegan Nellie—†	291	"	26	"
H	Brewer Elsie—†	292	housewife	35	"
K	Brewer Robert	292	engineer	40	"
L	McKinnon Catherine—†	292	maid	45	"
M	Wagner Sarah—†	292	"	46	"
N	Gray Francis C	293	lawyer	33	"
O	Gray Helen—†	293	housewife	32	"
P	Kioughan Mary—†	293	domestic	22	"
R	Baker Ezra H	294	banker	64	6 Gloucester
S	Baker Gertrude—†	294	housekeeper	27	6 "

Marlborough Street—Continued

T	Linde Alma—†	294	cook	64	6 Gloucester
U	Colleir Catherine—†	295	domestic	60	here
V	Fitzgerald Mary—†	295	"	22	"
W	Simpkins Olivia T—†	295	housewife	44	"
X	Brigham Ida M—†	296	nurse	46	"
Y	Coolidge Alice B—†	296	housewife	60	"
Z	Coolidge Francis L	296	retired	62	"
A	Kirby Annie—†	296	waitress	51	"
B	Mara Mary T—†	296	maid	40	"
C	Shea Hanna—†	296	cook	39	60 Pond
D	Cabot Elizabeth—†	297	housewife	50	here
E	Moran Margaret—†	297	domestic	26	"
F	Sheehan Julia—†	297	"	38	"
G	Crockett Elizabeth L—†	298	housewife	53	"
H	Hamlin Elizabeth—†	298	retired	40	"
K	Crowley Mary—†	299	domestic	26	"
L	Jackson Elizabeth—†	299	manager	29	"
M	Jackson Elizabeth P—†	299	housewife	64	"
N	Jackson Isaac	299	broker	70	"
O	Jackson Margaret—†	299	retired	30	"
P	McNulty Margaret—†	299	domestic	22	"
R	Remick John A	300	retired	90	"
S	Remick Lucretia S—†	300	housewife	67	"
T	Yerxa Ethel B—†	300	retired	46	"
U	Yerxa Herbert E	300	grocer	47	"
V	Fraser Christine—†	301	domestic	31	"
W	Jones Francis R	301	lawyer	58	"
X	Jones Helen S—†	301	housewife	53	"
Y	Munroe Christine—†	301	domestic	40	"
Z	Munroe Sarah—†	301	"	45	"
A	Connolly Delia—†	302	waitress	27	"
B	Griffith Ellen—†	302	cook	61	"
C	Lincoln Sereta—†	302	retired	66	"
D	Binney Alberta S—†	303	housewife	43	"
E	Binney Henry	303	banker	59	"
F	Gillis Margaret—†	304	cook	38	Wellesley
G	Joyce Julia—†	304	waitress	31	here
H	Musgrave Edith P—†	304	retired	53	"
K	Musgrave Eleanor—†	304	student	21	"
L	Musgrave Percy	304	"	20	"
M	Porter Hortense I—†	304	retired	55	"

Marlborough Street—Continued

	Letter	FULL NAME	Residence	Occupation	Age	Reported Residence
	N	Porter Rasamond—†	304	retired	49	here
	O	Woodland Edna—†	304	nurse	20	125 Parker Hill av
	P	Cronin Minnie—†	306	"	52	here
	R	Gill Earl	306	clerk	21	"
	S	Leahy Julia—†	306	cook	35	Milton
	T	Newell Margaret—†	306	waitress	28	1120 Beacon
	U	Sawyer Fred R	306	haberdasher	61	here
	V	Sawyer Hazel M—†	306	housewife	28	"
	W	Tenney Alice P—†	308	"	59	"
	X	Tenney Benjamin	308	physician	61	"
	Y	Tenney Benjamin, jr	308	student	24	"
	Z	Bradley Beatrice—†	309	domestic	28	"
	A	Millett Agnes—†	309	"	25	"
	B	Millett Margaret—†	309	"	27	"
	C	Clarke Hannah—†	310	"	30	"
	D	Clarke Mary—†	310	"	28	"
	E	Winslow Charles G	310	real estate	52	"
	F	Winslow Rosamond G—†	310	housewife	46	"
	G	Zinck Cora A—†	310	domestic	29	"
	H	Corcoran Teresa—†	311	"	28	"
	K	Huntington James L	311	physician	40	"
	L	Huntington Sarah H—†	311	housewife	35	"
	M	Soduland Dora—†	311	domestic	27	"
	N	Sullivan Elizabeth—†	311	"	32	"
	O	O'Brien Helen—†	312	"	48	"
	P	Perry Thomas G	312	retired	78	"
	R	Kelly Margaret—†	313	domestic	23	"
	S	Mason Harold	313	real estate	42	"
	T	Mason Junia—†	313	housewife	32	"
	U	O'Neil Catherine—†	313	domestic	32	"
	V	O'Neil Margaret—†	313	"	28	"
	W	Hopkinson George	314	physician	51	"
	X	Hopkinson Helen A—†	314	housewife	49	"
	Y	Murphy Frances—†	315	"	52	"
	Z	Fellows Harry A	317	salesman	43	Woburn
	A	Fellows Lelia G—†	317	housewife	41	"
	B	Sperd Flora E—†	317	domestic	55	263 Newbury
	C	Sperd Shirley C	317	agent	28	263 "
	D	Easley Alexander	319	janitor	52	here
	E	Easley Catherine—†	319	housewife	48	"
	G	Conroy Mary—†	321	domestic	40	"

Marlborough Street—Continued

H	Davison Nora—†	321	domestic	56	here
K	Driver Eleanor W R—†	321	housewife	85	"
L	Lyons Catherine—†	321	domestic	28	"
M	White Ethel B—†	322	housewife	45	"
N	White Franklin W	322	physician	50	"
O	Gilker Jane—†	323	housekeeper	50	"
P	Kirraine Bessie—†	323	domestic	48	"
R	Morse John W	323	lawyer	60	"
S	Sullivan Catherine—†	323	domestic	50	"
U	Brooks Agnes—†	336	retired	45	"
V	Brooks Gertrude—†	336	"	42	"
X	Bryant Adelaide B—†	338	housewife	37	"
Y	Bryant John	338	physician	43	"
Z	Carll Elizabeth—†	338	domestic	50	27 Cortes
A	McPherson Annie—†	338	"	55	317 "
B	Rosengren Hilna—†	338	"	24	157 Bay State rd
C	Remick Elizabeth—†	339	housekeeper	48	here
D	Remick Serena—†	339	bookkeeper	27	"
E	Campbell Lucy—†	340	domestic	45	"
F	Nyman Alexandra—†	340	"	44	"
G	Turner Cara L—†	340	retired	71	"
H	Turner Frederick A	340	lawyer	47	"
K	Yeo Elen—†	340	domestic	28	"
L	Holland Isabel—†	341	merchant	50	"
M	Trask Mary S—†	341	"	45	"
N	Trask William R	341	lawyer	58	"
O	Buckingham Edith W—†	342	housekeeper	45	"
P	Cahill Hannah—†	342	domestic	45	Brockton
R	Fish Emley G—†	342	secretary	46	here
R¹	Merritt Edward P	343	retired	64	"
S	Merritt Elizabeth—†	343	housewife	55	"
U	Hayes Margaret—†	345	domestic	23	"
V	MacNiel Mary—†	345	"	40	"
W	Woodbury Jennie R—†	345	housewife	68	"
X	Freeman Caroline S—†	346	clerk	50	"
Y	Sweeney Elizabeth †	346	domestic	40	"
Z	Wesson Isabel—†	346	"	48	"
A	Wesson James L	346	retired	78	"
B	Park Charles	347	clergyman	51	"
C	Park Mary E—†	347	housewife	45	"
D	Sabine Jane D—†	348	physician	60	"

Marlborough Street—Continued

E	Sabine Janet—†	348	student	20	here
F	Bryne Rose—†	349	domestic	54	64 Beacon
G	Hall Franas C	349	physician	33	here
H	Hall Priscilla—†	349	housewife	28	"
K	Kerr Isabella—†	349	domestic	25	"
L	Wats Helen—†	349	"	25	Medford
M	Chute Arthur L	350	physician	58	here
N	Chute Lila R—†	350	housewife	53	"
O	Chute Mary—†	350	student	21	"
P	Chute Richard	350	"	23	"
R	Clough Emma J—†	350	caretaker	69	"
S	Downey Katherine—†	350	domestic	33	"
T	Moylan Mary—†	350	cook	33	"
U	Scully Helen—†	350	domestic	23	"
V	Cunningham Henry W	351	retired	64	Milton
W	Cunningham Mary H—†	351	housewife	60	"
Y	Lavalle Alice C—†	353	retired	50	here
Z	Quilty Mary—†	353	domestic	36	"
A	Salmon Minnie—†	353	"	35	"
B	Cutler Harriet—†	354	teacher	40	"
C	Green Bell—†	354	retired	53	"
D	Howe Annie—†	354	"	50	"
E	Scanbough Adeline—†	354	cook	27	"
F	Vincent Elsie—†	354	maid	27	Newton
G	Williams James A	355	janitor	40	here
H	Williams Minnie—†	355	housewife	38	"
K	Gallagher Delia—†	356	cock	22	Cambridge
L	McKenna Mary—†	356	maid	22	here
M	Robbins Marion—†	356	housewife	42	"
N	Robbins William	356	physician	45	"
O	DeNormandie Alice W—†	357	housewife	40	"
P	DeNormandie Robert L	357	physician	48	"
R	Doherty Mary—†	358	cook	55	"
S	Dowler Beatrice—†	358	waitress	37	"
T	MacDonald Annie—†	358	domestic	45	"
U	Wendell Edith G—†	358	retired	64	"
V	Chadwick George W	360	director	68	"
W	Chadwick Ida M—†	360	housewife	66	"
X	Donelin Mary—†	360	domestic	27	"
Y	Quinn Mary A—†	360	cook	38	"
Z	Connell Elizabeth O—†	362	maid	44	"

Marlborough Street—Continued

A	Halligan Nora—†	362	maid	40	here
B	Hatfield Eliza S—†	362	housewife	63	"
C	Hatfield Hugh	362	physician	49	"
D	Mitchell Francis—†	362	domestic	30	Brookline
E	Cronin Margaret—†	363	"	50	here
F	Sherburne Kenneth	363	broker	45	"
G	Bacon George	364	student	26	"
H	McKittrick Gertrude—†	365	housekeeper	50	Brookline
A	Hines Nora—†	369	cook	45	here
B	McKenna Margaret—†	369	waitress	25	Manchester
C	McArthur George	370	janitor	45	here
D	McArthur Martha—†	370	housewife	40	"
E	Curran Susan—†	371	maid	32	"
F	Gilles Mary—†	371	"	26	89 Sawyer av
G	Hedge Alice—†	371	housewife	44	here
H	Hedge William R	371	broker	46	"
K	Holian Beatrice—†	371	cook	21	Brookline
L	McKinnon Jenny—†	372	housekeeper	40	here
M	Cryan Katherine—†	373	waitress	28	300 Beacon
N	Hecht Edith—†	373	housewife	35	340 "
O	Hecht Simond E	373	merchant	37	340 "
P	O'Brien Margaret—†	373	cook	48	340 "
R	Bachman George W	374	physician	32	here
S	Dodd Margaret B—†	374	housekeeper	40	"
T	Collins Grace E—†	375	practitioner	48	"
U	Lammard Christine—†	375	maid	22	Nova Scotia
V	Norton Elizabeth—†	375	practitioner	48	here
W	Dowling Mary—†	376	cook	35	459 Beacon
X	Finnegan Katherine—†	376	domestic	27	459 "
Y	Gillooly Mary—†	376	maid	27	459 "
Z	Rhoads Anna W—†	377	none	60	here
A	Shattuck Jane—†	377	school teacher	24	"
B	Billings Kenneth S	378	merchant	35	"
C	Billings Marjorie—†	378	housewife	33	"
D	Hesson Elizabeth—†	378	domestic	25	56 Com av
E	Higgins Marie—†	378	"	45	here
F	McKenzie Ada—†	378	"	27	"
G	Nagle Anna—†	378	"	27	"
H	Green Elizabeth—†	379	nurse	55	"
K	Mahoney Catherine—†	379	domestic	30	71 Marlboro
L	Noyes Helen—†	379	teacher	35	Cambridge

Marlborough Street—Continued

M	Noyes Marion—†	379	housewife	69	Cambridge
N	Upham Susan—†	379	none	64	here
O	Burns Hanna—†	380	domestic	22	"
P	Collings Catherine—†	380	"	60	"
R	Jackson Henry	380	physician	65	"
S	Jackson Lucy W—†	380	housewife	64	"
T	Kelley Catherine—†	380	domestic	50	"
U	Morgan Margaret—†	380	"	22	Brookline
V	Cronin Margaret—†	381	"	40	82 Com av
W	Hoar Helen—†	381	none	56	here
X	McDonald Elizabeth—†	381	domestic	40	Watertown
Y	Moran Sarah—†	381	cook	45	59 Marlboro
Z	Boyde Isabella—†	382	"	45	Canada
A	Cunniff Mary E—†	382	waitress	23	16 Lime
B	MacKiggan Sarah—†	382	maid	23	Canada
C	Sullivan Lucy W—†	382	retired	54	here
D	Wadsworth Eliot	382	banker	47	"
E	Wadsworth Nancy—†	382	housewife	37	"
F	Bartley Elizabeth—†	383	none	40	13 Hereford
G	Derby Sarah—†	383	"	79	13 "
H	Torpy Mary—†	383	domestic	35	506 Com av
L	Supple Alberta—†	385	housewife	35	409 Marlboro
M	Supple Edward	385	physician	40	409 "
N	Ayer Nathaniel	386	butler	43	here
O	Baritt Julia H—†	386	cook	30	"
P	Broadrick Mary—†	386	maid	55	"
R	Moriarty Mary S—†	386	retired	65	"
S	Chisholm Mary—†	387	cook	32	130 Marlboro
T	Sanford Kate—†	387	housewife	60	130 "
U	White Eleanor—†	387	maid	23	49 Burroughs
V	Boardman Mary B—†	388	retired	74	here
W	Boardman William P	388	physician	43	"
X	Motley Dorotya—†	389	housewife	27	Beverly
Y	Motley Edward P	389	merchant	38	"
Z	O'Leary Kathleen—†	389	waitress	30	91 Beacon
A	Rouse May—†	389	cook	42	New Jersey
B	Witzke Emma—†	389	nurse	40	Beverly
D	Ashworth Katherine—†	391	cook	47	Weston
E	Mason Sarah D—†	391	housewife	69	here
F	Stack Mabel—†	391	domestic	29	Newton
G	Hannon Mary T—†	392	housewife	21	63 Mountfort

Marlborough Street — Continued

H	Hannon Steven	392	insurance agent	45	63 Mountfort
K	Marsden Frederick A	392	chiropractor	35	here
L	Schopin Ernest	392	electrician	28	"
M	Schopin Leona — †	392	housewife	30	"
N	Fall Charles G	393	retired	78	"
O	Fall Emily B — †	393	housewife	70	"
P	Gillis Margaret — †	393	domestic	36	395 Marlboro
R	Cain Anna — †	394	nurse	24	New Hampshire
S	Cain Patrick	394	clerk	28	"
T	Callahan Idora — †	394	nurse	35	here
U	Campbell Cornelio — †	394	"	34	"
V	Ferrenson David	394	student	23	477 Com av
W	Fowler Helen — †	394	nurse	35	here
X	Lee Samuel	394	salesman	24	New York
Y	McDonough Louise — †	394	nurse	26	here
Z	McDonough Mary J — †	394	housekeeper	60	"
A	McDonough Thomas	394	retired	70	"
B	Meysenburg Edward	394	salesman	65	"
D	Paige Christine — †	394	lecturer	58	"
C	Papillon Fidelia — †	394	clerk	23	"
E	Poirier George H	394	physician	36	"
F	Boyd Effie — †	395	maid	25	Canada
G	Frothingham Channing	395	physician	45	here
H	Frothingham Clara R — †	395	housewife	41	"
L	MacKinnon Anna — †	395	waitress	30	Canada
K	McDonald Florence — †	395	domestic	26	here
M	Connelly Annie — †	396	waitress	34	"
N	Godsel Minnie — †	396	cook	40	"
O	Hall Elizebeth — †	396	housewife	39	"
P	Hall Gardner	396	physician	45	"
R	Goldsmith Fanney — †	397	housewife	63	"
S	Goldsmith Simon	397	real estate	69	"
T	Bailey Lothrop H	398	student	24	"
U	Batchelder Charles D	398	"	22	"
V	Clapp Channing P	398	"	23	"
W	De la Macorra Francesco	398	"	22	"
X	Fitts Harvey A	398	"	21	"
Y	Hammond Harry R	398	"	22	"
Z	Henninger John H	398	"	22	Cambridge
A	Le Clercq Robert R	398	"	25	here
B	Mossman Bruce M	398	salesman	22	"

Marlborough Street Continued

Letter	Full Name.	Residence April 1, 1924.	Occupation.	Supposed Age.	Reported Residence, April 1, 1923. Street and Number.
c	Moulton Edwin T	398	draughtsman	21	here
d	Sterling Royal	398	"	23	"
e	McLeod Christine—†	399	waitress	42	"
f	McLeod Mary C—†	399	cook	45	Canada
g	Rollins Miriam W—†	399	housewife	72	here
h	Rollins William H	399	physician	70	"
l	Christian Andreas F	401	"	57	"
m	Christian Hazel M—†	401	student	28	"
n	Christian Myrtle E—†	401	housewife	50	"
o	Hanson Anna—†	401	cook	60	"
p	Peterson Matilda—†	401	nurse	44	"
r	Carnargey John	402	student	28	Kentucky
s	Cheney Alden D	402	retired	82	465 Com av
t	Dystra Fred	402	student	22	Ohio
u	Edwards Jenney—†	402	housewife	65	Arkansas
v	Ekert Minna—†	402	student	26	Somerville
w	Knight Alton	402	"	22	Vermont
x	Morgan Ida—†	402	housewife	44	409 Marlboro
y	Reynolds Mabel—†	402	housekeeper	23	409 "
z	Woodside John W	402	retired	40	Watertown
a	Potter Harrison	403	teacher	32	here
b	Potter Mary E—†	403	housekeeper	60	"
c	Cotting Charles E	404	banker	33	"
d	Cotting Ruth—†	404	housewife	62	"
e	Gallagher Catherine—†	404	maid	34	"
f	Long Nora—†	404	"	32	"
g	Lordan Katherine—†	404	"	32	"
h	Sullivan Theresa—†	404	"	30	"
l	Curtain Emma—†	405	housekeeper	39	"
m	Clark Mildred L—†	405	housewife	32	"
n	Clark Walter B	405	salesman	49	"
o	Andrews Edwin G	405	manager	63	"
p	Andrews Fannie—†	405	housewife	56	"
r	Franklin Virginia A—†	405	"	30	61 Minot
s	Kane Cordelia—†	405	"	24	Maryland
t	Kane John D H	405	U S N	28	"
u	McClure Arabelle H—†	405	retired	65	186 Com av
v	O'Callahan Julia—†	405	maid	30	Beverly
w	Seavey Flora A—†	405	retired	66	363 Marlboro
x	Fisher Emma—†	405	housekeeper	56	here
y	Fisher William A	405	editor	58	"

Marlborough Street—Continued

		FULL NAME.	Residence	Occupation.	Age	Reported Residence
	A	Newton Josephine L—†	407	real estate	26	1423 Com av
	B	Rice Anna W—†	407	housewife	65	here
	C	Rice Barbara—†	407	student	28	"
	D	Rice Theodore H	407	banker	29	"
	E	Rice William M	407	merchant	76	"
	F	Rice William M, jr	407	clerk	24	"
	G	Beaulieu Eda H—†	407	housewife	36	Newton
	H	Hapgood Florence—†	407	"	69	Vermont
	K	Maynard Pheobe—†	407	maid	60	"
	L	Coblenz Miriam—†	407	student	23	583 Beacon
	M	Edwards Jennie—†	407	"	21	583 "
	N	Hurtle Agnes L—†	407	nurse	35	here
	O	Jacobs Isabel—†	407	student	21	583 Beacon
	P	Puckett Louise—†	407	"	21	Auburndale
	R	Satler Marion—†	407	"	20	New York
	S	Scheibler Helen—†	407	"	21	583 Beacon
	T	Ellis Ann J—†	407	retired	80	here
	U	Henderson Dolina—†	407	housewife	48	"
	V	Henderson Edgar	407	salesman	50	"
	W	White John	409	janitor	43	25 Rutland sq
	X	Bates Abby F C—†	409	housekeeper	42	Ohio
	Y	Gillis Emily—†	409	secretary	21	Montana
	Z	Knox Alberta V—†	409	student	22	Maine
	A	Louis Lydia D—†	409	"	20	Fall River
	B	Oliver Martha J—†	409	"	21	Newton
	C	Warren Eleanor L—†	409	"	21	40 Berkeley
	D	Curran Ann E—†	409	housewife	28	here
	E	Curran Louis F	409	physician	38	"
	F	Doherty Thomas F	409	"	49	61 Bernard
	G	McGillicuddy Cornelius J	409	"	53	193 Hunt'n av
	H	McGillicuddy Helen J—†	409	housewife	51	193 "
	K	Evans Albert	409	physician	53	here
	L	Gillespie Mabel—†	409	housewife	26	Canada
	M	Gillespie Marjorie—†	409	"	60	541 Com av
	N	Gillespie William G	409	salesman	33	Canada
	O	Ordway Ella A—†	409	housewife	40	here
	P	Hill Henrietta M—†	409	retired	88	"
	R	Jealous Grace H—†	409	housewife	50	"
	S	Jealous Horace C	409	merchant	57	"
	T	Harrington Josephine—†	409	housewife	68	57 Orchard
	U	Harrington Marguerite E—†	409	secretary	36	57 "

Marlborough Street—Continued

Letter	FULL NAME	Residence	Occupation	Age	Reported Residence
v	Abell Beatrice —†	409	student	22	14 Cedarlane
w	Hamer Dorothy —†	409	teacher	24	Newton
x	Peterson Ella—†	409	student	20	here
y	Slaughter Mary —†	409	social worker	23	Haverhill
z	Ward Doris—†	409	student	22	Brookline
a	Nye Margaret —†	409	housewife	38	here
b	Nye William H	409	manager	40	"
c	Stone Anna—†	409	domestic	61	Newton
d	Russell Katherine E—†	409	housewife	63	here
e	Kaiser Berwin	409	student	23	"
f	Kaiser Minerva B—†	409	housewife	48	"
g	Carroll John A	411	physician	66	"
h	Carroll Sarah H—†	411	housewife	60	"
k	McLennan Angus D	411	physician	44	"
l	McLennan Catherine—†	411	housewife	39	"
m	McDonald Annie—†	411	domestic	24	Nova Scotia
n	Blanchard Catherine B-†	411	housewife	36	here
o	Blanchard Stanley W	411	physician	45	"
p	Boylan Clara—†	411	domestic	30	Dorchester
r	Gill Matilda—†	411	retired	52	here
s	Woods Florence W—†	411	housekeeper	52	"
u	Dearbon George	411	merchant	50	"
v	Dearbon John L	411	retired	90	"
w	Dearbon Samuel	411	"	60	"
x	Wyght Mary—†	411	housekeeper	65	"
y	Little Bertha B—†	416	housewife	47	"
z	Little Otis	416	salesman	52	"
a	Cherry Arthur B	416	"	35	"
c	Gary Clara E—†	416	physician	55	"
d	Robinson Harriette L—†	416	nurse	33	"
e	Gumain Alice M—†	416	housewife	45	"
f	Gumain Harry H	416	physician	50	"
g	Willox Margaret—†	416	domestic	42	"
h	Hall William D	416	retired	68	"
k	Kingsley Victor J	416	dentist	35	"
l	Drury Dana W	416	physician	43	483 Beacon
m	Drury Elizabeth S—†	416	housewife	43	483 "
n	Everett Louise—†	416	retired	50	here
o	McCarthy Mary—†	416	domestic	52	"
p	Garrick Nathan H	416	physician	39	"
r	Garrick Rose D—†	416	housewife	33	"

Page	Letter	Full Name.	Residence, April 1, 1924.	Occupation.	Supposed Age.	Reported Residence, April 1, 1923. Street and Number.

Marlborough Street—Continued

s	Booth Harriette G—†	416	therapeutist	30	8 Fordham ct
t	Buckingham Emily A—†	416	retired	74	here
u	O'Brien Julia—†	416	domestic	34	Nova Scotia
v	Leonard Joseph T	416	manager	65	here
w	Leonard Pamelia A—†	416	retired	39	"
x	Leonard Sarah—†	416	housewife	61	"
y	Maloy Stella—†	416	buyer	36	22 Blagdon
z	Poore Grace R—†	416	retired	53	22 "
A	Dennie Mary H—†	416	"	84	here
B	Eustice Mary—†	416	nurse	40	New York
C	Feeley Annie M—†	416	domestic	73	here
D	Hasting Maria D—†	416	retired	80	"
E	Hasting Maria D—†	416	"	45	"
F	Mullen Hannah—†	416	maid	50	"
G	Shriner Iris B—†	416	housewife	45	"
H	Vedder Milton W	416	manager	32	"
L	Luce LeRoy A	416	physician	44	"
M	Herron Anna E—†	416	housewife	32	"
N	Herron Thomas J	416	manager	42	"
O	Horner Barbara—†	416	housewife	30	Weymouth
P	Horner Torr W	416	surgeon	42	here
S	Twombly Edward L	416	physician	45	"
R	Twombly Evelyn—†	416	housewife	41	"
T	Boardman Eliza D—†	416	retired	75	"
U	Higgins Margaret—†	416	domestic	55	"
V	Coriat Emma—†	416	housewife	45	"
W	Coriat Isadore H	416	physician	47	"
X	Regan Nora—†	416	domestic	22	434 Marlboro
Y	Young Ernest S	416	student	22	434 "
Z	Young Grace A—†	416	housewife	49	434 "
A	Tyrode Helen—†	416	"	36	here
B	Tyrode Morris V	416	physician	41	"
C	Becker Margaret S—†	416	retired	63	"
D	Riley Mary O—†	416	domestic	32	"
E	Moller Fannie C—†	416	housewife	67	"
F	Wardwell Mary E—†	416	retired	63	"
H	Dean Lucy—†	416	teacher	55	"
K	Graham Samuel L	416	student	28	"
L	James Jane E—†	416	housekeeper	53	"
M	Hewes Henry F	416	physician	56	"

Marlborough Street—Continued

N	Hewes Margaret W—†	416	housewife	28	here
O	Schultz Julia—†	416	domestic	50	"

Massachusetts Avenue

F	Dernier Edgar M	126	superintendent	57	here
G	Dernier Lena R—†	126	housewife	55	"

Newbury Street

L	Kingsley Blanche F—†	242	teacher	45	207 Newbury
M	Kingsley Estele L—†	242	housewife	72	207 "
N	Winsor Harry L	242	salesman	52	207 "
O	Harlow Arthur F	244	broker	51	here
P	Harlow Edith L—†	244	teacher	53	"
R	Harlow Mary P—†	244	housewife	78	"
S	Walker Diana—†	244	maid	50	"
T	Kenealy Nellie—†	245	"	38	"
U	Nash Herbert	245	merchant	70	"
V	Nash Herbert, jr	245	engineer	41	"
W	Nash Mary C B—†	245	housewife	65	"
X	Nash William B	245	salesman	33	"
Y	Scott Mary—†	245	maid	45	"
Z	Cambell Ines—†	246	housekeeper	36	"
A	Jackson Helen—†	246	teacher	40	24 Newbury
B	Ayer Mary T—†	247	artist	25	Somerville
C	Ball Jessie—†	247	dressmaker	48	72 Peterboro
D	Blanchard Rachel—†	247	secretary	25	Newton
E	Dearborn Sarah J—†	247	milliner	32	37 Peterboro
F	DeGroot Adrian M	247	artist	33	New York
G	Hughes William J	247	vocalist	25	105 Pinckney
H	Pape Alice—†	247	artist	25	Manchester
K	Pape Eric	247	"	50	"
L	Batchelor Chloe E—†	248	teacher	42	here

Newbury Street—Continued

M	Bush Sally—†	248	teacher	50	here
N	Dunn Florence P—†	248	housewife	38	"
O	Ellis Mary A—†	248	housekeeper	88	"
P	Palmer Anne—†	248	housewife	60	"
R	Parr Mary—†	248	dressmaker	40	"
S	Boardman Richard D	249	real estate	46	"
T	Shute Ida M—†	249	housewife	47	"
U	Shute Walter	249	valet	50	"
V	Dodge Edwin D	250	broker	52	236 Newbury
W	Lorimer Julia—†	250	manager	37	109 Myrtle
X	Thomas Helen—†	250	teacher	34	109 "
Y	Young Gladys—†	250	housewife	28	488 Beacon
Z	Young Roderick T	250	salesman	27	488 "
A	McGillivray Rebecca—†	251	maid	28	Chatham
B	McLeod Mary—†	251	housekeeper	60	here
C	Vaughn Nellie—†	251	cook	30	Maine
D	Abbott Claire—†	252	clerk	21	here
E	Abbott Fred L	252	physician	59	"
F	Abbott Mary—†	252	housewife	42	"
G	Hoare Mary B—†	252	cook	34	"
H	Laverly Bernard	253	caretaker	38	Taunton
K	Laverly Margaret—†	253	housewife	42	"
L	Gillis Sadie—†	254	maid	21	New York
M	Kelly Amanda—†	254	housewife	74	here
N	MacLain Annie—†	254	cook	50	New York
R	Butler Charles S	257	physician	53	here
S	Butler Margaret H—†	257	housewife	50	"
T	O'Keefe Nora—†	257	maid	30	Beverly
U	Toye Mary—†	257	"	29	"
V	Belanger Anglique—†	258	clerk	24	499 Beacon
W	Belanger Mary E—†	258	housekeeper	60	499 "
X	Belanger Victorine—†	258	writer	21	499 "
Y	Capron Mary H—†	259	housewife	54	here
Z	Capron William J	259	real estate	63	"
A	Rust Sarah—†	259	secretary	50	"
B	Sargent Nettie C—†	259	nurse	60	Brookline
C	Clasby Alice—†	260	"	31	here
D	Hinton Linda W—†	260	clerk	45	"
E	Johnson Jean—†	260	"	30	"
F	Smith Jennie M—†	260	housewife	62	"
G	Stewart Edward	260	salesman	45	"

Newbury Street—Continued

H	Todd Frank J	260	carpenter	35	here
K	Todd Vera M—†	260	housewife	26	"
L	Fredhof Oscar	261	student	22	"
M	Fuller Annie R—†	261	housekeeper	58	"
N	Parker Horace P	261	U S A	60	"
O	Hanscom Ford	262	salesman	44	New York
P	Hanscom Mary A—†	262	housewife	45	"
R	Pinkham Nellie L—†	262	housekeeper	35	Winthrop
S	Cash William	263	student	30	here
T	Devine Agnes—†	263	social worker	30	"
U	Mulhern Mary—†	263	housewife	47	"
V	Mulhern Mary C—†	263	collector	25	"
W	Prentiss Ruth—†	263	teacher	30	"
X	Slayton Foster	263	student	24	"
Y	Vidolli Alfred	263	"	24	"
Z	Fetis Jessie—†	264	clerk	45	"
A	Hanley Eva M—†	264	maid	30	1 Mystic
B	Robinson Helen T—†	264	housekeeper	42	here
C	Lawrence Arthur A	265	physician	50	"
D	Lawrence Susan E—†	265	housewife	50	"
F	Graff Eugene	267	manufacturer	50	"
G	Howes Mary E—†	267	companion	70	146 Mass av
H	Okeley Irene—†	267	dressmaker	65	here
K	Paul Frances M—†	267	housekeeper	65	"
L	Robinson Annie E—†	268	housewife	59	"
M	Robinson Charles A	268	broker	78	"
N	Baker Edward F	269	"	59	"
O	Smith Charles W	270	"	78	"
P	Smith Helen F—†	270	housekeeper	42	"
R	Smith Jerome C	270	lawyer	49	Newton
S	Drudy Mary—†	271	maid	24	18 Arundel
T	Sullivan George	271	housewife	42	here
U	Sullivan John F	271	proprietor	47	"
W	Crowell Lillian—†	273	nurse	56	215 Howard av
X	Larson Carl	273	student	25	New York
Y	Larson Pearl—†	273	"	24	"
Z	Booth Ida—†	274	clerk	40	here
A	Cornell Mildred—†	274	nurse	28	"
B	Grad Edel M—†	274	teacher	22	14 St Margaret
C	Gregg Charles M	274	salesman	40	24 Westland av
D	Gregg Penna—†	274	"	33	here

Page.	Letter.	FULL NAME.	Residence, April 1, 1924.	Occupation.	Supposed Age.	Reported Residence, April 1, 1923. Street and Number.

Newbury Street—Continued

	E	Holland Clara J—†	274	clerk	28	here
	F	Mullin John E	274	salesman	50	New York
	A	Mullin Mary A—†	274	housewife	40	"
	B	Pease Ellie J—†	274	"	65	here
	C	Pease Muriel C—†	274	clerk	31	"
	D	Putney Alice—†	274	nurse	35	"
	E	Rowell Mabel—†	274	clerk	38	"
	F	Stone Charles P	274	"	28	"
	G	Tucker Mildred L—†	274	"	31	"
	H	Whiteside Mary—†	274	"	45	"
	H¹	Goebel Marion—†	275	housewife	42	Berlin N H
	K	Carty Beatrice—†	276	clerk	40	here
	L	Carty Margaret—†	276	nurse	45	"
	M	Carver Alice M—†	276	teacher	36	"
	N	Carver Edgar N	276	retired	67	"
	O	Carver Florrie R—†	276	housewife	64	"
	P	Ingraham John W	276	retired	70	"
	R	Mitchell Lena—†	276	maid	36	"
	S	Northrop Hazel—†	276	nurse	35	247 Newbury
	T	Parritt Elizabeth—†	276	clerk	45	here
	U	Pratt Catherine—†	276	"	38	"
	V	Robinson Leda B—†	276	physician	24	Cambridge
	W	Robinson Maud B—†	276	student	46	"
	X	Small Ada M—†	276	nurse	51	247 Newbury
	Y	Tucker Amy—†	276	clerk	48	here
	Z	Tucker George G	276	jeweler	48	"
	A	Cresey Joseph	278	laborer	48	"
	B	Burbank Lillian C—†	280	teacher	45	288 Com av
	C	Burbank Margaret M—†	280	nurse	47	288 "
	D	Byrnes Edward	280	clerk	47	12 Newbury
	E	Byrnes Emma—†	280	retired	43	12 "
	F	Faison John M	280	clerk	26	12 "
	G	Murphy Madeline—†	280	waitress	25	Cambridge
	H	Pieplico Edward E	280	student	22	314 Newbury
	K	Plumer Emelyn S—†	280	housewife	48	12 "
	L	Plumer Marie E—†	280	clerk	27	12 "
	M	Saclis Henry N	280	student	21	285 "
	N	Siegel Harry	280	laborer	80	Winthrop
	O	Sprool Maynard E	280	chauffeur	23	Maine
	P	Taylor John	280	mechanic	21	Medford
	R	Thomas Theodore H	280	student	23	Lowell

Newbury Street—Continued

Letter.	FULL NAME.		Occupation.		Reported Residence
s	Thurston Alfred H	280	student	21	Lowell
T	Brackett Emma—†	281	housekeeper	50	Somerville
U	Leander Lorrie A—†	282	physician	30	here
V	Penniman Charles	282	janitor	37	"
W	Brammer Jessie—†	282	housekeeper	45	"
X	Houmann Louis F	282	salesman	32	"
Y	MacKay Mildred—†	282	clerk	31	"
Z	MacKay Wilson E	282	salesman	33	"
z¹	Lazarus Eva N—†	282	clerk	32	"
A	Lazarus Henry I	282	broker	35	"
C	Green Thomas	282	student	24	"
D	Hayford Jessamine—†	282	clerk	25	Springfield
E	McKnight Ida L—†	282	"	40	"
F	Penhallow Charles S, jr	282	bookkeeper	40	here
G	Wethered Frances M—†	282	waitress	60	Worcester
H	Corey Ada E—†	282	housekeeper	48	here
K	Curley Laura C—†	282	nurse	38	"
M	Baxter Charles S	282	lawyer	45	"
N	Baxter Grace—†	282	actress	50	"
O	Heffran Mary—†	282	housekeeper	45	"
R	Oddy James G	282	merchant	38	"
S	Ratigan Thomas J	282	insurance agent	45	"
T	Katium Gerald A	282	instructor	30	"
U	Katium Vera L—†	282	treasurer	50	"
V	Storer Ethel B—†	282	waitress	35	Bangor Me
W	Webber Ruth—†	282	clerk	22	"
X	Healy Kent T	282	student	22	here
Z	Healy Vera T—†	282	housewife	50	"
Y	Healy William	282	physician	55	"
A	White Donald H	283	manager	21	"
B	Anderson Carrie—†	284	cook	55	"
C	Gooding Ebenena Q—†	284	housewife	75	"
D	Gooding Theodore	284	retired	75	"
E	Tompson Johanna—†	284	waitress	30	"
F	Bond Edna Y—†	285	teacher	30	Ware
G	Brennan Joseph L	285	accountant	25	New York
H	Comesky Ethel T—†	285	housekeeper	38	Plymouth
K	Comesky Michael E	285	clerk	50	"
L	Hellar Harold	285	accountant	26	New York
M	Kingman Metcalf	285	salesman	35	New Bedford
N	Newton Chester	285	postal clerk	27	Vermont

Page	Letter	Full Name	Residence, April 1, 1924.	Occupation	Supposed Age	Reported Residence April 1, 1923. Street and Number.

Newbury Street— Continued

	o	Robertson Bayard	286	clerk	24	here
	p	Robertson Bernice—†	286	housewife	40	"
	r	Robertson Charles B	286	buyer	55	"
	s	Robertson Ruric	286	salesman	21	"
	t	Hersey Mary—†	287	housekeeper	80	"
	u	MacIsaac Effie M—†	287	cook	29	"
	v	Kayser Elizabeth—†	288	actress	26	"
	w	Kayser Eugene	288	retired	61	"
	x	Deery Patrick	289	bookkeeper	22	Rhode Island
	y	Flanagan George P	289	meatcutter	47	here
	z	Flanagan Sadie S—†	289	housekeeper	48	"
	A	Goddard Frank	289	bellboy	23	Rhode Island
	B	Halme Philip N	289	student	25	here
	C	Hanley John O	289	salesman	25	Rhode Island
	D	Hemmon Robert C	289	accountant	35	here
	E	Kelty James	289	auditor	40	"
	F	Lewis Elene—†	289	dressmaker	45	314 Newbury
	G	MacDonald Murray	289	clerk	40	here
	H	Metebier Henry	289	architect	25	Rhode Island
	K	Meunier Roland	289	student	24	"
	L	O'Connor James	289	clerk	30	Brookline
	M	Papadopolus Michaelus	289	merchant	40	314 Newbury
	N	Shaughnessey Charles	289	clerk	25	Rhode Island
	o	Shea Howard	289	student	25	here
	P	Baylor Emma—†	290	maid	32	"
	R	Rice Walter H	290	physician	50	"
	s	Laing Mary—†	291	maid	45	"
	T	Penhallow Thomas W	291	insurance agent	65	"
	U	Sherborn Evelyn—†	291	housekeeper	80	"
	V	Sullivan Elizabeth—†	291	maid	45	"
	w	Clasby Alice—†	292	nurse	22	"
	x	Dotten Hazel—†	292	"	21	27 Astor
	Y	Fallon Margaret—†	292	"	21	here
	z	Farrar Doris—†	292	"	21	Saugus
	A	Horan Beatrice—†	292	"	20	New Hampshire
	B	Larner Winifred—†	292	"	23	Newfoundland
	C	McKay Anna—†	292	"	21	Campello
	D	Moclair Helen—†	292	"	21	Dedham
	E	Packard Charlotte—†	292	"	20	71 Batavia
	F	Reed Julia—†	292	"	23	Nova Scotia
	G	Reed Minnie—†	292	"	31	"

Newbury Street—Continued

Letter.	Full Name.	Residence, April 1, 1924.	Occupation.	Supposed Age.	Reported Residence, April 1, 1923. Street and Number.
H	Riff Emma—†	292	nurse	21	here
K	Rogers Hannah—†	292	"	40	"
L	Shields Loretta—†	292	"	20	Winchester
L¹	Wright Alice P—†	292	"	21	Wollaston
M	Ackerman Harry	293	cook	40	Quincy
N	Burke Mary M—†	293	housekeeper	47	here
O	Burke Patrick J	293	detective	49	"
P	Creegan Catherine—†	293	hairdresser	25	1290 Com av
R	Doyle Ellen—†	293	"	20	Newburyport
S	Beckman Charles	295	chairmaker	53	here
T	Beckman Rose—†	295	housewife	44	"
U	Brown Catherine M—†	295	storekeeper	43	Maine
V	Brown Erma—†	295	teacher	22	here
W	Brown Mary A—†	295	housekeeper	48	"
X	Brown Walter A	295	mechanic	44	"
Y	Coe Charles A	295	manufacturer	71	"
Z	Kimball Gordon	295	student	21	"
A	Westerburg Alma—†	296	hairdresser	31	Somerville
B	Westerburg Oscar C	296	broker	28	"
C	Putnam Cordelia H—†	297	housewife	53	here
D	Putnam Henry H	297	journalist	55	"
E	Putnam Louise H—†	297	housekeeper	70	"
F	Smith Lillian A—†	297	teacher	57	"
G	Smith Marcia H—†	297	"	50	"
H	Boss Katherine—†	298	nurse	22	"
K	Pardi Annie—†	298	"	23	"
L	Prescott Alice—†	298	"	21	Cambridge
M	Richards Josephine—†	298	"	20	here
N	Griffin Norman J	299	salesman	32	819 Beacon
N¹	Keegan Mary H—†	299	housekeeper	21	819 "
O	Kinoshita Yokichi	299	artist	35	832 "
P	Corbett Elizabeth—†	301	nurse	30	here
R	Hanscom Inez—†	301	teacher	75	"
S	Hanscom Inez—†	301	secretary	35	"
T	Martin Genevieve F—†	301	clerk	35	43 Parker Hill av
U	Martin Gertrude—†	301	stenographer	29	43 "
V	Martin Lillian D—†	301	domestic	40	43 "
W	Martin Margaret A—†	301	housekeeper	45	43 "
X	Martin William F	301	merchant	81	43 "
Y	Sullivan Kate—†	301	bookkeeper	45	here
Z	Daniels Clara T—†	302	housewife	72	"

Newbury Street—Continued

A	Daniels Edwin A	302	physician	72	here
B	Doyle Cathrine—†	302	cook	35	Brookline
C	Kelley Nora—†	302	maid	25	here
D	Browne Harold S	304	engineer	35	"
E	Butler Percivil F	304	dentist	27	"
F	Dawson George H	304	engineer	40	"
G	Hardy Frank E	304	salesman	48	"
H	Henderson George B	304	banker	29	"
K	Jones Cecelia E—†	304	housewife	44	"
L	Jones George F	304	jeweler	45	"
M	McClellen John H	304	salesman	26	Hartford Ct
N	Stewart Charles E	304	physician	27	here
A	Thorndike Richard	304	writer	22	Providence R I
B	Threadwell Abbot	304	banker	27	New York
C	Richardson Carl	306	lawyer	50	here
D	Calatow Leon	308	engineer	28	"
E	Calaton Lola—†	308	clerk	21	"
F	Iffel Joseph	308	janitor	24	"
G	Jewell Harriette—†	308	teacher	22	"
H	Jewell Kate S—†	308	housekeeper	75	"
K	Jewell Saddie—†	308	stenographer	50	"
M	Degen Edith M—†	316	housewife	71	"
N	Degen George F	316	clergyman	75	"
O	Degen Jessie—†	316	teacher	48	"
R	Apollonio Adrienne—†	316	housewife	48	"
S	Apollonio Harold D	316	real estate	48	"
W	Clark Ada K—†	322	housewife	37	"
X	Clark James H	322	chauffeur	41	"
Y	Halstrick Cora R—†	322	retired	60	Malden
Z	Burgess George E	324	chauffeur	40	here
A	Burgess Lucy—†	324	housewife	36	"
B	Barry Edith G—†	325	clerk	24	382 Newbury
C	Barry Frances E—†	325	"	22	382 "
C¹	Denling Helen—†	325	"	22	here
D	Denling Marie H—†	325	nurse	26	"
E	Kelly Anna C—†	325	housewife	50	"
Y	Frazer Bettie—†	346	retired	55	"
Z	Frazer Bettie R—†	346	tel operator	24	"
D	Carlson Frank W	350	chauffeur	33	Lowell
E	Carlson Janet—†	350	housewife	31	"

Letter.	Full Name.	Residence, April 1, 1924.	Occupation.	Supposed Age.	Reported Residence, April 1, 1923. Street and Number.

Newbury Street—Continued

G	Fox Henry M	352	chauffeur	50	here
H	Fox Margaret—†	352	housewife	45	"
K	Fox Margaret E—†	352	student	21	"
L	Fox Ruth M—†	352	stenographer	22	"
M	Hillis William	353	chauffeur	46	"
N	Tedford Harry	353	houseman	42	"

Ward 8—Precinct 10

CITY OF BOSTON.

LIST OF RESIDENTS
20 YEARS OF AGE AND OVER

(FEMALES INDICATED BY DAGGER)

AS OF

APRIL 1, 1924

HERBERT A. WILSON, } Listing
JAMES F. EAGAN, } Board.

CITY OF BOSTON—PRINTING DEPARTMENT

Page.	Letter.	FULL NAME.	Residence, April 1, 1924.	Occupation.	Supposed Age.	Reported Residence, April 1, 1923. Street and Number.

Bay State Road

	A	Brooks George H	7	salesman	35	here
	B	Fraser Mable—†	9	cook	42	Newton
	c	George Arial W	9	physician	41	here
	D	George Sarah H—†	9	housewife	41	"
	E	Shepard Reta—†	9	maid	21	5 Elm Hill a
	F	Smith Anna—†	9	"	50	here
	G	Daly Agnes—†	11	"	29	Haverhill
	H	Johnson Charles H	11	retired	64	483 Beacon
	K	Johnson Margaret E—†	11	housewife	50	here
	L	Mahoney Abelia—†	11	maid	29	Brookline
	M	DesBrisay Lucy I—†	13	housekeeper	60	38 Newbury
	N	Donovan Paul J	13	superintendent	45	Brookline
	o	Morse George L	13	merchant	77	Melrose
	P	Sullivan Annie—†	13	nurse	35	38 Newbury
	R	Bangs Forrest T	15	dentist	25	New Hampshire
	s	Bangs Vera O—†	15	housewife	26	"
	T	Boutwell Leslie B	17	dentist	62	here
	U	Boutwell Madeline—†	17	housewife	50	"
	V	Kennedy Katherine—†	17	cook	60	"
	W	Scollard Julia B—†	19	housewife	42	1 Kenney
	X	Scollard Patrick	19	shipper	40	1 "
	Y	Roache Ellen—†	21	housewife	37	here
	z	Roache William	21	janitor	37	"
	A	Stafford Earl	23	"	31	91 Kendall
	B	Stafford Ruth—†	23	housewife	28	91 "
	c	Kaplan Abraham	25	student	22	Cambridge
	D	McKinnon Cora—†	25	housekeeper	33	here
	E	Sylvester Dorothy Y—†	25	housewife	30	"
	F	Sylvester Philip H	25	physician	42	"
	G	Young Charles F	25	retired	76	"
	H	Cleary William A	27	dentist	45	"
	K	Rinhardt Sarah—†	27	retired	60	"
	L	Butler Mary L—†	29	housekeeper	35	Brookline
	M	Raymond Arthur C	29	banker	60	"
	N	Raymond Dorothy—†	29	student	31	"
	o	Raymond Minnie—†	29	housewife	48	Florida
	R	Fineran George H	31	banker	52	here
	P	Fineran Kathlyn—†	31	housewife	50	"
	s	Saunders Charles H	31	banker	54	"
	T	Saunders Edith M—†	31	housewife	52	"

Bay State Road—Continued

Letter	Full Name	Residence	Occupation	Age	Reported Residence
U	Rowell Ida M—†	33	housekeeper	38	here
X	Butler Patrick F	35	physician	45	"
Y	Butler Teresa—†	35	housewife	42	"
V	Franklin David	35	janitor	35	"
W	Franklin Mattie—†	35	cook	35	"
Z	Rowe William	37	student	22	"
A	Sparrow Alfred	37	"	21	"
B	Chase Lewis M	39	broker	50	"
D	Mangu Dossie—†	43	housewife	38	"
E	Mangu Thompson B	43	caretaker	40	"
F	Reynolds Helen—†	45	housewife	30	"
G	Reynolds Hugh	45	janitor	28	"
H	Shearer Helen—†	47	housewife	40	"
K	Shearer William L	47	merchant	45	"
L	Eliiott Ruth—†	52	housekeeper	29	"
M	Parsons Emma S—†	52	domestic	27	"
N	Porter George A	52	physician	47	"
O	Porter Mary T—†	52	housekeeper	72	"
P	Hepburn Bessie F—†	56	housewife	36	"
R	Hepburn James J	56	physician	40	"
S	Murphy Mary A—†	56	nurse	32	"
T	Dumarsq Lillian S—†	58	retired	42	"
U	Dumarsq Philip	58	insurance agent	51	"
V	Dumarsq Sophie H—†	58	housekeeper	78	"
W	Whittington Georgie—†	58	maid	40	4 Turner
X	Fraser Annie—†	59	nurse	45	here
Y	Haywood Annie—†	59	cook	60	"
Z	Johnson Johanna—†	59	nurse	40	"
A	Landers Margaret—†	59	maid	37	"
B	McCarthy Mary—†	59	waitress	46	"
C	Olsen Ida—†	59	laundress	45	"
D	Patten Markeeta—†	59	nurse	30	"
E	Russell Frances—†	59	housekeeper	80	"
F	Curry Gladis B—†	60	"	29	"
G	Curry Haskell B	60	student	23	"
H	Montgomery Annie—†	61	cook	50	"
K	Moors Francis J	61	broker	60	"
L	Moors Marjorie S—†	61	housewife	50	"
M	Palin Mary—†	61	waitress	35	323 Marlboro
O	Curtis Frederick H	63	banker	50	New Hampshire
P	Curtis Helen—†	63	housewife	45	"

Bay State Road—Continued

R	Prendergast Sarah—†	63	waitress	30	Brookline
S	Kelley Margaret—†	64	maid	65	here
T	Powers Anna—†	64	"	28	"
U	Richardson Sidney K	64	retired	75	"
V	Richardson Ruth K—†	64	housekeeper	35	"
W	Windeler George H	65	insurance	62	Europe
X	Windeler Laura—†	65	housewife	55	"
Y	Kimpton Arthur R	66	physician	40	here
Z	Kimpton Elizabeth—†	66	housewife	42	"
A	Sullivan Anna—†	66	maid	31	164 Bay State rd
B	Mason Estelle H—†	67	housewife	46	here
C	Mason Henry L	67	manufacturer	59	"
F	Cummings Francis	70	tailor	50	"
G	Kehew Rose C—†	70	housekeeper	42	"
H	Murther Frank	70	clerk	30	340 Com av
K	Wasserman Harriot—†	70	retired	30	here
L	Brown Jonathon	71	broker	65	"
M	Brown Magdalen—†	71	housewife	45	"
N	Falls Esther—†	71	cook	28	161 Townser
O	Hermanson Elsa—†	71	maid	28	here
P	Nelson Corona—†	71	waitress	22	238 Beacon
R	Donovan Elizabeth—†	72	maid	29	here
S	Goulding Margaret—†	72	"	42	"
T	McIsaac Margaret—†	72	"	35	259 Marlbor
U	Ranney Fletcher	72	lawyer	61	here
V	Ranney Helen M—†	72	retired	62	"
W	Burns Mary—†	73	laundress	26	"
X	Lucey Mary F—†	73	maid	42	"
Y	McKeon Jane—†	73	cook	45	"
Z	Merriman Helen B—†	73	retired	80	"
A	Nearing Mary F—†	73	architect	30	"
B	Rice Ellen—†	73	waitress	41	"
C	Hawkins Phillip D	74	salesman	41	New York
D	Patterson Barbara B—†	74	housekeeper	45	here
E	Cloherty Mary C—†	75	waitress	23	Braintree
F	Connolly Margaret—†	75	cook	30	here
G	Hosmer Clara—†	75	housewife	60	"
H	Hosmer Sydney	75	engineer	55	"
L	Farrell Mary B—†	77	maid	27	238 Marlbor
M	Mahoney Nora T—†	77	waitress	29	313 "
N	Mayer Chrissie—†	77	maid	36	Brockton

Bay State Road—Continued

Letter.	Full Name.	Residence	Occupation.	Age	Reported Residence
o	McVittie Margaret—†	77	laundress	48	here
p	Ruhnburg Ebba—†	77	cook	49	56 Fenway
r	Thayer Ethel R—†	77	housekeeper	53	here
s	Thayer James B	77	student	24	"
t	Stockbridge Alfred E	78	treasurer	49	"
u	Stockbridge Irene V—†	78	housewife	51	"
v	Stockbridge Louise—†	78	student	21	"
w	Vaughan Grace—†	78	maid	36	"
x	Williams John L	78	chauffeur	25	"
y	Coppinger Margaret L—†	79	governess	39	Virginia
z	Johnson Margaret—†	79	maid	43	77 Mt Vernon
A	Johnson Sally—†	79	"	21	Sweden
B	Larson Augusta—†	79	cook	25	240 Beacon
C	Linkletter Jennie—†	79	nurse	45	here
D	Pierce Marie—†	79	housewife	40	"
E	Pierce Walwroth	79	broker	46	"
F	Turuse Kuma B	79	butler	50	300 Com av
G	Carter Cordelia—†	80	retired	73	here
H	Paine Alanzo K	80	physician	44	"
K	Paine Marjorie—†	80	housewife	43	"
L	Healy Jennie—†	81	waitress	40	"
M	Joslin Elizabeth D—†	81	housewife	55	"
N	Joslin Elliott P	81	physician	54	"
o	Leary Julia—†	81	cook	34	"
P	Lynch Mary—†	81	laundress	40	"
R	Dodge Alice A—†	82	housewife	47	390 Com av
s	Dodge Eleanor—†	82	student	21	New York
T	Dodge Katherine G—†	82	housekeeper	22	"
U	Dodge Robert G	82	lawyer	50	390 Com av
v	Garland Mary—†	82	maid	27	Ipswich
w	Garland Sarah—†	82	"	51	"
x	McDonough Agnes—†	82	"	29	291 Marlboro
y	Tyler Abbie L—†	83	retired	93	here
z	Tyler Charles H	83	lawyer	60	"
A	Ward Hannah—†	83	maid	42	"
B	Ward Katherine—†	83	"	45	"
C	Ward Marion—†	83	waitress	37	"
D	Halligan Winifred—†	84	maid	30	"
E	Hubbard Joshua C	84	physician	53	"
F	Hubbard Marion R—†	84	housekeeper	51	"
G	Hubbard Richard	84	student	20	"

Bay State Road—Continued

H	Toole Katheline—†	84	maid	24	England
K	Dysart Robert	86	accountant	45	here
L	Emerson Paul	86	physician	37	"
M	Horner Albert A	86	"	37	"
N	Phillips Arthur	86	janitor	43	"
O	Phillips Sarah T—†	86	housewife	43	"
P	Callahan Minnie—†	88	maid	45	"
R	Dooley Nellie—†	88	"	45	"
S	Pendergast Celia—†	88	"	22	Milton
T	Thomas Frances P—†	88	housewife	57	here
U	Thomas John G	88	student	21	"
V	Thomas John J	88	physician	62	"
W	Burns Mary—†	90	maid	42	"
X	Connolly Elizabeth—†	90	"	32	"
Y	Hawes Alice M—†	90	retired	73	"
Z	Hawes Marion A—†	90	"	68	"
A	Kidney Minnie—†	90	maid	52	"
D	Bogner Percival J	92	salesman	23	Chicago
E	Gordon Beale M	92	agent	27	44 Fairfield
F	Houghton Myron S	92	broker	23	Worcester
C	Huse Robert E	92	publicityman	24	83 Gainsboro
G	McPartlin Raymond F	92	editor	24	New Hampshire
H	Prentiss Nathan M	92	treasurer	37	44 Fairfield
K	Tillson Ernest F	92	bank teller	26	Plymouth
L	White Rose A—†	92	clerk	25	44 Fairfield
M	Courtney Joseph W	94	physician	55	here
N	Courtney Margaret C—†	94	housewife	52	"
O	Hastie Marie—†	94	maid	42	"
P	Peters Edith—†	94	"	25	Winchester
R	Narm Samuel	96	butler	21	New York
S	LaGabrick Elspeth—†	96	maid	41	"
T	Lewis Cora A—†	96	housewife	41	295 Com av
U	Lewis Mayland H	96	salesman	41	295 "
V	Keith Frank R	96	"	43	here
W	Keith Gertrude C—†	96	housewife	41	"
X	Bebee Eleanor H—†	96	"	58	"
Y	Bebee Junius	96	merchant	68	"
Z	Scammon Edith—†	96	retired	45	"
A	Scammon Elizabeth—†	96	"	49	"
B	Leckie Mary E—†	96	housewife	65	"
C	Pope Josephine—†	96	retired	33	"

Bay State Road—Continued

Letter.	FULL NAME.	Residence, April 1, 1924.	Occupation.	Supposed Age.	Reported Residence, April 1, 1923. Street and Number.
D	Alexander Georgiana M–†	96	retired	52	here
E	Sias Emily F—†	96	"	50	"
F	Thayer Caroline H—†	96	housewife	67	"
G	Thayer Nathaniel	96	retired	68	"
H	Welch Charles A	96	broker	23	58 Deerfield
K	Welch Ruth A—†	96	housewife	22	300 Marlboro
L	Prest Edward J	96	broker	55	here
M	Prest Sarah L—†	96	housewife	58	"
N	Covel Abbie W—†	96	secretary	51	"
O	Covel Helen—†	96	"	40	"
P	Burns Annie—†	96	maid	23	31 Lawrence
R	Brinsell Alice—†	96	"	40	here
S	Kelley Sarah J—†	96	"	40	"
T	Minor Edith F—†	96	"	25	48 Lancaster
U	Sullivan Mary A—†	96	"	40	here
V	Costello Mary—†	97	"	24	"
W	Crotty William H	97	butler	58	"
X	Danielson Helmer K—†	97	maid	35	Sweden
Y	Gaston Hope—†	97	student	22	here
Z	Gaston John	97	clerk	25	"
A	Gaston May L—†	97	housewife	58	"
B	Gaston William	97	student	27	"
C	Gaston William A	97	lawyer	64	"
D	Jenks Annie—†	97	laundress	55	"
E	O'Connor Bessie—†	97	"	60	249 Com av
F	Epstein Soloman	99	druggist	52	California
G	Fairbanks Leon H	99	real estate	40	153 Hemenway
H	Fairbanks Nellie A—†	99	housewife	37	153 "
K	Gallagher Edward	99	salesman	46	Somerville
L	Muir James F	99	mechanic	39	St Paul Minn
M	Muir Margaret—†	99	housewife	32	"
M¹	Small Agnes F—†	99	retired	67	Provincetown

Beacon Street

Letter.	FULL NAME.	Residence, April 1, 1924.	Occupation.	Supposed Age.	Reported Residence, April 1, 1923. Street and Number.
O	Byron Ellen—†	491	tel operator	23	263 W Newton
P	Hewey Harry R	491	salesman	35	263 "
R	Jeffery Katherine—†	491	nurse	36	Cambridge
S	Worster Charles H	491	broker	68	here
T	Worster Harriet A—†	491	housewife	56	"

Beacon Street—Continued

V	Perry Gerda Von B—†	497	dentist	43	141 Newbury
W	Bacon Ida J—†	497	secretary	56	here
X	Bates Alfred A	497	repairman	35	"
Y	Dougherty Abraham G	497	gateman	66	"
Z	Dodge Hattie M—†	497	companion	46	"
B	Murphy Joseph	499	janitor	35	Maine
C	Hersey Evelyn M—†	499	housewife	73	here
D	Hersey Freeman C	499	physician	80	"
E	Child Samuel M	499	lawyer	61	"
F	MacKenzie Alexander	499	clerk	20	54 Gloucester
G	Ayres Emma C—†	499	housewife	40	here
H	Ayres Muriel—†	499	student	21	"
K	O'Brien Edmond	501	retired	79	"
L	O'Brien Ellen M—†	501	housewife	77	"
M	O'Brien Thomas J	501	physician	51	"
N	Keegan Margaret—†	503	nurse	40	"
O	Moran Mary H—†	503	inst uctor	48	43 W Cedar
P	Peck Martin W	503	physician	43	here
R	Peck Wilda C—†	503	housewife	34	"
S	Webb Louise M—†	503	"	40	Cambridge
T	Williams Anna P—†	505	"	73	here
U	Williams Francis H	505	physician	71	"
V	Bowditch Olivia Y—†	506	housekeeper	82	"
W	Bowditch Vincent Y	506	physician	71	"
X	Loewe Mary E—†	506	housekeeper	65	"
Y	McClay Carrie—†	506	maid	26	"
Z	McDonald Katherine—†	506	"	21	"
A	Murray Nellie—†	506	"	52	"
B	O'Grady Annie E—†	507	housekeeper	46	"
C	O'Grady Thomas	507	houseman	52	Canada
D	Damon Ellen—†	508	housewife	75	here
E	Higgins Nellie—†	508	housekeeper	29	"
F	Morgan Celia—†	508	maid	28	"
G	Wheelwright Charles A	508	retired	60	"
H	Wheelwright Jessiah	508	electrician	35	"
K	Wheelwright Loretta—†	508	housewife	60	"
L	Allen Dorothy D—†	509	housekeeper	45	"
L¹	Allen Hannah D—†	509	housewife	79	Hingham
M	Carter Marjorie B—†	509	"	45	"
N	Collins Annie—†	509	maid	50	here
O	Woods Beatrice M—†	511	housewife	46	"

Beacon Street—Continued

Letter.	FULL NAME.	Residence, April 1, 1924.	Occupation.	Supposed Age.	Reported Residence
P	Woods Benard J	511	real estate	50	here
S	Cueon Julian	513	houseman	42	New Hampshire
T	Small Earl V	515	salesman	32	here
U	Small Marian M—†	515	housewife	32	"
V	Davis Robert .	517	inspector	28	New Jersey
W	Steele Vernon	517	steward	21	Medford
X	Ayer Nathaniel F	518	manufacturer	55	here
Y	Collins Kate—†	518	maid	60	"
Z	Keaveney Delia—†	518	"	50	"
A	Murphy Jennie—†	518	housekeeper	42	"
B	Cummings Ella P—†	519	"	59	"
C	Cummings Mary B—†	519	housewife	62	"
D	Lavin Mary C—†	519	waitress	46	"
E	Shukle Roy M	520	physician	38	39 E Concord
Z	Wilson Wilfred	520	dentist	42	here
C	Wood Nathaniel K	520	physician	48	"
N	Green Laura D—†	521	real estate	45	29 Mt Pleasant av
O	White Jenetta M—†	521	student	21	29 "
P	Brooks Anna—†	523	cook	32	here
R	Cummings Julia—†	523	housemaid	33	"
S	Murphy Mollie—†	523	"	33	"
T	Raymond Fairfield E	523	engineer	27	"
U	Raymond Franklin F	523	merchant	67	"
V	Raymond Gertrude C—†	523	retired	59	"
W	Brigham Elizabeth M—†	525	housekeeper	60	"
X	Buckley Katherine—†	525	maid	52	"
Y	Cunningham Katheryn—†	525	nurse	35	New York
Z	Davey Madge—†	525	companion	32	here
A	McGillicuddy Abbie—†	525	cook	42	"
B	Rockwell Annette J—†	525	nurse	50	"
C	Winslow Mary W—†	525	retired	50	"
D	Winslow William C	525	clergyman	84	"
F	Bennett Steven	527	broker	53	"
G	Donnelly Catherine—†	527	housewife	29	234 Marlboro
H	Donnelly Francis	527	janitor	38	234 "
K	Lund Charles C	527	physician	28	here
L	Brooks Albert S	528	student	20	"
M	Greonewold Bernard E	528	"	21	Ohio
N	Lund Edward	529	"	22	here
O	Lund Fred B	529	physician	59	"
P	Lund Zoe M—†	529	housewife	52	"

Beacon Street—Continued

R	Noone Catherine—†	529	maid	40	here
T	Haley Mary—†	531	housewife	40	"
U	Haley William T	531	physician	40	"
V	Webster Stella M—†	531	secretary	50	"
W	Burt Horace G	532	student	22	"
X	Byrne John C	532	"	22	"
Y	Fletcher Boynton J	532	"	22	"
Z	Alley George R	535	merchant	56	"
A	Alley Miriam S—†	535	housewife	51	"
B	Beebe Frederick	535	retired	59	"
C	Beebe Harold	535	merchant	35	"
D	Blaine Charles H	535	"	67	"
E	Blaine Emma F—†	535	retired	65	"
F	Blaine Margaret G—†	535	"	33	"
G	Bowers Frank	535	clerk	47	"
K	Brooks Florence H—†	535	housewife	52	"
L	Brooks Henry H	535	artist	56	"
M	Burrage Charles D	535	retired	51	"
N	Cheeney Charles A	535	"	51	"
O	Clark Caroline B—†	535	"	51	"
P	Codman Dorothy L—†	535	"	40	"
R	Codman Hugh	535	contractor	48	"
S	Cole Mollie R—†	535	retired	59	"
T	Connell Agnes—†	535	maid	59	"
U	Connolly Elizabeth—†	535	housekeeper	35	"
V	Devens Agnes L—†	535	housewife	41	"
W	Dexter Grace M—†	535	retired	51	"
X	Dexter Sydney	535	"	61	"
Y	Dorr Edith L—†	535	housewife	59	"
Z	Fitch Caroline T—†	535	retired	41	"
A	Frothingham Julia W—†	535	"	41	"
B	Gay Caroline I—†	535	"	64	"
C	Gay Harry H	535	"	64	"
D	Gill Elsie E—†	535	"	41	"
E	Gill William E	535	publisher	42	"
F	Guild Annie E—†	535	housewife	66	"
G	Guild Chester	535	trustee	67	"
H	Hatch Mary F—†	535	housewife	47	"
K	Hatch Roger C	535	salesman	45	"
L	Hyde Alice C—†	535	retired	52	"
M	Hyde Benjamin D	535	lawyer	54	"

Beacon Street—Continued

Letter.	FULL NAME.	Residence	Occupation	Age	Reported Residence
N	Hyde Lonvan W—†	535	retired	48	here
O	Libbey Sarah—†	535	"	83	"
P	McDonald Ora A—†	535	bookkeeper	34	"
R	Morse Margaret F—†	535	authoress	46	"
S	Moseley Ellen—†	535	retired	51	"
T	Murlin Lemuell	535	professor	56	"
U	Newcomb Warren	535	retired	64	"
V	Nolen William J	535	physician	51	"
W	Parker Runza B	535	retired	51	"
X	Patterson Alfred F	535	comptroller	53	"
Y	Patterson Alice E—†	535	housewife	49	"
Y1	Perkins Charles B	535	merchant	51	"
Z	Reece Robert H	535	architect	35	"
A	Reed Ella F—†	535	retired	68	"
C	Rice Ellen—†	535	"	41	"
D	Sheldon Clara P—†	535	"	71	"
E	Sheldon Henry M	535	"	77	"
F	Sherman Hellen H—†	535	"	64	"
G	Sherman Henry H	535	"	64	"
H	Stevens Lilla F—†	535	"	51	"
K	Sturdivant Florence—†	535	none	63	"
L	Thayer Alice M—†	535	housewife	44	"
M	Thayer Frank	535	retired	58	"
N	Tinkham Alice—†	535	"	75	"
O	Townsend Catherine W-†	535	teacher	26	"
P	Townsend Kate W—†	535	retired	69	"
R	Williams Elizabeth A—†	535	"	61	"
S	Williams Sarah D—†	535	"	54	"
T	Withington Georgiana B—†	535	housewife	64	"
U	Withington Margaret—†	535	librarian	35	"
V	Desmond John F	583	student	24	"
W	Desmond Katherine F—†	583	housewife	51	"
X	Macey Mercie W—†	585	retired	62	"
Y	Moody Martha—†	585	maid	58	9 Dilworth
Z	Watson Carl T	585	physician	52	here
A	Watson Eva B—†	585	none	51	"
B	Brown William A	587	physician	34	"
C	Thompson Carrie K—†	589	housewife	61	"
D	Thompson Charles O	589	physician	62	"
E	Thompson Howard K	589	"	30	"
F	Darlin Elmer E	591	cook	29	Providence

Beacon Street—Continued

G	Darlin Lillian—†	591	housekeeper	42	Providence
H	Ferguson Harry M	591	clerk	21	England
K	Ferguson Ina F	591	"	22	"
L	Ferguson James	591	"	24	"
M	Hayes Charles	591	"	35	464 Com av
N	Hoshenstein John R	591	examiner	29	Wash'n D C
O	Jacob Guy R	591	student	24	Lynn
P	Vockler James W	591	instructor	35	England
S	Hickey Elizabeth—†	601	domestic	40	329 Com av
T	Sheehan Catherine—†	601	"	39	329 "
U	Thorndike Alice A—†	601	housewife	58	here
V	Thorndike Augustus	601	retired	60	"
W	Boardman Edwin A	636–638	broker	50	"
X	Boardman Elvzra B—†	636–638	housewife	45	"
Y	Boardman Isabele—†	636–638	none	22	"
Z	Boysen Mable—†	636–638	maid	25	"
A	Buxbam Ellis—†	636–638	housewife	35	"
B	Buxbam Jacob	636–638	clerk	50	"
C	Cunningham Catherine—†	636–638	"	25	"
D	Gross Lewista—†	636–638	"	50	"
E	Mitchell Lewis R	636–638	janitor	44	"
F	Norton Harry A	636–638	salesman	55	"
F1	Norton Sidnie—†	636–638	housewife	47	"
G	Williams Maud F—†	636–638	retired	48	"

Boylston Street

A	DeMoucell Frederick	1069	chiropodist	50	here
B	Blanchard William H	1069	physician	36	"
C	Leach Mary F—†	1069	housekeeper	52	"
D	Stockwell Charles P	1069	real estate	57	"
E	Harding Nettie—†	1069	housekeeper	28	Cambridge
F	Josselson Israil	1069	physician	28	Somerville
G	Cunningham Frank	1069	metal worker	30	here
H	Hatch Lillian—†	1069	housekeeper	43	"
K	Hodgdon Eric	1069	teacher	24	"
L	Irving Harry W	1069	physician	43	"
M	Sylvester Caroline—†	1069	modiste	40	"
N	Dearborn Arthur	1069	clerk	60	"
O	Dearborn Lillian—†	1069	dressmaker	53	"

Boylston Street— Continued

P	Staines Albert G	1069	machinist	43	here
R	Staines Theresa F—†	1069	housewife	42	"
S	Whittimore Addie—†	1069	retired	76	"
T	Bianchi Frank	1069	student	23	409 Marlboro
U	Casanova Amelia—†	1069	housewife	38	409 "
V	Casanova Frank	1069	clerk	25	409 "
W	Mayorel Joaguin M	1069	student	21	409 "
X	Mayorel Maria—†	1069	housewife	40	409 "
Y	Bullins Catherine R—†	1069	housekeeper	54	here
Z	Ellis Frederick P	1069	retired	50	"
A	Ellis Martha E—†	1069	housewife	83	"
B	Luke Isabel—†	1069	author	40	"
C	Burke Thomas	1073	porter	33	Dover N H
D	Buehler George V	1073	physician	47	here
E	Dodge Sarah E—†	1073	dressmaker	70	"
F	Hall Charlotte A—†	1073	retired	60	Haverhill
G	Laskey Beatrice M—†	1073	housekeeper	31	here
H	Laskey Edwin J	1073	electrician	31	"
K	McDonald Alice—†	1073	housewife	59	"
L	McDonald Charles F	1073	physician	65	"
M	Allsion Alexander J	1073	superintendent	69	"
N	Allison Foster	1073	student	30	"
O	Allison Harriet M—†	1073	stenographer	40	"
R	Allison Margaret—†	1073	housekeeper	68	"
P	Allison Olive—†	1073	teacher	35	"
T	Nooman Deborah M—†	1073	housekeeper	45	"
U	Nooman Frank M	1073	storekeeper	44	"
V	Nooman Walter J	1073	"	25	"
W	Quinlan Lillian—†	1073	domestic	35	"
X	Gannon Margaret—†	1073	housekeeper	48	"
Y	Needham Mathew H	1073	salesman	49	"
Z	Saunders Catherine—†	1073	shoeworker	29	244 W Brookline
A	Smith James	1073	manager	43	Salem
B	Church Annie C—†	1073	housekeeper	48	here
C	Dunlap George W	1073	clerk	35	"
D	Lines James A	1073	manager	50	New Jersey
E	O'Hara Thomas	1073	contractor	32	here
F	Ramon Albert	1073	salesman	32	"
G	Gettings James H	1077	physician	46	"
H	Wolfe Idella—†	1077	dressmaker	33	"
K	King Eva C—†	1077	"	65	Wellesley

Page.	Letter.	FULL NAME.	Residence, April 1, 1924.	Occupation.	Supposed Age.	Reported Residence, April 1, 1923. Street and Number.

Boylston Street—Continued

L	Martin Joseph T	1077	student	28	Pennsylvania
M	Conant Florence A—†	1077	dentist's aid	44	here
N	Stowe Hellen H—†	1077	housewife	59	"
O	Stowe William H	1077	dentist	60	"
P	Crytzer J Sherman	1077	musician	22	Ohio
R	Morton Cornelia N—†	1077	housewife	34	here
S	Savage Rosalind E—†	1077	housekeeper	48	"
T	Hubbard Anna E—†	1077	housewife	62	Melrose
U	Hubbard Eben L	1077	conductor	64	"
V	Thompson Edith—†	1077	musician	40	here
W	Thompson Maria T—†	1077	housewife	70	"
X	Fanning Marshal B	1077	teacher	54	"
Y	Fanning Mary M—†	1077	"	50	"
Z	Gillis Mary—†	1077	domestic	22	Cambridge
A	Andrews Annie E—†	1081	housewife	48	here
B	Andrews Harold V	1081	physician	50	"
C	Carreiro Ernest	1081	chiropractor	35	"
D	Barker Norman	1081	teacher	35	"
E	Langille Mabel—†	1081	saleswoman	31	"
F	Shepherd Albert T	1081	violinist	29	"
G	Stewart Bertha—†	1081	housewife	43	"
H	Taylor Edith—†	1081	saleswoman	42	"
K	Auglie Minnie—†	1081	clerk	40	"
L	Carl Issac D	1081	physician	60	"
M	Carl Lizzie—†	1081	housewife	55	"
N	Kabley George W	1081	tailor	35	"
O	Gannon Mary V—†	1081	domestic	45	"
P	Hay Charles C	1081	retired	42	"
R	Hay Elizabeth—†	1081	housewife	40	"
S	Hay Marian P—†	1081	"	81	"
T	Jepson Hilda M—†	1081	bookkeeper	22	"
U	Jepson Lillian H—†	1081	clerk	25	"
V	Jepson Rose V—†	1081	bookkeeper	24	"
W	Matson Emily—†	1081	housewife	57	"
X	Matson Olaf	1081	tailor	60	"
Y	Flanders Mildred—†	1081	photographer	25	"
Z	Haley Gertrude—†	1081	housewife	50	"
A	Haley William T	1081	chauffeur	46	"
B	Cushing Mary A—†	1081	retired	57	"
D	Cox Ethel M—†	1085	housewife	32	"
E	Cox Oscar F, jr	1085	physician	37	"

Letter	Full Name	Residence, April 1, 1924.	Occupation.	Supposed Age.	Reported Residence, April 1, 1923. Street and Number.

Boylston Street—Continued

F	Mansway Charles G	1085	clerk	49	here
G	Waterman Fredrick M	1085	teacher	49	"
H	Cram Jane—†	1085	housekeeper	28	"
K	Marshall Fredrick R	1085	salesman	51	"
L	Marshall Ida N—†	1085	housewife	40	"
M	Arthur Cathryne C—†	1085	"	43	"
N	Clark Annie K—†	1085	clerk	46	"
O	Field Margaret—†	1085	housewife	30	829 Beacon
P	Prescott Grace—†	1085	"	28	Wash'n D C
R	Allen Clarence J	1085	student	35	here
S	Allen Jeanne B—†	1085	housewife	21	"
T	Murray Kathryne—†	1085	housekeeper	56	"
U	Summerhayes Martha—†	1085	housewife	65	"
V	DeLano Charles B	1089	salesman	50	"
W	DeLano Harriett—†	1089	housekeeper	49	"
X	Morris Gladys—†	1089	clerk	22	"
Y	Crawford Maude E—†	1089	saleswoman	54	82 Hunt'n av
Z	Pike Carl	1089	physician	55	82 "
A	Pike Rose—†	1089	housewife	48	82 "
B	Mahn Rosa—†	1089	"	55	Brookline
C	Rogers Alfred W	1089	physician	61	here
D	Rogers Alice—†	1089	housewife	45	407 Hunt'n av
E	Hunt Roy W	1089	manager	45	here
F	Tighe William A	1089	reporter	42	"
G	Westling Herman	1089	designer	54	"
H	Westling Mary—†	1089	housewife	44	"
K	Burrill Grace E—†	1089	"	50	"
L	Cox Townsend	1089	salesman	45	Newton
M	Castner Marion B—†	1089	housewife	29	10 Kenmore
N	Castner Ralph W	1089	manager	35	10 "
O	Martin Roy L	1089	clerk	20	New York
P	Wood Raymond A	1089	salesman	40	Newton
R	Rowland Samuel	1109	janitor	58	here
S	Kiff Flora—†	1109	hairdresser	40	"
T	Graves Josephine—†	1109	housewife	39	"
U	Foster Ella—†	1109	saleswoman	30	"
V	Mason Gilbert M	1109	physician	42	"
W	MacIntyre Mary—†	1109	saleswoman	40	"
X	Jenkins Bessie—†	1109	dressmaker	50	"
Y	McCarthy Francis	1109	physician	42	"
Z	Paraschos George	1109	merchant	40	"

Page.	Letter.	FULL NAME.	Residence, April 1, 1924.	Occupation.	Supposed Age.	Reported Residence April 1, 1923. Street and Number.

Boylston Street—Continued

	A	Goodale Helen—†	1109	hairdresser	48	here
	B	Arancio George	1109	merchant	37	"
	C	Cram Daniel	1199	contractor	50	390 Com av
	D	Nelson Julius	1109	lawyer	50	here
	E	Wehrle George	1109	salesman	50	"
	F	Bryant Myron	1109	dentist	39	"
	G	Arancio Frank	1109	merchant	40	"
	G¹	Elliot William	1109	banker	50	"
	H	Bailey Sarah—†	1109	dressmaker	50	"
	K	Brown Sarah—†	1109	teacher	40	"
	L	Lushins Max	1109	manager	40	"
	M	Campbell Harry	1109	"	48	Cambridge
	N	Hadley John	1111	janitor	65	here
	O	Wardwell James	1111	physician	42	"
	P	Ogden Frances—†	1111	hairdresser	31	"
	R	Shirley Edna—†	1111	demonstrator	30	"
	S	Walmsley Sarah—†	1111	saleswoman	30	"
	T	McGillicudy Frank	1111	physician	33	"
	U	Welles Franklin	1111	"	45	"
	V	Cuneen Anna—†	1111	stenographer	27	"
	W	Wanda Dorothy—†	1111	demonstrator	36	"
	X	Zeuch William	1111	salesman	45	"
	Y	Hall Ada—†	1111	saleswoman	39	"
	Z	Logue Sarah—†	1111	nurse	40	"
	A	McMillan Elisabeth—†	1111	saleswoman	41	"
	B	Holt Harry	1111	salesman	45	"
	C	Law Bernice—†	1111	stenographer	38	"
	D	Cunard Wilhelm	1111	manager	50	"
	E	Fay Frank	1111	salesman	48	"
	G	Kugell Simon H	1111	lawyer	31	"
	H	Dwyer Sarah—†	1111	housewife	55	Lynn
	K	Dodge Harry	1111	salesman	43	here
	L	Pontins William	1111	manager	45	"
	N	Bryant Gladys—†	1111	tel operator	25	"
	O	Goodman Joseph	1111	broker	48	"
	P	Cole Lawrence	1111	salesman	52	"
	R	Papineau Maude—†	1111	nurse	35	"
	S	Reynolds Charles	1111	broker	55	"
	T	DeForrest Mary—†	1111	bookkeeper	50	"
	U	Jones Clifford	1111	salesman	55	"
	V	Blair Frank	1111	manager	40	"

Boylston Street—Continued

Letter.	FULL NAME.	Residence	Occupation	Age	Reported Residence
w	Palmer Catherine—†	1111	stenographer	33	here
x	Boocock Jessie—†	1111	"	35	"
y	Malone Jean—†	1111	saleswoman	21	"
z	Thurlow Mary—†	1111	housewife	55	New Hampshire

Charlesgate East

Letter.	FULL NAME.	Residence	Occupation	Age	Reported Residence
A	Campbell Louise—†	24	maid	26	here
B	Gillispee Alexander	24	houseman	38	Wash'n D C
C	Johnson Helma—†	24	maid	45	here
D	MacLauchan Marjorie—†	24	nurse	35	"
E	McGillacudy Kate—†	24	cook	38	Brookline
F	Morss Edith S—†	24	housewife	42	here
G	Morss Henry A	24	manufacturer	52	"
H	Peterson Hilma—†	24	maid	34	Brookline
K	Robicheau Mary—†	24	governess	32	here
L	Jones John	50	janitor	40	"
M	Loring John	50	salesman	30	Reading
N	Burpee Ellen—†	50	housewife	40	140 Berkeley
O	Hirshman Louis	50	manager	35	Brookline
P	Brown Florence M—†	50	clerk	35	here
R	Banckman Marie—†	50	saleswoman	45	"
S	Dibble Rufus W	50	manager	40	"
T	Currier Ross	50	salesman	42	Cambridge
U	Nelson Edith—†	50	saleswoman	35	Brookline
V	Brackett Robert O	50	manager	48	Cambridge
W	Selfridge Arthur	50	lawyer	40	here
X	Drummond Emma—†	50	nurse	38	"
Y	Thomas John B	50	manager	45	"
Z	Hughes Eleanor—†	50	clerk	35	"
A	Rising Hawley K	50	lawyer	40	"
B	Olsson Marie L—†	50	manager	45	"
C	Chamberlain Julian	50	U S A	45	New York
D	McManus Mary—†	50	nurse	32	here
E	Thompson Walter	50	U S A	48	316 Hunt'n av
F	Abbott Martha—†	50	teacher	35	here
G	Shapira Samuel	50	salesman	38	Cambridge
H	Johnson Anna—†	50	teacher	35	Brookline
K	Adams Frank	50	manager	48	here
L	Congdon Louise—†	50	secretary	38	"

Charlesgate East—Continued

Letter	Full Name	Residence	Occupation	Age	Reported Residence
M	Woodman Alice—†	50	physician	40	here
N	Cooper Edwin C	50	manager	45	Somerville
O	Murphy Mary B—†	50	clerk	38	Brookline
P	Chick Ersla—†	50	"	28	Somerville
R	Conrade Anna—†	50	"	35	Brookline
S	Smith Gladys—†	50	nurse	30	here
T	Joyce Charles	52	janitor	35	"
V	Kochersperger Emma—†	52	housewife	65	"
W	Cummings Gladys—†	52	nurse	35	Brookline
X	MacDougall Derina W	52	lawyer	26	here
Y	MacDougall William T	52	electrician	34	"
Z	Manchester James A	52	manager	40	"
A	Burrows Mary—†	52	publisher	54	"
B	Goodwin Eva A—†	52	violin teacher	57	"
C	Nickerson James	52	salesman	40	"
D	Lewison Suzanne—†	52	housewife	50	"
E	O'Connor Eileen—†	52	clerk	28	Cambridge
F	Sewall William M	52	manager	45	here
G	Hayden Frank M	52	"	40	"
H	Coles Helen L—†	52	clerk	35	"
K	West Grace—†	52	saleswoman	35	Brookline
L	Dibbles Arthur W	52	manager	40	here
M	Gardner William	52	retired	60	Brookline
N	Haskell Edythe—†	52	tel operator	35	here
O	Ryan Lydia F—†	52	housewife	40	"
P	Davidson Mary—†	52	clerk	38	Cambridge
R	Haskell Grace I—†	52	"	38	here
S	Hickey Daniel F	52	salesman	45	Hull
T	Williams Edwin F	52	"	30	here
U	Nelligan Mary—†	52	nurse	35	"
V	McMurty Frank	52	salesman	30	Cambridge
W	Morse Myrtle—†	52	operator	30	here
X	Wyman Ethel—†	52	saleswoman	35	New York
Y	McPhee Joseph	56	janitor	45	here
Z	Remick Joseph	56	salesman	38	"
A	Thibodeau Rose—†	56	clerk	28	"
B	Pack Minnie—†	56	housewife	35	"
C	Eaton Loura J—†	56	clerk	35	"
D	Holden Sarah E—†	56	housekeeper	50	"
E	Holden Walter J	56	retired	60	"
F	Gardner Edward	56	salesman	40	Newton

Charlesgate East—Continued

Letter.	Full Name.	Residence, April 1, 1924.	Occupation.	Supposed Age.	Reported Residence, April 1, 1923.
G	Hunt May—†	56	clerk	32	here
H	Harris Sara—†	56	housewife	70	"
K	Houghton Madeline—†	56	clerk	30	"
L	Bent Arnold	56	salesman	45	Cambridge
M	Graham John	56	"	50	here
N	Rich Helen—†	56	clerk	40	"
O	Flenning Helen—†	56	housewife	60	"
P	McKay Mable—†	56	saleswoman	35	"
R	Skinner Clara—†	56	clerk	40	"
S	Sibley David F	56	lawyer	40	"
T	Holbrook Alice—†	56	housewife	45	"
U	Galbrith Stanley R	56	salesman	35	Brookline
V	Crawford May—†	56	saleswoman	30	here
V¹	Richards Elise—†	56	clerk	30	New York
W	Davidson Morris	56	salesman	38	Brookline
X	Sterns Alice—†	56	nurse	35	here
Y	Brabrook George H	56	salesman	45	Rochester N Y
Z	Johnsen George	56	"	40	New York
A	Rodway Charles B	60	janitor	56	here
B	Cousins Alice—†	60	housewife	40	"
C	Francis Sara—†	60	"	35	"
D	Babsker Joseph	60	salesman	38	"
E	Hinds Elizebeth—†	60	nurse	33	"
F	Buckley Sara—†	60	"	35	"
G	Morgan Edna—†	60	saleswoman	46	"
H	Kaufman Henry H	60	salesman	30	"
K	Fraser Sara—†	60	housewife	40	"
L	Madison Jennie—†	60	clerk	33	"
M	Abell Alice—†	60	housewife	38	New York
N	Barnum John	60	lawyer	40	here
O	Parker Mary—†	60	housewife	38	"
P	Tutle Cathryne—†	60	saleswoman	36	"
R	Traxler Anna M—†	60	"	40	"
S	Tully May—†	60	"	28	"
T	Wilson Ada—†	60	clerk	35	"
U	Fridler Enna V—†	60	housewife	65	"
V	Eveleth Helen F—†	60	teacher	45	"
W	Westcott Alice—†	60	clerk	35	"
X	Weimer Agnes—†	60	saleswoman	30	"
Y	Wells Amy—†	60	clerk	32	"
Z	Leahy Helen—†	60	saleswoman	45	"

Charlesgate East—Continued

B	Coggeshall Lydia—†	60	saleswoman	45	here
C	Abbott Anos	60	salesman	40	"
D	Turner Mary—†	60	housewife	50	"
E	Lipps Helen—†	60	clerk	40	"
F	LaCroix Henry	60	teacher	40	New York
G	Alber Herbert	64	janitor	40	52 Worcester sq
H	Farrar John A	64	lawyer	48	here
L	Little Charles A	64	salesman	50	"
M	Byrne Helen R—†	64	saleswoman	45	"
N	Nichols Herbert	64	salesman	35	"
O	Sinclair Charlotte—†	64	nurse	35	"
P	McGarry Frank J	64	druggist	44	"
R	McGarry Margaret—†	64	housewife	40	"
S	Jelal Jakob	64	manager	45	"
T	Swenson Carl J	64	salesman	38	"
U	Wallis Louis R	64	"	40	"
V	Gemms Charlott—†	64	housewife	55	"
W	Morse Blanche L—†	64	bookkeeper	45	"
X	Pindar Joseph L	64	manager	55	"
Y	Pindar Minnie E—†	64	housewife	62	"
Z	Ingalls Clara W—†	64	"	48	"
A	Stappls Edward	64	salesman	50	"
B	Scott Edward	64	"	48	"
C	Sterling Marire—†	64	nurse	40	"
D	Archer Harry	64	salesman	45	"
E	Hood Carolyn G—†	64	nurse	50	"
F	Wyeth Joseph R	64	salesman	45	"
G	Shipman Helen—†	64	housewife	48	"
H	Sibley Francis—†	64	teacher	40	"
K	Ferguson John	64	salesman	38	"
M	Hacker George	64	"	45	"
N	Newcomb Mable—†	64	saleswoman	35	"
O	Gromer Josephine—†	64	housewife	38	"
P	Bonner Mary R—†	64	"	60	"
R	McDonald Elizabeth A—†	64	nurse	40	Newton
S	Turner Margaret—†	64	saleswoman	35	Cambridge
T	Ham Colin E	64	manager	45	here
U	Sacker Amy—†	64	teacher	40	"
V	Scriven Marjorie—†	64	housewife	45	"

Commonwealth Avenue

w	Humphrey William	371	janitor	59	23 Warrenton
x	Winchester Walter F	371	dentist	40	here
y	Beatti Jennie—†	371	maid	40	Brookline
z	Catuna Harriet—†	371	cook	44	here
c	Perry John G	371	physician	84	"
d	Perry Martha D—†	371	housewife	83	"
a	Rellstab Barbare—†	371	nurse	33	14 Howland
b	Romkey Emma—†	371	maid	59	here
e	Bangs Mary F—†	371	secretary	61	"
f	Walker Sarah—†	371	retired	44	"
g	Harris Anna C—†	371	"	64	"
h	Sargent Edith A—†	371	secretary	34	"
k	Sargent Emilie—†	371	"	27	"
l	Sargent Emilie H—†	371	housewife	59	"
m	Sargent Margaret—†	371	secretary	24	"
n	Higgins Frank A	373	physician	56	"
o	Fuller Clara E—†	373	retired	59	"
p	Macmillan Janet—†	373	companion	70	"
r	Rogers Susie F—†	373	retired	77	"
s	Eaton Lucey H—†	373	housekeeper	80	"
u	Curtis Francis G	373	physician	65	"
v	Curtis Ruth D—†	373	housewife	64	"
x	Huntington Emma L—†	373	retired	72	"
y	Huntington Sarah E—†	373	"	65	"
a	Aslan Edward	373	"	40	"
b	Lerver Annie—†	373	housekeeper	43	"
d	Sanford George R	373	manager	51	"
e	Smith Alice E—†	373	retired	72	"
f	Williams Caroline A—†	373	"	79	"
k	Dodd George T	373	"	65	"
l	Brown Bertha G—†	373	"	69	"
m	Crosby Cora H—†	373	housewife	57	Cambridge
n	Crosby Isaac W	373	retired	60	"
o	Crosby Margaret D—†	373	"	30	"
r	Bradlee Thomas G	374	merchant	34	here
s	Grant Florence—†	374	housekeeper	45	"
t	Mower Penfield	374	broker	40	"
u	Smith Charles G, jr	374	lawyer	26	Brookline

Commonwealth Avenue—Continued

v	Hoyt George H	375	caretaker	60	Newton
w	Hoyt Ida M—†	375	housewife	55	"
x	Chenery Marion L—†	377	"	53	here
y	Chenery William E	377	physician	59	"
z	Connors Catherine—†	378	waitress	49	"
A	Donovan Norah—†	378	parlormaid	24	"
B	McDonald Sarah—†	378	cook	42	"
C	Pope Linder—†	378	housewife	73	"
D	Quigley James A	378	secretary	64	"
E	Weber Susan—†	378	chambermaid	58	199 Bay State rd
F	Fabyan Ellenor M—†	379	housewife	42	here
G	Fabyan Marshall	379	physician	45	"
H	Bingham Charles H	380	conductor	69	324 Com av
K	Bingham Elizabeth A—†	380	housewife	65	324 "
L	Payne Blanche—†	380	retired	55	324 "
M	Bird Charles S	381	"	39	England
N	Bird Julia—†	381	housewife	28	"
O	Davis Henry W	382	superintendent	46	here
P	Despradelle Leonora C—†	382	retired	64	"
R	Griffin Della E—†	382	maid	41	"
S	Hill Henry H	382	manufacturer	47	"
T	Hill Marian—†	382	housewife	45	"
U	Holbrook Mary D—†	382	"	50	"
V	Hunt Mary—†	382	"	38	"
W	Hunt Reed	382	professor	50	"
X	Boyden Dwight	382	retired	51	"
Y	Huse George H	382	merchant	64	"
Z	Huse Minnie W—†	382	housewife	53	"
A	Clunie John T J	382	broker	28	"
B	Clunie Suzette C—†	382	housewife	20	"
C	Reynolds Harriet G—†	382	"	25	"
D	Reynolds James	382	student	21	"
E	Sturgis Fannie T—†	382	housewife	66	"
F	Perera Gino L	382	artist	40	"
G	Nichols Elsie O—†	382	housewife	61	"
H	Nichols Henry G	382	treasurer	29	"
K	Collins Catherine—†	383	maid	34	395 Marlboro
L	Fahey Jane—†	383	waitress	25	here
M	Hall Anna B—†	383	none	22	"
N	Hall Anna K—†	383	housewife	49	"
O	Hall Henry L	383	salesman	23	"

Commonwealth Avenue—Continued

R	Davis Martha A—†	383	nurse	36	here
S	Erskine Alvan	384	merchant	30	Cambridge
T	Molberg Henry C	384	clerk	36	here
U	Moore George C	384	physician	48	"
V	McAllister Francis H	384	insurance agent	24	"
W	McAllister Laura H—†	384	teacher	58	"
X	Phisterer Frederick W	384	U S A	56	"
Y	Alden Craig	384	student	28	Milton
Z	Alden John W	384	retired	62	"
A	Alden Rachel—†	384	student	20	"
B	Alden Rachel C—†	384	housewife	58	"
C	Craig Josephine—†	384	"	48	Minnesota
D	Nears Florabel D—†	384	retired	59	here
E	Nears William N	384	broker	55	"
F	Clapp Freda—†	384	retired	50	"
G	Clapp George D	384	"	70	"
H	Knapp Bliss	385	reader	50	Brookline
K	Walker Frederick W	386	elevatorman	60	410 Mass av
L	Woods Bertha H—†	386	housewife	53	here
M	Woods Edward F	386	broker	60	"
N	Proctor Hazel—†	386	housewife	32	"
O	Proctor James O	386	broker	39	"
P	Boyle Edward J	386	merchant	66	"
R	Boyle Hannah A—†	386	retired	63	"
S	Dearborn Adelina—†	386	housewife	57	"
T	Dearborn John	386	constructor	57	"
W	Farmer Allen B	389	broker	43	653 Beacon
X	Farmer Natalia M—†	389	housewife	46	653 "
Y	Andrews Arthur C	390	manager	48	here
Z	Barrett Anna M—†	390	retired	47	"
A	Bartlett William O	390	physician	44	"
B	Briggs Frank H	390	merchant	67	"
C	Burdett Everett W	390	lawyer	69	"
D	Burdett Maud W—†	390	housewife	57	"
E	Colby Frank C	390	practitioner	53	"
F	Colby Mary B—†	390	"	47	"
G	Converse Charles H	390	retired	72	"
H	Converse Florence E—†	390	housewife	58	"
K	Currier Charles L	390	merchant	62	"
L	Currier Etta F—†	390	housewife	63	"
M	Ellis Amy F—†	390	"	46	"

Commonwealth Avenue—Continued

N	Ellis David A	390	lawyer	51	here
O	Goodwin Augustus	390	merchant	49	"
P	Hall Anthony D	390	manager	79	"
R	Hall Mary E—†	390	housewife	69	"
S	Hammond Eleanor P—†	390	teacher	58	"
T	Hayden Gertrude E—†	390	retired	70	"
U	Hoag Ella W—†	390	practitioner	67	"
V	Houghton Bertha—†	390	housewife	52	"
W	Houghton Elroy W	390	merchant	54	"
X	James Frank E	390	retired	66	"
Y	James Gertrude W—†	390	"	61	"
Z	Killen William V	390	"	66	"
A	Laskey Abbie G—†	390	"	59	"
B	Leonard Charles M	390	merchant	58	"
C	Leonard Elizabeth T—†	390	housewife	51	"
D	Leonard Julian T	390	salesman	29	"
E	Leonard Marian—†	390	student	24	"
F	Mackey William T	390	physician	44	"
G	Robinson Arthur L	390	merchant	65	Malden
H	Robinson Gertrude—†	390	none	26	"
K	Robinson Grace—†	390	"	37	"
L	Robinson Lovina P—†	390	"	59	"
M	Smith Carrie M—†	390	housewife	69	here
N	Smith Eugene H	390	dentist	70	"
O	Taber Gertrude L—†	390	retired	55	"
P	Thayer Harriet A—†	390	"	50	"
R	Cargill Mary—†	391	cook	49	39 Chestnut
S	Parker Hattie—†	391	housewife	55	here
T	Carey Ellen—†	393	cook	51	"
U	Dexter Josephine W—†	393	housewife	76	"
V	Farley Frances—†	393	maid	41	"
W	Maloney Catherine—†	393	housekeeper	57	"
Y	Abbott Waldo F	400–416	accountant	87	"
Z	Bacon Charles E	400–416	publisher	50	"
A	Bacon Pauline—†	400–416	housewife	33	"
B	Bennett Mary P—†	400–416	"	53	"
C	Cahill Eliza—†	400–416	physician	62	"
D	Cannon Henry P	400–416	merchant	62	"
E	Carleton Mary L—†	400–416	housewife	65	"
F	Chadwick Hanna M—†	400–416	"	54	"
G	Chapin Arthur B	400–416	banker	55	"

Commonwealth Avenue—Continued

Letter.	FULL NAME.	Residence, April 1, 1924.	Occupation.	Supposed Age.	Reported Residence, April 1, 1923.
H	Chapin Marion S M—†	400–416	housewife	41	here
K	Cohen Abraham K	400–416	lawyer	55	"
L	Cohen Sadie R—†	400–416	housewife	53	"
M	Cowles Ella H—†	400–416	"	77	"
N	Dabney Susanna R—†400–416	"	39	"
O	Duncan Frances S—†	400–416	"	59	"
P	Dustin Guy K	400–416	engineer	45	"
R	Dustin Marguerite M—†	400–416	housewife	37	"
S	Fairbanks Frank D	400–416	retired	64	"
T	Fairbanks Lucinda M—†	400–416	"	65	"
U	Fairbanks Mabel J—†	400–416	housewife	61	"
V	Gale Jessie N—†	400–416	"	47	Brookline
W	Gaskell Josephine A—†	400–416	retired	83	here
X	Glass James A	400–416	manufacturer	60	Brookline
Y	Hall Alwildia E—†	400–416	housewife	58	here
Z	Hall Frank C	400–416	manager	58	"
A	Hayden Josiah W	400–416	treasurer	77	"
B	Holmes Evelyn T—†	400–416	retired	65	"
C	Holmes Ida E—†	400–416	"	60	"
D	Johnson Annie E—†	400–416	housewife	42	"
E	Johnson George B	400–416	merchant	59	"
F	Jones Joseph G	400–416	broker	68	Brookline
G	Jordan Noah W	400–416	banker	78	here
H	Lord Elmer A	400–416	insurance agent	58	"
K	Lord Mary B—†	400–416	housewife	59	"
L	Lyle William P	400–416	manager	36	"
M	Mason Emma C—†	400–416	housewife	49	Illinois
N	Parker Charles L	400–416	broker	61	here
O	Parker Harold L	400–416	clerk	33	"
P	Pratt Marietta H—†	400–416	housewife	34	"
R	Pratt Walter M	400–416	treasurer	44	"
S	Reece John	400–416	manufacturer	40	34 Gloucester
T	Rice Clifford H	400–416	insurance	53	here
U	Shuman Sadie R W—†	400–416	housewife	43	"
V	Shuman Sidney E	400–416	merchant	57	"
W	Strecker Charles B	400–416	banker	60	"
X	Van Keuren Harold H	400–416	broker	42	Hotel Touraine
Y	West Anna S—†	400–416	housewife	57	here
Z	Cleere Anastasia—†	401	maid	36	"
A	Steinert Alexander	401	manufacturer	66	"
B	Steinert Bessie P—†	401	housewife	55	"

Commonwealth Avenue—Continued

c	Steinert Robert	401	manufacturer	79	here
d	Carr Susan W—†	403	housewife	74	"
e	DuBois Mary G—†	405	"	56	"
f	Amory Louise—†	407	"	61	"
g	Paine Dorothy B—†	409	student	23	"
h	Paine Francis W	409	banker	33	"
k	Paine Ruth W—†	409	housewife	56	"
l	Paine William A	409	banker	66	"
m	Bradley Robert S	411	manufacturer	66	"
n	Burke Bernard	411	butler	31	"
o	Chase Frances—†	411	housewife	29	132 Riverway
p	Chase Talbot	411	merchant	35	132 "
r	Newell Lavina—†	411	retired	62	330 Dartmout
s	Chandler Walter H	413	butler	55	306 "
t	Landstrom Ruth—†	413	maid	20	W Lynn
u	Carroll Julia—†	415	"	32	Southboro
v	Hayes Theresa—†	415	"	22	here
w	Hern Jessie—†	415	"	20	Brookline
x	Neilson Anna—†	415	"	45	148 Com av
y	Rust Florence P—†	415	housewife	43	here
z	Rust Paul D	415	merchant	49	"
a	Grandin Grace—†	461	housewife	74	"
b	Joyce Agnes—†	461	maid	35	"
c	Bunnell William S	463	student	22	"
f	Stodder Charles F	469	retired	61	"
g	Stodder Helen F—†	469	housewife	52	"
h	Biggers Geraldine—†	471	school teacher	22	S Carolina
k	Johnson Lena C—†	471	"	25	Brookline
l	Martin Eleanor—†	471	"	40	"
m	Martin Winona—†	471	"	42	"
n	Robinson Pauline—†	471	housekeeper	35	Mexico
o	Anderson William L	477	insurance agent	30	Quincy
p	Babb Charles H	477	broker	50	New York
r	Baker William F	477	student	38	Quincy
s	Bannon Francis	477	salesman	40	463 Com av
t	Carter Joseph W	477	"	40	Reading
u	Connors Margaret—†	477	stenographer	28	52 Queensberry
v	Gagnon Frederick	477	insurance agent	26	Gloucester
w	Hoe Robert M	477	salesman	35	New Jersey
x	Maroney Thomas H	477	marketman	45	462 Brookline av
y	Mills Hazel B—†	477	housewife	39	463 Com av

Commonwealth Avenue—Continued

z	Mills John J	477	hotelman	49	463 Com av
A	Cutler Alice R—†	479	housewife	52	here
B	Cutler Nathaniel R	479	merchant	26	"
C	Cutler William W	479	"	52	"
D	Cutler William W, jr	479	student	22	"
E	Rees Eliza M—†	481	housewife	26	Ohio
F	Rees Henry M	481	banker	33	"
G	Thorndike Augustus, jr	481	physician	28	here
H	Thorndike Olivia L—†	481	housewife	25	"
K	Crocker Lyneham	483	merchant	34	"
L	Crocker Mary T—†	483	housewife	32	"
N	Coolidge Algernon	487	physician	64	"
O	Coolidge Amy L—†	487	housewife	55	"
P	Coolidge Anne—†	487	social worker	26	"
R	Lydon Catherine—†	487	cook	32	"
S	Lydon Mary—†	487	maid	26	"
T	Quinn Josephine—†	487	"	30	284 Beacon
U	Balmain Margaret A—†	491	clerk	21	Winchester
V	Balmain Mary E—†	491	housekeeper	52	"
W	Prouty Arthur R	493	student	22	Worcester
Y	Rollins Charles H	497	secretary	68	here
Z	Rollins Helen M—†	497	housewife	74	"
D	Rollins Herbert	541	janitor	77	"
E	Berry Charles F	541	physician	53	"
F	Newell Adeline—†	541	housekeeper	55	"
G	Newell Marion—†	541	secretary	65	"
H	Brown Minnie G—†	541	housekeeper	60	Canada
K	Foley James	541	merchant	40	here
L	Ford Dorothy—†	541	student	23	Winthrop
M	Gross Breda—†	541	housewife	40	here
N	Joyce Gladys—†	541	"	24	16 Brainerd rd
O	Joyce Martin A	541	student	27	16 "
P	Stebbins Carrie A—†	541	housekeeper	57	here
R	Stebbins Edith M—†	541	"	60	"
T	Fellner Eugene	541	broker	56	"
U	Fellner Itta—†	541	housewife	56	"

Ipswich Street

B	Calleur Ethel B—†	30	artist	48	here
C	Nason Gertrude A—†	30	"	35	"

Page.	Letter.	FULL NAME.	Residence, April 1, 1921.	Occupation.	Supposed Age.	Reported Residence, April 1, 1923. Street and Number.

Ipswich Street—Continued

	G	Curtis Christine—†	30	artist	35	here
	L	Nordell Carl J	30	"	38	"
	M	Nordell Emma P—†	30	"	39	"
	N	Brett Harold M	30	"	40	"
	T	Titcomb Mary B—†	30	"	46	"
	U	Kirkpatrick William K	30	"	37	"
	V	Harstmeier Albert	30	"	50	"
	X	Pierce Margaret S—†	30	"	50	"
	B	Wallace Frederick E	30	"	30	"
	F	Major Ernest L	30	"	50	"
	G	Emerton James H	30	"	70	"
	K	Richardson Mary N—†	30	"	50	"
	L	Kauler Lee L	30	"	50	"
	M	Kauler William J	30	"	50	"
	O	Cook Leboron	30	"	37	"
	P	Perkins Harley	30	"	37	"
	S	Watson Elizabeth T—†	30	"	45	"
	T	Smith Rosamond L—†	30	"	40	"
	V	Kirkpatrick Marion P—†	30	"	37	"

Marlborough Street

	G	Clergy Charles	421	fireman	30	Brookline
	H	Cochran William	421	janitor	57	here
	K	Davies Edward A	421	insurance	28	"
	L	Weyse Arthur W	421	physician	57	"
	M	Suttan Gardner	421	clerk	24	N Andover
	N	Suttan Harry	421	superintendent	50	"
	O	Suttan Harry, jr	421	artist	26	"
	P	Lane Clarence G	421	physician	42	here
	R	Clark James H	421	retired	25	New York
	T	Gray Grace F—†	421	housewife	47	10 Gloucester
	U	Gray James C	421	decorator	47	10 "
	V	Ouadri Genevia B—†	423	housewife	48	Ohio
	W	Ouadri Virgil	432	student	23	"
	X	Granger Mary—†	423	retired	56	here
	Y	Mayberry Edith A—†	423	school teacher	48	"
	Z	Roundy Caroline M—†	423	housewife	68	"
	A	Roundy Franklin F	423	broker	66	"
	C	Brooks Florence M—†	425	nurse	50	"

Marlborough Street—Continued

D	deVeer Helena—†	425	nurse	55	here
E	Higgins Catherine—†	425	"	48	"
F	Kirkpatrick Agnes—†	425	"	37	"
G	McAdams Ruth—†	425	"	24	"
H	McCarthy Alice—†	425	"	42	"
K	McKay Annie—†	425	"	34	"
L	McKinnon Elizabeth—†	425	"	32	"
M	Milton Margery M—†	425	"	38	"
N	Ryan Florence—†	425	"	28	"
O	Taylor Mildred—†	425	"	26	Mass Gen Hosp
P	Tongring Signee—†	425	"	38	here
R	Blake Annie A—†	426	housewife	72	"
S	Blake Edward D	426	broker	73	"
T	Mulvaney Mary—†	426	cook	64	"
U	Everett Eugene E	427	physician	69	"
V	Everett Maude G—†	427	housewife	58	"
W	Morse Albert H, jr	428	broker	48	"
X	Coyle Margaret—†	429	cook	38	Plymouth
Y	Deuchy Mary—†	429	nurse	31	535 Beacon
Z	Waterbury Mildred C—†	429	housewife	37	535 "
A	Freeman Warren F	430	broker	52	Brookline
C	Dalton Marie L—†	430	teacher	51	here
D	Standish Myles	430	advertising	50	"
E	Smith William B	431	broker	45	"
F	Chatfield Anllia—†	432	housekeeper	45	"
G	Chatfield Charles K	432	pressfeeder	24	"
H	Chatfield Helen—†	432	housewife	27	Brookline
K	Whitman Marion—†	432	secretary	24	"
L	Southwick George R	433	physician	64	here
M	Brown Harriet—†	434	housewife	38	127 Pinckney
N	Brown Laurence A	434	lawyer	48	127 "
O	Badger George S C	435	physician	45	here
P	Badger Grace C—†	435	housewife	42	"
R	Grannum Cyril A	435	butler	30	14 Warwick
S	Grannum Louise M—†	435	housewife	27	14 "
T	Harbow Homer	436	teacher	40	here
U	Porter Ella F—†	436	housewife	70	"
V	Porter Lewis C	436	buyer	78	"
W	Harvey Elizabeth—†	437	cook	60	Atlanta Ga
X	Smith Charles M	437	physician	50	here
Y	Smith Mary L—†	437	housewife	48	"

Marlborough Street—Continued

z	Austin Caroline W—†	438	housekeeper	77	here
A	Austin Harriet—†	438	retired	92	"
B	Heard Adeline—†	439	housewife	65	"
C	Heard John, jr	439	clerk	34	"
D	Pickering Susan H—†	440	retired	60	"
F	Overlander Charles L	443	physician	50	520 Beacon
G	Overlander Ruth F—†	443	housewife	34	520 "
H	Emerson Frederick L	445	physician	63	here
K	Emerson Teckla H—†	445	housewife	53	"
L	Enos Angeline L—†	445	maid	38	"
M	Cabot William B	447	retired	66	"
N	Bransfield Anastasia—†	449	cook	45	"
O	Colby Harrison G O	449	retired	78	"
P	Eisen Elizabeth—†	449	maid	42	"
R	Walsh Mary—†	449	waitress	54	"
S	Appleton Francis H, jr	451	banker	48	"
T	Appleton Nathalie—†	451	housewife	35	"
U	Towle Alice M—†	453	"	57	"
V	Towle Elizabeth—†	453	student	21	"
W	Towle Harvey P	453	physician	57	"
X	Nye Helen C—†	455	housewife	50	"
Y	Nye William A	455	banker	56	"
Z	Southerland Mary E—†	455	housewife	60	25 St Germain
A	Taylor Ellise B—†	457	"	46	here
B	Taylor Ruth—†	457	housekeeper	23	"
C	Taylor Willis E	457	physician	47	529 Beacon

Massachusetts Avenue

D	Lawson James	9	janitor	41	here
E	Lawson Mary B—†	9	housewife	41	"
F	Bryant Alice G—†	9	physician	50	"
G	Tingley Louisa P—†	9	"	45	"
H	Williams Isaac	9	choreman	65	"
K	Boyd Adia—†	9	maid	40	"
L	McIntosh Christine—†	9	"	29	"
M	Reynolds Edward	9	physician	63	"
N	Reynolds George	9	"	25	"
O	Reynolds Harriet P—†	9	none	54	"
R	Aldrich Harry	9	lawyer	60	"

Massachusetts Avenue—Continued

Letter	Full Name	Residence April 1, 1924	Occupation	Supposed Age	Reported Residence April 1, 1923
s	Aldrich Henrietta—†	9	none	58	here
w	Daly Mary—†	9	maid	26	"
u	Thorndike Anna—†	9	none	32	"
v	Thorndike Paul	9	physician	60	"
y	Cummin Charlotte W—†	9	none	70	"
z	Cummin John W	9	physician	46	"
a	Dennesy Nellie—†	9	maid	50	"
c	Dolan Margaret—†	9	retired	70	"
d	Rosedale Anna—†	9	"	48	"
e	Rosedale Charles	9	physician	62	"
f	Rosedale Lillian, jr—†	9	none	22	"
l	Taylor Lila M—†	27	dressmaker	51	"
m	Fraser Ann R—†	27	bookkeeper	48	"
n	Murray Charles W	27	janitor	44	"
o	Murray Gertrude W—†	27	housewife	45	"
p	Timmerman Norman E	27	student	21	"
r	Brokemyr Eval	27	engineer	36	"
s	Gould Warren F	27	salesman	48	"
t	Raynor Margaret O—†	27	none	44	"
u	Rieley Marie E—†	27½	student	22	31 Mass av
w	Hafferty John J	27½	druggist	47	here
x	Hubbard Annie W—†	27½	teacher	45	"
y	Crowninshield Elizabeth—†	27½	housekeeper	68	"
z	Crowninshield Ethel F—†	27½	teacher	42	"
c	Evans John H	31	janitor	45	"
d	Daly Marguerite S—†	31	housewife	26	"
e	Daly William J	31	physician	50	"
f	Morrison Lillian—†	31	manicurist	31	Cambridge
g	Myers Anna—†	31	housewife	51	26 Evans way
h	Richards Else—†	31	retired	75	here
k	Cunningham Allan	31	broker	32	"
l	Cunningham Mary—†	31	piano teacher	32	"
m	Barker Augusta—†	31	housekeeper	50	"
n	Craven Lena—†	31	nurse	49	"
o	Wendell Constant	31	salesman	35	"
p	Wendell Helen S—†	31	housewife	71	"
r	Wendell Mark T	31	merchant	42	"
s	Wendell Percy L	31	salesman	34	"
t	Freeman Harold P	31	clerk	36	"
u	Freeman Katherine G—†	31	housekeeper	47	"
v	Burgess Edna S—†	31	housewife	36	"

Massachusetts Avenue—Continued

w	Burgess Robert S	31	broker	46	here
x	O'Shea Mary—†	31	maid	29	"
y	Le Moyne Mary M—†	31	retired	73	"
z	Haskell Francis H	31	insurance agent	60	Brookline
A	Haskell Sarah A—†	31	housewife	56	"
B	Hughes Mabel C—†	31	housekeeper	49	here
D	Stockford LeBaron B	47	proprietor	45	"
E	Greco Charles A	47	linguist	54	"
F	Griffin Agnes B—†	47	stenographer	30	Everett
G	Griffin Mary A—†	47	housekeeper	74	"
K	Blodgett John H	51	physician	51	here
L	Hanson Anna C—†	51	nurse	50	"
w	Hubley Frances—†	107	dressmaker	55	"
x	Young Charles H	107	salesman	40	"
E	Daley Marion L—†	119	teacher	38	"
F	Botsford Harry G	119	salesman	25	"
H	Anderson Theresa—†	119	dressmaker	37	"
K	Grant Laura L—†	119	housewife	48	"
L	Smith Blayden—†	119	nurse	28	"
M	Alander Marie—†	119	"	30	"
N	Pike Anna M—†	119	retired	74	137 Hamilton
O	Pike Anna M—†	119	clerk	37	137 "
P	Barry Mary—†	119	"	26	here
T	MacKenzie Daniel E	119	laborer	23	Nova Scotia
R	Murphy James F	119	chauffeur	29	1030 Boylston
S	Murphy Mary B—†	119	housewife	27	Halifax N S

Newbury Street

x	Betts Edwin	376	manufacturer	24	Canada
y	Elverkin Beulah E—†	376	housekeeper	34	30 Hemenway
z	Spicer Catherine S—†	376	clerk	32	Cambridge
A	Spicer Frederick C	376	upholsterer	33	"
B	Ferguson Melvin D	376	clerk	46	420 Mass av
C	Luthi William	376	salesman	56	Hotel Buckminster
D	Powers William	376	clerk	53	"
E	Rogers Isabel—†	376	vocalist	40	520 Mass av
F	Cahill Mary E—†	376	cashier	45	Cambridge
G	Nichols Ada E—†	376	housewife	65	here
H	Nichols Henry H	376	watchman	70	"

Newbury Street—Continued

K	Woodward Edward C	376	machinist	38	Georgia
L	Defresnes Julenne M—†	376	milliner	22	here
M	Defresnes Mary E—†	376	dressmaker	52	"
N	Bancroft Mary F—†	378	none	60	376 Newbury
O	Parsons Annie—†	378	saleswoman	40	Winchester
P	Cherry Marie J—†	378	none	25	here
R	Collins Alma—†	378	"	40	"
S	Lane Alice T—†	378	secretary	40	"
T	Lane Georgiana M—†	378	clerk	38	"
U	Lane John J	378	retired	78	"
V	Bailey Catherine B—†	378	housewife	60	"
W	Golding Frances A—†	380	"	25	Medford
X	Golding William T	380	salesman	33	"
Y	Narison William	380	musician	31	Brookline
Z	Mortell James	380	clerk	35	here
A	Mortell Louise—†	380	storekeeper	65	"
B	Jones Catherine J—†	380	housewife	50	"
C	Jones Marie G—†	380	clerk	27	"
D	Malley Anna T—†	380	bookkeeper	35	"
E	Swenson Oscar	380	chauffeur	47	Scituate
F	Gardener Mary L—†	380	none	50	here
G	Sullivan Edward F	380	dentist	32	149 Mass av
H	Little Colby—†	382	dressmaker	68	here
K	Bergstrom Lina E—†	382	manicurist	68	"
L	Larsen Elizabeth S—†	382	nurse	28	"
M	Phillips Eva S—†	382	dressmaker	36	"
N	Sprague Harold T	382	shipper	31	"
O	Kenney Michael	382	machinist	45	Cambridge
P	Kenney Thomas	382	"	55	"
R	Sullivan Marie P—†	382	teacher	28	9 Ellery
S	Valsecchi Beatrice—†	382	housewife	29	83 Westland av
T	Valsecchi John	382	salesman	31	83 "
U	Wiley Harriet L—†	382	housewife	50	here
V	Wiley Leanard J	382	engineer	42	"
W	Collins James J	382	orderly	42	32 Rutland sq
X	Collins Maude—†	382	housewife	41	32 "
Y	Gorden William J	382	engineer	44	here
Z	Rockwell Mildred B—†	382	hairdresser	24	Norwood
A	Ednester Florence M	382	clerk	36	193 St Botolph
B	Ednester Jennie—†	382	none	69	193 "
C	Ednester Sarah M—†	382	teacher	46	193 "

8—10

Newbury Street—Continued

D	Schaffer Sarah E—†	382	dressmaker	55	here
E	Burleigh Alice—†	382	clerk	31	"
F	Meservey Laura E—†	382	none	40	Waltham
G	Payzant Ida M—†	382	clerk	25	here
H	Snow Annabel—†	382	none	52	"
K	Payzant Marion—†	382	teacher	26	"
L	Tolliday Arthur W	382	bookkeeper	65	181 Perham
M	Tolliday Grace H—†	382	clerk	26	181 "
N	Tolliday Sarah I—†	382	housewife	53	181 "
O	Davidson Everett J	386	real estate	26	here
O¹	Davidson Lois C—†	386	director	45	"
P	Dana Bertha M—†	386	housewife	50	"
R	Dana James W	386	salesman	64	"
S	Ward George A	386	"	40	"
T	Baumgarten Cecile E—†	386	housewife	29	Lawrence
U	Baumgarten William B	386	optometrist	38	"
V	Quirie Ralph	386	carpenter	45	Cambridge
W	Selleck William R	386	mechanic	48	here
X	Spear Esther J—†	386	housewife	48	"
Y	Spear George H	386	wireworker	55	"
D	Laughman Leo B	399	steward	33	"
E	Laughman Pauline M—†	399	housewife	33	"
F	Le Blanc Lena—†	399	waitress	31	"
G	Macy Thomas	399	chauffeur	25	Hanover
H	McLoud John	399	doorman	65	here
K	Meany John	399	"	50	"
M	Griffin Anna—†	401	maid	34	here
N	Adams William H	403	student	21	Providence R I
O	Arana Julius	403	"	24	18 Batavia
P	Fleming Margaret J—†	403	housewife	50	Medford
R	Foale Arthur B S	403	student	23	324 Com av
S	Huston Dorothy—†	403	waitress	20	here
T	Partridge Benjamin	403	clerk	27	"
U	Paulin Frances—†	403	saleswoman	28	103 Norway
V	Paulin Phoebe—†	403	waitress	23	103 "
W	Potter Annie—†	403	dressmaker	50	here
X	Walker Richard F	403	lawyer	27	"
Y	Wirt Sidney H	403	salesman	26	"
Z	Campbell Ada—†	405	saleswoman	25	Cambridge
A	Campbell Eva—†	405	waitress	22	"
B	Campbell Mabel—†	405	nurse	26	"

Newbury Street—Continued

c	Gillis Catherine—†	405	dressmaker	45	here
d	Gillis Margaret—†	405	checker	52	"
e	Townsend Harry B	405	carpenter	53	"
f	Townsend Mary G—†	405	housewife	52	"
g	Townsend Mary J—†	405	checker	21	"
h	Zaitevsky Leon N	405	student	25	California
l	Cronin Bernard M	412	salesman	30	57 St Germain
m	Cronin Helen F—†	412	housewife	30	57 "
n	Lythgoe David H	412	teacher	45	81 Westland av
o	Diego Manuel	412	chef	29	1038 Boylston
p	Ricalde Jouquin	412	waiter	22	1038 "
r	Ricalde Raymond	412	vocalist	29	1038 "
s	Acrves Arthur	414	steward	30	23 Rutland sq
t	Bradford James G	414	salesman	25	Plymouth
u	Horton Clifford H	414	chauffeur	32	11 Dalton
v	Keaitly Caroline—†	414	housewife	50	Cambridge
w	Keaitly Robert	414	clerk	45	"
x	Lawrence Catherine S—†	414	dressmaker	38	11 Dalton
y	Ledue Henry J	414	dentist	28	95 Hunt'n av
z	Milen Charles R	414	salesman	29	Newton
a	Parmenter Eva—†	414	housewife	46	Hingham
b	Parmenter George	414	starter	56	"
c	Porter Howard	414	printer	30	20 Haviland
d	Ryan Joseph H	414	chef	24	Plymouth
e	Coaley Elizabeth P—†	415	housewife	35	here
f	Coaley Harry	415	superintendent	55	"
h	Babcock Adele—†	418	hairdresser	60	"
k	Glover Georgine W—†	418	teacher	45	"
l	Jeffery Hester C—†	418	housekeeper	75	"
m	Nelson Gertrude—†	418	nurse	35	"
n	Conors John	420	elevatorman	47	Wakefield
o	Dolan Elizabeth—†	420	maid	55	here
p	Frazier Norma—†	420	bookkeeper	26	Plymouth
r	Harkins Mary W—†	420	housekeeper	55	here
s	Malatesta Charles M	420	retired	70	"
t	Adams Charles	422	waiter	60	"
u	Cooney Charles D	422	salesman	29	"
v	Cooney Josephine M—†	422	typist	25	"
w	Cooeny Leo	422	inspector	24	"
x	Cooeny Nellie J—†	422	housewife	52	"
y	Howe Charles	422	steward	55	Cambridge

Newbury Street—Continued

z	Coggins Georgia L—†	424	dressmaker	55	here
A	Drummey Margaret—†	424	housewife	41	"
B	Drummey Richard	424	clerk	36	"
C	Duggan Charles J	424	waiter	33	"
D	Haley Florence A—†	424	dermatologist	66	"
E	McGlinchey John J	424	broker	60	"
F	Miller Stanley	424	watchman	56	"
G	Tyrell Catherine M—†	424	dressmaker	56	"
H	Tyrell Margaret—†	424	housekeeper	60	"
K	Cleveland William	426	salesman	60	"
L	Eaton Walter	426	chauffeur	31	Waterbury Ct
M	Garrity John	426	"	42	Framingham
N	Hoxie Ernest	426	salesman	42	E Weymouth
O	Meenan Margaret A—†	426	nurse	42	here
P	Meenan Mary E—†	426	housekeeper	40	"
R	Wade Gregory	426	salesman	28	"
S	Fraprie Frank R	428	publisher	49	Brookline
U	Bennett George S	440	salesman	57	here
V	Bennett Georgini M—†	440	housewife	56	"
W	Cameron Catherine—†	440	operator	38	Saxonville
X	Chisholm Bessie—†	440	"	27	41 Batavia
Y	Chisholm Jennie—†	440	"	26	41 "
A	Synder Michael G	440	clerk	34	here
C	Greenwood Tancred S	440	architect	25	Cambridge
D	Aitken Annie—†	440	housewife	40	Medford
E	Eliasen Martha—†	440	nurse	37	here
F	Shaw Catherine—†	440	housewife	62	66 Edgewood
G	Shaw Edward	440	janitor	64	66 "
H	Shaw Harold	440	"	32	66 "
K	Harrington Alice F—†	440	saleswoman	39	here
L	Miller James A	440	printer	24	Arlington
M	Miller Mary E—†	440	tel operator	29	"
N	Green Annie—†	440	saleswoman	43	Watertown
O	Craig Susan—†	440	secretary	35	here
P	Hall Helen M—†	440	nurse	75	"
R	Mitchell Merle—†	440	"	24	"
S	Snow Catherine—†	440	physician	25	"
T	Meuse Catherine—†	440	saleswoman	26	"
U	Sawyer Alice—†	440	cashier	38	"
V	Sawyer Margaret—†	440	musician	40	"
W	D'Avesne Alexander	440	teacher	60	246 Newbury

Newbury Street—Continued

Letter	Full Name	Res.	Occupation	Age	Reported Residence
x	Colby Frederick W	440	salesman	48	here
y	Gilbert Helen M—†	440	housewife	35	"
a	Coleman Nellie S—†	440	saleswoman	45	Quincy
b	Elliott Bertha—†	440	packer	46	here
c	Maynard Jean—†	440	teacher	45	"
d	Stevens Annie—†	440	housekeeper	61	Marblehead
e	Stevens Helen—†	440	"	36	"
f	Stevens William H	440	stationmaster	68	"
g	Fay Harry	440	auditor	44	Cambridge
h	Mulcahy Nora—†	440	cashier	32	here
k	Moran Mary—†	440	dressmaker	30	530 Newbury
l	Billings Marion	440	teacher	24	Stoughton
m	McLaughlin Catherine–†	440	clerk	25	Gloucester
n	Sipperley Ann—†	440	"	22	Troy N Y
o	Brereton William	440	salesman	46	here
p	Mason Mary E—†	440	printer	30	Cambridge
r	Mars Eva B—†	440	saleswoman	36	here
s	Marr Eva—†	440	clerk	35	"
t	Knox Mary—†	440	waitress	50	"
u	Swaelve Richard	440	salesman	50	England
v	Magee Richard	440	"	36	Brookline
w	Gillis Hugh A	440	machinist	29	here
x	Hergett Catherine—†	440	housewife	31	"

Raleigh Street

Letter	Full Name	Res.	Occupation	Age	Reported Residence
y	Ames Oliver—†	1	domestic	30	here
z	Fessenden Caroline—†	1	housewife	50	"
a	Fessenden Louise—†	1	student	23	"
b	Fessenden Sewel H	1	broker	55	"
c	Geegan Charles	1	chauffeur	20	Chicago Ill
d	Mulhill Julia—†	1	maid	32	Philadelphia
e	Todd Sarah—†	1	cook	30	here
f	Byrnes Annie—†	2	maid	30	"
g	Donohue Bridget—†	2	"	27	"
h	Ford Helen—†	2	"	30	"
k	Gleason Mary—†	2	cook	50	"
l	Hamlin George P	2	retired	55	"
m	Hamlin Mary—†	2	housewife	45	"
n	McGuire Catherine—†	2	waitress	35	"

Ward 8—Precinct 11

CITY OF BOSTON.

LIST OF RESIDENTS
20 YEARS OF AGE AND OVER

(FEMALES INDICATED BY DAGGER)

AS OF

APRIL 1, 1924

HERBERT A. WILSON, } *Listing*

JAMES F. EAGAN, } *Board.*

CITY OF BOSTON—PRINTING DEPARTMENT

Bay State Road

	Letter	Full Name	Residence	Occupation	Age	Reported Residence
	A	Barber Sarah H —†	110	teacher	36	here
	B	Green William H	110	operator	24	"
	C	Petrie Grace—†	110	maid	35	"
	D	Swift Walter B	110	physician	54	"
	E	Lockwood Caroline S—†	111	housekeeper	28	"
	F	Lockwood Dunbar	111	manufacturer	32	"
	G	Lockwood Emmline D-†	111	retired	71	"
	H	Manning Helen—†	111	maid	24	"
	L	Doherty Joseph E	114	broker	64	"
	M	Doherty Mary J—†	114	housewife	52	"
	N	Hannon Anna—†	114	maid	34	"
	O	MacIntosh Ellen A —†	114	retired	58	New York
	P	Gerle Anna—†	115	maid	44	here
	R	Peterson Hulda—†	115	"	49	"
	S	Sias Alice E—†	115	retired	66	"
	T	Swenson Emma—†	115	maid	54	"
	U	Jones Elenor—†	116	retired	46	"
	V	McManus Annie—†	117	cook	50	"
	W	Snow Fredrick E	117	lawyer	59	"
	X	Snow Lillian T—†	117	retired	42	"
	Y	Snow William T	117	lawyer	26	"
	Z	Sullivan Jane —†	117	maid	35	"
	A	Cooper Mary—†	118	cook	38	"
	B	Lahey Alice—†	118	housewife	38	"
	C	Lahey Frank H	118	physician	40	"
	D	Riley Annie—†	118	waitress	24	"
	E	Lefavour Anna B—†	119	retired	60	"
	F	Lefavour Henry	119	professor	60	"
	G	Bowen Florence —†	120	waitress	22	St John N B
	H	Cox Elizabeth K—†	120	cook	35	here
	K	Cunningham Minnie—†	120	nurse	50	"
	L	Rothwell Florence B —†	120	housewife	40	"
	M	Rothwell James M	120	real estate	51	"
	O	Leader Katherine—†	122	nurse	31	"
	P	O'Malley Mary —†	122	maid	30	"
	R	Smith Nora K —†	122	housewife	36	"
	S	Smith Stanley W	122	retired	54	"
	T	Hyde Mary—†	124	maid	38	"
	U	Ward Ellenor H —†	124	housewife	38	"
	V	Ward Lauriston	124	manager	40	"

2

Bay State Road—Continued

Letter.	FULL NAME.	Residence	Occupation.	Age	Street and Number.
w	Moen Sophie—†	125	retired	50	here
x	Clymer George	126	physician	40	"
y	Clymer Susan W—†	126	housewife	39	"
z	Shea Nellie—†	126	maid	32	259 Beacon
A	Farlow Annie H—†	127	retired	70	here
B	Farlow John W	127	physician	70	"
c	Swanson Eva—†	127	maid	33	"
D	Eldridge Clarence F	128	lawyer	62	"
E	Eldridge Helen—†	128	housewife	48	"
F	Eldridge Marion W—†	128	teacher	34	"
G	Powers Ida M—†	128	housekeeper	45	"
H	Curtis Margaret M—†	131	retired	50	"
K	Curtis Penlope—†	131	student	23	"
L	Ward Josephine—†	131	maid	26	413 Beacon
M	Guild Frederick	133	retired	72	76 Bay State rd
N	Guild Samuel	133	"	62	76 "
O	Halloran Margaret L—†	133	maid	64	76 "
P	Falvey Alice—†	135	retired	45	here
R	Falvey Mary J—†	135	"	35	"
S	Prendergast Julia C—†	135	"	60	"
T	Finlay Lillian B—†	137	maid	48	"
U	Jones Arthur M	137	clerk	48	"
V	Jones Mary W—†	137	housewife	46	"
W	Vaughan Frank M	139	physician	45	"
X	Vaughan Josephine—†	139	student	21	236 Bay State rd
Y	Vaughan Josephine E—†	139	housewife	47	236 "
Z	Gorman Minnie—†	141	maid	33	here
A	Mahoney Mary—†	141	"	45	"
B	McLeod Maude—†	141	housekeeper	43	"
C	Stetson Charles	141	lawyer	45	"
D	Burgess Mary—†	143	maid	29	"
E	Peters Amey D—†	143	retired	60	"
F	Peters Jane—†	143	"	26	"
G	Peters William Y	143	"	60	"
H	Peters William Y, jr	143	student	23	"
L	Giles Willis L	147	houseman	48	"
M	McAndrew Ellen K—†	147	maid	46	"
N	Burr Mary—†	152	cook	55	"
O	McAuley Katherine—†	152	maid	30	5 Brookline
P	Mitchell Florence—†	152	waitress	25	Cambridge
R	Noble James	152	laborer	35	here

Bay State Road—Continued

s	Stone Albert J	152	real estate	40	here
t	Stone Anna H—†	152	housewife	65	"
u	Stone Mary P—†	152	none	45	"
w	Duggan Mary—†	154	cook	55	"
x	Rust Dora D—†	154	housewife	71	"
y	Walsh Jane—†	154	maid	25	"
z	Harding Emor H	155	lawyer	69	"
A	Harding Helen B—†	155	housewife	58	"
B	Harding Helen B—†	155	nurse	29	"
c	Harding Madaline—†	155	clerk	32	"
D	Bosworth George F	156	architect	62	"
E	Bosworth Louise—†	156	housewife	55	"
F	Dale Margaret—†	156	maid	62	"
G	Orth John	156	teacher	72	"
H	Orth Syvilla—†	156	"	63	"
K	Young Royal B—†	156	"	50	"
L	Rotch Charles M	157	manager	45	"
M	Rotch Edith E—†	157	clerk	48	"
N	Rotch Mary E—†	157	retired	76	"
o	Rotch William	157	trustee	79	"
P	Hawkins Caroline—†	158	housewife	27	Australia
R	Hawkins Florence—†	158	"	48	here
s	Hawkins Frederick D	158	clerk	23	"
T	Hawkins Georgiana W–†	158	none	20	"
U	Hawkins Louis T	158	merchant	51	"
v	Bancroft Charles F	159	engineer	51	"
W	Bancroft Cornelia H—†	159	housewife	51	"
x	Horgan Julia—†	160	cook	32	"
y	McDonald Julia—†	160	waitress	20	"
z	O'Brien James T	160	manager	45	"
A	O'Brien Mary A—†	160	housewife	35	"
B	Patten Henry G	161	banker	60	"
c	Lacey Lucy—†	162	nurse	37	"
D	Lang Ethel R—†	162	housewife	36	"
E	Lang Malcom M	162	musician	41	"
F	Reagan Julia—†	162	waitress	25	New York
G	Sullivan Julia—†	162	maid	45	45 St James
H	Doyle Catherine M—†	163	"	33	here
K	Goodnow Ellen S—†	163	retired	60	"
L	Goodnow Philip S	163	salesman	33	"
M	Kelley Bridget F—†	163	maid	39	"

Bay State Road—Continued

Letter	Full Name.	Res.	Occupation.	Age	Reported Residence
N	Johnson Herbert S	164	clergyman	57	here
O	Johnson Mary C—†	164	housewife	54	"
P	Kelley Annie—†	164	cook	54	162 Bay State rd
R	Odlune Gretta—†	164	maid	22	141 Beacon
S	Davis Clara S—†	165	retired	53	here
T	Livingston Arlington M	165	caretaker	63	82 Chestnut
U	Livingston Katharine K—†	165	"	55	82 "
V	Prest Alice E—†	165	retired	46	here
W	Prest Bertha S—†	165	"	52	"
X	Prest William M	165	judge	62	"
Y	Bradley Eleanor C—†	166	housewife	30	"
Z	Bradley Ralph	166	merchant	35	"
A	MacPherson Mary—†	166	cook	24	Halifax N S
B	Southerland Isabel—†	166	waitress	35	here
D	Caspoil Elizabeth—†	168	maid	57	"
E	Foye Dorothy C—†	168	student	24	"
F	Foye Eugene E	168	broker	55	"
G	Foye Lura B—†	168	housewife	54	"
H	Bane Joseph H	169	janitor	66	"
K	Fuller Anna F—†	169	nurse	27	Laconia N H
L	Keegan Nancy S—†	169	"	24	here
M	Ross Mary J—†	169	"	40	"
N	Christensen Marie—†	171	maid	41	"
O	Logue Mary—†	171	"	26	143 Bay State rd
P	Wells Elizabeth D—†	171	student	22	here
R	Wells Wellington	171	lawyer	50	"
T	Joyce Annie—†	173	maid	27	Chestnut Hill
U	King Delia—†	173	"	35	here
V	Parker Chauncy D	173	banker	55	"
W	Parker Mary E—†	173	housewife	45	"
X	Fletcher Cuntis	174	salesman	63	"
X¹	Libbey Wilbur	174	retired	71	"
Y	McCorthy Hatie—†	174	maid	52	"
Z	Nickerson Alice—†	174	"	28	Gloucester
B	Simpson Marjorie—†	174	clerk	29	here
C	Dunne Alice—†	175	housekeeper	34	"
D	Dunne Duval	175	salesman	32	"
E	Dunne Frank L	175	merchant	72	"
F	Keating Margeret—†	175	maid	35	"
G	Magee Bridget—†	175	cook	31	"
H	Betts Ella J—†	176	retired	71	"

Bay State Road—Continued

K	Hagerty Annie—†	176	cook	28	here
L	Hagerty Suzen—†	176	maid	23	"
M	Talbot Edith—†	176	housewife	51	"
N	Talbot Edmund	176	lawyer	59	"
O	Brown Grace I—†	177	student	37	4 Short
P	Lawrence Madaline—†	177	housewife	40	here
R	Lawrence Robert M	177	physician	77	"
S	Holis Frederick	178	manager	57	"
T	Holis Helen B—†	178	housewife	50	"
U	Pricking Gertrude—†	178	retired	52	"
V	Bowers John W	179	student	22	Gloucester
W	Fiske Mary I—†	179	housekeeper	50	50 Ridgemon
X	Leary Harold	179	student	24	New York
Y	Moses Lucy L—†	179	"	35	"
Z	Carlton Georgie—†	180	housekeeper	51	8 Blackwood
A	Parmer Bertha—†	180	retired	55	England
B	Parmer Edward	180	lawyer	57	"
C	Jacques Mary F—†	181	maid	36	here
D	Mahoney Mary A—†	181	"	40	"
E	McInerney Bridget M—†	181	laundress	42	"
F	Watters Elizabeth S—†	181	housewife	56	"
G	Watters Walter F	181	vice president	60	"
H	Freeman Albert	182	retired	45	"
K	Hermon Josephine—†	182	housewife	50	"
L	Joyce Elizabeth—†	182	cook	27	Brookline
M	Sullivan Mary—†	182	maid	23	here
O	Dangan Delice—†	184	"	50	"
P	Mulcahy Hannah—†	184	"	40	"
R	Wood Elizabeth H—†	184	housewife	79	"
S	Bromwell Leitish—†	185	"	50	"
T	Bromwell Scott	185	student	26	Wash'n D C
U	Dwyer Mary—†	185	waitress	26	Ireland
V	Hunter Mary—†	185	maid	54	here
W	Kerr Margurie—†	185	cook	32	Hamilton
X	Robley Ellen—†	185	maid	24	here
X¹	Bumper Julia—†	186	"	33	"
Y	Donlan Helen—†	186	cook	23	"
Z	Noyes James	186	retired	53	"
A	Noyes Mary—†	186	housewife	50	"
C	Trip Edward	187	engraver	54	"
D	McCullagh Frances—†	188	housewife	45	429 Mass av

Bay State Road—Continued

		FULL NAME.	Residence, April 1, 1924	Occupation.	Supposed Age	Reported Residence, April 1, 1923. Street and Number.
E		McCullagh John	188	cook	56	429 Mass av
F		Roberts Nathanel	188	machinist	31	429 "
G		Cushman Henry	189	lawyer	70	here
H		Cushman Isabel—†	189	housewife	70	"
K		McPhee Amelia—†	189	maid	20	Canada
L		Mullen Julia—†	189	"	70	here
M		Washburn Amy—†	190	housewife	43	"
N		Washburn Fedrick	190	retired	54	"
O		Benton Louis E	191	"	63	"
P		Herbert Marion—†	191	cook	37	"
R		Hollander Theodore C	191	merchant	74	"
S		Cook Helena E—†	192	student	20	247 Newbury
T		Coulter Sally—†	192	"	22	11 E Newton
U		Crane Eleanor—†	192	"	20	New York
V		Dehendayer Madge V—†	192	"	24	247 Newbury
W		Demulin Marie M—†	192	"	23	247 "
X		Ralston Anna M—†	192	"	24	247 "
Y		Williams Kathrina—†	192	"	25	247 "
Z		Winter Audrey—†	192	"	21	Malden
A		Wyatt Ruth—†	192	"	21	475 Beacon
B		Bjooklund Selma—†	193	maid	30	New York
C		Romumles Matilda—†	193	"	35	here
D		Vose Dora E—†	193	housewife	34	"
E		Vose Frank T	193	real estate	64	"
F		Leary Johana—†	194	housewife	48	179 Bay State rd
G		Leary John J	194	laborer	45	179 "
H		Dutton Harry	195	retired	70	Cambridge
K		Gorgan Mary—†	195	cook	42	2 Plymouth
L		Morse Ervin P	195	president	42	320 Com av
M		Morse Marion—†	195	housewife	44	320 "
N		Small Alfonso	195	attendant	30	Cambridge
O		Sargent Porter	196	publisher	55	here
P		Sawyer Rachel—†	196	nurse	22	"
R		White Louise—†	196	teacher	21	"
S		Innes Charles H	197	lawyer	56	"
T		Innes Charles J	197	student	25	"
U		Innes Edna B—†	197	housewife	50	"
V		Innes Hiller	197	student	22	"
W		Karasawa Mary—†	197	maid	32	Salem
X		Karasawa Moksabro	197	butler	32	"
Y		McGinniss Bridget—†	198	housewife	45	22 Park Vale rd

Bay State Road—Continued

Y¹	McGinniss Francies	198	student	21	22 Parkvale rd
z	McGinniss Marguate—†	198	"	22	22 "
A	Cruft Eunice—†	199	retired	42	357 Com av
B	Cruft Frances—†	199	"	40	357 "
C	Devlin Catherine—†	199	maid	30	Waltham
D	Lee Nellie—†	199	"	46	127 Marlboro
E	McDonnall Annie—†	200	housewife	40	here
F	McDonnall Patrick	200	retired	45	"
G	Kennedy Mary—†	201	maid	25	17 Mechanic
H	Tuckerman Levert S	201	clerk	31	here
K	Tuckerman Linda S—†	201	housewife	31	"
L	Tuckerman Ruth A—†	201	"	66	"
M	Cass Joseph	202	nurse	48	"
N	Crowell Olive—†	202	"	28	"
N¹	Durkee Mary—†	202	"	26	"
O	Keefe Veronica—†	202	"	30	"
P	Kenneddy Jessey—†	202	"	26	"
R	Sawyer Frank	203	proprietor	40	"
S	Sawyer Samuel	203	retired	52	"
T	Sawyer William	203	manager	27	"
V	Capron Maude—†	205	maid	45	"
W	McLeod Annie—†	205	housewife	45	"
X	McLeod Evelyn E—†	205	secretary	24	"
Y	Driner Mollie—†	206	maid	24	"
Z	Fredman Elsie—†	206	social worker	43	"
B	Fredman Lee	206	lawyer	54	"
C	Fredman Sylvia—†	206	social worker	48	"
A	Fredman Tillie—†	206	housewife	73	"
D	O'Brien Mary—†	206	cook	35	"
E	Keenan George F	207	physician	45	"
F	Keenan Gertrude—†	207	housewife	35	"
G	McNeil Belle—†	207	maid	33	"
H	Boyle Mary—†	208	"	38	224 Marlboro
K	Hager Eugene	208	retired	74	here
L	Howe Elizabeth—†	208	housewife	75	"
M	Kelley Fannie—†	208	cook	44	"
N	Parsons Charles S	209	student	25	Milton
O	Sullivan Catherine—†	210	stenographer	22	here
P	Sullivan John	210	lawyer	55	"
R	Sullivan Mary—†	210	housewife	46	"
S	Sullivan Seause—†	210	teacher	24	"

Bay State Road—Continued

Letter.	FULL NAME.	Residence	Occupation.	Age	Street and Number.
T	Grant Amy G—†	211	housewife	64	here
U	Grant George R	211	publisher	72	"
V	Leary Katherine—†	211	waitress	22	Brookline
W	Monihan Mary—†	211	maid	27	"
X	Whalen Nellie—†	211	cook	21	"
Y	Boston Henry	212	manager	30	New York
Z	Fletcher Fredrick	212	"	50	74 Bay State rd
A	Smith Albertha—†	212	housekeeper	43	here
B	Smith Howard	212	salesman	52	"
C	Sampson Calvin	214	lawyer	70	"
D	Sampson Evelyn—†	214	housewife	32	"
E	Sampson Thompson S	214	insurance agent	38	"
F	Belfour Agnes—†	225	maid	55	"
G	Lindsay Annie—†	225	retired	59	"
K	Kenney Sarah—†	226	housekeeper	43	451 Meridian
L	Lane Lillian—†	226	retired	28	451 "
M	Cook Lura B—†	226	scalp specialist	35	63 Mountfort
N	Cook Sara J—†	226	housewife	74	63 "
P	Tully Juliet E—†	226	"	49	here
R	Tully Thomas F	226	salesman	55	"
S	Robinson Harold W	226	publisher	42	"
T	Robinson Lucille B—†	226	housewife	41	115 Hemenway
U	Murray Frances C—†	226	none	25	here
V	Murray Juliet M—†	226	housewife	60	"
W	Foss James O	226	accountant	41	"
X	Foss Mabel C—†	226	housewife	41	"
Y	Foss Wallace H	226	retired	70	Newton
Z	MacDonald Sarah—†	226	domestic	32	Canada
B	Hascall Florence C—†	226	housewife	47	here
C	Hascall Lee C	226	publisher	66	"
D	Woodbury Albert H	226	clerk	26	"
E	Woodbury Coburn P	226	"	22	"
F	Bennett Emily D—†	231	governess	29	"
G	Briggs Flora J—†	231	cook	36	"
H	Ransom Eliza T—†	231	physician	49	"
K	Ransom George W	231	retired	65	"
L	Hill Alice E—†	232	housewife	30	New Haven
M	Hill William J	232	janitor	32	"
N	George Alice C—†	232	clerk	35	10 Kenmore
O	Peters Anne G—†	232	housewife	42	10 "
P	Peters Charles A	232	manager	46	10 "

Bay State Road—Continued

	R	VanDeventer Howard	232	editor	40	here
	s	VanDeventer Lillian—†	232	housewife	36	"
	T	Smith Ellen J—†	232	"	45	"
	U	Smith Harold P	232	superintendent	50	"
	W	Voorhies Frank C	232	salesman	46	Salem
	X	Voorhies Lyda M—†	232	housewife	38	"
	Y	Hale Robert S	232	engineer	63	here
	Z	Rubenstein Bertha—†	232	housewife	39	"
	A	Rubenstein Rubin	232	engineer	38	"
	B	Thomsen Eli—†	232	nurse	38	"
	D	Bean Caroyn—†	232	housewife	40	"
	E	Bean Lemuel W	232	agent	57	"
	F	Dodge Florence A—†	232	nurse	24	280 Com av
	G	Cornwall Anna L—†	232	student	22	Melrose
	H	Cornwall George E	232	clerk	72	"
	K	Cornwall Mary A—†	232	housewife	60	"
	L	Barney Anne S—†	232	none	40	"
	M	Satterwhite David C	232	salesman	49	here
	N	Satterwhite Elizabeth—†	232	housewife	35	"
	O	Carr Gergia K—†	232	none	54	N Easton
	P	Kimball Augusta C	232	retired	81	Brookline
	R	Corner Ethel T—†	232	none	48	here
	s	Corner Josephine M—†	232	clerk	31	"
	T	Knight Ethel C—†	232	housewife	35	Virginia
	U	Knight Louis R	232	U S A	43	"
	V	Bateman Amy H—†	232	teacher	39	here
	W	Robertson Adele M—†	232	none	45	"
	X	Vialle Maud A—†	232	clerk	25	"
	Y	Lochman Annella—†	232	housewife	55	"
	Z	Lochman Dean E	232	salesman	55	"
	A	Lochman Evelyn F—†	232	student	25	"
	B	Macmahon Charles C	232	clerk	54	282 Newbury
	C	Macmahon Charles C. jr	232	bookkeeper	22	282 "
	D	Macmahon Elizabeth W—†	232	housewife	44	282 "
	E	La Montagne Agnes—†	232	"	48	here
	F	La Montagne Eloi	232	jeweler	50	"
	G	Ryan Helen—†	232	bookkeeper	22	"
	H	Munck Julia—†	232	housekeeper	58	California
	K	Sherry Elsie M—†	232	housewife	50	here
	L	Sherry Eugene C	232	merchant	60	"
	M	George Arthur W	232	salesman	24	"

Bay State Road—Continued

Letter	Full Name	Residence April 1, 1924	Occupation	Supposed Age	Reported Residence, April 1, 1925 Street and Number
x	George Jessie E—†	232	housewife	45	here
o	George Lawrence B	232	clerk	22	"
p	Cohen Nathaniel M	232	physician	34	"
r	Cohen Ruth O—†	232	housewife	29	"
s	Kulberg Charles	233	janitor	40	"
t	Upham George B	233	retired	70	"
u	Finley Charles	236	janitor	53	"
v	Finley Margaret—†	236	housewife	56	"
w	Pearson May W—†	236	secretary	36	"
x	McDermit Annie—†	236	student	20	Quincy
y	McDermit Emma—†	236	housewife	39	Brockton
z	Gray Charles	236	superintendent	43	here
A	Gray Emily—†	236	housewife	45	"
B	Gray Sidney G	236	operator	21	"
c	Kimball Grace L—†	236	housekeeper	43	"
D	Sealey Mary E—†	236	secretary	37	"
E	Washburn Martha C—†	236	housewife	50	"
F	Washburn Robert M	236	lawyer	56	"
G	Carlton Alice M—†	236	teacher	40	"
H	Carlton Eleanor—†	236	"	45	"
K	Sanderson Elizabeth—†	236	housewife	21	232 Bay State rd
L	Sanderson Jeffery	236	salesman	25	232 "
N	Way Charles L	236	superintendent	61	here
o	Way Idyl S—†	236	housewife	49	"
P	Butterfield Susan Y—†	236	"	64	"
R	Butterfield William A	236	retired	62	"
s	McInnis Frank A	236	engineer	66	23 Salcomb
T	McInnis Laura—†	236	housewife	58	23 "
U	Fahey Dorothy S—†	236	"	29	here
v	Fahey Michael L	236	lawyer	44	"
w	McInnis Frances—†	236	instructor	26	23 Salcomb
x	Byam Emma L—†	236	housekeeper	52	238 Hemenway
y	Pierce Annie—†	236	housewife	45	Florida
z	Pierce Joseph L	236	salesman	48	"
A	Geldert Nelson	236	buyer	60	here
B	Geldert Rose—†	236	housewife	46	"
c	Hopkins Emma—†	236	"	50	"
D	Hopkins Madeline B—†	236	secretary	26	"
E	Harding Maude—†	236	housekeeper	45	"
F	Shon Horriette A—†	236	"	68	"
G	Chase Clara—†	236	"	50	Brookline

Bay State Road —Continued

H	Fairbaine Laura—†	236	housekeeper	46	here
K	Filine Clara—†	236	housewife	92	"
L	Mulligan Blanche—†	236	housekeeper	25	New Brunswick
M	Brown Kennan K	264	janitor	26	39 Dell av
N	Graves Albert S	264	physician	52	here
O	Graves Frances S—†	264	housewife	49	"
P	Bisbee Alice M—†	264	student	21	"
R	Bisbee Helen—†	264	secretary	26	"
S	Bisbee Marion D—†	264	student	21	"
T	Briscoe Edith—†	264	secretary	22	Simmons College
U	Monett Margaret—†	264	"	26	here
V	Monett Martha—†	264	"	22	"
W	Seaver Nellie—†	264	matron	50	"
X	Wilson Gladys R—†	264	housewife	32	"
Y	Wilson Jessie S—†	264	insurance agent	37	"
Z	Greenwood Doris—†	264	secretary	27	"
A	Greenwood Eleanor—†	264	"	29	"
B	Greenwood Hannah L—†	264	housewife	40	"
C	Greenwood Lawrence B	264	evangelist	60	"
D	McKey Annie M—†	264	housewife	62	Hingham
E	McKey Eleanor G—†	264	cashier	32	"
F	Carter Esebelle W—†	264	retired	60	10 Kenmore
G	Carter Mary L—†	264	housewife	40	10 "
H	Peters Rena B—†	264	"	27	232 Bay State rd
K	Peters William C	264	manager	32	232 "
L	Sheppard Grace D—†	264	housewife	51	here
M	Sheppard Ruth—†	264	none	23	"
N	Bachrick John J	264	merchant	54	"
O	O'Niel Alice B—†	264	housewife	40	"
P	O'Niel Leo D	264	professor	42	"
R	Kates Anna E—†	264	secretary	30	"
S	Kates Helldegard C—†	264	decorator	28	"
T	Brooks Otis B	264	retired	43	"
U	Prescott Ella J—†	264	"	27	"
V	Donald Harry W	264	manager	42	"
W	Donald Lillian—†	264	housewife	26	"
X	MacJarle Carrie W—†	264	"	57	"
Y	MacJarle Francis J	264	dentist	64	"
Z	MacJarle Russell B	264	"	27	"
A	Hartman Helen N—†	264	housewife	29	226 Bay State rd
B	Hartman Lewis O	264	editor	47	226 "

Bay State Road—Continued

Letter.	FULL NAME.	Residence	Occupation	Age	Reported Residence
c	Harlow Marjorie L—†	264	retired	30	here
D	Harlow Willis A	264	inspector	55	"
E	Day Alice E—†	264	housewife	61	Holliston
F	Day Frank G	264	accountant	55	"
G	Jackson Florence G—†	264	dressmaker	50	here
H	Smith Sarah P—†	264	saleswoman	65	"
K	Waldron Reta—†	264	secretary	25	"
L	Betts Lillian M—†	264	housewife	41	Princeton Hotel
M	Betts William A	264	manager	48	"
N	Carney Anne A—†	264	social worker	38	"
O	Carney Maude E—†	264	secretary	39	"
P	Patron William J	264	lawyer	41	"
R	Sweeney Cecil—†	270	clerk	21	163 Hemenway
S	Sweeney Herman L	270	chauffeur	22	163 "
T	Sweeney Lewis W	270	janitor	54	163 "
U	Sweeney Mary E—†	270	housewife	42	163 "
V	Sweeney Rosco	270	janitor	23	163 "
W	O'Malley John	270	manager	42	here
X	O'Malley Nellie—†	270	housekeeper	40	"
Y	Carruth Martha G—†	270	housewife	48	"
Z	Carruth Thomas	270	manager	59	"
A	Willett Francis	270	clerk	26	Europe
B	Willett Katherine T—†	270	housewife	23	"
C	Appel Alice—†	270	"	25	here
D	Appel George	270	salesman	27	"
E	Currier Murrel—†	270	retired	41	"
F	Martin Cora R—†	270	housewife	65	"
G	Newhall Alfred L	270	cashier	40	"
H	Ames Louis	270	manager	47	"
K	Ames Margaret—†	270	housewife	30	"
L	King Donald S	270	physician	34	"
M	King Helen G—†	270	housewife	29	"
N	Lewis Alice B—†	270	"	57	712 Com av
O	Lewis Ralph	270	engineer	57	712 "
P	Armsted Adeline—†	270	housewife	44	here
R	Armsted Lewis	270	manager	52	"
S	McPherson Christine—†	270	housemaid	22	"
T	Dexter Nancy B—†	270	housewife	23	Pennsylvania
U	Dexter Sidney B	270	merchant	26	535 Beacon
V	Beckwith Fannie C—†	270	housekeeper	48	here
W	Hascall Henrietta—†	270	vocal teacher	59	"

Bay State Road—Continued

X	Hascall Wilber F	270	manager	69	here
Y	Bradstreet Laura A—†	270	housewife	52	"
Z	Wright Arthur M	270	truckman	57	"
A	Wright Edith G—†	270	housewife	57	"
B	Kellogg Foster	270	physician	39	"
C	Kellogg Rosalie—†	270	housewife	39	"
D	Gifford Stanley	270	salesman	22	114 Mt Vernon
E	Paseos Mabel—†	270	retired	50	182 Com av
F	Tenton Dorothy—†	270	stenographer	30	182 "
G	Thompson Angelia—†	270	housekeeper	71	182 "
H	Huot Lida A—†	270	housewife	54	Cuba
K	Huot Vilvon J	270	retired	71	"
L	Maelman George W	270	manager	55	here
M	Maelman Sadie W—†	270	housewife	34	"
N	Wright Joseph B	270	salesman	57	"
O	Wright Lillian—†	270	housewife	42	"
P	Carmer Dorothy B—†	270	"	33	"
R	Carmer Frederick V—†	270	agent	35	"
S	Lee Alice A—†	270	housewife	47	"
T	Lee Wesley T	270	physician	58	"

Beacon Street

W	Green George J	645	real estate	28	here
X	Kane Frank	645	"	31	"
Z	Gleason Edward F	645	physician	53	636 Beacon
A	Gleason Hattie C—†	645	housewife	49	636 "
E	Rogers Catherine L—†	645	retired	86	here
F	Harvey Agnes—†	645	housewife	49	"
G	Wadleigh Katherine M—†	645	housekeeper	40	Bermuda
H	Abbott George E	645	automobiles	51	97 St Stephen
K¹	Swan Seymour	645	merchant	53	here
L	Delano Henry C	645	broker	69	Rhode Island
M	Delano Lydia M—†	645	housewife	69	"
N	Sugarman Benjamin F	645	merchant	28	here
O	Sugarman Solomon M	645	retired	63	"
P	Goulston Leopold M	645	lawyer	45	"
R	Goulston Therese—†	645	retired	76	"

Beacon Street—Continued

Letter.	Full Name.	Residence	Occupation	Age	Reported Residence
v	Warren Paul D	645	manager	50	here
w	Dunbar Edward F	645	advertising	59	"
x	Einstein Alfred	645	salesman	52	"
z	Berkowitz Mortimer	645	advertising	36	Brookline
A	Berkowitz Ruth—†	645	housewife	35	"
B	Skilton Elizabeth A—†	645	retired	66	here
C	Skilton P Henry, jr	645	salesman	36	"
E	Moody Arthur M	645	merchant	52	Brookline
F	Noyes Joseph A	645	student	24	Maine
H	Mahoney Helena C—†	645	housewife	51	16 Garrison
K	Mahoney Joseph A	645	lawyer	52	16 "
M	Cohen Moses E	645	merchant	28	16 Rockland
N	Cohen Wolf	645	"	58	16 "
O	Dolbeare Fred T	645	agent	50	here
R	Whitney Miriam—†	645	social worker	28	New Hampshire
V	Martin Minnie E—†	645	housewife	49	Brookline
Y	Waters Elizabeth B—†	645	retired	58	here
Z	Waters Edith B—†	645	housewife	60	"
A	Parker George P	645	real estate	57	"
B	McNab Allen	645	student	22	Maryland
C	Larrabee Eleanor—†	645	retired	25	14 Charlesgate West
D	Larrabee Sarah C—†	645	"	91	14 "
G	Coats Lydia—†	645	lecturer	36	Michigan
N	Griffin Bartholomew F	645	editor	55	here
O	Niehus Oscar C	645	merchant	38	"
V	Price James R	645	secretary	62	New York
W	Monahan Edward J	645	physician	40	here
X	Tilton Warren N	645	"	33	"
Y	Sophian Lawrence	645	student	24	Wisconsin
Z	Barton Stephen E	645	insurance	75	here
C	Collamore Virginia D—†	645	retired	75	"
E	DelMonte Joseph P	645	manager	44	"
K	Eddington Frederick R	645	merchant	51	"
N	Williams Edward J	645	salesman	29	Meriden Ct
O	Campbell Catherine—†	645	retired	54	Wollaston
R	Twitchell Theolotia H—†	645	"	55	here
W	Reizenstein Carrie F—†	645	housewife	52	"
X	Reizenstein Emile	645	manufacturer	59	"
Y	Zuckernick Jacob B	645	lawyer	40	Cambridge
A	Wheeler Iza W—†	645	retired	78	Lexington
B	Burton James	645	merchant	27	Newtonville

Charlesgate West

k	Young Dexter	14	merchant	36	here
l	Francis Annie P—†	14	housewife	60	"
m	Francis William H	14	agent	70	"
n	Bawberger Leo P	14	manufacturer	45	"
x	Welcher Charles A	14	merchant	50	Allston
a	Hutchins Robert L	14	salesman	24	here
h	Odell James E	14	merchant	55	"
m	Harrison Solomon H	14	"	60	"
u	Knight Arthur S	14	accountant	55	"
v	Knight Jean A—†	14	housewife	50	"
x	Viets Henry R, jr	14	physician	34	Newton
c	Raymond Anna C—†	14	housewife	65	here
d	Raymond William H	14	retired	70	"
k	Swasey Emma B—†	14	"	50	"
n	Eaton Albert M	14	merchant	55	"
o	Eaton Edith C—†	14	housewife	50	"
s	Lamond Emma F—†	14	"	50	"
t	Lamond John P	14	merchant	55	"
u	Davis Anna P—†	14	retired	60	"
v	Hicks Anna F—†	14	housewife	50	"
w	Hicks Ellsworth H	14	merchant	55	"
x	Hicks Willard H	14	salesman	30	"
y	Mooar Lawrence A	14	treasurer	55	"
z	Noyes Curtis D	14	merchant	55	"
b	Frasse Hattie O—†	14	retired	55	"
c	Parker Jennie A—†	14	"	60	"
d	Grey Lena B—†	14	housewife	60	"
e	Grey Thomas H	14	retired	75	"
g	Wodelli Alice C—†	14	"	45	"
k	Brine Frederick	14	manager	44	"
l	Brine Harriett W—†	14	housewife	39	"
m	Brehaut Ellerstar	20	secretary	27	"
n	Gang Oliver	20	salesman	28	"
o	Howe Everett	20	"	26	"
p	Reynolds Samuel	20	"	25	"
r	Bakbaugh Jayson	20	engineer	22	"
s	Eacker Earl	20	"	25	37 Bay State rd
t	Eldredge Charles	20	chef	52	here
u	Lias Oswald	20	clerk	26	37 Bay State rd
v	Roger Arthur	20	salesman	25	37 "

Charlesgate West—Continued

Letter.	FULL NAME.	Residence, April 1, 1924.	Occupation.	Supposed Age.	Reported Residence, April 1, 1923. Street and Number.
w	Tinsenbarth Adolph	20	publisher	65	Cambridge
x	Luigi Stephen	20	lawyer	33	Norwood
y	Phillip Jessie—†	20	housewife	60	here
z	Magoun Fred	20	draughtsman	28	"
A	McElwell Leland	20	salesman	29	488 Com av
B	McKown Richard	20	"	29	here
C	Sprague Fred	20	"	28	"
D	Wolfe Charlotte—†	20	secretary	40	237 Berkeley
E	Gaylord Ella—†	20	housewife	43	448 Audubon rd
F	Gaylord Harry	20	professor	40	448 "
G	Hichborn Fred	20	salesman	36	448 "
H	Kennedy Lillian—†	20	student	23	96 Fenway
K	Marshall Althea—†	20	nurse	26	here
L	Campbell Katherine—†	20	teacher	42	"
M	Hart Eva—†	20	designer	28	"
N	Hatch Madeline—†	20	clerk	26	S Natick
O	Legare Eva—†	20	buyer	28	here
P	Lincoln Gladys—†	20	clerk	24	Braintree
R	Davenport Hilda—†	20	saleswoman	27	New Haven Ct
S	Free Florence—†	20	student	22	Ohio
T	Leighton Helen—†	20	secretary	30	New York
U	Brandt Athelsten—†	20	teacher	32	97 Francis
V	Gorden Josephine—†	20	nurse	45	here
W	Wilson Mable—†	20	clerk	38	"
X	Bruce Jessie—†	20	student	29	"
Y	Kelley Mary—†	20	nurse	40	"
Z	Ellis Anderson N	20	physician	82	"
A	Bailey William	20	"	50	"
B	Thorup Amelia—†	20	housewife	58	"
C	Bradshaw Mary—†	20	stenographer	23	Lawrence
D	Dale Helen—†	20	"	22	"
E	Gateley Emma—†	20	tel operator	25	here
F	Woodward Audrey—†	20	student	26	Needham
G	Woodward Emma—†	20	housewife	49	Connecticut
H	Campbell Frances—†	20	teacher	28	here
K	Fallon Mary—†	20	nurse	34	"
L	Murphy Stella—†	20	"	40	"
M	Wood Elizabeth—†	20	therapeutist	27	Portsmouth
N	Hall Clare—†	20	housewife	30	46 Mountfort
O	Hickey Anna—†	20	milliner	23	41 Allston
P	Kennedy Albertina—†	20	housewife	50	Florida

Charlesgate West—Continued

R	Atkinson Aloine—†	20	student	25	here
S	Benardi Jane—†	20	secretary	37	722 Com av
T	Keough Ellen—†	20	nurse	30	here
U	Mattes Helen—†	20	student	24	"
V	Whitnall Ernest A	20	manager	36	Cambridge
W	Whitnall Marion—†	20	housewife	28	"
X	Hornbrooke Dudley	20	salesman	48	here
Y	Dunn Emma—†	20	housewife	44	Newton Center
Z	Dunn Harris	20	manager	48	"
A	Movius Alice—†	20	housewife	43	here
B	Hawkes Laura—†	20	"	58	"
C	MacDonald Anne—†	20	student	30	Detroit Mich
D	MacDonald Margaret—†	20	housewife	50	"
E	Weeks Ella—†	20	"	50	"
F	Pierce Amy—†	20	"	54	New Jersey
G	Pierce Amy—†	20	clerk	30	Cambridge
H	Short Margaret—†	20	teacher	26	here
K	Tirrell Florence—†	20	retired	72	"
L	Brennan Wenona—†	20	saleswoman	27	"
M	Bryson Jean—†	20	housewife	40	92 Kilmarnoel
N	Powers Leary—†	20	manicurist	33	here
O	Wood Lavinia—†	20	nurse	40	"
P	Greene Delphine—†	20	clerk	29	"
R	Lawrence Fay—†	20	secretary	26	"
S	Lufkin Ida—†	20	housekeeper	50	"
T	Nichols Helen—†	20	nurse	34	"
U	Ober Truth—†	20	clerk	28	"
V	Bloom Harry	20	buyer	22	"
W	Cannell Marshall	20	manager	23	Cambridge
X	Harley Margaret—†	20	student	32	here
Y	Lyons Susie—†	20	nurse	50	"
Z	Butler Annie—†	20	housewife	42	Florida
A	Butler Leonard	20	real estate	42	"
B	Pipe Katherine—†	20	housewife	50	here
C	Pipe Margaret—†	20	student	21	"
D	Hersey Elizabeth—†	20	housewife	58	Brookline
E	Hersey Mark	20	U S A	60	"
F	Holmes Frances—†	20	housewife	48	Pennsylvania
G	Kloseman Alice—†	20	clerk	42	here
H	Barrows Mary—†	20	"	34	"

Charlesgate West—Continued

Letter.	FULL NAME.	Residence	Occupation	Age	Reported Residence
K	Betting Mildred—†	20	student	23	Pennsylvania
L	Cohen Ruth—†	20	clerk	24	here
M	Murphy Katherine—†	20	teacher	23	34 Fenway
N	O'Keefe Katherine—†	20	nurse	46	here
O	Wilson Esther—†	20	student	23	96 Fenway
P	Boos Josephine—†	20	clerk	50	here
R	Kennell Marie—†	20	student	23	Ohio
S	Schipin Carolyn—†	20	"	22	New York
T	Stanwood Marjorie—†	20	stenographer	26	here
U	Turnhill Ethel—†	20	nurse	38	"
V	Dexter Elizabeth—†	20	milliner	54	"
W	Dexter Marion—†	20	housewife	30	"
X	Dexter Pardon	20	salesman	33	"
Y	Seavey Maritta—†	20	housewife	60	"
Z	Patille Gilbert	20	manager	33	Brookline
A	Walter Ella—†	20	housewife	35	Portland Me
B	Walter Terry	20	physician	40	"
C	Ponsland David	20	banker	40	Carlisle
D	Ponsland Edith—†	20	housewife	50	"
E	Ponsland Edward	20	banker	30	"
F	Ponsland Fred	20	"	56	"
G	Hirsch Henry	20	student	20	Chicago Ill
H	Hull Franklin	20	architect	42	here
K	Besge Henry	20	manager	28	Florida
L	Colloten Frank	20	physician	40	here
M	Stewart Floyd	20	student	22	"
N	Hatfield Bessie—†	20	nurse	50	"
R	Hillman Ruby—†	20	student	23	"
O	Mulroy Mable—†	20	clerk	22	Cambridge
P	Osgood Ethel—†	20	nurse	40	here
S	Cotten Blanche—†	20	"	30	"
T	Hayden Fanny—†	20	teacher	31	"
U	McCarthy Frances—†	20	clerk	22	"
V	McQueen Mary—†	20	social worker	30	"
W	Sawyer Martina—†	20	examiner	22	25 Queensberry
X	Durkee Ida—†	20	clerk	21	New York
Y	Jillson Helen—†	20	manager	26	here
Z	McIntosh Jean—†	20	student	21	Brookline
A	Morse Elizabeth—†	20	secretary	22	here
B	Teeley Dorothy—†	20	"	21	78 Pilgrim rd

Commonwealth Avenue

Letter	Full Name	Residence, April 1, 1924	Occupation	Supposed Age	Reported Residence, April 1, 1923. Street and Number.
D	Buettner Marie O—†	464	saleswoman	38	Brookline
E	Hands Anna C—†	464	physician	63	here
F	Adams Alice F—†	464	retired	79	"
G	Romery Ethel C—†	464	healer	41	"
H	Lamb Eliza A—†	464	retired	71	"
M	Cutler Louis S	464	healer	32	"
N	Haben Arthur T	464	broker	40	"
O	Rathvon William R	464	trustee	70	"
R	Lawrence Mary H—†	464	retired	60	Cambridge
S	Mitchell Esther D—†	464	housewife	45	here
T	Mitchell Samuel H	464	merchant	45	"
U	Fleming Louise A—†	464	retired	59	"
V	Burke Annie T—†	464	"	61	"
W	Burke Frank P	464	salesman	24	"
X	Burke John W	464	"	34	"
Y	Griffeth Claude M	464	retired	51	20 Charlesgate West
Z	Griffeth Lucy Fay—†	464	housewife	53	20 "
A	MacLeod John	464	merchant	65	Brookline
B	Burton Robert P	464	salesman	55	Ohio
C	Jacobs Frederick W	464	merchant	51	here
D	Jacobs Hattie M—†	464	housewife	47	"
F	Ireson Charles L	464	merchant	73	"
G	Ireson Etta—†	464	retired	51	"
H	Hazen Harriet M—†	464	"	65	"
K	Jopp Harriet—†	464	"	50	"
L	Ireson Lilly J—†	464	salesman	23	"
M	Gold Samuel	464	merchant	56	"
N	Paul William M	464	"	75	"
P	Danforth Albion F	464	"	46	"
R	Danforth Bertha K—†	464	housewife	42	"
S	Carney Hannah M—†	464	retired	71	"
T	Blatchley Harry C	464	salesman	55	"
U	Nuremberg Charlotte—†	464	housewife	53	"
V	Nuremberg Fred	464	salesman	59	"
X	Seavey Elizabeth B—†	464	retired	42	"
Z	Crocker Mary C—†	464	"	40	"
A	Cushman Ella R—†	464	"	70	"
B	Cushman William F	464	"	74	"
C	Nicholson Annie Field—†	464	none	50	"
D	Nicholson Peter	464	broker	59	"

Commonwealth Avenue—Continued

F	Hewes Hazel E—†	464	retired	27	here
G	Dennison Joseph A	464	lawyer	55	"
H	Dennison Mary L—†	464	retired	56	"
K	Morse Katherine —†	464	housewife	47	"
L	Morse Simon A	464	merchant	52	24 Avery
M	Nowell Annie L—†	464	housewife	59	California
N	Nowell George M	464	lawyer	62	"
O	Maguire Susan L—†	464	school teacher	49	here
P	McKenney George P	466	manager	40	"
S	Marsters Blanche—†	466	retired	36	"
T	Marsters Emery H	466	merchant	46	"
U	Thompson Catherine—†	466	housewife	52	"
V	Thompson Clinton J	466	lawyer	54	"
W	Rich Pauline B—†	466	retired	59	"
X	Wilarsky Lily—†	466	hairdresser	40	"
Y	Bickford Mary—†	466	retired	61	"
A	Low Harruet P—†	466	housewife	45	645 Beacon
B	Low Joseph F	466	merchant	54	645 "
E	Rosencrantz George	466	broker	60	Brookline
F	Gray William H	466	manager	54	here
G	Clapp Gilmer	466	trustee	56	"
H	Mullin John C	466	salesman	50	"
K	Feibelman Emil	466	merchant	56	"
L	Feibelman Rebecca—†	466	housewife	51	"
O	Munroe Albert M	466	manager	41	"
P	McMullen Harriet G—†	466	retired	62	"
R	Plummer Edith—†	466	"	44	"
S	Plummer Marion C—†	466	"	67	"
T	Adrian Margaret—†	466	"	39	"
U	Perkins Mary D—†	466	housewife	40	"
V	Perkins Sumner R	466	salesman	47	"
Y	Ketchum Claude H	466	merchant	37	"
Z	Ketchum Georgia T—†	466	housewife	37	"
A	Wenz Mary P—†	466	manufacturer	46	"
B	Gilman Harry W	466	insurance	51	"
C	Gilman Helen D—†	466	housewife	49	"
E	Wheeler Gordon	466	student	21	"
F	Wheeler Harry A	466	manager	58	"
	Wheeler Maynard E	466	clerk	28	"
H	Lyle Ernest T	466	engineer	44	"
K	Lyle Grace B—†	466	housewife	46	"

Commonwealth Avenue— Continued

L	Rood Elizabeth N—†	466	retired	47	390 Com av
N	Warner Asa F	466	"	54	here
O	Lyons Harriet P—†	466	housewife	34	"
P	Lyons John M	466	salesman	37	"
R	Ruggles May C—†	466	retired	71	"
S	Shuman Julia—†	466	"	66	"
T	Ratchesky Harry F	466	insurance	47	"
U	Dean Charles K	466	salesman	38	Brookline
W	Patterson Lila—†	466	retired	42	here
X	Hill William D	466	student	24	"
Y	Sheehy Ambrose J	466	companion	37	"
Z	Moore Charles F	466	merchant	51	"
A	Peak Helen T—†	466	retired	67	"
B	Froham Philip H	466	architect	38	"
D	Smith Alder Holm	466	student	24	"
E	Smith Clifford P	466	lawyer	66	"
F	Smith Myrtle Holm—†	466	housewife	62	"
G	Pickert Amy R—†	466	retired	46	"
H	Pickert Bertha—†	466	"	77	"
K	Pickert Edna—†	466	"	44	"
L	Pickert Edwin S	466	"	42	"
M	Pickert Leo W	466	merchant	52	"
N	Gay Grace M—†	466	retired	61	"
O	Condon Frank C	466	manufacturer	75	"
P	Condon Mabel F—†	466	housewife	60	"
R	Creed Josephine—†	466	saleswoman	39	"
S	Collins Sarah—†	466	retired	64	"
T	Bennett Elizabeth—†	468	housekeeper	82	"
U	Johnson Arthur	468	chauffeur	26	"
V	Johnson Eva—†	468	laundress	30	"
W	Loring Homer	468	trustee	51	"
X	Loring May E—†	468	housewife	46	"
Y	Nelson Viola—†	468	cook	24	"
Z	Sundstrom Vera—†	468	maid	26	"
A	Maddox Ella—†	470	cook	40	11 Dartmouth pl
B	Maddox Warner	470	butler	50	11 "
C	Packard Horace	470	physician	71	here
D	Perry Ida—†	470	maid	30	560 Mass av
F	Hand Margaret—†	474	housekeeper	40	106 Marlboro
G	Traiser Richard E	474	merchant	60	here
H	Gluck Martha—†	476	waitress	25	Lexington

Commonwealth Avenue—Continued

K	Hackley Etta—†	476	nurse	26	New Haven Ct
L	Hanck Anna—†	476	cook	54	here
M	Leviseur Frederick J	476	merchant	32	"
N	Leviseur Lena F—†	476	housewife	53	"
O	Newman Helen L—†	476	retired	30	Connecticut
P	Ruf Christiania—†	476	laundress	45	"
R	Sonntag Marie—†	476	maid	45	"
T	Doherty Bridget—†	480	"	27	7 Gloucester
U	Gurgler Emmie—†	480	"	30	Brookline
V	Sheehan Annie—†	480	"	40	256 Com av
W	Stanwood Annie—†	480	housewife	60	New York
X	Carey Rose—†	482	cook	54	here
Y	Chamberlain Charlotte P—†	482	housewife	82	"
Z	Rice Florence E—†	482	housekeeper	70	"
A	Rowe Mera—†	484	maid	21	9 Com av
B	Wishek Habek	484	student	24	New York
C	Wishek Hafiya—†	484	physician	30	74 Tyler
D	Conant Ira M	486	clerk	35	Watertown
E	Conant Mary B—†	486	physician	63	here
F	Conant William M	486	"	68	"
G	Mahoney Mary—†	486	maid	49	"
H	Murphy Mary B—†	486	waitress	28	"
K	Rowe Nellie T—†	486	laundress	36	"
L	Neal Betty—†	488	maid	40	481 Beacon
M	Seymour Ethel—†	488	housewife	40	here
N	Seymout Malcolm	488	physician	48	"
O	Shrigley Emma—†	488	housekeeper	58	481 Beacon
P	Carlson Nancy—†	490	maid	30	E Brewster
R	Dalstrom Hannah—†	490	"	28	"
S	Nickerson Addie D—†	490	housewife	60	"
T	Peterson Mary—†	490	cook	65	"
U	Alexander Ruth—†	496	teacher	33	here
V	Barker Perry	496	engineer	51	"
W	Barker Amy L—†	496	retired	51	"
X	Bond Carrie—†	496	"	51	"
Y	Brown Marion—†	496	"	46	"
Z	Bruce Mary—†	496	housewife	33	"
A	Buckley William J	496	physician	39	"
B	Buerkel John F	496	engineer	61	"
C	Dalton Henry R	496	broker	51	"
D	Davis Alice H—†	496	housewife	46	"

Commonwealth Avenue— Continued

E	Davis Ernest L	496	merchant	51	here
F	Eiseman Sidney	496	"	41	"
G	Glaser Constance—†	496	student	23	"
H	Glaser Frances —†	496	"	22	"
K	Glaser Joseph	496	shoe dealer	56	"
L	Glaser Ruth—†	496	student	25	"
M	Glaser Violet—†	496	housewife	51	"
N	Goldsmith Esther—†	496	retired	56	"
O	Green Dorothy B—†	496	housewife	28	"
P	Green Robert M	496	physician	43	"
R	Hayman Abraham	496	retired	62	"
S	Hirsh Henry	496	physician	31	"
T	Jordan Grace—†	496	"	46	"
U	Kapf Anna—†	496	retired	59	"
V	Kapf Hattie L—†	496	clerk	36	"
Y	Mason Anna—†	496	retired	52	"
W	Moses George	496	jeweler	52	"
X	Moses Minnie—†	496	housewife	51	"
Z	Nickerson Herbert H	496	merchant	56	"
A	Pattern George E	496	manager	51	"
B	Schwarz Richard F	496	retired	81	"
C	Smith Conrad	496	physician	51	"
D	Smith Helen—†	496	housewife	46	"
E	Tyson George	496	merchant	61	"
F	Warner Alice—†	496	retired	48	"
G	Warner Clarence	496	broker	51	"
H	Webber Abraham	496	lawyer	41	"
K	Webber Sylvia—†	496	housewife	31	"
L	Young George A	496	broker	51	"
M	Cambell Mary—†	506	maid	30	Ireland
N	Caverly Hamah—†	506	cook	28	480 Beacon
O	Christian Lewis E	506	manager	56	here
P	Christian Minna —†	506	student	26	"
R	Whalen Threasea —†	506	waitress	29	480 . Beacon
U	Crocker Merle—†	508	housewife	35	here
V	Crocker Zenas	508	broker	35	"
W	Libby Hattie E —†	508	housewife	75	"
X	Libby Henry F	508	dentist	70	"
Y	Ray Elsie—†	508	housewife	30	"
Z	Ray Gilbert	508	dentist	30	"
A	Welton Ranna H	508	lawyer	40	Cohasset

Commonwealth Avenue—Continued

Letter.	Full Name.	Residence, April 1, 1924	Occupation.	Supposed Age.	Reported Residence, April 1, 1923. Street and Number.
B	Bell Elizabeth J —†	510	housewife	54	520 Beacon
C	Bell George H	510	manager	65	520 "
E	English Martin J	514	physician	42	here
F	McDonough Honor—†	514	none	64	"
G	Murtaugh Mary G—†	514	manager	31	"
H	Shortel Joseph H	514	physician	30	"
M	Dacy Anna J—†	520	secretary	50	"
O	Baxter Horace W	524	real estate	69	"
P	Donnelly Elizabeth—†	524	cook	33	6 Mountfort
R	Flynn Madge A—†	524	waitress	40	here
S	Taylor Mary C—†	524	housekeeper	60	"
W	Morrell Florence—†	536	housewife	26	Maine
X	Morrell Raymond	536	janitor	29	"
Y	Vogel George L	536	surgeon	49	here
Z	Vogel Mary J—†	536	housewife	35	"
A	Phelps Albert C	536	student	21	477 Com av
B	Greenberg Samuel L	536	physician	33	here
D	Bennett Grace J—†	536	operator	35	Wrentham
F	Barstaw Andrew T	536	physician	51	here
G	Barstaw Annie B—†	536	housewife	40	"
H	Burgess Harry H	536	physician	36	"
K	Perkins George Edward	536	"	45	"
N	Foyles Clara E—†	536	cashier	36	875 Hunt'n av
O	Beckwood Olive—†	536	hairdresser	25	here
P	Peterson Olive—†	536	"	26	"
R	Bruna Anjusto	536	student	24	Chile
S	DeAlmmada Maria A—†	536	retired	45	"
T	Little Edward C	536	manager	33	here
U	Gray Ethel S—†	536	nurse	42	"
V	Gray Frances—†	536	student	26	"
W	Kjerner Wahlborg C—†	536	nurse	45	"
A	Rabock Arthur	536	clerk	30	"
B	Johnson Bertha M—†	536	secretary	44	"
C	Johnson Robert K	536	accountant	42	"
D	Markell Abbot	536	salesman	35	Glenville av
F	Logan Viola—†	536	chemist	23	here
G	Hahn Gladys—†	536	housewife	30	1066 Com av
H	Hahn Myron	536	physician	29	1066 "
N	Donovan Lillian—†	536	stenographer	25	here
O	Stone Margaret—†	536	clerk	22	"
P	Bucknam Ralph	536	physician	30	"

Commonwealth Avenue—Continued

Letter	Full Name	Residence	Occupation	Age	Reported Residence
s	Lee Minnie D—†	536	housewife	47	here
t	Lee Morris	536	salesman	47	"
u	Wand Samuel	536	"	29	New York
v	Silver Mary—†	536	housewife	36	here
w	Silver William	536	physician	38	"
k	Hall Kathleen—†	580	housewife	33	Brookline
l	Hall Squire	580	janitor	45	"
m	Carney John H	580	molder	52	New Hampshire
n	Haynes Earle R	580	manager	31	109 Peterboro
o	Haynes Minnie E—†	580	housekeeper	59	109 "
p	Chambers Ethel—†	580	housewife	30	Lynn
r	Chambers John G	580	agent	34	"
s	Percy Catherine—†	580	dressmaker	40	here
t	Percy Margaret—†	580	bookbinder	45	"
u	Flagg George M	580	salesman	28	Worcester
v	Fox Ellen N—†	580	none	60	here
w	Fox May B—†	580	clerk	33	"
x	Rutledge Pearl A—†	580	"	30	Cambridge
z	Cnevas Armando D	580	interpreter	32	Everett
a	Cnevas Louise O—†	580	housewife	27	"
b	Fortini Charles J	580	elevatorman	23	Somerville
c	Fortini Jenney C—†	580	bookkeeper	28	"
d	Nash Mabelle—†	580	saleswoman	57	here
f	Ducharme Mary—†	580	nurse	28	Taunton
g	Morrison Marie—†	580	"	40	here
h	Allan Hettie—†	580	bookkeeper	35	"
k	Powers Catherine—†	580	housekeeper	65	"
l	Powers Mary T—†	580	stenographer	30	"
m	Rich Catherine M—†	580	broker	40	"
n	McPhee Elsie—†	580	bookkeeper	24	"
o	McPhee Olive—†	580	stenographer	22	"
p	McPhee Vina—†	580	bookkeeper	25	"
r	Lackey Ida M—†	580	secretary	21	Cambridge
s	McDonald Kenneth G	580	manager	30	1366 Com av
t	McDonald Nellie—†	580	none	47	1366 "
u	McNeil Laura—†	580	"	53	here
v	Rowell Albert L	580	manager	52	Pittsburgh
w	Rowell Melvina L—†	580	housewife	40	"
y	Lewis Charles A	580	printer	46	10 Guilford
z	Lewis Elizabeth—†	580	none	40	10 "
a	Gier Gunther	580	waiter	43	here

Commonwealth Avenue—Continued

Letter.	FULL NAME.	Residence, April 1, 1924.	Occupation.	Supposed Age.	Reported Residence, April 1, 1923. Street and Number.
B	Liedke Curt	580	waiter	32	here
C	Laird Charles T	580	salesman	55	"
D	Laird Elizabeth A—†	580	housewife	57	"
F	Boyce William S	580	manager	38	"
G	Burns Charles	580	barber	39	"
H	Burns Josephine—†	580	housewife	36	"
K	McShane Margaret L—†	580	waitress	33	"
L	Schlicting Bertha—†	580	"	32	Revere
M	Schlicting Walter	580	manufacturer	32	"
N	Place Georgia L—†	580	none	44	here
O	Gray Marion E—†	580	tel operator	30	"
P	Drew Edward H	580	foreman	44	"
R	Drew Emma M—†	580	housekeeper	38	"
S	Fitzgerald Mary E—†	580	dressmaker	46	"
T	Walker William P	580	broker	43	"
U	Deering Frederick A, jr	580	salesman	35	Holyoke
V	Deering Mabel F—†	580	housewife	32	"
W	Paine Adelaide M—†	580	nurse	50	Magnolia
X	Paine Thomas	580	salesman	55	24 Maverick sq
Y	Marshall Minnie M—†	580	matron	59	here
Z	Marshall Virginia—†	580	secretary	24	"
A	Ryan William	580	broker	37	"
B	Collins Marie G—†	580	tel operator	34	"
C	Tiernan Freida—†	580	cashier	31	New York
D	Daggett James H	580	merchant	54	here
E	Jewett Alice—†	580	stenographer	26	"
F	Stone James E	580	manufacturer	45	"
G	Briggs Edward W	580	fireman	58	"
H	Briggs Sarah A—†	580	housekeeper	54	"
K	Cunningham Lillian E—†	580	hairdresser	42	"
L	Carmichael Ethel B—†	580	housewife	37	"
M	Carmichael Mack	580	salesman	45	New York
T	Allen Beatrice R—†	609	housekeeper	49	here
U	Allen Steven J	609	retired	66	"
V	Sullivan Ella—†	609	maid	32	"
W	Sullivan Michael J	609	butler	31	"
Y	Buchanan John C	611	student	22	"
Z	Carroll Ellen E—†	611	retired	40	"
A	Delano Harry D	611	"	58	"
B	Delano Mary C—†	611	housewife	52	"
C	Ladensack Delia A—†	615	"	59	"

Commonwealth Avenue—Continued

Letter	Full Name	Res.	Occupation	Age	Reported Residence
D	Ladensack John N	615	salesman	27	here
E	Ladensack Olga—†	615	none	24	"
G	Dodge Irving P	617	superintendent	51	"
N	Johnston Nora M—†	623	maid	25	"
O	Hallian Carl A	625	machinist	38	Europe
P	Mackel Harry	625	salesman	50	New York
S	Wolf Alice L—†	627	housewife	50	here
T	Wolf Bernard	627	clothier	62	"
U	Wolf Junor	627	"	22	"
V	Wolf Robert	627	"	23	"
W	Conway Matilda—†	629	nurse	37	"
X	Curran Abbie—†	629	domestic	40	"
Y	Deacey Katie—†	629	"	58	"
Z	Linton Edna E—†	629	housewife	34	"
A	Linton Stanley H	629	merchant	40	"
B	Pantin Josephine—†	629	maid	29	"
C	Smith Bella—†	629	nurse	53	"
H	Duboyce Harold A	704	janitor	39	"
K	Duboyce Mae L—†	704	housewife	37	"
L	Richt Edward	704	manager	36	"
M	Richt Maragert—†	704	none	34	"
N	Burgess Earl	704	agent	38	"
O	Burgess Marion—†	704	none	34	"
P	Dennison Abbie M—†	704	"	74	"
R	Peters Edith G—†	704	clerk	33	"
S	Peter Mable F—†	704	retired	35	"
T	Dame Emma W—†	704	clerk	33	"
U	Potter Maud—†	704	designer	35	"
W	Barker Evelyn—†	794	none	37	"
X	Dodge Frank A	704	cashier	72	"
Y	Howes Nellie M—†	704	teacher	46	"
Z	Lockwood Sopha—†	704	merchant	45	"
Z¹	Merrill Bertha—†	704	clerk	40	"
A	Philips Joseph A	704	salesman	48	"
B	Stockwell Francis H—†	704	tel operator	38	"
C	Stockwell Harland E	704	salesman	42	"
D	Bailey Clara—†	704	none	54	"
E	Bailey Walter S	704	merchant	57	"
F	Mahoney John E	704	contractor	48	"
G	Lewis Henry B	704	merchant	57	"
H	Brown Edith S—†	704	secretary	29	"

Commonwealth Avenue—Continued

Letter.	FULL NAME.	Residence, April 1, 1924.	Occupation.	Supposed Age.	Reported Residence, April 1, 1923.
K	Clark Josephine —†	704	none	35	here
L	Clark Roy F	704	printer	35	"
M	DuBois Rachel—†	704	secretary	50	"
N	Andrews Mae P—†	704	"	46	"
O	Inman Grace B—†	704	"	40	"
P	Mitchell Helen—†	704	manicurist	28	"
R	Mitchell Louise—†	704	clerk	33	"
S	Gleason John M	704	manager	45	"
T	Gorman Josephine —†	704	none	55	"
U	Gorman Robert L	704	manager	54	"
V	Ball Olive A—†	704	secretary	40	"
W	Doherty Frederick	704	manager	35	"
X	Doherty Mary —†	704	none	33	"
Y	Maddock Catherine—†	704	secretary	50	"
Z	Clark Clara—†	704	none	50	"
A	Clark Samuel	704	salesman	28	"
B	Barnes Annette—†	704	accountant	38	"
C	Barnes Clara N—†	704	teacher	36	"
D	Gould Susan—†	704	none	60	"
E	Baker Elizabeth—†	704	clerk	50	"
F	Fay Rosina J—†	708	housekeeper	60	"
G	Hutchins Wilmer J	708	auto repairer	50	"
H	Park Frank S	708	salesman	26	Rumford Me
K	Kennedy Alexander G	710	physician	53	here
L	Kennedy Mary B—†	710	housewife	46	"
M	Plunkett Mary—†	710	maid	44	"
O	Perkins Henry B	710	cigar merchant	58	"
P	Sleeper Charles E	710	retired	71	"
R	Flood Margurite O—†	712	secretary	33	"
S	Flood Mary C—†	712	none	62	"
T	Miller Frank	712	janitor	45	"
U	Fulton Marie—†	714	nurse	22	"
V	Mathewson Jane E—†	714	"	22	"
W	Moore Jennett—†	714	"	22	"
X	Mullin May—†	714	"	22	"
Y	Vemotte Lolla—†	714	"	26	"
Z	Malloy Coleman C	718	janitor	44	"
A	Malloy Mary C—†	718	housewife	41	"
B	Lomasney Ethel—†	718	teacher	24	Winthrop
C	Lomasney Martin	718	factory worker	25	"
D	Lomasney Robert	718	clerk	22	"

Commonwealth Avenue—Continued

E	Young Margaret—†	718	housemaid	45	Brookline
F	Kennedy Elizabeth —†	718	bookkeeper	24	Revere
G	Corl John H	718	clerk	55	here
K	Granfield Elizabeth—†	718	bookkeeper	24	"
L	Granfield Gertrude—†	718	"	26	"
M	Robinson Cora—†	718	hairdresser	40	"
N	Knight Marie—†	718	"	30	"
O	Gaskell Earl B	718	garageman	36	Concord N H
P	Gaskell Hattie M—†	718	housewife	34	"
R	McLean Louise—†	718	bookkeeper	23	here
T	McLaughlin Anna—†	718	"	23	Malden
U	Egan Dora E—†	718	housewife	28	40 Ivy
V	Egan Walter J	718	chauffeur	38	40 "
W	Chapin Howard C	718	broker	50	here
X	Lucier Arthur J	718	salesman	28	"
Y	Lucier Margaret M—†	718	housewife	28	"
Z	Richardson Anna—†	718	bookkeeper	28	Brookline
B	Martin Isabella—†	718	clerk	35	here
C	Sherwood Jessie M—†	718	"	40	New York
D	Starr Alice W—†	718	hairdresser	40	"
E	Nutting Mertha—†	718	milliner	46	here
F	Wyman Harvey	718	salesman	39	"
G	Wyman Laura—†	718	housewife	37	"
H	Klagge David A	718	salesman	28	Winthrop
K	Sawyer Clayton	718	"	30	Belmont
L	Cox Anna—†	718	clerk	30	here
M	Cook Horace	718	broker	55	"
N	Gallagher Laura E—†	718	stenographer	25	"
O	Gallagher Madelene C—†	718	housekeeper	48	"
P	Amerman John	718	salesman	31	Connecticut
R	Reed Delle A—†	718	storekeeper	45	here
S	McLaughlin Anna —†	718	bookkeeper	23	"
T	McLaughlin Louise—†	718	teacher	25	"
U	Fish Alma J—†	718	housewife	48	"
V	Fish Constant P	718	manager	52	"
X	Downey Ina—†	718	bookkeeper	22	"
Y	Downey Micheal	718	chauffeur	21	"
A	Robillard Delia—†	722	housewife	44	"
B	Robillard Henry	722	janitor	48	"
C	Bornstein Edith —†	722	housekeeper	33	65 Audubon rd
D	Ewell Bessie —†	722	tel operator	28	115 Norway

Commonwealth Avenue—Continued

Letter	Full Name.	Residence, April 1, 1924.	Occupation.	Supposed Age.	Reported Residence, April 1, 1923.
E	Overall Annis V—†	722	housewife	43	Portland Me
F	Overall Charles A	722	salesman	54	"
H	Beckett Rachel C—†	722	tel operator	27	here
L	Duby John H	722	conductor	45	15 Rowell
K	Webber Lawrence E	722	sign painter	27	Pennsylvania
M	Mohn Nellie G—†	722	cashier	40	89 Union Park
N	Zellen Emily S—†	722	"	45	89 "
O	Morton Bessie H—†	722	housewife	32	here
P	Morton William A	722	manager	32	"
R	Quirin E Lafayette	722	student	21	"
S	Scripps William W	722	"	24	"
T	Allen Edgar	722	bookkeeper	24	1118 Hunt'n av
U	Allen Etta M—†	722	housewife	25	1118 "
V	Silverman Harry	722	salesman	35	here
W	Silverman Morris	722	"	30	"
X	Golding Arthur S	722	chauffeur	40	"
Y	Golding Edith—†	722	housekeeper	60	"
Z	Golding Phebe—†	722	secretary	38	"
A	Lingham Harriet E—†	722	clerk	47	"
B	McGiness Frank	722	cashier	47	"
C	Mellville Hazel R—†	722	housewife	27	"
D	Mellville Henry F	722	bookkeeper	37	"
E	Freeman Maud—†	722	nurse	28	"
F	Gray Katherine W—†	722	"	35	"
G	Rondeau Eleanor—†	722	housewife	23	Lynn
H	Rondeau Henry	722	salesman	27	"
K	Shumway Louise—†	722	dressmaker	36	here
L	Jacobus Frederick J	722	policeman	56	"
M	Paul Charles V S	722	superintendent	37	717 E Fourth
N	Pike Carroll M	722	salesman	52	here
O	McDonough Violet—†	722	waitress	26	26 Brook av
P	Powers Hilda—†	722	"	28	26 "
S	Everette Jacque	722	U S N	43	here
R	Everette Lillian H—†	722	housewife	41	"
T	Sagrin Mary—†	722	stenographer	30	"
U	Thomas Attossa B—†	722	nurse	32	"
V	Alley Catherine—†	722	"	30	"
W	Libby Margaret—†	722	"	35	"
X	McCarthy Leonora M—†	722	clerk	32	"
Y	Hall William B	722	manager	45	"
Z	Hughes Joseph	722	salesman	28	"

Commonwealth Avenue—Continued

A	Hughes Teresa—†	722	housewife	26	here	
B	Oman Mollie M—†	722	stenographer	34	24 Linwood s
C	Odabashian Arazy—†	722	housewife	25	Lynn
D	Odabashian Heratch	722	rug dealer	34	"
E	Parker Ida L—†	722	housewife	41	844 Beacon
F	Stjerstrum Elsa—†	722	dressmaker	35	here
G	Parker Kirk A	722	adjuster	47	Connecticut
H	Gallagher Rae E—†	722	retired	32	here
K	Campbell Merle—†	722	hairdresser	29	"
L	Levins Katherine—†	722	accountant	26	"
M	Wakefield Ethel P—†	722	stenographer	42	"
N	Ginn Louise A—†	722	housewife	37	"
O	Ginn Richard	722	dentist	37	"
P	Stites Edith M—†	722	housewife	44	"
R	Stites Harry F	722	salesman	47	"
T	Anderson Engla—†	722	hair specialist	44	"
U	Geissenhainer Hazel—†	722	housewife	30	"
V	Geissenhainer Louis R	722	salesman	30	"
W	Wood Carrie—†	722	housekeeper	50	"
X	Wood Horace I	722	manager	25	"
Z	Scranton Ward A	726	salesman	36	"
A	Garwood Marie—†	726	"	38	Reading
B	Markey John C	726	physician	35	here
C	Larson Frank B	726	accountant	28	Somerville
D	Larson Gertrude E—†	726	housewife	28	Cambridge
E	Rooney Margaret G—†	726	saleswoman	35	here
F	Blake George F	726	retired	55	"
G	Donahue Arthur	726	salesman	31	Beachmont
H	Donahue Elette—†	726	housewife	30	"
K	Berman Sarah—†	726	clerk	28	here
L	Root Ernest L	726	engineer	35	"
M	Root Laura G—†	726	housewife	35	"
N	Cassidy Georgia G—†	726	secretary	28	6 Westminster av
O	Roller Katherine B—†	726	housekeeper	34	here
P	Cushing Harry M	726	merchant	27	"
R	Cushing Jeannett C—†	726	housewife	24	"
S	Baxter John	726	auto mechanic	33	"
T	McMullin John H	726	merchant	45	Everett
U	McMullin Mabel A—†	726	housewife	39	Melrose
V	Estebrooks Minnie L—†	726	housekeeper	68	here
W	Foster Gustavus	726	salesman	31	722 Com av

Commonwealth Avenue—Continued

x	Foster Irene—†	726	housewife	26	722 Com av
y	Young Fred H	726	merchant	65	here
z	Somers Harold M	726	manager	32	Maine
A	Somers Laura G—†	726	housewife	32	"
B	Garvis Florence N—†	726	clerk	40	here
c	Miller Frances E—†	726	housekeeper	45	"
D	Miller George R	726	clerk	51	"
E	Miller Catherine—†	726	bookkeeper	41	"
F	Miller Julia—†	726	candyworker	37	"
G	Fredricks Genevieve—†	726	stenographer	29	120 Talbot av
H	O'Brien Jeremiah H	726	machinist	45	87 Mountfort
K	O'Brien Mary D—†	726	housewife	43	87 "
L	Cox Ernest C	726	salesman	46	here
M	Cox Lena L—†	726	housewife	47	"
N	Nichols Edna G—†	726	"	34	722 Com av
o	Nichols George C	726	dentist	49	722 "
P	Brown Alice M—†	726	corsetiere	55	here
R	Burnham Agnes B—†	726	housekeeper	55	"
s	Burnham Charles W	726	manager	58	"
T	Leighton Valtine—†	726	dressmaker	28	"
U	Amos Ethel—†	726	secretary	28	"
v	Miller Edna—†	726	nurse	27	"
x	Slack Harry C	726	manufacturer	53	"
Y	Slack Mary B—†	726	housewife	51	"
z	Slack Theodore W	726	student	21	"
A	Levin David	726	merchant	48	"
B	Thrope Harold	726	clerk	39	"
c	Thrope Mary—†	726	saleswoman	41	"
D	Thompson Alice—†	726	housewife	30	"
E	Thompson Thomas	726	merchant	40	"
F	Keddy Idella—†	726	manicurist	34	"
G	Boardman Russell N	726	salesman	35	"
K	Ewing Frank E	726	retired	55	Quincy
L	Magrath Ethel—†	726	clerk	38	here
M	Mullaney Mary—†	726	nurse	30	Malden
N	Sheehy Mildred—†	726	"	40	"
o	Harris Ella G—†	726	housekeeper	53	here
P	Morse Gertrude E—†	726	secretary	37	"
R	Gregory Joseph	728	janitor	45	"
s	Gregory William G	728	mechanic	24	"
T	Weeden Amy E—†	728	housekeeper	60	Hotel Buckminster

Page.	Letter.	FULL NAME.	Residence, April 1, 1924.	Occupation.	Supposed Age.	Reported Residence, April 1, 1923. Street and Number.

Commonwealth Avenue—Continued

u	Weeden Benjamin	728	retired	32	Hotel Buckminster
v	Fairbrother Katherine—†	728	housekeeper	35	here
w	Richards Charles G	728	hairdresser	54	"
x	Richards Julia M—†	728	housewife	48	"
y	Chase Annie B—†	728	bookkeeper	36	"
z	Hoyt Edward S	728	operator	49	Cambridge
A	Hoyt Marion K—†	728	housewife	41	"
B	White Bertha—†	728	clerk	40	Somerville
C	Farrell Mildred—†	728	housewife	23	4073 Wash'n
D	Mozer Abraham	728	tailor	38	here
E	Stone Benjamin F	728	policeman	28	"
F	Stone Elizibeth—†	728	housewife	32	"
G	Holmes Parker	728	broker	30	New Bedford
H	Wright Henry	728	merchant	30	Cambridge
K	Bruce Lulu H—†	728	housewife	42	here
L	Bruce Waldo A	728	painter	50	"
M	Delorey John	728	designer	32	Malden
O	Maguire Charles H	728	salesman	50	here
P	Maguire Mary H—†	728	housekeeper	68	"
N	McAnary Katherine G—†	728	manager	44	"
R	McMann Henry	728	salesman	28	"
S	McKissick Dorothy—†	728	secretary	26	"
T	Hambergur Isaac	728	salesman	63	Minnesota
U	Hambergur Sarah E—†	728	housewife	51	"
W	Heach Abraham	728	jeweler	26	Arlington
X	Hickman Lillian—†	728	manicurist	40	here
Y	Coffin Mabel—†	728	forewoman	32	"
Z	Ingals David	728	manufacturer	35	"
A	Hornbach Herbert J	728	salesman	42	"
B	Cotter Pauline—†	728	clerk	38	"
C	McLaughlin Jennie—†	728	"	35	"
D	Hutchins Alice—†	728	bookkeeper	45	"
E	Hutchins Sarah—†	728	"	43	"
F	Foster Henry	728	salesman	45	"
G	Manson James J	728	merchant	50	"
H	Carlton William B	728	"	55	"
K	Roden Ethel M—†	728	tel operator	30	"
L	Backerach Joseph	728	merchant	48	"
M	Fullock Charles	728	salesman	55	"
N	Fullock John	728	operator	26	"
O	Sutherland Charles	728	broker	30	Somerville

Commonwealth Avenue— Continued

P	McCutcheon Ida G—†	728	dressmaker	42	here
R	Gage George	728	merchant	50	Cambridge
S	Ettelson Anna—†	728	housewife	43	here
T	Ettelson Samuel W	728	dentist	51	"

Cummington Street

Z	Markey John C	26	veterinarian	49	here

Deerfield Street

V	Gately Catherine—†	2	maid	46	20 Gloucester
W	Gearghty Ella—†	2	"	24	here
X	Saltonstal Mary B—†	2	housewife	21	"
Y	Saltonstal Richard	2	banker	27	"
Z	Gibson Nancy J—†	58	maid	33	Winchester
A	Nelson Pauline—†	58	cook	62	here
B	Furner Rachael—†	58	maid	43	"
C	Welsh Frances C—†	58	housewife	65	"

Granby Street

D	Burke Francis A	25	clergyman	27	here
E	Desmond Bridget—†	25	maid	40	Ireland
F	Haberlin Richard J	25	clergyman	26	here
G	Hallahan Agnes—†	25	housekeeper	40	"
H	Lane Thomas	25	janitor	26	"
K	Laverty Anthony	25	clergyman	27	400 Wash'n
L	Lynch Elizabeth—†	25	maid	26	here
M	McGlinchey Joseph F	25	clergyman	26	"
N	O'Connell William H	25	archbishop	64	"

Kenmore Street

O	Becker Anne V—†	1	housekeeper	53	here
P	Conrad Gretchen—†	1	maid	32	Copley Plaza
R	Downing Julia—†	1	cook	36	here

Kenmore Street—Continued

s	Elliott William	1	butler	35	here
t	Irving Walter	1	houseman	20	202 W B'way
u	Vorenberg Frederick	1	treasurer	50	here
v	Vorenberg Samuel	1	buyer	46	"
w	Vorenberg Simon	1	merchant	74	"
y	Spaulding John P	10	physician	40	"
a	Chamberlain Agnes—†	10	retired	65	"
b	Chamberlain William	10	banker	35	"
e	Farmer Lewis G	10	lawyer	71	"
f	Farmer Mira—†	10	retired	70	"
g	Scribner June—†	10	physician	45	"
h	Martin Mabel I—†	10	manager	45	"
l	Gilbert George	10	broker	72	645 Beacon
m	Gilbert Joyce—†	10	housewife	70	645 "
n	Lee Catherine—†	10	retired	50	here
p	Dickinson Charles	10	lawyer	45	"
t	Collerd George R	10	salesman	45	Brookline
u	Collerd Mabel—†	10	housewife	45	"
x	Harrington Katherine—†	10	retired	45	here
w	Whitman Adelaide—†	10	"	55	"
z	Aspinwall Edward	10	broker	45	466 Com av
a	Else Clarence E	10	salesman	65	Brookline
d	Dobbins Henry, jr	10	real estate	35	"
e	Lowell Fannie—†	10	retired	70	here
f	Mullins William	10	merchant	45	"
g	West Charles	10	automobiles	55	"
k	Magill Joseph	10	retired	50	"
l	Button Hebert	10	salesman	30	"
m	Gordon Bernard C	10	retired	35	Swampscott
n	Gordon Jennie—†	10	housewife	28	"
o	Blackburne Ward	10	retired	55	here
r	Beal Herman	10	merchant	60	Brookline
s	Beal Maria—†	10	housewife	60	"
t	Langtery Albert P	10	newspaperman	60	here
u	Langtery Sallia—†	10	housewife	60	"
v	Fish Ira L	10	lawyer	55	"
w	Fish Irma—†	10	housewife	55	"
x	Litchfield Isaac W	10	engineer	55	"
y	Stevens Frank	10	lawyer	45	"
z	Cox Mabel—†	10	housewife	40	"
a	Cox Raymond B	10	banker	40	"

Letter.	FULL NAME.	Residence, April 1, 1924.	Occupation.	Supposed Age.	Reported Residence, April 1, 1923. Street and Number.

Kenmore Street—Continued

B	Hatch Frederick	10	merchant	55	here
D	Conniers Norman	10	teacher	65	"
E	Porter Harry L	10	agent	55	"
F	Porter Sarah—†	10	housewife	50	"
K	Koch Harry	10	merchant	40	Brookline
L	Koch Irma—†	10	housewife	35	"
M	Parker Carrie—†	10	retired	70	here
N	O'Meara Agnes—†	10	"	65	Lynn
O	Olmsted Ester—†	10	housewife	45	here
P	Olmsted Harry	10	physician	50	"

Newbury Street

S	Smith Bertha M—†	523	housewife	50	108 Hemenway
T	Smith Henry W	523	manager	63	108 "
U	Murphy John J	525	clerk	57	here
V	Murphy Margaret L—†	525	housewife	52	"
W	Mingo Anna M—†	526	"	32	"
X	Mingo Phillip V	526	janitor	30	"
Y	Rand Earl	526	merchant	32	"
Z	Rand Leah—†	526	housewife	31	"
A	Martin Elenor—†	526	waitress	26	"
B	Reed Georgia—†	526	"	26	"
C	Arsnow William	526	salesman	30	534 Newbury
D	Patterson Harry T	526	"	48	42 Belvidere
G	Devlin Agnes—†	526	waitress	23	619 Com av
F	McCue Margaret—†	526	"	25	Brookline
H	Armstrong Margaret—†	526	dressmaker	45	here
K	Holdridge Evelyn—†	526	"	51	"
L	Witton Charles J	526	boilermaker	30	"
M	Witton Dora—†	526	housewife	26	"
N	Bemis Sarah—†	526	housekeeper	63	"
O	Underwood Mary E—†	526	manicurist	45	"
P	Hunt Ella E—†	526	housewife	72	"
R	Taylor Carrie E—†	526	clerk	57	"
U	Menill Helen—†	526	"	23	"
S	O'Neil Catherine—†	526	"	35	"
T	O'Neil Ellen—†	526	housekeeper	77	"
V	Ryan Margaret W—†	526	bookkeeper	38	"
W	Boutet Anita—†	526	"	26	"

Page.	Letter.	Full Name	Residence, April 1, 1924.	Occupation.	Supposed Age.	Reported Residence April 1, 1923. Street and Number

Newbury Street—Continued

x	Boutet Della E—†	526	milliner	46	here
y	Anderson Esther E—†	526	housewife	51	"
z	Anderson Niels C	526	chauffeur	48	"
A	Clark Mary A—†	526	saleswoman	56	"
B	Ryan Mary—†	526	manager	51	"
c	Ryan Peter	526	shipper	40	"
D	Class Charles C	526	foreman	47	"
E	Class Lillian—†	526	housewife	36	"
F	Briggs George	526	chauffeur	30	548 Newbur
G	Moseley Charles B	526	clerk	62	here
H	Moseley Elizabeth L—†	526	housewife	63	"
K	Moseley Lucey M—†	526	social worker	34	"
L	Conere Estelle—†	526	cashier	29	"
M	Horton Eudora—†	526	housekeeper	66	"
N	Veizone Marie—†	526	dressmaker	28	"
O	Millis Ernest	526	salesman	27	Rockport
P	Pryor James E	526	policeman	32	103 Norway
R	Pryor Zelda B—†	526	housewife	24	103 "
S	Reed Charles	526	salesman	32	Brookline
T	Baldwin Chester D	529	"	47	here
U	Carpenter Victor H	529	physician	31	"
V	Jones James A	529	"	49	"
W	Goldstien Harry	530	bookkeeper	22	Malden
X	Rooff Joseph	530	salesman	30	"
Y	Rooff Mary—†	530	housewife	33	"
Z	McGail Ellen—†	530	dressmaker	45	here
A	McGail Sarah—†	530	"	50	"
B	Herman Emma—†	530	housewife	21	Newport R I
C	Herman Stanley	530	manager	32	"
D	Carter Matilda—†	530	waitress	35	Quincy
E	King Mary—†	530	checker	30	Plymouth
F	Neily Charles	530	chauffeur	37	here
G	Sangster Lucetta F—†	530	housekeeper	48	150 St Botol
H	Seldon Lillian—†	530	housewife	36	354 Mass av
K	Seldon Thomas	530	chauffeur	42	354 "
L	Shaw Alfred M	530	bookkeeper	22	150 St Botol
M	Hurley Edward A	530	salesman	36	here
N	Hussion James S	530	dyer	40	"
O	Alehin Alexander F	530	teacher	35	590 Newbury
P	Shah Nazaroff Leonid G	530	student	29	590 "
S	Bloom Ferdinand S	531	merchant	30	here

38

Newbury Street—Continued

Letter.	Full Name.	Res.	Occupation.	Age	Reported Residence
T	Bloom Marian S—†	531	housewife	58	here
U	Bloom William	531	merchant	62	"
R	LeBlanc Celenie—†	531	maid	35	Lynn
V	Saibel Martha—†	533	housewife	39	here
W	Saibel Robert	533	tailor	45	"
X	Sampson Julia B—†	533	secretary	30	"
Y	Berman Annie—†	534	housekeeper	32	Malden
B	Faucher Adelard	534	retired	70	341 Tremont
C	Grant Viola—†	534	teacher	35	341 "
D	Cote Annie—†	534	dressmaker	70	here
E	Williams Alma—†	534	housewife	54	"
F	Williams Frank	534	machinist	61	"
G	Wilbur Effie—†	534	housewife	42	Randolph
H	Wilbur Lester D	534	manager	50	"
L	Foster Nora B—†	534	housekeeper	54	here
M	Hill Lester S	534	chauffeur	41	"
N	McNally Robert R	534	"	26	160 St Botolph
O	Strout Roger	534	clerk	22	Portland Me
P	Lessen William	535	student	24	1697 Wash'n
R	Loring Herbert	535	"	21	918 Beacon
S	Schoenfeld Lester	535	"	22	Cambridge
T	Sohn Edward M	535	"	22	918 Beacon
U	Martin Helen—†	538	housekeeper	50	Brookline
V	Macdonald Louise—†	538	teacher	34	here
W	Oliver Charles M	538	barber	40	"
X	Oliver Isbelle—†	538	housewife	43	"
Z	Jarvins Maud—†	538	dressmaker	36	Newton
A	Somerville Alice M—†	538	buyer	40	here
E	Adams David	538	adjuster	28	Louisville Ky
F	Littlefield Stewart	538	salesman	22	Fall River
G	Walker William E	538	adjuster	24	New York
H	Whittum Charles H	538	"	24	Fall River
K	Coles James	540	student	23	Cambridge
L	Cowles Russell	540	"	24	Michigan
M	Eacmen Peter	540	"	20	Gardner
N	Farrell William J	540	clerk	23	27 St Botolph
O	Flannigan James	540	draughtsman	25	here
P	Hunt Milton L	540	shipper	21	Vermont
R	Price Joseph	540	engineer	30	Cambridge
S	Bean Blanche E—†	542	cashier	22	Maine
T	Joyce Margaret—†	542	housekeeper	38	here

Newbury Street—Continued

U	Magoun James E	542	clerk	29	here
V	Magoun Katherine—†	542	parlormaid	27	"
W	Scott James M	542	salesman	35	Cambridge
X	Snow Simon	542	manager	48	here
Y	Staples Anita—†	542	waitress	28	Waltham
Z	Bowers Mabel—†	544	housewife	38	here
A	Bowers Thomas	544	waiter	39	"
B	Chisolm Charles	544	clerk	48	"
C	Gorham William H	544	chauffeur	35	"
D	Sabourin Ovila	544	"	28	Rhode Island
E	Gelpke Anna S—†	546	housewife	39	Eastport Me
F	Gelpke Herbert A	546	chauffeur	38	"
G	McDonald Amelia—†	546	waitress	30	17 Rutland s
H	McDonald Laura—†	546	"	25	17 "
K	Rouillard Robert G	546	operator	24	Topsham Me
L	Batchelder Milton F	548	student	21	Vermont
M	Brady Jennie R—†	548	waitress	36	Florida
N	Cushay Anthony	548	barber	30	Revere
O	Eagan William F	548	agent	40	Natick
P	French George B	548	student	22	New Hampshire
R	Jones Frank A	548	auto tester	25	Salem
S	McGuire Joseph W	548	waiter	28	Florida
T	McPherson Ardithe—†	548	instructress	20	44 Falmouth
U	Perrault Rose A—†	548	housekeeper	40	Lynn
V	Rickert Clara—†	548	dressmaker	26	115 Mountfo
W	Rutterman Alfred	548	engineer	45	here
X	Scheirgols Harry	548	waiter	28	650 E Sixth
X¹	Nagle Anna M—†	550	retired	49	here
Y	Boswell Isaac	552	janitor	61	"
Z	Boswell Lydia M—†	552	dressmaker	50	"
A	Grevious Porthantheum	552	chauffeur	46	"
C	Nelson James	552	student	28	"
D	Stephens Ida—†	552	"	31	Cambridge
E	Baxter William N	554	agent	43	57 Mountfort
F	Binley Walter S	554	auditor	45	523 Newbury
G	Broughey Walter S	554	salesman	30	Salem
H	Lynch Margaret J—†	554	nurse	30	839 Boylston
K	Whitten Fredrick	554	waiter	50	here
L	Willensen Orsen	554	manufacturer	35	Worcester
M	Berwick Allen	556	student	21	here
N	Cohen Allen R	556	"	21	Leominster

Newbury Street—Continued

Letter	Full Name	Residence, April 1, 1924	Occupation	Supposed Age	Reported Residence, April 1, 1923
o	Delugach Gilbert L	556	student	20	here
p	Fine Henry R	556	"	20	"
r	Singer David	556	"	22	"
s	Tenney Polly—†	556	housekeeper	36	"
t	Benson Robert	558	waiter	26	"
u	Durgan Nellie—†	558	waitress	33	"
v	Kelly Delia—†	558	housekeeper	50	"
w	Lydon Patrick F	558	special police	48	"
x	McCabe Catherine A—†	558	housekeeper	52	"
y	Sullivan Gertrude E—†	560	"	26	"
z	Sullivan John J	560	manager	58	"
a	Sullivan Margaret V—†	560	housekeeper	48	"
b	Everett Jennie F—†	562	housewife	50	Denver Col
c	Everett William R, jr	562	mechanic	26	"
d	Everett William R	562	"	50	"
e	Snow Della—†	564	housekeeper	50	562 Newbury
f	Snow Robert	564	janitor	50	562 "
g	Hammond Allen D	566	clerk	27	Mattapoisett
h	Meier Emil K	566	bookkeeper	28	W Wareham
l	Chamberlain Alban	574	mechanic	26	13 Haviland
m	Chamberlain Alice K—†	574	housewife	25	13 "
n	Puttick Frances M—†	574	stenographer	36	here
o	Puttick John	574	caterer	66	"
p	Taylor Matilda J—†	574	cook	64	"
r	McCarthy Anna L—†	574	clerk	37	"
s	McCarthy Margaret—†	574	bookkeeper	42	"
t	Kyte Mary E—†	574	housewife	36	"
u	Kyte William H	574	conductor	39	"
v	Maxwell Bessie—†	574	dressmaker	65	"
w	Maxwell Sherman	574	student	21	"
x	Day Ganotte L	574	mechanic	30	89 Mountfort
y	Day Maebelle F—†	574	housewife	39	89 "
z	Beal Mildred F—†	574	dressmaker	52	here
a	David Daisey P—†	574	nurse	32	"
b	Jarves Frances H—†	574	dressmaker	51	Brookline
c	Titus Henry B	574	chauffeur	45	here
d	Titus Maria A—†	574	housewife	49	"
e	Morong Alton E	578	mechanic	29	75 Maple
f	Morong Gladys M—†	578	housewife	21	75 "
g	Neill Verne M	578	clerk	26	Eastport Me
h	Brothers Annette A—†	578	retired	48	here

Page.	Letter.	FULL NAME.	Residence, April 1, 1924.	Occupation.	Supposed Age.	Reported Residence, April 1, 1923. Street and Number.

Newbury Street—Continued

K	Brothers Margaret B—†	578	secretary	28	here
L	Flaherty Charles F	578	clerk	41	1427 Com av
M	Flaherty Helen M—†	578	housewife	30	1427 "
N	Sutcliffe Albert E	578	chauffeur	39	here
O	Sutcliffe Bertha A—†	578	housewife	37	"
P	Beckwith Charles F	578	optometrist	57	"
R	Beckwith Charles R	578	bookkeeper	24	"
S	Beckwith Minnie—†	578	housekeeper	50	"
T	deCordova Alice H—†	578	decorator	37	"
U	Miller Roxina B—†	578	retired	65	"
V	Boydick Harry B	578	printer	32	"
W	Boydick Laura—†	578	housewife	27	"
X	Tiberan Aaron	578	cutter	28	1025 Wash'n
Y	Gibson Carl	578	chauffeur	42	here
Z	Poulis Anthony	578	cook	38	"
A	Whitcher Fred J	578	chauffeur	40	"
B	Whitcher Jessie R—†	578	housewife	40	"
C	Dodge George B	582	tailor	66	"
D	Dodge Jane P—†	582	housekeeper	53	"
E	Perpoli Joseph	582	janitor	43	"
F	Perpoli Jurla—†	582	housewife	39	"
G	Bernard Hattie L—†	582	housekeeper	50	"
H	Lalley George W	582	clerk	47	"
K	Smith Abraham	582	mechanic	27	99 Mountfort
L	Halfacre George S	582	waiter	50	here
M	Halfacre Pauline A—†	582	housekeeper	49	"
N	Halfacre William E	582	student	21	"
O	Ingram Edwin J	582	salesman	56	"
P	Stover Lillian E—†	582	housekeeper	56	"
R	Fitzgerald Margaret E—†	582	"	50	580 Com av
S	Fortier Norman H	582	teacher	26	here
T	Kennedy Ermon L	582	salesman	35	"
U	Kennedy Mary—†	582	housewife	30	"
V	Lawrence Jane O—†	582	dressmaker	51	"
W	Anderson Alice S—†	586	clerk	49	50 Charlesgate East
X	Anderson Margaret—†	586	saleswoman	40	here
Y	Donough Agnes—†	586	"	38	78 Glenville av
Z	Egan Edith—†	586	housewife	29	78 "
A	Egan Michael	586	clerk	42	78 "
B	Howard Ana—†	586	tel operator	36	here
C	McLaughlin John C	586	porter	51	"

Newbury Street—Continued

	Letter.	Full Name.	Residence, April 1, 1924.	Occupation.	Supposed Age.	Reported Residence, April 1, 1923.
	D	Braun Gertrude—†	586	waitress	40	534 Newbury
	E	Schaefer Donald F	586	salesman	37	534 "
	F	Schaefer Ella M—†	586	housewife	42	534 "
	G	Cowan John C	586	manager	50	here
	H	Ducey Helen—†	586	dressmaker	38	"
	K	Landin Beda—†	586	housewife	42	"
	L	Landin Carl	586	manager	43	"
	M	Landin Eleanor—†	586	"	21	"
	N	Radigan Bernard J	586	chauffeur	53	Watertown
	O	Radigan Margaret V—†	586	housewife	43	"
	P	Brown Elizabeth V—†	590	"	37	here
	R	Brown Henry J	590	engineer	42	"
	S	Smith Ernest J	590	salesman	26	Haverhill
	T	Smith Mary L—†	590	housewife	55	"
	U	Floyd Nelson	590	chauffeur	31	101 Mountfort
	V	Floyd Ruth—†	590	housewife	26	11 Lakeville pl
	W	Cudworth Cora E—†	590	clerk	34	Lynnfield
	X	Renner Reta—†	590	housewife	34	544 Newbury
	Y	Renner Stanley J	590	U S A	39	here
	Z	Woods Harry A	590	salesman	42	Worcester
	A	McAvoy Edward J	590	"	30	Brookline
	B	Olin Blanche S—†	590	stenographer	32	here
	C	Olin Irene E—†	590	bookkeeper	27	"
	D	Olin John G	590	retired	80	"
	E	Goodwin Arthur B	590	salesman	28	Medford
	F	Goodwin Josephine—†	590	housewife	21	Everett
	G	Kent Charles	590	manager	30	here
	H	Kent Vera—†	590	housewife	35	"
	K	Fallon Cleo—†	590	waitress	32	"
	L	Fallon Thomas V	590	steward	38	"
	M	Madden Andrew	590	gardener	40	"

Ward 8—Precinct 12

CITY OF BOSTON.

LIST OF RESIDENTS
20 YEARS OF AGE AND OVER

(FEMALES INDICATED BY DAGGER)

AS OF

APRIL 1, 1924

HERBERT A. WILSON, } *Listing*

JAMES F. EAGAN, } *Board.*

CITY OF BOSTON—PRINTING DEPARTMENT

Aberdeen Street

A	Kimball Ethel E—†	7	secretary	48	Brookline
B	Vestagard Christy	7	gardener	67	here
C	Vestagard Maude A—†	7	secretary	35	"
D	Benson John	7	garagekeeper	44	"
E	Benson Meranda—†	7	housewife	35	"
F	Cook Frederick A	7	dentist	64	"
G	Cook Maud F—†	7	housewife	53	"
H	Cook Mildred—†	7	composer	22	"
K	Eastman Alman L	8	undertaker	65	"
L	Eastman Josephine E—†	8	housewife	60	"
M	Stowell John	9	chauffeur	34	627 Col av
N	Stowell Lillian—†	9	housewife	36	627 "
O	Mitchell Bertha—†	9	clerk	42	here
P	Wallace Jessie—†	9	"	52	"
R	Huggin Alfred	9	chauffeur	33	77 Mountfort
S	McPhee Celia—†	9	housewife	25	here
T	McPhee Charles H	9	chauffeur	29	"
U	Parks Catherine—†	10	housewife	43	"
V	Grant Mary—†	11	nurse	26	Brookline
W	MacLeod Maud—†	11	"	28	here
X	Allen Edward B	11	salesman	34	"
Y	Andrus Cora E—†	11	housekeeper	46	"
Z	Bostwick Charles S	11	bookkeeper	46	"
A	Ransom Allen M	11	clerk	33	Scituate
A¹	Gauvin Frank	11	"	21	Marlboro
B	Judson William A	11	blacksmith	60	"
C	Urquhart Agnes—†	11	housewife	41	here
D	Urquhart Milton S	11	clerk	40	"
E	Winthrop Andrew A	11	"	22	Cuba
F	Pembroke Arthur W	12	chauffeur	54	here
G	Pembroke Catherine—†	12	housewife	39	"
L	Guild Earl S	15	engineer	34	"
M	Guild Gertrude B—†	15	housewife	33	"
N	Clark Asa	15	clerk	27	"
O	Clark Clifford M	15	carpenter	23	"
P	Clark Olive M—†	15	housekeeper	49	"
R	Leaman Jesse—†	15	saleswoman	55	Nova Scotia
S	Adams Johnston	15	salesman	46	here
T	Brennan Hannah M—†	15	housewife	42	"
U	Brennan Joseph I	15	foreman	48	"

Aberdeen Street—Continued

Letter	Full Name	Residence, April 1, 1924	Occupation	Supposed Age	Reported Residence, April 1, 1923. Street and Number
v	Coffin Anna—†	17	musician	37	here
w	Wheeler Marie—†	17	bookkeeper	32	"
x	O'Keefe Charles I	17	printer	49	8 Maitland
y	O'Keefe Susan G—†	17	housewife	43	8 "
z	Klinor Hannah—†	17	"	40	Lawrence
a	Klinor Klieva	17	broker	50	"
b	Seymour Charles	19	chauffeur	40	8 Maitland
c	Seymour Minnie—†	19	housewife	38	8 "
d	Belden Alice—†	19	barber	26	New Hampshire
e	Doherty Helen—†	19	nurse	30	here
f	Brown Wallace	19	telegrapher	35	"
g	Epler Catherine—†	19	clerk·	22	"
h	Epler Leopoldin—†	19	housekeeper	58	"
k	Verat Alice—†	19	hairdresser	25	"
m	Quirk Agnes H—†	21	housewife	24	46 Mountfort
n	Quirk Joseph S	21	salesman	27	46 "
o	Quirk Mary E—†	21	housekeeper	69	46 "
r	Eldridge Ethel—†	21	bookkeeper	32	77 Westland av
s	Kett Emily B—†	23	tel operator	22	21 Aberdeen
t	Kett Johanna—†	23	housekeeper	58	21 "
u	Kett Mary F—†	23	bookkeeper	26	21 "
v	Kett Walter	23	foreman	24	21 "
w	Kett William	23	chauffeur	21	21 "
x	Fisher Emile	23	"	47	here
y	Fisher Lucy L—†	23	"	43	"
z	Fisher Lucy L—†	23	clerk	20	"
a	Beatty Francis	23	chauffeur	24	21 Aberdeen
b	Beatty James	23	engineer	50	21 "
c	Beatty James, jr	23	chauffeur	21	21 "
d	Beatty Mary—†	23	housewife	49	21 "
e	Beatty William	23	chauffeur	23	21 "
f	Achorn Carrie—†	25	dressmaker	40	6 Bailey
g	Blackburn Dorothy—†	25	none	26	Rhode Island
h	Blackburn James	25	draughtsman	31	"
k	Cassidy Charles	25	machinist	38	Quincy
l	Cassidy Elizabeth—†	25	housekeeper	50	"
m	Tone Carnelo	25	laborer	31	127 Vernon
n	Tone Frances—†	25	housewife	23	127 "
o	Swanson Steina—†	27	houseworker	35	here
p	Smith Fritz H	27	mailer	37	"
r	Bergeson Arthur J	27	chauffeur	38	8 Maitland

3

Page	Letter	Full Name.	Residence, April 1, 1924.	Occupation.	Supposed Age.	Reported Residence, April 1, 1923. Street and Number.

Aberdeen Street—Continued

	s	Bergeson Nicolina—†	27	housewife	45	8 Maitland
	t	Belle William	27	policeman	34	here
	u	Ryan Ellen G—†	27	housewife	48	"
	v	Ryan John S	27	salesman	30	"
	w	Ryan Maurice J	27	clerk	54	"

Arundel Street

	y	Davis Catherine A—†	12	bookkeeper	29	here
	z	Davis Harry O	12	salesman	42	"
	A	Getter Ruth S—†	12	none	24	42 Ivy
	B	Getter Seymour	12	manager	26	42 "
	c	Smith Alice M—†	16	housewife	26	here
	d	Smith Edger R	16	teacher	26	"
	E	Higgins Arthur A	16	salesman	38	76 Quint av
	F	Higgins Vivian—†	16	housewife	29	76 "
	G	Blanchard Azel	16	pianomaker	20	here
	H	Blanchard Edwin C	16	mechanic	22	"
	K	Blanchard Jesse C—†	16	bookkeeper	34	"
	L	Cameron Mabel A—†	16	nurse	38	"
	M	Gleason Dorothy—†	16	"	31	"
	N	Mayall Anna—†	16	housewife	60	"
	O	Mayall Eleanor—†	16	restaurateur	23	"
	P	Mayall John C	16	machinist	81	"
	R	McLeod Catherine—†	16	clerk	32	"
	S	Spears Catherine—†	16	saleswoman	39	"
	T	Spears Gordon R	16	chauffeur	37	"
	U	McElroy Dorothy—†	16	housewife	24	Cambridge
	V	McElroy Joseph T	16	surveyor	29	"
	W	MacNeil Florence—†	16	modiste	42	here

Audubon Road

	X	Auffrey Nellie—†	447	none	39	here
	Y	Cann Margery—†	447	clerk	33	"
	Z	Cann William	447	butler	38	"
	A	Marsh Alice—†	447	clerk	28	"
	B	Marsh Elizabeth—†	447	student	33	Plymouth
	C	Willson Alice T—†	447	none	38	Brookline

4

Audubon Road—Continued

D	Willson Walter J	447	editor	40	Brookline
E	Fera Viola —†	447	none	51	here
F	Robinson Eliza —†	447	"	73	"
G	Harding Elizabeth —†	447	social worker	36	"
H	Harding Margaret E —†	447	retired	70	"
K	Scanlon Martin	447	merchant	65	"
L	Taylor Ethel D —†	447	none	39	"
M	Taylor John C	447	trustee	43	"
N	Hiltz Joseph R	447	manager	23	"
O	Hiltz Mathilda —†	447	none	27	"
P	Lynch Rachel —†	447	maid	24	Barbadoes Isles
R	Clark Deverd	447	carpenter	47	Canada
S	Clark Minnie M —†	447	none	48	here
T	Dickens Nellie —†	447	cashier	45	1120 Boylston
U	Jessup George H	447	clerk	45	England
V	Driscoll Mary —†	447	maid	20	Ireland
W	Rintels Caroline —†	447	none	36	here
X	Rintels Sydney	447	druggist	50	"
Y	Tidd Jacob F	448	janitor	64	"
Z	Ross Annette —†	448	housewife	38	"
A	Ross Charles F	448	merchant	45	"
B	Souther Blanche —†	448	housewife	58	"
C	Souther Harrison A	448	physician	60	499 Audubon rd
D	Hovestad Evelyn M —†	448	housewife	24	here
E	Hovestad Frederick W	448	physician	33	"
F	Myers Bruce	448	manager	45	"
G	Myers Lydia C —†	448	housewife	48	"
H	Kempton Elvie	448	constructor	52	California
K	Kempton Katherine —†	448	housewife	52	"
L	Knight Henry B	448	druggist	52	here
M	Knight Rachel J —†	448	housewife	54	"
N	Doyle Henry K	448	steward	42	"
O	Washburn Anna A —†	448	housewife	38	39 Mountfort
P	Washburn Frank B	448	accountant	65	39 "
R	Bragdon Edith —†	448	nurse	29	Mass Gen Hosp
S	Gilmore Florence —†	448	"	35	here
T	Hodnett Mabel —†	448	"	37	"
U	Iverson Marie —†	448	"	35	"
V	Bryant Thomas B R	448	salesman	25	"
W	Eaton Dana H	448	"	27	"
X	Goodenow Charles H	448	"	27	"

Audubon Road—Continued

Y	Marsh Raymond	448	U S A	33	West Point
z	Pillsbury Elmer K	448	salesman	28	here
A	Kirby Edmund W	448	jewelry	40	"
B	Kirby Hilda F—†	448	housewife	35	"
D	McPherson Anna C—†	448	"	37	44 Cooper
E	West Dora A—†	448	"	48	146 Mass av
F	West Edward N	448	merchant	53	146 "
G	Webb Sarah G—†	448	housewife	50	here
H	Webb Walter G	448	salesman	55	"
K	Potter Leah F—†	448	merchant	36	"
L	Webster Jean—†	448	housewife	30	522 Audubon r
M	Webster Robert	448	manager	42	522 "
N	Keyes Clara S—†	448	housekeeper	44	here
O	Spear Lillian G—†	448	merchant	50	"
P	Palmer Henry F	448	real estate	50	"
R	Palmer Lillian H—†	448	actress	22	"
S	Palmer Lillian R—†	448	housewife	43	"
T	Squire Luella—†	449	none	58	"
U	Squire Walter J	449	teller	59	"
V	Metcalf Helen—†	449	nurse	30	36 Ivy
W	Fletcher Arthur	449	paymaster	41	here
X	Fletcher Blanche—†	449	none	30	"
Y	Stubbins Henrietta—†	449	dressmaker	32	44 Ivy
Z	Boudreau George	449	salesman	41	here
A	Boudreau Rose—†	449	dressmaker	24	"
B	Crowley John J	449	salesman	30	Indianapolis
C	Crowley Mary L—†	449	none	29	221 Cabot
D	Rosales Anna—†	449	"	29	here
E	Rosales Robert	449	chauffeur	32	"
F	Hess John S	449	physician	24	"
G	Shippy Harold W	449	draughtsman	26	"
H	Bundy Marion C—†	449	saleswoman	47	Cambridge
K	Connor Tillie—†	449	secretary	25	Fall River
L	Martin Catherine—†	449	student	24	Ohio
M	Farquhar Anna—†	449	none	55	here
N	Farquhar Frank C	449	roofer	60	"
O	Haskell Mabel—†	449	none	52	"
P	Haskell William N	449	manager	60	"
R	Heap Beatrice—†	449	stenographer	21	Avon
S	Heap Ralph G	449	clerk	21	Braintree
T	Burton Dorothy I—†	449	"	20	Connecticut

	Lettr.	FULL NAME.	Residence, April 1, 1921.	Occupation.	Supposed Age.	Reported Residence, April 1, 1923. Street and Number.

Audubon Road—Continued

	Lettr.	FULL NAME.	Res.	Occupation.	Age	Reported Residence
	U	Burton Eva J—†	449	housewife	52	Connecticut
	V	Burton Helen W—†	449	student	21	459 Audubon rd
	W	Luce Helen—†	449	none	32	here
	X	Luce John J	449	paymaster	44	"
	Y	Davis Ella—†	449	none	56	"
	Z	Lovely Louise—†	449	"	29	Brockton
	A	McKenzie Alice—†	449	housewife	28	here
	B	Brand Arthur A	449	broker	45	"
	C	Brand Bessie—†	449	none	26	"
	D	McCabe Anna—†	449	"	45	"
	E	McCabe Michael	449	merchant	47	"
	F	Daly Chester H	449	agent	28	"
	G	Vorenburg Frank	449	salesman	52	"
	H	Lewis Halsted	449	"	27	4 W Cedar
	K	Spalding Evans	449	broker	33	London
	L	Cummings John J	452	agent	41	here
	M	Downey Michael J	452	director	42	"
	N	Gould Arthur L	452	teacher	47	"
	O	Rose Walter J	452	merchant	42	"
	P	Ames Lillie M—†	452	retired	50	60 Fenway
	R	Garland Gladys—†	452	secretary	35	Somerville
	S	Ware Marjorie J—†	452	teacher	40	here
	T	Ries Emil D	452	professor	30	New Jersey
	U	Bragdon Edward A	452	mechanic	32	Maine
	V	Stockwell Clifford H	452	agent	50	82 Chestnut
	W	Stockwell Lilla M—†	452	housewife	45	82 "
	X	Hodgkinson Charles H	452	auditor	53	here
	Y	Hodgkinson Ethel M—†	452	housewife	41	"
	Z	Dunham Frederick H	452	manager	40	Springfield
	A	Dunham Meta—†	452	housewife	37	"
	B	Marsh Miriam T—†	452	"	30	New York
	C	Gallagher Alice R—†	452	secretary	28	Newton
	D	Chatman Lilian—†	452	housewife	54	here
	E	Samuels Leona—†	452	student	23	"
	F	Samuels Rose—†	452	housewife	44	"
	G	Marshall Emily H—†	452	"	54	"
	H	Fifield Gertrude A—†	452	bookkeeper	37	"
	K	Fraser Bertha—†	452	"	38	"
	L	Fraser Isabella—†	452	"	38	"
	M	Jenks Harvey P	452	merchant	27	Brookline
	N	Jenks Henrietta M—†	452	housewife	59	"

Page	Letter	Full Name.	Residence, April 1, 1924.	Occupation.	Supposed Age.	Reported Residence, April 1, 1923. Street and Number.	Page.

Audubon Road—Continued

o	Nickerson Emma S—†	452	retired	61	Brookline	
p	Hinson Bertha L F—†	452	"	60	here	
r	Hinson Leonard M	452	student	24	"	
s	Hays Eva H—†	452	housewife	41	"	
t	Hays John C	452	engineer	41	"	
u	Haslett Alice L—†	452	practitioner	60	"	
v	Austin Lucy M—†	452	merchant	50	"	
w	Nichols Marie—†	452	musician	40	"	
x	Lewis Carrie G—†	455	none	42	"	
y	Lawrence Harold W	455	janitor	33	"	
z	Lawrence Mae—†	455	none	28	463 Audubon rd	
A	McKenzie Jean P—†	455	nurse	50	463 "	
B	Walsh Helen B—†	455	"	30	463 "	
C	Lavin Catherine M—†	455	teacher	30	here	
D	Lavin Joseph L	455	manager	26	"	
E	Lavin Mary E—†	455	none	61	"	
F	Ross Annie—†	456	maid	55	"	
G	Stacey Alice M—†	456	housewife	55	"	
H	Stacey Charles F	456	physician	57	"	
K	Ladd John D	457	student	24	Chicago	
L	Ladd Lillian—†	457	"	23	"	
M	Munson Ada F—†	457	housekeeper	71	here	
N	Crosbie Arthur H	457	physician	46	"	
O	Rigby Agnes—†	457	housekeeper	26	Scotland	
P	Rigby Arthur	457	butler	33	"	
R	Spooner Leslie H	457	physician	42	here	
S	McVicar Christine—†	457	maid	38	"	
T	Mildram Elliot S	457	none	27	"	
U	Mildram Henry H	457	president	54	"	
V	Mildram Mary—†	457	clerk	52	"	
W	Piscopo John B	458	retired	46	"	
X	Davis Daisy E—†	459	none	44	"	
Y	Lacaillaide James O	459	physician	48	783 Hunt'n av	
Z	Lacaillaide Ruth E—†	459	none	31	783 "	
A	Preble Helen S—†	459	"	38	here	
B	Preble William E	459	physician	48	"	
C	Lomasney Joseph P	460	real estate	61	"	
D	Lomasney Nellie M—†	460	housewife	52	"	
E	Riley Rose L—†	460	none	38	"	
G	Blackwood Edith—†	461	nurse	34	162 Hunt'n av	
H	Cairns Lulu—†	461	"	38	394 Riverway	

Audubon Road—Continued

	Letter.	FULL NAME.	Residence, April 1, 1924.	Occupation.	Supposed Age.	Reported Residence, April 1, 1923.
	K	Huggard Gladys—†	461	nurse	28	394 Riverway
	L	Marion Carolina E—†	461	housekeeper	50	394 "
	M	Trull Elizabeth L—†	461	typist	21	394 "
	N	Donavan Emily A—†	461	housewife	55	here
	O	Donavan Minnie L—†	461	clerk	48	"
	P	Donavan William F	461	lawyer	52	"
	R	Ahearn Katherine—†	462	maid	28	"
	S	McLaughlin Edward A	462	lawyer	73	"
	T	McLaughlin Edward A, jr	462	"	28	"
	U	McLaughlin Raymond E	462	student	20	"
	V	McLaughlin Richard J	462	salesman	26	"
	W	Lucas Mary—†	463	housewife	38	59 Astor
	X	Lucas William	463	janitor	36	59 "
	Y	Allen Florence—†	463	housekeeper	48	here
	Z	Rice Elsie—†	463	dressmaker	45	"
	A	Hinchliffe George H	463	manager	49	"
	B	Hinchliffe Josephine R—†	463	housekeeper	47	"
	C	Auld Janet—†	463	clerk	38	Quincy
	D	Morgan Ruth—†	463	cook	23	Milton
	E	Simmons Allan	463	machinist	20	Somerville
	F	Jaquith Helene—†	463	clerk	23	here
	G	Macaulay Lauretta—†	463	"	33	"
	H	Macaulay Rose—†	463	housekeeper	72	"
	K	Buzzell Edith E—†	463	clerk	43	"
	L	Upham Edith E—†	463	"	41	"
	M	Flint Arline—†	463	teacher	25	New Hampshire
	N	Merrill Ethel C—†	463	buyer	39	"
	P	Deegan Hilda M—†	463	clerk	30	Cambridge
	R	Moran Erving	463	bookkeeper	38	308 Newbury
	S	Andrews Jeanette—†	463	housekeeper	36	here
	T	Noonan Joseph J	463	bookkeeper	37	Revere
	U	Hassen Mary K—†	463	manager	45	Hull
	V	Pooley Ree—†	463	"	28	"
	X	Adelson Julius	463	real estate	62	here
	Y	Adelson Lilliam—†	463	clerk	29	"
	B	Langill Eva E—†	463	housewife	44	"
	C	Langill James F	463	printer	43	"
	F	Connor Mary E—†	463	buyer	48	"
	G	Mulvihill Frances—†	463	clerk	36	"
	H	Dawe Josie M—†	464	housekeeper	52	"
	K	Higgins Lothrop C	464	merchant	61	"

Audubon Road—Continued

L	Whitehead Martha J—†	464	retired	94	here	
M	Layne Estella—†	465	housewife	34	"	
N	Layne Julian	465	janitor	30	"	
O	Esteabrook Emma R—†	465	housewife	56	"	
P	Esteabrook Frederick	465	merchant	66	"	
R	Shapira Ira W	465	real estate	52	640 Beacon	
S	Shapira Lena—†	465	housewife	45	640 "	
U	Kaffenburgh Ruth—†	465	"	35	here	
V	Kaffenburgh Walter A	465	farmer	37	"	
W	Winternitz Felix	465	teacher	52	61 Hemenway	
X	Winternitz Toni—†	465	housewife	56	61 "	
Y	Winters Kurt	465	manager	26	61 "	
Z	Hill Calvin C	466	practitioner	56	here	
A	Hill Frances T—†	466	housewife	37	"	
B	Williams Bessie—†	466	housekeeper	40	"	
C	Bradley Mildred—†	468	secretary	33	"	
D	Bradley Payson	468	merchant	76	"	
E	Foley Mary A—†	468	cook	48	"	
F	Murphy Bessie A—†	468	waitress	29	"	
H	Carlton Horace F	499	salesman	61	25 Hemenway	
K	Carlton Margaret A—†	499	housewife	60	25 "	
L	Bacheller John B	499	retired	77	here	
M	Giddings Helen A—†	499	housekeeper	45	"	
N	DeSelva Filomena M—†	499	"	43	Spain	
O	Tisdale Frank L	500	merchant	53	here	
P	Tisdale Grace R—†	500	housewife	45	"	
R	Wetherbee Lilla—†	500	retired	56	"	
S	Wetherbee Martha—†	500	"	53	"	
T	Lovett Esther P—†	500	housewife	32	"	
U	Lovett Sydney	500	clergyman	24	"	
W	Harnden Mary C—†	503	retired	80	"	
X	Koren Katherine O—†	503	"	50	"	
Z	Davis Ida M—†	504	housewife	61	"	
A	Pratt Frank B	504	salesman	75	"	
B	Thomas Harriet N—†	504	housewife	51	"	
C	Thomas James E	504	teacher	65	"	
D	MacDonald Dorothy F—†	504	accountant	23	New Hampshire	
E	MacDonald Helen I—†	504	nurse	23	"	
F	McDonald Isabelle R—†	504	housewife	52	"	
G	MacDonald Thomas A	504	insurance agent	57	"	
L	Robillard Jane—†	509	housewife	50	here	

Audubon Road—Continued

M	Robillard John	509	janitor	50	here
N	Adams Beatrice—†	509	stenographer	23	New Hampshire
O	Crydenwise Dorothy—†	509	social worker	22	35 Tyler
P	Parker Helen W—†	509	school teacher	23	Brookline
R	Webster Marion—†	509	"	26	"
S	Wells Elizabeth H—†	509	housekeeper	78	here
T	Wilby Katherine—†	509	none	48	"
U	Benson Louise M—†	509	housewife	28	"
V	Benson Warren E	509	manager	27	"
W	Skinner Clara E—†	509	housekeeper	53	"
X	Jones Ellen A—†	509	none	60	"
Y	Phillips Helen—†	509	instructor	32	Arlington
Z	Cowdery Eva—†	509	none	62	"
A	Griffin Margaret M—†	509	nurse	39	here
B	Beck Caroline E—†	509	housewife	64	"
C	Beck Shirley	509	banker	70	"
D	Smith Katherine—†	509	none	60	"
E	Wood Percy F	509	salesman	41	"
F	Cunningham Rose A—†	509	nurse	38	"
G	Rising Caroline E—†	509	social worker	50	Texas
H	Blanchard Beatrice C—†	509	school teacher	33	here
K	Blanchard Ruth—†	509	secretary	32	"
L	Mulvey Justin P	509	salesman	31	65 Audubon rd
M	Mulvey Marion H—†	509	housewife	28	65 "
N	Shuffler Lee	509	U S A	43	here
O	Shuffler Mary—†	509	housewife	40	"
P	Clifford Ethel M—†	509	bookkeeper	30	"
R	Finerty Anna M—†	509	nurse	47	"
S	Hersey Cora M—†	509	none	58	72 Peterboro
T	Makeever Madison M	509	merchant	53	here
U	Johnson Harriet J—†	509	student	32	Nova Scotia
V	Byrnes John F	509	accountant	42	here
W	Bryant Hattie H—†	509	pianist	35	"
X	Trainor Mary E—†	509	therapeutist	34	"
Y	Barnes Isabella F—†	509	secretary	38	"
Z	DeWolf Mary—†	509	nurse	30	Nova Scotia
A	Jacobs Sarah L—†	509	none	65	here
B	Warren Abbie—†	509	dressmaker	45	1325 Com av
C	Adams Ella F—†	509	housewife	42	here
D	Adams William	509	architect	44	"
E	Whitney Caroline B—†	509	none	65	"

Audubon Road—Continued

F	Jewett Arthur	509	superintendent	34	here
G	Jewett Mary E—†	509	housewife	30	"
H	Poole Edward G	509	cashier	59	"
K	Poole Jennie F—†	509	housewife	52	"
L	Haynes Frank L	509	engineer	40	"
M	Ford Annette E—†	509	housewife	53	"
N	Ford Frank T	509	manager	53	"
O	Bryant Charles A	509	salesman	43	"
P	Bryant Malvina—†	509	housewife	33	"
R	Crane Louise—†	509	stenographer	32	108 Redlands rd
S	Maguire Jane G—†	509	school teacher	30	108 "
T	Freeman Robert G	509	salesman	50	here
U	Green Lloyd	509	"	37	"
V	Richardson Conrad P	509	lawyer	36	"
W	Richardson Dorothy—†	509	housewife	27	"
Z	Averill Samuel M	514	buyer	56	"
A	Ames Annie C—†	514	none	65	"
B	Wilton George C	514	broker	54	48 Temple
C	Wilton Georgiana—†	514	none	41	here
D	Hendler Angie C—†	514	"	36	"
E	Hendler Charles A	514	manager	39	"
F	Gale Burt S	514	practitioner	60	"
G	Gale Hattie S—†	514	none	60	"
K	Hawes Joseph P	514	merchant	72	Brookline
L	Hawes Josephine C—†	514	none	41	"
P	Cunningham Mary—†	515	housekeeper	28	here
R	Doyle Polly—†	515	nurse	30	"
S	Roan Margaret—†	515	"	29	"
T	Leroy Peter C	515	salesman	35	558 Columbia rd
U	Reynolds Frank	515	florist	36	Brookline
V	McBurney Fanny—†	515	housewife	33	Newton
W	McBurney Joseph	515	chauffeur	49	41 Bickerstaff
X	Damon Ethel D—†	515	housewife	45	here
Y	Damon John W	515	manager	48	"
Z	Fay Leon B	515	repairman	32	Fitchburg
A	Higgins Elsie L—†	515	shoe stitcher	29	here
B	Higgins Parker G	515	mechanic	34	"
C	Perry Rose—†	515	shoe stitcher	21	Gardiner Me
D	Cook James E	516	janitor	46	5 Pelham
E	Cook Mary—†	516	housewife	38	5 "
F	Souther Helen D—†	516	none	42	here

Audubon Road—Continued

G	Souther Thoedore W	516	civil engineer	55	here
H	Crone Emma—†	516	none	46	"
K	Crone Michael	516	manager	51	"
L	Peabody Caroline—†	516	"	44	"
M	Peabody Caroline F—†	516	hairdresser	52	"
N	Bailey Helen—†	516	none	26	833 Beacon
O	Bailey John D	516	salesman	27	833 "
P	Hubbard Fannie M—†	516	none	69	here
R	Brin Leon M	516	salesman	25	"
S	Rose Alexander E	516	"	40	"
T	Saunders Rose—†	518	decorator	28	"
U	Shaw Anna G—†	518	none	54	"
V	Shaw Ira D	518	manufacturer	52	"
W	Batchelder John P	518	broker	58	"
X	Batchelder Luila L—†	518	housewife	60	"
Y	Aldridge Andrew T	518	lawyer	35	"
Z	Aldridge Emma C—†	518	housewife	34	"
A	Sutherland Elsie L—†	518	maid	23	"
B	Curry Adeline P—†	518	none	40	"
C	Curry Malcolm L	518	merchant	42	"
D	Van Amringe Elizabeth L—†	518	none	43	"
E	Van Amringe Robert C	518	lawyer	41	187 Bay State rd
F	O'Sullivan Edith—†	519	housewife	28	40 Ivy
G	O'Sullivan William	519	foreman	33	40 "
H	Sumner Florence—†	519	dressmaker	40	40 "
K	Gokey Edward P	519	chauffeur	35	32 Glenarm
M	Best Ralph E	519	"	36	here
N	Nagle Anna C—†	519	housekeeper	54	"
O	Nagle Robert C	519	clerk	24	"
P	Collins Alice M—†	519	housekeeper	25	40 Ivy
R	Collins Catherine—†	519	hairdresser	22	40 "
S	Collins Neil J	519	grocer	47	40 "
T	Costello Margaret—†	519	housewife	53	here
U	Irving Lillian—†	519	saleswoman	50	"
V	Promobost Edward	519	clerk	23	"
W	George Wallace B	519	mechanic	36	New Hampshire
X	Epps George	519	bookkeeper	55	here
Y	Epps Helen S—†	519	housewife	40	"
Z	Paige Blanche C—†	519	waitress	34	409 Marlboro
A	Cole Prentiss I	520	student	23	Chicago
B	Petze Edward S	520	"	24	Kansas City

Audubon Road—Continued

c	Wood Thomas S	520	student	28	Chicago Ill
d	Crawford Robert B	520	secretary	24	here
e	McKee Sara A—†	520	retired	70	"
f	Esterbrook Bertha S—†	520	"	61	"
g	Esterbrook Frank W	520	superintendent	64	"
h	Esterbrook Harriet W—†	520	clerk	21	"
k	Dempsey William A	520	salesman	35	"
l	Dempsey William M	520	"	34	"
m	Boyer Francis B	520	automobiles	42	"
n	Gardiner Walter	520	salesman	50	"
o	Dean Edward W	522	physician	43	"
p	Dean Ellen W—†	522	none	45	"
r	Dean Nellie M—†	522	"	50	"
s	Moore Abbey R—†	522	"	50	"
t	Moore Winthrop A	522	actor	47	"
u	Eaton Charles A	522	physician	43	"
v	Northey Edward A	522	retired	57	112 Pinckney
w	Welch Anna E—†	522	none	48	here

Beacon Street

a	Geary Nettie—†	776	housewife	57	here
b	Coomey Joseph	776	mechanic	32	Gloucester
c	McDonald Catherine L–†	776	housewife	50	here
d	McDonald Isabell R—†	776	musician	27	"
e	McDonald William A	776	shoemaker	51	"
f	Stevenson Stanford	776	clerk	27	Vermont
g	Tellier Augustus	776	mechanic	26	832 Beacon
h	Chute Paul J	776	teacher	38	here
k	Curran James J	776	lawyer	29	Lexington
l	Ryder George B	776	clerk	38	here
m	Paine Catherine F—†	776	retired	36	"
n	Waters Louise E—†	776	housewife	53	"
p	Chin Henry	778	laundryman	39	"
s	Perham Grace—†	780	housewife	22	Medford
t	Perham Price	780	carpenter	22	"
u	Perry Charles	780	janitor	38	here
v	Skinner Annie—†	780	housewife	59	"
w	Skinner Atlas	780	porter	37	"
x	Skinner Frances—†	780	housewife	23	"

Beacon Street—Continued

Letter.	FULL NAME.	Residence, April 1, 1924.	Occupation.	Supposed Age.	Reported Residence, April 1, 1923. Street and Number.
Y	Skinner Leslie	780	porter	23	here
A	Correa John F, jr	780	physician	32	"
B	Stanton Effie E—†	780	housewife	46	"
D	Lyons Katherine—†	780	stenographer	35	20 Queensberry
E	Oakes Georgianna—†	780	manager	45	Brookline
F	Cocoran William J	780	lawyer	49	"
G	Ginsburg Charles	780	salesman	40	"
H	Giroux May T—†	780	housewife	38	"
M	Crosbie Boynton	780	salesman	40	21 Aberdeen
N	Fish Carrie M—†	780	housekeeper	35	902 Beacon
O	Flemming Harry	780	machinist	41	139 Worcester
P	Owen Abram	780	"	26	139 "
T	King Clara P—†	780	musician	50	here
V	Watson George	784	laborer	77	"
W	Wright Agnes—†	784	housewife	39	"
X	Wright Willard L	784	physician	35	"
Z	Downing Henry	784	actor	28	"
A	Downing John G	784	physician	33	"
A¹	Downing Thomasine—†	784	housewife	65	"
B	Grant Herbert	784	steward	55	410 Com av
C	Hoff Frank S	784	engineer	36	51 Mountfort
D	Hoff Pearl A—†	784	housewife	36	51 "
E	Burke Carolyn—†	784	dressmaker	49	here
F	Langlois Beatrice—†	784	bookkeeper	29	"
G	Langlois Louise—†	784	stenographer	26	"
H	Cornell Arthur W	784	chemist	28	"
K	Cornell Ellen—†	784	housewife	64	"
L	Rogers Elizabeth F—†	784	"	57	"
M	Gannon Joseph	784	manager	40	"
N	Gannon Noel—†	784	housewife	30	"
O	McKinnon John	784	carpenter	53	"
P	McKinnon Margaret—†	784	housewife	39	"
R	Bradshaw Anna M—†	784	stenographer	20	"
S	Bradshaw Bentley R	784	carpenter	45	"
T	Bradshaw Mabel L—†	784	housewife	45	"
U	Kaulvourne Maude—†	784	manager	28	"
W	Wholley Dennis F	788	merchant	42	"
X	Wholley Katherine E—†	788	housewife	39	"
Y	Linnehan George W	788	physician	39	"
Z	Sullivan Corinne—†	788	housewife	49	"
A	Sullivan Harriet P—†	788	buyer	28	"

Beacon Street—Continued

B	Cuneo John F	788	masseur	44	here
C	Souther George C	788	auditor	55	Winthrop
D	Souther George H	788	student	28	"
E	Souther Minnie P—†	788	housewife	53	"
F	Avery Clyde	788	policeman	30	641 Hunt'n av
H	Avery Lillian—†	788	cashier	31	641 "
G	Avery Lydia—†	788	housewife	50	641 "
K	Gill Edward J	790	clerk	20	here
L	Meloon Herbert	790	"	35	"
M	Meloon Rennie	790	"	31	"
N	Dunlap Ernest M	790	salesman	24	Connecticut
O	Dunlap Isabel—†	790	housewife	24	"
P	Wadsworth Edna G—†	790	"	35	Brookline
R	Wallace Olive R—†	790	secretary	35	here
S	Eldredge Harry	790	salesman	50	"
T	Eldredge Josephine—†	790	housewife	45	"
U	Frost Benjamin	790	manager	48	New York
V	Frost Marion—†	790	housewife	45	"
W	Campbell Emily P—†	790	"	45	here
X	Stumpf Clayton	790	manufacturer	45	"
Y	Stumpf Mary—†	790	housewife	42	"
Z	Thomas Eva—†	792	"	30	"
A	Thomas Wallace B	792	salesman	37	"
B	Penny Jessie D—†	792	housewife	56	"
C	Penny John W	792	retired	76	"
D	Hardy Grace—†	792	secretary	35	"
E	Hardy Louise—†	792	clerk	20	"
F	McCrillis Ellen—†	792	"	22	"
G	Powers Helen—†	792	"	23	"
H	Litch Addie—†	792	housewife	46	"
K	Litch Joseph W	792	druggist	55	"
L	Cook George B	792	painter	60	"
M	Cook George L	792	"	29	"
N	McCarthy May M—†	792	housewife	26	"
O	McCarthy Thomas	792	dentist	35	"
P	Bedord Grover D	792	decorator	35	Minneapolis
R	Bedord Marie—†	792	housewife	30	"
S	Campbell Grace—†	792	"	32	Pennsylvania
T	Campbell James D	792	superintendent	25	"
U	Kain Albert H	792	salesman	35	Chicago Ill
V	Rush Charlotte—†	792	housewife	33	"

Beacon Street—Continued

W	Babbidge Catherine—†	792	housewife	45	here
X	Babbidge Douglas	792	student	22	"
Z	Otto Henry S	792	engineer	32	"
A	Otto Marie—†	792	housewife	30	"
B	Bryan Neil	792	foreman	35	Allentown Pa
C	Bryan Stella—†	792	housewife	30	"
E	Furlong John J	792	salesman	50	here
F	Furlong Rose B—†	792	housewife	46	"
G	Sisler Hilda—†	792	student	21	"
H	Lewis Marion—†	792	clerk	22	9 Pearl
K	Lewis Maude—†	792	housewife	50	9 "
L	Mackey Bessie L—†	792	saleswoman	35	9 "
N	Lonergen Catherin—†	792	housewife	28	here
O	Lonergen John E	792	clerk	35	"
U	Walsh Caroline—†	798 & 800	housewife	45	New Hampshire
V	Walsh John	798 & 800	janitor	39	"
W	Hamilton Elden H	798 & 800	clerk	75	Norwood
X	Hamilton Louella C—†	798 & 800	housewife	53	"
C	Bernstein Laura—†	798 & 800	"	35	Medford
D	Bernstein Morris	798 & 800	manager	55	"
E	Farnsworth Clinton S	798 & 800	nurse	38	10 Blackwood
F	Farnsworth Rose—†	798 & 800	housewife	35	10 "
G	Frisbie Abbie—†	798 & 800	seamstress	38	Rockport Me
K	Hyneman Ashur	798 & 800	merchant	71	here
L	Hyneman Helen—†	798 & 800	housewife	60	"
M	Nadien Harriet—†	798 & 800	"	29	99 Morris
N	Nadien Max	798 & 800	manager	33	99 "
O	Brant Lee	798 & 800	clerk	28	Somerville
P	Whittemore George	798 & 800	salesman	67	Winthrop
R	Whittemore Nellie S—†	798 & 800	housewife	62	"
S	Kelley Annie—†	798 & 800	housekeeper	40	236 Brighton av
T	Kelley Joseph	798 & 800	salesman	35	236 "
U	Kelley Mary—†	798 & 800	saleswoman	36	236 "
V	Wetherby Bertha-†	798 & 800	housekeeper	55	61 Louis Prang
W	Wetherby Madelin—†	798 & 800	bookkeeper	25	61 "
X	Rogers Margaret-†	798 & 800	stenographer	24	Dedham
Z	Geissler Arthur	798 & 800	piano teacher	27	24 Queensberry
A	Geissler Blanche—†	798 & 800	hairdresser	28	24 "
B	Foster Ella—†	798 & 800	housewife	38	56 Batavia
C	Foster Henry	798 & 800	engineer	45	56 "
E	Drabble Frances-†	798 & 800	housekeeper	45	England

Beacon Street—Continued

F	Drabble John J	798 & 800	salesman	25	England
G	Vanzant Margaret—†	798 & 800	saleswoman	42	58 St Germai
H	Briggs Anna G—†	798 & 800	dressmaker	46	739 Boylston
K	Drumny Catherine—†	798 & 800	saleswoman	34	35 Mountfort
M	Whitaker Alice E—†	798 & 800	retired	71	50 Peterboro
N	Whitaker Lillian—†	798 & 800	violinist	47	50 "
P	Shaw Carrie E—†	798 & 800	clerk	44	Maine
R	Mog John V	798 & 800	despatcher	30	50 Forsyth
S	Mog Phillis P—†	798 & 800	housewife	26	50 "
U	Everett Martha A P—†	798 & 800	retired	85	here
V	St John Martha E—†	798 & 800	housekeeper	60	"
Y	Vannine Augusta—†	798 & 800	violinist	52	99 Gainsboro
Z	Post Albert	798 & 800	manager	43	Lowell
A	Bragg Marian C—†	798 & 800	dressmaker	30	Brookline
B	Chase Mabel B—†	798 & 800	stenographer	22	"
C	Cole Gertrude S—†	798 & 800	reporter	38	here
D	Moore Myrtie L—†	798 & 800	housekeeper	57	118 Mt Vern
E	Stone Helen—†	798 & 800	saleswoman	36	118 "
F	Judy Marjorie—†	798 & 800	decorator	29	46 Cedarlane way
G	Judy Nannie—†	798 & 800	housekeeper	54	46 "
O	Johnston Mathilda C—†	811	housewife	52	here
P	Johnston Robert J	811	janitor	57	"
R	Condict Harold N	811	publisher	40	New York
S	Doucette Myron E	811	student	21	here
T	Heath Sargent D	811	"	22	"
U	Jones Irving R	811	salesman	44	"
V	Kingsley Donaldson W	811	student	25	New York
W	McGrath Philip	811	"	20	here
X	Turnbull Sarah E—†	811	housewife	43	"
Y	Turnbull William B	811	surgeon	60	"
Z	Hedesnkog Bertha A—†	811	housewife	62	"
A	Hedenshog Robert H	811	engineer	68	117 St Botol
B	Elson Arthur	811	teacher	49	here
C	Elson Bertha L—†	811	housewife	71	"
D	Gibson Fannie B—†	811	retired	55	"
E	Gibson Francis H	811	secretary	27	"
F	Rossman Elizabeth T—†	811	housewife	49	"
G	Balboni Thomas A, jr	813	nurse	21	Revere
H	Spears Clara M—†	813	housewife	63	106 Saratoga
K	Spears Elijah M	813	blacksmith	64	106 "
L	Spears Goldie P—†	813	housewife	37	Revere

Beacon Street—Continued

M	Spears Herbert A	813	agent	38	Revere
N	Lee Mary L—†	813	clerk	47	here
O	Sibley Charles S	813	grocer	62	"
P	Sibley Georgie E—†	813	housewife	62	"
R	Bailey Florence A—†	813	"	59	"
S	Bailey Fred H	813	storekeeper	58	"
T	Heinen Casper L	813	superintendent	47	"
U	Murphy John J	815	truckman	40	8 Maitland
V	Murphy Susanna—†	815	housewife	36	8 "
W	Philips Edward S	815	salesman	45	here
X	Philips John H	815	insurance agent	32	"
Y	Philips Mary A—†	815	none	45	"
Z	McKenzie Katherine—†	815	nurse	25	14 Idlewild
A	Murray Margaret—†	815	"	23	14 "
B	Norton Charles	815	postal clerk	25	8 Maitland
C	Perkins Mary A—†	815	housewife	59	here
D	Davis Gladys—†	815	seamstress	25	544 Hunt'n av
E	Mullane Mary E—†	815	nurse	25	here
F	Potter Ernestine S—†	815	milliner	45	"
G	Rudd Charles	815	treasurer	26	"
H	Donavan Florence E—†	817	clerk	20	"
K	Donavan Justin T	817	"	23	"
L	Donavan Mary E—†	817	dressmaker	52	"
M	Anthony Clarence S	817	salesman	40	"
N	Fitzpatrick Dorothy—†	817	hairdresser	35	"
O	Mason Vera—†	817	housekeeper	27	48 Astor
P	Robison Mary C—†	817	"	39	here
R	Salkeld Thomas F	817	salesman	70	"
S	Clinton Leo	817	foreman	24	"
T	Foley Michael	817	auto washer	41	"
U	Potter Agnes—†	817	housewife	41	"
V	Potter Thomas M	817	chauffeur	54	"
X	Kahofer Frank	819	waiter	36	"
Y	Kahofer Martha—†	819	housewife	32	"
Z	Brown Anna H—†	819	teacher	49	"
A	Fuller Ruth E—†	819	housewife	70	"
B	Fuller Samuel J	819	retired	73	"
C	Kingsbury George	819	tailor	40	"
D	Patterson Barbara—†	819	housekeeper	57	"
E	Russell Louise—†	819	dressmaker	57	"
F	Stetson Frederick	819	chemist	30	"

Beacon Street—Continued

G	Stetson Lois—†	819	stenographer	27	here
H	Harding Edward	819	chauffeur	53	California
K	Harding Elizabeth—†	819	housewife	44	S Maitland
L	Stetson Ethel—†	819	clerk	31	Brookline
N	Fortin Bernice—†	820	"	26	here
O	Fortin Pearl L—†	820	bookkeeper	30	"
P	Harbison Rallolickey	820	retired	45	Pittsburgh Pa
R	Clark Stella S—†	820	"	60	here
S	Flynn Delia J—†	820	housewife	55	"
T	Flynn Michael	820	janitor	56	"
U	Doty Harriet—†	820	saleswoman	33	"
V	Toulman Mary E—†	820	checker	31	57 Mountfort
W	Macomber Gladys—†	820	housewife	31	here
X	Macomber Roland W	820	druggist	32	"
Y	Lally Mary E—†	820	retired	34	"
Z	Sargent Catherine—†	820	housewife	30	"
A	Severance Josephine—†	820	retired	60	"
B	Smithers Marie—†	820	clerk	50	"
C	Smith Ruth E—†	820	manager	45	"
D	Fortescue James—†	820	secretary	78	"
E	Rudd Lillian K—†	820	retired	50	"
F	Lyons Edward D	820	letter carrier	33	"
G	Harrington Anna—†	820	clerk	46	"
H	Rhodes Lillian G—†	820	hairdresser	37	"
K	Tozier Josephine B—†	820	clerk	48	"
M	Hibbard Grace—†	820	"	40	"
N	Hibbard Lillian—†	820	dressmaker	50	"
O	Romelli Elizabeth—†	820	housewife	28	Worcester
P	Romelli Fred W	820	clerk	26	"
R	Barrett Helen—†	820	secretary	26	here
S	Bennett Frances—†	820	saleswoman	43	"
T	Dunbar Justin E	820	engineer	32	Springfield
U	Trueworthy Helen—†	820	housewife	76	here
V	Trueworthy Helen—†	820	student	26	"
W	Trueworthy Jessie—†	820	bookkeeper	30	"
X	Trueworthy Winifred—†	820	nurse	32	New York
Y	Fedderman Harry	821	janitor	43	here
Z	Fedderman Rose—†	821	housewife	34	"
A	Cram Blake	821	salesman	44	Iowa
B	Allen Elizabeth M—†	821	housewife	62	here
C	Hoover Mary H—†	821	retired	77	"

Beacon Street — Continued

D	Billings Carl W	821	salesman	29	here
E	Billings Ruth—†	821	housewife	24	"
F	Snow Ella F—†	821	"	60	"
G	Snow Gertrude—†	821	retired	50	"
H	McKinnon Alexander L	821	insurance agent	26	Medford
K	McKinnon Eleanor L—†	821	housewife	21	Brookline
L	Laurie Marie—†	821	"	50	here
M	Laurie Ossip R	821	physician	51	"
N	Boyer Adalaide—†	821	clerk	64	"
O	Prosser Grace—†	821	housewife	44	"
P	Prosser Robert S	821	agent	55	"
R	Hanson Albert E	821	cashier	25	152 Stratford
S	Hanson Beth—†	821	housewife	25	148 "
T	Eagan Frances—†	821	housekeeper	40	here
U	Eagan John C	821	salesman	45	"
V	Eagan Thomas E	821	retired	64	"
W	Decker George S	821	reporter	46	Norwell
X	Decker Mary E—†	821	housekeeper	43	"
Y	Pinkham Elizabeth—†	821	retired	65	"
Z	Cherkassky Aino—†	821	housewife	25	Finland
A	Cherkassky Paul	821	violinist	32	"
B	Perkins Jane—†	821	stenographer	26	1295 Com av
C	Ralphs Laura—†	821	nurse	26	429 Brookline
D	Eichbaum George R	821	mechanic	20	here
E	Eichbaum Julia—†	821	clerk	44	"
F	Eichbaum Marion—†	821	bookkeeper	22	"
G	Johnson Charlotte—†	821	housekeeper	60	"
H	Dutton Charles C	821	clerk	29	55 Ivy
K	Dutton Elvira A—†	821	housewife	49	55 "
L	Dutton Frank J	821	clerk	51	55 "
M	Farrington Edward F	821	agent	44	55 "
N	Pingree George S	821	broker	51	Brookline
O	Dickelman John	821	adjuster	53	487 Columbia rd
P	Dickelman Mary—†	821	housewife	45	487 "
R	Evennett Eileen—†	821	"	29	Canada
S	Evennett Harold	821	manager	29	"
T	Trapp Frank	821	lawyer	44	here
U	Sheehan Henry J	821	salesman	32	"
V	Sheehan Loretta—†	821	housewife	26	"
W	Sullivan Marie—†	821	student	28	"
X	Rand Charles B	821	optical	55	"

Beacon Street—Continued

y	Rand Ella—†	821	housekeeper	39	here
z	Scott Robert	821	merchant	57	444 Wash'n
A	Goode Walter P	821	agent	48	here
B	Ruiseau Florence—†	821	housekeeper	45	"
C	Diehl Alexandrine—†	821	housewife	31	New York
D	Diehl Browne	821	engineer	39	"
E	Hartney Gertrude C—†	821	clerk	37	here
F	Leighton Catherine—†	821	housekeeper	32	"
H	Webster Francis P—†	824	housewife	43	"
K	Webster Franklin A	824	treasurer	85	"
L	Oliver Mary E—†	826	retired	42	"
M	Bell Mary W—†	826	"	50	"
N	Mosher Harris P	828	physician	51	"
O	Mosher Helen A—†	828	housewife	52	"
P	Sherburne Anna—†	829	"	27	Rhode Island
R	Sherburne George	829	janitor	27	"
T	Cassidy John J	829	clerk	51	England
U	Hildreth George	829	inspector	24	here
V	Dog Wilberforce C	829	physician	72	"
W	Shattack Mary—†	829	hairdresser	44	"
Y	Levy Eli	829	salesman	48	"
Z	Wingersky Isaac W	829	"	45	"
A	Wingersky Rose—†	829	housekeeper	44	"
C	Roberts Charles W	829	salesman	41	15 Aberdeen
D	Roberts Frances—†	829	housewife	31	15 "
E	Small Charles G	829	salesman	58	800 Beacon
F	Small Lillian—†	829	housewife	60	800 "
G	Ordway Edith B—†	829	retired	46	here
H	Roberts Gertrude L—†	829	bookkeeper	37	"
K	Marwell Elizabeth—†	829	housekeeper	28	New York
L	Marwell Robert	829	salesman	35	"
M	Hildreth John H	829	clerk	62	here
N	Hildreth Mabel H—†	829	housewife	60	"
O	Libby Samuel	829	salesman	35	833 Beacon
P	Mottuz Etienne	829	cook	33	149 Audubon rd
R	Mottuz Mary—†	829	waitress	34	149 "
S	Winternitz Robert	829	salesman	30	104 Hemenway
T	Winternitz Sibyl—†	829	housewife	27	104 "
U	Paghera Angela	829	insurance agent	32	188 Webster
V	Paghera Angeline—†	829	housewife	31	188 "
W	Young Clara—†	829	housekeeper	65	New Hampshire

Beacon Street—Continued

Letter.	FULL NAME.	Residence, April 1, 1924.	Occupation.	Supposed Age.	Reported Residence, April 1, 1923.
x	Young Pearl —†	829	actress	33	New Hampshire
z	Poladieu Adaline —†	829	housewife	36	here
A	Poladieu George	829	shoeworker	36	"
B	Barrows Jennie E—†	829	housewife	63	"
c	Barrows Parlin L	829	retired	65	"
D	Silver Anna—†	829	chemist	26	"
E	Silver Margaret D—†	829	stenographer	31	"
F	Silver Michael	829	retired	63	"
G	Ciuffo Alice—†	829	saleswoman	33	"
H	Troy Mary—†	829	housewife	55	41 G
K	Krirnon Charles	829	salesman	32	here
L	Laws Ethel—†	829	actress	30	"
M	Cobe George E	829	clerk	52	"
N	Arnold William F	830	student	21	"
o	Chase Benjamin O	830	clerk	21	"
P	Chase Evelyn A—†	830	teacher	22	"
R	Chase Harrison G O	830	steward	24	"
s	Chase Harry G	830	quartermaster	43	"
T	Chase Mary F—†	830	housewife	45	"
U	Prendergast Annie M—†	832	"	53	"
V	Prendergast James	832	conductor	51	"
W	McKenny Lydin—†	833	housewife	25	"
X	McKenny William	833	foreman	30	"
Y	Albana Geanne—†	833	dressmaker	34	"
z	Albana Patrick	833	chauffeur	36	"
A	Nott Ellen—†	833	physician	55	"
B	Quinn Edward	833	manager	47	"
D	Jordan Chester	833	salesman	31	"
E	Jordan Marian R—†	833	housewife	26	"
F	Cass John T	833	salesman	31	"
G	McPride Anne—†	833	bookkeeper	44	"
H	Gotro Agnes—†	833	teacher	29	74 Brookline av
K	Jordan Anna—†	833	bookkeeper	40	1 Albemarle Chambers
L	Jordan William N	833	manager	46	1 "
M	Allen Minnie—†	833	hairdresser	23	here
N	Langley Dorothy—†	833	"	24	"
o	Davis John	833	salesman	47	Pennsylvania
P	Jellison Mabel—†	833	clerk	40	here
R	Griffin Ellen—†	833	housewife	31	Medford
s	Griffin Joseph	833	chauffeur	32	"
U	Penny Charles	833	salesman	73	here

Beacon Street—Continued

	Letter.	FULL NAME.	Residence	Occupation	Age	Reported Residence
	Y	Penny Jennie M—†	833	housewife	69	here
	X	Orister James	833	printer	26	"
	Y	Earle Fannie S—†	833	saleswoman	40	"
	Z	Brown Florence S—†	833	school teacher	36	Cambridge
	A	Sprague Lora E—†	833	"	34	"
	B	O'Hanely Harriet—†	833	housewife	43	here
	C	O'Hanley Ronald	833	manager	52	"
	D	Farren Flossie—†	833	housekeeper	33	"
	E	Schwamb Sylvia—†	833	housewife	23	Milton
	F	Schwamb Thomas A	833	salesman	25	"
	G	Boyce Earl W	833	clerk	24	Somerville
	H	Boyce Grace—†	833	housewife	21	"
	K	Starch Ida—†	833	"	48	"
	L	Starch Robert	833	chef	49	"
	M	Gilbert Nellie F—†	833	housekeeper	56	829 Beacon
	P	Lewis Catherine—†	833	housewife	24	30 Hemenway
	R	Lewis Edward	833	salesman	29	30 "
	S	Hannersley Helen E—†	833	nurse	31	here
	T	Mosher Margaret—†	833	bookkeeper	50	25 Astor
	U	Pratt Henrietta T—†	833	"	40	25 "
	V	Victorson Moses	833	salesman	58	here
	W	Raleigh Anna—†	833	housekeeper	60	"
	X	Raleigh William	833	mechanic	21	"
	A	Barton Eleanor—†	834	housewife	50	4 Lorraine ter
	C	Faulkner Clara A—†	836	saleswoman	31	175A Cambridge
	D	Swan Walter H	836	salesman	31	Iowa
	F	Mullen Ellen—†	838	merchant	40	780 Beacon
	K	Barnard Louis I	840	bank teller	34	here
	L	Barnard Simon	840	merchant	73	"
	M	Cawson Esther B—†	840	housewife	43	"
	N	Lubell Abraham	840	importer	36	"
	R	Stoffert Lucy—†	844	housewife	37	"
	S	Stoffert Rudolph	844	janitor	34	"
	T	Clark Charles H	844	retired	56	"
	U	Clark Deborah—†	844	housekeeper	81	"
	V	Howard Charles	844	manager	31	"
	W	Howard Helen A †	844	housewife	30	"
	X	Janney Edith—†	844	actress	38	New York
	Y	Prongnell Allan	844	manager	40	Wash'n D C
	Z	Silver Michael	844	salesman	40	Quincy
	A	May Raymond A	844	printer	35	871 Beacon

Beacon Street—Continued

B	Adolph Henry H	844	salesman	34	here
C	Sullivan Henry L	844	clerk	36	"
D	Seymour Bertha M—†	844	housekeeper	39	New York
E	Seymour Harry W	844	chauffeur	24	"
F	Miller Max	844	salesman	33	90 Pembroke
G	Winfield Morris	844	"	32	455 Col av
H	Winfield Pauline—†	844	housewife	27	455 "
K	Cooper Clinton B	844	salesman	30	here
L	Whitmarsh Henry F	844	retired	75	"
M	Gifford Ruth A—†	844	dressmaker	45	"
N	Kimball Harriett—†	844	"	55	"
P	Fletcher Isabell—†	844	housekeeper	63	"
R	Fletcher Mary A—†	844	school teacher	30	"
S	Malof Salum	844	salesman	38	New York
T	Malof Zebiva—†	844	housewife	38	"
V	Tebich Charles H	844	salesman	36	here
W	Tebich Margaret J—†	844	housewife	29	"
Y	Maynard Fay—†	844	"	22	New York
Z	Maynard William B	844	salesman	26	"
A	Bishope Margaret—†	844	housewife	35	here
B	Bishope Percy D	844	salesman	40	"
D	Packard Walter S	844	manager	24	"
E	Carlos Genita—†	844	saleswoman	30	"
F	Melrose Enid C—†	844	housekeeper	33	W Newton
G	Dreyfus Henry	844	retired	32	here
H	Rouleau Albert J	844	salesman	69	"
K	Rouleau Louis J	844	manager	37	"
L	Rouleau Marian—†	844	housewife	31	"
M	MacLeod Mary M—†	845	superintendent	45	"
N	Martin Mae—†	845	nurse	35	19 Joy
O	Braveman Charles	847	storekeeper	45	here
P	Dwyer Margaret—†	847	nurse	23	Somerville
R	Fenn Gertrude—†	847	"	28	Cambridge
S	Foisie Phillip	847	student	26	916 Beacon
T	Gray John	847	civil engineer	22	here
U	Harrington Catherine—†	847	housewife	23	"
V	Harrington John	847	clerk	35	"
W	Hogle Arthur B	847	draughtsman	55	"
X	Hogle Nellie B—†	847	housewife	45	"
Y	Osborn John E	847	clerk	28	Dayton O
Z	Osborn Zermal—†	847	housewife	25	"

Beacon Street—Continued

A	Osgood Evelyn S—†	847	stenographer	20	Somerville
B	Page Clinton	847	chauffeur	38	Magnolia
C	Page Julia —†	847	housewife	26	"
D	Symmes Althea—†	847	nurse	30	here
E	Tourtellott Arthur	847	painter	38	Worcester
F	Wood Donald E	847	manager	25	12 Somerset
G	Davoust Albert	848	engineer	34	Connecticut
H	Jordan Annise L—†	848	clerk	40	Worcester
K	Linzee Grace H—†	848	housewife	34	here
L	Linzee John W	848	engineer	55	"
M	Lyons Gertrude B—†	848	designer	24	Brookline
N	Moore Theresa E—†	848	housekeeper	54	here
O	Pease George B	848	engineer	24	Maine
P	Silverman Max	848	physician	35	here
R	Silverman Samuel	848	dentist	26	Pennsylvania
S	O'Neil Annie—†	849	maid	30	here
T	Pelletier Augustin S	849	accountant	47	"
U	Pettetier Louis S	849	instructor	48	"
V	Pelletier Victor M	849	broker	43	"
W	Whittemore William F	850	retired	74	"
X	Attwater George	851	salesman	60	"
Y	Attwater Hazel —†	851	housewife	35	"
A	Hatch Fannie—†	851	"	45	"
B	Hatch John	851	artist	45	"
C	Hawly Freeman	851	lawyer	47	"
C¹	Lilie Ferruccio A	851	clerk	23	Vermont
D	McKenzie Blanche —†	851	housewife	28	Dayton O
E	McKenzie John	851	manufacturer	30	"
F	Russell Lillian—†	851	housewife	25	here
G	Russell Raymond	851	reporter	30	"
H	Weaver Blanche †	851	housewife	50	"
K	Weaver Charles	851	salesman	50	"
L	Brickett Christina M—†	852	housewife	60	"
M	Brickett Rhoda C—†	852	stenographer	36	"
N	Brickett Stephen J	852	clerk	62	"
O	Sigilman Samuel	852	lawyer	46	"
P	Barnes Fannie —†	853	secretary	50	"
R	Clifton Raymond	853	salesman	27	220 Newbury
S	Fish Edwin E	853	printer	51	here
T	Kinard John	853	mechanic	25	Georgia
U	Kinard Jones	853	student	22	"

Beacon Street—Continued

Letter.	FULL NAME.	Residence, April 1, 1924.	Occupation.	Supposed Age.	Reported Residence, April 1, 1923. Street and Number.
v	LeMon Wilhelmeina —†	853	saleswoman	25	Pennsylvania
w	McSwain John	853	broker	50	here
x	McSwain Peter	853	mechanic	27	"
y	Milstead George	853	student	25	Cambridge
z	Moriarty James	853	retired	50	here
A	Morrill Clayton	853	clerk	23	220 Newbury
B	Norcross Leslie	853	bank teller	25	220 "
C	Stinson Charles	853	salesman	45	Pennsylvania
D	Stinson Cora—†	853	housewife	45	"
E	Stott Effie M—†	853	"	47	here
F	Stott Marion V—†	853	clerk	27	"
G	Stott Russell	853	printer	25	"
H	Cumming Rose—†	854	companion	69	"
K	Kellogg Edward B	854	physician	74	"
L	Kellogg Minnie B—†	854	housewife	69	"
M	Richardson Sarah M—†	855	housekeeper	50	"
N	Aheran James	856	superintendent	47	461 Audubon rd
O	Beck Edward S	856	engineer	29	here
P	Finnegan Catherine—†	856	housekeeper	48	"
R	Finnegan Helen G—†	856	clerk	23	"
S	Nolan Paul	856	student	26	"
T	Simpson Robert	856	salesman	29	"
U	Smith Norman	856	student	20	"
V	Toomey John	856	musician	50	"
W	Toomey Selma—†	856	housewife	46	"
X	Toomey Walter W	856	clerk	27	"
Y	Wellings Arline—†	856	student	20	"
Z	Gorman Michael P	857	janitor	66	"
A	Richardson Robina I—†	857	none	50	"
B	Pass Susan—†	857	housekeeper	52	909 Beacon
C	Shain Arthur I	857	physician	36	here
D	Shain Jacob	857	manager	26	"
E	Williams Agnes—†	857	housewife	28	"
F	Williams Malcolm	857	merchant	35	"
G	Rowell Jennie—†	857	housekeeper	50	"
H	Smith Carl D	857	jeweler	50	"
K	Schell Everleen—†	857	housewife	30	"
L	Schell William M	857	lawyer	35	"
M	Ranson Charles S	857	retired	40	"
N	Ranson Rose S—†	857	housewife	40	"
O	Damerest Jennie W—†	857	none	50	Cambridge

Beacon Street—Continued

P	Goldstein Ernest J	857	advertising	50	Cambridge	
R	Goldstein Frances—†	857	housewife	30	"	
S	Tobey Ella C—†	857	"	30	here	
T	Tobey Henry C	857	editor	45	"	
U	Barry Elizabeth—†	857	housewife	35	"	
V	Barry William J	857	lawyer	45	"	
W	Goodwin Ella C—†	857	housewife	45	"	
X	Goodwin Howard W	857	druggist	50	"	
Y	Buck Evelyn C—†	857	housekeeper	45	"	
Z	Buck Howard M	857	retired	50	"	
B	Pingree Celeste—†	858	"	76	"	
C	Pingree Frank	858	clerk	78	"	
D	Lull Henry C	858	retired	75	"	
E	Harriman Mattie B—†	858	housewife	59	"	
F	Means Arrie—†	858	"	56	"	
G	Lord Lyman L	858	coppersmith	63	"	
H	Wilson Daisy—†	858	housewife	48	"	
K	Wilson William	858	contractor	58	"	
L	Adley Wilhelmina—†	860	cook	39	"	
M	Courtney Mary—†	860	housekeeper	45	"	
N	Duggan Catherine—†	860	maid	32	"	
O	Booth James	862	salesman	30	"	
P	Cook Albert M	862	"	23	"	
R	Houston Marie—†	862	housekeeper	38	"	
S	Jenkins John	862	student	28	"	
T	Northrup Frank	862	accountant	30	"	
U	O'Rourke Cecelia—†	862	saleswoman	26	"	
V	Wilson Thomas	862	signalman	25	"	
W	Donoghue Francis D	864	physician	52	"	
X	Donoghue Merian F—†	864	housewife	47	"	
Y	Fisher Mary E—†	864	"	21	"	
Z	Barry Catherine—†	866	saleswoman	35	"	
A	Barry Elizabeth F—†	866	"	38	"	
B	Doyle Anna L—†	866	milliner	40	"	
C	Doyle Elizabeth—†	866	"	48	"	
D	Malloy Mary E—†	866	housekeeper	60	"	
E	Bachelder Minnie—†	867	nurse	50	"	
F	Boucher Doris—†	867	"	21	24 Old Harbor	
G	Buckley Katherine—†	867	"	22	24 "	
H	Cliff Lillian M—†	867	"	43	here	
K	Daley Beatrice—†	867	"	21	24 Old Harbor	

Letter	Full Name.	Residence, April 1, 1924.	Occupation.	Supposed Age.	Reported Residence, April 1, 1923. Street and Number.

Beacon Street—Continued

Letter	Full Name.	Residence, April 1, 1924.	Occupation.	Supposed Age.	Reported Residence, April 1, 1923. Street and Number.
L	Dowd Norah—†	867	nurse	30	here
M	Jones Mary—†	867	"	28	"
N	King Mary V—†	867	"	40	"
O	Ludden Hellen—†	867	"	29	"
P	McIntyre Alice M—†	867	student	20	"
R	McIsaac Agnes—†	867	nurse	25	Newton
S	Moore Mabel—†	867	"	23	"
T	Murphy Marion—†	867	"	25	"
U	Murphy Mary—†	867	student	20	"
V	O'Connor Katherine—†	867	"	21	Manchester
W	O'Donnell Irene—†	867	nurse	22	Newton
X	Staples Betty—†	867	"	21	24 Old Harbor
Y	Twohig Ella—†	867	"	22	24 "
Z	Webster Fannie—†	867	"	38	here
A	Wolfe Florence—†	867	"	35	"
B	Riley Augustus	868	physician	45	"
C	Donovan Alicia—†	869	milliner	59	"
D	O'Brien May—†	869	nurse	28	"
E	Tanzey Mary—†	869	houseworker	60	"
F	Churchill Louise F—†	869	retired	28	"
G	Ray Henryetta F—†	869	housewife	58	"
H	Ray Richard, jr	869	librarian	63	"
K	Garriety Nora A—†	870	maid	48	"
L	O'Brien Annie E—†	870	"	65	"
M	Martin Mary B—†	870	retired	65	"
N	Batt Nettie—†	871	housewife	26	"
O	Batt Philip	871	telegrapher	26	"
P	Bedford Chester	871	clerk	30	"
R	Bischoff Clifford	871	salesman	26	"
S	Finkler Jacob	871	tailor	28	"
T	Ham Annie—†	871	retired	55	"
U	Irving Lincoln	871	"	55	"
V	Irving Sarah J—†	871	housewife	55	"
W	Kieley Mary—†	871	companion	50	"
X	Klebert Mina—†	871	nurse	28	"
Y	Linares Aristides A	871	consul	38	Panama
Z	McDonald Ada—†	871	teacher	35	here
A	McDonald Winnie—†	871	"	32	"
B	Pollard Seth	871	insurance agent	25	Chicago Ill
C	Prout Mary—†	872	housewife	37	here
D	Prout William C	872	lawyer	42	"

Beacon Street—Continued

E	Melley Elizabeth F—†	873	housekeeper	61	here
F	Melley Francis B	873	real estate	27	"
H	Berenson Arthur	875	lawyer	45	"
K	Salagnarda Marie—†	875	cook	32	"
L	Dobbins Lucy—†	877	maid	30	"
M	Hattin Emma L—†	877	retired	76	"
N	McArt Sarah—†	877	maid	47	"
O	McCartin John E	877	physician	40	"
O¹	McCartin Laura L—†	877	housewife	35	"
P	Monroe Louise—†	877	retired	82	"
R	Deitch Elizabeth—†	879	housewife	32	"
S	Deitch Henry	879	janitor	34	"
T	Linton John F	879	investigator	51	"
U	Linton Melvin J	879	physician	25	"
V	Linton Sadie J—†	879	housewife	47	"
W	Deitch Elizabeth—†	879	"	33	"
X	Deitch Emanuel	879	musician	36	"
Z	Avery Ruth—†	879	salesman	69	"
Y	Barry Gertrude A—†	879	housewife	55	"
A	Marston Albion	879	salesman	55	"
B	Marston Emma—†	879	housewife	53	"
C	Rosenfield Lewis	879	manufacturer	57	"
D	Rosenfield Myer	879	"	84	"
E	Sweetser Edith—†	879	retired	64	"
H	Latham Annie—†	896	housewife	56	"
K	Latham Ernest I	896	undertaker	56	"
L	Latham Wayne H	896	student	20	"
M	Eastman Benjamin S	896	undertaker	35	"
N	Eastman Janet L—†	896	housewife	29	"
O	Landy Harold A	898	broker	26	"
P	Landy Lillian M—†	898	retired	38	"
R	Landy Mary E—†	898	"	55	"
T	Bloomberg Edythe C—†	900	stenographer	22	844 Beacon
U	Bronson Annie J—†	900	"	40	here
V	Gillooley Mary V—†	900	"	60	"
W	McDonough Mary E—†	900	housewife	45	"
X	Phelps Fanny—†	900	retired	78	"
Y	Phelps Lucy L—†	900	"	89	"
Z	Wilson Helen—†	900	"	80	"
A	Bragg Mary—†	901	"	60	"
B	Cowie Katherine—†	901	domestic	28	"

Beacon Street—Continued

c	Edgerly Emma A—†	901	retired	35	here
d	Parker Charles H	902	operator	44	115 Norway
e	Parker Nettie M—†	902	housewife	38	115 "
g	Condon Eva M—†	903	domestic	38	here
h	James Ruth D—†	903	housewife	40	"
k	James Thomas M	903	architect	45	"
l	Mann Frank C	904	broker	45	12–14 Somerset
m	Payne Arthur W	904	manager	50	Brookline
n	Payne Emma M—†	904	housewife	49	"
o	Payne Gerald B	904	salesman	21	"
p	Parks Nelly B—†	905	retired	59	here
r	Weston Marjorie—†	905	housewife	34	"
s	Weston William E	905	musician	36	"
t	Woodworth Helene—†	905	secretary	34	"
v	Rockwell George A	907	lawyer	49	"
w	Rockwell Maud M—†	907	housewife	52	"
x	Walton Alice E—†	907	retired	44	"
y	Duggan Margaret—†	908	nurse	28	"
z	McIssac William E	908	clerk	23	"
z¹	Thayer Mary C—†	908	manager	40	"
z²	Dana Anna M—†	909	housewife	42	"
z³	Dana Leon	909	masseur	45	"
a	Yerex Violet A—†	909	clerk	24	"
b	Cornwell Mary A—†	910	retired	53	New York
c	Herrick Margaret F—†	910	"	55	here
d	Herrick Sophia—†	910	"	85	"
e	McNeil Katherine—†	910	maid	30	"
f	Robson Elizabeth—†	910	"	35	Brookline
g	Larrabee Ada P M—†	912	housewife	55	here
h	Larrabee Ralph C	912	physician	53	"
k	Drinan Adelaide—†	914	none	50	"
l	Hervey Leonora—†	914	"	60	Brookline
m	Lothrop Josephine—†	914	"	60	here
n	Van Ness Addie—†	914	"	55	"
o	Van Ness Thomas	914	clergyman	60	"
p	Hughes Ada F—†	915	retired	48	"
r	Hughes Annie A—†	915	"	41	"
s	Barstow Chester A	916	salesman	40	"
t	Barstow Vivian A—†	916	housewife	29	"
u	Beverley Arthur B	916	retired	59	"
v	Beverley Effie R—†	916	secretary	28	"

Beacon Street—Continued

w	Beverley Freda B—†	916	milliner	30	here
x	Bigelow Russell	916	salesman	24	New Bedford
y	Kappius Meinloph	916	student	26	here
z	McCloud John	916	chauffeur	27	"
A	Munroe Donald	916	salesman	26	Rhode Island
B	Wheelock Emeline—†	917	retired	51	here
c	Wheelock Louis N	917	salesman	52	"
D	Healy Eleanor—†	918	dressmaker	45	"
E	Healy Jane E—†	918	none	40	"
F	Madden Josephine—†	918	nurse	42	S Weymouth
G	Brown Louis O	918A	confectioner	55	here
H	Benningham James W	919	salesman	64	"
H¹	Newhall Eldridge K	920	broker	52	"
K	Newhall Gertrude E—†	920	retired	50	"
L	Newhall Mary S—†	920	"	65	"
M	Lombard Annie S—†	921	"	26	"
N	Bengston Helene D—†	922	nurse	44	Texas
O	Cooper Carolyn—†	922	secretary	20	76 Gainsboro
P	DeMars Cora A—†	922	companion	48	9 Newbury
R	Douglas Walter L	922	salesman	45	Newton
T	Fairfield Harrison N	922	agent	23	Maine
U	Ferguson Eleanor B—†	922	physician	37	Weston
V	Garand Elizabeth N—†	922	none	34	Maine
W	Garand Oscar N	922	salesman	36	"
X	Goss Alice O—†	922	housekeeper	49	Gardner
Y	Hall Charles M	922	agent	50	here
Z	Hall Margaret—†	922	none	50	"
A	Henry Bessie H—†	922	"	45	Melrose
B	Lewis Charlotte I—†	922	lecturer	35	here
C	Marsh Fannie H—†	922	teller	27	25 Marlboro
D	Barnet Hannah—†	923	retired	70	here
E	Rentels Elizabeth B—†	923	none	23	"
F	Rentels Etta B—†	923	retired	48	"
G	Egecrone Ais	924	radio expert	30	Brookline
H	Egecrone Julie—†	924	housewife	28	"
L	Shepherd Elizabeth M—†	924	cashier	30	Northampton
M	Saunier Claude E	924	director	42	1018 Beacon
N	Saunier Elizabeth R—†	924	secretary	38	1018 "
O	Sawtelle Leslie—†	924	instructor	33	here
P	Hannigan Erdine—†	924	housewife	32	Lexington
R	Hannigan Judson	924	lawyer	31	"

Beacon Street—Continued

s	Hepworth Alma—†	924	retired	50	245 Audubon rd
T	Clewley Margaret B—†	924	housewife	26	here
U	Clewley William H	924	physician	29	"
V	Blair Olive S—†	924	housekeeper	39	"

Ivy Street

A	Gordon Florence—†	1	saleswoman	31	here
B	Smith Alfred F	1	machinist	45	Cambridge
C	Dillworth Margaret H—†	1	clerk	45	here
E	Smith Eleanor—†	1	saleswoman	48	"
F	Cooper David	1	clerk	35	Hull
G	Whall Catherine—†	1	housewife	26	here
H	Whall Clifton H	1	machinist	29	"
K	Adams Gertrude M—†	1	clerk	42	153 W Brookline
L	Rudd Alma M—†	1	housewife	31	here
M	Rudd Boland	1	draughtsman	27	"
O	Favier Ernest	1	electrician	36	"
P	Steele Alice M—†	1	waitress	33	"
R	Magan Anna L—†	1	housewife	29	"
S	Magan William S	1	engineer	33	"
T	DeMilo Mary—†	1	stenographer	22	Brookline
X	Dowling Florence E—†	1A	retired	40	here
Y	Foley Isabelle—†	1A	housewife	25	"
Z	Foley William J	1A	inspector	27	"
A	Kratt Dorothy—†	1A	typist	23	"
B	Lundberg Sofia—†	1A	dressmaker	65	786 Beacon
C	Donican Marion—†	1A	housewife	39	103 Charles
D	Donican Thomas F	1A	salesman	36	103 "
E	Knowlton Eva—†	1A	saleswoman	28	here
G	Blair Margaret—†	1A	retired	45	"
H	Suggat William P	1A	physician	67	"
K	Downey Florence E—†	1A	retired	45	"
L	Bracken Helen—†	1A	housewife	35	"
M	Bracken Thomas	1A	salesman	35	"
N	Guild Mabel—†	1A	clerk	30	"
O	Fultz Sophie—†	1A	stenographer	22	"
P	Crowley Joseph	2	carpenter	29	Brookline
R	Arnold Everett C	2	salesman	22	Braintree
S	Arnold Mildred L—†	2	housewife	24	Somerville

Ivy Street—Continued

T	Foss Clarence S	2	electrotyper	49	here
U	Foss Grace D—†	2	housewife	55	"
V	Mullen Catherine—†	2	housekeeper	45	1 Ivy
X	McGee James C	2	accountant	26	here
Y	McGee Rita—†	2	housewife	25	"
Z	Powell Stanley	2	foreman	38	"
A	Barrett Edward	2	manager	37	"
B	Costello John	3	electrician	47	"
C	Hanlon John	3	paperhanger	40	"
D	Mahan Catherine—†	3	housekeeper	33	455 Mass av
E	Armstrong Anna—†	5	"	43	94 Queensber
F	Small Harry	6	confectioner	34	15 Haviland
G	Small Hattie—†	6	housewife	27	15 "
H	King Alice—†	6	"	38	Cambridge
K	King Charles	6	foreman	63	"
L	Nickerson Harry	6	chauffeur	28	"
M	Morse Samuel	6	tailor	60	here
N	Warnke James	6	musician	50	"
O	Simmons Hazel M—†	6	student	20	26 Caspian w
P	Gleason Jerome J	6	salesman	34	Concord
R	Gleason Ruth E—†	6	housewife	25	"
S	Howard Eliza—†	6	"	55	65 Westland
T	Howard Irving	6	clerk	21	65 "
U	Howard James	6	real estate	57	65 "
V	Wilson Clara—†	6	housekeeper	58	here
Y	Hoye Bessie M—†	6	secretary	25	"
Z	Hoye Bridget—†	6	housekeeper	56	"
A	Opochinsky Jane—†	6	housewife	21	15 Haviland
B	Opochinsky Saul	6	salesman	21	15 "
C	Bates Ella M—†	6	housewife	43	here
D	Bates Harry L	6	manager	43	"
E	Raymond Ethel F—†	6	clerk	36	"
F	Raymond Georgia—†	6	housekeeper	63	"
G	Gagnon Exilda J—†	6	dressmaker	36	"
H	Marion John F	6	engineer	42	22 Ivy
K	Hackett Wallace	6	lawyer	60	here
L	MacKay Clara G—†	6	stenographer	24	"
M	MacKay Lelia C—†	6	nurse	26	"
N	Moss Beatrice J—†	6	"	33	"
O	Stevenson Annie T—†	6	"	33	"
P	Penniman Arthur L	6	mechanic	23	Cambridge

Page	Letter	Full Name	Residence, April 1, 1924.	Occupation	Supposed Age	Reported Residence, April 1, 1923. Street and Number.

Ivy Street—Continued

R	Penniman Marion D—†	6	housewife	24	127 Pembroke
s	Lill Louise A—†	6	"	25	N Carolina
T	Lill William J	6	salesman	33	"
U	Bond Freda R—†	6	nurse	31	Malden
V	Bond Marion I—†	6	clerk	24	"
W	Custance Florabell L—†	6	"	24	Lexington
X	Young Mary E—†	6	nurse	28	Malden
Y	Bamford Margaret—†	6	"	36	here
Z	Kattelle Laurie—†	6	housewife	36	4 Rollins pl
A	Kattelle Lawrence	6	draughtsman	33	4 "
B	Thompson Harry	6	instructor	25	2 Wadsworth
C	Thompson Marion—†	6	housewife	25	2 "
D	Hiland Henry	6	clerk	27	here
E	Sentpeters John	6	accountant	35	"
F	McCue Marguerite A—†	6	housewife	22	41 Hano
G	McCue Thomas J	6	foreman	22	41 "
H	Woods Isabelle B—†	7	housewife	52	here
K	Woods Thomas S	7	agent	54	"
L	Woods Thomas S, jr	7	salesman	27	"
M	Douglas Kate—†	9	artist	45	"
N	Gailbreath Agnes—†	9	dressmaker	48	"
O	Hunter Marion—†	9	saleswoman	25	"
P	McGourty Mary—†	9	housekeeper	39	Cambridge
R	Vernar John	9	checker	25	here
S	Whitney Helen—†	9	manager	33	"
T	Butler Minnie—†	11	cashier	27	"
U	Clark Esther F—†	11	secretary	22	"
V	Lawson Adolf	11	machinist	28	836 Beacon
W	Lee John F	11	clerk	55	here
X	O'Neil Mary N—†	11	housekeeper	45	"
Y	Carbonneau Herbert	13	salesman	34	"
Z	Cox Julia T—†	13	housewife	36	"
A	Cox Malcom W	13	chauffeur	41	"
B	Gassett Charles	13	salesman	35	6 Ivy
C	Girlick Edward C	13	operator	21	New York
D	Arsena Barrow R	15	actor	33	"
E	Arsena John	15	butcher	34	Brookline
F	Cunningham Florence—†	15	nurse	36	here
G	Manning Fredrick	15	salesman	35	Somerville
H	Toplain George	15	tailor	33	here
K	Weeks Harry	15	chauffeur	30	"

Ivy Street—Continued

Letter	Full Name	Residence	Occupation	Age	Reported Residence
L	Eason Grace—†	17	tel operator	28	here
M	Smith Sidney M—†	17	housewife	55	479 Mass av
N	Smith William B	17	school teacher	57	479 "
P	VanAttam Anna M—†	22	housewife	34	here
R	VanAttam Jasper	22	artist	21	"
S	VanAttam Slingerland	22	dentist	26	"
T	VanAttam William A	22	merchant	39	"
U	Daley Agnes—†	22	dressmaker	45	"
V	Daley Alice—†	22	nurse	25	"
W	Daley Ellen—†	22	retired	76	"
Y	Voss Julia—†	22	housewife	40	"
Z	Voss William J	22	manager	46	"
A	Kassman Luba—†	22	housewife	29	"
B	Kassman Nicholas	22	musician	37	"
C	Peyser Agnes—†	22	housewife	30	"
D	Peyser Harry	22	agent	50	"
F	Crawford Lucy M—†	22	housewife	31	Pennsylvania
G	Crawford Roy W	22	clerk	35	"
H	Bladet Gaston	22	musician	43	France
K	Bladet Louisa—†	22	housewife	40	"
L	Yukes Joseph A	22	mechanic	38	here
M	Yukes Lillian—†	22	housewife	38	"
N	Grant Marion—†	22	nurse	40	"
P	Costes Joseph F	22	steward	42	"
R	Costes Mary E—†	22	housewife	44	"
S	Ryan Frank H	22	toolmaker	53	"
T	Ryan Sarah A—†	22	housewife	49	"
U	Holmes Alexander	22	U S A	32	Cambridge
V	McLeod Emily—†	22	clerk	48	here
W	McLeod Eva M—†	22	"	20	"
X	McLeod Virginia—†	22	"	24	"
Y	Wheelock Harriet H—†	22	housekeeper	76	"
A	Keefe Marion J—†	24	bookkeeper	26	"
B	Keefe Sarah—†	24	housekeeper	57	"
C	Carey Julia—†	24	"	41	New York
D	Carey Selina—†	24	stitcher	23	"
F	Francke Gules	24	manager	52	here
G	Francke Stella—†	24	housewife	35	"
H	Smith Irene—†	24	bookkeeper	22	"
K	Pollack Elsia—†	24	cashier	35	"
L	Adcock Mary—†	24	housewife	30	"

Ivy Street—Continued

M	Adcock Ranald	24	manager	35	here
N	Elisen Alice—†	24	school teacher	27	Brookline
O	Elisen Edna—†	24	"	25	"
P	Jenson Frances—†	24	clerk	24	Gloucester
R	Lalley Anna T—†	24	housewife	34	Cambridge
S	Lalley Joseph F	24	engineer	33	"
T	McIntire Harry	24	salesman	48	here
U	McIntire Minnia—†	24	housewife	24	"
V	Wilds Richard C	24	manager	31	"
W	Boker Anna—†	24	dressmaker	50	"
X	Hodgkins Lyle	24	chauffeur	43	"
Y	Hodgkins Martha—†	24	housewife	48	"
Z	Caldwell Andrew A	24	foreman	66	"
A	Caldwell Lillian—†	24	stenographer	30	"
B	Burns John	24	chauffeur	45	"
C	Webb Mary—†	24	housekeeper	56	"
D	Sullivan Gulia—†	24	"	35	Gloucester
G	Bearse Caroline E—†	29	housewife	57	66 W Rutland sq
H	Bearse Charles G	29	watchmaker	62	66 "
K	Bearse Eleanor—†	29	clerk	25	66 "
L	Trayer Edgar	29	operator	25	New York
M	Head Anna S—†	31	retired	56	here
N	McCandlish Grace—†	31	clerk	39	"
O	Newell Mary W—†	31	nurse	50	Cambridge
P	Simmons Eliza T—†	31	housekeeper	72	here
R	Spiller Joseph B	31	retired	82	"
S	Reynolds Gertrude—†	33	housekeeper	40	Brookline
T	Wetherbee Alice—†	33	none	21	here
U	Wetherbee Winthrop	33	merchant	60	Manchester
V	Lubnick Abraham	34	agent	43	567 Tremont
W	Lubnick Edne—†	34	housewife	28	567 "
X	Dinsmore Clyde	34	bookkeeper	38	here
Y	Dinsmore Harriet H—†	34	housewife	37	"
Z	Young Maurice	34	chauffeur	35	52 Ivy
A	Young Ruth—†	34	housewife	31	52 "
B	Norton Francis	34	foreman	26	Canada
C	Norton Mary M—†	34	housewife	22	"
D	Brown Delmer	34	janitor	36	6 Ivy
E	Brown Harry T	34	chauffeur	40	6 "
F	Brown Mary A—†	34	dressmaker	60	6 "
G	Mack Edne—†	34	housewife	36	here

Page.	Letter	Full Name.	Residence, April 1, 1924.	Occupation.	Supposed Age.	Reported Residence, April 1, 1923. Street and Number.

Ivy Street—Continued

	H	Mack Grace B—†	34	housewife	38	here
	K	Mack Mathew	34	salesman	38	"
	L	Jenkins Minie C—†	34	housewife	30	"
	M	Jenkins Rudolph	34	policeman	34	"
	N	Jacobs Ire	34	janitor	38	Brookline
	O	Jacobs Mary—†	34	housewife	32	"
	P	Hazen Laura M—†	34	"	55	here
	R	Hazen Samuel F	34	agent	62	"
	S	Slamin Cornelius	34	chauffeur	32	30 St Germai
	T	Slamin Evelyn A—†	34	housewife	31	15 Bellvista r
	U	Norton Anna A—†	34	housekeeper	57	15 "
	V	Norton Mary A—†	34	school teacher	26	15 "
	W	Wall Edward T	34	manager	30	New York
	X	Widen Louise—†	34	milliner	30	Melrose
	Y	Brindisi Rocco B	34	physician	54	here
	Z	Gallagher Minnie—†	34	dressmaker	39	"
	A	Charles Anna B—†	34	retired	61	"
	B	Charles Buchanan	34	manager	26	"
	C	Charles Samuel B	34	pianist	36	"
	D	McKinnon Sarah—†	35	housemaid	65	Newton
	E	Thompson Nahun W	35	salesman	45	Florida
	F	Thompson Ruth H—†	35	housekeeper	74	here
	H	Bond Boyce C	38	chemist	32	"
	K	Bond Nellie—†	38	housewife	27	"
	L	Nye Nellie—†	38	bookkeeper	36	"
	M	Armstrong Edward M	38	chauffeur	46	"
	N	Armstrong Lillian A—†	38	housewife	34	"
	O	Bennett Henery	38	clerk	55	"
	P	King Richard B	38	student	22	New York
	R	Dinsmore Arthur	38	mechanic	40	Brookline
	S	Gatty Irene—†	38	social worker	23	here
	T	Gatty Irving	38	salesman	55	"
	U	Gatty Minnie—†	38	housewife	45	"
	V	Mulcahy Ellen—†	38	"	38	"
	W	Mulcahy Michael	38	salesman	55	"
	X	Christison Robert M	38	mechanic	38	Lynn
	Y	Fagan Gertrude—†	38	teacher	32	10 Albemarle
	Z	Fagan Robert J	38	steamfitter	32	10 "
	A	Harvey Mabel H—†	39	houseworker	44	here
	B	Harvey Norma—†	39	"	25	"
	C	Harvey Seward T	39	policeman	28	"

Ivy Street--Continued

	Letter.	FULL NAME.	Residence	Occupation.	Age	Reported Residence
	D	Leonard Edward T	39	mechanic	42	here
	E	Lovewell Clifford	39	salesman	28	55 Ivy
	F	Lovewell Phyllis—†	39	housewife	25	55 "
	G	Fox Mary—†	40	bookkeeper	40	Melrose
	H	Kosonowitz Samuel	40	janitor	43	here
	K	Kosonowitz Sarah—†	40	housewife	39	"
	L	Kitzmiller Charles	40	waiter	40	51 Queensberry
	M	Kitzmiller Marguerite—†	40	housewife	30	51 "
	N	MacCormack Leonard A	40	electrician	38	here
	O	MacCormack Vincent W	40	pilot	69	"
	P	Morton May—†	40	housekeeper	60	11 Ivory
	R	Smith Mary—†	40	"	35	here
	S	Samaras John	40	manager	56	378 Riverway
	T	Runso James	40	salesman	35	New York
	U	Runso Mary—†	40	nurse	22	"
	V	Burke James A	40	doorman	63	393 Mass av
	W	Lucas Laura—†	40	printer	23	Medford
	X	Story Wallace C	40	machinist	27	Brookline
	Y	Cobb Sylvanus	41	director	55	here
	Z	MacLeod Mary—†	41	housewife	42	"
	A	MacLeod Murdock	41	vocal teacher	62	"
	B	Hussey Albert R	42	salesman	45	"
	C	Hussey Martha V—†	42	housewife	35	"
	D	Connor Josephine—†	42	"	34	"
	E	Connor William J	42	salesman	44	"
	F	Folhege John	42	"	27	37 Ivy
	G	Holdgate Charles	42	"	50	here
	H	Holdgate Lucy J—†	42	housewife	48	"
	K	Holdgate Raymond C	42	student	20	"
	L	Crowell Albert F	42	retired	69	"
	M	Crowell Louise J—†	42	housewife	70	"
	N	Gross Joseph	42	electrician	30	New York
	O	Fabins John M	42	manufacturer	40	here
	P	Fabins Mary—†	42	housewife	36	"
	R	Tetreu Arthur	42	chauffeur	32	Cambridge
	S	Tetreu Ethlyn—†	42	housewife	27	"
	T	Robertson Anne—†	42	stenographer	21	here
	U	Robertson Ruth S—†	42	teacher	30	"
	V	Smith Ethelbert	42	carpenter	59	"
	W	Smith Kate—†	42	housewife	62	"
	X	Smith Rawland	42	carpenter	31	Shirley

Ivy Street—Continued

y	Gatter Bessie—†	42	housewife	48	here	
z	Gatter Henry	42	merchant	54	"	
a	Montgomery Evelyn M—†	42	housewife	47	"	
b	Montgomery Thomas A	42	electrician	46	"	
c	Gage Alve—†	42	housewife	23	"	
d	Gage Edger W	42	clerk	31	"	
e	Harris Fred F	42	salesman	46	"	
f	Fitzgerald Eleanor A—†	43	student	22	"	
g	Fitzgerald Ellen T—†	43	housewife	50	"	
h	Fitzgerald Miriam L—†	43	stenographer	20	"	
k	Fitzgerald Ruth M—†	43	student	21	"	
l	Fitzgerald William T	43	registrar	52	"	
m	Rhinestein Helda—†	44	housewife	51	"	
n	Rhinestein Ralph	44	merchant	39	"	
o	Mullen Meade	44	salesman	38	New York	
p	Rogers Julia T—†	44	housewife	47	here	
r	Rogers Merton T	44	manager	50	"	
s	Tripp Mary—†	44	clerk	22	Medford	
t	Tripp Ralph	44	accountant	23	"	
v	Condon Auther P	44	salesman	47	here	
w	Sadlers Gussie W—†	44	saleswoman	45	"	
x	Cohen Olga—†	44	housewife	33	"	
y	Cohen Samuel	44	salesman	34	"	
z	Betts Mary—†	44	saleswoman	40	"	
a	Branch Charles W	44	electrician	22	"	
b	Branch Myrtle—†	44	corsetfitter	45	"	
c	Artesani Belen A—†	44	housewife	48	"	
d	Artesani Dolores A—†	44	bookkeeper	20	"	
e	Artesani William N	44	pressman	56	"	
f	Kalberg Clara E—†	44	housewife	29	"	
g	Kalberg Frederick	44	letter carrier	34	"	
h	Comeau Emedee J	44	salesman	23	89 Alexander	
k	Bryant Abbot	45	chemist	35	here	
l	Garfield Frank P	45	supervisor	51	617 Tremont	
m	Garfield Mabel—†	45	housewife	40	617 "	
n	Collins Margret—†	47	housekeeper	40	Cambridge	
o	Coughlin Helen—†	47	"	50	Newton	
p	Lamb Charles	47	brushmaker	60	"	
r	McLean Douglas	47	student	21	Brookline	
s	McLean George	47	mechanic	25	"	
t	Farrell Helen A—†	48	housewife	32	here	

Ivy Street—Continued

u	Farrell William F	48	clerk	34	here
v	Garfield Edward	48	tiremaker	22	4 Dean way
w	Garfield Leonard D	48	egg tester	45	4 "
x	Garfield Melissa —†	48	dressmaker	45	4 "
y	Rodick Florence R—†	48	housewife	46	here
z	Holmes Bernardine—†	48	saleswoman	26	"
A	Jacobs Blanche L—†	48	housewife	29	"
B	Jacobs Sidney R	48	salesman	39	"
C	Bouve Pauline C—†	48	author	45	"
D	Cabell Marian F—†	48	housekeeper	89	"
E	Gillooly Catherine—†	48	"	33	"
F	Crosby Edwin H	48	broker	50	90 Beach
G	Brown Jennie C—†	48	housewife	48	here
H	Brown John L	48	manager	46	"
K	Cohen Lillian—†	48	housewife	35	"
L	Cohen Philip	48	manager	38	"
M	Luria Maurice	48	pressman	33	"
N	Julian Stephen	48	barber	41	"
O	Morrison Belle—†	48	bookkeeper	28	"
P	Morrison Mary—†	48	housewife	54	"
R	Dymsza Bronislaw—†	48	"	48	"
S	Dymsza Chester	48	upholsterer	25	"
T	Dymsza Edmund Z	48	lawyer	24	"
U	Dymsza Waldyslaw	48	upholsterer	49	"
V	Barry Mary W—†	48	demonstrator	43	"
W	Miller Winifred A—†	48	housekeeper	63	"
X	O'Reilly Catherine—†	50	stenographer	48	"
Y	Swanson Ella—†	50	waitress	30	107 Mountfort
Z	Williams Hazel—†	50	saleswoman	39	here
A	King Ethel O—†	50	nurse	35	"
B	Quinn Dorothy M—†	50	housewife	27	1325 Com av
C	Quinn William P	50	school teacher	31	1325 "
E	Titiev Oscar	50	druggist	32	Brookline
F	Olsen Agnes—†	50	stenographer	26	13 Lambert
G	Olsen Ragna—†	50	housewife	50	13 "
H	Brest Authur P	52	lawyer	36	Newton
L	Osterweil Cecil R	52	clerk	24	here
M	Osterweil Lillian E—†	52	photographer	25	"
N	Osterweil Mary—†	52	housewife	52	"
O	Rottenberg Julius	52	merchant	40	Melrose
P	Collingbourne Frederick W	52	retired	62	Squantum

Page.	Letter.	FULL NAME.	Residence, April 1, 1924.	Occupation.	Supposed Age.	Reported Residence, April 1, 1923. Street and Number.

Ivy Street—Continued

	R	Collingbourne Ruth—†	52	musician	31	Squantum
	T	Butter Edward J	52	merchant	46	here
	U	Rossyn George D	52	student	29	Cambridge
	V	Gardner Charles N	52	fireman	33	14 Welton rd
	W	Gardner Mary G—†	52	housewife	29	14 "
	X	Planesch John	52	machinist	43	Hingham
	Y	Church Christine—†	52	stenographer	30	Waltham
	Z	Mullane John J	52	salesman	32	Lynn
	A	King Elsie T—†	55	housewife	22	here
	B	King Marion C—†	55	companion	43	New York
	C	Densmore Albert A	55	constructor	45	here
	D	Densmore Charlotte—†	55	housewife	38	"
	E	Crowley Mary—†	55	housekeeper	45	"
	G	Broderick Anna M—†	55	saleswoman	32	"
	H	Leighton Caroline—†	55	nurse	27	"
	K	Kronberg Mary—†	55	housekeeper	40	"
	L	McLeod Florence—†	55	secretary	30	Canada
	M	Prior Elizabeth—†	55	housekeeper	45	here
	N	Ross Mary—†	55	secretary	35	"
	O	Spaulding Philip	55	"	23	New Hampshire
	P	Maginnis Mary E—†	55	housewife	30	46 Lindsey
	R	Maginnis Percy B	55	clerk	29	46 "

Keswick Street

	S	Ferry Isabelle G—†	5	housewife	65	here
	T	Ferry Manuel J	5	retired	65	"
	U	Ferry Mary I—†	5	musician	38	"
	W	Doherty Maria—†	7	housekeeper	40	Chelsea
	X	Sprague Frances W—†	7	retired	60	here
	Y	Bennett Marue—†	8	maid	40	367 Beacon
	Z	Gannett Margaret—†	8	"	40	Somerville
	A	Hollingsworth Amelia G—†	8	retired	70	here
	B	Newell Gertrude B—†	8	housewife	61	"
	C	Babson Eleanor—†	9	librarian	32	"
	D	Babson Helen S—†	9	housewife	71	"
	E	Babson Ruth S—†	9	saleswoman	29	"
	F	O'Brien Annie—†	9	maid	35	"
	G	Johnson Ann E—†	10	"	27	"

Keswick Street—Continued

H	Merrill Boynton	10	clergyman	32	here
K	Merrill Virginia—†	10	housewife	29	"
L	Barnet Sarah—†	11	"	41	"
M	Barnet Solomon J	11	manufacturer	46	"
N	Stinson Anna—†	11	domestic	26	"
O	Swanson Olga—†	11	cook	45	"
P	McDonald Ellen—†	12	maid	30	Ireland
R	O Meara Alice—†	12	musician	37	here
S	O Meara Frances—†	12	"	43	"
T	O Meara Isabella—†	12	housewife	69	"
U	O Meara Lucy—†	12	secretary	34	"
V	Connolly Lillian—†	14	maid	21	"
W	Jacobs Philip W	14	lawyer	40	"
X	Jacobs Ruth G—†	14	housewife	38	"
Y	Molloy Frances—†	14	maid	28	"
Z	Hale Irene—†	15	housewife	65	"
A	Hale Philip	15	journalist	70	"
B	Olson May—†	15	maid	48	"
C	McPherson Sarah—†	16	"	34	Brookline
D	Merrill Eliza L—†	16	housewife	53	"
E	Merrill Joshua	16	merchant	62	"
F	Connor Josephine—†	17	maid	28	here
G	Osborn Laura B—†	17	housewife	50	"

Maitland Street

H	Johnston Mitilda C—†	1	housewife	52	here
K	Johnston Robert J	1	janitor	57	"
L¹	Wilson Christine—†	8	housewife	32	94 Appleton
M	Wilson James	8	janitor	35	94 "
N	Bain Margaret—†	8	housekeeper	24	Norfolk
O	McIntosh Ina—†	8	"	41	183 Beach
P	Fielding Clara S—†	8	housewife	27	here
R	Fielding Henry	8	mechanic	27	"
S	Wood Mary J—†	8	clerk	32	111 Hamilton
T	Jordan Florence M—†	8	housewife	34	Brant Rock
U	Jordan Herbert E	8	carpenter	42	"
V	Trifiro John	8	barber	32	328 Mass av
W	Howe Geraldine B—†	8	housewife	28	27 Cumberland

43

Page.	Letter.	FULL NAME.	Residence, April 1, 1924.	Occupation.	Supposed Age.	Reported Residence, April 1, 1923. Street and Number.

Maitland Street—Continued

X	Howe Olin B, jr	8	clerk	30	27 Cumberland
Z	LeFerre Laura C—†	8	housewife	35	27 Harold
A	LeFerre Walter A	8	fireman	35	15 Madison
B	Stevenson Harry M	8	clerk	28	Vermont
C	Stevenson Mary M—†	8	housewife	41	"
D	Mulherin James A	8	bookbinder	42	Brookline
E	Mulherin Theresa D—†	8	housewife	40	"
F	Cook Alexander F	8	valet	33	17 Batavia
G	Cook Mildred J—†	8	housewife	29	17 "

Medfield Street

A	Danforth Anna—†	8	housewife	33	here
B	Danforth John C	8	superintendent	35	"
C	O'Brien Ellen—†	8	retired	62	71 Bickford
D	Fitzgerald Edward L	14	collector	40	here
E	Fitzgerald Isabella S—†	14	housewife	29	"
F	Fogarty William I	14	accountant	45	"
G	Cone Grace M—†	14	housewife	58	Harvard
H	Dakin Blanch B—†	14	"	54	here
K	Dakin George H	14	salesman	54	"
L	Hammond Harry G	14	"	27	"
M	Cunningham Isabella—†	14	student	28	Pennsylvania
N	Gleason Clara B—†	14	housewife	56	Pittsfield
O	Schall Leroy A	14	physician	31	here
P	Schall Mabel F—†	14	housewife	28	"
R	Higginson John B	18	manufacturer	30	Cohasset
S	Merrill Charles L	18	salesman	32	here
T	Merrill Hazel B—†	18	housewife	32	"
U	Tetlow Allen R	18	dentist	29	"
V	Tetlow Beatrice R—†	18	housewife	28	"
W	Wertheim Myer	18	salesman	56	"
X	Wertheim Rose—†	18	housewife	39	"
Y	Main Annie L—†	18	bookkeeper	39	"
Z	Smith Arthur C	18	advertising	40	"
A	Smith Mary B—†	18	housewife	65	"
B	Burke Laura M—†	18	"	37	50 Ivy
C	Burke Michael J	18	real estate	37	50 "
D	Bishop Haritte F—†	22	scalp specialist	43	here

44

Medfield Street—Continued

E	Impey Blanch A—†	22	housewife	43	here
F	Impey Harry W	22	salesman	43	"
G	Chandler Elizabeth—†	22	housewife	42	"
H	Carns Eliott G	22	agent	52	266 Brookline
K	Carns Lucey—†	22	housewife	48	266 "
L	Hawkins Edith M—†	22	"	34	here
M	Hawkins Ellsworth	22	manager	47	"
N	Langis Sarah—†	22	housewife	56	"
O	Lloyd Annette—†	22	"	64	"
P	Lloyd William	22	practitioner	63	"
R	Stoddard Lillian W—†	26	clerk	55	"
S	Stoddard Margurite W—†	26	saleswoman	30	"
T	Gross David	26	manager	28	93 Monroe
U	Gross Irene—†	26	housewife	26	93 "
V	Noone Leona M—†	26	dressmaker	34	18 Medfield
W	Cowan Clyde K	26	surgeon	39	here
X	Cowan Love E L—†	26	housewife	39	"
Y	Mackiernan Harold N	26	salesman	43	"
Z	Mackiernan Louise B—†	26	housewife	39	"
C	Martin Mary M—†	30	"	35	New York
D	Brodeur Adrian P	30	dentist	29	here
E	Brodeau Alma M—†	30	housewife	25	"
F	Campbell Anna M—†	30	"	35	41 Ivy
G	Campbell Warren L	30	druggist	36	463 Audubon rd
H	Cushing Charles	30	lawyer	31	here
K	Van Emden Ethel J—†	30	housewife	41	"
L	Van Emden John J	30	merchant	35	"
M	Millineaux James F	34	"	35	"
N	Flint Addie F—†	34	saleswoman	36	"
O	Crawley Edmond S	34	accountant	60	"
P	Crawley Lyda A—†	34	housewife	58	"
R	Dutton Clara P—†	34	"	31	Bedford
S	Dutton Lawrence F	34	student	29	"
T	Evans Howard T	34	engineer	30	Pennsylvania
U	Evans Ruth M—†	34	housewife	31	"
V	Albright Alberta—†	34	"	35	here
W	French Eisie—†	34	"	60	85 Glenville av
X	Farrar Gladys L—†	34	nurse	34	here
Y	Townsend Maude A—†	34	"	34	"

Page.	Letter.	FULL NAME.	Residence, April 1, 1924.	Occupation.	Supposed Age.	Reported Residence, April 1, 1923. Street and Number.

Miner Street

	z	Hutchinson Catherine E—†	1	housewife	70	here
	A	Hutchinson Jane—†	1	bookkeeper	69	"
	B	Hutchinson William	1	retired	70	"

Mountfort Street

	E	Harrington Anna—†	37	housewife	43	here
	F	Harrington Iva	37	janitor	42	"
	G	Martin William E	37	real estate	57	"
	H	Wood Mary—†	37	housekeeper	57	"
	K	Small Cora—†	37	housewife	67	"
	L	Small Doris E—†	37	clerk	29	"
	M	Small Edna—†	37	stenographer	38	"
	N	Small Hiram	37	retired	76	"
	O	Small Nettie—†	37	photographer	40	"
	P	Clough Raymond	39	salesman	30	Worcester
	R	Girard Adelia R—†	39	housewife	60	"
	S	Girard Jessie E—†	39	saleswoman	30	"
	T	Girard William C	39	optician	60	"
	U	Donoghue Mitildia—†	39	housewife	52	here
	V	Donoghue Timothy F	39	foreman	52	"
	W	Merriman Harold	39	clerk	21	"
	X	Saunders James P	39	"	20	"
	Y	Trimble Kenneth I	39	chauffeur	28	"
	z	Lake Harry E	39	civil engineer	38	Worcester
	A	Lund Camille—†	39	housewife	38	159 Hunt'n av
	B	Lund Charles O	39	lawyer	45	159 "
	C	Lindergren Frank E	43	real estate	56	here
	D	Sullivan Daniel J	43	laborer	60	1697 Com av
	E	Sullivan Mary T—†	43	housewife	58	1697 "
	F	Sullivan Michael	43	chauffeur	22	Lawrence
	G	Wright William B	43	U S A	30	Florida
	H	Gormley Minnie—†	45	housewife	40	Cambridge
	K	Gormley William	45	machinist	44	"
	L	Merlino Gruseppe	45	clergyman	50	780 Beacon
	M	Merlino Margherita—†	45	housewife	44	780 "
	N	Gallagher Elizabeth V—†	45	bookkeeper	29	34 E Brookline
	O	Gallagher William R	45	chauffeur	27	34 "
	P	Sullivan William C	45	clerk	43	34 "

Mountfort Street—Continued

R	Tamlyn Agnes—†	46	housewife	50	here
S	Tamlyn Walter B	46	janitor	51	"
T	Burchstead Lulu—†	46	bookkeeper	30	"
U	Vance Ida—†	46	"	28	"
V	Belling Angeline—†	46	housewife	48	538 Newbury
W	Belling Carl	46	school teacher	50	538 "
X	Weis Herbert H	46	salesman	29	here
Y	Weis Ruth K—†	46	housewife	27	"
A	Squires Frederick	46	butcher	31	"
B	Squires Selia—†	46	housewife	28	"
C	Rowan Elanor—†	46	school teacher	30	"
D	Rowan William	46	carpenter	26	"
E	Bingham William	46	"	35	"
F	Davenport Blanch—†	46	saleswoman	35	"
G	Cohen Louis	46	merchant	61	40 Peterboro
H	West Lillian—†	46	advertising	42	40 "
K	Eastman Annie H—†	46	housewife	56	36 Forest
L	Eastman Charles H	46	inventor	59	36 "
M	Eastman Viola C—†	46	housewife	26	36 "
N	Cotter Anne—†	46	bookkeeper	40	Somerville
O	Carter Daniel	46	supervisor	55	here
P	Carter Fannie M—†	46	housewife	45	"
R	Carter Jeannette—†	46	stenographer	27	"
S	Melliken Elbridge H	46	agent	59	"
T	Melliken Mary M—†	46	housewife	66	"
V	Dubois Earnest	46	foreman	40	"
W	Dubois Laura—†	46	housewife	35	"
X	Ascher Joseph	46	salesman	47	"
Y	Ascher Rae R—†	46	housewife	41	"
Z	Smith Louise—†	46	school teacher	28	"
A	Smith Phoebe—†	46	housewife	50	"
B	Smyth Alfred	46	reporter	53	"
C	Smyth Angeline—†	46	housewife	55	"
D	Shadwall George	46	salesman	40	881 Hunt'n av
E	Shadwall Mary—†	46	saleswoman	35	881 "
F	Bemis Cornelia H—†	46	secretary	51	Springfield
G	Medbury Helen G—†	46	"	47	here
H	Stuart Guilford B	46	real estate	25	92 Pinckney
K	Stuart Jessie—†	46	instructor	26	Alabama
L	Stuart Kathryn—†	46	stenographer	22	"
M	Hall Olive M—†	46	saleswoman	62	here

Page	Letter	FULL NAME.	Residence, April 1, 1924.	Occupation.	Supposed Age.	Reported Residence, April 1, 1923. Street and Number.

Mountfort Street—Continued

	N	Neilson Euric	46	carpenter	43	198 St Botolph
	O	Merrill Lola—†	46	stenographer	21	Maine
	P	Packard Evelyn—†	46	housewife	20	"
	R	Packard Royal D	46	student	22	"
	S	Green Mary M—†	46	nurse	35	"
	T	Stevens Emma—†	46	dressmaker	40	800 Beacon
	W	Emmons Florence E—†	49	housewife	50	here
	X	Emmons William R	49	foreman	54	"
	Y	Pendergast Mary E—†	49	housewife	32	314 Com av
	Z	Prendergast Thomas J	49	butler	42	314 "
	A	Shattuck Mary E—†	51	housewife	42	here
	B	Mahoney Margaret—†	51	cashier	38	"
	C	Galvin Brenda—†	51	housewife	60	"
	D	Fay Michael	53	janitor	40	"
	E	Peel Eva L—†	53	waitress	35	38 Ivy
	F	Ash Peter	53	cook	31	Lynn
	G	Ewing Robert	55	gardener	40	here
	H	Flodin Gustus	55	mechanic	38	"
	K	McFadden Bridget—†	55	housewife	51	"
	L	McFadden Ellen—†	55	bookkeeper	23	"
	M	McFadden William	55	gardener	52	"
	N	McFadden William J	55	salesman	21	"
	O	Morin Daniel	55	laborer	26	"
	P	Morin Martin	55	waiter	21	Ireland
	R	Morin William	55	garageman	23	"
	S	Morly Dominick	55	salesman	35	here
	T	O'Brien Timothy	55	chauffeur	31	"
	U	O'Brien Genevive—†	57	housewife	42	"
	V	O'Brien John	57	salesman	47	"
	W	Jennings Ellen G—†	59	retired	84	"
	X	Dill Edith S—†	61	housekeeper	57	"
	Y	Dill Fred G	61	elevatorman	28	"
	Z	Dill Gerald E	61	clerk	31	"
	C	Thorne Anna M—†	63	none	63	"
	D	Anderson Louise—†	65	laundress	40	"
	E	Donnelly Harriet—†	65	"	21	"
	F	Hanson Benjamin	65	laundryman	42	"
	G	Fisher Abram B	67	tailor	45	"
	H	Fisher Ella E—†	67	housewife	40	"
	K	Fisher Harry D	67	actor	26	"
	L	Day Elizabeth—†	69	maid	41	"

Mountfort Street—Continued

	Full Name	Residence April 1, 1924	Occupation	Age	Reported Residence
M	Kimball Albert T	69	manager	79	here
N	Kimball Florence A—†	69	retired	72	"
O	Bill Emma F—†	71	housekeeper	40	Revere
P	Bill Harrison W	71	mechanic	47	"
R	Abaghian Josephine—†	73	stenographer	20	here
S	Gensel Lloyd	73	student	25	Michigan
T	Jennings Charles H	73	broker	42	here
U	Jennings Grace H—†	73	housewife	38	"
V	Londino Saul	73	student	21	New York
W	Ginty Allen J	75	salesman	28	here
X	Ginty Flora A—†	75	housewife	57	"
Y	Ginty John A	75	coppersmith	62	"
Z	Ginty John A, jr	75	foreman	23	"
B	Shaw Albert J	79	physician	52	"
C	Shaw Arthur J	79	"	52	"
D	Shaw Flora H—†	79	none	46	"
E	Shaw Isadora T—†	79	"	72	"
F	Shaw Maud E—†	79	housewife	48	"
G	Dwyer Gertrude M—†	81	"	39	"
H	Dwyer William J	81	physician	40	"
K	Tenney Frank E	83 & 85	salesman	57	"
L	Tenney Isabella A—†	83 & 85	housewife	54	"
M	Beaudoin Frederic A	83 & 85	inspector	38	"
N	Beaudoin Helen T—†	83 & 85	housewife	34	"
O	Pratt Anna F—†	83 & 85	"	38	"
P	Bailey Phebe E—†	83 & 85	"	63	"
R	Bailey Walter B	83 & 85	chauffeur	64	"
S	Boyle Annie E—†	83 & 85	stitcher	52	"
T	Boyle Catherine—†	83 & 85	forewoman	51	"
U	Smith Gertrude C—†	83 & 85	stenographer	30	"
V	Smith Susie G—†	83 & 85	housewife	57	"
W	Ford Robert	83 & 85	chauffeur	30	"
X	Golman Dora E—†	83 & 85	housewife	55	"
Y	Ryan Katherine—†	87 & 89	saleswoman	57	"
Z	Ryan Margaret M—†	87 & 89	nurse	52	"
A	Ryan William F	87 & 89	insurance agent	66	"
B	Gale Louise P—†	87 & 89	housewife	31	"
C	Gale Waldo S	87 & 89	salesman	30	"
D	Bogan Charles F	87 & 89	conveyancer	46	"
E	Bogan Maragret E—†	87 & 89	housewife	41	"
F	Lawler Josephine M—†	87 & 89	nurse	28	"

8—12

Mountfort Street—Continued

G	Ward Frederick C	87 & 89	clerk	56	here
H	Silverstein Abraham	87 & 89	foreman	57	"
K	Silverstein Ella—†	87 & 89	housewife	46	"
L	Silverstein Nathan	87 & 89	manager	27	"
M	Murray Adelaide—†	87 & 89	housewife	45	"
N	Murray Alice—†	87 & 89	nurse	38	"
O	Murray Sadie—†	87 & 89	bookkeeper	42	"
P	Carpenger Lydia—†	87 & 89	housewife	45	122 Chandler
R	McLenen Daniel	93	shipper	45	here
S	McLenen Jennie—†	93	housewife	43	"
T	Bengham Bessie H—†	93	"	56	"
U	Hyde William	93	salesman	57	"
V	Gahagan Alma—†	93	housekeeper	69	"
W	Grady Catherine—†	93	housewife	40	"
X	Grady Joseph C	93	superintendent	45	"
Y	Grady William P	93	mechanic	21	"
A	Morrisey Mary—†	95	housewife	40	Lynn
B	Daly Julia A—†	95	"	60	here
C	Daly Patrick J	95	chef	65	"
D	Buckman Frank	96	elevatorman	48	"
E	Buckman Gladys—†	96	manicurist	43	"
F	Joyce Caroline—†	96	nurse	33	Natick
G	Gillis Susan—†	96	manicurist	35	here
H	Henerycot Frances—†	96	saleswoman	38	"
K	Mason Harriet—†	96	hairdresser	45	519 Audubon rd
L	Riley Agnes—†	96	"	40	519 "
M	Tellier Walter F	96	salesman	24	519 "
N	Crafts Fred N	96	chauffeur	47	here
O	Crafts Isabel N—†	96	housewife	45	"
P	Booth Florence M—†	96	school teacher	38	844 Beacon
R	Watson John	96	chauffeur	52	here
S	Foster Annie E—†	96	housewife	57	"
T	Foster Frank R	96	salesman	32	"
U	William Charles I	96	janitor	49	"
V	William Florence—†	96	housewife	45	"
W	Cunningham Gertrude C—†	97	"	42	"
X	Adolf Annie B—†	97	teacher	36	"
Y	Richardson Mary—†	97	clerk	38	"
Z	Hittinger Clara—†	97	housekeeper	57	"
A	Hoppe Fannie M—†	98	housewife	31	"
B	Jackson Bertha L—†	98	"	29	"

Page.	Letter.	FULL NAME.	Residence, April 1, 1924.	Occupation.	Supposed Age.	Reported Residence, April 1, 1923. Street and Number.

Mountfort Street—Continued

c	White Margaret—†	98	housewife	26	here
d	White Russell G	98	salesman	29	"
e	Tufts Harry M	98	appraiser	50	"
f	Maffitt Mary E—†	98	housewife	50	"
g	Tobey Margaret—†	98	"	34	"
h	Tobey Samuel	98	real estate	50	"
k	Besa Herman	98	agent	29	722 Com av
l	Besa Mary M—†	98	housewife	23	722 "
n	Levy Bertha—†	98	"	28	here
o	Levy Henry	98	manager	47	"
p	Carroll Frederick W	99	leather sorter	31	"
r	Carroll Winifred M—†	99	housewife	28	"
s	Doherty William	99	bookkeeper	24	Springfield
t	Levi Jacob N	99	salesman	53	New York
u	St Clair Nan J—†	99	housekeeper	62	here
v	Thorn Richard	99	conductor	38	Brookline
w	Kapstein Edward M	100	salesman	45	here
x	Kapstein Sybil—†	100	housewife	33	"
z	Gagnon Ida—†	100	"	33	98 Mountfort
A	Collins Margaret—†	100	stenographer	40	here
B	Hall Henry L	100	baggagemaster	40	"
C	Hall Mabelle N—†	100	housewife	34	"
D	Volke Marie K—†	101	dressmaker	36	"
E	Carroll Elizabeth—†	101	"	69	"
F	Cooper Harry	101	carpenter	40	Lynn
G	Dorenbaum John	101	clerk	28	here
H	Dean William	101	electrician	29	"
K	Emery Frank G	101	salesman	48	"
L	Emery Minnie A—†	101	housewife	42	"
M	Bouchier Josephine B—†	103	real estate	42	"
N	Knickle Blanche—†	103	housewife	35	"
O	Knickle Harris	103	moulder	44	"
P	Bowyer Grace E—†	103	housewife	35	"
R	Bowyer James T	103	mechanic	37	"
T	Davenport Ermimie A—†	105	housewife	57	"
U	Sandell Harry N	105	salesman	33	"
V	Pearson Helen R—†	105	tel operator	26	"
W	Sullivan Elizabeth—†	105	housewife	49	"
X	Sullivan James F	105	manager	46	"
Y	Larsen Grace—†	107	housewife	35	Cambridge
Z	Haynes John O	107	undertaker	53	here

Page.	Letter.	FULL NAME.	Residence, April 1, 1924.	Occupation.	Supposed Age.	Reported Residence, April 1, 1923. Street and Number.

Mountfort Street—Continued

A	Collins Mary—†	107	clerk	40	Newton
B	Boyd Fenwick C V	109	"	60	here
C	Boyd Vernon W	109	"	26	"
D	Phaneuf Joseph D	109	chauffeur	44	"
E	Young Mary—†	109	clerk	30	Cambridge
G	Black Charles A	111	painter	38	24 St Mary's
H	McAuliffe Sarah—†	111	housewife	51	1290 Wash'n
K	McAuliffe William	111	machinist	30	New York
L	Walker Anna E—†	111	housewife	43	here
M	Walker Samuel D	111	salesman	48	"
N	Walker Samuel D, jr	111	bookkeeper	22	"
O	Gaffney Edith M—†	111A	clerk	27	"
P	Goldie Ralph H	111A	packer	53	"
R	Gargan Candace C—†	111A	student	21	"
S	Gargan John J	111A	salesman	56	"
T	Gargan John R	111A	"	25	"
U	Gargan Mary C—†	111A	housewife	55	"
V	Russell Albert H	111A	salesman	40	"
W	Russell Erra F—†	111A	housewife	44	"
X	Smith Elise P—†	115	clerk	40	Cambridge
Y	Lynds Temple J	115	manager	36	13 Allston
Z	Guggenheim Bertha—†	115	cashier	30	here
A	Guggenheim Sadie—†	115	bookkeeper	32	"
B	Guggenheim Samuel	115	retired	81	"
C	Guggenheim Silas	115	shipper	46	"
D	Guggenheim Theresa—†	115	clerk	34	"
E	Fox May—†	119	housewife	29	Newton
F	Tilton Perley C	119	manager	47	here
H	Lewis Carrie—†	119	clerk	33	Newton
K	Gruber Florance—†	119	waitress	35	Milford
L	Punt Harry D	119	clerk	28	566 Col av
M	Prime Ada J—†	119	saleswoman	51	here
N	Williamson Alice B—†	119	housewife	47	"
O	Williamson Harry O	119	clerk	36	"
P	Blank Charles	119	"	40	"
R	Brown Charles E	119	machinist	50	"
S	Jones May—†	119	nurse	29	Cambridge
U	Whelan Anna—†	119	waitress	20	New York
V	Whelan Elizabeth—†	119	"	23	1006 Boylston
W	Whelan Nathen	119	clerk	22	New York

Mountfort Street—Continued

Letter.	Full Name.	Residence, April 1, 1924.	Occupation.	Supposed Age.	Reported Residence, April 1, 1923.
x	Brewer Lottie—†	119	waitress	48	New York
y	Woodhall James W	119	carpenter	45	"
z	Wing John E	119	chauffeur	32	here
a	Curtis Jennie—†	119	housewife	43	Maine
b	Bradford Henry	119	clerk	40	here
c	Dorherty Jennie—†	119	housewife	22	Newton
e	Condon Jennie—†	119	clerk	24	here
f	Young Mary—†	119	"	30	Brookline
g	Harris Grace—†	119	"	34	Cambridge
h	Peeler Minnie—†	119	waitress	28	here
k	Romkey Mildred—†	119	clerk	23	"
l	Young Jane P—†	119	waitress	30	Watertown
n	Goodman Daniel A	121	clerk	35	here
o	Goodman Sarah A—†	121	housewife	28	"
p	Whitfield John	121	clerk	48	Brookline
r	Gallipeau Catherine E—†	121	housewife	29	310 Col av
s	Gallipeau Joseph P	121	chauffeur	32	310 "
t	Pelton Alice—†	121	bookkeeper	32	here
u	Bushman Charles	121	salesman	39	Salem
v	Tutty James T	121	manager	30	here
w	Tutty Julia—†	121	housewife	31	"
x	Martin John	121	clerk	25	"
y	Martin Margaret—†	121	housewife	21	"
y¹	Johnson Grace L—†	121	retired	49	"
z	Stoddard Florence—†	121	pianist	36	"
b	Fuller Henery E	121	machinist	25	New York
c	Fuller Olive M—†	121	housewife	21	"
d	Hayes Sarah A—†	121	secretary	34	here
e	Heggarty Nellie—†	121	hairdresser	31	Brookline
f	Ball Alfred T	121	salesman	25	Weymouth
g	Ball Ella D—†	121	housewife	20	"
h	McKinnon Edward	121	machinist	31	Arlington
l	Wright Mary—†	121	secretary	51	here
m	Bates Mabel G—†	121	housekeeper	56	"
n	Saunders Vernon L	121	druggist	27	Medford
o	Sargent Mabel—†	121	secretary	32	Quincy
r	Frame James	121	clerk	29	Cambridge
s	Smart Joseph	121	chauffeur	39	Springfield

St Mary's Street

	Letter.	FULL NAME.	Residence, April 1, 1924.	Occupation.	Supposed Age.	Reported Residence April 1, 1923.
	C	Waters Bessie—†	24	saleswoman	43	696 Tremont
	D	Harvey Clide B	24	electrician	29	39 Ivy
	E	Harvey May—†	24	housewife	23	39 "
	F	Huskins Effie—†	24	saleswoman	37	1298 Com av
	H	Porter Frances—†	24	nurse	22	82 E Concor
	K	Young Grace—†	24	"	21	82 "
	L	Young Mary—†	24	retired	60	Cambridge
	N	Floyd Emma—†	24	saleswoman	58	here
	O	Wells Florence—†	24	"	38	"
	P	Stewart William F	24	accountant	37	76 Peterboro
	R	Peterson John	24	salesman	40	New York
	S	Manning Edwin	24	printer	33	40 Ivy
	T	Manning Helen—†	24	housewife	34	40 "
	U	Bunker Eileen—†	24	student	21	here
	V	Bunker Louise—†	24	housewife	46	"
	W	Hendrick Anna—†	24	"	31	"
	X	Hendrick John A	24	meatcutter	33	"
	Z	Hammond Arthur	24	photographer	42	Deerfield
	A	Fitzmaurice Frances—†	24	housewife	32	here
	B	Fitzmaurice Frank	24	postal clerk	38	"
	C	Pratt Charles A	24	salesman	36	"
	D	Pratt Hazel A—†	24	housewife	30	"
	E	Ford Frank	24	salesman	30	"
	F	Ruggles John A	24	shoeworker	45	"
	L	Costello Elizabeth—†	75	bookkeeper	33	"
	M	Costello Helen—†	75	hairdresser	35	"
	N	Whalen Margaret—†	75	waitress	35	Cambridge
	O	Philips Mabel E—†	75	housewife	44	306 Hyde Park av
	P	Philips William C	75	stereotyper	45	306 "
	R	Simpson Gladys—†	75	waitress	20	New Brunswick
	S	Thompson Joyce—†	75	"	22	440 Newbury
	T	Thompson Lucy—†	75	restaurateur	35	440 "
	U	Stevens Joseph W	90	janitor	69	here
	V	Stevens Nettie H—†	90	housewife	68	"
	W	Child Charlotte A—†	90	retired	82	"
	X	Child Sallie—†	90	"	41	"
	Y	Connolly Annie—†	90	houseworker	38	"
	Z	Guiler Gertrude—†	90	retired	50	"
	A	O'Connor Francis	90	merchant	61	"
	B	O'Connor Honor—†	90	housewife	50	"

Letter	Full Name	Residence, April 1, 1924.	Occupation.	Supposed Age.	Reported Residence, April 1, 1923. Street and Number.

St Mary's Street—Continued

C	Pinto Catherine—†	90	houseworker	20	here
D	Gay Grace—†	90	stenographer	29	Cambridge
E	MacBlair Henry	90	manager	35	here
F	Shaw Jessie E—†	90	housekeeper	32	"
G	Newsome Mary W—†	90	housewife	46	"
H	Newsome William	90	superintendent	55	"
K	Wylander Elin A—†	90	maid	30	"
M	Wright Amanda L—†	100	housewife	67	"
N	Wright Harry E	100	merchant	69	"
O	Hazelton Harriet—†	100	housekeeper	56	"
P	Corcoran Mary A—†	100	social worker	40	"
R	Kelliher Elizabeth M—†	100	housekeeper	50	"
T	Fletcher Emma E—†	100	housewife	47	"
U	Fletcher William B	100	provisions	50	"
V	Finlay Marie—†	100	housekeeper	36	"
W	Lorey Mary A—†	100	retired	67	"
Y	French Rena L—†	100	bookkeeper	37	394 Mass av
Z	Hazelton Bertha—†	100	pianist	35	here
B	Jones Ada R—†	124	housekeeper	68	"
C	McQueen Catherine A—†	126	maid	44	"
D	Reardon Mary K—†	126	"	61	"
E	Russell Dora W—†	126	housekeeper	62	"
F	Dowling Frank J	128	real estate	48	"
G	Dowling Sarah A—†	128	housewife	54	"
H	Dale Lydia J—†	130	"	73	"
K	Driscoll Margaret—†	130	cook	50	Milton
L	McCarthy Margaret—†	130	waitress	29	here
M	Howard Elizabeth—†	132	student	21	"
N	Howard Elizabeth—†	132	housewife	52	"
O	Howard Francis	132	clerk	24	"
P	Howard Francis G	132	merchant	60	"
R	Howard Margaret—†	132	student	21	"
S	Howard Thomas	132	engineer	24	"
T	McKinney Virginia—†	132	cook	50	Weston
U	Washburn Anna B—†	134	housewife	49	here
V	Washburn Roger D	134	teacher	25	"
W	Washburn Thomas G	134	real estate	52	"

Ward 8—Precinct 13

—

CITY OF BOSTON.

—

LIST OF RESIDENTS
20 YEARS OF AGE AND OVER

(FEMALES INDICATED BY DAGGER)

AS OF

APRIL 1, 1924

—

HERBERT A. WILSON, } *Listing*

JAMES F. EAGAN, } *Board.*

CITY OF BOSTON—PRINTING DEPARTMENT

Audubon Road

A	Rogers Clara M—†	11	housewife	31	51 Audubon rd
B	Rogers Wilfred A	11	janitor	31	51 "
C	Levens James	11	physician	38	Vermont
E	Lucy Helen—†	11	storekeeper	55	743 Tremont
F	Mann Grace T—†	11	nurse	43	145 Mass av
G	Cadosa Mary—†	11	saleswoman	35	24 Queensberry
H	Harlow George	11	salesman	45	31 "
K	Winchester Beulah—†	11	investigator	35	31 "
L	Cahoon Lester A	11	accountant	25	Cambridge
M	Cahoon Ruth S—†	11	clerk	25	"
N	Pelletier Josephine—†	11	dressmaker	29	65 Audubon r
O	Toohey Marjorie—†	11	housekeeper	24	1086 Com av
P	Holsberg Pearl L—†	11	housewife	31	645 Beacon
R	Holsberg Maurice B	11	lawyer	39	645 "
S	Veageq Carolyn—†	11	stenographer	35	54 Gainsboro
T	Burstin Bernard	11	physician	31	222 Mass av
U	Burstin Josephine—†	11	housewife	23	55 Esmond
V	Normser Edward	11	retired	60	98 Hemenway
W	Koslowsky Stanley	11	salesman	35	New York
Z	Deady Edward F	11	insurance	51	282 Newbury
A	Maclusky Lillian G—†	11	tel operator	28	282 "
B	Stevens Grace—†	11	cashier	40	51 Audubon
C	Littig Florence—†	11	housewife	47	149 Newbury
D	Littig Mark D	11	dentist	52	149 "
E	Silver Jeanette—†	11	artist	25	31 Queensberry
F	Hennessey Richard	11	salesman	37	Brookline
G	Marzynaski Dora—†	11	housewife	53	55 Esmond
H	Marzynaski Samuel	11	manager	53	55 "
L	DeMontreuil Blanche—†	11	housekeeper	30	60 Charlesgate East
M	Gorden Rose—†	11	saleswoman	25	60 "
O	Marzynaski Julian	11	superintendent	26	55 Esmond
P	Littig Betty—†	11	housewife	25	409 Hunt'n a
R	Littig Sibley	11	physician	26	409 "
T	Perry Christine—†	11	housewife	45	Newton
U	Perry Frederick	11	banker	45	"
V	Beaudet Eva—†	11	saleswoman	25	60 Charlesgate East
W	Saunders Emma—†	11	housewife	35	60 "
X	Saunders Frederick	11	salesman	35	60 "
Y	Ricker Anna C—†	11	stenographer	30	51 Audubon
Z	Adams Percy	11	salesman	25	64 Hemenwa

Audubon Road—Continued

Letter.	FULL NAME.	Residence, April 1, 1924.	Occupation.	Age.	Reported Residence, April 1, 1923.
A	Hamel Floyd	11	salesman	30	51 Audubon rd
B	Cahill Horace	11	"	30	77 "
C	Eaton Samuel	15	teamster	31	Cambridge
E	Donegan Carroll J	15	manager	30	Springfield
F	Donegan Grace L—†	15	housewife	27	"
G	Moulton Howard A	15	superintendent	35	8 Garrison
H	Moulton Louise—†	15	housewife	36	8 "
K	Porter James W	15	accountant	27	99 St Botolph
M	Lewis Hilda T—†	15	housewife	31	394 Riverway
N	Lewis Walter J	15	salesman	31	394 "
O	MacDonald Christie—†	15	saleswoman	35	36 Peterboro
P	MacDonald Christine—†	15	nurse	32	Florida
R	Lamont Jeanette—†	15	bookkeeper	40	Brookline
S	Conklin Georgiana—†	15	dressmaker	31	5) Charlesgate East
T	Nulty Charlotte—†	15	housewife	42	Cambridge
U	Nulty Daniel R	15	salesman	51	"
W	Mahoney Elizabeth—†	15	bookkeeper	25	35 Peterboro
X	O'Connell Elizabeth A—†	15	housewife	35	73 Audubon rd
Y	O'Connell Walter F	15	civil engineer	35	73 "
Z	Ludlum Christine—†	15	reporter	30	77 "
A	Boyd John	15	manager	30	Brookline
D	Crooker Foster	15	retired	56	Providence R I
E	Walker Lena B—†	15	none	30	"
F	Bradford William	15	chauffeur	39	50 Peterboro
G	Ellis Norma—†	15	saleswoman	25	85 Audubon rd
H	Coffin John	15	lawyer	40	25 "
K	Warren Mary—†	15	cashier	40	Brookline
M	Adelman Rose—†	15	none	50	1961 Com av
N	Downs Sarah E—†	15	"	80	1138 Boylston
O	Forbush Vinnie F—†	15	teacher	38	1138 "
P	Hubbard Jesse B	15	broker	43	51 Audubon rd
R	Summers Helen—†	15	nurse	30	72 Peterboro
S	Anderson Edna J—†	15	bookkeeper	31	61 Audubon rd
T	Fitzgerald Tabitha—†	15	teacher	45	282 Newbury
V	Murphy Mildred V—†	15	bookkeeper	28	51 Audubon rd
W	Phelphs James	15	baker	45	1111 Boylston
X	Wright Blanche—†	15	stenographer	45	16 Queensberry
Y	Ambrose Joseph V	15	druggist	35	here
Z	Granger Robert	15	salesman	35	Sharon
A	Eaton Annie B—†	15	housewife	63	15 Anderson
B	Eaton Harold B	15	retired	66	15 "

Audubon Road—Continued

c	Williams Gladys—†	15	nurse	23	25 Audubon rd
D	Rose Charles	25	janitor	38	here
E	Rose Effie—†	25	housewife	37	"
F	Ashley Edith—†	25	"	38	"
G	Ashley Thomas	25	insurance	50	"
K	Irish William H	25	lawyer	48	"
L	Keenan William	25	restaurateur	50	"
M	Turner Leona L—†	25	secretary	42	"
N	Harney Mary G—†	25	bookkeeper	45	"
O	Marsh Harriet—†	25	secretary	45	31 Audubon rd
P	Drew Susan A—†	25	none	60	here
R	Drew Wynette—†	25	bookkeeper	40	"
S	Whitehead Guy	25	druggist	38	"
T	Livingstone Lillian—†	25	housekeeper	30	"
U	Tilton Elizabeth—†	25	housewife	50	"
V	Tilton George P	25	secretary	55	"
W	Perkins Norton B	25	insurance	48	"
X	Badger Henry L	25	salesman	36	85 Audubon rd
Y	Badger Sarah L—†	25	housekeeper	73	85 "
Z	Sherman Annabelle—†	25	stenographer	40	here
A	Sherman Emma L—†	25	housekeeper	63	"
B	Canning Eva—†	25	bookkeeper	32	Brookline
C	Magee Isabel—†	25	housewife	30	here
D	Magee James H	25	treasurer	32	"
E	Deshon Dana, jr	25	salesman	42	"
F	Deshon Muriel—†	25	housewife	41	"
G	McNerny Henry J	25	superintendent	44	"
H	McNerny Laura J—†	25	housewife	43	"
K	Edwards Helen J—†	25	secretary	48	"
L	Seavey Hulda—†	25	bookkeeper	30	"
M	Seavey Rose—†	25	"	40	"
N	Marlowe Joseph	25	retired	69	"
O	Reilly Maud L—†	25	housekeeper	41	"
P	Maloney Johanna—†	25	retired	68	"
R	Maloney Theresa F—†	25	manicurist	28	"
S	Coy Annie F—†	25	secretary	38	"
U	Emerson Nellie—†	27	clerk	40	"
V	Simmons Mary—†	27	housekeeper	55	"
W	Wilson Mariaette—†	27	bookkeeper	30	"
X	Reed Mabel—†	27	"	40	"
Y	Smart Elizabeth—†	27	tel operator	41	"

4

Audubon Road—Continued

z	Howes Fred	27	salesman	45	here
A	Walton Ruth —†	27	secretary	25	Needham
B	Hopkins John	27	salesman	28	here
C	Wilder Clara—†	27	secretary	33	"
D	Chick Eva—†	27	manicurist	37	"
E	Nowell Joseph	27	salesman	50	"
F	Scherwin John	27	"	35	"
G	Scherwin Mary—†	27	housewife	33	"
H	Corbett Lawrence	27	civil engineer	30	"
K	Conley Mary—†	27	housekeeper	60	Lexington
L	McPeak Agnes—†	27	stenographer	47	"
M	McPeak Elizabeth—†	27	bookkeeper	45	"
N	White Marion—†	27	teacher	30	Lynn
O	Lanmen Mary—†	27	clerk	50	here
P	Ratigan Lillian—†	27	teacher	25	"
R	Ratigan Mary—†	27	saleswoman	50	"
S	Wagner Helen—†	27	housewife	23	52 St Stephen
T	Wagner Joseph	27	music teacher	28	52 "
U	Whitney Jesse—†	27	nurse	35	here
V	Maher Margaret—†	27	lawyer	50	"
W	Knowlton Arthur W	27	civil engineer	35	78 Peterboro
X	Hadlock Maud—†	27	clerk	40	here
Y	Gresley Geraldine—†	27	housekeeper	56	"
Z	Gresley Helen—†	27	clerk	29	"
A	Whitney Edward	27	physician	35	"
B	Towne Elenor—†	27	restaurateur	40	"
C	Dundas James	29	salesman	38	50 Peterboro
D	Gilbert Irene—†	29	bookkeeper	38	here
E	Wood Leon	29	salesman	42	"
F	Radcliffe Ralph P	29	broker	42	New Haven
G	Coffin Josephine—†	29	dressmaker	46	here
H	Knott Kate—†	29	housekeeper	44	20 Westland av
K	Edwards Mary—†	29	"	60	here
L	Ellsworth Cora E—†	29	manicurist	43	"
M	Newland Alice—†	29	housewife	21	Cambridge
N	Newland Earl F	29	teller	25	"
O	Cooley Matty—†	29	housekeeper	48	here
P	Swain Bernice C—†	29	clerk	30	"
S	Ray Guy J	29	"	50	"
T	Rose Helen K—†	29	bookkeeper	43	"
U	Munson Frederick L	29	butcher	46	"

Audubon Road—Continued

v	Ferguson Olive—†	29	nurse	30	here
w	McGlue John J. jr	29	teacher	31	"
x	Spike Mary—†	29	clerk	30	78 Peterboro
y	Parmenter Louise—†	29	"	25	11 E Newton
z	Qukes Mary L—†	29	"	25	11 "
A	Adler Alexander, jr	29	salesman	29	here
B	Adler Gwendoline W—†	29	housewife	29	"
c	Carlton Avis—†	29	teacher	35	"
D	Carlton Catherine—†	29	bookkeeper	32	"
E	Hodgkins Charles	29	salesman	35	"
F	Hodgkins George	29	"	45	"
G	Gordon Corrine M—†	29	teacher	45	"
H	Bradford Alaric P	29	superintendent	65	"
K	Bradford Elsie—†	29	housekeeper	28	"
L	Draper Carolyn—†	29	secretary	30	"
M	Macomber Ester—†	29	housekeeper	52	"
N	Macomber Pauline—†	29	clerk	25	"
O	Garrigan Mary—†	31	housewife	45	"
P	Garrigan Matthew	31	janitor	50	"
R	Lathis Mathew	31	broker	35	"
S	Kelley Agnes—†	31	clerk	30	"
T	Sides George	31	salesman	50	"
U	Sides Mary—†	31	nurse	47	"
V	Smith Edward A	31	superintendent	45	"
W	Sealander Charles	31	manager	46	"
X	Stanley Dorothea—†	31	clerk	30	"
Y	Stricker Emily—†	31	saleswoman	28	"
z	Emerson Luther	31	musician	40	"
A	Hayes Raymond	31	"	37	"
c	Witte Martin	31	lawyer	48	"
D	Mumford Elizabeth—†	31	nurse	55	"
E	Sexton Emily—†	31	buyer	40	"
F	Lund Gertrude—†	31	nurse	35	"
G	Lund Mabel—†	31	"	40	"
H	Eldridge Edward	31	teacher	60	"
K	Deaux Burton L	31	buyer	33	"
L	Thayer Hazel—†	31	hairdresser	25	78 Peterboro
M	Billings Thomas L	31	insurance	32	here
N	Hunt Edward	31	chauffeur	21	27 Audubon r
O	Hunt Lottie—†	31	salesman	28	27 "
P	Grainger Catherine—†	31	housekeeper	54	Brookline

Audubon Road—Continued

R	Craig Gertrude—†	31	teacher	40	here
S	Anderson Anna—†	31	bookkeeper	28	"
T	Cromstead Harry	31	electrician	30	"
U	Cromstead Marie—†	31	housewife	29	"
V	Dougal Jessie—†	31	saleswoman	44	"
W	Dougal Lorna—†	31	stenographer	25	"
X	Slade Wilfred J	31	salesman	50	Winchester
Y	Summerhayes Helen—†	35	housewife	38	here
Z	Summerhayes Robert	35	janitor	39	"
A	Lamm William	35	student	21	"
B	Valdes Augustin M	35	"	21	"
C	Harrington Helen—†	35	nurse	22	
D	Briand Alphonse	35	manager	49	137 Peterboro
E	Briand Annie M—†	35	housewife	45	137 "
F	Dyer Gladys E—†	35	saleswoman	22	84 Gainsboro
G	Ratzburg Elizabeth—†	35	student	24	84 "
H	Briand Fidella C—†	35	milliner	35	137 Peterboro
K	Briand Josephine R—†	35	"	28	137 "
L	Briand Leon T	35	retired	78	137 "
M	Livor John E	35	manager	47	Brookline
N	Malley Nancy—†	35	secretary	28	here
O	Taylor Mabel—†	35	saleswoman	35	"
P	Clash Donald	35	engineer	21	Delaware
R	Clash Josephine—†	35	housewife	21	New Jersey
S	Lakin Winifred—†	35	saleswoman	37	here
T	Ferill Louise—†	35	"	24	"
U	Kniffler Ida—†	35	housekeeper	60	"
V	Palmer William W	35	restaurateur	45	"
W	Coolidge Helen—†	35	clerk	35	151 Audubon rd
X	Leen Helen—†	35	"	25	42 Peterboro
Y	Leen Mary—†	35	"	23	42 "
Z	Chapin May—†	35	nurse	30	here
A	Werre Kay—†	35	saleswoman	23	New York City
B	Stone David J	35	manufacturer	40	here
C	Jones George R	35	lawyer	62	"
D	Jones Helen B—†	35	housewife	56	"
E	Renaud Louise—†	35	housekeeper	61	28 Queensberry
F	Woestman Frederick O	35	engineer	35	8 Irvington
G	Woestman Marie—†	35	housewife	34	New York City
H	Gaskell Frances—†	35	musician	35	here
K	Horseman Ernest	35	photographer	38	"

7

Audubon Road—Continued

	Letter	Full Name	Res.	Occupation	Age	Reported Residence
	L	Frost Thomas	35	teacher	30	133 Peterboro
	M	Hannaford Catherine—†	51	housewife	36	48 Rutland sq
	N	Hannaford Frank	51	janitor	43	48 "
	O	Delcourt Lucile—†	51	musician	30	409 Hunt'n a
	P	Haywood Laura—†	51	stenographer	38	Somerville
	R	Haywood William W	51	engineer	39	"
	S	Fiedler Arthur	51	musician	29	10 Parker
	T	Weiner Hans J	51	"	39	14 Westland a
	U	Lazarus Charlotte—†	51	housewife	22	New York Cit
	V	Lazarus Murray	51	salesman	28	"
	W	Ohliger Arthur	51	foreman	29	New Jersey
	X	Ohliger Mary A—†	51	housewife	21	"
	Y	Gibson Hazel L—†	51	saleswoman	30	New Hampshire
	Z	Buckley Sallie E—†	51	clerk	30	here
	A	White Kathiuke—†	51	housewife	64	"
	B	Giddens Claire—†	51	nurse	23	"
	C	Shay Caroline A—†	51	teacher	40	"
	D	Hanson Myra H—†	51	housewife	65	"
	E	Exley Corinne E—†	51	"	21	Allston
	F	Exley Elmer F	51	mechanic	28	"
	G	Godsman Charles J	51	salesman	28	Newton
	K	Partridge Henry E	51	merchant	40	here
	L	Partridge Mildred C—†	51	housewife	38	"
	M	Morley Elsie R—†	51	nurse	32	"
	N	Sadler Marie E—†	51	"	36	"
	O	Anderson Gertrude M—†	51	housewife	32	"
	P	Anderson Robert L	51	accountant	36	"
	R	Crane Blanche M—†	51	housewife	40	"
	S	Crane Hazel E—†	51	teacher	24	"
	T	Crane Joseph B	51	salesman	21	"
	U	Akin Donald A	51	broker	23	109 Gainsbor
	V	Akin Maron M—†	51	housewife	23	109 "
	W	Reitmeyer Henry	51	waiter	34	Haverhill
	X	Favorite Calvin F	51	merchant	30	Philadelphia
	Y	Morgan Effie A—†	51	milliner	22	115 Norway
	Z	Woods Gladys M †	51	bookkeeper	26	50 Peterboro
	A	Kelley Gertrude †	51	forewoman	50	here
	B	Swett Muriel A †	51	housewife	27	"
	C	Swett Norman W	51	dentist	26	"
	D	Foster Nassau	51	salesman	27	Georgia
	E	Wadsworth Lincoln	51	"	28	West Campton N H

Audubon Road—Continued

F	Wadsworth Marion D—†	51	stenographer	27	West Campton N H
G	Bronner Augusta F—†	51	psychologist	40	here
H	Stern Elsie B—†	51	housewife	37	"
K	Stern Jacob L	51	manufacturer	51	"
L	Stern John L	51	merchant	51	"
M	Kellar Alice B—†	51	forewoman	56	"
N	Dow Edith—†	51	stenographer	27	115 Norway
O	Dow Frances E—†	51	housewife	46	115 "
R	Wortman Vlair A	51	buyer	37	111 "
S	Wortman Gladys D—†	51	stenographer	22	Canada
T	Wortman Henrietta E—†	51	housewife	32	111 Norway
U	Connors Angus	51	merchant	40	here
V	Collins Marguerite —†	51	editor	26	"
W	Newton Elsie J—†	51	housewife	30	"
X	Sullivan James	55	janitor	50	Waltham
Y	Taylor Robert	55	salesman	36	here
Z	Mills Nellie—†	55	saleswoman	31	"
A	Hoornbeek Jansen K	55	student	29	New York
B	Tooley Louise B—†	55	clerk	23	here
C	Hinckley Benjamin L	55	merchant	30	New York
D	Cole Amey B—†	55	housewife	35	Providence R I
E	Kirby Catherine F—†	55	"	25	Springfield
F	Kirby Maurice F	55	salesman	25	Marlboro
G	Brown Charles W	55	"	29	here
H	Timmons John H	55	druggist	49	Belmont
K	Collins Susie P—†	55	clerk	26	here
L	Prescott Etta F—†	55	housewife	53	"
M	Brown Max	55	salesman	55	51 Audubon rd
N	Batts John F	55	"	37	New York
O	Doherty Ceclia J —†	55	housewife	27	Cambridge
P	Bucher William	55	salesman	40	here
R	Dull Ione—†	55	student	23	Salt Lake City
S	Smith Florence F—†	55	housewife	45	50 Peterboro
T	Whitaker Bessie B—†	55	"	69	50 "
U	Sawyer Agnes —†	55	nurse	31	here
X	Clare Robert W	55	salesman	26	51 Audubon rd
Y	Tibbetts John F. jr	55	"	30	609 Col av
Z	Pearlstein Samuel H	55	merchant	35	New York
A	Driscoll Thomas J	55	printer	30	Hyde Park
B	Driscoll Ellen F—†	55	housewife	30	"
C	Fay Blanche—†	61	"	33	Brookline

Audubon Road—Continued

D	Fay William	61	painter	38	Brookline
E	Worth Gunhild —†	61	housewife	32	Dover
F	Worth Jacob	61	salesman	34	"
G	Manning Peter	61	machinist	23	297 Wash'n
H	Manning Rebecca—†	61	housewife	28	1015 Com av
K	O'Reilly Thomas	61	fireman	31	21 St Germain
L	Whitehead Alice F—†	61	accountant	39	19 Queensberry
N	Earle Bessie E—†	61	none	45	here
O	Levine Jennie—†	61	housewife	25	6 Collins
P	Levine Leo	61	dentist	26	6 "
R	Amos Annie P—†	61	housewife	32	St John N B
S	Amos John B	61	carpenter	32	Brookline
U	Young Harold A	61	salesman	32	Indiana
V	Young Helen —†	61	housewife	28	"
W	Clark David W	61	student	22	Cambridge
X	Clark Nellie K—†	61	none	45	"
Y	Weaver Henry E	61	manager	47	New York City
Z	Weaver Katherine—†	61	housewife	47	"
A	Nrofsky Abram	61	real estate	52	12 Harold
B	Nrofsky Lizzie —†	61	housewife	50	12 "
D	Gunder Bessie B—†	61	"	40	Indiana
E	Gunder Claude A	61	manager	50	"
F	Burnham George E	61	editor	41	541 Com av
G	Burnham Grace E —†	61	housewife	39	541 "
H	Hall Letitia M—†	61	"	60	Putnam Ct
L	McDonnell John J	61	salesman	39	Wollaston
M	McDonnell Josephine—†	61	housewife	41	"
O	Cooper Pauline —†	61	clerk	25	here
R	Bowler George P	65	real estate	46	"
S	Bowler Isabel †	65	housewife	30	"
T	McHenry Hilda —†	65	"	21	Amesbury
U	McHenry Lawrence C	65	student	23	Brookline
V	Sadowski John	65	clerk	38	here
W	Rabinowich Mary †	65	housewife	28	Sharon
X	Rabinowich Nathan	65	electrician	29	"
Y	Harris Annie—†	65	housewife	38	here
Z	Harris Samuel C	65	merchant	50	"
A	Rogers Elsie. †	65	clerk	24	"
B	Perrin Alice B —†	65	housewife	54	"
C	Perrin Frank L	65	editor	61	"
E	Nielson Alice †	65	none	30	"

Page.	Letter	FULL NAME.	Residence, April 1, 1924.	Occupation.	Supposed Age.	Reported Residence, April 1, 1923. Street and Number.

Audubon Road—Continued

F	Moulton Fred	65	manager	40	77 Audubon rd
G	Birchard Alonzo D	65	publisher	51	124 Peterboro
H	Birchard Lillian H—†	65	housewife	50	124 "
M	Granthen Anna E—†	65	music teacher	23	Hull
N	Granthen Charlotte—†	65	housewife	48	"
O	Granthen Frederick W	65	salesman	61	"
P	Granthen Frederick W	65	student	22	"
R	Granthen John P	65	clerk	20	"
S	Hall Earl P	65	manager	29	Keene N H
T	Hall Verra I—†	65	housewife	23	"
U	Gordon Lewis	65	clerk	28	Georgia
W	Fitzgerald Joan S—†	65	housewife	30	here
X	Fitzgerald Leonard I	65	salesman	40	"
Y	Marano Frank	65	designer	44	"
Z	Marano Katherine—†	65	"	41	"
A	Drennan Virginia L—†	65	housewife	32	"
C	Sevigny Henry J	65	conductor	40	"
D	Farnsworth Arlene—†	65	housewife	22	Framingham
E	Farnsworth Kenneth G	65	musician	23	"
A	Simpson Bernard	69	janitor	34	77 Audubon rd
B	Simpson Gertrude—†	69	housewife	34	77 "
C	Simpson John	69	janitor	28	England
D	Demar Gertrude—†	69	housewife	26	158 St Botolph
E	Demar Michael	69	salesman	31	158 "
F	Whritner Alice—†	69	none	28	New Jersey
G	Whritner Harry C	69	clerk	53	"
H	Whritner Lillie E—†	69	housewife	52	"
K	Harold Myrtle S—†	69	"	27	Pittsburgh Pa
L	Harold Raymond P	69	clerk	25	"
M	Rice Herbert E	69	chauffeur	22	Worcester
N	Beans Chester	69	clerk	30	728 Com av
O	Newman Stanley	69	chemist	33	here
P	McAllister Harriet L—†	69	practitioner	45	"
R	Sellers Gertrude—†	69	clerk	35	"
S	Patrick Dora H—†	69	dressmaker	36	"
T	Amos George H	69	salesman	31	"
U	Amos Minnie—†	69	housewife	30	"
V	Farrell Eugenie—†	69	teacher	40	418 Mass av
W	Dermett Kate—†	69	finisher	30	here
X	Hammond Bessie C—†	69	housewife	59	Arlington
Y	Hammond William C	69	clerk	63	"

Page.	Letter.	Full Name.	Residence, April 1, 1924.	Occupation.	Supposed Age.	Reported Residence, April 1, 1923. Street and Number.

Audubon Road—Continued

z	Smith Eleanor L—†	69	housewife	27	here
A	Smith Warren S	69	editor	38	"
B	Carnard Karolina W—†	69	housewife	31	Worcester
C	Carnard Laurence N	69	teacher	32	"
D	Duffy Josephine I—†	69	housewife	32	here
E	Duffy Lawrence P	69	salesman	35	"
F	Keohane Alice M—†	69	housewife	26	Lowell
G	Keohane Jeremiah J	69	postal clerk	27	"
H	Williams Amanda—†	69	housewife	27	here
K	Williams Harry	69	salesman	28	"
L	Isenberg Harry	69	"	42	"
N	Ramsdell Albert E	69	engineer	47	Melrose
O	Burton Minnie G B—†	69	none	55	here
P	Donahue Anna F—†	69	retired	61	"
R	Donahue Catherine H—†	69	clerk	31	"
S	McAllister James E	69	"	45	7 Harvard pl
T	Edes Grace S—†	69	housewife	31	here
U	Edes Omar K	69	clerk	31	"
V	Flood Agnes—†	73	nurse	35	Cambridge
W	Campbell John C	73	salesman	25	Maine
X	Coderan John H	73	grocer	50	here
Y	Collins Mary R—†	73	teacher	25	Cambridge
A	Byrms Zelda G—†	73	buyer	35	here
B	Rockett Earl B	73	salesman	47	"
C	Rockett Margaret—†	73	housewife	50	"
D	Eliot Avis M—†	73	"	30	"
E	Eliot Charles B	73	chemist	30	"
F	Conway William	73	salesman	35	Springfield
G	Williams Winifred M—†	73	secretary	50	here
K	Johnson Fred R	73	master mariner	45	"
L	Evans Ralph P	73	real estate	32	"
M	Miller Philip W	73	salesman	40	"
N	Lindsey William E	73	manager	30	"
O	Fisher William	73	salesman	30	Cambridge
P	Marsters Alice F—†	73	housewife	27	58 Ruskin rd
R	Marsters Russell E	73	accountant	24	58 "
U	Grinell George H	73	compositor	34	Providence R I
V	Brown Emma—†	73	tel operator	30	here
W	Cooper Gertrude—†	73	saleswoman	35	"
X	Winslow Vera—†	73	"	25	Chelsea
Y	Baker Margaret E—†	73	"	30	here

12

Audubon Road—Continued

	z	Daley Peter	77	janitor	39	1125 Com av
	A	Daley Susan F—†	77	housewife	38	1125 "
	B	Neilson Lorina J—†	77	practitioner	60	New York
	C	Neilson Ruby—†	77	musician	21	"
	E	Goodhue Charles F	77	shipper	32	Lynn
	F	Goodhue Marion—†	77	housewife	32	"
	G	McGevern Harry	77	agent	30	Rhode Island
	H	Hannaford Josephine S—†	77	stenographer	32	here
	K	Burke Lizzie—†	77	housewife	40	"
	L	Burke William F	77	salesman	45	"
	N	Higgins Edna F—†	77	secretary	49	"
	O	Wing Lenora B—†	77	nurse	31	"
	P	Hobart James O	77	salesman	44	"
	R	Dyer Clarence F	77	teacher	35	"
	S	McCormick James	77	manager	32	New Haven
	U	Guthrie Percy A	77	lawyer	45	here
	V	Bradford Phillip	77	salesman	38	"
	W	Berkowitz Abraham	77	"	37	"
	X	Berkowitz Ollie—†	77	housewife	32	"
	Y	Gill Millicent—†	77	accountant	25	85 Audubon rd
	Z	Bernard Andrew	77	student	22	here
	B	Sedgwick Alfred	77	accountant	28	Cambridge
	C	Sedgwick Mabel—†	77	housewife	24	
	D	Perret Charlotte—†	77	"	29	65 Westland av
	E	Perret Gustave	77	musician	37	65 "
	F	Stacy Theresa—†	77	saleswoman	40	here
	G	Emerson Charles M	77	manager	41	New Jersey
	H	Emerson Kathleen M—†	77	housewife	30	"
	K	Howard Charles	77	salesman	50	Cambridge
	L	Duren Henrietta—†	81	buyer	35	here
	M	Krisher Dorothy L—†	81	student	23	Ohio
	N	Krisher Georgia M—†	81	housekeeper	46	"
	O	Forsell Anna M—†	81	dressmaker	33	here
	P	Jordan Evelyn—†	81	housewife	25	"
	R	Jordan Gerald	81	druggist	30	"
	S	Reid David G	81	seedsman	35	"
	T	Reid Mary A—†	81	housewife	33	"
	V	Hawkes Mabel—†	81	saleswoman	25	Brookline
	X	Evans Grace—†	81	teacher	22	New Hampshire
	Y	Evans Mary—†	81	stenographer	24	78 St Stephen
	Z	Evans Ruth—†	81	bookkeeper	26	78 "

13

Audubon Road—Continued

A	Rhodes Ruth—†	81	student	21	Bellingham
B	Hurwitz Benjamin	81	merchant	31	here
B¹	Hurwitz Rose—†	81	housewife	28	"
C	Watson Sarah B—†	81	housekeeper	40	"
D	Perkins Catherine—†	81	saleswoman	40	"
E	Tilton Clifford	81	salesman	30	"
F	Granger Dudley M	81	agent	22	184 Marlboro
G	Granger Sara D—†	81	housewife	23	New York
K	Haskins Clyde W	81	manager	33	here
L	Haskins Florence—†	81	housewife	33	"
M	McKenzie Mary—†	81	saleswoman	35	"
B	Champlain L Anna—†	81	housewife	22	"
O	Champlain Orrin, jr	81	photographer	25	"
P	Powers Mary—†	81	nurse	35	"
R	Currier George H	81	artist	70	"
S	Calnan Mary—†	81	salesman	35	19 Queensberry
T	Harris Laura—†	81	factory worker	32	55 Astor
U	Russell Virginia—†	81	nurse	30	Medford
W	Freeman Charles R	85	manufacturer	24	here
X	Freeman Margery H—†	85	housewife	25	"
Y	Blakeley Celia F—†	85	"	59	98 Hemenway
Z	Blakeley Frederick F	85	manager	40	98 "
A	Blakeley Warren A	85	chauffeur	36	98 "
B	Lorber Bertha T—†	85	housewife	25	here
C	Lorber Herman J	85	manager	27	"
E	Pulaski Albert M	85	salesman	43	"
F	Pulaski Louise T—†	85	housewife	38	"
H	Keleher Anna G—†	85	"	49	"
K	Keleher William J	85	real estate	49	"
L	Hughes Walter	85	salesman	30	Brookline
M	Hawkins Vera—†	85	saleswoman	35	here
N	Thomas James M	85	U S N	35	Florida
O	Thomas Nellie—†	85	housewife	37	"
P	McBride Ella G—†	85	housekeeper	50	Springfield
R	McBride Marion S—†	85	student	20	"
T	Pope Marie—†	85	dressmaker	30	here
U	Wallace Charles	85	student	30	New York
V	Sawyer Alice—†	85	buyer	30	Newton
W	Waterman Charles	85	salesman	30	Brookline
X	Waterman Margaret—†	85	housewife	25	"
Y	Newton Genevieve—†	85	"	56	here

Audubon Road—Continued

	Full Name	Res.	Occupation	Age	Reported Residence
z	Newton William H	85	salesman	60	here
A	Gordon Carrie—†	85	housewife	42	"
B	Gordon George L	85	broker	43	"
c	Elkhuyson Juliet—†	85	teacher	30	28 Appleton
D	Osburn Margeret R—†	85	model	52	26 St Stephen
E	Joel Benjamin	85	salesman	50	Somerville
F	Copeland Gertrude—†	85	cashier	32	Cambridge
G	Vincent Annie—†	85	housekeeper	63	19 Queensberry
H	McIsaac John	85	salesman	45	here
K	Davee Catherine—†	85	clerk	50	New York
M	MacLeon Mary—†	89	nurse	48	434 E Fifth
N	Ward Katherine—†	89	clerk	36	434 "
P	Wing Angeline—†	89	housewife	24	Newton
R	Wing Paul W	89	chauffeur	25	"
v	Berson Anna B—†	89	housewife	47	Pennsylvania
w	Berson Samuel	89	cigarmaker	49	"
A	Bruce Earl M	89	bookkeeper	36	22 Ivy
B	Bruce Sarah H—†	89	housewife	37	22 "
D	Schwamb Addie—†	89	"	37	81 Audubon rd
E	Schwamb Gilbert J	89	agent	36	81 "
H	Morgan Sarah E—†	89	stenographer	50	420 Peterboro
P	Mahan John L	89	pharmacist	26	462 Hunt'n av
R	Mahan Nellie M—†	89	housewife	26	Revere
T	Devine Sarah J—†	89	supervisor	32	590 Newbury
s	Donavan Catherine—†	89	"	24	590 "
u	Donavan Josephine M—†	89	tel operator	22	590 "
v	Pickering John R	95	clerk	23	Brookline
w	Woodward Mildred—†	95	housewife	33	212 Hemenway
x	Woodward Walter H	95	janitor	33	212 "
z	Wartman Charles	95	salesman	23	New York
A	Wartman Grace—†	95	housewife	21	"
B	Dehinger Isolde—†	95	"	30	Brookline
c	Dehinger Walter	95	teacher	35	"
D	Hull Robert W	95	salesman	22	195 Audubon rd
E	Barber Harry	95	"	32	360 Walnut av
F	Barber Jessie—†	95	housewife	26	Newton
G	Kelley Elizabeth—†	95	"	35	39 Peterboro
K	Swift Dorothy C—†	95	bookkeeper	31	Brookline
L	Swift Frances—†	95	secretary	30	"
M	Nesge Alice—†	95	clerk	26	New York
o	Cooper Harry E	95	"	30	81 Audubon rd

Audubon Road—Continued

P	Jones Maurice	95	salesman	32	81 Audubon r
R	Farrell Catherine—†	95	nurse	21	Brookline
S	Kennedy Margaret—†	95	"	22	"
T	Barstow Berten	95	salesman	40	"
V	White Frank J	95	machinist	35	Waverley
W	Jones Edna—†	95	housewife	24	New York
X	Jones Reginald	95	salesman	34	"
Y	Carver James C	95	student	23	"
Z	Carver Violet—†	95	housewife	22	"
A	Coburn Lucile—†	95	none	28	96 Hemenway
B	Coburn Mary A—†	95	"	50	96 "
D	Murphy Frances—†	95	hairdresser	36	9 Hendry
E	Murphy Margaret—†	95	none	65	9 "
F	Freeman Gertrude E—†	95	housewife	20	Groton
G	Freeman Joseph F	95	clerk	25	"
H	MacLeod Ethel S—†	95	housewife	35	115 Norway
L	Collins Margaret—†	107	maid	33	here
M	Dolan Annie—†	107	"	27	"
N	Dolan Mary—†	107	"	21	"
O	Eastwood Edith M—†	107	nurse	30	"
P	Harris Margaret—†	107	"	29	"
R	Higgins Julia—†	107	maid	30	"
S	Houston Margaret—†	107	nurse	24	"
T	Johanson Fannie—†	107	"	27	"
U	Johanson Victoria—†	107	"	33	"
V	Magrath Alice L—†	107	superintendent	32	"
W	Williams John	107	janitor	40	"
X	Osterman Annie—†	111	housewife	42	60 Westland a
Y	Osterman Joseph T	111	manager	46	60 "
Z	O'Neil Charles	111	"	35	Medford
B	Robinson John	111	salesman	50	Brookline
C	Manning John J	111	"	45	Newton
D	Baldwin Frolice—†	111	teacher	26	65 Audubon r
E	Mirek Martin	111	salesman	29	New York
F	Brunhiller William	111	broker	35	Cambridge
G	Molner Terrence	111	salesman	30	Quincy
H	Rutheford Catherine—†	111	dressmaker	60	Belmont
K	Kane Lester	111	retired	48	25 Queensberry
L	Silver Marie—†	111	none	60	85 Audubon r
M	Scates Adeline—†	111	"	50	Brookline
N	Loring Alice—†	111	"	55	Medford

Audubon Road—Continued

o	Crosen Edward	111	salesman	30	51 Audubon rd
p	Rodgers Edward T	111	"	26	Newton
r	Walch Edward D	111	"	28	New York
s	Randall Samuel	111	dentist	50	Milton
t	Denlow George	111	salesman	27	New York
u	Epple Louis	111	secretary	47	132 Hemenway
w	Bucull Phillip	111	salesman	35	New York
x	White Leslie B	111	physician	26	Cambridge
y	Bailey Jennie—†	111	none	60	Brookline
z	Stanley Margaret—†	111	"	31	New York
a	Dyer Alice—†	111	"	38	Newton
b	Trifton Edith—†	111	"	40	Brookline
c	Reed Mary—†	111	teacher	45	51 Audubon rd
d	Burns Walter E	111	salesman	50	61 Westland av
e	Janvrin Katherine—†	111	dressmaker	38	98 Hemenway
g	Leardon Charles	111	salesman	40	115 "
h	Smith George	111	"	30	Dover
k	Smith Frank	111	"	40	Brookline
l	Clark Leila—†	111	none	37	New York
m	Smith Charles	111	teacher	37	Medford
n	Bowditch Thomas	111	salesman	60	80 Peterboro
o	Finqueneisel Anita—†	111	bookkeeper	35	16 Westland av
p	Draney Thomas	111	physician	45	New York
r	Hennessey Walter F	111	salesman	35	Somerville
s	Sawyer Billee—†	111	none	32	Brookline
t	Neptune Edgar	111	physician	26	115 Hemenway
u	Phelps George	111	manager	28	Maine
v	Lawrence Dorothy C—†	111	none	26	Brookline
w	Hazen Josephine—†	111	retired	55	Milton
x	Fochtmann Anna—†	125	housewife	60	50 Copeland
y	Fochtman Charles	125	janitor	56	50 "
z	Wolf Elizabeth—†	125	housewife	32	California
a	Wolf Maurice N	125	manager	44	"
b	Osgood Nathaniel	125	retired	36	Brookline
c	Thommen Clara—†	125	secretary	24	5 Ivy
d	Cuddy Gertrude R—†	125	housewife	28	Texas
e	Cuddy Thomas S	125	physician	34	435 Columbia rd
f	Hanks Mary L—†	125	housewife	21	Wisconsin
g	Hanks William V	125	student	21	"
k	McKendrick Margaret-†	125	housewife	24	Springfield
h	McKendrick Ralph	125	salesman	28	"

Audubon Road—Continued

L	McAlister Charles	125	manager	35	here
M	McAlister Kathleen—†	125	housewife	30	Paris
N	Wells Dorothy C—†	125	"	36	Falmouth
O	Wells Ray D	125	broker	35	"
P	Hanson John L	125	physician	32	1069 Boylstor
R	McFarlane Katherine L—†	125	housewife	42	37 Mt Vernoı
S	McFarlane Thomas J	125	agent	52	37 "
T	Kingsley Walter H	125	salesman	25	Newton
U	Hooley Alice R—†	125	stenographer	23	"
V	Hooley Gladys G—†	125	clerk	25	"
W	Hooley William S	125	plasterer	54	"
Y	Ziegel Anthony	125	druggist	35	98 Hemenwa
Z	Ziegel Janette K—†	125	housewife	33	98 "
B	Cowan Harold	125	salesman	26	Brookline
C	Gaglione Charles	125	barber	32	106 St Botolp
D	Adams Frank R	125	manager	56	Connecticut
E	Adams Mildred D—†	125	housewife	39	"
F	Desaulniers Annette—†	125	secretary	31	97 Waldeck
G	Desaulniers Laura—†	125	housekeeper	40	97 "
H	Wayland Eileen—†	125	stenographer	25	97 "
K	Benire Frank W	125	manager	30	Milton
L	Benire Marion W—†	125	housewife	23	"
M	Walsh Harriet M—†	125	compositor	32	24 Mallet
N	Painting Ellen C—†	125	nurse	45	1289 Com av
O	Thornton Frances G—†	125	secretary	35	73 Audubon
P	Sharver Cecil H	125	agent	34	Weymouth
R	Sharver Della A—†	125	housewife	32	"
S	Dickson Edmund C	125	druggist	30	Maine
T	Dickson Mildred M—†	125	housewife	28	"
U	Cannon Olive M—†	125	"	28	39 Glenville ı
V	Cannon William F	125	clerk	33	39 "
W	Owens Mary B—†	125	"	26	Brookline
X	Sheehan Dorothy—†	125	"	25	Wash'n D C
A	Cooke Harry	125	buyer	55	Brookline
B	Phillips Russell A	125	bookkeeper	29	71 Batavia
C	Ganley Arnold L	125	teacher	23	Wilmington
D	Ganley Loraine S—†	125	housewife	24	Waltham
E	Sammet George V	125	manufacturer	43	8 Irvington
F	Quinn Helen V—†	125	clerk	30	Cambridge
G	Smith Franklin H	125	"	27	1842 Beacon
H	Smith Ruth D—†	125	housewife	26	1842 "

Audubon Road—Continued

Letter.	FULL NAME.	Residence, April 1, 1921	Occupation.	Supposed Age.	Reported Residence, April 1, 1923. Street and Number.
K	Lawton Lewis H	125	engineer	42	Maine
L	Lawton Mercedes M—†	125	housewife	24	"
M	Clark John T	125	engineer	49	10 Kenmore
N	Clark Reynolds G	125	salesman	21	Cambridge
O	Pomerory George	125	"	28	Newton
P	Cornwall Florence —†	125	housewife	22	New York
R	Cornwall Lawrence	125	engineer	23	"
S	Blagdon Edmond C	125	salesman	25	Greenfield
T	Blagdon Helen—†	125	housewife	21	"
U	Bradford May—†	125	clerk	28	Watertown
V	Robison Clara—†	125	housewife	34	25 Peterboro
W	Robison Rulon	125	musician	35	25 "
X	Newston Gertrude—†	125	housekeeper	24	4 May
Y	Beach Harry S	125	salesman	40	Cambridge
Z	Clark Zaidee—†	125	housewife	45	10 Kenmore
A	Hill Annie—†	131	"	52	64 Charlesgate East
B	Hill William	131	janitor	53	64 "
C	Creehan Alice F—†	131	housewife	27	91 Kilmarnock
D	Creehan Joseph	131	agent	21	91 "
E	McMillen Sarah J—†	131	housekeeper	37	26 Hemenway
F	Matheson Christina—†	131	nurse	30	Newton
G	Burgess Frances M—†	131	"	38	Philadelphia
H	Flanders Marion S—†	131	truant officer	33	94 Chestnut
K	Trainor Agnes J—†	131	nurse	36	Oklahoma
L	Connolly Josephine—†	131	manicurist	28	Everett
N	Basile John	131	editor	40	New York
P	Noyes Carrie I—†	131	housewife	64	Somerville
R	Noyes George W	131	clerk	66	"
T	Roberts Malva—†	131	student	23	26 Museum rd
U	Shorey Dorothy—†	131	"	22	26 "
V	Hollenbeck Mary—†	131	clerk	30	Quincy
W	Rich Louis	131	manager	31	"
X	Sperry Simon	131	watchman	69	Cambridge
Y	Kasson Margaret—†	131	social worker	40	Brookline
A	Hargraves Lucille —†	131	artist	26	22 Ivy
B	Jerry Leila—†	131	buyer	40	Wisconsin
C	Anderson Charles J	131	manager	34	New Hampshire
D	Anderson Christie C—†	131	housewife	32	"
E	Strauss George	131	merchant	50	Brookline
F	Louloff Jean	131	salesman	30	Springfield
G	Fenno George A	131	"	35	Lawrence

Audubon Road—Continued

H	Innis Robert	131	salesman	35	Winchester
K	Danielson Selma W—†	131	saleswoman	40	Worcester
L	Mulfred Frances—†	131	housewife	32	New Jersey
M	Mulfred Harry C	131	salesman	43	"
O	King Violet—†	131	nurse	28	Cambridge
P	Nevers Marion—†	131	"	30	"
R	Austin Edwin	131	clerk	21	Philadelphia
S	Fickett Harvey	131	"	25	95 St Botolph
T	Macomber Frederick	131	student	22	Maine
W	Jordan Irma E—†	131	retired	60	115 Hemenway
X	Devine George L	131	dentist	30	546 Mass av
Y	Saunders John T	131	"	29	4 Haviland
Z	Gropp Helen—†	131	housewife	24	Brookline
A	Gropp Otto H	131	salesman	24	"
B	Davis Marcia E—†	131	housekeeper	48	56 Cliff
C	Kenney Jennie L—†	131	retired	51	320 Longwood av
E	Olsen Albert T	131	bookkeeper	51	61 Neponset av
F	Olsen Anna M—†	131	housewife	45	63 "
G	Riley Helen—†	131	saleswoman	35	Somerville
H	White Joseph S	131	physician	32	Brookline
K	White Edith H—†	131	housewife	21	Cape Cod
L	White Henry G S	131	salesman	26	New York
M	Prince Dorothy E—†	131	housewife	35	226 Bay State rd
N	Prince William P	131	broker	35	226 "
O	Gootzeit Henry	131	civil engineer	29	Chicago
P	Gootzeit Sarah—†	131	housewife	25	"
S	McDonald Frances—†	131	dressmaker	32	580 Com av
T	Poole Florence—†	131	artist	28	580 "
U	McCarter Horace	131	clerk	28	Medford
V	Calabrese Louis J	131	musician	25	Milford
W	Marshall Gwendolyn—†	131	saleswoman	35	Somerville
A	Richardson Harold T	137	janitor	40	here
B	Richardson Nellie T—†	137	housewife	34	"
C	McNamara Joseph B	137	manufacturer	32	Haverhill
D	McNamara Mary B—†	137	housewife	30	"
F	Hynes Frank J	137	salesman	28	Natick
G	Mitchell John A	137	"	29	Florida
L	France Albert F	137	U S A	29	New York
M	Swett Lena S—†	137	clerk	47	"
N	Marshall Florence—†	137	housewife	35	222 Hunt'n av
O	Marshall Robert W	137	salesman	39	222 "

Audubon Road—Continued

P	Virgin Lilian—†	137	clerk	22	Concord N H
R	Foster Ina—†	137	manicurist	30	Maine
S	Johnson Edith—†	137	tel operator	23	6 Colon
T	James Morison C	137	clerk	23	Maine
U	Yorke Russell H	137	salesman	21	"
W	Goldstein Molly—†	137	housewife	32	New York
Y	Stanley Robert L	137	salesman	41	"
Z	Stanley Sadie M—†	137	housewife	38	"
B	Denison Clare M—†	137	"	35	232 Bay State rd
C	Hagel Henry	137	salesman	30	New York
D	Hagel Mary M—†	137	housewife	30	"
F	Phillips Phoebe—†	137	student	21	Atlanta Ga
H	Pfau Alice B—†	137	housewife	59	1019 South
K	Pfau Louis P	137	collector	69	1019 "
L	Pfau William V	137	salesman	32	1019 "
N	Kedie Evelin G—†	137	housewife	35	Medford
O	Kedie Solon	137	salesman	58	"
P	Bloch Louis	137	merchant	35	407 Hunt'n av
S	Kirios Anglos	137	"	35	Lynn
W	Gillis Marion—†	137	nurse	21	Somerville
X	Hubert Dora—†	137	housewife	28	3 Charlotte
Y	Hubert Samuel	137	manufacturer	32	3 "
Z	Smith Rachel—†	137	housekeeper	61	3 "
A	Lussier Henry E	137	compositor	56	121 St Stephen
B	Currier Katie A—†	137	housekeeper	86	Medford
C	Martin Eva M—†	137	housewife	48	"
D	Lewis Ida—†	137	clerk	34	Brookline
E	Webb Mae—†	137	cashier	31	"
F	Crown Harry A	137	salesman	36	"
G	Crown Sybil A—†	137	housewife	45	"
H	Work Georgia E—†	137	bookkeeper	31	Cambridge
N	Davis George	137	salesman	30	N Adams
O	Davis Gladys—†	137	housewife	28	"
P	Brenninger Alfred W	137	salesman	43	Providence R I
R	Brenninger Mary E—†	137	housewife	37	"
S	Voprsal Joseph	137	student	31	143 Hemenway
T	Fisher Amelia B—†	137	housekeeper	70	21 Fairfield
U	Jacobson Jacob	137	U S N	29	New York
W	Boines Annie—†	143	housewife	76	183 Mass av
X	Boines John	143	janitor	74	183 "
Y	Miller Charles G	143	manager	27	Swampscott

Audubon Road—Continued

z	Miller Vera—†	143	housewife	26	Swampscott
A	Stiles Beatrice—†	143	"	25	Minneapolis
B	Stiles Harry L	143	student	25	45 Norway
D	Soutsos Paul	143	restaurateur	28	99 Mountfort
E	O'Shea Edward	143	salesman	39	33 Champney
F	O'Shea Olive—†	143	housewife	35	33 "
G	Clark George E	143	manager	45	23 St Lukes i
H	Clark Helen L—†	143	housewife	40	23 "
K	Wood Fanny A—†	143	bookkeeper	50	2161 Wash'n
L	Albee Lois—†	143	housekeeper	62	New Hampshire
M	Southard Lillian M—†	143	secretary	28	238 Hemenwa
N	Southard Madge T—†	143	housekeeper	53	238 "
O	Bruns Charles	143	compositor	25	Revere
P	Bruns Mollie—†	143	housewife	23	"
R	Poole James A	143	painter	30	Medford
S	Poole Lillian C—†	143	nurse	25	"
T	Sargent Albert A	143	salesman	32	Waban
U	Sargent Harriette—†	143	housewife	32	"
V	Hebden Mildred—†	143	secretary	28	Newtonville
W	Ericson Augustus	143	carpenter	42	27 Cliff
X	Dider Glenna—†	143	housewife	25	Ohio
Y	Dider Paul A	143	manufacturer	27	"
Z	Goldinger Rose D—†	143	housewife	26	Brookline
A	Goldinger Sidney H	143	lawyer	34	"
B	Davis Florence—†	143	housewife	48	Philadelphia
C	Davis William K	143	salesman	49	"
D	Salmi Helnie—†	143	housewife	29	Springfield
E	Salmi Vaino	143	accountant	29	"
F	King George T	143	brakeman	33	36 Glenville
G	King Ina T—†	143	housewife	24	36 "
H	Bartlett Emma—†	143	"	23	114 Hemenw
K	Bartlett Willard	143	salesman	23	114 "
L	MacAuley Gertrude—†	143	nurse	20	785 Hunt'na
M	MacAuley Mary—†	143	housekeeper	40	785 "
N	Farmer James G	143	electrician	40	1330 Com a
O	Farmer Kate—†	143	housewife	34	1330 "
P	Schultes Caroline—†	143	"	31	72 Peterboro
R	Schultes Henry J	143	salesman	31	72 "
S	Connell Lucy—†	143	housewife	27	Iowa
T	Connell Walter	143	student	32	"
U	Hammond Sarah B—†	143	saleswoman	55	Ohio

Audubon Road—Continued

v	Kirkpatrick Glen N—†	143	clerk	20	41 St Stephen
w	Wilson Alice C—†	143	housekeeper	30	41 "
y	Coulter Nan—†	143	instructor	34	51 Charlesgate East
z	Linehan James H	143	bookkeeper	37	Fall River
a	Linehan Margaret P—†	143	housewife	29	Lynn
b	Boyce Walter P	143	nurse	35	Georgia
c	Reisman George	143	musician	26	60 Fenway
d	Reisman Lillian—†	143	housewife	24	60 "
e	Davis Cornela—†	143	stenographer	20	Arlington
f	Fraser Alice P—†	143	dressmaker	28	Malden
g	Rogers Sarah P—†	143	secretary	36	81 Pinckney
h	Knieczna Mary—†	143	student	22	Lowell
k	Feinburg David	143	salesman	37	New York City
l	Callaghan William J, jr	143	manager	27	Arlington
m	Hopkins Eleanor C—†	143	housekeeper	30	Ohio
o	Flewelling Ford N	143	salesman	24	196 St Botolph
p	Fleweling Lola—†	143	housewife	23	196 "
r	Cullen Charles J	143	broker	25	40 Glendale
s	Cullen Mary—†	143	housekeeper	58	40 "
t	Barber Louise—†	143	teacher	27	78 Gainsboro
u	Settle Frances B—†	143	"	30	78 "
v	Richie Oliver H	143	salesman	29	Utah
w	Spencer Charlotte—†	143	housewife	21	E Haven Ct
x	Spencer Henry, jr	143	salesman	24	"
y	Pastene Albert A	143	physician	49	Brookline
z	Pastene Susie B—†	143	housewife	43	"
a	Strong Mary E—†	143	accountant	40	134 Hunt'n av
b	Murphy Lillian—†	149	housewife	26	here
c	Murphy Thomas	149	superintendent	26	"
d	Carson Charles	149	foreman	28	Wollaston
e	Carson Hattie—†	149	housewife	22	"
f	Robertson Mary—†	149	"	55	Berlin N H
g	Robertson Robert	149	president	55	"
h	Atkins Jessica—†	149	student	25	Watertown
k	Bridges Josephine—†	149	"	25	"
l	Campbell Dorothy—†	149	"	25	"
m	Gilman Esther—†	149	"	25	"
n	Pitman Maud E—†	149	housewife	32	here
o	Pitman Stanton E	149	salesman	35	"
p	MacFarlane Florence A–†	149	elevatorwoman	27	Arlington
r	Wetherhead Ada F—†	149	housekeeper	58	"

Audubon Road—Continued

	s	Walton Annie—†	149	secretary	35	here
	T	Harding Marion—†	149	stenographer	30	"
	U	Porter Adeline—†	149	bookkeeper	30	"
	V	Fleming Margaret—†	149	dietitian	29	Moline Ill
	W	Fleming Pauline—†	149	school teacher	23	Cambridge
	X	Champagne Anna—†	149	housewife	32	Revere
	Y	Champagne Arthur	149	mechanic	35	"
	Z	Crapo Arthur	149	manager	35	325 Hunt'n a'
	A	Cooper Isaac	149	tailor	30	here
	B	Perlman Jacob	149	packer	40	"
	C	Weiss Henry	149	manufacturer	50	"
	D	Genzono Jerry	149	cutter	30	"
	E	Green Elizabeth—†	149	housekeeper	65	"
	F	Snyder Marion—†	149	housewife	30	"
	G	Snyder Victor	149	salesman	35	"
	H	Henry Edith—†	149	milliner	30	"
	N	Kelley John	149	detective	45	"
	L	Kelley Mary—†	149	housewife	38	"
	M	Goldsmith Helen—†	149	"	40	"
	N	Goldsmith Wallace	149	cartoonist	50	"
	O	Lewis Hazel L—†	149	housewife	30	"
	P	Lewis Lester T	149	banker	32	"
	R	Whitely Carl T	149	salesman	30	"
	S	Whitely May T—†	149	housewife	30	"
	T	Eldred Annie T—†	149	saleswoman	27	102 Queensberry
	U	Eldred Everett G	149	salesman	30	102 "
	V	Bartlett Carl	149	chauffeur	27	here
	W	Bartlett Julia—†	149	housewife	25	"
	X	Bowen Anna—†	149	saleswoman	26	"
	Z	Chipman Carl H	151	accountant	57	Fairhaven
	B	Chipman Mable N—†	151	housewife	47	"
	D	Daley Margie—†	151	"	30	"
	E	Daley William S	151	electrician	35	"
	F	Tyler John	151	compositor	55	Salem
	G	Stone Dorothy—†	151	student	21	Iowa
	H	Wheeler Edna—†	151	"	22	California
	K	Meehan Ruth—†	151	housewife	35	Ohio
	L	Dickerson Hettie S—†	151	"	32	England
	M	Dickerson Philip S	151	agent	45	"
	N	Francois Jane—†	151	housewife	60	here
	O	Francois Laura V—†	151	school teacher	25	"

Audubon Road—Continued

R	Cacley Corneiluis	151	salesman	45	here
S	Peterson Mildred—†	151	student	22	Ohio
T	Vandewort Esther—†	151	"	25	Minnesota
U	Belue Pauline—†	151	housewife	35	here
V	Belue Robert J	151	musician	40	"
W	Hopper Alice—†	151	housewife	40	310 Hunt'n av
X	Hopper John W	151	manager	45	325 "
Z	Roberts Helen G—†	151	"	38	here
A	Walter Elizabeth—†	151	housekeeper	35	"
C	Calhoun Margaret—†	151	saleswoman	38	"
D	Peirce Wilmot G	151	student	21	Brookline
E	Leary Thomas	151	policeman	28	here
F	Smith James B	151	"	28	"
G	Sloan George	151	artist	50	"
H	DeGolyer Anthony	151	engineer	35	New York
K	DeGolyer Isabelle—†	151	housewife	23	"
L	Nelson John	151	automobiles	40	here
M	Shinn Delphine—†	151	housewife	40	"
N	Shinn Paul H	151	dentist	48	"
O	Murphy Catherine—†	191	housewife	27	Beverly
P	Murphy George	191	bookkeeper	34	"
R	Durfee George F	191	superintendent	46	Salem Vt
S	Durfee Mary—†	191	housewife	36	"
T	Raymond Grace—†	191	"	22	Somerville
U	Raymond Roy	191	dentist	26	"
W	Burrows Winslow	191	student	26	New York
X	Smith George W	191	"	26	"
Y	Thomas Joseph	191	real estate	62	Quincy
Z	Thomas Mabel—†	191	housewife	50	"
A	Russell Nellie—†	191	"	50	here
B	Russell Warren	191	real estate	56	"
C	Fenwick Harold	191	student	28	Worcester
D	Fenwick Rita—†	191	housewife	25	"
E	Gladwin Catherine—†	191	manicurist	36	here
F	Chaplin Rita—†	191	student	24	"
G	Scottil Adelaid—†	191	practitioner	43	"
H	Cummings Abbie—†	191	teacher	55	365 Newbury
N	Scott Gilbert	191	"	34	here
L	Scott Maud—†	191	housewife	22	"
M	Chase Carrie—†	191	"	30	"
N	Chase Milton	191	builder	46	"

Audubon Road—Continued

	Letter	Full Name	Residence	Occupation	Age	Reported Residence
	o	Heath Ellen—†	191	bookkeeper	46	here
	p	Donovan Cora—†	191	housewife	38	"
	r	Donovan Joseph	191	lawyer	48	"
	s	Fowler William	191	U S gov't	50	Franklin N H
	t	Booth Edwin	191	clergyman	26	here
	u	Burdett Amy F—†	195	housewife	38	"
	v	Burdett William F	195	banker	50	"
	w	Huber Edward G	195	physician	40	California
	x	Huber Frances M—†	195	housewife	40	"
	y	Morris Mabelle H—†	195	bookkeeper	36	here
	z	Holgate Nellie—†	195	housewife	60	Springfield
	A	Douglas Helen †	195	"	36	here
	B	Loevy Ignace	195	retired	50	"
	C	Loevy Katherine—†	195	housewife	35	"
	D	Parke Harriet M—†	195	"	47	"
	E	Parke Percy H	195	advertising	49	"
	G	Bacheler Pauline—†	195	bookkeeper	30	"
	H	Cummings Carrie—†	195	saleswoman	25	Norwood
	K	MacKenzie Mary J—†	195	retired	80	here
	L	Palmer Harry	195	clerk	52	New York
	M	Palmer Louise—†	195	housewife	36	"
	N	Woodworth Alice S—†	195	"	53	here
	O	Woodworth Henry E	195	broker	53	"
	P	Woodworth Herbert S	195	saleswoman	30	"
	R	Kneedler Anne C—†	195	housewife	25	"
	S	Kneedler Weir M	195	student	27	"
	T	Emerson Mary—†	195	bookeeper	40	Norwood
	U	Rosenberg David	195	banker	35	New York
	V	Trefley Grace—†	195	clerk	22	"
	W	Oakman Ada D—†	195	"	53	"
	X	Oakman Clara E—†	195	teacher	31	"
	Y	Muldoon Agnes—†	195	housewife	35	"
	Z	Muldoon Charles	195	salesman	37	"
	A	Wales Eva—†	195	housewife	40	"
	B	Wales Thomas	195	broker	53	"
	C	Lawson George	195	salesman	44	"
	D	Saunders Peter	195	painter	40	Chelsea
	E	Nelson Agnes—†	195	hairdresser	24	here
	F	Powell Thomas	199	janitor	34	"
	G	Paige Marie—†	199	teacher	30	Maine
	H	Stevenson James	199	student	27	Chicago Ill

Audubon Road—Continued

K	Stevenson Mary—†	199	housewife	22	Chicago Ill
L	Bowdoin Galvin	199	salesman	30	here
M	Bowdoin Grace—†	199	hairdresser	21	"
N	Perry Harold	199	mechanic	31	"
O	Parkes Clifton	199	civil engineer	42	"
P	Parkes Henrietta—†	199	housewife	30	"
S	Moore Alice—†	199	"	30	New York
T	Moore Michael	199	mechanic	34	"
U	Borgasian Tessie—†	199	housewife	50	here
V	Morrison Rebecca—†	199	saleswoman	33	Brockton
W	Slater George	199	carpenter	33	Chicago Ill
X	Cleveland Harold	199	decorator	35	here
Y	Cleveland Mary—†	199	housewife	32	"
Z	Blaisdale Carrie—†	199	"	38	Brookline
A	Dunlap Catherine—†	199	"	30	Cleveland
B	Dunlap George	199	carpenter	34	"
D	Neil Harris	199	bookkeeper	32	here
E	Neil Mary—†	199	hairdresser	26	"
F	Cahoon Ada—†	199	housewife	30	Brockton
G	Cahoon Raymond	199	clerk	34	"
K	Meredith Thomas	199	broker	42	Canada
L	Leary Gertrude—†	199	bookkeeper	35	here
M	Leary Thomas	199	nurse	38	"
N	Allen Elsie—†	199	"	30	Medford
O	Chandler Arnold	199	architect	38	here
P	Chandler Ina—†	199	manicurist	32	"
R	Jones Elsie—†	199	model	27	"
S	Jones William	199	student	31	"
T	Ryan Frances—†	199	saleswoman	30	Everett
U	Ryan Frank	199	chauffeur	34	"
V	Drew Mary A—†	203	housewife	36	29 Audubon rd
W	Drew Warren C	203	janitor	31	29 "
X	Luby Edith M—†	203	housewife	24	15 Buckminster
Y	Luby Frank W	203	salesman	26	15 "
Z	McClung Edgar	203	U S N	36	here
A	McClung Henriette—†	203	housewife	30	"
B	Pellerin Aurore—†	203	saleswoman	35	"
D	Hukill Edith V—†	203	housewife	21	"
E	Hukill Edwin M, jr	203	clerk	53	"
F	Hukill Edwin M	203	salesman	23	"
G	Hukill Isabel—†	203	housewife	65	"

Audubon Road—Continued

H	Lake Charlotte A —†	203	clerk	70	here
K	Lake Elva M—†	203	"	33	"
L	Chase Gladys M—†	203	housewife	31	Buffalo N Y
M	Chase Walter H	203	builder	32	"
N	Coughlan Dorothy S—†	203	clerk	23	Watertown
O	Coughlan Maude D—†	203	housekeeper	52	"
P	Stewart William J	203	inspector	31	here
R	Stewart Winifred R —†	203	housewife	28	"
S	Barry Eliu A—†	203	teacher	35	"
T	Rosan Elinor G—†	203	housewife	40	329 Mass av
U	Rosan Sterling D	203	broker	50	329 "
V	Webster Donald M	203	clerk	47	329 "
X	Chamberlain Henry L	203	student	22	Memphis Tenn
Y	Day Agnes F—†	203	housewife	27	here
Z	Day George J	203	manager	32	"
A	Munsie Malcolm L	203	clerk	24	"
B	Munsie Marjorie D —†	203	housewife	26	"
D	Smith Frances D—†	203	housekeeper	50	"
E	Smith Henriette R—†	203	accountant	40	"
F	Host Frank J	203	salesman	40	Everett
G	Albee Albert S	203	clerk	33	Albany N Y
H	Blaunelt Arthur D	203	salesman	28	here
K	Blaunelt Laura—†	203	housewife	28	"
L	Swan G Dewey	203	draughtsman	27	Madison Wis
M	Swan Mary F—†	203	housewife	25	Melrose
O	Malmberg Harold T	203	salesman	35	New York
P	Vanderwood Charles F	207	dentist	30	here
R	Vanderwood Edith M—†	207	housewife	30	"
S	MacMillan Alexander	207	physician	30	"
T	MacMillan Leslie H—†	207	housewife	33	"
U	Bird Anna M—†	207	"	31	Wash'n D C
V	Melcher Elizabeth B—†	207	"	27	Maine
W	Melcher Richmond L, jr	207	salesman	35	"
Y	Peace Alma F—†	207	housewife	52	226 Wren
Z	Peace Muriel—†	207	stenographer	24	226 "
A	Davis Mary G—†	207	retired	55	N Carolina
B	Morningstar Florence D-†	207	housewife	24	New York
C	Morningstar Robert P	207	salesman	32	"
D	Eldridge June S—†	207	housewife	46	158 Hemenway
E	Steele Marion M †	207	secretary	22	Webster
F	Beck Abigal S †	207	clerk	39	Marlboro

Audubon Road—Continued

G	Carver Rachel—†	207	housewife	33	Detroit Mich
H	Carver Samuel	207	merchant	40	"
K	Orrell Elsie B—†	207	writer	27	77 Audubon rd
L	Wheeler Mary B—†	207	student	26	China
M	Brewer Samuel	207	U S N	27	Maryland
N	Brewer Dorothy—†	207	housewife	28	"
O	Peace John T	207	insurance	53	226 Wren
P	Dillon Elizabeth A—†	207	collector	33	19 Audubon rd
S	Ludwig Richard B	207	insurance agent	22	Hanover N H
T	Ludwig Vena B—†	207	housewife	22	Cambridge
U	Lonnquest Alice—†	207	"	23	Florida
V	Lonnquest Theodore	207	U S N	30	"
X	Coonan Mary F—†	207	bookkeeper	36	here
Y	Maddocks H Ross	207	manager	32	Brookline
Z	McLeod Anna M—†	207	stenographer	42	here
D	Lincoln Ethel H—†	211	teacher	39	149 Audubon rd
E	Lincoln Fredrick H	211	merchant	45	149 "
F	Nosarian Martha—†	211	housewife	55	Cambridge
G	Nosarian Martha—†	211	teacher	23	"
H	Gargan Thomas J	211	salesman	41	here
K	Greenleaf Harriett—†	211	housewife	63	Cambridge
L	Greenleaf William H	211	manager	34	"
M	Underhill John L	211	broker	22	"
N	Underhill Marion G—†	211	housewife	23	"
P	Flint Helen F—†	211	retired	48	Weymouth
R	Shaughnessy John P	211	plumber	42	Cambridge
S	Shaughnessy Katherine—†	211	housewife	42	Florida
T	O'Brien Frances C—†	211	artist	28	here
V	Gifford Margaret G—†	211	housekeeper	59	"
W	Scott Harry J	211	salesman	40	Brookline
X	O'Hearn Adelaide—†	211	housewife	45	1391 Com av
Y	O'Hearn John B	211	manager	52	1391 "
Z	Brooks Helena—†	211	clerk	27	233 Charles
A	Mooney Mary—†	211	hairdresser	33	20 Queensberry
B	White James R	211	physician	35	New Zealand
C	White Katherine—†	211	housewife	38	"
D	Batchler Henry H	211	salesman	47	Indianapolis
E	Batchler Merrill H—†	211	housewife	36	"
F	Schmidt Clotilda—†	211	"	57	here
G	Smith Hedwig—†	211	stenographer	30	"
H	Benson Florence G—†	211	retired	47	"

Audubon Road—Continued

K	Wilson Caroline—†	219	teacher	27	Brookline
L	Wilson Elsie—†	219	stenographer	35	"
M	Wilson Olive—†	219	accountant	22	"
N	Chipman Edina—†	219	bookkeeper	36	Lexington
O	Chipman Gilbert S	219	druggist	45	"
P	Rockwood Marion—†	219	teacher	47	Cambridge
R	Barnes Elizabeth L—†	219	secretary	20	82 St Stephen
S	Gifford Marion L—†	219	student	23	76 Gainsboro
T	Godfrey Marcia M—†	219	secretary	20	76 "
U	Kenney Marjorie—†	219	"	22	1126 Boylston
V	Lamb Mary—†	219	housekeeper	39	Braintree
W	Possiell Johana A—†	219	retired	52	Brookline
X	Possiell Rakenius J	219	student	21	"
Y	Bowler Catherine—†	219	retired	60	Dedham
Z	Bowler Marion—†	219	clerk	35	"
A	Early Agnes—†	219	teacher	35	Newton
B	Chase Alice M—†	219	retired	63	Somerville
C	Tilly Edith M—†	219	geneologist	48	6 Walnut
D	Pidgean Hannah—†	219	retired	63	Canada
E	Pidgean Walter D	219	musician	26	Brookline
F	Eastman Harry M	219	manager	50	21 Leroy
G	Eastman Susan P—†	219	housewife	48	21 "
H	Collingwood Morton	219	lawyer	42	46 Charles
K	Graves Bertha M—†	219	bookkeeper	41	82 Peterboro
L	Hayden Katherine—†	219	housekeeper	34	331 Beacon
M	Watson James B	219	secretary	41	Belmont
N	Watson Marion L—†	219	housewife	34	"
O	Allured Mary J—†	219	retired	50	30 Hemenway
P	Bainbridge Rose A—†	219	typist	50	30 "
R	Loomis Harvey N	219	editor	59	124 Peterboro
S	Maney Ethnie C—†	219	retired	42	115 Hemenwa
T	Burchard Charles C	219	merchant	50	Brookline
U	Chenery Fanny—†	219	retired	63	Terrace Falls
V	Perrin Irene—†	219	student	26	124 Gainsbor
W	Salmon Henry	219	"	20	Cambridge
X	Salmon Lucretia—†	219	teacher	27	124 Gainsbor
Y	Eisemann Maurice	223	merchant	38	119 Hemenwa
Z	Murray John J	223	salesman	34	Cambridge
A	Halberle Robert J	223	manager	45	41 Westbourn
B	Breed Arthur M	223	lawyer	50	Arlington
C	Breed Sarah S—†	223	housewife	50	"

Audubon Road—Continued

D	Eden Bernice H—†	223	chemist	27	Holliston
E	Eden Percy E	223	clerk	29	Newton
F	Ponulet John C	223	manager	34	Rhode Island
G	Cole Helena M—†	223	housewife	63	1706 Com av
H	Matheson Orpha—†	223	librarian	24	Cambridge
K	Phelan Mary—†	223	buyer	24	"
L	Meachen John W	223	physician	44	80 Peterboro
M	DeVolt Cora—†	223	dressmaker	40	Iowa
N	Somers Irene—†	223	teacher	25	Maine
O	Harty Corinne—†	223	housewife	24	144 Hemenway
P	Harty John J	223	engineer	34	144 "
R	Smith Mabel R—†	223	student	41	1409 Com av
S	Forbes Arthur	223	manager	35	146 Boylston
T	Povey Dorothy J—†	223	saleswoman	25	38 Hemenway
U	Putnam Eva—†	223	"	25	38 "
W	Arnold George B	223	operator	42	40 St Stephen
X	Grout Rosanna—†	223	buyer	24	Cambridge
Y	Young Anna—†	223	clerk	28	"
Z	Catlin Ruth—†	223	librarian	30	Newton
B	Wright Betty—†	227	saleswoman	34	111 Queensberry
C	Rothgeb Mabel R—†	227	housewife	35	Philadelphia
D	Rothgeb William C	227	manager	37	"
E	Berry Katherine—†	227	clerk	23	Dedham
F	Burdon Adelaide P—†	227	housewife	75	20 Glenville av
G	Burdon Marion L H—†	227	teacher	47	20 "
H	Jones Frank	227	physician	32	Brookline
K	Sparrell Elizabeth—†	227	housewife	34	24 Englewood av
L	Pratt Ella—†	227	"	52	Berkshire
M	Higgins Mary E—†	227	stenographer	24	24 St Mary's
N	Montgomery Achsah—†	227	housewife	43	390 Com av
O	Cushing Alice C—†	227	retired	62	92 Claybourne
P	Cushing Alice E—†	227	housekeeper	34	92 "
R	Quinn Mary M—†	227	nurse	28	California
S	Fairweather Grace F—†	227	housewife	39	Newton
T	Mitchel James J	227	salesman	29	81 Westland av
U	Mitchel Mary—†	227	housewife	24	81 "
V	Prowse Dorothy—†	227	stenographer	24	48 Astor
W	Hall Hellen L—†	227	housewife	25	Connecticut
X	Hall Raymond J	227	salesman	32	29 Charlesgate West
Y	Connolly Blanche F—†	227	manicurist	30	Malden
A	Shepard Henrietta—†	227	saleswoman	38	133 Peterboro

Page.	Letter.	FULL NAME.	Residence, April 1, 1924.	Occupation.	Supposed Age.	Reported Residence, April 1, 1923. Street and Number.

Audubon Road—Continued

	B	Macdonald Ruby—†	227	housewife	28	46 Adams
	C	Kelly Harry	227	brakeman	35	New Jersey
	D	Kelly Hellen—†	227	teacher	32	"

Boylston Street

	A	O'Reilley Jessie A—†	1175	housewife	30	Braintree
	B	Hess Katie S—†	1175	"	67	Brookline
	C	Horner Ethel M—†	1175	"	42	"
	D	Horner Robert H	1175	retired	44	"
	E	Weegar Harry E	1175	salesman	35	Maine
	F	Soucy Earnest	1175	"	38	10 Kenmore
	F¹	Soucy Joseph	1175	"	35	10 "
	G	Englehart Anna—†	1175	student	25	Kentucky
	H	Raymond George A	1175	dentist	29	Watertown
	K	Hersey Dwight	1175	manager	45	Cambridge
	N	Adams Anna—†	1175	student	20	"
	O	Mosher Mary—†	1175	"	20	S Carolina
	P	Jacobs Emily—†	1175	housewife	45	Newton
	U	Dove Alice T—†	1175	secretary	37	Melrose
	V	Donovan Mary—†	1175	school teacher	50	Newton
	X	Nash Abbie—†	1175	housewife	60	Malden
	Z	Spector Benjamin	1175	physician	30	69 Gainsboro
	A	Spector Bertha—†	1175	housewife	29	69 "
	C	Bullwinkle Richard	1175	mechanic	33	407 Hunt'n av
	E	Converse Agnes M—†	1175	real estate	35	Brookline
	F	Glendennin Martha A—†	1175	housewife	34	Maryland
	G	Lynch Mary—†	1175	saleswoman	45	Revere
	K	Scharton Julia—†	1175	housewife	37	54 Charlesgate
	L	Thom Florence L—†	1175	"	55	New Hampshire
	M	Lamb Edward	1175	manager	34	98 Bowdoin
	O	Sugarman Alice—†	1175	housewife	30	New York
	R	Dennis John	1175	student	26	"
	S	Crowley Grace A—†	1175	housewife	30	Florida
	T	Crowley Wallace	1175	lawyer	32	Brookline
	V	Zaler Rosanne—†	1175	clerk	36	266 Mass av
	X	Haynes Velma—†	1175	nurse	35	Brookline
	Y	Stevens Ruby—†	1175	"	30	"
	Z	Coyle Irving	1175	U S N	50	"
	A	Clark Annetta—†	1175	storekeeper	46	"

Boylston Street—Continued

B	Jordan Charlotte—†	1175	salesman	30	Revere
c	Kratt Dorothy—†	1175	student	23	1A Ivy
D	Kratt Hilda—†	1175	housewife	25	111 Norway
F	Winsor Bancroft	1175	salesman	38	New Bedford
G	Dowling Mark T	1175	"	45	New York
H	Southland Alice T—†	1175	housewife	62	64 Hemenway
K	Southland Orton L	1175	musician	70	64 "
L	Suydan Minnie—†	1175	stenographer	35	New York
N	Orton Lyman	1179	student	25	Cambridge
O	Holmberg Jeanette D–†	1179	real estate	48	"
P	Holmberg John F	1179	bookkeeper	50	"
R	Galligan Mary—†	1179	clerk	35	Randolph
S	Sadick Dorothy—†	1179	manicurist	33	Maine
T	Hayward Elizabeth—†	1179	housewife	27	Fitchburg
U	Hayward Roger	1179	draughtsman	25	"
V	Pfluger Sidney S	1179	salesman	30	New Jersey
W	Abbott Albert L	1179	"	27	New Hampshire
X	Greenwood Charles W	1179	"	20	"
Y	Leighton Philip H	1179	"	25	"
Z	Leighton Richard A	1179	student	23	83 Newbury
A	Lindsay Herbert	1179	mechanic	22	New Hampshire
B	Mahoney Joseph L	1179	student	23	Nebraska
C	O'Neil Frank D	1179	"	22	349 Com av
D	O'Neil Mary A—†	1179	housewife	45	Chicago Ill
E	O'Neil Walter G	1179	student	20	New Hampshire
G	Newton Minnie E—†	1179	housewife	41	Connecticut
H	Morehead William	1179	salesman	50	New York
K	Jones Arron E	1179	U S A	34	Wash'n D C
L	Edgecomb Catherine—†	1179	student	22	Maine
M	Evans George H	1179	manager	54	394 Mass av
N	Evans Katie P—†	1179	housewife	52	394 "
O	Gubanow Eugene	1179	teacher	27	Paris
P	Gubanow Natalie—†	1179	housewife	27	Europe
S	Quilley Thomas	1179	promotor	38	Newton
T	Leonard Benjamin F	1179	salesman	29	Medford
V	Barton Ida M—†	1179	housewife	37	455 Col av
W	Blaisdell Elma—†	1179	teacher	28	Maine
X	Larson Bengt H	1179	master mariner	37	Connecticut
Y	Larson Elizabeth M—†	1179	housewife	33	"
A	Hunter Elizabeth—†	1179	cashier	37	360 Riverway
B	Chapin Florence D—†	1179	housekeeper	36	Cambridge

Boylston Street—Continued

c	Hewitt Dorothy—†	1179	editress	25	Cambridge
E	Gamage Irwing E	1179	merchant	47	Newton
F	Davis Sadie—†	1179	housewife	40	New York
G	Crowson Fred F	1179	conductor	53	Vermont
H	Crowson Louise C—†	1179	housewife	43	"
L	Kennedy Emma—†	1179	"	45	Kentucky
M	Hart Edna—†	1179	"	23	Maine
N	Hart Vernon L	1179	banker	23	"
O	Hadlock Russell S	1179	salesman	23	Whitman
P	Hill Thomas M	1179	student	22	305 Bay State rd
R	Hampton Arthur C	1179	"	22	621 Com av
S	Nolte John O	1179	clerk	21	Florida
T	Bushman Victor	1179	salesman	35	New York
V	Richardson Jane R—†	1179	actress	34	"
X	Shipley John	1179	salesman	38	"
Y	Kennedy Mildred—†	1179	housekeeper	40	Concord
Z	Lyon George I	1179	superintendent	58	23 Westland av
A	Lyon Janet—†	1179	housewife	59	23 "
B	Davidson Edward F	1179	salesman	38	Connecticut
C	Morse Catherine—†	1179	clerk	35	Cambridge
E	Jennison Fannie—†	1179	school teacher	28	Framingham
G	Rideout Ezra M	1179	real estate	52	98 Hemenway
K	Henry William J	1185	janitor	46	1082 Com av
L	McEvoy May—†	1185	real estate	32	Somerville
M	Freeman Sadie—†	1185	saleswoman	34	Rhode Island
N	Davis Helen A—†	1185	housekeeper	38	26 Newbury
O	Davis Perley	1185	chauffeur	35	26 "
R	Hall Florence V—†	1185	saleswoman	31	133 Peterboro
S	Sears Gertrude E—†	1185	housewife	40	Weymouth
T	Sears John E	1185	banker	42	"
W	Best Gertrude M—†	1185	manager	30	133 Peterboro
X	Brewer Perley A	1185	"	36	1504 Com av
Y	Brewer Wilma S—†	1185	housewife	32	1504 "
D	Zilch George J	1185	chauffeur	42	147 Hemenway
E	Zilch Mary E—†	1185	housewife	39	147 "
G	Sanborn Anndora N—†	1185	housekeeper	31	1218 Com av
H	Sanborn James O	1185	retired	32	1218 "
K	Vanwick Herbert L	1185	manager	38	Connecticut
M	Hamlin Russell E	1185	broker	33	Newton
N	Sample Beatrice E—†	1185	student	26	Vermont
O	Amos George H	1185	salesman	31	69 Audubon rd

Boylston Street — Continued

P	Amos Minnie E —†	1185	housewife	30	69 Audubon rd
S	Ring Julia I— †	1185	bookkeeper	37	78 Peterboro
A	Fain Florence—†	1185	student	32	Georgia
B	Peherson Freida—†	1185	clerk	30	Cambridge
C	Murrow Marvin H	1185	salesman	47	8 Irvington
G	Burns Gladys—†	1185	housewife	23	73 Audubon rd
H	Burns Harry	1185	real estate	36	73 "
K	Helliwall Porter	1185	salesman	33	56 E Newton
L	Wennerlof Cecelia—†	1185	instructor	35	356 Com av
M	Benedict Cornelia G—†	1185	housewife	53	26 Evans way
N	Benedict Francis G	1185	physiologist	53	26 "
P	Novak John F	1185	manager	29	Brookline
R	Brothers George W	1185	engineer	24	Pennsylvania
S	Brothers Roselyne —†	1185	housewife	20	"
T	Collins Anna—†	1185	broker	30	Brookline
V	Wright Florence E—†	1185	housewife	32	50 Ivy
U	Wright George L	1185	clerk	35	50 "
W	Baldwin Hubert L	1185	reporter	30	Winthrop
X	DeCoucey Edith M—†	1185	housewife	26	New York
Y	Okerson Elizabeth—†	1185	clerk	35	356 Com av
A	Ware Eva—†	1191	housewife	45	Framingham
B	Ware Francis M	1191	retired	67	Lenox
C	Ware Robert	1191	student	25	Framingham
D	Mahoney Katherine—†	1191	tel operator	37	460 Hunt'n av
E	Triantafel Nichlos	1191	manager	32	40 Falmouth
L	King Christopher	1191	chauffeur	25	40 Porter
M	King Helen K—†	1191	housewife	28	40 "
N	Welch Anna A—†	1191	"	31	498 Com av
O	Welch Edward J	1191	florist	31	498 "
R	Fitzpatrick Rose M—†	1191	bookkeeper	22	New York
S	Seibert George R	1191	architect	27	"
T	Seibert Mildred —†	1191	housewife	27	"
U	Blocklock Ella F—†	1191	"	62	170 Hunt'n av
V	Blocklock Eugene	1191	agent	63	170 "
Y	Joseph William	1191	merchant	34	Revere
Z	Joseph Alice—†	1191	dressmaker	32	"
A	Joseph Jennie—†	1191	"	36	"
A¹	Joseph William	1191	merchant	34	"
B	Fitzpatrick Agnes G—†	1191	housewife	25	New York
C	Wier Anna M—†	1191	"	42	Washington
D	Wier Joseph S	1191	U S N	39	"

Boylston Street—Continued

F	Altekamp Adela—†	1191	writer	23	52 Charlesgate E
K	MacKinnon Alice F—†	1191	nurse	31	Swampscott
V	Donnell Carry S—†	1191	housekeeper	57	536 Com av
W	Furry Lewis	1191	vocalist	34	536 "
A	Urbon Emma—†	1191	housewife	50	1079 Boylston
D	Harding Lillian B—†	1191	agent	30	New York
E	Halsey Frank J	1191	salesman	37	Utah
F	Rudy Dorothy—†	1191	nurse	24	New York
G	Hossett Joseph J	1191	clerk	38	Quincy

Fullerton Street

A	Cutler Harry	28	fruit	42	here
B	Cutler Margaret—†	28	housewife	42	"
C	Chutjian Anna—†	30	"	35	"
D	Chutjian Dickron	30	rug dealer	30	"
E	Stavropolus Arthur	32	clerk	49	"
F	Stavropolus Jane—†	32	housewife	44	"
G	Stavropolus William	32	student	21	"

Jersey Street

D	Pike Edith I—†	107	manager	50	here
E	Pike Keneth	107	electrician	25	"
F	Witham Charles W	107	merchant	72	"
G	Witham Hattie E—†	107	housewife	68	"
H	Mooney Anna—†	107	"	45	"
K	Mooney George	107	secretary	40	"
L	Manning Clarice—†	107	"	22	Newton
M	Alley Gerard	107	professor	45	Chelsea
N	Arthur Edgar	107	accountant	36	here
O	Arthur Lina—†	107	housewife	39	"
P	Bowers Charles	107	merchant	38	"
R	Bowers Ruth—†	107	housewife	38	"
S	Kelly Madeline—†	107	seamstress	40	Somerville
T	Moran Eva—†	107	"	42	"
U	Framphton Gucia—†	107	housewife	40	163 Hemenw
V	Framphton Lionel	107	upholsterer	40	163 "
W	Dickenson Porter	107	student	24	209 Bay State rd

Jersey Street—Continued

Letter.	Full Name.	Residence	Occupation	Age	Reported Residence
x	Sharp May L—†	107	none	58	here
y	Landry Daniel A	107	clerk	30	Gloucester
z	MacDonald Sumner B	107	collector	28	California
a	Parker Roland H	107	clerk	27	Cuba
b	Estes Louise—†	107	none	25	here
c	Hill George H	107	manager	30	"
d	Hill Helen—†	107	housewife	24	"
e	Shepard Edith—†	107	none	41	55 Queensberry
f	Konkoly Annie—†	107	merchant	50	454 Centre
g	Konkoly Julia—†	107	clerk	21	454 "
h	Bender Stephen R	107	accountant	28	here
k	Hawes Emma J—†	107	housewife	25	"
l	Hawes Ralph	107	student	28	"
m	Catterall Mary—†	107	social worker	25	829 Beacon
n	Galt Mabel M—†	107	"	23	93 Tyler
o	Starbard Aarron C	108	janitor	63	1407 Com av
p	Starbard Katie L—†	108	housewife	57	1407 "
r	Hillstrom Albert	108	salesman	43	here
s	Hillstrom Henretta—†	108	housewife	42	"
t	Flaherty Lena—†	108	housekeeper	30	"
u	Haines James	108	agent	40	6 Warren
v	Haines Jeanette—†	108	housewife	30	here
w	Kirkpatrick Albert	108	packer	50	"
x	Kirkpatrick Bessie—†	108	housewife	40	"
y	Dempsey Mary—†	108	bookkeeper	50	"
z	Hunter Hellen—†	108	clerk	50	"
a	Lane Benjamin	108	salesman	66	"
b	Lane Mable F—†	108	housewife	64	"
c	Milholland Hellen R—†	108	"	34	New York
d	Milholland Robert J	108	salesman	37	"
e	Chase Lucy—†	108	retired	65	Melrose
f	Broughton Harry J	108	baker	40	here
g	Broughton Mary—†	108	housekeeper	35	"
h	Saunders Eva—†	108	retired	60	Waltham
k	Hamilton Mable—†	108	bookkeeper	22	Arlington
l	Nelson Lena—†	108	housekeeper	50	"
m	Bean Emily F—†	108	housewife	58	Somerville
n	Bean Marcus C	108	superintendent	64	"
o	Tufts Elizabeth C—†	108	housewife	26	here
p	Tufts William	108	salesman	28	"
r	Vinal Eva M—†	108	housewife	62	"

Jersey Street—Continued

s	Vinal George W	108	treasurer	58	here
T	Vinal Harold	108	editor	33	"
U	Williams Susan E—†	108	musician	24	80 Peterboro
V	Williams Susan E—†	108	housekeeper	45	80 "
W	Huntington Frank J	108	physician	30	Cambridge
X	Weeks Josiah W	108	"	30	"
Y	Clark Edward A L	111	teamster	55	here
Z	Clark Frank T	111	janitor	26	"
A	Clark Mary E—†	111	housewife	25	"
B	Clark Mary F—†	111	housemaid	55	"
C	Davol Lulu M—†	111	housekeeper	32	102 Queensberry
D	Osgood Florence M—†	111	housewife	47	here
E	Osgood Frederick M	111	salesman	57	"
F	Osgood Leslie S	111	clerk	31	"
G	Emerson Ada—†	111	saleswoman	25	"
H	Emerson Ralph	111	machinist	40	"
K	LaBlanc Mary—†	111	stenographer	23	Arlington
L	Slipp Ella—†	111	bookkeeper	30	here
M	Redican Nellie—†	111	tel operator	35	95 Waldeck
N	White Barney F	111	policeman	35	here
O	Beckwith Myron	111	secretary	27	136 Warren
P	Casteen Anna M—†	111	"	35	here
R	Downs Bessie—†	111	librarian	31	"
S	Johnson Elsie—†	111	nurse	25	"
T	McCarthy John P	111	lawyer	54	"
U	McCarthy Mary E—†	111	housewife	50	"
V	Campbell Grace E—†	111	"	47	"
W	Campbell Robert B	111	salesman	44	"
X	Hussey Anna—†	111	housewife	40	"
Y	Hussey Fred	111	shipper	60	"
Z	Driscoll Florence—†	111	school teacher	37	"
A	Sullivan Ida J—†	111	housewife	61	"
C	Upham Marion—†	111	"	30	Medford
B	Upham Munroe	111	bookkeeper	45	"
D	Wexler Isador	111	student	27	40 St Stephe
E	Wexler Minerva—†	111	housewife	36	382 Riverwa
F	Eck Arthur F	111	manager	22	84 Shepton
G	Eck Edith E—†	111	stenographer	20	Chelsea
H	Eastman Helen P—†	111	secretary	61	here
K	Stuart Charlotte B—†	111	"	35	"
L	Millett Anna—†	111	waitress	25	"

Jersey Street—Continued

M	Sands Lera—†	111	bookkeeper	35	here
N	Jones James L	112	student	31	"
O	Jones Marie—†	112	housewife	29	"
P	McDonald Allen J	112	dentist	48	"
R	McDonald Margaret—†	112	housewife	42	"
S	Wilkinson Georgiana—†	112	retired	50	"
T	Graham Arthur A	112	salesman	45	"
U	Rice Dorothy F—†	112	housewife	23	"
V	Rice Forrest D	112	chauffeur	25	"
W	Suffa George A	112	physician	66	"
X	Suffa Magrett A—†	112	housewife	64	"
Y	Tripp Bertha G—†	112	clerk	31	"
Z	Tripp Hellen J—†	112	secretary	26	"
A	Friese Hurbert C	112	electrician	34	27 Hancock
B	Friese Margaret A—†	112	housewife	36	27 "
C	Ladd Henry D. jr	112	real estate	28	here
D	Ladd Marie—†	112	housewife	23	"
E	Prior Fred V	112	merchant	60	"
F	Prior Jessie—†	112	housewife	45	"
H	Foram Fannie—†	112	nurse	25	Cambridge
K	Harvey Mary—†	112	"	30	"
L	Hallahan Ramond F	112	clerk	28	here
M	Hallahan Robert C	112	manager	38	"
N	Rupert Harold B	112	salesman	28	Vermont
O	Rupert Ramond L	112	"	26	"
P	Codding Isabel—†	112	housewife	46	here
R	Codding Joseph A	112	manager	44	"
S	Rogers Martha—†	112	bookkeeper	37	"
T	Carrigan Loretta—†	112	buyer	31	"

Kilmarnock Street

N	Lue King	73	laundryman	60	Cambridge
X	Whiting Charles A	91	clerk	32	here
Y	Gilson Elizabeth M—†	91	"	36	"
Z	Brownell Beulah O—†	91	stenographer	35	Melrose
A	Rogers Rebecca—†	91	"	42	here
B	Keiger Ida M—†	91	teacher	38	19 Queensberry
C	Talty Harry	91	lawyer	40	Malden

Page.	Letter.	FULL NAME.	Residence, April 1, 1924.	Occupation.	Supposed Age.	Reported Residence, April 1, 1923. Street and Number.

Kilmarnock Street—Continued

	D	Miller Beulah—†	91	housewife	28	Somerville
	E	Miller Winfred E	91	salesman	36	"
	F	MacDonald Annie C—†	91	clerk	37	here
	G	Dow Cynthia—†	91	none	50	"
	H	Dow Norma E—†	91	stenographer	30	"
	K	Gorman Dorothy—†	91	housewife	25	"
	L	Gorman Robert O	91	manager	30	"
	M	Kinlin Francis T	91	accountant	29	"
	N	Kinlin Georgina—†	91	housewife	24	"
	O	Walworth Madaline—†	91	"	25	Hartford Ct
	P	Walworth Walter F	91	teacher	31	"
	R	Lans Helen—†	91	housewife	36	here
	S	Lans John E	91	salesman	38	"
	T	Ricker Le Roy S	91	clerk	36	40 Queens' erry
	U	Marengo Elvira—†	91	housewife	25	Canada
	V	Marengo Maro	91	manager	35	"
	W	Rent Florence E—†	91	housewife	35	here

Peterborough Street

	A	Brown Norah—†	1	nurse	30	101 Mountfort
	B	Klimas Magdelane—†	1	"	29	98 Hunt'n av
	C	Foster Marie—†	1	stenographer	22	124 Peterboro
	D	Miranda Michael	1	salesman	30	New York City
	E	Miranda Mollie—†	1	housewife	26	25 Queens' erry
	F	Maloney Joseph F	1	broker	34	19 "
	G	Maloney Margurite M—†	1	housewife	31	19 "
	H	Polson Robert P	1	salesman	23	S Weymouth
	K	Armstrong Beatrice—†	1	dressmaker	45	59 Westland av
	L	French John T	1	salesman	30	Newton
	M	French Ruth I—†	1	housewife	26	Chicago
	N	Leavitt Clara—†	1	vocal teacher	38	94 Queensberry
	O	Lamb Marion E—†	1	bacteriologist	27	59 Westland av
	P	Lamb Mary A—†	1	housewife	63	59 "
	S	Isen Samuel A	1	musician	23	New York
	T	Webber Max.	1	antiques	30	29 Queensberry
	U	Charm Hannah—†	1	housewife	29	54 Clifford
	V	Charm Max J	1	electrician	39	54 "
	W	Doyle Mary T—†	1	secretary	32	Detroit

Peterborough Street—Continued

x	Childs Alice M—†	1	houseworker	64	590 Newbury
y	Childs Cynthia N—†	1	nurse	31	590 "
z	Childs Harold B	1	chauffeur	29	590 "
A	Bowen Caroline W—†	1	manager	47	76 Peterboro
B	Loy Mabel—†	1	buyer	42	18 Argyle
c	Sawyer Helen N—†	1	housewife	21	456 Benningt'n
D	Sawyer Robert B	1	testman	21	74 Westland av
E	Szepesi Alma—†	1	housewife	33	New York City
F	Szepesi Eugene	1	engineer	43	"
H	Morris George E	1	clerk	43	Providence R I
K	Morris Josephine A—†	1	housewife	36	"
L	Grant Harry H	1	salesman	30	Medford
M	Jouamnet Paul C	1	"	25	454 Hunt'n av
O	Bartlett Doris—†	1	stenographer	22	219 Newbury
P	Bushfield Dorothy—†	1	"	24	219 "
S	Donovan Thomas	5	janitor	30	109 Peterboro
T	Buchannan James R	5	salesman	26	Somerville
U	Kerr Charles G	5	"	31	12 Westland av
V	Mansfield Phillip B	5	engineer	24	Lynn
W	Matheuson Dana	5	"	28	12 Westland av
X	Allen Charles H	5	architect	43	36 Queensberry
Y	Allen Laura—†	5	housewife	29	36 "
Z	Mann Kathleen—†	5	"	24	Louisiana
A	Mann Walter	5	U S A	36	"
B	Nichols Corinne M—†	5	nurse	25	Haverhill
c	Williams David	5	newsdealer	33	51 Audubon rd
D	Williams Sarah—†	5	housewife	28	51 "
E	Aldrich Kathleen—†	5	secretary	24	Cambridge
F	Merchant Eva—†	5	nurse	24	"
G	Merchant Julia—†	5	dressmaker	26	Beverly
H	West Martha A—†	5	clerk	28	69 Pembroke
K	Frickey Edwin	5	statistician	30	Colorado
L	Frickey Helen—†	5	housewife	28	"
N	Noyes Alfred H	5	salesman	30	here
O	Ederton Joseph	5	"	32	100 Queensberry
P	Ederton Marge—†	5	housewife	29	100 "
R	Wood Manton A	5	merchant	43	640 Beacon
S	Wood Mary E—†	5	housewife	28	640 "
T	Burbank Marguerite P—†	5	secretary	27	115 Hemenway
U	Perry Gertrude—†	5	clerk	26	50 Peterboro
V	Farnsworth Leona E—†	5	housewife	26	Medford

Peterborough Street—Continued

w	Farnsworth Ora L	5	clerk	29	87 Worcester
x	Delaney Elizabeth—†	5	stenographer	21	Plymouth
y	Shinkwen Eva B—†	5	manager	31	209 Hunt'n a
z	Smith Charles A	5	broker	40	here
A	Dube Thersa W—†	5	manicurist	27	New York Cit
B	Barr Dorothy M—†	5	bookkeeper	30	25 Peterboro
C	Lewis Dorothy C—†	5	secretary	28	Cambridge
D	Hawes George M	5	teacher	46	46 Westland a
E	Morse Sadie M—†	5	clerk	50	Groton
F	DeCourcey Mary—†	5	tel operator	26	Clinton
G	Higgins Alice—†	5	cook	35	Maynard
H	Shea Rena—†	5	"	40	Hudson
K	Knight Florence O—†	5	secretary	42	109 Peterbor
M	Boudreau James	11	janitor	26	61 Audubon
N	Boudreau Mary H—†	11	housewife	23	61 "
P	Givens Helen—†	11	"	50	51 "
R	Hodge Nina—†	11	"	50	Cambridge
S	Webster George O	11	dentist	64	"
T	Webster Mary M—†	11	housewife	60	"
U	Frost Cora—†	11	clerk	24	Maine
V	McIntyre Esther—†	11	accountant	25	64 Hemenwa
W	Nilson Ada—†	11	teacher	35	Maine
X	Currier Abbie K—†	11	housewife	84	137 Peterbor
Y	Currier Elizabeth C—†	11	artist	47	137 "
Z	Farrell John	11	laborer	27	Cambridge
A	Fitzgerald Needa—†	11	saleswoman	26	9 Haviland
B	West Elsie—†	11	manicurist	27	26 Hemenwa
C	Biglin Nichols J	11	mechanic	46	New York
D	Conger Kenneth	11	student	20	153 Hemenwa
E	Weaver John H	11	"	20	153 "
F	McQueen Laura—†	11	bookkeeper	35	21 Astor
G	Holloway Josephine—†	11	nurse	26	818 Harris'n a
H	Carroll John	11	salesman	33	New York
K	Chase Elizabeth—†	11	teacher	32	20 Montvale
L	Schulz Laura—†	11	housewife	27	20 "
M	Lanigan Alice—†	11	saleswoman	45	Cambridge
N	Shelback Christina—†	11	housewife	45	"
R	Brightwell Helen—†	11	real estate	35	78 Peterboro
S	McKinnon Susie—†	11	housewife	33	61 Tower
T	McKinnon Walter A	11	carpenter	35	61 "
U	Margolis Angus	11	salesman	32	New York

Peterborough Street—Continued

v	Cox Helen—†	11	bookkeeper	27	728 Com av
z	Kimball Jane—†	19	milliner	28	New Hampshire
A	Kimball Nancy—†	19	housewife	58	"
B	Baldwin Frederick H	19	druggist	46	70 W Newton
D	Sherman Catherine—†	19	bookkeeper	30	Vermont
E	Marks Norman B	19	printer	27	153 Hemenway
F	Lupo Lewis	19	carpenter	28	35 Audubon rd
H	McRae Dorothy—†	19	nurse	26	10 Metcalf
K	White Viola—†	19	"	26	10 "
L	Cotton Levin	19	auditor	55	Providence R I
M	Griffith Fern—†	19	waitress	22	153 Hemenway
N	Moore Blanche—†	19	bookkeeper	23	133 Hunt'n av
O	Sawtell Margie—†	19	hairdresser	22	Maine
P	Ranagan Edna—†	19	housewife	23	37 Ivy
R	Ranagan Edwin C	19	salesman	26	37 "
S	Goldsmith Helen—†	19	bookkeeper	25	Revere
T	Goldsmith Henry I	19	salesman	52	"
U	Goldsmith Sadie—†	19	housewife	52	"
V	Murphy Viola—†	19	"	27	"
W	Sprague Bessie—†	19	saleswoman	30	"
X	Chelfin Morris	19	dentist	32	21 Astor
Y	Cattanach Gertrude L—†	19	housewife	22	3 Grant rd
Z	Cattanach John	19	chauffeur	24	3 "
A	Motz Harry	19	salesman	33	Brookline
B	Leonard Eleanor—†	19	housewife	55	"
C	Leonard Paul R	19	egg tester	20	"
D	Leonard Roland D	19	foreman	24	"
F	Mahr William	19	student	26	16 Westland av
H	Walke Evelyn—†	19	housewife	23	New Jersey
K	Walke Roger S	19	engineer	24	104 Hemenway
L	Austin Edna M—†	19	housewife	43	16 Queensberry
M	Delahanty Sarah—†	19	teacher	27	Fall River
N	Haskins Helen—†	19	bookkeeper	27	153 Hemenway
T	Kelly John	25	janitor	50	108 Jersey
U	Kelly Maragaret—†	25	housewife	41	108 "
V	Newcomb Marietta E—†	25	physician	56	here
W	Burchant Caroline—†	25	housewife	51	"
X	Peters Phebe—†	25	hairdresser	42	15 Bickerstaff
Y	Wallace Ethel—†	25	housewife	38	41 "
Z	Wallace Tidal T	25	clerk	38	41 "
A	Murray Laura—†	25	stenographer	36	here

Peterborough Street—Continued

B	Mathers Lawrence R	25	salesman	32	here
C	Murphy John C	25	policeman	49	"
D	Murphy Muriel—†	25	clerk	26	"
E	Murphy Susie—†	25	housewife	49	"
F	Griffin Anna J—†	25	"	25	60 Worcester
G	Griffin Lewis F	25	telegrapher	34	60 "
H	Harrington Harriette E—†	25	decorator	51	here
K	Harrington Herbert	25	salesman	28	"
L	Knowlton Mary R—†	25	stenographer	47	"
M	Frost Mabel—†	25	housewife	40	"
N	Smith Gabriel	25	teacher	30	"
O	Smith Greta—†	25	housewife	23	Worcester
P	Watson Isabella—†	25	nurse	41	here
R	Glasgow Celia—†	25	housewife	27	"
S	Glasgow Louise J	25	salesman	34	"
T	Howard Hannah—†	25	housewife	64	Peabody
U	Voight Herman B	25	dyemaker	39	"
V	Voight Mary C—†	25	housewife	39	"
W	Decker Mina S—†	25	"	41	Brookline
X	Decker Roland S	25	tester	20	"
Y	Boylan Catherine E—†	25	bookkeeper	23	Taunton
Z	Flye Velma M—†	25	nurse	32	here
A	Thomas Clara G—†	25	housewife	38	515 Audubon
B	Thomas Robert L	25	bookkeeper	40	515 "
C	Harrington Grace—†	25	housekeeper	76	here
D	Harrington Mary A—†	25	bookkeeper	37	"
E	Croucher Horace	25	salesman	22	469A Col av
F	Curry Norma—†	25	clerk	34	469A "
H	Bilodeau Mary V—†	25	operator	29	here
K	Nyhanen Ester—†	25	nurse	27	"
L	Rockwood Lillian P—†	25	operator	30	"
M	Quinlan Ella—†	25	teacher	34	"
N	Parson Robert G	25	teamster	70	"
O	Shanley Alice M—†	25	housewife	32	"
P	Shanley Edward M	25	bookkeeper	45	"
R	Chamberlin Robert C	25	teacher	42	"
S	Murphy Catherine—†	25	clerk	32	"
T	Murphy Margaret—†	25	"	30	"
U	Clemens Mary L—†	25	housewife	61	"
V	Clemens Stanley	25	bookkeeper	61	"
Y	Bostwick Richmond F	25	salesman	24	"

Peterborough Street Continued

z	Hart Glydes B—†	25	housewife	31	here
A	MacCool Mary L—†	25	clerk	44	"
E	Pearce Lillian—†	31	hairdresser	27	"
F	Holden Mary C—†	31	corsetiere	36	"
G	Bornestein Ruth—†	31	housewife	25	"
H	Montague Lazarus	31	cigarmaker	70	"
K	Edwards John P, jr	31	salesman	35	"
L	Whitcombe Isabel H—†	31	housekeeper	49	"
M	Chappelle Edward H	31	manufacturer	29	"
N	Albright Ruth—†	31	clerk	27	"
O	Avery Blanche—†	31	nurse	25	"
P	Williams Effie E—†	31	housewife	40	"
R	Dennis Lucy B—†	31	"	65	"
S	Albertson Elsie M—†	31	stenographer	35	"
T	Chabot George	31	salesman	34	"
U	Chabot Georgia—†	31	housewife	28	"
V	Haynes Harry E	31	photographer	45	"
W	McDonald Annie—†	31	clerk	35	"
X	Waldstein Rose—†	31	housewife	33	"
Y	Waldstein Samuel J	31	cigarmaker	42	"
Z	Sackmary Bessie—†	31	housewife	27	"
A	Sackmary Harry	31	printer	40	"
B	Donovan Mary F—†	31	nurse	45	"
C	Gallagher James E	31	salesman	30	"
D	Dow Amy G—†	31	housewife	83	"
F	McNally Mollie G—†	31	clerk	28	"
G	MacDonald Estelle G—†	31	housewife	35	"
H	MacDonald William A	31	journalist	34	"
K	Gill Ida P—†	31	agent	50	"
L	Kelly Eleanore A—†	31	housekeeper	28	"
M	Kelly Elizabeth—†	31	designer	32	"
N	Payne Bertha L—†	32	matron	58	"
O	MacDonnnell Leona—†	35	hairdresser	22	26 Whiting
P	Mathewe Lawrence, jr	35	salesman	30	Connecticut
S	Casey Anna L—†	35	housewife	21	here
T	Casey Edward L	35	salesman	29	"
U	Wood Earle D	35	manager	24	Newton
V	Welch Melissa—†	35	housewife	37	28 Westland av
W	Welch Roy C	35	salesman	41	28 "
X	Gans Albert E	35	"	32	Maine
Z	McKnight Clifford	35	garageman	21	Somerville

Peterborough Street—Continued

A	McKnight Susie H—†	35	real estate	50	Somerville
B	Murphy Alfred	35	salesman	33	Minnesota
C	Carlson Arthur	35	clerk	28	Somerville
D	Isenberg Albert	35	student	23	Ohio
E	Arey Florin G	35	lawyer	33	here
F	Arey Henry C	35	retired	63	"
G	Arey Rosalie—†	35	housewife	54	"
H	Perry Louis I	35	accountant	38	New York
K	Perry Mary L—†	35	housewife	30	"
M	Schneider Jasper	35	chauffeur	35	Eastham
A	Young Alice M—†	36	saleswoman	50	here
B	Murray Iris—†	36	housewife	29	"
C	Murray John	36	clerk	31	"
D	Kendall Walter J	36	architect	23	101 Mounfort
E	Young George F	36	"	37	98 Hemenway
F	Jefferson Florence W—†	36	saleswoman	41	here
G	Hardy Eliza A—†	36	cashier	52	"
H	Edmonds Edith—†	36	salesman	32	Worcester
K	Logue Daniel F	36	saleswoman	45	here
L	Smith Jacob G	36	buyer	45	"
M	Smith Mildred M—†	36	housewife	42	"
N	Ellns Henry	36	merchant	60	"
O	Sordito Amelia M—†	36	housewife	57	Newton
P	Sordito John L	36	towerman	54	"
R	MacDonald Margaret—†	36	saleswoman	32	here
R¹	MacDonald Rachel—†	36	"	31	"
S	Robinson Agnes—†	36	nurse	28	1080 Centre
T	Woleer Adeline—†	36	artist	37	here
U	McPeake Henry	36	dentist	50	"
V	McPeake Mary A—†	36	housewife	39	"
W	Lafon Alice M—†	36	clerk	45	"
X	Lafon Mary J—†	36	housekeeper	75	"
Y	Martin Helena—†	36	housewife	37	908 Beacon
Z	Martin John J	36	policeman	31	908 "
A	MacDonald Christine—†	36	nurse	27	here
B	MacNaughton Elizabeth—†	36	"	28	"
C	MacRae Bessie—†	36	"	27	"
F	Kelley Robert J	39	salesman	49	"
G	Hunt Ethel—†	39	manufacturer	47	"
H	Cohen Mary V—†	39	housewife	31	"
K	Cohen William J	39	manufacturer	33	"

Peterborough Street—Continued

	FULL NAME.	Res.	Occupation	Age	Reported Residence
L	Abrams Mark	39	real estate	42	here
M	Abrams Sadie —†	39	housewife	37	"
N	Levens Ralph	39	merchant	26	Brookline
O	Powers James	39	student	31	Nahant
R	Arnold Ethel—†	39	manager	43	83 Westland av
S	Loring Bentley E	39	student	36	6 Ivy
T	Loring Bernice E—†	39	housewife	39	6 "
U	Loring Hattie F—†	39	retired	62	6 "
V	Maiz William C	39	superintendent	53	here
W	Neal Maude—†	39	bookkeeper	38	"
X	McKenzie Ethel I—†	39	"	40	Arlington
Y	Snow Annette—†	39	"	30	here
Z	Allen Mable—†	39	nurse	40	Brookline
A	Leonard Leon P	39	U S A	40	Winthrop
B	Leonard Mabel C—†	39	housewife	35	"
C	Stevens Alice M—†	40	"	56	here
D	Stevens John F	40	janitor	55	"
E	Kennedy Linda—†	40	saleswoman	45	"
F	Chaffin Cora—†	40	clerk	45	"
G	Dakin Florence—†	40	"	36	"
H	Holstrom Grace—†	40	milliner	48	"
K	Dolliver Edward	40	nurse	32	"
L	Donaldson James	40	salesman	48	"
M	LaFord Winnifred—†	40	retired	27	"
N	McNamara Leo P	40	manager	29	Somerville
O	Taylor Minnie E—†	40	clerk	30	here
P	Skinner Alfred L—†	40	teacher	26	N Andover
R	Skinner Priscilla E—†	40	housewife	25	"
S	Dunhan Walter A	40	student	30	here
T	Callahan Grace—†	40	operator	28	"
V	O'Rourke Arthur N	40	fireman	34	146 Mass av
W	Scribner Beverly	40	chauffeur	35	here
X	Pegman Mary—†	40	clerk	25	"
Y	Donovan Emily—†	40	nurse	28	"
Z	Larsen Anna—†	41	housewife	45	"
A	Larsen Ross	41	janitor	43	"
B	Madore Elizabeth A—†	41	housewife	40	30 Hemenway
C	Madore John B	41	collector	40	30 "
D	Tarr Jessie H—†	41	clerk	40	Malden
E	Hall Florence V—†	41	"	35	here
F	Walker Lillian J—†	41	"	35	"

Peterborough Street—Continued

	Letter	FULL NAME	Residence April 1, 1924	Occupation	Supposed Age	Reported Residence Street and Number	
	G	Walker Lucy A—†	41	retired	74	here	
	H	Stahle Emma K—†	41	housewife	50	"	
	K	Stahle John A	41	engineer	44	"	
	L	Lyons Miriam—†	41	saleswoman	34	"	
	M	Brown Alice H—†	41	houseworker	53	39 Peterboro	
	N	Hahn Grethel L—†	41	clerk	26	39 "	
	O	Hall Emma P—†	41	secretary	45	here	
	P	Hall Margaret—†	41	housewife	50	"	
	R	Barrett Thomas W	41	student	21	105 Gainsboro	
	S	Johnson Alfred N	41	"	22	105 "	
	T	Griffin Ida—†	41	clerk	35	here	
	U	Pedrick Viola—†	41	stenographer	40	"	
	V	Allyn Harry O	41	salesman	41	"	
	W	Allyn Marie S—†	41	housewife	40	"	
	X	Wales Ardelle E—†	41	"	43	"	
	Y	Wales Moses S	41	engineer	49	"	
	Z	Pappas William	41	merchant	40	16 Westland a	
	A	Hallett Herbert A	41	chauffeur	25	134 Hunt'n a	
	B	Hallett Pearl—†	41	housewife	26	134 "	
	C	Deering Basil R	41	agent	35	here	
	D	Deering Edith C—†	41	housewife	30	"	
	E	Kroll Jennie C—†	41	saleswoman	27	"	
	F	Corson Jessie W—†	41	housewife	40	"	
	G	Corson Louise L—†	41	cashier	40	"	
	H	Corson Myron L	41	salesman	40	"	
	K	Bemis Cynthia O—†	42	housewife	60	"	
	L	Bemis Walter S	42	janitor	62	"	
	M	Gould Helen—†	42	housewife	42	"	
	N	Gilbert William	42	merchant	35	71 Batavia	
	O	Pulver Harold L	42	manager	25	115 Hemenwa	
	P	Mildream Samuel	42	engineer	45	here	
	R	Berry Etta A—†	42	housewife	58	16 Westland a	
	S	Berry Leonard F	42	engineer	65	16 "	
	T	Sealander Frank L	42	merchant	40	here	
	U	Webber Sewell M	42	clerk	29	"	
	V	Stanley Arthur	42	merchant	60	"	
	W	Maynard George S	42	clerk	57	"	
	X	Campbell Ethel L—†	42	housewife	45	"	
	Y	Campbell Ralph S	42	cashier	41	"	
	Z	Mackie William	42	salesman	45	"	
	A	Davy Caroline A—†	42	housewife	49	"	

Peterborough Street — Continued

	Letter.	FULL NAME.	Residence April 1, 1924	Occupation.	Supposed Age.	Reported Residence, April 1, 1923. Street and Number.
	B	Delaney Edwin F	42	salesman	28	here
	c	Doyle Agnes C—†	42	clerk	52	"
	D	Healy Mary A—†	42	housewife	63	"
	E	Olson George L	42	engineer	25	"
	F	Bixby Mabel C—†	42	saleswoman	55	"
	G	Brownell Evelyn H—†	42	housewife	79	"
	H	Hull Edward K	42	engineer	28	"
	K	Hull Mary C—†	42	housewife	45	"
	L	Hutchinson Grace—†	45	teacher	34	"
	M	Perrigo Lena—†	45	"	48	"
	N	Painchaud Agnes—†	45	corsetiere	47	"
	P	Lincoln Frederic G	45	machinist	69	"
	O	Lincoln Julia A—†	45	housewife	65	"
	R	Witham Lillian—†	45	clerk	36	"
	S	Fuller Caroline K—†	45	teacher	41	"
	T	Strout Mary—†	45	housewife	31	"
	U	Strout Thomas	45	chauffeur	34	"
	V	Dolliver Ernest W	45	salesman	36	"
	W	Dolliver Josephine—†	45	housewife	37	"
	Y	Martin Clifford M	45	manager	30	"
	Z	Boffice Caroline—†	45	nurse	25	"
	B	Wylie Francis H	45	clerk	30	"
	C	Scoville Annie G—†	45	"	36	"
	D	Smith William H	45	salesman	46	"
	E	Price Julius L	45	grocer	40	"
	F	Davis Walter A	45	manager	35	59 Astor
	G	Nourie Clara—†	45	saleswoman	42	here
	H	Armstrong Mary E—†	46	retired	75	"
	K	Leary John J	46	salesman	25	"
	M	Hoke Josephine M—†	46	housewife	37	"
	N	Hoke Perl H	46	salesman	39	"
	O	Kuyper George A	46	musician	25	"
	P	Kuyper Mildred B—†	46	housewife	26	"
	R	Haskell Harry	46	bookkeeper	54	"
	S	Craig Harold	46	actor	38	New York City
	T	Craig Theodore A	46	manager	32	90 St Mary's
	U	Gibbs Edee E—†	46	clerk	34	here
	V	Gibbs Mary L—†	46	housewife	76	"
	W	Bacon Howard K	46	manager	60	"
	X	Walsh Mable E—†	46	clerk	55	"
	Y	Montey Clare E—†	46	"	40	"

S—13

Page.	Letter.	FULL NAME.	Residence, April 1, 1924.	Occupation.	Supposed Age.	Reported Residence, April 1, 1923. Street and Number.

	z	Lancaster Henry S	46	merchant	42	here
	A	Kelly John W	46	engineer	32	42 Peterboro
	B	Kelliher Daniel A	46	clerk	35	here
	c	George Edith B—†	46	"	34	"
	D	George Pearle G—†	46	"	45	"
	E	Johnson Bessie S—†	46	housewife	43	"
	F	Johnson Willis C	46	teacher	33	"
	G	Shaughessy Joseph	50	janitor	33	Cambridge
	H	Vincent Walter J	50	retired	67	"
	K	Norton Agnes—†	50	housewife	22	83 Peterboro
	L	Norton Herbert	50	dentist	47	83 "
	M	Tippett Ernest H	50	clergyman	49	here
	N	Tippett Lillian I—†	50	housewife	45	"
	o	Tibbetts Ester—†	50	"	50	"
	P	Tibbetts John	50	clerk	52	"
	R	McLoud Daisy—†	50	manager	55	"
	s	Edell Ernest	50	"	46	Brookline
	v	Lanman Charles P	50	salesman	26	76 Peterboro
	W	Mackrile Caroline—†	50	housewife	48	here
	X	Mackrile John	50	chairmaker	47	"
	Y	Barlett Elizabeth—†	50	housewife	55	"
	z	Barlett Elizabeth—†	50	teacher	22	"
	A	Struab Otto	50	manager	28	535 Beacon
	B	Whitney Beulah—†	50	clerk	26	here
	c	Whitney Donald	50	student	21	"
	D	Whitney Helen—†	50	"	32	"
	E	Whitney Jessie—†	50	nurse	23	"
	F	Fisher Mary—†	50	teacher	29	"
	G	Rogers Mary F—†	50	"	44	"
	H	Covill Annie—†	50	waitress	35	"
	K	Covill John	50	salesman	46	"
	L	MacCarty Martha E—†	50	teacher	50	"
	M	MacCarty Rebecca E—†	50	housekeeper	82	"
	o	McLeod Bertha—†	50	clerk	32	"
	P	McLeod Maud—†	50	"	29	"
	R	Billings John	50	laborer	33	"
	s	Billings Mary—†	50	clerk	29	"
	T	Hannigan John	50	salesman	45	"
	U	Boot Henry J	50	clerk	28	Arlington
	v	Conroy Pearl—†	50	tel operator	33	Lowell
	W	Wilson Nellie J—†	50	housewife	59	here

Peterborough Street —Continued

X	Sissen Annie M—†	50	housekeeper	38	here
Y	Sisson Joseph M	50	druggist	40	"
Z	Olson Gertrude—†	50	student	22	"
A	Talmage Helen M—†	50	"	21	Brookline
B	Talmage Nelle A—†	50	housekeeper	30	"
C	Talmage Sterling B	50	student	34	"
D	Moore Edna—†	50	clerk	25	here
E	Moore Stanley E	50	manager	28	"
F	Byork Esther—†	50	clerk	26	"
G	Byork Olga—†	50	"	21	"
H	Lynch Henriette—†	50	secretary	24	"
K	Cohen Charles	50	salesman	41	530 Newbury
L	Cohen Elizabeth—†	50	tel operator	31	530 "
M	Taylor Ernest J	50	broker	51	here
N	Hovey Isabel—†	50	nurse	36	224 Newbury
O	Peterson Emma—†	50	"	50	35 Peterboro
P	Yerxa Albina—†	50	"	35	35 "
R	Black Joseph	50	salesman	35	here
S	Black Margaret M—†	50	waitress	30	"
T	Broad Blanche—†	50	housekeeper	42	Winthrop
U	Clarry Alice—†	50	operator	50	here
V	Wilson John K	50	steamfitter	40	"
W	Brown William G	50	manager	28	Virginia
X	Rodden Margaret F—†	50	clerk	55	here
Y	Rodden Mary G—†	50	"	50	"
Z	Northrop Lilian W—†	50	dressmaker	30	Maine
A	Kennedy Frank A	50	teacher	49	20 Queensberry
B	Kennedy Lorena—†	50	student	22	20 "
C	Kennedy Sadie B—†	50	housekeeper	49	20 "
D	Spaulding Dana	50	manager	45	here
E	Arnold Edward L	50	insurance agent	60	"
F	Mayer Theodore	50	storekeeper	48	"
G	Davis John	50	clerk	32	"
H	Davis Marion—†	50	housewife	28	"
L	Keeffe Joseph	50	salesman	30	"
M	Meloy Edward	50	"	28	"
N	Christopher John	50	manager	45	New Bedford
B	Johnson Everett E	72	carpenter	50	New York City
C	Johnson Mary—†	72	housewife	45	"
D	Hanes Agnes—†	72	clerk	30	Somerville
E	Doyle Lena R—†	72	dressmaker	28	59 Westland av

Peterborough Street—Continued

F	Green Louis J	72	student	28	Springfield
G	Green Mary—†	72	housewife	28	Somerville
K	Barney Louise H—†	72	clerk	45	here
L	Barney Mary E—†	72	retired	74	"
N	Burton Pearle—†	72	nurse	24	818 Harris'n av
O	Nunes Hellen—†	72	"	21	818 "
P	Nipoletta Bertha—†	72	retired	31	here
R	Nipoletta John	72	teamster	32	"
S	Tucker Dorothy C—†	72	housewife	26	Reading
T	Tucker Morris A	72	clerk	27	here
U	Jenkins Ada—†	72	housewife	26	"
V	Jenkins John	72	clerk	24	"
W	Quinn Lara A—†	72	nurse	22	"
X	Orbolar Edith—†	72	housewife	29	14 Queensberry
Y	Orbolar James	72	physician	31	14 "
Z	Tabor Margrett B—†	72	bookkeeper	36	here
A	Callansan Catherine—†	72	"	33	Brookline
B	Saunders Alice—†	72	model	22	"
C	Canniffe Elizabeth—†	72	bookkeeper	23	Winchester
D	St Thomas Loretta—†	72	clerk	23	Medford
E	St Thomas Xavier	72	salesman	26	Brookline
F	Droese Lucy M—†	72	secretary	42	"
G	Record Edward D	72	musician	40	21 W Canton
K	Norton Mary E—†	72	secretary	25	here
L	Gowey Herbert R	72	agent	30	Pittsfield
M	Gowey Lois—†	72	housewife	25	New York City
N	Deane Laurence	72	manager	45	80 Peterboro
O	Deane Ruth E—†	72	housewife	25	80 "
R	Burkholder Grace E—†	72	"	23	Kansas
S	Burkholder Theodore M	72	salesman	23	316 Hunt'n av
T	Orme William P	72	agent	66	11 Garrison
U	Schreiber Albert G	72	salesman	60	35 W Newton
V	Schreiber Maude E—†	72	housewife	50	35 "
X	Smith Anna L—†	72	cook	43	here
Z	Adams Carle H	72	teacher	37	Haverhill
A	Johnston Charles W	72	physician	35	here
B	Johnston Sadie—†	72	housewife	34	"
C	Nieluch Joseph	72	accountant	30	33 Bickerstaff
D	Nieluch Margrett—†	72	housewife	26	33 "
E	Greene Hellen—†	72	"	29	here
F	Greene Howard E	72	chauffeur	34	"

Peterborough Street — Continued

H	Whittier Edna S—†	72	stenographer	32	163 Hemenway
K	Wyght Florence—†	72	bookkeeper	34	163 "
R	Burlser Minola—†	72	student	23	Brookline
S	Burlser Richard	72	"	24	"
W	McGuyer Ellen—†	72	retired	50	here
V	McGuyer Hellen—†	72	secretary	24	"
Y	Laurence Gertrude E—†	72	hairdresser	38	Chelsea
Z	Chase Mary—†	72	clerk	22	here
A	Schumann Ellen C—†	72	secretary	27	"
B	Miller Dagmer	72	"	25	"
C	Miller John	72	manager	30	"
D	Foster Claudine—†	76	housewife	26	"
E	Foster Francis	76	janitor	35	"
F	Thomas Maud A—†	76	bookkeeper	35	"
G	Johnson Hurbert	76	salesman	40	"
H	Cook Chester S	76	musician	31	"
K	Cook Florence M—†	76	housewife	30	"
L	Harris Ruth—†	76	dressmaker	35	"
M	Roberts Delphine M—†	76	saleswoman	43	"
N	Rogers Harrold	76	bookkeeper	27	"
O	West William S	76	broker	40	"
P	Dorman Nan R—†	76	clerk	35	"
R	Dansforth Charles O	76	"	40	"
S	Jones Ethel—†	76	retired	36	"
T	Trundy Winnie—†	76	clerk	46	"
U	Altman William W	76	salesman	35	"
V	Tully Bernice—†	76	nurse	27	"
W	Durwan Thomas P	76	student	24	124 Peterboro
X	Starr Roland	76	"	23	New York
Y	Terry Sarah—†	76	saleswoman	40	here
Z	Adams Emila—†	76	housewife	25	25 Astor
A	Adams Harry E	76	gardener	50	25 "
B	Snooke James	76	chef	35	here
C	Buechner Carl A	76	salesman	45	Cambridge
D	Saunders Florence W—†	76	nurse	35	here
E	Saunders Frank	76	salesman	35	"
F	Rheinboldt Hjalmar	76	postal clerk	32	103 Norway
G	Rheinboldt Selma O—†	76	housewife	33	103 "
H	Martin Anna L—†	76	nurse	38	Brookline
K	Kraus Mary C—†	76	"	38	"
L	Walch William F	76	painter	42	here

Peterborough Street—Continued

M	Walch Gertrude M—†	76	housewife	32	here
N	Austin William A	76	carpenter	45	"
O	Gibson Frank	76	salesman	45	"
P	Drary William A	76	bookkeeper	35	"
R	McKee George R	76	student	40	"
S	Rydin Spencer	76	"	23	"
T	Ryan Margrette—†	78	housewife	35	"
U	McLaughlin Anna K—†	78	nurse	34	"
V	Cavert David	78	agent	40	"
W	Mareing Joel	78	student	36	Ohio
X	Mareing Pauline T—†	78	housewife	23	"
Y	Noyes Irena L—†	78	saleswoman	37	here
A	Farrell Margrett—†	78	tel operator	21	15 Mackin
B	Farrell Nora—†	78	retired	45	Hull
C	Assmer Martha G—†	78	housewife	24	here
D	Assmer Samuel L	78	manager	34	"
E	Moore Edith—†	78	maid	20	447 Talbot a'
F	Tierney John J	78	plasterer	26	Somerville
G	Tierney Mary A—†	78	housewife	29	8 Worcester s
M	Jones Frederick R	78	inspector	24	Hartford Ct
N	Jones Isabel—†	78	housewife	22	"
R	Elliott Edith—†	78	clerk	22	Somerville
S	Porter John M	78	student	24	here
T	Porter Mary L—†	78	housewife	24	"
Z	Rooney George T	78	civil engineer	33	Somerville
A	Rooney May—†	78	housewife	28	"
B	Dunne John J	78	salesman	28	here
C	Nickelson Helen—†	78	hairdresser	36	"
D	Doyle Grace—†	78	nurse	33	"
G	Richard Edna M—†	80	artist	26	"
H	Richard Edward H	80	salesman	52	"
L	Fox Annette C—†	80	housewife	34	"
M	Fox Edward H	80	salesman	35	"
N	Courtright Josephine—†	80	clerk	35	"
P	Anderson May—†	80	"	23	"
R	Howloway Howard J	80	student	24	25 Worcester
T	McCann Beatrice L—†	80	clerk	26	Watertown
U	McCann William H	80	"	24	139 P
V	Harrington Sadia—†	80	"	28	here
W	Fenton Charles	80	salesman	30	"
X	Maxwell James C	80	"	30	"

54

Peterborough Street—Continued

Y	Parker William	80	salesman	35	here
Z	Bowe Burton G	80	"	40	19 Myrtle
A	Martin John J	80	"	28	New York
B	Hersey William J	80	"	42	9 Mt Bowdoin ter
C	Rogers May—†	80	saleswoman	30	Cambridge
D	Garvey Gladys—†	80	clerk	30	"
F	Thomas Alice—†	80	"	30	Newton
G	Dowing Grace—†	80	"	25	here
H	Young Clara—†	80	"	30	"
K	Roach Kathryne—†	80	waitress	21	41 Fairfield
L	Roach May—†	80	"	30	41 "
M	Dunn Elizabeth—†	80	clerk	30	here
N	Hunter Kathryne—†	80	saleswoman	30	"
O	Monahan Charles	80	salesman	40	"
P	Parker Charles R	80	"	30	"
R	Leftin Louis	80	painter	31	"
A	DeRoche Ada—†	82	housewife	58	3 Lexington
B	Young Paul	82	janitor	50	3 "
C	Young Grace—†	82	clerk	30	here
D	Simpson Beverly	82	physician	30	New York
E	Lord Alice—†	82	bookkeeper	40	here
F	Ring Bertha—†	82	saleswoman	30	Maine
G	Aldrich Mary C—†	82	clerk	30	here
H	Skinner Bernice—†	82	"	32	"
K	Goldsmith Peter V	82	salesman	27	New York
L	Harris Harriette B—†	82	clerk	30	Newton
M	Turshman Fred	82	salesman	35	here
O	Avallone Anthony	82	chauffeur	27	717 E Seventh
P	Warren Fredrick	82	nurse	39	here
R	LaBatt Arthur A	82	teacher	37	"
S	Sigmon Charles	82	musician	38	"
T	Farrell Fredrick	82	salesman	31	"
U	Burns May—†	82	clerk	30	Watertown
V	Rogers Clara—†	82	"	30	here
W	Mumrill Mary—†	82	"	38	"
X	Sturtevant Henry	82	salesman	35	"
Y	Taylor May—†	82	clerk	35	Worcester
Z	Leo Albert	82	salesman	50	here
B	Deneen Grace—†	82	clerk	30	"
C	Grady Anna—†	82	"	35	"
D	Nichols Mary—†	82	"	32	"

Peterborough Street—Continued

E	VanTassel Karl R	82	salesman	33	here
F	Allard Alice—†	82	clerk	35	"
G	Lowell Mary—†	82	saleswoman	28	"
L	Chin Goey	88	laundryman	50	China
T	Lyman Carl E	105	salesman	46	here
V	Lyman Marguerite—†	105	housewife	37	"
W	Bowe Richard H	105	mechanic	40	"
X	Piper Jennie R—†	105	manager	50	"
Y	Piper Joseph E	105	watchmaker	55	"
Z	Humes Ada M—†	105	housewife	37	"
A	Humes Thomas L	105	clerk	36	"
B	Hilton Ella M—†	105	bookkeeper	46	"
C	Hilton Nellie—†	105	houseworker	71	"
D	Savage Abbie F—†	105	"	63	"
E	Savage Edith M—†	105	housewife	37	"
F	Savage Edland D	105	agent	37	"
G	Wright Gertrude—†	105	hairdresser	47	"
H	Mead Edwin C	105	U S A	36	New York
K	Mead Evelyn C—†	105	housewife	30	"
L	MacIntyre Isabel L—†	105	secretary	28	here
M	Beal Helen K—†	105	housewife	26	"
N	Beal Howard W	105	salesman	27	"
O	Carroll Anna—†	105	houseworker	78	"
P	Nickerson Florence T—†	105	housewife	36	"
R	Nickerson Lawrence C	105	salesman	32	"
S	Meagher Edward J	105	clerk	30	"
T	Meagher Margaret A—†	105	housewife	28	"
U	Lyons Harriet—†	105	"	36	"
V	Lyons Michael J	105	lawyer	36	"
W	Woodworth Viva E—†	105	housekeeper	47	"
X	Doctson Mary A—†	105	stenographer	51	"
Y	Ross Esther A—†	105	housewife	29	"
Z	Ross William L	105	auditor	33	"
A	McDonnell Helen A—†	105	retired	57	"
B	Doyle Alice F—†	105	milliner	40	"
C	Doyle Lorretta V—†	105	saleswoman	60	"
D	Reed Alonzo B	105	engineer	35	"
E	MacNichol David J	105	merchant	56	"
F	MacNichol Jessie—†	105	housewife	56	"
G	Fraser Arnold D	105	manager	25	Watertown
H	Fraser Beatrice M—†	105	housewife	25	"

Page.	Letter.	FULL NAME.	Residence, April 1, 1924.	Occupation.	Supposed Age.	Reported Residence, April 1, 1923. Street and Number.

Peterborough Street—Continued

K	Reichert Emma G—†	105	nurse	52	here
L	Reichert Karl	105	engineer	42	"
M	Buck Evelyn L—†	105	secretary	31	"
N	Hallet Elsie—†	105	housewife	32	"
O	Hallet Harold M	105	contractor	35	"
P	Johnson Charles	105	treasurer	73	"
R	Fisher Edith C—†	105	secretary	43	"
S	Fisher Henry E	105	treasurer	74	"
T	Green Minerva—†	105	stenographer	38	"
U	Dootsm Mary—†	105	teacher	50	"
V	Chandler Marjorie P—†	105	housewife	27	New York
W	Chandler Paul A	105	physician	27	"
X	Peers Caroline W—†	105	housewife	60	here
Y	Peers Kester J	105	accountant	58	"
Z	St Onge Estelle—†	105	stenographer	32	"
A	Johnson Charles	109	janitor	54	Chelsea
B	Herlihy Fred W	109	accountant	23	here
C	Herlihy Mary—†	109	housewife	46	"
D	Herlihy Mildred—†	109	stenographer	21	"
E	Herlihy William D	109	manager	49	"
F	Nickerson Henry W	109	auto mechanic	51	"
G	Nickerson Nellie A—†	109	housewife	37	"
H	McDevitt Daniel J	109	salesman	26	"
L	Bunnell Fred	109	chef	42	"
M	Reed Alice K—†	109	housewife	24	"
N	Reed Daniel J	109	engineer	24	"
O	Reed Della M—†	109	housekeeper	60	"
P	Reed Malcomb D	109	mech dentist	37	"
R	Cass James W	109	salesman	36	"
S	VonNieda Blanche L—†	109	housewife	51	"
T	VonNieda Charles K	109	manager	52	"
U	Mackay Catherine—†	109	nurse	48	"
V	Gougeon Mary E—†	109	saleswoman	35	66 Tower
W	Saunders Josephine—†	109	printing	27	21 Woodlawn
X	Seilig Gustave H	109	salesman	35	here
Y	Bullard Edith—†	109	vocal teacher	30	"
Z	Bullard Ida—†	109	retired	50	"
A	Ord Rodney D	109	salesman	37	"
B	Carstonson Annie C—†	109	nurse	40	"
C	Trader Helen M—†	109	clerk	26	"
D	Fenely James W	109	manager	36	"

Peterborough Street—Continued

F	George Nathan P, jr	109	professor	50	here
G	Tapley Rolland	109	musician	23	"
H	Whitmore Helen A—†	109	bookkeeper	39	"
K	Carling Willis C	109	salesman	28	"
L	Wilmot Claire S—†	109	chiropodist	45	"
M	Woodworth Vinia E—†	109	retired	48	"
N	Spence Alice E—†	109	housewife	52	"
O	Spence George W	109	merchant	64	"
P	Whittemore Helen A—†	109	bookkeeper	38	"
R	Whittemore Susan—†	109	retired	60	"
S	Bowler Marion E—†	109	teacher	40	Cambridge
T	Hardy Florence G—†	109	bookkeeper	30	Revere
U	Golden Nathaniel	109	lawyer	32	New York
V	Baker Marion F—†	109	hairdresser	28	here
W	Whelan Joseph M	109	ironworker	48	"
X	Whelan Nellie A—†	109	housewife	49	"
Y	Durfee Arthur F	120	janitor	44	"
Z	Durfee Lena A—†	120	housewife	43	"
A	Hall Herbert	120	machinist	28	Malden
B	Hall Lena—†	120	saleswoman	24	here
C	Hatch Esther—†	120	housewife	24	Maine
D	Hatch Gladstone F	120	engineer	27	"
E	Sawabini Elizabeth C—†	120	housewife	26	507 Beacon
F	Sawabini Mousa	120	manager	31	507 "
G	Clark Beatrice—†	120	housewife	20	Canada
H	Clark Walter	120	hostler	21	"
K	Bridge Florence B—†	120	none	35	here
L	Bridge Hollings	120	salesman	35	"
M	Lamson James J	120	retired	40	New Hampshire
N	Jackson Fredricka—†	120	none	25	Wrentham
O	Reagan Louise M—†	120	"	55	"
P	Richardson Henry	120	"	68	"
R	Douglas Edith M—†	120	housekeeper	47	119 Mountfort
S	Douglas Howard C	120	mechanic	27	119 "
T	Leonard Clare—†	120	manicurist	35	here
U	Hampton Helen—†	120	saleswoman	38	306 Hyde Park av
V	Reed Allen E	120	mechanic	43	New York
W	Sullivan Nora—†	120	saleswoman	43	306 Hyde Park av
X	Davis Emma—†	120	waitress	38	here
Z	Larkin Arline—†	120	housewife	32	469 Col av
A	Larkin Thomas	120	engineer	40	469 "

Page.	Letter.	Full Name.	Residence, April 1, 1924	Occupation.	Supposed Age.	Reported Residence, April 1, 1923. Street and Number.

Peterborough Street—Continued

	B	Bailey Frances—†	120	student	21	Needham
	C	Montague Queeda—†	120	"	28	68 Francis
	D	Houslin Josephine—†	120	checker	46	here
	E	McManus George F	120	printer	44	73 Montgomery
	F	McManus Perle	120	"	34	73 "
	G	Wilson Vera B—†	120	housewife	41	here
	H	Dame Bertha—†	120	"	44	Needham
	K	Dame Daniel	120	salesman	46	"
	L	Marshburn Noera—†	120	housewife	49	Virginia
	M	Marshburn Otis M	120	agent	50	"
	N	Campbell Edward G	120	miller	37	Minnesota
	O	Wylde Harry M	120	engineer	32	Somerville
	P	Wylde Lillian V—†	120	housewife	27	"
	R	MacPherson Edna—†	120	none	49	Reading
	S	Rice Grace E—†	120	bookkeeper	27	"
	V	Pinney Craige B	124	salesman	33	Maine
	W	Pinney Maude—†	124	housewife	31	"
	X	Ryan Anna M—†	124	housekeeper	32	here
	Y	Ryan John E	124	chauffeur	38	"
	Z	Tassara Rinaldo	124	salesman	36	"
	A	Williams Harley E	124	"	53	California
	B	Williams Lottie M—†	124	housewife	40	"
	C	Hinds Margaret E—†	124	nurse	35	137 Peterboro
	D	Curtis Ella G—†	124	none	68	here
	E	Curtis Margery—†	124	secretary	38	"
	F	Bishop Alice H—†	124	housewife	44	Canada
	G	LaVoie Catherine—†	124	"	37	120 Peterboro
	H	LaVoie William	124	chauffeur	37	120 "
	K	Vogel Joseph W	124	druggist	35	here
	L	Kinder Maeleine A—†	124	housewife	26	"
	M	Kinder William F	124	dentist's aid	27	"
	N	O'Brien Elizabeth—†	124	housewife	33	New York
	O	O'Brien Thomas H	124	salesman	41	"
	P	Richardson Dorothy—†	124	housewife	23	12 Sayward
	R	Richardson Forrest	124	student	28	12 "
	S	O'Neil Ada F—†	124	housewife	36	here
	T	O'Neil James J	124	clerk	34	"
	U	Mason Anna H—†	124	housewife	37	"
	V	Mason Clarence W	124	accountant	38	"
	W	Day Edith W—†	124	housewife	41	Watertown
	X	Day Jeremiah J	124	agent	53	"

Peterborough Street—Continued

Y	Cronkhite Schuyler E	124	salesman	48	Springfield
Z	Clemensson Carl A	124	chauffeur	44	here
A	Clemensson Clare I—†	124	housewife	44	"
B	Ordway Elizabeth—†	124	bookkeeper	28	Andover
C	Ordway Sarah—†	124	none	61	"
D	Vanness Ora—†	124	housewife	50	29 High
E	Vanness William	133	janitor	53	29 "
F	Duke Ellen—†	133	housewife	30	Springfield
G	Duke Robert H	133	engineer	35	"
H	Ryan Dennis	133	clerk	54	here
K	Ryan Mary F—†	133	housewife	52	"
L	Jackson Lillian—†	133	saleswoman	34	New Hampshire
M	Garrity Dorothy R—†	133	housewife	21	137 Peterboro
N	Garrity Hugh F	133	pianos	32	137 "
O	Fowler Bertram	133	clerk	30	96 Hemenway
P	Fowler Emily—†	133	housewife	30	96 "
R	Stanley Nina—†	133	dressmaker	36	15 Queensberry
S	Yates Elsie M—†	133	student	24	here
T	Yates Lillian A—†	133	housekeeper	48	"
U	Ely Emma—†	133	retired	56	"
V	Seeman Adam	133	"	77	"
W	Burchell Norman	133	nurse	25	New York
X	Drake William C	133	"	27	"
Y	Marshall Celia—†	133	retired	60	15 Queensberry
Z	Marshall George	133	student	28	15 "
C	Summers Alfred J	133	merchant	55	12 Somerset
D	Worden Helen A—†	133	housewife	33	here
E	Worden Robert	133	salesman	36	"
F	Jordan Arthur C	133	student	25	20 Fenwood rd
G	Jordan Esther—†	133	housewife	23	Malden
H	Watts David L	133	manager	30	Michigan
K	Watts Margaret—†	133	housewife	32	"
L	Caldwell Laura—†	133	saleswoman	38	4 Humboldt av
M	Woods Sally A—†	133	buyer	38	4 "
N	Conway Joseph A	133	lawyer	33	here
O	Conway Lillian M—†	133	housewife	28	"
P	St John Joseph L	133	salesman	27	Cambridge
R	St John Marjorie—†	133	housewife	27	"
S	Blome Henry A	133	salesman	33	here
T	Fleming Claude G	133	real estate	33	"
U	Fleming Mary B—†	133	housewife	28	"

Peterborough Street—Continued

v	Loungray Frances—†	133	hairdresser	22	2161 Wash'n
x	Peck Cady K	133	lumberman	25	here
y	Peck Ethel L—†	133	housewife	51	"
z	Peck Helen F—†	133	secretary	23	"
a	Lougee Stephanie Z—†	133	housewife	43	28 Queensbury
b	Lougee Walter	133	delicatessen	56	28 "
c	Zoeller Frederick K	133	retired	75	28 "
d	Miller Elizabeth C—†	133	housewife	22	here
e	Miller Joseph Q	133	salesman	31	"
f	Marsters Harry	133	clerk	27	68 Hunt'n av
g	Corn Alice B—†	133	housewife	40	Lynn
h	Smith Irene—†	133	"	21	Canada
k	Smith John D	133	salesman	29	"
l	Postings Emma—†	133	housewife	47	here
m	Postings Robert	133	clerk	43	"
n	Stewart Narval L	133	nurse	23	"
o	Busby May E—†	133	secretary	38	"
p	Almero Estella—†	137	houseworker	35	"
r	Colbert Jesse B	137	janitor	64	"
s	Colbert Mary A—†	137	housewife	54	"
t	Fajardo Megel	137	fireman	35	
u	Parkman Mary—†	137	housewife	28	Maine
v	Parkman Orin D	137	student	29	"
w	Rowe Louise L—†	137	hairdresser	50	Quincy
x	Rowe Muriel—†	137	clerk	23	here
y	Curtis Earle L	137	salesman	31	"
z	Curtis Florence D—†	137	housewife	29	"
a	Brown Edward T	137	steward	44	1734 Wash'n
b	Brown Ellen—†	137	housewife	44	1734 "
c	Tracy Daniel O	137	salesman	29	Brookline
d	Tracy Laura—†	137	housewife	27	"
f	Glazier Charles H	137	treasurer	60	here
g	Glazier Delia—†	137	retired	70	"
h	Sxiklas Adolf	137	laborer	56	Europe
k	Sxiklas Andra	137	student	22	"
l	Sxiklas Bela	137	clerk	26	"
m	Sxilas Rose—†	137	retired	56	"
n	Lemieux Bertha L—†	137	housewife	28	11 E Newton
o	Lemieux Theodore J	137	agent	39	42 Concord sq
p	Pitts Annette V—†	137	nurse	28	80 Peterboro
r	Fortney Grace—†	137	dressmaker	49	here

Peterborough Street—Continued

s	Taylor James C	137	B F D	46	here
t	Taylor Martha M—†	137	housewife	43	"
v	Wiswall Marie R —†	137	"	67	1 Mt Warren
w	Dodge Katherine—†	137	retired	83	Lincoln
x	Smith Dorothy M—†	137	stenographer	23	97 St Stephen
y	Quinland Anna F—†	137	housewife	43	here
z	Quinland John H	137	steward	46	"
A	Wood Ethel—†	137	truant officer	43	"
B	Wood Gertrude M—†	137	housewife	45	"
C	Wood W Hubert	137	lawyer	53	"
D	VonGroll Celeste—†	137	housewife	36	6 Humboldt av
E	VonGroll Maximallin	137	physician	50	6 "
F	Hussey Albert A	137	broker	47	here
G	Hussey Hattie F —†	137	housewife	43	"
H	Wilshire Cecil V	137	nurse	34	133 Peterboro
K	Wilshire Velmer K—†	137	housewife	32	133 "
L	Kemp Mary H—†	137	nurse	30	here
N	Smith Edwin A	137	U S A	31	Chicago Ill
O	Smith Mary H—†	137	housewife	26	"
P	Heinzen Henriette M—†	137	social worker	45	here
R	Prang Mary—†	137	retired	87	"
S	Prang Rosa—†	137	"	70	"
T	Rushen Chloa—†	137	bookkeeper	33	50 Peterboro
V	Grant Agnes—†	137	secretary	38	here
X	Hunt Frederick E	137	musician	26	Texas
Y	Hunt Josayle—†	137	housewife	25	"

Queensberry Street

A	Paramananda Swami	1	clergyman	40	here
B	Bennett A Willis	11	janitor	58	125 W Newton
C	Bennett Clara B—†	11	housewife	48	125 "
D	Thorndike Helen—†	11	"	38	here
E	Thorndike Rothchild	11	printer	38	"
F	Brimmer Jeanette —†	11	housekeeper	80	"
G	Brimmer Lydia—†	11	clerk	40	"
H	Clarke Helen A—†	11	authoress	55	"
K	Porter Charlotte—†	11	"	63	"
L	Percy Mary—†	11	nurse	40	"

Queensberry Street—Continued

M	Day Emma †	11	housewife	23	73 Gainsboro
N	Day Lester S	11	secretary	26	73 "
O	Leddy Joseph H	11	lawyer	25	here
P	Leddy Margaret J—†	11	housekeeper	72	"
S	Goodwin Carrie B—†	11	nurse	33	"
T	Thayer Harley P	11	manager	36	Somerville
U	Thayer Marjorie W—†	11	housewife	27	"
V	Roberts Emily C—†	11	housekeeper	70	here
W	Thompson Jessie E—†	11	teacher	57	"
X	Diamond Marie W—†	11	housewife	26	44 Moreland
Y	Diamond Paul T	11	decorator	26	2 Kearsarge av
Z	Judd Emelyn—†	11	clerk	60	here
A	Hardy Elizabeth—†	11	student	22	"
B	Wreczorek Francis T	11	salesman	27	Newton
C	Brigham Ella W—†	11	nurse	36	here
D	Frank Ethel M—†	11	clerk	38	"
E	Traband Katherine—†	11	"	34	114 Hemenway
F	May Maud A—†	11	housekeeper	50	here
G	May Viola S—†	11	clerk	25	"
K	Fletcher Carolyn—†	11	teacher	53	"
L	MacCullen Elizabeth—†	11	nurse	50	"
M	Rudd Ethel C—†	11	housewife	37	16 Garrison
N	Rudd Tracy P	11	artist	35	16 "
O	Chapman Clarence W	11	bookkeeper	47	here
P	Ladd Maria T—†	11	housekeeper	80	"
R	Laurent George	11	musician	38	36 Queensberry
S	Laurent Germaine—†	11	housewife	28	36 "
T	Whitten Carl	11	salesman	36	here
U	Whitten Hazel—†	11	housewife	34	"
W	Emerson Bertha C—†	11	manager	30	"
X	Ahern Hazel I—†	11	secretary	28	15 Woodville
Y	Clarke Ella M—†	11	clerk	45	here
Z	Ware Dorris M—†	11	"	27	31 Torrey
A	Ware Emily J—†	11	housekeeper	50	31 "
B	Latherbee Harold W	11	accountant	25	Milton
C	Inkley Alice M—†	11	stenographer	27	here
D	Inkley Ann B—†	11	"	31	"
E	Inkley Josephine N—†	11	"	23	"
F	Cleaves Evelyn—†	11	housewife	30	"
G	Cleaves Frederick	11	engineer	49	"
H	Carter Katherine—†	11	housekeeper	50	"

Queensberry Street—Continued

K Carter Mary—†	11	clerk	45	here
L Hay Jane—†	11	teacher	38	"
M Gauthier Rita—†	11	dressmaker	23	"
N Peterson Ruth—†	11	clerk	26	"
O DeWolfe Harry	11	salesman	45	"
P DeWolfe Naomi—†	11	dressmaker	47	"
R Thayer Zelpha—†	11	teacher	40	"
S McGloughlin David C	15	janitor	26	17 Worthington
T McGloughlin Frances A—†	15	housewife	25	17 "
U Bradley Bessie—†	15	dressmaker	38	here
V Bradley Louise S—†	15	housekeeper	71	"
W Bradley Lucy—†	15	dressmaker	41	"
X Attridge Burton	15	manager	25	"
Y Attridge Edith—†	15	housewife	22	"
Z Atkins Henrietta—†	15	student	30	Toledo Ohio
A Hussey Robert	15	salesman	30	here
B Shea Alfred	15	accountant	30	Newton
C Shea Dorothy—†	15	housewife	28	"
D Palumbo John	15	salesman	38	171 Hemenway
F Watson Bertha—†	15	teacher	45	here
G Briggs Martha—†	15	secretary	45	"
H Gunby Frederick M	15	engineer	40	"
L Murphy Alice—†	15	housekeeper	25	"
M Murphy John V	15	lawyer	31	"
N Warden Ralph P	15	salesman	26	"
P Scribner Carrie E—†	15	housewife	23	174 St Botolph
R Scribner Elmer	15	chauffeur	27	174 "
S Fentress Albert	15	salesman	40	here
T Fentress Mary—†	15	housekeeper	35	"
U Davy Louise—†	15	clerk	35	"
V Sgoberg John A	15	salesman	30	"
W Lord Ethana—†	15	housewife	48	"
X Lord Joseph W	15	bookkeeper	48	"
Y Kingston Agnes—†	15	nurse	35	"
Z Kingston Mary—†	15	bookkeeper	40	"
A Turner Catherine M—†	15	housewife	28	Pennsylvania
B Turner Edward W	15	chauffeur	30	"
D Creeley Evelyn—†	15	clerk	45	here
E Whitten Ida M—†	16	housewife	53	143 Hemenway
F Whitten Walter S	16	janitor	52	143 "
G Jacobs Alice—†	16	clerk	35	here

Queensberry Street—Continued

H	Scribner Sarah—†	16	housekeeper	75	here
K	Lord Charles E	16	clerk	27	36 Queensberry
L	Lord Charlotte P—†	16	housewife	25	36 "
M	Little David E	16	advertising	50	here
N	Floctor Minnie M—†	16	stenographer	47	"
O	Teft Mary E—†	16	clerk	30	"
P	Owen Walter D	16	manufacturer	47	Hull
R	Ingraham Martha—†	16	housekeeper	75	here
S	Lee Monville—†	16	"	80	"
T	Doil Renne M—†	16	housewife	42	74 Westland av
U	Doil William J	16	machinist	36	here
V	Kenyon Beatrice E—†	16	clerk	27	163 Hemenway
W	Kenyon Nellie C—†	16	housekeeper	60	163 "
X	Talmage Alice—†	16	clerk	35	here
Y	Harris Anita—†	16	housewife	35	51 Queensberry
Z	Harris Herbert S	16	caterer	36	51 "
A	Lovejoy Ethel M—†	16	housewife	42	51 "
B	Lovejoy Louis	16	mechanic	37	51 "
C	Combell Susan F—†	16	housekeeper	44	207 Audubon rd
D	Haggerty Susan W—†	16	clerk	30	here
E	Porter Sadie L—†	16	supervisor	35	"
F	Hayes Jessie—†	16	publisher	40	"
G	Richardson Helena S—†	16	housekeeper	53	Greenfield
H	Bolton Elizabeth—†	16	housewife	26	580 Com av
K	Bolton Hanley	16	agent	27	26 Dunreath
L	Orpen Mary—†	16	stenographer	32	here
M	Orpen Nora—†	16	dressmaker	40	"
N	Douglas Mary—†	16	saleswoman	40	"
O	Hall Blanche S—†	16	teacher	40	"
P	Ingraham Myrtie D—†	16	cashier	44	"
R	Mathewson Alexander J	16	manager	37	652 Hunt'n av
T	Tuttle Martha E—†	16	buyer	35	here
U	Carr Esther M—†	16	housewife	40	"
W	Frame Alice J—†	19	"	50	Medford
X	Frame Ruth J—†	19	typist	21	"
Y	Mori Kay	19	artist	35	here
Z	Potter Stoddard H	19	merchant	40	"
A	Caleman May—†	19	saleswoman	35	15 Queensberry
B	Coakley Frances—†	19	nurse	36	Queensberry s
D	Ross Ermine B—†	19	housewife	45	40 "
E	Ross James F	19	salesman	50	Canada

8—13

Queensberry Street—Continued

F	Dyer Beula—†	19	stenographer	26	here
G	Baker Stella—†	19	decorator	45	Winchester
H	Lewis Frank	19	salesman	48	"
K	Lewis Irene—†	19	housewife	45	"
L	Andrews Julia—†	19	"	30	"
M	Andrews Melvin	19	inventor	31	"
N	Owens Anna—†	19	masseuse	37	"
P	Curtis Katherine E—†	19	housewife	45	"
R	Simpson Emily—†	19	stenographer	32	"
S	Fabishio Ernest	19	musician	35	Brookline
T	Henderson Hazel—†	19	housewife	29	here
U	Henderson Lloyd	19	engineer	34	5 Cotter
V	Libby Caroline—†	19	housekeeper	45	here
W	Atherson Clara M—†	19	housewife	50	"
X	Atherson Hazel—†	19	secretary	27	"
Y	Atherson Mildred A—†	19	"	24	"
Z	Coleman May—†	19	housewife	42	"
A	Coleman William C	19	mechanic	45	"
B	Barnes Tyler L	19	manager	31	196 W Canto
C	Young Arthur W	19	"	30	73 Humboldt av
D	Lowery Ethel—†	19	stenographer	31	Winchester
E	Unitt Grace—†	19	"	30	41 Peterboro
F	Clifford Charles H	19	clerk	34	here
G	Clifford Mildred G—†	19	housewife	34	"
H	Beckett Martha E—†	19	stenographer	30	"
K	Barron George	20	real estate	48	Brookline
L	Barron Harriette—†	20	housewife	47	"
M	Gauvin Frances M—†	20	tel operator	32	Somerville
N	Wilkinson Margaret—†	20	"	28	Hamilton
O	Greenall Helen—†	20	housewife	32	here
P	Greenall Thomas W	20	advertising	46	"
S	Ernen Ella—†	20	housekeeper	37	Pittsburgh Pa
U	Wuest Carrie M—†	20	housewife	47	here
V	Wuest Phineas B	20	pharmacist	41	"
W	Shea Anna—†	20	housewife	27	Hartford Ct
X	Shea William T	20	tester	29	"
Y	Mills Ashley	20	tailor	49	here
Z	Mills Ashley E	20	student	24	"
A	Mills Laura A—†	20	housewife	48	"
B	Warren John	20	salesman	21	"
C	Morse Charles F	20	investigator	64	"

Queensberry Street—Continued

Letter.	FULL NAME.	Residence, April 1, 1924.	Occupation.	Supposed Age.	Reported Residence, April 1, 1923. Street and Number.
D	Jefferson Frances—†	20	secretary	29	here
E	Madden Hazel J—†	20	housewife	24	"
F	Madden John F	20	manager	36	"
G	Laman Edith—†	20	secretary	24	"
H	O'Keefe Margaret—†	20	"	29	"
K	Laurin Esther—†	20	nurse	55	"
L	Keefe Annie F—†	20	housewife	43	"
M	Keefe William J	20	salesman	43	"
N	Congdon Celia M—†	20	nurse	37	
O	Nason Wiltha—†	20	saleswoman	24	407 Hunt'n av
P	Smith Theressa—†	20	"	22	407 "
R	Courahall Edward	24	clerk	36	122 Roxbury
S	Courahall Mary—†	24	bookkeeper	27	122 "
T	Woodward Ethel B—†	24	housewife	31	55 St Stephen
U	Woodward Rufus S	24	reporter	29	55 "
V	Collins Frank	24	salesman	33	124 Amherst
W	Finn Charles A, jr	24	manager	27	120 Pleasant
X	Finn Margurite H—†	24	housewife	25	120 "
Z	Hogan John	24	student	23	Brookline
A	Hogan Margaret—†	24	bookkeeper	30	W Newbury
B	Follansbee Clara F—†	24	cashier	34	Haverhill
C	MacDonald Catherine—†	24	waitress	29	146 Hemenway
D	Danford Frances—†	24	housewife	34	1254 Com av
E	Danford Leo	24	salesman	35	1254 "
F	Kaplan Jacob	24	"	35	Revere
G	Gillis Helen—†	24	bookkeeper	27	124 Peterboro
H	Hallett Mildred—†	24	"	30	1126 Boylston
K	McCormack Della—†	24	"	27	115 Mountfort
L	Ashley Albert A	24	stagehand	50	11 Queensberry
M	Benson Dorothea M—†	24	clerk	47	here
N	Benson Emma J—†	24	housekeeper	74	"
O	Voss Edward	24	manager	29	New York
P	Andrews Arthur C	24	"	45	here
R	Andrews Harriet—†	24	housewife	45	"
S	Ward Cynthia—†	24	housekeeper	76	"
T	Fiske Margaret W—†	24	none	39	"
U	Burt David A	24	dentist	39	"
V	Burt Hattie E—†	24	housewife	34	"
W	Mahoney John A	24	clerk	56	147 Hemenw'y
X	Parker Charles S	24	painter	64	here
Y	Callahan Hattie M—†	25	operator	35	"

Queensberry Street—Continued

z	Callahan Jennie—†	25	housewife	74	here
A	Dexter Lena B—†	25	manicurist	28	"
B	Smith Stella S—†	25	"	31	"
D	Jordan George	25	salesman	35	"
E	Bounanfaut Loretta—†	25	operator	34	Brookline
F	Bounanfaut Theresa—†	25	dressmaker	35	"
G	Lucy Anna D—†	25	housewife	58	here
H	Lucy Charles F	25	manager	59	"
K	Thompson Agnes—†	25	housewife	50	"
L	Thompson Ephraim B	25	manager	52	"
M	Thompson Ephraim B	25	salesman	23	"
N	Lawrence Leroy	25	"	37	"
O	Lawrence Mabel—†	25	housewife	34	"
P	Cook Aubrey W	25	welder	26	New Haven
R	Cook Mary—†	25	housewife	21	"
S	Partridge George A	25	salesman	23	here
T	Partridge Lucy B—†	25	housewife	47	"
U	Fox Helen C—†	25	"	36	407 Marlbor
V	Fox Patrick L	25	student	34	407 "
X	Bentley Eileen H—†	25	clerk	35	here
Y	Peck Della H—†	25	nurse	36	"
Z	Davis Harlow M	25	salesman	35	"
A	Dibbell Julian E	25	accountant	35	"
B	Jones Martha—†	25	nurse	40	"
C	Dodge Hazel M—†	25	housewife	30	"
D	Dodge Howard M	25	advertising	46	"
E	MacMichael Jean—†	25	clerk	25	"
F	Conway Helen—†	25	saleswoman	43	"
G	Crocker Henry R	25	surveyor	30	"
H	McLaughlin Arnold	28	janitor	56	"
K	McLaughlin Mary—†	28	housewife	40	"
L	Moody Amos W	28	musician	32	"
M	Marble Bernice E—†	28	dietitian	34	"
N	Marble Helen—†	28	nurse	32	"
O	Blanchard Grace—†	28	teacher	45	Topsfield
P	Kloss Abbie C—†	28	housewife	64	here
R	Kloss Anna A—†	28	student	34	"
S	Mullen Madeleine M—†	28	housewife	24	Lynn
T	Mullen William G	28	engineer	25	"
U	Blake Annie M—†	28	retired	56	Brookline
V	Buffum Mary E—†	28	"	81	"

Queensberry Street—Continued

Letter.	FULL NAME.	Residence	Occupation	Age	Reported Residence
x	Webster Blanche H—†	28	housekeeper	41	here
y	Bingham Ralph F	28	clerk	35	Melrose
z	Davis Leora K—†	28	housekeeper	75	W Newton
a	Keith Henrietta—†	28	retired	65	"
c	Nettles Cora E—†	28	merchant	41	here
d	DesMarais Margaret—†	28	housewife	28	"
e	DesMarais Raphael M	28	salesman	30	"
f	Petrianos George	28	merchant	33	"
g	Petrianos Helen—†	28	housewife	32	"
h	Evans Florence A—†	28	"	40	181 Hunt'n av
k	Evans Horace M	28	physician	40	181 "
l	Hadley Elaine C—†	28	housewife	21	Alabama
m	Hadley Richard F	28	salesman	27	Arlington
n	Harris Harold C	28	"	30	here
o	Jackson George	29	janitor	45	127 Dartmouth
p	Mitchell Lillian —†	29	housewife	22	Somerville
r	Mitchell William B	29	salesman	25	Hull
s	Heindle Arthur	29	musician	37	here
t	Herrick Amelia N—†	29	housewife	28	"
u	Herrick Samuel	29	chemist	30	"
v	Caswell Viola—†	29	saleswoman	35	"
v	Rich Cecelia—†	29	housewife	36	"
x	Rich William B	29	physician	51	"
y	Dauber Lizzie J —†	29	seamstress	36	"
z	Stebner Wanda O—†	29	clerk	27	"
a	McFarlane Owen	29	salesman	52	"
b	Culp Ivan	29	mechanic	21	"
c	Culp Lena I—†	29	housewife	54	"
d	LeHuquet Elfrida—†	29	stenographer	23	"
e	LeHuquet Hilda L—†	29	housewife	40	"
f	Rosen George E	29	salesman	30	"
g	Rosen Gertrude—†	29	manager	25	"
h	Letournan Frank G	29	salesman	30	"
k	Letournan Susie—†	29	housewife	25	"
l	Riley Harriet—†	29	teacher	35	"
m	Riley Margaret—†	29	"	40	"
n	Reynolds Mary—†	29	housewife	23	"
o	Reynolds William G	29	chauffeur	25	"
p	Barr Thurston	29	salesman	23	"
r	Seaman Helen—†	29	housewife	27	"
s	Titus Mary—†	29	hairdresser	34	"

Page.	Letter.	FULL NAME	Residence, April 1, 1924.	Occupation.	Supposed Age.	Reported Residence, April 1, 1923. Street and Number.

Queensberry Street—Continued

	Letter	Full Name	Res.	Occupation	Age	Reported Residence
	T	Allen Woodward	29	clerk	35	here
	U	Hall George R	29	salesman	30	"
	V	Anderson Carl	29	merchant	28	"
	W	Thomas Earle L	29	"	27	"
	X	Fielding Irene—†	29	housewife	20	479 Mass av
	Y	Fielding Percy R	29	salesman	25	479 "
	Z	Gotts Josephine—†	29	retired	60	here
	A	Gotts Josephine A—†	29	demonstrator	43	"
	B	Faulknham Clarence	31	janitor	41	"
	C	Faulknham Mary—†	31	housewife	41	"
	D	Prendergast Agnes—†	31	"	30	Brookline
	E	Prendergast Michael	31	lawyer	35	"
	F	Logan Alma—†	31	secretary	30	Brockton
	G	Logan Elsie—†	31	clerk	25	"
	K	Rogers Daniel J	31	manager	38	here
	L	Rogers Eva J—†	31	housewife	37	"
	M	Patridge Clarence B	31	manager	38	29 Queensberry
	N	Patridge Hattie—†	31	housewife	35	29 "
	O	McKenzie Alice—†	31	clerk	35	Malden
	P	Peterson Gertrude C—†	31	housekeeper	65	here
	R	Peterson Gertrude D—†	31	saleswoman	35	"
	S	Dow Theresa—†	31	student	25	Portland Me
	T	Goodwillie Ethel M—†	31	secretary	43	here
	U	Lipschultz Emma—†	31	stenographer	38	"
	V	Esterling Edith—†	31	housewife	37	"
	W	Esterling Thomas L	31	teacher	40	"
	X	Romanesque Albert	31	musician	48	"
	Y	Cunningham Esther—†	31	housekeeper	62	"
	Z	Cunningham Marie—†	31	nurse	39	"
	A	Ringer Robert R	31	electrician	42	"
	B	Foster John P	31	clerk	48	"
	D	Burrill Arthur G	31	underwriter	31	"
	E	Burrill Myrtle F—†	31	housewife	28	"
	F	Belaskos Anthony P	31	cabinetmaker	31	280 Mass av
	G	Belaskos Mabel R—†	31	clerk	23	Cambridge
	H	Smith Minnie L—†	31	milliner	48	here
	K	Spencer Barbara E—†	31	"	55	"
	L	Mulholland William E	31	broker	31	"
	M	Thordeman Helen—†	31	buyer	38	"
	N	Donald Sadie A—†	31	stenographer	28	"
	O	Hardy Lillian J—†	31	clerk	30	"

Queensberry Street—Continued

P	Mondello Thomas	31	druggist	35	here
R	Douse Harry C	32	clerk	41	"
S	Mason Hattie O—†	32	housekeeper	62	"
T	Tyler Parker	32	clerk	56	"
U	Flinn Jeannette—†	32	housewife	30	Cambridge
V	Flinn Robert S	32	student	29	"
W	Morrison Lawrence S	32	miner	41	Mexico
X	Morrison Phoebe A—†	32	housekeeper	28	"
Y	Sawyer Anna L—†	32	hairdresser	44	here
Z	DeWolfe Margureite—†	32	nurse	28	"
A	Moran Mary A—†	32	"	28	"
B	Wachenfeld Alice—†	32	"	26	"
C	Beardsley Elliott G	32	insurance	55	"
D	Clements Albert J	32	manager	42	"
E	Clements Gertrude—†	32	housewife	35	"
F	Howard Arthur W	32	painter	26	"
G	Silva John E	32	"	42	"
H	Thompson Arthur J	32	clerk	26	"
L	McGaffey Elizabeth G—†	32	corsetiere	46	"
M	Lane Annie—†	32	housewife	29	"
N	Lane Bartley	32	tailor	43	"
O	Baker John W	32	chauffeur	36	Maine
P	Baker Sarah E—†	32	houskeeper	65	here
R	Putnam Charles B	32	clerk	55	"
S	Putnam Grace M—†	32	housewife	55	"
T	Artieres Louis	32	musician	29	"
U	Artieres Yvonne—†	32	housewife	27	"
V	Baker Mary E—†	32	clerk	33	"
A	Girvan John S	35	chauffeur	43	"
B	Girvan Lottie M—†	35	housewife	39	"
C	Clemens George	35	clerk	33	"
D	Prouty Robert	35	"	32	"
E	Hildreth Elizabeth J—†	35	secretary	35	"
F	Thiessen Dorothy M—†	35	bookkeeper	45	"
G	Bailey Catherine—†	35	secretary	35	"
H	Slayton Mary E—†	35	saleswoman	30	"
K	Goldsmith Meyer A	35	salesman	30	"
L	Mussells Nina P—†	35	buyer	31	"
M	Norton Catherine—†	35	saleswoman	41	"
N	Landers Clara—†	35	artist	38	"
O	Dunlary Jenny—†	35	milliner	38	"

71

Queensberry Street—Continued

	Letter	Full Name	Res.	Occupation	Age	Reported Residence
	P	Ferguson Fred A	35	salesman	31	29 Queensberry
	S	Salter Harry H	35	"	42	here
	T	Loeb Barron B	35	"	36	"
	U	Loeb Florence—†	35	housewife	34	"
	V	Hitchcock Gertrude M—†	35	superintendent	45	"
	W	Farrel Catherine—†	35	housewife	38	108 Jersey
	X	Farrel Lewis J	35	engineer	40	108 "
	Y	Knowles Mary A—†	35	milliner	44	here
	Z	Carlson Anna—†	35	stenographer	27	"
	A	Castelli Leonard	35	interpreter	50	153 Hemenway
	B	Bolton Ada—†	35	saleswoman	38	here
	C	Conway Anna—†	35	clerk	40	29 Queensberry
	D	Sullivan Bertha—†	35	saleswoman	46	here
	E	Henwood David D	35	merchant	39	"
	F	McKenna Daniel	36	janitor	42	"
	G	McKenna Mary—†	36	housewife	34	"
	H	Barlow Charles	36	salesman	54	55 Queensberry
	K	Barlow Minnie—†	36	housewife	52	55 "
	L	Gibbs Charles W	36	superintendent	32	New York
	M	Gibbs May E—†	36	housewife	26	"
	N	Bushard Eugenia—†	36	saleswoman	36	here
	O	Dickerson Donald I	36	student	23	Melrose
	P	Dickerson Lawton E	36	bookkeeper	20	"
	R	Dickerson Lois J—†	36	housewife	22	"
	S	Gardine Margaret—†	36	stenographer	27	24 Queensberry
	T	Thompson Ann—†	36	teacher	30	24 "
	U	Field Fred T	36	clerk	32	36 "
	W	Hayden Helen W—†	36	student	20	here
	X	Hayden Maud G—†	36	housewife	40	"
	A	Gardner Rosellia—†	36	clerk	46	"
	B	Hiriota Susamu	36	manager	25	Japan
	C	Toda Suehiro	36	clerk	23	"
	D	Takeda Rikugo	36	salesman	33	51 Queensberry
	E	Clark Charles P	36	repairer	53	Lowell
	F	Cornell Jennie L—†	36	hairdresser	57	here
	G	Morison Alice—†	36	housewife	31	Cambridge
	H	Morison Trueman G	36	salesman	29	Somerville
	K	Thomas Mary V—†	36	saleswoman	33	here
	L	Hardy Hazel G—†	36	clerk	27	Maine
	M	Hardy Ralph M	36	"	25	Cambridge
	N	McLaughlin Alice M—†	36	housewife	26	here

Queensberry Street—Continued

O	McLaughlin Frank A	36	clerk	28	here
R	Lynn Sarah—†	40	janitress	35	"
S	Blake Elsie M—†	40	teacher	55	"
T	Wright Charles	40	clerk	37	"
U	Newton Charles	40	trainman	37	"
V	Stetson Sarah L—†	40	housekeeper	53	"
W	Burlen Caroline—†	40	housewife	63	"
X	Burlen William	40	retired	75	"
Y	Anson Barry J	40	student	30	"
Z	Kennerie Florence—†	40	housewife	50	Quincy
A	Kennerie John B	40	electrician	55	"
C	Nichols Herbert	40	artist	30	here
D	Clark Mary L—†	40	librarian	50	"
E	White William D	40	salesman	35	"
F	Basham Alva T—†	40	housewife	30	"
G	Daum George M	40	salesman	62	"
H	Billings Louise—†	40	teacher	45	"
K	Baker John	40	printer	40	"
L	Marshall Ida—†	40	clerk	40	"
M	Emery Hazel—†	40	housekeeper	30	"
N	Davis Margaret P—†	40	buyer	35	"
O	Sears Catherine E—†	40	housewife	34	"
P	Bassett Leone P—†	40	stenographer	28	"
R	Fichord Amy H—†	40	bookkeeper	35	529 Wash'n
S	Morrison Hannah—†	40	housekeeper	55	here
T	Morrison Vera G—†	40	clerk	20	529 Wash'n
U	Gannon Grace—†	40	hairdresser	35	here
V	Atkinson Roy	40	editor	33	"
X	Holmes Agnes—†	51	housewife	22	Canton
Y	Holmes William C	51	steamfitter	22	"
B	Cook Earnest M	51	student	24	Maine
C	Cook Mary—†	51	housewife	23	"
D	Elder Edith—†	51	"	35	here
E	Elder George D	51	mechanic	38	"
G	Abo George B	51	merchant	41	"
H	Abo Taka—†	51	housewife	40	"
K	Whelpley Agnes—†	51	"	25	133 St Botolph
L	Whelpley George E	51	clerk	24	133 "
O	Watts Dorris—†	51	housewife	30	Minnesota
P	Watts William F	51	salesman	35	"
R	Dumas Marion—†	51	housewife	40	72 Peterboro

Queensberry Street—Continued

	Letter.	Full Name.	Residence, April 1, 1924.	Occupation.	Supposed Age.	Reported Residence, April 1, 1923. Street and Number.
	s	Dumas Nelson J	51	optician	45	72 Peterboro
	t	Whitside Alice—†	51	model	22	72 "
	u	Fitzpatrick Edward M	51	agent	34	Canada
	v	Fitzpatrick Marie—†	51	housewife	29	"
	w	Russell Anna—†	51	"	33	New Jersey
	x	Russell William A	51	salesman	35	"
	y	Fisk Louise W —†	51	nurse	34	here
	z	Hardy Hellen—†	51	teacher	25	Wellesley
	a	Greve Mary—†	51	waitress	45	here
	b	Darcy Daniel J	51	buyer	30	Fall River
	c	Nelligan Frank J	51	manager	30	1351 Com av
	d	Sullivan George F	51	accountant	29	Fall River
	e	Cushin George	51	operator	40	454 Hunt'n av
	f	Cushing Gertrude—†	51	housewife	26	454 "
	g	Vailini Virginia—†	51	"	60	here
	h	Emerson Hellen D—†	51	student	33	Hartford Ct
	k	Vallini Pietro	51	retired	66	here
	l	Davis Harry	55	chauffeur	27	"
	m	Davis Mary—†	55	housewife	25	"
	n	Smith Sylvester	55	salesman	55	"
	p	Redmon Artie M—†	55	housewife	24	Kentucky
	r	Redmon Roy S	55	engineer	25	"
	s	Suttie Guy	55	janitor	27	Canada
	t	Suttie Mildred—†	55	housewife	21	"
	v	Kaine Walter	55	student	25	here
	w	Leary William	55	"	22	"
	x	Smith Ralph	55	"	25	"
	y	Brogan Anna—†	55	bookkeeper	25	Franklin
	z	Brogan Kathleen—†	55	"	23	"
	a	Murdock Angus L	55	salesman	40	here
	b	Murdock Eugene H	55	housewife	35	"
	c	Dasher Mary—†	55	"	35	"
	d	Dasher Messa	55	cigarmaker	38	"
	f	Hoagland Lucy A—†	55	agent	43	"
	g	Howard Frank	55	salesman	40	Waltham
	h	McCue Hellen—†	55	stenographer	22	9 Follen
	k	McNamara Alice—†	55	"	22	9 "
	l	Brown Lydia E—†	55	housewife	46	here
	m	Brown Theodore	55	waiter	46	"
	n	Franklin Rebecca—†	55	retired	65	235 W Newton
	p	Kelley Frank J	55	lithographer	42	here

Page.	Letter.	Full Name.	Residence, April 1, 1924.	Occupation.	Supposed Age.	Reported Residence, April 1, 1923. Street and Number.

Queensberry Street—Continued

	T	Gerard William	55	chauffeur	29	here
	U	Marston Elizabeth—†	55	saleswoman	31	"
	V	Boyle John E	55	mechanic	35	Connecticut
	W	Regal Hellen T—†	55	housewife	27	here
	X	Regal William J	55	clerk	28	"
	Y	Dorsey Daniel C	94	janitor	53	"
	Z	Johnson Mary G—†	94	housekeeper	60	"
	B	Whitten Adelaide—†	94	stenographer	38	"
	C	Stidman Harold	94	salesman	32	104 Queensberry
	D	Stidman Irene—†	94	housekeeper	28	104 "
	E	Milspaw Lillian K—†	94	artist	38	here
	F	Sullivan Francis A	94	clerk	27	"
	G	Sullivan Gertrude M—†	94	housewife	26	"
	H	Murdock Hellen—†	94	saleswoman	28	55 Queensberry
	K	Murdock Jean—†	94	"	27	55 "
	L	Walters George	94	printer	45	here
	M	Foster Mildred	94	nurse	30	"
	N	White Jean—†	94	retired	30	"
	O	Beane Rose—†	94	bookkeeper	28	"
	P	Beane Virginia—†	94	tel operator	30	"
	R	Chapman Henry	94	printer	30	"
	S	Crump Alfred E	94	salesman	45	"
	T	Crump Dorothy—†	94	clerk	21	"
	U	Kurts Samuel B	94	printer	46	"
	V	Graham Eva M—†	94	cashier	40	"
	W	Taffier Edward	94	salesman	35	"
	X	Taffier Esther—†	94	stenographer	28	"
	Y	Deering Alfred	94	lineman	27	"
	Z	Walton Grenville	98	janitor	27	"
	A	Sullivan Viola—†	98	student	25	"
	B	Buford Charles	98	"	22	"
	C	Jackson Bertha—†	98	accountant	42	"
	D	Rall Frances—†	98	housewife	40	"
	E	Breer Anna—†	98	"	39	"
	F	Quincy Charles E	98	merchant	45	"
	G	Perkins Katherine S—†	98	retired	37	"
	H	Bradstreet Helen—†	98	teacher	37	"
	K	Nichols Loring P	98	merchant	27	"
	L	Nichols Marjorie E—†	98	housewife	24	"
	M	Malley Virginia—†	98	hairdresser	35	"
	N	Jacobs Sumner	98	clerk	35	"

Page.	Letter.	FULL NAME.	Residence, April 1, 1924.	Occupation.	Supposed Age.	Reported Residence, April 1, 1923. Street and Number.

Queensberry Street—Continued

	O	Wright Martha—†	98	housekeeper	40	here
	P	Curley James	98	merchant	40	"
	R	McCabe Anthony	98	student	22	"
	T	Morrison Frederick	98	salesman	35	"
	U	Morrison Marion—†	98	stenographer	27	16 Queensberry
	W	Murphy Edith A—†	100	housewife	34	19 Dawes
	X	Murphy John R	100	policeman	80	19 "
	Y	Gates Alice F—†	100	housewife	36	Braintree
	Z	Gates Burton T	100	real estate	27	"
	A	Dodge Louise T—†	100	nurse	28	Boxford
	B	Hanson Alice—†	100	clerk	42	here
	C	Hanson Anna D—†	100	housekeeper	72	"
	D	Raymond Fannie H—†	100	"	66	"
	E	Raymond Fannie M—†	100	clerk	45	"
	F	Wright Carl	100	salesman	28	"
	G	Boeck Laura—†	100	housewife	29	77 Audubon rd
	H	Boeck William C	100	student	30	77 "
	K	Daley Mary W—†	100	bookkeeper	40	here
	L	Gardner Clara M—†	100	clerk	47	"
	O	Alexander Charles W	100	salesman	32	107 Queensberry
	P	Decay John	100	student	32	here
	S	Franz Hazel—†	100	housewife	31	"
	T	Franz Robert	100	salesman	32	"
	U	Hamner Edith L—†	102	retired	40	"
	V	Moore Andrew J	102	"	40	S Carolina
	W	Moore Helen G—†	102	housewife	34	"
	X	Morrill Grace—†	102	"	27	Clinton
	Y	Morrill John	102	salesman	33	"
	A	Mates Benjamin	102	"	32	151 Audubon rd
	B	Mates Sylvia—†	102	housewife	22	151 "
	C	Lucey Jean—†	102	retired	44	here
	D	Smith Lucille—†	102	bookkeeper	35	"
	E	Sullivan Elizabeth—†	102	teacher	33	"
	F	Draper Rose—†	102	housewife	27	Malden
	G	Draper Stuart	102	salesman	30	"
	H	Lyons James D	102	dentist	45	96 Poplar
	K	Lyons Lucy—†	102	housewife	31	96 "
	L	Harriman Joseph	102	student	21	Maine
	M	Pray Arlie B—†	102	housewife	33	here
	N	Pray Wendall V	102	salesman	34	"
	O	Farwell Emma C—†	102	bookkeeper	44	"

76

Queensberry Street - Continued

P	Goss Irvin J	102	merchant	40	here
S	Root Mary—†	102	housewife	42	Georgetown
T	Root Raymond	102	physician	41	"
U	Koppelman Robert	102	florist	29	here
V	Koppleman Sarah—†	102	housewife	29	"
X	Limberg Ernest	102	salesman	40	104 Queensberry
Y	Donaldson Edith A—†	104	hairdresser	33	here
Z	Harlow Marion A—†	104	milliner	31	98 Queensberry
A	Reisig Jane C—†	104	housekeeper	35	here
B	Shannon Alexander	104	superintendent	35	"
C	Millbury Adeline—†	104	nurse	38	871 Beacon
D	Wilson Chester B	104	salesman	31	here
E	Wilson Helen F—†	104	housewife	24	"
F	Wright Frank H	104	salesman	40	Somerville
G	Barry Lillian M—†	104	housewife	27	85 Roxbury
H	Barry Thomas A	104	salesman	27	91 Belvidere
K	Sullivan Julia A—†	104	bookkeeper	29	here
L	Morris Ethel D—†	104	housewife	27	New York
M	Morris Maurice J	104	manager	31	"
N	Dyer Charles E	104	clerk	35	here
O	Joyce James E	104	salesman	27	58 Barry
P	Joyce Mabel E—†	104	housewife	31	58 "
R	Mullen John	104	salesman	40	Chelsea
S	Vose Frank C	104	teacher	28	here
T	Hayden Ella—†	104	housewife	28	"
U	Hayden Fredrick C	104	salesman	30	Waltham
V	Burke Laurence J	104	"	24	Cambridge
W	McCoy Grace—†	104	student	29	52 Queensberry
X	Olsen August	105	janitor	34	65 Hunt'n av
Y	Olsen Corinne—†	105	housewife	22	64 Hemenway
Z	Bridges Helen—†	105	"	34	here
A	Colby Georgia A—†	105	clerk	30	"
B	Lloyd Channing	105	salesman	35	"
C	Lloyd Margrett—†	105	housewife	23	"
D	Brown George	105	student	30	"
E	Roberts Dorothy—†	105	clerk	30	"
F	Roberts Josephine—†	105	housewife	50	"
G	Roberts Ruth—†	105	nurse	22	"
H	Andrews George F	105	salesman	45	"
K	Andrews Mary—†	105	housewife	40	"
L	Mitchell Agnes—†	105	"	28	Providence R I

Queensberry Street—Continued

M	Mitchell Ralph E	105	broker	34	Providence R I
N	Roberts Frank	105	salesman	50	here
O	Roberts Mary—†	105	housewife	40	"
P	Horrigan Charles D	105	salesman	33	"
R	Horrigan Marie—†	105	auditor	25	"
S	Gay Grant	105	salesman	35	"
U	Ross Pauline—†	105	nurse	35	"
V	Neidaur Henry	105	retired	70	"
W	Neidaur Lillian—†	105	clerk	33	"
X	Neidaur Mable—†	105	"	27	"
Y	Hillman Elizabeth—†	105	housewife	54	Somerville
Z	Hillman Esther—†	105	clerk	23	"
A	Coleman Henry	105	postal clerk	68	here
B	Coleman Mabel—†	105	housewife	65	"
C	Whitcomb Edna—†	105	"	34	"
D	Whitcomb Hednei	105	clerk	37	"
E	Young Isabelle—†	105	housewife	25	"
F	Young Ralph	105	salesman	32	"
G	Hodson Cardinal	106	janitor	31	"
H	Hodson Lottie P—†	106	housewife	24	"
K	Knighton Henry	106	agent	38	"
L	Knighton Sylvie	106	housewife	39	"
M	Lane Alice C—†	106	nurse	40	"
N	Rogers Frances—†	106	housewife	54	"
O	Rogers George L	106	lawyer	58	"
P	Marks Eva—†	106	housewife	28	Waltham
R	Marks John	106	salesman	28	"
S	Pierce Cora B—†	106	housekeeper	56	here
T	Pierce Marjorie—†	106	student	'23	"
U	Pierce Sumner T	106	buyer	57	"
W	Reeves Henry B	106	accountant	56	"
X	Reeves Marie—†	106	housewife	56	"
Y	St Armour Blanche—†	106	bookkeeper	32	Worcester
Z	Davis Irene A—†	106	housewife	33	here
A	Davis John R	106	demonstrator	35	"
B	Howard Arthur A	106	physician	42	56 Bay State rd
C	Howard Sarah J—†	106	retired	76	416 Marlboro
D	Potts Hattie E—†	106	housewife	59	here
E	Potts Vincent W	106	manager	65	"
F	Reardon Anastatia D—†	106	secretary	38	"
G	Wilson Hazel F—†	106	housewife	28	California

Queensberry Street—Continued

Letter.	FULL NAME.	Residence, April 1, 1924.	Occupation.	Supposed Age.	Reported Residence, April 1, 1923. Street and Number.
H	Addoria Florence—†	106	bookkeeper	35	Ayer
K	Estabrooks Grace E—†	106	housewife	37	here
L	Estabrooks John W	106	dentist	45	"
M	Gorgensen Augusta F—†	106	housewife	53	"
N	Lord Herbert	106	superintendent	34	"
O	Lord Inez—†	106	housewife	32	"
P	Lillemoen Carl A	106	mechanic	39	"
R	Lillemoen Edith—†	106	housewife	25	"
S	Sahlin George	106	mechanic	55	"
T	Sahlin Thelka—†	106	housewife	53	"
V	Matthews Ellen S—†	107	stenographer	24	Maine
W	Matthews Jessie—†	107	housewife	59	"
X	Webster Florence F—†	107	housekeeper	59	Springfield
Y	Webster Franklin	107	clerk	29	"
Z	Guinn Anna A—†	107	housewife	42	here
A	Guinn Burton R	107	carpenter	40	"
B	Hastings Alice M—†	107	housewife	32	California
	Hastings William W	107	U S N	35	"
D	Ellsion William	107	merchant	28	here
E	Horwitz Charles A	107	clerk	42	"
F	Horwitz Mildred A—†	107	housewife	37	"
G	Tobin George E	107	salesman	36	31 Newbury
H	Tobin Lula P—†	107	housewife	34	31 "
K	Bliss Ruth C—†	107	"	24	here
L	Bliss William B	107	clerk	28	"
M	Ribero Helen—†	107	bookkeeper	24	Franklin
N	Taylor Lilah A—†	107	housekeeper	64	Canada
O	Taylor Mertie M—†	107	masseuse	30	169 Hunt'n av
P	Taylor Viola M—†	107	nurse	23	169 "
R	Elis May—†	107	tel operator	35	here
S	Lyons Katherine—†	107	saleswoman	55	"
T	Miller Grace—†	107	technician	27	"
U	Gatchell Grace—†	107	teacher	37	"
V	Hounsell Clarence H	107	student	21	Lakeport N H
W	Philbrook Earl S	107	manager	20	New Jersey
X	Tibbetts Walter F	107	clerk	20	126 St Botolph
Y	Mashihara Hatsung—†	107	housewife	21	California
Z	Mashihara Taiji	107	dentist	32	74 Westland av
A	King Natalie R—†	107	social worker	32	508 E Fourth
B	Koehler Clemens	107	student	20	Lynn
C	Green Anne E—†	107	housekeeper	54	Abington

Queensberry Street—Continued

D	Green Carrie—†	107	bookkeeper	52	Abington
E	Mitchell Mary—†	107	housewife	22	Quincy
F	Mitchell Ralph	107	draughtsman	26	"
G	Peters Florence—†	107	stenographer	22	1202 Com av
K	Bensay Ernest P	109	superintendent	36	107 Queensberry
L	Bensay Grace N—†	109	housewife	36	107 "
M	Biganes Lena—†	109	"	26	N Carolina
N	Biganes Leon K	109	musician	26	"
O	Paul Jean M—†	109	"	31	here
P	Paul Mathew H	109	salesman	33	"
R	Grodnetsky Ernest	109	"	25	New York
S	Stone Mary W—†	109	student	40	Europe
T	Evans Harriett—†	109	none	62	here
U	Snow Pearl A—†	109	housewife	38	"
V	Snow Washington I	109	musician	38	"
W	Flanders Helen C—†	109	stenographer	38	Concord N H
X	Geldart Gertrude G—†	109	nurse	33	839 Boylston
A	Freeman Addison B	109	salesman	33	New York
B	Stansfield Norman	109	broker	33	here
C	Wilson Henry	109	salesman	35	"
D	Hunter Charlotte A—†	109	housewife	64	"
E	Coon Raymond	109	salesman	30	"
F	Perkins Josephine G—†	109	housewife	54	New Jersey
G	Perkins Kent	109	editor	63	139 Beacon
H	Tucker Bertha D—†	109	teacher	44	here
K	Hayes Alice S—†	109	clerk	49	Winthrop
L	Hayes Allison	109	student	29	"
M	Hayes Helen—†	109	tel operator	27	"
N	Bresnahan Elmira M—†	111	housewife	42	Hyannis
O	Bresnahan James E	111	janitor	36	"
P	Mulhern Elizabeth M—†	111	housewife	38	here
R	Mulhern James H	111	salesman	38	"
S	Lang Alfred	111	wool tester	32	"
T	Lang Marguerite—†	111	housewife	30	"
U	Duncan Gertrude—†	111	nurse	30	"
V	Mosher Rose—†	111	stenographer	35	"
W	Carstensen Andrew P	111	broker	37	105 Queensberry
X	Carstensen Mable V—†	111	housewife	28	105 "
Y	Hastings Atherton	111	broker	55	here
Z	Hastings Lola—†	111	housewife	36	"
A	Newkirk Mollie—†	111	waitress	23	153 Hemenway

Queensberry Street—Continued

B	Burnell Mattie M—†	111	bookkeeper	34	40 Berkeley
C	Long Ruth T—†	111	"	20	Cambridge
D	MacLeod Barbara M—†	111	"	29	40 Berkeley
E	Perkins Florence A—†	111	clerk	25	40 "
F	Walsh Irene H—†	111	bookkeeper	24	108 Jersey
G	Walsh Leah J—†	111	housewife	46	108 "
H	Walsh William	111	contractor	47	108 "
K	Potter John B	111	agent	51	here
L	Potter Mary E—†	111	housewife	54	"
M	Anderson Sonja L—†	111	bookkeeper	32	45 Batavia
N	Clare Elizabeth—†	111	housewife	29	56 Clarkwood
O	Clare Richard W	111	salesman	30	12 "
P	Foley Catherine A—†	111	housewife	36	11 Queensberry
R	Foley Paul H	111	real estate	44	11 "
S	Holmes Mary E—†	111	nurse	31	here
T	Webster Anna—†	111	"	34	"
V	Post Everett C	111	manager	35	"
W	Post Roberta L—†	111	housewife	29	"

Lightning Source UK Ltd.
Milton Keynes UK
UKHW030709270620
365625UK00012B/975